A THEORY OF INCENTIVES IN PROCUREMENT AND REGULATION

A THEORY OF INCENTIVES IN PROCUREMENT AND REGULATION

Jean-Jacques Laffont
and
Jean Tirole

The MIT Press
Cambridge, Massachusetts
London, England

Second printing, 1994

This book was set in Times Roman by Asco Trade Typesetting Ltd., Hong Kong, and was printed and bound in the United States of America.

Library of Congress Cataloging-in-Publication Data

Laffont, Jean-Jacques, 1947–
A theory of incentives in procurement and regulation / Jean-Jacques Laffont and Jean Tirole.
p. cm.
Includes bibliographical references and index.
ISBN 0-262-12174-3
1. Trade regulation. 2. Monopolies. 3. Industrial procurement. 4. Government purchasing. 5. Incentives in industry. 6. Contracts, Letting of. 7. Public utilities. I. Tirole, Jean. II. Title.
HD3612.L33 1993
338.8′2—dc20 92-21500
CIP

to Bénédicte, Bertrand, Cécile, Charlotte, Margot, and Naïs

CONTENTS

FOREWORD

During the 1970s and 1980s we witnessed a renewed interest in the regulation of natural monopolies and oligopolies. In the policy arena discontent was expressed with the price, quality, and cost performance of regulated firms and government contractors. The remedies sought in specific industries differed remarkably: More powerful incentive schemes were proposed and implemented, deregulation was encouraged to free up competition and entry, and in some countries changes in ownership (privatization) occurred. Meanwhile the academic debate attempted to shed light on some shortcomings of the generally accepted theory of regulation. Regulatory theory largely ignored incentive issues. Because exogenous constraints rather than the limited access to information of regulators were the source of inefficient regulatory outcomes, the theory of regulation did not meet the standards of the newly developed principal-agent theory, whose aim is to highlight the information limitations that impair agency relationships. Furthermore the considerably simplified formal models that assumed away imperfect information were less realistic in that they implied policy recommendations that require information not available to regulators in practice.

It is fair to say that despite much theoretical progress in the recent past, the field of regulation resembles that of industrial organization of the 1970s. Conventional wisdom and industry studies are often perceived as more enlightening than theoretical work. This situation may be linked with a suboptimal rate of diffusion of theoretical ideas in the academic and policy communities. But theorists probably still have a long way to go to make their models realistic and operational. We feel that the importance of the matter vindicates the effort to generate such models.

This book aims at developing a synthetic approach to the question of incentives in regulation and procurement. Although we will sometimes allow product market competition, our main focus is on the regulation of natural monopolies. Regulated firms, public enterprises, and government contractors are not scattered randomly over the industrial landscape. They often are firms that, because of increasing returns to scale, would enjoy substantial market power in the absence of regulation. Regulatory theory is thus meant to apply to military and nonmilitary contractors, to utilities (gas, electricity, telecommunications), and to transportation authorities (railroads, canals, local transit systems).

We are by no means not the first to analyze regulation as an agency relationship. In the early 1980s the pioneering work of Baron and Myerson (1982) and Sappington (1982, 1983), spurred by a paper of Loeb and Magat (1979), demonstrated that certain techniques (e.g., developed by Mirrlees 1971; Green and Laffont 1979; and Mussa and Rosen 1978) could be fruitfully employed to analyze the control of natural monopolies as an asymmetric information problem in which the firm has more information about its technology than the regulator. This work led the way to other very important contributions by researchers whose work we describe in the bibliographic notes. Because this book focuses on our work, we will try to explain the contributions of, and give due credit to, this vast literature in bibliographic notes located at the end of each chapter. Besides making substantial use of the insights obtained by these authors, we also borrow heavily from the less specific literatures on principal-agent theory and game theory developed in the 1970s and the 1980s. Our debt to those who fashioned those theories will become clear as we proceed.

The theoretical literature on regulation under asymmetric information has focused mostly on the use of demand data, more precisely on the control of prices charged by regulated firms to consumers. While this is an important dimension of regulation, many if not most regulatory schemes that have been tried also make use of observed accounting data such as costs or profits. Examples of such schemes are cost-reimbursement rules in procurement, cost-of-service pricing, and sliding scale plans in regulation.[1] Our approach presumes the observability of both accounting data and demand data and treats cost-reimbursement rules as central to the design of regulatory policy. As explained in section 4 of the introductory chapter, the regulator can reduce the rent derived by the regulated firm from its superior information by bearing part of the cost. Cost sharing between the government and the regulated firm, however, lowers the firm's motivation to reduce costs and generates an incentive problem that is absent when only demand data are observable. Much of our work is concerned with the sensitivity of the power (i.e., the fraction of costs born by the firm) of optimal incentive schemes to changes in factors such as uncertainty, product market competition, quality concerns, bidding competition, dynamics, and collusion.

The structure of the model will remain the same as we move along the chapters. This unified apparatus offers two advantages. Pedagogically, the reader will not need to invest in new modeling to study each economic issue. Conceptually, our work represents a controlled experiment. When studying a new chapter, the reader will not need to wonder whether the results are driven by modeling changes relative to previous chapters or by the economic phenomenon that is the focus of the chapter.

As its title indicates, this book is meant to develop a theory of incentives in regulation and procurement. By this, we do not mean that all chapters apply equally well to the two contexts. Subsection 1.4 of the introductory chapter lists some differences that will be refined in the other chapters. We feel, however, that regulation and procurement share enough features to vindicate a single approach. Nor is the analysis limited to government control of natural monopolies. Several conclusions apply, for example, to

1. The newly proposed price-cap scheme is not formally based on cost data, but previous costs or profits do influence regulatory reviews.

the design of managerial incentives within firms. Indeed we will at times use corporate analogies to strengthen the intuition. Thus, while focusing on regulation and procurement, this book can be used as part of either a graduate course on regulation or of a graduate course in contract theory.

The book is organized as follows: The introductory chapter summarizes regulatory practice, recounts the history of thought that led to the emergence of the "new regulatory economics," sets up the basic structure of our model and previews the economic questions tackled in the next seventeen chapters. Each chapter starts with a discussion of the economic issues, an informal description of the model, and an overview of the results and intuition. It then develops the formal analysis, including sufficient explanations for those with little training in information economics or game theory. Bibliographic notes provide the reader with an historical perspective of developments in the area and a description of complementary research. The bibliographic notes are not intended to provide a comprehensive survey of the literature on regulation. They merely attempt to describe papers in this literature that can be recast in the framework of this book. The concluding chapter discusses important areas for future work in regulatory economics. The reader will find a set of review problems at the end of the book.

How to Use the Book for Coursework

As mentioned above, the book can be used as part of a graduate course on regulation or contract theory. The material that we suggest can be assigned differs between the two courses.

A first graduate course on regulation might use sections 1 and 2 of the introductory chapter on the regulatory environment and institutions and section 4 of the introductory chapter on the methodology of the book. It could then move onto chapter 1 (putting particular emphasis on cost-reimbursement rules, yardstick competition, and underinvestment effects) and chapter 2 on pricing; develop the multiproduct and price discrimination analysis of chapter 3 in the simplified case of symmetric information between the regulator and the firm; mention a few principles of pricing in a competitive environment derived in chapter 5; go through the introduction of chapter 7 to discuss the costs and benefits of auctions; analyze the trade-off associated with second sourcing (chapter 8); and follow with chapter 11 to introduce regulatory capture and its effects. Some bibliographic notes (in particular those of chapter 2) ought to complement the presentation.

Needless to say, several topics that are often presented in a graduate regulation course are not covered, or are not fully covered, in this book. Our introduction to regulatory institutions could be usefully complemented by richer descriptions of institutional matters: for example, Scherer (1964), Peck and Scherer (1964), Stubbing (1986), Fox (1988), and Gansler (1989) on defense procurement; Kahn (1970), Breyer (1982), Berg and Tschirhart (1988), Sherman (1989), and Spulber (1989) on regulation. The books by Brown and Sibley (1986) and Wilson (1992) treat Ramsey pricing and price discrimination in greater depth than we do in chapter 3. Traditional approaches to utility behavior, such as the analysis of the Averch-Johnson effect, are more developed in the books on regulation cited above. Spulber (1989) contains a good discussion of several approaches not covered in this book. We also recommend using specific industry studies (there are too many books and articles to cite here). Finally, our book does not cover topics such as the regulation of environmental externalities, that of job safety, and that of more competitive industries such as health, banking, insurance, and airlines.[2] All of these topics are important in their own right, and we can only refer to standard reading lists and to the *Handbook of Industrial Organization* for references.

A first graduate contract theory course might make use of section 4 of the introductory chapter on the methodology, chapter 1, some of chapter 4, and chapters 7, 9, 10, and 11. Laffont (1989) offers the most extensive treatment of contract theory available. At a lower level, the book by Milgrom and Roberts (1992) will serve as a useful motivation and introduction. Let us also mention the surveys by Hart and Holmström (1987), which offers a good introduction to the methodology of moral hazard, labor contracts, and incomplete contracting theories; by Holmström and Tirole (1989), which covers a broader range of topics and is nontechnical; and by Fudenberg and Tirole (1991, ch. 7), which gives a self-contained exposition of mechanism design with single or multiple agents.

A set of review problems can be found at the end of the book. These review problems often study issues that were only mentioned in passing in this book. While some are straightforward, most are difficult. Solutions to the review problems, prepared by Peter Klibanoff, are available to instructors from The MIT Press. This booklet of solutions also contains a set of easier review exercises and questions that may be more appropriate for a first course.

Many of the chapters build on our previously published research:

Using cost observation to regulate firms. 1986. *Journal of Political Economy* 94: 614–641. (Chapters 1 and 2)

2. Besides the regulation of natural monopolies, Joskow and Noll (1981) consider regulation of price and entry in relatively competitive industries (e.g., airlines) and regulation for market failures (externalities, information) with applications to safety standards, health coverage, environmental issues, and so forth. A few insights obtained in this book are relevant to these "nonpersonnalized" forms of regulation to the extent that the industry is relatively cohesive.

The regulation of multiproduct firms. I: Theory. 1990. *Journal of Public Economics* 43: 1–36. (Chapters 2 and 3)

The regulation of multiproduct firms. II: Applications and policy analysis. 1990. *Journal of Public Economics* 43: 37–66. (Chapters 2 and 5)

Provision of quality and power of incentive schemes in regulated industries. 1991. In *Equilibrium Theory and Applications* (Proceedings of the Sixth International Symposium in Economic Theory and Econometrics), ed. by J. Gabszewicz and A. Mas-Colell. Cambridge University Press. (Chapter 4)

Bypass and cream skimming. 1990. *American Economic Review* 80: 1042–1061. (Chapter 6)

Auctioning incentive contracts. 1987. *Journal of Political Economy* 95: 921–937. (Chapter 7)

Repeated auctions of incentive contracts, investment and bidding parity. 1988. *Rand Journal of Economics* 19: 516–537. (Chapter 8)

Comparative statics of the optimal dynamic incentives contract. 1987. *European Economic Review* 31: 901–926. (Chapter 9)

The dynamics of incentive contracts. 1988. *Econometrica* 56: 1153–1175. (Chapter 9)

Adverse selection and renegotiation in procurement. 1990. *Review of Economic Studies* 75: 597–626. (Chapter 10)

The politics of government decision making: A theory of regulatory capture. 1991. *Quarterly Journal of Economics* 106: 1089–1127. (Chapter 11)

Cost padding, auditing and collusion. 1992. *Annales d'Économie et Statistique* 25–26: 205–226. (Chapter 12)

Auction design and favoritism. 1991. *International Journal of Industrial Organization* 9: 9–42. (Chapter 14)

The politics of government decision making: Regulatory institutions. 1990. *Journal of Law, Economics and Organization* 6: 1–32. (Chapter 15)

Should governments commit? 1992. *European Economic Review* 36: 345–353. (Chapter 16)

Privatization and incentives. 1991. *Journal of Law, Economics, and Organization* 6: 1–32. (Chapter 17)

REFERENCES

Baron, D., and R. Myerson. 1982. Regulating a monopolist with unknown costs. *Econometrica* 50:911–930.

Berg, S., and T. Tschirhart. 1988. *Natural Monopoly Regulation.* Cambridge: Cambridge University Press.

Breyer, S. 1982. *Regulation and Its Reform*. Cambridge, MA: Harvard University Press.

Brown, S., and D. Sibley. 1986. *The Theory of Public Utility Pricing*. Cambridge: Cambridge University Press.

Fox, R. 1988. *The Defense Management Challenge: Weapons Acquisition*. Cambridge, MA: Harvard Business School Press.

Fudenberg, D., and J. Tirole. 1991. *Game Theory*. Cambridge, MA: MIT Press.

Gansler, J. 1989. *Affording Defense*. Cambridge, MA: MIT Press.

Green, J., and J.-J. Laffont. 1979. *Incentives in Public Decision Making*. Amsterdam: North-Holland.

Hart, O., and B. Holmström. 1987. The theory of contracts. In *Advances in Economic Theory, Fifth World Congress*, ed. T. Bewley. Cambridge: Cambridge University Press.

Holmström, B., and J. Tirole. 1989. The theory of the firm. In *The Handbook of Industrial Organization*, ed. R. Schmalensee and R. Willig. Amsterdam: North-Holland.

Joskow, P., and R. Noll. 1981. Regulation in theory and practice: An overview. In *Studies in Public Regulation*, ed. G. Fromm. Cambridge, MA: MIT Press.

Kahn, A. 1971. *The Economics of Regulation: Principles and Institutions*. Vols. 1 and 2. New York: Wiley. Reprint Cambridge, MA: MIT Press, 1988.

Laffont, J.-J. 1989. *The Economics of Uncertainty and Information*. Cambridge, MA: MIT Press.

Loeb, M., and W. Magat. 1979. A decentralized method of utility regulation. *Journal of Law and Economics* 22:399–404.

Milgrom, P., and J. Roberts. 1992. *Economics, Organization and Management*. Englewood Cliffs, NJ: Prentice-Hall.

Mirrlees, J. 1971. An exploration in the theory of optimum income taxation. *Review of Economic Studies* 38:175–208.

Mussa, M., and S. Rosen. 1978. Monopoly and product quality. *Journal of Economic Theory* 18:301–317.

Peck, M., and F. Scherer. 1962. *The Weapons Acquisition Process: An Economic Analysis*. Cambridge, MA: Harvard Business School Press.

Sappington, D. 1982. Optimal regulation of research and development under imperfect information. *Bell Journal of Economics* 13:354–368.

Sappington, D. 1983. Optimal regulation of a multiproduct monopoly with unknown technological capabilities. *Bell Journal of Economics* 14:453–463.

Scherer, F. 1964. *The Weapons Acquisition Process: Economic Incentives*. Cambridge, MA: Harvard Business School Press.

Sherman, R. 1989. *The Regulation of Monopoly*. Cambridge: Cambridge University Press.

Spulber, D. 1989. *Regulation and Markets*. Cambridge, MA: MIT Press.

Stubbing, R. 1986. *The Defense Game*. New York: Harper and Row.

Waterson, M. 1988. *Regulation of the Firm and Natural Monopoly*. Cambridge, MA: Blackwell.

Wilson, R. 1992. *Nonlinear Pricing*. Oxford: Oxford University Press, forthcoming.

ACKNOWLEDGMENTS

In the decade that has elapsed between the conception of this book and its publication, many people have given us everyday support and advice. Those who helped improve the articles published in professional journals are too numerous to cite here. Special thanks, however, are due to Paul Joskow and Richard Schmalensee for regulatory theory and practice, and Drew Fudenberg, Jerry Green, Roger Guesnerie, Oliver Hart, Bengt Holmström, and Eric Maskin for contract theory.

Patrick Bolton, Mathias Dewatripont, Tracy Lewis, Mike Riordan, Stephan Reichelstein, David Sappington, and John Vickers made very detailed and useful comments on extensive parts of the penultimate manuscript. We thank Claude Crampes, Georges Dionne, Claude Fluet, Claude Henry, and Xavier Freixas for their comments as well.

We would especially like to thank Peter Klibanoff and Dimitri Vayanos for their excellent research assistance. Both read through most of the manuscript, corrected mistakes, and made expositional suggestions. Peter Klibanoff also wrote the answers to the review problems. We were very fortunate to have them work on the book. We are also grateful to our students at MIT (in the basic graduate regulation course and in advanced courses in regulation and contract theory) and at Toulouse (in the Ph.D. program). Many thanks go to our very skillful and cheerful typists, who did a beautiful job. Emily Gallagher typed many chapters, and Marie-Pierre Artigue and Pierrette Vaissade did the rest, all with much proficiency. Joel Gwynn drafted the figures with admirable precision and speed. Last, we would be remiss if we did not thank the staff at The MIT Press for their contributions—Terry Vaughn for his commitment to expediting the publication of this book, Dana Andrus for her high standards and graceful and diligent editing of the final manuscript, Sharon Warne and Mimi Ahmed for their sensitive preparation of the interior and cover designs.

We acknowledge the continuing support over the years of the Center for Energy Policy Research at MIT, the National Science Foundation, and the Pew Charitable Trust. Other institutions also provided financial support and facilities at crucial times in the writing of the book: the Sloan Foundation, the Guggenheim Foundation, the Ford Foundation, the MIT Telecommunications Business and Economics Research Program, the Taussig Visiting Professorship at Harvard, and the French Commissariat au Plan. Without the extremely generous support of all these institutions, we would not have been able to devote the time necessary for this undertaking.

A THEORY OF INCENTIVES IN PROCUREMENT AND REGULATION

INTRODUCTION

1 The Regulatory Environment and Institutions

A theory of regulation or procurement should reflect the regulatory environment. Although it need not fit with practice—commonly used schemes may not always be well conceived—it must be consistent with the firms' and regulators' information structures, constraints, and feasible instruments.

1.1 Regulatory Constraints

There are three types of regulatory constraints: informational, transactional, and administrative and political. In practice these constraints prevent the regulator from implementing his or her preferred policy (whatever it may be).

Informational Constraints

Regulators cannot rely on regulatory contracts that are contingent on information held only by the firm (or more generally on information not easily verifiable by a court). Informational constraints thus limit the efficiency of control of industries by government agencies. It is customary to distinguish between two types of informational constraints: moral hazard and adverse selection.

Moral hazard refers to *endogenous* variables that are not observed by the regulator. The firm takes discretionary actions that affect its cost or the quality of its products. The generic label for such discretionary actions is *effort*. It stands for the number of office hours put in by a firm's managers or for the intensity of their work. But it should be interpreted more broadly. Managers' allocation of perks (hiring personnel to lighten their work loads, inattention to excessive inventories of inputs, etc.), indulgence in activities that privilege their career potential over efficiency, delay of distasteful actions (e.g., layoffs during periods of low activity), purchase of materials and equipment at high prices, and hoarding of engineers or machines not required under current contracts but useful for commercial profits or for winning future contracts are examples of "negative effort."

Adverse selection arises when the firm has more information than the regulator about some *exogenous* variables. Most observers have emphasized the importance of adverse selection in regulation and procurement.[1]

1. How information can be manipulated by regulated firms is succinctly stated by Owen and Braeutigam (1978, p. 4):

> The ability to control the flow of information to the regulatory agency is a crucial element in affecting decisions. Agencies can be guided in the desired direction by making available carefully selected facts. Alternatively, the withholding of information can be used to compel a lawsuit for "production" when delay is advantageous. Delay can also be achieved by overresponse: flooding the agency with more information than it can absorb. Sometimes, when a specific item of information is requested and it is difficult or impossible to delay in providing it, the best tactic is to bury it in a mountain of irrelevant material. This is a familiar tactic of attorneys in antitrust suits. It is also sometimes useful to provide the

This asymmetry of information is likely to bear on the firm's technological possibilities or on the difficulty in implementing certain productive tasks. For instance, defense contractors are usually better informed than the Department of Defense about the likely cost of developing a new weapons system.[2] Similarly several authors have observed that AT&T, and not the Federal Communications Commission, has expertise to forecast the costs of telecommunication services,[3] that electric utilities know more than Public Utility Commissions.[4] But the firm's informational advantage can also bear on the demand curve in a regulatory context (in the case of government procurement the buyer is by definition the government itself, so the firm is less likely to have superior information about demand). Although the government can order demand studies whenever the informational asymmetry about demand imposes substantial inefficiencies in the regulatory outcome, frequent interaction with consumers (or wholesalers) may make such surveys less costly to the firm than to the regulator.[5]

In general, adverse selection allows the firm to extract a rent from its interaction with the government even if its bargaining power is poor.[6] Suppose that the firm's cost for a given level of cost-reducing activity can be high or low and that the firm knows which state of nature prevails. A regulator who must ensure that the firm supplies goods or services must guarantee that the firm is willing to participate in the production process even if it faces intrinsically high costs. That is, the firm must enjoy a nonnegative rent even if it is inefficient. Therefore the firm enjoys a rent when its intrinsic cost is low.[7] (A word on terminology: We will sometimes

> information but to deny its reliability and to commence a study to acquire more reliable data. Another option is to provide "accurate" information unofficially to selected personnel of the agency who are known to be sympathetic. If another party has supplied damaging information, it is important to supply contrary information in as technical a form as possible so that a hearing is necessary to settle the issues of "fact."

2. Robert Keller, former assistant comptroller general of the United States gives an archetypal assessment of informational asymmetries in procurement (quoted by Yuspeh 1976):

> The government negotiator generally is at a disadvantage in trying to negotiate, since the contractor knows not only all the facts and the assumptions underlying his estimates, the alternatives available to him, and the contingent areas, but he also knows the price at which he will be willing to accept the contract.

Similar assessments can be found in Scherer (1964, p. 227), for example.

3. For examples Breyer (1982, p. 307), Brock and Evans (1983, p. 76), and Owen and Braeutigam (1979, chs. 2, 7).

4. See Joskow and Schmalensee (1986, p. 12).

5. Such studies by regulator cannot use proprietary data.

6. Substantial rents are involved at the contracting stage; see, for example, Rogerson (1989) who estimates the value of winning an aerospace contract using event study methodology.

7. At worst the firm could lower its cost-reducing activity below the socially optimal level and produce at the high cost that would have been its cost had it been inefficient. This slack provides the firm with more utility than it would have had, had it been inefficient, and hence with a strictly positive rent. While the essence of the rent is the possibility of economizing on effort, we will see that the firm enjoys a monetary rent under optimal regulation; as Kahn (1970, vol. 2, p. 62) notes, asymmetric information gives rise to undesirable rents by rewarding good luck and favorable external developments.

speak of an "inefficient firm" or an "efficient firm" to signify "the firm when its intrinsic cost is high" and "the firm when its intrinsic cost is low." That is, unless otherwise specified, there is only one firm, but this firm can have several incarnations. In the tradition of the principal-agent literature, we will also talk about the firm's "type.")

The presence of moral hazard and adverse selection, and the concomitant loss of control for the regulator, create a demand for information gathering. In most countries public enterprises are periodically monitored by public audits. Similarly private regulated firms are subject to controls by agencies, and they sometimes have their cost disallowed. It is worth emphasizing the limits of such procedures. Audits can verify that costs are recorded according to standard accounting procedures and that no major improprieties (e.g., embezzlement) have been committed by the firm. They also measure the firm's total cost; they usually cannot disentangle its various components. Most dimensions of moral hazard and adverse selection do not show up in accounting statements. (An alternative way of putting this is that we will be concerned by the residual asymmetries of information left by the accounting process.)[8] Except in chapter 12, this book takes the auditing structure as given, but it will discuss alternative and more subtle ways of creating information to lessen the informational asymmetries: the promotion of competition (part III) and the involvement of watchdog supervisors (chapter 15).

Transactional Constraints

Contracts are costly to write and enforce and are likely to be somewhat incomplete (i.e., to omit some contingencies).[9] Williamson (1975) distinguished several kinds of "transaction costs." First, future contingencies must be considered; they may require long and costly studies. Second, contingencies must be unambiguously specified by the regulatory contract; the cost here is the time spent to instruct lawyers plus their legal fees. Third, the agreement must be monitored and enforced by a court.

Transaction costs are higher when contingencies are harder to foresee and formulate in a clear manner. For this reason one would expect the part of the contract concerning the near future to be more complete than that concerning the distant future. For instance, the contract may pre-

8. Public auditors sometimes make specific recommendations about the management of the firm. In the United States they recommended the closure of some unprofitable Amtrak train services. In France the Cour des Comptes sometimes suggests ways of cutting cost. But the recommendations do not need to be binding, and the small size of the staff of public auditing bodies, and their imperfect knowledge of the technology, considerably limit the scope of intervention. See Normanton (1966) for an extensive discussion of state audits in various countries.

9. Note the distinction between a complete (or comprehensive) contract and an incomplete contract. A contract that is not contingent on some (moral hazard or adverse selection) unobservable variables is nevertheless complete if it is contingent on all variables that are verifiable by a court.

cisely describe the product to be supplied in the next two-year production run but may leave unspecified the design adjustments for the future production runs. For the same reason one would expect contracts to be more incomplete in high-tech industries than in traditional industries. A case in point is defense contracting. The high uncertainty associated with a new weapons system naturally splits the acquisition cycle in several steps: preliminary studies, prototype building, full-scale development, and (possibly several stages of) production. Leaving aside the constraints on commitment to be discussed shortly, one would expect the production aspect of defense contracts covering prototype building and full-scale development to be poorly specified early in the acquisition cycle because ex ante the final product is hard to define.

Williamson (1975, 1985) and Grossman and Hart (1986) have shown that the governance structure (in particular, the pattern of ownership of assets) matters in the presence of transaction costs. The contingencies that are left out of the incomplete contract must be filled in. The authority relationship induced by the ownership of assets defines the status quo for the renegotiation about what is to be done when the unforeseen contingency occurs.

While chapters 9, 15, 16, and 17 incorporate transaction costs into the analysis, most of the book adopts the better-established methodology of complete contracting and emphasizes informational constraints over transactional constraints.

Administrative and Political Constraints

Regulators are constrained by federal codes of regulation, administrative procedure acts, or laws. First, the *scope* of regulation is limited. An agency such as the U.S. Federal Communications Commission has the authority to regulate telecommunications. Nevertheless, it cannot intervene in the computer industry, although the recent developments have brought together the two technologies and raised the question of their interface. As another example, the U.S. Environmental Protection Agency is allowed to regulate chemicals but not drugs or food additives.

Second, regulators cannot use any *instrument* they wish. The Environmental Protection Agency can only ban or allow some chemicals; it may use more sophisticated instruments such as tax incentives for some others. An instrument that is of much interest for our analysis is the transfer from the government to the regulated firm. Transfers to defense contractors are unavoidable because the buyer is the government. In the case of a regulated firm, costs can be paid through direct charges to consumers. For instance, while transfers (appropriations) are allowed in some regulated industries in Europe and in the railroad, subway, and postal systems in the United States, current U.S. legislation specifies that regulators cannot fine utilities or make payment subsidies to power and telecommunications industries.

Third, regulatory contracts extending beyond some specified *time horizon* may be illegal. In the United States electric utility regulators cannot sign binding long-term contracts with the firms they regulate. Also there has been much debate about allowing the Department of Defense (DOD) to engage in multiyear procurement (i.e., to commit funds for a substantial part of or the complete project).

These three constraints define a subset of feasible contracts in the set defined by the informational and transactional constraints. A fourth kind of administrative constraint involves *procedural requirements*. These requirements describe the way regulators can collect information and select and deal with the firms. The U.S. 1946 Administrative Procedures Act requires agencies to conduct regulatory hearings. They must warn, solicit comments, allow participation, and accept evidence. Similarly the Federal Acquisitions Regulation, Department of Defense directives, and services regulations specify in much detail source selection policies, including the draft solicitations to obtain comments, the identification and development of objective criteria (technical, cost, schedule, manufacturing, performance risks), the auction techniques, the organization of the selection committee, and the appropriateness of contacts with the industry. Agencies must also follow imposed standards of evidence (e.g., in the United States drugs must be proved safe to be marketed, while chemicals must be proved unsafe not to be marketed, which obviously makes a difference). Last, agencies may be constrained to formulate standards and follow their own rules; this may prevent them from discriminating between two distinct situations on the basis of soft (nonverifiable) information.

To this list of administrative constraints must be added political ones that may result from acts of Congress or local legislatures in the United States (i.e., the committees in charge of overseeing the regulatory agency) or of the executive branch in other countries. Politicians may be able to affect agency decisions by their control of appropriations of the agency and by the threats of shifting responsibilities of the agency and of impeaching its top officials or humiliating them during public hearings.

These administrative and political constraints have by and large been ignored by both the received theory and the new regulatory economics. Our philosophy, as developed in the last part of this book, is that such constraints are not exogenous but are driven by informational and transactional constraints. They have to do with the fact that regulators themselves are agents for other parties (politicians and more fundamentally their constituency). The welfare theory of agencies argues that they are created and given substantial powers because of the need to obtain information about regulatory trade-offs. However, regulators may have their own objectives and must be given incentives to implement the goals of the political principals.[10]

Thus the intent behind not letting an administration write long-term contracts with suppliers seems to be to limit externalities across administrations: By not letting the current administration bind future ones, the law reduces the efficiency of contracts but increases the accountability of each administration. Similarly the prohibition of transfers from the government to regulated firms could be traced to a fear that regulators might abuse this instrument. The procedural requirements are meant to restrain secret deals between the agency and the industry or other interest groups, to generate information for the political principals and to allow them to react to proposed policies; they are instruments for the control of agencies. Thus the study of "hierarchical regulation," as it pertains to the governance of multitiered regulatory and political structures, should be a central piece of the agenda for the new regulatory economics.

1.2 Regulatory Instruments and Incentive Schemes

Regulators use accounting and demand data to monitor a firm's performance. *Accounting data* are mainly the firm's aggregate cost or profit. Many incentive schemes are based on cost data (section 2 discusses commonly used schemes in more detail). A typical procurement contract has the government reimburse a fraction $b \in [0,1]$ of the firm's monetary expenditures C. We will adopt the convention that the government pays the firm's cost and then pays a net transfer t to the firm:

$$t = a - bC,$$

where a is a "fixed fee" and b is the fraction of costs born by the firm (alternatively, one could adopt the convention that the firm pays for its cost and that the government reimburses a fraction $1 - b$ of the cost and gives a fee a); b is the *power* of the incentive scheme. There are two common polar cases of such linear schemes:

1. The cost-plus-fixed-fee or *cost-plus* contract ($b = 0$). The firm does not bear any of its cost. The cost-plus contract is an extremely low-powered incentive scheme.

2. The *fixed-price* contract ($b = 1$). The firm is residual claimant for its cost savings. The government does not de facto reimburse any of the costs; it pays only a fixed fee. The fixed-price contract is an extremely high-powered incentive scheme.

Linear contracts with a slope b strictly between 0 and 1 are called "incentive contracts." Real-world contracts are often linear, but some have

10. Politicians should actually be given incentives to seek social welfare as they themselves have their own goals and are not perfect agents for the voters.

nonlinear features such as a ceiling on transfers from the government or a guarantee that the firm will not lose money. (Those contracts are then often piecewise linear. Another example of a piecewise linear contract is a managerial stock option, which rewards the manager linearly in the value of the firm beyond some threshold.)

Cost data play a similar role in some regulated industries' profit-sharing schemes such as the sliding scale mechanisms (in which prices are adjusted to move the firm's rate of return partly toward a target rate of return) or the related partial overall cost adjustment mechanisms (in which prices move up and down less than proportionally with changes in costs). Cost data also play an important role in cost-of-service (or average-cost-pricing) regulation, whereby (in theory) the regulator chooses prices so as to equate revenue from charges to consumers and cost.

Allocating aggregate cost among projects or product lines is generally considered difficult. On the one hand, several costs (facilities, machines, management, accounting, marketing, etc.) may be common to several activities. The firm can manipulate accounting procedures to reallocate costs to its advantage. On the other hand, the managers can also assign their best engineers to or exert their supervisory or cost-reducing effort in those activities with a smaller fraction of reimbursed cost. The "fully distributed cost schemes" used in some industries represent an attempt to allocate aggregate cost among activities. Their basic defect is that they use mechanical rules to determine the distribution of joint costs (e.g., allocation of joint costs proportionally to outputs). Such schemes are orthogonal to the efficiency concern of charging prices that reflect marginal costs; furthermore they introduce perverse incentives in the pattern of cost reduction.

Subcosts are sometimes used in formal incentive schemes when the accounting manipulations and input allocations are thought not to affect their measures too much. These subcosts can be "external," such as those of raw material, subcontracting, or the workers' hourly wage. Or they can be "internal" in the sense that they represent the performance of a cost center (design, manufacturing, distribution).

The *demand data* on which contracts can most easily be based are prices and quantities. To these must be added some verifiable dimensions of quality. For instance, there have been attempts to create objective measures of the punctuality and quality of services of Amtrak passenger trains.[11] Regulatory contracts with an electric utility can be based on the number of outages. Other commonly used demand data are delays in procurement, number of repeat buyers, number of customer complaints, and product image among customers. Note that formally the verifiable dimensions of quality can be treated as quantities of fictitious goods.

11. See, for example, Baumol (1975).

Hence we can lump outputs and verifiable quality together for modeling purposes.

1.3 Simple versus Informationally Demanding Regulatory Rule

We now discuss the informational requirements of regulatory recommendations. An interesting issue with a theory of regulation is whether its recommendations are simple. If by chance they are, their implementation is straightforward. It suffices that the agency be instructed to passively follow the rule prescribed by the economist. A simple rule can be described by an economist lacking detailed knowledge of the cost and demand functions, and yet is comprehensive enough to be readily applicable by—that is, leave no discretion to—regulators.[12] In contrast, an informationally demanding rule requires the regulator's knowledge of some demand and cost data and therefore leaves discretion to the regulator having these data.

It is worth emphasizing the distinction between "informationally demanding" and "complex." Complexity more vaguely refers to the degree of mathematical sophistication or subtlety of the rule. "Choose prices so as to equate revenue and cost over some regulatory period" or "charge marginal cost for each product" is not a complex rule, yet either one is informationally very demanding. While regulatory rules must be fully comprehended by agency personnel, the complexity of rules does not seem to be a major obstacle to efficient regulation.

An optimal regulatory rule is likely to use pieces of information about technology and demand held by the regulator. There is nothing wrong with the use of an informationally demanding rule. The economist can instruct the regulator to offer the firm the optimal regulatory scheme conditional on the regulator's information. But, unlike a simple rule, an informationally demanding rule is not always robust to the perversion of regulatory behavior. The agency may not exert enough effort to collect information about the industry, and it may use its information strategically to reach its own goals or to collude with the industry or other interest groups. If the optimal rule is not simple and if the agency is not benevolent and cannot be perfectly monitored, the model must be enriched to describe the agency's incentives and behavior.

1.4 Procurement versus Regulation

The relationship of government with its suppliers and the regulation of utilities are not subject to the same administrative and political constraints. The hierarchical structure of the regulatory body, its relationship with the executive, the hearing procedures, and the available instruments

12. A simple rule generally uses information held by the firm, but it can be fully deferential to the firm since it does not make use of information held by the regulator.

differ for the procurement of a weapons system and for the regulation of an electric utility. To grasp the rationale behind these points of departure, we must first understand more primitive differences that result from the very definition of procurement and regulation. Although taxonomies are always arbitrary, we find it instructive to refer to procurement when the firm supplies a good to the government and to regulation when it supplies a good to consumers on behalf of the government. Thus our definition of procurement is that the principal and the buyer coincide.

This distinction uncovers some important differences between procurement and regulation. First, as we noted earlier, the prohibition of transfers from the government to the firm is not a relevant option under procurement because the firm would be unable to recover any of its costs.

Second, it may be harder to give incentives to supply nonverifiable quality in procurement. If the quality can be observed by the consumer(s) before purchase (which does not imply that it can be costlessly described ex ante in a contract and verified ex post by a court), the demand for the (search) good is a proxy for its level of quality, and incentives to supply high quality can be provided by rewarding the firm more when sales are high. In a regulatory situation sales levels can be a useful, albeit imperfect, signal of quality because consumers have no individual incentive to distort their demand to affect the firm's reward. In a procurement context the regulator realizes that an increase in the demand for the good raises the reward to the firm and may thus have an incentive to distort the demand. This is not to say that sales incentives are impossible to create in procurement, but that their efficiency is lessened by the need to elicit the true demand for the good by the regulator. (This effect is only a conjecture and is not studied in this book.)

Third, the fact that consumers have no individual stake in procurement (the taxpayers do but are poorly organized) means that they are unlikely to be active in hearings and to act as watchdogs of the agency (unless the good procured is a local public good and local advocacy groups are well organized) This suggests that procurement agencies may be even freer to collude with the industry than their regulatory counterparts and that the procurement agencies may correspondingly be more bureaucratized (be given less discretion).

We should emphasize that the exact link between these primitive differences between procurement and regulation and the associated administrative and political constraints is still unknown to us or is in a state of conjecture. We only want to reiterate the point made in section 1.1 that institutions are endogenous and should as much as possible be explained by primitive considerations.

Another distinction between procurement and regulation is more circumstantial and less fundamental; it can be attributed to the fact that weapons acquisition is the procurement activity that draws the most attention. Defense contracting tends to involve more technologically complex and novel products than many regulatory activities. This may result (but we have no supporting evidence) in quantitative differences such as a higher degree of informational asymmetry or a higher difficulty to commit to long-term contracts because of the difficulty of giving a precise specification of the good in the future. We should note furthermore that one can easily find counterexamples to the proposition that procurement activities involve more technological uncertainty (compare the procurement of basic supplies like buildings or furniture for the government and the supply of telecommunication services).

2 Commonly Used Incentive Schemes

The purpose of this book is not to give a detailed analysis of actual incentive schemes used in regulation and procurement but rather to develop a normative theory that will shed some light on current practice and lead to ideas on how to improve upon it. To this end it is useful to briefly recall the main features of current schemes, for practice will guide modeling choices throughout this book: The schemes reveal feasible regulatory instruments, and together with regulatory institutions, they suggest the main problems confronted by regulation. This section will be useful to those who lack familiarity with regulatory institutions.

Current incentive schemes can be analyzed along two dividing lines. The first is whether the government is allowed to subsidize (or tax) regulated firms, that is, whether regulated firms can receive public funds and thus not cover all their costs through direct charges to private customers. Transfers can take several forms: direct subsidies, government loans at low interest rates or not meant to be repaid, free government guarantees when the firm borrows on the private market, transfers of public inputs at deflated prices, and so forth.

Such transfers to the firm necessarily take place in the procurement of public projects such as weapons acquisition: Since the government is the only buyer, costs cannot be covered through charges to private customers. Transfers are also quite common when the regulated firm is a state enterprise. For instance, U.S. railroads received subsidies after their nationalization in 1976. Similarly the U.S. Postal Service has received appropriations.[13]

In the case of public enterprises such as Électricité de France, which are not supposed to receive transfers from the government but can borrow

13. Unlike defense procurement, postal costs are covered partly by the government and partly by the private users. For instance, the 1970 U.S. Postal Reorganization Act states that postal rates must provide sufficient revenues so that total estimated income and appropriations equal total estimated costs.

Table 1
Power of commonly used incentive schemes

Power	Transfer allowed? Yes (procurement, most public enterprises)	No (most private regulated firms)
Very high (firm residual claimant)	Fixed-price contracts	Price caps
Intermediate (cost or profit sharing)	Incentive contracts	Incentive regulation
Very low (government or consumers residual claimants)	Cost-plus contracts	Cost-of-service regulation

subject to the approval of the Ministry of Finance, one should still reason as if the firm receives transfers as long as its intertemporal budget constraint is interpreted loosely, and the government otherwise conducts an optimal financial policy. In other words, when the firm borrows $1, the rest of the state would reduce its own borrowing by $1 and raise taxes by $1. At the margin of an optimal financial policy, welfare is unaffected by the reduction in borrowing and the increase in taxes, and everything is as if the firm received $1 from the government raised through taxes. Last, transfers can take place in some industries where firms are not public enterprises. A case in point is Medicare reimbursement.[14] Still in several other industries, in particular in the United States where most regulated firms are privately owned, regulators are not allowed by current legislation to fine utilities or make payment subsidies to them.

The second dividing line is the power of incentive schemes, that is, the link between the firm's transfer from the government and/or the firm's prices and its cost or profit performance. This dividing line is important because it underlies the philosophy of the three broad classes of incentive schemes encountered in practice and summarized in table 1. It is important, however, to note that there is a stark difference between the *spirit* of some incentive schemes and their *application*. As will be later discussed, economic and political considerations have induced some convergence between, for instance, price caps and cost-of-service regulation.[15]

14. Another example is given by operating franchises (see Schmalensee 1978, pp. 75–81), as in the Paris bus, trolley, and subway systems earlier in this century and in the dockyards in Britain. The assets of such franchises are government owned but privately managed. Franchise bidding among potential operators as well as incentive schemes lead to transfers between the government and regulated firms.

15. Another point worth noting is that the firm's reward for intermediate- and low-powered incentive schemes must depend on realized performance, and therefore transfers are necessarily retrospective. When transfers are allowed, whether the reward for the performance at date τ is transferred at date τ or (as auditing of performance requires) at $(\tau + 1)$ is irrelevant under perfect capital markets. The retrospective feature, however, matters when costs and rewards must be covered by direct charges to customers. While in theory the price p_τ charged to

2.1 Procurement Contracts[16]

This subsection describes some incentive schemes commonly used when transfers are allowed. While our definition of procurement (the government is the only buyer) does not encompass all industries in which transfers are allowed, procurement, and in particular defense procurement, offers a useful illustration of such schemes.

In the "cost-plus-fixed-fee contract" or, more simply, the "cost-plus contract," the government pays the contractor its realized cost and sets a fixed fee. The fixed fee is independent of actual performance, although its level is implicitly related to the size of the project.[17] At the opposite end of the spectrum is the "firm fixed-price contract" or, more simply, "fixed-price contract." In between these two extremes lie the "incentive contracts" (sometimes called the "fixed-price incentive contracts") in which the contractor and the government share realized costs according to some predetermined sharing rule. In the United States incentive contracts and fixed-price contracts are often subject to profit ceilings established by Congress and the DOD.

Scherer (1964, p. 134) reports that "historically, profit-sharing agreements have stipulated a contractor's share of from 10% to 30% in cost overruns or underruns, although recently the use of higher sharing proportions has been encouraged." In 1960, 40.9% of U.S. military procurement dollars involved cost-plus contracts, 13.6% incentive contracts, and 31.4% fixed-price contracts.[18] Reichelstein (1990), quoting a 1987 survey of the U.S. General Accounting Office, says that "for the period 1978–1984, firms' cost share parameters typically varied between 15% and 25%."

One must be careful to distinguish among stages of the procurement life cycle in this respect. A stylized fact is that low-powered contracts are employed much more in the early phase of the life cycle.[19] Another styl-

consumers at date τ ought to depend on the cost target C_τ for date τ, in practice p_τ is determined by past performance $C_{\tau-1}$ rather than by current performance. In other words, realized costs affect prices only with a lag.

16. Useful references concerning procurement practices include Fox (1974, 1988), Kovacic (1990), McAfee and McMillan (1987), Peck and Scherer (1962), Rogerson (1989), Scherer (1964), and Trueger (1966).

17. Before the 1960s fees set by the U.S. DOD were sometimes proportional to realized costs or to costs initially estimated by the firm. Little knowledge of incentive theory is required to understand why such schemes gave rise to perverse incentives: The firm is rewarded rather than penalized for raising its costs. A more current example of such perverse incentives is found in Germany, where pharmacists make more money, the more expensive the drugs they sell. Not surprisingly, "parallel imports" (i.e., drugs purchased cheaply in one country and sold at a higher price in another) have a low market share in Germany (*The Economist*, July 6, 1991, p. 73). Another example, still in Germany, is given by the use of cost-plus-proportional fee contracts for German defense contractors (see Reichelstein 1990).

18. Scherer (1964, p. 142); the rest involves hybrid contracts.

19. For instance, Scherer (1964, p. 145) reports that "in the 'major hard goods' category for fiscal year 1960, roughly 93% by dollar volume of Navy research and development contracts, but only 17% of production contracts were of the cost-reimbursement type."

ized fact is that low-powered contracts are also more employed for high technology than for nonstandard equipment.[20] Later in this book we will relate the theory to these observations about the low power of actual incentive schemes and about the differences in power along the life cycle and across technologies.

Remark Profit-sharing agreements similar to incentive contracts can also be found in some regulated industries (i.e., industries in which the government is not the final customer). For instance, in 1921 the Paris bus and trolley system came to be operated by a private franchisee. The franchisee received a low guaranteed return, a fraction of profits, and a fraction of gross revenues.[21]

2.2 Regulatory Incentive Schemes in the Absence of Government Transfers[22]

As we have already mentioned, many public utilities must cover their costs entirely through charges to customers. Historically the most important method of regulating prices in industries such as telecommunications, energy, and railroads has been cost-of-service regulation.[23] After a growing disenchantment with this form of regulation, attention has focused on alternative and presumably more efficient forms. The 1980s have seen the implementation of several new forms of regulatory mechanisms. In telecommunications, the Office of Telecommunications in Britain adopted price caps for British Telecom in 1984, followed in the United States in 1989 by the Federal Communications Commission for AT&T.[24] In the energy sector, price caps were adopted in 1986 for British Gas, while various forms of incentive regulation were implemented for electric utilities in the United States. Another example of experimentation with new incentive mechanisms is the U.S. Interstate Commerce Commission's allowing railroads to set prices as they wish, subject in particular to the constraints that total revenues must not exceed total costs over rolling four-year horizons

20. Again quoting Scherer (1964, p. 147): "For example, 83.6% of all expenditures on guided missiles during fiscal year 1960 were made under cost-reimbursement-type contracts, while only 9.1% of combat vehicle outlays and 1.6% of clothing outlays were covered by cost-reimbursement contracts."

21. See Schmalensee (1978, p. 76).

22. References about regulatory practices include Breyer (1982), Joskow (1989), Joskow and Schmalensee (1986), Kahn (1970), Spulber (1989), Srinagesh (1990), Vickers and Yarrow (1988), Vickers (1991), a report of the U.S. Federal Energy Regulatory Commission (1989), and a docket of the Federal Communications Commissions (1987). Useful descriptions of incentive regulation in the electric utility industry and in the telecommunications industry can be found in reports by the MIT Energy Laboratory (1984), Nera (1990), and Taylor (1990).

23. In the nineteenth century, that is in the early stages of regulation, price caps were not uncommon. The more general textbook expression for "cost-of-service regulation" is "rate-of-return regulation." We prefer "cost-of-service regulation" because it is more descriptive. Any regulatory regime, and not only cost-of-service regulation, determines some rate of return.

24. See FCC 89-91, CC Docket 87-313. An early example of adoption of price caps in the telecommunications industry is the Michigan Bell Telephone Company in 1980.

and that services that are not supplied competitively must be priced at less than 180% of their variable cost.

Cost-of-Service Regulation

The spirit of cost-of-service (COS) regulation is average cost pricing in that the prices chosen are determined by equating total revenue and total cost.

Revenue Requirement and Price Structure Typically the rates of a privately owned regulated firm (investor-owned utility) are determined in two stages. First, to arrive at the revenue requirement, the regulator looks at historical operating costs (labor, fuel, maintenance) over some reference period, often 12 months, and determines the level of capital stock, the so-called rate base, by estimating depreciation on previous investments. Costs are adjusted by disallowing some unjustified or imprudent expenditures (either input or capital)[25] and then by using projections on inflation and other exogenous future shocks. The regulator attempts to choose a "fair" and "reasonable" rate of return for capital. More precisely he or she tries to find out the alternative cost of the firm's invested capital (cost of debt plus the return on stocks with comparable risks). There is little downward flexibility in this choice in that the rate of return must be consistent with constitutional guarantees against the taking of private property without just compensation, but there is some upward flexibility in the setting of the rate of return (which is used in the alternative form of incentive regulation). The level of allowed cost plus the rate of return applied to the existing stock of capital determines the firm's revenue requirement.

The second stage consists in choosing the price level to equate revenue and revenue requirement, and in choosing the relative prices. A quasi-judicial regulatory hearing allows interested parties (e.g., industry, big customers and smaller consumers through their advocates or the attorney general) to bring relevant information to bear on the determination of the various variables in the two stages.

The first stage can give rise to substantial controversy about what costs to allow, and especially about the measurement of the stock of capital and about the cost of capital.[26] The second stage raises issues of price discrimination and cost allocation among product lines. Limited price discrimination might be allowed but with two constraints. First, some categories of consumers must be effectively insulated from high prices that might result either from a high cost of serving them or from a low elasticity of their demand. Examples for the United States include the prohibition of discrimination against persons or shippers or areas by the Interstate Commerce Act (1887), that of "undue and unreasonable discrimination among

25. For instance, a public utility commission may find that an electric utility purchased fuel at a price exceeding the market price, or that it has made poor investments in power plants (see, e.g., Joskow 1989).

26. See, for example, Kahn (1970) and Berg and Tschirhart (1988, ch. 8) for more details.

mail users" (Section 403c of the 1970 Postal Reorganization Act), and the ceiling on each rail price at 180% of variable cost in order to protect captive shippers such as coal producers and coal using utilities (Staggers Rail Act 1980). Similarly most telephone and electricity companies and post offices do not charge higher rates for rural users. Second, rates must reflect equal access to intermediate goods and services for industrial users. Such constraints on fairness in competition play an important role in the pricing of access to the local telephone network, to wheeling, and to rail bottlenecks. Similar considerations are also often present under incentive regulation or price caps.[27]

How to divvy up the revenue requirement, which determines the average price level, among the consumer groups or products to obtain the relative price structure is another difficult step in COS regulation. Some costs are easily attributable to some product. However, "common costs," such as the capital cost of electricity generation capacity, switches and circuits in telecommunications, or tracks and stations in the rail industry, are not associated with a single product. The regulatory commission generally allocates common costs according to arbitrary accounting rules that "fully distribute costs."[28] For instance, common costs might be allocated proportionally to the products' relative outputs, attributable costs, or revenues.

Once prices are determined, they are fixed until the next regulatory review up to some automatic adjustment clauses. Prices may be indexed to inflation, the price of inputs (e.g., the price of fuel purchased by other utilities), and so forth.

Regulatory Reviews and Regulatory Lags A crucial matter in determining the incentive properties of COS regulation is the length of time over which the output prices are fixed. Because prices are rigid and the firm is a residual claimant for its cost savings between reviews, the practice of COS regulation differs from its cost-plus spirit, which requires that prices track costs on a continuous basis. Indeed, with an infinite regulatory lag, COS regulation would have a fixed-price nature. In practice regulatory reviews are endogenous and can usually be initiated by the regulated firm or the regulatory agency. Quite often a firm facing rising costs of inputs applies to the agency for permission to raise its price. A hearing is held and information is collected on cost and revenue for a "test period" of one year, say. Rate filings, regulatory hearings, and decision making by agencies are lengthy. Price increases are strongly opposed by residential and industrial customers. Prices are quite sticky upward and downward.[29] Nevertheless,

27. Equity considerations are especially important when the supplier is vertically integrated. In the United States, for instance, electric utilities that are integrated backward into generation are required to purchase from qualifying cogenerators at pricing reflecting their "avoided cost." See chapter 5 for a discussion of access pricing.
28. See, for example, Braeutigam (1980).
29. See Joskow (1974).

given the cost of the process and especially the mediocre incentive properties of COS regulation with short regulatory lags, the resulting regulatory lag is often viewed not as a drawback but as an advantage.[30]

Incentive Regulation (Profit or Cost Sharing)

Incentive regulation grew in popularity considerably in the 1980s, but the concept is an old one. Consider, for instance, sliding scale plans, which adjust prices downward when the firm's rate of return exceeds the target rate and in which the adjustment is partial in order to let the firm keep part of the realized profit.[31] Such a plan was adopted in 1925 for the Potomac Electric Power Company (after some adjustments the plan was dropped in 1955 due to the effects of inflation). The price was lowered so as to reduce excess profits by 50% in each succeeding year (in contrast, a rate of return under the target gave rise to a full price adjustment to prevent revenue losses).

More recent examples are recorded in reports of the MIT Energy Laboratory (1984) and FERC (1989). In the case of the New York Telephone Company the 1986 plan stipulated that revenue requirements would be adjusted by an amount equivalent to $(r - 15\%)/2$ if $r > 15\%$ (downward adjustment), to $(13\% - r)/2$ if $r < 13\%$ (upward adjustment), and not adjusted if $13\% \leq r \leq 15\%$, where r is the realized rate of return. Many incentive plans for electric utilities link the companies' profits to their fuel cost savings/overruns,[32] construction costs, plant heat rate, and plant capacity factor.

Incentive contracts are often implemented using automatic rate adjustment mechanisms (ARAMs), whereby prices are adjusted every three or six months to changes in input prices without the lengthy proceedings associated with rate cases. To avoid cost-plus features, only a fraction of cost changes relative to some predetermined (historical or prospective) target are passed on.

Last, we should point out that incentive regulation can apply to other verifiable performance measures than cost.[33] Just as compensation in defense contracts is based on the respect of schedules or various quality dimensions of the procurement projects, price adjustments in regulatory contracts relate to outage rates, consumer energy conservation programs, consumer services, and so forth.[34]

30. See, for example, Kahn (1970, vol. 2, p. 48).

31. See FERC Report (1989, pp. 93–97) and Joskow and Schmalensee (1986, p. 29). The expected rate of return r_τ^e at the new prices given the current rate of return r_τ satisfies $r_\tau - r_\tau^e = b(r_\tau - r^*)$, where r^* is the target rate of return (e.g., the cost of capital).

32. In 1984 the California Public Utility Commission adopted a plan under which consumers and the firms share equally the fuel cost savings or excesses above or below a "dead-band" zone.

33. See chapter 3 for a discussion of the regulation of verifiable quality.

34. See Nera (1990) for a list of incentive regulation experiments in the U.S. electric utility industry.

Price Caps

Price-cap (PC) regulation does not make explicit use of accounting data. The regulator fixes ceiling prices for either all products or a basket of products (average or weighted price), and the firm is free to choose its prices at or below the ceilings.[35] An indexation clause adjusts these ceilings over the regulatory period.

Price-cap regulation in its pure form (infinite regulatory lag) rules out the contractual use of cost data and is therefore unlikely to be optimal. It also requires the regulator to have good knowledge of cost and demand conditions. Too high a price ceiling makes the firm an unregulated monopolist, too low a cap conflicts with viability, and in between the "right" price level is difficult to compute.

Like COS regulation, PC regulation fixes the firm's prices for some period of time. In spirit, however, it is different in three respects. First, PC regulation is meant to be prospective rather than retrospective. The firm's historical cost is not meant to be the basis for future prices; rather the price cap is intended to be the regulatory equivalent of a fixed-price contract and thus to be high powered. Second, the firm is granted a downward flexibility in its prices, which in particular allows it to adjust its structure of relative prices. Third, the distance between regulatory reviews is meant to be exogenous (usually four to five years).

The basic form of PC regulation, such as that used for British Telecom from 1984 on,[36] identifies baskets of goods and specifies a regulatory lag and an average price constraint for each basket. To account for a changing environment or productivity increases, the firm is allowed to choose the price structure within each basket[37] but not to raise the average price of the basket by more than a set percentage each year. The familiar RPI $-$ X formula sets the maximum rate of price increase at the growth rate of the retail price index minus some anticipated rate of technological progress X (e.g., 3% for the first regulatory period of British Telecom). British Gas, which has been subject to PC regulation since 1986, had until recently an RPI $- X + Y$ formula for domestic users, where the Y term allows a full pass through of the cost of gas supplies.

In the United States PC regulation is used for long-distance telecommunication services (the FCC has applied it to AT&T since 1989) and to intrastate telecommunication services (for the state regulation of local exchange carriers since 1991). For instance, three service baskets were identified for AT&T: residential and small businesses, 800 services, and

35. It faces the constraints $p_k \leq \bar{p}_k$ for all goods k under individual price caps, and the constraint $\sum_k \omega_k p_k \leq \bar{p}$ under an overall price cap, where $\bar{p}_k$ and $\bar{p}$ denote the caps, and the ω_k are weights ($\omega_k > 0, \sum_k \omega_k = 1$).

36. See Vickers and Yarrow (1988) and the FCC notice for proposed rule making (1987) for accounts of this experiment and related ones.

37. Price ceilings on some products are meant to protect specific classes of consumers and to prohibit some forms of price discrimination.

business services. The rate of growth of the price cap on each basket depends on the inflation rate minus an exogenously determined rate of technological progress (as is the case for British Telecom), on changes in access fees that AT&T must pay to local exchange carriers, and on various parameters measuring regulatory changes (accounting rules, tax laws, exogenous cost adjustments, etc.). AT&T can adjust its price on an individual service within some band on a two-week notice; the notice is a bit longer for price changes above the band (90 days) and below (45 days). If the firm wants its average price to exceed the cap, a lengthy regulatory process with full cost examination is launched that resembles COS regulatory reviews.

Hybrid Price-Cap–Incentive Regulation Mechanisms

Under a pure price cap the firm's realized profit or cost is not used explicitly in the regulatory contract (neither is it supposed to be used implicitly at the regulatory review). Some recent incentive schemes have tried to incorporate profit sharing into price caps. They are in effect incentive contracts with some price cap features (downward average price flexibility, exogenous determination of the regulatory lag). For instance, the "stabilizer proposal" for U.S. local exchange carriers is designed to let the users of telecommunications services share cost savings and overruns when the firm's rate of return differs from a target rate of return by more than 2%. The PC regulation introduced in California in 1990 sets a benchmark rate of return of 13%; earnings in excess of 13% are shared equally up to 18%, while earnings above 18% benefit consumers only.

Convergence of Regulatory Schemes

As many authors[38] have noted, it would be simpleminded to make a strong distinction between COS and PC regulations on the basis that one is very low powered and the other very high powered. After all in both regimes prices are set by the regulator for some length of time. Neither regime is a pure cost-plus or pure fixed-price contract in that the firm is residual claimant for its cost savings for some period of time.

What are the differences then? First, prices are rigid under COS and upwardly rigid under PC. The downward flexibility under PC is relevant more for the structure of relative prices within the basket than for the price level itself; indeed a nonbinding ceiling on average price suggests that the cap has been chosen above the monopoly level, which is certainly not the desired outcome of regulation.[39] In contrast, PC regulation implies that

38. For example, Joskow and Schmalensee (1986) and Vickers and Yarrow (1988).

39. Nonbinding price caps signal completely ineffective price regulation if the regulatory structure is fixed. If the regulated firm enjoys a high-powered incentive scheme such as PC regulation (for reasons to be discussed in this book), and if it is concerned that political pressure might push for a return to more traditional regulation such as COS, it may strategically charge prices below the ceiling even if the ceiling is below the monopoly price, while it would not do so in the absence of uncertainty about the mode of regulation.

individual prices reflect variable costs and demand elasticities more precisely than COS rules.

A second difference is, as we have noted, that the regulatory lag (except for ARAMs) is supposed to be exogenous under PCs. This is not quite so in practice. For instance, in Britain the regulator can initiate a review before the predetermined date. We also saw in our discussion of PC regulation for AT&T that the firm can ask for a traditional review if its costs are too high. All this is not surprising given that administrations have difficulties committing not to intervene when pressured to reduce prices in the face of large profits, or to increase prices when the firm shows signs of potential default.

A third potential distinction between COS and PC regulations is the prospective or retrospective character of price setting. In principle, price caps are not determined by previous costs or rate of returns. However, it is clear that the firm's past performance is (rationally, according to theory) used at PC reviews. Just as under COS regulation the firm is penalized for in the past having revealed that it is efficient or for having invested in cost-reducing technologies.[40] Actually it should be noted that with its constitutional guarantee of a fair rate of return, COS regulation may well offer more protection of measurable investment than PC regulation. Another difference between COS and PC is that *observable* and *nonpersistent* cost savings are not penalized under PC, even though they will tomorrow lead to a price decrease under COS. Still, overall COS and PC regulations have a lot in common. Besides the differences described above, the contrast between the two modes is mostly one of emphasis.

3 Received Theory and the Agenda for the New Regulatory Economics

Academics have traditionally emphasized institutional and empirical research on regulatory issues, but there is also a substantial and useful theoretical heritage in the area. By and large, the most successful contributions refer to the normative aspects of natural monopoly pricing, and, in this brief overview, we will emphasize them accordingly.[41]

3.1 Marginal Cost Pricing

The first contribution to marginal cost (MC) pricing came from Dupuit (1844). He measured the welfare loss generated when a firm's price deviates from its marginal cost. If price does not reflect marginal cost, consumers

40. See section 1.9 and chapters 9 and 16 for normative analyses of this phenomenon.

41. Berg and Tschirhart (1988), Brown and Sibley (1985), Drèze (1964), Spulber (1989), and Wilson (1991) contain much more thorough discussions of some of the themes of this section.

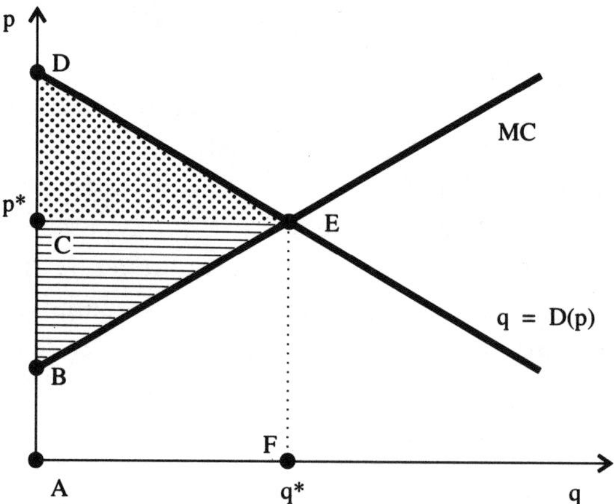

Figure 1
Marginal cost pricing

receive deceptive information about the societal cost of a marginal increase of demand. At a Pareto optimum, price must equal marginal cost, as illustrated in figure 1.

In the figure the consumer gross surplus is the area $ADEF$ (for consumption q^*) under the demand curve. To obtain the consumer net surplus, the area CDE (the dotted area), the income spent on the good, the area $ACEF$, is subtracted from the gross surplus. The firm's profit (up to a fixed production cost) is the area BCE (the hatched area) between price and marginal cost. Any price other than the MC price p^* does not yield as high a total surplus (consumer net surplus plus profit).

Since Dupuit's time many other authors such as Marshall, Pigou, Clark, Pareto, and Wicksell have discussed MC pricing, but the modern wave of enthusiasm for MC pricing started with Hotelling's (1938) article.[42] Meade (1944) and Fleming (1944) contributed to the interest in the British policy arena. Extensions by Boiteux (1949, 1951) paved the road for the first wide-scale application of a related concept at Électricité de France.

3.2 Peak-Load Pricing

Boiteux (1949) drew the implications of the Dupuit-Hotelling analysis for the "common capacity problem." In many regulated industries a facility (e.g., a power plant, a pipeline, a telephone switch, railroad tracks) is used to produce the same physical good at different times of the day or seasons. The marginal cost of production is then obviously not the same in periods when capacity use is saturated and when it is not. In the latter case only the variable or operating cost of production must be incurred to satisfy a

42. See Coase (1970) for an historical perspective.

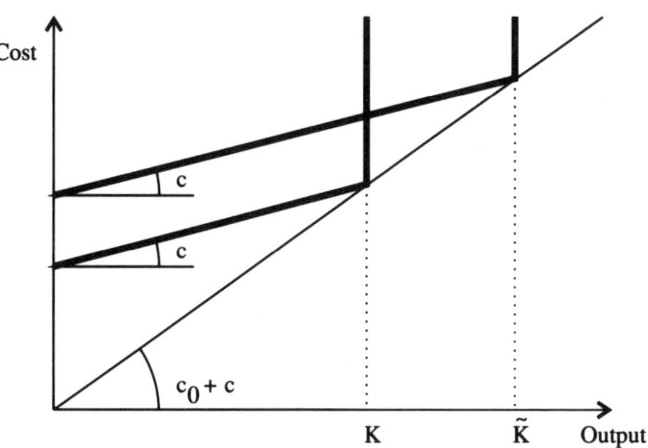

Figure 2
Short-term and long-term marginal costs

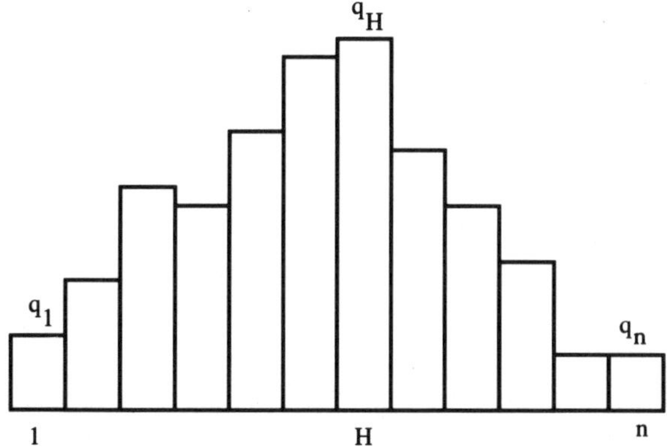

Figure 3
Load curve

marginal demand; in the former case capacity must be expanded. Prices should accordingly reflect the differences in marginal costs.

The simplest model of peak-load pricing is as follows: The firm chooses a capacity K to be used during n periods. The investment cost is $c_0 K$. At date $\tau \in \{1, \ldots, n\}$, the firm produces $q_\tau \leq K$ at variable cost cq_τ. The short-run marginal cost is thus c when $q_\tau < K$ and $+\infty$ when $q_\tau \geq K$. The long-run marginal cost is $[c_0 + c]$. Figure 2 shows the familiar tangency of the family of the short-term cost curves to the long-term cost curve in this example. Note that while the short-term production function exhibits decreasing returns to scale, the long-term production function has constant returns to scale.

Inelastic and Deterministic Demands

Suppose, in a first step, that the demands at all dates are known, and they are price inelastic. Figure 3 gives an example of a load curve for demand at every point in time. For simplicity we will assume that there is a single peak at time H. To satisfy demand, the capacity K must be equal to peak demand q_H. MC pricing requires that

$$p_\tau = c \qquad \text{for } \tau \neq H$$

and that

$$p_H = c_0 + c.$$

In the case of inelastic demand, pricing is not important, but it is worth noting that constant returns to scale and MC pricing ensure that the budget is balanced when capacity is equal to peak demand. The revenue is

$$c\left(\sum_{\tau \neq H} q_\tau\right) + (c + c_0)q_H,$$

and the sum of investment and variable cost is

$$c\left(\sum_{\tau} q_\tau\right) + c_0 K.$$

The budget is balanced when $q_H = K$.

Elastic, Deterministic, and Independent Demands

Assume now that demand at date τ depends only on that date's price and that the demand is downward sloping: $q_\tau = D_\tau(p_\tau)$. Demand is still assumed to be deterministic. We will consider two cases. The first is the simple case that arises when the peak demand is so high relative to other demands that applying MC pricing, assuming inelastic demands, does not shift the peak: namely $D_H(c_0 + c) > D_\tau(c)$ for all $\tau \neq H$. In this case the previous MC pricing rule can be used without changes. The second case is the more general one where the investment cost is high, so the peak shifts. MC pricing then serves to shift and depress the peaks. Pareto optimality requires both MC pricing and (because of constant returns to scale) a balanced budget. The capacity K and the prices p_τ must be simultaneously determined by the following system of equations. Let $T_1 \equiv \{\tau | D_\tau(c) \leq K\}$ and $T_2 \equiv \{\tau | D_\tau(c) > K\}$. For MC pricing

$$p_\tau = c \qquad \text{for } \tau \in T_1, \tag{1}$$

$$D_\tau(p_\tau) = K \qquad \text{for } \tau \in T_2. \tag{2}$$

For a balanced budget

$$\sum_{\tau \in T_2} (p_\tau - c) = c_0. \tag{3}$$

MC pricing requires prices to be at least equal to variable cost c. If $D_\tau(c) \leq K$, any price p_τ above c yields excess capacity at τ, implying a marginal cost of c and therefore a price above marginal cost. There often are several peak periods (periods in T_2). In those periods price is a priori indeterminate between c and $c_0 + c$, and it is chosen so as to equate supply K and demand $D_\tau(p_\tau)$; hence condition (2) prevails. Condition (3) is equivalent to the balanced budget, which results from

$$\sum_{\tau} (p_\tau - c)D_\tau(p_\tau) - c_0 K = \left[\sum_{\tau \in T_2} (p_\tau - c) - c_0 \right] K = 0.$$

A more natural way of viewing condition (3) would be from the perspective of optimal investment: One more unit of capacity accumulation costs c_0 and allows one more unit of consumption, valued p_τ at date τ, in each period where the capacity constraint binds.

Deterministic, Interdependent Demands

Often consumers delay or forward their consumption choices. The demand at date τ then depends on the vector of prices $\mathbf{p} = (p_1, \ldots, p_n)$. The optimum is still given by conditions (1) through (3), except that D_τ depends on $\mathbf{p}$ for all τ. The price adjustment that enables the peaks to shift is now simultaneous across periods.

Stochastic Demands

At each point in time firms generally face stochastic demand and possibly stochastic supply. Ideally in each time period prices should adjust to demand conditions to reflect state-contingent marginal costs. This is characteristic of "spot markets," but spot markets rarely exist in practice, if only because of the substantial transaction costs they would impose. Rather, within a given period prices tend to be rigid and not respond to demand or supply shocks. Fluctuations in demand are met either by using high marginal cost technologies (e.g., as gas turbines in electricity) as buffers or by rationing consumers (as is the case here in our fixed capacity formulation). Boiteux (1951) extended the model described above to allow for a normally distributed demand in each period (see Drèze 1964, pp. 18–24, for a full discussion). While the older literature has modeled the firm as constraining itself to satisfy demand with probability $1 - \varepsilon$ for $\varepsilon > 0$ or, alternatively, to incur a penalty for nonservice, the more recent literature (e.g., see Wilson 1989 and Spulber 1990) has considered more sophisticated rationing schemes. For instance, Wilson (1989) studied the practice of priority servicing in which electric utilities screen the customers for their willingness to pay not only for consumption but also for a low probability of this consumption being interrupted.

3.3 Marginal or Average Cost Pricing?

MC pricing has been debated on several grounds.

Criticism 1 Distinction between monetary and nonmonetary costs and benefits.

One of the earliest criticisms of MC pricing is related to the distortion brought about when government finances a firm's deficit. Meade (1944) first pointed out that in the absence of lump-sum transfers, the government must resort to distortionary taxes on income, capital, or consumption and that consequently the firm's monetary outlays and revenues ought not to be treated as the nonmonetary components such as consumer net surplus. In modern terms, public finance theory[43] shows that if the government raises \$1, society pays $\$(1+\lambda) > \$1$. The parameter λ is usually called the *shadow cost* of public funds. To compute the real cost incurred by a firm, the firm's cost and revenue are multiplied by $1+\lambda$.

To take an example, suppose that the firm produces a single output q at cost

$$C(q) = cq + \alpha,$$

where α is a fixed cost. Let $S(q)$ denote the consumer gross surplus and $P(\cdot)$ denote the inverse demand function. Optimal pricing in the presence of a shadow cost of public funds is given by

$$\max_q \{S(q) - P(q)q - (1+\lambda)[cq + \alpha - P(q)q]\}.$$

Let $\eta \equiv -(dq/dp)/(q/p)$ denote the elasticity of demand. Brief computations yield

$$\frac{p-c}{p} = \frac{\lambda}{1+\lambda}\frac{1}{\eta}. \tag{4}$$

Pricing is still closely related to marginal cost, but it also depends on the elasticity of demand. Because the firm's deficit is socially costly, pricing between marginal cost (which corresponds to $\lambda = 0$) and the monopoly price (which corresponds to $\lambda = \infty$, i.e., to monetary considerations weighting infinitely more than the consumer net surplus) obtains.

Note that this criticism is internal to the MC concept and does not lead to a fundamental departure from the MC principle. In particular, even though price exceeds marginal cost, pricing is unrelated to average cost pricing, since price is independent of the fixed cost.

Criticism 2 Coase and the social value of maintaining production.

A more fundamental criticism of MC pricing, due to Coase (1945, 1946; see also Wilson 1945) applies to a firm or a product whose existence is not a forgone conclusion. It may be an existing bus or railway line that runs a deficit and is a candidate for closure or a new product whose value added relative to the existing substitutes is being discussed. The basic idea is that unless the activity at least breaks even, MC pricing does not reveal

43. See, for example, section 3.9 and Atkinson and Stiglitz (1980).

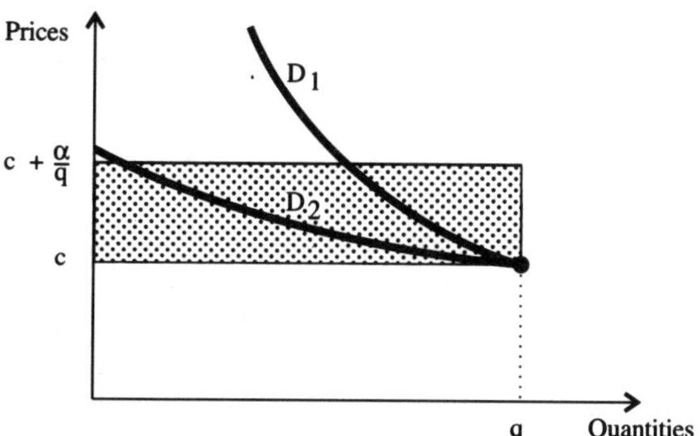

Figure 4
Marginal cost pricing and the value of maintaining production

whether for society it is worth incurring the fixed cost.[44] Coase thus argued that advocates of *MC* pricing assume that the government should decide for the consumers whether they would be willing to pay a sum of money that would cover the total cost and then, if they are willing to pay, not charge them the full cost. But the government may lack information to correctly implement this policy.[45]

Coase's point that a consumer should pay an amount equal to the total cost of supplying him is illustrated in figure 4, for cost function $C(q) = cq + \alpha$. In the figure production, which should be priced at mar-

44. Similar issues would arise even if the activity breaks even at a price equal to marginal cost, if either the activity exerts negative externalities or the activity makes the control of the regulated firm more difficult.

45. In a 1970 review, Coase summarizes his argument as follows:

> A consumer does not only have to decide whether to consume additional units of the product. He also has to decide whether it is worth his while to consume the product at all rather than spend his money in some other direction. This can be discovered if the consumer is asked to pay an amount equal to the total costs of supplying him. I suggested that the one way of doing this would be to have a charge independent of consumption to cover the cost not included in marginal cost. Note that marginal cost pricing makes it impossible for consumers to choose rationally between two alternative uses of the factors that are required for production but do not enter into marginal cost. In the one use, factors of production which do not enter into marginal cost would be free. In another use, providing that they enter into marginal cost in that use, they would have to be paid for.
>
> Apparently what the advocates of marginal cost pricing had in mind was that the Government should estimate for each consumer whether he would be willing to pay a sum of money which would cover the total cost. However, if it is decided that the consumer would have been willing to pay a sum of money equal to the total cost, then—and this strikes me as a very paradoxical feature of this argument—he will not be asked to do so. So the Government would estimate whether a consumer would be willing to pay, and if he is willing to pay, it does not charge him.
>
> I found this a very odd feature. But I do not see how it would be possible for any government, or anyone else for that matter, to make accurate estimates at low cost and without knowledge of what would have happened if consumers had been required to pay the cost. The way we discover whether people are willing to pay something is to ask them to pay it, and if we do not have such a system, it becomes extremely difficult to make estimates of whether they would be willing to pay. (p. 118)

ginal cost c if it takes place, is socially valuable for demand curve D_1 because the consumer net surplus exceeds the fixed cost (measured by the shaded area). Production ought to be abandoned if the demand curve is D_2. The regulator has no way of knowing whether D_1 or D_2 prevails if the consumer gets charged the marginal cost.

Coase does not supply a formal analysis, which would build on the theory about the Bayesian learning of the demand curve (see Aghion et al. 1991 for a recent contribution). Nevertheless, one can make the following observations: First, as Coase noted, MC pricing cannot reveal whether continued production or shutdown is desirable; the firm must experiment by setting price above marginal cost to obtain such information.[46] Second, the firm must make "large experiments." In general small increases above marginal cost can only reveal the valuations of consumers just above marginal cost; they say nothing about the valuations of high-demand consumers.[47] Third, the experiments should be such that the marginal information value of a price increase would equal its marginal cost in terms of lost demand. Fourth, during an experiment, pricing should reflect the fixed cost because the benefit (if any) of abandoning the activity grows with the fixed cost. Fifth, even though pricing during an experiment reflects the fixed cost, the ultimate goal is to return to MC pricing or to shut down the activity. Therefore permanent average cost pricing or some similar policy seems inappropriate unless, perhaps, the demand curve is imperfectly correlated over time.

Example To illustrate these points, consider the following example: There are two consumers (or more precisely two large groups of identical consumers). Each consumer has a unit demand for the good sold by the firm; the first has valuation v_1, and the second has valuation v_2. The firm's cost is $C(q) = cq + \alpha$, where $c < v_1 < v_2$. Suppose that the government knows v_1, but not v_2, and has prior distribution $G(\cdot)$, with density $g(\cdot)$ over $[v_1, \infty)$ for v_2. Assume further that $2(v_1 - c) < \alpha$ (production might not be socially desirable) and that $E(v_2) + v_1 - 2c > \alpha$ (production is on average desirable in the absence of experiment). This assumption rules out the case in which immediate shutdown is optimal. It is straightforward to extend the analysis when this assumption is violated. Let $\bar{p}_1 > c$ be defined by

$$E(v_2 | v_2 \leq \bar{p}_1) + v_1 - 2c = \alpha.$$

In words, the preceding equation states that government is indifferent between shutting down the firm and selling at marginal cost when it learns that the high-demand consumer's valuation is bounded above by $\bar{p}_1 > v_1$.

46. An alternative to experimentation is of course direct demand surveys.

47. See Jovanovic and Rob (1990) for an example of uncertainty that grows with "distance."

There are two periods, $\tau = 1, 2$. The good is nondurable, and a consumer consumes 0 or 1 in each period. The consumers do not act strategically and buy in a period if and only if their valuation exceeds the current price (this assumption is justified if there is a continuum of consumers of each type). The government cannot tell the consumers apart. In each period it first decides whether to operate and sink α, or else to shut down. It then charges a price to the consumers.

In period 2 experimentation is worthless, and the government either shuts down the firm or charges marginal cost. If the price p_1 charged in period 1 did not generate sales, the firm remains active if and only if

$$E(v_2|v_2 < p_1) + v_1 - 2c \geq \alpha.$$

Similarly, if p_1 generated sales, the firm remains active if and only if

$$E(v_2|v_2 > p_1) + v_1 - 2c \geq \alpha.$$

Clearly experimentation (in the sense of pricing above v_1 in period 1) can be optimal only if the firm is shut down in the event of bad news. Otherwise, sticking to marginal cost is a better policy. Therefore the price should not exceed $\bar{p}_1$. On the other hand, a price just above v_1 prevents consumption by the low-demand consumer and yields information leading to shutdown with negligible probability. The experimentation is therefore never local around v_1. Letting δ denote the discount factor, and charging marginal cost (or v_1 in this model) in both periods, yields intertemporal welfare:

$$(1 + \delta)[E(v_2) + v_1 - 2c - \alpha].$$

Alternatively, the firm can choose a price $p_1 < \bar{p}_1$ so as to maximize its expected profit:

$$\max_{p_1 < \bar{p}_1} \left\{ \int_{v_1}^{p_1} (-\alpha) g(v_2) dv_2 + \int_{p_1}^{\infty} [v_2 - c - \alpha + \delta(v_2 + v_1 - 2c - \alpha)] g(v_2) dv_2 \right\}.$$

Indeed, if $p_1 > v_2$, there is no sale in period 1. This results in a shutdown in period 2. If $p_1 < v_2$, one unit is sold in period 1, and two units are sold in period 2 at a price equal to marginal cost. Assuming that $p_1 < \bar{p}_1$, we can express the first-order condition as

$$p_1^* - c = \delta(\alpha + 2c - p_1^* - v_1), \tag{5}$$

or, equivalently,

$$p_1^* = c + \frac{\delta}{1 + \delta}[\alpha - (v_1 - c)]. \tag{6}$$

Equation (5) can be interpreted as follows: A unit increase in p_1 raises the probability that consumer 2 does not purchase, and at the margin it creates an extra first-period welfare loss proportional to $p_1 - c$ (which adds to that, $v_1 - c$, resulting from the low-demand consumer not purchasing). But, with equal probability, it saves the welfare loss of production $\alpha + 2c - p_1 - v_1$ in period 2. The left-hand side of (5) is thus (proportional to) the marginal cost of experimentation, while the right-hand side is (proportional to) its marginal benefit. Equation (6) shows that, as under average cost pricing, the optimal experimentation price increases with the fixed cost. Equation (6) can also be rewritten as

$$p_1^* - c = \frac{\delta}{1+\delta}[E(v_2|v_2 \leq \bar{p}_1) - c].$$

The optimal experimentation price is under $E(v_2|v_2 \leq \bar{p}_1)$ and therefore under $\bar{p}_1$. It converges to $E(v_2|v_2 \leq \bar{p}_1)$ when the first-period welfare loss is negligible relative to the information value (i.e., when $\delta \to \infty$).

Relevance of Coase's Criticism Because experimentation with prices way above marginal cost is socially costly, the regulator would ideally want to experiment only for a short period of time. If this is sufficient to learn whether production is socially desirable, then ex ante imperfect knowledge of the demand curve is not a serious matter. In practice there are several reasons why price experimentation cannot be performed rapidly. First, there is the cost of changing price: Prices must be widely advertised for the experiment to be successful. Delays in changing prices are further increased in the regulatory context by political interventions, hearings, and the like. Second, demand is noisy, and the regulator may need to keep the experimentation price fixed over some period of time to really learn the (expected) demand at that price. Third, consumers may arbitrage intertemporally. For example, if train fares are tripled, some consumers might choose to delay travel in the expectation that the regulator will bring the ticket prices down. Intertemporal arbitrage implies that the reduced demand today raises demand tomorrow and lowers the credibility of the shutdown option. It may easily give rise to multiple continuation equilibria for a given current price.[48] If in our example consumers have unit intertemporal demands (can delay their consumption), if there is a new inflow of consumers in period 2, and if the date 1 high-demand consumers expect that the firm will operate (at marginal cost) tomorrow, they may not consume today, but the firm may remain in operation tomorrow despite the absence of consumption, since some consumption has been delayed and since nonconsumption was not terribly bad news in terms of v_2. Thus strategic delaying of consumption and nonclosure of the activity can

48. See Fudenberg et al. (1987) for related ideas.

be self-fulfilling prophecies. Although a more detailed analysis would be warranted, the possibility of the public delaying consumption does make experimentation more difficult. In this connection it would be interesting to analyze the properties of a simpleminded constitution or law forcing government to track average cost (with a lag) as under standard cost-of-service regulation. Last, we note that strategic aspects come even more to the fore when the customers are large industrial buyers rather than atomistic consumers.

The alternative to experimentation of course is to order demand surveys. The advantage of surveys is that they do not involve large price distortions. However, there are two kinds of costs to consider with relation to surveys: First, there is the administrative cost of conducting the survey. Second, there is the potential cost of the survey's design being manipulated if the agency is captured by interest groups (the firm or the customers) having a stake in the activity being maintained through subsidies from the government. In this respect the information obtained by experimenting through high prices is much less manipulable.

Our overall assessment is that the issue of knowing the inframarginal consumers' surplus is well taken for activities whose existence is in question. This makes it an interesting question in regulation, although not a primordial one.

Criticism 3 Incentives.

Many economists such as Allais and Boiteux have supported *MC* pricing on theoretical grounds but have had reservations about it as a policy recommendation. For instance, Allais (1947) felt that the absence of a budget constraint would create inappropriate incentives for cost reduction. Indeed average cost (*AC*) pricing—that is, a balanced budget—is imposed in many regulated industries.

Being more precise about the relative incentive properties of *MC* and *AC* pricing requires an incentive model of regulation with cost observation of the sort developed in this book. Previewing our analysis, we will offer two reasons why incorporating the firm's fixed cost into the price may have desirable incentive properties.

The first reason, suggested to us by Patrick Bolton and studied in review problem 12, is that a balanced-budget rule may commit the government not to automatically subsidize an inefficient firm. That is, prohibiting such transfers from the government to firms would harden an inefficient firm's budget constraint and force the firm to bear more of the consequences of poor choices. For simplicity suppose that a firm through its current investment and maintenance policies can determine the future level of its fixed cost, and suppose that there is moral hazard in choosing this policy. If the firm does little to reduce its fixed cost and if the government can transfer money, then the government optimally will not pass increases in fixed cost into price hikes. Therefore the firm's level of output, which is a crucial determinant of the firm's rent, is unaffected. Given a balanced-budget rule, high fixed costs would be translated into high prices; this would lead to a contraction in output, which in turn would affect the firm. In short, a balanced-budget constraint forces the firm to pay more attention to its fixed cost.

The second reason, studied in chapter 15, is that passing the fixed costs along to taxpayers would not guarantee that costs would be closely monitored. Although the taxpayers may have a substantial collective stake in keeping fixed costs low, each taxpayer has a negligible stake in any regulatory issue, and taxpayers are often too dispersed to organize collectively. On the other hand, under some circumstances, charging the fixed cost to consumers gives them incentives to act as watchdogs. Close monitoring by consumers would make it more difficult for the firm to inflate fixed costs.

3.4 Balanced Budget and the Ramsey-Boiteux Model of Cost-of-Service Regulation

MC pricing will create a deficit if the firm operates under increasing returns to scale. Hotelling (1938), among others, suggested that the taxpayers be forced to absorb the deficit. If firms face a legal obligation to balance their budgets, this policy must be altered by introducing a discrepancy, or "toll," between price and marginal cost. Allais (1947), more for practical than theoretical purposes, advocated that all prices be proportional to marginal cost, with the coefficient of proportionality independent of the good and therefore of the elasticity of demand. This proportional price rule has, for instance, been used at Électricité de France. But more popular in the academic world is the Ramsey-Boiteux model, which can be summarized as follows:

Consider a multiproduct natural monopoly producing outputs $q_1, \ldots, q_n$ at cost $C(q_1, \ldots, q_n)$. Suppose that the demands for the goods are independent. Let $S_k(q_k)$ denote the consumer gross surplus associated with consumption q_k of good k, and let $p_k = P_k(q_k) = S'_k(q_k)$ denote the inverse demand curve.

In a contribution closely related to Ramsey's (1927) analysis of the optimal tax problem,[49] Boiteux (1956) posited that the regulator chooses outputs so as to maximize social welfare subject to the (budget) constraint that the firm's revenue from charges to consumers be sufficient to cover its cost. In this partial equilibrium framework Boiteux's postulate is equivalent to

$$\max_{\{q_1, \ldots, q_n\}} \left\{ \sum_k S_k(q_k) - C(q_1, \ldots, q_n) \right\}$$

subject to

49. See also Baumol and Bradford (1970).

$$\sum_k P_k(q_k)q_k \geq C(q_1,\ldots,q_n). \tag{7}$$

The important and celebrated insight of this model is that optimal prices are given by "Ramsey formulas": The Lerner index (or price–marginal cost ratio) on each good is inversely proportional to the elasticity of demand for the good. Letting $\mu \geq 0$ denote the shadow price of constraint (7), the reader should check that optimal prices satisfy

$$\frac{p_k - (\partial C/\partial q_k)}{p_k} = \frac{\mu}{1+\mu}\frac{1}{\eta_k(p_k)}, \tag{8}$$

where $\eta_k(p_k) = -(dq_k/dp_k)/(q_k/p_k)$ is the elasticity of demand for good k.

Note the analogy of (8) with (4). The difference between the two formulas is that the shadow price in (4) is exogenous to the firm because it is given by the economywide shadow cost of public funds. Boiteux's modeling is actually more general than its rendition here. First, it allows for dependent demands. Because we will review dependent demands and other extensions (e.g., product market competition) in chapters 3 and 5, we content ourselves here with the exposition of the case of independent demands. Second, Boiteux considers a general equilibrium framework in which the government optimizes over tolls and over lump-sum transfers to consumers. The elasticity equation (8) then applies to Hicksian *compensated* demand rather than to ordinary demand so that the income effects of pricing is taken into account.

Later research has unveiled the implications of Ramsey-Boiteux tolls for "cross-subsidization" in a multiproduct regulated firm. In particular, if entry of unregulated firms cannot be prohibited by the regulator, an entrant could find entry and price undercutting in a subset of markets profitable. This raises the question of when Ramsey prices are "sustainable" in the face of potential entry.

Faulhaber (1975) defines *cross-subsidies* in the following way: Let $\mathbf{q}$ denote the vector of the regulated firm's outputs $(q_1,\ldots,q_n)$, and let $\mathbf{q}_J$ denote a subvector of outputs $k \in J$. Let $C(\mathbf{q})$ and $C(\mathbf{q}_J)$ denote, respectively, the cost of producing a whole range of products and the cost of producing only a subset of products. [$C(\mathbf{q}_J)$ is called the "stand-alone cost."] A cost function[50] is subadditive (one formalization of increasing returns to scale) if $C(\mathbf{q}) \leq C(\mathbf{q}_J) + C(\mathbf{q}_{N-J})$, where N is the set of all goods and $N - J$ is the set of goods not in J. Faulhaber says that a regulated firm producing outputs $\mathbf{q}$ and selling at prices $\mathbf{p}$ does not cross-subsidize if, for all J, $\mathbf{p}_J \cdot \mathbf{q}_J \leq C(\mathbf{q}_J)$ (no subset of goods yields a net profit by itself to the firm, so entry by a firm with identical technology on markets J alone is not profitable). If the firm otherwise balances its budget, that is, if $\mathbf{p} \cdot \mathbf{q} = C(\mathbf{q})$, then the revenue on each subset of goods covers the incremental cost of

50. See Baumol et al. (1982) for a very thorough overview of properties of cost functions.

producing it: $\mathbf{p}_J \cdot \mathbf{q}_J \geq C(\mathbf{q}) - C(\mathbf{q}_{N-J})$. (Baumol et al. 1982 contains an extensive analysis of the sustainability of Ramsey prices in industries in which entry by firms with identical technology cannot be prevented.)[51]

Concerns with Ramsey-Boiteux Modeling The insights of the Ramsey-Boiteux model and of its many extensions are important. Yet there are several concerns with this model as a paradigm for regulation. In some sense the model is incomplete. Basic economic principles have taught us that efficient prices must be equal to marginal costs (with a possible correction to account for the shadow cost of public funds). To implement a socially efficient allocation, consumers must pay for each unit of a good the cost the production of this unit imposes on the firm—namely its marginal cost. Under linear pricing the firm's fixed cost should not enter the charges to consumers so as not to distort their consumption, and therefore it ought to be paid by the government. But the Ramsey-Boiteux model exogenously rules out transfers from the government to the firm, so prices in general exceed marginal costs. Now, one can rightly point out that in some countries and industries the law prohibits such transfers. However, once we wonder why such a law is even enacted, we uncover a tension between the assumptions that the regulator is benevolent, on the one hand, and that the regulator is not given free rein to operate transfers to the firm and to obtain efficiency, on the other. This suggests that the regulator's objective function may be misspecified in the presence of the legal constraint.

The second concern has less to do with the modeling than with the applicability of the paradigm. Implementing its price recommendations is much more complex than solving the model. The regulator needs a formidable knowledge of cost and demand conditions to compute the prices given by equation (8). The marginal cost depends on cost data, the elasticity of demand on demand data, and the shadow cost of the constraint on both. Not surprisingly actual cost-of-service regulation does not quite fit with the model. Regulators who are instructed to equate consumer charges and cost try to ensure an approximately balanced budget by using past cost and revenues and adjusting prices accordingly.[52]

51. See also Spulber (1989) for a good discussion.

52. Ramsey-Boiteux pricing is actually rarely implemented in practice. This may be due to a lack of knowledge of demand elasticities and of the shadow price μ (many regulated firms or public enterprises try to estimate their marginal costs). But there are also political reasons for the reluctancy to implement this principle. Take, for instance, the rule of nondiscrimination among consumers. This rule has often strangely been interpreted by charging identical prices to consumers with vastly different marginal cost of service (e.g. city and rural consumers). It has been suggested (e.g., by Owen and Braeutigam 1978, p. 5) that such cross-subsidies prevent entry in subsidized markets by other firms. The balanced budget, together with the loss of profitability in subsidized markets due to entry, requires an increase of prices in subsidized markets. This may create political opposition to the introduction of competition, which, if broad enough, can thwart deregulation. Similarly the existence of cross-subsidies among regions of a country is alleged to have the potential to prevent a regional breakup of the regulated firm.

The third concern is that this model, like the previous ones, presumes an exogenous cost function. In other words, the firm's managers and employees have no effect on cost. Similarly the demand function is independent of any effort by the firm's personnel to raise the quality or services of the products. In effect the Ramsey-Boiteux model has little to say about the incentives of regulated firms.

3.5 Input Choices

While MC and Ramsey-Boiteux pricing have been the leading normative models of rate making in regulated industries, the Averch and Johnson (1962) model[53] has been the leading input choice paradigm in received theory. This model examines how a regulated firm picks its inputs when the regulator exerts no control over this choice and the firm is permitted a rate of return on capital exceeding the cost of capital. The point of the analysis is that capital investment expends the rate base on which the firm is allowed an excess rate of return, and this induces the firm to select excessive capital–labor ratios. The Averch-Johnson model generated much interest in the profession because of some of its strong implications.[54] For instance, it implies that the regulated firm ought to resist peak-load pricing, leasing, power pooling, or any other policy that reduces the need for capacity and that, conversely, it ought to favor high standards of reliability or uninterruptability.

Consider a regulated monopolist producing a single output q from two inputs, capital K and labor L. Let $q = F(K, L)$ denote the (neoclassical) production function, r and w the unit costs of the capital and labor inputs, and $p = P(q)$ the inverse demand function. The firm's profit is thus

$$\pi = P(F(K,L))F(K,L) - wL - rK.$$

An unregulated firm would choose its capital–labor ratio so as to minimize total input cost, which requires that the marginal rate of transformation between the two inputs F_K/F_L be equal to the ratio of input prices r/w.

To study the influence of regulation on the input choice, Averch and Johnson (1962) posit that the regulator will not allow a rate of return on capital exceeding s, where $s > r$. The firm is otherwise unconstrained and chooses K and L so as to maximize profit subject to the rate-of-return constraint:

$$\max \pi$$

subject to

$$P(F(K,L))F(K,L) - wL \leq sK. \tag{9}$$

53. See also Wellisz (1963), and the review by Baumol and Klevorick (1970).

54. See chapter 2 of volume 2 of Kahn's (1970) classic text for a more complete list of implications.

The analysis goes on to demonstrate that if constraint (9) is binding, the firm adopts an inefficient production plan, whereby its capital-labor mix exceeds the cost-minimizing level: $F_K/F_L < r/w$. The firm accumulates an excessive amount of capital so as to relax the rate-of-return constraint (9).

For our purpose we are not particularly interested in the result, its extensions, or its much-discussed empirical relevance. Rather, we would like to evaluate the model as a theory of regulation. An oddity of the model is that the regulator, while actively enforcing the rate-of-return constraint, has no explicit objective function. The regulator's concern about the rate of return (which is realistic and will be an important building block of our analysis) suggests that leaving a rent to the firm is socially costly, though the social cost of the rent is not part of the model.

Furthermore, taking for granted that limiting the regulated firm's rent is a primary objective of the regulator, we may wonder why the allowed rate of return s is not set equal to the minimum rate of return r that induces the firm to produce. Somehow it must be the case that some unexplicit constraint prevents the regulator from extracting the firm's full rent. Could constraint (9) emerge as the "reduced form" of a more complex model? If so, wouldn't the reduced form be sensitive to changes in the structural form, which would make comparative statics exercises perilous?

3.6 The Agenda of the New Regulatory Economics

Despite some headway made by traditional theory, in particular on the pricing front, the institutional approach has remained the safest tool of the analysis kit for regulation. The traditional theoretical approach has stalled precisely where the new regulatory economics has sprung: the incentive front. To be certain, received theory implicitly touches on incentive issues: The Ramsey-Boiteux model rules out government transfers precisely because they might be abused, and the Averch-Johnson model describes a regulated firm's self-interested input choices. But received theory can only go so far. A more rigorous and realistic approach must adhere to the discipline of the broader principal-agent theory. Modeling must include a full description of the firm's and the regulator's objectives, information structures, instruments, and constraints. Information structures and the set of feasible regulatory schemes must as much as possible reflect real-world observational and contractual costs. Instruments and constraints must fit with property rights and laws, and when possible, property rights and laws should themselves be determined endogenously by the analysis.

From this perspective there are three reasons why regulation is not a simple exercise in second-best optimization theory: asymmetric information, lack of commitment, and imperfect regulators. As discussed earlier in this chapter, asymmetric information takes the form of moral hazard and adverse selection. It limits the control the regulator can exert over the firm. The difficulty for the regulator to commit to incentive schemes, for contractual or legal reasons, also reduces the efficiency of regulation. A benevolent regulator may want to act in the future in ways that he or she would like to prevent today. Last, the regulators or politicians may be incompetent, have their own hidden agendas, or simply be captured by interest groups; they may then not optimize social welfare.

Only a thorough investigation of these limits to perfect regulation can shed light on many issues of the traditional agenda of regulatory economics: power of incentive schemes, rate-of-return regulation, level and structure of rates, control of quality, entry regulation, access pricing and bypass, divestitures, privatizations, predation by regulated firms, franchise bidding and second sourcing, role of interest groups and regulatory institutions.

4 Methodology and Overview of the Book

4.1 The Controlled Experiment

This subsection introduces the common structure shared by all chapters of this book.

The Main Ingredients

Assumption 1 Regulation is subject to adverse selection and moral hazard.

The regulated firm has private information about its technology (or possibly demand) at the date of contracting, and its cost-reducing effort is unobserved by the regulator. The cost function will be written in the following form:

$$C = C(\beta, e, \ldots) + \varepsilon, \tag{10}$$

where β is a technological parameter (by convention $C_\beta > 0$;[55] a high β corresponds to an inefficient technology) and e is the effort or cost-reducing activity ($C_e < 0$ and $C_{ee} \geq 0$; effort reduces cost at a decreasing rate). The noise term ε stands for either forecast errors or accounting inaccuracies. In most of the book the adverse-selection parameter β and the moral hazard parameter e are one dimensional. We will let $\psi(e)$ denote the firm's managers' disutility of effort expressed in monetary terms. We will assume that $\psi' > 0$ (effort is costly), $\psi'' > 0$ (the cost of effort is convex), and for technical reasons $\psi''' \geq 0$ (which is a sufficient condition for the regulator's optimization programs to be concave and for the optimal incentive

55. Where there can be no confusion, subscripts will denote partial derivatives.

schemes to be deterministic).[56] Chapters 3 and 4 will consider multi-dimensional moral hazard and adverse selection variants. The variables omitted in the cost function may be the vector of outputs $q_1, \ldots, q_n$ of goods $1, \ldots, n$, the level of monetary services (quality) s, or current monetary investment I.

The model can be interpreted either as one of a public enterprise or else as one of a private regulated firm (or a contractor) in which shareholders and managers share private information and collude perfectly. Chapter 17 shows how the qualitative insights carry over to the case of a private regulated firm in which the managers' information (and goals) is not shared by the shareholders.[57]

As it stands, the model assumes that the regulator has incomplete information about the cost function but not about the disutility of effort function. The treatment of uncertainty about the disutility of effort is very similar to that of uncertainty about cost, as shown in the following simple example: Consider a fixed size project with cost $C = \beta_1 - e + \varepsilon$. Suppose that the disutility of effort is $\psi(\beta_2 + e)$ and that the firm has private information about both adverse selection parameters β_1 and β_2. Letting $\tilde{e} \equiv \beta_2 + e$ and $\beta = \beta_1 + \beta_2$, we can rewrite the cost and disutility functions as $C = \beta - \tilde{e} + \varepsilon$ and $\psi(\tilde{e})$. That is, we are back to the case in which the regulator has incomplete information about the cost function only.

The firm knows β, and the regulator has a (common knowledge) Bayesian distribution over β in an interval $[\underline{\beta}, \bar{\beta}]$. The cumulative distribution function is $F(\beta)$ [with $F(\underline{\beta}) = 0$, $F(\bar{\beta}) = 1$], and $F(\beta)$ has a continuous and strictly positive density $f(\beta)$ on $[\underline{\beta}, \bar{\beta}]$. Sometimes it will prove technically convenient to assume that the firm has only two possible types $\underline{\beta}$ and $\bar{\beta}$, with prior probabilities v and $1 - v$.

Assumption 2 The realized cost C, the outputs (and possibly some dimensions of quality), and the prices are verifiable. However, the regulator cannot disentangle the various components of cost.

Assumption 2 implies that the optimal regulatory contracts are based on aggregate cost and demand data (see the discussion at the beginning of this chapter) and that the regulator cannot allocate a multiproduct firm's cost among product lines (chapter 3), cannot disentangle the cost attributable to the provision of nonverifiable services from that associated to production (chapter 4) or operating expenditures and investment (chapter 8). Two exceptions to assumption 2 will be considered. In chapter 3 we will allow the firm's subcosts to be observable and will ask when subcost

56. Even if $\psi''' < 0$, the program is concave and optimal schemes are deterministic provided that either the uncertainty about β is small or the shadow cost of public funds (see assumption 8) is small.

57. Still another interpretation of the model, emphasized in Reichelstein (1990), is that the "disutility of effort" stands for the forgone revenues of the firm in unregulated lines of business (e.g., Western Electric for AT&T, or commercial projects for defense contractors).

observation does improve regulation. Chapter 12 will allow the firm to engage in accounting manipulations, so the measured cost may differ from the realized cost C.

Assumption 3 The firm (or its personnel) can refuse to produce if the regulatory contract does not guarantee it a minimum level of expected utility.

Assumption 3 forces the regulator to respect an "individual rationality" or "participation" constraint for the firm. We let U denote the firm's expected utility and normalize the individually rational level at zero. $U \geq 0$ will also be called the firm's "rent" or "surplus."

Assumption 4 The regulator can operate monetary transfers to the firm (except in sections 2.6, 2.7, 3.6, 5.4, 6.5, chapter 15, and review problem 12).

Assumption 4 is important and deserves comment. Its scope of validity is procurement, public enterprises with government appropriations, and public enterprises not receiving government transfers but able to borrow subject to the government's consent (see below).

What remains of the analysis in this book when the firm is subject to a strict budget constraint in which the firm's cost must be covered by charges to consumers? Optimal pricing and incentives are obtained from the same formulas, except that the shadow cost of public funds (see assumption 8) is replaced by the shadow cost of the budget constraint. This point was illustrated in a simple pricing example by the formal analogy between equations (4) and (8). Consider next the issue of providing rewards to managers that depend on their performance. The difference between prohibition and nonprohibition of transfers is who pays the reward at the margin: the consumer under balanced budget or the taxpayers under government transfers. In both cases the shadow cost of rewarding the firm by \$1 exceeds \$1. The trade-off between rent extraction and incentives discussed below is the same. Therefore, though not realistic in a number of industries, assumption 4 is not restrictive.

Other Modeling Options

The following assumptions are also made in the book:

Assumption 5 The firm and the regulator are risk neutral with respect to income.[58]

58. We will briefly study firm's risk aversion in chapter 1. The basic effect of risk aversion is to lower the optimal power of incentive schemes to give insurance to the firm. Our structure is ideally suited to analyze the trade-off between rent extraction and incentive (see subsection 4.2) but less well suited technically to study risk aversion. In this respect the pure moral hazard model of Holmström and Milgrom (1987), which, like ours, predicts linear incentive schemes in some circumstances, is more tractable.

Assumption 6 By accounting convention, the government receives the firm's revenue from charges to consumers $R(q)$, pays the firm's cost C, and pays a net transfer t to the firm.

Assumption 7 The firm cares about income and effort only.

We can write the firm's utility function as

$$U = t - \psi(e). \tag{11}$$

Assumption 8 The regulator faces a shadow cost of public funds $\lambda > 0$.

The idea behind assumption 8 is that each dollar spent by the government is raised through distortionary taxes (labor, capital, and excise taxes) and costs society \$$(1 + \lambda)$. In other words, ideal lump-sum taxes (which would imply that $\lambda = 0$) are not available. An important point is that the shadow cost of public funds is given by economywide data and is independent of the regulation of the industry under consideration as long as the latter is small relative to the economy. The measurement of the shadow cost of public funds results from the theory of public finance and from the estimation of the elasticities of demand and supply for consumption, labor, and capital. A reasonable mean estimate for the U.S. economy seems to be $\lambda = 0.3$ (see Ballard, Shoven, and Whalley 1985; Hausman and Poterba 1987). The shadow cost of public funds is likely to be higher in countries where the tax collection is less efficient.

Remark on leveraged public enterprises It might seem that the shadow cost of public funds, which is linked to taxation, is irrelevant to the measurement of costs and revenues of a public enterprise that cannot receive transfers from the government. This intuition might be incorrect if the firm is (as is usually the case) able to borrow on financial markets. The government can then adjust leverage to determine the de facto transfer to the firm. If the government is otherwise running an optimal dynamic fiscal policy, the firm's costs, revenues, and monetary rewards should be measured using the shadow cost of public funds. Suppose that at date τ the firm is allowed to borrow \$1 more. The government would then reduce its other debts by \$1 so as to keep total government debt constant. Next, ceteris paribus, the government would increase its taxes by \$1, which has cost \$$(1 + \lambda_\tau)$.[59]

Assumption 9 Except in parts V and VI, the regulator's objective is to maximize total surplus (consumers' plus firm's plus taxpayers') in society.

Assumption 9 can be called the "benevolent regulator assumption." In

59. This reasoning assumes that the government is unconstrained in the amount of leverage it can grant the firm. If a strict balanced intertemporal budget constraint were imposed (of the type $\lim_{\tau\to\infty} \exp(-\int_0^\tau r_s\, ds)\, D_\tau = 0$, where D_τ is the firm's debt and r_τ the interest rate at date τ), then the analysis would resemble that of a static balanced budget constraint.

parts V and VI we will assume that the regulator is self-interested and cannot be perfectly monitored.

The precise objective function of the regulator does not matter for the qualitative results. For instance, he or she might maximize the sum of consumer surplus and a fraction (between 0 and 1) of the firm's surplus as is posited in some contributions to the new regulatory economics.[60] What matters is that the regulator dislikes leaving a rent to the firm. In our framework, any dollar transferred to the firm costs $\$(1 + \lambda)$ to society and thus reduces social welfare by $\$[(1 + \lambda) - 1] = \$\lambda > 0$. This means that rent extraction is one of the regulatory goals. It is important to note that in our framework with quasi-linear utility functions and a utilitarian regulator (and therefore no redistributive objective), regulation would be straightforward if $\lambda = 0$. It would suffice to reward the firm with a transfer equal to consumer surplus plus a constant to reach the first best. See bibliographic note B1.1 of chapter 1.

Assumption 10 The regulator designs the regulatory contract.

Assumption 10 puts the whole bargaining power on the regulator's side, although generally the regulator and the firm bargain over the contract. Our assumption is not meant to be realistic but rather to avoid the signaling phenomena that arise in situations in which an informed party takes part in contract design.[61]

4.2 Overview of the Book

The book is divided into six parts. Part I focuses on the static control of a single firm by a benevolent regulator. Part II introduces product market competition. Part III treats competition for the natural monopoly position through auctioning. Part IV considers multiperiod regulation. Part V analyzes the politics of regulation and the control of regulators by legislatures and institutions. Last, part VI studies regulatory institutions. This section describes a few themes approached in these six parts.

To grasp a number of the results in the book, it is important to understand the basic trade-off between *incentives* and *rent extraction*. Recall that the regulator faces moral hazard and adverse selection. The regulator is unable to monitor the firm's effort to reduce cost and has less information than the firm about technology.

Ignoring for the moment output and quality decisions, the regulator has two goals: promote cost reduction and extract the firm's rent. To see why these two goals are necessarily in conflict, consider the two polar cases of

60. In private procurement it makes most sense to assume that the procuror is interested only in his or her own surplus (the equivalent of the consumers'/taxpayers' surplus here) and puts zero weight on the supplier's welfare in his or her objective function.

61. See Maskin and Tirole (1990) for a theory of the principal-agent relationship in which an informed party designs the contract.

Table 2
Incentives–rent extraction trade-off

	Goal	
Contract	Effort inducement	Rent extraction
Fixed-price	100%	0%
Cost-plus	0%	100%

cost-plus and fixed-price contracts. A fixed-price contract induces the right amount of effort because it makes the firm residual claimant for its cost savings. The firm has then the socially optimal incentive to reduce costs as it receives one dollar for any dollar saved. In contrast, a cost-plus contract offers no incentive for cost reduction, for the firm does not appropriate any of its cost savings.

The logic is reversed when it comes to rent extraction. Under a fixed-price contract any exogenous reduction in cost is received by the firm. The firm's rent thus is very sensitive to the technological environment. Because the firm must have a nonnegative rent when it has an intrinsically high cost, it obtains a substantial rent when facing an intrinsically low cost. In contrast, a cost-plus contract is ideal for rent extraction because any exogenous variation in cost is received by the government and not by the firm. We summarize the trade-off in table 2.

When the regulator has perfect information about the technology (moral hazard but no adverse selection), the optimal regulatory contract is a fixed-price contract. The fixed fee is optimally set at the lowest level consistent with the firm's participation provided that the firm chooses the cost-minimizing effort, that is, the effort that minimizes $C + \psi(e)$. When the firm has private information about its technology, the above analysis suggests that optimal contracts are incentive contracts trading off effort inducement, which calls for a fixed-price contract, and rent extraction, which calls for a cost-plus contract.

It is actually optimal for the regulator to offer a *menu of incentive contracts*. The reasoning is that the contract should be tailored to the firm's information. An inefficient firm should not be given the same contract as an efficient firm. This point will become clearer when we solve the complete model and give a corporate analogy of the menu of contracts. The reader at this stage should just note that the regulator offers a menu of contracts for exactly the same reason as a monopolist offers different price/quantity or quality combinations. The regulator discriminates among or screens the different potential types of the firm in the same way the monopolist price discriminates among consumers with different valuations for quantity or quality.

Chapter 1 formulates these considerations in the simplest framework of a firm producing a fixed output (normalized to one) of a single good. The firm thus implements a project with cost $C = C(\beta, e) + \varepsilon$. It shows that under some assumptions it is optimal for the regulator to offer a menu of contracts that are linear in cost ($t = a - bC$). We do not want to dwell on this result because, unlike the other results, it is not robust to perturbations in the modeling choices. For instance, the optimal contracts would not be quite linear if the firm were a bit risk averse. Similarly the linearity result is not robust to the repetition of regulation. The interest that this result holds for us is that, first, it shows that optimal contracts are not always complex. Second, and more important, it allows us to talk in a clean way about the slope or power of the incentive scheme (the optimal contracts are also linear in chapters 2 through 8).[62] One central concern of our analysis is how the slope b varies with some key parameters. When the optimal incentive schemes are not linear (as is the case in the repeated regulation framework), we will identify the power of the incentive scheme with the equilibrium level of cost-reducing activity by the firm.

After demonstrating the linearity of optimal incentive schemes, chapter 1 notes that moving from perfect information about technology to imperfect information reduces the power of incentive schemes. It then obtains the testable implication that the power of incentive schemes is positively correlated with the firm's cost performance and issues a warning concerning causal interpretations of this relationship. It also shows that the optimal cost-reimbursement rule, and more generally any scheme that gives incentives to reduce cost, are informationally demanding. Last, it shows how the basic model sheds light on standard regulatory issues such as yardstick competition, investment, and fair rate of return.

Chapter 2 studies pricing by a single-product firm. It extends the model of chapter 1 by allowing a continuously variable output [$C = C(\beta, e, q) + \varepsilon$] and a known elastic demand curve. The firm's incentive scheme depends on the two observable variables: realized cost and price (or, equivalently, realized cost and output). The optimal pricing rule is a Ramsey pricing rule. The existence of the shadow cost of public funds leads to a price in excess of marginal cost (but under the monopoly price). On the other hand, the cost-reimbursement rule follows the precepts of chapter 1. The study of the effect of a change in the demand curve on the regulated firm's price and rent serves as an introduction to the analysis of product market competition in part II.

62. The philosophy here is similar in spirit to that of Holmström and Milgrom (1987). They consider a pure moral hazard model and allow risk aversion. They show that if the agent has exponential utility, makes an effort to control a Brownian drift in cost, and observes the drift in real time, the optimal contract is linear in aggregate cost. This alternative linear model is very useful to study how the power of incentive schemes changes with key parameters in situations of moral hazard and risk aversion.

The rent extraction goal of our model and the insurance goal of theirs (which in both cases conflict with the incentive goal) are not dissimilar. One can view insurance as ex post rent extraction: Variations in ex post utility are socially wasteful if the firm is risk averse.

Chapter 2 then analyzes pricing and incentives when the regulator is legally prevented from transferring money to the firm. That is, for some unspecified reason, the benevolent regulator must choose pricing so as to equate the firm's revenue with its cost (including managerial compensation). To reflect the reality of most regulated industries in which transfers are legally prohibited, we first assume that the regulated firm charges a two-part tariff. The absence of government transfers does not preclude the use of incentive schemes. Indeed there is a sense in which the fixed charge in the two-part tariff acts as a costly transfer from the consumers. While the price differs from that that would obtain in the absence of prohibition of transfers, the incentive features described in the rest of the book are robust to the prohibition of transfers. We obtain similar conclusions under linear pricing (and balanced budget).

Chapter 3 extends the model to variable output of several goods [$C = C(\beta, e, q_1, \ldots, q_k, \ldots, q_n) + \varepsilon$]. Under symmetric information optimal prices are given by Ramsey rules. For instance, for independent demands the price of good k is given by the Ramsey formula (4). Do pricing rules under asymmetric information differ from the Ramsey rules? That is, is it worth distorting prices away from Ramsey prices to extract the firm's rent, or is the cost-reimbursement rule a sufficient instrument to do so? Chapter 3 provides necessary and sufficient conditions on the cost function for the pricing rules to be isolated from incentive issues. The pricing rules are then shown to be simple in the sense of subsection 1.3. The chapter proceeds to study the possibility of the firm's allocating its cost-reducing activity among product lines. It also derives conditions under which the observation of subcosts by the regulator is useless. Last, chapter 3 provides general equilibrium foundations for the shadow cost of public funds (this is the only place in the book where general equilibrium considerations are brought in). It shows how our formulas for cost reimbursement and pricing emerge naturally in a model with distortionary taxation, and it discusses conditions under which the regulator might want to use the prices of regulated firms to redistribute income among consumers.

Chapter 4 introduces unverifiable quality [$C = C(\beta, e, q, s) + \varepsilon$, where q is the output of a single product with quality s and $C_s > 0$] and considers the possibility of observing the quality of the good before purchasing (*search good*) or after purchasing (*experience good*). Because contracts cannot be made directly contingent on quality, the firm's incentive to provide quality is to preserve its reputation in the case of an experience good and to boost current sales in the case of a search good. We ask whether an increase in the valuation for quality results in high- or low-powered incentive schemes. The answer depends much on whether the good is a search or an experience good. For an experience good, current sales are not responsive to quality, and the cost-reimbursement rule is the only regulatory instrument; because the provision of services is induced by low-powered incentive schemes, an increase in the valuation for quality crowds out the cost-reducing activity. For a search good, consumption is a signal of quality, and incentives to provide quality can be disconnected from those to reduce cost if the firm is rewarded on the basis of sales.

Part II (chapters 5 and 6) studies pricing in a competitive environment. It posits the existence of an unregulated fringe with or without market power. In particular it analyzes some aspects of access pricing and bypass. The issue of access pricing arises when the regulated firm produces two complementary products A and B and faces competition for product B. The rival firms on market B, however, can compete only if they have access to the "bottleneck" product A that is monopolized by the regulated firm. For instance, before its divestiture AT&T's competitors on the long-distance market needed access to AT&T's local network. The issue in such a situation is how the bottleneck should be priced.

Bypass usually occurs when a firm practices second-degree price discrimination and an alternative technology is available to large consumers only (e.g., because of a large fixed cost of setting up this alternative technology). For instance, a university or a large firm could build direct access to long-distance carriers and bypass the local telephone company. The bypass activity "skims the cream" of the market and perturbs price discrimination. The issues are then optimal pricing by a regulated firm under the threat of bypass and its interaction with incentive schemes.

Parts I and II look at the control of a single firm. Part III analyzes the source selection process. We have in mind the Department of Defense's organizing an auction for the development or the production of a new weapons system or an agency putting up a franchise (e.g., for cable TV distribution) for bid. Even though the regulator picks a single firm, competition to become the source may lower the winning firm's rent.

Chapter 7 considers an auction between several firms for a natural monopoly position. At the date of the auction each firm i has private information about its technology parameter β^i. The winning firm engages in cost-reducing activity. The situation is similar to the familiar one of an auction of an indivisible object, with the difference that what is auctioned off is a complex object, namely an incentive contract. The optimal auction exhibits a simple separability. The slope of the winning firm, say, firm j's incentive scheme b^j, is the same as the one firm j would have faced in the absence of bidding competition. The only effect of competition is thus to lower the fixed fee a^j. The force of bidding competition is to reduce the regulator's range of uncertainty about the winning firm's technological parameter by truncating upward the distribution of uncertainty about this parameter at the level of the second bidder's uncertainty parameter.

In the case of a long-term monopoly position, it may be in the regulator's interest during the course of the relationship to replace the firm that initially received the contract if this firm's performance is not adequate or if a better alternative opportunity arises. Second sourcing or breakouts indeed occur in the reprocurement of defense contracts or at the renewal of franchises. While chapter 7 studies an auction for a once-and-for-all contract, chapter 8 considers a multiperiod auctioning process and focuses on the effect of future auctioning on the incumbent firm's incentive to invest. We recast the debate between the Chicago school, which argued that monopoly franchises should be awarded at each stage to the firm that offers to supply on the best terms, and Williamson (1976), who identified potential perverse effects of second sourcing on investment behavior. Our formal analysis lends support to Williamson's position and finds that investment myopia may considerably reduce the attractiveness of second sourcing. It finds that bidding parity ought to be distorted in the incumbent's favor and that the power of incentive schemes should increase over time to correct the pattern of investment.

Part IV is concerned with multiperiod regulation of a single firm. There are three possible forms of commitment in a repeated relationship. First, the parties may be able to commit to a long-term contract, whereby the terms of the contract are never questioned and the original contract is implemented as time passes on.[63] Second, the parties may be able to write a long-term contract that is enforced if any of the parties wants it to be enforced but may not be able to commit not to renegotiate if both parties find it advantageous to do so. The distinction matters because in a very general sense ex ante efficient contracts introduce for incentive reasons ex post inefficiencies that the parties will be tempted to renegotiate away. These two situations are ones of complete contracting (the future contingencies are fully specified in the initial contract), but there is the third possibility that only short-term (and therefore incomplete) contracts can be signed for transactional or legal reasons. The relationship between regulator and firm is then run by a sequence of short-term contracts.

These three forms of commitment (which we label "pure commitment," "commitment and renegotiation," and "noncommitment") are not inconsistent; they rather depict different situations. Clearly the regulator prefers pure commitment to commitment and renegotiation to noncommitment (at least when there are two periods). (Under pure commitment, the regulator can always compute and duplicate the renegotiation that would take place if renegotiation were possible. Under commitment and renegotiation, the regulator can always content him or herself with signing a short-term contract, thus duplicating the noncommitment situation.) But the regulator cannot choose among the three forms of commitment. The pure commitment situation represents an extreme case in which the regulator or the firm can commit to never sign in the future a contract that makes

63. Commitment does not imply inflexibility. The initial contract optimally allows the allocation to respond to new (private or public) information.

them better off. If the technology parameter is time invariant, the optimal commitment contract is to give the same incentive scheme in each regulatory period; the model is thus falsely dynamic (for this reason we will treat pure commitment in chapter 1). We find the cases of commitment and renegotiation and noncommitment more realistic in many situations. Whether one paradigm or the other obtains depends on whether complete long-term contracts can be signed and therefore on the transactional and legal environments referred to earlier. Part IV treats these two forms of commitment in the simplest framework [no output choice, no accounting or forecast errors, and time-invariant technology parameter, so that the date τ cost is $C_\tau = C(\beta, e_\tau)$].

Chapter 9 assumes noncommitment and formalizes the ratchet effect that is so pervasive in planned economies, regulated industries, and internal organization. If the firm performs well (produces at a low cost) early in the relationship, the regulator infers that the technological parameter is favorable and tries to extract the firm's rent by being more demanding during the regulatory review. The firm has thus an incentive to keep a low profile by not engaging in much cost-reducing activity. To induce the firm to produce at a low cost when efficient, the regulator must offer it a generous reward for good performance, and this may create a reverse incentive problem: The firm, even when it is inefficient, may want to take advantage of this generosity for a while and then quit the relationship. Technically the possibility of this "take-the-money-and-run" strategy implies that the incentive constraints may be binding in both directions under noncommitment. Chapter 9 shows that the cost performance slowly reveals the technological information over time and characterizes how this revelation of information is affected by the time preferences of the parties.

Chapter 10 studies the case of commitment and renegotiation. Technically the role of commitment is to prevent the firm from adopting the "take-the-money-and-run" strategy unveiled in chapter 9. The long-term relationship involves a weaker form of ratcheting than in chapter 9. Chapter 10 similarly analyzes the speed of revelation of information over time and demonstrates the circumstances under which the regulator strictly gains from committing beyond the short run.

Part V relaxes the assumption that the regulator is benevolent or can be perfectly monitored and develops an agency-theoretic approach to interest group politics. It studies the potential identification of a regulatory agency with the interests of the regulated firm and of nonindustry groups. The regulator is formalized as a supervisor who can use information strategically to collude with interest groups. The general insight is that to prevent collusion, regulatory schemes involve lower stakes of interest groups in regulatory decisions and less discretion for the regulator than the rest of the book would have predicted.

Chapter 11 takes up the model of chapters 1 and 2 and assumes that the regulator has more information about the technology parameter than the legislature or the public at large. It studies the effect of (potential) collusion on the cost-reimbursement rule and pricing. Low-powered incentive schemes, which were seen to reduce the firm's information rent (i.e., regulatory stake), are less sensitive to collusion between the regulator and the firm than high-powered incentive schemes, and they become more attractive in the presence of collusion. The threat of collusion also raises prices. The power of an interest group does not only depend on its stake in regulation and its degree of organization but also on the kind of influence it wants to exert.

Low-powered incentive schemes are appropriate when one is concerned about the capture of a regulatory agency, but high-powered ones may be needed to reduce the risk of capture of public accountants by the firm. Chapter 12 introduces the possibility of cost padding (diversion of money to unregulated product lines, unallowed compensation or charges, etc.). In the absence of collusion between the firm and its auditors, the possibility of cost padding makes high-powered incentive schemes more desirable: The firm is less tempted to inflate accounting cost if it bears a high fraction of this cost. But we show that the possibility of capture has ambiguous effects on the power of incentive schemes. Although fixed-price contracts require no audit and therefore are immune to capture, some cost sharing can still reduce rents. High-powered schemes create high rents and therefore make it more tempting for the firm to prevent the release of auditing information about cost padding.

Chapters 13 and 14 relate the threat of capture and the competitive structure of regulated industries. Chapter 13 builds on part II to analyze the regulation of product market competition. It is shown that the potential for "cartelization by regulation" may lead to the removal of the regulatory agencies' discretion in prohibiting or favoring entry. Similarly chapter 14 builds on part III to analyze the design of auctions. It first extends the auctioning model of chapter 7 to allow for a nonverifiable quality dimension. The focus of the analysis is on how the threat of favoritism leads to an apparently excessive emphasis of tangible criteria (like price) over less tangible ones (like quality) in the selection of government suppliers. Again, the fear of a collusive activity may lead to a reduction in the regulator's discretion, and thus to rigid regulatory rules.

While phenomena resembling rules can be generated from complete contracting models, rules have a broader scope. Part VI is an exploratory analysis of the idea that agencies are given a vague mandate (incomplete contract) to regulate industries. A priori restrictions on their instruments (see section 1) may then be desirable because they affect their incentives to achieve their own goals or to identify with interest groups, and the effectiveness of supervision by watchdogs (advocacy groups, legislators, etc.).

To illustrate this idea, chapter 15 returns to the puzzle posed in the discussion of the Ramsey-Boiteux model (see section 3). It compares two institutions: one where the regulator is allowed to transfer money to the firm and to regulate prices, in which case the mandate is to implement marginal cost pricing, and one where the regulator only controls prices, in which case the mandate is to implement average cost pricing. The regulator may identify with the industry, but a regulatory hearing offers the advocacy groups an opportunity to alter the proposed rule making. The comparison between the two mandates hinges on the deadweight loss associated with collusion and on the effectiveness of watchdog supervision.

Chapter 16 studies the possibility that regulators may not be able to commit to long-term contracts, not because the future characteristics of production and of its environment are hard to describe but rather because they are legally prohibited from committing the next administration. In the switching-administrations model of chapter 16, the lack of commitment has both a cost and a benefit. The cost is that the regulated firm is reluctant to invest to reduce its cost because the benefit of investment will be expropriated. The benefit is that future administrations will be able to reverse the regulatory policy if the current administration protects the industry. The analysis then endogenizes the probability of reelection of the current government by letting voters rationally update their beliefs about the government's integrity after observing its regulatory record.

Chapter 17 offers a first look at the effects of alternative ownership structures. It compares the incentives of a public enterprise with those of a privately owned regulated firm. It discusses some potential differences between the two structures and then sets up a formal model based on the allocation of residual rights of control. Private ownership generates a congruence between owners' objectives and managerial rewards and thereby limits the expropriation of managerial investments for nonprofit reasons (e.g., restricting imports or fighting unemployment). But it also creates a multimaster situation in which the managers must respond to the conflicting demands of the government and of the private shareholders. Finally, in the concluding chapter we offer some remarks about the directions for research. Review problems at the end of the book analyze some themes briefly mentioned or not covered in the book.

REFERENCES

Aghion, P., P. Bolton, C. Harris, and B. Jullien. 1991. Optimal learning by experimentation. *Review of Economic Studies* 58:621–654.

Allais, M. 1947. Le problème de la coordination des transports et la théorie economique. *Bulletin des Ponts et Chaussées et des Mines.*

Atkinson, A., and J. Stiglitz. 1980. *Lectures on Public Economics.* New York: McGraw-Hill.

Ballard, C., Shoven, J., and J. Whalley. 1985. General equilibrium computations of the marginal welfare costs of taxes in the United States. *American Economic Review* 75:128–138.

Baumol, W. J. 1975. Payment by performance in rail passenger transportation: An innovation in Amtrak's operations. *Bell Journal of Economics* 6:281–298.

Baumol, W., and A. Klevorick. 1970. Input choices and rate-of-return regulation: An overview of the discussion. *Bell Journal of Economics* 1:162–190.

Baumol, W., J. Panzar, and R. Willig. 1982. *Contestable Markets and the Theory of Industry Structure.* San Diego, CA: Harcourt Brace Jovanovich.

Berg, S., and T. Tschirhart. 1988. *Natural Monopoly Regulation.* Cambridge: Cambridge University Press.

Boiteux, M. 1949. La tarification des demandes en pointe. *Revue Générale de l'Électricité* 58: 321–340. Translated as "Peak-load pricing," *Journal of Business* 33 (1960): 157–179.

Boiteux, M. 1951. La tarification au coût marginal et les demandes aléatoires. *Cahiers du Séminaire d'Économétrie.*

Breyer, S. 1982. *Regulation and Its Reform.* Cambridge, MA: Harvard University Press.

Brown, S., and D. Sibley. 1986. *The Theory of Public Utility Pricing.* Cambridge: Cambridge University Press.

Coase, R. 1945. Price and output policy of state enterprise: A comment. *Economic Journal* 55:112–113.

Coase, R. 1946. The marginal cost controversy. *Economica* 13:169–182.

Coase, R. 1970. The theory of public utility pricing and its application. *Bell Journal of Economics* 1:113–128.

Drèze, J. 1964. Some postwar contributions of French economists to theory and public policy. *American Economic Review* 54:1–64.

Dupuit, J. 1844. De la mesure de l'utilité des travaux publics. *Annales des Ponts et Chaussées* 8. Translation in *AEA Readings in Welfare Economics*, ed. K. Arrow and T. Scitovsky.

Faulhaber, G. 1975. Cross-subsidization: Pricing in public enterprises. *American Economic Review* 65:966–977.

Federal Communications Commission. 1987. In the matter of policy and rules concerning rates for dominant carriers. CC Docket No. 87-313.

Federal Energy Regulatory Commission. 1989. Incentive regulation: A research report. Mimeo, Washington, DC. (Report written by L. Brown, M. Einhorn, and I. Vogelsang with the assistance of B. Porter.)

Fleming, J. 1944. Price and output policy of state enterprise: A comment. *Economic Journal* 54:328–337.

Fudenberg, D., D. Levine, and J. Tirole. 1987. Incomplete information bargaining with outside opportunities. *Quarterly Journal of Economics* 102:37–50.

Fox, R. 1974. *Arming America: How the US Buys Weapons.* Cambridge, MA: Harvard University Press.

Fox, R. 1988. *The Defense Management Challenge: Weapons Acquisition.* Cambridge, MA: Harvard Business School Press.

Grossman, S., and O. Hart. 1986. The costs and benefits of ownership: A theory of vertical and lateral integration. *Journal of Political Economy* 94:691–719.

Hausman, J., and J. Poterba. 1987. Household behavior and the tax reform act of 1986. *Journal of Economic Perspectives* 1:101–119.

Holmström, B., and P. Milgrom. 1987. Aggregation and linearity in the provision of intertemporal incentives. *Econometrica* 55:303–328.

Hotelling, H. 1938. The general welfare in relation to problems of taxation and of railway and utility rates. *Econometrica* 6:242–269.

Joskow, P. 1989. Regulatory failure, regulatory reform and structural change in the electric power industry. Mimeo, Massachusetts Institute of Technology.

Joskow, P., and R. Schmalensee. 1986. Incentive regulation for electric utilities. *Yale Journal on Regulation* 4:1–49.

Jovanovic, B., and R. Rob. 1990. Long waves and short waves: Growth through intensive and extensive search. *Econometrica* 58:1391–1410.

Kahn, A. 1971. *The Economics of Regulation: Principles and Institutions*. Vols. 1 and 2. New York: Wiley. Reprint Cambridge, MA: MIT Press, 1988.

Kovacic, W. 1990. The sorcerer's apprentice: Public regulation of the weapons acquisition process. In *Arms, Politics, and the Economy*, ed. R. Higgs. New York: Holmes and Meier.

McAfee, P., and J. McMillan. 1987. *Incentives in Government Contracting*. Toronto: University of Toronto Press.

Meade, J. 1944. Price and output policy of state enterprise. *Economic Journal* 54:321–328.

MIT Energy Laboratory. 1984. Incentive regulation in the electric utility industry. SR 84-03, Massachusetts Institute of Technology.

NERA. 1985. Incentive regulation in the electric utility industry. Mimeo, Cambridge, MA.

Normanton, E. 1966. *The Accountability and Audit of Governments*. Manchester, England: Manchester University Press.

Owen, B., and R. Braeutigam. 1978. *The Regulation Game: Strategic Use of the Administrative Process*. Cambridge, MA: Ballinger Books.

Peck, M., and F. Scherer. 1962. *The Weapons Acquisition Process: An Economic Analysis*. Cambridge, MA: Harvard Business School Press.

Reichelstein, S. 1990. Constructing incentive schemes for government contracts: An application of agency theory. Mimeo, University of California, Berkeley.

Rogerson, W. 1989a. An economic framework for analyzing DOD profit policy. Mimeo, Northwestern University.

Rogerson, W. 1989b. Profit regulation of defense contractors and prizes for innovation. *Journal of Political Economy* 97:1284–1305.

Schmalensee, R. 1979. *The Control of Natural Monopolies*. Lexington, MA: D. C. Heath, Lexington Books.

Spulber, D. 1989. *Regulation and Markets*. Cambridge, MA: MIT Press.

Spulber, D. 1990. Optimal nonlinear pricing and contingent contracts. Mimeo, Northwestern University.

Srinagesh, P. 1990. Incentive regulation in practice. Unpublished notes, Bellcore (Notes presented at Toulouse conference on regulation, September 1990.)

Taylor, W. 1990. Incentive regulation in telecommunications. Mimeo, NERA, Cambridge, MA.

Trueger, P. 1966. *Accounting Guide for Defense Contracts*. 5th ed. Chicago: Commerce Clearing House.

Vickers, J. 1991. Government regulatory policy. Mimeo, St. Catherine's College, Oxford.

Vickers, J., and G. Yarrow. 1988. *Privatization: An Economic Analysis*. Cambridge, MA: MIT Press.

Wellisz, S. 1963. Regulation of natural gas pipeline companies: An economic analysis. *Journal of Political Economy* 71:30–43.

Williamson, O. 1975. *Markets and Hierarchies: Analysis and Antitrust Implications*. New York: The Free Press.

Williamson, O. 1985. *The Economic Institutions of Capitalism*. New York: The Free Press.

Wilson, R. 1989. Efficient and competitive rationing. *Econometrica* 57:1–40.

Wilson, R. 1992. *Nonlinear Pricing*. Oxford: Oxford University Press.

Wilson, T. 1945. Price and outlay policy of state enterprise. *Economic Journal* 55:454–461.

Yuspeh, L. 1976. A case for increasing the use of competitive procurement in the department of defense. In *Bidding and Auctioning for Procurement and Allocation*, ed. Y. Amihud. New York: New York University Press.

I PRICE AND RATE-OF-RETURN REGULATION

1 COST-REIMBURSEMENT RULES

1.1 Some Background

Cost-reimbursement rules refer to the extent of cost sharing between the firm and either the taxpayers or the consumers. The power of an incentive scheme, namely the fraction of the realized cost that is borne by the firm, is a central notion in policy debates. This notion underlies views about the relative merits of cost-of-service regulation, profit-sharing schemes, and price caps (in regulation) and of cost-plus contracts, incentive contracts, and fixed-price contracts (in procurement). Section 4 of the introductory chapter (which is required reading for this chapter) pointed at a basic trade-off between rent extraction and incentives. Incentives are best provided if the firm bears a high fraction of its cost. But reimbursing the firm's cost limits its rent. In this chapter we begin by formalizing this trade-off and by studying some of its consequences.

We take the simplest regulatory situation: The regulator wants to realize a single, fixed-size project. The fixed output allows us to abstract from the issue of consumer prices. A single firm has the adequate technology. The regulator designs an incentive scheme so as to maximize social welfare. This is the basic framework that we will use to enrich the model in order to study variable size and multigood production (this part), product market competition (part II), auctioning (part III), repeated relationships (part IV), nonbenevolent regulators (part V), and regulatory institutions (part VI).

The chapter is divided into two parts. The first part (sections 1.2 through 1.6) formalizes the basic trade-off between rent extraction and incentives discussed in the introductory chapter. Because the present chapter provides the foundation for the rest of the book, its first sections emphasize methodology over economic insights. Sections 1.2 through 1.4 are rather formal. Our goal is to provide all the steps of reasoning for a reader unfamiliar with information economics. By taking the time to master those sections, the reader should be able to read almost any chapter in the book independently of the other chapters. Section 1.2 sets up the model, and sections 1.3 and 1.4 solve it in detail when the firm's technological information can take two values or a continuum of values. Despite its methodological function, section 1.4 already yields some interesting insights. Under some conditions it is optimal for the regulator to offer a menu of linear cost-reimbursement rules. The firm chooses a high-powered (low-powered) cost-reimbursement rule if it is confident that it will produce at low (high) cost. Furthermore asymmetric information about the technology pushes incentive schemes away from fixed-price contracts and toward cost-plus contracts. These results seem to fit with practical considerations as well as with evidence on procurement.

Section 1.5 summarizes some economic insights and obtains some results on the effect of changes in technological uncertainty on the firm's rent and on the expectation of the slope of its incentive scheme. This barebones version of our model also anticipates some of the main themes of the book. Section 1.6 discusses the relevance and informational requirements of menus of contracts and argues that the insights can be used to guide regulatory policy.

The second part of the chapter (its last five sections) combines our model with standard, but important, ideas of the literature on incentives. Section 1.7 explores the use of "yardstick competition" (also called "relative performance evaluation") as a way for the regulator to reduce the asymmetry of information about the firm's cost. The idea here is that the firm's cost should be compared with those of other firms (possibly in different geographical markets) facing a similar technology. This section shows how to modify the cost-reimbursement rules to account for yardstick competition.

Sections 1.8 and 1.9 examine the link between cost-reimbursement rules and investment. An investment stage is added prior to the production stage studied in the first part of this chapter. Section 1.8 assumes that the regulator and the firm can sign a (long-term) contract defining the cost-reimbursement rule for the production stage before the firm invests; it considers two polar cases in which the two parties can or cannot contract on investment. This section recasts the traditional policy debate on a "fair" and "reasonable" rate of return on investment as a problem of inducing the appropriate investment behavior from the firm. It derives the optimal setting of the rate of return on investment and analyzes the linkage between the incentive to invest and the incentive to reduce operating costs when the firm has superior knowledge about either the cost of investment or its effectiveness. Section 1.9 uses the model to study another familiar issue in regulatory economics: In the absence of a detailed long-term contract, the regulated firm may refrain from investing in the fear that once the investment is in place, the regulator would pay only for variable cost and would not allow the firm to recoup its sunk cost. The section demonstrates the link between the regulator's rent extraction concern and the underinvestment problem. It then studies the benefits and limits of four factors conducive to investment: indirect measurement of investment, long-term contracts, regulator's reputation, and existence of related commercial activities.

Section 1.10, to be reread before tackling chapters 9 and 10, shows the "false dynamics" of a repeated relationship in which the government and the firm can commit to a long-term contract but are unable to renegotiate it. The regulator optimally commits to the repetition of the optimal static contract. Section 1.11 analyzes the effect of firm's risk aversion on the power of the incentive schemes. Bibliographic notes and technical appendixes conclude the chapter.

1.2 The Model

We consider the simple case of an indivisible public project that has value S for consumers. A single firm can realize the project. Its cost function is

$$C = \beta - e, \tag{1.1}$$

where β is an efficiency parameter and e is the managers' effort. For expositional simplicity we will assume that efforts remain strictly positive over the relevant range of equilibrium efforts.[1] If the firm exerts effort level e, it decreases the (monetary) cost of the project by e and incurs a disutility (in monetary units) of $\psi(e)$. This disutility increases with effort $\psi' > 0$ for $e > 0$, at an increasing rate $\psi'' > 0$, and satisfies $\psi(0) = 0$, $\lim_{e \to \beta} \psi(e) = +\infty$.

We first assume that cost is observable by the regulator, and we take the accounting convention that cost is reimbursed to the firm by the regulator. To accept work for the regulator, the firm must be compensated by a net monetary transfer t in addition to the reimbursement of cost. Let U be the firm's utility level:

$$U = t - \psi(e). \tag{1.2}$$

In its relationship with the regulator the firm must obtain at least as much utility as outside the relationship. We normalize the firm's outside opportunity level of utility or "reservation utility" to 0.[2] The firm's individual rationality (IR) constraint is accordingly

$$t - \psi(e) \geq 0. \tag{1.3}$$

Let $\lambda > 0$ denote the shadow cost of public funds. That is, distortionary taxation inflicts disutility \$$(1 + \lambda)$ on taxpayers in order to levy \$1 for the state. The net surplus of consumers/taxpayers is

$$S - (1 + \lambda)(t + \beta - e). \tag{1.4}$$

For a utilitarian regulator, ex post social welfare is

$$S - (1 + \lambda)(t + \beta - e) + t - \psi(e) = S - (1 + \lambda)[\beta - e + \psi(e)] - \lambda U. \tag{1.5}$$

1. There is no difficulty in allowing zero or negative efforts; see appendix A9.9 in chapter 9 for an example.

2. In particular this assumption means that the outside opportunity level is independent of the efficiency parameter. The analysis is unchanged as long as the outside level does not decrease with β too quickly. See chapter 6 for an adverse-selection problem with a type-dependent reservation utility.

That is, social welfare is the difference between the consumer surplus attached to the project and (1) the total cost of the project $C + \psi(e)$ as perceived by the taxpayers plus (2) the firm's rent above its reservation utility times the shadow cost of public funds. The crucial feature of this social welfare function is that the regulator dislikes leaving a rent to the firm.

We assume that the regulator is a Stackelberg leader and makes a take-it-or-leave-it offer to the firm. Under *complete information*—that is, knowing β and observing e—the regulator would solve

$$\max_{\{U,e\}} \{S - (1 + \lambda)[\beta - e + \psi(e)] - \lambda U\} \tag{1.6}$$

subject to $U \geq 0$. The solution of this program is

$$\psi'(e) = 1 \quad \text{or} \quad e \equiv e^*, \tag{1.7}$$

$$U = 0 \quad \text{or} \quad t = \psi(e^*). \tag{1.8}$$

That is, the marginal disutility of effort, $\psi'(e)$, must be equal to marginal cost savings, 1 [equation (1.7)]. Furthermore the existence of a shadow cost of public funds implies that the firm receives no rent [equation (1.8)].

There are many contracts between the firm and the regulator that implement the optimal regulatory outcome defined by these two equations. For instance, the regulator could give the firm transfer $t = \psi(e^*)$ and ask the firm to exert effort e^* (or equivalently set a cost target $C = \beta - e^*$). If the firm accepts this contract and exerts less effort than e^*, it must pay a large penalty. More interesting for our purpose, the regulator can offer the firm a *fixed-price contract*:

$$t(C) = a - (C - C^*),$$

where $a \equiv \psi(e^*)$ and $C^* \equiv \beta - e^*$. The firm is then the residual claimant for its cost savings and therefore chooses e so as to maximize $a - (\beta - e - C^*) - \psi(e)$; that is, $e = e^*$. Its utility is then $U = 0$. A fixed-price contract gives the firm perfect incentives for cost reduction; furthermore the fixed payment a can be tailored to fully extract the firm's rent under complete information. Note also that this contract shows that the regulator need not observe effort. Indeed as long as the regulator knows β, he or she can infer effort $e = \beta - C$ from the observation of cost.

Our objective in this chapter is to alter only one assumption of the previous framework, namely that of complete information. The regulator observes realized cost but does not know the true value of β and does not monitor the level of effort. In section 1.3 we study the case where it is common knowledge that β can take one of two values $\{\underline{\beta}, \overline{\beta}\}$, and we obtain the optimal regulatory rule. The same analysis is carried out in section 1.4 for the case where β is a continuous parameter belonging to an interval $[\underline{\beta}, \overline{\beta}]$. Various exercises of comparative statics of the optimal regulation are performed in section 1.5: effects of a change in the value of the project, in the disutility of effort, in the uncertainty about β, and in the shadow cost of public funds.

1.3 The Two-Type Case

This section assumes that the regulator knows that β belongs to the two-point support $\{\underline{\beta}, \overline{\beta}\}$ with $\overline{\beta} > \underline{\beta}$. We let $\Delta\beta \equiv \overline{\beta} - \underline{\beta}$. The regulator observes the realized cost C and makes a net transfer t to the firm. A contract between the regulator and the firm can be based on these jointly observable variables. If we exclude stochastic contracts (which we can do without loss of generality; see appendix A1.1), a contract based on the observables t and C specifies a transfer-cost pair for each type of firm, namely $\{t(\underline{\beta}), C(\underline{\beta})\}$ for type $\underline{\beta}$ and $\{t(\overline{\beta}), C(\overline{\beta})\}$ for type $\overline{\beta}$. For notational simplicity let $\underline{t} \equiv t(\underline{\beta})$, $\underline{C} \equiv C(\underline{\beta})$, etc. We let $U(\beta) \equiv t(\beta) - \psi(\beta - C(\beta))$ denote the utility or rent of type β when it selects the transfer-cost pair designed for it. [So $\underline{U} \equiv \underline{t} - \psi(\underline{\beta} - \underline{C})$ and $\overline{U} \equiv \overline{t} - \psi(\overline{\beta} - \overline{C})$.]

Incentive compatibility (IC) says that the contract designed for type $\underline{\beta}$ (respectively type $\overline{\beta}$) is the one preferred by type $\underline{\beta}$ (resp. type $\overline{\beta}$) in the menu of transfer-cost pairs. Noting from (1.1) that $e = \beta - C$, incentive compatibility amounts to

$$\underline{t} - \psi(\underline{\beta} - \underline{C}) \geq \overline{t} - \psi(\underline{\beta} - \overline{C}), \tag{1.9}$$

$$\overline{t} - \psi(\overline{\beta} - \overline{C}) \geq \underline{t} - \psi(\overline{\beta} - \underline{C}). \tag{1.10}$$

Adding up (1.9) and (1.10) yields

$$\psi(\underline{\beta} - \overline{C}) + \psi(\overline{\beta} - \underline{C}) - \psi(\underline{\beta} - \underline{C}) - \psi(\overline{\beta} - \overline{C}) \geq 0, \tag{1.11}$$

or

$$\int_{\underline{C}}^{\overline{C}} \int_{\underline{\beta}}^{\overline{\beta}} \psi''(\beta - C) d\beta dC \geq 0 \tag{1.12}$$

which, together with $\psi'' > 0$ and $\overline{\beta} > \underline{\beta}$, implies that

$$\overline{C} \geq \underline{C}. \tag{1.13}$$

Thus a first implication of incentive compatibility is that C is nondecreasing in β.

Individual rationality (IR) for each type of firm amounts to

$$\underline{U} \geq 0, \tag{1.14}$$

$$\overline{U} \geq 0. \tag{1.15}$$

Note that incentive compatibility for the efficient type and individual rationality for the inefficient type imply individual rationality for the efficient type. To show this, we apply successively (1.9), (1.15), and the fact that ψ is increasing:

$$\begin{aligned}\underline{U} &\geq \underline{t} - \psi(\underline{\beta} - \overline{C}) \\ &\geq \psi(\overline{\beta} - \overline{C}) - \psi(\underline{\beta} - \overline{C}) \\ &\geq 0. \end{aligned} \tag{1.16}$$

That is, since the efficient type of firm can always mimic the inefficient one at a lower cost, we can ignore (1.14).

Ex post social welfare when the firm has type β becomes

$$\begin{aligned} W(\beta) &= S - (1 + \lambda)[t(\beta) + C(\beta)] + t(\beta) - \psi(\beta - C(\beta)) \\ &= S - (1 + \lambda)[C(\beta) + \psi(\beta - C(\beta))] - \lambda U(\beta). \end{aligned} \tag{1.17}$$

The regulator has a prior distribution on the values of β characterized by $\nu = \Pr(\beta = \underline{\beta})$ and selects the contract that maximizes expected social welfare $W \equiv \nu W(\underline{\beta}) + (1 - \nu) W(\overline{\beta})$ under the IC and IR constraints.

To maximize expected welfare under (1.9), (1.10), and (1.15), we momentarily neglect (1.10), and we later check that the solution of the maximization under (1.9) and (1.15) satisfies (1.10). Therefore we retain only the IR constraint of the inefficient type of firm and the IC constraint of the efficient type.

The IC constraint of the efficient type (1.9) can be rewritten

$$\begin{aligned}\underline{U} &\geq \overline{t} - \psi(\underline{\beta} - \overline{C}) \\ &\geq \overline{U} + \Phi(\overline{e}), \end{aligned} \tag{1.18}$$

where

$$\Phi(e) \equiv \psi(e) - \psi(e - \Delta\beta) \tag{1.19}$$

and

$$\overline{e} = \overline{\beta} - \overline{C}. \tag{1.20}$$

Since $\psi'' > 0$, $\Phi(\cdot)$ is increasing. Furthermore, if $\psi''' \geq 0$, $\Phi(\cdot)$ is convex, which ensures that the regulator's objective function is concave (see below). The assumption that $\psi''' \geq 0$ is generally not needed for comparative statics exercises, but it simplifies the exposition.

The function $\Phi(\cdot)$ plays a crucial role in what follows. It determines the rent of the efficient type of firm (relative to the inefficient type) by measuring the economy in disutility of effort associated with a better technology. The implication of the property that $\Phi(\cdot)$ is increasing is that the firm derives more informational rents under a high-powered incentive scheme (inducing high effort) than under a low-powered one.

The regulator's optimization problem is

$$\max_{\{\underline{C},\bar{C},\underline{U},\bar{U}\}} \{\nu[S - (1+\lambda)(\underline{C} + \psi(\underline{\beta} - \underline{C})) - \lambda\underline{U}]$$
$$+ (1-\nu)[S - (1+\lambda)(\bar{C} + \psi(\bar{\beta} - \bar{C})) - \lambda\bar{U}]\}, \tag{1.21}$$

subject to (1.15) and (1.18). Since the rents $U(\beta)$ are costly to the regulator, the constraints (1.15) and (1.18) are binding at the optimum. Substituting $\bar{U} = 0$ and $\underline{U} = \Phi(\bar{\beta} - \bar{C})$ in (1.21), we obtain

$$\psi'(\underline{\beta} - \underline{C}) = 1 \quad \text{or} \quad \underline{e} = e^*, \tag{1.22}$$

$$\psi'(\bar{\beta} - \bar{C}) = 1 - \frac{\lambda}{1+\lambda}\frac{\nu}{1-\nu}\Phi'(\bar{\beta} - \bar{C}), \quad \text{implying that } \bar{e} < e^*. \tag{1.23}$$

Note that the neglected constraint (1.10) is satisfied by this solution. This constraint can be written

$$\bar{U} \geq \underline{U} - \Phi(\bar{\beta} - \underline{C}) \tag{1.24}$$

or

$$0 \geq \Phi(\bar{\beta} - \bar{C}) - \Phi(\bar{\beta} - \underline{C}), \tag{1.25}$$

which is true since $\bar{e} < \underline{e}$ from (1.22) and (1.23) (and therefore $\bar{C} > \underline{C}$) and $\Phi' > 0$.

Thus far we have obtained the optimal deterministic contract. Appendix A1.1 shows that the contract is optimal under the additional assumption that $\psi''' \geq 0$, even in the class of stochastic contracts. Also we have assumed that it is worth realizing the project even with an inefficient firm. This is the case for S large enough. We will relax this assumption later. We gather our results in the following proposition:

Proposition 1.1 For S large enough and $\psi''' \geq 0$, optimal regulation under incomplete information is characterized by (1.22) and (1.23). It entails

i. an efficient level of effort and a positive rent for type $\underline{\beta}$,

ii. undereffort and no rent for type $\bar{\beta}$.

The ability of the efficient type to mimic the inefficient type forces the regulator to give up a rent to the efficient type if he or she wishes to have an active inefficient type. This rent $\Phi(\bar{e})$ is a function of the effort level required from the *inefficient* type. If the regulator were to insist on the first-best level of effort, or $\bar{C} = \bar{\beta} - e^*$, the result would be a high rent for the efficient type (since $\Phi' > 0$). To reduce the costly rent, the regulator lowers the effort level requested from the inefficient type.

We encounter here a crucial idea of this book. Asymmetric information forces principals to give up costly rents to their agents. To mitigate these costs, allocations are distorted away from first-best allocations and to-

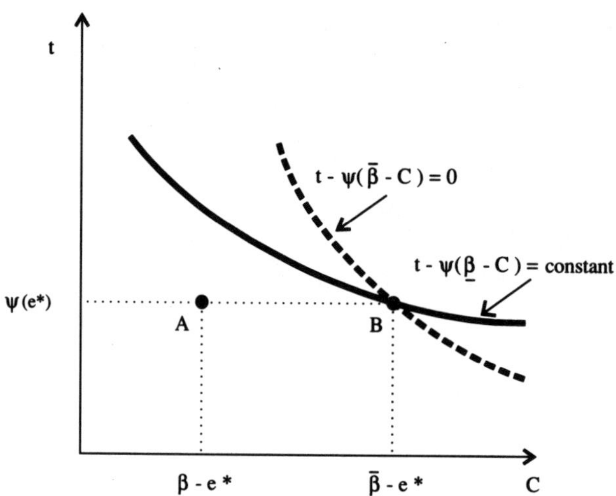

Figure 1.1
The complete information solution $\{A, B\}$ is not incentive compatible

ward low-powered schemes. These distortions constitute the regulatory response to the asymmetry of information.

Let us illustrate the solution in the transfer-cost space: In figure 1.1 the first-best $\{\underline{e} = \bar{e} = e^*, \underline{t} = \bar{t} = \psi(e^*)\}$ is not incentive compatible because both types prefer contract $\{\psi(e^*), \bar{\beta} - e^*\}$ (point B in the figure) to contract $\{\psi(e^*), \underline{\beta} - e^*\}$ (point A in the figure). Figure 1.2 illustrates the optimal solution. Type $\underline{\beta}$ is indifferent between contract $\{\underline{t}, \underline{C}\}$ (point D in figure 1.2) and contract $\{\bar{t}, \bar{C}\}$ (point E in figure 1.2). This illustrates the fact that type $\underline{\beta}$'s IC constraint is binding at the optimum. Type $\bar{\beta}$ strictly prefers point E to point D (its IC constraint is not binding), and it obtains no rent (its IR constraint is binding). Figure 1.2 illustrates why reducing the inefficient type's effort limits the efficient type's rent. Eliciting effort e^* from the inefficient type would correspond to giving this type point B rather than point E on its zero-utility indifference curve. But this would require moving the efficient type to a higher-utility indifference curve (moving from point D to point G). While the first-best *effort* levels can be implemented, for example by the menu $\{G, B\}$, it is optimal for the regulator to distort effort to extract rents.

Figure 1.2 also suggests the following intuitive derivation of $\bar{e}$: Increasing $\bar{C}$, or equivalently reducing $\bar{e}$ by one unit, has two effects. The net production cost of type $\bar{\beta}$ increases by $1 - \psi'(\bar{e})$. But type $\underline{\beta}$'s rent or transfer decreases by $\Phi'(\bar{e})$. The probability of type $\bar{\beta}$ is $1 - \nu$ so that the expected increase in production cost is

$$(1 - \nu)(1 + \lambda)[1 - \psi'(\bar{e})];$$

similarly the expected reduction in the social cost of transfer to type $\underline{\beta}$ is

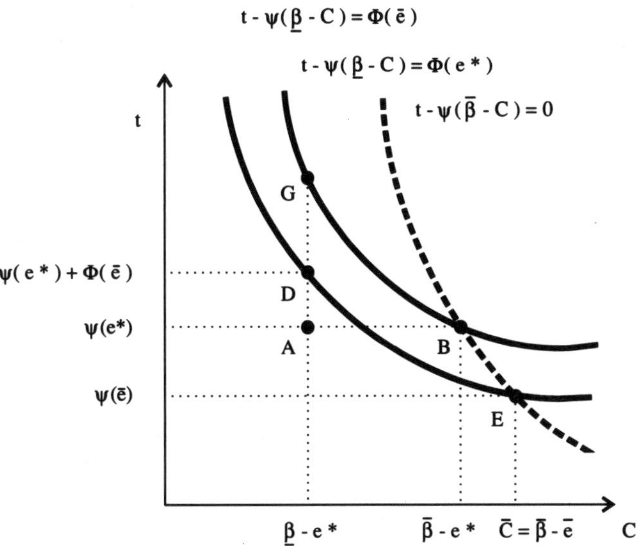

Figure 1.2
Guaranteeing incentive compatibility

$\nu\lambda\Phi'(\bar{e})$.

Point E in figure 1.2 is chosen so that a small move along type $\bar{\beta}$'s zero-utility curve generates an equal increase in expected production cost and a decrease in the expected social cost of transfer. This yields (1.23).

Remark (to be skipped in a first reading) By observing the contract selected by the firm, the regulator learns the cost characteristic β of the firm. Suppose, for instance, that he or she observes the choice of point D. Inferring that $\beta = \underline{\beta}$, the regulator would be tempted to keep requiring cost level $\underline{C} = \underline{\beta} - e^*$ and to reduce the transfer to $\psi(e^*)$ to extract the efficient type's rent. The crucial assumption made here is that the regulator cannot withdraw his or her initial offer once it is accepted. That is, either the contract is enforced by a court, or the regulator has developed a reputation for respecting agreements.

A more subtle issue arises in the application of the revelation principle. Suppose that the regulator can indeed commit to a contract, say, because contracts are enforceable. We mentioned two ways of implementing the optimal allocation. One is the use of an incentive scheme $t(C)$. That is, the regulator offers a contract $t(\cdot)$. If the firm accepts the contract, it produces. The realized cost C is observed and the regulator pays $t(C)$. Alternatively, the revelation principle (see appendix A1.2) says that the regulator can offer a direct mechanism $\{t(\beta), C(\beta)\}$. If the firm accepts this mechanism, it makes an announcement $\hat{\beta}$ of its parameter. The firm is then required to produce at cost level $C(\hat{\beta})$, and it receives transfer $t(\hat{\beta})$. Direct mechanisms suffer from the following drawback: After the firm announces $\hat{\beta}$ and before effort is exerted, the regulator and the firm could renegotiate their initial agreement. While $\{t(\hat{\beta}), C(\hat{\beta})\}$ can be enforced if one of the two parties wants it, both parties may find it mutually advantageous to void the initial agreement and design a new one. Such renegotiation would not arise should the firm announce $\underline{\beta}$ (chooses point D). Effort would then be efficient, and no renegotiation could improve the welfare of both parties. Suppose, however, that the firm announces type $\bar{\beta}$ (chooses point E). The effort would be suboptimal. It would then be optimal to renegotiate to ensure production at cost level $\bar{\beta} - e^*$ and share the gains from trade. For instance, if the regulator has all the bargaining power in the renegotiation, he or she will offer to alter contract E into contract B in figure 1.2. Anticipating this, type $\underline{\beta}$ will strictly prefer to choose contract E over contract D. In other words, the expectation of renegotiation destroys incentive compatibility.

While, by definition, renegotiation is beneficial ex post, it is never beneficial ex ante and may even be detrimental. Renegotiation is a concern in this model only if one uses direct revelation mechanisms. The problem is avoided in the more realistic incentive schemes $t(C)$ in which the regulator learns nothing about the firm's type until cost is realized, that is, until there is nothing to renegotiate about (except for the transfer, but no renegotiation can occur in this dimension only).[3] But, as we will see in chapter 10, in a multiperiod model renegotiation of long-term contracts is a serious issue.

Shutdown of the Firm

It is often reasonable to assume that a regulated firm cannot be shut down, since there are poor substitution opportunities for electricity, telephone, and other such basic products. However, in procurement, or in regulation at the level of a project, the regulator could decide to go ahead with production only if the cost is sufficiently low. If the regulator decides to shut down production of an inefficient firm, the optimal contract for type $\underline{\beta}$ would clearly be $\{t = \psi(e^*),\ C = \underline{\beta} - e^*\}$. In other words, because the efficient type now gets no rent by mimicking the inefficient one, the regulator can fully extract its rent. The gain is thus a lower rent for type $\underline{\beta}$ (note that not producing is an extreme instance of a low-powered incentive scheme); the loss is that the good is not produced if the firm has type $\bar{\beta}$. The regulator prefers to have the two types produce if and only if

$$\begin{aligned} &\nu\{S - (1 + \lambda)[\underline{\beta} - e^* + \psi(e^*)] - \lambda\Phi(\bar{e})\} \\ &\quad + (1 - \nu)\{S - (1 + \lambda)[\bar{\beta} - \bar{e} + \psi(\bar{e})]\} \\ &\geq \nu\{S - (1 + \lambda)[\underline{\beta} - e^* + \psi(e^*)]\}. \end{aligned} \tag{1.26}$$

3. However, it may be useful to have the firm reveal information before performing so that the regulator could coordinate its activity with that of other firms, or the regulator might want to shut the firm down, as is studied next.

Because the derivative of the left-hand side of (1.26) with respect to S is 1 and that of the right-hand side is only ν, shutdown occurs only for low values of S. For instance, when S is small because there exist substitutes, shutting down type $\bar{\beta}$ becomes an attractive option. This suggests that the firm is hurt by the introduction of competition on its product market. Competition reduces the social surplus attached to its production and makes it more likely that the regulator would shut down the inefficient type. Competition thus reduces the efficient type's rent. Regulated firms derive more rents when they are indispensable. Similarly there exists $\nu_0 \in (0,1)$ such that the regulator shuts down type $\bar{\beta}$ if and only if $\nu > \nu_0$.

1.4 Continuum of Types

We now assume that β is a continuous parameter that belongs to the interval $[\underline{\beta}, \bar{\beta}]$. From the revelation principle (see appendix A1.2) we know that any regulatory mechanism is equivalent to a direct revelation mechanism that induces truthful revelation of the firm's cost parameter.

Let $\{t(\hat{\beta}), C(\hat{\beta})\}_{\hat{\beta} \in [\underline{\beta}, \bar{\beta}]}$ be such a revelation mechanism, where $\hat{\beta}$ denotes the announcement. That is, if the firm announces a cost parameter $\hat{\beta}$, it must realize a cost $C(\hat{\beta})$, and it will receive a net transfer $t(\hat{\beta})$. The firm's utility as a function of the true parameter β and the announced one $\hat{\beta}$ is

$$\varphi(\beta, \hat{\beta}) \equiv t(\hat{\beta}) - \psi(\beta - C(\hat{\beta})). \tag{1.27}$$

The truth-telling requirement in particular implies that for any pair of values β and β' in $[\underline{\beta}, \bar{\beta}]$,

$$t(\beta) - \psi(\beta - C(\beta)) \geq t(\beta') - \psi(\beta - C(\beta')), \tag{1.28}$$

$$t(\beta') - \psi(\beta' - C(\beta')) \geq t(\beta) - \psi(\beta' - C(\beta)). \tag{1.29}$$

Adding up (1.28) and (1.29) gives

$$\psi(\beta' - C(\beta)) - \psi(\beta - C(\beta)) \geq \psi(\beta' - C(\beta')) - \psi(\beta - C(\beta')), \tag{1.30}$$

or

$$\int_{\beta}^{\beta'} \int_{C(\beta)}^{C(\beta')} \psi''(x - y)\,dx\,dy \geq 0. \tag{1.31}$$

Therefore, if $\beta' > \beta$, $C(\beta') \geq C(\beta)$. Incentive compatibility thus implies that $C(\cdot)$ is a nondecreasing function. Hence $C(\cdot)$ is differentiable almost everywhere. Actually we will focus on a smaller class of functions, the class of piecewise differentiable functions in order to use optimal control theory (a piecewise differentiable function admits a continuous derivative except at a finite number of points, and when the derivative does not exist, the function still admits left and right derivatives). At a point of differentiability of C, (1.28) and (1.29) imply that t is also differentiable (see appendix A1.3).

The first-order condition for truth telling ($\hat{\beta} = \beta$ maximizes $\varphi(\beta, \hat{\beta})$) can be written

$$\varphi_2(\beta, \beta) = 0 \qquad \text{almost everywhere,} \tag{1.32}$$

or equivalently

$$\dot{t}(\beta) = -\psi'(\beta - C(\beta))\dot{C}(\beta) \qquad \text{almost everywhere.} \tag{1.33}$$

(From now on, we will omit the qualifier "almost everywhere" for notational simplicity.)

Let $U(\beta) \equiv \varphi(\beta, \beta)$ denote type β's rent. Equation (1.32) [or the envelope theorem applied to the maximization of (1.27) with respect to $\hat{\beta}$] yields

$$\dot{U}(\beta) = -\psi'(\beta - C(\beta)). \tag{1.34}$$

Appendix A1.4 shows that if this first-order condition is satisfied and if $C(\cdot)$ is nondecreasing, these necessary conditions are sufficient, and incentive compatibility is achieved.

We summarize the previous steps by the next proposition.

Proposition 1.2 If $\beta \in [\underline{\beta}, \bar{\beta}]$, a pair of piecewise differentiable functions $U(\cdot)$ and $C(\cdot)$ is incentive compatible if and only if

$$\dot{U}(\beta) = -\psi'(\beta - C(\beta)), \tag{1.34}$$

$$\dot{C}(\beta) \geq 0. \tag{1.35}$$

Assumption 1.1 Let $F(\cdot)$ be the absolutely continuous distribution function, with density $f(\cdot)$, that describes the prior of the regulator on the interval $[\underline{\beta}, \bar{\beta}]$: $f(\beta) > 0$ for all $\beta \in [\underline{\beta}, \bar{\beta}]$.

The regulator maximizes expected social welfare under the IC and IR constraints:

$$\max_{\{e(\cdot), U(\cdot)\}} \int_{\underline{\beta}}^{\bar{\beta}} [S - (1 + \lambda)[\beta - e(\beta) + \psi(e(\beta))] - \lambda U(\beta)] dF(\beta) \tag{1.36}$$

subject to

$$\dot{U}(\beta) = -\psi'(e(\beta)), \tag{1.34}$$

$$\dot{e}(\beta) \leq 1, \tag{1.37}$$

$$U(\beta) \geq 0 \qquad \text{for all } \beta. \tag{1.38}$$

Note that we take $e(\cdot)$ as the control variable; this is equivalent to using $C(\beta) = \beta - e(\beta)$ as the control variable as we have done until now.

The constraint $\dot{e}(\beta) \leq 1$ is the rewriting of the second-order condition $\dot{C}(\beta) \geq 0$. Because $U(\cdot)$ is nonincreasing from (1.34), inequalities (1.38) can be replaced by

$$U(\bar{\beta}) \geq 0. \tag{1.39}$$

We will usually solve this type of problem using optimal control.[4] The reader unfamiliar with optimal control can use the following technique: Integrating (1.34), we get

$$U(\beta) = \int_{\beta}^{\bar{\beta}} \psi'(e(\tilde{\beta}))d\tilde{\beta} + U(\bar{\beta}). \tag{1.40}$$

Since rents are socially costly, the regulator sets $U(\bar{\beta}) = 0$. Integrating by parts, the expected rent to be given up by the regulator is

$$\begin{aligned}\int_{\underline{\beta}}^{\bar{\beta}} U(\beta)dF(\beta) &= \int_{\underline{\beta}}^{\bar{\beta}} \int_{\beta}^{\bar{\beta}} \psi'(e(\tilde{\beta}))d\tilde{\beta}dF(\beta) \\ &= \left[F(\beta)\int_{\beta}^{\bar{\beta}} \psi'(e(\tilde{\beta}))d\tilde{\beta}\right]\Bigg|_{\underline{\beta}}^{\bar{\beta}} + \int_{\underline{\beta}}^{\bar{\beta}} F(\beta)\psi'(e(\beta))d\beta \\ &= \int_{\underline{\beta}}^{\bar{\beta}} F(\beta)\psi'(e(\beta))d\beta = \int_{\underline{\beta}}^{\bar{\beta}} \frac{F(\beta)}{f(\beta)}\psi'(e(\beta))dF(\beta).\end{aligned} \tag{1.41}$$

Substituting (1.41) into (1.36), we obtain the regulator's optimization problem:

$$\max_{\{e(\cdot)\}} \int_{\underline{\beta}}^{\bar{\beta}} \left\{S - (1 + \lambda)[\beta - e(\beta) + \psi(e(\beta))] - \lambda\frac{F(\beta)}{f(\beta)}\psi'(e(\beta))\right\}dF(\beta) \tag{1.42}$$

subject to

$$\dot{e}(\beta) \leq 1. \tag{1.43}$$

Note that the integrand in (1.42) is concave in $e(\beta)$ if $\psi''' \geq 0$. Ignoring constraint (1.43) for the moment, we get

$$\psi'(e(\beta)) = 1 - \frac{\lambda}{1 + \lambda}\frac{F(\beta)}{f(\beta)}\psi''(e(\beta)). \tag{1.44}$$

Equation (1.44) has a straightforward interpretation. Raise effort of types in $[\beta, \beta + d\beta]$ [in number $f(\beta)d\beta$] by δe. Productive efficiency increases by $[1 - \psi'(e(\beta))]\delta e$ for these types, which yields social gain $(1 + \lambda)[1 - \psi'(e(\beta))]\delta e f(\beta)d\beta$. However, this also raises the rent of types in $[\underline{\beta}, \beta]$ [in number $F(\beta)$]. From (1.34) the rent of type β is increased by

4. Some good introductions to optimal control theory are Arrow and Kurz (1970), Bryson and Ho (1975), Hadley and Kemp (1971), Kamien and Schwartz (1981), and Seierstad and Sydsaeter (1987).

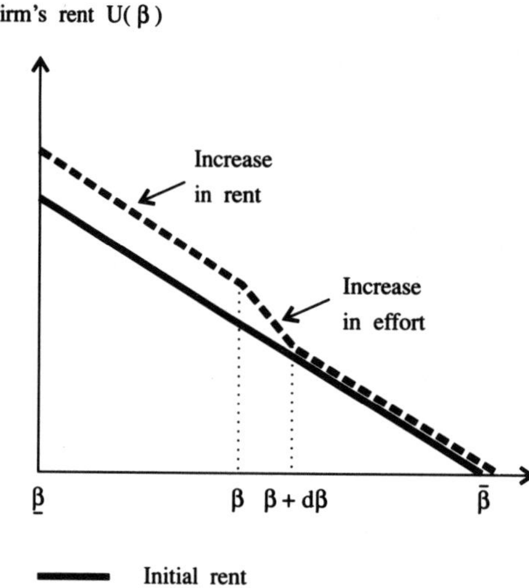

Figure 1.3
Trade-off between incentives and rent extraction

$\psi''(e(\beta))\delta e d\beta$, and so is the rent of types $\tilde{\beta} < \beta$. The social cost of the extra rents is $\lambda\psi''(e(\beta))(\delta e)(d\beta)F(\beta)$. At the optimum the marginal cost must equal the marginal benefit, which yields (1.44). This reasoning is illustrated in figure 1.3.

Differentiating (1.44), we get

$$\dot{e}(\beta) = -\frac{[\lambda/(1+\lambda)]\psi''(e(\beta))(d/d\beta)[F(\beta)/f(\beta)]}{\psi''(e(\beta)) + [\lambda/(1+\lambda)][F(\beta)/f(\beta)]\psi'''(e(\beta))}. \tag{1.45}$$

At an interior maximum the denominator of (1.45) is positive. [As we already noted, the assumption $\psi''' \geq 0$, used to discard stochastic mechanisms, ensures the global concavity of the problem.] To give the sign of the numerator, we make the following assumption:

Assumption 1.2 *Monotone hazard rate or log concavity of F:* $d[F(\beta)/f(\beta)]/d\beta \geq 0$.

This condition is satisfied by most usual distributions—uniform, normal, logistic, chi-squared, exponential, and Laplace.[5] One interpretation in our context is as follows: The basic technology, known to everyone, is characterized by parameter $\bar{\beta}$. There can be "improvements" on this technology. In our notation $\bar{\beta} - \beta$ is a measure of the number of improvements. $F(\beta)$ is the probability that there are at least $\bar{\beta} - \beta$ improve-

5. See Bagnoli and Bergström (1989) for a more complete list and for results allowing the identification of distributions with monotone hazard rates.

ments. The probability that there are more than $\overline{\beta} - \beta$ improvements and less than $\overline{\beta} - \beta + d\beta$ improvements is thus $f(\beta)d\beta$. Decreasing β from $\overline{\beta}$, $f(\beta)/F(\beta)$ is the conditional probability that there are no more improvements given that there have already been $\overline{\beta} - \beta$ improvements. Assumption 1.2 states that this conditional probability increases as the firm becomes more efficient; in this sense assumption 1.2 is a decreasing returns assumption. Together with (1.45) it implies that at any interior maximum, $\dot{e}(\beta) \leq 0$. A fortiori the agent's global second-order condition (1.37) is satisfied.[6]

We now use optimal control for an alternative derivation of the optimum. Let U be the state variable and e the control variable. The hamiltonian is

$$H = (S - (1 + \lambda)[\beta - e(\beta) + \psi(e(\beta))] - \lambda U(\beta))f(\beta) - \mu(\beta)\psi'(e(\beta)), \tag{1.46}$$

where $\mu(\cdot)$ is the Pontryagin multiplier. By the maximum principle

$$\dot{\mu} = -\frac{\partial H}{\partial U} = \lambda f(\beta). \tag{1.47}$$

The boundary $\beta = \underline{\beta}$ is unconstrained. Hence the transversality condition at $\beta = \underline{\beta}$ is

$$\mu(\underline{\beta}) = 0. \tag{1.48}$$

Integrating (1.47) yields

$$\mu(\beta) = \lambda F(\beta). \tag{1.49}$$

Last, maximizing H with respect to e gives (1.44).

Let $e^*(\beta)$ be the solution of (1.44). The firm's rent and transfer are

$$U^*(\beta) = \int_{\beta}^{\overline{\beta}} \psi'(e^*(\tilde{\beta}))d\tilde{\beta}, \tag{1.50}$$

and

$$t^*(\beta) = \psi(e^*(\beta)) + U^*(\beta). \tag{1.51}$$

We gather our results in proposition 1.3.

Proposition 1.3 Under assumption 1.2 the optimal regulatory allocation is given by

$$C^*(\beta) = \beta - e^*(\beta),$$

6. If assumption 1.2 does not hold, the regulator may want to induce different types to produce at the same cost, that is, to "bunch." For techniques on solving for the optimal mechanism in such circumstances, see appendix A1.5 and Guesnerie and Laffont (1984).

$$\psi'(e^*(\beta)) = 1 - \frac{\lambda}{1+\lambda}\frac{F(\beta)}{f(\beta)}\psi''(e^*(\beta)),$$

$$U^*(\beta) = \int_{\beta}^{\bar{\beta}} \psi'(e^*(\tilde{\beta}))d\tilde{\beta},$$

$$t^*(\beta) = \psi(e^*(\beta)) + U^*(\beta).$$

Effort decreases with β, and cost increases with β.

Proposition 1.3 defines only implicitly the transfer as a function of cost. Because $C^*(\cdot)$ is a strictly increasing function under assumption 1.2, it can be inverted to yield a function $\beta = \beta^*(C)$. Substituting this function into (1.51) gives the optimal net transfer as a function of the observed cost level:

$$T^*(C) \equiv \psi(e^*(\beta^*(C))) + U^*(\beta^*(C)). \tag{1.52}$$

We now show that $T^*(\cdot)$ is a convex function:

$$\frac{dT^*}{dC} = \frac{dt^*}{d\beta}\frac{1}{dC^*/d\beta} = -\psi'(\beta^*(C) - C), \tag{1.53}$$

$$\frac{d^2T^*}{dC^2} = -\psi''(\beta - C^*(\beta))\left(\frac{1}{dC^*/d\beta} - 1\right) = -\psi''(e^*(\beta))\frac{\dot{e}^*(\beta)}{\dot{C}^*(\beta)} \geq 0, \tag{1.55}$$

using the facts that $\dot{e}^* \leq 0$ and $\dot{C}^* > 0$. Since $T^*(\cdot)$ is convex, it can be replaced by the family of its tangents. These tangents represent a menu of contracts that are linear in realized costs:

$$t(\hat{\beta}, C) = t^*(\hat{\beta}) - \psi'(e^*(\hat{\beta}))(C - C^*(\hat{\beta})). \tag{1.56}$$

Let us check that (1.56) induces truth telling ($\hat{\beta} = \beta$) and the appropriate effort level ($e(\beta) = e^*(\beta)$). Consider the firm's optimization program when facing this menu of linear contracts:

$$\max_{\{\hat{\beta}, e\}} \{t^*(\hat{\beta}) - \psi'(e^*(\hat{\beta}))[\beta - e - \hat{\beta} + e^*(\hat{\beta})] - \psi(e)\}. \tag{1.57}$$

The first-order conditions are

$$\begin{aligned} &-\psi'(e^*(\hat{\beta}))[1 - \dot{e}^*(\hat{\beta})] - \psi'(e^*(\hat{\beta}))[\dot{e}^*(\hat{\beta}) - 1] \\ &\quad -\psi''(e^*(\hat{\beta}))[\beta - e - \hat{\beta} + e^*(\hat{\beta})]\dot{e}^*(\hat{\beta}) = 0, \end{aligned} \tag{1.58}$$

$$\psi'(e) = \psi'(e^*(\hat{\beta})). \tag{1.59}$$

Equation (1.59) implies that $e = e^*(\hat{\beta})$ and (1.58) that $\hat{\beta} = \beta$. Moreover the optimization program (1.57) is concave in $(\hat{\beta}, e)$, and therefore the first-order conditions are sufficient.

Figure 1.4 illustrates the implementation by a menu of linear contracts. The function $T^*(\cdot)$ represented by the bold curve is convex and so are the

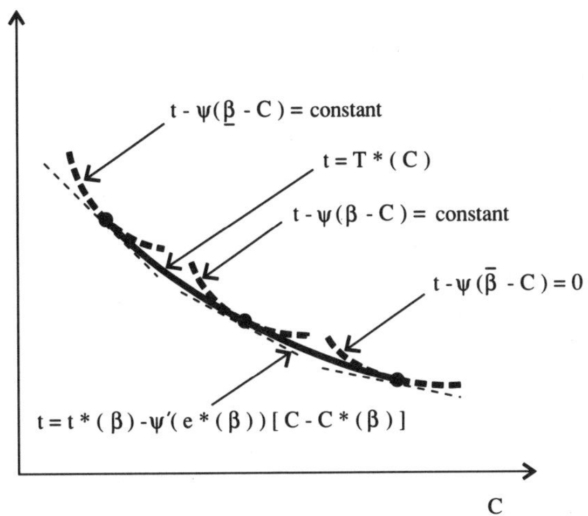

Figure 1.4
Implementation by a menu of linear contracts

firm's isoutility curves (the dashed curves). The firm selects the same {cost, transfer} pair whether it faces $T^*(\cdot)$ or the menu of its tangents (depicted by light lines).

Proposition 1.4 Under assumption 1.2 the optimal regulatory mechanism can be implemented by the menu of linear contracts defined by (1.56).

1.4.1 Decentralization through a Menu of Linear Contracts[7]

We can rewrite the menu of linear contracts in the following way: The firm chooses the share b of cost that it will bear and a fixed payment a. That is, the net transfer is

$$t = a - bC. \tag{1.60}$$

Type β must choose $(a(\beta), b(\beta))$ such that

$$a(\beta) = t^*(\beta) + \psi'(e^*(\beta))C^*(\beta) \tag{1.61}$$

and

$$b(\beta) = \psi'(e^*(\beta)). \tag{1.62}$$

Eliminating β, we can derive a relationship between the fixed payment and the coefficient of cost sharing that satisfies

$$\frac{da}{db} = C. \tag{1.63}$$

7. Reichelstein (1989) derives a finite approximation to the optimal menu of linear incentive schemes for some parameterized distributions and utility functions.

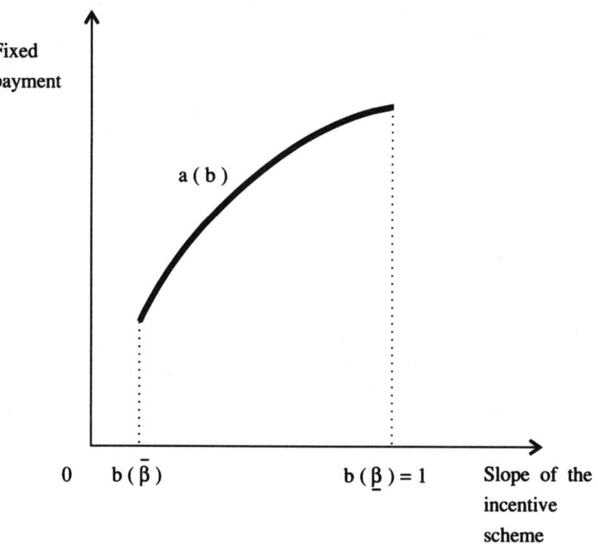

Figure 1.5
Characterization of the menu of contracts

That is, a unit increase in the slope must be compensated by the extra cost to the firm. We conclude that

$$\frac{d^2a}{db^2} = \frac{d(da/db)/d\beta}{(db/d\beta)} = \frac{1-\dot{e}}{\psi''\dot{e}} < 0. \tag{1.64}$$

The fixed payment is thus a *concave* function of the slope of the incentive scheme, as depicted in figure 1.5. Note in the figure that the most efficient type faces a *fixed-price contract* [since $\psi'(e^*(\underline{\beta})) = b(\underline{\beta}) = 1$] and is therefore residual claimant for its cost savings. The other types are given incentive contracts that are intermediate between the fixed-price contract and the cost-plus contract, corresponding to $b = 0$.

Alternatively, the regulator can ask for a cost estimate C^a and give slope $\tilde{b}(C^a)$ and expected reward $\tilde{a}(C^a)$; the linear scheme given in (1.60) can then be rewritten[8]

$$t(C^a, C) = \tilde{a}(C^a) - \tilde{b}(C^a)(C - C^a). \tag{1.60'}$$

We can interpret the coefficient $\tilde{b}$ as the coefficient of sharing of cost overruns. The firm is given a lower expected reward $\tilde{a}$ and shares a lower fraction $\tilde{b}$ of overruns when it announces a higher cost estimate.[9]

8. We have $b(\beta) = \tilde{b}(C^*(\beta))$ and $a(\beta) = \tilde{a}(C^*(\beta)) + \tilde{b}(C^*(\beta))C^*(\beta)$. Inverting $C^*(\cdot)$ yields $\tilde{b}(\cdot)$ and $\tilde{a}(\cdot)$.
9. Again $d\tilde{a}/d\tilde{b} > 0$.

1.4.2 Parameters of the Incentive Scheme and Performance

The relationship between parameters of the incentive scheme and performance $-C$ is summarized in proposition 1.5.

Proposition 1.5 The performance $-C$ of the firm is positively correlated with the slope b of the incentive scheme and with the fixed payment a.

Proposition 1.5 results from $dC/d\beta > 0$, $db/d\beta < 0$, and $da/d\beta < 0$. It is important not to interpret the proposition as a causal relationship. Otherwise, one could conclude that high-powered incentive schemes (b high) are better because they induce better performance. While the second statement is correct, the first ignores the desirability of rent extraction. Optimal screening of the firm's technology yields over the sample good performances and high-powered schemes together with poor performances and low-powered schemes. One application of this idea is to the interesting evidence gathered by Mathios and Rogers (1989). They look at prices of intrastate interlata telephone services in the United States. (There are 161 local access and transportation areas—latas—in the United States. Therefore intrastate long-distance services are provided either inter- or intralata.) Such services are regulated differently in different states. They show that states that have adopted price-cap regulation have on average lower rates than those that have stuck to cost-of-service regulation. If one views the possibility of moving from COS regulation to PC regulation as part of a bargain between the state regulators and the telephone companies, the model predicts that efficient telephone companies (those with the lowest rates) are more eager to push for or to accept PC regulation, which is a more powerful incentive scheme. It does not by itself imply that some states have acted suboptimally by not adopting price caps.[10]

The basis for proposition 1.5 is that more efficient types choose high-powered schemes because they produce at a lower cost and therefore do not mind bearing their cost in exchange for a high fixed fee. An analogy of this behavior in the corporate world is Lee Iacocca's bargaining with Chrysler's board for a token salary of $1 and very high stock options, a behavior consistent with his belief that he would be a successful chief executive. The selection of high-powered incentive schemes by defense contractors that have favorable information is reported in Scherer (1964, p. 227). He writes:

> When contractors believe that cost targets will be tight (i.e., when there is an overrun bias), they bargain successfully for low sharing proportions and high price ceilings, while when loose targets (i.e., an underrun bias) are expected, they accept

10. Another reason why the left- and right-hand side of a regression of telephone prices on (among other things) regulatory structure might be determined by a joint omitted variable may be that states with more energetic and efficient regulators may also have engaged earlier in regulatory innovation.

a high share of overruns and (more likely) underruns and relatively low price ceilings. Or when relatively high sharing proportions are agreed upon in advance of cost negotiations, contractors hold out for pessimistic cost targets. On the other hand, the causality could conceivably run in another direction—high shares and low ceilings could provide stronger incentives for cost control and cost reduction, and hence lead to larger underruns. Both explanations may be valid, but the qualitative evidence from our case studies lends greater support to the first (bargaining) hypothesis.

Scherer (1964, p. 150) also documents that high-powered incentive schemes are correlated with higher rents, as our theory implies:

Profit rates actually realized (as opposed to initially negotiated) have followed a similar distribution by contract type, as the following Renegotiation Board data for 25 major contractors show:

Type of Contract	*Average Profit as % of Sales, before Renegotiation*
Firm fixed-price	18.3%
Redeterminable fixed-price	10.6
Fixed-price incentive	8.8
Cost-plus-fixed-fee and cost-plus-incentive-fee	4.9

Likewise, John Perry Miller found that during World War II the average realized rate of profit before negotiation on Navy fixed-price type contracts was 13.6%, while the average on cost-plus-fixed-fee contracts was 4.8%.

There is some evidence of the pattern of covariance in performance, slope, and rewards in the corporate world.[11]

1.4.3 Additive Noise and Linear Contracts

The possibility of decentralizing through a menu of linear contracts shows that introducing noise (accounting or forecast errors) in the cost function $C = \beta - e + \varepsilon$ has no effect. The intuition for this result is that the introduction of noise does not affect expected cost. But additive noise may make the control of the firm more difficult, and therefore it cannot raise social welfare. The regulator can nevertheless obtain the same welfare as in the absence of noise by using linear incentive schemes: $E_\varepsilon\ (a - b(\beta - e + \varepsilon)) = a - b(\beta - e)$ (here the firm and the regulator are risk neutral, so their utilities are left unaffected). More formally, consider an incentive scheme $\mathring{t}(C, \hat{\beta})$ describing the transfer as a function of announced type $\hat{\beta}$ and realized cost C. Let $C^e = E_\varepsilon C = \beta - e$ denote the expected cost. Expected social welfare is still given by

11. For example, Brickley et al. (1985) and Tehranian and Waegelian (1985) show that stock prices rise on announcements of introduction of performance-based incentive schemes. In our model this corresponds to the principal's welfare increasing when the manager signals an efficient technology by sharing cost—or in the corporate world by taking stock options.

$$\int_{\underline{\beta}}^{\bar{\beta}} [S - (1 + \lambda)[(\beta - e(\beta)) + \psi(e(\beta))] - \lambda U(\beta)]dF(\beta).$$

Since

$$U(\beta) = \max_{\hat{\beta}} E_\varepsilon[\mathring{t}(C^e(\hat{\beta}) + \varepsilon, \hat{\beta}) - \psi(\beta - C^e(\hat{\beta}))],$$

and from the envelope theorem, the slope of the rent function still satisfies $\dot{U}(\beta) = -\psi'(e(\beta))$. Since the new program has the same objective function as in the noiseless case, and faces the same IC constraint, the same IR constraint $[U(\bar{\beta}) = 0]$, and possibly some additional constraints, the welfare under noisy cost is bounded above by that in the noiseless case. To see that the regulator can do as well in the noisy case, it suffices to take $\mathring{t}(C, \hat{\beta}) = a(\hat{\beta}) - b(\hat{\beta})C$, where $a(\cdot)$ and $b(\cdot)$ are defined in (1.61) and (1.62). Since the firm obtains the same expected utility from a given choice of $\hat{\beta}$ and e in the noisy and noiseless cases, its choices of $\hat{\beta}$ and e are unaffected by the presence of noise.

Last, we should note that the linear schemes are robust in that they are *optimal regardless of the distribution of accounting or forecast errors* (more on this in bibliographic notes B1.2 and B1.3). It can be shown that *only* a menu of linear contracts has the property of being optimal if the noise term can have any distribution with mean zero (see Caillaud et al. 1992). Linear contracts are thus important because of their *robustness* property.

1.4.4 The Two-Type Case and Nonlinearity of Optimal Contracts

It is interesting to note that the use of linear contracts does not carry over to the two-type case, as can be seen in figure 1.2. To induce type $\bar{\beta}$ to choose point E, the regulator would need to offer the linear scheme through E tangent to type $\bar{\beta}$'s indifference curve at this point. But in this case point D is no longer optimal for type $\underline{\beta}$, which prefers a point to the northwest of E on the straight line just defined.[12]

The technical reason for this difference between the continuum and discrete models is that the two-type distribution is poorly behaved; it does not satisfy the monotone hazard rate property. To see why this is so, it suffices to approximate the discrete distribution by a continuous one as in figure 1.6 [to the left of the spikes at $\underline{\beta}$ and $\bar{\beta}$, the density grows very fast, and (F/f) is not weakly increasing].

1.4.5 Shutdown of the Firm

As in the two-type case we consider the possibility that the project is not realized for all types. Let β^* denote the "cutoff" type; that is, type β in

12. The optimal allocation in the two-type case can be implemented by a piecewise linear contract (with one kink).

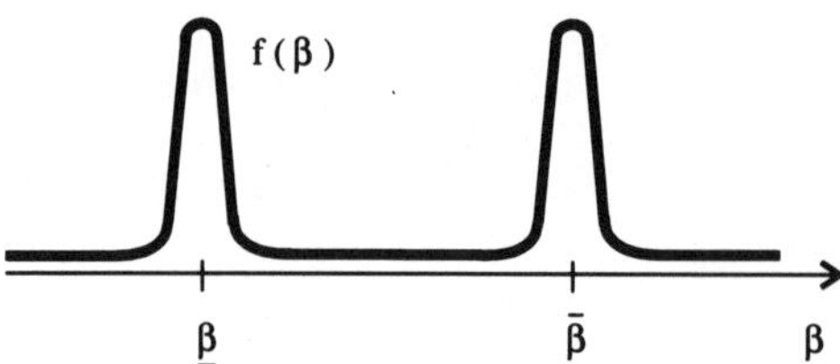

Figure 1.6
Approximation of the two-type case by a continuous density

$[\underline{\beta}, \beta^*]$ produce and types β in $(\beta^*, \bar{\beta}]$ do not. Let $U(\beta, \beta^*)$ be type β's rent when the cutoff type is β^*. Social welfare is then

$$W(\beta^*, S) = \int_{\underline{\beta}}^{\beta^*} \{S - (1+\lambda)[\beta - e^*(\beta) + \psi(e^*(\beta))] - \lambda U(\beta, \beta^*)\} dF(\beta). \tag{1.65}$$

Note two important properties. First, the optimal effort at $\beta < \beta^*$ is independent of the truncation point β^*. This can be seen from (1.44) and the fact that the hazard rate is invariant to an upward truncation of the distribution: For $\beta \leq \beta^*$, $[f(\beta)/F(\beta^*)]/[F(\beta)/F(\beta^*)] = f(\beta)/F(\beta)$. The economic interpretation is that the optimal effort is determined by the trade-off between the local distortion in effort and the extra rent to be left to more efficient types. This trade-off is not affected by upward truncations of the probability distribution. Second, the rent U does depend on the truncation point: $U(\beta^*, \beta^*) = 0$, and (1.34) imply that for $\beta \leq \beta^*$,

$$U(\beta, \beta^*) = \int_{\beta}^{\beta^*} \psi'(e^*(\tilde{\beta})) d\tilde{\beta}. \tag{1.66}$$

Integrating by parts [see (1.41)] and taking the derivative of expected social welfare with respect to β^* yields

$$f(\beta^*)\{S - (1+\lambda)[\beta^* - e^*(\beta^*) + \psi(e^*(\beta^*))]\} = \lambda F(\beta^*)\psi'(e^*(\beta^*)), \tag{1.67}$$

if we assume an interior solution ($\beta^* < \bar{\beta}$). The left-hand side of (1.67) is the net surplus attached to keeping type β^*. The right-hand side is the cost of the extra rent for the more efficient types.

To see how β^* depends on S, let β_0^* and β_1^* denote optima for surpluses S_0 and S_1, respectively. Revealed preference implies that $W(\beta_0^*, S_0) \geq W(\beta_1^*, S_0)$ and that $W(\beta_1^*, S_1) \geq W(\beta_0^*, S_1)$. Adding up these two inequalities shows that

$$\int_{\beta_0^*}^{\beta_1^*} \int_{S_0}^{S_1} \frac{\partial^2 W}{\partial S \partial \beta^*} dS d\beta^* \geq 0. \tag{1.68}$$

But $\partial^2 W/\partial S \partial \beta^* = f(\beta^*) > 0$. Hence

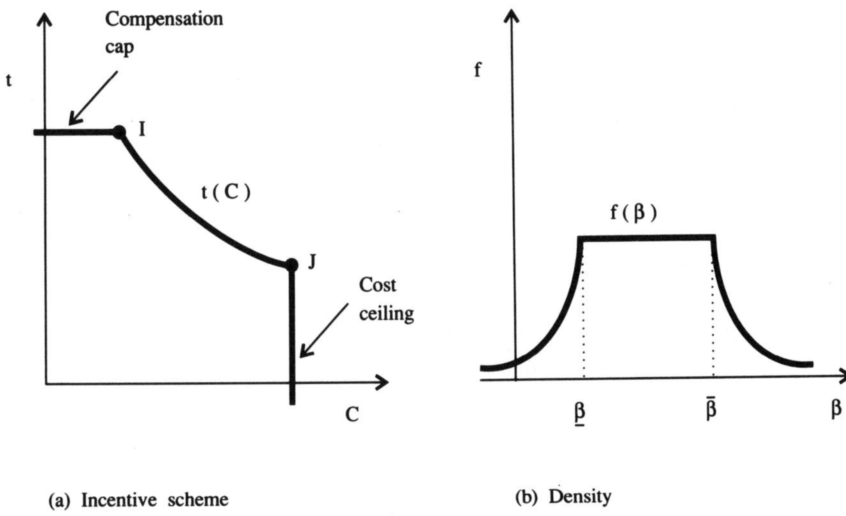

Figure 1.7
Compensation caps and cost ceilings: (a) incentive scheme; (b) density of the technology parameter

$$S_1 > S_0 \Rightarrow \beta_1^* \geq \beta_0^*, \tag{1.69}$$

as expected. If S is sufficiently large, the project is realized for all types ($\beta^* = \bar{\beta}$).

1.4.6 Compensation Caps and Cost Ceilings

Procurement contracts and managerial compensation schemes often include a compensation cap as well as a cost ceiling (for procurers) or profit floor (for divisional managers). A compensation cap denies any further net compensation to the procurer below some cost level (or any further bonus above some profit level for a division manager). That is, the incentive contract reverts to a low-powered scheme in the range of exceptional performances. Conversely, an upper bound on cost (or lower bound on profits) is imposed. Compensation caps and cost ceilings are illustrated in figure 1.7. This figure builds on figure 1.4 through the addition of a horizontal half-line to the left of point I and a vertical half-line below point J.

Compensation caps are rationalized in the following way: Suppose that the efficiency parameter β falls "normally" in the segment $[\underline{\beta}, \bar{\beta}]$, and suppose that the distribution over this interval has a decreasing hazard rate f/F (assumption 1.2). The distribution, however, has a larger support; in particular the efficiency parameter can take values below $\underline{\beta}$. Suppose that the density f increases rapidly below $\underline{\beta}$ in such a way that the hazard rate itself increases rapidly. For example, let

$$F(\beta) = h(\beta_0 - \beta)^{-k} \qquad \text{for } \beta \in (-\infty, \underline{\beta}],$$

where $\beta_0 > \underline{\beta}$, $h > 0$, $k > 0$ (see figure 1.7b).[13] The inverse hazard rate $F/f = (\beta_0 - \beta)/k$ is decreasing, and it decreases quickly for k small. Thus, for k sufficiently small,[14] the solution in equation (1.44) satisfies $\dot{e}(\beta) > 1$, or, equivalently, $\dot{C}(\beta) < 0$ on $(-\infty, \underline{\beta}]$. The solution does not satisfy the incentive constraint $\dot{C}(\beta) \geq 0$.

We conclude that there is a conflict between incentive compatibility—the realized cost must increase with the firm's type—and optimality—the realized cost ought to decrease with the firm's type—over the range $(-\infty, \underline{\beta}]$. A proper resolution of this conflict follows the lines of the study of bunching in appendix A1.5 of this chapter, but it is easy to guess its outcome. The constant cost allocation, $\dot{C}(\beta) = 0$ on $(-\infty, \hat{\beta}]$, with $\hat{\beta} > \underline{\beta}$, is the policy that approximates the optimal solution best while still being implementable. Therefore there is bunching of all types in $(-\infty, \hat{\beta}]$ at the cost level of type $\hat{\beta}$. This (constrained) optimum can be implemented by a compensation cap at the level $t(C(\hat{\beta}))$ as in figure 1.7a.

The previous analysis for $\beta \geq \hat{\beta}$ remains unchanged. A *cost ceiling* is rationalized by our analysis of the shutdown option. For an efficiency parameter above some cutoff value β^*, it is not worth letting the firm produce.[15]

1.5 The Main Economic Conclusions

We now collect some main results and show how a careful reading of these results allows us to anticipate some latter themes of this book.

Result 1.1 Asymmetric information allows the regulated firm to enjoy a rent.

Result 1.2 Asymmetric information reduces the power of the incentive schemes (effort decreases).

It is interesting to note that the power of procurement contracts is quite sensitive to uncertainty. As noted in section 2 of the introductory chapter, fixed-price contracts tend to be used for either production contracts or low-tech projects, while cost-plus contracts are more popular for development contracts or high-tech projects. Thus contracts are more low-powered when technologies are not standard. An alternative explanation for this fact is that the firms are risk averse and seek insurance when

13. Note that for given (β_0, k), $F(\underline{\beta}) = h(\beta_0 - \underline{\beta})^{-k}$ can be made as small as desired by choosing h small. The following reasoning does not rely on $F(\underline{\beta})$ being small but rather hinges on the increasing hazard rate property below $\underline{\beta}$.

14. When $\psi(e) = e^2/2$, $k < \lambda/(1 + \lambda)$ yields $\dot{\bar{e}}(\beta) > 1$.

15. Consider, for instance, the distribution in figure 1.7b. Suppose that production is very valuable so that type $\bar{\beta}$ should not be shut down, and that the density is rapidly decreasing beyond $\bar{\beta}$. Then β^* lies just beyond $\bar{\beta}$.

forecast errors are substantial. Since the magnitudes of ex ante informational asymmetries and ex post forecast errors are likely to be highly correlated, such practice does not distinguish between the screening and insurance explanations. But the importance of informational asymmetries and rent extraction concerns suggests that part of the explanation is the difficulty in extracting rents when technologies are not standard.

Results 1.1 and 1.2 compare the asymmetric and symmetric information situations; they were proved in sections 1.3 and 1.4. More generally we would want to compare different degrees of asymmetric information. Appendix A1.6 compares the expected slopes of incentive schemes for two structures of information that are comparable in the sense of Blackwell (1951). Another kind of comparison of distributions will prove more relevant for the purpose of this book:

Definition 1.1

i. *Two-type case.* The distribution $(\tilde{v}, 1 - \tilde{v})$ is more favorable than distribution $(v, 1 - v)$ if $\tilde{v} \geq v$.

ii. *Continuum case.* The distribution G on $[\underline{\beta}, \overline{\beta}]$ is more favorable than the distribution F on the same interval if

$$G(\beta) \geq F(\beta) \qquad \text{for all } \beta \text{ (first-order stochastic dominance)}$$

and

$$\frac{g(\beta)}{G(\beta)} \leq \frac{f(\beta)}{F(\beta)} \qquad \text{for all } \beta \text{ (hazard rate dominance).}$$

In other words, one distribution is more favorable than another if it puts more weight on more efficient types. In the two-type case this simply means that the probability of type $\underline{\beta}$ is higher. We require the analogous property in the continuum case (first-order stochastic dominance) and impose the regularity condition that G has a lower hazard rate. Returning to the interpretation of the hazard rate, the conditional probability that there is no more improvement relative to the basic technology when there are already $[\overline{\beta} - \beta]$ improvements is smaller for G than for F. Properties of part ii are satisfied, for instance, for G uniform on $[\underline{\beta}, \tilde{\beta}]$ and F uniform on $[\underline{\beta}, \overline{\beta}]$, where $\tilde{\beta} \leq \overline{\beta}$. More generally they are satisfied by any two cumulative distribution functions G and F such that $G = M(F)$, where M is increasing and concave.[16]

16. As noted by Maskin and Riley (1986). First, M concave, $M(0) = 0$, and $M(1) = 1$ [because $G(\underline{\beta}) = F(\underline{\beta}) = 0$ and $G(\overline{\beta}) = F(\overline{\beta}) = 1$] imply that $G(\beta) \geq F(\beta)$ for all β. Second,

$$\frac{f}{F} - \frac{g}{G} \propto \frac{d}{d\beta}\left(\frac{F}{G}\right) \propto [M - FM']f,$$

where $\propto$ means "proportional to." But $(M - FM')(\underline{\beta}) = 0$, and $(M - FM')' = -FM''f \geq 0$.

Results 1.3 and 1.4 are similar to results 1.1 and 1.2 but compare distributions that are more or less favorable.

Result 1.3 A firm with type β enjoys a higher rent when the regulator's probability distribution is less favorable.

Proof

i. For the two-type case, let $\mathcal{U}(\nu)$ denote the (reduced-form) rent of type $\underline{\beta}$ when the regulator's beliefs are ν. Consider two probabilities ν and $\tilde{\nu}$ such that $\tilde{\nu} > \nu$. Suppose first that the regulator keeps type $\bar{\beta}$ for beliefs $\tilde{\nu}$ and therefore for probability ν. Equation (1.23) implies that $\bar{e}(\tilde{\nu}) < \bar{e}(\nu)$ because Φ is convex. Since $\mathcal{U}(\nu) = \Phi(\bar{e}(\nu))$ and $\Phi(\cdot)$ is increasing, $\mathcal{U}(\nu) > \mathcal{U}(\tilde{\nu})$. When $\tilde{\nu}$ is such that the regulator shuts down type $\bar{\beta}$, then $\mathcal{U}(\tilde{\nu}) = 0$, and the result holds automatically.

ii. For the continuum case, let $\mathcal{U}(\beta, F)$ denote type β's rent when the regulator's beliefs are F, and similarly for distribution G. With notation as before, equation (1.44) implies that $e^*(\beta, F) \geq e^*(\beta, G)$ if the hazard rate condition holds. We leave it to the reader to check that the cutoff points satisfy $\beta^*(F) \geq \beta^*(G)$ from equation (1.67). If $\beta \leq \beta^*(G)$, then

$$\begin{aligned}\mathcal{U}(\beta, G) &= \int_{\beta}^{\beta^*(G)} \psi'(e^*(\tilde{\beta}, G))d\tilde{\beta} \\ &\leq \int_{\beta}^{\beta^*(F)} \psi'(e^*(\tilde{\beta}, F))d\tilde{\beta} = \mathcal{U}(\beta, F).\end{aligned}$$

If $\beta > \beta^*(G)$, then $\mathcal{U}(\beta, G) = 0$, and the result automatically holds. ■

Result 1.4

i. The effort of type β is lower when the regulator's probability distribution is more favorable. (Furthermore any type $\beta > \underline{\beta}$ will eventually be shut off if the probability distribution becomes favorable enough.)

ii. If F and G are continuous distributions satisfying assumption 1.2, and if $\psi''(\cdot)$ is constant, the expected slope of the incentive scheme is lower for the more favorable distribution provided that the firm is indispensable (i.e., the cutoff must be $\bar{\beta}$ for both distributions). When the firm is not indispensable, the cutoff type is smaller for the more favorable distribution; this effect increases the average slope of the incentive scheme for the more favorable distribution relative to that of the less favorable one and makes the comparison of the average slopes ambiguous.

Part i does not imply that an outside observer will observe on average more powerful incentive schemes when the distribution is less favorable because the distribution puts more weight on inefficient types, who choose low-powered incentives, as we have seen. Part ii of the result is an attempt to say something about the expected slope.

Proof

i. The proof follows the same lines as that of result 1.3.

ii. Since the slope of the incentive scheme is equal to $\psi'(e)$, equation (1.44) implies that

$$E_F b = 1 - \frac{\lambda}{1+\lambda} \frac{\int_{\underline{\beta}}^{\beta^*(F)} F(\beta)\psi''(e^*(\beta, F))d\beta}{F(\beta^*(F))},$$

and similarly for distribution G. Thus, for $\psi''(\cdot)$ constant, $E_F b \leq E_G b$ if and only if

$$\frac{\int_{\underline{\beta}}^{\beta^*(F)} F(\beta)d\beta}{F(\beta^*(F))} \geq \frac{\int_{\underline{\beta}}^{\beta^*(G)} G(\beta)d\beta}{G(\beta^*(G))}.$$

Consider a family of log-concave distributions $H(\cdot, \rho)$ with $H(\beta, 0) = F(\beta), H(\beta, 1) = G(\beta)$ for all β, $\partial(h/H)/\partial\beta \leq 0$, $\partial H/\partial\rho \geq 0$, and $\partial(h/H)/\partial\rho \leq 0$ (where h is the density of H). We require that H_ρ be strictly positive for a set of β's of positive measure. The derivative of $[\int_{\underline{\beta}}^{\beta^*(H)} H(\beta)d\beta]/H(\beta^*(H))$ with respect to ρ is equal to

$$\frac{1}{H^2}A + \frac{1}{H^2}\frac{d\beta^*}{d\rho}B,$$

where

$$A \equiv H(\beta^*(H)) \int_{\underline{\beta}}^{\beta^*(H)} H_\rho(\beta)d\beta - H_\rho(\beta^*(H)) \int_{\underline{\beta}}^{\beta^*(H)} H(\beta)d\beta$$

and

$$B = H^2(\beta^*(H)) - h(\beta^*(H)) \int_{\underline{\beta}}^{\beta^*(H)} H(\beta)d\beta.$$

That B is positive results from Prekova's (1973) theorem: A sufficient condition for a strictly monotonic function on an interval $[\underline{\beta}, \bar{\beta}]$ taking value 0 at either $\underline{\beta}$ or $\bar{\beta}$ to be log concave on this interval is that its derivative is log concave. Here $B \geq 0$ is implied by $\int_{\underline{\beta}}^{\beta} H(\tilde{\beta})d\tilde{\beta}$ log concave in β. From Prekova's theorem this in turn is implied by $H(\cdot)$ log concave, which is assumption 1.2.

We also noted in the proof of result 1.3 that $d\beta^*/d\rho \leq 0$. Hence it remains to be shown that $A \geq 0$. Let

$$A(\beta) \equiv H(\beta) \int_{\underline{\beta}}^{\beta} H_\rho - H_\rho(\beta) \int_{\underline{\beta}}^{\beta} H.$$

Clearly $A(\underline{\beta}) = 0$, and $A(\bar{\beta}) > 0$ since $H_\rho \geq 0$, $H_\rho > 0$ on a set of positive measure and $H_\rho(\bar{\beta}) = 0$. The derivative of A is

$$\frac{dA}{d\beta} = h \int_{\underline{\beta}}^{\beta} H_\rho - h_\rho \int_{\underline{\beta}}^{\beta} H.$$

We know that $H_\rho \geq 0$. Hence, if $h_\rho \leq 0$, $dA/d\beta \geq 0$. If $h_\rho(\beta) \geq 0$ and $A(\beta) = 0$,

$$\frac{dA}{d\beta} = h_\rho \left(\int_{\underline{\beta}}^{\beta} H_\rho \right) \left[\frac{h}{h_\rho} - \frac{\int_{\underline{\beta}}^{\beta} H}{\int_{\underline{\beta}}^{\beta} H_\rho} \right]$$

$$\geq h_\rho \left(\int_{\underline{\beta}}^{\beta} H_\rho \right) \left[\frac{H}{H_\rho} - \frac{\int_{\underline{\beta}}^{\beta} H}{\int_{\underline{\beta}}^{\beta} H_\rho} \right] = 0,$$

using $\partial(h/H)/\partial\rho \leq 0$. Hence $dA/d\beta \geq 0$ whenever $A(\beta) = 0$, and since $A(\bar{\beta}) > 0$, $A(\beta) \geq 0$ for all β.

The proof of part ii has revealed three effects: First, a more favorable distribution lowers the cutoff type and therefore raises the average slope of the incentive scheme (less efficient types have lower slopes). Second, the more favorable distribution puts more weight on more efficient types, resulting again in higher slopes. Third, the regulator is more eager to extract rents because the hazard rate is smaller; this reduces the slope of the incentive scheme for a given β. The third effect dominates the second, as shown by the property $A \geq 0$. ■

Results 1.1 through 1.4 suggest a number of insights for further analysis:

Result 1.1 shows that the firm is better off under asymmetric information. It will therefore want to keep secret information about its technology. We will make much use of this idea when providing agency-theoretic foundations for the phenomenon of regulatory capture in chapter 11. The firm will benefit from the retention of information that would allow the extraction of its rent.

Result 1.2 shows that the concern for rent extraction reduces the power of incentive schemes and moves them toward cost-plus contract. An important theme of this book is the determination of other factors (risk aversion, quality concerns, competition, dynamics, auditing, politics, etc.) that increase or decrease the power of incentive schemes.

Result 1.3 is the foundation for the ratchet effect studied in part IV of this book. An efficient type has an incentive to convince the regulator that it is inefficient. As we will see, this implies that it is more difficult to elicit the firm's information in a multiperiod context than in a single-period one. Result 1.5 below refines result 1.3 by comparing the relative gain of two types of convincing the regulator that the distribution is less favorable.

Result 1.3 also provides a foundation for the phenomenon of regulatory capture studied in part V of the book. Suppose that the prior distribution on $[\underline{\beta}, \bar{\beta}]$ is $F(\cdot)$. The regulator obtains some signal ρ, and signals are ordered in the sense that a higher ρ yields a more favorable posterior distribution $H(\cdot, \rho)$. The firm would like to induce the regulator to announce a low signal in order to enjoy a higher rent.

Result 1.5 A type gains more from the regulator's distribution being less favorable than a less efficient type.

Proof Let us prove a stronger result. Suppose that the firm does not necessarily know its type. It simply knows from which distribution F or G it will be drawn, where G is more favorable than F.

The gain Δ_1 for a firm with "type" F (i.e., knowing β will be drawn from F) from having the regulator believe that the distribution is $\tilde{F}$ rather than $\tilde{G}$, where $\tilde{G}$ is more favorable than $\tilde{F}$, is

$$\Delta_1 = \int_{\underline{\beta}}^{\beta^*(\tilde{F})} \mathscr{U}(\beta, \tilde{F}) dF(\beta) - \int_{\underline{\beta}}^{\beta^*(\tilde{G})} \mathscr{U}(\beta, \tilde{G}) dF(\beta).$$

Similarly the gain Δ_2 for a firm with type G from having the regulator believe that the distribution is $\tilde{F}$ rather than $\tilde{G}$ is

$$\Delta_2 = \int_{\underline{\beta}}^{\beta^*(\tilde{F})} \mathscr{U}(\beta, \tilde{F}) dG(\beta) - \int_{\underline{\beta}}^{\beta^*(\tilde{G})} \mathscr{U}(\beta, \tilde{G}) dG(\beta).$$

Integrating by parts yields

$$\Delta_2 - \Delta_1 = \int_{\underline{\beta}}^{\beta^*(\tilde{F})} \psi'(e^*_{\tilde{F}}(\beta))[G(\beta) - F(\beta)]d\beta - \int_{\underline{\beta}}^{\beta^*(\tilde{G})} \psi'(e^*_{\tilde{G}}(\beta))[G(\beta) - F(\beta)]d\beta.$$

Last, $G \geq F$, $\beta^*(\tilde{F}) \geq \beta^*(\tilde{G})$, and $e^*_{\tilde{F}}(\cdot) \geq e^*_{\tilde{G}}(\cdot)$ imply that $\Delta_2 \geq \Delta_1$. The proof is similar in the two-type case. ∎

Result 1.5 implies that in a multiperiod context in which the firm's type is positively correlated over time, an efficient type has more incentive than an inefficient type to convince the regulator that it is inefficient. This indicates that it will be quite difficult to learn the type of an inefficient firm.

Result 1.6 An increase in the gross surplus S raises the firm's rent.

Result 1.6 follows directly from section 1.3 and 1.4, where we showed that the cutoff type (weakly) increases with S and that the rent of a given type increases with the cutoff type. In chapter 2 we will show more generally that an increase in demand raises the firm's rent. This suggests that the firm does not like to face product market competition. This idea is central to our study of access pricing (chapter 5), cartelization (chapter 13), and favoritism (chapter 14).[17]

Several regulatory issues are related to the firm's engaging in multiple activities. Besides exerting effort, it may invest or increase the quality of its

17. In chapter 6 we will encounter the bizarre case of competition by a substitute product that raises the firm's demand. But there is no contradiction with the general rule because we will show then that competition also increases the firm's rent.

product. These activities interact with effort because they jointly determine cost. Let us for the moment index the disutility of effort function by a parameter ζ, which is a proxy for an activity: $\psi(e,\zeta)$. We assume that $\partial\psi/\partial\zeta > 0$ (the activity ζ increases the disutility of effort) and that $\partial^2\psi/\partial e\partial\zeta > 0$ (the activity ζ increases the marginal disutility of effort). That is, e and ζ are substitute activities.

Result 1.7 If λ is small, if there is little uncertainty, or if $\partial^3\psi/\partial^2 e\partial\zeta$ is nonnegative, an increase in the intensity ζ of the substitute activity reduces the power of optimal incentive schemes: $\partial e^*(\beta)/\partial\zeta < 0$.

The assumptions $\partial\psi/\partial\zeta > 0$, $\partial^2\psi/\partial e\partial\zeta > 0$, and $\partial^3\psi/\partial^2 e\partial\zeta \geq 0$ are quite easy to interpret when the substitute activity (e.g., investment or increase in quality) increases cost in an additive way: $C = (\beta - e) + \zeta$ and the disutility of effort is $\psi(\cdot)$. Substituting $e = \beta - C + \zeta$, the disutility of effort becomes $\psi(\beta - C + \zeta)$. The assumptions then boil down to $\psi' > 0$, $\psi'' > 0$, $\psi''' \geq 0$.

Result 1.7 is stated in terms of effort being crowded out by the substitute activity. Another way of interpreting the result is that low-powered incentive schemes are needed to encourage the production of the substitute activity. We will make use of this idea in models in which the firm chooses its quality (chapter 4) and invest in long-term capital (chapter 8).

1.6 Implementation: Relevance and Informational Requirements of Menus

In this section we discuss two issues concerning the application of the optimal incentive scheme: Is the idea of menus incongruous? What information do they require? We saw that in the presence of informational asymmetries, the regulator optimally offers a menu of contracts to the firm. It can be argued that we do not observe regulators offering menus of contracts in practice. We can respond to this in three ways. First, we might observe only the final contract signed by the firm, and not the bargaining process that gives rise to this contract. When bargaining over cost sharing and pricing, regulators are likely to screen the firm's information about technology. Second, there exist examples of explicit menus of managerial incentive schemes in corporations. For instance, many managers are given the choice of cashing their bonuses or stock options or transforming them into stocks or stock options. They thus face a menu. The option of cashing in on rewards for past performance can be viewed as a low-powered incentive scheme in which the manager decides not to be rewarded according to performance in the future (at least not beyond the extent defined by his or her other holdings of stocks and stock options). The option of buying (further) stocks or stock options can be viewed as choosing a high-powered incentive scheme. Presumably the second option has a higher expected reward than the first and will be selected by those managers who are confident about the firm's future profits. Thus menus are not as incongruous as they might seem.[18] Third, some recent proposals for regulation have advocated the explicit use of menus. For instance, Kwerel[19] has suggested that utilities could be given the choice between sliding scale plans and a price cap.[20] As in this chapter the utility would share more of its costs if it forecasts a better performance (a higher productivity increase in the context of this proposal). Similarly Lewis and Sappington (1989) have analyzed the effects of a simple menu composed of cost-of-service regulation and a price cap. An optimistic firm will prefer a price cap to cost-of-service regulation, while a pessimistic firm will make the opposite choice. Including the cost-of-service option guarantees that the firm's individual rationality constraint is satisfied. That is, the firm is willing to choose cost-of-service regulation over shutting down, whatever its efficiency. This is particularly valuable in situations where the regulator can err in formulating the distribution of uncertainty and, as is often the case in regulation, cannot afford a shutdown.

Let us also point at two current experiments with menus of linear contracts, one in procurement and the other in regulation. Both are designed to fit the theory. Naturally the continuum of linear contracts is approximated by a finite number of them (7 and 6, respectively). One was commissioned by the German Department of Defense to examine the applicability of such schemes; see Reichelstein's 1991 paper. An adjustment that Reichelstein makes to the theory is to vary the slopes of the menus between 0.15 and 0.5 so that the highest slope is not 1. But, as we will see (e.g., in section 1.11 and chapters 4 and 11), there are several reasons why it is not always optimal to include a fixed-price contract in the menu. Two pilot projects were set up in Germany in 1990 and were scheduled to be completed in 1992. The other experiment recommended the adoption by Michigan state regulators of such a menu for Palisades, a nuclear generating plant; see Brown's 1990 testimony on behalf of the U.S. Federal Energy Regulatory Commission.[21] At the time of this writing, the menu has been drafted and tabulated and is awaiting final approval by state regulators. Needless to say, the calibration of the menus is industry specific, and we refer to Reichelstein's and Brown's contributions for details.

The informational requirements of the optimal cost-reimbursement rule are substantial (in contrast, we will see in chapter 2 that informational

18. Even if the regulators did not screen, one might ask why they would be less sophisticated than the managers of private firms, who, for a very long time, have practiced nonlinear pricing to screen customers. Although one may argue that firms can more easily learn about the benefits of screening because they face many customers, the difference in rationality assumed from the two parties seems too convenient.

19. See FERC (1989) report, p. 76.

20. See the section 2 of the introductory chapter for definitions.

21. October 2, 1990. Palisades Generating Company/Consumers Power Company. Docket Nos. ER89-256-000, ER90-333-000, EC89-10-000.

requirements for pricing are smaller). This is the case not so much because the function ψ may not be known (as discussed in section 4 of the introductory chapter, the uncertainty on ψ can be subsumed in that about β under some conditions) but because the optimal incentive scheme depends on the subjective distribution $F(\cdot)$. There are two related concerns. First, the regulator may not have the motivation or incentive to apply the optimal rule. Second, the regulator may distort his or her subjective distribution to benefit the firm or other interest groups.

The sensitivity of the optimal scheme to the distribution of uncertainty is characteristic of schemes that try to extract the firm's rent while providing adequate incentives. A scheme that does not give rise to a concern about poor implementation because it is independent of the distribution is the cost-plus contract in which the regulator reimburses any level of cost (see chapter 12, however). But cost-plus contracts have poor incentive properties and are thus unattractive. We will pursue this theme of sensitivity of optimal schemes to the distribution of uncertainty in chapter 11 in which we allow regulators to manipulate their information. There it is shown that the threat of manipulations moves optimal schemes toward cost-plus contracts. The discussion also points out that the relevant range for possible costs is more likely to be computed from objective engineering data and past performance of the firm or similar firms than from subjective evaluations by the regulator.

Last, we note that the informational requirements for optimal *menus* of linear contracts are the same as those for optimal contracts in the restricted class of *single* contracts (e.g., of the type $t = a - bC$) and that regulators routinely offer (at least) one contract (incentive contracts in procurement and regulation, price caps, and fixed-price contracts) that has the potential of leaving a rent to the firm.

1.7 Using Yardstick "Competition" to Reduce Informational Asymmetries

Because informational asymmetries between the regulator and the firm reduce the efficacy of regulation, the regulator ought to use all available information to reduce these asymmetries. One way of learning about the technology parameter is to compare the firm's performance to that of other firms facing a similar technological environment. Suppose that a regulator is responsible for two public utilities located in separate geographic areas.[22] Each utility produces a fixed amount of output normalized at 1. In particular the utilities do not compete in the product market (unlike in part II); nor do they compete to be the sole supplier (unlike in part III). Utility i, $i = 1, 2$, has cost function

22. The reasoning would remain the same if the two uncoordinated regulators were in charge of one utility each.

$$C^i = \beta^a + \beta^i - e^i,$$

where β^a is an aggregate shock common to both firms and β^i is an idiosyncratic shock independent of β^j. Letting $U^i = t^i - \psi(e^i)$ denote firm i's rent, social welfare is

$$\sum_i \{S - (1 + \lambda)[C^i + \psi(e^i)] - \lambda U^i\}.$$

The regulator observes only realized costs. Firm i learns the realizations of β^a and β^i before contracting.

In the case of *purely idiosyncratic shocks*, $\beta^a \equiv 0$, the firms are unrelated and the regulator optimally regulates them individually as in sections 1.3 and 1.4. In the case of *purely aggregate shocks*, $\beta^i \equiv 0$, the symmetric information (first-best) outcome can be obtained despite the fact that the regulator has a priori less information about the technology than the firms. It suffices that the regulator offer both firms a fixed-price contract with "relative performance evaluation" or "yardstick competition":

$$t^i = \psi(e^*) - (C^i - C^j).$$

Firm i then maximizes $\{\psi(e^*) - [(\beta^a - e^i) - (\beta^a - e^j)]\} - \psi(e^i)$ and chooses $e^i = e^*$. Since the other firm also chooses e^*, the firm earns no rent whatever the realization of the aggregate shock. Filtering aggregate uncertainty out of each firm's performance thus yields the first best.

Finally, in the case of *general shocks*, it is easy to see that welfare is the same as if the regulator could observe the aggregate shock but not the idiosyncratic shocks. The reasoning is simply a generalization of that for purely aggregate shocks. For instance, for the continuum of types studied in section 1.4, the regulator can offer the following menu of incentive schemes:

$$t^i(\hat{\beta}^i, C^i, C^j) \equiv a(\hat{\beta}^i) - b(\hat{\beta}^i)(C^i - C^j) - b(\hat{\beta}^i)E_{\beta^j}(\beta^j - e^*(\beta^j)),$$

where $a(\cdot)$, $b(\cdot)$, and $e^*(\cdot)$ are given by (1.61), (1.62), and (1.44). Firm i's expected utility when having type β^i and reporting type $\hat{\beta}^i$ is then equal to

$$a(\hat{\beta}^i) - b(\hat{\beta}^i)(\beta^i - e^i) - \psi(e^i).$$

It thus faces the same decision making as in section 1.4. Again the aggregate shock has been filtered out through relative performance evaluation.[23]

Relative performance evaluation is used in the United States for Medicare, whereby the reimbursement received by a hospital for a given treatment is based on the average cost of the treatment in similar hospitals. Similarly clauses indexing an electric utility's price to the fuel cost of other

23. The theory of yardstick competition was developed by Baiman and Demski (1980), Holmström (1982), and others. An application to regulation is in Shleifer (1985).

electric utilities are meant to filter out the common shocks in the price of fuel and encourage the utility to purchase its fuel at a low cost. However, despite its attractive properties, relative performance evaluation has not been used much in regulation.[24] The problem is that regulated firms are often not comparable. That is, idiosyncracies often prevail over common features.[25]

Nevertheless, we can expect an increased use of yardstick competition in segments of regulated industries such as water and electricity distribution. For instance, the application of yardstick competition on bulk electricity purchase costs (and other costs) for the British Regional Electricity Companies is the object of a lively debate in Britain.[26] More use of yardstick competition has also been advocated in the United States. Joskow and Schmalensee (1986) argue:

> Cost norms based on the statistical yardstick notion could be developed by applying econometric techniques to data on hundreds of plants and utilities, along with indices of local wages and raw material prices; such norms could be used as a basis for incentive payments. This type of approach could be incorporated with performance norms and fuel price norms to provide a more comprehensive incentive system that operates on total generating costs, exclusive of capital costs. (p. 45)

1.8 Adding Investment to the Model

An important theme in industrial organization is that parties to a long-term relationship (e.g., involving a supplier and a buyer) often sink investments that are specific to their relationship: The supplier designs equipment and a product to meet the needs of the customer, while the customer commits investments whose value is contingent on the supplier abiding by his or her promises.

A classic example[27] is that of a coal mine and a power plant. The mine digs with the prospect of supplying coal to the power plant. The power plant buys a burner that is efficient for the kind of coal supplied by the mine but less efficient for other kinds of coal. The power plant may also locate near the coal mine (forming a "mine-mouth" plant), thereby increasing transportation costs for alternative sources of supply.

Investment is an important issue in many regulated industries. Telephone and electricity companies, for instance, sink substantial investments

24. The "Marco Estable" regulatory scheme for the Spanish electricity industry is one of the rare attempts to implement explicit yardstick competition. Another example is the indexing in 1985 of Illinois Power's rate based on an index of 24 other midwestern utilities.

25. Another potential limitation of relative performance evaluation is the potential for collusion among the firms. This potential is weaker when there are many firms in the comparison group.

26. See Vickers and Yarrow (1991) for a good description and discussion of the British electricity experiment.

27. See Joskow (1985, 1987).

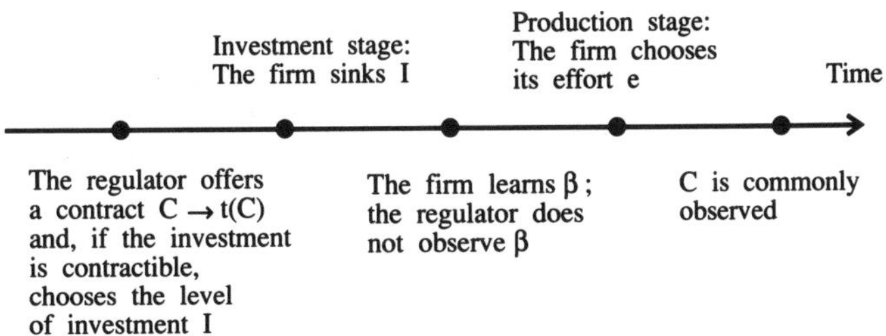

Figure 1.8
Investment choice under a long-term contract

before serving their customers. The purpose of this section and the next is to extend our basic model by introducing an investment decision prior to the production stage in order to study some issues related to rate-of-return on investment and investment control and expropriation.

Suppose that before learning its efficiency parameter β, the firm commits some investment $I \geq 0$. The investment determines a probability distribution $F(\beta|I)$ for the efficiency parameter $\beta \in [\underline{\beta}, \bar{\beta}]$. We assume that a higher investment makes it more likely that the firm is efficient. That is, we presume first-order stochastic dominance: $F_I \equiv \partial F/\partial I > 0$ for $\beta \in (\underline{\beta}, \bar{\beta})$. We also assume decreasing returns in investment: $F_{II} < 0$. The firm's ex post cost is $C = \beta - e$. The timing is summarized in figure 1.8. The *socially optimal investment* level $\hat{I}$ minimizes the sum of the investment cost and the ex post cost:

$$\hat{I} \text{ minimizes} \left\{ I + \int_{\underline{\beta}}^{\bar{\beta}} \beta dF(\beta|I) \right\},$$

or, after an integration by parts,

$$\hat{I} \text{ minimizes} \left\{ I - \int_{\underline{\beta}}^{\bar{\beta}} F(\beta|I) d\beta + \bar{\beta} \right\}.$$

The socially optimal level of effort is $e(\beta) = e^*$ for all β, where $\psi'(e^*) = 1$, and the socially optimal rent is $U(\beta) = 0$ for all β. These three prescriptions will be referred to as the "social optimum." (More generally the rent at the social optimum needs to be equal to 0 only in expectation over the firm's types. This fact will be used in subsection 1.8.1.)

We can make one of two assumptions concerning investment. In the first, investment is *contractible*. The regulator can then choose the level of investment and can also offer a cost-reimbursement rule: $C \to t(C)$ for production, where t is the net transfer. More generally, if the regulator has less information than the firm about the efficiency or cost of investment (see subsection 1.8.3), the regulator ought to delegate the choice of investment level to the firm and offer an incentive scheme: $(I, C) \to t(I, C)$, where

t is the net transfer after reimbursement of the total cost $I + C$.[28] The second possible assumption is that the regulator *cannot observe and contract* on investment.[29] The regulator must restrict attention to cost-reimbursement rules: $C \to t(C)$ or $C \to t(I + C)$ (depending on whether investment is nonmonetary or enters the firm's accounts). The firm then freely chooses the level of investment.

In practice there are dimensions of investment that are contractible (the monetary expense) and others that are not (the level of care exerted to choose the investment or its quality). The quality dimension is hard to assess for a given monetary investment. Even monetary investments create some measurement problems. There is a long tradition of regulated firms paying excessive prices to affiliated, unregulated companies for various inputs, including investments (see Kahn 1970, vol. I, pp. 28–30). For instance, there has been an ongoing concern about the relationship between AT&T and its equipment supplier, Western Electric, which is also its subsidiary. It is therefore important to study both contractible and noncontractible investments. Subsections 1.8.1 and 1.8.2 analyze contractible and noncontractible investments when the firm and the regulator have symmetric information at the contracting date. In contrast, subsection 1.8.3 assumes that the firm has private information about the effectiveness or private cost of investment. These subsections all assume that the regulator can commit in advance to a cost-reimbursement rule. Section 1.9 will study the implications of a lack of commitment to a cost-reimbursement rule.

1.8.1 Contractible Investment

As mentioned above, when investment is contractible and information is symmetric at the contracting date, we can assume without loss of generality that the regulator imposes some level I and, by accounting convention, reimburses it. The firm's ex post utility is then

$$U = t - \psi(e),$$

where t is the net transfer after the investment I and the production cost C are reimbursed. Let $U(\beta)$ denote the rent of type β. Section 1.4 has shown that

$$\dot{U}(\beta) = -\psi'(e(\beta)),$$

28. Note again that when there is symmetric information about the efficiency or cost of investment, the regulator can, without loss of generality, restrict attention to incentive schemes of the form $t(I, C) = -\infty$ if $I \neq \bar{I}$, where $\bar{I}$ is the desired level of investment.

29. There is actually a third possibility that will not be considered here: The regulator might observe investment but not be able to provide evidence that is accurate enough for a court in charge of enforcing the regulatory contract. In information economics such investment is said to be "observable," though "noncontractible" or "unverifiable." See Tirole (1986) and Riordan (1987) for studies of observable, noncontractible investments in the context of noncommitment to future incentive schemes for production.

and therefore that

$$U(\beta) = U(\bar{\beta}) + \int_{\beta}^{\bar{\beta}} \psi'(e(x))dx.$$

No Ex post Participation Constraint

Suppose that the firm's manager can commit in the initial contract not to quit the relationship even for a bad realization of the technological parameter β. The manager's willingness to enter a contract ex ante can be expressed as

$$\int_{\underline{\beta}}^{\bar{\beta}} U(\beta)dF(\beta|I) \geq 0.$$

In such circumstances the regulator can obtain the *socially optimal allocation* by offering a *fixed-price contract*:

$$t(C) = a - C.$$

Indeed the regulator can even afford to delegate the investment decision to, rather than impose it on, the firm. To see this, consider the firm's choice of investment and effort under a fixed-price contract (in which neither the investment nor the production cost are reimbursed). The firm maximizes

$$\max_{\{I, e(\cdot)\}} \left\{ \int_{\underline{\beta}}^{\bar{\beta}} [a - (\beta - e(\beta)) - I - \psi(e(\beta))] dF(\beta|I) \right\}.$$

This yields

$$\psi'(e(\beta)) = 1 \quad \text{or} \quad e(\beta) = e^* \qquad \text{for all } \beta,$$

and

$$I \text{ minimizes} \left\{ I + \int_{\underline{\beta}}^{\bar{\beta}} \beta dF(\beta|I) \right\} \quad \text{or} \quad I = \hat{I}.$$

To obtain the social optimum, it then suffices to offer a fixed price a equal to the firm's total expected cost so as to fully capture the expected rent:

$$a = \int_{\underline{\beta}}^{\bar{\beta}} \beta dF(\beta|\hat{I}) - e^* + \psi(e^*) + \hat{I}.$$

The idea is thus to make the firm residual claimant for all its decisions, be they investment or effort. The firm then fully internalizes the consequences of these decisions.[30] Rent extraction is no concern because the contract is signed under symmetric information and the fixed price can be chosen so as to leave no *expected* rent to the firm.

30. This reasoning is reminiscent of that developed in the context of collective decision making to show that "expected externality payments" lead to socially optimal behavior; see, in particular, Arrow (1979) and d'Aspremont and Gerard Varet (1979).

Ex post Participation Constraint

Suppose, in contrast, that the firm's manager cannot commit not to quit the relationship once he or she learns the realization of β. In this case the regulator must ensure (as in this chapter) that $U(\beta)$ is nonnegative for all β, that is, that $U(\bar{\beta}) \geq 0$. There are two motivations for such an ex post individual rationality constraint. First, the law may specify that the firm's employees cannot be obliged to remain in the firm. Second, the employees may exhibit risk aversion. In particular, if they have very negative utility when their ex post rent falls below zero, the regulator must offer a contract such that $U(\bar{\beta}) \geq 0$ for it to be accepted. This motivation is sometimes referred to as "infinite risk aversion below zero."

Assuming that the manager is risk neutral in the range of nonnegative rents, the expected social welfare function can be written

$$\int_{\underline{\beta}}^{\bar{\beta}} [S - (1 + \lambda)(I + \beta - e(\beta) + \psi(e(\beta))) - \lambda U(\beta)]dF(\beta|I),$$

where

$$\dot{U}(\beta) = -\psi'(e(\beta))$$

and

$$U(\bar{\beta}) \geq 0.$$

Except for the added investment choice, the maximization of this expected social welfare is identical to program (1.36) (ignoring, as usual, the second-order condition $\dot{e}(\beta) \leq 1$). The counterpart of (1.42) is

$$\max_{\{I, e(\cdot)\}} \left\{ S - (1 + \lambda)I - \int_{\underline{\beta}}^{\bar{\beta}} \left[(1 + \lambda)(\beta - e(\beta) + \psi(e(\beta))) + \lambda \frac{F(\beta|I)}{f(\beta|I)} \psi'(e(\beta)) \right] dF(\beta|I) \right\}. \tag{1.70}$$

Thus effort is still given by equation (1.44). Of more interest is the first-order condition for investment:

$$1 + \lambda + \int_{\underline{\beta}}^{\bar{\beta}} \left[[(1 + \lambda)(\beta - e + \psi(e)) + \lambda \frac{F}{f} \psi'(e)] f_I + \lambda \frac{\partial}{\partial I}\left(\frac{F}{f}\right) \psi'(e) f \right] d\beta = 0.$$

Integrating by parts and using the fact that the social welfare function, given by (1.70), is maximized with respect to $e(\beta)$ for all β, this first-order condition can be rewritten as

$$1 + \lambda = (1 + \lambda) \int_{\underline{\beta}}^{\bar{\beta}} F_I d\beta + \lambda \int_{\underline{\beta}}^{\bar{\beta}} \psi'(e) \left[\frac{F_I}{f} \frac{\partial}{\partial \beta}\left(\frac{F}{f}\right) - \frac{\partial}{\partial I}\left(\frac{F}{f}\right) \right] dF. \tag{1.71}$$

The left-hand side of (1.71) is the marginal (social) cost of investment. The first term on the right-hand side is the marginal cost savings due to investment. Relative to the determination of $\hat{I}$, there is a new term, the second term on the right-hand side, associated with the incentive problem at the production stage. Note that if rents have no social cost ($\lambda = 0$), one obtains the level of investment $\hat{I}$ of the social optimum (similarly we saw that in the absence of ex post participation constraint, investment was socially optimal because ex post rents could be captured ex ante and therefore had no social cost). This correction of investment due to imperfect incentives at the production stage itself reflects two effects. First, an increase in investment shifts the distribution toward low β's ($F_I > 0$), for which incentive corrections are small $\partial(F/f)/\partial\beta > 0$). This effect pushes toward more investment. On the other hand, if investment makes the distribution of β's more favorable in the sense of definition 1.1 [i.e., $\partial(F/f)/\partial I > 0$, given that $F_I > 0$], investment makes rent extraction more necessary, and we have a second effect pushing toward less investment. When investment does not increase the hazard rate, then we can unambiguously conclude that investment is higher than in the absence of ex post incentive problems.[31]

1.8.2 Noncontractible Investment

We observed in the previous subsection that in the absence of the ex post participation constraint, the noncontractibility of investment imposes no cost. This is not the case when the firm must be given nonnegative rent for each realization of β. At the optimum with contractible investment, the firm is given a cost-reimbursement rule that has the government and the firm share the production cost. When investment becomes noncontractible, but the same incentive scheme is kept, the firm may not choose the appropriate level of investment because it does not internalize the share of production cost borne by the government. This raises the question of how the cost-reimbursement rule ought to be adjusted to reflect the noncontractibility of investment.

Suppose that the investment I is nonmonetary and that the firm's disutility of effort is $I + \psi(e)$. The firm's utility is then

$$U = t - I - \psi(e),$$

and social welfare

$$S - (1 + \lambda)(t + C) + U = S - (1 + \lambda)[I + C + \psi(e)] - \lambda U.$$

31. A family of distributions for which investment increases the hazard rate and where the two effects cancel is

$$F(\beta|I) = H(\beta + l(I)),$$

with $l' > 0$. (This family has moving support in general.)

For I given, the firm's rent as a function of β satisfies

$$\dot{U}(\beta) = -\psi'(e(\beta)).$$

The firm chooses its investment so as to maximize

$$-I + \int_{\underline{\beta}}^{\bar{\beta}} U(\beta) dF(\beta|I),$$

which, after an integration by parts, yields the moral hazard constraint:

$$\int_{\underline{\beta}}^{\bar{\beta}} U(\beta) dF_I(\beta|I) = \int_{\underline{\beta}}^{\bar{\beta}} \psi'(e(\beta)) F_I(\beta|I) d\beta = 1.$$

Maximizing expected social welfare is equivalent to

$$\max_{\{I, e(\cdot)\}} \left\{ \int_{\underline{\beta}}^{\bar{\beta}} \left[S - (1+\lambda)(\beta - e + \psi(e) + I) - \lambda \frac{F(\beta|I)}{f(\beta|I)} \psi'(e) \right] dF(\beta|I) \right.$$
$$\left. + \nu \left(\int_{\underline{\beta}}^{\bar{\beta}} \psi'(e) F_I(\beta|I) d\beta - 1 \right) \right\},$$

where ν is the shadow price of the moral hazard in investment constraint. This yields the first-order conditions for $e(\beta)$ and I:

$$\psi'(e) = 1 - \frac{\lambda}{1+\lambda} \frac{F(\beta|I)}{f(\beta|I)} \psi''(e) + \frac{\nu}{1+\lambda} \frac{F_I(\beta|I)}{f(\beta|I)} \psi''(e), \tag{1.72}$$

and

$$\int_{\underline{\beta}}^{\bar{\beta}} F_I d\beta = 1 - \frac{\lambda}{1+\lambda} \int_{\underline{\beta}}^{\bar{\beta}} \psi'(e) \left[\frac{F_I}{f} \frac{\partial}{\partial \beta} \left(\frac{F}{f} \right) - \frac{\partial}{\partial I} \left(\frac{F}{f} \right) \right] dF(\beta|I)$$
$$- \frac{\nu}{1+\lambda} \int_{\underline{\beta}}^{\bar{\beta}} F_{II} \psi'(e) d\beta. \tag{1.73}$$

If

$$\left[\frac{F_I}{f} \frac{\partial}{\partial \beta} \left(\frac{F}{f} \right) - \frac{\partial}{\partial I} \left(\frac{F}{f} \right) \right] \geq 0,$$

underinvestment relative to the first-best would not occur under contractible investment, as we saw in the last section, and the shadow price ν can be shown to be positive.[32] We conclude that if investment is to be encouraged when contractible, noncontractibility of investment generates a new and positive term in the cost-reimbursement rule (1.72), which pushes toward high-powered incentives.

32. Because $F_{II} < 0$, (1.73) then implies that $\int_{\underline{\beta}}^{\bar{\beta}} F_I d\beta \leq 1$, if $\nu \leq 0$. But $\nu \leq 0$, together with (1.72), also implies that $\psi'(e(\beta)) < 1$ for all $\beta > \underline{\beta}$. Therefore $\int_{\underline{\beta}}^{\bar{\beta}} F_I \psi'(e) d\beta < 1$, which contradicts the incentive compatibility constraint.

1.8.3 Private Information on the Desirability of Investment: Rate of Return on Investment, Incentives, and the Averch-Johnson Model

By their design the previous two subsections have sidestepped the issue of the determination of contracted rate of return on investment. In the last subsection the noncontractibility of investment made it impossible for the government and the firm to share the cost of investment. In subsection 1.8.1 the regulator and the firm had symmetric information about the desirability of investment, and therefore the regulator could impose the level of investment and fully reimburse it. This section also assumes that investment is contractible, but it introduces private information of the firm about the desirability of investment as well as the cost of production. The regulator then delegates the investment choice to the firm and keeps some control over it through a policy of rate of return on investment. This allows us to connect the analysis with standard debates concerning the rate of return on investment to be granted to the firm.

Should a regulated firm's rate of return on (measurable) investment be tied to that on alternative assets in financial markets? Should the cost of investment be shared by government or the ratepayers? Various regulation and procurement policies have responded to these questions differently. In the United States, at least until the 1980s, cost-of-service regulation has generally guaranteed a fair rate of return on the capital of public utilities. While there have been lengthy debates about the measurement of the rate base and of the cost of capital, few departures from the principle of a fair rate of return occurred.[33] The 1980s witnessed more frequent cost disallowances, for instance, the disallowance of investment in nuclear power plants. Price-cap regulation, in contrast, does not include a formal guarantee of a rate of return on investments, although it is understood that the firm ought not lose money. Concerns about investment expropriation of the kind studied in section 1.9 are therefore strong under price caps.[34] Last, while the regulatory arena exhibits the use of different rate-of-return policies, the procurement world illustrates the use of investment subsidies. For instance, the U.S. Department of Defense shares the contractor's expenses in defense-related R&D.[35]

33. See Berg and Tshirhart (1988, pp. 300–301) for some exceptions.

34. Naturally there are also cost-sharing schemes on investment. For instance, in 1983 the New Jersey Board of Public Utilities set up the following incentive scheme for the construction of the Hope Creek nuclear power plant: The electric utility, Jersey Central Power and Light Company, would recover 80% and then 70% of construction beyond a "dead-band" range. Conversely, it would keep 20% of cost savings under the dead-band range.

35. The subsidy mechanism is the so-called independent R&D program. R&D expenses that are not part of a contract or a grant can nevertheless be included as indirect costs in other Department of Defense contracts, up to a ceiling (see Lichtenberg 1988, 1990). While most defense contractors spend more on R&D than the allowed ceiling on such government subsidies, which suggests that the marginal government subsidy is zero, the negotiated ceiling increases with past R&D expenditures and the marginal subsidy rate is positive. Lichtenberg (1990) estimates the implicit government subsidy at around 40% of private military investment.

There are two possible attitudes toward policies regarding the rate of return on investment: either pass investment costs along to taxpayers and ratepayers or sensitize the firm to its investment choices.

Pass Investment Costs along to Taxpayers or Ratepayers
The pass-through attitude is based on the perception that agency problems on investment are small (so that the main incentive issue is to limit the level of operating costs). That is, while the regulator may not know the optimal level of investment, the firm may have little control over investment expenditures and therefore not be able to derive much rent from purchasing equipment, at least as long as it purchases it from unaffiliated suppliers. There is then little need for concern and the policy of paying the market rate on capital (the equivalent of a cost-plus contract on capital) may be appropriate.

Sensitize the Firm to Its Investment Choices
A different (and we think more appropriate) view is that investment choices are subject to adverse selection and moral hazard. First, the firm may have private information about the likely *cost* of the investment and can try to bring this cost down. Second, the firm may have superior knowledge about the *effectiveness* of the investment. In the latter case the firm, even if it has no discretion on the investment cost and thus cannot derive any rent just from the act of investing, has a stake in the choice of investment as it determines its future rent. In both cases the firm must be given incentives to choose an appropriate level of investment.

The firm can be sensitized by either *fiat* or *contracts*. A fiat consists in letting the regulator (or, in less extreme form, the regulator subject to court control) choose the firm's rate of return on investment on the basis of a discretionary ex post assessment of the firm's performance in this respect. This occurs to a limited extent when a regulator disallows a nuclear power plant on "prudency" grounds.[36] The fiat solution, however, confronts the problem of selective intervention. Ideally one would want to allow the regulator to punish the firm when the regulator observes moral hazard in the choice of investment, and to deprive the regulator of the right to punish in other circumstances, in order to prevent the regulator from expropriating proper investments of the firm. But it is in general hard to specify ex ante when the regulator rightfully or wrongfully refuses to compensate the firm for its investment.[37]

This subsection emphasizes the contractual method of sensitizing the firm. As discussed above, the regulator can either ex ante subsidize the firm or make promises as to the ex post rate of return. In the context of the

36. See chapter 12 for a study of ex post auditing of cost and effort.

37. There is a current concern that U.S. electric utilities do not want to invest, or that, when they invest, they exhibit short termism (e.g., by purchasing low-investment-cost, high-marginal-cost gas turbines). See, for example, Kolbe and Tye (1991).

traditional agenda of regulatory economics, the questions are then: Should there be a *linkage* between ex post incentive schemes and the level of investment? For instance, should a high investment today be tied to a promise of future price-cap or cost-of-service regulation? Or should sensitization be performed only through subsidies and taxes on investment? Should excess returns on investment be permitted, as is presumed in the Averch-Johnson model (see section 3 of the introductory chapter)? Is an Averch-Johnson overinvestment a concern in an optimal regulatory scheme? The clarity of the theoretical answers to these questions depends on the context, as we now see.

Uncertainty about the Cost of Investment

Suppose first that the firm is to undertake a given investment project, say, building a nuclear power plant. The realized investment cost I depends on the firm's effort e to bring the price of inputs down, to coordinate the subprojects, and to choose appropriate technologies. It also depends on the difficulty, indexed by a parameter β, of keeping investment cost down. Let

$$I = \beta - e.$$

The analysis of investment is then a trivial reinterpretation of that of operating costs in this chapter, where the operating cost C is replaced by the investment cost I. In this reinterpretation the net transfer or rate of return $t^*(I)$ is given by equation (1.52) in the case of a continuum of efficiency parameters. While the theoretical analysis is straightforward, its implications for the debate on rates of return are worth noting.

First, the marginal rate of return on investment is negative [$dt^*/dI \leq 0$ or, equivalently, $d(I + t^*(I))/dI \leq 1$]. This must be contrasted with the Averch-Johnson assumption that the firm's revenue grows with its investment ($s > r$ in the notation of section 3 of the introductory chapter). Here the firm and the taxpayers (or in the model of sections 2.6 and 2.7 the ratepayers) must share the investment cost.

Second, investment sharing implies that the firm underinvests relative to the social optimum. This again is inconsistent with the Averch-Johnson model.

Third, and more in line with the Averch-Johnson model, the firm derives some rents from its exercise of discretion over the investment level. Its net transfer $t^*(I)$ is positive. Even if the nonmeasured cost $\psi(e)$ is included in the profitability measure (e.g., think of a defense contractor who forgoes profits $\psi(e)$ in unregulated commercial activities), the firm's rent $U^* = t^*(I) - \psi(e)$ is strictly positive for almost all β.

Fourth, there is no necessary linkage between current investment and future incentive schemes. Suppose that the firm's future rents depend on the nuclear power plant being built but not on its construction cost so that future rents are independent of the investment problem under consideration. Then all investment incentives would be created by the sharing of the investment cost between the firm and the taxpayers (in procurement) or the ratepayers (in regulation). The absence of linkage is the topic of the following two remarks.

Remark 1 For a regulated firm that operates under a budget constraint, the share of investment borne by the consumers would be smoothed over time. It is suboptimal to impose a large toll at the date of investment and a much smaller toll later on. This intertemporal smoothing of rates is performed for a public enterprise such as Électricité de France through the borrowing mechanism, and in the case of a private regulated firm by the accounting transformation of capital stocks into flows; in both cases investment is charged to consumers over several periods. We can conclude that, in the case of budget balance regulation, there is an indirect linkage between current investment scheme and future incentive schemes through price smoothing.

Remark 2 If the firm is also engaged in reducing *current* regulated operating costs and if it allocates its effort between the two activities, then the regulator should link the incentive schemes relative to investment and operating expenditures.[38] For instance, as we will see in chapter 3, in some circumstances auditing the firm's subcost does not bring any welfare gain. In this context the firm's incentive scheme need depend only on total cost (investment plus operating). The two activities are then perfectly linked through a single incentive scheme.

Uncertainty about the Effectiveness of Investment

Suppose now that the cost of achieving a certain investment size is given (the firm has no discretion over it) but that the firm has superior information about its effectiveness. For instance, let the firm produce tomorrow at operating cost,

$$C = \beta - e,$$

where β is private information and is learned tomorrow by the firm and e is the effort to reduce operating cost. As in subsections 1.8.1 and 1.8.2 the firm must commit today some investment I that (partially) determines the ex post efficiency parameter β. We assume that the regulator and the firm can contract on this investment.

If the firm has no private information about the effectiveness of the investment (the extent to which it reduces operating cost), then the firm and the regulator agree on some investment level, and the main issue

38. Related ideas on competing activities can be found in chapters 3, 4, 8, and review problem 13.

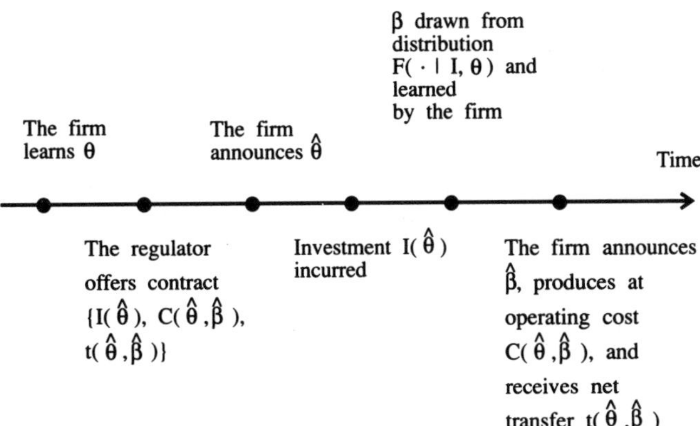

Figure 1.9
Timing when the firm has private information about the effectiveness of its investment

pertains to the ex post cost-reimbursement rule. But suppose, in contrast, that the firm ex ante has private information about an efficiency parameter θ. Let the ex post cumulative distribution of β on $[\underline{\beta}, \bar{\beta}]$ be denoted by $F(\cdot|I,\theta)$, with density $f(\cdot|I,\theta)$. We assume that $F_I \geq 0$ (investment reduces the operating cost, in the sense of first-order stochastic dominance), $F_{II} < 0$ (decreasing returns), and $F_\theta \geq 0$ (a high θ is good news about the future operating cost). The effect of θ on the desirability of investment is measured by the cross-partial derivative $F_{I\theta}$ and can be positive or negative. For instance, a currently inefficient firm may have a pressing need for investment because its capital is obsolete, in which case $F_{I\theta} < 0$. Or, a firm with efficient managers may be able to make better use of a new investment than if its managers were inefficient, and then $F_{I\theta} > 0$. Let the regulator have prior cumulative distribution $G(\cdot)$ with density $g(\cdot)$ over θ on $[\underline{\theta}, \bar{\theta}]$. This uncertainty of the regulator about the effectiveness of investment will give rise to variations in investment levels and incentive schemes over the sample and will enable us to discuss the linkage between the two. We assume that the regulator and the firm can fully commit to an incentive scheme. Figure 1.9 summarizes the timing.

As before, we make the accounting convention that the costs (of investment and production) are paid by the regulator who then gives a net transfer to the firm. The description of the timing makes also implicit use of the revelation principle, according to which the regulator can restrict attention to contracts that induce the firm to reveal its true technological parameters. Let $U(\beta,\hat{\theta})$ and $e(\beta,\hat{\theta})$ denote the rent and effort of the firm when its operating cost parameter is β and it has announced $\hat{\theta}$ at the investment stage. Letting $\dot{U}$ denote the partial derivative of U with respect to β, we have the usual incentive compatibility condition for each $\hat{\theta}$:

$$\dot{U}(\beta,\hat{\theta}) = -\psi'(e(\beta,\hat{\theta})).$$

Let $V(\theta) \equiv \sup_{\hat{\theta}}\{\int_{\underline{\beta}}^{\bar{\beta}} U(\beta,\hat{\theta})f(\beta|I(\hat{\theta}),\theta)d\beta\}$ denote the firm's expected rent when it has ex ante type θ. As is now usual, individual rationality need only be satisfied at the least efficient type:[39]

$$V(\underline{\theta}) \geq 0.$$

For simplicity we assume that there is no ex post participation constraint (when the firm cannot commit to produce for all realizations of β, the analysis combines the features unveiled in this subsection and in subsection 1.8.1). From the envelope theorem the incentive constraint is

$$\dot{V}(\theta) = \int_{\underline{\beta}}^{\bar{\beta}} U(\beta,\theta)f_\theta(\beta|I(\theta),\theta)d\beta = \int_{\underline{\beta}}^{\bar{\beta}} \psi'(e(\beta,\theta))F_\theta(\beta|I(\theta),\theta)d\beta,$$

after an integration by parts and using $F_\theta(\underline{\beta}|I,\theta) = F_\theta(\bar{\beta}|I,\theta) = 0$ for all (I,θ). By ignoring, as before, the firm's second-order condition, we find that social welfare maximization is equivalent to

$$\max_{\{e(\cdot),I(\cdot)\}} \left\{\int_{\underline{\theta}}^{\bar{\theta}} g(\theta)\Big[-(1+\lambda)I(\theta) - \lambda V(\theta) + \int_{\underline{\beta}}^{\bar{\beta}} [S-(1+\lambda)(\beta - e(\beta,\theta) + \psi(e(\beta,\theta)))]f(\beta|I(\theta),\theta)d\beta\Big]d\theta\right\}$$

subject to the incentive compatibility constraint.

We let the reader check that the effort to reduce operating costs is given by

$$\psi'(e(\beta,\theta)) = 1 - \frac{\lambda}{1+\lambda}\frac{1-G(\theta)}{g(\theta)}\frac{F_\theta(\beta|I(\theta),\theta)}{f(\beta|I(\theta),\theta)}\psi''(e(\beta,\theta)).$$

The first conclusion is that the regulator does not offer a fixed-price contract because ex ante the firm has private information about the operating cost through the correlation of θ and β.[40]

Next suppose that $[(1-G)/g](F_\theta/f)$ is decreasing in θ.[41] Then the firm is given a more powerful incentive scheme when its θ is high. The optimal investment $I(\theta)$ is given by

$$\int_{\underline{\beta}}^{\bar{\beta}} [S-(1+\lambda)(\beta - e + \psi(e))]f_I d\beta = (1+\lambda) + \lambda\frac{1-G}{g}\int_{\underline{\beta}}^{\bar{\beta}} \psi'(e)F_{I\theta}d\beta.$$

39. We assume that the firm and the regulator do not trade if they fail to sign a contract at the investment stage. Alternatively, one could introduce a sufficiently large minimal investment level; the expropriation of the firm's investment in the absence of a long-term contract (see section 1.9) would then guarantee that the firm would not want to invest and therefore would be unable to trade ex post.

40. On the role of intertemporal correlation in the absence of investment, see bibliographic note B1.4.

41. Nonincreasing $(1-G)/g$ is nothing but the monotone hazard rate condition on the distribution of θ. An example of a distribution F that then yields the above assumption is $F = \beta^{h(I,\theta)}$ on $[0,1]$, with $h_I < 0$, $h_\theta < 0$, and h_θ/h increasing.

The left-hand side of this equation would be equal to the marginal social benefit of investment if this investment did not affect the firm's rent. The first term on the right-hand side is the unit investment cost measured at the shadow cost of public funds. The second term on the right-hand side reflects the effect of investment on the firm's rent. This effect is positive if investment benefits most those types (high θ's) whose rent is hard to capture (i.e., if $F_{I\theta} > 0$) and negative if the investment benefits most the inefficient types (i.e., if $F_{I\theta} < 0$). Investment must thus be corrected to contribute to rent extraction.

The analysis of how the investment changes with θ is complex and is left to the reader. Let us simply point out that at the optimum, high investments may be linked with high or low θ's (if only because $F_{I\theta}$ can be positive or negative). From this observation and the previous observation that high θ's are given high-powered incentives under some condition, we conclude that there is indeed a correlation between the level of investment chosen by the firm and its ex post incentive scheme but that the exact linkage depends on fine details of the technological and informational environment. For instance, in the restricted context where attention is limited to cost-of-service and price-cap regulations, the regulator may optimally tie future price-cap regulation to a high current investment in some circumstances and to a low current investment in some others.

1.9 Investment under Noncommitment

This section analyzes the effect on investment of the absence of a long-term contract for the production stage. As was recognized by Williamson (1975), an absence of a long-term contract between the two parties and the resulting ex post bargaining about the terms of trade may create distortions in the relationship. The first distortion is an inefficiency in bargaining. A well-known result in contract theory[42] states that under some weak conditions, bargaining between two parties, each having private information about his or her willingness to trade, is bound to be inefficient. For example, a coal mine with private information about incremental digging costs and a power plant with private information about the operating cost of its burner or about the cost of alternative supplies are unlikely to fully exploit their potential gains from trade. In particular the two parties may, by being too greedy, refrain from trade in situations where there is a surplus to be divided.

The second distortion is that the two parties in general choose a socially inappropriate specific investment: They often invest too little and do not specialize their investment enough. They invest too little because part of

42. This result is due to Myerson and Satterthwaite (1983). A closely related result is in Laffont and Maskin (1979).

the value added generated by their investment is expropriated in the bargaining process. For example, the power plant may well assert (with outrage) that it invested so many dollars in a specialized burner; the two parties will nevertheless correctly reason that this investment is sunk at the time of bargaining and is therefore irrelevant (except for the ex post technologies that it generated).[43] Similarly the parties do not specialize their investments as much as would be socially optimal. They preserve their "outside opportunities" by picking general purpose technologies. In this way they create the credible threat to trade with an alternative partner if they do not find the bargaining outcome satisfactory. For example, in the absence of a long-term contract, a power plant might buy an expensive burner that can take many types of coal.

This theory, often developed in the context of two private firms, applies with a vengeance to the regulated environment, since the regulator/regulated firm relationship is very often one of monopsony/monopoly. The two distortions discussed above therefore apply to regulated industries. The bargaining inefficiency has been studied in detail in this chapter:[44] The firm produces at higher cost than under symmetric information. Let us now show why the regulated firm has an incentive to underinvest.[45]

1.9.1 Rent Extraction Generating Underinvestment

The underinvestment effect in the absence of a long-term contract is wholly demonstrated in the symmetric information variant of the model in which the regulator observes β before offering a production contract. The regulator optimally extracts the firm's rent: $U(\beta) = 0$ for all β. Therefore the firm has no incentive to invest: $I = 0$.

Despite its triviality the symmetric information variant already makes the following interesting point: The regulator's benevolence is a virtue when the regulator can commit but not necessarily when he or she cannot commit; then the expropriation of the firm's investment is socially optimal ex post but not ex ante. Indeed, when commitment is impossible, welfare might be higher were the regulator corrupt! The idea is that the prospect of being able to convince the regulator to take a proindustry stance will

43. An example closer to home (but hopefully hypothetical) is that of a house that a prospective buyer builds on a tract of land still owned by the seller. If the two parties have not signed a contract specifying in advance the price of land, it is unlikely that the price of land be set ex post at the market price of unbuilt land.

44. The Laffont-Maskin/Myerson-Satterthwaite result does not apply when only one party —here, the firm—has private information. However, in the specific bargaining process we considered—the uninformed regulator makes a take-it-or-leave-it offer to the informed firm —bargaining inefficiencies arise.

45. The first formal model of underinvestment when the parties have symmetric information is due to Grout (1984). For models of investments when the parties have asymmetric information, see Klibanoff (1991) and Tirole (1986). These papers, however, do not consider regulated industries. The application to such industries was first laid out by Riordan (1987) and Vickers and Yarrow (1988, pp. 88–91). See also Vickers (1991).

give the firm some incentive to invest, and this welfare gain will offset the welfare loss associated with the regulatory capture (see review problem 15 for a demonstration of this). When the regulator does not observe β before offering a contract, the firm is somewhat protected from expropriation of its investment. We may therefore ask whether the regulator's imperfect knowledge suffices to prevent underinvestment.

In a pure strategy equilibrium the regulator correctly anticipates the equilibrium investment I^*. The regulator offers the incentive scheme defined in proposition 1.3 for cumulative distribution $F(\cdot|I^*)$. Let $U^*(\beta;I^*)$ denote type β's associated ex post rent (also given in proposition 1.3). Ex ante the firm chooses its investment so as to maximize its expected ex post rent minus its investment cost:

$$I^* \text{ maximizes } \left\{\int_{\underline{\beta}}^{\bar{\beta}} U^*(\beta;I^*)dF(\beta|I) - I\right\},$$

or, by integrating by parts and using $\dot{U}^*(\beta;I^*) = -\psi'(e^*(\beta;I^*))$ and $U^*(\bar{\beta};I^*) = 0$, we have

$$I^* \text{ maximizes } \left\{\int_{\underline{\beta}}^{\bar{\beta}} \psi'(e^*(\beta;I^*))F(\beta|I)d\beta - I\right\}.$$

Since $F_I > 0$, the firm now has an incentive to invest. However, since $\psi'(e^*(\beta;I^*)) \leq 1$ for all β, the firm invests less than is socially optimal: $I^* < \hat{I}$.[46] Since the firm's rent increases by less than \$1 when it reduces its cost parameter by \$1, the firm underinvests. The firm would face the socially optimal incentive to invest if it were given a fixed-price contract (and the regulator did not shut down any type): There would then be no split in cost savings between the firm and the consumers/taxpayers. But fixed-price contracts are not optimal because they leave too much rent to the firm.

1.9.2 Four Mechanisms Mitigating the Underinvestment Effect

The underinvestment effect is a serious issue in regulation. But there exist (imperfect) mechanisms that alleviate it somewhat. First, it often happens

46. For a formal proof, we use a revealed preference argument:

$$\int_{\underline{\beta}}^{\bar{\beta}} \psi'(e^*(\beta;I^*))F(\beta|I^*)d\beta - I^* \geq \int_{\underline{\beta}}^{\bar{\beta}} \psi'(e^*(\beta;I^*))F(\beta|\hat{I})d\beta - \hat{I}$$

and

$$\hat{I} - \int_{\underline{\beta}}^{\bar{\beta}} F(\beta|\hat{I})d\beta \leq I^* - \int_{\underline{\beta}}^{\bar{\beta}} F(\beta|I^*)d\beta.$$

Adding up these two inequalities, we obtain

$$\int_{\underline{\beta}}^{\bar{\beta}} [1 - \psi'(e^*(\beta;I^*))][F(\beta|\hat{I}) - F(\beta|I^*)]d\beta \geq 0.$$

First-order stochastic dominance then implies that $\hat{I} \geq I^*$.

that investment cannot be measured because it cannot be disentangled from some (here unmodeled) operating costs at the investment stage. Yet in this case investment is "partially" or "imperfectly" measurable because there exists some accounting variable at the investment stage that includes investment as well as other costs. We will see in chapter 8 (see also review problem 18) that because investment then competes with other tasks of the firm such as the reduction of current operating costs, incentives for investment can be created by reimbursing a high fraction of the firm's total (investment plus operating) cost at the investment stage.

The second mechanism fostering investment (analyzed in subsection 1.8.1) can be the existence of a *long-term contract* for production signed before the firm sinks its investment. By promising more ex post incentives to exert effort (i.e., by committing to less rent extraction), the regulator can induce more investment by the firm. For instance, the promise of a fixed-price contract would create the proper incentive to invest, although it generally is suboptimal for rent extraction purposes.

Commitment through a long-term contract, however, has its limits. The regulator and the firm must be able to draft a detailed contract before investment is sunk, which may prove to be difficult or costly. What is more, letting regulators commit the state for the long run could be hazardous if regulators do not need to be benevolent. As we will see in chapter 16, legal prohibitions on governmental commitment may allow proindustry policies to be rectified.

The third mechanism arises from the *repetition* of the relationship between the regulator and the firm. A regulator may be involved in a couple of rate hearings with a regulated firm, or else in the rate hearings of several regulated firms, during his or her tenure in the administration. The regulator may then be able to develop a reputation for being fair, namely for not expropriating the firm's investment. As Croker and Reynolds (1989), Gilbert and Newbery (1988), and Salant and Woroch (1988, 1991) have argued, such repetition may substitute for long-term contracts and guarantee appropriate levels of investment. One would expect these reputation effects to be stronger when the regulator's tenure, and therefore the number of rate hearings in which the regulator is involved would increase.[47]

A fourth alleviating mechanism is the existence of *nongovernmental opportunities* for the firm. If the firm is legally allowed to engage in commercial activities, if its investment can be used indifferently for governmental or commercial purposes, and if the firm cannot be forced to give priority to government contracting, the regulator has a harder time ex-

47. See Hart and Holmström (1987, sec. 3) for a reputation model determining the extent of underinvestment as a function of the length of the relationship between a supplier and a buyer. It should also be noted that in the private sector there are few long-term contracts when the parties interact very frequently (or, more generally, have reputations to defend in their markets); see MaCaulay (1963).

propriating the firm's investment, for the firm can focus on its commercial activity instead of accepting low government prices. Letting the firm engage in commercial activities, however, is not without cost. First, the firm has an incentive to underspecialize its investment in order to boost its bargaining power against the government (see review problem 17). Second, the firm, which bears the full cost of its commercial activities and only a fraction of the cost of its government activities (due to cost sharing), has an incentive to arbitrage between the two and charge commercial costs to the government. It may do so through mere accounting manipulations, although much has been attempted to prevent this in practice, for example, in defense procurement. It may also allocate its best engineers or the general office's attention to its commercial activities. This puts constraints on the extent to which the regulator can reimburse the firm's cost attributed to the government projects (on this, see review problem 13). We conclude that these four mechanisms alleviate but do not eliminate the underinvestment effect.

1.10 Multiperiod Relationship under Commitment: False Dynamics

Suppose that the firm can realize a succession of identical projects at dates $\tau = 1, \ldots, T$. The cost at date τ is

$$C_\tau = \beta - e_\tau.$$

Let t_τ denote the net transfer to the firm at date τ. This transfer generally depends on the sequence of costs $C_1, \ldots, C_\tau$ up to date τ (the firm might not want to produce at some dates, but this would not affect the analysis). The firm's utility and the regulator's welfare are

$$U = \sum_{\tau=1}^{T} \delta^{\tau-1}(t_\tau - \psi(e_\tau))$$

and

$$W = S(1 + \delta + \cdots + \delta^{T-1}) - (1 + \lambda)\left[\sum_{\tau=1}^{T} \delta^{\tau-1}(C_\tau + t_\tau)\right] + U.$$

We now show that this model is only superficially dynamic. It is optimal for the regulator to offer the optimal static scheme in each period. We show that an upper bound on $E_\beta W$ is $1 + \delta + \cdots + \delta^{T-1}$ times the optimal one-period welfare. It then suffices to note that the regulator obtains this upper bound if he or she commits to letting the firm choose in the optimal static menu in each period. Let $\{C_\tau(\beta) = \beta - e_\tau(\beta), t_\tau(\beta)\}_{\tau=1,\ldots,T}$ denote an intertemporal allocation. We assume it is deterministic for notational simplicity, but nothing would be affected if it were a random allocation. This allocation must satisfy the following constraints:

$$\sum_{\tau=1}^{T} \delta^{\tau-1}(t_\tau(\beta) - \psi(e_\tau(\beta))) \geq 0 \text{ for all } \beta \qquad \text{(IR constraint)}$$

and

$$\sum_{\tau=1}^{T} \delta^{\tau-1}(t_\tau(\beta) - \psi(e_\tau(\beta)))$$

$$\geq \sum_{\tau=1}^{T} \delta^{\tau-1}(t_\tau(\tilde{\beta}) - \psi(e_\tau(\tilde{\beta}) + (\beta - \tilde{\beta}))) \qquad \text{for all } (\beta, \tilde{\beta}) \text{ (IC constraint).}$$

In other words, the firm could refuse to produce at all and guarantee itself a zero utility. Hence, whatever its type, its rent cannot be negative. Furthermore type β can mimic type $\tilde{\beta}$, which explains IC.

Now suppose that the regulator obtains more (per period) in the multiperiod than in the one-period relationship. Letting $\{C^*(\beta) = \beta - e^*(\beta), t^*(\beta)\}$ denote the optimal static allocation (derived in the two-type case in section 1.3 and in the continuum case in section 1.4), we obtain

$$E_\beta\left[(1+\lambda)\sum_{\tau=1}^{T} \delta^{\tau-1}(C_\tau(\beta) + t_\tau(\beta)) + \sum_{\tau=1}^{T} \delta^{\tau-1}(\psi(e_\tau(\beta)) - t_\tau(\beta))\right]$$

$$< E_\beta\left[(1+\lambda)(1 + \delta + \cdots + \delta^{T-1})(C^*(\beta) + t^*(\beta))\right.$$

$$\left. + \sum_{\tau=1}^{T} \delta^{\tau-1}(\psi(e^*(\beta)) - t^*(\beta))\right].$$

Consider the *static* random revelation mechanism in which the regulator asks the firm to announce its type $\hat{\beta}$ and the allocation is determined by a public randomizing device: With probability $1/(1 + \cdots + \delta^{T-1})$, the cost target is $C_1(\hat{\beta})$, and the transfer is $t_1(\hat{\beta}); \ldots$; with probability $\delta^{T-1}/(1 + \cdots + \delta^{T-1})$, the cost target is $C_T(\hat{\beta})$, and the transfer is $t_T(\hat{\beta})$. This static mechanism is individually rational from IR and incentive compatible from IC. Furthermore it yields a higher expected welfare to the regulator than $\{C^*(\cdot), t^*(\cdot)\}$ and thus contradicts the optimality of the latter mechanism in the static context. Clearly the regulator cannot do better in the repeated relationship than in the one-period one. This concludes the proof that the regulator cannot do better than offering the optimal static contract in each period.

By offering T times the optimal static scheme, the regulator in a sense commits not to learn the firm's information. That is, the firm still faces a choice in $\{C^*(\cdot), t^*(\cdot)\}$ in period 2 as if the regulator had not learned anything from first-period performance. Yet, if the regulator observes C_1 (or equivalently $\hat{\beta}$), he or she learns the firm's type, and it is no longer certain that the two parties will not want to renegotiate away from the contract $\{C^*(\cdot), t^*(\cdot)\}$ for period 2. The commitment effort in period 2 therefore will be suboptimal in order to limit the firm's rent; this issue is the topic of chapter 10.

One interpretation of the optimal intertemporal contract when assumption 1.2 is satisfied is that the firm chooses a slope b of sharing of *intertemporal* cost (since the optimal scheme is stationary, the cost-sharing coefficient in each period is time invariant) and receives some net transfer $A(b) = a(b)(1 + \delta + \cdots + \delta^{T-1})$ [see section 1.4 for the definition of $a(\cdot)$]. The firm thus chooses b and $\{e_1, \ldots, e_T\}$ so as to maximize

$$U = A(b) - \sum_{\tau=1}^{T} \delta^{\tau-1}[b(\beta - e_\tau) + \psi(e_\tau)].$$

Let us now add an investment decision by the firm. The firm chooses a sequence of (positive or negative) costs from investment $(I_1, \ldots, I_T)$ subject to an investment technology $g(I_1, \ldots, I_T) \leq 0$ (a two-period-investment example is $I_1 = +1$ and $I_2 = -2$). Assume that investment enters the cost function in a separable way:

$$C_\tau = \beta - e_\tau + I_\tau.$$

The firm chooses investment so as to minimize $b(\sum_{\tau=1}^{T} \delta^{\tau-1} I_\tau)$ subject to $g(I_1, \ldots, I_T) \leq 0$, which amounts to minimizing $(\sum_{\tau=1}^{T} \delta^{\tau-1} I_\tau)$ subject to $g(I_1, \ldots, I_T) \leq 0$. Thus the socially optimal choice of investment is obtained even if the regulator observes only aggregate cost and does not monitor investment.[48] The intuition is that while the firm bears only a fraction b of the cost of the investment, it also appropriates only a fraction b of its benefits. Its choice is thus undistorted. Chapters 4 and 8 study situations in which the firm invests and the slope of the optimal incentive schemes is not time invariant.

1.11 Risk Aversion

Let us briefly explore the consequences of risk aversion on the firm's behavior and on the incentive scheme. Let us assume that the firm has "mean-variance" preferences:

$$U = Et - r \operatorname{var} t - \psi(e),$$

where var t is the variance of the transfer.

If there is no noise in cost observation ($C = \beta - e$), nothing changes in sections 1.3 and 1.4 (the optimal schemes we derived there are deterministic). When cost observation is noisy ($C = \beta - e + \varepsilon$), the analysis becomes more complex. Optimal cost-reimbursement rules are no longer

48. $A(b)$ must be corrected by $b(\sum_{\tau=1}^{T} \delta^{\tau-1} I_\tau^*)$, where $\{I_\tau^*\}$ is the optimal sequence of investments.

linear in cost. We will not derive the optimal mechanism but content ourselves with studying the optimal menu of linear schemes $t = a(\hat{\beta}) - b(\hat{\beta})C$. As expected, risk aversion leads to a decrease in the fraction of cost borne by the firm.[49] The slope $b(\beta)$ chosen by type β decreases with the coefficient r of risk aversion.

BIBLIOGRAPHIC NOTES

B1.1 Mechanism Design

In the absence of accounting or forecast errors, our basic model is technically one of adverse selection even though it apparently mixes adverse selection and moral hazard elements: Substituting $e = \beta - C$, the firm's and the regulator's objective functions depend only on the observable variables (t, C) and on the private information parameter β.

The seminal paper on contract design under adverse selection (mechanism design) is Mirrlees (1971). While Mirrlees was concerned with optimal taxation, his techniques and intuition proved to carry over to many different economic applications. The theory was further developed by Mussa and Rosen (1978), Green and Laffont (1979), Baron and Myerson (1982), Guesnerie and Laffont (1984), and Maskin and Riley (1984), and later extended in many directions.[50] A survey of the techniques of mechanism design is chapter 7 of Fudenberg and Tirole (1991).

The first paper to view regulation as a mechanism design problem was Loeb and Magat (1979). Loeb and Magat considered the special case in which there is no social cost of leaving rents to the firm. To obtain the first-best level of welfare, it then suffices to give the firm a reward equal to the net surplus of other parties (here, the consumers). For example, in the model of this chapter, when the shadow cost of public funds is equal to zero, it suffices to pay the firm the consumers' surplus S if the firm implements the project, and 0 otherwise. The firm then perfectly internalizes the other parties' utilities and makes the right decision concerning effort ($e = e^*$) and production [produce if and only if $S - (1 + \lambda)(\beta - e^* + \psi(e^*)) \geq 0$].

The first-best result of Loeb and Magat is, however, in conflict with the conventional wisdom that leaving rents to the firm is costly. For this rea-

49. This result is drawn from a slightly more general one in Laffont and Tirole (1986).
50. For instance, when the agent's utility is not monotonic in his or her type or if the agent has type-contingent reservation utility the individual rationality constraint is not necessarily binding in the conventional way (see, e.g., Champsaur and Rochet 1989, Lewis and Sappington 1989a, b, and chapters 6 and 10).

son the literature applying mechanism design to regulation really began with the papers of Baron and Myerson (1982) and Sappington (1982). We will discuss the contribution of Baron and Myerson on price regulation under cost unobservability in the bibliographic notes of chapter 2. The model of Sappington is a precursor to the one in this chapter. It allows asymmetric information at the contracting stage (adverse selection) and postcontractual learning by the firm (hidden knowledge), and it derives the optimal incentive scheme in the class of menus of linear contracts.

B1.2 The Linearity Result

We showed that with a continuum of types and under some conditions, the optimal transfer function is convex in cost, which is a necessary and sufficient condition for being able to use a menu of linear contracts. Linear contracts are attractive because they are robust; they are still optimal when any additive accounting or forecast error is added.

Rogerson (1987) generalized the linearity result to the following class of adverse-selection problems: Let θ denote an adverse-selection parameter distributed on $[\underline{\theta},\bar{\theta}]$ with density g and cumulative distribution function G. Let the agent's utility be $U = t - v(\theta, y)$ and the principal's utility be $V = w(y) - t$ (in our model, the adverse-selection parameter θ enters w, but this does not alter Rogerson's analysis). Rogerson's main assumptions are that the hazard rate is monotonic ($(g(\theta)/(1 - G(\theta))$ nondecreasing) and that $v_{yy\theta} \le 0$, $v_{y\theta\theta} \ge 0$ (both of which are implied by $\psi''' \ge 0$ in our model).[51] Rogerson shows that a necessary and sufficient condition

$$v_{y\theta}\gamma' + v_{yy} \ge 0, \tag{B1.1}$$

where $\gamma(y)$ is the inverse function of $y(\theta)$ and its derivative is given by

$$\gamma'(y) = \frac{-w''(y) + v_{yy}(y,\gamma(y)) - H(\gamma(y))v_{yy\theta}(y,\gamma(y))}{-[1 - H'(\gamma(\theta))]v_{y\theta}(y,\gamma(y)) + H(\gamma(y))v_{y\theta\theta}(y,\gamma(y))},$$

and $H(\theta) \equiv (1 - G(\theta))/g(\theta)$.

As Rogerson shows on some examples, condition (B1.1) is actually quite strong. (This generalizes the observation that in our model the linearity result holds only if ψ''' is not too negative and the hazard rate is monotonic.) We thus should not consider the linearity result as a general rule but rather as defining a class of environments in which one can conveniently work with linear incentive schemes. The linearity result also sug-

51. The other assumptions are standard or technical; see Rogerson's 1987 paper for details. In particular $v_y > 0$, $v_{yy} > 0$, $v_\theta < 0$, $v_{\theta y} < 0$. In our model $\theta = -\beta$, $y = -C$, $U = t - \psi(\beta - C)$, and $V = [S - (1 + \lambda)C - \psi(\beta - C)]/\lambda - t$.

gests that using a menu of linear schemes may be a good approximation of the optimal policy in some circumstances.

It should also be pointed out that Melumad et al. (1991) proposed an alternative set of sufficient assumptions for the optimality of a menu of linear contracts. The agent produces output y with cost parameter θ. Let the disutility of effort have the multiplicative form $v(\theta, y) = h(\theta)l(y)$, with l increasing and convex and h decreasing and convex. Then a menu of linear contracts is optimal if the ratio $r(\theta) = (-h'(\theta)/h(\theta))[(1 - G(\theta))/g(\theta)]$ decreases with θ. The sharing coefficients are then $[1 + r(\theta)]^{-1}$.

What can be said if the transfer function is not convex in cost? A menu of linear schemes cannot be used to implement the optimum, but Picard (1987) shows that a menu of appropriately chosen *quadratic* schemes does. Let

$$C = \beta - e + \varepsilon,$$

where the noise ε has variance σ^2. As in section 1.4 let the firm announce its parameter $\hat{\beta}$ [or equivalently its expected cost $C^*(\hat{\beta})$, where $C^*(\hat{\beta})$ is defined implicitly by (1.44)]. The firm then receives the quadratic scheme

$$t(C, \hat{\beta}) = a(\hat{\beta}) - b(\hat{\beta})(C - C^*(\hat{\beta})) - d[(C - C^*(\hat{\beta}))^2 - \sigma^2],$$

where $a(\cdot)$ and $b(\cdot)$ are as in equations (1.60) and (1.61). Let $C^e = \beta - e$ denote the expected cost chosen by the firm. Then

$$Et = a(\hat{\beta}) - b(\hat{\beta})(C^e - C^*(\hat{\beta})) - d(C^e - C^*(\hat{\beta}))^2.$$

Noise is now irrelevant to the firm, which maximizes $\{Et - \psi(\beta - C^e)\}$. Figure 1.10 shows why choosing d high guarantees that the firm behaves

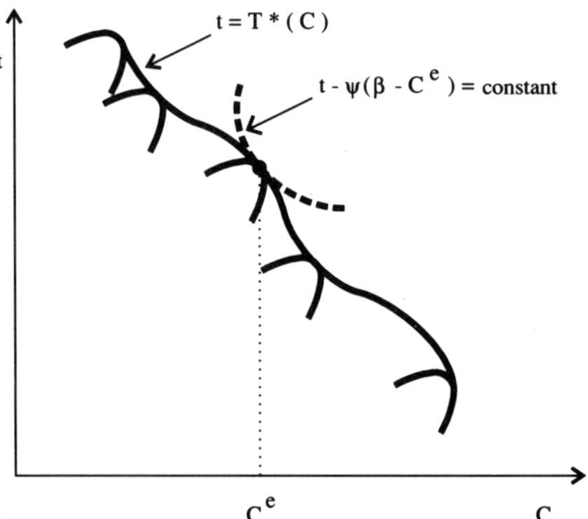

Figure 1.10
Quadratic schemes when the transfer function is not convex

in the same way as under the optimal $t(C)$ function. For d sufficiently large, it does not pay to choose $C^e \neq C^*(\hat{\beta})$. Last, note that Picard's quadratic schemes require knowledge of the variance of the noise. This requirement is not needed when linear schemes are optimal.

B1.3 The Value of Communication

We saw that with a continuum of types and under our assumptions, the optimal allocation can be implemented through a menu of linear contracts. This method of implementing the optimum requires ex ante communication from the agent to the principal. Caillaud, Guesnerie, and Rey (1992), Demougin (1989), and Melumad and Reichelstein (1989) have independently studied whether communication is necessary when cost observation is noisy (Guesnerie, Picard, and Rey 1988 discuss and compare the first and third papers). [Of course no menu is needed in the noiseless case: Any menu $t(\beta, C)$ can be replaced equivalently by the incentive scheme $t^*(C) = \max_\beta t(\beta, C)$.]

The problem with noisy cost observation can be posed as follows: Let the agent's utility be

$$U = t - \psi(\beta, C^e),$$

where C^e is the some cost target chosen by the agent and the disutility of effort ψ depends in an arbitrary way on β and C^e. The outcome, or realized cost, has some conditional cumulative distribution $G(C|C^e)$ (so in our model $C - C^e = \varepsilon$). The principal is risk neutral with respect to the outcome C. Suppose first that C^e is observed; that is, either there is no noise or else the principal can observe the noise. Let $T^*(C^e)$ denote the optimal transfer function [given by (1.52) in our model].

Suppose now that the principal only observes C, but that there exist transfers $\{\hat{t}(C)\}$ such that for all C^e in the relevant range,

$$T^*(C^e) = \int \hat{t}(C) dG(C|C^e). \tag{B1.2}$$

In this case the optimal allocation when the principal can observe C^e can also be implemented through the transfer function $\hat{t}(\cdot)$ when the principal only observes the realization C. This then shows two things. First, there is *no cost to noisy observation* in this risk-neutral world. [This result generalizes the linearity result of this chapter. But there is a sense in which it is weaker: The $\hat{t}(\cdot)$ function depends on the specific distribution of noise, while the linear contracts are optimal for any distribution of additive noise.] Second, there is *no value to communication.* That is, the optimum can be implemented by basing the agent's reward on realized cost only, and not on a message sent by the agent.

A transfer function $\hat{t}(\cdot)$ satisfying equation (B1.2) exists under fairly weak conditions. Basically what is needed is for the principal to be able to stochastically tell any two cost targets C^e and $\tilde{C}^e$ apart. When the spaces of cost targets and cost realizations are discrete, this requires a "spanning" or "full rank" condition allowing the inversion of the matrix of conditional probabilities in (B1.2) to obtain the $\hat{t}$ transfers. When the spaces of cost targets and realizations are continuous, this matrix inversion can be generalized, as was first studied by Vitto Volterra and Ivor Fredholm.

Remark 1 The idea that noise in observations does not matter in certain classes of agency problems dates back to Mirrlees (1975). Mirrlees showed that in a moral hazard context, the nonobservability of effort does not matter if there exist outcomes that reveal with probability equal to 1, or arbitrarily close to 1, that the agent defected from the prescribed effort. Closer to the work discussed here is the literature on auctions with correlated values; with various degrees of generality, Crémer and McLean (1985, 1988), McAfee, McMillan, and Reny (1992), and Maskin and Riley (1980) show that a principal can extract a risk neutral bidder's informational rent as long as there exists another bidder whose valuation is correlated with the first bidder's valuation. Related contributions in adverse selection models include Johnson, Pratt, and Zeckhauser (1990) and Riordan and Sappington (1988). Last, a full-rank condition is also invoked in infinitely repeated games with imperfect public information. Fudenberg, Levine, and Maskin (1990) prove a folk theorem for games in which the players' actions are unobservable, but a publicly observable outcome stochastically reveals a player's deviation (in that the vectors of probabilities of outcomes for two different actions of the player, fixing the other players' strategies, are linearly independent).

Remark 2 McAfee and McMillan (1986) and Picard and Rey (1990) have generalized the results of this chapter to teams. Suppose that there are two agents who choose cost levels C^1 and C^2 and that the principal's total cost is $C(C^1, C^2)$. Agent i's utility is, as before, $t^i - \psi(\beta^i, C^i)$, where t^i is his or her net transfer. Each agent has private information about his or her cost parameter. McAfee and McMillan and Picard and Rey show that the principal's expected welfare is the same whether he or she observes individual performances C^i or only aggregate performance C (or, even as pointed out above, a garbled version of C). The idea is that the principal can see through the distribution of C^j (as a function of β^j) when giving incentives to agent i.[52]

52. Picard and Rey show that the result does not require Bayesian implementation, and carries over to the more demanding concept of posterior implementation (Green and Laffont 1987).

B1.4 Dynamics under Full Commitment: Extension to Imperfect Intertemporal Correlation

Section 1.10 showed how to solve for the optimal intertemporal incentive scheme when the firm's type is perfectly correlated over time. Baron and Besanko (1984) have extended the analysis to imperfect correlation. We discuss their generalization in a two-period version of the model of this chapter. The presentation will be heuristic in that we ignore second-order conditions.

The timing is as in section 1.10 except that the firm learns its second-period type β_2 only at the beginning of period 2. Given first-period type β_1, the conditional cumulative distribution is $F_2(\beta_2|\beta_1)$ on $[\underline{\beta}_2, \overline{\beta}_2]$ with density $f_2(\beta_2|\beta_1)$. Positive correlation means that given two types $\beta_1 < \tilde{\beta}_1$, the second-period distribution conditional on β_1 first-order stochastically dominates that conditional on $\tilde{\beta}_1$. That is, $F_2(\beta_2|\beta_1) \geq F_2(\beta_2|\tilde{\beta}_1)$ for all β_2 (the distribution puts more weight on low realizations of β_2 for β_1 than for $\tilde{\beta}_1$). Thus we assume that $\partial F_2/\partial\beta_1 \leq 0$ for all β_2. The distribution of the first-period type is $F_1(\beta_1)$ on $[\underline{\beta}_1, \overline{\beta}_1]$. The firm knows its type before contracting in period 1. Letting $U(\beta_1)$ denote the firm's expected intertemporal rent given type β_1, and δ denote the discount factor, we have[53]

$$\dot{U}(\beta_1) = -\psi'(e_1(\beta_1)) + \delta \int_{\underline{\beta}_2}^{\overline{\beta}_2} \left(\int_{\beta_2}^{\overline{\beta}_2} \psi'(e_2(x))dx \right) \frac{\partial f_2(\beta_2|\beta_1)}{\partial \beta_1} d\beta_2.$$

Assuming that shutting down the firm is never optimal, the regulator maximizes expected intertemporal welfare:

$$\begin{aligned} S - (1 + \lambda)\Bigg\{ \int_{\underline{\beta}_1}^{\overline{\beta}_1} \Bigg[& \beta_1 - e_1(\beta_1) + \psi(e_1(\beta_1)) \\ & + \int_{\underline{\beta}_2}^{\overline{\beta}_2} [\beta_2 - e_2(\beta_1, \beta_2) + \psi(e_2(\beta_1, \beta_2))] f_2(\beta_2|\beta_1) d\beta_2 \Bigg] f_1(\beta_1) d\beta_1 \Bigg\} \\ & - \lambda \int_{\underline{\beta}_1}^{\overline{\beta}_1} U(\beta_1) f_1(\beta_1) d\beta_1. \end{aligned}$$

Following the steps of section 1.4 [integrating by parts and using $\partial F_2/\partial\beta_1 = 0$ at $\beta_2 = \underline{\beta}_2$ and $\overline{\beta}_2$ and $U(\overline{\beta}_1) = 0$] yields

$$\psi'(e_1(\beta_1)) = 1 - \frac{\lambda}{1 + \lambda} \frac{F_1(\beta_1)}{f_1(\beta_1)} \psi''(e_1(\beta_1)),$$

and

$$\psi'(e_2(\beta_1, \beta_2)) = 1 - \frac{\lambda}{1 + \lambda} \left(- \frac{\partial F_2(\beta_2|\beta_1)/\partial\beta_1}{f_2(\beta_2|\beta_1)} \right) \frac{F_1(\beta_1)}{f_1(\beta_1)} \psi''(e_2(\beta_1, \beta_2)).$$

53. We normalize the second-period rent to be 0 at $\overline{\beta}_2$, without loss of generality.

The trade-off between incentives and rent extraction in period 1 is the same as in the static framework, and so the first-period effort is as in equation (1.44).

To understand the expression for the second-period effort, consider first the cases of perfect correlation and independence. If β_2 and β_1 are almost perfectly correlated, $-(\partial F_2/\partial \beta_1)/f_2$ is almost equal to 1 and the stationarity result of section 1.10 obtains approximately. If β_2 and β_1 are independent, $\partial F_2/\partial \beta_1 = 0$ and the second-period effort is the socially optimal level e^*. This is natural, for the second-period contract is then signed in the first period under symmetric information about second-period cost. Therefore it is optimal for the regulator to commit to a fixed-price contract for period 2 and extract the expected second-period rent (which is independent of β_1) in period 1. More generally, since $(-\partial F_2/\partial \beta_1)/f_2$ is a measure of the informativeness of β_2 about β_1, it guides the use of second-period distortions to extract the firm's informational rent associated with its knowledge of β_1.

B1.5 Stopping Rules in Multistage Projects, Buying-in, and Cost Overruns

Consider a defense project that evolves in two stages (the generalization to N stages is straightforward). The social surplus S is realized only if each of the two stages is completed. Suppose that the contractor has cost $C_\tau = \beta_\tau - e_\tau$, $\tau = 1, 2$. The two stages of the project are sufficiently different that the private information parameters β_1 and β_2 are independent (chapters 9 and 10 study intertemporal correlation). We make the (strong) assumption that β_1 and β_2 are drawn from the same continuous distribution $F(\cdot)$ on $[\underline{\beta}, \bar{\beta}]$. The timing is as follows: In each period the firm learns its type β_τ and the regulator offers an incentive scheme $t_\tau(C_\tau)$ for that period. There is no intertemporal commitment; that is, the relationship is run by a sequence of short-term contracts.

Arvan and Leite (1989) show that the regulator is more lenient as time passes, in that the price paid to the contractor for a given cost performance increases over time. The intuition is that the value for the regulator of continuing the project increases over time as sunk costs are irrelevant for current decision making. The cutoff type therefore increases over time, which raises the firm's transfer and instantaneous rent. To show this, consider period 2. The expected rent at the end of period 1 is

$$\bar{U}_2 = E_{\beta_2} U(\beta_2, \beta_2^*),$$

where, from (1.66),

$$U(\beta_2, \beta_2^*) = \int_{\beta_2}^{\beta_2^*} \psi'(e^*(\tilde{\beta}))d\tilde{\beta},$$

and the cutoff type β_2^* is given by (1.67) and $e^*(\beta)$ is given by (1.44). The expected welfare in period 2 is given by (1.65):

$$\overline{W}_2 = \int_{\underline{\beta}}^{\beta_2^*} [S - (1 + \lambda)(\beta_2 - e^*(\beta_2) + \psi(e^*(\beta_2))) - \lambda U(\beta_2, \beta_2^*)] dF(\beta_2).$$

Consider now the first period. Let $U_1(\beta_1)$ denote the first-period rent of type β_1. Expected social welfare in period 1 is

$$\int_{\underline{\beta}}^{\beta_1^*} [\delta \overline{W}_2 - (1 + \lambda)[\beta_1 - e_1(\beta_1) + \psi(e_1(\beta_1))] - \lambda U_1(\beta_1)] dF(\beta_1),$$

where β_1^* is the first-period cutoff type. Letting $\delta \leq 1$ denote the common discount factor, the first-period individual rationality constraint for the firm is

$$U(\beta_1) \equiv U_1(\beta_1) + \delta \overline{U}_2 \geq 0.$$

The incentive compatibility constraint is, as before,

$$\dot{U}(\beta_1) = \dot{U}_1(\beta_1) = -\psi'(e_1(\beta_1)).$$

Brief inspection of the problem shows that $e_1(\beta_1) = e^*(\beta_1)$, and therefore $U_1(\beta_1) = U_1(\beta_1^*) + U(\beta_1, \beta_1^*)$. Furthermore $U_1(\beta_1^*) = -\delta \overline{U}_2$. Expected social welfare is thus

$$\int_{\underline{\beta}}^{\beta_1^*} \{[\delta(\overline{W}_2 + \lambda \overline{U}_2)] - (1 + \lambda)[\beta_1 - e^*(\beta_1) + \psi(e^*(\beta_1))] - \lambda U(\beta_1, \beta_1^*)\} dF(\beta_1)$$

Note that this social welfare function is the same as in the static (or second-period) problem except that the surplus S is replaced by $\delta(\overline{W}_2 + \lambda \overline{U}_2) < S$.[54] Section 1.4 then implies that $\beta_1^* \leq \beta_2^*$, which may be interpreted as a *lock-in effect*. Since for a given type the rent is higher in period 2 than in period 1 and the cost is the same, the transfer is higher in period 2. Therefore the transfer for a given cost level is higher in period 2.

The assumptions that the distributions of technological uncertainty in periods 1 and 2 are the same and that $\delta \leq 1$ are of course strong. Suppose, for instance, that the scale of the second-period activity much exceeds that of the first period. Descaling the utility functions of the two parties then yields a discount factor greater than 1 even if the parties exhibit impatience. In the extreme case where the first-period activity is negligible relative to the second-period's, it is optimal never to shut down the firm before period 2 ($\beta_1^* = \overline{\beta} \geq \beta_2^*$). Therefore we should exercise caution in interpreting the result. Yet Arvan and Leite make the interesting point that as time

54. Assuming that the cost $\beta - e^*(\beta)$ is positive for all β, which is reasonable.

elapses, the regulator's demand for the project goes up, which puts the firm in a better position.[55]

The previous example shows that in a multistage relationship run by short-term contracts, it may pay for the firm to lose money early in the relationship in order to "get a foothold in" and derive rents in the future.[56] In the example there is a single firm willing to sacrifice short-term profits to get the project going. The same phenomenon can occur in a situation where the future of the project is not necessarily in doubt but where there are several potential firms that bid in the first stage to be the sole supplier. A well-known practice in defense procurement is *low-ball bidding* in which the firms submit very low bids to win the initial contract in the hope of reaping high profits from follow-on contracts.[57] This practice is also known under the name of *buying in.* Buying-in results are common in multistage models of procurement.[58]

A related, but distinct, issue is that of *cost overruns.* Realized costs often exceed initial cost estimates in defense procurement.[59] The phenomenon of cost overruns is at first sight surprising. *Predictions* about cost realizations must follow a martingale in a rational-expectations world; indeed it would be surprising if the firms, the Department of Defense, and Congress would systematically be wrong in their cost predictions. Thus somehow the costs that are *announced* or written down in initial contracts must underestimate the parties' prediction of expected cost.

55. See also Lewis (1986) for a reputation model in which the government's net value for the project increases over time. Lewis uses this property to show that, at the end of their relationship, the firm has less incentive to keep a reputation for being a low-cost producer as the continuation of the project is less in question.
56. Since $U_1(\beta_1^*) + \delta \bar{U}_2 = 0$, types below but close to β_1^* have a negative first-period rent $U_1(\beta_1)$.
57. According to Scherer (1964, p. 156),

> to sell their efforts contractors commonly submit (and buying agencies encourage) unrealistically low cost estimates. This practice may require accepting a low realized rate of profit on development work, but contractors have generally been willing to sacrifice initial development contract profits for the chance of earning substantial production follow-on contract profits once they are locked together with the government in a relationship analogous to bilateral monopoly.

Stubbing (1986, p. 177) reports:

> Thus, the incentive given to contractors is to win the early contract, even at a financial sacrifice, in order to reach the placid waters of lucrative follow-on contracts negotiated in a sole-source atmosphere.

58. See, for example, Marshall (1989), Riordan and Sappington (1989), and chapter 4.
59. For instance, Scherer (1964, p. 27) reports that

> actual costs in the 12 weapon system developments covered by our case studies exceeded original contractor predictions by 220% on the average. Actual costs turned out to be less than original predictions in only one program—the program initiated under the least competitive circumstances.

For more recent examples, see Fox (1988).

One explanation for cost overruns is that for bad realizations of the technological uncertainty the firm can threaten to go out of business, and the government is then forced to renegotiate price upward. The government is not fooled because it knows that the initial price will prevail only in good states of nature. According to this explanation the difference between announced and predicted expected costs is, for the government, similar to that between nominal and real values of debt for creditors of a firm that has positive probability of going bankrupt.

A second explanation for cost overruns is that the government keeps adding design changes that raise the cost of the project independently of any agency problem. That is, the government commits to paying a certain amount for a basic technology and then raises costs by upgrading this technology. This explanation assumes that the technology adjustments involve more often upgradings than downgradings or simplifications.

This second explanation, which abstracts from agency problems, does not quite deliver the prediction of buy-in behavior. To combine buy-ins and cost overruns, we can mix the model discussed above and the idea of design changes by the government.[60] For instance, we can alter the two-period model above in the following way. With some probability the second-period project uses a known technology and is the continuation of the first-period project; the second-period cost parameter is $\beta_2 = \beta_1$. With some probability the government will desire an upgrade in the technology. The technological cost parameter for period 2 is then $\beta_2 = \beta_1 + \tilde{\beta}_2$, where $\tilde{\beta}_2$ is learned by the firm at the beginning of period 2 (e.g., is independent of β_1). Suppose further that at date 1 the two parties can sign a long-term contract covering the known technology, that is, the relationship in period 1 and that for period 2 if no upgrading is requested. But the potential change in design in period 2 cannot be described in period 1, so negotiation will have to occur if the upgrading opportunity occurs in period 2. Such a situation will generate both cost overruns—because of the probability of upgrading—and buying-in—because the firm is willing to lose some money on the long-term contract in the hope that the government will want to change the design, in which case the firm will enjoy a new informational rent.

The fourth explanation is that contract supervisors themselves encourage cost underestimates in order to get support from headquarters or Congress.[61] Such an explanation seems to involve some myopia some-

60. See Lewis (1986), Marshall (1989), and Tirole (1986).

61. In Scherer's (1964, p. 28) words,

> and as the advocates of new programs, government operating agencies have often encouraged contractors to estimate costs optimistically, recognizing that higher headquarters might be shocked out of supporting a program where true costs were revealed at the outset. They have sought to disclose cost increases only gradually, after programs have gained momentum and cancellation has become difficult.

where in the agency ladder (voters, Congress, or headquarters), and we are not aware of formal modeling of this commonly mentioned idea.

B1.6 Risk Aversion: Forecast versus Accounting Errors

Our discussion of the robustness of linear contracts to noise under risk neutrality applies equally well to forecast and accounting errors. Baron and Besanko (1988) make the interesting point that the two types of errors have markedly different consequences under risk aversion. To see why this is so, suppose that the measured cost is

$$C = C^e + \varepsilon_f + \varepsilon_a.$$

The firm's expected cost is C^e $(=\beta - e)$. The forecast error is ε_f with mean 0 and variance σ_f^2; so the realized cost is $(C^e + \varepsilon_f)$. Government accountants make a random accounting error ε_a with mean 0 and variance σ_a^2. With the mean-variance preferences of section 1.11 and *gross* transfer function $t = a + dC$, the firm's utility is $a - bC^e - \psi(\beta - C^e) - r[b^2\sigma_f^2 + (1-b)^2\sigma_a^2]$, where $b \equiv 1 - d$. That is, the firm bears real cost $(C^e + \varepsilon_f)$ and is reimbursed a fraction d of measured cost. It is thus residual claimant for a fraction b of forecast errors and $(1 - b)$ of accounting errors. While forecast errors and risk aversion push optimal schemes toward cost-plus contracts ($b = 0$), accounting errors and risk aversion push optimal schemes toward fixed-price contracts ($b = 1$); after all, cost accounting plays no role if the firm is residual claimant for its cost.

B1.7 Subcontracting and Delegation

Subcontracting is pervasive in defense and aerospace contracts, but it is also very common in regulated industries. For instance, an electric utility buys fuel, power plants, and even electricity from other utilities or qualified facilities. Subcontracting raises new issues relative to in-house production if the regulator is better able to observe the specific cost associated with the subcontracted activity. The general approach to regulation when the regulator observes variables other than total cost (here the subcontracting cost) will be developed in chapter 3. But the simplicity of the specific subcontracting structure allows us to treat the problem already here.

Consider a variant of the model of this chapter, in which part of the regulated firm's task is performed by a subcontractor. Assume that the regulated firm's and the subcontractor's activities are separate and perfectly complementary and that their two costs can be measured. Should the regulator entirely delegate subcontracting to the regulated firm and pay it on the basis of total cost (internal cost plus subcontracting cost)?[62] Should the regulator reward the two units on the basis of the two realized costs? Should he or she design the subcontract? The answer is that the regulator should *not* delegate subcontracting to the regulated firm, unless one of the following conditions holds:

1. The subcontractor is a foreign firm whose welfare does not enter the social welfare function.
2. The subcontractor has no private information.

The preceding argument is developed in review problem 19, but the intuition for why delegation generally is not optimal is simple: When designing a contract for the subcontractor the regulated firm tries to extract too much rent from its subcontractor (or, equivalently, offers a too low-powered incentive scheme). Under a centralized set of contracts designed by the regulator, the formula for the subcontractor would be given by equation (1.44) applied to the appropriate distribution of uncertainty about the subcontractor's cost parameter. In contrast, the contract designed by the regulated firm for the subcontractor under delegation is given by a modification of equation (1.44) in which "$\lambda/(1+\lambda)$" is replaced by "1." Except in case 1 the social welfare oriented regulator internalizes part of the subcontractor's surplus, while the regulated firm does not. The regulated firm is thus "too tough" toward the subcontractor from the regulator's point of view. That case 2 also constitutes an exception to the general rule against delegation is equally clear: In the absence of private information for the subcontractor, there is no rent extraction under either delegation or no delegation.

To delegate the design of the subcontract to the regulated firm, the regulator must use a "scoring rule" for C_2, the cost of the subcontractor. Under some assumptions "delegation" is costless if the regulator can offer a menu of linear incentive schemes to the regulated firm (firm 1) of the type

$$t_1 = a_1 - b_1(C_1 + t_2 + \hat{C}_2(C_2)),$$

where $\hat{C}_2$ is a convex function of C_2 (with slope 1 at the lowest equilibrium cost). The convexity of $\hat{C}_2$ is meant to punish the regulated firm's for granting low-powered incentives. But this of course is a perverted use of the concept of delegation.

The result that delegation (without scoring rule) does not reduce welfare if the subcontractor is a foreign firm is actually well known in the literature in another context. Melumad et al. (1991) consider private hierarchies in which the principal does not internalize his or her agents' welfares. They

62. That is, if 1 and 2 index the regulated firm and the subcontractor, and if t_i denotes firm i's net revenue, should the net transfer t_1 from the government to the regulated firm depend only on the total cost $[C_1 + (t_2 + C_2)]$ that it declares?

show that delegation is (weakly) optimal; hence the concept of "responsibility center" within the hierarchy. Baron and Besanko (1992) also compare centralized and delegated contracting and look at the effect of the observability of the communication between the contractor and the subcontractor by the regulator. They in particular show that the principal can contract with one of the agents only if he or she can observe the contracting between the agents.

Another result, due to Melumad et al. (1990) and McAfee and McMillan (1990),[63] is that delegation generally is not optimal in a private hierarchy when the principal cannot measure the payment the contractor makes to the subcontractor (which in the case of cost performance rules out payment to the contractor based on the contractor's total cost). In this case it can be shown that the contractor distorts the production assignment for the subcontractor in his or her favor.[64]

B1.8 Informed Regulator

We assumed that the regulator's objective function is common knowledge. In practice, the regulator may well have private information about demand (e.g., his or her own demand in procurement) or the availability of substitute products. Keeping the framework of this chapter and assuming that the regulator's information does not directly enter the firm's utility function (as seems plausible in the two examples just given), it can be shown that none of the analysis is affected by the privacy of the regulator's information. That is, the optimal contract and the regulatory outcome are the same as if the firm knew the regulator's information.

The intuition for this irrelevance of the asymmetry of information about the regulator's objectives is twofold. First, the regulator can guarantee the same welfare when he or she has private information by offering the same incentive contract as when information about the regulator's preferences is symmetric. Because the regulator's information does not enter the firm's utility function, none of the firm's incentive and individual rationality constraints is affected. Second, this leaves open the question of whether the regulator cannot do better when he or she has private information. Different types of regulator could pool at the contract design stage and reveal their information only during the execution of the contract. By so doing, they would pool the firm's individual rationality and incentive constraints. In other words, the firm's constraints would no longer need to be satisfied for

63. See also the related work of Demski and Sappington (1989).

64. Melumad et al. (1990, 1991) also consider delegation in hierarchies in which communication is limited. Delegation can then be strictly advantageous, as it allows a more flexible use of the contractor's private information.

each type of regulator, but only on average over the types of regulator. Such a pooling of constraints can be profitable for the regulator only if the shadow prices of the firm's constraints are contingent on the regulator's type. However, with quasi-linear preferences these shadow prices are the same whatever the regulator's preferences and thus there is no gain to pooling.

In contrast, when the parties' preferences are not quasi-linear, the regulator (generically) obtains a higher welfare than when his or her preferences are known to the firm. The regulator gains by delaying the revelation of his or her private information until the execution of the contract with the firm. These two results can be found in Maskin and Tirole (1990).[65]

Last, in some cases the regulator has private information that is directly relevant to the firm. For instance, the regulator might have experience with some component of the project through his or her own research labs or through interaction with the firm's competitors. The design of a contract by the regulator then signals information that affects the firm's willingness to accept the contract and to reach certain levels of performance. See Maskin and Tirole (1992) for the resolution of this case.

APPENDIXES

A1.1 Nonoptimality of Stochastic Contracts

We show in this appendix that under the assumption $\psi''' \geq 0$, it is not worth considering stochastic mechanisms, that is mechanisms that for a given announcement of type draw from a nondegenerate distribution the transfer and the cost target. Suppose, on the contrary, that the optimal contract involves randomization for both types. Type $\underline{\beta}$'s allocation is chosen randomly among

$$(t^1, C^1), \ldots, (t^m, C^m),$$

and type $\bar{\beta}$'s among

$$(t^{m+1}, C^{m+1}), \ldots, (t^n, C^n).$$

Note that since $\psi'' \geq 0$, both the regulator's and the firm's utility functions are concave in (t, C). Both the regulator and the firm, whatever its type, gain by replacing these random contracts by their expectations taken with the probability distributions corresponding to the randomizations. Let α^k denote the probability of (t^k, C^k) (so $\sum_{k \leq m} \alpha^k = \sum_{k \geq m+1} \alpha^k = 1$), $\bar{C} \equiv \sum_{k>m} \alpha^k C^k$, and $\bar{t} - \psi(\bar{\beta} - \bar{C}) \equiv \sum_{k>m} \alpha^k [t^k - \psi(\bar{\beta} - C^k)]$. In words, the inefficient type is given the expected cost target and a new transfer that keeps its utility constant. Type $\underline{\beta}$ does not want to mimic type $\bar{\beta}$ because

65. Tan (1991) develops similar ideas in the context of an auction designed by an informed procuror. With risk-averse suppliers, the procuror may for instance prefer to conceal the reserve price.

$$\sum_{k<m+1} \alpha^k[t^k - \psi(\underline{\beta} - C^k)] \geq \sum_{k>m} \alpha^k[t^k - \psi(\underline{\beta} - C^k)]$$
$$\geq \sum_{k>m} \alpha^k[\psi(\overline{\beta} - C^k) - \psi(\underline{\beta} - C^k)]$$
$$- [\psi(\overline{\beta} - \overline{C}) - \psi(\underline{\beta} - \overline{C})]$$
$$+ [\bar{t} - \psi(\underline{\beta} - \overline{C})]$$
$$\geq \bar{t} - \psi(\underline{\beta} - \overline{C}),$$

where the first inequality describes incentive compatibility of the initial allocation, the second uses the definition of $\bar{t}$, and the third uses the convexity of the function $C \to [\psi(\overline{\beta} - C) - \psi(\underline{\beta} - C)]$ (due to $\psi''' \geq 0$) and Jensen's inequality. We leave it to the reader to show that type $\overline{\beta}$'s allocation can similarly be replaced by a deterministic one. We conclude that stochastic schemes are suboptimal.

The proof with a continuum of types is related to this. The key step consists in noting that $E(\psi'(\beta - C)) \geq \psi'(\beta - EC)$, where E denotes an expectation. Since $\dot{U}(\beta) = -E(\psi'(\beta - C))$, the rate at which the rent grows with efficiency can be reduced by the use of a deterministic scheme. ■

A1.2 The Revelation Principle

The revelation principle is a general result of incentive theory, which we will use repeatedly throughout this book. Let us prove this principle in the context of our model. The two observable variables for the regulator are cost C and the net transfer t. For type β a deterministic regulatory mechanism implies realized cost $C(\beta)$ and transfer $t(\beta)$. We can view any regulatory mechanism as a game in which the firm plays some strategy σ (any strategy by the regulator can be subsumed in the definition of the mechanism). Let us call σ^* (β) the optimal strategy of type β faced with the regulatory mechanism, which associates to each realized pure strategy σ cost $C(\sigma)$ and transfer $t(\sigma)$.

Consider now the direct revelation mechanism which associates with the announcement of $\hat{\beta}$ the pair $\{C(\sigma^*(\hat{\beta})), t(\sigma^*(\hat{\beta}))\}$. That is, the regulator commits to use the optimal strategy of the agent in the original mechanism. Of course it is in the interest of the agent to announce $\hat{\beta} = \beta$. Suppose, on the contrary, that there exists $\beta' \neq \beta$ such that

$$t(\sigma^*(\beta')) - \psi(\beta - C(\sigma^*(\beta'))) > t(\sigma^*(\beta)) - \psi(\beta - C(\sigma^*(\beta))).$$

Then there exists $\sigma' = \sigma^*(\beta') \neq \sigma^*(\beta)$ such that

$$t(\sigma') - \psi(\beta - C(\sigma')) > t(\sigma^*(\beta)) - \psi(\beta - C(\sigma^*(\beta))),$$

which contradicts the optimality of $\sigma^*(\cdot)$. The proof is similar for stochastic mechanisms. ■

A1.3 Differentiability Almost Everywhere of the Transfer Function

Let β be a point of differentiability of $C(\cdot)$. From (1.28) and (1.29), and for $\beta' > \beta$,

$$\frac{\psi(\beta - C(\beta')) - \psi(\beta - C(\beta))}{\beta' - \beta} \geq \frac{t(\beta') - t(\beta)}{\beta' - \beta} \geq \frac{\psi(\beta' - C(\beta')) - \psi(\beta' - C(\beta))}{\beta' - \beta}.$$

As $\beta' \to \beta$, the left-hand side and the right-hand side converge to $-\psi'(\beta - C(\beta))\dot{C}(\beta)$. Therefore

$$\left.\frac{dt}{d\beta}\right|_{+} = -\psi'(\beta - C(\beta))\dot{C}(\beta).$$

Similarly, taking $\beta' < \beta$, we get

$$\left.\frac{dt}{d\beta}\right|_{-} = -\psi'(\beta - C(\beta))\dot{C}(\beta).$$

Therefore, at any point where C is differentiable, $t(\cdot)$ is differentiable and

$$\dot{t}(\beta) = -\psi'(\beta - C(\beta))\dot{C}(\beta). \qquad \blacksquare$$

A1.4 Sufficiency of the Monotonicity Condition

In the continuum model of section 1.4, monotonicity of $C(\cdot)$ (i.e., that it be nondecreasing) and the first-order condition (1.32) imply that $\hat{\beta} = \beta$ is a global optimum for type β. To show this, assume to the contrary that type β strictly prefers to announce $\hat{\beta} \neq \beta$:

$$\varphi(\beta, \hat{\beta}) > \varphi(\beta, \beta),$$

or

$$\int_{\beta}^{\hat{\beta}} \varphi_2(\beta, x)dx > 0.$$

Using (1.32), this is equivalent to

$$\int_{\beta}^{\hat{\beta}} (\varphi_2(\beta, x) - \varphi_2(x, x))dx > 0$$

or

$$\int_{\beta}^{\hat{\beta}} \int_{x}^{\beta} \varphi_{12}(y, x)dydx > 0.$$

φ_{12} exists almost everywhere and satisfies

$$\varphi_{12}(y, x) = \frac{\partial}{\partial x}[-\psi'(y - C(x))] = \psi''(y - C(x))\dot{C}(x) \geq 0.$$

If $\hat{\beta} > \beta$, $x \geq \beta$ for all $x \in [\beta, \hat{\beta}]$, and the inequality cannot hold. Similarly, if $\hat{\beta} < \beta$, $x \leq \beta$ for all $x \in [\hat{\beta}, \beta]$, and again we obtain a contradiction. $\blacksquare$

A1.5 Bunching

In this appendix we study optimal regulation when the solution to (1.44) does not yield a monotonic cost function. We must then reintroduce the monotonicity constraint into the regulator's program:

$$\max \int_{\underline{\beta}}^{\bar{\beta}} \left\{ S - (1 + \lambda)(\beta - e(\beta) + \psi(e(\beta)) - \lambda \frac{F(\beta)}{f(\beta)} \psi'(e(\beta)) \right\} dF(\beta),$$

subject to

$$\dot{e}(\beta) - 1 \leq 0.$$

Let $y(\beta) \equiv \dot{e}(\beta)$. Then the constraint can be written

$$\dot{e}(\beta) = y(\beta) \text{ and } y(\beta) \leq 1.$$

We can treat this problem as an optimal control problem with e as the state variable and y as the control variable. The hamiltonian is

$$H = \left(S - (1 + \lambda)(\beta - e(\beta) + \psi(e(\beta))) - \frac{\lambda F(\beta)}{f(\beta)} \psi'(e(\beta)) \right) f(\beta) + \theta(\beta) y(\beta),$$

where $\theta(\beta)$ is the Pontryagin multiplier of $\dot{e}(\beta) = y(\beta)$. Thus

$$\dot{\theta}(\beta) = -\frac{\partial H}{\partial e} = (1 + \lambda)(\psi'(e(\beta)) - 1) + \frac{\lambda F(\beta)}{f(\beta)} \psi''(e(\beta)).$$

Maximizing with respect to $y(\beta)$ yields for all β,

$$\theta(\beta) \leq 0,$$

and if $\theta(\beta) < 0$,

$$y(\beta) = 1.$$

Consider an interval where the monotonicity constraint is not binding. Then $\theta(\beta) \equiv 0$ in this interval and the optimal solution $\hat{e}(\beta)$ coincides with $e^*(\beta)$. Consider now an interval (β_0, β_1) where the monotonicity constraint is binding. Because it is not binding to the left of β_0, $\theta(\beta) = 0$ for $\beta \uparrow \beta_0$ and by continuity $\theta(\beta_0) = 0$. Similarly $\theta(\beta_1) = 0$. Integrating yields

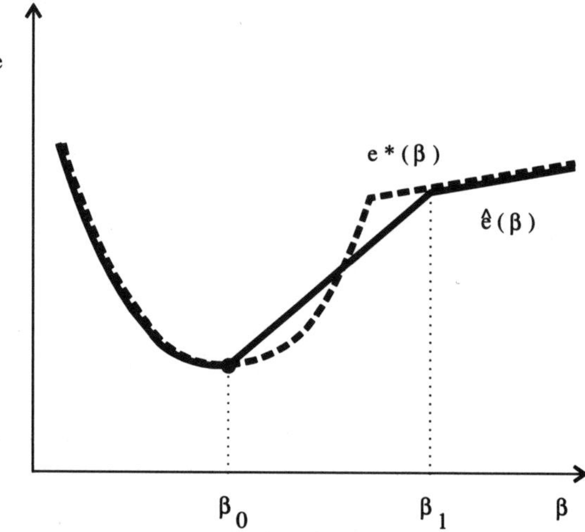

Figure 1.11
Bunching

$$\int_{\beta_0}^{\beta_1}\left[(1+\lambda)(\psi'(\beta+k)-1)+\lambda\frac{F(\beta)}{f(\beta)}\psi''(\beta+k)\right]dF(\beta)=0,$$

where $e(\beta)=\beta+k$ for some k since $\dot{e}=1$. To determine β_0, β_1, and k, we also use

$$\hat{e}(\beta_0)=e^*(\beta_0)=\beta_0+k,$$

$$\hat{e}(\beta_1)=e^*(\beta_1)=\beta_1+k.$$

We thus have three equations with three unknowns β_0, β_1, k. Figure 1.11 gives an example of an optimal solution when the monotonicity constraint is binding.

A1.6 Comparison of Information Structures in the Sense of Blackwell

An information structure is finer than another if it corresponds to a finer partition of the set of states of nature. Obviously a (single) decision maker (in our context, the regulator) always prefers a finer information structure to a coarser one. The effect on the firm's rent or slope of incentive scheme is less clear as we now demonstrate. Fix a prior distribution $F(\cdot)$ on the interval $[\underline{\beta},\bar{\beta}]$, and let the regulator receive a signal ρ_k, $k=1,\ldots,K$, with probability x_k such that $\sum_k x_k=1$. Let $f_k(\cdot)$ and $F_k(\cdot)$ denote the associated posterior "densities" and "cumulative distributions" (the actual densities and cumulative distributions are $f_k(\cdot)/F_k(\bar{\beta})$ and $F_k(\cdot)/F_k(\bar{\beta})$, where $F_k(\bar{\beta})=x_k$): For all β,

$$F(\beta)=\sum_k F_k(\beta)$$

and

$$f(\beta)=\sum_k f_k(\beta).$$

[As is well known, this is one way of writing that the latter (posterior) information structure is finer than the former (prior)]. We will assume that all conditional distributions satisfy the monotone hazard rate property.

Let us assume that $\psi''(\cdot)$ is constant (e.g., is equal to 1). In this case when the regulator receives no signal and lets the firm produce, the expected slope of the incentive scheme is

$$Eb\equiv 1-\frac{\lambda}{1+\lambda}\int_{\underline{\beta}}^{\beta^*}\frac{F(\beta)}{f(\beta)}\frac{f(\beta)}{F(\beta^*)}d\beta,$$

where β^* is the cutoff level for distribution F. Similarly let β_k^* denote the cutoff level for conditional distribution F_k. When the regulator obtains a signal before choosing an incentive scheme, we write the expected slope as

$$\tilde{E}b=1-\frac{\lambda}{1+\lambda}\sum_k x_k\int_{\underline{\beta}}^{\beta_k^*}\frac{F_k(\beta)}{f_k(\beta)}\frac{f_k(\beta)}{F_k(\beta_k^*)}d\beta.$$

Knowing that the move from asymmetric information about β to full information (ρ yields a degenerate distribution at the true value of β) raises the slope of the incentive scheme, we might wonder whether the same property holds more generally for a move from a coarse to a fine information structure. That this need not be the case is demonstrated in the following example. Suppose that the social surplus S is big and the signals not precise enough so that $\beta_k^*=\bar{\beta}$ for all k. Then

$$\tilde{E}b = 1 - \frac{\lambda}{1+\lambda}\sum_k \int_{\underline{\beta}}^{\overline{\beta}} F_k(\beta)d\beta = Eb.$$

We now study a class of information structures such that a finer information structure raises the average slope of the incentive scheme. Suppose that signal ρ_k amounts to a truncation of the interval $[\underline{\beta}, \overline{\beta}]$ into K subintervals. That is, the regulator learns that β belongs to $[\beta_k, \beta_{k-1}]$ where $\beta_k < \beta_{k-1}$, $\beta_K = \underline{\beta}$, $\beta_0 = \overline{\beta}$ (the numbering follows the convention that higher ρ's correspond to more favorable signals). The interpretation of this signal is as follows: Recall that $(\overline{\beta} - \beta)$ can be thought of as being the number of improvements on the basic technology $\overline{\beta}$. When the regulator learns that some of the $(\overline{\beta} - \beta)$ improvements are not feasible, the distribution is truncated downward. Similarly when the regulator learns that some of these improvements are feasible, the distribution is truncated upward. The resulting support is thus a subinterval.

Assume that S is sufficiently large so that $\beta_k^* = \beta_{k-1}$. Then

$$\tilde{E}b = 1 - \frac{\lambda}{1+\lambda}\left\{\int_{\underline{\beta}}^{\beta_{K-1}} F(\beta)d\beta + \int_{\beta_{K-1}}^{\beta_{K-2}} [F(\beta) - F(\beta_{K-1})]d\beta + \cdots \right.$$
$$\left. + \int_{\beta_1}^{\overline{\beta}} [F(\beta) - F(\beta_1)]d\beta \right\} > Eb.$$

It is difficult to compare the effects of alternative information structures without specializing the class of signals as we have done here.

REFERENCES

Arrow, K. 1979. The property rights doctrine and demand revelation under incomplete information. In *Economies and Human Welfare*. San Diego, CA: Academic Press.

Arrow, K., and M. Kurz. 1970. *Public Investment, the Rate of Return, and Optimal Fiscal Policy*. Baltimore, MD: Johns Hopkins University Press.

Arvan, L., and A. Leite. 1989. Cost overruns in long-term projects. Mimeo, University of Illinois and Universidade Nova de Lisboa.

Bagnoli, M., and T. Bergstrom. 1989. Log-concave probability and its applications. CREST WP #89–23, University of Michigan.

Baiman, S., and J. Demski. 1980. Economically optimal performance evaluation and control systems. *Journal of Accounting Research* (supp.) 18:184–234.

Baron, D., and D. Besanko. 1984. Regulation and information in a continuing relationship. *Information Economics and Policy* 1:447–470.

Baron, D., and D. Besanko. 1988. Monitoring of performance in organizational contracting: The case of defense procurement. *Scandinavian Journal of Economics* 90:329–356.

Baron, D., and D. Besanko. 1992. Information, control, and organizational structure. RP #1207, Stanford Graduate School of Business. Forthcoming, *Journal of Economics and Management Strategy*.

Baron, D., and R. Myerson. 1982. Regulating a monopolist with unknown costs. *Econometrica* 50:911–930.

Berg, S., and T. Tschirhart. 1988. *Natural Monopoly Regulation*. Cambridge: Cambridge University Press.

Breyer, S. 1982. *Regulation and Its Reform*. Cambridge, MA: Harvard University Press.

Brickley, J., S. Bhagat, and R. Lease. 1985. The impact of long-range managerial compensation plans on shareholder wealth. *Journal of Accounting Research* 7:115–130.

Brown, S., and D. Sibley. 1986. *The Theory of Public Utility Pricing*, Cambridge: Cambridge University Press.

Bryson, A., and Y. C. Ho. 1975. *Applied Optimal Control*. New York: Hemisphere.

Caillaud, B., R. Guesnerie, and P. Rey. 1992. Noisy observation in adverse selection models. *Review of Economic Studies* 59:595–615.

Champsaur, P., and J.-C. Rochet. 1989. Multiproduct duopolists. *Econometrica* 57:533–558.

Crémer, J., and R. McLean. 1985. Optimal selling strategies under uncertainty for a discriminating monopolist when demands are interdependent. *Econometrica* 53:345–361.

Crémer, J., and R. McLean. 1988. Full extraction of the surplus in Bayesian and dominant strategy auctions. *Econometrica* 56:1247–1258.

Croker, K., and K. Reynolds. 1989. Efficient contract design in long-term relationships: The case of air force engine procurement. Working Paper 10-89-1, Pennsylvania State University.

d'Aspremont, C., and L. A. Gerard Varet. 1979. Incentives and incomplete information. *Journal of Public Economics* 11:25–45.

Demougin, D. 1989. A renegotiation-proof mechanism for a principal-agent model with moral hazard and adverse selection. *Rand Journal of Economics* 20:256–267.

Demski, J., and D. Sappington. 1989. Hierarchical structure and responsibility accounting. *Journal of Accounting Research* 27:40–58.

Federal Energy Regulatory Commission. 1989. Incentive regulation. Research Report #89-3. Washington, DC.

Fox, R. 1988. *The Defense Management Challenge: Weapons Acquisition*. Cambridge, MA: Harvard Business School Press.

Fudenberg, D., D. Levine, and E. Maskin. 1990. The folk theorem in repeated games with imperfect public information. Mimeo, Massachusetts Institute of Technology.

Fudenberg, D., and J. Tirole. 1991. *Game Theory*. Cambridge, MA: MIT Press.

Gilbert, R., and D. Newbery. 1988. Regulation games. WP 88-79, University of California, Berkeley.

Green, J., and J.-J. Laffont. 1979. *Incentives in Public Decision Making*. Amsterdam: North-Holland.

Green, J., and J.-J. Laffont. 1987. Posterior implementability in a two-person decision problem. *Econometrica* 55:95–115.

Grout, P. 1984. Investment and wages in the absence of binding contracts: A Nash bargaining approach. *Econometrica* 52:449–460.

Guesnerie, R., and J.-J. Laffont. 1984. A complete solution to a class of principal-agent problems with an application to the control of a self-managed firm. *Journal of Public Economics* 25:329–369.

Guesnerie, R., Picard P., and P. Rey. 1988. Adverse selection and moral hazard with risk neutral agents. *European Economic Review* 33:807–823.

Hadley, G., and M. Kemp. 1971. *Variational Methods in Economics*. Amsterdam: North-Holland.

Hart, O., and B. Holmström. 1987. The theory of contracts. In *Advances in Economic Theory, Fifth World Congress*, ed. T. Bewley. Cambridge: Cambridge University Press.

Holmström, B. 1982. Moral hazard in teams. *Bell Journal of Economics* 13:324–340.

Johnson, S., J. Pratt, and R. Zeckhauser. 1990. Efficiency despite mutually payoff-relevant private information: The finite case. *Econometrica* 58:873–900.

Joskow, P. 1985. Vertical integration and long term contracts: The case of coal-burning electric generating plants. *Journal of Law, Economics, and Organization* 1:33–79.

Joskow, P. 1987. Contract duration and relationship-specific investments: The case of coal. *American Economic Review* 77:168–185.

Joskow, P., and R. Schmalensee. 1986. Incentive regulation for electric utilities. *Yale Journal of Regulation* 4:1–49.

Kamien, M., and N. Schwartz. 1981. *Dynamic Optimization: The Calculus of Variations and Optimal Control in Economics and Management*. Amsterdam: North-Holland.

Klibanoff, P. 1991. Risk aversion and underinvestment in procurement. Mimeo, Department of Economics, Massachusetts Institute of Technology.

Kolbe, L., and W. Tye. 1991. The Duquesne opinion: How much "hope" is there for investors in regulated firms? *Yale Journal on Regulation* 8:113–170.

Laffont, J.-J., and E. Maskin. 1979. A differentiable approach to expected utility maximizing mechanisms. In *Aggregation and Revelation of Preferences*, ed. J.-J. Laffont. Amsterdam: North-Holland.

Laffont, J.-J., and J. Tirole. 1986. Using cost observation to regulate firms. *Journal of Political Economy* 94:614–641.

Lewis, T. 1986. Reputation and contractual performance in long-term projects. *Rand Journal of Economics* 17:141–157.

Lewis, T., and D. Sappington. 1989a. Inflexible rules in incentive problems. *American Economic Review* 79:69–84.

Lewis, T., and D. Sappington. 1989b. Countervailing incentives in agency problems. *Journal of Economic Theory* 49:294–313.

Lewis, T., and D. Sappington. 1989c. Regulatory options and price-cap regulation. *Rand Journal of Economics* 20:405–416.

Lichtenberg, F. 1988. The private R&D investment response to federal design and technical competitions. *American Economic Review* 78:550–559.

Lichtenberg, F. 1990. US government subsidies to private military R&D investment: The defense department's independent R&D policy. *Defence Economics* 1:149–158.

Loeb, M., and W. Magat. 1979. A decentralized method of utility regulation. *Journal of Law and Economics* 22:399–404.

McAfee, R. P., and J. McMillan. 1986. Optimal contracts for teams. Mimeo, University of Western Ontario.

McAfee, R. P., and J. McMillan. 1989. Multidimensional incentive compatibility and mechanism design. *Journal of Economic Theory* 46:335–354.

McAfee, R. P., and J. McMillan. 1990. Organizational diseconomies of scale. Mimeo, University of California, San Diego.

McAfee, R. P., McMillan, J., and P. Reny. 1992. Correlated information and mechanism design. *Econometrica* 60:395–422.

MaCaulay, S. 1963. Non-contractual relations in business. *American Sociological Review* 28:55–70.

Marshall, R. 1989. Weapons procurement—an economics perspective. Mimeo, Duke University.

Maskin, E., and J. Riley. 1980. Auction design with correlated values. Mimeo, University of California, Los Angeles.

Maskin, E., and J. Riley. 1984. Monopoly with incomplete information. *Rand Journal of Economics* 15:171–196.

Maskin, E., and J. Tirole. 1990. The principal-agent relationship with an informed principal: The case of private values. *Econometrica* 58:379–410.

Maskin, E., and J. Tirole. 1992. The principal-agent relationship with an informed principal, II: Common values. *Econometrica* 60:1–42.

Mathios, A., and R. Rogers. 1989. The impact of alternative forms of state regulation of AT&T on direct-dial, long-distance telephone rates. *Rand Journal of Economics* 20:437–453.

Melumad, N., D. Mookherjee, and S. Reichelstein. 1990. Hierarchical decentralization of incentive contracts. Mimeo, Stanford University.

Melumad, N., D. Mookherjee, and S. Reichelstein. 1991. A theory of responsibility centers. Mimeo, Stanford University.

Melumad, N., and S. Reichelstein. 1989. Value of communication in agencies. *Journal of Economic Theory* 47:334–368.

Mirrlees, J. 1971. An exploration in the theory of optimum income taxation. *Review of Economic Studies* 38:175–208.

Mirrlees, J. 1975. The theory of moral hazard and unobservable behavior—part I. Mimeo, Nuffield College, Oxford.

Mussa, M., and S. Rosen. 1978. Monopoly and product quality. *Journal of Economic Theory* 18:301–317.

Picard, P. 1987. On the design of incentive schemes under moral hazard and adverse selection. *Journal of Public Economics* 33:305–331.

Picard, P., and P. Rey. 1990. Incentives in cooperative research and development. In *Essays in Honor of Edmond Malinvaud*. Vol. 1. Cambridge, MA: MIT Press.

Prekova, A. 1973. On logarithmic concave measures and functions. *Act. Sci. Math.* (Szeged) 34:335–343.

Reichelstein, S. 1991. Constructing incentive schemes for government contracts: An application of agency theory. Mimeo, University of California, Berkeley. Forthcoming, *The Accounting Review*.

Riordan, M. 1987. Hierarchical control and investment incentives in procurement. WP E-87–44, Hoover Institution, Stanford University.

Riordan, M., and D. Sappington. 1988. Optimal contracts with public ex post information. *Journal of Economic Theory* 45:189–199.

Rogerson, W. 1987. On the optimality of menus of linear contracts. Mimeo, Northwestern University.

Salant, D., and G. Woroch. 1988. Trigger price regulation. Forthcoming, *Rand Journal of Economics*.

Salant, D., and G. Woroch. 1991. Promoting capital improvements by public utilities: A supergame approach. Mimeo, GTE Laboratories, Waltham.

Sappington, D. 1982. Optimal regulation of research and development under imperfect information. *Bell Journal of Economics*, 354–368.

Scherer, M. 1964. *The Weapons Acquisition Process: Economic Incentives*. Cambridge, MA: Harvard Business School Press.

Seierstad, A., and K. Sydsaeter. 1987. *Optimal Control Theory with Economic Applications*. Amsterdam: North-Holland.

Shleifer, A. 1985. A theory of yardstick competition. *Rand Journal of Economics* 16:319–327.

Spulber, D. 1989. *Regulation and Markets*. Cambridge, MA: MIT Press.

Stubbing, R. 1986. *The Defense Game*. New York: Harper and Row.

Tan, G. 1991. Auctioning procurement contracts by an informed buyer. DP 91–24, University of British Columbia.

Tehranian, H., and J. Waegelian. 1985. Market reaction to short-term executive compensation plan adoption. *Journal of Accounting and Economics* 7:131–144.

Tirole, J. 1986. Procurement and renegotiation. *Journal of Political Economy* 94:235–259.

Vickers, J. 1991. Privatization and the risk of expropriation. Mimeo, St. Catherine's College, Oxford.

Vickers, J., and G. Yarrow. 1991. The British electricity experiment. *Economic Policy*: 189–232.

Williamson, O. 1975. *Markets and Hierarchies: Analysis and Antitrust Implications*. New York: The Free Press.

2 PRICING BY A SINGLE-PRODUCT FIRM WITH AND WITHOUT BUDGET BALANCE

2.1 Some Background

Reimbursing cost is only one dimension of procurement and regulation. Another important dimension, especially in regulation, is the choice of output and price. Pricing affects the firm, its customers, and—when the firm does not need to balance its budget—taxpayers. It is therefore natural that much attention is devoted to the determination of prices. This chapter is an introduction to the economic analysis of regulated prices when the government can or cannot legally transfer money to the firm—that is, when balance of the budget is or is not imposed.

Chapter 1 derived the optimal cost-reimbursement rule for a fixed-size project. This chapter introduces variable size and the concomitant issue of pricing. For pedagogical purposes we content ourselves with the case of a regulated monopolist with a single product and choose a very specific cost function: Total cost C is equal to marginal cost $(\beta - e)$ times the output q plus known fixed cost (which we will normalize at zero). As in chapter 1, β stands for a technological variable known by the firm, though not by the regulator, and e is the level of (marginal) cost-reducing activity. The regulator observes total cost and output, and from this can infer and regulate marginal cost $c \equiv \beta - e$. This simple framework enables us to use the acquired knowledge of chapter 1 and allows a smooth transition into pricing issues. Chapter 3 studies regulated monopolies with multiple products and allows general cost functions.

Introductory economics textbooks tell the merits of marginal cost pricing and point out that a motivation for regulating natural monopolies is to avoid the deadweight loss associated with (monopoly) pricing above marginal cost. The price paid by consumers ought to reflect the seller's opportunity cost of supplying the good. We ask whether marginal cost is indeed the right benchmark for pricing by a regulated firm when transfers from the government to the firm are feasible. Ignoring in a first step incentive issues (all components of the firm's cost function are perfectly monitored), it is easily seen that marginal cost pricing is indeed appropriate if the good is a private good and if the firm can perfectly price discriminate (e.g., consumers all have the same preferences and the firm can use a two-part tariff). Marginal cost evaluated at the social cost of public funds is the correct benchmark if the good is a public good. Last, pricing above marginal cost, but below the monopoly price, is optimal if the good is a private good and the firm cannot perfectly price discriminate (it charges either a linear price or a two-part tariff to a set of heterogeneous consumers).

These recommendations are straightforward. Take, for instance, the leading case of a private good and linear pricing. Raising the price slightly above marginal cost introduces a minor distortion in allocative efficiency but increases the firm's revenue and reduces the deadweight loss associated with the taxation needed to finance the firm's deficit. The optimal pricing formula is then of the "Ramsey type": The Lerner index—the ratio of price minus marginal cost over price—is equal to $\lambda/(1 + \lambda)$ times the inverse of the elasticity of demand. Note in particular that since the shadow price of public funds λ is determined by economywide data, the relationship between price and marginal cost depends only on the elasticity of demand, and not on the cost function. We make use of this fact in section 2.5 where we develop an algorithm that decentralizes the choice of the price to the firm. (We leave it to the reader to obtain the intuition in the other cases.)

Section 2.3, in the two-type case, and section 2.4, in the continuum-of-types case, show that these simple pricing rules still hold when the regulator does not know the firm's technology. That is, the regulator ought not bias the Ramsey pricing rules in order to extract the firm's rent or (this is the opposite side of the same coin) to give incentives to reduce cost. Incentive concerns are reflected in the cost-reimbursement rule and not in pricing. The generality of this "dichotomy" between incentives and pricing is studied in chapter 3. We should warn the reader that the technical analysis in sections 2.3 and 2.4 proceeds at a quick pace, given that it duplicates that of chapter 1. But the reader familiar with the first chapter will have no difficulty following the argument.

A frequent objection to incentive models as models of regulation (but of course not as models of procurement) is that they ignore institutional realities by presuming that the state can subsidize or tax the regulated firms. For instance, in the United States, regulated telephone and electricity companies are not allowed to receive subsidies from the government. In section 2.6 we examine the optimal pricing and incentives when (1) the firm's revenue from sales to consumers must exactly cover its cost (including managerial rewards) and (2) the firm charges a two-part tariff. The motivation for 2 is that industries in which the government is prohibited from transferring money to the regulated firms often also exhibit two-part tariffs (as the telephone and electricity examples demonstrate). Joskow and Schmalensee (1986) have conjectured that the fixed premium paid by consumers would play a similar role to that played by the (missing) transfer from the government. We study the validity of this conjecture.

How do the economic conclusions differ from those when transfers are legal? In a nutshell, the recommendations about incentives are quite similar. The economywide shadow cost of public funds is replaced by the marginal deadweight loss associated with an increase in the fixed premium, which kicks marginal consumers out of the market. In contrast, recommendations about pricing, although they can be given a Ramsey interpretation, are quite different. Thus the main incentive issues of this book (e.g., relative to the effect of product market competition, auctioning, dynamics, and capture) are robust to legal constraints on transfers, while pricing issues (the core of chapters 2, 3, and part of chapter 4) are not.

Section 2.7 performs a similar analysis for the case in which arbitrage among consumers forces the regulated firm to charge a linear price, and the firm's budget must be balanced (another motivation for considering linear pricing is the willingness to provide universal service and thus not to exclude consumers through a fixed premium). The analysis of linear pricing is naturally somewhat simpler than that of two-part tariffs. The results otherwise corroborate those obtained for two-part pricing. The formula determining the power of the firm's incentive scheme has the same interpretation as in chapter 1, except for the interpretation of the "shadow cost of public funds." An increase in the firm's reward is no longer paid for by taxpayers. Rather, it requires an increase in the consumer price away from marginal cost and toward the monopoly price. The shadow cost of public funds, which is linked with the distortions brought about by taxation, is replaced by the shadow cost of rewards, which is the marginal deadweight loss of the price increase associated with the reward.

We show that the optimal incentive scheme is (a static form of) a sliding scale plan. The firm is allowed to charge a price $p^*(c)$ that depends on its announced average cost target. There is cost sharing between consumers and the firm in that an increase in cost is not fully reflected in an equal reduction in the firm's reward.

The unregulated monopoly and price-cap regulation are particular cases of the class of regulatory schemes without transfer. In those mechanisms effort is optimal conditionally on the production levels, but these production levels are too low and leave high rents to the firm. Any further decrease of these rents, and therefore of prices, must be achieved by decreasing effort levels below the conditionally optimal levels. We briefly discuss the relationship of these two suboptimal mechanisms with the optimal mechanism derived in section 2.7.

Sections 2.6 and 2.7 do not investigate the foundations of the prohibition of transfers from the government. Such foundations will be studied in chapter 15, which takes a critical view of models with welfare-maximizing regulators and exogenous budget constraints for regulated firms. Sections 2.6 and 2.7 thus depict the following situation: For an unknown reason the law (unwisely) deprives the regulator from the transfer instrument; the regulator structures pricing and incentives so as to maximize expected social welfare.

2.2 The Model

2.2.1 Description

Unlike in chapter 1, we assume that the project has a variable scale. Let q denote the output (in another interpretation, q could be the verifiable quality of a fixed-size project, e.g., the inverse of the development time).

Total cost is

$$C = (\beta - e)q + \alpha. \tag{2.1}$$

We assume that the fixed cost is known, and for notational simplicity we normalize it at zero: $\alpha = 0$. Let $c \equiv \beta - e$ denote marginal cost.[1]

We make the accounting convention that the cost is paid by the government who also receives the revenue from sales, if any. The government pays a net transfer t to the firm, whose utility is

$$U = t - \psi(e). \tag{2.2}$$

The disutility of effort function $\psi(\cdot)$ satisfies the same assumptions as in chapter 1. Similarly the firm's reservation utility is normalized to be zero.

To allow the study of several situations (public or private good, linear or two-part pricing), let $V(q)$ denote the social surplus brought about by the production of output q. We assume that $V(0) = 0$, $V' > 0$, and $V'' < 0$. Social welfare is then

$$\begin{aligned} W &= V(q) - (1 + \lambda)(C + t) + U \\ &= V(q) - (1 + \lambda)[C + \psi(e)] - \lambda U. \end{aligned} \tag{2.3}$$

Examples of functions $V(\cdot)$ are

1. *Public good.* Let $S(q)$ denote the consumer surplus associated with production of output q. Since the public good is not sold, it generates no revenue, and

$$V(q) = S(q).$$

2. *Private good.* Let the good be private and be sold at (linear) price p. The gross consumer surplus, the inverse demand function, the regular demand function, and the firm's revenue are $S(q)$, $p = P(q) = S'(q)$, $q = D(p)$, and $R(q) = qP(q)$, respectively. In this case $V(q)$ is the sum of the consumers' net surplus plus the revenue for the government, computed at the shadow price of public funds (because the revenue helps cover the firm's cost and reduces the need for distortionary taxation):

$$\begin{aligned} V(q) &= [S(q) - R(q)] + (1 + \lambda)R(q) \\ &= S(q) + \lambda R(q) \\ &= S(q) + \lambda qP(q). \end{aligned}$$

Sufficient conditions for $V(\cdot)$ to be concave given a downward-sloping demand are here either $P(\cdot)$ concave or λ small.

3. *Perfect price discrimination.* Suppose that all consumers have the same

1. See chapter 3 for more general functional forms.

preferences. We can thus formalize demand as that of a representative consumer with gross consumer surplus $S(\cdot)$. The firm charges a two-part tariff $A + pq$. The consumer chooses q so as to maximize $S(q) - A - pq$ or $p = P(q)$. As in the case of linear pricing

$$V(q) = S(q) + \lambda R(q).$$

But now $R(q) = A + P(q)q$. Furthermore A is chosen optimally so as to make the consumer be indifferent between buying and not buying: $A \equiv S(q) - P(q)q$. Hence

$$V(q) = (1 + \lambda)S(q).$$

Perfect price discrimination allows the firm to extract the entire consumer surplus, which is valued at the social cost of public funds.

Section 2.6 derives $V(\cdot)$ when the firm charges a two-part tariff and cannot perfectly price discriminate because of consumers' heterogeneity.

2.2.2 Full Information

Consider the benchmark case in which the regulator knows all components of the cost function. Maximizing (2.3) with respect to U, e, and q yields[2]

$$U = 0 \tag{2.4}$$

(the regulator leaves no rent to the firm),

$$\psi'(e) = q \tag{2.5}$$

(marginal disutility of effort = marginal cost saving), and

$$V'(q) = (1 + \lambda)(\beta - e) \tag{2.6}$$

(marginal social value of output = marginal cost for taxpayers).
Equation (2.5) generalizes (1.7) to variable output. Of particular interest is the pricing equation (2.6). Its application to the cases mentioned above yields the following: For the *public good* case, in which the good is not sold to consumers, the marginal consumer surplus is $S'(q)$, and (2.6) becomes

$$S'(q) = (1 + \lambda)c. \tag{2.7}$$

In the case of a *private good* with linear pricing, equation (2.6) yields

$$P(q) + \lambda P(q) + \lambda q P'(q) = (1 + \lambda)c$$

or

2. The objective function is concave if $-V''\psi'' > (1 + \lambda)$.

$$L \equiv \frac{p-c}{p} = \frac{\lambda}{1+\lambda}\frac{1}{\eta}, \tag{2.8}$$

where $\eta \equiv -(dq/dp)/(q/p)$ is the elasticity of demand. In words, the Lerner index is equal to a number between 0 and 1 times the inverse of the elasticity of demand. When taxation is not distortionary, λ is equal to 0, and price is equal to marginal cost. When the shadow cost of public funds becomes very large, the price tends to the monopoly price. More generally revenue considerations imply that the firm's pricing behavior lies between those of a competitive firm and of an unregulated monopoly.

In the case of *perfect price discrimination*, equation (2.6) yields

$$S'(q) = p = c. \tag{2.9}$$

We let $q^*(c)$ denote the solution to (2.5) and (2.6), and $p^*(c) \equiv P(q^*(c))$. The standard revealed preference argument shows that $q^*(\cdot)$ and $p^*(\cdot)$ are nonincreasing and nondecreasing, respectively. Since our main focus is on the case of a private good and imperfect price discrimination, we will call $q^*(c)$ and $p^*(c)$ the *Ramsey output* and *price*, respectively, for marginal cost c.

We now assume that the regulator observes only total cost and output (or price, since we will assume that the demand function is known). As in chapter 1 we start with the case of two potential technological parameters and then move on to the continuum case. We leave to chapter 3 the treatment of general cost functions and multiple products. Also from now on we will focus on the case of a private good (with linear pricing except in section 2.6) for expositional purposes.

2.3 The Two-Type Case

Let β be equal to $\underline{\beta}$ with probability ν and to $\bar{\beta}$ with probability $1-\nu$. The firm knows β, but the regulator does not.

In this model the regulator observes average cost $c = \beta - e$. In a sense we are back to the model of chapter 1 with C replaced by c.[3] Let $\{(\underline{t}, \underline{q}, \underline{C}, \underline{c}, \underline{U}), (\bar{t}, \bar{q}, \bar{C}, \bar{c}, \bar{U})\}$ denote the equilibrium transfer, output, cost, marginal cost, and utility of the two types. Assume that the regulator wants to keep both types. The binding individual rationality constraint is that the inefficient type has a nonnegative utility. Because transfers are socially costly,

$$\bar{U} = \bar{t} - \psi(\bar{\beta} - \bar{c}) = 0. \tag{2.10}$$

As in chapter 1 we guess that the binding incentive compatibility constraint

3. If we reintroduced the fixed cost α, the regulator would observe $(C-\alpha)/q = \beta - e$, and the analysis would carry over.

is the efficient type's (the proof that the other incentive compatibility constraint is not binding is the same as in chapter 1).

$$\begin{aligned} \underline{U} &= \underline{t} - \psi(\underline{\beta} - \underline{c}) = \bar{t} - \psi(\underline{\beta} - \bar{c}) \\ &= \bar{U} + \psi(\bar{\beta} - \bar{c}) - \psi(\underline{\beta} - \bar{c}) \\ &= \Phi(\bar{\beta} - \bar{c}) = \Phi(\bar{e}), \end{aligned} \tag{2.11}$$

where $\Phi(\cdot)$, an increasing function, is defined by (1.19):

$$\Phi(e) \equiv \psi(e) - \psi(e - \Delta\beta).$$

The efficient type's rent is entirely determined by the inefficient type's marginal cost or, equivalently, effort.

Expected social welfare is thus

$$\begin{aligned} W = \nu[V(\underline{q}) - (1 + \lambda)[(\underline{\beta} - \underline{e})\underline{q} + \psi(\underline{e})] - \lambda\Phi(\bar{e})] \\ + (1 - \nu)[V(\bar{q}) - (1 + \lambda)[(\bar{\beta} - \bar{e})\bar{q} + \psi(\bar{e})]]. \end{aligned} \tag{2.12}$$

The maximization[4] is the same as for full information (more precisely, for the technology-contingent optimum), except for the expected cost of the rent $\nu\lambda\Phi(\bar{e})$. Since this new term depends only on $\bar{e}$, the levels of $\underline{q}$ and $\underline{e}$ are the same as under full information, and $\bar{q}$ is equal to $q^*(\bar{\beta} - \bar{e})$:

$$\underline{q} = q^*(\underline{\beta} - \underline{e}), \tag{2.13}$$

$$\psi'(\underline{e}) = \underline{q}, \tag{2.14}$$

$$\bar{q} = q^*(\bar{\beta} - \bar{e}), \tag{2.15}$$

$$\psi'(\bar{e}) = \bar{q} - \frac{\lambda}{1 + \lambda}\frac{\nu}{1 - \nu}\Phi'(\bar{e}). \tag{2.16}$$

Equations (2.13) and (2.15) show that the optimal price for either type is the Ramsey price given the marginal cost. That is, the rule giving price as a function of marginal cost is the same as under full information. This means that prices are not distorted for rent extraction or, equivalently, incentives purposes. Incentives concerns are entirely taken care of by the cost-reimbursement rule.

Equations (2.13) and (2.14) together show that the output and effort of the efficient type are the same as under full information, but type $\underline{\beta}$ now enjoys an informational rent. In contrast, we will show that the inefficient type's effort is lower under asymmetric information [note that (1.43) is a special case of (2.16), with $\bar{q} = 1$]. As in chapter 1 a low-powered incentive scheme is given to the inefficient type to limit the efficient type's rent.

Let us now compare the optimal costs and outputs of the two types. First, we show that $\underline{c} \leqslant \bar{c}$ (which implies that the monotonicity condi-

4. The objective function is concave if $\psi''' \geq 0$ and $-V''\psi'' > (1 + \lambda)$.

tion that is necessary and sufficient for the allocation to satisfy the firm's second-order condition is satisfied; see chapter 1): $\underline{c}$ and $\bar{c}$ maximize

$$\mathscr{W}(c, \beta, \xi) \equiv V(q^*(c)) - (1 + \lambda)[cq^*(c) + \psi(\beta - c)] - \xi\frac{\nu}{1-\nu}\lambda\Phi(\beta - c)$$

for $(\beta = \underline{\beta}, \xi = 0)$ and $(\beta = \bar{\beta}, \xi = 1)$, respectively. Revealed preference implies that

$$\mathscr{W}(\underline{c}, \underline{\beta}, 0) \geq \mathscr{W}(\bar{c}, \underline{\beta}, 0) \qquad (\text{type } \underline{\beta})$$

and

$$\mathscr{W}(\bar{c}, \bar{\beta}, 1) \geq \mathscr{W}(\underline{c}, \bar{\beta}, 1) \qquad (\text{type } \bar{\beta}).$$

Adding up these two inequalities yields

$$\left[(1 + \lambda) + \lambda\frac{\nu}{1-\nu}\right][\Phi(\bar{\beta} - \underline{c}) - \Phi(\bar{\beta} - \bar{c})] \geq 0,$$

or

$$\bar{c} \geq \underline{c}. \tag{2.17}$$

Monotonicity of marginal cost with respect to type, together with (2.13) and (2.15), in turn yields

$$\bar{q} \leq \underline{q}. \tag{2.18}$$

Next we check that the effort $\bar{e}$ and the output $\bar{q}$ of the inefficient type are smaller under asymmetric information than under full information ($\underline{e}$ and $\underline{q}$ are not affected by the asymmetry of information, as we have seen). Let $\bar{c}$ and $\bar{c}^*$ denote the inefficient type's cost levels under asymmetric and full information, and let $\bar{q}$ and $\bar{q}^*$ denote the associated outputs. From revealed preference we have

$$\mathscr{W}(\bar{c}^*, \bar{\beta}, 0) \geq \mathscr{W}(\bar{c}, \bar{\beta}, 0) \qquad (\text{full information})$$

and

$$\mathscr{W}(\bar{c}, \bar{\beta}, 1) \geq \mathscr{W}(\bar{c}^*, \bar{\beta}, 1) \qquad (\text{asymmetric information}).$$

Adding up these two inequalities yields

$$\lambda\frac{\nu}{1-\nu}[\Phi(\bar{\beta} - \bar{c}^*) - \Phi(\bar{\beta} - \bar{c})] \geq 0,$$

or

$$\bar{c} \geq \bar{c}^*. \tag{2.19}$$

Equation (2.15) then implies that

$$\bar{q} \leq \bar{q}^*. \tag{2.20}$$

We summarize our conclusions in proposition 2.1.

Proposition 2.1 With two types and government transfers, the optimum exhibits the dichotomy property that pricing conditional on marginal cost is not affected by the asymmetry of information. Pricing is given by the Ramsey formula $(p - c)/p = [\lambda/(1 + \lambda)](1/\eta)$ in the case of a private good and linear pricing. The cost-reimbursement rule is affected by informational asymmetries. The inefficient type's average cost exceeds that under full information. Consequently the inefficient type's output is lower under asymmetric information.

Note that asymmetric information not only creates a rent for the firm in state of nature $\underline{\beta}$ but also benefits those who dislike production (e.g., if it pollutes) in state of nature $\bar{\beta}$. In the latter state of nature it hurts the consumers of the good because they face a higher price.

Next we refine result 1.6 concerning an increase in demand on the efficient type's rent. Suppose that the social value of output $V(q, \theta)$ depends on demand parameter θ such that $V_{q\theta} > 0$ (an increase in θ raises the marginal social value of output). Let $q^*(c, \theta)$ maximize $\{V(q, \theta) - (1 + \lambda)cq\}$. The efficient type's rent is equal to $\Phi(\bar{\beta} - \bar{c}(\theta))$, where $\bar{c}(\theta)$ maximizes

$$Z(c, \theta) \equiv V(q^*(c, \theta), \theta) - (1 + \lambda)[cq^*(c, \theta) + \psi(\bar{\beta} - c)] - \lambda \frac{v}{1 - v} \Phi(\bar{\beta} - c).$$

Take two values $\theta < \theta'$, and let $\bar{c}(\theta)$ and $\bar{c}(\theta')$ denote the corresponding optima. It can be checked that $Z(\bar{c}(\theta), \theta) \geq Z(\bar{c}(\theta'), \theta)$ and $Z(\bar{c}(\theta'), \theta') \geq Z(\bar{c}(\theta), \theta')$ imply that $\bar{c}(\theta) \geq \bar{c}(\theta')$. This yields result 1.6′.

Result 1.6′ An increase in demand (i.e., in θ) raises the firm's rent.

Result 1.6′ has strong implications for the effect of product market competition on the firm.

2.4 Continuum of Types

We now assume that β is continuously distributed on $[\underline{\beta}, \bar{\beta}]$ with cumulative distribution function $F(\cdot)$ and strictly positive density $f(\cdot)$. As in chapter 1, $F(\cdot)$ is assumed to satisfy the monotone hazard rate condition; that is, F/f is nondecreasing. As in the two-type case the firm's rent is determined by the marginal cost function $c(\beta) = C(\beta)/q(\beta)$. Because type β can mimic the marginal cost of type $\beta + d\beta$, one has (as in chapter 1)

$$\dot{U}(\beta) = -\psi'(e(\beta)) = -\psi'(\beta - c(\beta)). \tag{2.21}$$

The regulator maximizes expected social welfare subject to the incentive compatibility and individual rationality constraints:[5]

$$\max_{\{q(\cdot),e(\cdot),U(\cdot)\}} \int_{\underline{\beta}}^{\bar{\beta}} \{V(q) - (1+\lambda)[(\beta - e)q + \psi(e)] - \lambda U\} f(\beta) d\beta \quad (2.22)$$

subject to

$$\dot{U} = -\psi'(e), \quad (2.21)$$

$$[\beta - e(\beta)] \text{ nondecreasing}, \quad (2.23)$$

and

$$U(\bar{\beta}) = 0. \quad (2.24)$$

The analysis of program (2.22) is the same as that of program (1.35) in chapter 1. We therefore content ourselves with a statement of the results:

$$q(\beta) = q^*(\beta - e(\beta)) \qquad \text{(Ramsey pricing)} \quad (2.25)$$

and

$$\psi'(e(\beta)) = q(\beta) - \frac{\lambda}{1+\lambda}\frac{F(\beta)}{f(\beta)}\psi''(e(\beta)) \quad (2.26)$$

(the effort of type β is distorted downward to limit the rent of more efficient types). Note that (2.26) generalizes (1.44) in which $q(\beta) = 1$. Following the discussion in sections 1.4 and 2.3, the reader should check, first, that $e(\cdot)$ is nonincreasing [and therefore (2.23) is satisfied], second, that $q(\cdot)$ is nonincreasing, and third, that an increase in demand [i.e., an increase in θ when the social value of output is $V(\cdot,\theta)$ with $V_{q\theta} > 0$] raises output, effort, and rent. (It raises the firm's rent for two related reasons: It raises effort for a given β, and it raises the cutoff type if the latter differs from $\bar{\beta}$.)

Last, we investigate whether the optimal incentive scheme can be replaced by a menu of linear schemes. In chapter 1 we showed that if $e(\cdot)$ is nonincreasing in β (as we just pointed out), the regulator can give a menu of schemes that are linear in (here, marginal) cost:

$$t(\beta, c) = a(\beta) - b(\beta)c, \quad (2.27)$$

where $b(\cdot)$ and $a(\cdot)$ are decreasing. Note that since output is costly, the firm is rewarded on the basis of average or *corrected* cost $c = C/q$ rather than total cost C. Note that the firm is indifferent as to the choice of price as long as its compensation is based on average cost. On the other hand, one can reward the firm as a function of total cost: Replacing c by C/q in (2.27) yields

5. This program is concave if the conditions of footnote 4 are satisfied.

$$\tilde{t}(\beta, C) = a(\beta) - \tilde{b}(\beta)C, \tag{2.28}$$

where, from (2.26),

$$\tilde{b}(\beta) \equiv \frac{b(\beta)}{q(\beta)} \leq 1. \tag{2.29}$$

In this case one must also check that the output is consistent with the firm's choice of linear contract, that is, that the firm produces $q(\beta)$ when it chooses contract $\{a(\beta), \tilde{b}(\beta)\}$.[6] Otherwise, the firm would clearly prefer to produce no output in order to have the lowest possible cost. This problem does not arise when the firm's reward is based on average cost, for the firm's utility depends only on the level of c.

Proposition 2.2 With government transfers and a continuum of types, the dichotomy property still holds and the price is given by the Ramsey formula. The firm's effort, except for the most efficient type, is distorted downward to limit rents. Furthermore under some conditions the transfer to the firm can be chosen to be linear in realized cost, with a coefficient lower than 1.

2.5 Delegation of Pricing to the Firm

Section 2.4 has shown that the rent of type β is $U(\beta) = \int_{\beta}^{\bar{\beta}} \psi'(e^*(\tilde{\beta}))d\tilde{\beta}$. It depends only on the profile of effort (or, equivalently, average cost) that is implemented. The firm is indifferent as to the choice of the production level $q(\beta)$ as long as this output is associated with a cost target $C(\beta)$ such that $C(\beta)/q(\beta) = c(\beta)$. Consequently it is indifferent as to the choice of the pricing rule $p(\beta)$ as long as the average cost target is chosen appropriately. The optimal regulation is then composed of a transfer function that depends only on the average cost target and of a recommendation to choose a production level desired by the regulator. This section develops several rules that allow the decentralization of the pricing decision for a private good to the regulated firm. We emphasize the informational requirements and the amount of agency discretion for each of these rules.

2.5.1 An Introduction to Price Taxes

Consider the case of a private good and linear pricing. Letting $V(q) = S(q) + \lambda R(q)$ be the social value of output, we saw that the optimal output satisfies

$$S_q + \lambda R_q = (1 + \lambda)C_q. \tag{2.30}$$

6. Note also that it is no longer clear that the slope with respect to total cost is decreasing in β (it is if ψ''' is not too large; see chapter 4). An increasing $\tilde{b}(\cdot)$ might still be consistent with a decreasing $e(\cdot)$ as long as $q(\cdot)$ is decreasing.

Suppose that the regulated firm receives from the government a benefit

$$B(q) = \frac{S(q) + \lambda R(q)}{1 + \lambda}. \tag{2.31}$$

From our accounting convention the government receives $R(q)$ and pays $B(q)$ to the firm. But the firm is no longer reimbursed for its cost (in this section only we assume that benefit is regulated, but not cost). Its profit is then $\pi(q) = B(q) - C(q)$ and the maximization of profit leads to (2.30). That is, the reward function $B(\cdot)$ allows the decentralization of pricing to the firm.

It is worth emphasizing the reason why the optimal prices can be obtained without the regulator's information about cost, unlike in the Ramsey-Boiteux approach to cost-of-service pricing reviewed in subsection 3.4 of the introductory chapter: λ is an economywide shadow cost of public funds, while the shadow cost of the firm's budget constraint in the Ramsey-Boiteux model depends on the cost function.

The reward function $B(\cdot)$, however, requires knowing the demand function. That is, an economist would be unable to decentralize the pricing decision to the firm without first estimating this function. We now grope toward decentralization rules that are even less informationally demanding. To this end we describe a related pricing rule that does not formally require knowledge of the demand side but requires estimates of the quantity to be produced by the regulated firm. Knowing this quantity even approximately is of course informationally demanding, and the main interest of this rule is to offer a useful introduction to the historical scheme described in subsection 2.5.2 and to indicate the domain of validity of this historical scheme.

The regulator forms a *rough* estimate of the demand $\bar{q}$ for the firm's product at the optimal price. $\bar{q}$ can result from survey data. The regulator then measures the estimated demand at some price in the likely price range and imposes a price tax equal to $p\bar{q}/(1 + \lambda)$. He or she otherwise gives entire price freedom to the firm. The firm maximizes its profit π like a monopolist subject to the price tax. Thus

$$\pi = \max_p \left\{ pD(p) - cD(p) - \frac{p\bar{q}}{1 + \lambda} \right\}, \tag{2.32}$$

The firm's privately optimal price is obtained by the maximization in (2.32):

$$(p - c)D' + q - \frac{\bar{q}}{1 + \lambda} = 0. \tag{2.33}$$

In contrast, equation (2.30) yields the socially optimal price:

$$(1 + \lambda)(p - c) + \lambda P'q = 0. \tag{2.34}$$

Suppose that $\bar{q} \simeq q$. Then since $P'D' = 1$, equation (2.33) coincides with equation (2.34), and the pricing structure is socially optimal. In practice the regulator may not estimate the demand function as well as the firm. But he or she might complement rough guesses or even survey data by some historical scheme such as the one developed in the next subsection.

Remark on quality In this chapter we ignore quality issues or, equivalently, assume that the regulator perfectly controls quality. We will consider quality issues in chapter 4. But it is worth noting at this point that any incentive scheme that penalizes the firm for high prices could give rise to a deterioration in quality. Clearly, if the firm cannot quite translate quality improvements into higher prices, it will have lower incentives to provide quality.

One such concern with price-cap regulation is that the firm might evade a binding price cap by an unverifiable cut in product quality. Indeed, Vickers and Yarrow (1988, p. 228) using the British regulatory agency Oftel's quality-of-service indicators note that "British Telecom's quality of service has not deteriorated since privatization, but that it had not improved much either. Given the rate of advance of telecommunications technology, this record is poor."[7]

A similar problem may arise for our price tax regulation. Suppose that demand depends on a noncontractible level of services s chosen by the firm, $D(p, s)$, and that cost also depends on quality, such as $C = (\beta - c + s)q$. A regulated firm subject to the price tax defined above maximizes

$$\max_{\{p,s\}} \left\{ pD(p,s) - \frac{p\bar{q}}{1+\lambda} - (\beta - e + s)D(p,s) \right\} \tag{2.35}$$

over the price p and the quality of service s.

Under our scheme (and under a price cap) there is a case in which the firm clearly undersupplies quality. Suppose that price reductions and quality increases are perfect substitutes for both the consumers and the firm:

$$D(p,s) = \tilde{D}(p - s) \quad \text{and} \quad C = (\beta - e + s)q.$$

Program (2.35) then yields the monopoly outcome. The firm has an incentive to drive p to 0 in order to escape the price tax and to choose a quality level equal to minus the monopoly price[8] if such a low level of quality is feasible and unverifiable by the regulatory agency. The allocation (in-

7. Some dimensions of quality subsequently became the objects of monetary incentives.
8. The monopoly price is the price that maximizes $\{pD(p) - (\beta - e)D(p)\}$.

cluding the firm's profit) is the same under a price cap.[9] All this is not surprising. If the regulator cannot monitor quality and if quality is a perfect substitute for price, everything is as if the price were not regulated.

More generally we conclude that noncontractible quality reduces the efficacy of a price tax scheme. Chapter 4 shows that in such a situation finer regulatory schemes that base rewards on sales allow a better control of quality.

2.5.2 Using Historical Data to Construct the Price Tax

An alternative to basing the price tax on a rough estimate $\bar{q}$ is to use past quantity observations, if such exist. One would be tempted to replace $\bar{q}_\tau$, the reference output for the date τ price tax, by $\bar{q}_{\tau-1}$, the observed output at date $\tau - 1$. Yet the regulator must be careful not to offer perverse incentives to a foresighted firm. Indeed this price scheme can be shown to lead to excessive prices (at least in the long run). A better scheme based on historical data consists in taxing *price changes*. More precisely let

$$T(p_\tau, p_{\tau-1}, q_{\tau-1}) \equiv \frac{(p_\tau - p_{\tau-1})q_{\tau-1}}{(1+\lambda)(1-\delta)} \tag{2.36}$$

be the tax levied on the firm at date τ, where $q_{\tau-1} = D(p_{\tau-1})$ is the date $\tau - 1$ sale and δ denotes the discount factor. Faced with this price tax, the firm maximizes

$$\sum_{\tau=0}^{\infty} \delta^\tau \{b_\tau[p_\tau D(p_\tau) - T(p_\tau, p_{\tau-1}, D(p_{\tau-1})) - (\beta - e_\tau)D(p_\tau)] - \psi(e_\tau)\}, \tag{2.37}$$

where b_τ is the slope of the firm's incentive scheme at date τ.

The normative analysis implies that the incentive scheme should be time invariant (the proof is the same as in section 1.10). Of course keeping the slope of the incentive scheme constant need not be optimal once the firm chooses its price in response to an ad hoc rule such as (2.36). But this suggests that invariant slopes do not perform too badly in such circumstances, particularly in the long run when prices converge to the Ramsey price. So let us complete our tax-on-price-changes scheme by a time-invariant–rate-of-return rule; in particular let $b_\tau = b$ for all τ. The first-order condition with respect to p_τ in (2.37) yields

$$(p_\tau - c_\tau)D'(p_\tau) + D(p_\tau) - \frac{D(p_{\tau-1})}{(1+\lambda)(1-\delta)} - \frac{\delta((p_{\tau+1} - p_\tau)D'(p_\tau) - D(p_\tau))}{(1+\lambda)(1-\delta)} = 0, \tag{2.38}$$

where $c_\tau \equiv \beta - e_\tau$. In steady state $p_{\tau-1} = p_\tau = p_{\tau+1}$, and hence

9. Under a price cap $\bar{p}$ the profit is obtained by maximizing $\pi = pD(p, s) - (\beta - e + s)D(p, s)$ subject to $p \leq \bar{p}$. The two schemes yield a generalized price $p - s$ equal to the monopoly generalized price and a profit π equal to the monopoly profit.

$$(p - c)D' + \frac{\lambda D}{1 + \lambda} = 0, \tag{2.39}$$

which is the socially optimal pricing policy.

The dynamic behavior of price p_τ is given by (2.38), the initial price p_{-1} and demand $q_{-1} = D(p_{-1})$ at date -1 and the transversality condition. Let us make the following assumption:

Assumption 2.1 $D(p) = \alpha - \gamma p$; $\psi(e) = e^2/2$.

Given a slope b of the incentive scheme, the date τ effort is given by $\psi'(e_\tau) = bq_\tau$ or $e_\tau = b(\alpha - \gamma p_\tau)$. Substituting e_τ into (2.38) yields a second-order linear difference equation in the price. The study of this difference equation leads to proposition 2.3.

Proposition 2.3 Under assumption 2.1 the optimal price is given by

$$p_\tau = p^* + (p_{-1} - p^*)r^{\tau-1},$$

where p^* is the steady state solution given by (2.30) (i.e., the socially optimal price) and

$$r = \frac{1 + \lambda(1-\delta) - \frac{\gamma b}{2}(1+\lambda)(1-\delta) - \sqrt{\left[1 + \lambda(1-\delta) - \frac{\gamma b}{2}(1+\lambda)(1-\delta)\right]^2 - \delta}}{\delta}.$$

In proposition 2.3 a sufficient condition for r to be less than 1 is that $(1 - \delta)(1 + \lambda) < 1$. So for $\lambda = 0.3$, $\delta > 0.23$ is sufficient for $r < 1$. We conclude that the delegated price converges in a nonoscillatory way toward the socially optimal price.

The price tax schemes based on survey data and on historical data can be used jointly. Particularly for new products the survey data can be used to initiate the price tax (to yield a $\bar{q}_0$), with the price tax later determined by (2.36). This procedure can yield faster convergence than a price tax initiated by the historical output.

Technological Progress

Our mechanism is tailored to a stationary environment. To be more realistic, it ought to be adapted to environments with changing technology.[10] An obvious difficulty in doing this is that in contrast to the stationary case, the optimal policy may involve time variations in the slope of the incentive scheme: Since the optimal output increases as cost decreases and since technological progress can interact with the marginal productivity of ef-

10. That technological progress ought to be reflected in regulatory design is apparent, for example, in the British Telecom "RPI-3 %" rule, which indexes the price caps to the retail price index and to an anticipated rate of technological progress equal to 3%. But it should also be noted that with average cost pricing and scale economies, the "X" in the "RPI-X" formulas should also reflect demand growth.

fort in the cost function in subtle ways, the effort to be required from managers—and thus the slope of the incentive scheme—changes over time. Although a general analysis can be conducted, we will content ourselves with a simple case in which a straightforward extension of (2.36) can be obtained. Let us assume a single product supplied at cost:

$$C_\tau(\beta, e_\tau, q_\tau) = \alpha^\tau c q_\tau + \beta - e_\tau, \tag{2.40}$$

where $0 < \alpha < 1$. The cost function in (2.40) exhibits not only the dichotomy property (the optimal relationship between price and marginal cost is unaffected by incentives considerations) but also a separability between pricing and effort decisions (the optimal price is independent of the effort level and conversely), since the incentive problem concerns only the fixed cost. It is easily verified (1) that the optimal effort and slope of the incentive scheme are time independent and (2) that the optimal price is given by the Ramsey formula

$$\frac{p_\tau - \alpha^\tau c}{p_\tau} = \frac{\lambda}{(1+\lambda)\eta_\tau}, \tag{2.41}$$

where η_τ is the elasticity of demand at date τ.

We further assume that the demand function has constant elasticity:

$$q_\tau = D(p_\tau) = d p_\tau^{-\eta}, \tag{2.42}$$

where $\eta > 1$. Suppose that the regulator imposes a price tax

$$T(p_\tau, p_{\tau-1}, q_{\tau-1}) = (x p_\tau - y p_{\tau-1}) q_{\tau-1}, \tag{2.43}$$

where x and y are to be determined, and gives an incentive scheme leaving a bonus $a + b(p_\tau q_\tau - C_\tau - T_\tau)$ at date τ to the firm, where a and b are two positive constants. The firm then maximizes

$$\sum_{\tau=0}^{\infty} \delta^\tau \{a + b[p_\tau q_\tau - \alpha^\tau c q_\tau - (\beta - e_\tau) - (x p_\tau - y p_{\tau-1}) q_{\tau-1}] - \psi(e_\tau)\}. \tag{2.44}$$

Let x and y be given by

$$x = \frac{1}{(1+\lambda)(\alpha^{-1/\eta} - \delta\alpha)}, \tag{2.45}$$

$$y = \alpha x. \tag{2.46}$$

We leave it to the reader to check that in "steady state" the firm charges the optimal price given by equation (2.41).

Formula (2.43) thus generalizes (2.36) to account for technological progress. It is worth noting that the price tax is based not on the change in price $p_\tau - p_{\tau-1}$ but on the *corrected change in price* $p_\tau - \alpha p_{\tau-1}$. As in the absence of technological progress, the steady-state price is optimal even if the slope b of the incentive scheme is not chosen optimally. However, we should note that the price tax becomes informationally more demanding in the presence of technological progress. While (2.36) does not require any information about cost and demand functions (beyond the fact that they are stationary), (2.43) makes use of the rate of technological progress and of the elasticity of demand. Although assuming knowledge of these two data is much weaker than assuming knowledge of the demand and cost functions, the algorithm based on historical data is no longer simple in that it leaves discretion to the regulator.

Inflation

Correcting for inflation is a simple matter. The formulas derived above are expressed in real prices. Let X be equal to one plus the rate of inflation. Thus, if p_τ denotes the real price and $\tilde{p}_\tau$ the nominal price, $\tilde{p}_\tau = X^\tau p_\tau$. Formula (2.43) gives the price tax in real terms. The nominal price tax $\tilde{T}_\tau$ is thus

$$\tilde{T}_\tau = X^\tau T = X^\tau(xp_\tau - yp_{\tau-1})q_{\tau-1} = (x\tilde{p}_\tau - yX\tilde{p}_{\tau-1})q_{\tau-1}.$$

We can conclude that as one would expect, the price tax must be based on the corrected difference $\tilde{p}_\tau - (\alpha X)\tilde{p}_{\tau-1}$.

In practice it often makes sense to index regulatory schemes not on the overall rate of inflation but on the rate of inflation of a basket of key inputs of the firm (e.g., fuel for electric utilities), as is done in "automatic rate adjustment mechanisms." The derivation of the appropriate price tax follows the lines of the one for technological progress and overall inflation and is left to the reader.

2.6 Two-Part Tariffs in the Absence of Government Transfer

We now assume that the government is prohibited from exchanging money with the regulated firm. Its cost, including managerial compensation, must be covered by direct charges to consumers. We assume that the firm offers a two-part tariff: $A + pq$ for $q > 0$, where A and p are positive.

Consumers are heterogeneous. The gross surplus of a consumer with type θ from consuming q units of the good $S(q,\theta)$ satisfies $S_q > 0$, $S_{qq} < 0$, $S_\theta > 0$, and $S_{q\theta} > 0$ (a higher θ implies both a higher gross surplus and a higher willingness to pay for an extra unit. A high θ thus indicates a high demand for the good). There is a continuum of consumers, with preferences indexed by $\theta \in [\underline{\theta}, \bar{\theta}]$ according to the cumulative distribution function $G(\cdot)$ with density $g(\cdot)$.

Let $q(p,\theta) \equiv \arg\max_q\{S(q,\theta) - A - pq\}$. For a given two-part tariff (A,p), the "cutoff type" $\theta^* = \theta^*(A,p)$ is the type who is indifferent between purchasing and not purchasing:

$$S(q(p,\theta^*),\theta^*) - A - pq(p,\theta^*) = 0. \tag{2.47}$$

All consumers with type $\theta > \theta^*$ purchase a positive amount and those with type $\theta < \theta^*$ do not consume.

Let c denote the firm's marginal cost (as earlier, we ignore the fixed cost for notational simplicity). We assume that the firm's revenue must cover its cost, *including managerial compensation* t (since government transfers are prohibited in this industry, the use of the notation t for managerial reward should not create any confusion):

$$A(1 - G(\theta^*(A,p))) + (p - c)\int_{\theta^*(A,p)}^{\bar{\theta}} q(p,\theta)g(\theta)d\theta \geq t. \tag{2.48}$$

Consider the problem of maximizing consumers' net welfare subject to the budget constraint:

Program I

$$\mathscr{V}(c,t) = \max_{\{A,p\}} \int_{\theta^*(A,p)}^{\bar{\theta}} [S(q(p,\theta),\theta) - A - pq(p,\theta)]g(\theta)d\theta$$

subject to (2.48).

We let $1 + \tilde{\lambda} = 1 + \tilde{\lambda}(c,t)$ denote the shadow price of the budget constraint (2.48) in program I. Thus

$$\frac{\partial \mathscr{V}}{\partial t} = -(1 + \tilde{\lambda}) \tag{2.49}$$

and

$$\frac{\partial \mathscr{V}}{\partial c} = -(1 + \tilde{\lambda})D(A,p), \tag{2.50}$$

where

$$D(A,p) \equiv \int_{\theta^*(A,p)}^{\bar{\theta}} q(p,\theta)g(\theta)d\theta \tag{2.51}$$

is the aggregate demand function.

As a reference we compare program I with the derivation of the optimal two-part tariff when transfers with the government are feasible. Any revenue or expense is then valued at shadow price $1 + \lambda$, and the optimal two-part tariff is given by

$$\max_{\{A,p\}} \left\{ \int_{\theta^*(A,p)}^{\bar{\theta}} [S(q(p,\theta),\theta) - A - pq(p,\theta)]g(\theta)d\theta \right.$$
$$\left. + (1 + \lambda)\left[A(1 - G(\theta^*(A,p))) + (p - c)\int_{\theta^*(A,p)}^{\bar{\theta}} q(p,\theta)g(\theta)d\theta \right] \right\}. \tag{2.52}$$

Thus the only difference between program I and the program in the presence of government transfers is that the shadow price $\tilde{\lambda}$ depends on c and t instead of being determined by economywide data (and thus constant in c and t).

2.6.1 The Optimal Two-Part Tariff

This subsection analyzes the solution to program I. It can be skipped in a first reading. The one thing that the reader ought to know for the rest of the section is that $\tilde{\lambda} > 0$. The intuition is that the budget constraint forces the firm to foreclose access to some low-demand consumers whose consumption would otherwise be socially desirable.

Differentiating (2.47) and using the envelope theorem yields

$$\frac{\partial \theta^*}{\partial A}(A, p) = \frac{1}{(\partial S/\partial \theta)(q(p, \theta^*), \theta^*)} > 0 \tag{2.53}$$

and

$$\frac{\partial \theta^*}{\partial p}(A, p) = q(p, \theta^*)\frac{\partial \theta^*}{\partial A}(A, p) > 0. \tag{2.54}$$

From (2.47), the first-order conditions of program I with respect to p and A are, respectively,

$$\begin{aligned} &-\int_{\theta^*}^{\bar{\theta}} q(p, \theta)g(\theta)d\theta + (1 + \tilde{\lambda})\left[(p - c)\int_{\theta^*}^{\bar{\theta}} \frac{\partial q}{\partial p}(p, \theta)g(\theta)d\theta \right.\\ &\quad \left. + \int_{\theta^*}^{\bar{\theta}} q(p, \theta)g(\theta)d\theta\right] - [(p - c)q(p, \theta^*) + A]g(\theta^*)\frac{\partial \theta^*}{\partial p} = 0 \end{aligned} \tag{2.55}$$

and

$$\tilde{\lambda}(1 - G(\theta^*)) - (1 + \tilde{\lambda})[(p - c)q(p, \theta^*) + A]g(\theta^*)\frac{\partial \theta^*}{\partial A} = 0. \tag{2.56}$$

Let

$$Q(p, \theta^*) \equiv \int_{\theta^*}^{\bar{\theta}} q(p, \theta)g(\theta)d\theta$$

and

$$\frac{\partial Q}{\partial p}(p, \theta^*) \equiv \int_{\theta^*}^{\bar{\theta}} \frac{\partial q}{\partial p}(p, \theta)g(\theta)d\theta$$

denote the aggregate demand and the derivative of the aggregate demand *for a fixed participation or cutoff level* θ^*. Let $e_p(p, \theta^*) = -(\partial Q/\partial p)(p, \theta^*)p/Q(p, \theta^*)$, the price elasticity *for a fixed participation level.*

Combining (2.55), (2.56), and (2.54) yields

$$L = \frac{p - c}{p} = \frac{\tilde{\lambda}}{1 + \tilde{\lambda}} \frac{1}{e_p(p, \theta^*)} \left[1 - \frac{q(p, \theta^*)}{Q(p, \theta^*)} (1 - G(\theta^*)) \right]$$

or

$$L = \frac{\tilde{\lambda}}{1 + \tilde{\lambda}} \frac{1}{e_p(p, \theta^*)} \left[1 - \frac{q(p, \theta^*)}{\bar{Q}(p, \theta^*)} \right], \tag{2.57}$$

where

$$\bar{Q}(p, \theta) = \frac{\int_{\theta^*}^{\bar{\theta}} q(p, \theta) g(\theta) d\theta}{\int_{\theta^*}^{\bar{\theta}} g(\theta) d\theta}$$

denotes the average consumption. Under the single crossing property ($S_{q\theta} > 0$), $q(\cdot, \cdot)$ is increasing in θ, and therefore the consumption of the marginal consumer is less than average consumption.

The Lerner index is equal to $\tilde{\lambda}/(1 + \tilde{\lambda})$ times a term that is the two-part tariff analogue of the inverse elasticity of demand for linear pricing. When reducing price by dp, the firm can keep the same participation by increasing A by $q(p, \theta^*)dp$. Since the price decrease applies to average consumption and the fixed fee's increase is based on the consumption of the marginal consumer, the relative revenue loss incurred by lowering price is

$$\frac{\bar{Q}(p, \theta^*)dp - q(p, \theta^*)dp}{\bar{Q}(p, \theta^*)dp} = 1 - \left[\frac{q(p, \theta^*)}{\bar{Q}(p, \theta^*)} \right].$$

Under a linear tariff this relative revenue loss would be equal to 1 because the decrease in price would not be compensated by an increase in fixed fee. With a two-part tariff it is less because the marginal and average consumers differ and the relationship between Lerner index and inverse elasticity of ("compensated") demand must be corrected by $1 - q/\bar{Q}$. Finally note that unlike in the case of homogeneous consumers and perfect price discrimination, the price exceeds marginal cost. The intuition is that a small increase in price above marginal cost introduces a second-order effect in allocative efficiency and increases revenue to the first-order which is socially desirable since we have assumed that the budget constraint is binding.

Using (2.53), we can rewrite (2.56) as

$$(p - c)q(p, \theta^*) + A = \frac{\tilde{\lambda}}{1 + \tilde{\lambda}} \frac{(1 - G(\theta^*))}{g(\theta^*)} \frac{\partial S}{\partial \theta}(q(p, \theta^*), \theta^*). \tag{2.58}$$

Let

$$E = \frac{1 - G(\theta^*)}{g(\theta^*)(\partial\theta^*/\partial A)A} = \frac{-(1 - G(\theta^*))}{[d(1 - G(\theta^*))/d\theta^*](\partial\theta^*/\partial A)A}$$

be the price elasticity of participation. Then (2.58) can be interpreted as optimal pricing of the commodity "right to participate" if written as

$$\frac{A + (p - c)q(p, \theta^*)}{A} = \frac{\tilde{\lambda}}{1 + \tilde{\lambda}} \frac{1}{E}. \tag{2.59}$$

To see that the left-hand side of (2.59) is a Lerner index, note that A is the price of access and that the cost to the firm of giving access to a marginal consumer is $-(p - c)q(p, \theta^*)$ (since $p > c$, the firm makes a marginal profit on the marginal consumer). We can now show that $\tilde{\lambda} > 0$. Suppose that $\tilde{\lambda} = 0$ (the multiplier of the budget constraint must be nonnegative). Then $p = c$ from (2.57) and $A = 0$ from (2.59). The budget balance constraint (2.48) is therefore violated.

2.6.2 Optimal Cost-of-Service Regulation

We now analyze the optimal regulation when the regulator is prevented from transferring money to the firm. As before, the regulator does not know the value of the technological parameter β, which is distributed according to the cumulative distribution function $F(\cdot)$ on $[\underline{\beta}, \overline{\beta}]$ satisfying the monotone hazard rate property. A mechanism is a quadruple $\{A(\beta), p(\beta), c(\beta), t(\beta)\}$ specifying a fixed premium, a usage price, a marginal cost, and a managerial compensation for each value of the technological parameter. The firm's utility is then $U(\beta) = t(\beta) - \psi(e(\beta))$, where $e(\beta) = \beta - c(\beta)$. The mechanism is feasible if it satisfies the budget constraint (2.47) for each β. Assume that the regulator maximizes expected social welfare. Thus

$$\max_{\{c(\cdot), U(\cdot), t(\cdot)\}} \int_{\underline{\beta}}^{\overline{\beta}} (\mathscr{V}(c(\beta), t(\beta)) + U(\beta)) f(\beta) d\beta \tag{2.60}$$

subject to (2.2),

$$\dot{U}(\beta) = -\psi'(e(\beta)) = -\psi'(\beta - c(\beta)), \tag{2.61}$$

$$c(\cdot) \text{ nondecreasing,} \tag{2.62}$$

$$U(\overline{\beta}) = 0. \tag{2.63}$$

As we saw in section 2.4, (2.61) and (2.62) are the first- and second-order conditions for incentive compatibility and (2.63) is the individual rationality constraint. As is now usual, we take U as the state variable and e as the control variable and ignore the monotonicity constraint (2.62), which then needs to be checked ex post.

Program II

$$\max_{\{e(\cdot), U(\cdot)\}} \int_{\underline{\beta}}^{\overline{\beta}} [\mathscr{V}(\beta - e(\beta), U(\beta) + \psi(e(\beta))) + U(\beta)] f(\beta) d\beta$$

subject to

$$\dot{U}(\beta) = -\psi'(e(\beta))$$

$$U(\bar{\beta}) = 0.$$

Its hamiltonian is

$$H = [\mathscr{V}(\beta - e, U + \psi(e)) + U]\mathrm{f} - \mu\psi'(e),$$

which yields first-order conditions

$$\frac{\partial H}{\partial e} = 0 = \left[-\frac{\partial \mathscr{V}}{\partial c} + \frac{\partial \mathscr{V}}{\partial t}\psi'(e) \right] f - \mu\psi''(e) \tag{2.64}$$

and

$$\dot{\mu} = -\frac{\partial H}{\partial U} = -\left(\frac{\partial \mathscr{V}}{\partial t} + 1\right) f. \tag{2.65}$$

Integrating (2.65), using the free boundary condition $\mu(\underline{\beta}) = 0$, and recalling that $\partial\mathscr{V}/\partial c = -(1 + \tilde{\lambda}(\beta))Q(\beta)$ and $\partial\mathscr{V}/\partial t = -(1 + \tilde{\lambda}(\beta))$, where $Q(\beta) \equiv D(A(\beta), p(\beta)), \tilde{\lambda}(\beta) \equiv \tilde{\lambda}(c(\beta), t(\beta))$, we obtain

$$\psi'(e(\beta)) = Q(\beta) - \frac{\int_{\underline{\beta}}^{\beta} \tilde{\lambda}(x) f(x) dx}{(1 + \tilde{\lambda}(\beta)) f(\beta)} \psi''(e(\beta)). \tag{2.66}$$

Note the link between (2.66) and (2.26). When transfers are allowed, $\tilde{\lambda}(\beta) = \lambda$, and (2.66) yields (2.26). The analogy with the case of an exogenous λ is clear. Effort is lower under asymmetric information and the informational rent increases with efficiency. The difference in the case of government transfers is that the "shadow cost of public funds," or now the "shadow cost of rewards," is type contingent. Since the power of the incentive scheme for a given type is related to the extraction of the rent of the more efficient types, this power depends on the shadow costs of this type as well as the more efficient types. The logic of the basic incentive–rent extraction trade-off is otherwise unchanged.

Let us conclude this section with a caveat: As in the case of government transfers, some conditions are needed to ensure that the average cost is indeed nondecreasing in the cost parameter [condition (2.62)]. We leave the derivation of such conditions on the utility functions and the distribution of consumer and firm types for future research.

Proposition 2.4 Under budget balance and two-part pricing, the fixed premium and the usage price are given by Ramsey formulas. The power of the firm's incentive scheme is given by the same equation as in the absence of budget constraint, except that the shadow cost of public funds is replaced by a shadow cost of the budget constraint or shadow cost of rewards. This shadow cost is now type contingent and reflects the deadweight loss of reduced participation when the premium is raised, or equivalently, of reduced consumption when the usage price is increased.

2.7 Linear Pricing in the Absence of Government Transfer

2.7.1 Optimal Linear Prices as Sliding Scale Plans

Universal service is often imposed on regulated monopolies. In the last section we saw that optimal two-part tariffs exclude some consumers. A linear price is the only two-part tariff that ensures universal service. Linear pricing is thus optimal when the marginal utility of the service is infinite at zero consumption and when simultaneously no information is available about agents' resources. More generally optimal linear pricing is a good approximation to optimal two-part pricing when there is concern that a nonnegligible fixed premium would exclude either too many customers or customers with low incomes whose welfare is given substantial weight in the social welfare function.[12] Alternatively, linear prices can, in some industries, be justified by the possibility of arbitrage. We perform in this section an analysis similar to the one of section 2.6 when the firm charges a linear price instead of a two-part tariff.

Let $q = D(p)$ denote the demand function, with inverse demand $p = P(q)$. The consumer *net* surplus $S^n(p)$ is given by $S^n(p) = \int_p^\infty D(x)dx$. The firm's cost function is $C = (\beta - e)q$. The *full information* optimum in the absence of government transfer leaves no rent to the firm; individual rationality then requires that

$$[p - (\beta - e)]D(p) = \psi(e), \tag{2.67}$$

because the firm must be rewarded from direct charges to consumers. The optimal choice of effort minimizes total production cost:

$$\psi'(e) = q.$$

The price is then given by the (lowest) solution to (2.67).

Under *asymmetric information* the regulator must leave a rent $U(\beta)$ to the firm. The regulator can offer a menu $\{t(\beta), p(\beta), c(\beta)\}_{\beta \in [\underline{\beta}, \bar{\beta}]}$ specifying a reward, a price, and a marginal cost target for each level of β. The menu satisfies the balanced-budget constraint for each β:

$$(p(\beta) - c(\beta))D(p(\beta)) = t(\beta), \tag{2.68}$$

or

$$(p(\beta) - c(\beta))D(p(\beta)) = U(\beta) + \psi(e(\beta)). \tag{2.69}$$

12. Note that we do not formally introduce redistributive considerations in the social welfare function. The analysis could easily be amended along the lines of section 3.9.

Let $\mathscr{P}(c, t)$ denote the lowest price satisfying (2.68). We assume that over the relevant range, $\mathscr{P}$ is differentiable and increasing in c and t.[12] The regulator's program is thus

$$\max \int_{\underline{\beta}}^{\bar{\beta}} [S^n[\mathscr{P}(\beta - e(\beta), U(\beta) + \psi(e(\beta))] + U(\beta)]f(\beta)d\beta \tag{2.70}$$

subject to

$$\dot{U}(\beta) = -\psi'(e(\beta))$$

if we ignore the firm's second-order condition ($\dot{c}(\beta) \geq 0$) in program (2.70).[13] Letting μ denote the multiplier of the constraint in program (2.70), the first-order conditions for this program are

$$\dot{\mu} = f\left[q\frac{\partial \mathscr{P}}{\partial t} - 1\right]$$

and

$$q\left[\frac{\partial \mathscr{P}}{\partial c} - \frac{\partial \mathscr{P}}{\partial t}\psi'(e)\right]f = \mu\psi''(e).$$

Using the transversality condition $\mu(\underline{\beta}) = 0$ and the fact that $\partial\mathscr{P}/\partial c = q\partial\mathscr{P}/\partial t$, we obtain the optimal effort level:

$$\psi'(e(\beta)) = q(\beta) - \frac{\int_{\underline{\beta}}^{\beta}[(\partial\mathscr{P}/\partial c)(\tilde{\beta}) - 1]f(\tilde{\beta})d\tilde{\beta}}{(\partial\mathscr{P}/\partial c)(\beta)f(\beta)}\psi''(e(\beta)). \tag{2.71}$$

Note the similarity of equation (2.71) with equations (2.26) (no budget constraint) and (2.66) (budget constraint and two-part tariff). The type-contingent shadow cost of rewards is now $\tilde{\tilde{\lambda}}(\beta) = (\partial\mathscr{P}/\partial c)(\beta) - 1 = q(\partial\mathscr{P}/\partial t)(\beta) - 1$. The interpretation is that a unit increase in the firm's reward costs $q(\partial\mathscr{P}/\partial t)$ to consumers, and $q(\partial\mathscr{P}/\partial t) - 1 = \partial\mathscr{P}/\partial c - 1$ to society. Note that $\partial\mathscr{P}/\partial c > 1$ from (2.68): Since price exceeds marginal cost, a price increase has a negative indirect impact on revenue by reducing demand, and therefore an increase in marginal cost must be offset by an even greater increase in price to keep revenue constant. In this way

12. This is the case if the demand function is differentiable and if the profit function is a strictly concave function of price (see Guesnerie and Laffont 1978 for a relaxation of this hypothesis). Then $\mathscr{P}(c, t)$ is differentiable and strictly increasing in t and c in the (relevant) range in which the profit is increasing in price.

13. Let us further assume that demand goes to infinity but the net surplus is bounded if the price goes to zero, that $\psi'(e)$ goes to $+\infty$ if e goes to $\underline{\beta}$, and that for strictly positive production levels the net surplus is large at the optimal effort level ($\psi'(e) = q$) so that a zero effort level and zero production level can never be optimal. Then the solution of (2.70) must be an interior solution and it satisfies the first-order conditions. However, the objective function being quite generally a convex function, discontinuities may occur in the optimal solution. If the optimal solution of (2.70) is nondecreasing, it is the solution we are looking for. If it has downward discontinuities or more generally decreasing pieces, bunching occurs.

we obtain the familiar trade-off between rent extraction and incentives. The regulator reduces incentives to lower transfers and thus equilibrium prices.

The optimal mechanism decreases effort from the conditionally optimal level $\hat{e}(q(\beta))$ defined by $\psi'(\hat{e}(q(\beta))) \equiv q(\beta)$ [see (2.71)], decreasing the "fixed cost" $U(\beta) + \psi(e(\beta))$ and allowing a decrease of price. This further move must satisfy a delicate incentive constraint because monopolies like to respond with a higher price to a lower effort (i.e., a higher cost).

The optimum can be implemented through a kind of (static) *sliding scale plan*: The regulator offers price $p^*(c)$, which is obtained by eliminating β and $e(\beta)$ using (2.69), (2.71), and $U(\beta) = \int_{\beta}^{\bar{\beta}} \psi'(e(\tilde{\beta}))d\tilde{\beta}$. Incentive compatibility requires that p^* be increasing over the relevant range (as revenue must be increasing in price). That there is *cost sharing between consumers and the firm* is demonstrated by differentiating the identity

$$t(c) \equiv (p^*(c) - c)D(p^*(c)),$$

or

$$d[cD(p^*(c))] - [-dt] = d[p^*(c)D(p^*(c))].$$

When cost increases, so does price and revenue pD. Therefore the increase in cost is not fully reflected in the reduction $-dt$ of the firm's reward. For the most efficient type which produces at the lowest average cost $\underline{c} = c^*(\underline{\beta})$, we can show that $(dp^*/dc)(\underline{c}) = 0$, so small cost increases are not shared by consumers.

Proposition 2.5 Under budget balance and linear pricing, the price is chosen so as to equate revenue and the firm's total cost (including its reward). As under two-part pricing the power of the firm's incentive scheme is determined by the same equation as in the absence of budget constraint, except that the shadow cost of public funds is replaced by a type-dependent shadow cost of rewards that reflects the marginal deadweight loss associated with a move toward the monopoly price. The optimum can be implemented through a sliding scale plan in which the consumers and the firm share cost increases. In this plan a small cost increase for the most efficient type is not reflected in a price increase.

It would be interesting to extend this theory to allow for cost or demand uncertainty. Uncertainty creates the same problem for the balance of the budget in theory and practice. There is no way to guarantee that the firm breaks even over a given period. The firm must absorb the difference between revenue and cost either through borrowing (e.g., for a public enterprise) or through equity gains or losses (e.g., for a private utility). That is, the budget constraint is satisfied at best intertemporally.

2.7.2 Relationship to Monopoly Pricing and Price Caps

Unregulated monopoly pricing belongs to the family of pricing mechanisms without government transfer. A constant price is also such a mechanism as is a price cap $\bar{p}$. A price cap leads to monopoly pricing for β less than some β^* and to price $\bar{p}$ above β^*.

Consider first *monopoly pricing*. The firm chooses its price $p^M(\beta)$ and effort $e^M(\beta)$ so as to maximize

$$U(\beta) = \max_{\{p,e\}} \{[p - (\beta - e)]D(p) - \psi(e)\}.$$

Monopoly pricing can be interpreted as average cost pricing with a fixed cost equal to the disutility of effort [for the monopoly effort level that is the optimal level $\hat{e}(D(p^M(\beta)))$ conditionally on the production level] plus a rent $U(\beta) = \int_\beta^{\bar{\beta}} \psi'(e^M(\tilde{\beta}))d\tilde{\beta} + U(\bar{\beta})$. The rent is socially costly because it forces the price higher than the average cost with a zero rent which is itself higher than the marginal cost.

Turn next to a *price cap* $\bar{p}$ which is binding for and leaves no rent to the most inefficient type. Such a price cap must satisfy

$$\begin{aligned} U(\bar{\beta}) &= \max_{\{e\}} \{[\bar{p} - (\bar{\beta} - e)]D(\bar{p}) - \psi(e)\} \\ &= 0 \\ &\geq \max_{\{p \leq \bar{p}, e\}} \{[p - (\bar{\beta} - e)]D(p) - \psi(e)\}. \end{aligned}$$

The inequality implies that the price cap is below the monopoly price corresponding to marginal cost $[\bar{\beta} - \hat{e}(D(\bar{p}))]$. Indeed a move from the monopoly price to a lower price cap $\bar{p}$ that is individually rational for the firm raises social welfare by

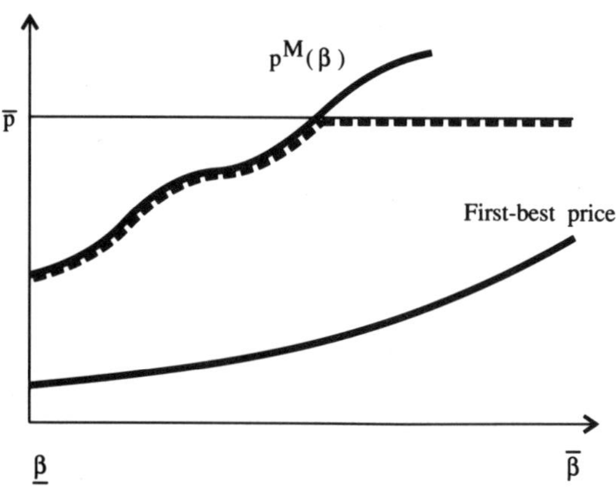

Figure 2.1
Price-cap and monopoly pricing

$$-\int_{\bar{p}}^{p^M(\beta)} \frac{d}{dp}(S^n + U)dp = \int_{\bar{p}}^{p^M(\beta)} [-[p - (\beta - \hat{e}(D(p)))]D'(p)]dp > 0,$$

for any type β for which the price cap is binding. (A standard revealed preference argument shows that the monopoly price is nondecreasing in β. This implies that a price cap is binding for types above some threshold type β^*, as illustrated in figure 2.1.) Last, note that further decreases in the price level can be obtained only by decreasing the firm's rent and therefore lowering the effort level from the conditionally efficient effort profile $\hat{e}(\cdot)$. This requires measuring accounting data.

2.8 Concluding Remarks

This chapter has examined pricing by a regulated natural monopoly using a simple example. It has served as an introduction to the systematic study of Ramsey pricing presented in chapters 3 and 5. It has also pointed out that incentive issues are very similar whether or not there is a budget constraint. The analysis is a bit more complex, however, under a budget constraint because of the endogeneity of the shadow cost; much work remains to be done in this case. For example, it would be worthwhile to further analyze the properties of and to calibrate the optimal sliding scale plan that arises as the optimal incentive contract under budget balance.

BIBLIOGRAPHIC NOTES

B2.1 Price Regulation When Cost Is Not Observable: The Model of Baron and Myerson

B2.1.1 Price Distortions as a Rent Extraction Device

Baron and Myerson (1982) assume that the regulator cannot observe cost. As we will see, the nonobservability of cost has important consequences for optimal pricing.

Suppose that the firm has cost

$$C = \beta q$$

and that the regulator only observes output q. [Cost unobservability is a special case of the general model of chapter 3. Suppose that cost is observable, but $C = \beta q - e$, and $\psi(e) = e$. Then the firm can "steal" money as it wants, because a unit decrease in e increases the firm's cost and utility by one.] Since cost is unobservable, we let t denote the *gross* transfer from the regulator to the firm; we make the convention that the firm receives the revenue from sales plus the transfer t from the regulator: $U = t + P(q)q - \beta q$, where $P(\cdot)$ is the inverse demand function. Note that we do not introduce moral hazard. Since cost is unobservable, the contract given to the firm is necessarily a fixed-price contract, and therefore the regulator has no control over the power of the incentive scheme and the level of cost-reducing activity. Adding moral hazard thus complicates the notation and derivations without creating new insights.[14]

Let the firm's private information parameter be distributed on $[\underline{\beta}, \bar{\beta}]$ according to the cumulative distribution function $F(\beta)$ with strictly positive density $f(\beta)$. It is assumed that this distribution has a monotone hazard rate. The social welfare function is equal to the sum of the consumer's net surplus and the firm's utility minus the cost for taxpayers of the transfer to the firm:[15]

$$W = S(q) - P(q)q - (1 + \lambda)t + U$$

or

$$W = S(q) + \lambda P(q)q - (1 + \lambda)\beta q - \lambda U. \tag{B2.1}$$

Under *full information* the regulator would capture the firm's rent ($U = 0$) and choose output so that

$$p + \lambda(P'q + p) = (1 + \lambda)\beta$$

or

$$L = \frac{p - \beta}{p} = \frac{\lambda}{1 + \lambda}\frac{1}{\eta}.$$

As in equation (2.8) the Lerner index is equal to $\lambda/(1 + \lambda)$ times the inverse elasticity of demand. This is not surprising because the absence of cost observability is irrelevant under full information (i.e., the full information allocation can be implemented by a fixed-price contract and therefore does not require cost observability).

Under *asymmetric information* the regulator offers a mechanism $\{t(\hat{\beta}), q(\hat{\beta})\}$, and the firm chooses its announcement so as to maximize $U(\beta, \hat{\beta}) \equiv t(\hat{\beta}) + P(q(\hat{\beta}))q(\hat{\beta}) - \beta q(\hat{\beta})$. The envelope theorem implies that

$$\dot{U}(\beta) = -q(\beta); \tag{B2.2}$$

14. If we had posited $C = (\beta - e)q$ and $U = t + P(q)q - (\beta - e)q - \psi(e)$, then the firm would have chosen $\psi'(e) = q$, defining a function $e^*(q)$. We could then have replaced the cost function by a new cost function that exhibits only adverse selection: $\tilde{C} \equiv (\beta - e^*(q))q + \psi(e^*(q))$. The treatment would have followed the lines of the Baron-Myerson model.

15. Baron and Myerson do not have a shadow cost of public funds, but they assume that the regulator discounts the firm's utility relatively to consumer surplus. This assumption introduces only minor differences; the main difference is that the full information benchmark in Baron and Myerson is marginal cost while it is Ramsey pricing here.

that is, a unit increase in marginal cost increases cost and decreases utility by q units.

The local second-order condition for the firm is obtained as in chapter 1 (we refer to chapter 1 for the proof of differentiability): From the identity $U_{\hat{\beta}}(\beta, \beta) = 0$, we derive the second-order condition:

$$0 \geq U_{\hat{\beta}\hat{\beta}}(\beta, \beta) = -U_{\hat{\beta}\beta}(\beta, \beta) = \dot{q}(\beta).$$

The firm's output must thus be nonincreasing in marginal cost. As usual, we ignore the local second-order condition and check ex post that it is satisfied by the solution to the relaxed program. Furthermore the local second-order condition turns out to imply the global second-order condition.[16] The regulator solves

$$\max \int_{\underline{\beta}}^{\bar{\beta}} W(\beta) f(\beta) d\beta$$

subject to constraint (B2.2).

The hamiltonian is

$$H = [S(q) + \lambda P(q)q - (1+\lambda)\beta q - \lambda U]f - \mu q.$$

The first-order conditions are

$$\frac{\partial H}{\partial q} = [p(1+\lambda) + \lambda P'q - (1+\lambda)\beta]f - \mu = 0$$

and

$$\dot{\mu} = -\frac{\partial H}{\partial U} = \lambda f.$$

The transversality condition $\mu(\underline{\beta}) = 0$ therefore implies that $\mu(\beta) = \lambda F(\beta)$ and that

$$L \equiv \frac{p(\beta) - \beta}{p(\beta)} = \frac{\lambda}{1+\lambda} \frac{1}{\eta(\beta)} + \frac{\lambda}{1+\lambda} \frac{F(\beta)}{f(\beta)p(\beta)}. \tag{B2.3}$$

We let the reader check that q is indeed decreasing in β.

16. Suppose that $U(\beta, \hat{\beta}) > U(\beta, \beta)$, or $\int_{\beta}^{\hat{\beta}} U_{\beta}(\beta, x)dx > 0$. Using the first-order condition, this implies that

$$\int_{\beta}^{\hat{\beta}} [U_{\hat{\beta}}(\beta, x) - U_{\hat{\beta}}(x, x)]dx > 0,$$

or

$$\int_{\beta}^{\hat{\beta}} \int_{x}^{\beta} U_{\beta\hat{\beta}}(y, x)dydx = \int_{\beta}^{\hat{\beta}} \int_{\beta}^{x} \dot{q}(x)dx > 0$$

which is ruled out by $\dot{q} \leq 0$.

Clearly the price exceeds its Ramsey level. The distortion at β reflects the trade-off between the inefficiency cost at β, proportional to the density, and the expected amount of rent extracted, proportional to the cumulative distribution. As mentioned above, this conclusion would remain if we introduced moral hazard, that is, if $C = (\beta - e)q$.

There are thus two related differences between the cases of cost observation and cost unobservability. First, we already noted that selecting the power of the incentive scheme is not an instrument when cost is not observable. Second, price is always distorted beyond the Ramsey price when cost is not observable, while it is equal to the Ramsey price in equation (2.25) (chapter 3 will investigate general conditions under which this property holds). The point is that the cost-reimbursement rules are, under some conditions, a sufficient instrument to limit the firm's rent, so the regulator does not need to distort the price. Deprived of the cost-reimbursement instrument, the regulator must resort to reductions in output to limit rents.

The intuition for (B2.3) can be readily obtained from (B2.2). Low quantities reduce the influence of variations in marginal cost on the firm's rent. (Indeed, if the firm did not produce, i.e., $q(\beta) = 0$ for all β, the rent would identically equal 0.) The analogue of figure 1.3 for the Baron-Myerson model is figure 2.2.

B2.1.2 Cost Measurement in the Absence of Moral Hazard

Baron and Besanko (1984) have extended the Baron-Myerson model to allow random audits of cost. Suppose that at cost K the regulator can observe a garbled version of the true cost:

$$C^m = \beta q + \varepsilon,$$

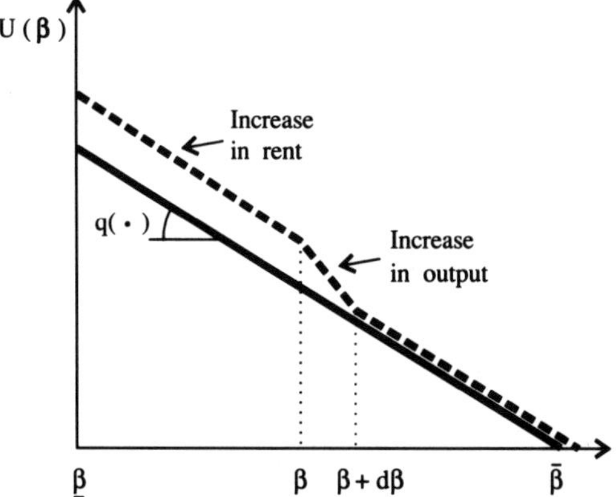

Figure 2.2
The firm's rent $[U(\beta) = \int_{\beta}^{\bar{\beta}} q(\tilde{\beta})d\tilde{\beta}]$ in the Baron-Myerson model

where ε is an ex post noise unobserved by the parties with mean 0. To be more specific, assume that ε has symmetric distribution $G(\varepsilon)$ on $(-\infty, +\infty)$ around 0, with differentiable density g. For the moment we assume costless auditing ($K = 0$), and later we indicate how the optimal policy changes when auditing is costly. Note that we do not allow moral hazard. As we will see, conclusions are quite different under moral hazard, in contrast with the previous case where audits were not feasible and moral hazard was qualitatively irrelevant.

Baron and Besanko assume that the regulator ex ante transfers $t(\hat{\beta})$ that depends on the firm's announcement and ex post imposes penalty $Z(\hat{\beta}, C^m) \in [0, \bar{Z}]$, where $\bar{Z}$ is an exogenous upper bound on the penalty.[17]

The firm's utility is

$$U(\beta) = \max_{\hat{\beta}} \left\{ t(\hat{\beta}) - \beta q(\hat{\beta}) - \int_{-\infty}^{+\infty} Z(\hat{\beta}, C^m) g(C^m - \beta q(\hat{\beta})) dC^m \right\}.$$

The envelope theorem and truth telling imply that

$$\dot{U}(\beta) = -q(\beta) + \int_{-\infty}^{+\infty} Z(\beta, C^m) q(\beta) g'(C^m - \beta q(\beta)) dC^m.$$

To simplify the analysis, suppose that g is normal with mean 0 and variance 1. Then $g'(\varepsilon) = -\varepsilon g(\varepsilon)$. Therefore

$$\dot{U}(\beta) = -q(\beta) - E[Zq(C^m - \beta q)], \tag{B2.4}$$

where the expectation operator is with respect to ε. We will ignore the second-order conditions for the firm (the global second-order condition is quite complex). The regulator maximizes

$$\int_{\underline{\beta}}^{\bar{\beta}} [S(q) + \lambda P(q)q - (1 + \lambda)\beta q - \lambda U] f(\beta) d\beta \tag{B2.5}$$

subject to constraint (B2.4).

The hamiltonian is

$$H = [S(q) + \lambda P(q)q - (1 + \lambda)\beta q - \lambda U]f - \mu[q + E(Zq(C^m - \beta q))].$$

As usual $\mu(\beta) = \lambda F(\beta)$. We also have

$$[(1 + \lambda)p + \lambda P'q - (1 + \lambda)\beta]f$$
$$- \lambda F[1 + E(Z(C^m - 2\beta q)) + E[Z\beta q(C^m - \beta q)^2]] = 0.$$

17. Two comments are in order here. First, the regulator could implement the first best if penalties were not bounded (the reader can obtain intuition about this from bibliographic notes B1.3 of chapter 1). Second, the modeling is not equivalent to a limited liability constraint. If the constraint on penalties were that the firm could not receive negative transfers, it would be optimal for the regulator to delay any reward until measurement accrues. The constraint would then be $t(\hat{\beta}, C^m) \geq 0$. The results are a bit different in this alternative formulation of limited punishments (see the discussion of the section on effort monitoring in chapter 12).

Last, the choice of the optimal penalty is bang-bang because the hamiltonian is linear in penalties:

$$Z = \begin{cases} 0 & \textit{if } C^m \geq \beta q, \\ \bar{Z} & \text{if } C^m < \beta q. \end{cases}$$

In this model the firm is penalized with probability 1/2. Four points are worth making:

First, optimal penalties penalize the firm when the measured cost is *low*. The intuition for this is that the regulator is concerned about the firm pretending to have a high cost. Low costs thus signal that the firm may have lied. Note also that the optimal punishment policy is no longer sustainable if the firm can increase its cost. Indeed we saw that under moral hazard low costs are rewarded rather than punished.

The second point to note is that in absolute value $\dot{U}$ is lower than its no-audit level q. To keep the individual rationality constraint satisfied while using extreme punishments, $\bar{Z}$ must be kept small enough (so that $\dot{U}$ does not become positive). For larger $\bar{Z}$, the regulator can implement the first best.

Third, it can be shown that the price is smaller than the price in the absence of an audit. The intuition is that the regulator can partly extract the firm's rent through the audit and therefore can reduce the price distortion.

Fourth, what if there is a cost K of audit? Then the regulator optimally specifies a probability of audit as a function of the report $\hat{\beta}$. Baron and Besanko show that the firm is more likely to be audited if it forecasts a *high* cost. Because the regulator is concerned about the firm falsely reporting high costs, it makes sense to audit high-cost estimates more than low ones.

B2.1.3 Private Information about Demand

Lewis and Sappington (1988a) assume that the firm has more information about demand rather than cost.[18] The firm has known cost function $C(q)$. Neither C nor q is observable by the regulator. But the firm must serve all customers at the established price. The demand is $q = D(p, \theta)$, where θ is known by the firm while the regulator has prior cumulative distribution $G(\theta)$ on some interval $[\underline{\theta}, \bar{\theta}]$. Assume that $\partial D/\partial p < 0$ and that $\partial D/\partial \theta > 0$. The regulator can observe price and make a transfer. A regulatory mechanism is thus a pair of functions $\{t(\theta), p(\theta)\}_{\theta \in [\underline{\theta}, \bar{\theta}]}$. The firm's utility is $U = t + pD(p, \theta) - C(D(p, \theta))$ (recall the assumption that quantity is unobservable; this assumption requires that revenue accrue to the firm).

18. They extend their analysis to private information about demand and cost in Lewis and Sappington (1988b). An early paper on asymmetries of information about demand is Riordan (1984). See also Spulber (1988).

Lewis and Sappington, following Baron and Myerson, assume that the regulator discounts the firm's utility but that there is no shadow cost of public funds:

$$W = S(q,\theta) - pD(p,\theta) - t + \alpha U$$
$$= S(q,\theta) - C(D(p,\theta)) - (1-\alpha)U,$$

where $\alpha \in [0,1)$. (Unlike what we did in B2.1.1 and B2.1.2, we do not reformulate the social welfare function in terms of a shadow cost of public funds, because even the qualitative results differ slightly in the two cases.) Under full information the regulator sets $U = 0$ and charges a price equal to marginal cost: Let

$$p^*(\theta) = C'(D(p^*(\theta),\theta)).$$

Asymmetric information about demand has different implications than asymmetric information about cost.

First, under decreasing returns to scale ($C'' \geq 0$), the regulator can implement the first best by offering price $p^*(\hat{\theta})$ and transfer $t(\hat{\theta}) = C(D(p^*(\hat{\theta}),\hat{\theta})) - p^*(\hat{\theta})D(p^*(\hat{\theta}),\hat{\theta})$. The firm thus obtains no rent if it tells the truth about θ. Yet it cannot gain by lying because, for all $\hat{\theta}$,

$$0 \geq t(\hat{\theta}) + p^*(\hat{\theta})D(p^*(\hat{\theta}),\theta) - C(D(p^*(\hat{\theta}),\theta))$$
$$= \int_{\hat{\theta}}^{\theta} \frac{\partial D}{\partial \theta}(p^*(\hat{\theta}),x)[p^*(\hat{\theta}) - C'(D(p^*(\hat{\theta}),x))]dx,$$

where use is made of the fact that $p^*(\hat{\theta}) = C'(D(p^*(\hat{\theta}),\hat{\theta}))$ and of decreasing returns.

The intuition for this result is that, first, direct price effects are offset by changes in transfer, and, second, by lying to increase the price, say, the firm contracts demand and forgoes sales on units for which marginal cost was under the price (and conversely, for price decreases). Note that the result does not hold with a shadow cost of public funds. The full information benchmark is then the Ramsey price, so $p^*(\hat{\theta}) > C'(D(p^*(\hat{\theta}),\hat{\theta}))$. The firm has an incentive to expand demand (by asking for a low price) because the price exceeds its marginal cost.

Second, consider increasing returns to scale ($C'' < 0$). Suppose, for instance, that demand is separable: $D(p,\theta) = \tilde{D}(p) + \theta$. Assume that returns to scale are moderate ($1 - C''\tilde{D}' > 0$). The regulator would then want $p(\theta)$ to *decrease* with θ: A higher demand lowers marginal cost and thus vindicates a lower price. We let the reader check that incentive compatibility requires that $p(\theta)$ *increase* with θ. The optimal policy is then to induce a constant price, an instance of the phenomenon of "nonresponsiveness" of the allocation with respect to private information first exhibited in Guesnerie and Laffont (1984).

B2.2 Pricing Schemes Based on Historical Data

The mechanism using historical data described in subsection 2.5.2. bears some resemblance to those of Finsinger and Vogelsang (1979, 1981, 1982) and Tam (1981).[19] We briefly review these mechanisms in the single-good context.

Finsinger and Vogelsang offer to give regulated firms a bonus

$$B_\tau = a + \pi_\tau - \pi_{\tau-1} + (p_{\tau-1} - p_\tau)q_{\tau-1}, \tag{B2.6}$$

where $\pi_\tau \equiv p_\tau q_\tau - C(q_\tau)$ and a is a constant. Finsinger and Vogelsang's major insight was that this scheme, which depends only on historically observable data (profit, quantity, and price) yields in the long run Ramsey prices. However, as Sappington (1980) pointed out, this scheme has perverse incentive properties (see also Gravelle 1985). If the cost function C depends on a cost-reducing activity, the cost-reducing activity is vastly undersupplied. This can be seen intuitively from (B2.6). In a steady state $\pi_\tau = \pi_{\tau-1}$, and the firm does not gain from reducing its cost.

Tam (1981) proposed the following bonus:

$$\tilde{B}_\tau = a + b(\pi_\tau - p_\tau q_{\tau-1}). \tag{B2.7}$$

Tam shows that if the firm behaves myopically (i.e., maximizes its current bonus instead of the present discounted value of the bonus), the firm's price converges to marginal cost in the long run. One drawback of this mechanism is that the long-run steady state is marginal cost pricing rather than Ramsey pricing. Another, and more important one, is that when the firm does not behave myopically there is no convergence to marginal cost pricing (Finsinger and Vogelsang 1985).

The link between our mechanism and those of Finsinger and Vogelsang and Tam is that they all are negative price incentive schemes. The firm is penalized for increases in its current price. Our mechanism can be seen as combining the positive aspects of the two other schemes. Like Finsinger and Vogelsang's, it is based on a taxation of price changes rather than of price levels. Like Tam's, it lets the firm retain (at least part of) its long-term profit and thus has desirable incentive properties. Finsinger and Vogelsang introduced rewards based on changes in profits to obtain convergence to Ramsey prices. The fact that under optimal regulation Ramsey prices depend on the economywide shadow cost of public funds allows us to finely compute the tax on price changes and base rewards on profit levels rather than on changes of profit levels.

19. For discussions of the properties of these mechanisms, see the 1985 *QJE* papers by Finsinger and Vogelsang, Gravelle, and Tam.

Last, Vogelsang (1989, 1990) designs a subsidy mechanism very much in the spirit of (2.36). The mechanism differs from ours[20] in terms of prices it implements, but by making the firm residual claimant for its cost savings, it has good incentive properties.

B2.3 Pricing and Incentives in the Presence of a Budget Constraint

Section 2.6, on two-part pricing under a budget constraint follows a suggestion made in Joskow and Schmalensee (1986) that the transfer from the regulator in the model of section 2.4 might be thought of as being the fixed charge to consumers in a budget-balance situation. Section 2.6 formalizes the extent to which the deadweight loss associated with depriving some consumers of service is akin to a shadow cost of transferring money to the firm.

Section 2.7, on linear pricing under a budget constraint, is related to work by Schmalensee (1989). The two models are identical. Schmalensee constrains the price charged by the firm to be linear is realized marginal cost ($p = a + dc$) and performs some numerical simulations. We allow general incentive schemes, and we solve for the optimal scheme $p^*(c)$. It might be worth performing numerical simulations similar to those of Schmalensee to investigate the shape of $p^*(\cdot)$ and to analyze its sensitivity to the parameters of the model. Gasmi, Ivaldi, and Laffont (1991) compare numerically the optimal regulation mechanism, the Schmalensee linear rule, and price-cap rules with redistribution of excessive profits.

REFERENCES

Baron, D., and R. Myerson. 1982. Regulating a monopolist with unknown costs. *Econometrica* 50:911–930.

Baron, D., and D. Besanko. 1984. Regulation, asymmetric information and auditing. *Rand Journal of Economics* 15:447–470.

Finsinger, J., and I. Vogelsang. 1979. Regulatory adjustment process for optimal pricing by multiproduct monopoly firms. *Bell Journal of Economics* 10:157–171.

Finsinger, J., and I. Vogelsang. 1981. Alternative institutional framework for price-incentive mechanisms: Some comments. *Kyklos* 34:388–404.

Finsinger, J., and I. Vogelsang. 1982. Performance indices for public enterprise. In *Public Enterprise in Less-Developed Countries*, ed. L. P. Jones. Cambridge: Cambridge University Press.

20. Letting $\lambda_g > 1$ denote the government's transfer cost (to use Vogelsang's notation), Vogelsang suggests giving a subsidy

$$S_\tau = S_{\tau-1} + \left(\frac{q_{\tau-1}}{\lambda_g - 1}\right)(p_{\tau-1} - p_\tau)$$

to the firm (so that the firm's total income at date τ is $p_\tau q_\tau - C_\tau + S_\tau$). This formula differs from (2.36) in the coefficient of the price tax and in its autoregressive character.

Finsinger, J., and I. Vogelsang. 1985. Strategic management behavior under reward structures in a planned economy. *The Quarterly Journal of Economics* 100:263–270.

Gravelle, H. 1985. Reward structures in a planned economy: Some difficulties. *The Quarterly Journal of Economics* 100:271–278.

Guesnerie, R., and J. J. Laffont. 1978. Taxing price makers. *Journal of Economic Theory* 19:423–455.

Guesnerie, R., and J. J. Laffont. 1984. A complete solution to a class of principal-agent problems with an application to the control of a self-managed firm. *Journal of Public Economics* 25:329–369.

Joskow, P., and R. Schmalensee. 1986. Incentive regulation for electric utilities. *Yale Journal on Regulation* 4:1–49.

Lewis, T., and D. Sappington. 1988a. Regulating a monopolist with unknown demand. *American Economic Review* 78:986–998.

Lewis, T., and D. Sappington. 1988b. Regulating a monopolist with unknown demand and cost functions. *Rand Journal of Economics* 19:438–457.

Riordan, M. 1984. On delegating price authority to a regulated firm. *Rand Journal of Economics* 15:108–115.

Sappington, D. 1980. Strategic firm behavior under a dynamic regulatory adjustment process. *Bell Journal of Economics* 11:360–372.

Sappington, D. 1982. Optimal regulation of research and development under imperfect information. *Bell Journal of Economics* 13:354–368.

Schmalensee, R. 1989. Good regulatory regimes. *Rand Journal of Economics* 20:417–436.

Spulber, D. 1988. Bargaining and regulation with asymmetric information about demand and supply. *Journal of Economic Theory* 44:251–268.

Tam, M. 1981. Reward structures in a planned economy: The problem of incentives and efficient allocation of resources. *The Quarterly Journal of Economics* 96:111–128.

Vogelsang, I. 1990. Public enterprise in monopolistic and oligopolistic industries. In *Fundamentals of Pure and Applied Economics*, ed. J. Lesourne and H. Sonnenschein, London: Harwood.

Vogelsang, I. 1989. Two-part tariffs as regulatory constraints. *Journal of Public Economics* 39:45–66.

3 PRICING AND INCENTIVES IN A MULTIPRODUCT FIRM

3.1 Some Background

Most regulated firms and government contractors supply a range of products. Railroads offer freight and passenger services. Electric utilities generate power at different times of the day or seasons of the year, and for both residential and industrial customers. Similarly telephone companies serve residential consumers, small and big businesses, offer 800 services, and can transmit video signals or data. Government contractors often work on several public or private projects.

The multiproduct framework is also relevant when the firm supplies a single product with a variable and verifiable quality. For instance, contracts for weapons acquisition include provisions for delivery time and performance at the delivery date such as the speed or fuel efficiency of an airplane. Regulatory examples include attempts to tie railroads' rewards to the timeliness of trains,[1] the telephone industry's,[2] and the electricity industry's[3] experiments with quality incentives. Verifiable dimensions of quality can be treated as quantities of fictitious outputs and are thus amenable to the multiproduct analysis.

Not surprisingly over the last 20 years in several industries policy discussion has emphasized multiproduct issues in the regulation of natural monopolies. Take the move from cost-of-service regulation to price caps. This move has witnessed debates about whether it would promote incentives, reduce prices, remove "cross-subsidization," or influence the regulated firms' competitors. Concurrently the theory of multiproduct cost functions and sustainability of natural monopolies developed, culminating in the book by Baumol, Panzar, and Willig (1982). By and large this theoretical literature has ignored the regulators' informational environment.

There are two kinds of issues in the regulation of multiproduct firms: pricing and incentives. The main pricing issue is how to price discriminate, and how to price goods in the presence of competitors or when the firm's

1. See Baumol (1975).

2. Noam (1989) draws up a list of quality dimensions in the telephone industry that can be subject to regulatory incentives. Examples include dial-tone delay, call completion time, installation lag and repair service, operator response time, and directory assistance.

Another interesting example (communicated to us by John Vickers) is the 1988 contractual agreement between the British director general of telecommunications and British Telecom. British Telecom accepted contractual liability for fault repair and provision of new service, forcing it to compensate customers to a minimum extent of £5.00 per day if it is more than two days late in providing a line or if it takes more than two days to repair a fault (see the statement issued by the director general of telecommunications in July 1988 on "The Control of British Telecom's prices").

3. See the MIT Energy Laboratory's extensive report (1984) on programs, existing or under consideration at the time, for power companies. Those programs are designed to give incentives to increase the consumers' welfare (e.g., reduce the number of outages) or achieve other goals (encourage coal conversions, promote conservation of energy by the firm or by its customers). Contracts between electric utilities and independent cogenerators also include many quality dimensions, which we will discuss in chapter 14.

goods are substitutes or complements. There are three important incentive issues:

1. Should pricing be used to promote the firm's incentives, or should this job be left entirely to the cost-reimbursement rule?
2. How should one account for the firm's task allocation among its product lines or activities?
3. Should subcosts of some activities, if observable, be used in the incentive scheme, or should the firm face uniform incentive schemes across all activities?

This chapter extends the analysis of chapter 2 by considering a multiproduct firm with private information about its technology and exerting effort to reduce cost. The regulatory instruments are the firm's total cost and prices; in particular the regulator cannot fully distribute costs to particular products, except through an arbitrary accounting procedure. The regulator chooses an optimal regulatory policy subject to his or her informational gap.

Section 3.2 considers a general model and derives the optimal rate-of-return and price regulation. It derives the optimal cost-reimbursement rule and gives sufficient conditions for the optimal regulatory allocation to be implementable through a menu of linear contracts. Mainly it demonstrates that the regulated price of good k satisfies the equation

$$L_k = R_k + I_k,$$

where L_k is the Lerner index (price-cost margin), R_k is a Ramsey index, and I_k is the "incentive correction for good k."

In contrast with the Ramsey index obtained in the conventional cost-of-service regulation model,[4] our Ramsey index can be computed from publicly available data and requires no knowledge of the firm's cost function. Applications to linear pricing of several commodities, to second-degree price discrimination for a single commodity, and to the regulation of verifiable quality are given in sections 3.3 through 3.5. Applications to competitive environments will be given in chapter 5.

The incentive correction, if any, reflects the regulator's desire to limit the firm's rent without destroying incentives and, more specifically, depends on whether an increase in good k's price helps raise incentives. A fundamental theoretical question is whether the incentive and pricing issues can be disconnected ($I_k = 0$) or not ($I_k \neq 0$); that is, is the optimal rate-of-return regulation (which under some assumptions turns out to be linear in

4. The conventional cost-of-service regulation model imposes a somewhat ad hoc budget constraint for the regulated firm, as discussed in subsection 3.4 of the introductory chapter and in chapter 15.

the firm's performance) a sufficient instrument to promote incentives?[5] Using familiar techniques from the theory of aggregation, section 3.6 gives necessary and sufficient conditions for the dichotomy between incentives and pricing to hold in the case of a one-dimensional cost-reducing activity. Section 3.7 allows the firm to allocate its cost-reducing activity among the diverse (unobserved) components of the cost function, assuming one of two functional forms: the shared fixed-cost function in which the n goods share a joint cost and otherwise have individual subcost functions, and the shared variable-cost function in which a cost-reducing activity affects the marginal cost of producing each good, as is the case in the peak-load-pricing model. Section 3.7 also contains some technical conditions on when a multidimensional parameter space can be treated by the usual techniques developed for a one-dimensional parameter.

Section 3.8 introduces subcost observation. The firm is free to allocate its effort among activities. This "allocative arbitrage" may mean that the regulator cannot do better than when only total cost is observed. Section 3.8 develops the counterpart of the incentive-pricing dichotomy for subcosts; that is, it obtains sufficient conditions for the regulator not intervening in the efficient allocation of effort among activities.

Section 3.9 analyzes the validity of the partial equilibrium approach in a simple imperfect-income-taxation, general equilibrium model. It shows that the partial equilibrium approach yields the right qualitative Ramsey, incentive, and effort corrections. The partial and general equilibrium results coincide in the absence of redistributive concerns. In the presence of redistributive concerns the Ramsey term depends on the relative social weights of consumers in the social welfare function. In contrast, the incentive and effort corrections depend on the relative weights of the regulated firms' insiders and outsiders. Section 3.10 summarizes the major insights of the chapter.

Last, we cast our analysis in the context of the existence of government transfers. Our results carry over when the government is prohibited from transferring money to the firm. Rather than rederive all results in the latter context, we content ourselves with obtaining the characterization of the incentive-pricing dichotomy in the absence of government transfers in section 3.6.

3.2 Optimal Regulation

This section sets up the model of a multiproduct firm with a general cost function, derives the optimal regulatory policy, and obtains sufficient con-

5. Incentives and pricing were disconnected for the single-product technology assumed in chapter 2.

ditions under which it can be implemented through a menu of linear cost-reimbursement rules.

3.2.1 The Model

Consider a regulated firm with aggregate cost function

$$C = C(\beta, e, \mathbf{q}), \tag{3.1}$$

where

β is a technological parameter or firm's "type" ($C_\beta > 0$),[6]
e is its managers' cost-reducing effort ($C_e < 0$),
$\mathbf{q} \equiv (q_1, \ldots, q_n)$ is the firm's output vector ($C_{q_k} > 0$).

(Vectors are denoted by bold letters.)

The technological parameter β and the effort level e are one-dimensional. In sections 3.7 and 3.8 we show how the analysis applies when managers allocate their effort among product lines; there we also give conditions under which a multidimensional parameter space (with one parameter β_k per product line) can be reduced to our one-dimensional representation.

We let $E(\beta, C, \mathbf{q})$ denote the effort required for a firm of type β to produce $\mathbf{q}$ at cost C:

$$C \equiv C(\beta, E(\beta, C, \mathbf{q}), \mathbf{q}). \tag{3.2}$$

The partial derivatives of this effort function with respect to its arguments are denoted E_β, E_C, and E_{q_k} ($E_\beta > 0, E_C < 0, E_{q_k} > 0$).

As in chapter 2 we make the accounting convention that the revenue $R(\mathbf{q})$ (if any) generated by the sale of the outputs is received by the state and that the cost is reimbursed to the firm. Letting t denote the net monetary transfer from the regulator to the firm and $\psi(\cdot)$ denote the disutility of effort, the firm's objective function is

$$U = t - \psi(e). \tag{3.3}$$

The firm is willing to participate in the regulatory process if and only if $U \geq 0$.

Let $V(\mathbf{q})$ denote the social value associated with the production of vector $\mathbf{q}$. This value is assumed increasing and concave in $\mathbf{q}$. For example, if the goods are private goods, and if $S(\mathbf{q})$ denotes the gross consumer surplus attached to their consumption, then $V(\mathbf{q})$ is equal to the sum of net consumer surplus $\{S(\mathbf{q}) - R(\mathbf{q})\}$ and of the social value of tax savings for taxpayers generated by the sale of the goods, $(1 + \lambda)R(\mathbf{q})$ (where λ is the shadow cost of public funds). That is, $V(\mathbf{q}) = S(\mathbf{q}) + \lambda R(\mathbf{q})$. But we wish to

6. Subscripts other than those indexing goods (k, l) denote partial derivatives: $C_\beta \equiv \partial C / \partial \beta$.

apply optimal regulation formulas to other situations (e.g., the case of public goods or, as in chapter 5, the case of a regulated monopolist facing regulated or unregulated competition). To cover a wide spectrum of applications, we thus keep the function $V(\cdot)$ general.

The utilitarian social welfare function is the sum of consumer welfare and the firm's welfare:

$$W = [V(\mathbf{q}) - (1 + \lambda)(t + C(\beta, e, \mathbf{q}))] + U \tag{3.4}$$

or, using (3.3),

$$W = V(\mathbf{q}) - (1 + \lambda)(\psi(e) + C(\beta, e, \mathbf{q})) - \lambda U. \tag{3.5}$$

Equation (3.5) shows that W can be decomposed into three terms: the social value V of outputs, the total cost $\psi + C$ of operating the firm times the shadow price of this cost, and the social cost λU of leaving a rent to the firm.

The regulator observes the firm's cost C and quantities $\mathbf{q}$ [or equivalently, prices $\mathbf{p} \equiv (p_1, \ldots, p_n)$]. Unless otherwise stated, he or she regulates the firm's n outputs. The firm has private information about (knows) its technology parameter β, which from the regulator's viewpoint is drawn from a cumulative distribution $F(\cdot)$ on $[\underline{\beta}, \overline{\beta}]$ with density $f(\cdot)$. We make assumption 1.2 of chapter 1 that the hazard rate $f(\beta)/F(\beta)$ of the distribution is monotonic: $d(F/f)/d\beta \geq 0$ and the assumption that no type is shut down. The cost-reducing effort e is also unobservable by the regulator.

3.2.2 The Optimal Regulatory Allocation

The regulator maximizes the expectation over β of the social welfare function given by (3.5), over $\{\mathbf{q}(\beta), e(\beta), U(\beta)\}$ (which amounts to maximizing with respect to $\{\mathbf{q}(\beta), e(\beta), t(\beta)\}$):

$$E_\beta W = \int_{\underline{\beta}}^{\overline{\beta}} [V(\mathbf{q}) - (1 + \lambda)(\psi(e) + C(\beta, e, \mathbf{q})) - \lambda U] f(\beta) d\beta, \tag{3.6}$$

subject to the individual rationality and incentive constraints. Because the firm's rent is necessarily decreasing in β and because [from (3.5)], the regulator does not wish to leave rents to the firm, the individual rationality constraint can be written:

$$U(\overline{\beta}) = 0. \tag{3.7}$$

The derivation of the incentive constraint is standard (see chapter 1). An intuitive argument is as follows: A firm with type $\beta - d\beta$ ($d\beta > 0$) can produce the same output vector at the same cost as a firm with type β and therefore obtains the same revenue and transfer by reducing its effort relative to that of type β by $de = E_\beta(\beta, C(\beta, e, \mathbf{q}), \mathbf{q}) d\beta$. This implies that the gradient of the firm's rent with respect to β, $\dot{U}(\beta) \equiv dU/d\beta = -\psi'(e) de/d\beta$, is given by

$$\dot{U}(\beta) = -\psi'(e)E_\beta(\beta, C(\beta, e, \mathbf{q}), \mathbf{q}). \tag{3.8}$$

Equation (3.8) is the first-order condition of incentive compatibility for the firm; it gives the rate at which the firm's rent must grow to elicit its information.

Taking $e(\beta)$ and $\mathbf{q}(\beta)$ as control variables and $U(\beta)$ as a state variable, the regulator maximizes (3.6) subject to (3.7) and (3.8). Appendix A3.1 shows that under standard technological assumptions, $dC/d\beta \geq 0$ and $dq_k/d\beta \leq 0$ for all k are sufficient conditions for the firm's second-order conditions to be satisfied. Whether those conditions hold for the solution to the first-order conditions must be checked in each application of our model.

The optimal regulatory policy is derived in appendix A3.1. Here we content ourselves with its statement and intuition.

Proposition 3.1 The first-order conditions of the regulator's program with respect to effort e and output q_k are

$$\psi'(e) = -C_e - \frac{\lambda}{1+\lambda}\frac{F(\beta)}{f(\beta)}[\psi''(e)E_\beta + \psi'(e)E_{\beta C}C_e], \tag{3.9}$$

$$V_{q_k} = (1+\lambda)C_{q_k} + \lambda\frac{F(\beta)}{f(\beta)}\psi'(e)\frac{d}{dq_k}(E_\beta). \tag{3.10}$$

To understand equation (3.9), note that in a symmetric information (first-best) world the marginal disutility of effort $\psi'(e)$ should be equal to the marginal cost savings $(-C_e)$. The last term in equation (3.9) is due to the regulator's desire to extract the firm's informational rent. The term in brackets

$$A \equiv \psi''(e)E_\beta + \psi'(e)E_{\beta C}C_e$$

is the derivative with respect to e of $|\dot{U}(\beta)|$. A sufficient condition for A to be positive is that $C_{ee} \geq 0$ (there are decreasing returns in the cost reducing technology) and that $C_{\beta e} \geq 0$ (the marginal cost reduction is not higher for inefficient types). From equation (3.8), A is also the increase in the rent of all types in $[\underline{\beta}, \beta]$ [which have probability $F(\beta)$], when the effort of type β is increased by one. From equation (3.6), the social cost of the extra rent for the types in $[\underline{\beta}, \beta]$ is $\lambda F(\beta)A$. On the other hand, the distortion in effort for type β relative to the first-best level $[\psi'(e) + C_e]$ has social cost $(1+\lambda)(\psi'(e) + C_e)$ from equation (3.5) and occurs with probability $f(\beta)$. The trade-off between rent extraction and efficient effort thus yields equation (3.9). An implication of equation (3.9) that we develop below is that the regulator can use cost-reimbursement rules that are intermediate between the cost-plus contract [which induces $\psi'(e) = 0$] and the fixed-price contract [which induces $\psi'(e) = -C_e$].

Of particular interest for the subsequent analysis of this chapter is the "modified Ramsey equation" (3.10). Under symmetric information the marginal generalized gross surplus $\partial V/\partial q_k$ is equal to the marginal social cost of production $\partial((1 + \lambda)C)/\partial q_k$. Under asymmetric information there may exist an incentive correction associated with the regulator's desire to extract the firm's rent. From equation (3.8) a unit increase in output k affects the rent by $\psi'(e)[dE_\beta/dq_k]$, where

$$\frac{d}{dq_k}(E_\beta) = E_{\beta C}C_{q_k} + E_{\beta q_k} \tag{3.11}$$

is a total derivative and is a measure of how output k affects the potential effort savings associated with an increase in efficiency. As in equation (3.9) the gain in reducing $|\dot{U}|$ is proportional to the probability $F(\beta)$ that the firm is more efficient than type β, and the cost of the distortion relative to the first best is proportional to the probability $f(\beta)$ that the firm has type β, which explains equation (3.10).

When the incentive correction is equal to zero (see proposition 3.4 below for a necessary and sufficient condition), the incentive-pricing dichotomy holds as equation (3.10) determines pricing as a function of marginal costs independently of informational (control) problems.

3.2.3 Linearity of Cost-Reimbursement Rules

Linear cost (or profit-) sharing rules have the attractive property that they are still optimal under an additive cost disturbance or accounting error $[C \equiv C(\beta, e, \mathbf{q}) + \varepsilon]$ as long as the parties are risk neutral. One might wonder whether the optimal regulatory policy can be implemented through a menu of linear cost-reimbursement rules as in chapters 1 and 2. Strong assumptions are likely to be needed to get exact linearity. Finding the minimal such assumptions is a difficult task, and we content ourselves with stating a sufficient condition for a menu of linear contracts to be optimal.

Proposition 3.2 Assume that

i. $C(\beta, e, \mathbf{q}) = G(\beta - e)H(\mathbf{q})$, where $G' > 0$, $G'' > 0$, and the curvature of G is "not too high":

$$\max_\beta \left(\frac{G''}{G'}\right) \leq \min_\beta \left(\frac{d(F/f)/d\beta}{F/f}\right);$$

ii. $\psi''' \geq 0$;

iii. for all β,

$$\frac{d}{d\beta}G(\beta - e(\beta)) \geq 0 \quad \text{and} \quad \frac{d}{d\beta}q_k(\beta) \leq 0$$

where $\{e(\beta), \mathbf{q}(\beta)\}$ denote the solution to equations (3.9) and (3.10). Then the optimal regulatory policy can be implemented through a menu of linear contracts.

Assumption iii in proposition 3.2 is reasonable. For the optimal policy a firm with a higher β is likely to produce less ($dq_k/d\beta \leq 0$) and to have a higher $G(\beta - e(\beta))$. (It is easy to find sufficient conditions for these to hold.) Assumption ii is technical and is much stronger than necessary. It ensures that the optimal regulatory scheme is not stochastic. Assumption i is strong. The proof of proposition 3.2 can be found in appendix A3.2. Note that proposition 3.2 implies proposition 1.3.

In the next three sections we examine special cases of equation (3.10).

3.3 Third-Degree Price Discrimination

In this section we adapt the general formulas obtained above to two well-known cases of third-degree price discrimination. First, we consider the case of linear prices with a shadow cost of public funds $1 + \lambda$, which we call Ramsey pricing. We generalize the famous Ramsey-Boiteux pricing equations with the addition of an incentive correction due to asymmetric information. Similarly we then generalize the Boiteux-Steiner formulas of optimal peak-load pricing.

3.3.1 Ramsey Pricing

Suppose that the social value $V(\mathbf{q})$ is simply the consumers' gross surplus plus the social value of revenue, $S(\mathbf{q}) + \lambda R(\mathbf{q})$, and that linear pricing is used. Then the revenue function is $R(\mathbf{q}) = \sum_k p_k q_k = \sum_k S'_k(\mathbf{q}) q_k$, where $S'_k(\mathbf{q})$ is the partial derivative of S with respect to q_k. Let $q_k(\mathbf{p})$ be the demand functions [defined by $p_k = S'_k(\mathbf{q})$], and let $\eta_{kl} \equiv (\partial q_k/\partial p_l)(p_l/q_k)$ and $\eta_k \equiv -(\partial q_k/\partial p_k)(p_k/q_k) = -\eta_{kk}$ denote the cross and own elasticities of demand.

For this case equation (3.10) can be written

$$p_k + \lambda\left(p_k + \sum_l \frac{\partial p_l}{\partial q_k} q_l\right) - (1 + \lambda) C_{q_k} - \lambda \frac{F(\beta)}{f(\beta)} \psi'(e) \frac{d}{dq_k}(E_\beta) = 0, \quad (3.12)$$

or

$$L_k = R_k + I_k, \quad (3.13)$$

where

$$L_k \equiv \frac{p_k - C_{q_k}}{p_k} \quad \text{(good } k\text{'s Lerner index)}, \quad (3.14)$$

$$R_k \equiv -\frac{\lambda}{1 + \lambda}\left(\sum_l \frac{\partial p_l}{\partial q_k} \frac{q_l}{p_k}\right) \quad \text{(good } k\text{'s Ramsey index)}, \quad (3.15)$$

$$I_k \equiv \left[\frac{\lambda F(\beta)\psi'(e)}{(1+\lambda)f(\beta)p_k}\right]\frac{d}{dq_k}(E_\beta) \qquad \text{(good } k\text{'s incentive correction).} \tag{3.16}$$

Possibly up to the incentive correction, the pricing structure is determined by a familiar Ramsey formula. For instance, for independent demands,

$$R_k = \frac{\lambda}{1+\lambda}\frac{1}{\eta_k}.$$

As mentioned earlier, a difference with the traditional Ramsey formula is that the "Ramsey number" $\lambda/(1+\lambda)$ is determined economywide and in particular does not depend on the unknown technology, in contrast with the traditional cost-of-service theory of Ramsey, Boiteux, and Baumol-Bradford.[7]

There are other familiar expressions for the Ramsey index. We can, for instance, rewrite equation (3.10) by taking the derivatives of the social welfare function with respect to prices instead of quantities. This yields

$$(1+\lambda)\sum_{l=1}^{n}(p_l - C_{q_l})\frac{\partial q_l}{\partial p_k} + \lambda q_k - \lambda\frac{F(\beta)}{f(\beta)}\psi'(e)\left[\sum_{l=1}^{n}\left(\frac{d}{dq_l}(E_\beta)\right)\frac{\partial q_l}{\partial p_k}\right] = 0. \tag{3.17}$$

For instance, for $n = 2$, it can be shown that

$$R_k = \frac{\lambda}{1+\lambda}\frac{1}{\hat{\eta}_k}, \qquad k = 1, 2,$$

where

$$\hat{\eta}_1 \equiv \eta_1\left[\frac{1-(\eta_{12}\eta_{21}/\eta_1\eta_2)}{1+(p_2q_2/p_1q_1)(\eta_{21}/\eta_2)}\right]$$

and symmetrically for $\hat{\eta}_2$. The "superelasticities" $\hat{\eta}_k$ were first derived by Boiteux (1956) (see Brown and Sibley 1985 for a general exposition and chapter 5 for examples of analytical derivations of such formulas). Thus with substitutes ($\eta_{kl} > 0$ for $k \neq l$) the price of good k should be adjusted upward to account for the fact that such an increase raises the revenue received on good $l \neq k$.

3.3.2 Peak-Load Pricing

The above Ramsey analysis emphasized demand interdependencies among products. Another famous third-degree price-discrimination paradigm—the peak-load model—emphasizes cost interdependencies.

Consider a simple peak-load pricing problem with independent demands in which the peak demand function is $q_2 = D_2(p_2)$ and the off-peak

7. See subsection 3.4 of the introductory chapter.

demand function is $q_1 = D_1(p_1)$; let $C(\beta, e, q_1, q_2)$ denote the cost function. We obtain a generalization of the formula of Boiteux (1949) and Steiner (1957):

$$\frac{p_1 - (\partial C/\partial q_1)}{p_1} = \frac{\lambda}{1+\lambda}\frac{1}{\eta_1} + I_1,$$

$$\frac{p_2 - (\partial C/\partial q_2)}{p_2} = \frac{\lambda}{1+\lambda}\frac{1}{\eta_2} + I_2,$$

where

$$I_k = \frac{\lambda}{1+\lambda}\frac{F(\beta)\psi'(e)}{f(\beta)p_k}\frac{d}{dq_k}\left(-\frac{\partial C/\partial \beta}{\partial C/\partial e}\right), \qquad k = 1, 2.$$

Let us consider two special cases in which we assume that off-peak demand is strictly lower than capacity at the optimal policy:[8] unknown capacity cost function and known marginal cost, on the one hand, and unknown variable cost and known constant capacity cost, on the other.

Unknown Capacity Cost Function and Known Marginal Cost
Let

$$C(\beta, e, q_1, q_2) = c(q_1 + q_2) + G(\beta, e, q_2).$$

Then

$$\frac{p_1 - c}{p_1} = \frac{\lambda}{1+\lambda}\frac{1}{\eta_1},$$

$$\frac{p_2 - c - (\partial G/\partial q_2)}{p_2} = \frac{\lambda}{1+\lambda}\frac{1}{\eta_2} + \frac{\lambda}{1+\lambda}\frac{F(\beta)}{f(\beta)}\frac{\psi'(e)}{p_2}\frac{d}{dq_2}\left(-\frac{\partial G/\partial \beta}{\partial G/\partial e}\right).$$

The incentive-pricing dichotomy here always holds for the off-peak good. It holds for the peak good if and only if $G(\beta, e, q_2) \equiv G(\zeta(\beta, e), q_2)$, as we show in proposition 3.4.

Unknown Variable Cost and Known Constant Capacity Cost
Let

$$C(\beta, e, q_1, q_2) = v(\beta, e, q_1 + q_2) + dq_2.$$

Then the (generalized) Boiteux-Steiner formula holds for both peak- and off-peak demands:

$$\frac{p_1 - (\partial v/\partial Q)}{p_1} = \frac{\lambda}{1+\lambda}\frac{1}{\eta_1} + I_1.$$

8. That is, we abstract from the "shifting peak" problem. Our analysis can be straightforwardly extended to shifting peaks as well as to interdependent demands. See subsection 3.2 of the introductory chapter.

$$\frac{p_2 - [(\partial v/\partial Q) + d]}{p_2} = \frac{\lambda}{1+\lambda}\frac{1}{\eta_2} + I_2,$$

where $\partial v/\partial Q$ is the marginal variable cost, $Q \equiv q_1 + q_2$, and

$$I_k = \frac{\lambda}{1+\lambda}\frac{F(\beta)\psi'(e)}{f(\beta)p_k}\frac{d}{dQ}\left(-\frac{\partial v/\partial \beta}{\partial v/\partial e}\right).$$

These two examples show that in contrast with cost-of-service regulation (Bailey 1973), which induces the firm to distort the pricing rule toward low peak prices (because such prices raise the demand for capacity, a familiar Averch-Johnson excess accumulation of capital), the distortions here depend on the ability of price distortions to help reduce the rents associated with asymmetric information.

3.4 Second-Degree Price Discrimination

Let us now assume that the regulated firm produces a single physical good and practices nonlinear pricing. To see why we can apply the general multiproduct framework to this situation, consider two types of consumers, $k = 1, 2$. Consumers of type k, who are in proportion α_k (such that $\alpha_1 + \alpha_2 = 1$), have gross surplus function $S_k(q_k)$, with $S_k(0) = 0$ and $S_2' > S_1'$ (where $S_k' = dS_k/dq_k$). Consumers of type 2 are thus the "high-demand consumers." The consumers' gross surplus function is then

$$S(\mathbf{q}) = \alpha_1 S_1(q_1) + \alpha_2 S_2(q_2).$$

The cost function can be written $C(\beta, e, Q)$, where $Q \equiv \alpha_1 q_1 + \alpha_2 q_2$ is total output. We analyze fully nonlinear price in subsection 3.4.1 and two-part pricing in subsection 3.4.2.

3.4.1 Fully Nonlinear Pricing

Let $\{T_1, q_1\}$ and $\{T_2, q_2\}$ denote the payment-quantity pairs for the two types of consumers. Incentive compatibility requires that high-demand consumers do not pretend they have low demand:

$$S_2(q_2) - T_2 \geq S_2(q_1) - T_1. \tag{3.18}$$

Furthermore we assume that even the low-demand consumers consume the good:[9]

$$S_1(q_1) - T_1 \geq 0. \tag{3.19}$$

Since public funds are costly, inequalities (3.18) and (3.19) are binding. The revenue function can then be written

9. By a familiar reasoning, the other incentive compatibility and individual rationality constraints are not binding.

$$R(\mathbf{q}) = \alpha_1 T_1 + \alpha_2 T_2 = S_1(q_1) + \alpha_2(S_2(q_2) - S_2(q_1)). \tag{3.20}$$

Letting $p_k \equiv S_k'(q_k)$, we can now apply equation (3.10):

$$\alpha_1 p_1 + \lambda[p_1 - \alpha_2 S_2'(q_1)] = \alpha_1(1+\lambda)C_Q + \tilde{I} \tag{3.21}$$

and

$$\alpha_2 p_2 + \lambda \alpha_2 p_2 = \alpha_2(1+\lambda)C_Q + \tilde{I}, \tag{3.22}$$

where $\tilde{I} \equiv [\lambda F(\beta)\psi'(e)/f(\beta)](dE_\beta/dQ)$ is the *common* incentive correction. The Ramsey indices $R_k \equiv (p_k - C_Q)/p_k$ for the two types of consumers are therefore given by

$$R_1 = \frac{\alpha_2}{\alpha_1}\frac{\lambda}{1+\lambda}\left[\frac{S_2'(q_1) - S_1'(q_1)}{S_1'(q_1)}\right] > 0, \tag{3.23}$$

$$R_2 = 0. \tag{3.24}$$

In words, we obtain the familiar result that high consumption should not be distorted, and that low consumption is lower than the one when the firm has perfect information about preferences. The shadow cost of public funds induces the regulated firm to behave somewhat like a monopolist and to distort the consumption vector.

There are several interesting extensions of the general approach. For instance, chapter 6 allows for outside competition in this second-degree price discrimination model. The possibility of bypass in general puts other constraints on the above maximization problem (e.g., high-demand consumers of long-distance services can build their own access to the long-distance carriers and bypass the local exchanges).

3.4.2 Two-Part Tariffs

We next restrict attention to combinations of a fixed fee and a marginal price: $T(q) = A + pq$. Let $S_i(p)$ and $S_i^n(p)$ denote the gross and net surpluses of consumers of type i for marginal price p $[dS_i/dp = pD_i'(p), dS_i^n/dp = -D_i(p)]$. For a given marginal price p the fixed fee is optimally chosen equal to the low-demand consumers' net surplus: $A = S_1^n(p)$. Thus the firm's revenue is

$$R(p) = S_1^n(p) + pD(p),$$

where $D(p) \equiv \alpha_1 D_1(p) + \alpha_2 D_2(p)$ is total demand at price p. It is easily checked that the Ramsey index is given by

$$R = \left(\frac{\lambda}{1+\lambda}\frac{1}{\eta}\right)\left[\frac{\alpha_2(D_2 - D_1)}{\alpha_1 D_1 + \alpha_2 D_2}\right], \tag{3.25}$$

where η is the elasticity of total demand; $\eta \equiv -(dD/dp)/(D/p)$. In the absence of incentive correction, the marginal price should lie between marginal cost and the optimal linear price, which satisfies $L = (\lambda/(1+\lambda))(1/\eta)$. Its location between these two values depends on the relative demands of the two types of consumers.

3.5 Verifiable Quality

As mentioned in section 3.1, there are dimensions of quality that can be specified in a contract and enforced. Such verifiable dimensions of quality can be treated as outputs of fictitious goods, and they therefore are subject to the analysis of this section. That the good "quality" does not have a standard demand curve is not a problem, since formulas (3.9) and (3.10) are derived for general social value and revenue functions. In this subsection we give two examples of application of these formulas; the issue of unverifiable quality is tackled in chapter 4.

3.5.1 A Procurement Example

Suppose that a contractor produces q units of a single dimensional output of quality s at cost $C(\beta, e, q, s)$. This situation is formally equivalent to the case of a two-dimensional output ($q_1 = q, q_2 = s$). In a procurement context $R(q,s) = 0$. Let $S(q,s)$ denote the government's surplus, with partial derivatives S_q and S_s. Applying equation (3.10) yields

$$S_q = (1+\lambda)C_q + \lambda\frac{F(\beta)}{f(\beta)}\psi'(e)\frac{\partial}{\partial q}\left(-\frac{C_\beta}{C_e}\right) \tag{3.26}$$

and

$$S_s = (1+\lambda)C_s + \lambda\frac{F(\beta)}{f(\beta)}\psi'(e)\frac{\partial}{\partial s}\left(-\frac{C_\beta}{C_e}\right). \tag{3.27}$$

In particular, when the incentive-pricing dichotomy holds [$C = C(\zeta(\beta, e), q, s)$; see proposition 3.4 below], the marginal benefits of output and quality are equal to their social marginal costs.

3.5.2 A Regulation Example

As in subsection 3.5.1 consider one-dimensional output q and quality s, yielding a social surplus $S(q,s)$ and produced at cost $C(\beta, e, q, s)$. However, unlike in subsection 3.5.1, assume that the good is sold to consumers and is subject to arbitrage among them. The revenue function is then $R(q,s) = P(q,s)q$, where $P(q,s) = S_q(q,s)$ is the inverse demand function. Assuming that the incentive-pricing dichotomy holds [the incentive corrections, if any, are the same as in equations (3.26) and (3.27)], equation (3.10) yields

$$\frac{p - C_q}{p} = \frac{\lambda}{1+\lambda}\frac{1}{\eta} \tag{3.28}$$

and

$$S_s + \lambda P_s q = (1 + \lambda)C_s, \tag{3.29}$$

where η is the price elasticity of demand.

Equation (3.28) is the classic "Lerner index equal to Ramsey index" equation. Of more interest is equation (3.29), which states that at the optimum the marginal surplus of quality (S_s) exceeds the marginal cost of quality (C_s) if and only if the average consumer values marginal increases in quality more than the marginal consumer does ($S_s/q > P_s$).[10]

3.6 The Incentive-Pricing Dichotomy

3.6.1 Necessary and Sufficient Conditions

Equation (3.10) yields a simple conclusion: Incentives and pricing of good k are disconnected if and only if $d(E_\beta)/dq_k = 0$. In this case the regulator uses only the cost-reimbursement rule [implicit in equation (3.9)] to extract the firm's rent while preserving incentives. If $d(E_\beta)/dq_k > 0$ (resp., <0), the price of good k exceeds (resp., is lower than) its symmetric information level, ceteris paribus. Proposition 3.3 below states that the incentive correction favors a high price (a low quantity) for good k if an increase in the output k increases the marginal rate of transformation between effort and efficiency in the cost function, that is, if this increase in output makes it easier for the firm to transform exogenous cost changes into rent.

Proposition 3.3 Ceteris paribus, the price of good k exceeds its symmetric information level if and only if

$$\frac{\partial}{\partial q_k}\left(-\frac{C_\beta}{C_e}\right) > 0.$$

Proof Differentiating equation (3.2) with respect to β yields

$$0 = C_\beta + C_e E_\beta.$$

Hence

$$\frac{d}{dq_k}(E_\beta) = \frac{\partial}{\partial q_k}\left(-\frac{C_\beta}{C_e}\right).$$

Substituting into equation (3.10) shows that $[V_{q_k} - (1 + \lambda)C_{q_k}]$ is positive if and only if

$$\frac{\partial}{\partial q_k}\left(-\frac{C_\beta}{C_e}\right) > 0. \qquad \blacksquare$$

10. See Tirole (1988, sec. 2.2.1) for a discussion of when the average consumer values quality more than the marginal consumer.

As mentioned earlier, a central issue is whether pricing should be used to promote incentives (or to extract the firm's rent). Leontief's (1947) well-known aggregation theorem and proposition 3.3 yield the next proposition.

Proposition 3.4 The incentive-pricing dichotomy $[d(E_\beta)/dq_k = 0$ for all $k]$ holds if and only if there exists a function ζ such that

$$C = C(\zeta(\beta, e), \mathbf{q}). \tag{3.30}$$

Proposition 3.4 is both important and straightforward. If efficiency and effort can be aggregated in the cost function, changing q_k does not affect the extent to which the firm can convert exogenous productivity increases into rent, which is entirely determined by the ζ function. Proposition 3.4 holds in particular for the single-product technology assumed in chapter 2, namely $C = (\beta - e)q$. This is the reason why optimal pricing was simply Ramsey pricing in chapter 2.

Corollary If the cost function is separable in the sense of (3.30), the firm can be rewarded as a function of the realization ζ of $\zeta(\beta, e)$ only: $t = T(\zeta)$.

The corollary results from the facts that the firm's utility depends on the net transfer and the disutility of effort and that the firm's effort depends on its type and on ζ only. A trivial application of the corollary is to the single-product technology of chapter 2. There $\zeta = C/q$, and therefore it suffices to reward the firm as a function of average cost only. We will later give more interesting applications.

When the incentive-pricing dichotomy does not hold, it is interesting to know whether the incentive corrections have the same signs for all goods. A sufficient condition for this is given in proposition 3.5.

Proposition 3.5 Suppose that there exists a function $\Gamma(q_1, \ldots, q_n)$ such that

$$C = C(\beta, e, \Gamma(\mathbf{q})). \tag{3.31}$$

Then the incentive correction has the same sign for all goods.

Proof For the functional form (3.31),

$$\frac{\partial}{\partial q_k}\left(-\frac{C_\beta}{C_e}\right) = \left[\frac{\partial}{\partial \Gamma}\left(-\frac{C_\beta}{C_e}\right)\right]\Gamma_{q_k}. \tag{3.32}$$

Proposition 3.5 follows from the fact that all the Γ_{q_k} have the same (positive) sign. ■

An example in which proposition 3.5 applies is the case of second-degree price discrimination (see section 3.4). Then there is only one good produced, and the vector $\mathbf{q}$ is the vector of quantities of the good consumed by the various types of consumers.

3.6.2 Example of Nondichotomy

Consider the procurement of satellites for which cost C and delay d in production are the crucial dimensions of performance. Let $V(d)$ denote the social value of delay, with $V_d < 0$. Delay and cost are related by

$$d = \beta - r(e, C),$$

with $r_e > 0$ (where e is the attention or effort devoted to reducing delay), $r_C > 0$ (by buying inputs or sacrificing cost-reducing activities, one reduces delay), $r_{ee} < 0$, $r_{CC} < 0$, $r_{eC} < 0$ (effort and cost are substitutes to produce delay reductions).

Here we have

$$E_\beta(\beta, C(\beta, e, d), d) = \frac{1}{r_e(e, C(\beta, e, d))},$$

so

$$\frac{d(E_\beta)}{dd} = \left[-\frac{r_{eC}}{(r_e)^2}\right]C_d = \frac{r_{eC}}{r_e^2 r_C}.$$

From (3.10) we get

$$V_d = (1+\lambda)\left(-\frac{1}{r_C}\right) + \lambda\frac{F}{f}\psi'(e)\left(\frac{r_{eC}}{r_e^2 r_C}\right).$$

From (3.9) we have

$$\psi'(e) = \frac{r_e}{r_C} - \frac{\lambda}{1+\lambda}\frac{F}{f}\left[\frac{\psi''}{r_e} + \psi'\left(\frac{r_{eC}}{r_C r_e}\right)\right].$$

The dichotomy obtains when $r_{eC} = 0$. Then only the cost-reimbursement rule is used to decrease rents by reducing effort. When cost and effort become substitutes in reducing delays, higher delays become an instrument to decrease the rent by decreasing the rate at which the firm can substitute effort for lies in β (see the expression for dE_β/dd). Furthermore, since effort and cost are substitutes, higher delays, which imply lower costs, call for more effort. This is achieved by giving more incentives for effort through the cost-reimbursement rule. On the contrary, if effort and cost are complements in reducing delays ($r_{eC} > 0$), lower delays help reduce rents. Lower delays call for less effort.

3.6.3 The Incentive-Pricing Dichotomy in the Absence of Government Transfer

We now extend the results of subsection 3.6.1 to the case in which the government is prohibited from transferring money to the firm. The analysis parallels that of sections 2.6 and 2.7 and is only sketched here. Using $t(\beta) \equiv \psi(e(\beta)) + U(\beta)$, and letting $S(q_1, \ldots, q_n)$ and $R(q_1, \ldots, q_n)$ denote the consumer's gross surplus and the firm's revenue, the regulator solves

$$\max \int_{\underline{\beta}}^{\bar{\beta}} [S(q_1,\ldots,q_n) - R(q_1,\ldots,q_n) + U]f(\beta)d\beta$$

subject to

$$R(q_1,\ldots,q_n) - C(\beta, e, q_1,\ldots,q_n) = \psi(e) + U,$$

$$\dot{U} = -\psi'(e)E_\beta,$$

$$U(\bar{\beta}) = 0.$$

Let $(1 + \tilde{\lambda}(\beta))f(\beta)$ denote the multiplier of the budget constraint and $\mu(\beta)$ denote that of the incentive constraint; the first-order condition with respect to q_k is

$$\frac{\partial S}{\partial q_k} = (1 + \tilde{\lambda})\frac{\partial C}{\partial q_k} - \tilde{\lambda}\frac{\partial R}{\partial q_k} + \frac{\mu}{f}\psi'(e)\frac{d}{dq_k}(E_\beta). \qquad (3.10')$$

Since $\mu(\beta) \neq 0$ if the budget constraint is binding,[11] the incentive-pricing dichotomy holds if and only if $(dE_\beta/dq_k) = 0$ for all k.

Proposition 3.4′ In the absence of government transfer to the firm, the incentive-pricing dichotomy holds if and only if there exists a function ζ such that

$$C = C(\zeta(\beta, e), \mathbf{q}).$$

For instance, under this separable cost function, for marketed goods $(\partial S/\partial q_k = p_k$ and $R(\mathbf{q}) = \sum_{k=1}^n p_k q_k)$ and independent demands,

$$\frac{L_k}{L_l} = \frac{\eta_l}{\eta_k} \qquad \text{for all } (k, l).$$

Similarly proposition 3.5 and the other results of this chapter can be extended to the absence of government transfer.

3.7 Multidimensional Effort and Characteristics

3.7.1 Effort Allocation: The Shared-Fixed-Cost Model

In this section we make more specific assumptions about the cost function. Our first paradigm is that of a joint fixed cost shared by several product lines, along with a variable cost for each product line (this paradigm might depict the case of switches used for several telecommunications services):

11. $\mu(\underline{\beta}) = 0$ and $\dot{\mu}(\beta) = \tilde{\lambda}(\beta)f(\beta) > 0$ if the budget constraint is binding. Thus $\mu(\beta) > 0$ except at $\beta = \underline{\beta}$.

$$C = \mathscr{C}(\beta, e_0, \ldots, e_n, \mathbf{q}) = \sum_{k=1}^{n} C^k(\beta, e_k, q_k) + C^0(\beta, e_0). \tag{3.33}$$

In (3.33), C^k is the subcost or variable cost of good k. C^0 is the fixed cost. The fixed cost and the subcosts cannot be disentangled from accounting data (an often reasonable assumption), so only the total cost C can be contracted on. The firm's managers allocate their cost-reducing activity e among the product lines and the joint activity

$$e = \sum_{k=0}^{n} e_k \tag{3.34}$$

so as to minimize $\mathscr{C}$ (this behavior is optimal as long as regulation is based on total cost):

$$C(\beta, e, \mathbf{q}) = \min_{\{e_0, \ldots, e_n\}} \mathscr{C}(\beta, e_0, \ldots, e_n, \mathbf{q}), \tag{3.35}$$

subject to (3.34).

Let $\{e_l^*(\beta, e, \mathbf{q})\}_{l=0}^{n}$ denote the solution to (3.35). The goal of this subsection is to obtain the analogues of propositions 3.4 and 3.5 for this model. That is, we look for conditions on the subcost and joint cost functions so that the dichotomy holds or at least that all incentive corrections have the same sign when the firm allocates its cost reducing activity.

Proposition 3.6 Assume an interior solution to program (3.35). The incentive-pricing dichotomy holds in the shared-fixed-cost model if and only if[12]

$$\sum_{l=0}^{n} \frac{\partial}{\partial e_l}\left(\frac{C_\beta^l}{C_{e_l}^l}\right)\frac{\partial e_l^*}{\partial q_k} + \frac{\partial}{\partial q_k}\left(\frac{C_\beta^k}{C_{e_k}^k}\right) = 0 \qquad \text{for all } k. \tag{3.36}$$

Proof From proposition 3.4, a necessary and sufficient condition for the dichotomy to hold is that $\partial(C_\beta/C_e)/\partial q_k = 0$ for all k. We have

$$C_\beta = \sum_{k=0}^{n} \left(C_\beta^k + C_{e_k}^k \frac{\partial e_k^*}{\partial \beta}\right).$$

Furthermore program (3.35) implies that

$$C_e = C_{e_k}^k \qquad \text{for all } k.$$

Hence

$$C_\beta = \sum_{k=0}^{n} C_\beta^k,$$

12. $\partial e_l^*/\partial q_k$, the change in effort $e_l^*(\beta, e, \mathbf{q})$ resulting from a unit increase in output k, is obtained by totally differentiating the $n+1$ equation system $\{C_{e_l}^l = C_{e_k}^k$ for all l in $\{0, \ldots, k-1, k+1, \ldots, n\}$ and $\sum_{l=0}^{n} e_l = e\}$ with respect to q_k.

using $\sum_k (\partial e_k^* / \partial \beta) = 0$. This implies that

$$\frac{C_\beta}{C_e} = \sum_{k=0}^{n} \left(\frac{C_\beta^k}{C_{e_k}^k} \right).$$

Hence C_β / C_e is independent of outputs if and only if (3.36) holds. ■

Example Adopting the convention that $q_0 \equiv 1$, the following functional form

$$C^k(\beta, e_k, q_k) = [\exp(-\mu_k e_k)] r^k(\beta) z^k(q_k) \qquad \text{for } k = 0, 1, \ldots, n \qquad (3.37)$$

satisfies (3.36) because $C_\beta^k / C_{e_k}^k$ depends only on β. Hence for the cost function described by (3.37), the incentive-pricing dichotomy holds. An example of a functional form for which $C_\beta^k / C_{e_k}^k$ is constant, and thus for which the dichotomy holds, is

$$C^k(\beta, e_k, q_k) = (\beta - a_k e_k)^b z^k(q_k) \qquad \text{for } k = 0, 1, \ldots, n.$$

Remark A difference between the fixed effort allocation model (which can be thought of as allocating effort in fixed proportions among the product lines and joint cost) and this flexible effort allocation model is that *the regulator may lose some power to extract rent through price distortions when the firm can allocate effort among product lines.* For example, assume that $n = 1$ and that

$$C = [\exp(-\alpha_1 e)] r^1(\beta) z^1(q_1) + [\exp(-\alpha_0 e)] r^0(\beta), \qquad (3.38)$$

with $\alpha_0 + \alpha_1 = 1$ (so $e_0 = \alpha_0 e$ and $e_1 = \alpha_1 e$, where α_0 and α_1 are positive and predetermined). (This technology can be viewed as a two-product cost function in which one of the "products"—with associated subcost the fixed cost—is produced in quantity one.) From proposition 3.4, the dichotomy always fails for the cost function described in (3.38). However, from proposition 3.6, it holds for the analogous cost function with flexible effort allocation:

$$C = [\exp(-e_1)] r^1(\beta) z^1(q_1) + [\exp(-e_0)] r^0(\beta). \qquad (3.37')$$

To understand why this is so, suppose, for instance, that $r^0(\beta) = r^0$ [β might then be the quality or price of an input and $\exp(-e_1)$ a measure of the efficiency of the transformation of the input into the output]. The incentive correction for (3.38) (whose sign is given in proposition 3.3) consists in lowering q_1 relative to the symmetric information case. This reduces $|(de/d\beta)|_{q \text{ and } C \text{ constant}}$ and thus the firm's rent. In contrast, for the technology described by (3.37′), the firm can lower e_1 without lowering e_0 when β decreases (and is indifferent to doing so at the margin), so marginal changes in q_1 do not affect the slope of the rent function.

More generally, when do all incentive corrections have the same sign in the shared-fixed-cost model? From proposition 3.5 a sufficient condition for this is that there exist a function Γ such that the solution to (3.35) can be written $C = C(\beta, e, \Gamma(\mathbf{q}))$.

Formally the existence of such a Γ is equivalent to the possibility of partially aggregating capital goods in the production function of a firm that allocates labor optimally to capitals of different vintages. (The outputs q_k correspond to the vintages of aggregated capital $K_{1,k}$, the efforts e_k correspond to the labor inputs L_k allocated to machines of vintage k, $\beta_k = \beta$ is the analogue of a vintage specific capital $K_{2,k}$ that is not aggregated.) The necessary and sufficient condition for the partial aggregation of capital goods was developed by Fisher (1965).[13] Applied to our context, theorem 5.1 in Fisher (1965) yields proposition 3.7.

Proposition 3.7 The necessary and sufficient conditions for the indirect cost function obtained in (3.35) to have the form $C(\beta, e, \Gamma(\mathbf{q}))$ are that

$$\frac{\partial^2 C^k}{\partial q_k \partial \beta} - \frac{(\partial^2 C^k/\partial q_k \partial e_k)(\partial^2 C^k/\partial e_k \partial \beta)}{\partial^2 C^k/\partial e_k^2} = 0 \qquad \text{for all } k \text{ in } \{1,\ldots,n\}, \tag{3.39}$$

and that there exists a function $g(\cdot)$ such that

$$\frac{(\partial C^k/\partial q_k)(\partial^2 C^k/\partial e_k^2)}{\partial^2 C^k/\partial e_k \partial q_k} = g\left(\frac{\partial C^k}{\partial e_k}\right) \qquad \text{for all } k \text{ in } \{1,\ldots,n\}. \tag{3.40}$$

Hence, if (3.39) and (3.40) hold, all incentive corrections have the same sign.

Example The conditions stated in proposition 3.7 are obviously very strong, but they allow us, for instance, to find classes of cost functions such that all incentive corrections have the same sign. Suppose that the subcost functions have the following multiplicative form:

$$C^k = r^k(\beta) s^k(e_k, q_k) \qquad \text{for all } k \text{ in } \{1,\ldots,n\}. \tag{3.41}$$

The reader can check that conditions (3.39) and (3.40) hold if and only if

$$\frac{\partial}{\partial e_k}\left(\frac{\partial s^k/\partial q_k}{\partial s^k/\partial e_k}\right) = 0 \qquad \text{for all } k \text{ in } \{1,\ldots,n\}$$

[e.g., as is the case if $s^k(e_k, q_k) = z^k(q_k)\exp(-\mu_k e_k)$].

3.7.2 Multidimensional Type

The same techniques of partial aggregation of capital goods can be applied to the question of when a vector of cost parameters can be reduced to a one-dimensional cost parameter. To this purpose, it suffices to reverse the roles of the exogenous cost parameters and quantities in proposition 3.7. More specifically suppose that each product line is affected by a

13. See also Gorman (1968). More general results have been developed by Blackorby and Schworm (1984, 1988).

specific cost parameter:

$$C = C(\beta_0, \ldots, \beta_n, e, \mathbf{q}) = \min_{\{e_0, \ldots, e_n\}} \left[\sum_{k=1}^{n} C^k(\beta_k, e_k, q_k) + C^0(\beta_0, e_0) \right] \quad (3.42)$$

subject to

$$\sum_{k=0}^{n} e_k \leq e.$$

The set of technological parameters $(\beta_0, \ldots, \beta_n)$ is now $(n + 1)$-dimensional. We allow the joint distribution over $(\beta_0, \ldots, \beta_n)$ to be arbitrary. The manager knows all parameters, while the regulator knows none.

The validity of the single-parameter representation in this case depends on the possibility of partially aggregating technological parameters in the cost function. Suppose that there is a function $\Lambda(\cdot)$ satisfying

$$C(\beta_0, \ldots, \beta_n, e, \mathbf{q}) = C(\Lambda(\beta_0, \ldots, \beta_n), e, \mathbf{q}). \quad (3.43)$$

We define $\beta \equiv \Lambda(\beta_0, \ldots, \beta_n)$. The distribution over β results from the joint distribution over $(\beta_0, \ldots, \beta_n)$. All the results obtained so far in the one-dimensional case can then be applied as long as the distribution of β satisfies the monotone-hazard-rate property: $d(F(\beta)/f(\beta))/d\beta > 0$.

Thus Fisher's (1965) theorem 5.1 also yields proposition 3.8.

Proposition 3.8 Assuming an interior solution to (3.42), necessary conditions for the cost function thus obtained to have the form $C(\Lambda(\beta_0, \ldots, \beta_n), e, \mathbf{q})$ are that

$$\frac{\partial^2 C^k}{\partial q_k \partial \beta_k} \frac{\partial^2 C^k}{\partial e_k^2} = \frac{\partial^2 C^k}{\partial q_k \partial e_k} \frac{\partial^2 C^k}{\partial e_k \partial \beta_k} \quad \text{for all } k \text{ in } \{1, \ldots, n\}. \quad (3.44)$$

and that there exists a function $h(\cdot)$ such that

$$\frac{(\partial C^k/\partial \beta_k)(\partial^2 C^k/\partial e_k^2)}{\partial^2 C^k/\partial e_k \partial \beta_k} = h\left(\frac{\partial C^k}{\partial e_k}\right) \quad \text{for all } k \text{ in } \{0, \ldots, n\}. \quad (3.45)$$

Example The subcost functions

$$C^k(\beta_k, e_k, q_k) = (\beta_k - e_k)^{\alpha_k} z^k(q_k), \quad (3.46)$$

with $\alpha_k > 1$ and z^k increasing, satisfy the conditions of proposition 3.8 [if an interior solution to (3.42) prevails] so that the technological parameters can be aggregated into a one-dimensional parameter.

A further aggregation result for types can be obtained by using theorem 3 of Blackorby and Schworm (1984).[14]

Proposition 3.9 Suppose that $C = min_{\{e_0, \ldots, e_n\}} \{\sum_{k=0}^{n} C^k(\beta_k, e_k, q_k)\}$ and that

14. We are grateful to Charles Blackorby for pointing this out to us.

$$C^k = \min_{\{e_k^M, e_k^N\}} \{M(B^k(\beta_k), e_k^M, q_k) + N^k(e_k^N, q_k) | e_k^M + e_k^N = e_k\},$$

where M is linearly homogeneous in its first two arguments and is independent of k. Then total cost can be written

$$C(\beta, e, \mathbf{q}) = \min_{\{e^M, e^N\}} \{M(B(\beta), e^M, \mathbf{q}) + N(e^N, \mathbf{q}) | e^M + e^N = e\},$$

where

$$B(\beta) = \sum_{k=0}^{n} B^k(\beta_k),$$

$$e^M = \sum_{k=0}^{n} e_k^M,$$

$$e^N = \sum_{k=0}^{n} e_k^N.$$

3.7.3 Effort Allocation: The Shared-Marginal-Cost Model

In several regulated industries the same physical good is sold at different points of time (or in different geographical areas). A reduction in the marginal cost of producing one good (e.g., where a good is the physical good indexed by time) cannot be separated from a reduction in the marginal cost of producing other goods, in contrast with the technology considered in subsection 3.7.1.

Consider an electric utility facing time-varying demand for electricity. During a fraction $x_k \in (0, 1)$ of the time, the demand for electricity is q_k (which depends on the prices charged at different points of time). We have $\sum_{k=1}^{n} x_k = 1$. Without loss of generality let us assume that $q_1 < \cdots < q_n$ (so n denotes the peak period). The firm installs capacity for each incremental output $(q_k - q_{k-1})$: q_1 units of base capacity, $q_2 - q_1$ units to supplement the base capacity in period 2, and so on. Let us set $q_0 \equiv 0$. Let $X_k \equiv \sum_{l=k}^{n} x_l$ denote the load factor of capacity of type k. The optimal investment policy implies that the marginal production costs (assumed constant) associated with all types of capacity satisfy $c_1 \leq c_2 \leq \cdots \leq c_n$. Let $G(q_1, q_2 - q_1, \ldots, q_n - q_{n-1})$ denote the total cost of installing the different types of capacities, and let $\tilde{c}_k \equiv c_k X_k$. The firm's cost function can be written

$$\begin{aligned} C &= \mathscr{C}(\beta, e_1, \ldots, e_n, \mathbf{q}) \\ &= c_1(\beta, e_1) q_1 X_1 + c_2(\beta, e_2)(q_2 - q_1) X_2 + \cdots + c_n(\beta, e_n)(q_n - q_{n-1}) X_n \\ &\quad + G(q_1, q_2 - q_1, \ldots, q_n - q_{n-1}) \\ &= \sum_{k=1}^{n} \tilde{c}_k(\beta, e_k)(q_k - q_{k-1}) + G(q_1, q_2 - q_1, \ldots, q_n - q_{n-1}). \end{aligned} \tag{3.47}$$

To give an example with $n = 2$, e_1 and e_2 can be thought of as the managers' efforts to supervise or improve the technology of the nuclear power division (which supplies both peak and off-peak demands) and the coal division (which supplies peak demand only).

As before we define

$$C(\beta, e, \mathbf{q}) = \min_{\{e_1,\ldots,e_n\}} \mathscr{C}(\beta, e_1, \ldots, e_n, \mathbf{q}) \tag{3.48}$$

subject to

$$\sum_{k=1}^{n} e_k = e.$$

Proposition 3.10 Assume an interior solution to program (3.48). The incentive-pricing dichotomy holds for the shared-marginal-cost model if and only if, for all k,

$$\sum_{l=1}^{n} \frac{\partial}{\partial e_l}\left(\frac{\partial \tilde{c}_l/\partial \beta}{\partial \tilde{c}_l/\partial e_l}\right)\frac{\partial e_l^*}{\partial q_k} = 0, \tag{3.49}$$

where the functions $\{e_l^*\}_{l=1}^n$ are the solutions of (3.48).

Proof The proof is essentially the same as that of proposition 3.4. From (3.48) we know that $(\partial[\tilde{c}_k(\beta, e_k)]/\partial e_k)(q_k - q_{k-1}) = C_e$ for all k. Therefore

$$\frac{\partial}{\partial q_k}\left(-\frac{C_\beta}{C_e}\right) = -\sum_l \frac{\partial}{\partial q_k}\left(\frac{\partial \tilde{c}_l/\partial \beta}{\partial \tilde{c}_l/\partial e_l}\right).$$

Because of constant returns to scale, $\tilde{c}_l$ and its partial derivatives depend on q_k only through the effect of q_k on e_l^*. Together with proposition 3.3 this yields (3.49). ∎

Example Equation (3.49), and therefore the incentive-pricing dichotomy, holds for the marginal cost functions

$$c_k(\beta, e_k) = (\beta - e_k)^{b_k}, \tag{3.50}$$

$$c_k(\beta, e_k) = \beta - \log e_k. \tag{3.51}$$

[For marginal cost function (3.50), $(\partial/\partial e_l)[(\partial \tilde{c}_l/\partial \beta)/(\partial \tilde{c}_l/\partial e_l)] = 0$ for all l. For marginal cost function (3.51), the same term is equal to -1 for all l. The equality $\sum_{l=1}^n (\partial e_l^*/\partial q_k) = 0$ then yields (3.49).]

3.8 Is Subcost Observation Useful?

When the firm engages in multiple activities, the observability of the subcost associated with each activity in principle makes it easier for the regulator to control the firm. The issue of subcost observation arises, for instance, when deciding on the price of access for competing firms to a bottleneck controlled by the regulated firm (local network for a telephone company, distribution for a gas or electricity company). The measurement of subcosts is costly, and it is important to know when it is useful.

The limit to the use of subcosts in incentive schemes is arbitrage among activities by the firm. Suppose that the firm bears marginal fractions b_1 and $b_2 > b_1$ of its subcosts on activities 1 and 2. Then the firm has an incentive to shift expenses from activity 2 to activity 1 and gains $\$(b_2 - b_1)$ on each dollar thus transferred. There are two ways in which the firm can reallocate its expenses:

1. *Accounting arbitrage.* The firm engages in accounting manipulations. Labor, raw materials, and other inputs are imputed to an activity for which they were not used. The transfer prices for intermediate goods traded between divisions is set at the wrong level.

2. *Allocative arbitrage.* The general office allocates its effort or attention to those activities that face the most powerful incentive schemes rather than to minimize total cost. To these activities are also dedicated the best engineers or inputs. There is no imputation of expenses of one activity on another, but rather more attention is paid to certain activities.

We will come back to accounting manipulations in chapter 12. Let us simply note that in its purest form it involves no allocative cost, except possibly for the time spent by internal accountants. We also note that it may be limited by large enough (and costly) external accounting. Indeed such external accounting of subcost is routine in procurement in which firms often produce for the government and at the same time engage in commercial activities with steeper incentives.[15]

The focus of this section is on allocative arbitrage. Intuitively the observation of subcosts is useful only if subcosts are not reimbursed in the same fraction. Since different cost-reimbursement rules for different subcosts imply allocative arbitrage by the firm, and therefore cost inefficiency, such discrimination among subcosts can only be justified if it contributes to rent extraction. We now introduce conditions under which subcost observation does nothing to extract the rent and therefore is useless.

The shared-fixed-cost model introduced in subsections 3.7.1 and 3.7.2 is a natural framework to study the use of subcosts. We consider both the case of a one-dimensional type,

$$C_k = C^k(\beta, e_k, q_k), \qquad k = 0, 1, \ldots, n,$$

and that of a multidimensional type,

$$C_k = C^k(\beta_k, e_k, q_k), \qquad k = 0, 1, \ldots, n.$$

15. For the implications of the existence of a commercial activity for the power of incentive schemes under allocative arbitrage, see review problem 13.

The subcosts, for instance, might relate to the purchase costs of different inputs. The private information parameter(s) then correspond to the market conditions for these inputs. The effort e_k measures the time or energy spent to obtain price reductions on input k. When inputs are unrelated (labor, computers, switches, power plants, etc.), a multidimensional-type-space representation is more appropriate. In contrast, for inputs that face similar market conditions (different supplies of oil, different categories of labor, etc.), the one-dimensional-type-space representation may not be too misleading.

Technically the one-dimensional case is straightforward because it suffices to treat each subcost as one particular output [so the new output vector is $\mathbf{Q} = (\mathbf{q}, \mathbf{C})$, where $\mathbf{q} = (q_1, \ldots, q_n)$ and $\mathbf{C} = (C_0, C_1, \ldots, C_n)$]. The multidimensional case will be handled by the aggregation techniques of section 3.7.

3.8.1 One-Dimensional Type

Let $e_k \equiv E^k(\beta, C_k, q_k)$ denote the effort (which we assume exists) required to reach subcost C_k when producing output q_k with cost parameter β. Total effort is thus

$$e = \sum_{k=0}^{n} E^k(\beta, C_k, q_k) = E(\beta, \mathbf{C}, \mathbf{q}).$$

The firm's rent grows at rate

$$\dot{U} = -\psi'(e)\left[\sum_{k=0}^{n} \frac{\partial E^k}{\partial \beta}\right].$$

The regulator observes the subcosts C_k and the outputs q_k. Treating the subcosts as particular outputs, we obtain the following first-order condition for the maximization of social welfare with respect to C_k:

$$\left[(1+\lambda)\psi' f + \lambda F \psi'' \frac{\partial E}{\partial \beta}\right]\left(-\frac{\partial E^k}{\partial C_k}\right) = (1+\lambda) f + \lambda F \psi' \frac{\partial^2 E^k}{\partial C_k \partial \beta}. \tag{3.52}$$

A *high-powered scheme on activity* k corresponds to a high value of $(-\partial E^k/\partial C_k)$ (recall that E^k is a decreasing function of C_k). If $\partial E^k/\partial C_k$ is high in absolute value, marginal cost reductions on activity k per unit of effort are small, and therefore the firm is already induced to exert a large effort on activity k.

Note that if subcosts were not observable, the firm would minimize its effort for any cost target; that is, it would choose $\{e_k\}$ so as to minimize $\sum_{k=0}^{n} E^k(\beta, C_k, q_k)$ subject to $\sum_{k=0}^{n} C_k = C$. Hence, in the absence of subcost observation, the marginal efforts to reduce subcosts $-\partial E^k/\partial C_k$ would be equalized. The question is then whether under subcost observation the firm faces higher-powered incentives on some activities than on others, or whether it faces uniform incentives. In the latter case subcost observation turns out to be useless (under weak conditions).

Whether the regulator wants to give differentiated incentives on different activities hinges on the cross-partial derivatives $\partial^2 E^k/\partial C_k \partial \beta$. These derivatives have a natural interpretation: $\partial E^k/\partial \beta$ measures the economy of effort on activity k per unit reduction in the efficiency parameter. It thus determines how the firm's rent is affected by the efficiency parameter. The cross-partial derivative $\partial^2 E^k/\partial C_k \partial \beta$ measures the effect of the target subcost on the firm's rent. The reader will notice here the similarity in reasoning with that in the discussion of the incentive correction and the dichotomy for outputs.

We make the assumption that the minimization of total effort $\sum_{k=0}^n E^k(\beta, C_k, q_k)$ subject to $\sum_{k=0}^n C_k = C$ has a unique solution $e_k = \hat{E}^k(\beta, C, \mathbf{q})$, which is the solution to the system $\{\partial E^k/\partial C_k = \partial E^l/\partial C_l$ for all (k, l), and $\sum_{k=0}^n C_k = C\}$.

Proposition 3.11 Consider subcost observation in the case of a one-dimensional type:

i. The firm faces higher-powered incentives on those activities for which low costs reduce rents ($\partial^2 E^k/\partial C_k \partial \beta$ large).

ii. The firm faces uniform incentives on all activities if $\partial^2 E^k/\partial C_k \partial \beta \equiv K$ for some K and for all $k \in \{0, \ldots, n\}$. Subcost observation then does not raise welfare.

Proof Part i results from (3.52). To prove that subcost observation is useless when $\partial^2 E^k/\partial C_k \partial \beta = K$ for all k, note that at the optimal regulatory policy, $-\partial E^k/\partial C_k$ is the same for all k. That is, the firm is induced to allocate its effort so as to minimize total cost. Now, for a given incentive scheme $\beta \to \{t(\beta), C_0(\beta), \ldots, C_n(\beta), q_1(\beta), \ldots, q_n(\beta)\}$ under subcost observability, consider the associated incentive scheme $\beta \to \{t(\beta), C(\beta), q_1(\beta), \ldots, q_n(\beta)\}$ under subcost unobservability, where $C(\beta) \equiv \sum_{k=0}^n C_k(\beta)$. This incentive scheme is incentive compatible. For this it suffices to show that if type β announces $\hat{\beta}$, it will choose the subcost allocation $\{C_0(\hat{\beta}), \ldots, C_n(\hat{\beta})\}$ corresponding to its announcement, even though the regulator cannot control subcosts. Note that from (3.52) there exists α such that

$$\frac{\partial E^k}{\partial C_k}(\hat{\beta}, C_k(\hat{\beta}), q_k(\hat{\beta})) = \alpha \qquad \text{for all } k$$

and

$$\sum_{k=0}^{n} C_k(\hat{\beta}) = C(\hat{\beta}).$$

But the condition $\partial^2 E^k/\partial C_k \partial \beta \equiv K$ for all k implies that

$$\frac{\partial E^k}{\partial C_k}(\beta, C_k(\hat{\beta}), q_k(\hat{\beta})) = \alpha' \qquad \text{for all } k \text{, as well.}$$

From our assumption $\{C_0(\hat{\beta}), \ldots, C_n(\hat{\beta})\}$ is the unique effort minimizer for type β when it announces $\hat{\beta}$. We can thus implement the same allocation when subcosts are unobservable as when they are. ■

Example The subcost functions

$$C^k(\beta, e_k, q_k) = (\gamma_k \beta - e_k)^{\alpha_k} z_k(q_k),$$

with $\gamma_k > 0$ and $\alpha_k > 1$ (to guarantee an interior solution to effort minimization) satisfy condition ii of proposition 3.11 and therefore exhibit no role for subcost observability.

3.8.2 Multidimensional Type

Proposition 3.12 Assume that

i. The effort $e = \sum_{k=0}^{n} e_k$ required to produce the output vector $\mathbf{q} \equiv (q_1, \ldots, q_n)$ at subcost vector $\mathbf{C} \equiv (C_0, \ldots, C_n)$ under parameter vector $\boldsymbol{\beta} \equiv (\beta_0, \ldots, \beta_n)$ has the following separable form:

$$e = \mathscr{E}(\Lambda(\boldsymbol{\beta}), H(\mathbf{C}, \mathbf{q})), \tag{3.53}$$

with $\partial\mathscr{E}/\partial\Lambda > 0$, $\partial\mathscr{E}/\partial H > 0$, and $\partial^2\mathscr{E}/\partial\Lambda\partial H \geq 0$.

ii. The efficient allocation of effort

$$\min_{\{C_0, \ldots, C_n\}} \quad \mathscr{E}(\Lambda(\boldsymbol{\beta}), H(C_0, \ldots, C_n, \mathbf{q}))$$

subject to $\sum_{k=0}^{n} C_k = C$ has a unique solution $\{\hat{C}^k(C, \mathbf{q})\}$ for all $\mathbf{q}$, satisfying $\partial H/\partial C_k = \partial H/\partial C_l$ for all (k, l).

iii. When only total cost is observable, the solution to the regulatory problem, which from (3.53) depends only on $\beta \equiv \Lambda(\boldsymbol{\beta})$, is monotonic:

$$\frac{dC}{d\beta} \geq 0, \quad \frac{dq_k}{d\beta} \leq 0.$$

Under i, ii, and iii, expected social welfare is the same whether the regulator observes the subcosts C_k or only total cost C.

Proof Suppose that subcosts are observable. A revelation mechanism is then a $(2n + 2)$-uple $\{C_0(\boldsymbol{\beta}), \ldots, C_n(\boldsymbol{\beta}), q_1(\boldsymbol{\beta}), \ldots, q_n(\boldsymbol{\beta}), t(\boldsymbol{\beta})\}$. It is easily seen that the firm's rent $U(\boldsymbol{\beta})$ depends only on the aggregate $\beta = \Lambda(\boldsymbol{\beta})$: If $\Lambda(\boldsymbol{\beta}) = \Lambda(\tilde{\boldsymbol{\beta}})$ and $U(\boldsymbol{\beta}) > U(\tilde{\boldsymbol{\beta}})$, then the firm with the vector of parameters $\tilde{\boldsymbol{\beta}}$ can always choose $\{\mathbf{C}(\boldsymbol{\beta}), \mathbf{q}(\boldsymbol{\beta})\}$, exert the same effort as for vector $\boldsymbol{\beta}$ [from (3.53)], and obtain the same rent as for vector $\boldsymbol{\beta}$, which is a contradiction.

Following the usual reasoning, the firm's rent satisfies

$$\dot{U}(\beta) = -\psi'(e)\frac{\partial \mathscr{E}}{\partial \beta}(\beta, H(\mathbf{C}, \mathbf{q})), \tag{3.54}$$

where, by an abuse of notation, U (as well as the other components of the allocation) becomes a function of β. The local and global second-order condition is

$$U_{\beta\hat{\beta}} = (-\psi''\mathscr{E}_\beta\mathscr{E}_H - \psi'\mathscr{E}_{\beta H})H_\beta \geq 0$$

or, more simply, $H_\beta \leq 0$; that is,

$$\sum_{k=0}^{n}\left(\frac{\partial H}{\partial C_k}\frac{dC_k}{d\beta} + \frac{\partial H}{\partial q_k}\frac{dq_k}{d\beta}\right) \leq 0. \tag{3.55}$$

The expected social welfare is

$$\int_{\underline{\beta}}^{\bar{\beta}}\left\{V(\mathbf{q}(\beta)) - (1+\lambda)\left[\sum_{k=0}^{n} C_k(\beta) + \psi(\mathscr{E}(\beta, H(\mathbf{C}(\beta), \mathbf{q}(\beta))))\right]\right.$$
$$\left. - \lambda U(\beta)\right\} f(\beta)d\beta.$$

To maximize expected social welfare subject to the incentive constraints (3.54) and (3.55) and to the individual rationality constraint $U(\bar{\beta}) = 0$, we first ignore the second-order condition (3.55). The first-order condition with respect to C_k is then, for all k,

$$-(1+\lambda)\left[1 + \psi'\frac{\partial \mathscr{E}}{\partial H}\frac{\partial H}{\partial C_k}\right]f(\beta)$$
$$- \lambda F(\beta)\left[\psi''\frac{\partial \mathscr{E}}{\partial H}\frac{\partial H}{\partial C_k}\frac{\partial \mathscr{E}}{\partial \beta} + \psi'\frac{\partial^2 \mathscr{E}}{\partial \beta \partial H}\frac{\partial H}{\partial C_k}\right] = 0. \tag{3.56}$$

This implies that $\partial H/\partial C_k$ is independent of k and, using assumption ii of the proposition, that $C_k = \hat{C}^k(C, \mathbf{q})$.

Now define

$$\hat{H}(C, \mathbf{q}) \equiv H(\hat{C}^0(C, \mathbf{q}), \ldots, \hat{C}^n(C, \mathbf{q}), \mathbf{q}).$$

The incentive constraint under subcost observability for the optimal incentive scheme can then be rewritten

$$t(\beta) - \psi(\mathscr{E}(\beta, \hat{H}(C(\beta), \mathbf{q}(\beta)))) \geq t(\hat{\beta}) - \psi(\mathscr{E}(\beta, \hat{H}(C(\hat{\beta}), \mathbf{q}(\hat{\beta}))))$$
$$\text{for all } (\beta, \hat{\beta}). \tag{3.57}$$

Suppose that only total cost is observable. Let us give the firm the incentive scheme $\{t(\beta), C(\beta) = \sum_{k=0}^{n} C_k(\beta), \mathbf{q}(\beta)\}$, where the functions $\{t(\cdot), C_k(\cdot), \mathbf{q}(\cdot)\}$ correspond to the optimal incentive scheme under subcost observability. Suppose next that the firm has type β and announces $\hat{\beta}$.

It then allocates its effort, or equivalently chooses its subcosts, so as to minimize

$$\mathscr{E}(\beta, H(C_0, \ldots, C_n, \mathbf{q}))$$

subject to

$$\sum_{k=0}^{n} C_k = C(\hat{\beta}).$$

The firm chooses $C_k = \hat{C}^k(C, \mathbf{q})$. Its utility from announcing $\hat{\beta}$ is $t(\hat{\beta}) - \psi(\mathscr{E}(\beta, \hat{H}(C(\hat{\beta}), \mathbf{q}(\hat{\beta}))))$. Incentive compatibility under subcost unobservability then results from (3.57). We can thus implement the same allocation under subcost unobservability as under subcost observability.

Last, our reasoning is valid only if the optimal regulatory scheme under subcost observability satisfies (3.55), that is, if we were right in ignoring the firm's second-order condition. Assumption iii of the proposition, which ensures that the firm's second-order condition under subcost unobservability is satisfied, also guarantees that it is satisfied under subcost observability, since (3.56) implies that the two conditions are the same:

$$\sum_{k=0}^{n} \left(\frac{\partial H}{\partial C_k} \frac{dC_k}{d\beta} + \frac{\partial H}{\partial q_k} \frac{dq_k}{d\beta} \right) = \frac{\partial H}{\partial C_0} \frac{dC}{d\beta} + \sum_{k=0}^{n} \frac{\partial H}{\partial q_k} \frac{dq_k}{d\beta}. \qquad \blacksquare$$

The conditions underlying proposition 3.12 are of course strong. Proposition 3.12, however, shows that there may be no benefit to subcost observation even if the firm cannot engage in accounting contrivances. In such cases the regulated firm should be treated as a single responsibility center.

Example The subcost functions given by (3.46) satisfy the conditions of proposition 3.12: First, note that

$$\mathscr{E}(\Lambda(\boldsymbol{\beta}), H(\mathbf{C}, \mathbf{q})) = \sum_{k=0}^{n} \beta_k - \sum_{k=0}^{n} \left[\frac{C_k}{z^k(q_k)} \right]^{1/\alpha_k} = \Lambda(\boldsymbol{\beta}) + H(\mathbf{C}, \mathbf{q}),$$

and that condition i is satisfied. Second, the system

$$\frac{\partial H}{\partial C_k} = - \frac{1}{\alpha_k z^k(q_k)} \left[\frac{C_k}{z^k(q_k)} \right]^{1/\alpha_k - 1} = \alpha$$

and

$$\sum_{k=0}^{n} C_k = C$$

has a unique solution (for $\alpha < 0$). So, if $\alpha_k > 1$ for all k, H is convex and effort minimization leads to a unique solution; then condition ii is satisfied. Condition iii depends on the program of optimization of social welfare and is quite reasonable. We omit the more primitive assumptions that yield this condition.

Remark The role of condition i is clear: The firm's rent is determined by its type β and the function $\mathscr{H}(\beta) = H(\mathbf{C}(\beta), \mathbf{q}(\beta))$. For a given function $\mathscr{H}(\cdot)$ there is no point distorting the cost minimization process in order to extract rents.[16] The role of condition ii is to guarantee that allocative arbitrage indeed takes place. Suppose, for instance, that the firm produces one unit of outputs 1 and 2 at subcosts

$$C_1 = \beta_1,$$

$$C_2 = \beta_2 - e_2.$$

Under subcost observation the firm has private information about β_2 only, while under subcost unobservability the regulator observes only $C = \beta - e$, where $e \equiv e_2$, and the firm has private information about $\beta \equiv \beta_1 + \beta_2$. This example satisfies condition i ($e = e_2 = \beta_2 - C_2$) but not condition ii ($\partial H/\partial C_1 = 0 \neq \partial H/\partial C_2 = -1$). (The minimization of effort subject to $C_1 + C_2 = C$ has no interior solution.)

3.9 General Equilibrium Analysis: Foundations of the Shadow Cost of Public Funds and Taxation by Regulation

3.9.1 Motivation

This book follows the partial equilibrium tradition of the regulation literature. This raises two potential issues.

First, recall that in our formulation of the social welfare function, we multiplied the firm's cost, transfer, and revenue by a factor $1 + \lambda$ and stated that $\lambda > 0$ (the shadow cost of public funds) is determined by economywide considerations. The factor $\lambda/(1 + \lambda)$, which measures the relative social cost of transfers and real expenses, plays a crucial role in the effort correction [equation (3.9)], in the Ramsey index [e.g., equation (3.15)], and in the incentive correction [e.g., equation (3.16)]. Clearly the existence of a shadow cost of public funds and the validity of the partial equilibrium approach to incentives and pricing can be ascertained only in a general equilibrium model.

Second, the gross consumer surplus was taken to be the unweighted sum of individual gross consumer surpluses. In practice the distribution of income is not socially optimal, and one might wonder whether regulation

16. Note that it is important here that the regulator puts equal weights on all subcosts. If for some reason the prices of the firm's inputs were distorted relative to their social value so that the regulator would put different weights on different costs, equation (3.56) would not hold, and therefore subcost observation would be useful even under the conditions of proposition 3.12.

should be used as a substitute for a (nonexistent) perfect taxation system. In more technical terms, should the Lerner index differ from the sum of the Ramsey index and the incentive correction for specific goods? Posner (1971) has argued that "existing views of regulation do not explain well the important phenomenon of internal subsidization" (p. 28) and offers to "modify existing views by admitting that one of the functions of regulation is to perform distributive and allocative chores usually associated with the taxing or financial branch of government" (p. 23). Examples of regulated pricing that seem to be motivated by redistributive concerns are the use of uniform rates for mail and telephone, avoiding cost-based price discrimination between rural and urban areas, or British Telecom's license agreement preventing low-usage residential customers' line rental charges from growing faster than the retail price index plus 2% per year.

This issue of "demand-side cross-subsidization" closely relates to the debate on direct versus indirect taxation in public finance about whether the responsibility for redistribution should be assumed by income taxation only or by differential excise taxes as well. One of the main findings of this literature (Atkinson and Stiglitz 1976; Mirrlees 1976) is that using indirect taxation to redistribute income is a less obvious policy than one might have thought. Indeed the government need not use indirect taxation if (1) consumers differ in their ability (or wage w earned per unit of labor), (2) consumers' utility function exhibits weak separability between consumption and labor [$U = U(A(q_1, \ldots, q_n), L)$, where L is labor], and (3) the government uses optimal excise taxes on goods and optimal nonlinear income taxation [so taxes paid by a consumer of "type" w have the form $\sum_{k=1}^{n} \tau_k q_k + T(wL)$]. (That is, the government can pick $\tau_k = \tau$ for all k, and, without loss of generality, τ can be taken to be zero from the homogeneity of the consumers' budget constraints.)

This result does not imply that taxation by regulation (i.e., pricing driven by redistributive concerns) is socially inefficient, simply that it is not a forgone conclusion. There are several ways to reintroduce motives for such "demand-side cross-subsidization." First, the strong assumption of weak separability could be relaxed; however, as Atkinson and Stiglitz (1980, p. 437) note, nearly all empirical studies of demand and labor supply functions have made this assumption and are therefore of little guidance for our purpose. Second, one could assume that income is imperfectly observable because of perks, domestic production, or tax evasion (e.g., Deaton 1977 takes this route). Third, consumers could differ with respect to other attributes than ability. To these three reasons listed by Atkinson and Stiglitz (1980, p. 440) can be added a fourth. There could exist situations in which commodity taxation can be based on information not available for income taxation because of different arbitrage possibilities. For instance, it may be costly to make income taxation contingent on the rural or urban character of the consumer's place of residence because of potential manipulation of fiscal address. However, the consumptions of electricity or telephone in urban and rural areas are less subject to arbitrage. So, for instance, if the distribution of the unit wage w profile in urban areas first-order stochastically dominates that for rural areas, one could show that under some conditions on preferences, the prices of electricity and telephone in rural areas should be subsidized relative to those in the urban areas.

3.9.2 An Imperfect Income Taxation Model

We now show how foundations for the shadow cost of public funds and for taxation by regulation can be obtained in a general equilibrium framework. We follow Deaton's line of analyzing imperfect income taxation. To keep the model as simple as possible and to focus on essentials, we assume away income taxation. This situation corresponds to the extreme case in which the consumers' incomes are not observable by the government.

The model has $(n + 1)$ goods. Good 0, the numéraire, is a privately produced good. Goods 1 through n are produced by the regulated sector and have prices $p_1, \ldots, p_n$.

Consumers

There are m categories of consumers (e.g., imagine a continuum of consumers in each category). Consumers of type i have quasi-linear preferences

$$S^i(Q_1^i, \ldots, Q_n^i) + Q_0^i,$$

where Q_0^i and $(Q_1^i, \ldots, Q_n^i)$ are the consumptions of private and regulated goods. They have endowment $\bar{Q}_0^i$ of the numéraire and no endowment of the regulated goods. Their net surplus is

$$S^i(Q_1^i, \ldots, Q_n^i) + \bar{Q}_0^i - \sum_{k=1}^{n} p_k Q_k^i.$$

Regulated Firms

To remove aggregate uncertainty and simplify the exposition of the government balanced-budget condition, we assume that there is a continuum of regulated firms producing goods 1 through n. (Alternatively, there could be a single firm, and the government budget constraint would be interpreted in expectation; see section 6.5 for the resolution of a similar problem when there is a single firm and the budget constraint must be satisfied for each realization of β.) A regulated firm is indexed by its efficiency parameter β in $[\underline{\beta}, \bar{\beta}]$, and it has cost function $C = C(\beta, e, \mathbf{q})$ in terms of numéraire. The managers of the regulated firms know their firm's β, but the government only knows the distribution $F(\beta)$ of parameters (and views all firms as ex ante identical). Each regulated firm is run by a manager with utility function $U = t - \psi(e)$, where t is the transfer from the government and $\psi(e)$ the disutility of effort, both expressed in terms of numéraire. The functions C and ψ are assumed to satisfy the assumptions of section 3.2. For notational simplicity we assume that the managers of regulated firms consume only the numéraire; nothing would be altered if they consumed also regulated goods. Last, recall from section 3.2 that the individual rationality and incentive compatibility constraints are

$$U(\bar{\beta}) = 0 \tag{3.7}$$

and

$$\dot{U}(\beta) = -\psi'(e)E_\beta(\beta, C(\beta, e, \mathbf{q}), \mathbf{q}). \tag{3.8}$$

Budget Constraint

The government must balance its budget. In our framework the revenue from regulated goods must exceed the total cost (cost plus managerial income) of running the regulated firms. Using the fact that $t(\beta) = U(\beta) + \psi(e(\beta))$, and expressing the budget constraint in terms of numéraire, we have

$$\sum_{k=1}^{n} p_k\left(\sum_{i=1}^{m} Q_k^i\right) \geq \int_{\underline{\beta}}^{\bar{\beta}} [C(\beta, e(\beta), \mathbf{q}(\beta)) + U(\beta) + \psi(e(\beta))]f(\beta)d\beta. \tag{3.58}$$

Market Clearing

The demand for regulated goods must not exceed supply:

$$\int_{\underline{\beta}}^{\bar{\beta}} q_k(\beta)f(\beta)d\beta \geq \sum_{i=1}^{m} Q_k^i \qquad \text{for all } k = 1, \ldots, n. \tag{3.59}$$

Social Welfare Function

The government maximizes a weighted average of the consumers' and managers' net surpluses. Let w^i and w^0 denote the weights on consumers of type i and managers. Thus

$$W = \sum_{i=1}^{m} w^i\left[S^i(Q_1^i, \ldots, Q_n^i) + \bar{Q}_0^i - \sum_{k=1}^{n} p_k Q_k^i\right] + w^0 \int_{\underline{\beta}}^{\bar{\beta}} U(\beta)f(\beta)d\beta. \tag{3.60}$$

Let $Q_k \equiv \sum_{i=1}^{m} Q_k^i$, and let $p_k(Q_1, \ldots, Q_n)$ denote the inverse demand for regulated good k. The social optimum is obtained by maximizing (3.60) with respect to the control variables Q_k^i, $q_k(\beta)$, and $e(\beta)$, and the state variable $U(\beta)$ subject to constraints (3.7), (3.8), (3.58), and (3.59). Let $\mu(\beta)$, γ, and v_k denote the multipliers associated with constraints (3.8), (3.58), and (3.59); the first-order conditions are

$$\sum_i w^i\left(-\sum_l \frac{\partial p_l}{\partial Q_k} Q_l^i\right) + \gamma\left(\sum_l \frac{\partial p_l}{\partial Q_k} Q_l + p_k\right) - v_k = 0, \tag{3.61}$$

$$-\mu(\beta)\psi'(e)\frac{d}{dq_k}(E_\beta) - \gamma C_{q_k} f + v_k f = 0, \tag{3.62}$$

$$-\mu(\beta)\frac{d}{de}(\psi'(e)E_\beta) - \gamma(C_e + \psi'(e)) = 0, \tag{3.63}$$

$$\dot{\mu}(\beta) = (\gamma - w^0)f(\beta). \tag{3.64}$$

Using the fact that $\underline{\beta}$ is a free boundary, we find that (3.64) implies that

$$\mu(\beta) = (\gamma - w^0)F(\beta). \tag{3.65}$$

Substituting (3.62) into (3.61) yields

$$L_k = R_k + I_k, \tag{3.66}$$

where

$$L_k \equiv \frac{p_k - C_{q_k}}{p_k} \quad \text{(good } k\text{'s Lerner index)},$$

$$R_k \equiv -\sum_l \frac{1}{p_k}\frac{\partial p_l}{\partial Q_k}\left(\frac{\gamma Q_l - \Sigma_i w^i Q_l^i}{\gamma}\right) \quad \text{(good } k\text{'s Ramsey index)},$$

$$I_k \equiv \frac{\gamma - w^0}{\gamma}\frac{F(\beta)}{f(\beta)p_k}\psi'(e)\frac{d}{dq_k}(E_\beta) \quad \text{(good } k\text{'s incentive correction)}.$$

Equation (3.63) yields the optimal effort:

$$\psi'(e) = -C_e - \frac{\gamma - w^0}{\gamma}\frac{F(\beta)}{f(\beta)}\frac{d}{de}(\psi'(e)E_\beta). \tag{3.67}$$

Clearly (3.66) and (3.67) bear a strong resemblance to (3.13) and (3.9). The effort correction is still proportional to $[F(\beta)/f(\beta)][d(\psi'(e)E_\beta)/de]$. The incentive correction is equal to zero if and only if the cost function is separable $d(E_\beta)/dq_k = 0$ for all k or $C = C(\zeta(\beta, e), \mathbf{q})$). Proposition 3.13 provides the exact link between partial and general equilibrium results.

Proposition 3.13

i. Suppose that the social welfare function puts equal weight on all parties ($w^i = w$ for all $i = 0, \ldots, m$). Then

ia. the shadow cost of public funds expressed in terms of numéraire is given by $\lambda = (\gamma - w)/w$ (i.e., $1 + \lambda = \gamma/w$),

ib. the partial and general equilibrium approaches coincide [(3.66) and (3.67) coincide with (3.13) and (3.9)].

ii. If the weights in the social welfare function differ, the partial and general equilibrium results still coincide as long as iia. one defines "consumer-specific shadow costs of public funds": $\gamma^i \equiv (\gamma - w^i)/w^i$ for consumers $i = 1, \ldots, m$ and $\lambda^0 \equiv (\gamma - w^0)/w^0$ for managers,

iib. the shadow cost of public funds that applies to the effort equation (3.9) and the incentive correction (3.16) is the cost λ^0 of public funds collected from managers.

iic. (taxation by regulation) the coefficient $(\lambda/1 + \lambda)Q_l$ in the Ramsey index (3.15) is taken equal to $[1 - \sum_{i=1}^m x_l^i/(1 + \lambda^i)]Q_l$, where $x_l^i \equiv Q_l^i/Q_l$ is consumer i's share of consumption of good l.

The intuition for proposition 3.13 is straightforward. If all parties are weighted equally, there is no redistributive concern among consumers or between consumers and managers. The partial equilibrium approach need not be amended. To understand the definition of the shadow cost of public funds, suppose that for some exogenous reason the government must collect one more unit of numéraire, which is thrown away. By definition, the loss in social welfare is equal to the multiplier γ of the government's budget constraint. Since one unit of numéraire for any party has value w in the social welfare function, the welfare loss caused by this extra budgetary need is $1 + \lambda = \gamma/w$.

When weights in the social welfare function differ, formulas must be amended slightly. First, when managers and consumers are weighted differently, what matters in equations (3.9) and (3.16) is the shadow cost of public funds collected from managers. The reason is that the reduction in the power of incentive schemes [equation (3.9)] and the incentive correction on prices [equation (3.16)] are two alternative ways of extracting managerial rents. Their social cost thus relates to λ^0.

Second, when consumers are weighted differently among themselves, the Ramsey index must take into account redistributive concerns (taxation by regulation). In particular, goods that are much consumed by consumers whose utility matters a lot in the social welfare function (x_k^i high, w^i high) have low Ramsey indices and therefore low prices.[17]

A special case of taxation by regulation is that of third-degree price discrimination. Suppose that the regulated firms produce a single physical good (electricity) that in equilibrium is consumed in equal amounts by city inhabitants (consumers 1) and rural inhabitants (consumers 2). Let p_1 and p_2 be the prices charged in urban and rural areas. If incomes are lower in rural areas so that $w^2 > w^1$, the fact that $x_1^1 = x_2^2 = 1$ together with (3.66) yields $p_1 > p_2$.

17. The reader may be surprised by the fact that λ^i is low when w^i is high. Recall, however, that the λ^i in the Ramsey index corresponds to the social *value* of raising revenue to cover the regulated firms' costs. Raising revenue from poor consumers (w^i high) yields low social welfare.

3.10 Concluding Remarks

Let us summarize the main findings of this chapter:

1. Optimal pricing requires that each product's Lerner index be equal to the sum of a Ramsey term and an incentive correction.

2. In the absence of a budget constraint, the Ramsey term is entirely determined by the industry demand data and the economywide shadow cost of public funds, and it may reflect redistributive concerns. In contrast to the Ramsey-Boiteux model, the Ramsey term is independent of the firm's cost structure.

3. The possibility of using pricing to extract the firm's informational rent may give rise to an incentive correction. Incentive corrections are entirely cost determined (independent of the demand function) and can be analyzed by using aggregation techniques. But prices should not necessarily be used to promote incentives (in which case the incentive correction would be equal to zero) because cost-reimbursement (or profit-sharing) rules may alone be sufficient. Indeed we view the dichotomy between the cost-reimbursement rule as an incentive device and pricing as an allocation device as a good benchmark. A strong case must be built that the cost technology is conducive to incentive corrections if one were to add such corrections.

4. The study of the dichotomy between pricing and incentives can be extended to allow for the firm's effort allocation across its product lines or activities.

5. Some models with a multidimensional-type space can be treated by the techniques developed for a one-dimensional-type space.

6. Accurate measurement of the firm's subcosts is useful only if it helps the regulator to extract the firm's rent. But effort reallocation across activities may imply that the regulator does not want to interfere with the firm's cost minimization process through discrimination in the power of incentives among activities. In such a case observing only the firm's total cost involves no welfare loss.

7. The inception of general equilibrium considerations in a partial equilibrium framework can be given foundations through an optimal taxation model. The general equilibrium approach unveils the existence of a shadow cost of public funds and, possibly, a motivation for taxation by regulation.

The main contribution of the chapter is the derivation of conditions under which the regulator should not interfere with Ramsey pricing and cost minimization despite the existence of incentive problems. The chapter has otherwise remained quite orthodox in its Ramsey prescriptions. In this respect it has followed an old and rich literature on multiproduct Ramsey pricing by a regulated firm, and on price discrimination by a monopolist (see bibliographic notes for some references). The chapter only superficially touches on the question of why Ramsey pricing is so little used in practice. Regulated firms often refrain from discriminating according to marginal costs or to the elasticities of demand. For example, we mentioned that rural consumers pay prices similar to those paid by urban consumers despite large differences in the cost of service. As another example, Électricité de France, whose staff has made pioneering contributions to the theory of Ramsey pricing, has long had for official policy the "Allais rule" of equating the Lerner indices across goods. That is, the prices of Électricité de France have in principle been determined by multiplying marginal costs by a uniform coefficient, when Ramsey pricing would yield a higher multiplicative coefficient for goods with a lower elasticity of demand.

Unless such discrepancies from Ramsey pricing were motivated by incentive corrections, which seems doubtful, this chapter leaves us with the general equilibrium analysis of taxation by regulation as the only explanation for this widespread phenomenon. Redistributive concerns certainly are an important element, but they are not the only one.

Several other reasons have been mentioned. Their validity is worth exploring. First, it is sometimes argued that regulated firms avoid peak-load pricing in order to justify higher investments in capacity, which presumably bring them higher rents. It remains to be understood why regulators would not force firms to practice peak-load pricing. Asymmetric information about marginal costs or demands, and possibly regulatory capture by consumer groups, may play a role here. Second, one could argue, as in section 11.7, that uniform pricing reduces the stakes consumer groups have in regulatory decisions and thus reduces the extent of their lobbying and the risk of regulatory capture. Third, it is sometimes mentioned that cross-subsidizations among consumer groups can help the firm build a constituency against a possible break up (e.g., in different geographical units) because some consumers will lose their implicit subsidy in the firm's breakup. Again it remains to be examined why the firm wants to prevent the divestiture and why the regulators would delegate pricing to the firm in such a situation. Fourth, it may be that distortions arise from the existence of multiple jurisdictions, such as state versus federal. For instance, state regulators of a telephone company have an incentive to add as much as possible to the price of interstate calls, which are paid partly by out-of-state residents, and to lower the price of intrastate calls, which are paid entirely by state residents. Such behavior is no evidence against Ramsey pricing per se; rather it may be Ramsey pricing with the wrong objective function, which does not internalize the consumer surplus of other states. Last, but not least, we should not forget the transaction costs of practicing Ramsey pricing rather than uniform pricing; such transaction costs are often substantial when selling to nonindustrial or noncommercial customers.

BIBLIOGRAPHIC NOTES

B3.1 Definitions of Cross-subsidization

Equation (3.13), $L_k = R_k + I_k$, sheds light on two alternative viewpoints on cross-subsidization.

The first point of view is normative. The characterization of optimal prices defines, by comparison with reference prices, optimal cross-subsidizations. If the reference prices are marginal cost prices C_{q_k}, we say that good k must be cross-subsidized if and only if $L_k = R_k + I_k < 0$. If the reference prices are Ramsey prices, we say that good k must be cross-subsidized (for incentive reasons) if and only if $L_k - R_k = I_k < 0$. If the reference prices are the prices given by (3.13), which are optimal in the absence of redistributive concern, we say that good k is cross-subsidized if and only if $L_k - (R_k + I_k) < 0$. As shown in section 3.9, this kind of cross-subsidization is optimal when prices are distorted to favor a targeted class of consumers (demand-side cross-subsidization). Formally what Posner (1971) has dubbed "taxation by regulation" would correspond to a discrepancy between a good's Lerner index and the Lerner index that emerges from a regulatory policy that maximizes the unweighted sum of consumers' surpluses and the firm's utility. Demand-side cross-subsidization may also stem from the different powers of the various interest groups, as emphasized by the political science literature. See chapter 11 for a political theory of cross-subsidization.

The second definition of cross-subsidization encountered in the literature is positive or strategic. It relates to the existence of prices that are viable for the firm and that prevent the entry by an unregulated competitor with an identical technology. Cross-taxation is said to occur for a subset of goods if the cost of producing those goods only (the "stand-alone cost") is lower than the revenue associated with that subset of goods. Then there is a danger of entry on the associated markets. The definition of cross-subsidization is thus related to the possibility for entrants to make money when the firm cannot change its prices in the face of entry.

This point of view has been taken in the contestability literature. Faulhaber (1975) asks whether a given production plan and given (inflexible) prices for a firm may trigger (hit and run) entry by a competitor who faces the same technology. If they do, the production plan and the prices exhibit *competitive* cross-subsidization.

The work of Baumol et al. (1982) is an attempt to combine the positive and normative approaches. They investigate when Ramsey pricing (presumed to be optimal) is consistent with the absence of competitive cross-subsidization (sustainability). Then optimal prices are robust to the threat of entry (for this particular entry game), and this obviates the need for regulating entry.

In part II (on product market competition) we will abstract from the concerns of the contestability literature by assuming that the market is not contestable; that is, even though other firms may produce similar or differentiated products, the technology facing the regulated firm is unique and cannot be costlessly duplicated. In various entry situations we will derive optimal prices when entry can or cannot be regulated, and we will derive the optimal prices in the presence of competition.

Finally, let us note that except in section 3.8, we also abstract from what could be called *cost-side* cross-subsidization. Such cross-subsidization occurs when the firm's managers allocate investments and their time and energy inefficiently among the firm's product lines. In effect, when the marginal productivity of a cost-reducing activity applied to some product exceeds that for another product, the former product subsidizes the latter. Any regulation based on aggregate cost avoids cost-side cross-subsidization, as it induces managers to allocate (given levels of) investment and effort so as to minimize cost. In contrast, fully distributed cost pricing, which allocates joint costs to services in an arbitrary accounting manner, is a natural breeding ground for such cross-subsidies (see Brennan 1987).

But fully distributed cost pricing is only one cause of cost-side cross-subsidization. An alternative and common cause of such cross-subsidization is the coexistence of two activities with different cost-reimbursement rules. The firm then has an incentive to manipulate accounting so as to charge costs incurred for the activity with high-powered incentives (e.g., under a fixed-price contract) to the activity with low-powered incentives (e.g., under a cost-plus contract).[18] The firm also has an incentive to allocate its best engineers and the attention of the general office to the activity with high-powered incentives. On this, see section 3.8.

18. A recent illustration is supplied by the proposal of Consumers Power, a US electric utility, to sell its Palisades nuclear-generating plant to a consortium, 4/9 of which Consumers Power would own. It was further proposed that the new company, Palisades Generating Company, would sell all its power to Consumers Power under a price-cap contract. Brown (1990, Palisades Generating Company, Docket No. ER89-256000) on behalf of the Federal Energy Regulatory Commission argued (among other things) that Consumers Power would have an incentive to charge operation and maintenance done at Palisades Generating Company to Consumers Power, and thus to let Consumers Power's ratepayers subsidize such expenses.

B3.2 Optimal Pricing When Cost Is Not Observable

It is worth comparing our approach with Sappington's (1983) early work in incentives in multiproduct firms. Sappington, along the lines of Baron and Myerson's (1982) single-product contribution (see bibliographic notes in chapter 2), shows that prices are generally distorted to limit the firm's informational rent. There are two differences between his results and ours. First, Sappington's (like Baron-Myerson's) symmetric information benchmark is marginal cost pricing and not Ramsey pricing because of the absence of a cost of public funds. Second, and mainly, Sappington finds that pricing cannot be disconnected from incentives as long as the uncertainty parameter affects marginal costs.

For instance, suppose that

$$C = \zeta(\beta, e)\left(\sum_{k=1}^{n} q_k\right). \tag{B3.1}$$

Equation (B3.1) describes a technology in which efficiency and effort determine the constant marginal cost of a common output to be distributed in n different markets. From proposition 3.4, the price of good k is set at the symmetric information level in our model, while it is set above the symmetric information level in Sappington's model. This second discrepancy is due to Sappington's assumption that the firm's cost (or a garbled version of it) is not observable. Thus the regulator cannot use cost-reimbursement rules to extract rents and is forced to use price distortion as a substitute.[19] While the condition for the dichotomy is strong in our model, it leads us to view the dichotomy as a benchmark from which a case must be built that price manipulations do promote incentives.

B3.3 Ramsey Pricing and Price Discrimination

There is nothing new to the expressions of the Ramsey terms derived in this chapter. These expressions are borrowed from the vast and closely related literatures on price discrimination by an unregulated monopoly and on Ramsey pricing by a regulated monopoly. Surveys on monopoly second-degree and third-degree price discrimination include Phlips (1983), Tirole (1988, ch. 3), and Varian (1989). Ramsey pricing by a regulated

19. Sappington's analysis assumes a single-dimensional cost parameter. See Dana (1987) for an example of regulation (without cost observation) when the firm's subcosts are determined by different (although possibly correlated) parameters. See also proposition 3.8, as well as the literature on regulation with multiple adverse-selection parameters (Laffont, Maskin, and Rochet 1987; McAfee and McMillan 1988; Rochet 1985; Lewis and Sappington 1988).

monopoly is reviewed, for instance, in Brown and Sibley (1985) and Sheshinski (1986). Wilson (1992) contains much material on both topics. We have kept the social surplus function $V(\cdot)$ general enough to be able to accommodate all results in the literature, not only those derived in this chapter.

There is also a large literature, initiated by Vogelsang and Finsinger (1979), that shows that pricing under an average price constraint, rather than a budget constraint, leads to Ramsey pricing as well. This literature has generated renewed interest with the use of price caps on baskets of goods (see, e.g., Armstrong and Vickers 1991). Consider, for instance, the case of a monopolist subject to an average price constraint, $\sum_{k=1}^{n} \alpha_k p_k \leq \bar{p}$ (where $\alpha_k > 0$), and facing independent demands. This monopolist maximizes

$$\sum_{k=1}^{n} P_k(q_k)q_k - C(q_1, \ldots, q_n)$$

subject to

$$\sum_{k=1}^{n} \alpha_k P_k(q_k) \leq \bar{p}.$$

Letting θ denote the shadow price of the constraint, we obtain

$$L_k = \frac{1 - (\theta\alpha_k/q_k)}{\eta_k}.$$

In particular, if the coefficients α_k are chosen proportional to q_k, the pricing structure is a Ramsey structure:

$$\frac{L_k}{L_l} = \frac{\eta_l}{\eta_k} \qquad \text{for all } (k, l).$$

The questions raised by the endogeneity of q_k have been discussed in section 2.5.

B3.4 Aggregation Results

Although, to the best of our knowledge, the use of Leontief's theorem is new in the theory of regulation, it underlies an important result in optimal taxation due to Mirrlees (1976) and Atkinson and Stiglitz (1976) and reviewed in section 3.9. The transposition of results on the aggregation of capital goods to incentive problems is, we believe, new to the literature.

APPENDIXES

A3.1 Proof of Proposition 3.1

Assuming differentiability, we first derive the first-order condition of incentive compatibility for the firm:

$$U(\beta) = \max_{\hat{\beta}} \mathscr{U}(\beta, \hat{\beta}) \equiv \max_{\hat{\beta}} [t(\hat{\beta}) - \psi(E(\beta, C(\hat{\beta}), \mathbf{q}(\hat{\beta})))]$$

yields the first-order condition (at $\hat{\beta} = \beta$),

$$\frac{d}{d\beta}(t(\beta)) - \psi'\left(E_C \frac{dC}{d\beta} + \sum_k E_{q_k} \frac{dq_k}{d\beta}\right) = 0.$$

By the same proof as in chapter 1, a sufficient second-order condition is $\partial^2 \mathscr{U}/\partial\beta\partial\hat{\beta} \geq 0$; that is,

$$\frac{\partial}{\partial\hat{\beta}}(-\psi'(E(\beta, C(\hat{\beta}), \mathbf{q}(\hat{\beta}))E_\beta(\beta, C(\hat{\beta}), \mathbf{q}(\hat{\beta}))) \geq 0,$$

or

$$-\psi'' E_\beta\left(E_C \frac{dC}{d\beta} + \sum_k E_{q_k} \frac{dq_k}{d\beta}\right) - \psi'\left(E_{C\beta} \frac{dC}{d\beta} + \sum_k E_{q_k\beta} \frac{dq_k}{d\beta}\right) \geq 0.$$

From our assumptions on the cost function $E_\beta > 0$, $E_C < 0$, $E_{q_k} > 0$ for all k. If furthermore C_{ee}, $C_{e\beta}$, C_{eq_k}, and $C_{\beta q_k}$ are nonnegative, $E_{C\beta} \leq 0$, and $E_{q_k\beta} \geq 0$ for all k. Then $dC/d\beta \geq 0$, and $dq_k/d\beta \leq 0$ for all k ensure that the second-order conditions are satisfied. As before, we do not impose these inequality constraints but check that they are satisfied by our solutions. Otherwise, bunching *may* occur.

Letting $U(\beta)$ denote the rent of the firm, we can rewrite the first-order condition:

$$\dot{U}(\beta) = -\psi'(e)E_\beta(\beta, C(\beta, e, \mathbf{q}), \mathbf{q}) < 0. \tag{A3.1}$$

Since $U(\beta)$ is decreasing, the individual rationality constraint of the firm is achieved by imposing

$$U(\bar{\beta}) \geq 0. \tag{A3.2}$$

The regulator maximizes (3.6) under (A3.1) and (A3.2) with respect to $e(\beta)$, $q_k(\beta)$ for all k, treating U as the state variable. The hamiltonian is

$$H = [V(\mathbf{q}) - (1 + \lambda)(\psi(e) + C(\beta, e, \mathbf{q})) - \lambda U]f(\beta)$$
$$- \mu(\beta)\psi'(e)E_\beta(\beta, C(\beta, e, \mathbf{q}), \mathbf{q}).$$

We have: $\dot{\mu}(\beta) = -\partial H/\partial U = \lambda f(\beta)$. Since $\mu(\underline{\beta}) = 0$, $\mu(\beta) = \lambda F(\beta)$. Substituting $\mu(\beta)$ into H, the first-order conditions $\partial H/\partial e = 0$ and $\partial H/\partial q_k = 0$ for all k yield (3.9) and (3.10). ■

A3.2 Proof of Proposition 3.2

Let $\overline{C} \equiv C/H(\mathbf{q})$ and $I \equiv G^{-1}$ (with $I' = 1/G' > 0$ and $I'' = -G''/G'^3 < 0$). Thus

$$\beta - e = I(\overline{C}).$$

Since $\overline{C}$ is a "sufficient statistic" for e given β, the transfer function can be made contingent on $\overline{C}$ only: $t(\overline{C})$. Linearity with respect to C is equivalent to linearity with respect to $\overline{C}$. The firm chooses $\overline{C}$ so as to maximize

$$t(\overline{C}) - \psi(\beta - I(\overline{C})),$$

yielding the first-order condition

$$\frac{dt}{d\overline{C}} = -\psi' I'$$

and the second-order condition (with the first-order condition used as an identity)

$$I' \frac{d}{d\beta}(\overline{C}) \geq 0$$

or

$$\frac{d}{d\beta}\left(\frac{C(\beta)}{H(\mathbf{q}(\beta))}\right) \geq 0.$$

Condition iii in proposition 3.2 thus guarantees that the firm's second-order condition is satisfied.

The regulator can use a menu of linear cost-reimbursement rules if and only if the transfer function $t(\overline{C})$ is convex (the linear cost-reimbursement rules are then given by the tangents to the convex curve). But

$$\frac{d^2 t}{d\overline{C}^2} = -\psi''\left(\frac{d\beta}{d\overline{C}} - I'\right)I' - \psi' I''.$$

Using the definition of $\overline{C} \equiv G(\beta - e)$ and $I' = 1/G'$, we have

$$\frac{d\beta}{d\overline{C}} - I' = \frac{\dot{e}}{(1 - \dot{e})G'},$$

where $\dot{e} \equiv de/d\beta$. Differentiating (3.9) yields

$$\dot{e} = \frac{HG'' - [\lambda/(1+\lambda)][d(F/f)/d\beta]\psi'' + (\Sigma H_k \dot{q}_k)G'}{\psi'' + HG'' + [\lambda/(1+\lambda)](F/f)\psi'''}$$

Now, if $\psi''' \geq 0$ and $\dot{q}_k < 0$ for all k, either $\dot{e} \leq 0$ and $d^2 t/d\overline{C}^2 \geq 0$ follow immediately or $\dot{e} > 0$ and

$$\frac{\dot{e}}{1 - \dot{e}} \leq \frac{HG'' - [\lambda/(1+\lambda)][d(F/f)/d\beta]\psi'' + (\Sigma H_k \dot{q}_k)G'}{\psi''}$$

so that, using $d(F/f)/d\beta \geq 0$,

$$\frac{d^2 t}{d\overline{C}^2} \geq \frac{\psi' G''}{G'^3} - \frac{HG'' - [\lambda/(1+\lambda)]d(F/f)/d\beta]\psi''}{G'^2}.$$

Using (3.9) to replace ψ' yields, after some simplifications,

$$\frac{d^2t}{d\bar{C}^2} \geq \frac{\lambda}{1+\lambda}\left(\frac{\psi''}{G'^3}\right)\left[G'\frac{d(F/f)}{d\beta} - G''\frac{F}{f}\right].$$

Hence, if the condition i in proposition 3.2 holds, $d^2t/d\bar{C}^2 \geq 0$ (recall that the hazard rate is monotonic). This implies that the regulator can use a menu of linear contracts. The slope of each incentive contract is given by the firm's first-order condition

$$\frac{dt}{d\bar{C}} + \psi'(\beta - I(\bar{C}))I'(\bar{C}) = 0;$$

it suffices to invert the equilibrium function $\bar{C} = \bar{C}(\beta)$ into $\beta = \beta(\bar{C})$ and eliminate β in the previous equation. ■

REFERENCES

Armstrong, M., and J. Vickers. 1991. Welfare effects of price discrimination by a regulated monopolist. Mimeo, Oxford University.

Atkinson, A., and J. Stiglitz. 1976. The design of tax structure: Direct and indirect taxation. *Journal of Public Economics* 6:55–75.

Atkinson, A., and J. Stiglitz. 1980. *Lectures on Public Economics.* New York: McGraw-Hill.

Bailey, E. 1973. *Economic Theory of Regulatory Constraint.* Lexington, MA: D.C. Heath, Lexington Books.

Ballard, C., J. Shoven, and J. Whalley. 1985. General equilibrium computations of the marginal welfare costs of taxes in the United States. *American Economic Review* 75:128–138.

Baron, D., and R. Myerson. 1982. Regulating a monopolist with unknown costs. *Econometrica* 50:911–930.

Baumol, W. 1975. Payment by performance in rail passenger transportation: an innovation in Amtrak's operations. *Bell Journal of Economics* 6:281–298.

Baumol, W., and D. Bradford. 1970. Optimal departures from marginal cost pricing. *American Economic Review* 60:265–283.

Baumol, W., J. Panzar, and R. Willig. 1982. *Contestable Markets and the Theory of Industry Structure.* San Diego, CA: Harcourt Brace Jovanovich.

Blackorby, C., and W. Schworm. 1984. The structure of economies with aggregate measures of capital: A complete characterization. *Review of Economic Studies* 51:633–650.

Blackorby, C. and W. Schworm. 1988. The existence of input and output aggregates in aggregate production functions. *Econometrica* 56:613–643.

Boiteux, M. 1949. La tarification des demandes en pointe. *Revue Générale de l'Électricité* 58:321–340. Translated as Peak-load pricing, *Journal of Business* 33 (1960):157–179.

Boiteux, M. 1956. Sur la gestion des monopoles publics astreints à l'equilibre budgétaire. *Econometrica* 24:22–40.

Brennan, T. 1987. Cross subsidization and discrimination by regulated monopolists. EAG DP# 87-2, U.S. Department of Justice.

Brown, S., and D. Sibley. 1985. *The Theory of Public Utility Pricing.* Cambridge: Cambridge University Press.

Dana, J. 1987. The organization and scope of monitored agents: Regulating multiproduct industries. Mimeo, Massachusetts Institute of Technology.

Deaton, A. 1977. Equity, efficiency and the structure of indirect taxation. *Journal of Public Economics* 8:299–312.

Faulhaber, G. 1975. Cross-subsidization: Pricing in public enterprises. *American Economic Review* 75:966–977.

Fisher, F. 1965. Embodied technical change and the existence of an aggregate capital stock. *Review of Economic Studies* 35:263–288.

Gorman, W. 1968. Reviewing the quantities of fixed factors. In *Value, Capital and Growth: Essays in Honor of Sir John Hicks*, ed. J. N. Wolfe. Edinburgh: Edinburgh University Press, ch. 5.

Hausman, J., and J. Poterba. 1987. Household behavior and the tax reform act of 1986. *Journal of Economic Perspectives* 1:101–119.

Laffont, J.-J., E. Maskin, and J.-C. Rochet. 1987. Optimal nonlinear pricing: The case of buyers with several characteristics. In *Information, Incentives and Economic Mechanisms: In Honor of L. Hurwicz*, ed. T. Groves, R. Radner, and S. Reiter. Minneapolis: University of Minnesota Press.

Leontief, W. 1947. Introduction to a theory of the internal structure of functional relationships. *Econometrica* 15:361–373.

Lewis, T., and D. Sappington. 1988. Regulating a monopolist with unknown demand and cost functions. *Rand Journal of Economics* 19:438–457.

McAfee, P., and J. McMillan. 1988. Multidimensional incentive compatibility and mechanism design. *Journal of Economic Theory* 46:335–354.

Mirrlees, J. 1976. Optimal tax theory: A synthesis. *Journal of Public Economics* 6:327–358.

MIT Energy Laboratory. 1984. Incentive regulation in the electric utility industry. SR84-03, Massachusetts Institute of Technology.

Noam, E. 1989. The quality of regulation in regulating quality: A proposal for an integrated incentive approach to telephone service performance. Mimeo, New York State Public Service Commission.

Phlips, L. 1983. *The Economics of Price Discrimination.* Cambridge: Cambridge University Press.

Posner, R. 1971. Taxation by regulation. *Bell Journal of Economics* 2:22–50.

Ramsey, F. 1927. A contribution to the theory of taxation. *Economic Journal* 37:47–61.

Rochet, J.-C. 1985. The taxation principle and multi-time Hamilton-Jacobi equations. *Journal of Mathematical Economics* 14:113–128.

Sappington, D. 1983. Optimal regulation of a multiproduct monopoly with unknown technological capabilities. *Bell Journal of Economics* 14:453–463.

Sharkey, W. 1982. *The Theory of Natural Monopoly.* Cambridge: Cambridge University Press.

Sheshinski, E. 1986. Positive second best theory: A brief survey of the theory of Ramsey pricing. In *The Handbook of Mathematical Economics*, vol. 3, ed. K. Arrow and M. Intriligator. Amsterdam: North-Holland, ch. 5.

Steiner, P. 1957. Peak loads and efficient pricing. *The Quarterly Journal of Economics* 71:585–610.

Tirole, J. 1988. *The Theory of Industrial Organization.* Cambridge, MA: MIT Press.

Varian, H. 1989. Price discrimination. In *The Handbook of Industrial Organization*, vol. 1, ed. R. Schmalensee and R. Willig. Amsterdam: North-Holland, ch. 10.

Wilson, R. 1992. *Nonlinear Pricing.* Oxford: Oxford University Press.

Vogelsang, I., and J. Finsinger. 1979. A regulatory adjustment process for optimal pricing by multiproduct monopoly firms. *Bell Journal of Economics* 10:157–171.

4 REGULATION OF QUALITY

4.1 Some Background

An unregulated monopolist has two incentives to provide quality: a sales incentive and a reputation incentive. When quality is observed by consumers before purchasing (*search good*), a reduction in quality reduces sales, and thus revenue as the monopoly price exceeds marginal cost. In contrast, when quality is observed by consumers only after purchasing (*experience good*), the monopolist has no incentive to supply quality unless consumers may repeat their purchases in the future. The provision of quality is then linked with the monopolist's desire to keep its reputation and preserve future profits.

In this chapter we investigate whether similar incentives to provide quality exist in a regulated environment. Before doing so, it is useful to distinguish between *observable* and *verifiable* qualities. Quality is usually observable by consumers before or after consumption. Quality is verifiable if its level can be (costlessly) described ex ante in a contract and ascertained ex post by a court. When quality is verifiable, the regulator can impose a quality target on the regulated firm, or more generally reward or punish the firm directly as a function of the level of quality. For instance, a regulatory commission can dictate the heating value of gas or can punish an electric utility on the basis of the number and intensity of outages. Formally the regulation of verifiable quality is analogous to the regulation of a multiproduct firm, since the level of quality on a given product can be treated as the quantity of another, fictitious product (see chapter 3).

This chapter is concerned with observable but *unverifiable* quality. The effectiveness of a new weapons system, the quality of programs broadcast by a regulated television station, the range of services enjoyed by a railroad passenger, or the threat of a core meltdown at a nuclear plant are hard to quantify and include in a formal contract. As Kahn (1988, p. 22) argues:

> But it is far more true of quality of service than of price that the primary responsibility remains with the supplying company instead of with the regulatory agency, and that the agencies, in turn, have devoted much more attention to the latter than to the former. The reasons for this are fairly clear. Service standards are often much more difficult to specify by the promulgation of rules.

When quality is unverifiable, the regulator must recreate the incentives of an unregulated firm to provide quality without throwing away the benefits of regulation. First, it must reward the regulated firm on the basis of sales. Second, the possibility of nonrenewal of a regulatory license, of second sourcing, of deregulation, or of missing future sales-contingent rewards makes the regulated firm concerned about its reputation as a supplier of quality.

The focus of our analysis is the relationship between quality concern and the power of optimal incentive schemes. Recall that an incentive scheme is high (low) powered if the firm bears a high (low) fraction of its realized costs. Thus a fixed-price contract is very high powered, and a cost-plus contract is very low powered.

The link between quality and the power of incentive schemes has been widely discussed. For instance, there has been a concern that "incentive regulation" (understand: high-powered incentive schemes) conflicts with the safe operation of nuclear power plants by forcing management to hurry work, take shortcuts, and delay safety investments. There have been accounts that the switch to a high-powered incentive scheme for British Telecom (price caps) after its privatization produced a poor record on the quality front (Vickers and Yarrow 1988, p. 228).[1] A related concern has been expressed about the effect of yardstick competition on cost. It is feared that firms would concentrate their efforts on reducing cost and would sacrifice quality. To the extent that yardstick competition makes high-powered schemes more attractive (see chapter 1), the concern about yardstick competition resembles those about incentive regulation.

Similarly Kahn (1988, I, p. 24) contends that in the matter of quality under cost-of-service regulation (a very low-powered incentive scheme) "far more than in the matter of price, the interest of the monopolist, on the one hand, and the consumer, on the other, are more nearly coincident than in conflict." Kahn's intuition is that the regulated monopolist does not suffer from incurring monetary costs to enhance quality because these costs are paid by consumers through direct charges. This intuition is incomplete. First, some components of quality involve nonmonetary costs. Second, and more important, under pure cost-of-service regulation the regulated firm does not gain from providing costly services either, so a low perceived cost of supplying quality does not imply a high incentive to supply quality.[2] Last, in the context of military procurement, Scherer (1964, pp. 165–166) has suggested:

> There is reason to believe that the use of fixed-price contracts would not greatly reduce the emphasis placed on quality in weapons development projects, although it might affect certain marginal trade-off decisions with only a minor expected impact on future sales.

1. It is not surprising that the dissatisfaction with the quality performance subsequently led to the costly development and monitoring of quality indices to be included in the incentive schemes.

2. In practice one does not observe pure cost-of-service regulation. Due to the regulatory lag the regulated firm is, like an unregulated monopolist, the residual claimant for the revenue it generates and costs it incurs between rate reviews (the differences being that the prices are fixed and that the regulated monopolist is concerned about the ratchet effect); thus actual cost-of-service incentive schemes are not as low powered as one might believe. We will not try to study (variants of) cost-of-service regulation but will rather focus on optimal regulation. See Joskow and Rose (1989) for empirical evidence on the level of services under cost-of-service regulation.

To give formal arguments that would assess the relevance of these perceptions, we introduce two related natural monopoly models of an experience good and of a search good. Whether the power of regulatory contracts decreases when quality becomes more desirable depends crucially on whether contractual incentives can be based on sales (on top of cost), that is, on whether the regulated firm supplies a search or an experience good. In our two-period model of an experience good, the regulator purchases a fixed amount from the regulated firm in the first period. Since quality is ex ante unverifiable, the regulator has no alternative other than to accept the product. The supplier's incentive to provide quality is then the reputation incentive, that is, the possibility of losing future sales. In contrast, our static search good model has the firm sell to consumers who observe quality before purchasing. The former model is best thought of as a procurement model, and the latter as a regulation model, although other interpretations are possible (in particular some regulated products are experience goods).

In the case of an *experience good*, we argue that incentives to supply quality and those to reduce cost are inherently in conflict. The regulator has a single instrument—the cost-reimbursement rule—to provide both types of incentives. High-powered incentive schemes induce cost reduction but increase the firm's perceived cost of providing quality. This *crowding-out effect* implies that the more important quality is, the lower will be the power of the optimal incentive scheme. We also show that when the firm becomes more concerned about the future, its perceived cost of supplying quality decreases, and this induces the regulator to offer more powerful incentive schemes. We thus find Scherer's suggestion quite perceptive.

In the case of a *search good*, the crowding-out effect is latent but has no influence on the power of incentive schemes. In our model the regulator can separate the two incentive problems because he or she has two instruments: the cost-reimbursement rule and the sales incentive. The incentive to maintain quality is provided through a reward based on a quality index, which is the level of sales corrected by the price charged by the firm. As for an experience good, the cost-reducing activity is encouraged through the cost-reimbursement rule, which is now freed from the concern of providing the right quality incentives. This dichotomy does not, however, imply that an increase in the desirability of quality has no effect on the power of incentive schemes; it has an indirect effect because higher services may increase or decrease the optimal level of output, which in turn changes the value of reducing marginal cost and thus affects the regulator's arbitrage between incentives and rent extraction.

Before proceeding, we should comment on the possibility of having (search) goods whose quality is observable by consumers but is not verifiable by regulators. We have in mind the case of a television station or of a railroad, whose services are hard to measure objectively and yet are relatively well-perceived by the consumers. It is important, however, to realize that regulators can in practice resort to user panels. For instance, a wide range of consumer satisfaction variables in telecommunications services has been collected in the states of New York and Florida (percentage call completions, consumer trouble reports, missed repair appointments, accuracy of billing, operator response time, etc.; see, e.g., Noam 1989). Very generally regulators face a trade-off between developing costly quality performance measures and giving the firm monetary incentives of the sort described in the search good section of this chapter (or using both methods).

The chapter is organized as follows. Section 4.2 develops a single-product, static model of sales incentive. The regulator observes the total cost, price, and output of a natural monopoly. The regulator's imperfect knowledge of the production technology and of the demand function makes the problems of inducing cost-reducing activities and the provision of quality/services nontrivial. Services are monetary or nonmonetary; monetary services enter total cost but cannot be disentangled from other costs (i.e., cannot be recovered from the aggregate accounting data). Section 4.3 solves for the optimal incentive scheme. Section 4.4 shows that the optimum can be implemented by a scheme that is linear in both realized cost and a quality index that is computed from price and sales data. Section 4.5 links variations in the quality concern and the slope (power) of incentive schemes.

Section 4.6 discusses reputation incentives. It develops a model of an experience good in which a quality choice by the firm has permanent effects. The observation of quality today reveals information about future quality. This model is one of moral hazard (unverifiable intertemporal choice of quality). In contrast, many models of reputation in the industrial organization literature have assumed that the firm can be "born" a high- or low-quality producer and can, at a cost, masquerade as a high-quality producer if it is a low-quality producer. Appendix A4.9 stages a variant of the reputation models of Kreps and Wilson (1982), Milgrom and Roberts (1982), and Holmström (1982) in a regulatory context and obtains results similar to those in the moral hazard model. Section 4.7 concludes the chapter and suggests some desirable extensions.

4.2 The Model with a Search Good

We begin this section by considering a special case in which the cost-reducing activity can be perfectly monitored and incentive issues arise only for the provision of quality. We then extend the model to analyze the interaction between the incentives to supply quality and those to reduce cost.

4.2.1 Incentives to Provide Quality

We first consider a natural monopoly producing a single commodity in quantity q with observable but unverifiable quality/services. We assume that the firm's cost function depends only on quantity and is common knowledge:

$$C = C(q)$$

(since we assume away issues of incentives for cost reduction, we can without loss of generality ignore any effort to reduce cost).

On the demand side we assume that the regulator does not perfectly know the demand curve, which depends on the level of quality s. Otherwise, he or she would be able to infer the exact level of services provided by the firm from the price and output data. Thus we posit an inverse demand function

$$p = P(q, s, \theta),$$

where P decreases with q and (by convention) with θ, and increases with s. Let η denote the elasticity of demand. θ is a demand parameter known by the firm only and is drawn from the cumulative distribution F with a strictly positive density f on $[\underline{\theta}, \bar{\theta}]$. The consumer's gross surplus function is denoted $S^g(q, s, \theta)$.

Quantity and quality are *net complements* if an increase in quality raises the net marginal willingness to pay, that is, the difference between price and marginal cost:

$$\frac{\partial^2(S^g - C)}{\partial s \partial q} = \frac{\partial(p - C_q)}{\partial s} > 0.$$

Similarly quantity and quality are *net substitutes* if $\partial^2(S^g - C)/\partial s \partial q < 0$. Quality is provided by the firm that has a (nonmonetary) disutility of $\psi(s)$ with $\psi' > 0$, $\psi'' > 0$, $\psi''' \geq 0$. Making the accounting convention that the regulator reimburses the cost C and receives the revenue from sales, the firm's utility level is $U = t - \psi(s)$, and social welfare is

$$W = S^g(q, s, \theta) + \lambda P(q, s, \theta)q - (1 + \lambda)[\psi(s) + C(q)] - \lambda U.$$

We assume that W is concave in (q, s).

From a methodological point of view, the model closely resembles those of chapters 2 and 3, with θ replacing β and s replacing e. Consequently calculations are left to the reader, and technicalities are skipped. Under *complete information* optimal regulation is characterized by the equality of the marginal benefits and costs of output and quality:

$$\frac{p - C'}{p} = \frac{\lambda}{1 + \lambda}\frac{1}{\eta},$$

and

$$S_s^g + \lambda P_s q = (1 + \lambda)\psi'.$$

Consider now the case of *incomplete information*, where the regulator observes only the price, the output, and the realized cost. Let $s = \chi(p, q, \theta)$ denote the solution in s of $p = P(q, s, \theta)$. Then

$$U = t - \psi(\chi(p, q, \theta)).$$

The incentive and individual rationality constraints can be written

$$\dot{U} \equiv \frac{dU}{d\theta} = -\psi'(s)\chi_\theta(P(q, s, \theta), q, \theta)$$

(using the envelope theorem) and

$$U(\bar{\theta}) \geq 0.$$

Note that the convention $P_\theta < 0$ implies that $\chi_\theta > 0$ and that $\dot{U} < 0$.

Neglecting second-order conditions, we characterize optimal regulation by

$$\frac{p - C'}{p} = \frac{\lambda}{1 + \lambda}\frac{1}{\eta} + \frac{\lambda}{p(1 + \lambda)}\frac{F}{f}\psi'(\chi_{\theta p}P_q + \chi_{\theta q})$$

and

$$S_s^g + \lambda P_s q = (1 + \lambda)\psi' + \lambda\frac{F}{f}(\psi''\chi_\theta + \psi'\chi_{\theta p}P_s).$$

If χ_θ is independent of p and q [i.e., if $p = P(q, \zeta(s, \theta))$], the dichotomy obtains; then the Ramsey pricing rule is unaffected by incentives.

The simple case $s = \xi(p, q) + \theta$ can be reinterpreted in the framework of chapter 1 by setting $s \equiv e$, $\beta \equiv \theta$, and $C \equiv -\xi(p, q)$ and by replacing the marginal social value of service $S_s + \lambda P_s q$ by the marginal social value of cost savings $1 + \lambda$. Thus

$$\psi'(s) = \frac{S_s^g + \lambda P_s q}{1 + \lambda} - \frac{\lambda}{1 + \lambda}\frac{F}{f}\psi''(s).$$

Incomplete information affects the quality and quantity variables and increases the cost of supplying quality. Since rents are increasing in the level of quality obtained, it is desirable to decrease quality. This is achieved by giving lower incentives for quality than under complete information.

Considering the special case $s = \xi(p, q) + \theta$, the optimal regulation can be implemented by a nonlinear transfer that is a function of the aggregate or "price-adjusted output" $\xi(p, q)$. This nonlinear function can itself be replaced by a menu of linear contracts, as in chapters 1 and 2. Sales are used as an index of quality, since consumers discover the quality of the search good before purchasing.

4.2.2 Incentives for Quality and Cost Reduction

We now extend the model to a more general (variable) cost function

$$C = C(q, s, e, \beta),$$

which depends on the level of quality s, on the level of cost-reducing effort e, and on the parameter of private information β. The model is thus one of two-dimensional moral hazard (e and s) and two-dimensional adverse selection (β and θ). To obtain a closed-form solution, we specialize it to *linear* cost and demand functions. This enables us to reduce the problem to a one-dimensional adverse selection one.

Let us now describe the model in more detail. The cost function is

$$C = (\beta + s - e)q. \tag{4.1}$$

Note that (4.1) now assumes that the cost of providing quality is monetary. However, the remark that follows shows that a relabeling of variables allows the cost of providing quality to be nonmonetary as in subsection 4.2.1. Note also that as in chapter 2, a scale effect is built into the cost function. The higher the production level, the more valuable is effort. Other notation and conventions follow those of chapter 3. The firm's rent is

$$U = t - \psi(e). \tag{4.2}$$

Consumers observe the quality before purchasing the (search) good and derive from the consumption of the commodity a gross surplus:

$$S^g(q, s, \theta) = (A + ks - h\theta)q - \frac{B}{2}q^2 - \frac{(ks - h\theta)^2}{2}, \tag{4.3}$$

where A, B, h, and k are known positive constants and θ in $[\underline{\theta}, \bar{\theta}]$ is a demand parameter.[3]

The inverse demand curve is then

$$p = \frac{\partial S^g}{\partial q} = A + ks - h\theta - Bq. \tag{4.4}$$

3. Note that S^g differs from 0 at $q = 0$. One could think of S^g as a local approximation in the relevant range. Or one might allow services to affect consumers even in the absence of consumption. The reader should be aware that the Spencian comparison between the marginal willingnesses to pay for quality of the marginal and the average consumers under unregulated monopoly requires that S^g be equal to zero at $q = 0$.

Quantity and quality are net complements if $k > 1$ and net substitutes if $k < 1$. We will of course focus on parameters that put the problem in the relevant range ($\partial S^g/\partial q > 0, \partial S^g/\partial s > 0$).

The consumers'/taxpayers' net surplus is

$$S^n = (A + ks - h\theta)q - \frac{B}{2}q^2 - \frac{(ks - h\theta)^2}{2} - pq - (1 + \lambda)(C - pq + t). \tag{4.5}$$

From (4.4), (4.5) can be rewritten

$$S^n = (A + ks - h\theta)q - \frac{B}{2}q^2 - \frac{(ks - h\theta)^2}{2} + \lambda(A + ks - h\theta - Bq)q - (1 + \lambda)(C + t). \tag{4.6}$$

Remark As mentioned before, our model covers the case of a nonmonetary cost of providing quality. Suppose that the accounting cost is $C = (\beta - \tilde{e})q$, where $\tilde{e}$ is the effort to reduce cost. Suppose further that the firm exerts a second type of effort s per unit of output that provides services to consumers. Then the disutility of effort is $\psi(\tilde{e} + s)$. By letting $e \equiv \tilde{e} + s$, the accounting cost becomes $C = (\beta + s - e)q$ and the disutility of effort is $\psi(e)$. This remark shows vividly that cost-reducing activities $\tilde{e}$ and the provision of services s are *substitutes*: An increase in services raises the marginal disutility $\psi'(\tilde{e} + s)$ of exerting effort to reduce cost.

Under *complete information* a utilitarian regulator maximizes the sum of consumer and producer surpluses under the constraint that the firm be willing to participate:

$$\max_{\{q,s,e\}} \left\{ W = (1 + \lambda)(A + ks - h\theta)q - B\left(\frac{1}{2} + \lambda\right)q^2 - \frac{(ks - h\theta)^2}{2} - (1 + \lambda)[(\beta + s - e)q + t] + t - \psi(e) \right\} \tag{4.7}$$

such that

$$t - \psi(e) \geq 0, \tag{4.8}$$

where equation (4.8) normalizes the firm's reservation utility to be zero. For B large enough, the program $\{(4.7), (4.8)\}$ is concave and its (interior) maximum is characterized by the first-order conditions:

$$(1 + \lambda)p - \lambda Bq = (1 + \lambda)(\beta + s - e), \tag{4.9}$$

$$(1 + \lambda)kq - k(ks - h\theta) = (1 + \lambda)q, \tag{4.10}$$

$$\psi'(e) = q, \tag{4.11}$$

$$t = \psi(e). \tag{4.12}$$

Equation (4.9) equates the marginal social utility of the commodity [composed of the marginal utility of the commodity to consumers S^g_q and the marginal financial gain $d(\lambda pq)/dq$] to its marginal social cost $(1 + \lambda)C_q$. Similarly equation (4.10) equates the marginal social utility of service quality to its marginal social cost. Equation (4.11) equates the marginal disutility of effort $\psi'(e)$ to its marginal utility q. And equation (4.12) says that no rent is left to the firm.

Equations (4.9) and (4.10) are most easily interpreted in the following forms:

$$\frac{p - C_q}{p} = \frac{\lambda}{1 + \lambda}\frac{1}{\eta}, \tag{4.9'}$$

$$\frac{\partial S^g}{\partial s} + \lambda\frac{\partial P}{\partial s}q = (1 + \lambda)\frac{\partial C}{\partial s}, \tag{4.10'}$$

where $\eta \equiv p/Bq$. The Lerner index—or price–marginal cost ratio—is equal to a Ramsey index (a number between 0 and 1) times the inverse of the elasticity of demand. The optimal level of services equates the marginal gross surplus plus the shadow cost of public funds times the increase in revenue to the social marginal cost of quality.

For the record it is worth comparing the regulated level of quality with that chosen by an unregulated monopoly. Since the cost and demand functions are linear in services, the monopoly solution is "bang-bang." Quality is either zero if quantity and quality are net substitutes or maximal (if an upper bound on quality exists) if quantity and quality are net complements. As in Spence (1975) an unregulated monopolist may over- or undersupply quality for a given quantity.

4.3 Optimal Regulation under Asymmetric Information

We now assume that the regulator faces a multidimensional asymmetry of information. The regulator knows neither β nor θ and cannot observe e and s. However, he or she observes C, p, and q. Faced with this informational gap, the regulator is assumed to behave as a Bayesian statistician who maximizes expected social welfare and has a prior cumulative distribution F_1 on $\beta \in [\underline{\beta}, \bar{\beta}]$ and a prior cumulative distribution F_2 on $\theta \in [\underline{\theta}, \bar{\theta}]$. The firm knows β and θ before contracting.

The regulator knows that consumers equate their marginal utility of the commodity to the price; hence

$$p = A + ks - h\theta - Bq. \tag{4.13}$$

Using the observability of p and q, it is possible to eliminate the unobservable service quality level s in the consumers' gross valuation of the commodity, which becomes

$$S^g(p,q) = \frac{B}{2}q^2 + pq - \frac{1}{2}(p - A + Bq)^2. \tag{4.14}$$

Similarly the cost function becomes

$$C = \left(\beta + \frac{h\theta}{k} - e\right)q + q\left(\frac{p - A + Bq}{k}\right). \tag{4.15}$$

Note that β and θ enter the cost function only through the linear combination $\gamma \equiv \beta + h\theta/k$. This feature, which also holds for the firm's and regulator's objective functions (see below), reduces the model to a one-dimensional adverse-selection problem, and it will enable us to obtain a closed-form solution.[4]

Consider now the firm's objective function (recalling our accounting convention that the regulator pays the cost and receives the revenue):

$$U = t - \psi(e) = t - \psi\left(\gamma + \frac{p - A + Bq}{k} - \frac{C}{q}\right). \tag{4.16}$$

The regulator wishes to maximize expected social welfare under the incentive and individual rationality constraints of the firm. From the revelation principle we can restrict the problem of control of the firm to the analysis of direct and truthful revelation mechanisms.

For simplicity we assume that the cumulative distribution function $F(\cdot)$ of γ on $[\underline{\gamma}, \bar{\gamma}] = [\underline{\beta} + h\underline{\theta}/k, \bar{\beta} + h\bar{\theta}/k]$ (the convolution of F_1 and F_2) satisfies the monotone hazard rate property $d(F(\gamma)/f(\gamma))/d\gamma > 0$. Appendix A4.1 computes the hazard rate of the convolution. The monotone-hazard-rate assumption avoids bunching without significant loss for the economics of the problem. The firm is faced with a revelation mechanism $\{t(\gamma), c(\gamma), p(\gamma), q(\gamma)\}$ that specifies for each announced value of γ a net transfer to the firm $t(\gamma)$, an average cost to realize $c(\gamma)$, a price to charge $p(\gamma)$, and a quantity to sell $q(\gamma)$. Truth telling is caused by the first- and second-order conditions of incentive compatibility (see appendix A4.2):

$$\dot{t} = \left[\frac{\dot{p} + B\dot{q}}{k} - \left(\frac{\dot{C}}{q}\right)\right]\psi', \tag{4.17}$$

$$\frac{\dot{p} + B\dot{q}}{k} - \left(\frac{\dot{C}}{q}\right) \le 0, \tag{4.18}$$

where $\dot{t} \equiv dt/d\gamma$, and so on.

4. A more general formulation of the consumers' tastes would lead to a truly two-dimensional adverse-selection problem. The qualitative results would be similar, but the technical analysis would be greatly complicated (e.g., see Laffont, Maskin, and Rochet 1987).

Using (4.13) to substitute out quality, the social welfare function (4.7) can be written

$$W = \frac{B}{2}q^2 + (1+\lambda)pq - \frac{1}{2}(p - A + Bq)^2$$
$$- (1+\lambda)\left[(\gamma - e)q + q\left(\frac{p - A + Bq}{k}\right) + \psi(e)\right] - \lambda U. \tag{4.19}$$

The regulator maximizes the expected social welfare function under the incentive compatibility conditions {(4.17), (4.18)} and the individual rationality constraint of the firm:

$$U(\gamma) \geq 0 \qquad \text{for any } \gamma.^5 \tag{4.20}$$

Using U as a state variable, we obtain the maximization program:

$$\max_{\{p(\cdot), q(\cdot), e(\cdot), U(\cdot)\}} \int_{\underline{\gamma}}^{\bar{\gamma}} \left\{\frac{B}{2}q^2 + (1+\lambda)pq - \frac{1}{2}(p - A + Bq)^2\right.$$
$$\left. - (1+\lambda)\left[(\gamma - e)q + q\left(\frac{p - A + Bq}{k}\right) + \psi(e)\right] - \lambda U\right\} dF(\gamma) \tag{4.21}$$

such that

$$\dot{U}(\gamma) = -\psi'(e), \tag{4.22}$$

$$\dot{e} - 1 \leq 0, \tag{4.23}$$

$$U(\bar{\gamma}) \geq 0. \tag{4.24}$$

Equation (4.22) is another version of the first-order incentive compatibility constraint (4.17). Moreover, since $U(\gamma)$ is decreasing, the IR constraint (4.20) reduces to the boundary condition (4.24). From appendix A4.2, (4.23) is a rewriting of the second-order condition (4.18). We ignore it in a first step and later check that it is indeed satisfied by the solution of the subconstrained program. For A and B large enough, the program is concave and the optimum is characterized by its first-order conditions (see appendix A4.3). Let $\mu(\gamma)$ denote the Pontryagin multiplier associated with (4.22) and H the hamiltonian associated with the program {(4.21), (4.22), (4.24)}. From the Pontryagin principle we have

$$\dot{\mu}(\gamma) = -\frac{\partial H}{\partial U} = \lambda f(\gamma). \tag{4.25}$$

From the transversality condition and (4.25) we derive

$$\mu(\gamma) = \lambda F(\gamma). \tag{4.26}$$

5. We implicitly assume here that it is worth producing for any γ in $[\underline{\gamma}, \bar{\gamma}]$.

Maximizing the hamiltonian with respect to q, p, e, we get after some algebraic manipulations:

$$(1 + \lambda)p - \lambda Bq = (1 + \lambda)\left(\gamma - e + \frac{p - A + Bq}{k}\right), \tag{4.27}$$

$$(1 + \lambda)kq - k(p - A + Bq) = (1 + \lambda)q, \tag{4.28}$$

$$\psi'(e) = q - \frac{\lambda}{1 + \lambda}\frac{F(\gamma)}{f(\gamma)}\psi''(e). \tag{4.29}$$

Equations (4.27) and (4.28), which correspond to the maximizations with respect to q and p, coincide with (4.9) and (4.10). That is, for a given effort e the price, quantity, and quality are the same as under complete information about the technology and demand parameter. This result is reminiscent of the incentive-pricing dichotomy result for multiproduct firms obtained in chapter 3. From (4.22) we see that p and q do not affect the rate at which the rent must be given up to the firm. There is no point in distorting p or q for incentive purposes. Appendix A4.4 derives a more general class of cost functions for which the dichotomy holds in this quality problem.

To extract part of the firm's rent, the effort is distorted downward for a given output level [compare (4.29) and (4.11)], except when $\gamma = \underline{\gamma}$. Appendix A4.3 shows that for the solution to $\{(4.27), (4.28), (4.29)\}$, $\dot{p}(\gamma) > 0$, $\dot{q}(\gamma) < 0$ and $\dot{e}(\gamma) < 0$. In particular the neglected second-order condition for the firm $[1 - \dot{e}(\gamma) \geq 0]$ is satisfied. Next, we compare the levels of quality under complete and incomplete information about β and θ.

Proposition 4.1 The level of quality is lower under incomplete information than under complete information if and only if quantity and quality are net complements.

Proof See appendix A4.5.

Incomplete information makes rent extraction difficult and reduces the power of incentive schemes, that is, leads to a decrease in effort. This raises marginal cost and reduces output. If quantity and quality are net complements, lower services are desirable, and conversely for net substitutes. Note that asymmetric information lowers quality exactly when the unregulated monopolist oversupplies quality.

To conclude this section, note that for a search good, sales are an indicator of quality in the same way cost is an indicator of effort (and quality). The regulation of quality and effort under asymmetric information is therefore in the spirit of the regulation of a multiproduct firm (see chapter 3).

4.4 Implementation of the Optimal Regulatory Mechanism

For each announcement of the firm's technological parameter and of the consumers' taste parameter, the regulator imposes a level of average cost to achieve, a quantity to produce, and a market price to charge. An appropriate net transfer $t(\gamma)$ is offered to induce truthful behavior.

This transfer can be reinterpreted as follows: Let $z \equiv C/q - (p - A + Bq)/k$. The first-order incentive compatibility condition is (see appendix A4.2)

$$\frac{dt}{d\gamma} + \psi'(\gamma - z)\frac{dz}{d\gamma} = 0 \tag{4.30}$$

or

$$\frac{dt}{dz} = -\psi'(\gamma - z) < 0. \tag{4.31}$$

Differentiating (4.31), we obtain

$$\frac{d^2t}{dz^2} = -\psi''(\gamma - z)\left(\frac{1}{dz/d\gamma} - 1\right). \tag{4.32}$$

From the second-order condition $dz/d\gamma \geq 0$ and $1 - dz/d\gamma = de/d\gamma < 0$ from appendix A4.3. Therefore $d^2t/dz^2 > 0$; in words, the transfer as a function of z is a convex and decreasing function (see figure 4.1).

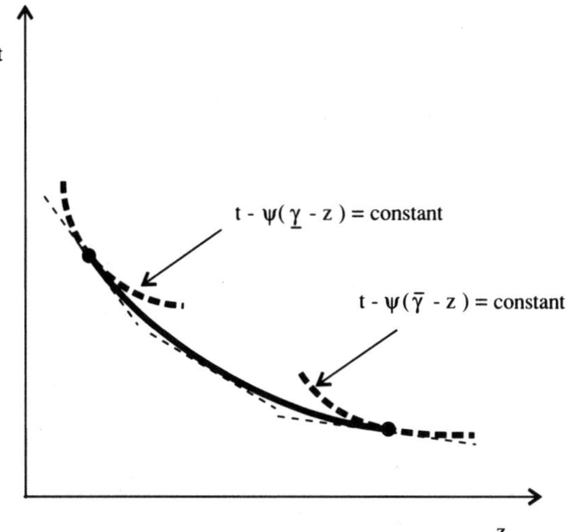

Figure 4.1
Incentive scheme for a search good

As in chapter 2 the convex nonlinear transfer function $t(z)$ can be replaced by a menu of linear contracts

$$t(z,\gamma) = a(\gamma) + b(\gamma)[z(\gamma) - z],$$

where $z(\gamma)$ is the announced value of $C/q - (p - A + Bq)/k$ and z is the observed ex post value. The transfer is therefore a function of a performance index that subtracts from the realized average cost an approximation of the service quality inferred from market data. In other words, the firm is offered a choice in a menu of linear contracts and is rewarded or penalized according to deviations from an index aggregating cost data and service quality data inferred from the observation of market price and quantity and from a priori knowledge of the demand function.

The coefficient $b(\gamma)$ sharing the overrun in the performance index is $\psi'(e^*(\gamma))$, where $e^*(\gamma)$ is the solution of the regulator's optimization program. Indeed

$$\max_{\{e,\tilde{\gamma}\}} \{a(\tilde{\gamma}) + \psi'(e^*(\tilde{\gamma}))[z(\tilde{\gamma}) - \gamma + e] - \psi(e)\}$$

implies that $\psi'(e^*(\tilde{\gamma})) = \psi'(e)$ and therefore that $e = e^*(\tilde{\gamma})$ and $\dot{a}(\tilde{\gamma}) + \psi''\dot{e}^*(\tilde{\gamma})[z(\tilde{\gamma}) - z] + \psi'(e^*(\tilde{\gamma}))\dot{z}(\tilde{\gamma}) = 0$. If $a(\cdot)$ is chosen so that $\dot{a}(\gamma) + \psi'(e^*(\gamma))\dot{z}(\gamma) = 0$ for any γ or $\dot{a}(\gamma) = \dot{t}(\gamma)$, then $\tilde{\gamma} = \gamma$.

Alternatively, the menu of linear contracts can be decomposed into a linear sharing of total cost overruns with a coefficient $b_1(\gamma) = \psi'(e^*(\gamma))/q^*(\gamma)$ and a linear sharing of overruns in the service quality index with a coefficient $b_2(\gamma) = \psi'(e^*(\gamma))$, or

$$t = a(\gamma) + b_1(\gamma)[C(\gamma) - C] + b_2(\gamma)\left[\frac{p + Bq}{k} - \frac{p(\gamma) + Bq(\gamma)}{k}\right].$$

Since the firm is risk neutral, we see that our analysis extends immediately to the case in which random additive disturbances affect total cost and the inverse demand function.

Proposition 4.2 The optimal regulatory scheme can be implemented through a menu of contracts that are linear in realized cost and in a quality index equal to sales corrected by the price level:

$$t = \tilde{a} - b_1 C + b_2 \frac{p + Bq}{k}.$$

Clearly the parameters characterizing the power of the incentive schemes $b_1(\gamma) = \psi'(e^*(\gamma))/q^*(\gamma)$ and $b_2(\gamma) = q^*(\gamma)b_1(\gamma)$ are related. If we study the comparative statics of these coefficients with respect to a parameter x, we have

$$\frac{d}{dx}\left[\frac{\psi'(e)}{q}\right] = \frac{\psi'' e_x q - \psi' q_x}{q^2}.$$

From

$$\psi'(e) = q - \frac{\lambda}{1+\lambda}\frac{F}{f}\psi''(e),$$

$$q_x = \left(\psi'' + \frac{\lambda}{1+\lambda}\frac{F}{f}\psi'''\right)e_x$$

and

$$\frac{d}{dx}\left[\frac{\psi'(e)}{q}\right] = e_x\frac{\lambda}{1+\lambda}\frac{F}{f}\frac{\psi''^2 - \psi'\psi'''}{q^2}.$$

The comparative statics of $b_2(\gamma) = \psi'(e^*(\gamma))$ is the same as the comparative statics of $e^*(\gamma)$, and the comparative statics of $b_1(\gamma)$ is identical as long as ψ''' is not too large, which we will assume in section 4.5. Note that b_1 and b_2 are then positively correlated over the sample of types.

Remark Our recommendation of rewarding the firm as a function of sales could have perverse effects if the firm were also required to take measures that are meant to reduce sales. For instance, an electric utility might be encouraged to promote energy conservation (there is much debate about whether the utilities have enough of a comparative advantage in promoting conservation to justify the conflict of interest associated with their receiving this mission; e.g., contrast Joskow 1990 and Lewis and Sappington 1991b). The regulated firm must then both raise sales through high quality and lower sales through conservation measures. If expenses incurred in promoting conservation are not separately measurable, incentives based on sales are likely to be less effective in implementing the social optimum.

4.5 Concern for Quality and the Power of Incentive Schemes

This section studies the effects of an increase in the consumers' marginal surplus from quality ($\partial S^g/\partial s$) and of an increase in the marginal cost of supplying quality ($\partial C/\partial s$) on the power of incentive schemes. For a clean analysis of these effects, the change must not affect the structure of information, in particular the information revealed by the demand data about the level of quality or by the cost data about cost-reducing effort. The three changes we consider yield identical results (the proofs for them are provided in appendix A4.6).

First, suppose that the consumers' gross surplus S^g is replaced by $\tilde{S}^g = S^g + l(ks - h\theta, v)$, where $l_{11} < 0$ and $l_{12} > 0$.[6] Note that a change in v, the parameter indexing the marginal gross surplus with respect to

6. l_{ij} denotes the second derivative of l with respect to its ith and jth arguments.

quality, does not affect the inverse demand curve and therefore does not change the information revealed by q and p about s. The first-order conditions (4.27) to (4.29) are unchanged except that $\{\partial l/\partial s\}$ must be added to the left-hand side of (4.28). Differentiating (4.27) to (4.29) totally with respect to v yields proposition 4.3.

Proposition 4.3 An increase in the concern for quality (in the sense of an increase in v) raises the power of incentive schemes if quantity and quality are net complements and lowers the power of incentive schemes if they are net substitutes.

Next, let us consider an increase in the marginal cost of quality. To keep the structure of information constant, we transform the cost function into $\tilde{C} \equiv C + m(ks - h\theta, \rho)$, where $m_{11} > 0$ and $m_{12} > 0$ (an increase in ρ corresponds to an increase in marginal cost; the structure of information is kept unchanged because the term $ks - h\theta$ is equal to $p - A + Bq$ and is therefore verifiable).

Proposition 4.4 An increase in the marginal cost of supplying quality (in the sense of an increase in ρ) lowers the power of incentive schemes if quantity and quality are net complements and raises the power of incentive schemes if they are net substitutes.

Last, let us consider an increase in k keeping h/k constant. The point of keeping h/k constant is to leave the asymmetry of information unaffected: When facing demand parameter θ, the firm can claim that the demand parameter is $\hat{\theta}$ by choosing services s satisfying $ks - h\theta = ks(\hat{\theta}) - h\hat{\theta}$ without being detected through the demand data p and q. Thus the "concealment set" is invariant.

Proposition 4.5 An increase in k keeping h/k constant raises the power of incentive schemes if quantity and quality are net complements and lowers the power of incentive schemes if they are net substitutes.

An increase in k corresponds to an increase in the marginal willingness to pay for the good p if and only if $k > 1$. To see this, note that $\partial p/\partial k \propto ks - h\theta = (1 + \lambda)(k - 1)q/k$ from (4.28). Proposition 4.5 thus says that increases in the marginal willingness to pay for the good tilt the optimal contracts toward a fixed price contract for all k.[7]

The intuitions for all these propositions are similar. An increase in the concern for quality (or a decrease in the marginal cost of supplying quality) makes higher quality socially desirable. If quality and quantity are net complements, higher quantity is also socially more desirable. Effort

7. This result is similar to the one obtained when unverifiable quality is not an issue (see chapter 2).

becomes then more effective because it affects more units of the product. To encourage effort, more powerful incentive schemes are used.

4.6 Reputation Incentives for an Experience Good

In some industries the sales incentive is limited because the quantity purchased is fixed or inelastic (e.g., the good is an experience good) or because the buyer is the regulator, as in the case in procurement, or both. Suppose that the buyer (regulator) buys a fixed amount from the firm. The firm's main incentive to provide quality is then the threat of jeopardizing future trading opportunities with the buyer rather than current ones. In general terms, one could think of two mechanisms that link current quality and future sales. First, the buyer could develop a reputation for punishing the firm, for instance, by not trading with it if the firm has supplied low quality in the past. This mechanism might be especially powerful if the buyer oversees many firms and thus has had an opportunity to develop such a reputation. Second, and closer to the industrial organization tradition, the buyer could infer information about the profitability of future trade from the observation of current quality. We focus on this second mechanism.

The industrial organization literature has identified two informational reasons why a buyer could find future trade undesirable after observing poor quality. On the one hand, the quality of the product supplied by the seller might have permanent characteristics, as is the case when the seller commits long-term investments that affect the quality level over several periods. On the other hand, the intertemporal link might be human capital rather than technological investment. The seller's competence or diligence is then signaled through today's choice of quality which conveys information about tomorrow's quality, even though the seller will probably manufacture a brand-new product using new machines. In this section we focus on a permanent and unverifiable choice of technology. Appendix A4.9 develops a model of reputation for being a high-quality producer. The two models yield similar results. We emphasize the new insights added by the human-capital model in appendix A4.9.

For the seller to care about future trade, it must be the case that this trade creates a rent. This rent will be an informational rent, but other types of rents (e.g., due to bargaining power of the seller, to a private benefit associated with production, or to the necessity for the buyer to offer an "efficiency wage" scheme to create incentives) are consistent with the model. Thus in our model complete information about period 2 destroys the possibility of creating incentives for quality provision in period 1.

The model has two periods, $\tau = 1, 2$. In period 1 the seller (regulated firm) produces one unit of the good for the buyer (regulator) at cost

$$C_1 = \beta_1 - e_1 + s, \tag{4.33}$$

where C_1 is the first-period verifiable cost, β_1 an efficiency parameter, e_1 the firm's effort to reduce the first-period cost, and s the level of "care." As in the sales incentive model of sections 4.2 through 4.5, s is formalized as a monetary cost but, alternatively, can be interpreted as a nonmonetary cost. The variables β_1, e_1, and s are private information to the firm; the regulator has a prior cumulative distribution $F(\beta_1)$ on $[\underline{\beta}_1, \overline{\beta}_1]$ with density $f(\beta_1)$ that satisfies the monotone-hazard-rate property $d[F(\beta_1)/f(\beta_1)]/d\beta_1 \geq 0$. Effort e_1 involves disutility $\psi(e_1)$ (with $\psi' > 0$, $\psi'' > 0$, $\psi''' \geq 0$). With probability $\pi(s) \in [0, 1]$ the product "works" and yields a gross social surplus S_1; with probability $1 - \pi(s)$ the product is defective and yields gross social surplus 0. We will say that the firm produces a high- or low-quality item, respectively. We assume that $\pi' > 0$ and that $\pi'' < 0$, as well as that $\pi'(0) = +\infty$ (in order to avoid a corner solution at $s = 0$) and that $\pi''' \leq 0$ (which is a sufficient condition for the regulator's program to be concave). Whether the product works or is defective is observed at the end of period 1 by the regulator. But it is not verifiable by a court, so the regulatory contract cannot be contingent on the quality outcome.

Parties have a discount factor $\delta > 0$ between the two periods. To obtain the simplest model, we assume that the firm's second-period product is defective if and only if the first-period product is defective (i.e., the first- and second-period quality outcomes are both determined by the first-period level of care and are perfectly correlated—as is easily seen, what matters for the results is that a higher s in period 1 raises the expected quality level in period 2). Our assumption implies that the firm will not be asked to produce in period 2 if its product is defective in period 1; in this case the second-period social welfare and firm's rent are normalized to be zero. Let $\overline{U}_2 > 0$ and $\overline{W}_2 > 0$ denote the second-period expected rent for the firm and expected social welfare when the product works. For simplicity we assume that $\overline{U}_2$ and $\overline{W}_2$ are independent of β_1.[8]

Let $\{s(\beta_1), e_1(\beta_1)\}$ denote the firm's first-period care and effort levels, $U_1(\beta_1)$ denote the firm's first-period rent, and $U(\beta_1) \equiv U_1(\beta_1) + \delta\overline{U}_2\pi(s(\beta_1))$ denote the firm's intertemporal rent. Note that a firm with type β_1 can always duplicate the cost and probability of high quality of a firm with type $(\beta_1 - d\beta_1)$ by choosing levels $\{s(\beta_1 - d\beta_1), e_1(\beta_1 - d\beta_1) + d\beta_1\}$ so

8. To give an example, suppose that (1) the firm produces one unit of the same good or a related good in period 2 at cost $C_2 = \beta_2 - e_2$, where $\beta_2 \in [\underline{\beta}_2, \overline{\beta}_2]$ is the second-period efficiency parameter, is uncorrelated with β_1, and is learned (by the firm only) between the two periods (β_2 might reflect the new input costs); (2) the second-period gross surplus is equal to S_2 (possibly equal to S_1) if the firm has produced a high-quality item in period 1, and zero otherwise; and (3) the regulator offers the second-period contract at the beginning of period 2 (no commitment). In this simple example $\overline{U}_2$ and $\overline{W}_2$ are computed as in chapter 1. Furthermore, if S_2 is sufficiently large relative to $\overline{\beta}_2$, $\overline{U}_2$ is independent of S_2.

that the incentive compatibility constraint for effort is

$$\dot{U}(\beta_1) = -\psi'(e_1(\beta_1)). \tag{4.34}$$

Next, consider the firm's choice of care. Suppose that it raises the level of care by 1. To reach the same cost, the firm must increase its effort by 1. At the margin such changes do not affect the firm's rent. The incentive compatibility constraint with respect to care is thus

$$\delta\pi'(s(\beta_1))\bar{U}_2 - \psi'(e_1(\beta_1)) = 0. \tag{4.35}$$

Now suppose that the firm cannot produce in period 2 if it has not produced (and thus invested) in period 1. The individual rationality constraint says that the firm must obtain at least its reservation utility, which we normalize at zero: For all β_1,

$$U_1(\beta_1) + \delta\bar{U}_2\pi(s(\beta_1)) \geq 0. \tag{4.36}$$

As usual, the individual rationality constraint is binding at $\beta_1 = \bar{\beta}_1$ only:[9]

$$U_1(\bar{\beta}_1) + \delta\bar{U}_2\pi(s(\bar{\beta}_1)) = 0. \tag{4.37}$$

Note that type $\bar{\beta}_1$ "buys in"; that is, type $\bar{\beta}_1$ is willing to trade a negative first-period rent for an expected second-period rent.[10] Expected social welfare can then be written

$$\int_{\underline{\beta}_1}^{\bar{\beta}_1} [\pi(s)(S_1 + \delta\bar{W}_2) - (1+\lambda)[\beta_1 - e_1 + s + \psi(e_1)] - \lambda(U(\beta_1) - \delta\pi(s)\bar{U}_2)]f(\beta_1)d\beta_1. \tag{4.38}$$

The regulator maximizes (4.38) subject to (4.34), (4.35), and (4.37). Let $\mu(\beta_1)$ and $v(\beta_1)f(\beta_1)$ denote the multipliers of constraints (4.34) and (4.35), respectively. The hamiltonian is

$$H = [\pi(s)(S_1 + \delta\bar{W}_2) - (1+\lambda)(\beta_1 - e_1 + s + \psi(e_1)) - \lambda U + \lambda\delta\bar{U}_2\pi(s)]f - \mu\psi'(e_1) + vf[\delta\pi'(s)\bar{U}_2 - \psi'(e_1)]. \tag{4.39}$$

We have

$$\dot{\mu} \equiv \frac{d\mu}{d\beta_1} = -\frac{\partial\mathscr{H}}{\partial U} = \lambda f. \tag{4.40}$$

Since $\underline{\beta}_1$ is a free boundary and $F(\underline{\beta}_1) = 0$, we obtain

$$\mu(\beta_1) = \lambda F(\beta_1). \tag{4.41}$$

9. This results from equation (4.34).
10. Such "buy-in" phenomena are typical of noncommitment models, in which firms trade off current losses and future rents. See, for example, Riordan-Sappington (1989).

Taking the derivatives of H with respect to the control variables e_1 and s yields

$$\psi'(e_1) = 1 - \frac{\lambda}{1+\lambda}\frac{F(\beta_1)}{f(\beta_1)}\psi''(e_1) - \frac{\nu}{1+\lambda}\psi''(e_1), \tag{4.42}$$

$$\pi'(s)(S_1 + \delta\overline{W}_2 + \lambda\delta\overline{U}_2) - (1+\lambda) + \nu\delta\pi''(s)\overline{U}_2 = 0. \tag{4.43}$$

Equation (4.42) tells us that the need to give incentives for care induces the regulator to alter the power of the incentive contract [term $[\nu/(1+\lambda)]\psi''(e_1)$]. Whether incentives are more or less powerful than when quality s is verifiable (i.e., whether $\nu \lesseqgtr 0$) is ambiguous. On the one hand, the firm does not internalize the externality of an increase in quality on the welfare of the rest of society ($S_1 + \delta\overline{W}_2 + \lambda\delta\overline{U}_2 > \delta\overline{U}_2$). This externality calls for a subsidization of investments in quality, that is, for a decrease in the power of the incentive scheme. On the other hand, incomplete information about technology already yields low-powered incentives; since its investment is subsidized, the firm has an incentive (aggravated by $\lambda > 0$) to overinvest in quality. When S_1 is small (or δ is large) and the firm captures a high fraction of future rents, the second effect dominates; for small asymmetries of information, i.e., F/f small, or for β_1 close to $\underline{\beta}_1$, the firm's contract when quality is verifiable is close to a fixed-price contract, and the first effect dominates at least for small λ.

As shown in appendix A4.8, the second-order conditions for maximization are satisfied. The solution $\{e_1(\beta_1), s(\beta_1), \nu(\beta_1)\}$ is thus given by (4.35), (4.42), and (4.43). We now derive the comparative-statics results using the interpretation of the optimal incentive scheme as a menu of linear contracts (see appendix A4.7).

Proposition 4.6 There exists $\delta_0 > 0$ such that for all $\delta \geq \delta_0$, investment in quality must be encouraged, in the sense that the shadow price ν of the moral hazard constraint is positive. For $\delta \geq \delta_0$ optimal cost-reimbursement rules are linear. The first-period contract moves toward a fixed-price contract (the slope of the incentive scheme increases for all β_1) when

i. the discount factor δ increases,

ii. the social value of quality S_1 decreases (if $\partial\overline{W}_2/\partial S_1 \geq 0$ and $\partial\overline{U}_2/\partial S_1 = 0$; e.g., see footnote 8).

For lower discount factors the firm may invest too much in quality because of the investment subsidy provided by the rent-extracting, low-powered incentive schemes. The shadow price of the moral hazard constraint (4.35) is negative, and the conclusions become accordingly ambiguous.

Proof See appendix A4.8.

Thus, when the future matters a lot ($\delta \geq \delta_0$) and when quality becomes very important, the firm must be given a low-powered incentive scheme to supply more care (result ii). This illustrates the crowding-out effect. In the crowding-out effect care and effort are substitutes, so the production of more quality is obtained at the expense of cost-reducing activities. Result i formalizes the reputation argument. Farsighted firms can be given high-powered incentive schemes.

Finally, the firm exerts more care when it is less efficient. This can be shown using a revealed preference argument in which the level of care in the firm's utility function is replaced by the optimal (type-independent) $s(e_1)$ given by equation (4.35). The intuition can be gleaned from the linearity of the cost-reimbursement rules: The firm chooses the fixed fee a and the slope b of its incentive scheme in the menu offered by the regulator and then picks e_1 and s so as to maximize

$$a - b(\beta - e_1 + s) + \delta\pi(s)\overline{U}_2 - \psi(e_1).$$

A less efficient firm chooses a low-powered scheme (a low b), and a high level of care as care is highly subsidized.

4.7 Concluding Remarks

We have analyzed the circumstances under which quality concerns call for low-powered incentive schemes. For an experience good the lack of informational value of the current sale indicator makes the cost-reimbursement rule the only instrument to achieve the conflicting goals of quality provision and cost reduction. A high concern for quality leads to low-powered incentive schemes. We have also argued that steeper incentive schemes are optimal if the supplier is sufficiently eager to preserve his or her reputation. For a search good there is no "crowding-out effect," since direct sales incentives can be provided. There is, however, a new "scale effect" of quality concern on the power of incentive schemes; a high concern for quality leads to low-powered incentive schemes if and only if quantity and quality are net substitutes.

The chapter has considered the important polar cases of a search good with scale effects (in which a higher output makes cost reduction more valuable) and of an experience good without scale effects (for which output was taken as given). Understanding the crowding-out and the scale effects makes it easy to extend the theory to cover the other two polar cases. Consider, first, a search good and assume that the cost-reducing activity affects the fixed cost rather than the marginal cost: $C = cq + \beta - e + s$.[11]

11. This technology is chosen so as to keep the adverse selection one-dimensional and as to yield a closed-form solution. The analysis, which follows the lines of section 4.3, is left to the reader.

	Search good	Experience good
Effort reduces marginal cost	+ if q and s net complements – if q and s net substitutes	Ambiguous
Effort reduces fixed cost	0	–

Figure 4.2
Effect of an increase in the marginal social value of quality on the power of incentive schemes

When quality becomes more desirable, output changes,[12] but the optimal effort is unaffected. Because direct sales incentives can be given and because there is no scale effect, the power of incentive schemes is independent of the demand for quality. Second, consider an experience good with variable scale such that (1) an (observable) increase in quality today raises the demand for the good tomorrow and (2) the effort reduces the marginal cost. For such a good a higher valuation for quality today leads to an increase in demand for the good tomorrow; this creates a scale effect that can offset the crowding-out effect today (see figure 4.2).

We should also note that scale effects can take forms other than that obtained in this chapter. If the two moral hazard variables s and e interact in the cost function ($\partial^2 C/\partial s \partial e \neq 0$), an increase in the demand for quality has both direct and indirect effects on effort through the complementarity (or substitutability) of quality and output. Although ruling out this interaction is a good working hypothesis, one could think of situations in which effort produces a new technology that reduces the marginal cost of providing services ($\partial^2 C/\partial s \partial e < 0$). We conjecture that in such situations there is a new scale effect that leads to high-powered incentive schemes when the demand for quality is high.

Our model of an experience good was cast in a procurement framework. Consider its regulatory counterpart in which consumers use their observation of quality today to decide tomorrow on whether to repeat their purchase. If the parties could commit to a long-term contract, the regulator could promise rewards for high consumption tomorrow in order to promote quality today; the mechanism is then similar to that discussed in our static search good model except that the sales reward is delayed. Under noncommitment the regulator cannot promise delayed rewards. The firm's incentive to provide quality may be weakened, but it does not vanish; as

12. Output increases for the above cost function because quantity and quality are then net complements as long as they are gross complements.

in section 4.6 a good reputation boosts future sales and therefore future informational rents.

Our theory may also shed some light on the behavior of more complex regulatory hierarchies, for instance, ones in which regulators have other objectives than maximizing welfare. For instance, suppose that the regulator derives perks from the supplier's delivering high-quality products. That is, the regulator values quality more than the public at large. The regulator will then lobby in favor of low-powered incentive schemes if the good is an experience good. Our theory thus offers a clue as to why Department of Defense officials who value quality highly sometimes manage to transform fixed-price contracts into cost-plus contracts.[13]

Last, the distinction between verifiable and unverifiable quality is extreme. More generally one would want to allow quality to be verifiable at a cost. It would be worthwhile to analyze the relationship among expenses to monitor quality, quality and reputation concerns, and power of incentive schemes.

BIBLIOGRAPHIC NOTES

B4.1 Regulation of Quality

While there exists a vast literature on the provision of quality by an unregulated monopoly,[14] surprisingly little theoretical research has been devoted to this issue in a regulated environment. Besanko et al. (1987) assume that the monopolist offers a range of verifiable qualities to discriminate among consumers with different tastes for quality (à la Mussa and Rosen 1978) and investigate the effect of imposing minimum quality standards or price ceilings (see also Laffont 1987). Closer to this chapter is the work of Lewis and Sappington (1988), who examine both verifiable and unverifiable quality. Sales depend on a demand parameter, price, and quality. When quality is not verifiable, Lewis and Sappington assume that the regulator monitors prices (but not cost, quantity, or quality) and operates transfers to the firm. To give incentives to provide quality the regulator allows prices in excess of the (known) marginal cost. A higher markup above marginal cost raises the deadweight loss due to pricing but also raises quality. Lewis and Sappington show that the rent derived by the firm from its private information about the demand parameter is higher when quality is verifiable than when it is not. Our work differs from theirs

13. See also Scherer (1964, pp. 33–34, 236–239). DOD officials are well known to favor performance over cost. They often feel that fixed-price contracts encourage contractors to make "uneconomic" reliability trade-offs and be reluctant to make design improvements.
14. See, for example, Tirole (1988, ch. 2).

in that, among other things, we allow cost observation and focus on the effect of quality concerns on the power of incentives schemes.

B4.2 Task Allocation

Holmström and Milgrom (1991) have independently obtained conclusions similar to the crowding-out effect of the experience good model. Their multitask principal-agent analysis (here, the two tasks are cost reduction and quality provision) is conducted in a risk-aversion rather than an adverse-selection framework. There are also extensive literatures on decision substitutes and complements in various fields, such as optimal taxation (see Holmström-Milgrom for references, and chapter 3 for applications to Ramsey questions).

APPENDIXES

A4.1 The Hazard Rate of a Convolution of Distributions

Let $\gamma = \beta + h\theta/k$, and for notational simplicity assume that $h = k$. It is reasonable in this problem to assume that the distributions of β and θ, $F_1(\cdot)$ and $F_2(\cdot)$, are independent. Then

$$F(\gamma) \equiv \text{Prob}(\tilde{\gamma} \leq \gamma) = \int_{-\infty}^{+\infty} \text{Prob}(\theta \leq \tilde{\theta} \leq \theta + d\theta)\,\text{Prob}(\beta \leq \gamma - \theta)$$

$$= \int_{-\infty}^{+\infty} f_2(\theta) F_1(\gamma - \theta) d\theta,$$

$$f(\gamma) = \int_{-\infty}^{+\infty} f_2(\theta) f_1(\gamma - \theta) d\theta,$$

and

$$\frac{d}{d\gamma}\left[\frac{F(\gamma)}{f(\gamma)}\right] = 1 - \frac{\int_{-\infty}^{+\infty} f_2(\theta) F_1(\gamma - \theta) d\theta \int_{-\infty}^{+\infty} f_2(\theta) f_1'(\gamma - \theta) d\theta}{\left[\int_{-\infty}^{+\infty} f_2(\theta) f_1(\gamma - \theta) d\theta\right]^2}.$$

Some care must be taken when dealing with distributions with supports in bounded intervals because of the discontinuities of F/f.

A4.2 First- and Second-Order Conditions of Incentive Compatibility in the Search Model

The firm is faced with the revelation mechanism $\{t(\tilde{\gamma}), p(\tilde{\gamma}), q(\tilde{\gamma}), (C/q)(\tilde{\gamma})\}$. For simplicity we assume that the mechanism is almost everywhere differentiable (see chapter 1). The firm chooses the announcement $\tilde{\gamma}$ that maximizes its objective function, that is, solves

$$\max_{\tilde{\gamma}} \left\{ t(\tilde{\gamma}) - \psi\left(\gamma + \frac{p(\tilde{\gamma}) - A + Bq(\tilde{\gamma})}{k} - \frac{C}{q}(\tilde{\gamma}) \right) \right\}$$

$$\Leftrightarrow \quad \max_{\tilde{\gamma}} \{t(\tilde{\gamma}) - \psi(\gamma - z(\tilde{\gamma}))\}, \tag{A4.1}$$

where

$$z(\tilde{\gamma}) \equiv \frac{C}{q}(\tilde{\gamma}) - \frac{p(\tilde{\gamma}) - A + Bq(\tilde{\gamma})}{k}.$$

The first-order condition of incentive compatibility is

$$\dot{t}(\gamma) + \psi'(\gamma - z(\gamma))\dot{z}(\gamma) = 0, \tag{A4.2}$$

and the second-order condition is

$$\dot{z}(\gamma) \geq 0. \tag{A4.3}$$

Formulas (A4.2) and (A4.3) constitute necessary and sufficient conditions for incentive compatibility (see chapter 2). Note that $z(\gamma) = \gamma - e(\gamma)$. So the second-order condition can be rewritten

$$\dot{e}(\gamma) - 1 \leq 0. \tag{A4.4}$$

■

A4.3 Concavity of the Social Welfare Maximization Program

The regulator maximizes H with respect to $\{q, p, e\}$. The matrix of second-derivatives of H with respect to these variables is (divided by f)

$$\begin{bmatrix} B - B^2 - \dfrac{2(1+\lambda)B}{k} & (1+\lambda) - B - \dfrac{(1+\lambda)}{k} & 1+\lambda \\ (1+\lambda) - B - \dfrac{(1+\lambda)}{k} & -1 & 0 \\ 1+\lambda & 0 & -(1+\lambda)\psi'' - \dfrac{\lambda F \psi'''}{f} \end{bmatrix}.$$

[This matrix differs from the jacobian of equations (4.27) through (4.29) in that (4.28) was used to obtain equation (4.27).] For the submatrix in $\{q, p\}$ to be negative semidefinite it must be the case that

$$B > 1 - \frac{2(1+\lambda)}{k} \tag{A4.5}$$

and

$$B(1 + 2\lambda) > (1+\lambda)^2 \left(1 - \frac{1}{k}\right)^2. \tag{A4.6}$$

The determinant is

$$\Delta = -\left[(1+\lambda)\psi'' + \frac{\lambda F \psi'''}{f}\right]\Delta_1 + (1+\lambda)^2,$$

where Δ_1 is the determinant of the submatrix in $\{q, p\}$. Or

$$\Delta < 0 \quad \Leftrightarrow \quad \left[(1+\lambda)\psi'' + \frac{\lambda F \psi'''}{f}\right]\Delta_1 > (1+\lambda)^2,$$

which is satisfied if and only if

$$B > \frac{(1+\lambda)^2}{(1+2\lambda)[(1+\lambda)\psi'' + (\lambda F/f)\psi''']} + \frac{(1+\lambda)^2(1-1/k)^2}{1+2\lambda}.$$

To sum up, sufficient conditions for the second-order conditions to be satisfied are

$$B > \max\left\{1 - \frac{2(1+\lambda)}{k}, \frac{(1+\lambda)^2}{1+2\lambda}\left(1-\frac{1}{k}\right)^2, \right.$$
$$\left.\frac{(1+\lambda)^2}{(1+2\lambda)[(1+\lambda)\psi'' + (\lambda F/f)\psi'''} + \frac{(1+\lambda)^2(1-1/k)^2}{1+2\lambda}\right\}.$$

The solution obtained in section 4.3 is valid if the second-order incentive constraint $\dot{e} \leq 1$ is satisfied by the solution of the previous first-order equation.

Differentiating (4.27), (4.28), and (4.29), we obtain

$$-\left(\lambda + \frac{1+\lambda}{k}\right)B\dot{q} + (1+\lambda)\left(1-\frac{1}{k}\right)\dot{p} + (1+\lambda)\dot{e} = 1+\lambda, \tag{A4.7}$$

$$((1+\lambda)(k-1) - Bk)\dot{q} - k\dot{p} = 0, \tag{A4.8}$$

$$\dot{q} - \left[\psi''(e) + \frac{\lambda}{1+\lambda}\frac{F(\gamma)}{f(\gamma)}\psi'''(e)\right]\dot{e} = \frac{\lambda}{1+\lambda}\psi''(e)\frac{d}{d\gamma}\left[\frac{F(\gamma)}{f(\gamma)}\right]. \tag{A4.9}$$

Hence

$$\dot{p} = \frac{1}{\Delta}[(1+\lambda)(k-1) - Bk](1+\lambda)$$
$$\times \left\{\psi''(e) + \frac{\lambda}{1+\lambda}\frac{F(\gamma)}{f(\gamma)}\psi'''(e) + \frac{\lambda}{1+\lambda}\psi''(e)\frac{d}{d\gamma}\left[\frac{F(\gamma)}{f(\gamma)}\right]\right\},$$

where Δ is the determinant of the system, which is negative because we are at a maximum. Since $\psi'' > 0$, $\psi''' \geq 0$, and $d[F(\gamma)/f(\gamma)]/d\gamma > 0$, $\dot{p} > 0$ for $B > (1+\lambda)(k-1)/k$, which is automatically satisfied in the relevant range if $B > 1$: Formula (4.28) and $\partial S^g/\partial s > 0$ imply that $kq[(B - (1+\lambda)(1-1/k)] > 0$. From (A4.8), $\dot{q} < 0$, and $\dot{e} < 0$ from (A4.9). In that case the second-order condition of incentive compatibility is satisfied. ■

A4.4 A Class of Cost Functions for Which the Dichotomy Property Holds

The dichotomy result between optimal pricing and quality and optimal incentive schemes obtained in section 4.3 can be generalized as follows: Let $\tilde{C}(\beta, e, q, s)$ denote a general cost function, and let $s = \chi(p, q, \theta)$ be obtained by inverting the demand function $q = D(p, s, \theta)$. The derived cost function is

$$C(\beta, \theta, e, q, p) = \tilde{C}(\beta, e, q, \chi(p, q, \theta)).$$

Let $e = E(\beta, \theta, C, q, p)$ be the solution of

$$C(\beta, \theta, e, q, p) = C.$$

The problem here is genuinely two-dimensional. The first-order incentive constraints can be written

$$U_\beta = -\psi'(e)E_\beta,$$

$$U_\theta = -\psi'(e)E_\theta$$

$$U_{\beta\theta} = U_{\theta\beta},$$

where subscripts denote partial derivatives. A sufficient condition for the dichotomy result is[15]

$$\frac{\partial E_\beta}{\partial q} = \frac{\partial E_\beta}{\partial p} = \frac{\partial E_\theta}{\partial q} = \frac{\partial E_\theta}{\partial p} = 0,$$

which requires (from Leontief's theorem) that there exist $\Lambda(\cdot,\cdot)$, $\Gamma(\cdot,\cdot)$ such that

$$C = C(\Lambda(\beta, e), \Gamma(\theta, e), p, q).$$

A special case of this is

$$C = C(\xi(\beta, \theta, e), p, q).$$

In our example we have $\xi(\beta, \theta, e) = \beta + (h\theta/k) - e$.

A4.5 Proof of Proposition 4.1

Since the equations defining quality and price are the same as under complete information (dichotomy result) the comparison between complete and incomplete information can be easily obtained by observing that incomplete information gives a lower level of effort conditionally on the level of production [equation (4.29)]. This decrease of effort itself leads, from (4.27) and (4.28), to a decrease of q (reinforcing the initial decrease of effort which is therefore an unconditional decrease of effort) and to an increase in p.

For any γ, let de denote an infinitesimal decrease in effort. Differentiating (4.27) and (4.28) yields

$$k\frac{ds}{de} = \frac{dp}{de} + B\frac{dq}{de} = (1 + \lambda)\left(1 - \frac{1}{k}\right)\frac{dq}{de}.$$

The conclusion follows from the fact that e and q are lower under incomplete information from the first- and second-order conditions. ■

A4.6 Proof of Propositions 4.3, 4.4, and 4.5

We offer a single proof to the three propositions. After substituting for the shadow price of (4.22) [see (4.26)], the hamiltonian becomes

15. If these conditions hold, the derivatives of the hamiltonian with respect to p and q involve no terms associated with the incentive constraints and therefore with asymmetric information.

$$H = \frac{B}{2}q^2 + (1+\lambda)pq - \frac{1}{2}(p - A + Bq)^2 + l(p - A + Bq, v) - (1+\lambda)$$
$$\times \left[(\gamma - e)q + q\left(\frac{p - A + Bq}{k}\right) + m(p - A + Bq, \rho) + \psi(e)\right] - \lambda\frac{F}{f}\psi'(e). \qquad \text{(A4.10)}$$

Letting $\Delta < 0$ denote the determinant of the jacobian with respect to the control variables $\{q, p, e\}$, we have

$$\frac{de}{dx} = -\frac{1}{\Delta}\begin{vmatrix} \frac{\partial^2 H}{\partial q^2} & \frac{\partial^2 H}{\partial q \partial p} & \frac{\partial^2 H}{\partial q \partial x} \\ \frac{\partial^2 H}{\partial q \partial p} & \frac{\partial^2 H}{\partial p^2} & \frac{\partial^2 H}{\partial p \partial x} \\ \frac{\partial^2 H}{\partial e \partial q} & \frac{\partial^2 H}{\partial e \partial p} & \frac{\partial^2 H}{\partial e \partial x} \end{vmatrix} \qquad \text{for } x = v, \rho, k.$$

But $\partial^2 H/\partial e \partial q = (1+\lambda)$, $\partial^2 H/\partial e \partial p = 0$, and $\partial^2 H/\partial e \partial x = 0$ for $x = v, \rho, k$. Hence

$$\text{sign}\left(\frac{de}{dx}\right) = \text{sign}\begin{vmatrix} \frac{\partial^2 H}{\partial q \partial p} & \frac{\partial^2 H}{\partial q \partial x} \\ \frac{\partial^2 H}{\partial p^2} & \frac{\partial^2 H}{\partial p \partial x} \end{vmatrix}. \qquad \text{(A4.12)}$$

The propositions follow from

$$\frac{\partial^2 H}{\partial q \partial p} = (1+\lambda)\left(1 - \frac{1}{k}\right) - B(1 + m_{11}(1+\lambda) - l_{11}),$$

$$\frac{\partial^2 H}{\partial p^2} = -(1 + m_{11}(1+\lambda) - l_{11}),$$

$$\frac{\partial^2 H}{\partial q \partial v} = Bl_{12} = B\frac{\partial^2 H}{\partial p \partial v}, \quad \frac{\partial^2 H}{\partial q \partial \rho} = -(1+\lambda)Bm_{12} = B\frac{\partial^2 H}{\partial p \partial \rho},$$

$$\frac{\partial^2 H}{\partial q \partial k} = \frac{1+\lambda}{k^2}(p - A + 2Bq), \quad \frac{\partial^2 H}{\partial p \partial k} = \frac{1+\lambda}{k^2}q.$$

[To obtain proposition 4.5, use (4.28) to substitute for $p - A + Bq$]. ∎

A4.7 The Linearity of Contracts in the Experience Good Model

From chapter 1 we know that we can decentralize a nonlinear contract with a menu of linear contracts if the transfer $t(C_1)$ is convex. From the first-order conditions of incentive compatibility,

$$\frac{dt}{d\beta_1} + \psi'(e_1)\frac{dC_1}{d\beta_1} = 0 \qquad \text{with } \frac{dC_1}{d\beta_1} \geq 0$$

from second-order incentive compatibility conditions. Hence

$$\frac{dt}{dC_1} = -\psi'(e_1) \quad \text{and} \quad \frac{d^2t}{dC_1^2} = -\psi''\dot{e}_1\frac{1}{dC_1/d\beta_1}.$$

$t(C_1)$ is convex if and only if $\dot{e}_1 < 0$. Differentiating the first-order conditions we get

$$\dot{e}_1 = \frac{-(\delta\pi''\overline{U}_2)^2\lambda\psi''[d(F(\beta_1)/f(\beta_1))/d\beta_1]}{(\delta\pi''\overline{U}_2)^2[(1+\lambda)\psi'' + \lambda(F(\beta_1)/f(\beta_1))\psi''' + \nu\psi'''] - [\pi''(S_1 + \delta\overline{W}_2 + \lambda\delta\overline{U}_2) + \nu\delta\pi'''\overline{U}_2](\psi'')^2}$$

$$< 0$$

if $\nu \geq 0$. ■

A4.8 Proof of Proposition 4.6

Differentiating (4.42), (4.43), and (4.35) totally yields

$$\left[\psi'' + \left(\frac{\lambda}{1+\lambda}\frac{F}{f} + \frac{\nu}{1+\lambda}\right)\psi'''\right]de_1 = -\frac{\psi''}{1+\lambda}d\nu, \tag{A4.13}$$

$$[\pi''(S_1 + \delta\overline{W}_2 + \lambda\delta\overline{U}_2) + \nu\delta\overline{U}_2\pi''']ds + \left[\pi'\left(1 + \delta\frac{\partial\overline{W}_2}{\partial S_1}\right)\right]dS_1$$

$$+ [\nu\pi''\overline{U}_2 + \pi'\overline{W}_2 + \lambda\overline{U}_2\pi']d\delta + \delta\pi''\overline{U}_2 d\nu = 0, \tag{A4.14}$$

$$\psi''de_1 = (\pi'\overline{U}_2)d\delta + (\delta\overline{U}_2\pi'')ds. \tag{A4.15}$$

Substituting, using (4.43), $\psi''' \geq 0$, and $\pi''' \leq 0$, we obtain

$$\text{sign}\left(\frac{\partial e_1}{\partial S_1}\right) = \text{sign}\left[-\pi'\left(1 + \delta\frac{\partial\overline{W}_2}{\partial S_1}\right)\right] < 0, \tag{A4.16}$$

$$\text{sign}\left(\frac{\partial e_1}{\partial\delta}\right) = \text{sign}(-\pi''\pi'\overline{U}_2 S_1 - \delta\nu\overline{U}_2^2\pi'''\pi' + \delta\overline{U}_2^2(\pi'')^2\nu) > 0. \tag{A4.17}$$

It is easily seen that the assumptions $\psi''' \geq 0$ and $\pi''' \leq 0$ guarantee that the second-order conditions are satisfied if $\nu \geq 0$. ■

A4.9 Quality, Asymmetric Information, and Reputation

We consider a two-period model in which, with probability x, the firm is a high-quality producer; that is, it generates a social surplus S^H when producing. With probability $1 - x$ it is a low-quality producer; that is, it generates a social surplus $S^L < S^H$ unless it applies some effort $s > 0$, in which case the social surplus is S^H.

To avoid signaling issues that would complicate the analysis, we assume that the firm does not know in period 1 if it is a high- or a low-quality producer. (Thus the model is closer to Holmström's 1982 than to Kreps-Wilson's 1982 or Milgrom-Roberts's 1982.) Moreover quality cannot be contracted upon. At the end of period 1, if production occurs, the regulator discovers the quality level.

In period 1 the firm has a cost function

$$C_1 = \beta_1 - e,$$

where β_1 is known to and C_1 observed by the regulator, and e is a cost-reducing effort. Total effort for the firm is $e_1 = e$ or $e_1 = e + s$ when the firm is putting the extra effort s to make sure that first-period quality is high. Let t_1 be the transfer given to the firm in period 1.

The regulator cannot commit for period 2. In period 2 the firm has a cost parameter $\beta_2 \in [\underline{\beta}, \bar{\beta}]$ with a (common knowledge) distribution $F(\cdot)$ and a cost function

$$C_2 = \beta_2 - e_2.$$

β_2 will be learned by the firm at the beginning of date 2. At that time we will be in a one-period, adverse-selection problem.

For any expected social surplus S in period 2, the second-period welfare is

$$W^*(S) = \int_{\underline{\beta}}^{\beta_2^*} \{S - (1 + \lambda)(\psi(e^*(\beta_2)) + \beta_2 - e^*(\beta_2)) - \lambda U^*(\beta_2)\} dF(\beta_2),$$

where β_2^* is the cutoff type for surplus S, and, according to chapter 1,

$$\psi'(e^*(\beta_2)) = 1 - \frac{\lambda}{1 + \lambda} \frac{F(\beta_2)}{f(\beta_2)} \psi''(e^*(\beta_2)),$$

$$U^*(\beta_2) = \int_{\beta_2}^{\beta_2^*} \psi'(e^*(\tilde{\beta}_2)) d\tilde{\beta}_2.$$

Let t^*, C^*, U^* be the *expected* transfer, cost, and rent, respectively, in this optimal second-period mechanism when $\beta_2^* = \bar{\beta}$. To limit the analysis to the most interesting cases, we postulate the following assumptions:

Assumption 4.1 If $S = xS^H + (1 - x)S^L$, then $\beta_2^* = \bar{\beta}$. Furthermore $S^L - (1 + \lambda)[\psi(e^*) + \underline{\beta} - e^*] < 0$.

Assumption 4.1 says that for an expected quality defined by the prior, it is worth realizing the project whatever β. This, together with subsection 1.4.5, implies that the cutoff type is $\bar{\beta}$ whenever the posterior probability of high quality exceeds the prior probability. However, if the firm is known to be a low-quality firm, it is not worth contracting with it even if attention is restricted to the best types (close to $\underline{\beta}$). Assumption 4.1 requires that $(\bar{\beta} - \underline{\beta})$ not be "too large."

Assumption 4.2 $s < [(1 - \delta)(1 - x)/(1 + \lambda)](S^H - S^L)$.

Assumption 4.2 says that the extra effort needed to upgrade quality is not too high compared to the social gain $(S^H - S^L)$. Without this assumption, it is never optimal to induce upgrading of quality in the first period.

Two policies must be considered. In policy A, s is not induced, and in policy B, s is induced (inducing randomization by the firm is never optimal).

Policy A

Social welfare is

$$W = xS^H + (1 - x)S^L - (1 + \lambda)(\beta_1 - e_1 + t_1) + \delta x(S^H - (1 + \lambda)(t^* + C^*)) + U,$$

where U is the firm's intertemporal rent, and we use the fact that in period 2 the regulator knows whether he or she is facing a high-quality firm.

Social welfare must be maximized under the individual rationality (IR) and incentive compatibility (IC) constraints. If the firm does not produce in period 1, the regulator learns nothing and the firm can expect a rent U^* in period 2. Accordingly the IR constraint takes the form

$$t_1 - \psi(e_1) + \delta x U^* \geq \delta U^* \qquad (\mathrm{IR_A}).$$

The IC constraint is

$$t_1 - \psi(e_1) + \delta x U^* \geq t_1 - \psi(e_1 + s) + \delta U^* \qquad (\mathrm{IC_A}).$$

In regime I, $(\mathrm{IC_A})$ is not binding and therefore

$$\psi'(e_1) = 1 \quad \text{or} \quad e_1 = e^*,$$

$$t_1 = \psi(e_1) + \delta(1 - x)U^*,$$

$$U = \delta U^*.$$

$(\mathrm{IC_A})$ can be rewritten with $\tilde{\Phi}(e) \equiv \psi(e + s) - \psi(e)$,

$$\tilde{\Phi}(e_1) \geq \delta(1 - x)U^* \quad \text{or} \quad \delta \leq \delta_1,$$

where $\tilde{\Phi}(e^*) \equiv \delta_1(1 - x)U^*$.

In regime II, $(\mathrm{IC_A})$ is binding, and effort is defined by

$$\tilde{\Phi}(e(\delta)) = \delta(1 - x)U^*,$$

with $de/d\delta > 0$ and $e(\delta) > e^*$. Welfare is then

$$W^{\mathrm{I}} = xS^H + (1 - x)S^L - (1 + \lambda)(\beta_1 - e^* + \psi(e^*)) + \delta x W^*(S^H) - \lambda(1 - x)\delta U^*,$$

$$W^{\mathrm{II}} = xS^H + (1 - x)S^L - (1 + \lambda)(\beta_1 - e(\delta) + \psi(e(\delta))) + \delta x W^*(S^H) - \lambda(1 - x)\delta U^*.$$

$W^I \geq W^{\mathrm{II}}$, but regime I is not feasible for $\delta > \delta_1$.

Policy B

Social welfare is now

$$W = S^H - (1 + \lambda)[\beta_1 - (e_1 - s) + t_1] + \delta[S^H - (1 - x)(S^H - S^L) - (1 + \lambda)(t^* + C^*)] + U$$

with the constraints

$$t_1 - \psi(e_1) + \delta U^* \geq \delta U^* \qquad (\mathrm{IR_B}),$$

$$t_1 - \psi(e_1) + \delta U^* \geq t_1 - \psi(e_1 - s) + \delta x U^* \qquad (\mathrm{IC_B}).$$

In regime III, $(\mathrm{IC_B})$ is not binding, and $e_1 = e^*$, $t_1 = \psi(e_1)$. Regime III prevails as long as

$$\tilde{\Phi}(e^* - s) = \psi(e^*) - \psi(e^* - s) \leq \delta(1 - x)U^*$$

or $\delta > \delta_0$ with $\delta_1 > \delta_0$. If $\delta < \delta_0$, $(\mathrm{IC_B})$ is binding, and e_1 is defined by

$$\tilde{\Phi}(e_1 - s) = \delta(1 - x)U^*$$

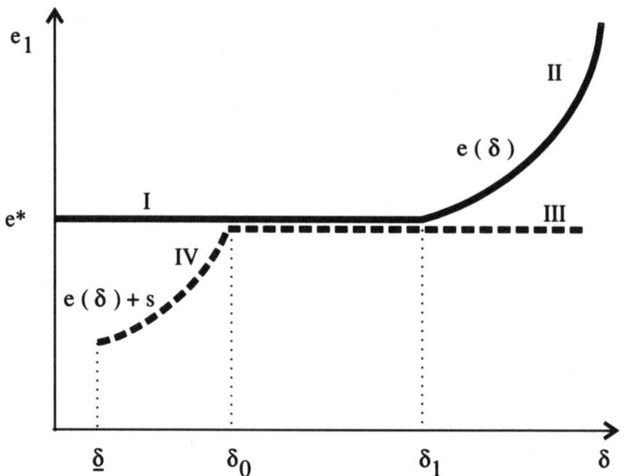

Figure 4.3
Power of the incentive scheme for an experience good

or $e_1 = e(\delta) + s$ with $s + e(\delta) < e^*$ (regime IV). For $\delta \leq \underline{\delta}$ defined by $s = e(\underline{\delta})$, it is *not possible* to induce quality.

Welfares are

$$W^{\mathrm{III}} = S^H - (1 + \lambda)[\beta_1 - e^* + s + \psi(e^*)] + \delta(W^*(S^H) - (1 - x)(S^H - S^L)),$$

$$W^{\mathrm{IV}} = S^H - (1 + \lambda)[\beta_1 - e(\delta) + \psi(e(\delta) + s)] + \delta(W^*(S^H) - (1 - x)(S^H - S^L)).$$

Effort levels are summarized in figure 4.3.

Lemma 4.1 $W^{\mathrm{III}} > W^{\mathrm{I}}$.

Proof

$$W^{\mathrm{III}} - W^{\mathrm{I}} = (1 - \delta)(1 - x)(S^H - S^L) - (1 + \lambda)s + (1 - x)\delta(S^H - (1 + \lambda)E(\psi(e^*(\beta_2)) + \beta_2 - e^*(\beta_2))).$$

The sum of the first two terms is positive in view of assumption 4.2, and the third term is positive in view of assumption 4.1. ■

Since $W^{\mathrm{II}} < W^{\mathrm{I}}$, regime III is optimal for $\delta \geq \delta_0$. For $\delta < \underline{\delta}$, regime I is clearly optimal.

Lemma 4.2

i. There exists $\hat{\delta} \in [\underline{\delta}, \delta_0)$ such that for $\delta > \hat{\delta}$ the optimum is to induce quality and

$$e_1 = \begin{cases} e(\delta) + s < e^* & \text{if } \hat{\delta} < \delta \leq \delta_0, \\ e^* & \text{if } \delta > \delta_0. \end{cases}$$

ii. If $S^H - S^L < \lambda U^*$ for $\delta < \hat{\delta}$, the optimum is not to induce quality, and $e_1 = e^*$.

Proof

i. At $\delta = \delta_0$, $W^{\mathrm{III}} = W^{\mathrm{IV}}$. Apply lemma 4.1.

ii. $\dfrac{dW^{\mathrm{I}}}{d\delta} = xW^*(S^H) - \lambda(1-x)U^*,$

$$\frac{dW^{\mathrm{IV}}}{d\delta} = W^*(S^H) - (1-x)(S^H - S^L) - (1+\lambda)(\psi'(e(\delta)+s) - 1)\frac{de}{d\delta},$$

and

$$\frac{de}{d\delta} = \frac{(1-x)U^*}{\psi'(e(\delta)+s) - \psi'(e(\delta))},$$

$$\frac{dW^{\mathrm{IV}}}{d\delta} = W^*(S^H) + \frac{(1+\lambda)(1-x)U^*(1-\psi'(e(\delta)+s))}{\psi'(e(\delta)+s) - \psi'(e(\delta))} - (1-x)(S^H - S^L).$$

If $S^H - S^L < \lambda U^*$, $dW^{\mathrm{IV}}/d\delta > dW^{\mathrm{I}}/d\delta$; hence the result. ■

Thus we get proposition 4.7.

Proposition 4.7

i. Incentives are higher when one does not want to induce quality.

ii. Conditional on inducing quality, the incentive scheme becomes more high-powered when δ increases.

Proof Part i follows from the fact that $e_1 \leq e^*$ when quality is induced. Part ii follows from $de/d\delta > 0$. ■

The results are thus very similar to those of the moral hazard model of section 4.6. As in section 4.6 incentives are not monotonic in the discount factor. For a low discount factor an extremely low-powered incentive scheme is needed for the firm to exert s. The loss of incentive to reduce cost is too costly, so the optimum is a corner solution: Because the firm is not induced to provide quality and β_1 is common knowledge, the first-period contract is a fixed-price contract. But as long as the discount factor is sufficiently high to make it worthwhile to induce quality, cost-reducing incentives increase with the discount factor.

REFERENCES

Besanko, D., S. Donnenfeld, and L. White. 1987. Monopoly and quality distortion: Effects and remedies. *Quarterly Journal of Economics* 102:743–768.

Holmström, B. 1982. Managerial incentive problems: A dynamic perspective. In *Essays in Economics and Management in Honor of Lars Wahlbeck.* Helsinki: Swedish School of Economics.

Holmström, B., and P. Milgrom. 1991. Multi-task principal agent analysis: Incentive contracts, asset ownership and job design. *Journal of Law, Economics and Organization* 7:26–52.

Joskow, P. 1990. Should conservation proposals be included in competitive bidding programs? In *Competition in Electricity: New Markets and New Structures*, ed. J. Plummer and S. Troppman, 235–280. Public Utility Reports and QED Research, Inc.

Joskow, P., and N. Rose. 1989. The effects of economic regulation. In *The Handbook of Industrial Organization*, vol. 2, ed. R. Schmalensee and R. Willig. Amsterdam: North-Holland.

Kahn, A. 1971. *The Economics of Regulation: Principles and Institutions.* New York: Wiley. Cambridge, MA: MIT Press, 1988.

Kreps, D., and R. Wilson. 1982. Reputation and imperfect information. *Journal of Economic Theory* 27:253–279.

Laffont, J.-J. 1987. Optimal taxation of a non linear pricing monopolist. *Journal of Public Economics* 33:137–155.

Laffont, J.-J., E. Maskin, and J.-C. Rochet. 1987. Optimal nonlinear pricing with two-dimensional characteristics. In *Information, Incentives and Economic Mechanisms: In Honor of L. Hurwicz*, ed. T. Groves, R. Radner, and S. Reiter. Minneapolis: University of Minnesota Press.

Lewis, T., and D. Sappington. 1988. Regulating a monopolist with unknown demand. *American Economic Review* 78:986–998.

Lewis, T., and D. Sappington. 1991a. Incentives for monitoring quality. *Rand Journal of Economics*, Winter issue.

Lewis, T., and D. Sappington. 1991b. Incentives for conservation and quality improvement by public utilities. Mimeo, University of Florida.

Milgrom, P., and J. Roberts. 1982. Predation, reputation and entry deterrence. *Journal of Economic Theory* 27:280–312.

Riordan, M., and D. Sappington. 1989. Second sourcing. *Rand Journal of Economics* 20:41–58.

Mussa, M., and S. Rosen. 1978. Monopoly and product quality. *Journal of Economic Theory* 23:301–317.

Noam, E. 1989. The quality of regulation in regulating quality: A proposal for an integrated incentive approach to telephone service performance. New York State Public Service Commission.

Sappington, D. 1983. Optimal regulation of a multiproduct monopoly with unknown technological capabilities. *Bell Journal of Economics* 14:453–463.

Scherer, F. 1964. *The Weapons Acquisition Process: Economic Incentives*, Graduate School of Business Administration, Harvard University.

Spence, A. M. 1975. Monopoly, quality and regulation. *Bell Journal of Economics* 6:417–429.

Tirole, J. 1988. *The Theory of Industrial Organization*. Cambridge, MA: MIT Press.

Vickers, J., and G. Yarrow. 1988. *Privatization: An Economic Analysis*. Cambridge, MA: MIT Press.

II PRODUCT MARKET COMPETITION

5 COMPETITIVE RAMSEY FORMULAS AND ACCESS PRICING

5.1 Some Background

Regulated firms often operate in a competitive environment. Indeed the deregulation wave of the 1970s and 1980s has tried to create the scope for a challenge of regulated firms by other regulated firms and often by unregulated ones. AT&T must now share the U.S. long-distance market with Sprint, MCI, and other companies. British Telecom faces some rivalry from Mercury. Electric utilities must compete with independent generators as well as with substitute energies. Several transportation modes, some of them regulated, compete among themselves.

This chapter analyzes pricing by a regulated firm in a competitive product market. It considers both the pricing of a final good and that of an intermediate good that allows rivals to compete with the regulated firm on a final output market (access pricing). As we saw in chapter 3, pricing by a regulated firm must reflect two considerations. The first consideration is the effect of prices on the customers' consumption of goods and on the firm's budget, and it is embodied in the Ramsey index. The second consideration is the effect of pricing on agency costs, and it can give rise to an incentive correction. Chapter 3 derived necessary and sufficient conditions for the absence of incentive correction. The first focus of this chapter is on the expression of the Ramsey index in the presence of product market competition.

Equation (3.10) in chapter 3 shows very generally that, in the absence of incentive correction, the optimal price of good k is given by the equality between its marginal social value and its marginal cost evaluated at the shadow cost of public funds:

$$V_{q_k} = (1 + \lambda)C_{q_k}.$$

To analyze pricing in a competitive environment, it thus suffices to correctly define the social value of output k of the regulated firm. As we will see, this social value must reflect not only the marginal surplus for the consumers but also the effect on other regulated firms' profits, or that on the distortions in pricing of unregulated firms due to market power or environmental externalities. Section 5.2 derives the economic implications of the general pricing formula.

The rest of this chapter pursues the investigation of pricing in a competitive environment by studying the issue of access pricing. In several industries (telecommunications, railroads, energy, airlines) a regulated firm must supply an input (local access, trackage services, transportation of energy, computer reservation systems, airport facilities, routes) to a competitor in order for the latter to be able to compete on the product market. For instance, before its divestiture AT&T, a regulated firm, had monopoly over the local exchange and competed with a couple of unregulated companies on the long-distance market; the rivals needed access to AT&T's local network to supply toll calls. A railroad might have a monopoly position from location A to location B but compete with trucks or another railroad from B to C; to carry freight from A to C, the competitors would need access to the segment AB. In the energy field British Gas' rivals need access to British Gas' distribution network to compete for gas customers. Similarly the U.S. Public Utility Regulatory Policy Act of 1978 gave access to "qualified" independent suppliers by requiring electric utilities to purchase power generated by these firms.[1]

The feasibility of access is a central issue in regulation and has been the subject of much legal and regulatory activity lately. There has been concern that rivals would not have fair access to the input and thus would be unable to compete with the regulated firm producing this input. There are two traditional responses to this concern. First, one could try to create fair access for competitors to the input by imposing mandatory trade or interconnection with competitors. For instance, trackage rights could be extended to railroads with no ownership rights on the tracks. This policy is not specific to a regulated firm. For instance, in 1984 the Civil Aeronautics Board imposed equal access to the Computer Reservation Systems for the (unregulated) parent airlines and for nonintegrated airlines. Whether the outcome of an antitrust action or of a regulatory decision, or whether it applies to a regulated or unregulated firm, the main question associated with this first policy has been to finely define the input in question (in particular its quality) and then to determine an appropriate "access price" to be paid by competitors to the integrated firm.

Second, regulators could break up the integrated firm in an attempt to avoid favorable treatment of the internal consumer of the input by the supplier of the input. This divestiture is accompanied by a line-of-business restriction meant to prevent the supplier of the input from reintegrating back into the competitive sector. For example, the Bell Operating Companies, when separated in 1984 from their parent company AT&T, were prohibited from entering the competitive long-distance telephone market, from carrying television signals down their lines, and from manufacturing equipment.[2]

This chapter focuses on the first policy, that is, the regulation of access prices in the absence of divestiture. The regulation of access has two dimensions.

First, putting aside incentive issues, one must analyze the optimal access price to be charged to the competitor; a key to the understanding of this pricing problem is to view the intermediate good supplied to the competi-

1. See Tye (1987) for more details.
2. European regulators often adopt a much milder version of the American divestiture approach by requiring that the integrated firm establish a subsidiary with separate accounts.

tor and the final good of the regulated firm as substitutes. The pricing of the intermediate good then follows standard Ramsey principles (section 5.3).

Second, there is the incentive issue of whether the regulated firm can gain by foreclosing the market for the final good through an excessive access price. Since the firm's rent from producing the final output increases with the demand it faces for this final good (see chapter 2), the firm is tempted to overstate the cost of supplying access to competitors and thus to reduce their presence on the final good market. This suggests, as is confirmed in this chapter, that the regulated firm's incentive scheme should depend not only on the firm's cost and outputs but also on the output produced by its competitors.

We argue as well that the difficulty in eliciting the appropriate access price from the regulated firm depends on the technology. If the regulated firm and its competitor have identical requirements of the intermediate good to produce their final outputs, the firm cannot claim that the production of the intermediate good is costly without making a case against its own final output. The regulator can detect anticompetitive access pricing by comparing a high access price and a low price for the final output of the regulated firm. Suppose, in contrast, that the regulated firm must produce a distinct intermediate good for its competitor (or must add to its existing capacity at a privately known cost to supply its competitor); the regulated firm has then an incentive to charge an excessive access price to restrict competition and increase its informational rent on the final good market. Section 5.4 analyzes the effect of such foreclosure on the power of the regulated firm's incentive scheme and on welfare and compares the access pricing problem with the bypass problem studied in chapter 6. Section 5.5 concludes with a discussion of some open questions.

5.2 Pricing and Competition

This section obtains the Ramsey index for some competitive variants of the third-degree price discrimination model: regulated competition, unregulated competitive fringe, and unregulated competition with distorted pricing. The following analysis is simple and often will only state the results, yet it contains some pitfalls. Its general goal is to explain how to compute elasticities correctly. To simplify, we will assume that the demands for the regulated firm's n products are independent and that a competitor produces a good $n+1$ that is an imperfect substitute for good n. Thus the consumer gross surplus can be written

$$S(\mathbf{q}, q_{n+1}) = \sum_{k=1}^{n-1} S^k(q_k) + \tilde{S}(q_n, q_{n+1}).$$

The competitor produces with cost function $C^{n+1}(q_{n+1})$. (We abstract from possible incentive issues for the competition. The absence of uncertainty about the competitor also implies that the regulator cannot learn from the quantities traded information not contained in the regulated firm's choice of prices. The regulator could learn from outputs if the two firms' technologies were correlated.)

Before proceeding, we should discuss the social value of a unit profit of the competitor. We will assume that \$1 of the competitor's profit has social value \$$(1 + \lambda)$ if the competitor is regulated, and \$1 if it is not. The assumption in the regulated competitor case is easy to justify: Any dollar in its revenue reduces the cost of regulation by \$1 and thus reduces the deadweight loss of distortionary taxation by \$$(1 + \lambda)$. In contrast, the assumption in the unregulated firm's case depicts only a particular situation in which none of the profits is redistributed to the government. If a fraction τ of the competitor's profit were captured by the government (e.g., through a profit tax), the social value of the competitor's unit of profit would be \$$(1 + \lambda\tau)$. Thus we are in a sense restricting attention to the polar cases $\tau = 1$ and $\tau = 0$, but it is straightforward to extend our formulas to general social values of the competitor's profit (we will do so in section 5.3 on access pricing).

We also will use the following notation for elasticities: $\eta_{kl} = (\partial q_k/\partial p_l)/(q_k/p_l)$ is the elasticity of good k relative to the price of good l. And $\eta_k = -\eta_{kk}$ is the own elasticity of demand of good k. We start with the case in which the competitor is regulated.

5.2.1 Regulated Competition

The notation for the main regulated firm follows that of chapter 3, and we assume the incentive-pricing dichotomy holds; that is, $C = C(\zeta(\beta, e), \mathbf{q})$ with $\mathbf{q} = (q_1, \ldots, q_n)$. Suppose further that good $n + 1$ is produced by another regulated firm. For instance, electricity and local gas distribution are both regulated at the state level in the United States and are substitutes for heating and cooking. The competitor's revenue has then social value $\lambda p_{n+1} q_{n+1} = \lambda q_{n+1}(\partial \tilde{S}/\partial q_{n+1})$. Hence, in the notation of chapter 3, the social value of output is

$$V(\mathbf{q}) = S(\mathbf{q}, q_{n+1}) + \lambda \sum_{k=1}^{n+1} p_k q_k - (1 + \lambda)C^{n+1}(q_{n+1}).$$

Then the nth Ramsey index for the multiproduct firm is given by a superelasticity formula:[3]

$$R_n = \frac{\lambda}{(1 + \lambda)\eta_n}\left[\frac{1 + (p_{n+1}q_{n+1}/p_n q_n)(\eta_{n+1,n}/\eta_{n+1})}{1 - (\eta_{n,n+1}\eta_{n+1,n}/\eta_n \eta_{n+1})}\right]. \tag{5.1}$$

That is, aside from the incentive correction (which is here equal to zero

3. See appendix A5.1 for a proof.

from our technological assumption), the price of good n should be regulated as if the two firms were merged (see chapter 3). A regulated firm must be induced to internalize the loss in another regulated firm's revenue due to its pricing behavior. This conclusion is very natural, yet it does not hold in the traditional cost-of-service model (see the bibliographic notes). The conclusion is more subtle than it appears, for it hinges on the shadow price of public funds being firm independent.

Proposition 5.1 In the absence of incentive corrections, the optimal prices of competing regulated firms are determined as if the competing firms formed a single firm. That is, they ought to apply the superelasticity formulas obtained in chapter 3 for the horizontally integrated unit.

5.2.2 Unregulated Competitive Fringe

We now suppose that the competitor is *unregulated*. We maintain the assumption that goods n and $n + 1$ are substitutes (e.g., as in AT&T vs. unregulated long-distance carriers, or railway vs. road freight; the case of complements, e.g., as in public transportation vs. private hotel accommodations, can be treated analogously). We assume that the regulated and the unregulated firms compete in prices, and we consider both the sequential and simultaneous timing. In the sequential timing the regulator is able to choose a regulatory scheme and induce price setting by the regulated firm before the unregulated competitor chooses its price. In the other timing the two decisions are simultaneous, so the regulator loses his or her commitment power. Needless to say, conclusions that are insensitive to the timing are more attractive.

In the social welfare function the competitor's revenue has no weight because it cancels with the consumers' expenditure on good $n + 1$:

$$V(\mathbf{q}) = S(\mathbf{q}, q_{n+1}) + \lambda \sum_{k=1}^{n} p_k q_k - C^{n+1}(q_{n+1}).$$

Suppose that the fringe is a price-taker ($p_{n+1} = \partial\tilde{S}/\partial q_{n+1} = dC^{n+1}/dq_{n+1}$), and consider first *simultaneous timing*. The optimal regulatory policy then yields

$$L_n = \frac{\lambda}{1+\lambda}\frac{1}{\eta_n}. \tag{5.2}$$

That is, the regulated firm should "ignore" the competitive fringe [i.e., contrary to (5.1), not internalize the effect of its pricing]. The intuition is that the marginal cost of producing good $n + 1$ is equal to its marginal social value for the consumers, so there is no externality within the private sector associated with a unit change in the consumption of that good. The regulated firm should not worry about the effect of its price on the consumption of the privately produced good and should simply reason in terms of residual demand (demand for good n given the price of good $n+1$).

When the regulator is a Stackelberg leader (*sequential timing*), p_n has an effect on p_{n+1}. We let

$$\varepsilon \equiv \frac{dp_{n+1}/dp_n}{p_{n+1}/p_n}$$

denote the elasticity of the fringe's price reaction. We define the "generalized or net elasticity of demand for good n" (which takes into account the fringe's reaction) as

$$\tilde{\eta}_n \equiv -\frac{(\partial q_n/p_n) + (\partial q_n/\partial p_{n+1})(dp_{n+1}/dp_n)}{q_n/p_n} = \eta_n - \eta_{n,n+1}\varepsilon.$$

For strategic complements ($\varepsilon > 0$) and demand substitutes ($\eta_{n,n+1} > 0$), $\tilde{\eta}_n < \eta_n$. The optimal regulatory policy for the sequential timing yields

$$L_n = \frac{\lambda}{1+\lambda}\frac{1}{\tilde{\eta}_n}. \tag{5.3}$$

That is, the price of good n is higher under sequential timing because a high p_n induces the fringe to raise its price, which increases the regulated firm's revenue.

A useful conclusion is that both cases can be summarized in a single recommendation. The relevant elasticity of demand is the net elasticity of demand, which may or may not coincide with the ordinary elasticity of demand. This result is useful because, together with the price tax analysis of chapter 2, it implies that the optimal price decision can be delegated to the firm. That is, the regulator need not know the exact game firms are playing (sequential or simultaneous) as long as the regulated firm knows it. The regulated firm will automatically adopt the net elasticity as the correct measure of a change in price on its demand.[4]

Proposition 5.2 In the absence of incentive correction, if the regulated firm faces a competitive, untaxed, and unregulated fringe, the regulated firm should charge the optimal Ramsey price without internalizing the effects of its pricing on the fringe's profit. The Ramsey index is equal to $\lambda/(1+\lambda)$ times the inverse of the perceived elasticity of demand for the regulated firm's product.

i. If the regulated firm and the fringe choose prices simultaneously, the perceived elasticity of demand is equal to the ordinary elasticity of demand.

4. Knowledge of the game's timing could help the regulator to better initialize the historical scheme studied in chapter 2 and thus obtain faster convergence toward optimal prices.

ii. If the regulator and the firm can commit to a price before the competitive fringe chooses its price, the perceived elasticity of demand includes the effect of the regulated price on the fringe's price. The perceived elasticity of demand is lower than the ordinary elasticity of demand for strategic complements and demand substitutes.

5.2.3 Unregulated Competition with Distorted Pricing

Subsection 5.2.2 assumed that the producer of good $n + 1$ charges the social marginal cost. In practice the price could be distorted because of either market power or subsidies.

Competitor with Market Power

Suppose that the competitor is a monopolist and equates marginal revenue and marginal cost:

$$q_{n+1} + p_{n+1}\frac{\partial q_{n+1}}{\partial p_{n+1}} = \frac{dC^{n+1}}{dq_{n+1}}\frac{\partial q_{n+1}}{\partial p_{n+1}}.$$

$V(\mathbf{q})$ is as in subsection 5.2.2, but the choice of p_{n+1} is defined by the above constraint; the optimization with respect to p_n takes this constraint into account.

Under *simultaneous competition* the optimal Lerner index for good n is

$$L_n = \frac{\lambda}{(1+\lambda)\eta_n} + \frac{(p_{n+1}q_{n+1})\eta_{n+1,n}}{(p_n q_n)(1+\lambda)\eta_n\eta_{n+1}}. \tag{5.4}$$

Equation (5.4) implies that, if goods n and $n + 1$ are substitutes, the price of good n should exceed the level corresponding to the ordinary elasticity of demand. This conclusion is not surprising. A standard result is that the demand for a monopolized product should be encouraged by a commodity subsidy. Here, reducing the demand for good n has a similar effect as a (missing) commodity subsidy on good $n + 1$, in that both encourage consumption of good $n + 1$.[5] There is a minor difference between the two situations: Under a commodity subsidy the demand curve does not move, and the monopoly price is reduced (as the monopolist de facto faces a new marginal cost equal to the old marginal cost minus the unit subsidy). In contrast, when the price of a substitute increases, the monopolist's demand curve shifts outward. But under simultaneous competition, the regulator takes the monopolist's price p_{n+1} as given; so, an increase in the price of the substitute raises demand for the monopolized good. Thus in both cases the effect of the policy is to raise the consumption of the monopolized good. Things differ, however, under sequential competition, since the increase in the price of the substitute leads to a countervailing

5. Note that our framework implies that commodity subsidies are an imperfect instrument because of the existence of a shadow cost of public funds.

effect through an increase in the price of the monopolized good if the two goods are strategic complements.

Under *sequential competition* $V(\mathbf{q})$ is determined as in subsection 5.2.2, but the optimization takes the *pricing rule* of the competitor as given. The optimal Lerner index for good n is

$$L_n = \frac{[\lambda/(1+\lambda)\eta_n] + [(p_{n+1}q_{n+1})(\eta_{n+1,n} - \eta_{n+1}\varepsilon)]/(p_n q_n)(1+\lambda)\eta_n\eta_{n+1}}{1 - (\eta_{n,n+1}\varepsilon/\eta_n)}. \tag{5.5}$$

Equation (5.5) unveils two new, straightforward effects that correspond to the terms in the elasticity of the private monopolist's price reaction ε. By raising p_n, the regulated firm induces the competitor to raise p_{n+1}, which induces a further distortion in the consumption of good $n+1$; this effect shows up in the numerator of (5.5). But the increase in p_{n+1} also raises the regulated firm's revenue, which has a social value;[6] this explains the new term in the denominator.

Proposition 5.3 A regulated firm ought to internalize the effect of its pricing on the demand for unregulated, substitute goods sold under market power. In the absence of incentive correction, and under simultaneous pricing, the regulated firm should raise its price above the Ramsey price corresponding to the ordinary elasticity of demand in order to boost the demand for unregulated goods. Two strategic effects have to be added under sequential pricing.

Subsidized Competition

It may happen that the unregulated competitor's pricing is distorted by subsidies. For instance, it is often asserted that railroads face "unfair competition" from subsidized competitors (barges which do not pay for the use of facilities and trucks which do not pay for congestion costs or highway maintenance) and that subway tokens should be subsidized to account for the fact that charging congestion and pollution costs to city drivers is too costly.

Let us assume that the competitor is a price-taker and that the subsidy in question is the absence of payment of some social cost proportional to production (pollution, congestion cost). Then

$$V(\mathbf{q}) = S(\mathbf{q}, q_{n+1}) + \lambda \sum_{k=1}^{n} p_k q_k - C^{n+1}(q_{n+1}) - \tau_{n+1} q_{n+1},$$

where τ_{n+1} is the implicit subsidy on good $n+1$. The competitor produces until p_{n+1} equals his or her private marginal cost (dC^{n+1}/dq_{n+1}). The opti-

6. As long as the previous effect is not so powerful that it induces the regulated firm to charge below marginal cost (an unlikely occurrence).

mal Lerner index for good n in the simultaneous mode is given by

$$L_n = \frac{\lambda}{(1+\lambda)\eta_n} - \frac{(\tau_{n+1} q_{n+1})\eta_{n+1,n}}{(p_n q_n)(1+\lambda)\eta_n}. \tag{5.6}$$

Thus, if the goods are demand substitutes, the price of good n is lowered to reduce the demand for, and hence the negative externality created by, good $n + 1$.

In the sequential mode the formula is the same as (5.6), except that the elasticities must be replaced by the net elasticities [which includes the elasticity $\varepsilon = (dp_{n+1}/dp_n)/(p_{n+1}/p_n)$ of reaction of the competitive fringe]

$$\tilde{\eta}_n = \eta_n - \eta_{n,n+1}\varepsilon$$

and

$$\tilde{\eta}_{n+1,n} = \eta_{n+1,n} - \eta_{n+1}\varepsilon.$$

Assuming that (5.6) yields pricing above marginal cost (which is not guaranteed) and that the goods are strategic complements and demand substitutes, the fringe's reaction lowers the net elasticity of demand for good n, and thus calls for a higher price p_n. Furthermore the fringe's reaction to an increase in p_n reduces demand for the subsidized good $n + 1$, a socially useful effect. Hence the two effects have the same sign, and the sequential timing calls for a higher price p_n than the simultaneous timing.

Proposition 5.4 A regulated firm ought to internalize the effect of its pricing on the demand for unregulated substitutes that exert negative, say, externalities on society. In the absence of incentive correction, and under simultaneous pricing, the regulated firm ought to lower its price below the Ramsey price corresponding to the ordinary elasticity of demand in order to reduce the demand for the unregulated goods. (Sequential pricing weakens the case for low regulated prices.)

5.3 Access Pricing: Pricing in the Absence of Incentive Correction

We now analyze a variant of the unregulated competitive fringe model of subsection 5.2.2 to study the pricing of an input by a regulated multiproduct firm to a firm producing a good that competes with another product of the regulated firm. To abstract from the incentive issue, this section assumes that the dichotomy holds (in order that prices are not used to provide incentives) and derives the optimal pricing rule.

Suppose that one unit of good 1, an intermediate good produced by the regulated firm, is consumed to produce each unit of good n (produced by the regulated firm) or of good $n + 1$ (produced by the fringe). Total production of good 1 is thus $q_n + q_{n+1}$. Letting p_1 denote the transfer price, the fringe's cost is $[C^{n+1}(q_{n+1}) + p_1 q_{n+1}]$, while the regulated firm's cost is $C(\zeta(\beta, e), q_n + q_{n+1}, q_2, \ldots, q_n)$.

We will assume that the fringe's profit has social value $1 + \tilde{\lambda}$ per unit, where $0 \leq \tilde{\lambda} \leq \lambda$. As discussed in section 5.2, $\tilde{\lambda}$ might, for instance, be equal to $\lambda\tau$ if a fraction τ of the fringe's profit is recouped by the government through profit taxation.

We will also assume that $d^2 C^{n+1}/dq_{n+1}^2 \geq 0$ (the fringe has convex costs). The fringe's price is determined by the prices p_1 and p_n using

$$p_{n+1} = \frac{dC^{n+1}}{dq_{n+1}}(q_{n+1}(p_n, p_{n+1})) + p_1.$$

Weighting the fringe's profit by $1 + \tilde{\lambda}$, we obtain the social welfare function:

$$\begin{aligned} W = {} & S^2(q_2(p_2)) + \cdots + S^{n-1}(q_{n-1}(p_{n-1})) + \tilde{S}(q_n(p_n, p_{n+1}), q_{n+1}(p_n, p_{n+1})) \\ & + \lambda \sum_{k=2}^{n-1} p_k q_k(p_k) + \lambda p_n q_n(p_n, p_{n+1}) - \lambda U \\ & - (1 + \lambda)[\psi(e) + C(\zeta(\beta, e), q_n(p_n, p_{n+1}) \\ & + q_{n+1}(p_n, p_{n+1}), q_2(p_2), \ldots, q_n(p_n, p_{n+1}))] \\ & + \lambda q_{n+1}(p_n, p_{n+1})[p_{n+1} - \frac{(\lambda - \tilde{\lambda})}{\lambda} \frac{dC^{n+1}}{dq_{n+1}}(q_{n+1}(p_n, p_{n+1}))] \\ & - (1 + \tilde{\lambda}) C^{n+1}(q_{n+1}(p_n, p_{n+1})), \end{aligned}$$

where the last two terms in W are rewritings of the social value $(1 + \lambda)p_1 q_{n+1}$ of the sale of the intermediate good to the competitive sector, plus the social value $(1 + \tilde{\lambda})[(dC^{n+1}/dq_{n+1})q_{n+1} - C^{n+1}(q_{n+1})]$ of this sector's profit, minus the consumers' expenditure on good $n + 1$, $p_{n+1} q_{n+1}$. The term U is the regulated firm's rent (see chapter 3 for its determination).

Maximizing with respect to p_k, $k = 2, \ldots, n - 1$, we obtain the usual Ramsey formula for goods 2 through $n - 1$:

$$L_k = \frac{\lambda}{1 + \lambda} \frac{1}{\eta_k} \qquad k = 2, \ldots, n - 1. \tag{5.7}$$

Maximizing with respect to p_n and p_{n+1} yields

$$\begin{aligned} & p_n \frac{\partial q_n}{\partial p_n} + p_{n+1} \frac{\partial q_{n+1}}{\partial p_n} + \lambda q_n + \lambda p_n \frac{\partial q_n}{\partial p_n} \\ & \quad - (1 + \lambda)\left[\frac{\partial C}{\partial q_1}\left(\frac{\partial q_n}{\partial p_n} + \frac{\partial q_{n+1}}{\partial p_n}\right) + \frac{\partial C}{\partial q_n}\frac{\partial q_n}{\partial p_n}\right] \end{aligned}$$

$$+ \lambda \frac{\partial q_{n+1}}{\partial p_n}\left(p_{n+1} - \frac{(\lambda - \tilde{\lambda})}{\lambda}\frac{dC^{n+1}}{dq_{n+1}}(q_{n+1})\right)$$

$$- \lambda q_{n+1}\left(\frac{\lambda - \tilde{\lambda}}{\lambda}\right)\frac{d^2C^{n+1}}{dq_{n+1}^2}(q_{n+1})\frac{\partial q_{n+1}}{\partial p_n} - (1 + \tilde{\lambda})\frac{dC^{n+1}}{dq_{n+1}}\frac{\partial q_{n+1}}{\partial p_n} = 0. \quad (5.8)$$

$$p_n \frac{\partial q_n}{\partial p_{n+1}} + p_{n+1}\frac{\partial q_{n+1}}{\partial p_{n+1}} + \lambda p_n \frac{\partial q_n}{\partial p_{n+1}}$$

$$- (1 + \lambda)\left[\frac{\partial C}{\partial q_1}\left(\frac{\partial q_n}{\partial p_{n+1}} + \frac{\partial q_{n+1}}{\partial p_{n+1}}\right) + \frac{\partial C}{\partial q_n}\frac{\partial q_n}{\partial p_{n+1}}\right]$$

$$+ \lambda \frac{\partial q_{n+1}}{\partial p_{n+1}}\left(p_{n+1} - \frac{(\lambda - \tilde{\lambda})}{\lambda}\frac{dC^{n+1}}{dq_{n+1}}(q_{n+1})\right)$$

$$+ \lambda q_{n+1}\left(1 - \frac{(\lambda - \tilde{\lambda})}{\lambda}\frac{d^2C^{n+1}}{dq_{n+1}^2}(q_{n+1})\frac{\partial q_{n+1}}{\partial p_{n+1}}\right) - (1 + \tilde{\lambda})\frac{dC^{n+1}}{dq_{n+1}}\frac{\partial q_{n+1}}{\partial p_{n+1}} = 0. \quad (5.9)$$

Algebraic manipulations yield

$$L_n \equiv \frac{p_n - [(\partial C/\partial q_1) + (\partial C/\partial q_n)]}{p_n} = \frac{\lambda}{1 + \lambda}\frac{1}{\hat{\eta}_n}, \quad (5.10)$$

where

$$\hat{\eta}_n \equiv \eta_n \frac{1 - (\eta_{n,n+1}\eta_{n+1,n}/\eta_n\eta_{n+1})}{1 + (p_{n+1}q_{n+1}/p_nq_n)(\eta_{n+1,n}/\eta_{n+1})} < \eta_n \quad (5.11)$$

is good n's superelasticity, and

$$L_1 \equiv \frac{p_1 - (\partial C/\partial q_1)}{p_1} = \frac{\lambda}{1 + \lambda}\frac{1}{\hat{\eta}_1}, \quad (5.12)$$

where

$$\hat{\eta}_1 \equiv \frac{\eta_1}{[(p_{n+1}q_{n+1}\eta_n\eta_1 + p_nq_n\eta_{n,n+1}\eta_1)/p_1q_1(\eta_n\eta_{n+1} - \eta_{n,n+1}\eta_{n+1,n})] + [\lambda - \tilde{\lambda}][1 - (dp_{n+1}/dp_1)]/\lambda} \quad (5.13)$$

and

$$\frac{dp_{n+1}}{dp_1} = \frac{1}{1 - (\partial q_{n+1}/\partial p_{n+1})(d^2C^{n+1}/dq_{n+1}^2)} \in (0, 1]. \quad (5.14)$$

The key to understanding equations (5.10) and (5.12) is to view goods 1 and n as substitutes. An increase in p_n raises the demand for good $n + 1$, which in turn raises the demand for the access good by an equal amount.

It is therefore not surprising that the Lerner index for good n is given by a familiar superelasticity formula. Equation (5.11) reflects the fact that a unit decrease in q_{n+1} implies a unit decrease in q_1 and thus a loss of revenue for the regulated firm.

Of particular interest is equation (5.12) which determines the access price p_1. Note first that $\hat{\eta}_1 > 0$, so the price of the "access good" must exceed its marginal cost. Observing an external transfer price in excess of the internal transfer price is no evidence that the regulated firm has too much incentive to weaken competition, since this pricing formula must hold even when the regulator has full information about, and therefore perfectly controls, the firm.

An interesting case is that of a fringe operating under *constant returns to scale* ($d^2C^{n+1}/dq_{n+1}^2 = 0$). Then $dp_{n+1}/dp_1 = 1$, and (5.13) can be written as a superelasticity formula:

$$\hat{\eta}_1 = \eta_1 \frac{1 - (\eta_{n,n+1}\eta_{n+1,n}/\eta_n\eta_{n+1})}{1 + (p_n q_n/p_{n+1}q_{n+1})(\eta_{n+1,n}/\eta_n)} < \eta_1. \tag{5.15}$$

Because of constant marginal cost the fringe makes no profit, and therefore the social value of its profit $\tilde{\lambda}$ is irrelevant. Good 1 can just be treated as a substitute for good n, and its pricing is given by the usual Ramsey rule. Note in particular that the access price exceeds not only the marginal cost of providing access but also the "myopic" Ramsey price $\lambda/(1+\lambda)\eta_1$ associated with good 1's elasticity of demand.

Proposition 5.5 In the absence of incentive considerations, the choice of a regulated firm's price of an intermediate good to unregulated competitors on a final good's market should reflect the fact that the intermediate good supplied to competitors and the regulated firm's final product are (indirect) substitutes. The access price exceeds marginal cost. If the competitive fringe operates under constant returns to scale, the access price even exceeds the Ramsey price implied by the ordinary elasticity of demand for the intermediate good.

5.4 Access Pricing and Incentives

Section 5.3 has studied pricing of access independently of incentives, as is legitimate under the dichotomy property. In practice incentive considerations play an important role in the determination of access policies. This section analyzes the incentives of the integrated regulated firm to provide access to its downstream competitors in two polar cases: In the first, the regulated firm's unit cost of producing the intermediate good demanded by the competitors is the same as that of producing the intermediate good for internal consumption. This *common network* case is analyzed in subsection 5.4.1. An important feature is that the regulated firm cannot claim that the production of the intermediate good is costly in order to hurt its competitors without making a case against the production of its own final good. As we will see, the regulator can call the regulated firm's bluff of a high access price for the intermediate good by imposing a low level of the regulated firm's final output. In the second case, labeled *network expansion* and studied in subsection 5.4.2, the regulated firm must build new facilities, transportation capacities, or interconnections to give access to its competitors. The cost of these additions to the regulated firm's network may differ from the cost of providing access to itself. Indeed in our polar case we will assume that the cost of giving access to competitors is unrelated to that of self-access. The regulated firm then has more leeway than in the case of a (purely) common network because it can claim to have a high cost of giving access to its competitors without necessarily producing a low output itself on the final product market. The high access price squeezes out the fringe and allows the regulated firm to enjoy an increased informational rent on its private information concerning downstream production.

5.4.1 Common Network

A regulated firm operates a network of size Q at subcost

$$C_0 = C^0(\beta, e_0, Q).$$

The technological parameter β is private information to the firm and is drawn from cumulative distribution $F(\cdot)$, with strictly positive density $f(\cdot)$ on $[\underline{\beta}, \overline{\beta}]$. The firm's effort to reduce the network's subcost is denoted e_0. The subcost function satisfies $C^0_\beta > 0$, $C^0_{e_0} < 0$, $C^0_Q > 0$.

The level Q of network activity is allocated to three uses. First, the regulated firm supplies a quantity q_0 of a monopolized commodity (e.g., local telephone). Let $S(q_0)$ denote the consumers' gross surplus from this good, with $S' > 0$, $S'' < 0$.

The regulated firm also produces q_1 units of good 1 (long-distance telephone). A competitive fringe produces a quantity q_2 of an imperfect substitute to good 1. Let $V(q_1, q_2)$ denote the associated consumers' gross surplus. These outputs require one unit of utilization of the common network per unit of output:

$$Q = q_0 + q_1 + q_2.$$

The regulated firm's subcost for producting q_1 is denoted

$$C_1 = C^1(\beta, e_1, q_1),$$

where e_1 is the effort allocated by the firm to its competitive activity. The subcost function satisfies $C^1_\beta > 0$, $C^1_{e_1} < 0$, $C^1_{q_1} > 0$. The firm's disutility of effort is $\psi(e_0 + e_1)$, with $\psi' > 0, \psi'' > 0, \psi''' \geq 0$. We make the convention that the government receives the regulated firm's revenue $p_0q_0 + p_1q_1 + aq_2$, where p_k is the price of good k ($k = 0,1,2$) and a is the unit access charge paid by the fringe for access to the network. Let t denote the net transfer to the regulated firm, whose utility is $U = t - \psi(e_0 + e_1)$. The production of q_2 units by the competitive fringe has cost cq_2, where c is common knowledge. The fringe thus charges its total marginal cost: $p_2 = c + a$.

Let us start with the benchmark of *complete information*. Using the fact that the fringe makes no profit, the regulator's objective function is

$$S(q_0) + V(q_1, q_2) + \lambda(p_0q_0 + p_1q_1 + p_2q_2)$$
$$- (1 + \lambda)(C_0 + C_1 + cq_2 + \psi(e_0 + e_1)) - \lambda U.$$

The regulator extracts the firm's rent: $U = 0$. The pricing choices parallel those obtained in section 5.3. Let $\eta_0 = -(dq_0/dp_0)(p_0/q_0)$ denote the price elasticity of the monopolized good. Using the traditional notation: $\eta_{kl} \equiv (dq_k/dp_l)(p_l/q_k)$ ($k \neq l$; $k = 1, 2$; $l = 1,2$) and $\eta_k \equiv -\eta_{kk}$, we can introduce the superelasticities

$$\hat{\eta}_1 = \eta_1 \frac{\eta_1\eta_2 - \eta_{12}\eta_{21}}{\eta_1\eta_2 + (p_2q_2/p_1q_1)\eta_1\eta_{21}}$$

and

$$\hat{\eta}_2 = \eta_2 \frac{\eta_1\eta_2 - \eta_{12}\eta_{21}}{\eta_1\eta_2 + (p_1q_1/p_2q_2)\eta_2\eta_{12}}.$$

We have

$$L_0 \equiv \frac{p_0 - C_Q^0}{p_0} = \frac{\lambda}{1+\lambda}\frac{1}{\eta_0}, \tag{5.16}$$

$$L_1 \equiv \frac{p_1 - (C_Q^0 + C_{q_1}^1)}{p_1} = \frac{\lambda}{1+\lambda}\frac{1}{\hat{\eta}_1}, \tag{5.17}$$

and

$$L_2 \equiv \frac{p_2 - (C_Q^0 + c)}{p_2} = \frac{\lambda}{1+\lambda}\frac{1}{\hat{\eta}_2}. \tag{5.18}$$

Note that the access charge can be rewritten, using $p_2 = c + a$, as

$$a = \frac{C_Q^0 + [\lambda/(1+\lambda)](c/\hat{\eta}_2)}{1 - [\lambda/(1+\lambda)](c/\hat{\eta}_2)}. \tag{5.19}$$

Unless the shadow cost of public funds equals 0, the access price exceeds the marginal cost of providing access.

Last, the marginal disutility of effort on each activity is equal to marginal cost savings:

$$\psi'(e_0 + e_1) = -C^0_{e_0} = -C^1_{e_1}. \tag{5.20}$$

Let us now assume that the regulator has *incomplete information* about β and does not observe efforts e_0 and e_1. For the moment we assume that the regulator observes subcosts C_0 and C_1 separately. Let $E^0(\beta, C_0, Q)$ denote the effort required to produce Q units of network activity at subcost C_0 under technology β: That is, $C_0 = C^0(\beta, E^0(\beta, C_0, Q), Q)$. Similarly let $E^1(\beta, C_1, q_1)$ denote the effort required to produce q_1 units of final good 1 at subcost C_1 under technology β: $C_1 = C^1(\beta, E^1(\beta, C_1, q_1), q_1)$. The firm's utility can be written:

$$U = t - \psi(E^0(\beta, C_0, Q) + E^1(\beta, C_1, q_1)).$$

The envelope theorem implies that

$$\dot{U} = -\psi'(E^0_\beta + E^1_\beta).$$

Since $E^0_\beta > 0$ and $E^1_\beta > 0$, the individual rationality constraint binds at $\bar{\beta}$ only:

$$U(\bar{\beta}) \geq 0.$$

The regulator maximizes

$$\int_{\underline{\beta}}^{\bar{\beta}} [S(q_0) + V(q_1, q_2) + \lambda(p_0 q_0 + p_1 q_1 + p_2 q_2) - (1 + \lambda)(C_0 + C_1 + cq_2 + \psi) - \lambda U] f(\beta) d\beta$$

subject to the incentive and participation constraints just derived. We leave it to the reader to show that the corrected pricing rules are

$$\frac{p_0 - C^0_Q}{p_0} = \frac{\lambda}{1+\lambda}\frac{1}{\eta_0} + \frac{\lambda}{1+\lambda}\frac{F}{f}\frac{\psi'}{p_0}\frac{d}{dQ}\left(-\frac{C^0_\beta}{C^0_{e_0}}\right) \tag{5.21}$$

$$\frac{p_1 - (C^0_Q + C^1_{q_1})}{p_1} = \frac{\lambda}{1+\lambda}\frac{1}{\hat{\eta}_1} + \frac{\lambda}{1+\lambda}\frac{F}{f}\frac{\psi'}{p_1}\left[-\frac{d}{dQ}\left(\frac{C^0_\beta}{C^0_{e_0}}\right) - \frac{d}{dq_1}\left(\frac{C^1_\beta}{C^1_{e_1}}\right)\right], \tag{5.22}$$

and

$$\frac{p_2 - (C^0_Q + c)}{p_2} = \frac{\lambda}{1+\lambda}\frac{1}{\hat{\eta}_2} + \frac{\lambda}{1+\lambda}\frac{F}{f}\frac{\psi'}{p_2}\frac{d}{dQ}\left(-\frac{C^0_\beta}{C^0_{e_0}}\right). \tag{5.23}$$

All prices are modified by the incentive correction corresponding to the network activity. Good 1 has an additional correction associated with the firm's private information on subcost C_1. The access charge is given by

$$a = \frac{C_Q^0 + [\lambda/(1+\lambda)](c/\hat{\eta}_2) + [\lambda/(1+\lambda)](F/f)\psi'(d/dQ)(-C_\beta^0/C_{e_0}^0)}{1 - [\lambda/(1+\lambda)](1/\hat{\eta}_2)} \tag{5.24}$$

Note that the new term (incentive correction) in this access charge is equal to zero for the most efficient type, since $F(\underline{\beta}) = 0$. The expression $d(-C_\beta^0/C_{e_0}^0)/dQ = dE_\beta^0/dQ$ measures the rate at which the firm can substitute low effort for improved productivity on the production of the network good. If $dE_\beta^0/dQ > 0$, an increase in the production of the network good raises rents, and it is optimal to raise the access price (as well as the other prices) for incentive purposes, and conversely, for $dE_\beta^0/dQ < 0$. The dichotomy property (see chapter 3) obtains when $C_0 = C^0(\zeta(\beta, e_0), Q)$ for some function $\zeta(\cdot,\cdot)$.

These pricing conclusions suggest that the commonality of access to the network limits the gain made by the firm when misrepresenting its cost of giving access to its competitors. The marginal cost C_Q^0 and the incentive correction $d(-C_\beta^0/C_{e_0}^0)/dQ$ affect the pricing of access and that of good 1 in qualitatively equivalent ways.

Last, the cost-reimbursement rule is given in implicit form by

$$\begin{aligned}\psi'(e_0 + e_1) &= -C_{e_0}^0 - \frac{\lambda}{1+\lambda}\frac{F}{f}[\psi''(E_\beta^0 + E_\beta^1) + \psi' E_{\beta C_0}^0 C_{e_0}^0] \\ &= -C_{e_1}^1 - \frac{\lambda}{1+\lambda}\frac{F}{f}[\psi''(E_\beta^0 + E_\beta^1) + \psi' E_{\beta C_1}^1 C_{e_1}^1]\end{aligned} \tag{5.25}$$

Example Let

$$C_0 = (\beta - e_0)(q_0 + q_1 + q_2) \tag{5.26}$$

and

$$C_1 = (\beta - e_1)q_1. \tag{5.27}$$

Then

$$E^0 + E^1 = 2\beta - \frac{C_0}{q_0 + q_1 + q_2} - \frac{C_1}{q_1}.$$

Therefore the firm can be rewarded on the basis of a *performance indicator*:

$$t = T\left(\frac{C_0}{q_0 + q_1 + q_2} + \frac{C_1}{q_1}\right), \qquad \text{with } T' < 0. \tag{5.28}$$

The firm can then be granted freedom to choose the access price. The point is that it knows that a high access price cuts the demand for good 2 and therefore deteriorates the performance indicator. Note that with respect to the competitive market, *the regulated firm's reward increases with both its own output* q_1 *and the industry output* $q_1 + q_2$. Writing q_2 as a function of q_1 and the access price, we can also express the transfer to the firm as a function of C_0, C_1, q_0, q_1, and the access price a.

Remark on nonobservability of subcosts We assumed that the regulator can audit and separate the costs of the network and of the competitive activity. As in chapter 3, we can alternatively consider the case in which subcosts cannot be disentangled and only aggregate cost is observable. Subcost observability is irrelevant if $\partial E_\beta^k/\partial C_k = K$ for $k = 0, 1$ (from proposition 3.11). We could also easily consider a multidimensional parameter space and thus completely disconnect the technological characteristics of the network and competitive activities as long as proposition 3.12 can be applied [e.g., the performance indicator would be unchanged in the previous example if $C_0 = (\beta_0 - e_0)(q_0 + q_1 + q_2)$ and $C_1 = (\beta_1 - e_1)q_1$, where β_0 and β_1 are two independent parameters]. We also know that when subcost observability is relevant, it leads to the adoption of higher-powered incentives on that activity for which a low subcost reduces rent more ($\partial E_\beta^k/\partial C_k$ larger).

Remark on budget balance As in the previous chapters the analysis can straightforwardly be extended to the case in which the government is prohibited from making transfers to the regulated firm. The "shadow price of public funds" is now type contingent, $\tilde{\lambda}(\beta)$. The ratio $\lambda/(1 + \lambda)$ in the Ramsey terms must be replaced by $\tilde{\lambda}(\beta)/[1 + \tilde{\lambda}(\beta)]$. The incentive correction term $\lambda F/[(1 + \lambda)f]$ for prices and effort choices must be replaced by $[\int_{\underline{\beta}}^{\beta} \tilde{\lambda}(x)f(x)dx]/[(1 + \tilde{\lambda}(\beta))f(\beta)]$.

We summarize our conclusions in proposition 5.6.

Proposition 5.6 (Common Network) A regulated firm producing a monopolized intermediate good at the same marginal cost for itself and for its downstream competitors cannot inflate the access price without making a case against its own downstream production. Prices are given by formulas (5.21) through (5.24). The regulated firm's reward should increase with the downstream competitors' output or, equivalently, decrease with the level of the access price.

5.4.2 Network Expansion

Suppose now that to provide access to its competitors, the regulated firm must add new capacity or connections, unrelated to existing self-access capacity or connection. We already noted that under such circumstances the regulated firm can claim to have a high cost of giving access without necessarily producing a low output on the final product market(s). The high access price squeezes out the fringe and allows the regulated firm to enjoy a high informational rent on its second technological parameter. We will content ourselves with a highly stylized example to illustrate the idea.

A Two-Dimensional Example

Let the regulated firm and the fringe produce the same final output. There are Q customers with unit demands and reservation price r per unit, so total output is Q. The regulated firm's cost is

$$C = (\beta_0 - e_0)x + (\beta - e)q + \alpha,$$

where α is a fixed cost, β_0 and β are two independent adverse-selection parameters, Δq is the firm's output, and $x = 1$ if access is given to the fringe and $x = 0$ otherwise. The disutility of effort is $\psi(e_0 + e)$. If the fringe is given access, it can produce any amount at constant unit cost $c < r$. We assume that β_0 can take only two values: β_0^L (low) with probability $1 - y$ or β_0^H (high) with probability y, while β is drawn from the distribution $F(\beta)$ on $[\underline{\beta}, \bar{\beta}]$ with density $f(\beta)$ [with the usual properties that $f(\beta) > 0$ and $d(F/f)/d\beta \geq 0$ for all β].

We assume that β_0^H is very large ("infinite"), so all output should be produced by the regulated firm when $\beta_0 = \beta_0^H$, and we assume that when $\beta_0 = \beta_0^L$, it would be optimal to let the fringe supply the entire market if the regulator had full information about the adverse-selection parameters (i.e., c and β_0^L are sufficiently small; see below).

Full Information

First, consider the case in which the regulator knows β_0 and β. If $\beta_0 = \beta_0^L$, the regulator gives access to the fringe at price $r - c$ per unit of output, and requires effort $e_0 = \hat{e}$ such that $\psi'(\hat{e}) = 1$ (marginal disutility of effort equals marginal cost reduction). The firm receives a net income equal to $\psi(\hat{e})$. Social welfare is

$$W^L = (1 + \lambda)[(r - c)Q - [\beta_0^L - \hat{e} + \alpha + \psi(\hat{e})]].$$

If $\beta_0 = \beta_0^H$, no access is granted to the fringe. The regulator requires effort $e = e^*$ such that $\psi'(e^*) = Q$ (marginal disutility of effort equals marginal cost reduction) and gives net transfer $\psi(e^*)$ to the firm. Social welfare is

$$W^H(\beta) = (1 + \lambda)[rQ - [(\beta - e^*)Q + \alpha + \psi(e^*)]].$$

We assume that $W^L > W^H(\underline{\beta})$, so it is always optimal to use the fringe if $\beta_0 = \beta_0^L$.

Asymmetric Information

Under asymmetric information the regulator must elicit the information about cost. Appendix A5.2 shows that

1. No access is given to the fringe when $\beta_0 = \beta_0^H$.
2. There exists $\beta^* \in [\underline{\beta}, \bar{\beta}]$ [independent of $y = \text{Prob}(\beta_0 = \beta_0^H)$] such that, when $\beta_0 = \beta_0^L$, types in $[\underline{\beta}, \beta^*]$ do not give access (i.e., might as well claim that $\beta_0 = \beta_0^H$) and types in $(\beta^*, \bar{\beta}]$ give access and do not produce the final output. The later types receive a lump-sum transfer to allow access giving

them rent equal to the rent of type β^* under the no-access policy (then even type $\bar{\beta}$ gets a strictly positive rent when $\beta_0 = \beta_0^L$). There is less access than under full information ($\beta^* > \underline{\beta}$) unless the cost differential between the regulated firm and the fringe is so high that there is the same amount of access ($\beta^* = \underline{\beta}$).

Asymmetric information makes the use of the regulated firm's intermediate good more costly than under complete information. Consequently *less* access is given. This result can be contrasted with that for the bypass problem. In chapter 6 it will be shown that asymmetric information about the regulated firm leads to *more* bypass. The apparent conflict between these two conclusions (asymmetric information yields less competition in one case and more in the other) is easily resolved: In both cases incentives issues raise the cost of the regulated firm's goods. In the access-pricing problem, the good is an input for a competitor, while it is a final good in the bypass problem.

3. The regulated firm's slope of the incentive scheme and rent are lower than under full information when $\beta_0 = \beta_0^H$. There is thus a spillover between the two revelation problems. To discourage the regulated firm from refusing access to the fringe when it is optimal to grant it, the regulator lowers the rents in the no-access policy and to this purpose lowers the incentives. One can actually show the stronger result, that the regulated firm's rent in the no-access policy decreases with the probability that access is feasible (i.e., with the probability that $\beta_0 = \beta_0^L$).

4. The effect of an increased possibility of access on the regulated firm's rent is ambiguous. While we already noted that types β close to $\bar{\beta}$ gain when the probability $1 - y$ that access is feasible is positive rather than 0, the rent of types β in $[\underline{\beta}, \beta^*]$ decreases with $1 - y$.

Proposition 5.7 A regulated firm with private information about the additional cost of giving access to a rival is tempted to exaggerate this cost to face less competition and earn higher rents on the final product market. In our example less access is given than under full information. Low-powered incentive schemes are given to reduce the temptation to inflate the access price, but the regulated firm may gain or lose from the possibility of access.

Finally it is clear that if the marginal costs of access for the regulated firm and fringe were strongly correlated, the firm would not be able to derive much rent from private information about the access costs. An extreme example of this phenomenon occurs in our above example when the regulated firm also needs access and when

$$C = (\beta_0 - e_0)(x_1 + x_2) + (\beta - e)q_1 + \alpha,$$

where

$x_1 = 1$ for access of the regulated firm,
$x_2 = 1$ for access of the fringe.

Then the regulated firm never produces the final good ($q_1 = 0$) and does not benefit from its private information about β.

5.5 Concluding Remarks

This chapter has set itself two tasks. First, it adjusted the monopoly Ramsey formulas to account for the effects of the regulated firm's pricing on its competitors. The logic of such adjustments is by now intuitive and straightforward. Second, the chapter took a first look at the access-pricing issue. There is no doubt that access pricing is and will remain one of the central questions in regulation (and antitrust). Because of the importance of the matter, it is regrettable that our analysis here does not go beyond a couple of insightful examples. A central item on the regulatory research agenda is thus the development of a general theory of access pricing.

Besides this need for more generality, let us point at two important issues related to access pricing that are not tackled in this book. First, in an intertemporal context the number of competitors and their size are not fixed. In particular the lower the competitors' profit today, the more they need to borrow to expand or remain in the market. Since capital markets are imperfect (e.g., due to asymmetries of information), competitors may be financially constrained and prevented from expanding or forced to quit the market. This, together with the fact that the regulated firm derives a higher rent in the absence of competition, suggests that the regulated firm might benefit from strategies that reduce its competitors' retained earnings.[7]

The regulated firm has two instruments with which to prey on its competitors: It can claim a low marginal cost of producing the final output to vindicate a low final price or a high marginal cost of giving access to justify a high access price. We think that these two instruments differ in attractiveness and make the following conjecture:

Conjecture If the regulatory relationship is run by a sequence of short-term contracts (the regulator and the firm can commit only in the short run), predation through a high access price is more attractive to the regulated firm than predation through a low price on the final good market.

7. Although we couch the argument in terms of the "long purse story," we could have described it using the signaling model in which the incumbent firm tries to deter entry or induce exit by signaling a low production cost. See Tirole (1988, ch. 9) for a discussion of these two approaches to predation. Recent developments on the "long purse story" include Bolton and Scharfstein (1990) and Poitevin (1989).

The intuition for this conjecture is as follows: Suppose that the regulated firm manipulates its information so as to produce a high final output today. The regulator then believes that the firm can produce this output at low cost, and tomorrow will insist on a high output and a small cost reimbursement. This is the ratchet effect studied in chapter 9. In contrast, when the firm pretends to have a high cost of giving access to its competitors, the regulator will not reduce transfers tomorrow, since the firm is not revealing any favorable realization of the technological uncertainty. That is, predation via high access prices is not subject to the ratchet effect associated with predation via low final output prices.

Second, we have assumed that the only way to obtain fair access for the regulated firm's competitors is to control the access price (or more generally access price and quality). An alternative route, such as that followed by Judge Greene in the 1984 divestiture of AT&T, is to separate the production of the intermediate good from that of the final product in the hope that the intermediate good producer behaves more fairly than under vertical integration.[8]

An important research question in regulatory theory is to identify the costs and benefits of breakups in a regulatory situation.[9] Among these costs are those emphasized in the literature on incomplete contracts and ownership structure in unregulated industries: reduction of coordination, possible expropriation of specific investment. Divestiture could enlarge control possibilities for the regulator (on the cost of delegating the choice of incentive schemes in hierarchies, see bibliographic notes B1.7 of chapter 1), but mainly it would reduce the incentives of the producer of the intermediate good to favor one final good producer over the others. We feel that the integration of the literatures on market foreclosure and on regulation will help reframe the policy debate.

BIBLIOGRAPHIC NOTES

B5.1 Cost-of-Service Pricing in the Presence of Several Regulated Firms

In the cost-of-service model, that is when both the main regulated firm and its competitors must balance their budgets, the definition of social

8. Contrast the AT&T decision with another important access decision taken the same year. The U.S. Civil Aeronautics Board decided against forcing the main airlines to divest their computer reservation system divisions. Rather, it chose to regulate the access price and quality.
9. See Hart and Tirole (1990) for an analysis of foreclosure via vertical integration in unregulated industries. Other papers on the topic include Bolton and Whinston (1992), which mainly addresses other issues but contains material on monopolization; Ordover et al. (1990); and Salinger (1988).

surplus can be modified to include the externality on the competitor, by adding the term $\mu_{n+1} p_{n+1} q_{n+1}$ where μ_{n+1} is the shadow cost of the competitor's budget constraint. Nevertheless, there is no reason why a formula like (5.1) should hold given that the shadow price of the multiproduct firm's budget constraint μ in general differs from μ_{n+1}. See Brauetigam (1984).

The correct superelasticity is obtained in the COS model only in Boiteux's (1956) analysis of a single budget constraint for the public sector (as opposed to the individual budget constraints of the traditional COS model) or in Brauetigam's (1984) "viable industry Ramsey optimum" in which the regulator can impose lump-sum transfers among the regulated firms.

Brauetigam (1979) considers a model of an increasing returns-to-scale firm facing constant-returns-to-scale competitors. In the "totally regulated second-best environment," the increasing-returns firm is regulated in a Ramsey-Boiteux fashion, and the competitors are taxed. However, the taxes do not enter the social welfare function, since the shadow cost of public funds is assumed equal to zero. The resulting conclusion therefore differs from that obtained in equation (5.1). The Ramsey-Boiteux firm in Brauetigam is instructed to behave as if there were no competition [in our notation, $R_n = \lambda/(1+\lambda)\eta_n$].

Last, part i of proposition 5.2, which states that a regulated firm facing a competitive fringe ought to charge the Ramsey price corresponding to the ordinary demand curve, was first obtained by Brauetigam (1979) in a Ramsey-Boiteux framework.

APPENDIXES

A5.1 How to Obtain Superelasticity Formulas

We consider the case where the competitor's production level can be regulated and all its profits captured by the government. The consumers-taxpayers' utility is

$$\sum_{k=1}^{n-1} S^k(q_k) + \tilde{S}(q_n, q_{n+1}) + \lambda \sum_{k=1}^{n} p_k q_k - p_{n+1} q_{n+1}$$
$$- (1+\lambda)[t + C(\zeta(\beta, e), \mathbf{q}) + C^{n+1}(q_{n+1}) - p_{n+1} q_{n+1}].$$

Adding to this utility the regulated firm's utility level $U = t - \psi(e)$, we obtain social welfare:

$$\sum_{k=1}^{n-1} S^k(q_k) + \tilde{S}(q_n, q_{n+1}) + \lambda \sum_{k=1}^{n} p_k q_k + \lambda p_{n+1} q_{n+1}$$
$$- (1+\lambda)[\psi(e) + C(\zeta(\beta, e), \mathbf{q}) + C^{n+1}(q_{n+1})] - \lambda U.$$

Note that if we had not assumed the competitor's rents to be zero, we would have had an additional term representing the utility of the competitor. Because of the incentive-pricing dichotomy the optimal pricing rules are simply obtained by maximizing this expression *with respect to prices*, taking into account correctly the interdependencies between products in the demand functions.

Now we rewrite the relevant part of the welfare function as a function of prices $\mathbf{p} = (p_1, \ldots, p_n)$ and p_{n+1}. The separability of the utility function implies that we can focus on products n and $n+1$, the formulas for products 1 through $n-1$ being identical to those obtained in chapter 3. Welfare is (up to some additive terms that are irrelevant to the pricing decision)

$$\tilde{S}(q_n(p_n, p_{n+1}), q_{n+1}(p_n, p_{n+1})) + \lambda[p_n q_n(p_n, p_{n+1}) + p_{n+1} q_{n+1}(p_n, p_{n+1})]$$
$$- (1+\lambda)[C(\zeta(\beta, e), q_1(p_1), \ldots, q_{n-1}(p_{n-1}), q_n(p_n, p_{n+1})) + C^{n+1}(q_{n+1}(p_n, p_{n+1}))].$$

Maximizing the welfare with respect to (p_n, p_{n+1}), we obtain

$$\frac{\partial \tilde{S}}{\partial q_n}\frac{\partial q_n}{\partial p_n} + \frac{\partial \tilde{S}}{\partial q_{n+1}}\frac{\partial q_{n+1}}{\partial p_n} + \lambda\left[q_n + p_n\frac{\partial q_n}{\partial p_n} + p_{n+1}\frac{\partial q_{n+1}}{\partial p_n}\right] - (1+\lambda)\frac{\partial C}{\partial q_n}\frac{\partial q_n}{\partial p_n}$$
$$- (1+\lambda)\frac{\partial C^{n+1}}{\partial q_{n+1}}\frac{\partial q_{n+1}}{\partial p_n} = 0,$$

$$\frac{\partial \tilde{S}}{\partial q_n}\frac{\partial q_n}{\partial p_{n+1}} + \frac{\partial \tilde{S}}{\partial q_{n+1}}\frac{\partial q_{n+1}}{\partial p_{n+1}} + \lambda\left[p_n\frac{\partial q_n}{\partial p_{n+1}} + q_{n+1} + p_{n+1}\frac{\partial q_{n+1}}{\partial p_{n+1}}\right] - (1+\lambda)\frac{\partial C}{\partial q_n}\frac{\partial q_n}{\partial p_{n+1}}$$
$$- (1+\lambda)\frac{\partial C^{n+1}}{\partial q_{n+1}}\frac{\partial q_{n+1}}{\partial p_{n+1}} = 0.$$

Noting that $\partial\tilde{S}/\partial q_n = p_n$ and that $\partial\tilde{S}/\partial q_{n+1} = p_{n+1}$, these two equations can be rewritten

$$(1+\lambda)\begin{bmatrix} \dfrac{\partial q_n}{\partial p_n} & \dfrac{\partial q_{n+1}}{\partial p_n} \\[2ex] \dfrac{\partial q_n}{\partial p_{n+1}} & \dfrac{\partial q_{n+1}}{\partial p_{n+1}} \end{bmatrix}\begin{bmatrix} p_n - \dfrac{\partial C}{\partial q_n} \\[2ex] p_{n+1} - \dfrac{\partial C^{n+1}}{\partial q_{n+1}} \end{bmatrix} = \begin{bmatrix} -\lambda q_n \\ -\lambda q_{n+1} \end{bmatrix}$$

or (by Cramer's rule)

$$p_n - \frac{\partial C}{\partial q_n} = -\frac{\lambda}{1+\lambda}\frac{\begin{vmatrix} q_n & \dfrac{\partial q_{n+1}}{\partial p_n} \\[2ex] q_{n+1} & \dfrac{\partial q_{n+1}}{\partial p_{n+1}} \end{vmatrix}}{\begin{vmatrix} \dfrac{\partial q_n}{\partial p_n} & \dfrac{\partial q_{n+1}}{\partial p_n} \\[2ex] \dfrac{\partial q_n}{\partial p_{n+1}} & \dfrac{\partial q_{n+1}}{\partial p_{n+1}} \end{vmatrix}}.$$

$$p_{n+1} - \frac{\partial C^{n+1}}{\partial q_{n+1}} = -\frac{\lambda}{1+\lambda} \frac{\begin{vmatrix} \dfrac{\partial q_n}{\partial p_n} & q_n \\ \dfrac{\partial q_n}{\partial p_{n+1}} & q_{n+1} \end{vmatrix}}{\begin{vmatrix} \dfrac{\partial q_n}{\partial p_n} & \dfrac{\partial q_{n+1}}{\partial p_n} \\ \dfrac{\partial q_n}{\partial p_{n+1}} & \dfrac{\partial q_{n+1}}{\partial p_{n+1}} \end{vmatrix}}.$$

In particular

$$\frac{p_n - (\partial C/\partial q_n)}{p_n} = -\frac{\lambda}{1+\lambda}\left[\frac{q_n(\partial q_{n+1}/\partial p_{n+1}) - q_{n+1}(\partial q_{n+1}/\partial p_n)}{p_n[(\partial q_n/\partial p_n)(\partial q_{n+1}/\partial p_{n+1}) - (\partial q_n/\partial p_{n+1})(\partial q_{n+1}/\partial p_n)]}\right].$$

Using our conventions for denoting elasticities, we immediately obtain

$$L_n = R_n = \frac{p_n - (\partial C/\partial q_n)}{p_n} = \frac{\lambda}{(1+\lambda)\eta_n}\left[\frac{1 + (p_{n+1}q_{n+1}/p_n q_n)(\eta_{n+1,n}/\eta_{n+1})}{1 - (\eta_{n,n+1}\eta_{n+1,n}/\eta_n\eta_{n+1})}\right],$$

and likewise we obtain a symmetric expression for L_{n+1}. ■

A5.2 Access Pricing and Incentives

This appendix proves the results listed in subsection 5.4.2. From the revelation principle we know that the regulator can restrict attention to mechanisms in which the firm announces its parameters truthfully.

First, if $\beta_0 = \beta_0^H$, the firm is a monopolist, since giving access to the fringe is too expensive. Let $e^*(\beta)$ be the effort of type β and $U^*(\beta) = \int_\beta^{\bar\beta} \psi'(e^*(\tilde\beta))d\tilde\beta$ its rent.

Second, if $\beta_0 = \beta_0^L$, the regulator has two options: either to give access to the fringe and let the fringe supply total output or not to give access.[10] By incentive compatibility, it is easily seen that for types $\beta \in [\underline\beta, \beta^*]$ no access is given and for types $\beta \in (\beta^*, \bar\beta]$ access is given (because lower-cost types enjoy a higher rent under the no-access policy, while all types enjoy the same rent under the access policy). To induce types $\beta \in (\beta^*, \bar\beta]$ to give access (i.e., not to announce β_0^H), the regulator must give a lump-sum transfer $U^*(\beta^*)$ beyond the compensation for the effort $e_0 = \hat e$ when giving access.

Let $y \equiv \text{Prob}(\beta_0 = \beta_0^H)$. Social welfare then is

$$W = \max\left\{ y \int_{\underline\beta}^{\bar\beta} [(1+\lambda)(rQ - (\beta - e^*(\beta))Q - \alpha - \psi(e^*(\beta))) - \lambda U^*(\beta)]f(\beta)d\beta \right.$$

$$+ (1-y)\left[\int_{\underline\beta}^{\beta^*} [(1+\lambda)(rQ - (\beta - e^*(\beta))Q - \alpha - \psi(e^*(\beta))\right.$$

10. The policy of giving access and sharing the market of the final good is dominated. If access is given to the fringe, choosing $q = 0$ is optimal because, first, the fringe has lower marginal cost and, second, $q = 0$ allows the regulator to perfectly control e_0.

$$- \lambda U^*(\beta)]f(\beta)d\beta + \int_{\beta^*}^{\bar{\beta}} [(1+\lambda)((r-c)Q - \beta_0^L + \hat{e} - \alpha - \psi(\hat{e}))$$

$$\left. \left. - \lambda U^*(\beta^*)]f(\beta)d\beta \right] \right\} \tag{A5.1}$$

subject to $U^*(\bar{\beta}) = 0$ and $\dot{U}^*(\beta) = -\psi'(e^*(\beta))$. Integrating by parts, and optimizing, yields

$$\psi'(e^*(\beta)) = Q - \frac{\lambda}{1+\lambda}\frac{F(\beta)}{f(\beta)}\psi''(e^*(\beta)) \qquad \text{for } \beta \leq \beta^*. \tag{A5.2}$$

$$\psi'(e^*(\beta)) = Q - \frac{\lambda}{1+\lambda}\frac{F(\beta) + (1-y)/y}{f(\beta)}\psi''(e^*(\beta)) \qquad \text{for } \beta > \beta^*. \tag{A5.3}$$

The interpretation of these equations is as follows: Equation (A5.2) is the version of equation (3.9) of chapter 3 for this model. Because types under β^* do not give access whatever β_0, the trade-off between bringing marginal benefit and marginal disutility closer together (lowering $Q - \psi'$) and leaving more rent to better types is resolved in the standard way. In contrast, types above β^* give access when $\beta_0 = \beta_0^L$. An increase in $e^*(\beta)$ for such types not only raises the rent of more efficient types but also, with probability $1 - y$, raises the rent of types in $[\beta^*, \bar{\beta}]$ who get the lump-sum transfer $U^*(\beta^*)$ for giving access. This results in lower incentives than those predicted by equation (A5.2).

We now optimize with respect to β^*. Assuming an interior solution, we have

$$\begin{aligned} &\lambda(1 - F(\beta^*))\psi'(e^*(\beta^*)) \\ &\quad = (1+\lambda)f(\beta^*)[(\beta^* - e^*(\beta^*))Q + \psi(e^*(\beta^*)) - cQ - \beta_0^L \\ &\qquad - \psi(\hat{e}) + \hat{e}], \end{aligned} \tag{A5.4}$$

where $e^*(\beta^*)$ denotes the value in the no-access policy [equation (A5.2)]. The assumption that $W^L > W^H(\beta)$ and the fact that $e^*(\beta^*) \leq e^*$ imply that the right-hand side of (A5.4) is positive. Equation (A5.4) expresses the equality between the marginal benefit of increasing access—by raising β^* by $d\beta^*$, one lowers the rent of types in $[\beta^*, \bar{\beta}]$ when access is given by $\psi'(e^*(\beta^*))d\beta^*$—and the marginal cost of production associated with more access. Note that β^* is independent of y. The possibility of using linear contracts when F/f is increasing and no access is granted follows the usual lines. ■

REFERENCES

Boiteux, M. 1956. Sur la gestion des monopoles publics astreints à l'équilibre budgétaire. *Econometrica* 24:22–40.

Bolton, P., and D. Scharfstein. 1990. A theory of predation based on agency problems in financial contracting. *American Economic Review* 80:94–106.

Bolton, P., and M. Whinston. 1992. Incomplete contracts, vertical integration, and supply insurance. Forthcoming, *Review of Economic Studies*.

Brauetigam, R. 1979. Optimal pricing with intermodal competition. *American Economic Review* 69:38–49.

Brauetigam, R. 1984. Socially optimal pricing with rivalry and economies of scale. *Rand Journal of Economics* 15:127–134.

Hart, O., and J. Tirole. 1990. Vertical integration and market foreclosure. *Brookings Papers on Economic Activity: Microeconomics 1990*, 205–276, 285–286.

Ordover, J., G. Saloner, and S. Salop. 1990. Equilibrium market foreclosure. *American Economic Review* 80:127–142.

Poitevin, M. 1989. Financial signalling and the "deep pocket" argument. *Rand Journal of Economics* 20:26–40.

Salinger, M. 1988. Vertical mergers and market foreclosure. *Quarterly Journal of Economics* 103:345–356.

Tirole, J. 1988. *The Theory of Industrial Organization.* Cambridge, MA: MIT Press.

Tye, W. 1987. Competitive access: A comparative industry approach to the essential facility doctrine. *Energy Law Journal* 8:337–379.

Vickers, J. 1989. Competition and regulation in vertically related markets. Mimeo, Oxford University.

6 BYPASS AND CREAM SKIMMING

6.1 Some Background

The regulation of "natural monopolies" is often associated with policies toward competition, including restrictions on entry. This chapter is concerned with a common form of competition that threatens the regulated firm in its most lucrative markets. Examples abound. In the telecommunications industry the development of microwave radio and communication satellites in the 1960s introduced the possibility that big telecommunication customers could bypass the major common carrier AT&T and, for instance, deal directly with a satellite company. More recently some large firms have bypassed the local telephone networks and have acquired direct links to long-distance carriers. Similar issues arise in the energy sector. Big industrial consumers of electricity can generate their own power. The 1978 Natural Gas Policy Act in the United States has created the possibility for industrial plants to bypass the local distribution utilities by building direct connections to the pipelines, gas producers, or intermediaries.

What distinguishes these examples from other situations in which a regulated firm faces competition is that the competitive pressure focuses on the high-demand customers (the "cream") and not on low-demand ones (the "skimmed milk"). That is, entry interferes with second-degree price discrimination by the regulated monopolist.[1]

As one would expect, cream skimming has been the object of much regulatory attention. Regulated monopolies have repeatedly called for entry restrictions. For instance, AT&T has assailed MCI as a cream-skimmer, lapping up the profits on favorable routes and eschewing high-cost, low-return service and has accused Comsat of syphoning the most profitable part of the business. More recently local distribution companies have made similar charges against bypass. In both cases the regulated monopoly has argued that because of economies of scale, bypass would raise the rates of small-volume commercial and residential users or would reduce the quality of their service. Historically the case for restriction on entry into the market of a natural monopoly has often been supported on such cream-skimming grounds. Conversely, some have held the view that bypass is the outcome of a healthy competition and can only result in efficiency gains when it occurs. For instance, the Federal Energy Regulatory Commission has argued against the denial of certificates to competitors on the basis that local distribution companies are in a position to compete aggressively.[2]

1. Cream skimming is also often discussed in the context of a multiproduct firm where some of the regulated firm's most valuable products are skimmed off by competitors. The case of third-degree price discrimination is simpler to analyze than that of second-degree because different customers are offered different terms, and therefore there are no incentive constraints of consumers to satisfy.

2. See Kahn (1971, chs. 1, 4, 6) for a discussion of the economic arguments in favor of and against cream skimming.

This chapter develops a normative model of regulatory policy toward bypass and cream skimming. It posits a double asymmetry of information. First, the regulated firm is ignorant of the demand characteristics of individual customers and must thus practice second-degree price discrimination.[3] As before, there are two types of customers: high demand and low demand. The high-demand customers have the opportunity of using an alternative, competitively supplied technology. The fixed cost associated with this alternative technology (e.g., the cost of building an interconnection or an own generator) makes bypass unattractive to low-demand customers. Second, the regulated firm knows more about its own technology than the regulator. The firm's rent is affected by the policy toward bypass. Although the cost function is assumed linear in total output, it exhibits increasing returns to scale, since a bigger output makes reductions in marginal cost more desirable. The regulator chooses the pricing, cost reimbursement, and possibly bypass policies so as to maximize social welfare.

The chapter's technical contribution is two fold. First, the theory of nonlinear pricing has focused on "downward-binding" incentive constraints; that is, a monopolist must design a pricing scheme that prevents high-demand customers from consuming the low-demand customers' bundle.[4] In the presence of bypass, the monopolist may have to offer advantageous terms to high-demand customers in order to retain them. This could lead low-demand customers to consume the high-demand customers' bundle, even though they would not use the bypass technology. This chapter studies the effect of "upward-binding" incentive constraints. Second, the bypass technology introduces discontinuities in the control of the regulated firm. We show how to deal with such discontinuities and extend results obtained with more conventional net-demand functions, in particular the linearity of optimal cost-reimbursement rules.

The economic contribution is a welfare analysis of cream skimming. We ask (1) whether asymmetric information between the regulator and the regulated firm increases the amount of bypass, (2) how in a situation of asymmetric information the regulator can ask the firm to substantiate its claim that bypass should either be prohibited or prevented through price cuts, (3) whether a marginal price under marginal cost is an appropriate response to the threat of bypass, (4) whether low-demand customers are hurt by the possibility of bypass, (5) whether there is socially too much or too little bypass, and (6) whether the regulated firm is necessarily hurt by the possibility of bypass.

3. Imperfect information about consumers' incomes may justify cross-subsidization for redistributional purposes (see chapter 3). A normative analysis of entry in such circumstances is carried out in section 6.5. Preventing entry may facilitate redistribution in the same way it may facilitate second-degree price discrimination.
4. See Maskin and Riley (1984) and Mussa and Rosen (1978).

Section 6.2 describes the model. Section 6.3 derives the optimal regulatory scheme. Section 6.4 asks whether there is too much bypass and how bypass affects consumers. Section 6.5 introduces redistributive concerns and budget constraints. Section 6.6 summarizes the main findings.

6.2 The Model

The regulated firm serves two types of consumers ($i = 1,2$) in numbers α_1 and α_2. Let q_1 (resp. q_2) be the consumption of type-1 (resp. type-2) consumers. Total consumption is $Q = \alpha_1 q_1 + \alpha_2 q_2$. Let $S_i(q_i)$ be the utility derived by a type-i consumer from consuming the regulated firm's good. To facilitate the analysis,[5] we make the assumption that $S_1(q) = S(q)$ and that $S_2(q) = \theta S(q)$ with $\theta > 1$.

The technology of the regulated firm is defined by its cost function

$$C = (\beta - e)Q, \tag{6.1}$$

with the usual assumptions. The cost parameter β belongs to $[\underline{\beta}, \bar{\beta}]$.

The regulator observes the firm's outputs q_1 and q_2, cost C, and revenue $R(q_1, q_2)$. We make the usual accounting convention that the regulator receives $R(q_1, q_2)$, reimburses cost C, and pays a net transfer t to the firm. The regulatory scheme must satisfy the individual rationality (IR) constraint of the firm:[6]

$$U = t - \psi(e) \geq 0 \qquad \text{for all } \beta \in [\underline{\beta}, \bar{\beta}]. \tag{6.2}$$

In addition there exists an alternative (*bypass*) technology to which each consumer has access if he or she pays a fixed cost σ. Then, the constant marginal cost of this alternative technology is d.[7]

We make an assumption that ensures that type-1 consumers (the low-valuation consumers) never find it advantageous to use the bypass technology. Let

$$S_1^* \equiv \max_q \, [S(q) - \sigma - dq]$$

denote the utility level of a type-1 consumer using the bypass technology. We postulate that the bypass alternative is never an optimal choice for low-demand consumers: $S_1^* \leq 0$. We further assume that α_1/α_2 is not too small so that it is always optimal for the regulated firm to serve the low-demand customers. However, in some circumstances the type-2 (high-

5. This assumption guarantees that the welfare optimization programs are convex so that necessary and sufficient conditions for characterizing the optimal solution are available.

6. We assume implicitly that it is never optimal to shut down the regulated firm.

7. Our analysis would be unchanged if the regulated firm could also offer the alternative technology and Bertrand competition with zero profits on the high-demand consumers took place.

valuation) consumers may want to quit the regulated firm and use the bypass technology.

To fit the examples given in the introduction, we assume that individual consumption of the regulated product can be monitored by the regulated firm so that nonlinear pricing is feasible. Let $\{(T_1, q_1), (T_2, q_2)\}$ be a nonlinear schedule. Then $R(q_1, q_2) = \alpha_1 T_1 + \alpha_2 T_2$.

The regulator is utilitarian and wishes to maximize the sum of consumers' welfares and of the firm's utility level, taking into account that the social cost of public funds is $1 + \lambda > 1$ (because of distortive taxation). When all consumers consume the regulated firm's good, social welfare is

$$\begin{aligned} W &= \alpha_1 S(q_1) + \alpha_2 \theta S(q_2) - (\alpha_1 T_1 + \alpha_2 T_2) \\ &\quad - (1 + \lambda)(C + t - \alpha_1 T_1 - \alpha_2 T_2) + U \\ &= \alpha_1 S(q_1) + \alpha_2 \theta S(q_2) - (1 + \lambda)[(\beta - e)(\alpha_1 q_1 + \alpha_2 q_2) + \psi(e)] \\ &\quad - \lambda U + \lambda(\alpha_1 T_1 + \alpha_2 T_2). \end{aligned} \tag{6.3}$$

When type-2 consumers use the bypass technology, their utility level is $S_2^* = \max_q(\theta S(q) - \sigma - dq)$, and social welfare is

$$W^b = \alpha_1 S(q_1) + \alpha_2 S_2^* - (1 + \lambda)[(\beta - e)\alpha_1 q_1 + \psi(e)] - \lambda U + \lambda \alpha_1 T_1. \tag{6.4}$$

The transfers T_1, T_2 will be seen to be linear combinations of $S(q_1)$ and $S(q_2)$. So, if we denote $S(q_1) \equiv s_1$, $S(q_2) \equiv s_2$, the concavity of the objective function W relies on the concavity in (e, s_1, s_2) of $\Gamma(e, s_1, s_2) \equiv -(1 + \lambda)[(\beta - e)(\alpha_1 \zeta(s_1) + \alpha_2 \zeta(s_2)) + \psi(e)]$, where ζ is the inverse function of S. Throughout the chapter we assume that $\Gamma(\cdot)$ is strictly concave in the relevant domain of (e, s_1, s_2).[8] This will ensure a unique solution for (e, q_1, q_2) in each regime considered in the chapter.

The regulator does not observe e and has incomplete information about β. The regulator has a prior on $[\underline{\beta}, \bar{\beta}]$ represented by the cumulative distribution function $F(\beta)$, which satisfies the monotone hazard rate property $d(F/f)/d\beta > 0$. The first step of our analysis is to characterize the regulator's optimal pricing rule and optimal incentive schemes under incomplete information.

6.3 Optimal Pricing Rules and Optimal Incentive Schemes

Our first observation is that incentive compatibility implies that the marginal cost $c(\beta)$ is a nondecreasing function of the intrinsic cost parameter β. Moreover the cost function we postulated for the regulated firm implies that the rent of asymmetric information $U(\beta)$ which must be given up

8. If we assume that $\psi'(e) \to \infty$, as $e \to \bar{e}$ and $\beta - \bar{e} > 0$ for all β, concavity is obtained if S'' is large enough.

to type β depends only on the marginal cost schedule $c(\cdot)$ being implemented. These facts, which follow from arguments similar to those in chapters 1 and 2, are proved in appendix A6.1. The intuition as to why the firm's rent depends only on the marginal cost schedule $c(\cdot)$ can be grasped from the cost function (6.1). The regulator observes C and Q and therefore knows the realized marginal cost. Thus the scope for the firm to transform good technological conditions (low β) into a slack rent (low e) is determined by the marginal cost schedule. The intuition as to why c is nondecreasing in β is that it is less costly for a low β firm to produce at a low cost. Hence, if type β prefers to produce at cost c rather than cost $\tilde{c} < c$, type $\beta' > \beta$ cannot prefer to produce at cost $\tilde{c}$ rather than cost c.

These two facts justify the two-step procedure that we use to characterize the optimal solution. For a given value of β and a given average (or marginal cost) c, social welfare is

$$W(c, q_1, q_2, T_1, T_2, \beta) = V(c, q_1, q_2, T_1, T_2) + Z(\beta, c), \tag{6.5}$$

where

$$Z \equiv -(1 + \lambda)\psi(\beta - c) - \lambda U(\beta)$$

and

$$V \equiv \alpha_1 S(q_1) + \alpha_2 \theta S(q_2) - (1 + \lambda)c(\alpha_1 q_1 + \alpha_2 q_2) + \lambda(\alpha_1 T_1 + \alpha_2 T_2)$$

when the bypass technology is not used by type-2 consumers, and

$$V \equiv \alpha_1 S(q_1) + \alpha_2 S_2^* - (1 + \lambda)c\alpha_1 q_1 + \lambda\alpha_1 T_1$$

when it is.

The constraints imposed on the regulator's maximization program are of two kinds: the firm's incentive and participation constraints (see appendix A6.1) are

$$\begin{aligned} \dot{U}(\beta) &= -\psi'(\beta - c(\beta)), \\ \dot{c}(\beta) &\geq 0, \end{aligned} \tag{6.6}$$

$$U(\bar{\beta}) \geq 0 \tag{6.7}$$

[the constraints in (6.6) must hold almost everywhere, but we omit the "almost everywhere" qualifier for notational simplicity]. The consumers' incentive constraints come from the fact that the firm cannot distinguish ex ante between the two types of consumers. Type-1 consumers' individual rationality constraint (IR_1) is

$$S(q_1) - T_1 \geq 0 \qquad (\text{IR}_1). \tag{6.8}$$

Type-2 consumers must obtain a utility level as large as in the bypass alternative to remain with the regulated firm:

$$\theta S(q_2) - T_2 \geq S_2^* \qquad (\text{IR}_2). \tag{6.9}$$

When the type-2 consumers use the bypass technology, (IR_2) becomes irrelevant. In the absence of bypass self-selection by consumers also imposes the incentive constraints:

$$S(q_1) - T_1 \geq S(q_2) - T_2 \qquad (\text{IC}_1), \tag{6.10}$$

$$\theta S(q_2) - T_2 \geq \theta S(q_1) - T_1 \qquad (\text{IC}_2). \tag{6.11}$$

The optimization of expected social welfare under the constraints (6.6) through (6.11) can be decomposed, in view of the decomposition obtained in (6.5), into a maximization of V subject to (6.8) through (6.11) with respect to q_1, q_2, T_1, and T_2 for each value of c (which determines optimal pricing) and a maximization of the expected value of social welfare with respect to $c(\cdot)$ for those values of q_1, q_2, T_1, and T_2 and under the constraints (6.6) and (6.7).

Let us now consider the first maximization. Straightforward arguments show that constraints (6.8) through (6.11) define six possible regimes characterized by the binding constraints in (6.8) through (6.11) and the occurrence of the bypass regime (see appendix A6.2 for a proof). These regimes are

Regime	Constraints		
1	(IC_2) (IR_1)	Binding	No bypass
2	(IC_2) (IR_1) (IR_2)	Binding	No bypass
3	(IR_1) (IR_2)	Binding	No bypass
4	(IR_1) (IR_2) (IC_1)	Binding	No bypass
5	(IR_2) (IC_1)	Binding	No bypass
6	(IR_1)	Binding	Bypass

In each of the six regimes optimal pricing is determined by

$$\max V(c, q_1, q_2, T_1, T_2)$$

subject to the binding constraints of regime i.

Let $\tilde{V}^i(c)$ be the optimal value of this program in regime i and $q_j^i(c)$ the consumption of type j in regime i, $i = 1, \ldots, 6$. The results of these maximizations are gathered in the next proposition. Let $p_1 \equiv S'(q_1)$ and $p_2 \equiv \theta S'(q_2)$ denote the marginal prices for the type-1 and type-2 consumers, respectively. We obtain proposition 6.1.

Proposition 6.1 In regimes 1 and 2, $p_1 > c$ and $p_2 = c$ with $dp_1/dc > 0$ in regime 1 and $dp_1/dc = 0$ in regime 2. In regime 3, $p_1 = p_2 = c$. In regimes 4 and 5, $p_1 = c$ and $p_2 < c$, with $dp_2/dc = 0$ in regime 4 and $dp_2/dc > 0$ in regime 5. In regime 6, $p_1 = c$.

See appendix A6.3 for a proof of this proposition and for the formulas defining optimal prices. Later in proposition 6.2 we show that regimes are ordered from 1 through 6 as c [or equivalently β from (6.6)] increases.

For a very efficient regulated firm (very low β), the net surplus obtained by high-valuation consumers is strictly higher than what they could obtain with the bypass, even when the firm uses optimal second-degree price discrimination. The classical "no-distortion-at-the-top" result amounts to the equality of marginal price and marginal cost for the high-valuation consumers (regime 1). For low-valuation consumers the marginal price exceeds marginal cost to prevent high-valuation consumers from buying the low-valuation buyers' bundle (since the shadow cost of public funds is positive, the regulated firm behaves qualitatively like a monopolist and tries to limit the rent enjoyed by high-valuation consumers). As the efficiency of the regulated firm decreases, the bypass constraint becomes binding. The allocation is then distorted in several steps. The payment T_2 that can be obtained from the high-valuation consumers must be limited; this relaxes IC_2 and thus allows the regulator to bring the low-valuation consumers' marginal price closer to marginal cost (regime 2). When β increases further, IC_2 becomes nonbinding, and the regulator equates marginal cost and marginal price for both types (regime 3). But when β still increases, the limit put on the payment made by type-2 consumers makes type-1 consumers' incentive constraint IC_1 binding. They wish to take the contract offered to type 2. To prevent that, consumption of type-2 consumers is increased beyond the first-best level by lowering the marginal price below marginal cost; this relaxes IC_1 because type-2 consumers have a higher marginal utility for the good (regime 4). Finally, the payment made by the type-1 consumers is lowered to satisfy their incentive constraint, which leaves them with a surplus. Because of the unmonitored bypass, when this regime (regime 5) is obtained, we have the interesting result that optimal regulation requires leaving a rent to low-valuation consumers in order to offer to high-valuation consumers a deal good enough that they do not use the bypass. Last, in the bypass regime (regime 6), the firm serves a single category of consumers and thus imposes no distortion in consumption.

Remark 1 Note that all the conclusions obtained in proposition 6.1 hold for any β, in that they are due only to the asymmetry of information with respect to consumers' tastes.

Remark 2 For a given marginal cost c, the consumptions of low-demand customers in regime 2, q_1^2, and of high-demand customers in regime 4, q_2^4, are equal. This is due to the facts that $\theta S(q_1^2) - T_1 = S_2^*$ (from IC_2 and IR_2) and $T_1 = S(q_1^2)$ (from IR_1), on the one hand, and $\theta S(q_2^4) - T_2 = S_2^*$ (from IR_2) and $T_2 = S(q_2^4)$ (from IC_1 and IR_1), on the other hand,

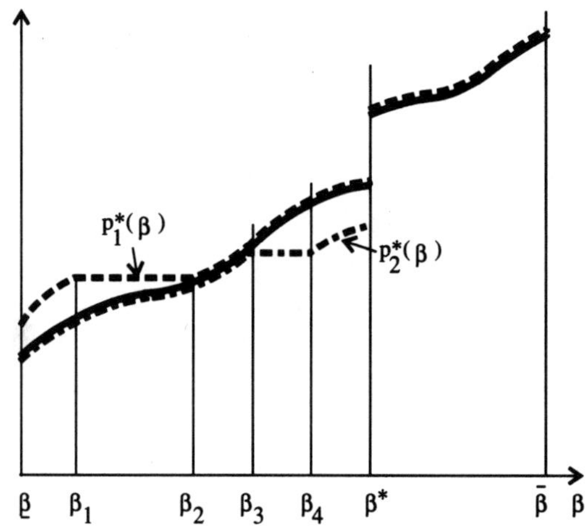

Regime	1	2	3	4	5	6
Binding constraints	IR_1 IC_2	IR_1 IC_2 IR_2	IR_1 IR_2	IR_1 IR_2 IC_1	IR_2 IC_1	IR_1
Bypass?	No bypass					Bypass

Figure 6.1
Price profiles (*solid line*: marginal cost $\beta - e^*(\beta)$)

yield the same solution $q_1^2 = q_2^4 = S^{-1}(S_2^*/(\theta - 1))$. (This is not an artifact of the particular surplus functions we chose.)

We next show that the bypass regime can only occur for an interval $[\beta^*, \bar{\beta}]$ of values of β,[9] and more generally the regimes (when they exist) are ordered from 1 to 6 when β increases:

Proposition 6.2
i. There exists $\beta^* \in [\underline{\beta}, \bar{\beta}]$ such that the bypass regime occurs iff $\beta > \beta^*$.
ii. There exist $\{\beta_i\}_{i=0,\ldots,6}$ with $\beta_i \leq \beta_{i+1}$, $\beta_0 = \underline{\beta}$, $\beta_5 = \beta^*$, $\beta_6 = \bar{\beta}$ such that regime i prevails iff $\beta \in [\beta_{i-1}, \beta_i]$.

See appendix A6.4 for a proof.

The intuition for property i is simply that, if the regulated firm becomes more inefficient, letting the high-demand customers use the bypass becomes more attractive. The idea behind the proof of property ii is that given the concavity of our problem, variables that satisfy the first-order conditions for maximizing expected social welfare and yield continuous control variables form a solution. Moving from regime 1 to regime 5 yields a continuous solution on $[\underline{\beta}, \beta^*]$. Figures 6.1 and 6.2 summarize our findings up to now.

9. This observation is of interest only when $\bar{\beta}$ is sufficiently large. For small $\bar{\beta}$, $\beta^* = \bar{\beta}$ and bypass never occurs (although it may be binding).

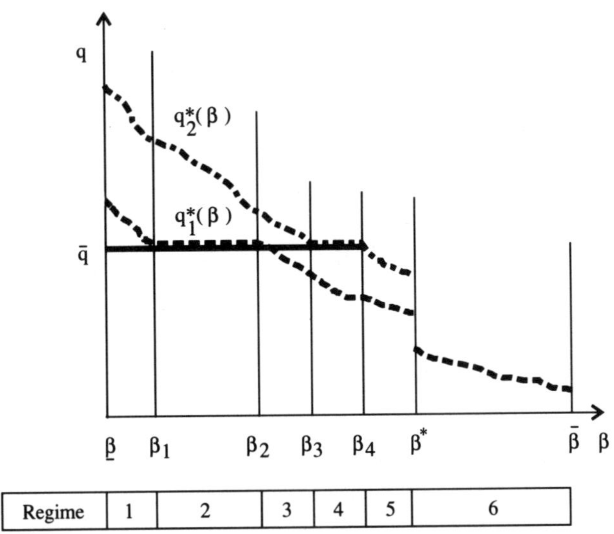

Regime	1	2	3	4	5	6

Figure 6.2
Quantity profiles

We next look for a solution to the maximization over $[\underline{\beta}, \beta^*]$ with the ordering of regimes 1, 2, 3, 4, 5 along the β-axis. Let us call $\tilde{V}(c)$ the function obtained by piecing together the functions $\tilde{V}^1(c), \ldots, \tilde{V}^5(c)$ on the intervals $[\underline{\beta}, \beta_1], [\beta_1, \beta_2], \ldots, [\beta_4, \beta^*]$, with $\underline{\beta} \leq \beta_1 \leq \beta_2 \leq \beta_3 \leq \beta_4 \leq \beta^* \leq \bar{\beta}$ (all regimes need not exist). That is, $\tilde{V}(c) = \max_{i \in \{1,\ldots,5\}} \tilde{V}^i(c)$.

In view of proposition 6.2 the program for the overall maximization of expected welfare can be written

$$\max_{\{c(\cdot), c^6(\cdot), U(\cdot)\}} \int_{\underline{\beta}}^{\beta^*} [\tilde{V}(c(\beta)) - (1+\lambda)\psi(\beta - c(\beta)) - \lambda U(\beta)] dF(\beta)$$

$$+ \int_{\beta^*}^{\bar{\beta}} [\tilde{V}^6(c^6(\beta)) - (1+\lambda)\psi(\beta - c^6(\beta)) - \lambda U(\beta)] dF(\beta) \tag{6.12}$$

subject to[10]

$$\dot{U}(\beta) = -\psi'(\beta - c(\beta)),$$

$$U(\bar{\beta}) \geq 0,$$

and

$$\dot{c}(\beta) \geq 0.$$

Fixing β^* and $U(\beta^*) \equiv \bar{U} \equiv \int_{\beta^*}^{\bar{\beta}} \psi'(\tilde{\beta} - c^{6*}(\tilde{\beta})) d\tilde{\beta}$, we first look for a solution to the maximization over $[\underline{\beta}, \beta^*]$ using the fact that the ordering

10. The last constraint will be ignored in a first step, and checked ex post.

of regimes is 1, 2, 3, 4, 5 along the β-axis. We have

$$\max_{\{c(\cdot),U(\cdot)\}} \int_{\underline{\beta}}^{\beta_1} \tilde{V}^1(c(\beta))dF(\beta) + \int_{\beta_1}^{\beta_2} \tilde{V}^2(c(\beta))dF(\beta) + \int_{\beta_2}^{\beta_3} \tilde{V}^3(c(\beta))dF(\beta)$$
$$+ \int_{\beta_3}^{\beta_4} \tilde{V}^4(c(\beta))dF(\beta) + \int_{\beta_4}^{\beta^*} \tilde{V}^5(c(\beta))dF(\beta)$$
$$- \int_{\underline{\beta}}^{\beta^*} [(1+\lambda)\psi(\beta - c(\beta)) + \lambda U(\beta)]dF(\beta) \tag{6.13}$$

subject to

$$\dot{U}(\beta) = -\psi'(\beta - c(\beta)),$$
$$U(\beta^*) = \overline{U}.$$

Using $d\tilde{V}^i/dc = -(1+\lambda)(\alpha_1 q_1^i + \alpha_2 q_2^i)$, and letting $q_j^{i*}(c)$ denote the optimal consumption of type-j consumers in regime i when marginal cost is c (see proposition 6.1), we apply the Pontryagin principle in each regime:

$$\psi'(\beta - c^{i*}(\beta)) = \alpha_1 q_1^{i*}(c^{i*}(\beta)) + \alpha_2 q_2^{i*}(c^{i*}(\beta))$$
$$- \frac{\lambda}{1+\lambda}\frac{F(\beta)}{f(\beta)}\psi''(\beta - c^{i*}(\beta)), \tag{6.14}$$

which has a unique solution from our concavity assumptions.

Finally, the characterizations of the (possibly degenerate) intervals defining regimes are obtained by maximizing (6.13) with respect to β_1, β_2, β_3, β_4. Since the firm's rent, the outputs, and marginal cost are continuous in the firm's type in the absence of bypass [see appendix A6.3 and (6.14)], we have

$$\begin{aligned}
\tilde{V}^1(c^{1*}(\beta_1)) &= \tilde{V}^2(c^{2*}(\beta_1)),\\
\tilde{V}^2(c^{2*}(\beta_2)) &= \tilde{V}^3(c^{3*}(\beta_2)),\\
\tilde{V}^3(c^{3*}(\beta_3)) &= \tilde{V}^4(c^{4*}(\beta_3)),\\
\tilde{V}^4(c^{4*}(\beta_4)) &= \tilde{V}^5(c^{5*}(\beta_4)).
\end{aligned} \tag{6.15}$$

The derivative of the value of the program (6.13) with respect to $\overline{U} = U(\beta^*)$ is equal to $\lambda F(\beta^*)$ (a unit increase in $\overline{U}$ translates into a unit increase in the rent of all types that are more efficient than β^*, which has social cost λ).

Next, with β^* still fixed, we look for a solution to

$$\max_{\{c(\cdot),U(\cdot)\}} \int_{\beta^*}^{\overline{\beta}} [\tilde{V}^6(c(\beta)) - (1+\lambda)\psi(\beta - c(\beta)) - \lambda U(\beta)]dF(\beta)$$
$$- \lambda F(\beta^*)U(\beta^*) \tag{6.16}$$

subject to

$$\dot{U}(\beta) = -\psi'(\beta - c(\beta))$$

and

$$U(\bar{\beta}) \geq 0.$$

As before, the shadow price of the incentive constraint $\mu(\beta)$ satisfies $\dot{\mu}(\beta) = \lambda f(\beta)$. We know that $\mu(\beta^*) = \lambda F(\beta^*)$, so we have $\mu(\beta) = \lambda F(\beta)$. Since $d\tilde{V}^6/dc = -(1+\lambda)q_1^6(c)$, the Pontryagin principle gives

$$\psi'(\beta - c^{6*}(\beta)) = \alpha_1 q_1^6(c^{6*}(\beta)) - \frac{\lambda}{1+\lambda}\frac{F(\beta)}{f(\beta)}\psi''(\beta - c^{6*}(\beta)), \qquad (6.17)$$

with

$$U(\beta^*) = \int_{\beta^*}^{\bar{\beta}} \psi'(\tilde{\beta} - c^{6*}(\tilde{\beta}))d\tilde{\beta}.$$

Using the expression for q_1^6 given in proposition 6.1, our concavity assumptions of section 6.2 imply that (6.17) has a unique solution $\{q_1^{6*}(\beta), c^{6*}(\beta)\}$. The rents are obtained by backward induction from regime 6 to regime 1:

$$U(\beta) = \int_{\beta}^{\bar{\beta}} \psi'(\tilde{\beta} - c^{6*}(\tilde{\beta}))d\tilde{\beta} \qquad \text{for } \beta \in [\beta^*, \bar{\beta}],$$

$$U(\beta) = \int_{\beta}^{\beta^*} \psi'(\tilde{\beta} - c^{5*}(\tilde{\beta}))d\tilde{\beta} + U(\beta^*) \qquad \text{for } \beta \in [\beta_4, \beta^*], \qquad (6.18)$$

....

$$U(\beta) = \int_{\beta}^{\beta_1} \psi'(\tilde{\beta} - c^{1*}(\tilde{\beta}))d\tilde{\beta} + U(\beta_1) \qquad \text{for } \beta \in [\underline{\beta}, \beta_1].$$

It remains for us to optimize welfare with respect to β^*. For λ small enough, the problem is strictly concave in β^* (appendix A6.5). Assuming that β^* is the upper bound of regime $i \in \{1, \ldots, 5\}$, the continuity of the rent at β^* implies that

$$\tilde{V}^i(c^i(\beta^*)) - (1+\lambda)\psi(\beta^* - c^i(\beta^*))$$
$$= \tilde{V}^6(c^6(\beta^*)) - (1+\lambda)\psi(\beta^* - c^6(\beta^*)). \qquad (6.19)$$

(Figures 6.1 and 6.2 depict the case in which all five regimes exist to the left of β^*.) Since the objective function is concave in β^* for all i, there exists a unique solution. Which regime i occurs before bypass occurs depends on the values of the parameters (see appendix A6.6).

Remark on two-part tariffs A similar analysis can be performed when the firm is constrained to charging a two-part tariff: $T(q) = A + pq$.[11] The number of relevant regimes is lower because there are no longer incentive constraints for the two types of customers (each type of customer chooses his or her preferred point along the tariff's straight line). So IR_1 alone, IR_2 alone, or both individual rationality constraints[12] could be binding. Results similar to those for nonlinear pricing can then be obtained. For instance, if only the bypass constraint IR_2 is binding (which can be shown to be optimal for some values of the parameters), the optimal slope of the two-part tariff is given by

$$(p - (\beta - e))\left(\alpha_1 \frac{dq_1}{dp} + \alpha_2 \frac{dq_2}{dp}\right) = \alpha_1(q_2(p) - q_1(p))\frac{\lambda}{1 + \lambda}.$$

This condition can be interpreted as follows: A unit increase in the usage price p decreases consumption by $|\alpha_1(dq_1/dp) + \alpha_2(dq_2/dp)|$. The welfare loss per unit of forgone consumption is equal to the difference between price and marginal cost. The left-hand side of the condition is thus equal (in absolute value) to the welfare loss brought about by a unit price increase. But a unit price increase requires a reduction in the fixed premium A of $q_2(p)$ in order to keep the high-demand consumers from using the bypass technology. So the net reduction in the transfer from the consumers to the firm associated with a unit price increase is equal to $(\alpha_1 + \alpha_2)q_2(p) - [\alpha_1 q_1(p) + \alpha_2 q_2(p)] = \alpha_1[q_2(p) - q_1(p)]$. The right-hand side of the condition reflects the relative weight of transfers in the social welfare function. Since $q_2(p) > q_1(p)$, and $dq_i/dp < 0$ for all p and i, $p < \beta - e$: The regulated firm's marginal price is below marginal cost.

Returning now to general tariffs, let us show that the optimal transfer schedule can be implemented through a menu of linear contracts. Type β^* is indifferent between the bypass regime and the no-bypass regime. From chapter 2 we know that in the bypass and no-bypass regions the nonlinear transfer schedule $t(c)$ is convex.[13] It is therefore also globally convex across regimes (see figure 6.3). This implies that this schedule can be replaced by a menu of linear contracts with slope $\psi'(\beta(c) - c)$, where $\beta(c)$ is the type that produces at marginal cost c. The interest of this result is that

11. We maintain our assumption that the regulator chooses an incentive scheme $t(c)$ for the firm. As before, the firm's revenue is not necessarily raised entirely through the direct charges to final consumers.

12. In the latter case A and p, and therefore $q_1(p)$ and $q_2(p)$, are completely determined by the two constraints.

13. The concavity of $t(c)$ in $[\underline{\beta}, \beta^*]$ results directly from chapter 2. The proof must be slightly extended in $[\beta^*, \bar{\beta}]$ because of the term $\lambda F(\beta^*)U(\beta^*)$ in program (6.16), which represents the shadow cost of the rent at the left of the inverval. But the shadow cost, and therefore the allocation on $[\beta^*, \bar{\beta}]$, are the same as if regime 6 obtained on $[\underline{\beta}, \bar{\beta}]$. So, again as in chapter 2, $t(c)$ is convex on $[\beta^*, \bar{\beta}]$.

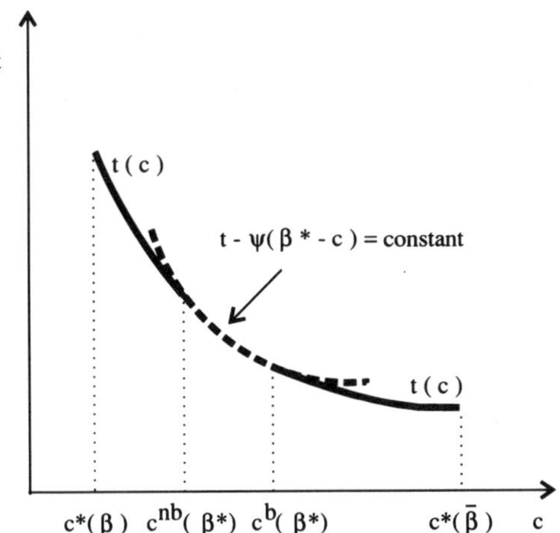

Figure 6.3
Implementation through linear schemes: c = marginal cost; nb = no bypass; b = bypass

an additive noise can be added in the cost function (6.1) without any effect on our results.

6.4 Bypass and Cream Skimming

In this section we compare the optimal regulatory mechanism characterized in section 6.3 with the one obtained when the regulator can in addition monitor the access to the bypass technology. We assume that the regulator's new instrument is the possibility of prohibiting bypass (i.e., bypass is only partially regulated). The regulator's objective function is unchanged, but the constraints are now

$$\theta S(q_2(\beta)) - T_2(\beta) \geq \theta S(q_1(\beta)) - T_1(\beta), \tag{6.20}$$

$$S(q_1(\beta)) - T_1(\beta) \geq S(q_2(\beta)) - T_2(\beta), \tag{6.21}$$

$$S(q_1(\beta)) - T_1(\beta) \geq 0, \tag{6.22}$$

$$\theta S(q_2(\beta)) - T_2(\beta) \geq 0, \tag{6.23}$$

when the bypass technology is not used. When the bypass technology is used by high-valuation consumers, the only constraint is (6.22).

As in traditional adverse-selection problems, only the high-valuation incentive constraint and the low-valuation individual rationality constraint are binding. For $\beta \leq \beta^{c*}$ we are in regime 1 of section 6.3. For $\beta \geq \beta^{c*}$ we are in regime 6 of section 6.3. The pricing policy is illustrated in figure 6.4. Optimization with respect to the value β^{c*} at which bypass starts being allowed yields (the superscript c identifies this case of "con-

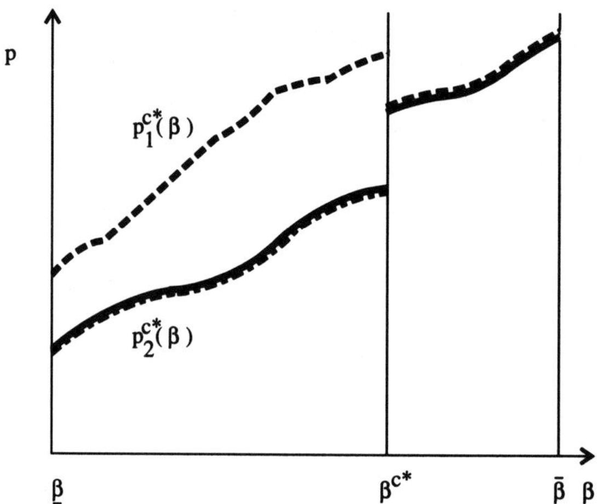

Regime	1	6
Binding constraints	IR_1 IC_2	IR_1
Bypass?	No bypass	Bypass

Figure 6.4
Price profiles when bypass is monitored (*solid line*: marginal cost)

trol" of access to bypass)

$$\tilde{V}^1(c^1(\beta^{c*})) - (1+\lambda)\psi(\beta^{c*} - c^1(\beta^{c*}))$$
$$= \tilde{V}^6(c^6(\beta^{c*})) - (1+\lambda)\psi(\beta^{c*} - c^6(\beta^{c*})). \tag{6.24}$$

Proposition 6.3 $\beta^{c*} \geq \beta^*$: There is excessive bypass when bypass cannot be prohibited.

Proof Suppose that $\beta^{c*} < \beta^*$. From the definition of β^* we have

$$\int_{\beta^{c*}}^{\beta^*} (\tilde{V}(\tilde{c}(\beta)) - (1+\lambda)\psi(\beta - \tilde{c}(\beta)) - \lambda\tilde{U}(\beta))f(\beta)d\beta - \lambda F(\beta^{c*})\tilde{U}(\beta^{c*})$$
$$\geq \int_{\beta^{c*}}^{\beta^*} (V^6(c^6(\beta)) - (1+\lambda)\psi(\beta - c^6(\beta)) - \lambda U^6(\beta))f(\beta)d\beta$$
$$- \lambda F(\beta^{c*})U^6(\beta^{c*}), \tag{6.25}$$

where

$$U^6(\beta) \equiv \int_\beta^{\bar{\beta}} \psi'(\tilde{\beta} - c^6(\tilde{\beta}))d\tilde{\beta}, \tag{6.26}$$

$$\tilde{U}(\beta) \equiv \int_\beta^{\beta^*} \psi'(\tilde{\beta} - \tilde{c}(\tilde{\beta}))d\tilde{\beta} + U^6(\beta^*), \tag{6.27}$$

and $\tilde{c}$ and $\tilde{V}$ refer to c^i and $\tilde{V}^i$ for the optimal regime $i \in \{1,\ldots,5\}$ (as in section 6.3). In words, when bypass cannot be prohibited, the regulator could have used regime 6 on $[\beta^{c*}, \beta^*]$ but elected not to do so. Now (6.25) is satisfied a fortiori if $\tilde{V}(\tilde{c}(\beta))$ is replaced by $V^1(\tilde{c}(\beta))$ because $V^1(c) \geq \tilde{V}(c)$ for all c (there are fewer constraints when bypass can be prohibited). This means that when bypass can be prohibited, the regulator would be better off prohibiting bypass on $[\beta^{c*}, \beta^*]$ even if he or she chose the suboptimal function $\tilde{c}(\cdot)$ instead of $c^1(\cdot)$ on that interval, a contradiction. ■

The intuition for proposition 6.3 is that when the regulated firm supplies high-demand consumers, the threat of bypass imposes an additional constraint that reduces welfare relative to the one (V^1) that can be obtained when bypass is prohibited. Since the prohibition of bypass eliminates this constraint and raises welfare in the no-bypass region, it becomes optimal to expand the latter region. Next we compare the firm's rents $U(\beta)$ and $U^c(\beta)$ when bypass cannot and can be prohibited.

Proposition 6.4 There exists $\beta_0 \geq \underline{\beta}$ such that

$$U^c(\beta) < U(\beta) \qquad \text{for } \beta < \beta_0,$$

$$U^c(\beta) > U(\beta) \qquad \text{for } \beta_0 < \beta < \beta^{c*},$$

$$U^c(\beta) = U(\beta) \qquad \text{for } \beta \geq \beta^{c*}.$$

Furthermore $\beta_0 \geq \beta_1$ if $\beta_0 > \underline{\beta}$.

Proof The rent in both cases is given by $\int_{\beta}^{\bar{\beta}} \psi'(e(\tilde{\beta}))d\tilde{\beta}$, where

$$\psi'(e(\tilde{\beta})) = Q(\tilde{\beta}) - \frac{\lambda}{1+\lambda}\frac{F(\tilde{\beta})}{f(\tilde{\beta})}\psi''(e(\tilde{\beta})). \tag{6.28}$$

We note that $Q^i(c) \geq Q^1(c) > Q^6(c)$ for $i \in \{1,\ldots,5\}$ and for all c.[14] This results from proposition 6.1: In regimes 2 and 3, q_2 is the same as in regime 1 (for the *given* marginal cost c), while q_1 is higher. In regimes 4 and 5 both q_1 and q_2 are higher than in regime 1. Since in all regimes

$$\psi'(\beta - c^i(\beta)) = Q^i(c^i(\beta)) - \frac{\lambda}{1+\lambda}\frac{F(\beta)}{f(\beta)}\psi''(\beta - c^i(\beta)), \tag{6.29}$$

and since the objective function is concave, we get $c^i(\beta) \leq c^1(\beta)$ for all $i \in \{1,\ldots,5\}$. Hence $Q^i(\beta) \equiv Q^i(c^i(\beta)) \geq Q^i(c^1(\beta)) \geq Q^1(c^1(\beta)) \equiv Q^1(\beta)$.

Consequently equation (6.28) implies that $\psi'(e(\beta))$ (which is also the slope of the incentive scheme at β) is higher on $[\beta_1, \beta^*]$ and smaller

14. Note the parallel between bypass and the "shutdown option" studied in sections 1.3 and 1.4. In a shutdown region the firm's rent does not increase with its efficiency. Here it increases at a slower rate in the bypass region ($Q^i > Q^6$).

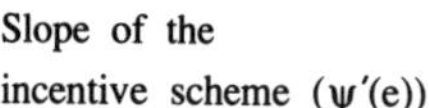

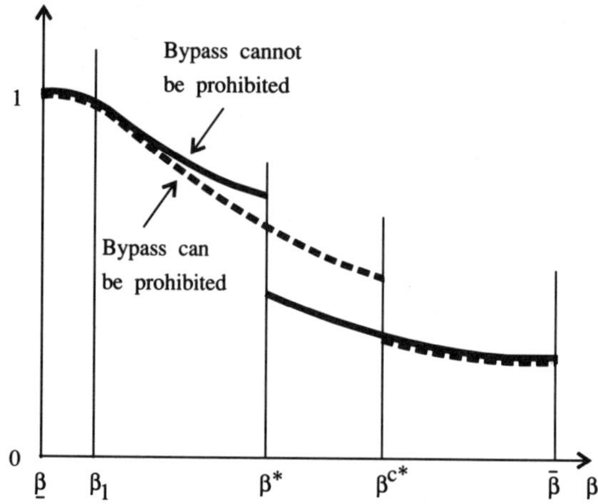

Figure 6.5
Slope of the incentive scheme

on $[\beta^*, \beta^{c*}]$ when bypass cannot be prohibited. The slopes coincide on $[\underline{\beta}, \beta_1]$ and on $[\beta^{c*}, \bar{\beta}]$. See figure 6.5. Proposition 6.4 follows immediately. ■

The intuition for proposition 6.4 is as follows. The bypass region is smaller when bypass can be prohibited. Thus in $[\beta^*, \beta^{c*}]$, where bypass is now avoided, the regulated firm supplies the high-demand customers, which raises demand and makes marginal cost reduction more desirable. More incentives are given to the firm to reduce costs, which raises the rent of types in $[\beta^*, \beta^{c*}]$. However, in former regimes 2 through 5 (if such regimes exist), keeping the high-demand customers no longer requires the high outputs characterized in proposition 6.1, since bypass can be prohibited. The regulator reduces the incentives for cost reduction and thus the firm's rent. That is, as β decreases under β^*, $U^c(\beta) - U(\beta)$ decreases and may become negative. The firm need not gain from the prohibition of bypass because the threat of bypass was a "good excuse" for low prices, high outputs, and therefore a high rent.

Let us next consider the effect of a change of information on the extent of bypass when access to bypass is controlled. We index the inverse of the hazard rate (F/f) by a parameter v, $H(\beta, v)$. Differentiating (6.24), we get

$$\frac{d\beta^{c*}}{dv} = \frac{\lambda}{1+\lambda}\frac{H(\beta, v)}{Q^1 - Q^6}\left[\frac{d}{dv}(\psi'(e^1(\beta^{c*}))) - \frac{d}{dv}(\psi'(e^6(\beta^{c*})))\right]. \tag{6.30}$$

Intuitively an increase of v creates more bypass if at β^{c*} the rate of increase of the (costly) rent ψ' is less affected in the no-bypass regime than in the bypass regime.

Differentiating the first-order conditions defining quantities and effort [see (6.31) as well as regimes 1 and 6 in appendix A6.3], we obtain

$$\frac{de^1}{dv} = -H_v \frac{\lambda}{1+\lambda} \frac{\psi''(e^1)}{\psi''(e^1) + [\lambda/(1+\lambda)]\psi'''(e^1)H + dQ^1/dc}, \tag{6.31}$$

$$\frac{de^6}{dv} = -H_v \frac{\lambda}{1+\lambda} \frac{\psi''(e^6)}{\psi''(e^6) + [\lambda/(1+\lambda)]\psi'''(e^6)H + dQ^6/dc}. \tag{6.32}$$

We now assume that $H_v < 0$ (i.e., the hazard rate increases with v). For some families of distributions an increase in the hazard rate corresponds to an improvement in information. For instance, for a uniform distribution on $[\underline{\beta}, \bar{\beta}]$, $H = \beta - \underline{\beta}$, so that when $\underline{\beta}$ increases, the support of the uniform distribution shrinks (in this example, $v = \underline{\beta}$).

Proposition 6.5 Assume that ψ'' is constant, and that either λ is small or demand functions are concave. Then an increase in v that increases the hazard rate f/F around β^{c*} increases β^{c*}.[15]

Proof We know from appendix A6.4 that $Q^1 > Q^6$. Hence $e^1 > e^6$ from (6.14) and the associated second-order condition. Next λ small or concave demand functions imply that $dQ^1/dc < dQ^6/dc < 0$ (see the expressions in appendix A6.3). Thus (6.30), (6.31), and (6.32) imply that $d\beta^{c*}/dv > 0$. ■

The intuition for proposition 6.5 is that as f/F increases, the concern with the firm's rent in the no-bypass region (which has probability F) decreases relative to the concern for the distortion at β^{c*} (which consists in imposing bypass to reduce the rent of better types and has probability f). The need for assumptions in proposition 6.5 comes from the fact that output, and not only the firm's rent and cost, matters. Without such assumptions the result might be reversed. In the case where bypass cannot be prohibited, the result is similar and true even more often because the slope $|dQ/dc|$ is higher in that case (at least for regimes 3, 4, and 5).

Finally, let us note that at least for small λ, bypass increases with λ both with and without control of access to bypass. Intuitively more costly transfers make bypass more desirable by increasing the incentive costs of the regulated firm. This holds at least for small λ. For large λ the social gain stemming from the firm's revenue $\lambda R(q)$ might upset this result. We now prove this result in the case where bypass is controlled, but a similar reasoning holds in the other case.

15. The probability of bypass is equal to $1 - F(\beta^{c*}, v)$. The total effect of an increase in v is in general ambiguous as F decreases with v but increases with β^{c*}, which itself increases with v.

Proposition 6.6 Bypass increases with λ, for λ small.

Proof Let $SC(\beta) \equiv (\beta - e)Q + \psi(e)$ denote total social cost and $R(\beta) \equiv \alpha_1 T_1 + \alpha_2 T_2$ total revenue. Differentiating (6.24) gives

$$\left.\frac{d\beta^{c*}}{d\lambda}\right|_{\lambda=0} = \frac{[R^1(\beta^{c*}) - SC^1(\beta^{c*})] - [R^6(\beta^{c*}) - SC^6(\beta^{c*})]}{Q^1(\beta^{c*}) - Q^6(\beta^{c*})}. \tag{6.33}$$

At $\lambda = 0$,

$$R^1(\beta^{c*}) - SC^1(\beta^{c*}) = W^1(\beta^{c*}) - (\theta - 1)\alpha_2 S(q_1^1(\beta^{c*})),$$

$$R^6(\beta^{c*}) - SC^6(\beta^{c*}) = W^6(\beta^{c*}) + \alpha_2 S_2^*.$$

Since social welfare is continuous at β^{c*} and $Q^1(\beta^{c*}) > Q^6(\beta^{c*})$, the result follows. ∎

6.5 Some Further Considerations about Bypass: Redistribution and Budget Constraint

The analysis has up to now focused on some facets of the bypass question. First, why does bypass occur? We have argued that the alternative technology often involves large installation costs. Returns to scale in the bypass technology make it attractive to high-demand but not to low-demand consumers. In some industries there is a second reason why some consumers are more eager to use a bypass technology than others: The regulated firm might pursue redistributional objectives and practice third-degree price discrimination that favors the latter to the detriment of the former. Then those consumers who are charged high prices would be tempted to bypass the regulated firm. Typical examples include the cross-subsidization of rural areas by urban ones, and of residential customers by commercial ones.

Second, why does bypass hurt some customers? Our analysis attributes negative effects of bypass of some customers on other customers to increasing returns to scale in the production of the regulated firm: The defection of some customers raises the firm's marginal cost and therefore prices. To be certain, no one was hurt in our two-consumer-type model: The low-demand consumers have no surplus in the absence of a bypass technology and therefore cannot complain when such a technology is introduced. If the high-demand consumers were made worse off, their utility from using the bypass technology, which does not exceed that obtained when bypass is feasible, would be smaller than that obtained in the absence of a bypass technology. Therefore the regulator should simply ignore the threat of bypass and offer the same allocation as when bypass is not feasible. The threat of bypass would then not bind. That is, in the terminology of the literature on barriers to entry, bypass would be "blockaded." However, with more than two types of consumers some types would be hurt by the desertion of other types.[16]

An alternative reason why some consumers would be hurt by an impending bypass (even if there are only two consumer types) is that the firm is subject to a budget constraint. When some categories of consumers desert for the bypass technology or else must be granted lower prices to remain clients of the regulated firm, other customers must bear the associated revenue loss.

This section combines these two new themes—redistributive concerns and budget constraint. It analyzes a major argument put forward to justify the regulation of entry: Bypass activities undermine the redistributive goals of regulators.

Our simple model maintains the basic structure of section 6.2 except that $S_2(\cdot) = S_1(\cdot) = S(\cdot)$. The regulator engages in third- rather than second-degree price discrimination. The regulator is able to tell apart type-1 consumers (city dwellers, commercial customers) from type-2 customers (rural inhabitants, residential customers) and to charge them differentiated linear prices p_1 and p_2.[17] For notational simplicity type-1 and type-2 consumers are in equal numbers ($\alpha_1 = \alpha_2$).

All consumers have the same quasi-linear preferences

$$S(q) + x,$$

where q is their consumption of the commodity produced by the regulated firm, $S(q)$ the associated gross surplus, and x the disposable income. We let $S^n(q) = S(q) - pq$ denote a consumer's net surplus when facing price p.

Redistributive concerns arise from different distributions of incomes in each class of consumers. The endowment $\bar{x}$ of a type-i consumer is drawn from distribution $G_i(\bar{x})$ with support $[0, \infty)$. We assume that class 1 is richer than class 2 in that $G_1(\bar{x}) < G_2(\bar{x})$ for $\bar{x} > 0$. That is, the endowment distribution for class 1 dominates in the sense of first-order stochastic dominance that for class 2.

As in section 3.9 we want to formalize the idea that income taxation is imperfect. We consider the polar case in which income is unobservable. In this case the regulator can at most impose a poll tax (i.e, a lump-sum transfer from the consumers to the government), but our assumption that the smallest income in each class is zero guarantees that no such poll tax is feasible.

16. Suppose that there are three types of customers. If type-3 (high-demand) customers use the bypass technology, the cost of producing for the remaining two types increases because of returns to scale, which may reduce the net consumer surplus of type-2 customers.

17. The study of two-part tariffs is uninteresting here because all consumers in the same class have the same preferences, and the regulator can thus perfectly capture their surplus through a fixed fee. The study of two-part tariffs with heterogeneous consumer preferences within each class yields similar results to the case of linear pricing with homogeneous preferences studied in this section.

Let p denote the price charged to a consumer. The consumer maximizes

$$S(q) + \bar{x} - pq.$$

Let $S^n(p)$ denote the net consumer surplus. The consumer's utility is thus $\bar{x} + S^n(p)$.[18]

The regulator has redistributive concern in that he or she values consumer utility $\bar{x} + S^n(p)$ at $V(\bar{x} + S^n(p))$ where $V' > 0$, $V'' < 0$. The regulator's assessment of consumer welfare is thus

$$\int_0^\infty V(\bar{x} + S^n(p_1))dG_1(\bar{x}) + \int_0^\infty V(\bar{x} + S^n(p_2))dG_2(\bar{x}).$$

Let us now assume that the regulated good is a small determinant of consumer utility. Using a Taylor expansion, we have

$$V(\bar{x} + S^n(p)) \simeq V(\bar{x}) + V'(\bar{x})S^n(p).$$

The regulator's assessment of social welfare is then equivalent to

$$w_1 S^n(p_1) + w_2 S^n(p_2),$$

where

$$w_1 \equiv \int_0^\infty V'(\bar{x})dG_1(\bar{x}) = V'(\infty) - \int_0^\infty V''(\bar{x})G_1(\bar{x})d\bar{x}$$

$$< w_2 \equiv \int_0^\infty V'(\bar{x})dG_2(\bar{x}) = V'(\infty) - \int_0^\infty V''(\bar{x})G_2(\bar{x})d\bar{x}.$$

We now introduce the producer side. We maintain the simple cost function

$$C = (\beta - e)(q_1 + q_2),$$

where q_i is the aggregate consumption of class i. As in chapter 2 and section 6.2, the firm's incentive and individual rationality constraints reduce to

$$\dot{U}(\beta) = -\psi'(e(\beta))$$

and

$$U(\bar{\beta}) \geq 0.$$

Following section 3.9 and the above analysis, we consider the social welfare function

18. We ignore the possibility that the expenditure on the regulated good $pD(p)$ can exceed $\bar{x}$. Later we make the assumption that the expenditure on the good is small; hence a non-negativity constraint on net income will bind only for a negligible fraction of (very poor) consumers. Thus, our treatment is correct up to the neglect of this negligible fraction.

$$w_1 S^n(p_1) + w_2 S^n(p_2) + w_0 U.$$

We assume that the firm is constrained to balance its budget (note that we have a single firm here and thus ex ante uncertainty about the equilibrium allocation; alternatively, one could have followed section 3.9 in assuming a continuum of firms and no aggregate uncertainty):

$$p_1(\beta)q_1(\beta) + p_2(\beta)q_2(\beta) \geq (\beta - e(\beta))(q_1(\beta) + q_2(\beta)) + U(\beta) + \psi(e(\beta)).$$

In the absence of bypass technology the optimal allocation is obtained by solving the following program:

$$\max_{\{q_1(\cdot),q_2(\cdot),e(\cdot),U(\cdot)\}} \int_{\underline{\beta}}^{\bar{\beta}} [w_1 S^n(P(q_1(\beta))) + w_2 S^n(P(q_2(\beta))) + w_0 U(\beta)] f(\beta) d\beta$$

subject to

$$\dot{U}(\beta) = -\psi'(e(\beta)),$$

$$U(\bar{\beta}) = 0,$$

$$P(q_1(\beta))q_1(\beta) + P(q_2(\beta))q_2(\beta)$$
$$\geq (\beta - e(\beta))(q_1(\beta) + q_2(\beta)) + U(\beta) + \psi(e(\beta)).$$

Let μ denote the Pontryagin multiplier associated with the state variable U, and let γf denote the multiplier of the firm's budget constraint. The first-order conditions of this program are

$$w_1[-P'(q_1(\beta))q_1(\beta)] + \gamma(\beta)[P(q_1(\beta)) + P'(q_1(\beta))q_1(\beta) - (\beta - e(\beta))] = 0,$$

$$w_2[-P'(q_2(\beta))q_2(\beta)] + \gamma(\beta)[P(q_2(\beta)) + P'(q_2(\beta))q_2(\beta) - (\beta - e(\beta))] = 0,$$

$$-\mu(\beta)\psi''(e(\beta)) + \gamma(\beta)[q_1(\beta) + q_2(\beta) - \psi'(e(\beta))]f(\beta) = 0,$$

$$\dot{\mu}(\beta) = -w_0 f(\beta) + \gamma(\beta) f(\beta),$$

and

$$\mu(\underline{\beta}) = 0.$$

Therefore

$$\mu(\beta) = \int_{\underline{\beta}}^{\beta} [\gamma(\tilde{\beta}) - w_0] f(\tilde{\beta}) d\tilde{\beta}$$

and

$$\psi'(e(\beta)) = [q_1(\beta) + q_2(\beta)] - \frac{\int_{\underline{\beta}}^{\beta} [\gamma(\tilde{\beta}) - w_0] f(\tilde{\beta}) d\tilde{\beta}}{\gamma(\beta) f(\beta)} \psi''(e(\beta)).$$

Furthermore

$$\frac{p_1(\beta) - (\beta - e(\beta))}{p_1(\beta)} = \frac{\gamma(\beta) - w_1}{\gamma(\beta)} \frac{1}{\eta(p_1(\beta))}$$

and

$$\frac{p_2(\beta) - (\beta - e(\beta))}{p_2(\beta)} = \frac{\gamma(\beta) - w_2}{\gamma(\beta)} \frac{1}{\eta(p_2(\beta))}.$$

γ is the multiplier of the budget constraint. It is the analog of $1 + \lambda$ in our partial equilibrium theory (see also chapter 2). If $w_1 = w_2 = 1$ and $\gamma(\beta) = \lambda$, we would be back to Ramsey pricing. But $w_1 < w_2$, and consumers of type 1 are discriminated against: $p_1 \geq p_2$.[19] Note that because of the dichotomy (see chapter 3), the weight w_0 of the firm's utility in social welfare does not directly affect pricing. It only affects the distortion of effort, which reflects the optimal trade-off between efficiency and rent extraction of the firm.

Suppose now that a *bypass technology is available* as in section 6.2, and let

$$S^* = \max_q \{S(q) - \sigma - dq\}.$$

Assume that for $w_1 = w_2$, no consumer finds it advantageous to use the bypass technology. As w_1 becomes smaller than w_2 and p_1 larger than p_2, there comes a point where type-1 consumers want to use the bypass technology. If type-1 consumers use the bypass technology, no redistribution is possible between type-1 and type-2 consumers.

We want to obtain the optimal regulation under the constraint that the bypass technology is not used. We must add the constraint

$$S^n(p_1(\beta)) \geq S^*.$$

Let $\tau(\beta)$ be the multiplier of this constraint. The analysis is unchanged except that the pricing rules become

$$\frac{p_1(\beta) - (\beta - e(\beta))}{p_1(\beta)} = \frac{\gamma(\beta) - (w_1 + \tau(\beta))}{\gamma(\beta)} \frac{1}{\eta(p_1(\beta))},$$

and

$$\frac{p_2(\beta) - (\beta - e(\beta))}{p_2(\beta)} = \frac{\gamma(\beta) - w_2}{\gamma(\beta)} \frac{1}{\eta(p_2(\beta))}.$$

Clearly the bypass constraint puts a limit to price discrimination. The shadow price $\gamma(\beta)$ of the budget constraint is higher than when bypass is infeasible. Otherwise, both prices would be lower than before, and welfare

19. Were it the case that $p_1 < p_2$, prices ($p_1' = p_2$ and $p_2' = p_1$) would also balance the budget and would yield a higher social welfare.

higher, which would contradict the fact that we have added one constraint. We thus conclude that $p_2(\beta)$ has increased. Type-2 consumers are hurt by the availability of the bypass technology.

6.6 Concluding Remarks

We summarize and discuss our main economic findings:

1. Asymmetric information between the regulator and the firm raises the actual cost of the regulated firm and increases the probability of bypass.

2. High-demand customers ought to be given incentives not to bypass when the regulated firm is efficient. An efficient firm is screened through its choice of a steep (high-slope) incentive scheme. Hence the slope of the regulated firm's incentive scheme is positively correlated with its success in counteracting bypass.

3. It may be optimal to charge marginal prices below marginal cost for high-demand customers. Advantageous terms are granted to high-demand customers in order to retain them; high-demand customers are charged a high fixed fee and a low marginal price in order to dissuade the low-demand customers from buying the high-demand customers' bundle.

4. Low-demand customers are not necessarily hurt by the threat of bypass. In our model low-demand customers may enjoy a positive net consumer surplus when the regulated firm constrained by bypass does not let the bypass operate. (This cannot occur when bypass is controlled by the regulator.) Low-demand customers indirectly benefit from the advantageous terms offered to high-demand customers. With more than two customer types, it can be shown that some customers may be hurt by bypass even in the absence of a budget constraint. Our point here is that the effect of bypass on low-demand customers is ambiguous; contrary to conventional wisdom, "skimmed milk" need not be made worse off by bypass.

5. There is excessive bypass if bypass cannot be controlled by the regulator. Bypass interferes with optimal second-degree price discrimination.

6. A mediocre regulated firm will be hurt by bypass. An efficient regulated firm may benefit from the threat of bypass because it can use it to justify high levels of production.

Caution should be exercised in particular when applying the last two conclusions. We compared two regulatory institutions in which the regulator has or does not have the authority to prohibit the competitive technology. The analysis is restrictive for two (related) reasons. First, in principle, government has at its disposal a vast array of intervention instruments with which to control competition, among these, direct regulation, subsidies, and taxation. Second, government has limited authority in the competitive sector. Although we did not make explicit the reasons why there exists this limitation in scope of authority, presumably it stems from the costs of regulation or from the fear that the extension of regulatory authority from the dominant firm to the whole industry would result in producer protection. Despite these caveats we believe that a normative analysis, such as the one performed here, is a first step toward understanding the policy trade-offs with regard to bypass and cream skimming.

Caution should also be exercised in the study of particular industries. While the conclusions above refer to optimal regulation, transfers from the regulators to the firms are sometimes legally prohibited (e.g., in the telecommunications and electricity industries in the United States). A regulated firm's cost is then entirely paid by direct charges to consumers. As observed in section 6.5, some of our conclusions may be affected by the impossibility of transfers. (See chapter 15 for an attempt at explaining the prohibition of transfers.) For instance, low-demand consumers are more likely to be hurt by bypass when consumers are obligated to pay the firm's full cost.

Last, several additional issues could be addressed within our normative framework. For instance, if ex ante the regulated firm were to choose among technologies, would it prefer a high-investment–low marginal cost technology to counteract bypass or a low-investment–high marginal cost technology to focus on low-demand customers, and how would this affect high- and low-demand customers? We have likewise ignored some potential benefits of competition. If the bypass technology is similar to the regulated firm's, the regulator could use bypass as a yardstick to further monitor the firm. What is more, bypass could enhance product variety by making available goods that cannot be produced by the regulated firm. These and other questions are left open for future research.

BIBLIOGRAPHIC NOTES

B6.1 Nonstandard Incentive Constraints

In standard price-discrimination models (Mussa and Rosen 1978; Maskin and Riley 1984), incentive constraints are "downward binding." The issue for the monopolist is to prevent high-demand consumers from pretending they have low demand. Low-demand consumers generally are not tempted to mimic high-demand consumers. In the presence of bypass, the monopolist must offer a good deal to high-demand consumers in order to retain them. This may induce low-demand consumers to pretend they have high demand, even though they would not consider using the bypass technology. Incentive constraints would then be "upward binding." Similar considerations appear in Champsaur and Rochet's (1989) model of duopoly competition in prices and qualities and, in a somewhat different context, in Lewis and Sappington's (1989) work on countervailing incentives.[20] Nonstandard binding incentive constraints can also arise in dynamic incentive models without commitment (see chapter 9); then a "good type" must be given a sufficiently good deal to reveal its information, which might again induce a "bad type" to pretend it is a good type.

B6.2 Product Market Competition and Incentives of Regulated Firms

We have examined the effect of the residual demand curve associated with the bypass activity on regulatory incentive schemes. Caillaud (1990) studies the effect of an unregulated competitive fringe on the regulation of a natural monopoly. As demonstrated in this chapter, the possibility of substitution for consumers introduces discontinuities in the regulated firm's control problem. Caillaud focuses on the role of correlation between the technologies of the regulated firm and the competitive fringe, rather than on the issue of second-degree price discrimination (in Caillaud's model, arbitrage constrains firms to practice linear pricing).

Einhorn (1987) provides an analysis of bypass in a model without asymmetric information about the firm's technology. He obtains the result that marginal price may be below marginal cost for some consumers in the absence of incentive constraints for consumers. In our analysis price may be below marginal cost because the regulated firm cannot identify high-valuation consumers and use third-degree price discrimination. Einhorn finds that customers make efficient choices when deciding to use the bypass technology. We have shown, on the contrary, that bypass is used too often compared to a situation where the regulator could monitor the access to bypass.

The conclusion that asymmetric information between the regulator and the firm raises the actual cost of the regulated firm and increases the

20. Lewis and Sappington (1991) draw an interesting implication of outside opportunities that rise quickly with the agent's efficiency. In a regulatory context their insight might go something like this. Suppose that, as in section 1.9, the firm commits an investment I that determines the distribution $F(\beta|I)$ of the firm's efficiency parameter, that the firm and the regulator are not bound by a long-term contract, that the firm chooses between the government contract and a commercial activity, and that the firm's profit $\bar{U}(\beta)$ in the commercial activity decreases steeply with β. Under such conditions the regulator prefers that the firm invest *little*, if government contracting is always preferred to the commercial activity in the end. A higher investment increases the ex post gains from trade between the government and the firm and also the payment the government must pay to the firm to compensate for the loss of the commercial activity. If $d\bar{U}/d\beta$ is sufficiently negative, the second effect dominates. Therefore, in the terminology of Lewis and Sappington, "the principal may prefer a less able agent." (Contrast this result with that of section 1.9 and review problem 16, where the firm has no outside opportunity. In that case ex post welfare increases with the firm's investment.)

probability of bypass is familiar from the incentive literature. It is similar to the conclusion in chapter 1 that the cutoff cost parameter β^*, above which an indivisible project is not realized, is smaller under asymmetric information. The "project not being implemented" in chapter 1 is analogous to the "monopolist not serving high-demand consumers" in this chapter. Similarly the role of bypass in providing discipline for the regulated firm is related to the role played by entry and auditing in Demski, Sappington, and Spiller (1987) and Scharfstein (1988).

B6.3 Link with the Contestability Literature

Our approach differs from that of the contestability literature (e.g., Baumol, Panzar, and Willig 1982) in several respects. First, we allow transfers between the regulator and the firm. Second, the regulated firm and its competitors (here, the bypass producers) do not face the same cost functions. Third, the regulated firm's technology is unknown to the regulator.

APPENDIXES

A6.1 Incentive Compatibility for the Firm

From the revelation principle a regulation mechanism can be represented by a revelation mechanism that specifies for each announcement of the cost characteristic $\hat{\beta}$ a level of production for a type-1 (resp. type-2) consumer $q_1(\hat{\beta})$ (resp. $q_2(\hat{\beta})$), a total cost target $C(\hat{\beta})$, and a net transfer received by the firm from the regulator $t(\hat{\beta})$.

Incentive compatibility at β and β' requires that

$$U(\beta,\beta) \equiv t(\beta) - \psi\left(\beta - \frac{C(\beta)}{\alpha_1 q_1(\beta) + \alpha_2 q_2(\beta)}\right)$$

$$\geq U(\beta,\beta') = t(\beta') - \psi\left(\beta - \frac{C(\beta')}{\alpha_1 q_1(\beta') + \alpha_2 q_2(\beta')}\right), \tag{A6.1}$$

$$U(\beta',\beta') = t(\beta') - \psi\left(\beta' - \frac{C(\beta')}{\alpha_1 q_1(\beta') + \alpha_2 q_2(\beta')}\right)$$

$$\geq U(\beta',\beta) = t(\beta) - \psi\left(\beta' - \frac{C(\beta)}{\alpha_1 q_1(\beta) + \alpha_2 q_2(\beta)}\right). \tag{A6.2}$$

Adding (A6.1) and (A6.2) and denoting $c(\beta) \equiv C(\beta)/[\alpha_1 q_1(\beta) + \alpha_2 q_2(\beta)]$ (the average cost), we get

$$\psi(\beta' - c(\beta)) - \psi(\beta - c(\beta)) \geq \psi(\beta' - c(\beta')) - \psi(\beta - c(\beta')). \tag{A6.3}$$

Consider the function $\Phi(x) \equiv \psi(\beta' - x) - \psi(\beta - x)$. For $\beta < \beta'$, $\Phi'(x) < 0$, since $\psi'' > 0$. Therefore (A6.3) implies that $c(\beta) \leq c(\beta')$.

The revelation mechanism can alternatively be represented by the functions $q_1(\cdot)$, $q_2(\cdot)$, $c(\cdot)$, and $t(\cdot)$. Let $U(\beta)$ be the rent captured by type β. Incentive compatibility implies that $U(\beta)$ be continuous and nonincreasing, since type β with $\beta < \beta'$ can always mimic type β' at smaller cost. $U(\beta)$ is therefore almost everywhere differentiable. Similarly $c(\beta)$ is a.e. differentiable. $\dot{U}(\beta)$ exists a.e. and is given by

$$\dot{U}(\beta) = -\psi'(\beta - c(\beta)) \qquad \text{a.e.}$$

and the rent of type β is

$$U(\beta) = \int_{\beta}^{\bar{\beta}} \psi'(\beta - c(\beta))d\beta.$$

Necessary and sufficient second-order conditions are (see chapter 2)

$$\dot{c}(\beta) \geq 0.$$

Since $\dot{U}(\beta) < 0$, the firm's individual rationality constraint reduces to $U(\bar{\beta}) \geq 0$. ■

A6.2 Taxonomy of Regimes of Consumer Behavior

In addition to the bypass regime, we have potentially as many regimes as combinations of binding constraints among (6.8) through (6.11). However, the following lemmas cut down the number of cases to five.

Lemma 6.1 If the two consumers' types are offered two different contracts, the two incentive constraints cannot be simultaneously binding.

Proof Suppose the contrary. If the type-1 constraint is binding $T_2 - T_1 = S(q_2) - S(q_1)$. If the type-2 incentive constraint is also binding, we have $\theta(S(q_2) - S(q_1)) = S(q_2) - S(q_1)$ a contradiction unless $q_1 = q_2$. But then $T_1 = T_2$, contradicting the fact that we have two distinct contracts. ■

Lemma 6.2 If type-i's incentive constraint is not binding, then type-i's individual rationality constraint is binding.

Proof If type-i's IC and IR constraints are not binding, T_i can be increased slightly without perturbing these constraints. Increasing T_i also relaxes type-j's incentive constraint ($j \neq i$). ■

Lemma 6.3 A pooling contract can never be optimal.

Proof Note first that, in a pooling contract (q, T) both types' incentive constraints are automatically satisfied.

i. If $p_2 = \theta S'(q) > (\beta - e)$, increase q_2 by ε positive and small and the transfer by $dT_2 = \theta S'(q)\varepsilon$ so that type-2 consumers remain indifferent. Let type-2 consumers choose $(q + \varepsilon, T + \theta S'(q)\varepsilon)$, and let type-1 consumers choose (q, T). Since at (q, T) the marginal rate of substitution between q and T is higher for type-2 consumers, this new allocation is incentive compatible. This raises welfare by $\alpha_2[(1 + \lambda)\theta S'(q) - (1 + \lambda)(\beta - e)]\varepsilon$.

ii. If $p_2 \leq (\beta - e)$, $p_1 < (\beta - e)$. Decrease q_1 by ε positive and small, adjusting T_1 so that type-1 consumers remain on the same indifference curve; that is, $dT_1 = -S'(q)\varepsilon$. Note that type-2 consumers prefer (q, T) to $(q - \varepsilon, T - S'(q)\varepsilon)$. Then the total welfare change is $-(1 + \lambda)\alpha_1 S'(q)\varepsilon + (1 + \lambda)\alpha_1(\beta - e)\varepsilon$ which is positive by assumption, a contradiction. ■

Combining lemmas 6.1, 6.2, and 6.3, we have only the five regimes described in the text in addition to the bypass regime.

A6.3 Proof of Proposition 6.1

The relevant transfers are deduced from the relevant binding constraints.

Regime 1

$$\max\{\alpha_1 S(q_1) + \alpha_2 \theta S(q_2) - (1 + \lambda)c(\alpha_1 q_1 + \alpha_2 q_2) + \lambda[\alpha_1 S(q_1) + \alpha_2(\theta S(q_2) - \theta S(q_1) + S(q_1))]\}$$

yields [letting $p_1 \equiv S'(q_1)$ and $p_2 \equiv \theta S'(q_2)$]

$$\frac{p_1 - c}{p_1} = \frac{\lambda}{1 + \lambda}\frac{\alpha_2}{\alpha_1}(\theta - 1),$$

$$p_2 = c.$$

Note that $dp_1/dc > 0$.

Regime 2

$$\max\{\alpha_1 S(q_1) + \alpha_2 \theta S(q_2) - (1 + \lambda)c(\alpha_1 q_1 + \alpha_2 q_2) + \lambda[\alpha_1 S(q_1) + \alpha_2(\theta S(q_2) - S_2^*)]\}$$

subject to

$$(\theta - 1)S(q_1) = S_2^*$$

yields

$$p_2 = c,$$

$$q_1 = \bar{q} \equiv S^{-1}\left(\frac{S_2^*}{\theta - 1}\right),$$

implying that $dp_1/dc = 0$.

Regime 3

$$\max\{\alpha_1 S(q_1) + \alpha_2 \theta S(q_2) - (1 + \lambda)c(\alpha_1 q_1 + \alpha_2 q_2) + \lambda[\alpha_1 S(q_1) + \alpha_2(\theta S(q_2) - S_2^*)]\}$$

yields

$$p_1 = p_2 = c.$$

Regime 4

$$\max\{\alpha_1 S(q_1) + \alpha_2\theta S(q_2) - (1+\lambda)c(\alpha_1 q_1 + \alpha_2 q_2) + \lambda[\alpha_1 S(q_1) + \alpha_2(\theta S(q_2) - S_2^*)]\}$$

subject to

$$\theta S(q_2) - S(q_2) = S_2^*$$

yields

$$p_1 = c,$$

$$q_2 = \bar{q} = S^{-1}\left(\frac{S_2^*}{\theta - 1}\right),$$

implying that $dp_2/dc = 0$.

Regime 5

$$\max\{\alpha_1 S(q_1) + \alpha_2\theta S(q_2) - (1+\lambda)c(\alpha_1 q_1 + \alpha_2 q_2) + \lambda[\alpha_1(S(q_1) - S(q_2) + \theta S(q_2) - S_2^*) + \alpha_2(\theta S(q_2) - S_2^*))]\}$$

yields

$$p_1 = c,$$

$$\frac{p_2 - c}{p_2} = -\frac{\lambda}{1+\lambda}\frac{\alpha_1}{\alpha_2}\left(\frac{\theta - 1}{\theta}\right),$$

implying that $dp_2/dc > 0$.

Regime 6

$$\max\{\alpha_1 S(q_1) + \alpha_2 S_2^* - (1+\lambda)c\alpha_1 q_1 + \lambda\alpha_1 S(q_1)\}$$

yields

$$p_1 = c.$$

Note that since in all regimes individual prices p_1, p_2 are nondecreasing, individual quantities q_1, q_2 (and also aggregate quantity Q) are nonincreasing in c. ∎

A6.4 Proof of Proposition 6.2

i. Let Q^i denote aggregate production in regime i. Note that $Q^i > Q^6$ for $i = 1, \ldots, 5$ and for any marginal cost c. From appendix A6.3, under bypass $p_1 = c$ and $q_2 = 0$.

For $i = 3, 4, 5$, $p_1 = c$ so that q_1 is the same as in regime 6. But since $q_2 > 0$ in any regime i, $i \le 5$, $Q^i > Q^6$. For $i = 1, 2$, constraints IC_2 and IR_1 are strictly binding, and no bypass occurs. Hence $(\theta - 1)S(q_1^1) \ge S_2^*$. In regime 6, IR_1 is strictly binding, and bypass occurs. Hence $(\theta - 1)S(q_1^6) \le S_2^*$. This implies that $Q^i > Q^6$ for $i = 1, 2$.

From the envelope theorem, for any i, $(d/dc)\tilde{V}_1^i(c) = -(1+\lambda)Q^i$. Therefore

$$\frac{d}{dc}[\tilde{V}^i(c) - \tilde{V}^6(c)] = -(1+\lambda)(Q^i - Q^6) < 0, \qquad i = 1, \ldots, 5.$$

Consequently there exists $c^* \in [0, +\infty)$ such that regime 6 corresponds to c levels above c^*. Since c is a nonincreasing function of β from (6.6), there exists an interval $[\beta^*, \bar{\beta}]$ (possibly degenerated) in which bypass occurs. Note that at β^* there is a discontinuity in total production, since in regime 6,

$$S'(q_1) = (\beta^* - e),$$

$$\psi'(e) = \alpha_1 q_1 - \frac{\lambda}{1+\lambda}\frac{F(\beta^*)}{f(\beta^*)}\psi''(e),$$

$$Q^6 = \alpha_1 q_1,$$

and in regime 5,

$$S'(q_1) = (\beta^* - e),$$

$$\theta S'(q_2) = \frac{\beta^* - e}{1 + [\lambda/(1+\lambda)](\alpha_1/\alpha_2)[(\theta - 1)/\theta]},$$

$$\psi'(e) = \alpha_1 q_1 + \alpha_2 q_2 - \frac{\lambda}{1+\lambda}\frac{F(\beta^*)}{f(\beta^*)}\psi''(e).$$

The discontinuity in Q and e translates into a discontinuity in marginal cost at β^*.

ii. Since by the change of variables $S(q_1) \equiv s_1$, $S(q_2) \equiv s_2$, the constraints define a convex set in the space of control variables, and since $\psi''' \geq 0$, the function of the control variable c, $-\psi(\beta - c)$, is concave and the objective function is concave in control and state variables, the Pontryagin conditions are sufficient and yield continuous controls on $[\underline{\beta}, \beta^*]$ and $[\beta^*, \bar{\beta}]$ (see Seierstad and Sydsaeter 1987, thm. 5, p. 28). By ordering the regimes according to 1, 2, 3, 4, 5, we exhibit a continuous solution that satisfies the Pontryagin conditions and is therefore a solution. ■

A6.5 Concavity of the Welfare-Maximization Program

Suppose that we have regime i ($i \leq 5$) at the left of β^*. The second derivative of the objective function with respect to β^* is, using $d\tilde{V}^i/dc = -(1+\lambda)Q^i$,

$$-(1+\lambda)Q^i\frac{dc^i}{d\beta} - (1+\lambda)\psi'(\beta^* - c^i(\beta^*))\left(1 - \frac{dc^i}{d\beta}\right) + \lambda\psi'(\beta^* - c^i(\beta^*))$$
$$+ (1+\lambda)Q^6\frac{dc^6}{d\beta} + (1+\lambda)\psi'(\beta^* - c^6(\beta^*))\left(1 - \frac{dc^6}{d\beta}\right) - \lambda\psi'(\beta^* - c^6(\beta^*)). \tag{A6.4}$$

Using the fact that

$$\psi'(\beta^* - c^i(\beta^*)) = Q^i - \frac{\lambda}{1+\lambda}\frac{F(\beta^*)}{f(\beta^*)}\psi''(\beta^* - c^i(\beta^*)),$$

(A6.4) becomes

$$- [\psi'(\beta^* - c^i(\beta^*)) - \psi'(\beta^* - c^6(\beta^*))] - \lambda \frac{F(\beta^*)}{f(\beta^*)}$$

$$\times \left[\psi''(\beta^* - c^i(\beta^*)) \frac{dc^i}{d\beta} - \psi''(\beta^* - c^6(\beta^*)) \frac{dc^6}{d\beta} \right]. \quad \text{(A6.5)}$$

Since $\beta^* - c^i(\beta^*) > \beta^* - c^6(\beta^*)$ for all i, (A6.5) is negative for $\lambda = 0$. The objective function is therefore concave in β^* in a neighborhood of $\lambda = 0$. ■

A6.6 Regime 5 (Low-Demand Consumers Have a Rent) Can Be Optimal

It can be checked that each of the regimes is relevant for some values of the parameters. Of particular interest for our analysis is the possibility of existence of regime 5. To do so, let us construct economies for which regime 5 is optimal among regimes $i \in \{1, \ldots, 5\}$ for all $\beta \in [\underline{\beta}, \overline{\beta}]$ (and therefore is globally optimal for small βs). Suppose that $S(q) = q^{1-(1/\varepsilon)}/[1 - (1/\varepsilon)]$, where $\varepsilon > 1$. That is, the demand functions have constant elasticity ε. Consider a sequence of economies indexed by θ in which θ tends to 1 (the consumers become more and more alike). The bypass technology has cost $\sigma(\theta) + d(\theta)q$, where $\sigma(\cdot)$ and $d(\cdot)$ are to be determined. All other data are fixed. Straightforward computations show that

$$S_2^* - S_1^* = \frac{(d(\theta))^{1-\varepsilon}(\theta^\varepsilon - 1)}{1 - (1/\varepsilon)}$$

and

$$S_2^* = \frac{(d(\theta))^{1-\varepsilon}\theta^\varepsilon}{1 - (1/\varepsilon)} - \sigma(\theta).$$

Now choose $d(\theta)$ converging to 0 sufficiently fast with θ so that $S_2^* - S_1^* \to +\infty$, and $\sigma(\theta)$ so as to keep S_2^* constant. The analysis in the text is unchanged, since S_2^* is constant along the sequence and S_1^* is negative. However, $p_1(\theta)$ and $p_2(\theta)$ converge to the marginal cost $(\beta - e)$ in all regimes. Because the difference $\theta S(q_2) - S(q_1)$ converges to 0 when θ converges to 1 (as long as the marginal cost $\beta - e$ does not converge to 0, which is guaranteed if $\underline{\beta}$ is not too small and ψ is sufficiently steep), in the limit $S(q_1) \simeq S_2^* > 0$. So the type-1 customers' IR constraint is not binding, which indicates that regime 5 is obtained in the limit [if bypass is prevented, which will be the case for an appropriate $\psi(\cdot)$ function].

REFERENCES

Baumol, W., J. Panzar, and R. Willig. 1982. *Contestable Markets and the Theory of Industry Structure*. San Diego, CA: Harcourt Brace Jovanovich.

Caillaud, B. 1990. Regulation, competition and asymmetric information. *Journal of Economic Theory* 52:87–110.

Champsaur, P., and J.-C. Rochet. 1989. Multiproduct duopolists. *Econometrica* 57:533–558.

Demski, J., D. Sappington, and P. Spiller. 1987. Managing supplier switching. *Rand Journal of Economics* 18:77–97.

Einhorn, M. 1987. Optimality and sustainability: Regulation and intermodal competition in telecommunications. *Rand Journal of Economics* 18:550–563.

Guesnerie, R., and J.-J. Laffont. 1984. A complete solution to a class of principal-agent problems with an application to the control of a self-managed firm. *Journal of Public Economics* 25:329–369.

Kahn, A. 1971. *The Economics of Regulation: Principles and Institutions.* Vol. 2, *Institutional Issues.* New York: Wiley. Reprint Cambridge, MA: MIT Press, 1988.

Lewis, T., and D. Sappington. 1989. Countervailing incentives in agency problems. *Journal of Economic Theory* 49:294–313.

Lewis, T., and D. Sappington. 1991. Choosing workers' qualifications: No experience necessary? Forthcoming, *International Economic Review.*

Maskin, E., and J. Riley. 1984. Monopoly with incomplete information. *Rand Journal of Economics* 15: 171–196.

Mussa, M., and S. Rosen. 1978. Monopoly and product quality. *Journal of Economic Theory* 18:301–317.

Scharfstein, D. 1988. The disciplinary role of takeovers. *Review of Economic Studies* 55:185–200.

Seierstad, A., and K. Sydsaeter. 1987. *Optimal Control Theory with Economic Applications.* Amsterdam: North-Holland.

III BIDDING FOR NATURAL MONOPOLY

7 AUCTIONING INCENTIVE CONTRACTS

7.1 Some Background

An important dimension of a procurement policy in a natural monopoly context is the selection of the contractor and its contract. Think of a city looking for a private franchisee to operate its bus network, its cable TV, or its garbage collection; of the Department of Defense setting up an auction for the development of a new fighter plane; or of a big industrial customer choosing among long-distance telephone companies. Demsetz (1968) and others have argued that competitive bids should be elicited when several firms are possible candidates to realize a project.[1] The idea is to ensure production efficiency and a low cost by selecting the most efficient firm.

Organizing auctions, however, is costly. Procurors incur the "processing cost" of writing requests for proposals and reading the proposals, making sure that the language and terms of the proposals are unambiguous. Potential suppliers also spend substantial amounts of time preparing contracts in industries with widely opened procurement policies. To this must be added the lengthy assessment of subjective attributes of bids: When evaluating suppliers, procurers often do not compare only their price and output. They also inquire about the financial viability of the suppliers, since they are concerned that the project might not be completed. They also look at the suppliers' reputation, industrial capability, and availability. Properly assessing such attributes is time-consuming. Certainly such transaction costs exist with a single potential supplier, but they tend to grow with the number of bidders.

These processing costs are only one component of the total cost of setting up auctions. As we will discuss later in this book, procurors, who are often themselves agents (e.g., for the public), might favor one supplier over the others; this possibility often gives rise to cumbersome institutional checks on the procurement process such as the creation of multiple independent evaluation teams, the design of rigid weights and definitions for the various attributes of bids for transparency purposes, and voluntary distortions in the trade-offs among attributes. Again, we do not assess that such "capture costs" do not exist with a single potential supplier because, even then, the procurer could be too lenient in designing a contract. But, as we will see, bidding competition gives rise to specific possibilities for the procurer to identify with suppliers. This can reduce the benefits of auctions.

1. Demsetz's (1968) original suggestion is in the context of allocating a natural monopoly position for a commercial activity when the government cannot transfer money to the franchisee. This suggestion, first made by Sir Edwin Chadwick, is to choose the firm offering the lowest consumer price (under identical technologies price competition among firms yields average cost pricing). Demsetz also suggested the use of nonlinear prices when feasible in order to reduce the inefficiencies associated with average cost pricing. For further discussions of franchise bidding, see Goldberg (1977), Schmalensee (1979, ch. 5), Waterson (1988, ch. 6), and Williamson (1976).

Last, Williamson (1976) pointed out the existence of "dynamic costs" of auctions in situations where auctioning is repeated over time. Suppose that the potential suppliers' relative efficiency can change; for instance, the loser of an auction may reorganize its management, invest in capacity (or equivalently be freed from previous commitments), or discover new production technologies. The logic of selecting the most efficient supplier at each point of time requires that the natural monopoly position be put up for bid periodically. This may induce "short-termism" in the investment behavior of the incumbent firm, as we will analyze in chapter 8.

The natural first step in the analysis of auctions is to ignore their processing, capture, and dynamic costs and study their benefits. To this purpose received auction theory must be generalized to "multidimensional bidding." Unless one exogenously restricts attention to fixed-price contracts and automatically selects the supplier who offers to produce at the lowest price, an incentive contract is not auctioned off like a painting or a treasury bill. In practice the procurer also often wants to audit the winner's realized cost. As we will see, bids can then be interpreted as the choice of an expected price and of a coefficient of sharing of cost overruns in a menu offered by the procurer. This chapter extends our analysis to the case of multiple firms. It studies a one-shot project, and leaves to chapter 8 the questions raised by the auctioning of an activity repeated over time and to chapter 14 those raised by the subjectivity of some bid attributes.

In section 7.2 we set up a natural monopoly model; m firms can realize a project that has a fixed, large value for society. Under complete information the regulator would select the most efficient firm and impose an optimal level of effort. Section 7.3 characterizes the optimal Bayesian auction for a utilitarian government under asymmetric information in the simple case of two firms with two possible cost parameters. Section 7.4 characterizes the optimal Bayesian auction with m firms and a continuous distribution for their cost parameters. In both cases the best auction awards the project to the firm that announces the smallest expected cost. The contract between the regulator and the selected firm is then the same as that derived (in chapters 1 and 2) in the case of a single firm, except for a reduced fixed payment. In the case of a continuous distribution, the contract can be written as the sum of a fixed payment function of the announced cost and of a linear sharing of overruns; the coefficient characterizing this sharing rule is a function of the announced cost. The separation property, that the winner faces the same slope and same incentives as if there had been no bidding competition, is the main result of this chapter (the reader should refer to chapters 1 and 2 for a detailed study of the optimal contract). Section 7.5 constructs a dominant strategy auction that implements the optimum, section 7.6 demonstrates the optimality of linear contracts, section 7.7 extends the analysis to regulation, and section 7.8 makes some concluding observations.

Before turning to the formal analysis, we give a heuristic explanation of the separation property for a continuous distribution. For a single firm, as we showed in section 1.4, the optimal incentive scheme is $[1 - \psi'(e(\beta))]f(\beta) = \lambda F(\beta)\psi''(e(\beta))/(1 + \lambda)$. The effort and therefore the slope of the incentive scheme that induces it are determined by the hazard rate $f(\beta)/F(\beta)$, which reflects the trade-off between reducing the distortion at type β [which has probability $f(\beta)$] and raising the rent of all more efficient types [which have probability $F(\beta)$].

Now consider an auction. Let β denote the winner's cost parameter. Bidding changes the government's opportunity cost of controlling the winner. The government could replace the winner by the second most efficient firm, with cost parameter $\beta^* > \beta$. Everything is as if the winner were regulated under a smaller extent of asymmetric information, with the government knowing that it has a parameter in $[\underline{\beta}, \beta^*]$ instead of $[\underline{\beta}, \bar{\beta}]$ But note that the hazard rate is invariant to *upward* truncations of the distribution: $(f(\beta)/F(\beta^*))/(F(\beta)/F(\beta^*)) = f(\beta)/F(\beta)$. Hence there is no gain from changing the slope of the incentive scheme faced by the winner. Bidding only reduces the fixed transfer.

7.2 The Model

We assume that any one of m firms can realize the project. Firm i has cost

$$C^i = \beta^i - e^i, \tag{7.1}$$

where e^i is manager i's ex post effort level and β^i is firm i's efficiency parameter. Manager i, $i = 1, \ldots, m$, has utility function

$$U^i = t^i - \psi(e^i), \tag{7.2}$$

where t^i is the net monetary transfer received from the regulator and $\psi(e^i)$ is firm i's disutility of effort e^i with $\psi' > 0$, $\psi'' > 0$, $\psi''' \geq 0$, and $\psi(0) = 0$. As before, $\psi''' > 0$ facilitates the analysis by ensuring that there is no need for using stochastic incentive schemes.

Let S be the social utility of the project. Under complete information the regulator selects the firm with the lowest parameter β, firm i, say, and makes a transfer t^i only to that firm. Social net utility for a utilitarian regulator is

$$S - (1 + \lambda)(t^i + C^i) + t^i - \psi(e^i) = S - (1 + \lambda)(C^i + \psi(e^i)) - \lambda U^i, \tag{7.3}$$

where U^i denotes the selected firm's utility level. Each firm has outside opportunities normalized to zero. Under complete information the optimal level of effort of the selected firm is e^* determined by $\psi'(e^*) = 1$, and the net transfer equals $\psi(e^*)$.

However, the regulator observes neither the technological parameters nor the effort chosen by the winner. Ex post he or she observes the realized cost of the firm that has been chosen to carry out the project. To select a firm and regulate it, the regulator organizes an auction, as explained below. We consider the "two-firm, two-type case" in section 7.3. This case is conceptually very simple but notationally cumbersome. We recommend that the reader unfamiliar with auction theory go through the steps of the analysis of this case.[2] The more advanced reader may skip this section and proceed directly to the more elegant analysis of section 7.4.

7.3 The Optimal Bayesian Auction in the Two-Firm, Two-Type Case

Consider the case of two firms, each with two possible cost characteristics $\underline{\beta}$ and $\bar{\beta}$. Let ν be the probability that firm i has type $\underline{\beta}$. The cost parameters are drawn independently.

In a given auction let $x^i(\beta^1, \beta^2)$, $i = 1, 2$, be the probability that firm i is selected to carry out the project when firm 1 (resp. firm 2) has characteristics β^1 (resp. β^2). We must have

$$x^1(\beta^1, \beta^2) + x^2(\beta^1, \beta^2) \leq 1 \qquad \text{for any } (\beta^1, \beta^2), \tag{7.4}$$

$$x^i(\beta^1, \beta^2) \geq 0 \qquad i = 1, 2, \text{ for any } (\beta^1, \beta^2). \tag{7.5}$$

Suppose for simplicity that it is always desirable to realize the project under complete information:

$$S - (1 + \lambda)(\bar{\beta} - e^* + \psi(e^*)) > 0. \tag{7.6}$$

Then, still in the complete information case, efficiency requires that the lowest cost firm be selected:

$$x^1(\underline{\beta}, \bar{\beta}) = x^2(\bar{\beta}, \underline{\beta}) = 1, \tag{7.7}$$

$$x^1(\underline{\beta}, \underline{\beta}) + x^2(\underline{\beta}, \underline{\beta}) = 1, \tag{7.8}$$

$$x^1(\bar{\beta}, \bar{\beta}) + x^2(\bar{\beta}, \bar{\beta}) = 1. \tag{7.9}$$

Consider now the case of incomplete information. From the revelation principle, we can restrict the analysis to revelation mechanisms. The argument is similar to that in chapter 1 and excludes the need for considering stochastic mechanisms.

A (deterministic) revelation mechanism is here a set of functions $x^i(\tilde{\boldsymbol{\beta}})$, $C^i(\tilde{\boldsymbol{\beta}})$, $t^i(\tilde{\boldsymbol{\beta}})$ inducing truth telling. $\tilde{\boldsymbol{\beta}}$ is the vector of announced characteristics $(\tilde{\beta}^1, \tilde{\beta}^2)$, $x^i(\tilde{\boldsymbol{\beta}})$ is the probability that firm i is selected, $C^i(\tilde{\boldsymbol{\beta}})$ is the

2. The two-firm, two-type case will also be used in chapter 14, where we introduce quality differences between the firms as well as the possibility of favoritism by the regulator.

cost that firm i must realize if it is selected, and $t^i(\tilde{\boldsymbol{\beta}})$ is the net monetary transfer that firm i receives.[3]

For truth telling to form a Bayesian Nash equilibrium it must be the case that $\tilde{\beta}^1 = \beta^1$ maximizes firm 1's expected utility when it anticipates that firm 2 is telling the truth:

$$\beta^1 \in \arg\max_{\tilde{\beta}^1} \{\nu[t^1(\tilde{\beta}^1, \underline{\beta}) - x^1(\tilde{\beta}^1, \underline{\beta})\psi(\beta^1 - C^1(\tilde{\beta}^1, \underline{\beta}))]$$

$$+ (1 - \nu)[t^1(\tilde{\beta}^1, \bar{\beta}) - x^1(\tilde{\beta}^1, \bar{\beta})\psi(\beta^1 - C^1(\tilde{\beta}^1, \bar{\beta}))]\}$$

or

$$\beta^1 \in \arg\max_{\tilde{\beta}^1} E_{\beta^2}\{t^1(\tilde{\beta}^1, \beta^2) - x^1(\tilde{\beta}^1, \beta^2)\psi(\beta^1 - C^1(\tilde{\beta}^1, \beta^2))\}.$$

This condition can be rewritten as two incentive constraints for firm 1, namely

$$E_{\beta^2}\{t^1(\underline{\beta}, \beta^2) - x^1(\underline{\beta}, \beta^2)\psi(\underline{\beta} - C^1(\underline{\beta}, \beta^2))\}$$
$$\geq E_{\beta^2}\{t^1(\bar{\beta}, \beta^2) - x^1(\bar{\beta}, \beta^2)\psi(\underline{\beta} - C^1(\bar{\beta}, \beta^2))\}, \tag{7.10}$$

$$E_{\beta^2}\{t^1(\bar{\beta}, \beta^2) - x^1(\bar{\beta}, \beta^2)\psi(\bar{\beta} - C^1(\bar{\beta}, \beta^2))\}$$
$$\geq E_{\beta^2}\{t^1(\underline{\beta}, \beta^2) - x^1(\underline{\beta}, \beta^2)\psi(\bar{\beta} - C^1(\underline{\beta}, \beta^2))\}, \tag{7.11}$$

with similar constraints for firm 2. The individual rationality constraints are

$$E_{\beta^2}\{t^1(\underline{\beta}, \beta^2) - x^1(\underline{\beta}, \beta^2)\psi(\underline{\beta} - C^1(\underline{\beta}, \beta^2))\} \geq 0, \tag{7.12}$$

$$E_{\beta^2}\{t^1(\bar{\beta}, \beta^2) - x^1(\bar{\beta}, \beta^2)\psi(\bar{\beta} - C^1(\bar{\beta}, \beta^2))\} \geq 0, \tag{7.13}$$

with similar constraints for firm 2. Clearly (7.10) and (7.13) imply (7.12). From chapter 1 we can guess that (7.11) is not binding (and check later that this constraint is satisfied) and that (7.13) is binding.

The regulator wishes to maximize expected social welfare under the individual rationality and incentive compatibility constraints and the feasibility constraints (7.4) and (7.5). Expected social welfare is the sum of the consumers' expected utility

$$E_{\beta^1,\beta^2}\{[x^1(\beta^1, \beta^2) + x^2(\beta^1, \beta^2)]S - (1 + \lambda)[t^1(\beta^1, \beta^2) + t^2(\beta^1, \beta^2)]$$
$$-(1 + \lambda)[x^1(\beta^1, \beta^2)C^1(\beta^1, \beta^2) + x^2(\beta^1, \beta^2)C^2(\beta^1, \beta^2)]\} \tag{7.14}$$

and of the firms' expected rents

$$E_{\beta^1,\beta^2}\{t^1(\beta^1, \beta^2) - x^1(\beta^1, \beta^2)\psi(\beta^1 - C^1(\beta^1, \beta^2))\} \equiv E_{\beta^1,\beta^2} U^1(\beta^1, \beta^2) \tag{7.15}$$

3. As was mentioned earlier, the mechanism is restricted (without loss of generality) to be deterministic in transfers and cost targets. We still allow the selection to be random ($x^i \in [0, 1]$).

and

$$E_{\beta^1,\beta^2}\{t^2(\beta^1,\beta^2) - x^2(\beta^1,\beta^2)\psi(\beta^2 - C^2(\beta^1,\beta^2))\} \equiv E_{\beta^1,\beta^2}U^2(\beta^1,\beta^2). \tag{7.16}$$

Using equations (7.15) and (7.16) to eliminate the transfers $t^i(\beta^1,\beta^2)$ from equation (7.14), expected social welfare can be rewritten as

$$\begin{aligned}E_{\beta^1,\beta^2}\{&[x^1(\beta^1,\beta^2)+x^2(\beta^1,\beta^2)]S\\ &-(1+\lambda)x^1(\beta^1,\beta^2)[C^1(\beta^1,\beta^2)+\psi(\beta^1 - C^1(\beta^1,\beta^2))]\\ &-(1+\lambda)x^2(\beta^1,\beta^2)[C^2(\beta^1,\beta^2)+\psi(\beta^2 - C^2(\beta^1,\beta^2))]\\ &-\lambda U^1(\beta^1,\beta^2) - \lambda U^2(\beta^1,\beta^2)\}.\end{aligned} \tag{7.17}$$

Since (7.13) is binding, $E_{\beta^2}U^1(\bar{\beta},\beta^2) = 0$, and since (7.10) is binding,

$$\begin{aligned}E_{\beta^2}U^1(\underline{\beta},\beta^2) &= E_{\beta^2}x^1(\bar{\beta},\beta^2)[\psi(\bar{\beta} - C^1(\bar{\beta},\beta^2)) - \psi(\underline{\beta} - C^1(\bar{\beta},\beta^2))]\\ &= \nu x^1(\bar{\beta},\underline{\beta})[\psi(\bar{\beta} - C^1(\bar{\beta},\underline{\beta})) - \psi(\underline{\beta} - C^1(\bar{\beta},\underline{\beta}))]\\ &\quad + (1-\nu)x^1(\bar{\beta},\bar{\beta})[\psi(\bar{\beta} - C^1(\bar{\beta},\bar{\beta})) - \psi(\underline{\beta} - C^1(\bar{\beta},\bar{\beta}))].\end{aligned} \tag{7.18}$$

Let $e^i(\beta^1,\beta^2) \equiv \beta^i - C^i(\beta^1,\beta^2)$, and let $\Phi(e) \equiv \psi(e) - \psi(e - \Delta\beta)$, where $\Delta\beta \equiv \bar{\beta} - \underline{\beta}$. The expected rent of firm 1 with type $\underline{\beta}$ can be rewritten

$$E_{\beta^2}U^1(\underline{\beta},\beta^2) = \nu x^1(\bar{\beta},\underline{\beta})\Phi(e^1(\bar{\beta},\underline{\beta})) + (1-\nu)x^1(\bar{\beta},\bar{\beta})\Phi(e^1(\bar{\beta},\bar{\beta})), \tag{7.19}$$

and a similar expression obtains for firm 2.

Using (7.19) and factoring the terms in x^i, expected social welfare takes the final form:

$$\begin{aligned}&\nu^2[x^1(\underline{\beta},\underline{\beta})(S - (1+\lambda)(\underline{\beta} - e^1(\underline{\beta},\underline{\beta}) + \psi(e^1(\underline{\beta},\underline{\beta}))))\\ &\qquad\qquad + x^2(\underline{\beta},\underline{\beta})(S - (1+\lambda)(\underline{\beta} - e^2(\underline{\beta},\underline{\beta}) + \psi(e^2(\underline{\beta},\underline{\beta}))))]\\ &+\nu(1-\nu)[x^1(\underline{\beta},\bar{\beta})(S - (1+\lambda)(\underline{\beta} - e^1(\underline{\beta},\bar{\beta}) + \psi(e^1(\underline{\beta},\bar{\beta}))))\\ &+x^2(\underline{\beta},\bar{\beta})(S - (1+\lambda)(\bar{\beta} - e^2(\underline{\beta},\bar{\beta}) + \psi(e^2(\underline{\beta},\bar{\beta}))) - \frac{\lambda\nu}{1-\nu}\Phi(e^2(\underline{\beta},\bar{\beta})))]\\ &+\nu(1-\nu)[x^1(\bar{\beta},\underline{\beta})(S-(1+\lambda)(\bar{\beta} - e^1(\bar{\beta},\underline{\beta}) + \psi(e^1(\bar{\beta},\underline{\beta}))) - \frac{\lambda\nu}{1-\nu}\Phi(e^1(\bar{\beta},\underline{\beta})))\\ &\qquad\qquad + x^2(\bar{\beta},\underline{\beta})(S - (1+\lambda)(\underline{\beta} - e^2(\bar{\beta},\underline{\beta}) + \psi(e^2(\bar{\beta},\underline{\beta}))))]\\ &+(1-\nu)^2[x^1(\bar{\beta},\bar{\beta})(S-(1+\lambda)(\bar{\beta} - e^1(\bar{\beta},\bar{\beta}) + \psi(e^1(\bar{\beta},\bar{\beta}))) - \frac{\lambda\nu}{1-\nu}\Phi(e^1(\bar{\beta},\bar{\beta})))\\ &+x^2(\bar{\beta},\bar{\beta})(S - (1+\lambda)(\bar{\beta} - e^2(\bar{\beta},\bar{\beta}) + \psi(e^2(\bar{\beta},\bar{\beta}))) - \frac{\lambda\nu}{1-\nu}\Phi(e^2(\bar{\beta},\bar{\beta})))].\end{aligned} \tag{7.20}$$

The maximization of this program with respect to (x^i) and (e^i) is now straightforward. The optimal effort levels are[4]

$$e^1(\underline{\beta},\underline{\beta}) = e^2(\underline{\beta},\underline{\beta}) = e^2(\bar{\beta},\underline{\beta}) = e^1(\underline{\beta},\bar{\beta}) = e^*, \tag{7.21}$$

$$e^2(\underline{\beta},\bar{\beta}) = e^1(\bar{\beta},\underline{\beta}) = e^1(\bar{\beta},\bar{\beta}) = e^2(\bar{\beta},\bar{\beta}) = \bar{e}, \tag{7.22}$$

with $\bar{e}$ defined as in equation (1.23) by

$$\psi'(\bar{e}) = 1 - \frac{\lambda}{1+\lambda}\frac{\nu}{1-\nu}\Phi'(\bar{e}).$$

The optimal probabilities satisfy

$$x^1(\underline{\beta},\underline{\beta}) + x^2(\underline{\beta},\underline{\beta}) = 1,$$

$$x^1(\underline{\beta},\bar{\beta}) = 1, \quad x^1(\bar{\beta},\underline{\beta}) = 1,$$

$$x^1(\bar{\beta},\bar{\beta})+x^2(\bar{\beta},\bar{\beta})=\begin{cases} 1 \text{ if } S-(1+\lambda)[\bar{\beta}-\bar{e}+\psi(\bar{e})+\dfrac{\lambda}{1+\lambda}\dfrac{\nu}{1-\nu}\Phi(\bar{e})]\geq 0, \\ 0 \text{ if } S-(1+\lambda)[\bar{\beta}-\bar{e}+\psi(\bar{e})+\dfrac{\lambda}{1+\lambda}\dfrac{\nu}{1-\nu}\Phi(\bar{e})]<0. \end{cases} \tag{7.23}$$

The optimal auction always picks the best firm but may fail to realize the project if

$$(1+\lambda)[\bar{\beta}-e^*+\psi(e^*)] < S < (1+\lambda)[\bar{\beta}-\bar{e}+\psi(\bar{e}) + \frac{\lambda}{1+\lambda}\frac{\nu}{1-\nu}\Phi(\bar{e})].$$

This is due to the fact that the rent of asymmetric information introduces an additional cost, $[\lambda/(1+\lambda)][\nu/(1-\nu)]\Phi(\bar{e})$, which may make the project socially nonprofitable. Note that the right-hand inequality, which says that the surplus is smaller than the generalized cost of type $\bar{\beta}$, is nothing but inequality (1.26). The effort level of a selected efficient firm is always optimal and the effort of the selected inefficient firm is biased downward.

Note that the distortion of the inefficient firm is the same as if there were a single firm (chapter 1). The auction does not change the effort level of the winning firm but decreases its rent. Indeed suppose that we use the symmetric auction

$$x^1(\bar{\beta},\bar{\beta}) = x^2(\bar{\beta},\bar{\beta}) = x^1(\underline{\beta},\underline{\beta}) = x^2(\underline{\beta},\underline{\beta}) = \tfrac{1}{2}.$$

Equation (7.19) implies that the expected rent of a firm with type $\underline{\beta}$ is $\frac{1}{2}(1-\nu)\Phi(\bar{e})$ instead of the rent $\Phi(\bar{e})$ that the firm would obtain if it faced no competition (this assumes that the project is always implemented).

We gather our results in proposition 7.1.

4. The first-order conditions are sufficient, since the program is concave in view of $\psi''' \geq 0$.

Proposition 7.1 With two firms and two types per firm,

i. the optimal auction always selects the most efficient firm but realizes the project less often than under complete information,

ii. the effort level of the winning firm is as in the monopoly case (separation property),

iii. competition lowers the rent of the winning firm.

7.4 The Optimal Bayesian Auction in the Continuum Case

Suppose now that the efficiency parameters β^i of the m bidders are drawn independently from the same distribution with a cumulative distribution function $F(\cdot)$ on the interval $[\underline{\beta}, \bar{\beta}]$ and a density function f that is bounded below by a strictly positive number on $[\underline{\beta}, \bar{\beta}]$. Moreover $F(\cdot)$ is common knowledge and has a monotone hazard rate (F/f is nondecreasing).

Firms bid simultaneously by announcing efficiency parameters $(\tilde{\beta}^1, \ldots, \tilde{\beta}^m) = \tilde{\boldsymbol{\beta}}$. Let $x^i(\tilde{\boldsymbol{\beta}})$ be the probability that firm i is selected to carry out the project. We must have

$$\sum_{i=1}^{m} x^i(\tilde{\boldsymbol{\beta}}) \leq 1 \qquad \text{for any } \tilde{\boldsymbol{\beta}}, \tag{7.24}$$

$$x^i(\tilde{\boldsymbol{\beta}}) \geq 0 \qquad \text{for any } 1, \ldots, m, \text{ and for any } \tilde{\boldsymbol{\beta}}. \tag{7.25}$$

7.4.1 The Firm's Bidding Behavior

Let $t^i(\tilde{\boldsymbol{\beta}})$ be firm i's transfer as a function of the announced bids. Ex ante firm i's expected utility is

$$E_{\tilde{\boldsymbol{\beta}}^{-i}}[t^i(\tilde{\boldsymbol{\beta}}) - x^i(\tilde{\boldsymbol{\beta}})\psi(e^i(\tilde{\boldsymbol{\beta}}))], \tag{7.26}$$

where $\tilde{\boldsymbol{\beta}}^{-i} \equiv (\tilde{\beta}^1, \ldots, \tilde{\beta}^{i-1}, \tilde{\beta}^{i+1}, \ldots, \tilde{\beta}^m)$. The ex post observability of cost enables us to rewrite (7.26) as

$$E_{\tilde{\boldsymbol{\beta}}^{-i}}\{t^i(\tilde{\boldsymbol{\beta}}) - x^i(\tilde{\boldsymbol{\beta}})\psi(\beta^i - C^i(\tilde{\boldsymbol{\beta}}))\}, \tag{7.27}$$

where $C^i(\tilde{\boldsymbol{\beta}})$ is the cost level that the regulator requires the firm to reach given announcements $\tilde{\boldsymbol{\beta}}$.

We look for mechanisms $(x^i(\tilde{\boldsymbol{\beta}}), C^i(\tilde{\boldsymbol{\beta}}), t^i(\tilde{\boldsymbol{\beta}}))$ that induce a truth-telling Bayesian Nash equilibrium. A necessary condition for truth telling is, at $\tilde{\beta}^i = \beta^i$,

$$\frac{\partial}{\partial \tilde{\beta}^i} E_{\boldsymbol{\beta}^{-i}} t^i(\boldsymbol{\beta}) = \frac{\partial}{\partial \tilde{\beta}^i} E_{\boldsymbol{\beta}^{-i}}\{x^i(\boldsymbol{\beta})\psi(\beta^i - C^i(\boldsymbol{\beta}))\} \tag{7.28}$$

almost everywhere for $i = 1, \ldots, m$, where the derivatives in (7.28) are partial derivatives with respect to firm i's announcement $\tilde{\beta}^i$ taken at the true parameter values $\boldsymbol{\beta}$. (Differentiability of these expectations almost everywhere results from their monotonicity, which in turn stems from incentive compatibility; see appendix A7.1.)

We will later show that $C^i(\boldsymbol{\beta})$ only depends on β^i (lemma 7.1). So, by abuse of notation, we will denote it by $C^i(\beta^i)$. If the following condition (7.29) is satisfied, (7.28) can be shown to be sufficient:[5]

$$\frac{dC^i}{d\beta^i} \geq 0, \quad \frac{d}{d\beta^i} E_{\boldsymbol{\beta}_{-i}} x^i(\boldsymbol{\beta}) \leq 0. \tag{7.29}$$

In what follows we first ignore the second-order conditions (7.29) and check later that they are indeed satisfied at the optimum.

Let $U^i(\beta^i)$ be firm i's expected utility level when telling the truth:

$$U^i(\beta^i) = E_{\boldsymbol{\beta}_{-i}}\{t^i(\boldsymbol{\beta}) - x^i(\boldsymbol{\beta})\psi(\beta^i - C^i(\boldsymbol{\beta}))\}. \tag{7.30}$$

From (7.27) and (7.28), we have

$$\dot{U}^i(\beta^i) = -E_{\boldsymbol{\beta}_{-i}}\{x^i(\boldsymbol{\beta})\psi'(\beta^i - C^i(\boldsymbol{\beta}))\}. \tag{7.31}$$

7.4.2 The Optimal Auction

The maximand of a utilitarian regulator is the expectation of

$$\left(\sum_{i=1}^m x^i\right)S - (1+\lambda)\sum_{i=1}^m t^i - (1+\lambda)\sum_{i=1}^m x^i C^i + \sum_{i=1}^m (t^i - x^i\psi(e^i))$$
$$= \left(\sum_{i=1}^m x^i\right)S - \lambda\sum_{i=1}^m U^i - (1+\lambda)\sum_{i=1}^m x^i(C^i + \psi(e^i)). \tag{7.32}$$

The first term on the left-hand side of (7.32) is the expected surplus from the project, the second the social cost of transfers, the third the social cost of the expected production cost (the sum of these three terms is equal to the net expected consumer surplus), and the fourth the expected sum of the firms' rents.

From (7.31) we see that U^i is nonincreasing in β^i, so firm i's individual rationality constraint is satisfied if it is satisfied at $\beta^i = \bar{\beta}$. Since the regulator's objective function is decreasing in U^i, the constraint will be tight at $\bar{\beta}$; that is,

$$U^i(\bar{\beta}) = 0, \qquad i = 1, \ldots, m. \tag{7.33}$$

The regulator's optimization problem under incomplete information is

$$\max_{\{x^i(\cdot), C^i(\cdot), U^i(\cdot)\}} \left\{ E_{\boldsymbol{\beta}}\left(\left[\sum_{i=1}^m x^i(\boldsymbol{\beta})\right] S - \lambda \sum_{i=1}^m U^i(\beta^i) - (1+\lambda)\sum_{i=1}^m x^i(\boldsymbol{\beta})[C^i(\boldsymbol{\beta}) + \psi(\beta^i - C^i(\boldsymbol{\beta}))] \right)\right\} \tag{7.34}$$

5. The proof mimics that of appendix A1.4 of chapter 1.

subject to

$$\dot{U}^i(\beta^i) = -E_{\boldsymbol{\beta}^{-i}}\{x^i(\boldsymbol{\beta})\psi'(\beta^i - C^i(\boldsymbol{\beta}))\}, \tag{7.35}$$

almost everywhere, $i = 1, \ldots, m$,

$$U^i(\bar{\beta}) = 0, \qquad i = 1, \ldots, m, \tag{7.36}$$

$$-\sum_{i=1}^{m} x^i(\boldsymbol{\beta}) + 1 \geq 0 \qquad \text{for any } \boldsymbol{\beta}, \tag{7.37}$$

$$x^i(\boldsymbol{\beta}) \geq 0 \qquad \text{for any } \boldsymbol{\beta}, i = 1, \ldots, m. \tag{7.38}$$

Suppose for simplicity that S is so large that it is worth producing for any realization of $\boldsymbol{\beta}$. Then (7.37) is satisfied with equality. We now show that program (7.34) can be simplified by considering functions $C^i(\boldsymbol{\beta})$ that are functions of β^i only.

Lemma 7.1 At the optimum (denoted by a star) $C^{*i}(\boldsymbol{\beta})$ is a function of β^i only, $i = 1, \ldots, m$.

The proof of lemma 7.1 is provided in appendix A7.2. The intuition is that in the absence of correlation among the parameters, making $C^{*i}(\boldsymbol{\beta})$ depend on announcements other than β^i amounts to a stochastic incentive scheme. Such a stochastic incentive scheme has two drawbacks. First, the manager, whose disutility of effort function is convex, dislikes randomness in effort. So the objective function (7.34) is decreased. Second, if $\psi''' \geq 0$, ψ' is convex, and the slope of the manager's rent as a function of the firm's efficiency [given by (7.35)] increases.

For given $x^i(\cdot)$ and therefore given $X^i(\cdot)$, where $X^i(\beta^i) \equiv E_{\boldsymbol{\beta}^{-i}}[x^i(\boldsymbol{\beta})]$, the optimization with respect to $C^i(\beta^i)$ is equivalent to

$$\max_{\{C^i(\cdot), U^i(\cdot)\}} \left\{\int_{\underline{\beta}}^{\bar{\beta}} \{-\lambda U^i(\beta^i) - (1 + \lambda)X^i(\beta^i)[C^i(\beta^i) + \psi(\beta^i - C^i(\beta^i))]\} f(\beta^i)\, d\beta^i\right\} \tag{7.39}$$

subject to

$$\dot{U}^i(\beta^i) = -X^i(\beta^i)\psi'(\beta^i - C^i(\beta^i)), \tag{7.40}$$

$$U^i(\bar{\beta}) = 0. \tag{7.41}$$

When U^i is considered as the state variable and C^i as the control variable, the hamiltonian of this program is

$$H^i = \{-\lambda U^i(\beta^i) - (1 + \lambda)X^i(\beta^i)[C^i(\beta^i) + \psi(\beta^i - C^i(\beta^i))]\} f(\beta^i) + \mu^i(\beta^i)[-X^i(\beta^i)\psi'(\beta^i - C^i(\beta^i))]. \tag{7.42}$$

The Pontryagin principle gives

$$\dot{\mu}^i(\beta^i) = \lambda f(\beta^i), \tag{7.43}$$

$$(1 + \lambda)[1 - \psi'(\beta^i - C^i(\beta^i))]f(\beta^i) = \mu^i(\beta^i)\psi''(\beta^i - C^i(\beta^i)), \tag{7.44}$$

$$\mu^i(\underline{\beta}) = 0. \tag{7.45}$$

Integrating (7.43) and using the transversality condition (7.45), we get

$$\mu^i(\beta^i) = \lambda F(\beta^i). \tag{7.46}$$

The optimal cost function $C^{*i}(\beta^i)$ is therefore determined by

$$(1 + \lambda)[1 - \psi'(\beta^i - C^{*i}(\beta^i))] = \lambda \frac{F(\beta^i)}{f(\beta^i)}\psi''(\beta^i - C^{*i}(\beta^i)). \tag{7.47}$$

Note that we obtain the same formula as in the monopoly case. This is the analytical basis for the separation property discussed in the introduction to this chapter.

We then substitute the $C^{*i}(\beta^i)$ into (7.34) to solve for the optimal $x^i(\boldsymbol{\beta})$. Integrating (7.40), we can write the lagrangian as

$$\int \left\{ \left[\sum_{i=1}^{m} x^i(\boldsymbol{\beta}) \right] S - \lambda \int_{\beta^i}^{\bar{\beta}} x^i(\tilde{\beta}^i, \boldsymbol{\beta}^{-i})\psi'(\tilde{\beta}^i - C^{*i}(\tilde{\beta}^i))\, d\tilde{\beta}^i \right.$$

$$\left. -(1+\lambda) \sum_{i=1}^{m} x^i(\boldsymbol{\beta})[C^{*i}(\beta^i) + \psi(\beta^i - C^{*i}(\beta^i))] \right\} f(\beta^1)\dots f(\beta^m)\, d\beta^1 \dots d\beta^m. \tag{7.48}$$

Integrating the second integral by parts for given $\boldsymbol{\beta}^{-i}$, we have

$$\int_{\underline{\beta}}^{\bar{\beta}} \int_{\beta^i}^{\bar{\beta}} x^i(\tilde{\beta}^i, \boldsymbol{\beta}^{-i})\psi'(\tilde{\beta}^i - C^{*i}(\tilde{\beta}^i))\, d\tilde{\beta}^i\, dF(\beta^i)$$

$$= \left[F(\beta^i) \int_{\beta^i}^{\bar{\beta}} x^i(\tilde{\beta}^i, \boldsymbol{\beta}^{-i})\psi'(\tilde{\beta}^i - C^{*i}(\tilde{\beta}^i))\, d\tilde{\beta}^i \right] \Bigg|_{\underline{\beta}}^{\bar{\beta}}$$

$$+ \int_{\underline{\beta}}^{\bar{\beta}} F(\beta^i) x^i(\boldsymbol{\beta})\psi'(\beta^i - C^{*i}(\beta^i))\, d\beta^i$$

$$= \int_{\underline{\beta}}^{\bar{\beta}} x^i(\boldsymbol{\beta}) \frac{F(\beta^i)}{f(\beta^i)} \psi'(\beta^i - C^{*i}(\beta^i))\, dF(\beta^i). \tag{7.49}$$

The objective function can be rewritten

$$\int \sum_{i=1}^{m} x^i(\boldsymbol{\beta}) \left\{ S - (1 + \lambda)[C^{*i}(\beta^i) + \psi(\beta^i - C^{*i}(\beta^i)) \right.$$

$$\left. + \frac{\lambda}{1 + \lambda} \frac{F(\beta^i)}{f(\beta^i)} \psi'(\beta^i - C^{*i}(\beta^i))] \right\} dF(\beta^1) \dots dF(\beta^m). \tag{7.50}$$

Differentiating (7.47) and using the convexity of ψ', we see that the monotone hazard rate assumption implies that C^{*i} is nondecreasing in β^i. Consequently

$$S - (1 + \lambda)\left[C^{*i}(\beta^i) + \psi(\beta^i - C^{*i}(\beta^i)) + \frac{\lambda}{1 + \lambda}\frac{F(\beta^i)}{f(\beta^i)}\psi'(\beta^i - C^{*i}(\beta^i))\right]$$

is nonincreasing in β^i.

We must choose

$$\begin{aligned} x^{*i}(\boldsymbol{\beta}) &= 1 \qquad \text{if } \beta^i < \min_{k \neq i} \beta^k, \\ x^{*i}(\boldsymbol{\beta}) &= 0 \qquad \text{if } \beta^i > \min_{k \neq i} \beta^k. \end{aligned} \tag{7.51}$$

Hence $X^{*i}(\beta^i)$ is nonincreasing almost everywhere, and $C^{*i}(\beta^i)$ is nondecreasing almost everywhere. The neglected second-order conditions (7.29) are therefore satisfied. We have obtained the following proposition:

Proposition 7.2 With m firms, whose types are drawn independently from the same continuous distribution with a monotone hazard rate, an optimal auction awards the contract to the firm with the lowest cost parameter. The cost level required from the selected firm is the solution of (7.47). The transfer to the firm solves (7.28) and (7.33).

Proposition 7.2 deserves some comment. The optimal auction is deterministic. The level of effort determined by equation (7.47) is below the optimal level and is decreasing in the cost parameter. Actually the effort level is identical to the one we obtained in the monopoly case [equation (1.44)]. Competition in the auction amounts to a truncation of the interval $[\underline{\beta}, \overline{\beta}]$ to $[\underline{\beta}, \beta^j]$, where β^j is the second-lowest bid. This is the separation property.

As m grows, the winner's productivity parameter β^i converges (in probability) to $\underline{\beta}$, $F(\beta^i)$ converges to zero, and the effort level is close to the optimal one. Competition asymptotically solves the moral hazard problem by solving the adverse-selection problem (this extreme result clearly relies on risk neutrality). Proposition 7.2 can be viewed as a formalization of Demsetz's (1968) intuition.

Remark It is straightforward to allow for the possibility that the project is not implemented at all. Let β^* be defined as in equation (1.67):

$$S - (1 + \lambda)\left[\beta^* - e^*(\beta^*) + \psi(e^*(\beta^*)) + \frac{\lambda}{1 + \lambda}\frac{F(\beta^*)}{f(\beta^*)}\psi'(e^*(\beta^*))\right] = 0.$$

Assuming that $\beta^* < \overline{\beta}$ (i.e., that S is not too large), the optimal selection rule becomes

$$x^{*i}(\boldsymbol{\beta}) = 1 \quad \text{if and only if} \quad \beta^i < \min\left(\min_{k \neq i} \beta^k, \beta^*\right).$$

7.5 Implementation by a Dominant Strategy Auction

From (7.30) the system of transfers of the optimal Bayesian auction is such that

$$t^{*i}(\beta^i) \equiv E_{\boldsymbol{\beta}_{-i}} t^{*i}(\boldsymbol{\beta}) = U^{*i}(\beta^i) + X^{*i}(\beta^i)\psi(\beta^i - C^{*i}(\beta^i)). \tag{7.52}$$

Using (7.31) and (7.33), we have

$$t^{*i}(\beta^i) = X^{*i}(\beta^i)\psi(\beta^i - C^{*i}(\beta^i)) + \int_{\beta^i}^{\bar{\beta}} X^{*i}(\tilde{\beta}^i)\psi'(\tilde{\beta}^i - C^{*i}(\tilde{\beta}^i))\,d\tilde{\beta}^i. \tag{7.53}$$

We now construct a dominant strategy auction of the Vickrey type that implements the same cost function (and effort function) and the same rents and also selects the most efficient firm. (A dominant strategy auction is an auction in which each bidder has a strategy that is optimal for any bids of its opponents. In contrast, we have assumed until now that the bidder's strategy is optimal only "on average" given the other bidders' strategies.) For simplicity we maintain the assumption that S is large enough that the project is always implemented. The analysis below is easily generalized by replacing β^j by $\min(\beta^j, \beta^*)$ in what follows. Let

$$\tilde{t}^i(\boldsymbol{\beta}) = \psi(\beta^i - C^{*i}(\beta^i)) + \int_{\beta^i}^{\beta^j} \psi'(\tilde{\beta}^i - C^{*i}(\tilde{\beta}^i))\,d\tilde{\beta}^i \tag{7.54}$$

if $\quad \beta^i = \min_k \beta^k \quad$ and $\quad \beta^j = \min_{k \neq i} \beta^k$,

$$\tilde{t}^i(\boldsymbol{\beta}) = 0 \qquad \text{otherwise.} \tag{7.55}$$

When firm i wins the auction, its transfer is equal to the individually rational transfer plus the rent the firm gets when the distribution is truncated at β^j. Therefore we are back to the monopoly case, except that the truncation point β^j is random. But for any truncation point, truth telling is optimal in the monopoly case. Clearly truth telling is a dominant strategy in the auction (see appendix A7.3).

If $\beta^i = \bar{\beta}$, (7.54) implies that firm i gets no rent for any β^j and therefore also in expectation. The dominant strategy auction is individually rational. Let us check that the dominant strategy auction costs the same in expected transfers as the optimal Bayesian auction: Since $X^{*i}(\beta^i) = [1 - F(\beta^i)]^{m-1}$, from (7.53) we know that the expected transfer of type β^i in the optimal Bayesian auction is

$$t^{*i}(\beta^i) = [1 - F(\beta^i)]^{m-1}\psi(\beta^i - C^{*i}(\beta^i))$$
$$+ \int_{\beta^i}^{\bar{\beta}} [1 - F(\tilde{\beta}^i)]^{m-1}\psi'(\tilde{\beta}^i - C^{*i}(\tilde{\beta}^i))\,d\tilde{\beta}^i.$$

Consider now the transfers of the dominant strategy auction given by (7.54) and (7.55). To compute $E_{\boldsymbol{\beta}_{-i}}\tilde{t}^i(\boldsymbol{\beta})$, we treat β^j as the first-order statistic in a sample of size $m-1$ and observe that the transfer is zero if β^j is less than β^i and is given by (7.54) if β^j is greater than β^i. An integration by parts yields

$$\begin{aligned} E_{\boldsymbol{\beta}_{-i}}\tilde{t}^i(\boldsymbol{\beta}) &= \int_{\beta^i}^{\bar{\beta}} [\psi(\beta^i - C^{*i}(\beta^i)) \\ &\quad + \int_{\beta^i}^{x} \psi'(\tilde{\beta}^i - C^{*i}(\tilde{\beta}^i))\, d\tilde{\beta}^i]\, d(-(1-F(x))^{m-1}) \\ &= [1 - F(\beta^i)]^{m-1}\psi(\beta^i - C^{*i}(\beta^i)) \\ &\quad + \int_{\beta^i}^{\bar{\beta}} [1 - F(\tilde{\beta}^i)]^{m-1}\psi'(\tilde{\beta}^i - C^{*i}(\tilde{\beta}^i))\, d\tilde{\beta}^i \\ &= t^{*i}(\beta^i). \end{aligned}$$

7.5.1 Reduction in Transfer

Equation (7.54) enables us to compute the gain in expected transfer from having an auction. Consider the following thought experiment: Fix the distribution of the winner's cost parameter, and take two situations in which the winner must bid against other bidders or be regulated as a monopoly. The gain in transfer from the auction is equal to

$$G = \int_{\beta^j}^{\bar{\beta}} \psi'(\tilde{\beta}^i - C^{*i}(\tilde{\beta}^i))\, d\tilde{\beta}^i.$$

The expected gain is $E_{\beta^j}G$. The second-order statistic in the sample of m parameters, β^j, has distribution given by

$$\text{Prob}(\beta^j \leq x) = 1 - [1 - F(x)]^m - mF(x)[1 - F(x)]^{m-1}.$$

For instance, for a uniform distribution on $[\underline{\beta}, \bar{\beta}]$ and quadratic disutility of effort $\psi(e) = e^2/2$, it can be shown that

$$E_{\beta^j}G = \Delta\beta - \frac{2\Delta\beta}{m+1} - \frac{\lambda}{2(1+\lambda)}\Delta\beta^2\left[1 - \frac{6}{(m+1)(m+2)}\right],$$

where $\Delta\beta = \bar{\beta} - \underline{\beta}$.

7.5.2 Equivalent Dominant Strategy Auction

An alternative, two-stage way of implementing the optimal allocation is to ask the firms how much they are willing to pay to be regulated as a monopolist, that is, to be offered in the second stage the monopoly menu derived in chapter 1. In the second stage the winner is asked to reveal its β (or, alternatively, it is reimbursed as a function of observed cost). To see that this procedure is equivalent to the dominant strategy auction above, suppose that the first stage is a Vickrey auction. A firm with type β is willing to pay

$$\int_{\beta}^{\bar{\beta}} \psi'(\tilde{\beta} - C^*(\tilde{\beta}))\, d\tilde{\beta}$$

to become a monopolist. This number is therefore its bid in the Vickrey auction. The first-stage price to be paid by the winner is the second bid; that is,

$$\int_{\beta^j}^{\bar{\beta}} \psi'(\tilde{\beta} - C^*(\tilde{\beta}))\, d\tilde{\beta},$$

which yields the same overall transfer as (7.54).

7.5.3 On the Revelation Principle in an Auction

We noted in chapter 1 that mechanisms that make literal use of the revelation principle (i.e., that have a firm announce its type directly before producing) are not renegotiation-proof. Once the regulator learns the firm's type, the regulator and the firm have an incentive to renegotiate away the allocative inefficiency, which was introduced to limit rents, and to choose a fixed-price contract. We also observed that if worried by the renegotiation problem, the regulator could equivalently offer a contract specifying a transfer as a function of realized cost (or else, as concerns a menu of linear contracts, to have this choice made and sealed by the firm and disclosed only after performing.)

In an auction the winning firm must be selected before it performs, which suggests that the optimal allocation is not renegotiation-proof. However, the separation property guarantees that the optimal allocation can be implemented, even though *some* information about the firms' types must be revealed before any production. Let the firms announce their types to a third party (a machine?), which then selects the lowest type as the winner and announces only the name of the winner i, say, and the type β^j of the best loser. Let the auction specify that the winner must produce and is rewarded according to the transfer function $C^i \to T^*(C^i)$, which is optimal for a monopoly with cost distributed according to the truncated distribution on $[\underline{\beta}, \beta^j]$ (this incentive scheme was derived in chapter 1). By definition, the incentive scheme is optimal for the regulator given his or her information that the winner's type is distributed according to cumulative distribution $F(\cdot)/F(\beta^j)$ on $[\underline{\beta}, \beta^j]$. (In information economics the allocation induced by this incentive scheme is said to be "interim efficient.") So the regulator has no incentive to offer an alternative contract.

In the absence of a third party or a machine programmed to receive and send messages, the optimal allocation can no longer be implemented. To always select the winning firm efficiently, the regulator must learn all firms' types perfectly, and renegotiation cannot be prevented. Based on work done by Boïton and Farrell (1990; see also chapter 10), we would then expect substantial pooling of types and/or delay in the selection of the winning firm.

7.6 Optimality of Linear Contracts

Implicit in the mechanisms of our approach is the fact that if the selected firm's ex post cost differs from $C^{*i}(\beta^i)$, the firm incurs an infinite penalty. However, this mechanism is not robust to the introduction of a random disturbance ε^i (uncorrelated with β^i in the cost function $C^i = \beta^i - e^i + \varepsilon^i$).

We now rewrite the transfer function in a form that is closer to actual practice and is robust to cost disturbances. Let

$$t^i(\boldsymbol{\beta}, C) = a^i(\boldsymbol{\beta}) - b(\beta^i)[C - C^*(\beta^i)], \tag{7.56}$$

where $a^i(\boldsymbol{\beta}) \equiv \tilde{t}^i(\boldsymbol{\beta})$ is defined in (7.54) and $b(\beta^i) \equiv \psi'(\beta^i - C^*(\beta^i)) \in [0, 1]$, noting that the optimal cost function C^* is independent of i. It is easy to check that (7.56) still induces the appropriate ex post effort level and truth telling. The transfer is now decomposed into a transfer $a^i(\boldsymbol{\beta})$ computed at the time of the auction and into a sharing of overruns (meaningful when costs are random) determined by the coefficient $b(\beta^i)$.

The auction selects the most efficient firm and awards the winner an incentive contract to induce a second-best level of effort. Thus we generalize the result in chapter 1 that the optimal allocation can be implemented by offering the firm(s) a menu of linear contracts. In particular, using equation (7.54), the fixed transfer a^i decreases with the winner's bid (β^i) and increases with the second bid (β^j). The slope of the incentive scheme b decreases with the winner's bid. So the contract moves toward a fixed-price contract when the winning bid decreases.

Finally, we note that firm i's expected cost $C^*(\beta^i)$, if it is chosen, is an increasing function of β^i. This implies that announcing β^i is equivalent to announcing an expected cost and that therefore the optimal auction can have the firm make an announcement C^{ai} of its expected cost. Equation (7.56) can then be rewritten as

$$t^i(C^a, C) = a(C^{ai}, C^{aj}) - b(C^{ai})(C - C^{ai}), \tag{7.57}$$

where $C^{ai} \le C^{aj} \le C^{ak}$ for all $k \ne i, j$.

7.7 Auctions in Regulation

The auction theory developed above for procurement can be immediately extended to the regulation framework where any of m firms can become the sole producer of a commodity sold to consumers. For simplicity we consider only the case in which the regulator can transfer money to the firm. Let $C^i = (\beta^i - e^i)q^i$ be the cost function of firm i, where q^i is firm i's production level and where the same assumptions as in section 7.4 apply to the average cost $\beta^i - e^i$.[6] Let $P(\cdot)$ be the inverse demand function.

A revelation mechanism is now a set of functions $\{x^i(\tilde{\boldsymbol{\beta}}), q^i(\tilde{\boldsymbol{\beta}}), c^i(\tilde{\boldsymbol{\beta}}), t^i(\tilde{\boldsymbol{\beta}})\}$, where $q^i(\tilde{\boldsymbol{\beta}})$ and $c^i(\tilde{\boldsymbol{\beta}})$ are, respectively, the production level and the average cost level to be achieved by the winning firm when announcements are $\tilde{\boldsymbol{\beta}}$. The same arguments as in section 7.4 lead to the following regulator's optimization problem (under the same assumptions as in section 7.4):

$$\max_{\{x^i(\cdot),q^i(\cdot),c^i(\cdot),U^i(\cdot)\}} \left\{ E_{\boldsymbol{\beta}}\left[\sum_{i=1}^{m} x^i(\boldsymbol{\beta})[S(q^i(\boldsymbol{\beta})) + \lambda P(q^i(\boldsymbol{\beta}))q^i(\boldsymbol{\beta})] \right.\right.$$

$$\left.\left. -(1+\lambda)\sum_{i=1}^{m} x^i(\boldsymbol{\beta})[c^i(\boldsymbol{\beta})q^i(\boldsymbol{\beta}) + \psi(\beta^i - c^i(\boldsymbol{\beta}))] - \lambda \sum_{i=1}^{m} U^i(\beta^i) \right]\right\}$$

subject to

$$\dot{U}^i(\beta^i) = -E_{\boldsymbol{\beta}_{-i}}[x^i(\boldsymbol{\beta})\psi'(\beta^i - c^i(\boldsymbol{\beta}))] \qquad \text{a.e., } i = 1, \ldots, m,$$

$$U^i(\bar{\beta}) = 0, \qquad i = 1, \ldots, m,$$

$$-\sum_{i=1}^{m} x^i(\boldsymbol{\beta}) + 1 \geq 0 \qquad \text{for any } \beta,$$

$$x^i(\boldsymbol{\beta}) \geq 0 \qquad \text{for any } \beta,\ i = 1, \ldots, m.$$

Since cost functions exhibit the separability property of proposition 3.4, the incentive-pricing dichotomy holds, and the optimal pricing of the winning firm must be Ramsey pricing for the effort level, as defined in equations (2.8) and (2.26):

$$\psi'(e^{*i}(\beta^i)) = q^{*i}(\beta^i) - \frac{\lambda}{1+\lambda}\frac{F(\beta^i)}{f(\beta^i)}\psi''(e^{*i}(\beta^i))$$

and

$$\frac{P(q^{*i}(\beta^i)) - (\beta^i - e^{*i}(\beta^i))}{P(q^{*i}(\beta^i))} = \frac{\lambda}{1+\lambda}\frac{1}{\eta(P(q^{*i}(\beta^i)))}.$$

The firm selected by the optimal auction is the one producing the highest "welfare":

$$H^i(\beta^i) = S(q^{*i}(\beta^i)) + \lambda P(q^{*i}(\beta^i))q^{*i}(\beta^i)$$

$$-(1+\lambda)[c^{*i}(\beta^i)q^{*i}(\beta^i) + \psi(\beta^i - c^{*i}(\beta^i))$$

$$+\frac{\lambda}{1+\lambda}\frac{F(\beta^i)}{f(\beta^i)}\psi'(\beta^i - c^{*i}(\beta^i))].$$

6. We omit any fixed cost for notational simplicity, and assume that only one firm produces (see bibliographic notes B.75 for an analysis of dual sourcing).

Since $H^i(\beta^i)$ is decreasing in β^i, the firm with the lowest β^i is selected. The other results are also straightforwardly generalized.

7.8 Concluding Remarks

This chapter has drawn a remarkably simple bridge between auction theory and incentive theory. The optimal auction truncates the uncertainty range for the successful bidder's intrinsic cost from $[\underline{\beta}, \bar{\beta}]$ to $[\underline{\beta}, \beta^j]$, where β^j is the second bidder's intrinsic cost. The principal offers the successful bidder the optimal incentive contract for a monopolist with unknown cost in $[\underline{\beta}, \beta^j]$. Previous work then implies that the successful bidder faces a linear cost-reimbursement contract, the slope of which depends only on its bid, and not on the other bidders' bids.

Technically the optimal auction can be viewed by each bidder as the optimal monopoly contract with a random upward truncation point. This trivially implies that the auction is a dominant strategy auction. Our separability—the slope of the successful bidder's incentive scheme depends only on the first bid—comes from the fact that the incentive constraint is downward binding while bidding leads to an upward truncation of the conditional distribution. Finally, we should note that the optimal allocation can be implemented by a dominant strategy auction that uses information about the first and second bids.

Whether actual auctions resemble optimal ones is a question worthy of further study. In practice it is difficult to observe or find proxies for some variables (e.g., preferences), although some others are available, such as the number of bidders, the distribution of bids, or proxies for the degree of asymmetric information. For instance, our model indicates that, ceteris paribus, the contract resembles more a fixed-price contract, the higher the number of bidders and the lower the degree of asymmetric information. This observation fits well with the feeling of most regulators that it is appropriate to award fixed-price contracts rather than cost-based contracts when there is substantial competition.

Of course the number of bidders is not always exogenous. If it depends on a fixed cost of obtaining a private estimate of β and being able to produce, the previous conclusion carries over: If several auctions are differentiated only by different such fixed costs, they will yield different numbers of bidders, and the ones with the lowest fixed costs will have on average lower realized costs and higher cost sharing by the winning firm. But the number of bidders also may increase with the uncertainty (because the firm's rent is higher, the higher the asymmetry of information). Then the degree of uncertainty directly increases the probability that a contract resembles a cost-plus one but indirectly reduces the latter probability through the effect on the number of bidders.

As mentioned in its introduction, this chapter has analyzed the benefits of auctions and has ignored their transaction costs, their capture costs (analyzed in chapter 14), and their dynamic costs (studied in chapter 8). Let us issue two further caveats concerning the results of this chapter.

First, we emphasized the benefits of selecting the most efficient firm.[7] In practice the firm with the most attractive bid is not always selected because of the following industrial policy considerations: the regulator's objective of keeping capacity utilization and learning by doing approximately equal across firms in order to preserve competition in future auctions, and exogenous political constraints on the "fair distribution" of contracts and subcontracts across regions or countries (e.g., as with contracts signed by the European Space Agency).

Second, we have assumed that the firms bid noncooperatively. In reality there is ample evidence of collusion in some industries, for instance, with regard to municipal procurement contracts. The theory of bid rigging, despite recent progress,[8] is still in its infancy. Let us only note that the assumption of competitive bids is a serious limitation of our analysis in some cases.

BIBLIOGRAPHIC NOTES

B7.1 Auction Theory

Following Vickrey's (1961) pionneering article and the development by Harsanyi of the concept of Bayesian Nash equilibrium, auction theory has quickly progressed in the decade 1975 to 1985. The surveys by Milgrom (1987) and McAfee and McMillan (1987a) provide adequate summaries of most of the results. Since then, progress has been slower on issues such as dynamic auctions, asymmetric auctions, and collusion.

In this book we consider only the case of risk-neutral firms and the independent value paradigm in which the firms' valuations are drawn independently from the same distribution. In the case of standard auctions for indivisible goods, the revenue equivalence theorem asserts that the first price auction and the second price auction (or Vickrey's auction) are equivalent and optimal from the point of view of the seller (in our framework, the "seller" is the procurer, and the "buyers" the firms). However, the second price auction is a dominant strategy auction, whereas the equi-

7. The theory can be straightforwardly extended to allow asymmetric distributions of firms' costs, along the lines of Myerson (1981) and McAfee and McMillan (1987a). In this case the a priori less efficient firms, (i.e., the firms with the least favorable distributions) must be favored in the auction. The regulator then need not select the ex post most efficient firm.
8. See chapter 14 for references and for a discussion.

libria considered in the first price auction are the symmetric Bayesian Nash equilibria.

Ignoring risk aversion is an important limitation of our work suited to explore moral hazard–adverse-selection models with risk-neutral agents. Even without moral hazard the study of optimal auctions is very complex when risk aversion is introduced (see Maskin and Riley 1984). This complexity is a strong barrier to the generalization of our normative approach to the risk aversion case (see McAfee and McMillan 1986 for a study of procurement that encompasses risk aversion, moral hazard, and adverse selection, but with the a priori restriction to linear contracts).

Another limitation of our analysis is the assumption of independent types. One would in practice expect the firms' costs of implementing a given task to be somewhat correlated. To see what correlation implies, suppose that the cost parameters β^i are correlated and that each firm knows its β^i only. Then, in our context, a standard result in auction theory[9] is that if the firms are risk neutral and under an additional very weak condition, the procurer can guarantee him or herself the same welfare as if he or she knew the firms' types. In a sense information is not really private with risk-neutral firms and correlated types. The intuition for this result is that the procurer can ask the firms for their types. Each firm's true type is the best predictor for the other firms' types. By choosing arbitrarily large rewards and penalties for good and bad predictions, the regulator can make lies about one's type arbitrarily costly. These large costs of lying swamp any gain of lying in the auction. Furthermore the large penalties and rewards have no social cost with risk-neutral parties. Note that the de facto absence of adverse selection implies that the winning firm can be given a fixed-price contract.

This first-best result is clearly extreme when the costs are weakly correlated (indeed most of the literature on correlated values has studied and compared first- and second-bid auctions; see the Milgrom 1987 and McAfee and McMillan 1987a surveys for references). This is because we do not believe in the feasibility of the arbitrarily large penalties that are implied by small amounts of correlation among types. Such penalties conflict with risk aversion or with limited liability constraints. Another reason to be suspicious of the result for small correlations is that small mistakes in assessing the distribution of types, or the absence of common knowledge of this distribution, can have dramatic consequences. However, it has proved difficult to introduce risk aversion, limited liability, or robustness considerations into the analysis of optimal auctions, and we therefore have little more to offer beyond the analysis of this chapter.

On the other hand, note that if $\beta^i = \theta + \xi^i$, where θ is a common shock

9. See remark 1 in bibliographic notes B1.3 of chapter 1 for references.

on cost parameters, if firm i knows both θ and ξ^i, and if the ξ^i are independently distributed, the logic of correlated information being de facto common information under risk neutrality implies that the procurer need only worry about the private information about ξ^i; that is, the procurer can learn θ at no cost (see Auriol and Laffont 1991 where this observation is exploited and review problem 11).

In a similar spirit Branco (1991) considers a common-value model where (in the context of procurement) firm i has cost

$$C^i = \xi^i + \sum_{j \neq i} \alpha_{ij} \xi^j - e^i,$$

where $\alpha_{ij} \geq 0$, say. ξ^i is firm i's private information parameter. Assuming that losers cannot be held liable for cost misrepresentations (limited liability), the optimal auction is one in which the winner i, say, has private information about ξ^i but not about $\sum_{j \neq i} \alpha_{ij} \xi^j$, which is revealed by the other firms' bids. Three conclusions then emerge. First; the separation property carries over; the effort of the winner i, say, is determined by the hazard rate of ξ^i. Second, a firm's cutoff type (above which the firm is not taken to implement the project even if it offers the best bid) is contingent on the other bids. Third, care must be exerted in implementing the optimal auction; for example, any ascending method (in which ever lower-powered incentive schemes are offered until one firm accepts the scheme) cannot implement the optimal allocation because it does not reveal the losers' types and therefore cannot yield a cutoff rule that is contingent on all types.

When $C^i = \sum_j \xi^j - e^i$, the required cost for the winning firm i takes the form

$$C^i = h(\xi^i) + \sum_{j \neq i} \xi^j,$$

where $h(\xi^i) \equiv \xi^i - e^*(\xi^i)$ and $e^*(\cdot)$ is as defined in this chapter. Branco then shows that the optimal auction can be implemented by having firms announce cost estimates C^{ai}, by choosing the firm with the lowest cost estimate, and by asking the winner to produce at a cost that depends on the average losing cost estimate

$$C^i = \hat{h}\left(\frac{C^{ai}}{n}\right) + \sum_{j \neq i} \frac{C^{aj}}{n}$$

for an appropriately constructed function $\hat{h}(\cdot)$. This Bayesian auction is not in dominant strategies but satisfies the intermediate requirement that a firm's optimal strategy does not depend on the firm's beliefs about the other firms' distributions of types.

B7.2 The Separation Property

One of the main results of this chapter is the separation property: The winner's cost is the same as the one that obtains if the winner faced no bidding competition; the presence of alternative sources simply reduces the transfer given to the winner.[10] This result has been obtained independently by Riordan and Sappington (1987) and McAfee and McMillan (1987c).

Riordan and Sappington (1987) consider a framework complementary to ours. Bidders submit bids, and then the winner sinks some fixed cost and learns its true marginal cost. Each firm's private information at the bidding stage is a signal correlated with the final marginal cost it will incur if selected. Thus Riordan and Sappington are interested in repeated adverse selection (under commitment) as opposed to ex ante adverse selection and ex post moral hazard. The model is otherwise of the Baron-Myerson kind (unobservable cost, screening on quantity). They show that a first-price auction, in which the successful bidder's allocation depends only on its bid, and not on the other bidders' bids, is optimal and exhibits the separation property.

McAfee and McMillan (1987c) have independently extended the model of chapter 1 to competitive bidding.[11] They focus on the equivalent of a first-bid auction in which the incentive scheme of the winner depends only on its bid. They show that the effort level is identical to the monopoly one. Together with our optimality and dominant strategy results, their result demonstrates the analog of the revenue equivalence theorem (which says that for auctions on a good rather than a contract, the optimum can be implemented by an auction using only information about the high bid as well as by a dominant strategy auction using information about the first and second bids).

B7.3 Dominant Strategy Auction

Another major result of the chapter is that the regulator can implement the optimal allocation through a Vickrey-style dominant strategy auction. This result has been substantially generalized by Mookherjee and

10. This result is similar in spirit to that obtained in chapter 1 when we varied the gross surplus attached to the monopolist's project.

11. A precursor to this chapter and to McAfee and McMillan (1987c) is McAfee and McMillan (1986) (see also Fishe and McAfee 1983). Their paper looks at the trade-off among giving the selected agent incentives for cost reduction, stimulating bidding competition, and sharing risk. They restrict the contract to be linear in observed cost and in the successful bidder's bid ("first-bid auction"). This chapter shows that under risk neutrality the optimal contract can indeed be taken to be linear in observed costs. However, the coefficient of risk sharing should decrease with the successful bidder's bid.

Reichelstein (1992). They ask, When can an optimal Bayesian allocation with multiple agents be implemented through a dominant strategy mechanism? They come up with the following sufficient conditions. The agents $i = 1, \ldots, n$ have quasi-linear preferences

$$U^i(\mathbf{x}, t^i, \beta^i) = V^i(\mathbf{x}, \beta^i) + t^i,$$

where $\mathbf{x}$ is a multidimensional, contractible variable and t^i is the principal's transfer to agent i. [In the framework of this chapter, $\mathbf{x} = (C^1, \ldots, C^n)$ with the conventions that $C^i = +\infty$ if firm i is not selected (so that $n-1$ costs are equal to $+\infty$) and that the principal's gross surplus depends only on the minimum of the n components of $\mathbf{x}$.] While $\mathbf{x}$ is multidimensional, the agent's surplus is required to depend on $\mathbf{x}$ only through a one-dimensional statistic $h^i(\mathbf{x})$:

$$V^i(\mathbf{x}, \beta^i) = \tilde{V}^i(h^i(\mathbf{x}), \beta^i).$$

[Using the conventions that $C^i = +\infty$ if firm i is not selected and that $\psi(e) = 0$ if $e \leq 0$, then in our framework $\tilde{V}^i = -\psi(\beta^i - C^i)$, $\mathbf{x} = (C^1, \ldots, C^n)$, and $h^i(\mathbf{x}) = C^i$.]

Mookherjee and Reichelstein further assume that types are drawn independently, that the distributions of types satisfy the monotone-hazard-rate property $[F^i(\beta^i)/f^i(\beta^i)$ nondecreasing], and that preferences satisfy the sorting assumption $\partial^2 \tilde{V}^i/\partial h^i \partial \beta^i \geq 0$ and the condition that $\partial^2 \tilde{V}^i/\partial h^i \partial \beta^i$ is increasing in β^i. Under these assumptions they show that an allocation that maximizes the principal's expected utility

$$E_{\boldsymbol{\beta}}\left[V^0(\mathbf{x}, \boldsymbol{\beta}) - \sum_{i=1}^{n} t^i(\boldsymbol{\beta})\right],$$

subject to the constraints of individual rationality, $E_{\boldsymbol{\beta}^{-i}}[V^i(\mathbf{x}, \beta^i) + t^i] \geq 0$, and Bayesian incentive compatibility, can be implemented in dominant strategies with the same expected transfers.

The intuition for this result is as follows: With quasi-linear preferences and the sorting condition assumed for the sufficient statistic $h^i(\mathbf{x})$, the allocation rule $\mathbf{x}(\boldsymbol{\beta})$ that solves the above maximization problem is weakly monotonic in β^i and therefore dominant strategy implementable for agent i, for all i (fixing $\boldsymbol{\beta}^{-i}$, one can apply the results of chapter 1 to demonstrate that monotonicity implies implementability). Furthermore a Bayesian mechanism cannot economize on transfers, since the transfers of the Bayesian mechanisms are, up to some constants, the expectations of the transfers required in the dominant strategy mechanisms.

In the auction example the optimal Bayesian mechanism selects the bidder with the lowest characteristic β^i and is therefore monotonic. The previous result implies that it is dominant strategy implementable (and the expected transfers are the same because the constants referred to above are determined by individual rationality at $\bar{\beta}$ in both cases).

B7.4 Scoring Rules[12]

One way of looking at the optimal auction is that the firms can submit a two-dimensional bid (t^i, C^i), where t^i is the net transfer and C^i is their proposed cost target. It may be convenient to design a scoring rule that aggregates the components of a bid into a single number so that the regulator picks the offer with the lowest score.

A natural scoring rule to consider is *total or gross transfer*: $z^i = t^i + C^i$. Unfortunately, using this scoring rule and picking the firm with the lowest z^i (and transferring t^1 if the winner 1, say, abides by its promise to produce at cost C^1) does not implement the optimal allocation. To see this, consider, for instance, a second-bid auction in which the winner, firm 1, say, receives the gross transfer demanded by the second-best offer, z^2, say. Firm 1 then maximizes $\{t^1 - \psi(\beta^1 - C^1)\}$ subject to $\{t^1 + C^1 \leq z^2\}$. Firm 1 then chooses the first-best effort: $C^1 = \beta^1 - e^*$. In other words, choosing the gross-transfer scoring rule amounts to restricting attention to fixed-price contracts. The gross-transfer scoring rule is a suboptimal scoring rule for the same reason that not allowing cost sharing is suboptimal in the monopoly problem of chapter 1.

What is needed is a *modified-gross-transfer scoring rule*. Let $\beta^*(C)$ denote, as defined implicitly in equation (1.44) or (7.47), the type that chooses cost C in the optimal monopoly scheme. Consider the adjusted cost $\hat{C}$ as a function of the target cost C:

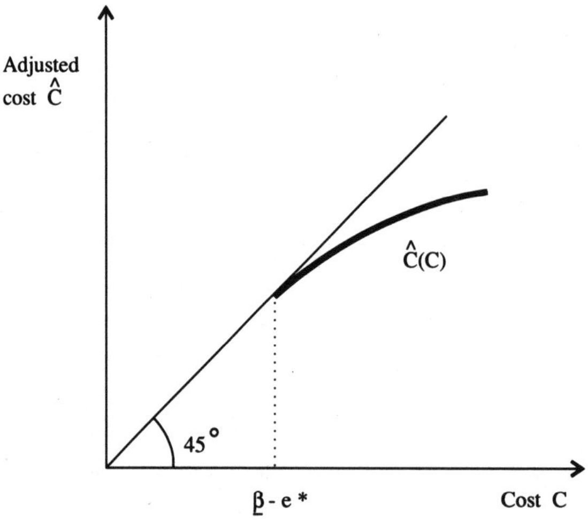

Figure 7.1
Scoring rule

12. This section borrows heavily from Che (1990).

$$\hat{C}(C) \equiv \int_{\underline{\beta}-e^*}^{C} \psi'(\beta^*(\tilde{C}) - \tilde{C})\, d\tilde{C} + (\underline{\beta} - e^*).$$

This adjusted cost, depicted in figure 7.1, is lower than the target cost C, since $\psi' \leq 1$ at the optimum. For instance, in the uniform-quadratic case (β uniformly distributed on $[1,2]$ and $\psi(e) = e^2/2$), one can show that $\underline{\beta} - e^* = 0$ and that

$$\hat{C}(C) = C - \frac{\lambda}{2(1 + 2\lambda)} C^2.$$

The modified-gross-transfer scoring rule associates with any bid (t^i, C^i) a score equal to the modified gross transfer

$$z^i \equiv t^i + \hat{C}(C^i).$$

Consider, for example, the Vickrey-style second-bid auction in which the regulator chooses the firm with the lowest score and pays a net transfer corresponding to the second score. That is, if the bids (t^i, C^i) satisfy $z^1 < z^2 < \cdots < z^n$, firm 1 wins the auction and receives net transfer $\hat{t}^1$ such that the modified gross transfer is equal to the losers' lowest modified gross transfer:

$$\hat{t}^1 + \hat{C}(C^1) = z^2.$$

Note that the winner's utility is

$$\hat{t}^1 - \psi(\beta^1 - C^1) = z^2 - [\hat{C}(C^1) + \psi(\beta^1 - C^1)].$$

Thus everything is as in a standard Vickrey auction except that each firm's generalized cost is $\min_{C^i}\{\hat{C}(C^i) + \psi(\beta^i - C^i)\}$. A firm's optimal cost target thus satisfies

$$\psi'(\beta^i - C^i) = \frac{d\hat{C}}{dC^i} = \psi'(\beta^*(C^i) - C^i)$$

and is the optimal cost given in equation (1.44) or (7.47). Furthermore a dominant strategy for each firm is to bid a score equal to its generalized cost.

The interpretation of this scoring rule is that the regulator discounts cost reductions: A unit decrease in cost is not valued as much as a unit decrease in net transfer. This unequal weighting of cost and net transfer is of course intended to limit the firm's rent.[13]

13. Similarly in a Baron-Myerson model in which the regulator screens the firm's type through the choice of (verifiable) quality or quantity (see bibliographic notes of chapter 2), the optimal scoring rule deflates the regulator's marginal valuation for quality or quantity. See Che (1990).

B7.5 Dual Sourcing with Independent Activities

This chapter has considered only the winner-take-all rule. In practice the production is sometimes divided among several bidders. Such "split auctions"—or "dual sourcing"—have been used, for instance, in the "Great Engine War" in the United States in which General Electric and Pratt and Whitney submitted bids for splits of the total requirement as well as for the entire requirement.[14] Similarly regulated health services are routinely provided by several hospitals in the same city. One motivation for dual sourcing is the desire to keep several firms alive and thus promote competition in later auctions. Another motivation is that in a static context dual sourcing would allow product variety or reduce production costs if firms face decreasing returns to scale. But dual sourcing also has specific incentive properties. Anton and Yao (1992) and McGuire and Riordan (1991) have developed various models to study the link between dual (or multiple) sourcing and incentives in auctions.

Anton and Yao do not consider optimal auctions, but McGuire and Riordan solve for the optimal auction between two firms when two units of a good are purchased by the regulator. So, in the model of McGuire and Riordan, each firm can produce 0, 1, or 2 units. Each firm i's cost includes a fixed cost $\alpha \geq 0$ if the firm produces at all, and marginal cost $c^i = \beta^i - e^i$ per unit produced. The model has thus two elements of increasing returns that in a symmetric information world would make dual sourcing inefficient:[15] the fixed cost, and the fact that marginal cost reductions are more desirable if the firm produces more units.

Let us assume that consumers' surplus is S if both units are produced and zero otherwise. Let $x^1(\beta^1, \beta^2)$, $x^2(\beta^1, \beta^2)$, $y(\beta^1, \beta^2)$ be, respectively, the probabilities that firm 1 produces both units, firm 2 produces both units, or each firm produces one unit. Let $e^1(\beta^1, \beta^2)$, $e^2(\beta^1, \beta^2)$, $e_1^1 \beta^1, \beta^2)$, $e_1^2(\beta^1, \beta^2)$ be, respectively, the effort level of firm 1 if it produces both units, firm 2 if it produces both units, firm 1 if it produces one unit, and firm 2 if it produces one unit.

Expected social welfare is

$$\begin{aligned}
&x^1\{S - (1 + \lambda)[2(\beta^1 - e^1) + \psi(e^1)]\} \\
&+ x^2\{S - (1 + \lambda)[2(\beta^2 - e^2) + \psi(e^2)]\} \\
&+ y\{S - (1 + \lambda)[(\beta^1 - e^1) + \psi(e_1^1) + (\beta^2 - e^2) + \psi(e_1^2)]\} \\
&- \lambda U^1 - \lambda U^2.
\end{aligned}$$

14. See Anton and Yao (1990) for other examples.
15. While dual sourcing under symmetric information is inefficient here, it may be efficient in the McGuire-Riordan model in which the two firms' products are differentiated.

Under incomplete information and the usual monotone-hazard-rate assumption, maximization of expected welfare under incentive and individual rationality constraints shows that the interdependence between firms is only through outputs and transfers. The separation property holds in the sense that conditional on the chosen production level, the effort level is determined by the familiar monopoly equation

$$\psi'(e^i) = q^i - \frac{\lambda}{1+\lambda}\frac{F(\beta^i)}{f(\beta^i)}\psi''(e^i).$$

In each case (single sourcing by firm 1 or firm 2, and dual sourcing) effort levels depend only on the type of the firm, and clearly from the above equation

$$e^1(\beta^1) > e_1^1(\beta^1),$$

$$e^2(\beta^2) > e_1^2(\beta^2).$$

The incentive constraint, for firm 1, say, reduces to

$$\dot{U}(\beta^1) = -E_{\beta^2}[x^1(\beta^1,\beta^2)\psi'(e^1(\beta^1)) + y(\beta^1,\beta^2)\psi'(e_1^1(\beta^1))].$$

Dual sourcing, allocating one unit to each firm instead of buying both units from firm 1, say, has two effects. First, it reduces firm 1's rent as $\psi'(e^1\beta^1)) > \psi'(e_1^1(\beta^1))$, but it raises firm 2's rent as $\psi'(e_1^2(\beta^2)) > 0$. This second effect is called the cushion effect by McGuire and Riordan (1991). It decreases the cost of not being selected as a single source.

Appropriate sourcing is chosen on the basis of generalized or virtual costs, which are

$$(1+\lambda)[2(\beta^i - e^i(\beta^i)) + \psi(e^i(\beta^i))] + \lambda\frac{F(\beta^i)}{f(\beta^i)}\psi'(e^i(\beta^i)),$$

with firm i as the single source, and

$$(1+\lambda)[\beta^1 - e_1^1(\beta^1) + \psi(e_1^1(\beta^1))] + \lambda\frac{F(\beta^1)}{f(\beta^1)}\psi'(e_1^1(\beta^1))$$

$$+ (1+\lambda)[\beta^2 - e_1^2(\beta^2) + \psi(e_1^2(\beta^2))] + \lambda\frac{F(\beta^2)}{f(\beta^2)}\psi'(e_1^2(\beta^2)),$$

for dual sourcing.

For small λ, effort levels are almost optimal conditional on output levels, and therefore informational costs are essentially proportional to output levels. They are $[\min_{\beta^i} \lambda(F(\beta^i)/f(\beta^i))] \times 2$ in the best single source instead of $\lambda[F(\beta^1)/f(\beta^1)] + \lambda[F(\beta^2)/f(\beta^2)]$. The informational costs of dual sourcing are therefore higher than the informational cost of single sourcing.

For large λ, effort levels are suboptimal, and this may work in favor of dual sourcing. Take, for example, the case $\psi(e) = e^2/2$, and consider the most favorable case for dual sourcing, that is, when $\beta^1 = \beta^2$. Then the information cost of single sourcing is $2\lambda(F/f) - \lambda^2(F/f)^2/[2(1 + \lambda)]$ instead of $2\lambda(F/f) - [\lambda^2(F/f)^2/(1 + \lambda)]$ in the case of dual sourcing. The second terms in these expressions may make dual sourcing optimal.

In their model McGuire and Riordan introduce imperfect substitution between the commodities of both firms, creating circumstances in which dual sourcing may be desirable under complete information. Therefore incomplete information improves the case for single sourcing for small λ and may improve the case for dual sourcing for large λ.

Slama (1990) extends chapter 7 in various ways, in particular in treating the case where the monotone-hazard-rate property does not hold and the case where firms are not drawn from identical distributions. She also treats the case where incomplete information may affect simultaneously marginal cost and fixed cost. She finds that with a negative correlation between marginal and fixed costs, dual sourcing can occur despite increasing returns.

Finally, Auriol and Laffont (1991), in the context of a Baron-Myerson model, show how dual sourcing may be motivated by the correlation of types (yardstick competition), by decreasing returns once fixed costs are incurred, or by imperfect substitutability of goods.

B7.6 Dual Sourcing with Competing Activities

In the split auction example considered in section B7.5, the firms compete for production. But, once the allocation of production is determined, the activities of the two firms are "separable," or "independent," and the separation property holds. The separation property does not hold if the firms' activities enter nonseparably in the regulator's objective function, as is shown in Olsen (1991). Suppose, for instance, that the regulator has objective function

$$S(\gamma^1, \gamma^2) - (1 + \lambda)(t^1 + t^2) + U^1 + U^2,$$

where the gross surplus depends on the observable performances γ^i of the two firms, t^i is the transfer to firm i, and U^i is firm i's rent. Let $\gamma^i = \beta^i - e^i$, where firm i's effort e^i costs $\psi(e^i)$, and firm i's type β^i is drawn from distribution F_i on $[\underline{\beta}, \bar{\beta}]$.

Suppose that dual sourcing is always used and, most crucially, that $\partial^2 S/\partial\gamma^1\partial\gamma^2 > 0$ (complement activities) or < 0 (substitute activities). For instance, suppose with Olsen that the two firms try to discover an innovation. The discovery time for firm i is $\gamma^i + \varepsilon^i$, where ε^i is a random variable distributed on $[0, +\infty)$ according to some distribution G_i. Normalizing the social value of the innovation to 1 and letting $r > 0$ denote the rate of interest, the gross surplus function is

$$S(\gamma^1, \gamma^2) = E_{\varepsilon^1, \varepsilon^2}(e^{-r \min(\gamma^1 + \varepsilon^1, \gamma^2 + \varepsilon^2)}).$$

It is easy to show that $\partial S/\partial \gamma^i < 0$ (later discoveries reduce surplus) and that $\partial^2 S/\partial \gamma^1 \partial \gamma^2 < 0$ (effort by firm i to reduce the discovery time is less valuable if firm j discovers fast on average). We focus on these sign conditions in our comments. We assume that γ^i is contractible (this is without loss of generality as long as the firms are risk neutral and at least the real discovery time, $\gamma^i + \varepsilon^i$, is contractible. For similar ideas, see bibliographic notes B1.3 in chapter 1).

The generalization of equation (2.26) is in this context

$$(1 + \lambda)\psi'(e^i) = -\frac{\partial S}{\partial \gamma^i}(\gamma^1(\beta^1), \gamma^2(\beta^2)) - \lambda \frac{F_i(\beta^i)}{f_i(\beta^i)} \psi''(e^i).$$

The important point is that the optimal effort is affected by the asymmetry of information in two opposite ways: First, as before, effort is reduced to extract firm i's rent, as indicated by the second term of the right-hand side, and, second, firm i's effort is now indirectly affected by the asymmetry of information about firm j. Because γ^j increases due to the rent extraction concern, a decrease in γ^i becomes more desirable, which raises the effort of firm i.

It is easy to see that the second effect can dominate the first. For instance, suppose that only firm 1 has private information. The first effect then does not exist for firm 2. Firm 1's effort is lower than under symmetric information (except when $\beta^1 = \underline{\beta}$), and firm 2's effort *exceeds* its symmetric information level. Olsen also shows that the gross surplus function S may exceed the symmetric information level, another property that would be ruled out by independent activities.

B7.7 Auctions and Technology Transfers

The chapter has also ruled out the possibility that one of the firms produces with the technology of another firm. But consider a procurement situation in which a firm, say, firm 1, has developed a new technology. At the production stage the requirement may be met by firm 1 or by firm 2 using either its own technology or firm 1's technology. The implications of the transfer of the technology between firms are analyzed in Riordan and Sappington (1989) and Stole (1991).

Let us sketch Stole's model. For simplicity we ignore moral hazard considerations (or, equivalently, we focus on fixed price contracts). Firm 1's (private) production cost β^1 is distributed according to distribution F_1. Firm 2's production cost β^2, if it uses its own technology, is distributed according to distribution F_2. As a special case of Stole's transfer technology, let us assume that firm 2's cost if it uses firm 1's technology is

$$l(\beta^1, \beta^2) = k\beta^1 + (1-k)\beta^2 + \alpha,$$

where $k \in [0,1]$ and $\alpha \geq 0$ (firm 2 need not know β^1 before the transfer is made).[16] The technology is perfectly transferable if $k = 1$ and $\alpha = 0$.

The regulator must choose among three alternatives (the project cannot be split): developer, second source without technology transfer, or second source with technology transfer. Under symmetric information the regulator's optimal choice is given by

$$\min\{\beta^1, \beta^2, k\beta^1 + (1-k)\beta^2 + \alpha\}.$$

In particular a technology transfer is here never optimal under symmetric information. This is no longer so under asymmetric information. As is intuitive, the regulator then compares the three virtual costs (which include the costs of giving informational rents to the better types):

$$\min\left\{\beta^1 + \frac{F_1(\beta^1)}{f_1(\beta^1)}, \beta^2 + \frac{F_2(\beta^2)}{f_2(\beta^2)}, k\beta^1 + (1-k)\beta^2 + \alpha + (1-k)\frac{F_2(\beta^2)}{f_2(\beta^2)}\right\}.$$

Note that firm 2's informational rent grows only at rate $1-k$ under licensing, which explains the third term. (Firm 2 cannot enjoy an informational rent on β^1 under licensing because firm 1 announces β^1 truthfully to the regulator.) For example, when $k = 1$ and $\alpha = 0$, licensing always dominates production by firm 1. The idea is simply that firm 2 cannot enjoy an informational rent on firm 1's technology while firm 1 can. We thus conclude that technology transfers (when feasible) may help reduce informational rents.

Stole also points out that technology transfer looks less advantageous if the developer must invest to reduce β^1 before the auction. Transferable investments are unfortunately best promoted by favoring the firm that commits those investments, a theme we will come back to in chapter 8.

B7.8 Research and Development prior to Procurement

Defense contractors or architects often sink substantial investments before bidding on a contract. Tan (1991), in a Baron-Myerson model with unobservable cost $C^i = \beta^i$, assumes that prior to bidding, the firms commit investments, I^i for firm i; the cost parameter is then drawn from distribution $F(\beta^i | I^i)$ (see also Dasgupta and Spulber 1989; Rob 1986).

16. Stole further assumes limited liability so that the regulator cannot punish firm 1 if licensing occurs and firm 2 discovers that the true value of β^1 differs from the one announced by firm 1. (We let the reader check that in the absence of limited liability, everything would be as if the regulator knew β^1.)

As in sections 1.8 and 1.9, which consider a single bidder, one can in the case of several bidders consider the polar cases in which investments are unobservable and in which investments are contractible. Tan analyzes the first- and second-price auctions with and without free entry under the assumption of unobservable investments.

APPENDIXES

A7.1 Characterization of Truth Telling

To minimize technicalities, we assume that the allocation is almost everywhere differentiable. The proof that it is indeed the case is essentially the same as that in chapter 1 (in particular in appendix A1.3). For truth telling to be a best strategy for firm i, β^i must be the best response for firm i when it assumes that the other firms are truthful; that is, it must be the solution of

$$\max_{\tilde{\beta}^i} \{E_{\boldsymbol{\beta}^{-i}}[t^i(\tilde{\beta}^i, \boldsymbol{\beta}^{-i}) - x^i(\tilde{\beta}^i, \boldsymbol{\beta}^{-i})\psi(\beta^i - C^i(\tilde{\beta}^i, \boldsymbol{\beta}^{-i}))]\}.$$

Transfers must satisfy the first-order condition of incentive compatibility:

$$\frac{\partial}{\partial \tilde{\beta}^i}(E_{\boldsymbol{\beta}^{-i}} t^i(\boldsymbol{\beta})) = \frac{\partial}{\partial \tilde{\beta}^i}(E_{\boldsymbol{\beta}^{-i}}\{x^i(\boldsymbol{\beta})\psi(\beta^i - C^i(\boldsymbol{\beta}))\}). \tag{A7.1}$$

[On the right-hand side of (A7.1), the differentiation $\partial/\partial\tilde{\beta}^i$ means differentiation with respect to β^i in $x^i(\boldsymbol{\beta})$ and in $C^i(\boldsymbol{\beta})$ only.]

If C^i is nondecreasing in β^i almost everywhere and if $E_{\boldsymbol{\beta}^{-i}} x^i(\boldsymbol{\beta})$ is nonincreasing in β^i almost everywhere, then following the proof in Guesnerie and Laffont (1984, thm. 2), we show that the functions $x^i(\cdot)$ and $C^i(\cdot)$ can be implemented by transfers solutions of (A7.1). ■

A7.2 Proof of Lemma 7.1

Suppose that C^{*i} is not a function only of β^i. We show that the optimal value of program (7.34) can be increased, a contradiction. Denote $X^i(\beta^i) \equiv E_{\boldsymbol{\beta}^{-i}}[x^i(\boldsymbol{\beta})]$, and choose $C^i(\beta^i)$ such that

$$C^i(\beta^i) = E_{[\boldsymbol{\beta}^{-i}|x^i(\boldsymbol{\beta})=1]} C^i(\boldsymbol{\beta}).$$

Observe that from the linearity of the program in $x^i(\boldsymbol{\beta})$, the optimum can be chosen so that the $x^i(\boldsymbol{\beta})$ are zeros and ones. Then, since $\psi(0) = 0$,

$$E_{\boldsymbol{\beta}^{-i}}[x^i(\boldsymbol{\beta})\psi(\beta^i - C^i(\boldsymbol{\beta}))] = X^i(\beta^i) E_{[\boldsymbol{\beta}^{-i}|x^i(\boldsymbol{\beta})=1]}\psi(\beta^i - C^i(\boldsymbol{\beta})). \tag{A7.2}$$

Since $\psi'' > 0$, by Jensen's inequality, the expression in (A7.2) exceeds

$$X^i(\beta^i)\psi(E_{[\boldsymbol{\beta}^{-i}|x^i(\boldsymbol{\beta})=1]}[\beta^i - C^i(\boldsymbol{\beta})]) = X^i(\beta^i)\psi(\beta^i - C^i(\beta^i)).$$

The maximand of (7.34) can therefore be replaced by the larger quantity

$$E_{\boldsymbol{\beta}}\left(\sum_{i=1}^{m} x^i\right)S - \sum_{i=1}^{m} E_{\boldsymbol{\beta}^{-i}}\{\lambda U^i(\beta^i) + (1+\lambda)X^i(\beta^i)[C^i(\beta^i) + \psi(\beta^i - C^i(\beta^i))]\}.$$

Moreover the constraints can be relaxed. Since $\psi'(0) = 0$ and $\psi''' \geq 0$, we have similarly

$$E_{\boldsymbol{\beta}^{-i}}\{x^i(\boldsymbol{\beta})\psi'(\beta^i - C^i(\boldsymbol{\beta}))\} \geq X^i(\beta^i)\psi'(\beta^i - C^i(\beta^i)).$$

Therefore, since the objective function is decreasing in U^i, the constraints are relaxed if we replace (7.35) by

$$\dot{U}^i(\beta^i) = -X^i(\beta^i)\psi'(\beta^i - C^i(\beta^i)).$$

■

A7.3 Implementation in Dominant Strategy

Let us check that truth telling is indeed a dominant strategy in the auction defined in (7.54) and (7.55). Suppose first that by announcing the truth, firm i wins the auction. Since the auction is individually rational and losers get nothing, firm i cannot gain by lying and losing the auction. Consider an announcement $\tilde{\beta}^i$ such that $\tilde{\beta}^i < min_{k \neq i} \beta^k$.

Firm i's program is

$$\max_{\{\tilde{\beta}^i \leq \min_{k \neq i} \beta^k\}} \{\tilde{t}^i(\tilde{\beta}^i, \boldsymbol{\beta}^{-i}) - \psi(\beta^i - C^{*i}(\tilde{\beta}^i))\}.$$

The first-order condition for an interior solution is

$$\psi'(\tilde{\beta}^i - C^{*i}(\tilde{\beta}^i))\left[1 - \frac{dC^{*i}}{d\beta^i}(\tilde{\beta}^i)\right] - \psi(\tilde{\beta}^i - C^{*i}(\tilde{\beta}^i))$$
$$+ \psi'(\beta^i - C^{*i}(\tilde{\beta}^i))\frac{dC^{*i}}{d\beta^i}(\tilde{\beta}^i) = 0.$$

Hence $\tilde{\beta}^i = \beta^i$ is the only solution of the first-order condition. The second-order condition at $\tilde{\beta}^i = \beta^i$ is satisfied since $dC^{*i}/d\beta^i \geq 0$.

Finally, observe that a loser of the auction does not want to bid less than its true parameter. If the firm still loses the auction, its utility is unchanged. If the firm wins the auction, its transfer does not compensate it for its disutility of effort. Let β^i be the loser's true parameter, and let its announcement $\tilde{\beta}^i$ be smaller than the smallest announcement β^j:

$$U^i(\beta^i, \tilde{\beta}^i) = \psi(\tilde{\beta}^i - C^{*i}(\tilde{\beta}^i)) + \int_{\tilde{\beta}^i}^{\beta^j} \psi'(\hat{\beta}^i - C^{*i}(\hat{\beta}^i))\, d\hat{\beta}^i$$
$$- \psi(\beta^i - \tilde{\beta}^i + \tilde{\beta}^i - C^{*i}(\tilde{\beta}^i))$$
$$\leq -(\beta^i - \tilde{\beta}^i)\psi'(\tilde{\beta}^i - C^{*i}(\tilde{\beta}^i)) + \int_{\tilde{\beta}}^{\beta^j} \psi'(\hat{\beta}^i - C^{*i}(\hat{\beta}^i))\, d\hat{\beta}^i$$
$$\leq -(\beta^i - \tilde{\beta}^i)\psi'(\tilde{\beta}^i - C^{*i}(\tilde{\beta}^i)) + (\beta^j - \tilde{\beta}^i)\psi'(\tilde{\beta}^i - C^{*i}(\tilde{\beta}^i)),$$

since, from (7.47),

$$\frac{de^{*i}}{d\beta^i} = 1 - \frac{dC^{*i}}{d\beta^i} \leq 0.$$

Since $\beta^i \geq \beta^j$, $U^i(\beta^i, \tilde{\beta}^i) \leq 0$. ■

REFERENCES

Anton, J., and D. Yao. 1990. Coordination in split-award auctions. *Quarterly Journal of Economics* 107:681–708.

Auriol, E., and J.-J. Laffont. 1991. Regulation by duopoly. Mimeo, IDEI, Université de Toulouse.

Baron, D., and D. Besanko. 1987. Monitoring, moral hazard, asymmetric information and risk-sharing in procurement contracting. *Rand Journal of Economics* 18:509–532.

Bolton, P., and J. Farrell. 1990. Decentralization, duplication and delay. *Journal of Political Economy* 98:803–826.

Branco, F. 1991. Auctioning an indivisible good. Mimeo, Massachusetts Institute of Technology.

Che, Y.K. 1990. Design competition through multi-dimensional bidding. Mimeo, Stanford University.

Dasgupta, S., and D. F. Spulber. 1989. Managing procurement auctions. *Information Economics and Policy* 4:5–29.

Demsetz, H. 1968. Why regulate utilities? *Journal of Law and Economics* 11:55–65.

Fishe, R., and R. P. McAfee. 1983. Contract design under uncertainty. Mimeo, University of Western Ontario.

Goldberg, V. 1977. Competitive bidding and the production of pre-contract information. *Bell Journal of Economics* 8:250–261.

Guesnerie, R., and J.-J. Laffont. 1984. A complete solution to a class of principal-agent problems with an application to the control of a self-managed firm. *Journal of Public Economics* 25:329–369.

McAfee, R. P., and J. McMillan. 1986. Bidding for contracts: A principal-agent analysis. *Rand Journal of Economics* 17:326–338.

McAfee, R. P., and J. McMillan. 1987a. Auctions and bidding. *Journal of Economic Literature* 25:699–738.

McAfee, R. P., and J. McMillan. 1987b. *Incentives in Government Contracting*. Toronto: University of Toronto Press.

McAfee, R. P., and J. McMillan. 1987c. A reformulation of the principal-agent model. *Rand Journal of Economics* 18:296–307.

McGuire, T., and M. Riordan. 1991. Incomplete information and optimal market structure: Public purchases from private providers. Mimeo, Boston University.

Maskin, E., and J. Riley. 1984. Optimal auctions with risk-averse buyers. *Econometrica* 52: 1473–1518.

Milgrom, P. 1987. Auction theory. In *Advances in Economic Theory*, ed. T. Bewley. Cambridge: Cambridge University Press.

Mookherjee, D., and S. Reichelstein. 1992. Dominant strategy implementation of Bayesian incentive compatible allocation rules. *Journal of Economic Theory* 56:378–399.

Myerson, R. 1981. Optimal auction design. *Mathematics of Operations Research* 6:619–632.

Olsen, T. 1991. Regulation of multi-agent R&D under asymmetric information. Mimeo, Norwegian Research Centre in Organization and Management, Bergen.

Riordan, M., and D. Sappington. 1987. Awarding monopoly franchises. *American Economic Review* 77:375–387.

Riordan, M., and D. Sappington. 1989. Second sourcing. *Rand Journal of Economics* 20:41–58.

Rob, R. 1986. The design of procurement contracts. *American Economic Review* 76:378–389.

Schmalensee, R. 1979. *The Control of Natural Monopolies*. Lexington, MA: D.C. Heath, Lexington Books.

Slama, S. 1990. Théorie des enchères et des appels d'offres pour des marchés publics, Ph.D. dissertation, University of Tunis.

Stole, L. 1991. Information expropriation and moral hazard in optimal second-source auctions. In *Essays on the Economics of Contracts.* Ph.D. dissertation, Massachusetts Institute of Technology.

Tan, G. 1991. Entry and R&D in procurement contracting. Mimeo, University of British Columbia.

Vickrey, U. 1961. Counterspeculation, auctions, and competitive sealed tenders. *Journal of Finance* 16:8–37.

Waterson, M. 1988. *Regulation of the Firm and Natural Monopoly.* Oxford: Blackwell.

Williamson, O. 1976. Franchise bidding for natural monopolies—in general and with respect to CATV. *Bell Journal of Economics* 7:73–104.

8 REPEATED AUCTIONS OF INCENTIVE CONTRACTS, INVESTMENT, AND BIDDING PARITY

8.1 Some Background

The regulation of a natural monopoly is often a repeated game. If the regulated monopoly's performance is not adequate, it may be in the regulator's interest to look for another firm (or team of managers) to replace the incumbent. Second sourcing indeed occurs in the reprocurement of defense contracts, in the repeated bidding for franchises, and in private contracting. Should auctions be set up that sequentially select the regulated firm? Should such auctions be concerned with bidding parity between the incumbent and the entrants? What is the incumbent firm's incentive to invest in physical capital? In human capital? The determination of the optimal breakout policy and its interaction with incentive schemes are the topics of this chapter.

The "Chicago approach" to regulating a natural monopoly (Demsetz 1968; Stigler 1968; Posner 1972) suggests that a monopoly franchise should be awarded to the firm that offers to supply the product on the best terms. Franchise bidding can also be repeated over time to adjust for new, noncontracted-for circumstances or to encourage entry of another, more efficient, firm. It allows the regulator to select the most efficient supplier at any point in time. Williamson (1976), responding to this approach, has forcefully made the following points:

1. Physical capital, and even human capital, are not always easily transferable from firm to firm. Hence symmetry between the firms is unusual at the franchise renewal stage. The incumbent firm enjoys an advantage over its competitors.
2. Even when the incumbent's capital is transferable, the corresponding investment is hard to measure. This is clearly true for nonmonetary investments; for instance, the quality of past investment choices admits no monetary measure. Furthermore accounting manipulations garble the measurement of monetary investments. For instance, the incumbent firm could integrate into supply, arrange kickbacks from the equipment suppliers, or adjust depreciation charges. The prospect of being replaced by an entrant would lower the incumbent's incentive to invest in capital that it would not be able to transfer at the right price.

These two points form the building blocks of our model. We assume that part of the incumbent's investment is transferable (general) and that part is nontransferable (specific)—point 1. Furthermore we assume that the regulator can observe the regulated firm's cost or profit but is unable to recover the precise amount of investment from aggregate accounting data—point 2.

Our model has two periods. In the first the regulator offers an incentive contract to a single firm (the incumbent, the first source). The incumbent's cost, which is the only variable observed by the regulator, is a function of the firm's intrinsic productivity or efficiency, the firm's first-period "effort," and a monetary investment. By a simple relabeling of variables, the model also allows for a nonmonetary investment. The firm knows its productivity and chooses both effort and investment. In the second period (reprocurement stage) the regulator can keep the incumbent or invite another firm (the entrant, the second source) to replace the incumbent. The entrant's intrinsic productivity is known to the entrant only and can be higher or lower than the incumbent's. The second-period cost of the selected firm depends on its efficiency, its second-period effort, and the first-period investment (the entire investment for the incumbent but only the transferable part for the entrant). We assume that the incumbent's and the entrant's efficiency parameters are drawn from a common distribution; any ex ante intrinsic discrepancy in second-period efficiency is attributable only to nontransferable investment.

We focus on the interaction between the breakout rule and the intertemporal evolution of the slope of the incumbent's incentive scheme. (Optimal incentive schemes turn out to be linear in cost.) We say that *bidding parity* obtains when the regulator selects the entrant if and only if the entrant's *second-period* efficiency exceeds the incumbent's; these efficiencies include the effect of the first-period investment. The regulator favors the incumbent when the entrant is selected only if it is sufficiently more efficient than the incumbent, and vice versa. The Chicago school recommendation alluded to above is tantamount to advocating bidding parity.

In the case of a *transferable* investment, any cost savings from the investment become savings for the second source if the first source is replaced. Since the investment is not observable[1] and so cannot be compensated directly, the incumbent has too little incentive to invest; with some positive probability the fruits of this costly investment will accrue to the second source. The regulator optimally uses both the breakout rule at the reprocurement stage and the intertemporal evolution of the incumbent firm's incentive scheme to increase its incentive to invest. The regulator favors the incumbent at the reprocurement stage. To see why this is optimal, note that a small departure from bidding parity implies only a negligible loss in ex post productive efficiency and increases investment if the incumbent is favored. Second, the regulator provides for time-increasing incentives. The incumbent firm bears a small fraction of its first-period cost and therefore perceives investment as cheap. In contrast, it bears a high fraction of its second-period cost (if its contract is renewed), which ex ante gives it much incentive to invest.

The policy recommendations are quite different in the case of a *non-*

1. Alternatively, we could assume that the investment is not verifiable. The important point is that investment should be noncontractible.

transferable investment. In this case the incumbent fully internalizes the realized social value of its cost savings, so the previous externality does not exist. There is, however, a new effect: The incumbent has "on average" a cost advantage at the reprocurement stage. Our result, reminiscent of the theory of auctions with asymmetric bidders, is that if the distribution of potential efficiencies satisfies the classic monotone-hazard-rate property, the auction should be biased in favor of the higher-cost firm—the entrant. But the slope of the incumbent's incentive scheme should be, as in section 1.10, time invariant because the absence of externality creates no special need for investment incentives.

In section 8.2 we set up the model, and in section 8.3 we solve for the optimal breakout rule and incentive schemes. Next we study a variant of the model in which the first-period effort to reduce first-period cost also reduces the second-period cost. This "learning-by-doing" investment does not increase the first-period cost, in contrast with the basic model. It leads the regulator to favor the incumbent at the reprocurement stage: An increase in the probability of being selected in the second period encourages the incumbent to learn by doing in the first period and thus to reduce first-period costs, which are partly borne by the regulator (section 8.4). Section 8.5 summarizes the results obtained thus far and assesses their relevance. In section 8.6 we focus on transferable investment and obtain a rich set of policy recommendations and testable implications. We also show how the optimal regulatory policy can be implemented through the setup of a second-period auction combined with a simple incentive package composed of "performance related incentives" (cost-reimbursement rules) and "switching incentives" (cancellation fee or entry fee).

8.2 The Model

We consider a two-period natural monopoly model. Each period a project valued S by consumers must be realized by a single firm, but the identity of the firm can change over time. In period 1 there is a single firm, the incumbent, with cost function:

$$C_1 = \beta - e_1 + d(i). \tag{8.1}$$

Here $\beta \in [\underline{\beta}, \bar{\beta}]$ is the incumbent's intrinsic cost parameter, e_1 is the level of effort exerted by the firm's manager, and $d(i)(d' > 0, d'' > 0)$ is the cost of a first-period (monetary) investment that lowers the incumbent's second-period cost by i. The disutility of effort for the incumbent is $\psi(e_1)$ with $\psi' > 0$, $\psi'' > 0$, $\psi''' \geq 0$. Note that there is no bidding in period 1. The interpretation is that other potential firms are very inefficient in period 1. One could generalize our model to situations in which other firms compete unsuccessfully with the "incumbent" in period 1, and some of them possibly improve their technology or phase out previous commitments and become more competitive in the second period.

The incumbent's second-period cost function is

$$C_2 = \beta - e_2 - i. \tag{8.2}$$

where β is the same parameter as in period 1 and e_2 is the effort exerted in period 2, at disutility $\psi(e_2)$.

The investment $d(i)$ in period 1 also lowers the entrant's (second-period) cost by ki, where $k \in [0, 1]$. If $k = 0$, the investment is nontransferable (or specific). If $k = 1$, the investment is transferable (or general). More generally we allow the investment to be partly transferable and partly specific. Hence the (potential) entrant has in period 2 a cost function

$$C' = \beta' - e' - ki, \tag{8.3}$$

where $\beta' \in [\underline{\beta}, \overline{\beta}]$ is the entrant's intrinsic cost parameter, which is learned at the beginning of period 2, and e' is its level of effort. The entrant has the same function of disutility of effort as the incumbent. All costs are accounting costs, which are commonly observed. The parameters β and β' are independently drawn from the same distribution with cumulative distribution function $F(\beta)$ and density function $f(\beta)$ continuous and positive on $[\underline{\beta}, \overline{\beta}]$ with $d[F(\beta)/f(\beta)]/d\beta \geq 0$.

Remark on nonmonetary investments In the introduction we claimed that our model depicts both monetary and nonmonetary investments. The formulation above assumes a monetary investment, since $d(i)$ increases the first-period cost. To substantiate our claim, suppose that there is no monetary investment. The first-period cost is then

$$C_1 = \beta - \tilde{e},$$

where $\tilde{e}$ is the effort expended to reduce the first-period cost. The incumbent's managers exert a second type of effort that reduces the incumbent's second-period cost by $\tilde{\tilde{e}}$ and the entrant's cost by $k\tilde{\tilde{e}}$. The first-period effort to obtain this cost reduction is $d(\tilde{\tilde{e}})$, so the total first-period disutility of effort is $\psi(\tilde{e} + d(\tilde{\tilde{e}}))$. One could think of $d(\tilde{\tilde{e}})$ as the number of hours spent in the first period on finding the right technology for the second period. A simple change in variables shows that this model is formally equivalent to the monetary investment model set up above: Let $e_1 \equiv \tilde{e} + d(\tilde{\tilde{e}})$ denote the total first-period effort and $i \equiv \tilde{\tilde{e}}$. Then the first-period cost can be written

$$C_1 = \beta - [e_1 - d(\tilde{\tilde{e}})] = \beta - e_1 + d(i).$$

The regulator's problem is to organize production and transfers so as to maximize social welfare. The incumbent's expected utility level is

$$U = t - \psi(e_1) - \delta\pi\psi(e_2), \tag{8.4}$$

where δ is the discount factor, π is the probability that the incumbent will remain active in period 2, and $t \equiv t_1 + \delta t_2$ is the net expected (present discounted) transfer received by the firm from the regulator. The firm receives t in addition to the payment of realized costs by the regulator. We will assume that the regulator has the ability to commit to two-period regulatory schemes.[2] To obtain the incumbent's participation, the regulator must ensure that[3]

$$U \geq 0 \tag{8.5}$$

where the individual rationality (IR) level has been normalized to zero.

The entrant's utility level, if the entrant is active in period 2, is

$$V = t' - \psi(e'), \tag{8.6}$$

where t' is the (expected) net transfer received from the regulator. The entrant's IR constraint is

$$V \geq 0. \tag{8.7}$$

A utilitarian regulator wishes to maximize the sum of expected utilities of consumers and firms. *Under complete information* his or her instruments are the levels of investment, efforts, transfers, and the breakout rule (i.e., the choice of who is active in period 2). Complete information implies that the (potential) entrant should be allowed to enter if and only if $\beta' < \beta^*(\beta, i) = \beta - (1 - k)i$.

Letting λ denote the shadow cost of public funds, the consumers' expected utility level is

$$S - (1 + \lambda)(C_1 + t_1) + \delta(1 - F(\beta^*(\beta, i)))[S - (1 + \lambda)(C_2 + t_2)]$$
$$+ \delta \int_{\underline{\beta}}^{\beta^*(\beta, i)} [S - (1 + \lambda)(C'(\beta') + t'(\beta'))]f(\beta')d\beta', \tag{8.8}$$

where we assume that consumers have the same discount factor as the incumbent. Since $\lambda > 0$, the individual rationality constraints (8.5) and (8.7) are binding in the regulator's optimization program. The regulator's program thus reduces to

$$\max_{\{e_1, e_2, e', i\}} \Big\{ S(1 + \delta) - (1 + \lambda)[\beta - e_1 + d(i) + \psi(e_1)]$$
$$- \delta(1 - F(\beta - (1 - k)i))(1 + \lambda)[\beta - e_2 - i + \psi(e_2)]$$
$$- \delta(1 + \lambda) \int_{\underline{\beta}}^{\beta - (1-k)i} [\beta' - e' - ki + \psi(e')]f(\beta')d\beta' \Big\}, \tag{8.9}$$

2. See chapters 9 and 10 for analyses of procurement with short-term contracts and long-term commitment and renegotiation, respectively.

3. Because of our assumption about two-period commitment, we need to consider only an intertemporal individual rationality constraint.

where e_1, e_2, and i are functions of β, and e' is a function of β'. This is a quasi-concave problem[4] with first-order conditions

$$\psi'(e_1) = \psi'(e_2) = \psi'(e') = 1, \tag{8.10}$$

$$d'(i) = \delta[(1 - F(\beta - (1 - k)i)) + kF(\beta - (1 - k)i)]. \tag{8.11}$$

Equation (8.11) tells us that investment should be set at the level that equates its marginal cost $d'(i)$ with its expected social marginal utility, which is δ if the investment is transferable ($k = 1$) but only $\delta(1 - F(\beta - i))$ if it is not ($k = 0$). The *positive externality* of the first-period investment on the entrant's cost must be internalized when it exists. Equation (8.10) indicates that the marginal disutility of each type of effort must be equated to its marginal benefit. In the next section we solve the regulator's optimization problem under incomplete information.

8.3 Optimal Regulation under Asymmetric Information

Suppose that the regulator observes costs but does not know the parameters β and β' (even though he or she knows their distribution) and cannot observe effort levels. We also assume that the investment is unobservable by the regulator. (The case of observable investment will be treated as a special case).

The regulator's instruments are now cost-reimbursement rules as well as a breakout rule. This regulatory procedure can be viewed as a revelation mechanism for the incumbent composed of a contract $(C_1(\beta), C_2(\beta), t(\beta))$ and a breakout rule $\beta^*(\beta)$ and as a revelation mechanism for the entrant $(C'(\beta'|\beta), t'(\beta'|\beta))$. In this section we use the abstract framework provided by the revelation principle to characterize the optimal allocation (efforts, investment, breakout rule). In section 8.6 we show how this optimal allocation can be implemented through familiar mechanisms like linear cost-reimbursement rules, auctions, and cancellation fees, and we develop some further empirical implications of the optimal regulatory scheme.

Digression on the Methodology The reader might be concerned that our interpretation of the revelation principle is too restrictive. We now make two methodological comments that ought to be skipped by those mainly interested in regulation (a third methodological comment is in remark 2 below). First, the revelation principle more generally would imply that the incumbent's contract should depend on both announcements of β and β'. Since the incumbent does not know β', and since the two types are uncorrelated, making C_1, C_2 or t contingent on β' amounts to using β' as a

4. For $k = 1$, the problem is always quasi-concave. For $k \neq 1$, a sufficient condition for quasi-concavity is that the marginal cost of the investment is high enough (see Laffont and Tirole 1988).

randomizing device in the incumbent's scheme. By a reasoning familiar from chapters 1 and 7, randomized schemes do not improve on deterministic ones, and therefore there is no loss of generality in assuming that the incumbent's contract is independent of β'. The reader might also wonder whether our "cutoff formulation" of the breakout rule is not restrictive. It is easy to show that it is not: The incumbent's incentive compatibility and individual rationality constraints depend only on the probability of breakout and not on the type of the entrant in case of breakout. For a given probability of breakout, it is optimal for the regulator to break out only in favor of the most efficient types of the entrant.

Second, we should also make a methodological point concerning the amount of information received by the entrant about the incumbent's productivity. The revelation principle tells us that without loss of generality the principal can ask the incumbent to (truthfully) announce its type: $\tilde{\beta} = \beta$. Should $\tilde{\beta}$ be revealed to the entrant? Note that even if it is not, the incumbent's first-period cost still reveals information about the incumbent's productivity. Is it worth distorting the first-period allocation to garble the entrant's information about β? For instance, if the optimal first-period regulation implies that C_1 perfectly reveals β (as will be the case here), would one want to induce some first-period pooling so that the entrant would possess less information about β than the principal and possibly would bid more aggressively? Fortunately the answer is no. Maskin and Tirole (1990), in their study of contracts designed by an informed principal (here the regulator), show that if preferences are quasi-linear (as is the case in this chapter), the design of the optimal contract for the entrant is independent of how much the agent (here the entrant) knows about the principal's information.[5] Hence there is no point hiding the announcement $\tilde{\beta}$ from the entrant or distorting the first-period allocation.[6]

5. The relevance of the informed principal framework for this situation can be seen as follows: Myerson's (1982) generalized revelation principle implies that without loss of generality the regulator can ask in period 1 the incumbent for its true type, and that the regulator can send a message to the entrant which, together with the date 1 observable (the realized cost), will form the entrant's information at the beginning of date 2. One can describe this situation as one in which a regulator informed about the incumbent's type builds a mechanism for the entrant. The one, irrelevant, difference with the Maskin-Tirole framework is that here the regulator can commit to a mechanism (that is contingent on the incumbent's type) before knowing this information.

6. It should be noted that when one of the parties' preferences is not quasi-linear, an informed principal (regulator) strictly gains by not revealing his or her information to the agent (entrant) at or before the contract proposal stage. That is, by pooling at the contract proposal stage, the different types of principal (a misnomer that refers here to the possible values of β) can trade the slack variables corresponding to the agent's individual rationality and incentive compatibility constraints. This may introduce a tension between first-period efficiency and optimal regulation of the entrant. Also the Maskin-Tirole result applies as long as the principal's information does not enter the agent's utility function; in particular the agent's information can enter the principal's objective function, as is the case here.

Let $U(\beta)$ be the rent extracted by an incumbent of type β. The incumbent's incentive compatibility and individual rationality constraints can be written

$$\dot{U}(\beta) = -\psi'(\beta - C_1(\beta) + d(i)) - \delta(1 - F(\beta^*(\beta)))\psi'(\beta - C_2(\beta) - i), \tag{8.12}$$

$$U(\bar{\beta}) = 0, \tag{8.13}$$

with sufficient second-order conditions[7]

$$\frac{dC_1}{d\beta} \geq 0, \quad \frac{dC_2}{d\beta} \geq 0, \quad \frac{d\beta^*}{d\beta} \geq 0. \tag{8.14}$$

Equation (8.12) results from the fact that when the incumbent's intrinsic cost parameter is reduced by 1, the incumbent can reduce its effort by 1 in each period and obtain the same transfers. Its rent is thus increased by $[\psi'(e_1) + \delta\pi\psi'(e_2)]$, where $\pi = (1 - F(\beta^*(\beta)))$ is the probability of no breakout. Equation (8.13) states that the least efficient type gets no rent at the optimum.

Moreover, since investment is nonobservable, we must consider the (moral hazard) constraint[8] describing the incumbent's choice of investment:

$$d'(i)\psi'(\beta - C_1(\beta) + d(i)) - \delta(1 - F(\beta^*(\beta)))\psi'(\beta - i - C_2(\beta)) = 0. \tag{8.15}$$

Suppose that the firm contemplates a unit increase in investment. The extra investment cost is $d'(i)$. To keep the first-period cost (and thus reward) constant, effort must be increased by the same amount, thereby engendering additional disutility $\psi'(e_1)d'(i)$. In turn the second-period effort can be reduced by 1, saving disutility $\psi'(e_2)$, with probability $1 - F(\beta^*(\beta))$. At the optimum the firm cannot gain by increasing or decreasing its investment slightly, and therefore equation (8.15) must hold.

Similarly let $V(\beta'|\beta)$ be the rent extracted by an entrant of cost characteristic β' when the incumbent's type is β. The entrant's incentive and individual rationality constraints can be written[9]

$$\frac{\partial V(\beta'|\beta)}{\partial \beta'} = -\psi'(\beta' - ki - C'(\beta'|\beta)), \tag{8.16}$$

$$V(\beta^*(\beta)|\beta) = 0, \tag{8.17}$$

with the second-order condition $dC'/d\beta' \geq 0$. Integrating (8.16) with (8.17) as a boundary condition yields, for $\beta' \leq \beta^*(\beta)$,

7. See chapter 3.

8. If the marginal cost of investment is high enough, the first-order approach we take in this moral hazard problem is valid.

9. The incentive constraint (8.16) is valid for parameters where the entrant is selected, that is, for $\beta' < \beta^*(\beta)$. For $\beta' > \beta^*(\beta)$, we have $\partial V/\partial \beta' = 0$.

$$V(\beta'|\beta) = \int_{\beta'}^{\beta^*(\beta)} \psi'(\tilde{\beta} - ki - C'(\tilde{\beta}|\beta))d\tilde{\beta}. \tag{8.18}$$

Using U and V as state variables, and C_1, C_2, C', and i as control variables, the regulator's maximization problem can be written as the following optimal control problem:

$$\max \int_{\underline{\beta}}^{\bar{\beta}} \Big\{ S(1 + \delta) - (1 + \lambda)[C_1(\beta) + \psi(\beta - C_1(\beta) + d(i(\beta)))] - \lambda U(\beta)$$
$$- \delta(1 - F(\beta^*(\beta))(1 + \lambda)[C_2(\beta) + \psi(\beta - i(\beta) - C_2(\beta))]$$
$$- \delta \int_{\underline{\beta}}^{\beta^*(\beta)} [(1 + \lambda)(C'(\beta'|\beta) + \psi(\beta' - ki(\beta) - C'(\beta'|\beta))$$
$$+ \lambda V(\beta'|\beta)]f(\beta')d\beta' \Big\} f(\beta)d\beta \tag{8.19}$$

subject to (8.12), (8.13), (8.15), (8.16), and (8.17). In this formulation the regulator's objective function has been rewritten to separate the "efficiency" costs of the form $(1 + \lambda)(C + \psi)$ and the "distributional" costs λU and λV.

Remark 1 Since some second-order conditions are only sufficient, we do not impose them but rather check later that they are satisfied by our solution.

Remark 2 We do not allow the incumbent's contract to depend on the entrant's realized cost C' following a breakout. In the case of nontransferable investment, this does not involve any loss of generality because C' does not contain any information about i. It does involve a loss of generality, however, for transferable investments (an artifact of the risk neutrality framework is that such a dependence would enable the second best level of investment to be achieved with sufficiently large penalties[10]). Excluding such a dependence of t on C' is a good approximation to reality for several reasons. First, this dependence would create a delayed transfer or penalty. The displaced incumbent would be required, for instance, to pay a penalty five or ten years after the breakout, and this raises the issue of the feasibility of such long-run contracts; in contrast, our transfers can follow production immediately. Second, and perhaps more important, the entrant's

10. Take, for instance, the case in which the entrant does not observe i before announcing β' and choosing e'. Let the regulator ask the incumbent to invest some i^*. If the entrant's realized cost C' differs from $\beta' - e'(\beta') - ki^*$, the regulator imposes an infinite penalty on the incumbent. An arbitrarily small probability of second sourcing then suffices to deter the incumbent from deviating from i^*. (More precisely there exists an equilibrium in which the entrant correctly anticipates i^* and the incumbent chooses i^*.) If the entrant's cost is random, then the techniques mentioned in bibliographic notes B1.3 of chapter 1 can be used to show that perfect control of investment again is no problem.

cost might be subject to manipulation. Indeed ex post the entrant and the regulator have an incentive to tinker with accounting data on C' so as to force the incumbent to pay a penalty. Hence letting the incumbent's reward depend on the entrant's cost may not be feasible after all. Third, in the presence of cost uncertainty and risk aversion (or, alternatively, limited penalties), the incumbent would not bear a large fraction of its successor's realized cost. To summarize, although some dependence of the incumbent's reward on post-termination performance may be feasible in some instances, it is at most a limited instrument, which leaves ample scope for the policies described in this chapter.[11]

Solving the problem in (8.19), we obtain proposition 8.1.

Proposition 8.1 With transferable and unobservable investment, the optimal breakout rule favors the incumbent ($\beta^*(\beta) < \beta$) except at $\beta = \underline{\beta}$, where bidding parity obtains: $\beta^*(\underline{\beta}) = \underline{\beta}$. Bidding parity ($\beta^*(\beta) = \beta$) holds when the investment is transferable and observable.

Proof See appendix A8.1.

The intuition behind this result is straightforward. When investment is transferable and observable, the regulator can directly force the incumbent to internalize the positive externality on the entrant's cost by imposing the right level of investment. Since the firms' efficiencies are drawn from the same distributions, bidding parity should hold. Incentive questions remain separate from the breakout rule. If investment is not observable, there is underinvestment because the incumbent has no reason to internalize the externality. The regulator can then mitigate this inefficiency by raising the probability that the incumbent remains active in period 2. This is achieved by favoring the incumbent in the breakout rule. An incumbent of type $\underline{\beta}$ has a zero probability of being replaced. It thus invests the socially optimal amount, and the selection rule need not be biased to encourage investment.

The next result is that the regulator alters the incentive schemes as well as the breakout rule to remedy this externality problem. This is best explained by replacing the nonlinear transfer functions $t(C)$ by linear contracts as in chapter 1. The transfers can then be written (see proof of proposition 8.2)

$$t(C_1^a, C_1) = a_1(C_1^a) - b_1(C_1^a)(C_1 - C_1^a)$$

for the incumbent in period 1,

$$t_2(C_2^a, C_2, C_1^a) = a_2(C_2^a, C_1^a) - b_2(C_2^a)(C_2 - C_2^a)$$

for the incumbent in period 2 (in the case of no breakout), and

11. Note also that common auctions for contract renewal belong to the class of mechanisms considered here.

$$t'(C'^a, C', C_1^a) = a'(C'^a, C_1^a) - b'(C'^a)(C' - C'^a)$$

for the entrant in period 2 (in the case of breakout); t_1, t_2, and t' are the net transfers (after cost reimbursement); a_1, a_2, and a' are the fixed components of the transfers; b_1, b_2, and b' are the slopes of the incentive schemes with respect to the realized costs; the superscripts a refer to announced values of costs. As in chapter 1 the implementation of the optimal contract by a menu of linear schemes is particularly valuable when the cost functions include random terms: The linear schemes are still optimal for any distributions of the cost uncertainties.

The interesting questions refer to the slopes of the incentive schemes. We obtain proposition 8.2.

Proposition 8.2 With unobservable and at least partly transferable investment ($k > 0$), the incumbent's first-period incentive scheme is "low-powered" relative to the second-period one ($b_1 < b_2$). Because the slope with observable investment is time invariant and lies between b_1 and b_2, unobservability calls for a flatter incentive scheme in the first period and a steeper incentive scheme in the second period than does the observable-investment scheme.

Proof See appendix A8.2.

The intuition is that a contract resembling more a cost-plus contract in the first period lowers the incumbent's perceived investment cost, while a contract closer to a fixed-price contract in the second period allows the incumbent to capture the proceeds of the investment. The results are quite different when investment is specific.

Proposition 8.3

i. With unobservable nontransferable investment, the optimal breakout rule favors the entrant ($\beta^*(\beta) > \beta - i$).

ii. The unobservability of nontransferable investment imposes no cost on the regulator.

Proof See appendix A8.3.

Part ii of proposition 8.3 is not surprising. A classical result is that the slope of the incumbent's incentive scheme must be time invariant if investment is observable (see section 1.10). Since there is no externality between the incumbent and the entrant when investment is nontransferable, and since the incumbent's and the regulator's intertemporal preferences coincide (due to the constant slope and identical discount factors), the incumbent correctly selects the socially optimal investment; that is, unobservability of investment imposes no social loss.

Part i of proposition 8.3 is more subtle and relies on the monotone-hazard-rate assumption. To understand it, recall the static, single-firm regulatory problem. Let β be drawn from a cumulative distribution function $F(\cdot)$, with density $f(\cdot)$ on $[\underline{\beta}, \overline{\beta}]$. When choosing an incentive scheme for the firm, the regulator must trade off efficiency (which would call for a fixed-price contract) and minimization of the firm's informational rent (which would call for a cost-plus contract). This trade-off yields a distortion in the effort allocation for all $\beta > \underline{\beta}$. By reducing the distortion in effort for parameter β, the regulator realizes a gain proportional to $f(\beta)$. At the same time it must give a higher rent to all types of firms that are more efficient than β, in proportion $F(\beta)$, because the latter can always mimic the behavior of a less efficient firm. At the optimum the marginal gain in efficiency must equal the marginal cost associated with the firm's expected rent. Now consider our two-period model. Suppose that the incumbent's and the entrant's productivity parameters β and β' are independently drawn from the same distribution $F(\cdot)$; that is, any observable discrepancy in intrinsic efficiency is attributable to the incumbency advantage. Suppose that in the second period the regulator does not favor the incumbent or the entrant, and consider parameters β and β' such that the two firms have the same second-period intrinsic efficiency. In the presence of specific investment, the "cutoff point" is $\beta' = \beta^*(\beta) = \beta - i < \beta$. Thus, if we make the classic assumption that the inverse hazard rate F/f is an increasing function, we have $F(\beta^*)/f(\beta^*) < F(\beta)/f(\beta)$. This means that at equal second-period intrinsic efficiency, the optimal regulation of the entrant calls for less distortion of effort than does regulation of the incumbent. Another way of phrasing this intuition begins by noticing that the selection of a firm amounts to an upward truncation of the distribution of its productivity parameter. Thus, at equal second-period intrinsic efficiency, the regulator is less uncertain about the entrant's productivity than about the incumbent's and therefore can regulate the entrant more efficiently. Specific investments thus call for favoring the entrant at the reprocurement stage. We call this effect the *rent differential effect*.

Two final observations conclude this section. First, despite the incentives to invest described in propositions 8.1 and 8.2, it is still the case that the incumbent *underinvests relative to the social optimum.*[12] Second, a reasonable conjecture is that the bias in the breakout rule $(\beta - i) - (\beta^*(\beta) - ki)$ is an increasing function of k. We have proved this result only in the case of observable investment and k in a neighborhood of 1. We suspect the property holds more generally.

8.4 Learning by Doing

An interesting variant of our model allows learning by doing rather than investment to reduce the second-period cost. We now assume that the

12. Apply the lemma in appendix A8.1 to equation (A8.10).

incumbent's effort in period 1, e_1, affects costs in period 2 so that

$$C_2 = \beta - e_2 - (g + h)e_1 \tag{8.20}$$

and

$$C' = \beta' - e' - ge_1, \tag{8.21}$$

where g, $h \geq 0$. That is, the fraction $\tilde{k} \equiv g/(g + h)$ of such learning is transferable to the entrant. The first-period cost of the incumbent is $C_1 = \beta - e_1$. The effort exerted by the incumbent firm generates tricks or technologies that reduce its first-period production cost and that can still be used in period 2.

Under complete information the breakout rule is $\beta^*(\beta) = \beta - he_1$. The optimal effort levels would be determined by the program

$$\max_{\{e_1, e_2, e'\}} \Bigg\{ S(1 + \delta) - (1 + \lambda)[\beta - e_1 + \psi(e_1)] - \delta(1 - F(\beta - he_1))(1 + \lambda)[\beta - e_2 - (g + h)e_1 + \psi(e_2)] - \delta(1 + \lambda) \int_{\underline{\beta}}^{\beta - he_1} [\beta' - e' - ge_1 + \psi(e')]f(\beta')d\beta' \Bigg\}. \tag{8.22}$$

The first-order conditions are[13]

$$\psi'(e_1) = 1 + \delta g + \delta h(1 - F(\beta - he_1)), \tag{8.23}$$

$$\psi'(e_2) = 1, \tag{8.24}$$

$$\psi'(e') = 1. \tag{8.25}$$

In particular equation (8.23) equates the marginal disutility of effort to its total marginal social benefit, which is the first-period benefit, 1, plus the transferable effect on the second period, δg, plus the expected specific effect, $\delta h(1 - F(\beta - he_1))$.

Under incomplete information we must add the incentive constraint in the regulator's optimization program. Intuitively type $\beta - d\beta$ can obtain the same cost as type β by exerting $de_1 = d\beta$ less in terms of effort. The difference in efficiency between the two types in period 2 is then only $d\beta - de_1(h + g) = d\beta(1 - h - g)$. Therefore

$$\dot{U}(\beta) = -\psi'(e_1(\beta)) - \delta(1 - g - h)[1 - F(\beta^*(\beta))]\psi'(e_2(\beta)).$$

Following the same lines of argument as in section 8.3 we obtain proposition 8.4.

Proposition 8.4 With unobservable and fully transferable learning by doing ($h = 0$), the breakout rule favors the incumbent ($\beta^*(\beta) < \beta$).

13. These conditions are sufficient for $h^2\delta$ small.

Proof See appendix A8.4.

There are now two effects favoring the incumbent: the externality effect of proposition 8.1 and the *learning-by-doing effect.* Recall that the incumbent's informational rent comes from the possibility of mimicking a less efficient type's cost by exerting less effort. Under learning by doing, a reduction in the first-period effort reduces the second-period efficiency and rent, and this all the more that the probability of keeping the franchise is high. Hence, by increasing the probability of choosing the incumbent in the second period, the regulator makes it more costly for the incumbent to hide its efficiency in the first period. This effect, which does not exist for monetary investment, calls for favoring the incumbent.

When learning is partly specific, the relevant comparison for $\beta^*(\beta)$ is with $\beta - he_1$. Now at $\beta^*(\beta) = \beta - he_1$ the rent obtained by the incumbent is higher at the parity point, and this calls for favoring the entrant as in proposition 8.3. It can be shown that either effect can dominate.[14] In particular, when the learning is purely specific ($g = 0$), we have two opposite incentive effects, the learning-by-doing effect and the rent differential effect.

A striking feature of the analysis in section 8.3 is that the slope of the incumbent's incentive scheme must be increasing in time to encourage it to invest. In contrast, when investment is embodied in the first-period effort, we have two opposite effects. Considering for simplicity the case $\psi'' =$ constant, we obtain

$$b_1(\beta) - b_2(\beta) = \delta g F(\beta^*(\beta)) - \frac{\lambda F(\beta)}{(1 + \lambda) f(\beta)} \times [1 - (1 - (g + h))(1 + \delta(g + h)(1 - F))].$$

First, we note that for the most efficient type ($\beta = \underline{\beta}$), $b_1 = b_2 = 1$. Second, for $g > 0$, there is an *externality effect*, $\delta g F(\beta^*(\beta))$. To encourage the internalization of this external effect, incentives for effort in period 1 are increased ($b_1 > b_2$). This is the dominating effect if λ is small.

There is also a *rent extraction effect*

$$-\frac{\lambda F(\beta)}{(1 + \lambda) f(\beta)} [1 - (1 - g - h)(1 + \delta(g + h)(1 - F))],$$

which is always negative, since $1 - (1 - g - h)[1 + \delta(g + h)(1 - F)]$ is always positive. Raising b_2 raises the marginal benefit of e_1 and makes it more costly to conceal efficiency in period 1. This rent extraction effect dominates when the externality effect is negligible ($g \approx 0$). We gather these remarks in the next proposition.

14. See Laffont and Tirole (1988).

Proposition 8.5 With unobservable learning by doing, in the quadratic case the first-period incentive scheme is steeper (resp. less steep) than the second-period one if λ is small enough and learning by doing is transferable (resp. if learning by doing is essentially nontransferable).

8.5 Assessment of the Model

Table 8.1 summarizes the analysis of the optimal allocation. The previous analysis aimed at generality and allowed many technological patterns. Before proceeding, it is worth assessing the relevance of the various effects leading the regulator to bias the bidding process. It should be clear that our focus is on sizable, nonobservable investment. When investments matter, breakouts are most likely to be observed (and to be socially desirable) when the entrant is not at too much of a cost disadvantage (i.e., when it benefits from the incumbent's investment). But the incumbent should be favored at the reprocurement stage, however, precisely when investment is transferable. That a second source may not be of much use when investment is transferable leads us to a somewhat pessimistic assessment of how much regulators can hope to gain by using second sourcing in a natural monopoly situation involving substantial investments. Although substantial intrinsic cost differences between the firms may justify breakouts, our recommendations are more likely to apply to industries with transferable investments. In the rest of the chapter, we focus on such industries. Section

Table 8.1
Characteristics of the optimal allocation

Nature of investment	Breakout rule	Time invariance of slope of incentive schemes
Transferable		
Observable	Bidding parity	Yes
Unobservable monetary or nonmonetary	Incumbent favored (externality effect)	No ($b_1 < b_2$)
Learning by doing	Incumbent favored (externality effect + learning effect)	No
Nontransferable		
Observable, or unobservable monetary or nonmonetary	Entrant favored (rent differential effect)	Yes
Learning by doing	Ambiguous (two opposite effects: learning and rent differential)	No

8.6 derives some further recommendations and testable implications of our model.[15]

8.6 Transferable Investment

We now specialize the model of section 8.3 to transferable investment, a quadratic disutility of effort, and a uniform distribution of cost parameters:

Assumption 8.1

i. $k = 1$.

ii. $\psi(e) = e^2/2$.

iii. $F(\cdot)$ is uniform on $[0, 1]$.

iv. $1 > \lambda$.

Part iv of assumption 8.1 is technical and is consistent with the second-order conditions, which require that λ not be too large. We can now state proposition 8.6.

Proposition 8.6 Under assumption 8.1

i. the bias in favor of the incumbent is higher, the less efficient the incumbent is; that is,

$$\frac{d}{d\beta}[\beta - \beta^*(\beta)] > 0,$$

ii. the incumbent exerts more effort in the second period than the type of entrant that makes entry socially indifferent; that is,

$$e_2(\beta) > e'(\beta^*(\beta)).$$

Proof See appendix A8.5.

Part i of proposition 8.6 conveys an important intuition. An inefficient incumbent is replaced with high probability and therefore invests little. The bidding process must then be biased considerably so as to encourage it to invest. Part ii compares $e_2(\beta)$ and $e'(\beta^*(\beta))$. We knew that $e_2(\beta) > e'(\beta)$. There is a second effect, however, coming from the fact that $\beta^*(\beta) < \beta$ and that e' is decreasing. The two effects work in opposite directions, but the first dominates.

We saw in section 8.3 that transferable investments call for special incentives to invest: bias in the breakout rule and time-increasing incentives.

15. In the bibliographic notes we point out that our results apply to takeovers where, we would argue, most of the firm's assets are transferable to a second source, that is, to a raider.

An inefficient incumbent exerts a particularly high externality because of a high probability of breakout. Proposition 8.6 showed that the breakout rule is more distorted for inefficient incumbents. Proposition 8.7 is its counterpart for the distortion in the slopes of the incentive scheme. An inefficient incumbent should face incentives that rise sharply over time.

Proposition 8.7 Under assumption 8.1, if λ is "not too large," then

$$\frac{d}{d\beta}[b_2(\beta) - b_1(\beta)] > 0.$$

Proof The proof is straightforward.

To derive the optimal regulation, we assumed that the incumbent reports β once and for all in period 1. But the optimal allocation can also be implemented by, first, regulating the incumbent in period 1 and, second, organizing an auction between the two firms in period 2. Proposition 8.6 enables us to obtain some interesting results on the second-period bidding process. As in chapter 7 we can view this bidding process as a first- or second-bid auction in which each bidder (here, each firm) bids for the right to choose from a menu of monopoly linear incentive contracts. Unlike in chapter 7 the menus of contracts differ between the two competitors because of the asymmetry of the problem. Let $U_2(\beta)$ denote the incumbent's second-period rent associated with the right to choose from its menu of contracts. Similarly let $U'(\beta')$ denote the entrant's second-period rent. From incentive compatibility we know that

$$\frac{dU_2}{d\beta} = -\psi'(e_2(\beta))$$

and that

$$\frac{dU'}{d\beta'} = -\psi'(e'(\beta')).$$

The rents $U_2(\cdot)$ and $U'(\cdot)$ are defined up to positive constants. Although we will be mainly interested in their derivatives, we normalize these functions by imposing second-period individual rationality constraints

$$U_2(\bar{\beta}) = 0$$

and

$$U'(\beta^*(\bar{\beta})) = 0.$$

Recall that the highest β' who may be allowed to produce is $\beta^*(\bar{\beta})$.

Now consider a second-price auction in which each firm bids for the right to choose from its menu of linear incentive schemes. Then the incumbent bids $U_2(\beta)$, and the entrant bids $U'(\beta')$. In general the equation

$U_2(\beta) = U'(\beta')$ yields $\beta' \neq \beta^*(\beta)$ so that the second-price auction does not necessarily select the right firm. *The auction must thus be biased.* One way of doing so is to introduce a "cancellation fee" $G(\beta)$ to be paid to the incumbent if it is replaced (G is like the "golden parachute" paid to managers of a firm who are dismissed after a takeover). Hence one could envision a first-period contracting process in which the incumbent chooses a first-period incentive scheme and a second-period cancellation fee. The second-period allocation is determined by the auction described above.

For the right firm to be selected, the cancellation fee must satisfy

$$U_2(\beta) - G(\beta) = U'(\beta^*(\beta)),$$

since the incumbent shades its second-period bid by $G(\beta)$. Thus

$$G(\beta) = \int_{\beta}^{\bar{\beta}} \psi'(e_2(x))dx - \int_{\beta^*(\beta)}^{\beta^*(\bar{\beta})} \psi'(e'(x))dx,$$

or

$$G(\beta) = \int_{\beta}^{\bar{\beta}} \left[\psi'(e_2(x)) - \psi'(e'(\beta^*(x)))\frac{d\beta^*}{d\beta}(x) \right] dx,$$

and we have proposition 8.8.

Proposition 8.8 Under assumption 8.1 the cancellation fee is positive, and it increases with the incumbent' s efficiency (i.e., $G(\beta) \geq 0$, $\dot{G}(\beta) < 0$).

Proof For a quadratic disutility of effort, we have

$$G(\beta) = \int_{\beta}^{\bar{\beta}} \left(e_2 - e'\frac{d\beta^*}{d\beta} \right) dx.$$

Proposition 8.6 implies that $e_2 > e'(d\beta^*/d\beta)$. ■

As we mentioned earlier, the important result in proposition 8.8 is that the cancellation fee increases with the firm's efficiency.

To summarize, the optimal allocation can be implemented by a second-period auction in which each firm bids for the right to be the monopoly supplier. Efficient selection is obtained by offering in the first period a cancellation fee together with a first-period incentive scheme. This is the cancellation fee characterized in proposition 8.8.

Rather than using cancellation fees, the regulator could have the entrant pay an entry fee to bias the auction. Let $P(\beta)$ denote this entry fee,[16] where P stands for "poison pill" (roughly a poison pill forces a raider to pay an extra price to acquire the firm). In the context of our model, an entry fee is equivalent to a negative cancellation fee, though in a more general model the two instruments would not be perfect substitutes. Reinterpreting prop-

16. $P(\beta)$ must satisfy: $U'(\beta^*(\beta)) - P(\beta) = U_2(\beta)$.

Table 8.2
Summary of implications for transferable investments

Class A	Class B
Incumbent's performance (minus cost, profit)	Probability of second sourcing
Slopes of the incumbent's incentive schemes (b_1, b_2)	Intertemporal increase in the slope of the incumbent's incentive scheme $(b_2 - b_1)$
Cancellation fee	Entry fee

osition 8.8, we see that the entry fee should decrease with the incumbent's efficiency ($\dot{P}(\beta) > 0$): An efficient incumbent should be protected relatively less than an inefficient one.

We summarize in table 8.2 our recommendations and testable implications for transferable investments. The variables in class A are positively correlated with each other and negatively correlated with the variables in class B.

8.7 Concluding Remarks

In this chapter we have provided answers to some questions that Williamson (1976) and the Chicago school placed on the research agenda concerning the optimal organization of franchise bidding for natural monopolies. We showed that a rich yet tractable model can be built that yields testable equilibrium relationships among switching incentives, managerial incentive schemes, probability of second sourcing, and incumbent performance.

We arrived at a relatively pessimistic assessment of the virtues of second sourcing (or takeover) when substantial investments are at stake.[17] The incumbent should be favored at the reprocurement stage precisely when the investment is transferable, that is, when the second source is at not too much of a cost disadvantage. Indeed the incumbent should be favored more the higher the probability of second sourcing. To pursue this research, it seems desirable to study various forms of noncommitment due either to incomplete contracting and renegotiation[18] or to the possibility of mutually advantageous renegotiation.[19]

In an incomplete contracting setting, property rights do serve as switching incentives together with cancellation and entry fees. For instance, in

17. We considered the case in which the number of potential entrants was exogenous (actually equal to one, but the analysis generalizes straightforwardly to any number). When this number is endogenous and increases with the expected rent to be gained in the second-period auction, new effects should be taken into account. Favoring entrants now increases the competitiveness of the second-period auction.
18. See section 1.9 and Grossman and Hart (1986), Klein et al. (1978), Tirole (1986), and Williamson (1975) for investment concerns, and chapter 9 for the ratcheting problem.
19. See chapter 10 and the references therein.

defense procurement the government sometimes owns the property rights to data and technological information. Leaving the property rights to the defense contractor can be viewed as a way of biasing the reprocurement stage in its favor, for the government must bargain with and pay some money (the equivalent of a cancellation fee) to the defense contractor for the right to supply the relevant information to a second source. Property rights have thus some of the features of the switching incentives considered in this chapter.[20]

BIBLIOGRAPHIC NOTES

B8.1 Relationship to the Literature

There is an earlier literature on intertemporal procurement of a single firm under commitment (Baron and Besanko 1984), second-sourcing (Anton and Yao 1987; Caillaud 1990; Demski et al. 1987; Scharfstein 1988), and auctions of incentive contracts (see chapter 7 and the references therein). Although none of these papers considers simultaneously intertemporal regulation, investment, and second sourcing, and therefore is apt to address the issue of bidding parity, this chapter makes considerable use of their insights.

For instance, we can draw an interesting analogy between part i of proposition 8.3 (with nontransferable investment, the optimal breakout rule favors the entrant) with the literature. Demski, Sappington, and Spiller (1987) offer a second-sourcing example in which the purchaser selects the entrant rather than the incumbent to be the producer, even though he or she knows that the incumbent has lower production costs (corollary 5, p. 91; for similar results, see Caillaud 1990 and, in the classic context of auctioning of an object, Myerson 1981 and McAfee-McMillan 1984). The Demski et al. model does not allow any investment but assumes that the incumbent's and the entrant's production costs are drawn from asymmetric distributions, and that the incumbent's cost distribution stochastically dominates the entrant's. Our model presumes identical cost distributions ex ante, but the existence of specific investment confers a (statistical) superiority on the incumbent ex post. Like Demski et al., we find that this stochastic dominance by the incumbent calls for favoring the entrant.

Sen's (1991) model of second sourcing differs from the one in this chapter in the following respects. First, the incumbent does not invest. Second, the two firms are a priori equally efficient. The types are positively corre-

20. Similar ideas about property rights were expressed independently by Riordan and Sappington (1989, pp. 42–43).

lated across time and across firms. Third, there are two possible types ($\beta_\tau^i \in \{\underline{\beta}, \overline{\beta}\}$ for all i, τ). Fourth, a firm learns (privately) its type at date τ only after having been selected (a limited liability or ex post individual rationality constraint prevents the symmetric information allocation from being implemented). Note, however, that the positive intertemporal correlation together with imperfect interfirm correlation imply that more is known at the beginning of period 2 about the type of the "incumbent" (the firm that was selected in period 1) than about the type of the "entrant" (the firm that was not selected in period 1). That the type is revealed after firm selection implies two things: In period 1 it does not matter which firm is selected due to the ex ante symmetry, and in period 2 the probability of breakout can be contingent only on the incumbent's first-period performance. A main result of Sen's analysis is that it is optimal to terminate the relationship with the incumbent when the latter has announced type $\overline{\beta}$ in period 1, and this for two reasons. The "efficiency reason" is that given the bad news about the incumbent, the entrant is on average more efficient than the incumbent. The "incentive reason" is that a higher probability of breakout deters an efficient incumbent from pretending to be inefficient.

Riordan and Sappington (1989) consider a second-sourcing model with limited commitment of the regulator. There are two stages: a development stage and a production stage. The choice between single sourcing or second sourcing is the only commitment that the regulator can make. Under single sourcing the incumbent knows that it will enjoy for sure an informational rent in the second period, and it has strong incentives to invest in R&D in the first period. Under second sourcing the entrant has a cost disadvantage but does not retain any rent. An auction with bidding parity is organized at the production stage. Second sourcing decreases the rent given up by the regulator but also reduces the incumbent's incentives for R&D.

The motivation for second sourcing in the Riordan-Sappington model is the desire to reduce the incumbent's rent. Farrell and Gallini (1988) and Shepard (1987) develop models of second sourcing in which competition is meant to guarantee the buyer against expropriation of its investment by a monopoly supplier. In their models, which are based on specific investment by the buyer and noncommitment (as in section 1.9 where one party committed an investment before negotiating a contract), the existence of two suppliers raises the buyer's incentives to invest. These authors conclude that a monopoly supplier may have an incentive to license its technology and thus create its own competition in order to encourage investment in specific assets by a buyer (as long as the monopolist can recoup some of the newly created gains from trade).

Last, Cabral and Greenstein (1990) consider a case where second sourcing imposes switching costs. These costs create an asymmetry between the bidders' costs. They compare two nonoptimal auctions. They first assume that the procurer commits to a symmetric auction that takes nonoptimal ex post decisions but encourages aggressive bidding. Cabral and Greenstein then analyze an auction in which the ex post optimal choice of a source is made (which corresponds to noncommitment).

B8.2 A Reinterpretation: Takeovers and Managerial Myopia

As mentioned in the text, our model of second sourcing can shed some light on the desirability of takeovers. The entrant can be reinterpreted as a raider, and the incumbent as the current managerial team. The accounting cost stands for per-period performance (profit or stock value). The cost parameter β is a measure of the inefficiency of current management, and the effort variable e refers to the possibility of self-dealing management (appropriation of profits, luxurious offices, personal jets, golf playing, etc.). The reprocurement stage can be thought of as a tender offer. The rigging of bidding parity in favor of the incumbent or the entrant is a rough formalization of defensive tactics and protakeover measures, respectively.[21]

Our assumption that the incumbent's incentive scheme is not contingent on the entrant's performance translates into the assumption that the displaced managerial team does not keep substantial stock options in the firm after leaving. This assumption is made in most of the literature on the market for corporate control (e.g., Blair et al. 1986; Grossman and Hart 1988; Harris and Raviv 1988). Theoretical reasons can be found to motivate it. Although the arguments advanced in the context of regulation (in particular the collusion argument in section 8.3) fare less well in this context, the raider and displaced managers have an ex post incentive to renegotiate former contracts if the managers are risk averse, and they may agree to let the displaced managers resell stock options, which no longer serve an incentive purpose and create an excessive risk in the displaced managers' portfolio.[22]

Another effect limiting the role of post-termination stock options is that if there is no merger (so that the firm's stock remains traded), minority

21. There are of course a large number of different ways to acquire firms, from friendly mergers to proxy fights. The view that managerial teams bid against each other can be a good first approximation and is taken in Blair et al. (1986), Grossman and Hart (1988), and Harris and Raviv (1988), among others. It should be noted that other reasonable descriptions of the auctioning process would yield results similar to those we derive. For instance, suppose that the raider buys the whole firm, which then goes private. The auction is then equivalent to offering a fixed-price contract to the second source; the raider is made the residual claimant for the firm's second-period profit. Redoing the analysis by assuming that only a fixed-price contract can be offered to the entrant does not alter our intuition.

Note also that our allowing discrimination among the raider's types yields the result that after a takeover the firm goes private ($b' \simeq 1$) when the raider is very efficient (β close to $\underline{\beta}$) and does not when the raider is less efficient ($b' < 1$ for higher βs).

22. See Fudenberg and Tirole (1990) for a formal analysis of this issue in a model without takeovers.

freeze-out problems are very acute. In this case covenants must be imposed that greatly reduce the information value of the firm. (See Holmström and Tirole 1989 for an informal development of this point). At a more empirical level this assumption also makes some sense. First, since many acquired firms do not have outstanding shares after the takeover, the incumbent managers automatically exercise their stock options. Second, even if the raider acquires only control, many managerial contracts specify that the managers must exercise their options within 90 days if their employment is terminated. (Hence, in the context of our model, the options are exercised well before the investment pays off.) We believe that stock options encourage the incumbent managers to internalize the positive externality of *observable* investment on the raiders' post-takeover performance. Our point is that stock options provide very insufficient incentives to induce managers to internalize the effect of investments that are *not observable* by the market.[23]

Some implications of our model in the takeover context are (assuming that investment is transferred to the raider and is not of the learning-by-doing type):[24]

1. Firm performance and the probability of takeover are negatively correlated.

2. The use of defensive tactics to disadvantage the raider benefits the firm's shareholders.

3. The managers are given linear incentive schemes, which can be interpreted as salary plus stocks. Their incentive package also includes golden parachutes or poison pills.

4. The incumbent managers' stock holdings increase over time.

5. The size of the golden parachute is positively related to the number of stock holdings.

23. Although the process of investing per se is likely to be observed by the market, the derivation of investment expenditure from accounting data may not be as straightforward (recall Williamson's argument), and the quality of the investment may be hard to assess. In a similar spirit Ruback (1986, p. 72) argues that "the management of most corporations has private information about the future prospects of the firm. This information usually includes plans, strategies, ideas, and patents that cannot be made public. Even if they are efficient, market prices cannot include the value of information that the market does not have." To the extent that plans, strategies, ideas, and patents result from investments, Ruback's argument fits with the notion that a nonnegligible fraction of investment is not reflected in the market valuation of the firm. Hence we believe that post-termination stock options, although they cannot be completely excluded, are at most a limited instrument to induce managers to invest.

24. Our view that the shareholders organize a bidding contest between managerial teams may be too simplistic, so caution should be exercised when applying our conclusions. But it is worth noting that Walking and Long (1986) found that managers with large stock holdings are less likely to oppose takeovers than managers with small stock holdings and that Malatesta and Walking (1986) provided evidence that firms that adopt poison pill defenses are relatively unprofitable. Such empirical evidence is consistent with our normative analysis.

6. The size of the golden parachute is positively related to the firm's performance.[25]

7. The size of the poison pill is negatively correlated with the incumbent managers' stock holdings.

8. The size of the poison pill is negatively correlated with the firm's performance.

Conclusion 2 suggests that defensive tactics are not necessarily harmful.[26] Although most of the incentive literature on the topic views takeovers as a managerial discipline device, we believe that the popular fear of managerial myopia should not be neglected by economists. Our argument supplies an *efficiency* reason for foreclosing entry. That is, a social planner, whose objective function puts equal weight on the incumbent and the entrant, biases the auctioning process against the entrant. When the principal is a private entity (as is the case for shareholders), the contract signed between the principal and the incumbent does not internalize its effect on the entrant's welfare. Aghion and Bolton (1987) have shown that the desire to extract the entrant's rent leads the two initial parties to sign a contract that favors the incumbent because it induces too little "trade" between the initial vertical structure and the entrant; there is socially too much foreclosure. Note that both our theory and theirs yield the same positive implication: The incumbent is favored at the reprocurement stage. In our model poison pills, for instance, have *efficiency* justifications rather than Aghion-Bolton's *anticompetitive* motives.[27]

25. It is worth recalling the intuition of why the golden parachute (resp. the poison pill) should increase (resp. decrease) with the manager's ability and performance. A first guess might have been that bad managers should be encouraged to leave with large golden parachutes and small poison pills. This, however, is not correct because bidding between managers already selects the best managers. Our point is that the auction should be rigged to encourage managers to invest. A (good) manager with probability 0.9 of keeping his or her job selects roughly the right amount of investment, and further incentives are not needed. A (bad) manager with probability 0.1 of keeping his or her job chooses an inefficiently low investment, since with probability 0.9 this investment goes to a rival manager. A small golden parachute or a large poison pill increases a manager's probability of keeping his or her job and incentive to invest.

26. We suspect that the many shark repellents are far from being substitutes and involve fairly different social costs. It would be worthwhile to investigate how each favors the incumbent managerial team.

27. Hermalin (1987) and Stein (1988) also analyze the popular argument that the takeover threat could lead to underinvestment. Their models differ from ours in many respects and can be thought of as complementary. In these analyses the investment pays off before the raider enters the market for corporate control (i.e., period 1 in our model). Incumbent managers may not invest even in the presence of profitable opportunities because the probability of success of the investment is positively correlated with the manager's ability, and a failure signals a low ability and may encourage a takeover. These papers emphasize how signaling (managerial career concerns) distorts managerial decisions (more generally than investments) that might convey information about managers. We assume, on the contrary, that investment has long-delayed effects, and we focus on the intertemporal evolution of managerial profit-sharing schemes. Closer in spirit to our work is the signal-jamming model of Stein (1989) in which a manager overborrows to mislead the market about the firm's worth. See also Bebchuk and Stole (1992).

APPENDIXES

A8.1 Proof of Proposition 8.1

The optimization problem is quasi-concave (for λ small enough) and separable. For given β and $\beta^*(\beta)$, we can maximize the inside integral with respect to C' under the constraints (8.16) and (8.17). The first-order condition of this control problem yields effort $e'(\beta') = e^*(\beta')$, where $e^*(\beta')$ is given by

$$\psi'(e^*(\beta')) = 1 - \frac{\lambda}{1+\lambda}\frac{F(\beta')}{f(\beta')}\psi''(e^*(\beta')) \tag{A8.1}$$

for any $\beta' < \beta^*(\beta)$. Equation (A8.1) defines the optimal effort level and therefore the optimal C' function:

$$C'(\beta'|\beta) = \beta' - ki(\beta) - e^*(\beta'). \tag{A8.2}$$

If the entrant is selected ($\beta' < \beta^*(\beta)$), it has rent

$$V^*(\beta'|\beta) = \int_{\beta'}^{\beta^*(\beta)} \psi'(e^*(\tilde{\beta}))d\tilde{\beta}. \tag{A8.3}$$

We can now maximize (8.19) with respect to $C_1(\beta)$, $C_2(\beta)$, $\beta^*(\beta)$, and $i(\beta)$ subject to (8.12), (8.13), and (8.15). Let $\mu(\beta)$ [resp. $\nu(\beta)$] be the multiplier of the constraint (8.12) [resp. (8.15)]. The Pontryagin principle yields

$$\dot{\mu}(\beta) = -\frac{\partial H}{\partial U} = \lambda f(\beta). \tag{A8.4}$$

Using the transversality condition at $\underline{\beta}$, we have

$$\mu(\beta) = \lambda F(\beta). \tag{A8.5}$$

Maximization with respect to C_1, C_2, β^*, i gives

$$\psi'(e_1(\beta)) = 1 - \frac{\lambda F(\beta)}{(1+\lambda)f(\beta)}\psi''(e_1(\beta)) + \frac{\nu(\beta)d'(i)}{(1+\lambda)f(\beta)}\psi''(e_1(\beta)), \tag{A8.6}$$

$$\psi'(e_2(\beta)) = 1 - \frac{\lambda}{1+\lambda}\frac{F(\beta)}{f(\beta)}\psi''(e_2(\beta)) - \frac{\nu(\beta)}{(1+\lambda)f(\beta)}\psi''(e_2(\beta)), \tag{A8.7}$$

$$\begin{aligned}&[\beta - i - e_2(\beta) + \psi(e_2(\beta))] - [\beta^* - ki - e'(\beta^*) + \psi(e'(\beta^*))]\\ &= \frac{\lambda}{1+\lambda}\left[\frac{F(\beta^*)}{f(\beta^*)}\psi'(e'(\beta^*)) - \frac{F(\beta)}{f(\beta)}\psi'(e_2(\beta))\right] - \frac{\nu(\beta)}{(1+\lambda)f(\beta)}\psi'(e_2(\beta)),\end{aligned} \tag{A8.8}$$

$$\begin{aligned}0 = &-(1+\lambda)f(\beta)d'(i)\psi'(e_1(\beta)) + (1+\lambda)\delta(1 - F(\beta^*(\beta)))\psi'(e_2(\beta))f(\beta)\\ &- \lambda F(\beta)[d'(i)\psi''(e_1(\beta)) - \delta(1 - F(\beta^*(\beta)))\psi''(e_2(\beta))]\\ &+ \nu(\beta)[d'(i)^2\psi''(e_1(\beta)) + \psi'(e_1(\beta))d''(i) + \delta(1 - F(\beta^*(\beta)))\psi''(e_2(\beta))]\end{aligned}$$

$$+ f(\beta)k\delta\left[\int_{\underline{\beta}}^{\beta^*(\beta)} (1+\lambda)\psi'(e'(\beta'))f(\beta')d\beta' + \lambda\int_{\underline{\beta}}^{\beta^*(\beta)}\int_{\beta'}^{\beta^*(\beta)} \psi''(e'(\tilde{\beta}))d\tilde{\beta}f(\beta')d\beta'\right]. \tag{A8.9}$$

Integrating the last term of (A8.9) and using the first-order condition with respect to C', we can replace the last two terms by $f(\beta)\delta kF(\beta^*(\beta))(1+\lambda)$. Using the other first-order conditions (A8.9) reduces to

$$v(\beta) = \frac{(1+\lambda)f(\beta)[d'(i) - \delta((1-F(\beta^*(\beta)) + kF(\beta^*(\beta)))]}{\psi'(e_1(\beta))d''(i)}. \tag{A8.10}$$

We first show that the following result holds:

Lemma $v(\beta) \leq 0$ for any β. $v(\beta) = 0$ if and only if $k = 0$ or $\beta = \underline{\beta}$.

Proof Substituting (8.15) in (A8.10) yields

$$v(\beta) = \frac{(1+\lambda)f(\beta)}{[\psi'(e_1(\beta))]^2}\frac{\delta(1-F(\beta^*(\beta)))}{d''(i)}\left[\psi'(e_2(\beta)) - \psi'(e_1(\beta)) - k\frac{F(\beta^*(\beta))}{1-F(\beta^*(\beta))}\psi'(e_1(\beta))\right]. \tag{A8.11}$$

Suppose, on the contrary, that $v(\beta) > 0$. From (A8.11) and $\psi'' > 0$,

$$e_2(\beta) > e_1(\beta). \tag{A8.12}$$

From $\psi''' > 0$, we have

$$\psi''(e_2(\beta)) > \psi''(e_1(\beta)). \tag{A8.13}$$

Let us now rewrite the first-order conditions relative to C_1 and C_2 as follows:

$$\psi'(e_1(\beta)) + \frac{\lambda}{1+\lambda}\frac{F(\beta)}{f(\beta)}\psi''(e_1(\beta)) = 1 + \frac{v(\beta)d'(i)}{(1+\lambda)f(\beta)}\psi''(e_1(\beta)), \tag{A8.14}$$

$$\psi'(e_2(\beta)) + \frac{\lambda}{1+\lambda}\frac{F(\beta)}{f(\beta)}\psi''(e_2(\beta)) = 1 - \frac{v(\beta)}{(1+\lambda)f(\beta)}\psi''(e_2(\beta)). \tag{A8.15}$$

If $v(\beta) > 0$, the left-hand side of (A8.14) is larger than the left-hand side of (A8.15), implying that $e_1(\beta) > e_2(\beta)$, a contradiction. Note further that $v(\beta) = 0$ if and only if $k = 0$ or $\beta = \underline{\beta}$ [from (A8.11), (A8.14), and (A8.15)]. ■

We see from this lemma and (A8.6) and (A8.7) that $b_1 < b_2$ [since $\psi'(e_1(\beta)) < \psi'(e_2(\beta))$]. The first-period contract is closer to a cost-plus contract than the contract of the second period.

We show now that the incumbent is favored. Let

$$\Delta(\beta, \beta^*) \equiv (\beta^* - ki) - (\beta - i),$$

$$h(\beta, e_2) \equiv \psi(e_2) - e_2 + \frac{\lambda}{1+\lambda}\frac{F(\beta)}{f(\beta)}\psi'(e_2) + \frac{v(\beta)}{(1+\lambda)f(\beta)}\psi'(e_2),$$

and

$$g(\beta^*, e') \equiv \psi(e') - e' + \frac{\lambda}{1+\lambda} \frac{F(\beta^*)}{f(\beta^*)} \psi'(e').$$

Using (A8.6) and (A8.7), (A8.8) can be written

$$\Delta(\beta, \beta^*) = \max_{e_2} \{h(\beta, e_2)\} - \max_{e'} \{g(\beta^*, e')\}. \tag{A8.16}$$

Equation (A8.16) implies that $\Delta(\beta, \beta) < 0$, since $v(\beta) < 0$ implies that $h(\beta, e) < g(\beta, e)$ for all e. But the definition of Δ yields $\Delta(\beta, \beta) \geq 0$, a contradiction, if $\beta^* = \beta$ were the solution. Instead we have

$$\frac{\partial}{\partial \beta^*}\left[\Delta(\beta, \beta^*) - \max_{e_2} \{h(\beta, e_2)\} + \max_{e'} \{g(\beta^*, e')\}\right]$$

$$= 1 + \frac{\lambda}{1+\lambda} \psi'(e') \frac{d}{d\beta^*}\left(\frac{F(\beta^*)}{f(\beta^*)}\right) > 0. \tag{A8.17}$$

Hence, for (A8.16) to be satisfied, we need $\beta^* < \beta$, which for $k = 1$ implies that the incumbent is favored.

When investment is observable or when $\beta = \underline{\beta}$, $v(\beta) = 0$. From (A8.6) and (A8.7), the incumbent's effort is identical in periods 1 and 2. Equation (A8.8) then yields $\beta^*(\beta) = \beta$. ■

A8.2 Proof of Proposition 8.2

From chapter 1 we know that under slightly stronger assumptions ensuring second-order conditions, we can rewrite the incentive contract of the entrant as a menu of incentive schemes that are linear in the cost overrun:

$$t'(C', \beta', \beta) = \tilde{a}(\beta', \beta) - \tilde{b}(\beta')(C' - C'^*(\beta'|\beta)), \tag{A8.18}$$

with $\tilde{b}(\beta') = \psi'(e^*(\beta'))$ and $C'^*(\beta'|\beta) = \beta' - e^*(\beta') - ki(\beta)$.

Recall that $dC'^*/d\beta' > 0$ and $dC_1^*/d\beta > 0$. We can rewrite the transfer as

$$t'(C', C'^a) = a(C'^a, C_1^a) - b(C'^a)(C' - C'^a),$$

with

$$b(C'^a) \equiv \psi'(e^*(\beta')) = \psi'(e^*(\beta'^{-1}(C'^a))).$$

We can now extend the reasoning to the case of the incumbent. The transfer to the incumbent can be decomposed into two menus of linear incentive schemes, one for each period:

$$t_1(C_1, C_1^a) = a_1(C_1^a) - b_1(C_1^a)(C_1 - C_1^a),$$

$$t_2(C_2, C_2^a, C_1^a) = a_2(C_1^a, C_2^a) - b_2(C_2^a)(C_2 - C_2^a),$$

with

$$b_1(C_1^a) \equiv \psi'(e_1^*(\beta)) = \psi'(e_1^*(\beta_1^{-1}(C_1^a))),$$

$$b_2(C_2^a) \equiv \psi'(e_2^*(\beta)) = \psi'(e_2^*(\beta_2^{-1}(C_2^a))),$$

and the decomposition between a_1 and a_2 is arbitrary with a joint constraint (only their discounted sum matters, but one can choose a_1 and a_2 so that the individual rationality constraint is binding in each period). From (A8.6) and (A8.7) and $\nu(\beta) < 0$ we see that $b_1 < b_2$, since $\psi'(e_1(\beta)) < \psi'(e_2(\beta))$. When investment is observable $\nu(\beta) = 0$ and $b_1 = b_2$. ■

A8.3 Proof of Proposition 8.3

The intuition for the proof is that the incumbent fully internalizes the benefits of his investment when $k = 0$. Hence, the shadow price of the first-order condition for investment $\nu(\beta)$ should be equal to zero even when investment is unobservable. If $\nu(\beta) = 0$, then $e_1(\beta) = e_2(\beta) = e^*(\beta)$ from (A8.6) and (A8.7). Equation (A8.10) yields

$$d'(i(\beta)) = \delta(1 - F(\beta^*(\beta))), \tag{A8.19}$$

and (A8.9) is then satisfied. The functions $i(\beta)$ and $\beta^*(\beta)$ are defined by equations (A8.8) and (A8.19). Note that (A8.8) can be rewritten as

$$\beta^* - (\beta - i) = \max_e \{g(\beta, e)\} - \max_e \{g(\beta^*, e)\}, \tag{A8.20}$$

where

$$g(\beta, e) \equiv \psi(e) - e + \frac{\lambda}{1+\lambda}\frac{F(\beta)}{f(\beta)}\psi'(e).$$

From the envelope theorem and the monotone-hazard-rate condition, the right-hand side of (A8.20) is decreasing in β^* and is thus positive for $\beta^* < \beta$. Now suppose that $\beta^* \leq \beta - i$. Then $\beta^* < \beta$, and thus the right-hand side of (A8.20) is strictly positive, while the left-hand side is nonpositive, a contradiction. We conclude that $\beta^* > \beta - i$. ■

A8.4 Proof of Proposition 8.4

The first-order conditions of the regulator's quasi-concave maximization problem are

$$\psi'(e'(\beta')) = 1 - \frac{\lambda}{1+\lambda}\frac{F(\beta')}{f(\beta')}\psi''(e'(\beta')), \tag{A8.21}$$

$$\psi'(e_1(\beta)) = 1 + \delta g + \delta h(1 - F(\beta^*(\beta))) - \frac{\lambda}{1+\lambda}\frac{F(\beta)}{f(\beta)}\psi''(e_1(\beta)), \tag{A8.22}$$

$$\psi'(e_2(\beta)) = 1 - \frac{\lambda}{1+\lambda}\frac{F(\beta)}{f(\beta)}(1 - g - h)\psi''(e_2(\beta)), \tag{A8.23}$$

$$\begin{aligned} &\beta - he_1(\beta) - e_2(\beta) + \psi(e_2(\beta)) - (\beta^* - e'(\beta^*) + \psi(e'(\beta^*))) \\ &= \frac{\lambda}{1+\lambda}\left[\frac{F(\beta^*)}{f(\beta^*)}\psi'(e'(\beta^*)) - (1 - g - h)\frac{F(\beta)}{f(\beta)}\psi'(e_2(\beta))\right]. \end{aligned} \tag{A8.24}$$

At $h = g = 0$, $\beta^* = \beta$. Differentiating (A8.24) and using (A8.21) and (A8.23) gives $\partial\beta^*/\partial g < 0$ for any g, which proves proposition 8.4. ■

A8.5 Proof of Proposition 8.6

We will assume that $\beta^*(\beta)$ and $v(\beta)$ are differentiable. This can be proved by using the implicit function theorem and the first-order conditions.

Let us first note that $(d\beta^*/d\beta)(\underline{\beta}) < 1$. This is due to the fact that $\beta^*(\underline{\beta}) = \underline{\beta}$ and $\beta^*(\beta) < \beta$ for $\beta > \underline{\beta}$ (from proposition 8.1). Second, we know that $e' \equiv e'(\beta^*(\overline{\beta}))$ is equal to $e_2 \equiv e_2(\overline{\beta})$ at $\beta = \underline{\beta}$ (from proposition 8.1). Hence, at $\underline{\beta}$, we have $e_2 > e'(d\beta^*/d\beta)$. But differentiating (A8.8) in the uniform-quadratic case, and using the first-order conditions (A8.6) and (A8.7), yields

$$1 - \frac{d\beta^*}{d\beta} = \frac{\lambda}{1+\lambda}\left(e'\frac{d\beta^*}{d\beta} - e_2\right) - \frac{e_2}{1+\lambda}\frac{dv}{d\beta}. \tag{A8.25}$$

This implies that at $\beta = \underline{\beta}$, $dv/d\beta$ is negative. Now

$$\frac{d}{d\beta}(e' - e_2) = \frac{de'}{d\beta'}\frac{d\beta^*}{d\beta} - \frac{de_2}{d\beta}.$$

Using (A8.6) and (A8.7) in the linear-quadratic case yields

$$\frac{d}{d\beta}(e' - e_2) = \frac{\lambda}{1+\lambda}\left(1 - \frac{d\beta^*}{d\beta}\right) + \frac{1}{1+\lambda}\frac{dv}{d\beta}. \tag{A8.26}$$

But (A8.25) implies that, at $\beta = \underline{\beta}$,

$$1 - \frac{d\beta^*}{d\beta} < -\frac{e_2}{1+\lambda}\frac{dv}{d\beta}$$

so that

$$\frac{d}{d\beta}(e' - e_2) < \frac{1}{1+\lambda}\frac{dv}{d\beta}\left(1 - \frac{\lambda e_2}{1+\lambda}\right) < 0,$$

since $e_2(\overline{\beta}) = 1$ and $1 > \lambda/(1+\lambda)$. So $e' < e_2$ in a neighborhood of $\underline{\beta}$. Now consider the lowest $\beta > \underline{\beta}$ such that one of these three conditions holds:

Condition A,

$$e'(\beta)\frac{d\beta^*}{d\beta}(\beta) = e_2(\beta).$$

Condition B,

$$e'(\beta) = e_2(\beta).$$

Condition C,

$$\frac{d\beta^*}{d\beta}(\beta) = 1.$$

Condition A cannot be satisfied strictly before condition B or condition C, since $d\beta^*/d\beta < 1$ and $e' < e_2$ in a neighborhood of $\underline{\beta}$.

Suppose that condition B is satisfied. So, at this β, $e'(d\beta^*/d\beta) \le e_2$ and $d\beta^*/d\beta \le 1$. The first inequality, together with (A8.25) implies that

$$1 - \frac{d\beta^*}{d\beta} \le -\frac{e_2}{1+\lambda}\frac{dv}{d\beta}, \tag{A8.27}$$

so $dv/d\beta \le 0$. Using (A8.26), and the same reasoning as before, we obtain

$$\frac{d}{d\beta}(e' - e_2) \le \frac{1}{1+\lambda}\frac{dv}{d\beta}\left(1 - \frac{\lambda e_2}{1+\lambda}\right) \le 0 \tag{A8.28}$$

[since $e_2(\beta) = e'(\beta^*(\beta)) < 1$, from equation (A8.1)]. So the function $e' - e_2$ cannot become positive at β, since it is negative earlier and has a negative slope.

Last, suppose that condition C is satisfied. Equation (A8.25) can be rewritten

$$\frac{\lambda}{1+\lambda}(e' - e_2) = \frac{e_2}{1+\lambda}\frac{dv}{d\beta}. \tag{A8.29}$$

But (A8.6) and (A8.7) yield

$$e' - e_2 = \frac{1}{1+\lambda}\frac{dv}{d\beta}. \tag{A8.30}$$

It is easy to see that (A8.29) and (A8.30) are inconsistent unless $e_2 = \lambda/(1+\lambda)$. Rather, from (A8.6) and the fact that $v(\beta) < 0$, $e_2 > 1 - \lambda/(1+\lambda)$. Since we assumed that $1 > 2\lambda/(1+\lambda)$, we obtain a contradiction. Thus none of the three conditions A, B, or C can obtain to the right of $\underline{\beta}$. This proves proposition 8.6. ■

REFERENCES

Aghion, P., and P. Bolton. 1987. Contracts as a barrier to entry. *American Economic Review* 77:388–401.

Anton, J., and D. Yao. 1987. Second sourcing and the experience curve: Price competition in defense procurement. *Rand Journal of Economics* 18:57–76.

Baron, D., and D. Besanko. 1984. Regulation and information in a continuing relationship. *Information Economics and Policy* 1:267–302.

Bebchuk, L., and L. Stole. 1992. Do short-term objectives lead to under- or over-investment in long-term projects? Forthcoming, *Journal of Finance*.

Blair, D., J. Gerard, and D. Golbe. 1986. Unbundling the voting rights and the residual profit claims of common shares. Mimeo, Rutgers University.

Cabral, L., and S. Greenstein. 1990. Switching costs and bidding parity in government procurement of computer systems. Working Paper, University of Illinois.

Caillaud, B. 1990. Regulation, competition, and asymmetric information. *Journal of Economic Theory* 52:87–110.

Demsetz, H. 1968. Why regulate utilities? *Journal of Law and Economics* 11:55–66.

Demski, J., D. Sappington, and P. Spiller. 1987. Managing supplier switching. *Rand Journal of Economics* 18:77–97.

Farrell, J., and N. Gallini. 1988. Second sourcing as a commitment: Monopoly incentives to attract competition. *Quarterly Journal of Economics* 103:673–694.

Fudenberg, D., and J. Tirole. 1990. Moral hazard and renegotiation in agency contracts. *Econometrica* 58:1279–1320.

Goldberg, V. 1976. Regulation and administered contracts. *Bell Journal of Economics* 7:426–452.

Goldberg, V. 1981. Pigou on complex contracts and welfare economics. *Research in Law and Economics* 3:39–51.

Grossman, S., and O. Hart. 1986. The costs and benefits of ownership: A theory of vertical and lateral integration. *Journal of Political Economy* 94:691–719.

Grossman, S., and O. Hart. 1988. One share/one vote and the market for corporate control. *Journal of Financial Economics* 20:175–202.

Harris, M., and A. Raviv. 1988. Corporate governance: Voting rights and majority rules. *Journal of Financial Economics* 20:203–235.

Hart, O., and J. Moore. 1988. Incomplete contracts and renegotiation. *Econometrica* 56:755–786.

Hermalin, B. 1987. Adverse effects of the threat of takeovers. Mimeo, Massachusetts Institute of Technology.

Holmström, B., and J. Tirole. 1989. The theory of the firm. In *The Handbook of Industrial Organization*, vol. 1, ed. R. Schmalensee and R. Willig. Amsterdam: North-Holland, ch. 2.

Joskow, P., and R. Schmalensee. 1983. *Markets for Power*. Cambridge, MA: MIT Press.

Klein, B., R. Crawford, and A. Alchian. 1978. Vertical integration, appropriable rents and the competitive contracting process. *Journal of Law and Economics* 21:297–326.

Laffont, J.-J., and J. Tirole. 1988. Repeated auctions of incentive contracts, investment and bidding parity, with an application to takeovers. *Rand Journal of Economics* 19:516–537.

McAfee, P., and J. McMillan. 1984. Discrimination in auctions. Mimeo, University of Western Ontario.

Malatesta, P., and R. Walking. 1986. Poison pill securities: stockholder wealth, profitability, and ownership structure. Mimeo, University of Washington and Ohio State University.

Maskin, E., and J. Tirole. 1990. The principal-agent relationship with an informed principal: The case of private values. *Econometrica* 58:379–410.

Myerson, R. 1981. Optimal auction design. *Mathematics of Operations Research* 6:58–73.

Pigou, A. D. 1920. *The Economics of Welfare*. New York: Macmillan.

Posner, R. 1972. The appropriate scope of regulation in the cable television industry. *Bell Journal of Economics* 3:98–129.

Riordan, M., and D. Sappington. 1989. Second sourcing. *Rand Journal of Economics* 20:41–58.

Ruback, R. 1986. An overview of takeover defenses. In *Mergers and Acquisitions*, ed. A. Auerbach. National Bureau for Economic Research prepublication report.

Scharfstein, D. 1988. The disciplinary role of takeovers. *Review of Economic Studies* 55:185–200.

Shepard, A. 1987. Licensing to enhance demand for a new technology. *Rand Journal of Economics* 18:360–368.

Stein, J. 1988. Takeover threats and managerial myopia. *Journal of Political Economy* 96:61–80.

Stein, J. 1989. Efficient stock prices, inefficient firms: A signal-jamming model of myopic corporate behavior. *Quarterly Journal of Economics* 104:655–669.

Stigler, G. 1968. *The Organization of Industry*. Homewood, IL: Richard D. Irwin.

Tirole, J. 1986. Procurement and renegotiation. *Journal of Political Economy* 94:235–259.

Walking, R., and M. Long. 1984. Agency theory, managerial welfare, and takeover bid resistance. *Rand Journal of Economics* 15:54–68.

Williamson, O. 1975. *Markets and Hierarchies: Analysis and Antitrust Implications*. New York: The Free Press.

Williamson, O. 1976. Franchise bidding for natural monopolies—in general and with respect to CATV. *Bell Journal of Economics* 7:73–104.

Williamson, O. 1985. *The Economic Institutions of Capitalism*. New York: The Free Press.

IV THE DYNAMICS OF REGULATION

9 DYNAMICS WITHOUT COMMITMENT AND THE RATCHET EFFECT

9.1 Some Background

Regulated firms and their agencies or ministries often repeatedly interact. In the procurement arena, multistage production processes and related orders create repeated interactions between suppliers and buyers. Ideally such relationships are governed by extensive long-term contracts: If the two parties can sign full long-term contracts, they can always contractually duplicate how they would behave in the absence of such contracts, and in general they can do better.

In practice, however, regulatory and procurement relationships are often run by a series of short-term contracts, for two reasons. First, most countries have legal prohibitions on long-term commitment; that is, the current administrations are allowed to bind future ones only to a limited extent. Some of the debate on the relative merits of cost-of-service and price-cap regulations has focused on the length of time over which the regulated firm's prices are fixed.[1] While regulatory reviews can be initiated by the firm or the agency under cost-of-service regulation, price caps are determined for four or five years, say. That is, the spirit of price-cap regulation is to allow a longer commitment to prices determined in regulatory hearings. There are also sempiternal debates in the U.S. procurement arena about whether the Department of Defense and Congress should be allowed to engage in multiyear procurement, that is, to commit to fund projects over the long run. Legal prohibitions on commitment are also prominent in France where ministries or parliament cannot allocate money to public enterprises over an horizon exceeding their annual budget. (Chapter 16 will attempt to derive foundations in a changing administration framework for the noncommitment assumption, which we take as given in this chapter.) The second motivation for noncommitment is that future production or technologies cannot be perfectly described contractually today, and that changes in the environment or the design may make current long-term contracts meaningless. This is the "incomplete contracting" motivation.

The lack of commitment and the concommitant repeated bargaining between firms and regulators is perceived as having two perverse effects. First (as analyzed in section 1.9), the regulator might not compensate the firm adequately for its investments and the firm therefore would be reluctant to invest. Second, and the object of this chapter, the regulated firm might be concerned about the "ratchet effect": If it produces at a low cost today, the regulator might infer that low costs are not that hard to achieve

1. See the introductory chapter for more detail. It is interesting to note that cost-of-service regulation has a partial commitment mechanism through the firm's legal right to a "fair" rate of return on capital for "prudent" investment. The courts define the degree of commitment by determining the regulators' discretion in deciding what is fair and what is prudent.

and tomorrow offer a demanding incentive scheme. That is, the firm jeopardizes future rents by being efficient. The ratchet effect is often perceived as a serious problem in regulated industries, procurement, planned economies, and private organizations.

To put the ratchet effect in perspective, recall from section 1.10 that, if the two parties can commit to a long-term contract at the beginning of their relationship, the regulator optimally commits to use each period the optimal static contract. That is, it is optimal for the regulator to commit not to exploit the information acquired from observing the firm's performance. Commitment is crucial for this outcome because the regulator would want to fully extract the firm's rent from the second period on after the firm reveals its efficiency in the first period.

This chapter analyzes the ratchet effect in regulatory relationships run by a series of short-term contracts. For simplicity it studies a two-period version of the model in chapter 1, in which the regulator can commit to a single-period mechanism in period 1 but cannot at the beginning of period 1 commit not to renege in period 2 on a period-2 contract specified in period 1.

In equilibrium there may be substantial pooling in the first period. Efficient types conceal their productivity and mimic inefficient ones. Because the regulator is aware of this strategy, he or she may induce more effort than the first-best level for some types. More specifically we show that with a continuum of potential efficiencies (types) for the firm, and for any first-period incentive scheme, no separating equilibrium exists. Furthermore, when the range of potential efficiencies is small, the regulator can do no better in the first period than impose "much pooling." In this case the most inefficient types exert more effort than in the first best. This holds even when, in the static framework, full separation is optimal. These two results are derived in section 9.3. Section 9.3 also gives necessary and sufficient conditions for the existence of partition equilibria, namely equilibria in which each level of cost chosen in period 1 is associated with a subinterval of the interval of potential efficiencies $[\underline{\beta}, \bar{\beta}]$. Section 9.3 also shows the existence of nonpartition equilibria and gives an example of inexistence of partition equilibria. The extremely complex nature of equilibria makes it hard to characterize the optimal incentive scheme.

To somewhat simplify the problem, section 9.4 analyzes the two-type case, that is, $\beta \in \{\underline{\beta}, \bar{\beta}\}$. Nevertheless, the family of equilibria remains quite complex unless we restrict the regulator to offering no more than two contracts in period 1. But we can completely describe the types of equilibria and perform numerical and analytical comparative statics of the optimal contract in this restricted class. The class is rich enough to exhibit the main economic facts: first, the importance of pooling and, second, the possibility that the inefficient type's incentive constraint would be binding at the optimum. Indeed, contrary to the standard one-period framework (see chapter 1) where, at the optimum, only the efficient type's incentive constraint is binding, here any incentive constraint could turn out to be binding at the optimum. This phenomenon and the complexity of the equilibria we obtain in this chapter are due to the *take-the-money-and-run strategy*. To induce the good type to reveal its efficiency, the regulator must give it a large transfer in period 1. However, this large transfer may attract the bad type which finds it advantageous in period 1 to select the contract designed for the good type. When period 2 comes, the regulator believing that the firm is a good type, is very demanding, but the bad type then quits the relationship. This possibility may well lead to an optimum where both types's incentive constraints are binding.

This last result is the most unexpected one of this chapter. It implies that the lack of commitment in repeated adverse-selection situations leads to substantial difficulties for contract theory. (The next chapter will show that the alternative restriction on commitment, where it is assumed that the regulator can commit to a long-term contract but cannot commit not to renegotiate it, fortunately yields simpler results.)

Despite this gloomy picture of our knowledge of incentive schemes in a repeated relationship run by short-term contracts, there are *two robust results* in the two-type case that are worth emphasizing. First, for small discount factors, the optimal first-period contract separates the two types. This result is intuitive but nontrivial: While the firm substantially discounts the future and needs only small incentives to reveal its information, the regulator also attaches in period 1 a low value to having information in period 2. Second, for large discount factors the first-period regulatory outcome cannot be empirically distinguished from a pure pooling (uninformative) outcome.

We conclude this introduction by a heuristic discussion of the ratchet effect and the take-the-money-and-run strategy in the case of two efficiency levels, $\underline{\beta} < \bar{\beta}$. Figure 9.1 builds on figure 1.2. The optimal static allocation (which from section 1.10 is also the optimal allocation in each period when the parties can sign a long-term contract) is depicted by points D for type $\underline{\beta}$ and E for type $\bar{\beta}$ (the notation follows that of figure 1.2). The efficient type's incentive compatibility constraint and the inefficient type's individual rationality constraint are binding. Obviously the (D, E) allocation is also feasible and optimal in the first period of a long-run relationship when the firm has discount factor 0. More generally we ought to ask: Is (D, E) still incentive compatible in the first period of a two-period relationship? If it is, then it ought to be offered by the regulator because it maximizes first-period welfare and generates perfect information for the regulator in period 2. Alas, (D, E) is not incentive compatible for discount factor $\delta > 0$. By choosing D, type $\underline{\beta}$ reveals its efficiency, enjoys no second-period rent, and has intertemporal rent $\Phi(\bar{e})$. By choos-

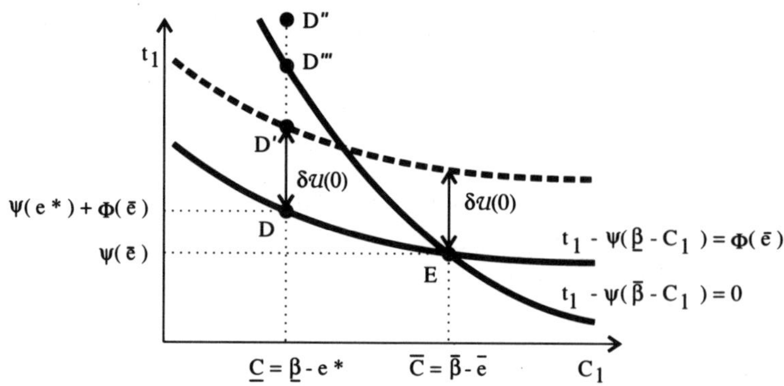

Figure 9.1
Ratcheting and the take-the-money-and-run strategy

ing E, this type is mistaken for type $\bar{\beta}$ and therefore enjoys rent $\mathcal{U}(0) > 0$[2] in period 2. So choosing E yields intertemporal rent $\Phi(\bar{e}) + \delta\mathcal{U}(0) > \Phi(\bar{e})$ to type $\underline{\beta}$. To restore incentive compatibility, the regulator must raise the first-period transfer associated with cost $\underline{C} = (\underline{\beta} - e^*)$ by $\delta\mathcal{U}(0)$ and thus offer first-period menu (D', E). Note that in figure 9.1 type $\bar{\beta}$, which never enjoys a second-period rent and therefore chooses the allocation that maximizes its first-period utility, prefers E to D'. We will show that the first-period allocation (D', E) is optimal for the regulator (given the constraint of no commitment) when the discount factor is small.

The take-the-money-and-run strategy can be illustrated by considering large discount factors. The first-period transfer associated with cost $\underline{C}$ must then be high. The resulting point D'' now lies above type $\bar{\beta}$'s indifference curve through E. That is, type $\bar{\beta}$ would be better off producing at cost $\underline{C}$ in the first period and refusing to produce later on.[3] If the regulator sticks to the first-period menu of costs $(\underline{C}, \bar{C})$, he or she must offer allocation (D''', E). But the regulator must then tolerate some pooling, since, in case of separation, type $\underline{\beta}$ would strictly prefer E to D'''. Type $\underline{\beta}$'s randomizing between D''' and E reduces type $\underline{\beta}$'s rent of choosing E; similarly type $\bar{\beta}$'s randomizing between D''' and E may raise type $\underline{\beta}$'s rent when choosing D'''. Both randomizations may raise type $\underline{\beta}$'s incentive to choose D''', and in equilibrium this type must be indifferent between D''' and E. Alternatively, the regulator could preserve separation by lowering $\underline{C}$ or raising $\bar{C}$, as can be seen in figure 9.1. That is, he or she could give more incentives to the efficient type in order to increase the cost of the take-the-money-and-run strategy for the inefficient type, or fewer incentives to the

2. $\mathcal{U}(\nu)$, in the notation of section 1.5, is the efficient type's rent when the regulator puts probability ν on the firm's having type $\bar{\beta}$. Note that $\mathcal{U}(0) = \Phi(e^*)$.

3. Following cost $\underline{C}$, the regulator, who believes the firm has type $\underline{\beta}$, demands cost $\underline{C}$ again but offers transfer $\psi(e^*)$ only. So type $\bar{\beta}$ is better off not producing in period 2.

inefficient type in order to reduce the payment to be handed to the efficient type, again making the take-the-money-and-run strategy less attractive.

9.2 The Model

We consider the two-period repetition of the static model: The firm must implement in each period a project at cost

$$C_\tau = \beta - e_\tau, \qquad \tau = 1, 2, \tag{9.1}$$

where e_τ is the level of cost reduction or "effort" performed by the firm's manager in period τ and β is a time-invariant parameter known only to the firm.[4]

Social welfare at date τ is

$$W_\tau = S - (1 + \lambda)(C_\tau + t_\tau) + U_\tau,$$

where

$$U_\tau = t_\tau - \psi(e_\tau).$$

Both parties have discount factor δ.[5]

Section 1.10 showed that the optimal mechanism with commitment is the repetition of the optimal static mechanism. Under complete information the optimal stationary solution is clearly

$$t_\tau = \psi(e_\tau), \tag{9.2}$$

$$e_\tau = e^*, \tag{9.3}$$

where $\psi'(e^*) = 1$. The intent of this chapter is to consider the case where the regulator cannot commit him- or herself to a second-period incentive scheme. The regulator chooses the second-period incentive scheme optimally given his or her beliefs about the firm's type at that date. These beliefs depend on the realized first-period cost and the first-period incentive scheme. In the case of two types ($\underline{\beta} < \bar{\beta}$), we let ν_1 and ν_2 denote the prior and the posterior probability that $\beta = \underline{\beta}$. In the continuum case ($\beta \in [\underline{\beta}, \bar{\beta}]$), $F_1(\cdot)$, and $F_2(\cdot)$ will denote the prior and posterior cumulative distribution functions. We will model the equilibrium of the game between

4. The analysis of the effect of cost uncertainty is left for future research.

5. There is no difficulty in allowing different discount factors for the regulator and the firm in our analysis. In particular it would seem that a lower discount factor for the regulator than for the firm may be more descriptive of the changing-administration framework, which is one of the motivations for the absence of long-term contract. Note, however, that even so, our model is not a perfect rendition of the changing-administration framework, since a fundamentalist approach would attribute the prohibition of long-term contracts to a probability that administrations are corrupt or incompetent (see chapter 16). Relative to the motivation of changing administrations, our model thus only unveils some strategic aspects.

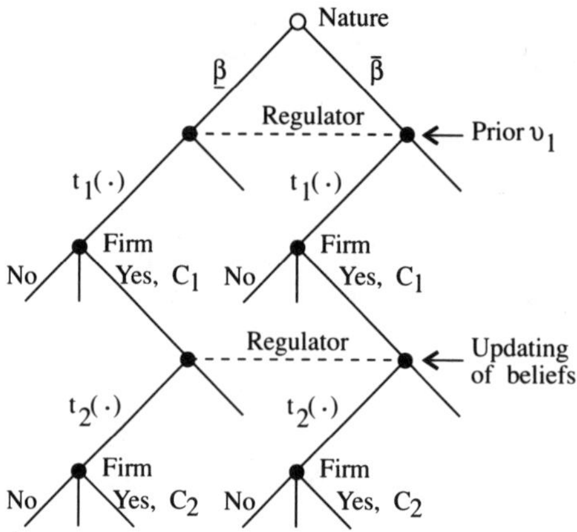

Figure 9.2
Extensive form

the regulator and the firm as a perfect Bayesian equilibrium (PBE). (See figure 9.2 for the game tree in the case of two types $\underline{\beta}$ and $\overline{\beta}$.)

The regulator's strategy is an incentive scheme $C_1 \to t_1(C_1)$ in period 1 and an incentive scheme $C_2 \to t_2(C_2; t_1(\cdot), C_1)$ in period 2. We allow the firm to quit the relationship (and to obtain its reservation utility 0) at any moment. Let $\chi_\tau = 1$ if the firm accepts the incentive scheme at date τ, and let $\chi_\tau = 0$ if it quits. The firm's strategy is a choice of participation and effort level in period 1,

$$\chi_1(\beta, t_1(\cdot)), \qquad e_1(\beta, t_1(\cdot)),$$

and in period 2,

$$\chi_2(\beta, t_1(\cdot), t_2(\cdot), C_1), \qquad e_2(\beta, t_1(\cdot), t_2(\cdot), C_1).$$

These strategies and beliefs form a PBE iff

(P1) $\{e_2(\cdot), \chi_2(\cdot)\}$ is optimal for the firm given $t_2(\cdot)$,

(P2) $t_2(\cdot)$ is optimal for the regulator given his or her posterior beliefs,

(P3) $\{e_1(\cdot), \chi_1(\cdot)\}$ is optimal for the firm given $t_1(\cdot)$ and the fact that the regulator's second-period scheme depends on C_1,

(P4) $t_1(\cdot)$ is optimal for the regulator given subsequent strategies,

(B) the posterior is derived from the prior, the firm's strategy given by (P3), the first-period incentive scheme $t_1(\cdot)$, and the observed cost C_1 using Bayes's rule.

Conditions (P1) through (P4) call for "perfection," namely optimization by each player at any history of the game. Condition (B) requires that the updating of the regulator's beliefs about the firm's type follow Bayes's rule. Note that (P2) requires the regulator to choose in the second period an optimal static incentive scheme relative to his or her posterior beliefs, even off the equilibrium path. Similarly we require that the firm play optimally at any history of the game.

Last, consider an arbitrary first-period incentive scheme $t_1(\cdot)$. A *continuation equilibrium* is a set of strategies [excluding $t_1(\cdot)$] with an updating rule that satisfies (P1), (P2), (P3), and (B). In other words, it is an equilibrium for an exogenously given first-period incentive scheme. It is fully separating if the function $\beta \to C_1(\beta) = \beta - e_1(\beta)$ is one to one.

9.3 Ratcheting and Pooling in the Continuum Case

We consider here the case of a continuum of values $[\underline{\beta}, \overline{\beta}]$ with a prior $F_1(\cdot)$ with density $f_1(\cdot)$ strictly positive on $[\underline{\beta}, \overline{\beta}]$ and satisfying assumption 1.2 of chapter 1: $d(F_1(\beta)/f_1(\beta))/d\beta > 0$. Remember that under this assumption the optimal static mechanism is fully separating. The main result of the continuum case is as described in proposition 9.1.

Proposition 9.1 For *any* first-period incentive scheme $t_1(\cdot)$, there exists no fully separating continuation equilibrium.

Proposition 9.1 (which does not require the monotone-hazard-rate assumption) shows that while in the static case full separation is feasible and desirable, it is not even feasible in the dynamic case. The intuition behind the proof of this proposition is the following: If the firm fully reveals its information in the first period, it enjoys no second-period rent. Thus it must maximize its first-period payoff. Now suppose that type β deviates from its equilibrium strategy and produces at the same cost as if it had type $\beta + d\beta$, where $d\beta > 0$. By the envelope theorem, it loses only a second-order profit in the first period. On the other hand, it enjoys a first-order rent in the second period because the regulator is convinced it has type $\beta + d\beta$. Thus type β would like to pool with type $\beta + d\beta$. The proof makes this intuition rigorous.

Proof We drop the index relative to date 1 in the proof. Consider two types: $\beta < \beta'$. Type β produces at cost C and receives t. Type β' produces at cost $C' \neq C$ and receives t'. (If strategies are mixed, C and C' are realizations of the optima for types β and β'.) If the equilibrium is separating, C signals that the firm has type β, and similarly for (β', C'). So in the second period the firm is put at its individual rationality level (i.e., obtains no rent). Imagine that type β' deviates and chooses to produce at cost C. In the second period this type obtains no rent because the second-period incentive scheme is designed to extract all the surplus from the more efficient type β and type β' quits. In contrast, if type β deviates in the first period and produces at cost C', then it will receive a strictly positive rent in the second period (since the less efficient type obtains no rent). We denote this rent $U(\beta|\beta') > 0$. Optimization by both types requires that

$$t - \psi(\beta - C) \geq t' - \psi(\beta - C') + \delta U(\beta|\beta') \tag{9.4}$$

and

$$t' - \psi(\beta' - C') \geq t - \psi(\beta' - C). \tag{9.5}$$

Adding (9.4) and (9.5), we obtain

$$[\psi(\beta - C') + \psi(\beta' - C)] - [\psi(\beta - C) + \psi(\beta' - C')] \geq 0. \tag{9.6}$$

Convexity of ψ and (9.6) then imply that $C < C'$ (since $C \neq C'$).

If $\{C(\beta), t(\beta)\}$ denotes the first-period allocation, C must be an increasing function of β. Therefore C is differentiable almost everywhere. On the other hand, t must be decreasing (otherwise, some type β would imitate some type β'; $\beta' > \beta$), so it is differentiable almost everywhere. Consider now a point of differentiability β, say. If type β deviates and behaves like type $\beta - d\beta$, $d\beta > 0$, it does not get a rent in the second period. Thus

$$t(\beta) - \psi(\beta - C(\beta)) \geq t(\beta - d\beta) - \psi(\beta - C(\beta - d\beta)). \tag{9.7}$$

Taking the limit as $d\beta$ goes to zero,

$$\frac{dt(\beta)}{d\beta} + \psi'(\beta - C(\beta))\frac{dC(\beta)}{d\beta} \geq 0. \tag{9.8}$$

If type β deviates and behaves like type $\beta + d\beta$, it obtains a second-period surplus. Although its magnitude turns out to be irrelevant, this second-period surplus is easy to compute: In the second period type β must mimic the outcome of type $\beta + d\beta$. Thus it saves $d\beta$ on effort. Since the regulator believes that he or she has complete information about the firm, the marginal disutility of effort is equal to one. Consequently $U(\beta|\beta + d\beta) = d\beta$. We obtain

$$t(\beta) - \psi(\beta - C(\beta)) \geq t(\beta + d\beta) - \psi(\beta - C(\beta + d\beta)) + \delta d\beta, \tag{9.9}$$

or by taking the limit as $d\beta$ goes to zero,

$$0 \geq \frac{dt(\beta)}{d\beta} + \psi'(\beta - C(\beta))\frac{dC(\beta)}{d\beta} + \delta, \tag{9.10}$$

which contradicts (9.8). ■

The proof of proposition 9.1 shows more generally that there exists no nondegenerate subinterval of $[\underline{\beta}, \overline{\beta}]$ over which separation occurs. The impossibility of separation is an extreme illustration of the general fact that the revelation principle (in its usual form, in which the agent reveals the true parameter(s) to the principal) does not apply to repeated relationships in the absence of commitment. The next proposition shows that for small uncertainty ($|\bar{\beta} - \underline{\beta}|$ small), the regulator imposes "much pooling," in the sense defined below. (The analysis in the rest of this section is technical, and some readers may want to skip it and move on to section 9.4.)

We will say that a continuation equilibrium exhibits infinite reswitching if there exist two equilibrium cost levels C^0 and C^1 and an infinite ordered sequence in $[\underline{\beta}, \bar{\beta}]: \{\beta_k\}_{k \in N}$ such that producing at cost C^0 (resp. C^1) is an optimal action for β_{2k} (resp. β_{2k+1}) for all k. (In this definition and in the next, "an optimal action" must be taken to mean that the action is in the support of the type's equilibrium strategy, not just that it is a weak best response.) An equilibrium that exhibits infinite reswitching is thus very complex; in particular an increasing well-ordered partition of the interval $[\underline{\beta}, \bar{\beta}]$ into subintervals such that every type in a given subinterval chooses the same cost level (partition equilibrium) does not exist. An example of an equilibrium exhibiting infinite reswitching is provided in appendix A9.1.

We will say that for a given (small) ε, a continuation equilibrium exhibits pooling over a large scale $(1 - \varepsilon)$ if there exist a cost level C and two values $\beta_1 < \beta_2$ such that $(\beta_2 - \beta_1)/(\bar{\beta} - \underline{\beta}) \geq 1 - \varepsilon$, and C is an optimal action for types β_1 and β_2. In words, one can find two types that are arbitrarily far apart (i.e., "arbitrary" in the choice of ε) and pool. A full pooling equilibrium (all types choose the same cost target) of course involves pooling over a large scale (for $\varepsilon = 0$).

We can now state proposition 9.2. For it let us consider a sequence of economies with fixed $\bar{\beta}$. We let the lower bound of the interval $\underline{\beta}_n$ converge to $\bar{\beta}$ [the density is thus obtained by successive truncations of the initial density: $f_1^n(\beta) = f_1(\beta)/(1 - F_1(\underline{\beta}_n))$, defined on $[\underline{\beta}_n, \bar{\beta}]$].

Proposition 9.2 (Small Uncertainty) Consider an arbitrary first-period incentive scheme $t_1(\cdot)$, and assume that ψ' is bounded below by a positive number. For any $\varepsilon > 0$ there exists $\beta_\varepsilon < \bar{\beta}$ such that for all n with $\underline{\beta}_n \geq \beta_\varepsilon$, there exists no continuation equilibrium that yields the regulator a higher payoff than the optimal full pooling contract and that either (i) involves less than a fraction $(1 - \varepsilon)$ of firms producing at the same cost or (ii) does not exhibit both infinite reswitching and pooling over a large scale $(1 - \varepsilon)$.

Proof See appendix A9.2.

Let us discuss proposition 9.2. For small uncertainty the regulator must either create almost full pooling or resort to a continuation equilibrium with an infinite amount of reswitching and still much pooling. Appendix A9.1 constructs such a continuation equilibrium, which is depicted in figure 9.3. The principal offers two (cost, transfer) pairs. The two costs are C and $\tilde{C}$. Firms in $[\underline{\beta}, \tilde{\beta}]$ strictly prefer C. Firms in $[\tilde{\beta}, \bar{\beta}]$ are indifferent between C and $\tilde{C}$ and randomize between these two costs. Appendix A9.1 shows that this first-period randomization can be chosen so that the regulator's posterior, and thus the firm's second-period rent, maintain the

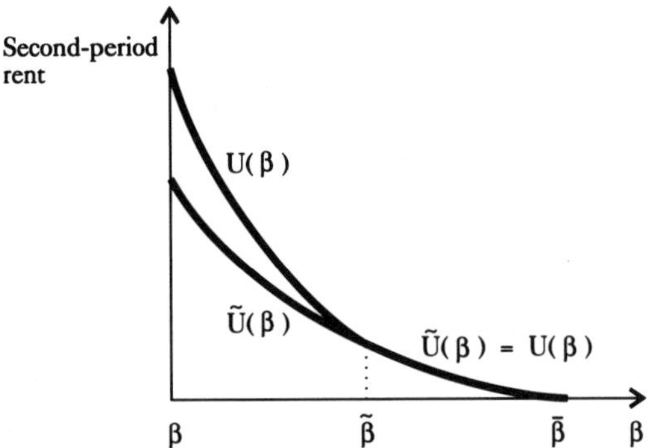

Figure 9.3
Nonpartition equilibrium

equality between the second-period rents U and $\tilde{U}$ over this interval. It can also be shown that C and $\tilde{C}$ can be chosen close (by choosing $\tilde{\beta}$ close to $\underline{\beta}$); hence a priori this equilibrium need not be suboptimal for small uncertainty.

In the class of full pooling equilibria, the best cost target is easy to characterize (see the proof of proposition 9.2). If such a cost target is imposed, the firm's first-period effort decreases with efficiency (while it increases with efficiency in the static model). Furthermore despite the ratchet effect there is no underprovision of effort in the first period. Indeed it is possible to show that under a quadratic disutility of effort and a uniform prior, the average marginal disutility of first-period effort over the population of types is the same as in the static (or full commitment) incomplete information case. What is more, for β close to $\bar{\beta}$ the firm works harder than in the first best. This is due to the fact that the regulator, when offering a pooling contract, forces the less efficient types to work very hard to avoid an excessive amount of shirking by the efficient types. Last, the most efficient types work harder in the second period, while the least efficient types work harder in the first period. The variance of earnings t_τ over the population of types grows over time (while it is constant under commitment). The optimal full pooling equilibrium in the uniform-quadratic case is represented in figure 9.4 for the disutility of effort function $\psi(e) = \alpha e^2/2$. The symmetric information effort level is then $e^* = 1/\alpha$. The areas between the effort function under commitment and that under the optimal full pooling in the first period are denoted by A_1 and A_2 in figure 9.4 and are equal in the quadratic-uniform case.

We conclude this section by a discussion of a subclass of equilibria. The natural type of continuation equilibrium to look for in dynamic incentive problems like this is the *partition equilibrium*. In a partition equilibrium $[\underline{\beta}, \bar{\beta}]$ can be divided into a (countable) number of ordered intervals such

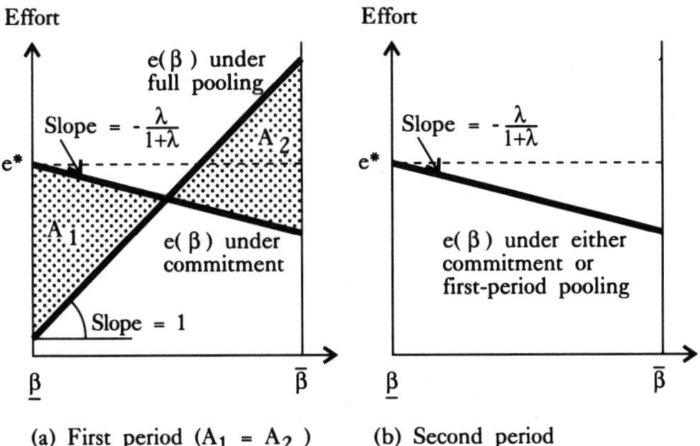

Figure 9.4
Quadratic-uniform small uncertainty case: (a) first period, $A_1 = A_2$; (b) second period

that in the first period all types in an interval choose the same cost level, and two types in two different intervals choose different cost levels.[6] The case of full pooling is a degenerate partition equilibrium in which there is only one such interval. Before proceeding, we make the following change in our notation: Since in the rest of the section all cost levels pertain to the first period, we no longer indicate time. Rather, we use superscripts to differentiate first-period cost levels.

We now derive necessary and sufficient conditions for arbitrary first-period incentive schemes to admit a nondegenerate partition equilibrium in the continuation game, when the disutility of effort is quadratic (or, more generally, α-convex, whereby $\psi'' \geq \alpha$ everywhere, as the reader will see).

Proposition 9.3 (Necessary Condition) Assume that ψ is quadratic $[\psi(e) = \alpha e^2/2]$ and that the equilibrium is a partition equilibrium. If C^k and C^l are two equilibrium first-period cost levels, $|C^k - C^l| \geq \delta/\alpha$.

Proof See appendix A9.3.

Proposition 9.3 states that the minimum distance between two equilibrium costs in a partition equilibrium is equal to the discount factor divided by the curvature of the disutility of effort.

Since the regulator can impose large negative transfers when the firm's cost is not an equilibrium cost, we define a set of "allowed cost-transfer pairs" among which all types must choose. We now state the following proposition:

6. For examples of partition equilibria in sender-receiver games, see Crawford and Sobel (1982).

Proposition 9.4 (Sufficient Condition) Assume that ψ is quadratic $[\psi(e) = \alpha e^2/2]$ and that assumption 1.2 is satisfied. If the principal offers a finite set of allowed cost-transfer pairs $\{t^k, C^k\}$ such that $|C^k - C^l| \geq \delta/\alpha$ for all (k, l), there exists a partition equilibrium in the continuation game.

The proof of proposition 9.4 is provided in appendix A9.4. It is a constructive proof that works by backward induction from $\overline{\beta}$. It starts by noticing that type $\overline{\beta}$, which never enjoys a second-period rent, maximizes its first-period utility. It then constructs the cutoff points of the partition equilibrium by moving toward $\underline{\beta}$. (Note that in this construction not all $\{t^k, C^k\}$ pairs need be chosen in equilibrium.)

We thus see that, contrary to the case in which sending a message is costless,[7] the existence of a partition equilibrium requires some stringent assumptions. Indeed it is possible to construct first-period incentive schemes for which there exists neither a partition equilibrium nor a full pooling (degenerate partition) equilibrium in the continuation game (see appendix A9.5).

We have verified that the intuition and the characterization results obtained for the continuous case also hold for the *large, but finite case* (finite number of types for the firm and finite number of potential cost-transfer pairs for the regulator). For instance, proposition 9.1 can be restated informally:

Proposition 9.1′ Let $[\underline{C}, \overline{C}]$ denote an arbitrary cost range and $[\underline{\beta}, \overline{\beta}]$ the uncertainty range. Assume that the set of potential efficiencies in the uncertainty range is finite and that the regulator must offer a finite number of (cost, transfer) pairs, where the costs belong to the cost range. For any first-period incentive scheme $t_1(\cdot)$ and for a sufficiently large number of potential efficiencies, there exists no separating equilibrium.

Proof See appendix A9.6.

Thus, with a finite number of types, separation may be feasible, but as the grid becomes finer, equilibrium costs must go to $\pm\infty$ to allow separation. This clearly cannot be optimal for the regulator. We checked that (the natural analogues of) propositions 9.2, 9.3, and 9.4 also hold in the finite case, but the statements would be cumbersome.

We have assumed that the firm's characteristic is invariant over time. More generally we could consider a second-period conditional cumulative distribution $G(\beta_2|\beta_1)$ [not to be confused with the regulator's posterior beliefs as a function of $t_1(\cdot)$ and C_1]. To keep emphasizing the ratchet effect in its extreme form, we focus on the case of almost perfect correlation. More precisely we fix the first-period cumulative distribution $F_1(\beta_1)$, and we consider a sequence of second-period conditional cumulative dis-

7. As in Crawford and Sobel (1982).

tributions $G^n(\beta_2|\beta_1)$ indexed by n (n tending to infinity), such that there exists $\varepsilon(n) > 0$ satisfying $\lim_{n\to\infty}\varepsilon(n) = 0$ and $\lim_{n\to\infty}[G^n(\beta_1 + \varepsilon(n)|\beta_1) - G^n(\beta_1 - \varepsilon(n)|\beta_1)] = 1$ uniformly over β_1. Thus the second-period distribution puts most of its weight around the first-period value. β_2 is learned (by the firm only) at the beginning of the second period.

Proposition 9.5 Under almost perfect correlation a separating equilibrium is not optimal. That is, there exists n_0 such that for $n \geq n_0$ any separating equilibrium is dominated by the optimal full pooling equilibrium.

Note that proposition 9.5 does not say that full pooling is optimal in the general class of incentive schemes but that it dominates any separating equilibrium. Its proof, which is very similar to that of proposition 9.1, is provided in appendix A9.7.

Despite the insights gained in this section, the complexity of equilibria makes it difficult to fully characterize the optimum. We now move to the two-type case in the hope of simplifying the problem.

9.4 The Two-Type Case

Consider the case where β can take only two values $\underline{\beta}$ and $\overline{\beta}$ with $\overline{\beta} > \underline{\beta}$. Let $\Delta\beta = \overline{\beta} - \underline{\beta}$. Each period the firm's utility level is $t - \psi(e)$. Unless $\Delta\beta$ is large and the probability that $\beta = \underline{\beta}$ is high, the regulator does not want to shut down the inefficient type in the one-period model. However, in the dynamic analysis, posterior (second-period) beliefs are endogenous, and we need to allow for the possibility of shutdown. To improve the readability of this section, we will ignore this possibility in the derivations. Of course in the numerical simulations shutdown must be allowed (see appendix A9.9).

It is convenient to introduce the following notation: Let $W^{FI}(v)$ be the optimal expected one-period social welfare under full information when the regulator's belief that $\beta = \underline{\beta}$ is v. From chapter 1 we know that

$$W^{FI}(v) = S - (1 + \lambda)[v\underline{\beta} + (1 - v)\overline{\beta} - e^* + \psi(e^*)]$$

with $e^* = \arg\max_e[e - \psi(e)]$.

Let $W^{AI}(v)$ be the optimal expected one-period social welfare under incomplete information with the same prior. Again from chapter 1 we have

$$W^{AI}(v) = S - v[(1 + \lambda)(\underline{\beta} - e^* + \psi(e^*)) + \lambda\Phi(\bar{e})] - (1 - v)(1 + \lambda)(\overline{\beta} - \bar{e} + \psi(\bar{e})),$$

where the inefficient type's effort level $\bar{e}$ is defined by

$$\psi'(\bar{e}) = 1 - \frac{\lambda}{1+\lambda}\frac{v}{1-v}\Phi'(\bar{e}) \quad \text{or} \quad \bar{e} = \bar{e}^S(v).$$

The superscript S is a reminder for the fact that the static optimum separates the two types, and $\Phi(\cdot)$ is defined in equation (1.19).

Finally, let $W^P(v)$ be the optimal expected one-period social welfare when the regulator is constrained to offer a single (pooling) contract. By definition, we have

$$W^P(v) = \max_C \{S - v[(1+\lambda)(C + \psi(\underline{\beta} - C)) + \lambda\Phi(\bar{\beta} - C)]$$
$$- (1-v)(1+\lambda)(C + \psi(\bar{\beta} - C))\}.$$

The optimal cost target is defined by the first-order condition

$$1 = v\psi'(\underline{\beta} - C) + (1-v)\psi'(\bar{\beta} - C) + v\frac{\lambda}{1+\lambda}\Phi'(\bar{\beta} - C).$$

Alternatively, if we denote by $e^P(v)$ the effort level of the inefficient type in this pooling allocation, we have

$$1 = v\psi'(e^P(v) - \Delta\beta) + (1-v)\psi'(e^P(v)) + v\frac{\lambda}{1+\lambda}\Phi'(e^P(v)),$$

from which it is easily seen that $e^P(v) \in (e^*, e^* + \Delta\beta)$.

We consider now the two-period version of this model. As in the continuum case the equilibria often involve some form of pooling, but unlike in the continuum case, separation can occur. The nature of pooling can be very complex. We will restrict our analysis to two steps. First we will assume that a finite number of contracts is offered in period 1, and we will characterize menus that can yield the upper bound on welfare subject to equilibrium behavior. Then we will discuss the structure of continuation equilibria when the number of contracts offered in period 1 is the number of types (i.e., two). We will prove that we have only two types of continuation equilibria. We next relax the restrictions and ask what the robust results are. First we show that as δ goes to zero, the separating equilibrium gets as close as desired to the optimum and that, as δ goes to infinity, the pooling equilibrium gets as close as desired to the optimum. Then we show that there exists δ_0 such that for $\delta < \delta_0$ the optimum is a separating equilibrium and that for any large δ the optimum is close but never equal to the pooling equilibrium.

9.4.1 Characterization of Finite First-Period Menus That Induce the Upper Bound on Welfare

Consider a finite set of contracts that are offered and used in period 1: $(C^0, t^0), (C^1, t^1), \ldots, (C^K, t^K)$, with $C^0 < C^1 < \cdots < C^K$. Let $A^0, \ldots, A^K$ denote the associated points in the (C, t) space.

Let $(x^0, x^1, \ldots, x^K)$, with $x^k \geq 0$ for all k and $\sum_{k=0}^{K} x^k = 1$, be the probabilities that the efficient type selects in period 1 these contracts, and similarly let $(y^0, y^1, \ldots, y^K)$ denote the corresponding probabilities for the inefficient type, with $x^k + y^k > 0$ for all k. With the choice of A^k by the firm in period 1 is associated the regulator's posterior probability v^k that the firm is efficient:

$$v^k = \frac{x^k v}{x^k v + y^k(1 - v)}.$$

The second-period contract is the optimal static contract derived in chapter 1 for the beliefs v^k. It yields no rent for type $\bar{\beta}$ and rent $\mathscr{U}(v^k)$ for type $\underline{\beta}$ with

$$\mathscr{U}(v^k) = \Phi(e_{v^k}),$$

$$\psi'(e_{v^k}) = 1 - \frac{\lambda}{1 + \lambda} \frac{v^k}{1 - v^k} \psi''(e_{v^k})$$

[as long as v^k does not exceed the cutoff beliefs; otherwise, $\mathscr{U}(v^k) = 0$. See chapter 1.]

Proposition 9.6 provides a first characterization of the first-period menu that yields the upper bound on intertemporal welfare subject to the constraint that the allocation results from a continuation equilibrium for this menu. A word of explanation is in order here. At this stage we are not saying that the regulator actually offers in the first period a menu satisfying the property stated in proposition 9.6 below. It might be the case that the menu associated with the upper bound gives rise to other, lower-welfare, continuation equilibria. Indeed, if a welfare suboptimal equilibrium prevailed for this menu, the regulator might want to offer an alternative menu that does not yield the upper bound on intertemporal welfare. The appropriate methodology is then to compute the menu that (for some continuation equilibrium) yields the upper bound on welfare by using characterizations such as that of proposition 9.6, and then to see if the resulting continuation equilibrium is unique (chapter 10 also uses this methodology).

Proposition 9.6 A first-period menu that (for some continuation equilibrium) yields the upper bound on intertemporal welfare must satisfy the following property: There exists $\underline{U} \geq \bar{U} \geq 0$ such that

i. $x^k > 0$, $k = 0, \ldots, K - 1$,

ii. $y^k > 0$, $k = 1, \ldots, K$,

iii. $t^k - \psi(\bar{\beta} - C^k) = \bar{U}$, $k = 1, \ldots, K$,

iv. $t^k - \psi(\underline{\beta} - C^k) + \delta\mathscr{U}(v^k) = \underline{U}$, $k = 0, \ldots, K - 1$.

Proof See appendix A9.8.

Thus at the upper bound the efficient type separates with probability at most x^0; the inefficient type separates with probability at most y^K; and, with probability at least $\nu(1-x^0)+(1-\nu)(1-y^K)$, pooling contracts are chosen leading to posterior beliefs ν^k (see figure 9.5). The fact that the utilities of the two types are constant on the support of their strategies (properties iii and iv) simply results from the definition of a continuation equilibrium. The real force of proposition 9.6 is that the upper bound on the regulator's welfare can be obtained by having a single separating allocation per type.

Note that from properties iii and iv for $k = 1, \ldots, K-1$, $\psi(\bar{\beta}-C^k) - \psi(\underline{\beta}-C^k) + \delta\mathscr{U}(\nu^k) = \underline{U} - \bar{U}$. Differentiating this expression and using the definition of $\mathscr{U}(\nu^k)$ and ν^k, it is easily seen that ν^k must decrease with k: Since the first-period rent $\psi(\bar{\beta}-C^k)-\psi(\underline{\beta}-C^k)$ decreases with C^k and therefore k, the second-period rent $\mathscr{U}(\nu^k)$ must increase with k, which means that the higher the k, the more confident the regulator is that the firm is inefficient. Proposition 9.6 is illustrated in figure 9.5.

The optimization by the regulator in the set defined by proposition 9.6 is an involved nonconcave programming problem. We did not find any argument to exclude generally menus with more than two contracts. However, to confirm the view that continuation equilibria can be complex, we restrict our analysis to two-contract menus ($K = 1$) and identify three types of equilibria. We prove that "type II equilibria" cannot be optimal, and we study by simulation the comparative statics of the optimal contract.

9.4.2 Preliminary Analysis: Two-Contract Menus

If $K = 1$, two contracts (t^0, C^0) and (t^1, C^1) are offered. Without loss of generality, assume that type $\underline{\beta}$ chooses (t^0, C^0) with positive probability and that type $\bar{\beta}$ chooses (t^1, C^1) with positive probability. There are at

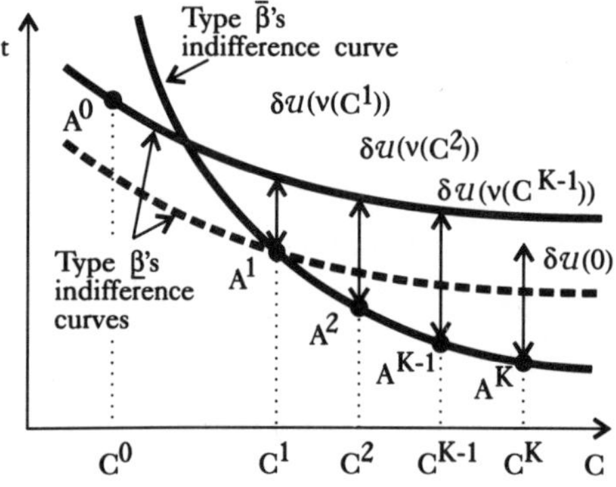

Figure 9.5
Dynamic incentive compatibility

least four constraints for the regulator, two IR constraints and two IC constraints:

$$t^0 - \psi(\underline{\beta} - C^0) + \delta\mathscr{U}(v^0) \geq t^1 - \psi(\underline{\beta} - C^1) + \delta\mathscr{U}(v^1) \qquad (\underline{\text{IC}}),$$

$$t^1 - \psi(\bar{\beta} - C^1) \geq t^0 - \psi(\bar{\beta} - C^0) \qquad (\overline{\text{IC}}),$$

$$t^0 - \psi(\underline{\beta} - C^0) + \delta\mathscr{U}(v^0) \geq 0 \qquad (\underline{\text{IR}}),$$

$$t^1 - \psi(\bar{\beta} - C^1) \geq 0 \qquad (\overline{\text{IR}}).$$

Clearly $(\overline{\text{IR}})$ and $(\underline{\text{IC}})$ imply $(\underline{\text{IR}})$. To obtain the upper bound on welfare, $(\overline{\text{IR}})$ must be binding. [This property could alternatively be derived from a "Markov principle": If $(\overline{\text{IR}})$ were not binding, the regulator could reduce t^0 and t^1 by the same small positive amount and keep all constraints satisfied; if one assumes that the same continuation equilibrium prevails after this lump-sum reduction in the firm's income as before, social welfare is increased due to the presence of the shadow cost of public funds. It is difficult to rule out a positive rent for both types because the reduction in income described above could bring about a change in the continuation equilibrium if there exist several such equilibria. We, however, find our restriction reasonable.] Therefore at the optimum we have at most three types of equilibria [with $(\overline{\text{IR}})$ binding]:

Type I: $(\underline{\text{IC}})$ alone is binding.

Type II: $(\overline{\text{IC}})$ alone is binding.

Type III: Both incentive constraints are binding.

Note that an equilibrium with full pooling in the first period is a degenerate version of any of the three equilibrium types.

Equilibrium of Type I: Incentive Constraint of Only the Efficient Type Binding

In a type I equilibrium the inefficient type strictly prefers to choose (t^1, C^1), while the efficient type is indifferent between (t^0, C^0) and (t^1, C^1) and chooses (t^0, C^0) with probability x^0. If the efficient type does not randomize, we have a separating equilibrium. A separating type I equilibrium is depicted in figure 9.6.

Let $\underline{e}$ denote type $\underline{\beta}$'s effort when choosing contract (t^0, C^0) (i.e., $C^0 = \underline{\beta} - \underline{e}$), and let $\bar{e}$ denote type $\bar{\beta}$'s effort when choosing contract (t^1, C^1) (i.e., $C^1 = \bar{\beta} - \bar{e}$). Social welfare for a type I equilibrium is

$$\begin{aligned} S &- v_1 x^0(1+\lambda)[\underline{\beta} - \underline{e} + \psi(\underline{e})] - v_1(1-x^0)(1+\lambda)[\bar{\beta} - \bar{e} + \psi(\bar{e} - \Delta\beta)] \\ &- (1-v_1)(1+\lambda)[\bar{\beta} - \bar{e} + \psi(\bar{e})] - v_1\lambda\Phi(\bar{e}) \\ &+ \delta v_1 x^0[W^{FI}(1) - \lambda\mathscr{U}(v^1)] + \delta[v_1(1-x^0) + (1-v_1)]W^{AI}(v^1), \end{aligned} \tag{9.11}$$

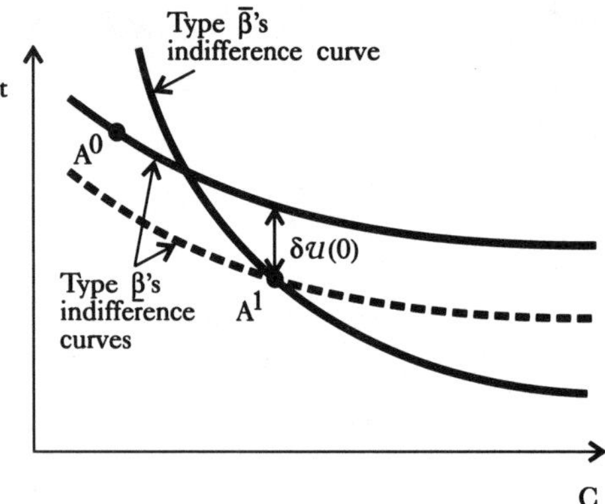

Figure 9.6
Incentive constraint of type $\underline{\beta}$ binding

where

$$v^1 \equiv \frac{v_1(1 - x^0)}{(1 - v_1) + v_1(1 - x^0)}.$$

The second-period terms in this social welfare can be interpreted as follows: With probability $v_1 x^0$ the firm has type $\underline{\beta}$ and reveals it; the second-period welfare is then the full information one corresponding to the efficient type except that the efficient type must be compensated in period 1 for not choosing C^1 and obtaining rent $\Phi(\bar{e}) + \delta\mathscr{U}(v^1)$. With probability $v_1(1 - x^0) + (1 - v_1)$, the firm chooses C^1, and the second-period expected welfare is $W^{AI}(v^1)$, which already embodies the social cost of the efficient type's second-period rent. Maximization of (9.11) with respect to $\underline{e}$ and $\bar{e}$ yields

$$\underline{e} = e^*,$$

$$\psi'(\bar{e}) = 1 - \frac{\lambda}{1+\lambda}\frac{v_1}{1-v_1}\Phi'(\bar{e}) + \frac{v_1}{1-v_1}(1 - x^0)(1 - \psi'(\bar{e} - \Delta\beta)),$$

with $e^P(v_1) \geq \bar{e} \geq \bar{e}^S(v_1)$. The pooling solution (resp. the separating solution) corresponds to $x^0 = 0$ (resp. $x^0 = 1$). In the special case of a separating equilibrium ($x^0 = 1$), social welfare reduces to

$$W^{AI}(v_1) - v_1\lambda\delta\mathscr{U}(0) + \delta W^{FI}(v_1).$$

In a semiseparating or pooling equilibrium ($x^0 < 1$), the ratchet effect leads to more powerful incentives than in the static model. The intuition is that distorting the inefficient type's effort $\bar{e}$ toward low effort also distorts the efficient type's effort when the latter pools with the inefficient type. The inefficient type may even work harder than in the first-best level of effort, since $e^P(v_1) > e^*$.

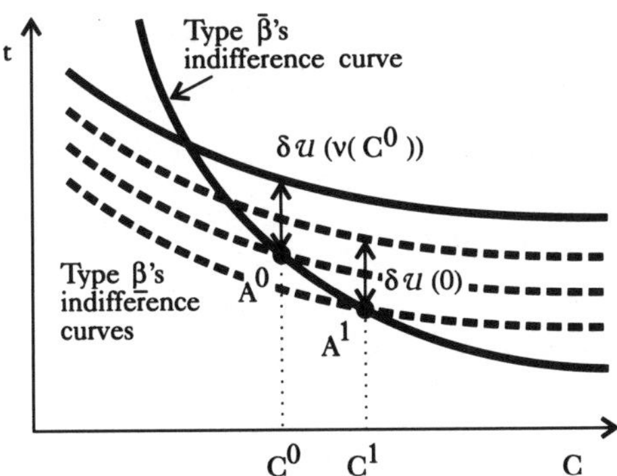

Figure 9.7
Incentive constraint of type $\overline{\beta}$ binding

Equilibrium of Type II: Incentive Constraint of Only the Inefficient Type Binding

In a type II equilibrium the efficient type strictly prefers to select contract (t^0, C^0) (or strictly prefers to reveal its true type), while the inefficient type is indifferent between the contracts (t^0, C^0) and (t^1, C^1) and may or may not randomize. A type II equilibrium is depicted in figure 9.7.

Let y^0 denote the probability that type $\overline{\beta}$ chooses cost C^0. Let $\underline{e}$ denote type $\underline{\beta}$'s effort (so $C^0 = \underline{\beta} - \underline{e}$), and let $\bar{e}$ denote type $\overline{\beta}$'s effort when choosing C^1 (so $C^1 = \overline{\beta} - \bar{e}$). Note that the efficient type's rent is $\Phi(\underline{e} + \Delta\beta)$ in period 1 (since type $\overline{\beta}$ exerts effort $\underline{e} + \Delta\beta$ when choosing cost C^0) and $\mathscr{U}(v^0)$ in period 2 where $v^0 \equiv v_1/[v_1 + (1 - v_1)y^0]$. Social welfare for a type II equilibrium is

$$\begin{aligned} S &- v_1(1+\lambda)[\underline{\beta} - \underline{e} + \psi(\underline{e})] - (1 - v_1)y^0(1+\lambda)[\underline{\beta} - \underline{e} + \psi(\underline{e} + \Delta\beta)] \\ &- (1 - v_1)(1 - y^0)(1+\lambda)[\overline{\beta} - \bar{e} + \psi(\bar{e})] - v_1\lambda\Phi(\underline{e} + \Delta\beta) \\ &+ \delta\{[v_1 + y^0(1 - v_1)]W^{AI}(v^0) + (1 - v_1)(1 - y^0)W^{FI}(0)\}. \end{aligned}$$

The maximization of social welfare with respect to $\underline{e}$ and $\bar{e}$ leads to

$$\bar{e} = e^*,$$

$$\psi'(\underline{e}) = 1 - \frac{\lambda}{1+\lambda}\Phi'(\underline{e} + \Delta\beta) + \frac{1 - v_1}{v_1}y^0(1 - \psi'(\underline{e} + \Delta\beta)),$$

where $\underline{e}$ lies between the pooling solution corresponding to $y^0 = 1$ and the "separating" solution corresponding to $y^0 = 0$. Moreover $\underline{e} < e^*$ (since at e^* the derivative of social welfare with respect to $\underline{e}$ is negative).

The following lemma enables us to eliminate type II equilibria from further analysis:

Lemma 9.1 A type II equilibrium cannot be optimal.

Proof Let us compute the derivative of social welfare with respect to y^0 and show that it is always negative for $y^0 > 0$: This derivative is

$$(1 - \nu_1)(1 + \lambda)[\bar{\beta} - \bar{e} + \psi(\bar{e}) - (\bar{\beta} - (\underline{e} + \Delta\beta) + \psi(\underline{e} + \Delta\beta))]$$

$$+ \delta(1 - \nu_1)\left[W^{AI}(v^0) - W^{AI}(0) + \frac{\nu_1 + y^0(1 - \nu_1)}{1 - \nu_1}\frac{dW^{AI}}{dv^0}\frac{dv^0}{dy^0}\right].$$

The first term is negative since $\bar{e} = e^*$ in an optimal type II equilibrium. Furthermore

$$\frac{\nu_1 + y^0(1 - \nu_1)}{1 - \nu_1}\frac{dW^{AI}}{dv^0}\frac{dv^0}{dy^0} = -v^0\frac{dW^{AI}}{dv^0}(v^0).$$

The second term in the derivative of social welfare is negative because $W^{AI}(v^0)$ is increasing and convex, as is easily checked. Last, either $y^0 = 0$ yields an incentive compatible allocation and the optimum is separating, though the best separating equilibrium is a type I equilibrium, or the incentive constraint of the efficient type becomes binding before y^0 reaches 0, and our initial allocation is dominated by a type III equilibrium. ■

The intuition for lemma 9.1 is that increasing the probability that type $\bar{e}$ chooses first-period cost $\bar{\beta} - \bar{e} = \bar{\beta} - e^*$ raises first-period welfare. It also raises second-period welfare because the regulator is then better informed. It does not undermine incentive compatibility if the incentive constraint of type $\underline{\beta}$ is not binding.

Equilibrium of Type III: Both Incentive Constraints Binding

In a type III equilibrium both types are indifferent between the two contracts (t^0, C^0) and (t^1, C^1). None, one, or both types can randomize. A type III equilibrium is depicted in figure 9.8. Using the same notational conventions as for the other types of equilibrium, social welfare for a type III equilibrium is

$$\begin{aligned}
S &- \nu_1 x^0(1 + \lambda)(\underline{\beta} - \underline{e} + \psi(\underline{e})) - \nu_1(1 - x^0)(1 + \lambda)(\bar{\beta} - \bar{e} + \psi(\bar{e} - \Delta\beta)) \\
&- (1 - \nu_1)(1 - y^0)(1 + \lambda)(\bar{\beta} - \bar{e} + \psi(\bar{e})) \\
&- (1 - \nu_1)y^0(1 + \lambda)(\underline{\beta} - \underline{e} + \psi(\underline{e} + \Delta\beta)) \\
&- \nu_1 x^0 \lambda \Phi(\underline{e} + \Delta\beta) - \nu_1(1 - x^0)\lambda\Phi(\bar{e}) \\
&+ \delta[(\nu_1 x^0 + (1 - \nu_1)y^0)W^{AI}(v^0) \\
&+ (\nu_1(1 - x^0) + (1 - \nu_1)(1 - y^0))W^{AI}(v^1)].
\end{aligned}$$

$\underline{e}$ and $\bar{e}$ are obtained in this regime by maximizing social welfare under the constraint $\Phi(\underline{e} + \Delta\beta) + \delta\mathscr{U}(v^0) = \Phi(\bar{e}) + \delta\mathscr{U}(v^1)$.

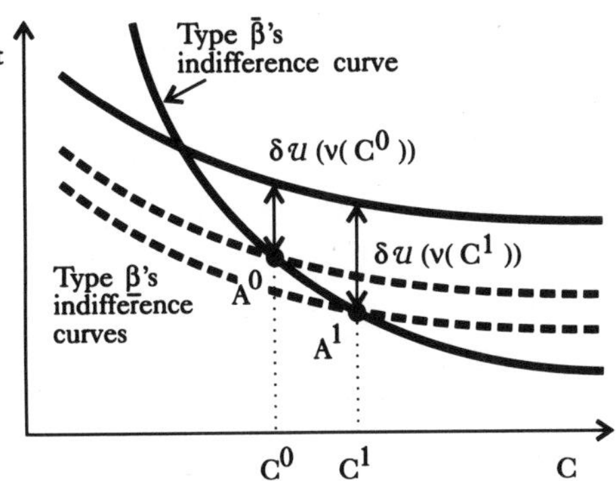

Figure 9.8
Both incentive constraints binding

Some Comparisons

If attention is reduced to (the best) separating and (the best) pooling first-period allocations, we have the simple proposition 9.7.

Proposition 9.7 There exists $\delta_0 > 0$ such that for $\delta \leq \delta_0$, separation is better than pooling, and for $\delta \geq \delta_0$, pooling is better than separation.

Proof Let W^P, W^{FI}, and W^{AI} denote, respectively, the best one-period welfare under pooling, the full information one-period welfare, and the asymmetric information one-period welfare (obtained in chapter 1). All are relative to a static context with beliefs v_1. Note that

$$W^{AI} > W^{FI} - v_1 \lambda \Phi(e^*).$$

Under asymmetric information and in a static context, the regulator could offer a fixed-price contract [i.e., $t(C) = \psi(e^*) - (C - (\bar{\beta} - e^*))$] and obtain the full information welfare except that this contract would leave rent $\Phi(e^*)$, and the regulator can do strictly better than this.

Now consider the two-period context. Welfare under the optimal pooling allocation is

$$\mathscr{W}^P = W^P + \delta W^{AI}.$$

Welfare under the optimal separating allocation is

$$\mathscr{W}^S = \max_{\{\underline{e},\bar{e}\}} \{S - v_1[(1+\lambda)(\underline{\beta} - \underline{e} + \psi(\underline{e})) + \lambda(\Phi(\bar{e}) + \delta\Phi(e^*))]$$
$$- (1 - v_1)(1+\lambda)(\bar{\beta} - \bar{e} + \psi(\bar{e})) + \delta W^{FI}\}$$

subject to

$$\Phi(\underline{e} + \Delta\beta) \geq \Phi(\bar{e}) + \delta\Phi(e^*) \qquad (\gamma)(\overline{\text{IC}}).$$

To obtain the incentive constraint ($\overline{\text{IC}}$) of the inefficient type, note that the efficient type's rent $\underline{t} - \psi(\underline{e}) + \delta \cdot 0$ is equal to $\Phi(\bar{e}) + \delta\Phi(e^*)$. Constraint ($\overline{\text{IC}}$) can be written

$$\underline{t} - \psi(\underline{e} + \Delta\beta) \leq 0,$$

which yields the expression above. [In passing, for δ small, ($\overline{\text{IC}}$) is not binding, and the solution $\{\underline{e}, \bar{e}\}$ is the optimal static solution. For larger δ's, $\underline{e}$ is increased and $\bar{e}$ further decreased to ensure that ($\overline{\text{IC}}$) is satisfied.]

We thus have

$$\frac{\partial}{\partial\delta}(\mathscr{W}^P - \mathscr{W}^S) = W^{AI} + v_1\lambda\Phi(e^*) - W^{FI} + \gamma\Phi(e^*) > 0.$$

Last, $\mathscr{W}^S > \mathscr{W}^P$ for $\delta = 0$. It is trivial to show that $\mathscr{W}^P > \mathscr{W}^S$ for large δ: The per-period welfare $\mathscr{W}^P/(1+\delta)$ converges to the commitment welfare W^{AI}, while $\mathscr{W}^S/(1+\delta)$ does not. ∎

Proposition 9.8 If ψ' is bounded away from zero (e.g., by α), there exists $\eta > 0$ such that, if $\Delta\beta \leq \eta$, the regulator is better off fully pooling the two types than fully separating them.

Proof For the optimal full pooling welfare, the welfare distortion relative to the commitment welfare (which is equal to the first-period distortion) converges to zero with $\Delta\beta$. Let us consider a separating equilibrium and the associated incentive constraints:

$$\underline{t} - \psi(\underline{\beta} - \underline{C}) \geq \bar{t} - \psi(\underline{\beta} - \bar{C}) + \delta\mathscr{U}(0),$$

$$\bar{t} - \psi(\bar{\beta} - \bar{C}) \geq \underline{t} - \psi(\bar{\beta} - \underline{C}),$$

where use is made of the facts that under full information a firm's rent is zero and that when type $\bar{\beta}$ lies in the first period, it can quit in the second period and get a zero rent. Furthermore we know that for small $\Delta\beta$, $\mathscr{U}(0) \approx \Delta\beta$. Adding up the two incentive constraints and using the convexity of ψ, we obtain

$$\psi(\bar{\beta} - \bar{C} - \Delta\beta) - \psi(\bar{\beta} - \bar{C}) + \psi(\underline{\beta} - \underline{C} + \Delta\beta) - \psi(\underline{\beta} - \underline{C}) \geq \delta\mathscr{U}(0),$$

or

$$\Delta\beta[\psi'(\underline{\beta} - \underline{C}) - \psi'(\underline{\beta} - \underline{C} + \Delta\beta - (\bar{C} - \underline{C}))] \gtrsim \delta\Delta\beta,$$

or

$$[(\bar{C} - \underline{C}) - \Delta\beta]\alpha \gtrsim \delta,$$

or

$$\bar{C} - \underline{C} \gtrsim \Delta\beta + \frac{\delta}{\alpha}.$$

Thus we see that the cost differential cannot converge to zero with $\Delta\beta$. The welfare distortion in a separating equilibrium is bounded away from zero. ■

9.4.3 Comparative Statics of the Optimal Contract in an Example

To explore some comparative statics properties of the optimal contract, we consider the special case of a quadratic disutility of effort function $\psi(e) = \frac{1}{2}[\max(0, e)]^2$. For this function, $e^* = 1$. From section 9.4.2. and lemma 9.1, we know that only a type I equilibrium or a type III equilibrium can be optimal.

Table 9.1 shows how the optimal equilibrium depends on δ. If $\delta = 0$, the model is isomorphic to the static case. When δ is positive and small, we still have a separating equilibrium. As δ increases, equilibria of type III in which both types' incentive constraints are binding become optimal. Note also that when δ is large, the effort level of the inefficient type exceeds the first best level (recall that this should be so in a pooling equilibrium).

We see in table 9.2 that as the prior probability ν_1 of the efficient type increases, fewer and fewer transfers are made to induce the inefficient type to provide a high level of effort. Moreover the expected rent of the firm decreases as the regulator becomes more and more convinced that the firm is efficient.

As the opportunity cost of public funds increases, fewer expenses are incurred to induce effort, and effort levels decrease (see table 9.3). As $\Delta\beta$ decreases, full separation is no longer optimal. The firm's rent increases with $\Delta\beta$ (see table 9.4).

9.4.4 General Results

At this point in our analysis we remove the restriction that the regulator can offer only two contracts. We also no longer require that the inefficient type's individual rationality constraint be binding.

Table 9.1
Varying the discount factor ($\underline{\beta} = 1.5$, $\bar{\beta} = 2$, $S = 100$, $\nu_1 = 0.5$, $\lambda = 0.1$)

	$\delta = 0.01$	$\delta = 0.1$	$\delta = 1$	$\delta = 10$
Type of equilibrium	I	I	III	III
yielding the upper bound	$x^0 = 1$	$x^0 = 1$	$x^0 = 1$	$x^0 = 0.9$
			$y^0 = 0$	$y^0 = 0.9$
$\underline{e}_1$	1	1	1.10	0.72
$\bar{e}_1$	0.95	0.95	0.85	1.23
$\underline{t}_1$	0.85	0.89	1.28	0.75
$\bar{t}_1$	0.45	0.45	0.36	0.75
Expected welfare/$(1 + \delta)$	98.6	98.6	98.6	98.6
Expected rent/$(1 + \delta)$	0.35	0.38	0.34	0.36

Table 9.2
Varying the prior ($\underline{\beta} = 1, \bar{\beta} = 2, S = 100, \delta = 0.5, \lambda = 0.1$)

	$v_1 = 0.1$	$v_1 = 0.3$	$v_1 = 0.5$	$v_1 = 0.7$
Type of equilibrium	I	I	I	I
yielding the upper bound	$x^0 = 1$	$x^0 = 1$	$x^0 = 1$	$x^0 = 1$
$\underline{e}_1$	1	1	1	1
$\bar{e}_1$	0.99	0.96	0.90	0.79
$\underline{t}_1$	1.24	1.21	1.15	1.04
$\bar{t}_1$	0.49	0.46	0.41	0.31
Expected welfare	147.7	148.0	148.3	148.6
Expected rent	0.74	0.71	0.66	0.53

Table 9.3
Varying the shadow cost of public funds ($\underline{\beta} = 1.5, \bar{\beta} = 2, S = 100, \delta = 0.5, v_1 = 0.5$)

	$\lambda = 0.01$	$\lambda = 0.1$	$\lambda = 1$
Type of equilibrium	I	I	I
yielding the upper bound			
$\underline{e}_1$	1	1	1
$\bar{e}_1$	0.99	0.91	0.50
$\underline{t}_1$	1.24	1.15	0.75
$\bar{t}_1$	0.49	0.41	0.12
Expected welfare	148.5	148.3	146.8
Expected rent	0.74	0.66	0.25

Table 9.4
Varying the uncertainty ($\underline{\beta} = 1, S = 100, \delta = 0.5, \lambda = 0.1, v_1 = 0.5$)

	$\bar{\beta} = 1.01$	$\bar{\beta} = 1.1$	$\bar{\beta} = 1.5$
Type of equilibrium	III	III	I
yielding the upper bound	$x^0 = 0.1$	$x^0 = 0.9$	
	$y^0 = 0.2$	$y^0 = 0.1$	
$\underline{e}_1$	0.99	0.96	1
$\bar{e}_1$	1.00	1.02	0.95
$\underline{t}_1$	0.50	0.57	1.04
$\bar{t}_1$	0.50	0.53	0.45
Expected welfare	149.2	149.1	148.7
Expected rent	0.01	0.04	0.54

Small Discount Factor

The optimal contract with commitment is the repetition of the optimal static contract. Suppose that the regulator picks the optimal static cost-transfer pairs but adds $\delta\mathscr{U}(0)$ to the firm's transfer $\underline{t}$ when it announces $\underline{\beta}$. That is, let the regulator offer the contracts $\{\underline{t} = \psi(\underline{e}) + \mathscr{U}(v_1) + \delta\mathscr{U}(0), \underline{C} = \underline{\beta} - e^*\}$ for type $\underline{\beta}$ and $\{\bar{t} = \psi(\bar{e}(v_1)), \bar{C} = \bar{\beta} - \bar{e}(v_1)\}$ for type $\bar{\beta}$. Because δ is small, this allocation (called henceforth the "separating one") is incentive compatible. Clearly, by construction, type $\underline{\beta}$ weakly prefers to announce $\underline{\beta}$, and since δ is small and since type $\bar{\beta}$'s incentive constraint is not binding in the optimal static mechanism, type $\bar{\beta}$ still tells the truth. This first-period separating allocation is followed by the complete-information allocation in the second period. In period 1 it yields a distortion of $\lambda v_1 \delta\mathscr{U}(0)$ relative to the optimal incomplete information static welfare. Intertemporal social welfare with this separating allocation is then

$$W^{AI}(v_1) - \lambda v_1 \delta\mathscr{U}(0) + \delta W^{FI}(v_1),$$

so the total distortion relative to the commitment situation is equal to

$$\delta[\lambda v_1 \mathscr{U}(0) - (W^{FI}(v_1) - W^{AI}(v_1))].$$

For small δ this distortion is negligible. If δ is chosen small enough, the separating allocation yields a social welfare as close as desired to the optimal social welfare. Actually we can show more:

Proposition 9.9 If ψ'' is bounded away from zero (e.g., by α), the optimal first-period incentive scheme induces full separation between the types and yields in period 1 the same effort levels as in the optimal static mechanism.

Proof See appendix A9.10.

Intuitively, pooling in period 1 must be infinitesimal as δ goes to zero; otherwise, contrary to what happens with the separating solution, the distortion relative to the commitment solution cannot go to zero. But any type of pooling creates an ε misallocation in period 1 and only a $\delta\varepsilon$ gain in rent reduction.

We know that the regulator loses from his or her inability to commit. We may wonder whether the firm is also worse off under no commitment. The answer is provided by a simple corollary of proposition 9.9.

Corollary For δ small, the firm prefers the noncommitment situation.

Proof Note that type $\bar{\beta}$ has a zero rent in both cases. Suppose that δ is close to zero. From proposition 9.9 type $\underline{\beta}$'s equilibrium rent under noncommitment is equal to $\mathscr{U}(v_1) + \delta\mathscr{U}(0)$ instead of $(1 + \delta)\mathscr{U}(v_1)$ in the commitment case. ∎

We saw in subsection 9.4.3 that if attention is restricted to two-contract menus, and for larger δ's, the firm may prefer the commitment solution. We conjecture that this also may be the case without any restriction to two contracts.

Large Discount Factor

We now look at the other polar case of a large discount factor. A large discount factor is not uncommon: The accounting period in the second production stage could exceed that for the first production stage or the second-period project could be much more important than the first-period one. For a large discount factor the firm is very wary of the ratchet effect, so it is quite costly to induce it to reveal its type. Yet, because the future matters a lot to the regulator as well, revelation of information has a high value.

For a large δ, the first-period welfare is negligible. By offering a single contract in period 1, the regulator "commits" not to update his or her beliefs and ensures the optimal static mechanism in period 2. So, if we consider the best pooling allocation in period 1 followed by the optimal static mechanism, the loss relative to the optimal commitment solution can be made as small as we wish. (On the other hand, the welfare under the separating allocation of proposition 9.9, which actually is no longer incentive compatible, stays away from optimal social welfare in the sense that the distortion relative to global welfare does not converge to zero.) However, it is not the case that for δ large, full pooling becomes optimal. The asymptotic behavior of the optimal contract for δ large is described by proposition 9.10.

Proposition 9.10 For δ large, a perfect Bayesian equilibrium of the overall game is empirically indistinguishable from a full pooling equilibrium in the following sense: Consider a sequence $\delta \to \infty$ and a selection of equilibrium strategy profiles σ_δ. The ex ante probability that posterior beliefs are close to prior beliefs converges to 1: For all ε_1,

$$\mathrm{Prob}_{\sigma_\delta}(|\nu_2 - \nu_1| > \varepsilon_1) \xrightarrow[\delta \to \infty]{} 0.$$

The proof of proposition 9.10 is straightforward: If ν_2 differed from ν_1 with nonnegligible probability, the second-period allocation would differ from the optimal static allocation with nonnegligible probability. By strict concavity of the static program (1.21), the resulting distortion, which is proportional to δ, would dominate any first-period gain over full pooling. Finally, we conjecture that the ex ante probability that the firm chooses a cost C_1 close to the optimal full pooling cost converges to 1: For all $\varepsilon_2 > 0$,

$$\text{Prob}_{\sigma_\delta}(|C_1 - C^P(v_1)| > \varepsilon_2) \xrightarrow[\delta \to \infty]{} 0.$$

9.5 Concluding Remarks

The analysis in this chapter has been quite complex. We have focused on technical aspects, but a number of economic implications emerge. For instance, the regulator learns the firm's technology slowly when both parties are patient. This is true even though the principal gains much from learning the information and could use transfers to elicit it. Also, contrary to what intuition first suggests, the ratcheting effect may not lower incentives. In fact incentives are likely to be quite high powered for inefficient types.

The results of our game-theoretic approach differ from those obtained by positing a rule in which the incentive scheme is updated in a mechanistic way as a function of past performance.[8] Such a mechanistic approach would predict type-independent behavior, immediate revelation of the technology, and low-powered incentives; it would also offer little guidance as to the time pattern of the incentive scheme.

BIBLIOGRAPHIC NOTES

B9.1 Passive Target Setting

Several papers have analyzed the behavior of a regulated firm facing an incentive scheme that moves according to some exogenous, backward-looking revision rule. Perhaps the best-known work in this area is by Weitzman (1980).

Weitzman's analysis proceeds as follows: A regulated firm has cost $C_\tau = \beta - e_\tau$ at dates $\tau = 1, 2, \ldots$. The private cost of effort at date τ is $\psi(e_\tau)$. The firm faces the incentive scheme

$$t_\tau = b(\overline{C}_\tau - C_\tau),$$

where $\overline{C}_\tau$ is date τ "target." The slope b of the incentive scheme is time invariant, but the intercept $b\overline{C}_\tau$ need not be.

8. See bibliographic notes B9.1.

If $\overline{C}_\tau$ were not backward looking, the firm would choose effort $e_\tau = e^*(b)$, where $\psi'(e^*(b)) = b$, regardless of its efficiency parameter β. But suppose instead that the cost target is revised on the basis of past performance:

$$\overline{C}_\tau = kC_{\tau-1} + (1-k)\overline{C}_{\tau-1} + h,$$

where $k \in [0, 1]$. Then the firm maximizes

$$\sum_{\tau=1}^{\infty} \delta^{\tau-1}[b(\overline{C}_\tau - C_\tau) - \psi(e_\tau)]$$

subject to the feedback adjustment rule for the target. The solution equates, for each τ, the marginal disutility of effort and the present discounted value of a current unit reduction in cost on current and future rewards:

$$\psi'(e_\tau) = b - b\delta k(1 + \delta(1-k) + \delta^2(1-k)^2 + \cdots) = \frac{b}{1 + (k/r)} \quad \text{for all } \tau,$$

where r is the interest rate, $\delta = 1/(1+r)$. Thus effort is type and time independent and is lower than when the intercept of the incentive scheme is independent of past performance: A lower cost today reduces the payment tomorrow and is less profitable for the firm. The model thus exhibits a form of the ratchet effect, in that the firm is concerned that a good performance today will make future schemes more demanding.

In Weitzman's model the regulator's behavior and updating of beliefs are blackboxed and subsumed in the revision rule for the incentive scheme. Game theory endogenizes the revision of the incentive scheme. The results are accordingly different. For instance, the firm's behavior depends on its technology and the firm does not reveal its technology immediately, the power of the incentive scheme varies over time, and effort need not be lower than under a non-backward-looking revision rule.

B9.2 Game-Theoretic Approach: The Restriction to Linear Schemes

Freixas et al. (1985) developed a game-theoretic analysis of the revision of linear incentive schemes. They did so in a simple case: The firm has two types, and the relationship lasts two periods. Quite crucially the restriction of incentive schemes to linear schemes, $t_\tau = a_\tau - b_\tau C_\tau$, is maintained. As we will see, the linearity restriction considerably simplifies the analysis by eliminating the problems associated with multiple optimal choices for the inefficient type and by ruling out the take-the-money-and-run strategy emphasized in this chapter.

Consider the framework of section 9.4. The firm has two potential types $\underline{\beta}$ and $\overline{\beta}$ and cost function $C_\tau = \beta - e_\tau$, $\tau = 1, 2$. The disutility of effort is

$\psi(e_\tau)$. Denote the date 1 and date 2 probabilities of an efficient type by v_1 and v_2. In period 2, when facing incentive scheme (a_2, b_2), the firm solves

$$\max_{e_2} \{a_2 - b_2(\beta - e_2) - \psi(e_2)\}$$

and thus chooses (type independent) effort $e_2 = e^*(b_2)$ where (as in B9.1) $\psi'(e^*(b)) \equiv b$. The efficient type's second-period rent is $b_2 \Delta\beta = b_2(\bar{\beta} - \underline{\beta})$.

The regulator chooses the second-period slope b_2 so as to solve

$$\max_{b_2} \{S - (1 + \lambda)[\psi(e^*(b_2)) + (v_2\underline{\beta} + (1 - v_2)\bar{\beta} - e^*(b_2))] - \lambda v_2 b_2 \Delta\beta\}.$$

A revealed preference argument shows that the optimal slope $b_2(v_2)$ is nonincreasing in v_2. (Note that the cross-partial derivative of the maximand in v_2 and b_2 is negative. We make the maintained assumption that the regulator does not shut down the inefficient type.) The efficient type's rent under linear schemes, $\mathscr{U}^L(v_2)$ is thus given by

$$\mathscr{U}^L(v_2) = b_2(v_2)\Delta\beta$$

and is a decreasing function of the posterior probability of an efficient type (e.g., $\mathscr{U}^L(0) = \Delta\beta$).

Consider now the firm's first-period reaction to an arbitrary incentive scheme $t_1 = a_1 - b_1 C_1$. As in this chapter, type $\bar{\beta}$ knows that it will never enjoy a second-period rent and therefore maximizes its first-period utility. But, in contrast to this chapter, its optimal choice, point A in figure 9.9, is unique. This gives rise to drastically different analyses for linear and nonlinear incentive schemes. Consider now the efficient type. We first claim that the support of type $\underline{\beta}$'s optimal strategy is included in the two-point set $\{\underline{C}_1, \bar{C}_1\}$ corresponding to points B and A in figure 9.9. Any equilibrium cost that is not equal to $\bar{C}_1$ reveals that the firm is efficient. Thus type $\underline{\beta}$ gets no rent anytime it chooses an equilibrium cost different from $\bar{C}_1$. Type $\underline{\beta}$ might as well choose the cost $\underline{C}_1$ that maximizes its first-period utility. So we have reduced type $\underline{\beta}$'s choice to the two-point set $\{A, B\}$. By mimicking type $\bar{\beta}$ (i.e., by choosing point A rather than point B), type $\underline{\beta}$ loses

$$\begin{aligned}\mathscr{L}(b_1) &\equiv \{a_1 - b_1[\underline{\beta} - e^*(b_1)] - \psi(e^*(b_1))\} \\ &\quad - \{a_1 - b_1[\bar{\beta} - e^*(b_1)] - \psi(e^*(b_1) - \Delta\beta)\}. \\ &= b_1 \Delta\beta - \Phi[e^*(b_1)],\end{aligned}$$

where, as usual, $\Phi(e) \equiv \psi(e) - \psi(e - \Delta\beta)$. Under our assumptions $\mathscr{L}$ is increasing.[9]

For any first-period incentive scheme (a_1, b_1), the continuation equilibrium is unique.

9. $d\mathscr{L}/db_1 = \Delta\beta - [\psi'(e^*(b_1)) - \psi'(e^*(b_1) - \Delta\beta)]/\psi''(e^*(b_1)) \geq 0$, since $\psi''' \geq 0$.

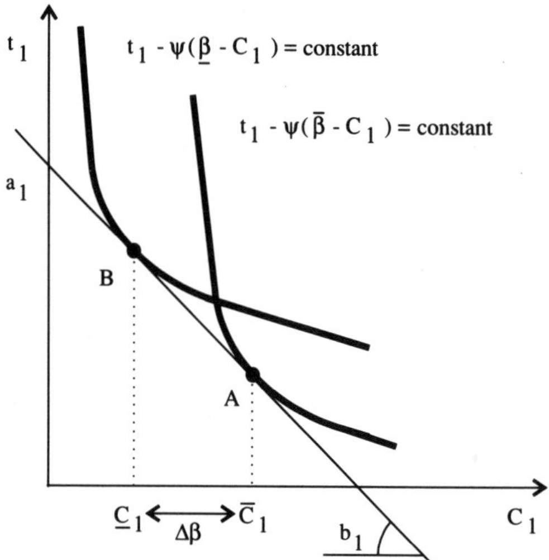

Figure 9.9
Linear scheme

Case 1. $\mathscr{L}(b_1) \geq \delta\mathscr{U}^L(0)$.
The equilibrium is then separating. The efficient type prefers point B to point A in figure 9.9.

Case 2. $\mathscr{L}(b_1) \leq \delta\mathscr{U}^L(v_1)$.
The equilibrium is pooling. Both types choose A.

Case 3. $\delta\mathscr{U}^L(v_1) < \mathscr{L}(b_1) < \delta\mathscr{U}^L(0)$.
The equilibrium is semiseparating. The efficient type randomizes between A and B.

Note that, since $\mathscr{L}$ is strictly increasing, the regulator obtains more separation in period 1 by giving a high powered (high b_1) incentive scheme. The optimal first-period incentive scheme may induce the types to pool, semiseparate or separate. Furthermore the optimal first-period slope exceeds the optimal static slope; in that sense the regulator is led to high-powered schemes by the ratchet effect.

Zou (1989) shows that linear schemes yield a lower social welfare than piecewise linear schemes with a maximum cost, defined by $t_\tau = a_\tau - b_\tau C_\tau$ for $C_\tau \leq C_\tau^*$ (and $t_\tau = -\infty$ for $C_\tau > C_\tau^*$). Such schemes are clearly superior to linear schemes in a static framework because the regulator has three instruments (intercept, slope, and maximum cost) instead of two (i.e., the regulator can always mimic a linear scheme by setting $C_\tau^* = +\infty$). What is less obvious is that they dominate linear schemes in a dynamic environment without commitment as they might aggravate the ratchet effect. But it turns out that piecewise linear schemes leave lower second-period informational rents to the firm and therefore reduce the efficient type's incentive to mimic the inefficient type in period 1. (The intuition can be gleaned from figure 9.9. Starting from the optimal first-period linear incentive scheme, the regulator can rotate the incentive scheme counterclockwise around point A, reduce type $\underline{\beta}$'s rent by reducing the slope of the incentive scheme, and keep type $\bar{\beta}$ at point A by imposing the upper bound $C_1^* = \bar{C}_1$ on cost.) Thus piecewise linear schemes dominate linear schemes on two counts.

Zou's analysis illustrates the fact that the rent that the firm obtains from hiding its type is the engine of the ratchet effect. Another paper that emphasizes the size of future rents is Richardson's (1989). Richardson considers the relevant extension in which the regulator has private information about the marginal social valuation of the output produced by the firm (alternatively, the regulator could have private information about the shadow cost of public funds). It can be shown that in a static framework the regulator's having private information is irrelevant. That is, the regulator offers the same scheme to the firm as if the firm knew his or her information. This is no longer so in a repeated relationship without commitment. The analysis is involved because of bilateral asymmetric information, but the intuition is that a high-valuation regulator may want to pretend to have a low valuation. Since the firm enjoys a higher informational rent in period 2 when the regulator has a high valuation (is "desperate") for the good (on this, see chapters 1 and 2), the firm is more tempted to hide its type in period 1 if it learns that the regulator has a high valuation.

When the firm responds to several principals (e.g., regulator and private owners), the principals exert negative externalities on each other by trying to extract the firm's rent. The outcome is an excessive rent extraction and too low-powered incentive schemes (see chapter 17). Olsen and Torsvik (1991) observe that this cost of common agency may become a blessing in a dynamic setting under noncommitment: The large rent extraction created by common agency reduces the firm's benefit of hiding its type. Olsen and Torsvik consider the two-type linear-incentive-schemes framework with either one or two principals (i.e., single or common agency). They first observe that the set of bonuses that induce separation of the two types (where the bonus faced by the firm in the case of common agency is the sum of the two bonuses offered by the principals) is the same for single and common agency: Since the firm enjoys no second-period rent in a separating equilibrium, it does not matter whether it has one master or two. In contrast, common agency expands the semiseparating region and shrinks the pooling region. This is the first sense in which common agency alleviates the ratchet effect. Furthermore, fixing a first-period bonus b_1 in the semiseparating region under single agency (which, from the previous characterization, also belongs to the semiseparating region under common agency), welfare is higher under common agency: Since the efficient type's first-period loss of concealing the type, $\mathscr{L}(b_1)$, depends only on the bonus, and therefore is the same in both cases, the gain from concealing one's type is also the same. What is more, since for given second-period beliefs, the firm's rent is lower under common agency, the efficient type's indifference between revelation and concealment implies that when concealing, beliefs put more weight on the inefficient type under common agency. That is, there must be more first-period revelation. This is the second sense in which common agency alleviates the ratchet effect. Olsen and Torsvik show that intertemporal welfare may be higher under common agency.

Extensions of the ratchet analysis to more than two periods have been derived by Zhou (1986), Litwack (1987), and Skillman (1988). Litwack (1987) has extended the above framework to allow for the regulator's coordination problem with other firms. He shows that greater costs of coordination of outputs increase the likelihood of a pooling equilibrium.[10]

One of the first game-theoretic analyses of the ratchet effect is Yao (1988), who considers a two-period model of emission standard setting by the Environmental Protection Agency. As in this section it is assumed that the regulator's instruments are limited. The EPA sets standards but does not directly reward pollution abatement or tax emissions.

B9.3 Fixed-Price Contracts

Section B9.2 discussed one way of simplifying the analysis of the ratchet effect, namely exogenously focusing on linear schemes. Another special case studied in the literature is that of fixed-price contracts. Fixed-price contracts are the only feasible contracts when cost is not observable (or, equivalently, when cost $C = \beta - e$ is observable but $\psi(e) = e$). As discussed in section B2.1, we can then ignore moral hazard without loss of generality. Let the firm have private cost $C_\tau = \beta$ of realizing the project at date $\tau = 1, \ldots, T$. Under noncommitment the regulator offers a price t_τ at the beginning of period τ for realization of the date τ project. The per-period and overall objective functions of the firm and the regulator are

$$U_\tau = t_\tau - \beta \quad \text{and} \quad W_\tau = S - (1 + \lambda)t_\tau + U_\tau$$

if the date τ project is realized,

$$U_\tau = W_\tau = 0$$

otherwise, and

10. Yet another extension of the ratchet effect with linear schemes is due to Vincent (1989), who allows imperfect correlation of the type over time.

$$U = \sum_{\tau=1}^{T} \delta^{\tau-1} U_\tau \quad \text{and} \quad W = \sum_{\tau=1}^{T} \delta^{\tau-1} W_\tau.$$

The outcome of the game is easy to characterize if T is finite and large and if $\delta > \frac{1}{2}$:

If the firm's type can take two values ($\underline{\beta}$ and $\bar{\beta}$), there exist T_0 and T_1 such that for any $T \geq T_0$ and any perfect Bayesian equilibrium, the regulator offers $t_\tau = \bar{\beta}$ for all $\tau = 1, 2, \ldots, T - T_1$ (Hart and Tirole 1988).

If the firm's type can take an arbitrary number of values ($\beta_1 = \underline{\beta} < \beta_2 < \cdots < \beta_m = \bar{\beta}$), there exist T_0 and T_1 such that for any $T \geq T_0$ and any Markov perfect Bayesian equilibrium, the regulator offers $t_\tau = \bar{\beta}$ for all $\tau = 1, 2, \ldots, T - T_1$ (Schmidt 1990).

In words, this no-screening result says that when the horizon is long the regulator offers the high price and production occurs in all periods except, perhaps, the last ones. The intuition is that if the regulator offers less than $\bar{\beta}$ in some period, the efficient type $\underline{\beta}$ gains at most $\bar{\beta} - \underline{\beta}$ today by accepting to produce and loses future rents almost equal to $(\delta + \delta^2 + \cdots)(\bar{\beta} - \underline{\beta}) = \delta(\bar{\beta} - \underline{\beta})/(1 - \delta)$ if the remaining horizon is long. Thus the efficient type rejects offers that are also rejected by the inefficient type, as long as $\delta > \frac{1}{2}$ and the remaining horizon is long. This implies that the regulator should not attempt to learn information about the firm's type except maybe in the last periods. It would be interesting to prove a similar result when regulatory contracts are not restricted to be fixed price contracts. Note that our result of convergence toward the pooling equilibrium when δ goes to infinity is closely related to this conjecture.

Little is known about the equilibrium path for arbitrary horizons. The no-screening result indicates that for T large, the firm always implements the project except, perhaps in the last periods. We thus infer that the firm's production may decrease in some period. (This conclusion is similar to the observation in this chapter that effort need not be increasing over time.)

Fernandez-Arias and Kofman (1989) have made some progress in studying the equilibrium dynamics under fixed-price contracts. For instance, they show that with a continuum of types, at least three periods, and a discount factor $\delta \leq 1$, a partition equilibrium may not exist. The intuition for their result can be gleaned from the following example: Assume that $T = 2$, $\delta > 1$ (the second-period project is bigger or lasts longer than the first-period one) and that β is uniformly distributed on $[0, 1]$. For notational simplicity consider the modified welfare function $W_\tau = 1 - t_\tau$ when the firm accepts offer t_τ, and $W_\tau = 0$ otherwise (this is the objective function of a private monopsonist). Fix a first-period price t_1. Consider a candidate partition equilibrium in which types $\beta < \beta^*$ accept t_1 and types $\beta > \beta^*$ reject it, for some cutoff $\beta^* \in (0, 1)$. The optimal second-period price given posterior beliefs is $\min(\frac{1}{2}, \beta^*)$ if t_1 has been accepted, and $(1+\beta^*)/2$ if t_1 has been rejected. A type β slightly above β^* thus obtains intertemporal utility $t_1 - \beta + \delta(0)$ by accepting t_1, and $0 + \delta[(1+\beta^*)/2 - \beta]$ by rejecting it. For δ greater than 1, the payoff to rejecting decreases faster with β than the payoff to accepting, and thus the types just above β^* are more tempted to accept t_1 than type β^* who by assumption is indifferent between the two, a contradiction. On the other hand, that types above some β^* accept t_1 and those under β^* reject it is also impossible because the payoff from accepting t_1 for β just above β^*, which is $t_1 - \beta + \delta[(1+\beta^*)/2 - \beta]$, decreases faster with β than the payoff from rejecting t_1, which is 0. Thus no partition equilibrium exists in general. With $\delta < 1$, one needs at least three periods to build an example of nonexistence of a partition equilibrium, so in period 1 the future will outweigh the present.

We conclude that despite the simplification brought about by fixed-price contracts, little is known about ratchet dynamics except for long horizons or two-period relationships.

B9.4 Intermediate Commitments, Fairness, and Third Party Monitoring of Long-Term Relationships

This chapter has assumed that the regulator is unconstrained in his or her choice of second-period incentive scheme and that the firm is free to leave the relationship when it is not bound by a contract. This contrasts with full commitment in which both parties are committed to a second-period incentive scheme in advance. Baron and Besanko (1987) have studied an intermediate form of commitment based on the following two assumptions:[11]

1. The firm cannot leave the relationship in period 2; that is, it must accept the regulator's second-period incentive scheme as long as it is "fair."

2. The regulator must be fair in period 2 in the following sense: If the first-period incentive scheme $\{t_1(\hat{\beta}_1), C_1(\hat{\beta}_1)\}$ specifies a different allocation for each first-period report $\hat{\beta}_1$ (is "statically separating"), the firm must be given a second-period transfer and cost target such that it derives nonnegative second-period utility if it told the truth in period 1: $t_2 - \psi(\hat{\beta}_1 - C_2) \geq 0$. If $t_1(\hat{\beta}_1)$ and $C_1(\hat{\beta}_1)$ are invariant over some subset $\mathscr{B}$ of the interval $[\underline{\beta}, \bar{\beta}]$ (the first-period scheme is "statically pooling"), the second-period scheme must give a nonnegative second-period utility to the upper bound of $\mathscr{B}$.

11. Baron and Besanko use a repeated Baron-Myerson model. As before, we adapt their contribution to the framework of this book.

One possible interpretation for assumption 1, given that managers may be protected by nonslavery laws,[12] is that the firm is a private firm and that its owners have the same information as the managers and are prohibited by law from taking their assets away. Given assumption 1, the regulator must be constrained in choosing the second-period incentive scheme; otherwise, he or she would demand a huge transfer from the firm because of the existence of a shadow cost of public funds, and the firm, anticipating this, would not enter the relationship in period 1. A possible interpretation for assumption 2 is that a court with limited powers checks that the firm is guaranteed a nonnegative second-period rent assuming it has responded truthfully to the first-period incentive scheme. Assumption 2 thus introduces a third player, the court, into the picture. In contradistinction to the framework of this chapter, the court does not content itself with mechanically enforcing existing contracts but also puts constraints on the way contracts are designed.

Since the firm cannot exit, the take-the-money-and-run strategy is infeasible, and separating equilibria exist despite the assumption of a continuum of types. The optimal first-period incentive scheme in the class of separating schemes is actually simple to characterize: It is the optimal static scheme, except that the transfer function must be steeper in cost because type β obtains second-period gain $\delta d\beta$ by pretending to be type $\beta + d\beta$ ($d\beta \gtrless 0$) in period 1.[13] Baron and Besanko also characterize partition equilibria and show that it is always optimal to induce separation at $\beta = \underline{\beta}$.

Baron and Besanko have opened a fruitful alley of research by introducing the possibility of third party arbitrage (the arbitrator could alternatively be a hierarchical superior). Further developments would require a theory of bounded rationality that would determine what the court can or cannot be instructed to do. For instance, it may be transactionally no more complex for a court to impose the repetition of the first-period allocation (a possibility that would enable the regulator to obtain the full commitment solution) than to monitor that the second-period incentive scheme satisfies assumption 2.

B9.5 Reasons for Noncommitment

We mentioned at the beginning of the chapter two reasons why the regulator may not be able to commit. First, there may exist an (optimal) prohibi-

12. However, Gibbons (1987), who compares the implications of noncommitment and intermediate commitment in a labor context, points out that employees may post a bond in the firm.

13. Hence $dt/dC = -\psi'(\beta^*(C) - C) - \delta(d\beta^*/dC)$, where $\beta^*(C)$ is given implicitly by equation (1.44).

tion of commitment motivated by a lack of confidence in the regulator's benevolence. This foundation for noncommitment is studied in chapter 16. Second, the regulator may be unable to design a complete contract. This chapter has taken the extreme point of view that the second-period good or project cannot be described, and therefore contracted upon, in period 1 (as in Grossman and Hart 1986). That is, only short-term contracts are assumed feasible. Some contributions have compared various degrees of commitment by taking a less extreme position and allowing classes of incomplete long-term contracts. For instance, the second-period good or project can be described in period 1, but some other relevant parameters cannot. Due to contract incompleteness short-term contracts may dominate some forms of rigid long-term contracts.

Dearden (1990) assumes that a parameter of the regulator's valuation of the second-period project unknown at date 1 is revealed to all at date 2 but cannot be contracted upon. Long-term contracts are assumed not to be responsive to the new information about the regulator's demand (in particular the regulator cannot pick from a menu in period 2). There is then a trade-off between short-term and long-term contracting. Short-term contracting allows the second-period allocation to reflect the new information, but it gives rise to ratcheting.

In a different context, Amstrong, Rees, and Vickers (1991) look at the optimal regulatory lag when the regulator cannot transfer money to the firm and there is no cost sharing between the firm and consumers. The firm's production cost parameter is commonly observable and follows a controlled Markov process in which the firm's investment reduces on average its production cost. The class of long-term contracts considered is the class of T-period contracts, in which the consumer price is kept constant for T periods (the regulatory lag), after which the regulator chooses the price anew. A longer regulatory lag implies that the price does not track cost well; however, it does give the firm more incentives to invest.

Two branches of contract theory emphasize motivations for short-term contracting that differ from those discussed above. Several contributions have argued that a party to a long-term relationship might want to signal private information by signing a short-term contract if this information is at least partially revealed (in a noncontractible way) during the relationship. Hermalin (1988) shows that an efficient worker attempts to signal his or her ability by signing an employment contract with no penalty for breach or severance pay, despite the fact that this contract induces suboptimal on-the-job training by the employer. A short-term contract (or, rather, a long-term contract without penalty for breach) signals that the worker is not afraid of going back into the labor market once his or her intermediate performance is observed. It allows the worker to obtain a higher wage initially. In Aghion and Bolton (1987) an incumbent supplier has an initial monopoly position and receives private information about the likelihood of future entry in its market. The supplier offers contracts to buyers with low penalties for switching to a new supplier. The incumbent supplier could impose a higher penalty for breach if the probability of entry is common knowledge but prefers to signal that it is not worried about the possibility of entry in order to extract better terms from the buyers. In Diamond (1992) an entrepreneur borrows to finance a long-term project and uses a similar strategy. Under symmetric information between the entrepreneur and the creditors, the debt would have the same maturity as the project, namely be a long-term debt, since it is not optimal to liquidate the firm once the initial investment is sunk. However, Diamond's entrepreneur is superiorly informed about the project's probability of success and uses short-term debt to signal that she is not worried about going back to the capital market to refinance this short-term debt, as long as some information about the probability of success is publically revealed by that time. It is easy to see how the reasoning in these three papers can be applied to the case of public procurement.

Another literature (notably the contributions of Fellingham, Newman, and Suh 1985; Fudenberg, Holmström, and Milgrom 1990; Malcomson and Spinnewyn 1988; and Rey and Salanié 1990) studies the principal-agent relationship with repeated moral hazard. The agent is risk averse, and shocks are independently and identically distributed. Under some conditions (including exponential utility, to eliminate income effects) the optimal long-term contract can be duplicated by a sequence of short-term contracts, namely the repetition of the optimal static contract. This literature therefore emphasizes that long-term contracting is motivated by asymmetric information (at the contracting date or arising during the relationship) or by incomplete contracting, but not by pure moral hazard.

B9.6 The Firm Has Outside Opportunities in Period 2

Suppose now that the firm can switch to another principal in period 2 if it chooses to do so. Such situations are particularly relevant in labor economics where they have mostly been studied.[14] But imagine that a defense contractor could elect to focus on civilian activities or to supply foreign governments rather than the home ministry of defense.

We can distinguish two polar behaviors when the firm is concerned about the principals' interference about its efficiency:

1. The firm has an incentive to look inefficient in order not to face demanding incentive schemes in the future from the current principal (as in this chapter).

14. See Holmström (1982), Aron (1987), Gibbons (1987), and Kanemoto and MacLeod (1990) for various models of reputation in labor markets.

2. The firm has an incentive to look efficient to generate attractive offers through competition among the principals.

Which of these two behaviors obtains depends on whether the firm incurs a cost of switching to a different principal and on what assumptions are made on the effect of the firm's type on the principals' objective functions. Reputations for inefficiency are likely to prevail when switching costs are high (they are infinite in this chapter) and when the alternative principals care about the terms of the contract but not about the firm's type per se. In contrast, reputations for efficiency are likely to prevail when switching costs are low and when alternative principals are concerned about the agent's type, as shown in Holmström's (1982) well-known work on career concerns in labor markets.

Holmström assumes that the agent, a worker, faces no mobility cost and that each period he is offered by the labor market—namely the current employer and alternative employers—a fixed wage (the equivalent of a cost-plus contract in regulation). All employers are identical. The worker's ability is unknown to the worker and to the employers (the principals).[15] The commonly observable marginal productivity of the worker in a period depends on his ability, the period's effort, and noise. Despite being on a fixed wage, the worker exerts effort in a (vain) attempt to fool the labor market about his ability and to thereby generate high wage offers in the future. Holmström's worker, unlike our regulated firm, tries to build a reputation for efficiency.

Kanemoto and Macleod (1990) consider another interesting situation in which employers can offer incentive schemes to the worker and care about the worker's performance but not about his type per se (i.e., the employer's profit depends only on the contractible output and transfer). The outside employers thus offer the worker in period 2 the first-best output combined with a transfer leaving no profit to the employer (this is the equivalent in regulation of a fixed-price contract designed by the firm). However, the worker must pay a mobility cost to switch from the incumbent employer to an alternative employer; employers are otherwise undifferentiated. In period 2 the first-period employer offers an incentive scheme, taking into account the fact that the worker will leave if he does not obtain the first-best surplus associated with his productivity, minus the mobility cost. Although the worker never moves in equilibrium, the threat of switching firms affects the analysis of this ratchet model (unlike Holmström's model, the worker has no incentive to build a reputation for efficiency as the firms' profit depend on his contractible performance and not on his efficiency; in contrast, the mobility cost gives him an incentive to develop a

15. The study of career concerns becomes much more complex when the worker knows his type, because it then mixes the subtleties of the Rothschild-Stiglitz-Wilson analysis of market screening with reputation concerns. See Aron (1987).

reputation for inefficiency). Kanemoto and Macleod consider the two-type case.

The technical difference with the model of this chapter is that in period 2 the incumbent principal must give the agent a reservation utility that is increasing (and not constant) in the agent's efficiency, at least if the mobility cost is not too high.[16] Kanemoto and Macleod show that in period 2 there is still no distortion for the efficient type and a distortion for the inefficient type. The first-period analysis is also altered by the presence of competition among employers. For small mobility costs the worker reveals his efficiency in period 1. For larger mobility costs the equilibrium may be semiseparating or even pooling as in the analysis in bibliographic notes B9.2. The ratchet effect is more severe, the higher the mobility cost.

B9.7 The Regulator Has Outside Opportunities in Period 2

If the regulator can replace the incumbent firm by a second source with a similar technology, the incumbent firm has a shorter horizon and is less concerned about disclosing its efficiency. As in the case of outside opportunities for the firm (see bibliographic notes B9.6), this possibility is particularly relevant in labor economics. Ickes and Samuelson (1987) have shown that by using frequent job rotation, employers can learn each task's difficulty and thus avoid costly informational rents (as long as "rate busters" are not ostracized by their subsequent coworkers). Job rotation thus thwarts the ratchet effect.

Sen (1991) developed the point that the ratchet effect can also be alleviated by the possibility of second sourcing (as in chapter 8) even when the technologies of the first and second sources are uncorrelated. The idea that second sourcing can alleviate the ratchet effect was suggested by Anton and Yao (1987). Consider the two-type model of section 9.4. Suppose that it is ex post optimal for the regulator to replace in period 2 the incumbent by an entrant if the incumbent has a high cost parameter. The efficient type then does not benefit much from claiming to be inefficient even though it misleads the regulator. It just won't be around to enjoy the second-period informational rent! To illustrate this point in a trivial manner, assume that it is known in period 1 that an entrant with deterministic cost parameter $\beta^2 \in [\underline{\beta}, \bar{\beta}]$ will enter in period 2. Then suppose that the regulator offers the optimal static menu (D, E) in figure 9.1, and in period 2 offers the first-best rent-extracting contract A (see figure 1.2) if contract D was chosen in period 1, and switches to the second source if E was chosen. [One could argue that the regulator would actually offer a menu in period 2 just in case type $\underline{\beta}$ has "trembled" and chosen E in

16. See chapters 6 and 10 for other examples of type-contingent reservation utilities.

period 1 (or in case correlation is imperfect across time). But type $\underline{\beta}$ enjoys no rent even if a menu is offered, and the results are unchanged.] The incumbent's type $\underline{\beta}$ choosing D and type $\bar{\beta}$ choosing E is then obviously incentive compatible because no type can enjoy a second-period rent. Noncommitment imposes no welfare cost in this extreme example.

B9.8 Imperfect Correlation

Section 9.3 studied almost perfect correlation in the continuum-of-types case and showed that full separation is feasible, though not desirable. Riordan and Sappington (1988), in a different context, offer a more detailed analysis of the class of separating contracts for arbitrary degrees of correlation. In the first period there is no production, but several firms bid for the right to produce in period 2. The winner of the auction then sinks some investment. The bidders have private information about the second-period production cost, but their signal and the production cost are imperfectly correlated. The winner's first-period bid reveals information about its second-period efficiency, which in the absence of commitment gives rise to a ratchet effect.

An open question is that of the optimality of separating schemes. An obvious conjecture based on the extreme cases of no correlation (separation is optimal) and perfect or almost perfect correlation (separation is dominated) is that separating schemes fare better when the correlation between periods is small, but we are unaware of formal treatments of this question.

B9.9 More Cooperative Behaviors

This chapter and the next take the point of view of a conflictual relationship between the regulator and the firm. When the two parties are engaged in a long relationship, the regulator may succeed in building a reputation for being "fair,"[17] in the sense of not opportunistically expropriating the firm's quasi-rents. (This idea may apply to several contexts. The regulator might not use information revealed by the firm in the past, as in this chapter, might refrain from expropriating past investments, as in chapter 16, or even not induce inefficient trade by screening the firm's type.) Croker and Reynolds (1989), Gilbert and Newbery (1988) and Salant and Woroch (1988) have developed models of infinitely repeated contracting in which some collusive equilibria do not exhibit the trading inefficiencies associated with shorter horizons.

17. "Fairness" is here self-enforceable and thus differs from the concept defined by Baron and Besanko and reviewed in section B9.4, where limits on expropriation are enforced by a court.

APPENDIXES

A9.1 Example of a Nonpartition Equilibrium

The nonpartition equilibrium constructed in this appendix is depicted in figure 9.3. The first-period incentive scheme offers two levels of cost $C < \tilde{C}$, and associated transfers $t > \tilde{t}$. Let $U(\beta|C)$ and $U(\beta|\tilde{C})$ denote type β's second-period rent when it has chosen C or $\tilde{C}$ in the first period. Let

$$U(\beta) \equiv t - \psi(\beta - C) + \delta U(\beta|C)$$

and

$$\tilde{U}(\beta) \equiv \tilde{t} - \psi(\beta - \tilde{C}) + \delta U(\beta|\tilde{C}).$$

Assume that ψ is quadratic: $\psi(e) = e^2/2$, that $\bar{\beta} - \underline{\beta} = 1$, and that the prior f is uniform on $[\underline{\beta}, \bar{\beta}]$: $f = 1$.

The continuation equilibrium we construct has the following property: Types in $[\underline{\beta}, \tilde{\beta}]$ produce at cost C. Types in $[\tilde{\beta}, \bar{\beta}]$ are indifferent between producing at C and producing at $\tilde{C}$. They randomize in such a way that the posterior distributions on $[\tilde{\beta}, \bar{\beta}]$ given C and $\tilde{C}$, are uniform on this interval.

Let us introduce some more notation before constructing the equilibrium. Types in $[\tilde{\beta}, \bar{\beta}]$ choose C with (constant) probability g and $\tilde{C}$ with (constant) probability $\tilde{g}$, where $g + \tilde{g} = 1$. Let h and $\tilde{h}$ denote the conditional (posterior) densities given that C and $\tilde{C}$ have been chosen in the first period. Since the densities are uniform, we have, if $\beta \in [\underline{\beta}, \tilde{\beta}]$,

$$h(\beta) = \frac{1}{(\tilde{\beta} - \underline{\beta}) + (\bar{\beta} - \tilde{\beta})g},$$

$$\tilde{h}(\beta) = 0,$$

and, if $\beta \in [\tilde{\beta}, \bar{\beta}]$,

$$h(\beta) = \frac{g}{(\tilde{\beta} - \underline{\beta}) + (\bar{\beta} - \tilde{\beta})g},$$

$$\tilde{h}(\beta) = \frac{1}{\bar{\beta} - \tilde{\beta}}.$$

We now put conditions on the parameters g (the uniform unconditional density given C is chosen), $\tilde{\beta}$, and the cost and transfer levels so that the strategies described above indeed form an equilibrium. These conditions are

$$t - \psi(\bar{\beta} - C) = \tilde{t} - \psi(\bar{\beta} - \tilde{C}) = 0, \tag{A9.1}$$

$$\tilde{C} - C = \frac{\delta\lambda}{1 + \lambda}\left(\frac{\tilde{\beta} - \underline{\beta}}{g}\right). \tag{A9.2}$$

Condition (A9.1) says that type $\bar{\beta}$ is indifferent between the two cost levels (remember that type $\bar{\beta}$ never has any second-period rent). Condition (A9.2) ensures that the indifference between costs C and $\tilde{C}$ is kept from $\bar{\beta}$ to $\tilde{\beta}$, as we now show. Let $e(\beta)$ and $\tilde{e}(\beta)$ denote type β's second-period effort when it has chosen cost C or $\tilde{C}$.

Let us show that for all β in $[\tilde{\beta}, \bar{\beta}]$, $U(\beta) = \tilde{U}(\beta)$. Given (A9.1), it suffices to show that for all β in $[\tilde{\beta}, \bar{\beta}]$, $\dot{U}(\beta) = \dot{\tilde{U}}(\beta)$, or

$$-\psi'(\beta - C) - \delta\psi'(e(\beta)) = -\psi'(\beta - \tilde{C}) - \delta\psi'(\tilde{e}(\beta)), \tag{A9.3}$$

where we use the fact that the derivative of the second-period rent is equal to minus the marginal disutility of effort. Next the posterior densities satisfy assumption 1.2 (monotone hazard rate) on $[\underline{\beta}, \bar{\beta}]$. Using the fact that ψ is quadratic, we know that

$$\psi'(e(\beta)) = 1 - \frac{\lambda}{1+\lambda}\frac{H(\beta)}{h(\beta)},$$

and

$$\psi'(\tilde{e}(\beta)) = 1 - \frac{\lambda}{1+\lambda}\frac{\tilde{H}(\beta)}{\tilde{h}(\beta)},$$

where H and $\tilde{H}$ are the cumulative distributions corresponding to h and $\tilde{h}$; on $[\tilde{\beta}, \bar{\beta}]$,

$$H(\beta) = \frac{(\tilde{\beta} - \underline{\beta}) + (\beta - \tilde{\beta})g}{(\tilde{\beta} - \underline{\beta}) + (\bar{\beta} - \tilde{\beta})g}$$

and

$$\tilde{H}(\beta) = \frac{\beta - \tilde{\beta}}{\bar{\beta} - \tilde{\beta}}.$$

So, on $[\tilde{\beta}, \bar{\beta}]$,

$$\psi'(e(\beta)) = 1 - \frac{\lambda}{1+\lambda}\left[\left(\frac{\tilde{\beta} - \underline{\beta}}{g}\right) + (\beta - \tilde{\beta})\right]$$

and

$$\psi'(\tilde{e}(\beta)) = 1 - \frac{\lambda}{1+\lambda}(\beta - \tilde{\beta}).$$

Using the fact that ψ is quadratic, equation (A9.3) then becomes

$$\frac{\delta\lambda}{1+\lambda}\frac{\tilde{\beta} - \underline{\beta}}{g} = \tilde{C} - C,$$

which is nothing but condition (A9.2).

To complete the proof that this is indeed an equilibrium, we must show that the parameters can be chosen so that g is less than 1 and that for β in $[\underline{\beta}, \tilde{\beta})$, $U(\beta) > \tilde{U}(\beta)$.

It is easy to ensure that

$$g = \frac{\delta\lambda}{1+\lambda}\frac{\tilde{\beta} - \underline{\beta}}{\tilde{C} - C}$$

is less than one. It suffices to take $\tilde{\beta}$ close to $\underline{\beta}$. To check that types in $[\underline{\beta}, \tilde{\beta})$

prefer to choose C, it suffices to show that on this interval, $\dot{U}(\beta) \leq \dot{\tilde{U}}(\beta)$, or

$$-\psi'(\beta - C) - \delta\psi'(e(\beta)) \leq -\psi'(\beta - \tilde{C}) - \delta\psi'(\tilde{e}(\beta)).$$

Since assumption 1.2 is satisfied for the posterior distribution given C, we have, for β in $[\underline{\beta}, \tilde{\beta}]$,

$$\psi'(e(\beta)) = 1 - \frac{\lambda}{1+\lambda}(\beta - \underline{\beta}).$$

On the other hand, $\tilde{e}(\beta) = \tilde{e}(\tilde{\beta}) - (\tilde{\beta} - \beta)$ (in the second period, type β, which is to the left of the lower bound $\tilde{\beta}$ of the posterior distribution, does produce at the same cost as $\tilde{\beta}$). So

$$\psi'(\tilde{e}(\beta)) = \psi'(\tilde{e}(\tilde{\beta}) - (\tilde{\beta} - \beta)).$$

Using the fact that ψ is quadratic, the condition for $\dot{U}(\beta) \leq \dot{\tilde{U}}(\beta)$ becomes, for any β in $[\underline{\beta}, \tilde{\beta}]$,

$$\tilde{C} - C \geq \delta\left(\frac{\lambda}{1+\lambda}\right)(\tilde{\beta} - \underline{\beta}),$$

which is satisfied from (A9.2) and the fact that $g < 1$. ■

A9.2 Proof of Proposition 9.2

We drop the index relative to period 1 in the proof. The starting point of the proof consists in noticing that when $\underline{\beta}_n$ tends to $\overline{\beta}$, the distortion in the regulator's welfare relative to full information and associated with the best (full) pooling scheme tends to 0. For instance, the regulator can require a cost target $C = \overline{\beta} - e^*$ and give transfer $t = \psi(e^*)$. The first-period distortion (which exceeds the second-period one) is equal to

$$E[(1+\lambda)(-\psi(e^*) + \psi(e^* - (\overline{\beta} - \beta)) + (\overline{\beta} - \beta))$$
$$+ \lambda(\psi(e^*) - \psi(e^* - (\overline{\beta} - \beta)))] \to 0,$$

when $\underline{\beta}_n$ goes to $\overline{\beta}$.

We can show that the optimal full pooling cost target C satisfies

$$\int_{\underline{\beta}}^{\overline{\beta}} \psi'(\beta - C)f(\beta)d\beta = 1 - \frac{\lambda}{1+\lambda}\int_{\underline{\beta}}^{\overline{\beta}} [\psi'(\overline{\beta} - C) - \psi'(\beta - C)]f(\beta)d\beta$$

(here $\underline{\beta} = \underline{\beta}_n$). To prove the theorem, it suffices to prove that the distortion remains bounded away from zero as long as the continuation equilibrium does not satisfy either condition i or ii.

Consider a first-period incentive scheme $t(C)$, and two distinct levels of cost C^0 and C^1 that are best strategies for some types, for some n (we will delete the subscript n in what follows). Let β^i $(i = 0, 1)$ denote the supremum of types β for which playing C^i is optimal, and which are still active in the second period (i.e., are willing not to exercise their exit option) when they play C^i. β^i will be called the "supremum for C^i." β^i does not obtain any second-period rent when playing C^i. Assume for the moment that $\beta^0 > \beta^1$. Thus type β^0 does not obtain any second-period rent when playing C^1 either. Letting $U(\beta|C^i)$ denote type β's second-period rent when it has played C^i in the first period, we have

$$t(C^0) - \psi(\beta^0 - C^0) \geq t(C^1) - \psi(\beta^0 - C^1) \tag{A9.4}$$

and

$$t(C^1) - \psi(\beta^1 - C^1) \geq t(C^0) - \psi(\beta^1 - C^0) + \delta U(\beta^1|C^0). \tag{A9.5}$$

Adding (A9.4) and (A9.5), we get

$$\psi(\beta^0 - C^1) - \psi(\beta^1 - C^1) + \psi(\beta^1 - C^0) - \psi(\beta^0 - C^0) \geq \delta U(\beta^1|C^0). \tag{A9.6}$$

Type β^1, if it chooses C^0, can always duplicate what type β^0 does. Thus, if $e(\beta^0|C^0)$ denotes type β^0's effort in the second period, we have

$$\begin{aligned} U(\beta^1|C^0) &\geq \psi(e(\beta^0|C^0)) - \psi(e(\beta^0|C^0) - (\beta^0 - \beta^1)) \\ &\geq \psi'(e(\beta^0|C^0) - (\beta^0 - \beta^1))(\beta^0 - \beta^1) \\ &\geq \alpha(\beta^0 - \beta^1), \end{aligned} \tag{A9.7}$$

which follows from the convexity of ψ and the assumption that ψ' is bounded below by some α. Combining (A9.6) and (A9.7), we obtain

$$\frac{\psi(\beta^0 - C^1) - \psi(\beta^1 - C^1) + \psi(\beta^1 - C^0) - \psi(\beta^0 - C^0)}{\beta^0 - \beta^1} \geq \alpha > 0. \tag{A9.8}$$

Let us now come back to the sequence of economies. Consider a sequence of costs and suprema of types that choose these costs: $(C_n^0, C_n^1, \beta_n^0, \beta_n^1)$. We want to show that in the limit, C_n^0 and C_n^1 must be "sufficiently far apart." Using a Taylor expansion since β_n^0 and β_n^1 are close to $\overline{\beta}$, and inequality (A9.8), we get

$$\psi'(\overline{\beta} - C_n^1) - \psi'(\overline{\beta} - C_n^0) \geq k > 0 \tag{A9.9}$$

for some k. Equation (A9.9) implies that there can be at most one of the two cost levels that belongs to the equilibrium path as well as to the interval $[\overline{\beta} - e^* - \zeta, \overline{\beta} - e^* + \zeta]$, where $(\overline{\beta} - e^*)$ is the optimal effort in the limit (when n goes to infinity) and ζ is a given strictly positive constant. Thus the fraction of types that choose the other cost level must be negligible if the distortion relative to the first best is to converge to zero (which must be the case if the equilibrium dominates the full pooling optimum).

More generally we must allow for the possibility that the suprema of types playing some costs and still active in the second period are equal. Equation (A9.9) applies only when these suprema differ pairwise. However, it tells us that, for a given n, there exists β_n and a set $\mathscr{C}_n$ of equilibrium cost levels such that the corresponding suprema for all these cost levels coincide and are equal to β_n, and these cost levels are chosen by a fraction $(1 - \varepsilon)$ of types, where ε can be taken arbitrarily small if the equilibrium dominates the full pooling optimum.

That the equilibrium must exhibit pooling on a large scale follows: Since cost levels in $\mathscr{C}_n$ are chosen by a fraction $(1 - \varepsilon)$ of types and all cost levels have the same supremum, there exists at least one cost level that is an optimal strategy for two types sufficiently far apart.

Last, if the equilibrium does not exhibit infinite reswitching, for any two cost levels C^0 and C^1 in $\mathscr{C}_n$, C^0, say, is strictly preferred to C^1 in an interval (β, β_n), where β_n is the supremum for C^0, and β_n cannot be the supremum for C^1. Hence there can exist only one cost in $\mathscr{C}_n$, which means that the equilibrium is, up to ε, a full pooling equilibrium. ■

A9.3 Proof of Proposition 9.3

Let $\{\beta^k\}$ denote the cutoff points and $\{C^k\}$ the equilibrium costs in a partition equilibrium. Types in (β^k, β^{k+1}) choose cost C^k (where $\beta^k < \beta^{k+1}$). Type β^k is indifferent between C^k and C^{k-1}. It is easily seen that C^k increases with k. Observe that type β^{k+1} does not have a second-period rent when it chooses C^k or C^{k-1}:

$$t(C^k) - \psi(\beta^{k+1} - C^k) \geq t(C^{k-1}) - \psi(\beta^{k+1} - C^{k-1}).$$

Also type β^k does not enjoy a second-period rent when it chooses C^{k-1} but enjoys a strictly positive rent when it chooses C^k. Thus

$$t(C^{k-1}) - \psi(\beta^k - C^{k-1}) > t(C^k) - \psi(\beta^k - C^k).$$

Adding these two inequalities and using the convexity of ψ leads to $C^k > C^{k-1}$.

Next define the function $\Delta_k(\beta)$ on $[\beta^k, \beta^{k+1}]$:

$$\Delta_k(\beta) \equiv \{t(C^k) - \psi(\beta - C^k) + \delta U(\beta | C^k)\} - \{t(C^{k-1}) - \psi(\beta - C^{k-1})\}.$$

To interpret $\Delta_k(\beta)$, remember that the regulator's posterior beliefs when the firm chooses C^{k-1} are the prior truncated on $[\beta^{k-1}, \beta^k]$. Thus type β^k, and a fortiori type $\beta > \beta^k$, enjoy no second-period rent when they choose C^{k-1}. When the firm chooses C^k, however, the posterior puts all the weight on $[\beta^k, \beta^{k+1}]$ and type $\beta \in [\beta^k, \beta^{k+1})$ enjoys a rent which we denote $U(\beta | C^k)$. Thus $\Delta_k(\beta)$ is the difference in intertemporal profits for type β in $[\beta^k, \beta^{k+1})$ when it chooses C^k and C^{k-1}. By definition, $\Delta_k(\beta^k) = 0$. If we want type $(\beta^k + \varepsilon)$ to choose C^k, it must be the case that $\Delta_k'(\beta^k) \geq 0$, or

$$-\psi'(\beta^k - C^k) + \delta U'(\beta^k | C^k) + \psi'(\beta^k - C^{k-1}) \geq 0. \tag{A9.10}$$

From the "no-distortion-at-the-top" result we know that $U'(\beta^k | C^k) = -\psi'(e^*) = -1$. Thus a necessary condition is

$$\alpha(C^k - C^{k-1}) - \delta \geq 0. \tag{A9.11}$$

■

A9.4 Proof of Proposition 9.4

Let C^0 denote the arg $\max_C \{t(C) - \psi(\bar{\beta} - C)\}$, where $C \in \Gamma$, the set of allowed costs. If there are ties, take C^0 to be the lowest of the arg max. Type $\bar{\beta}$ chooses C^0, since it will get a zero surplus in period 2 regardless of the regulator's posterior beliefs. Let $\beta^0 = \bar{\beta}$.

Let $U(\beta | [\beta, \beta^0])$ denote type β's second-period rent when the regulator's posterior distribution is the prior distribution truncated at β (i.e., the regulator knows that the firm's type belongs to the interval $[\beta, \bar{\beta}]$). U is continuous in β, and is equal to 0 for $\beta = \beta^0$. Define the function $h^0(\beta)$:

$$h^0(\beta) = t^0 - \psi(\beta - C^0) + \delta U(\beta | [\beta, \beta^0]) - \max_{C < C^0} \{t(C) - \psi(\beta - C)\}. \tag{A9.12}$$

We know that h^0 is continuous and that from the definition of C^0, $h^0(\beta)$ is strictly positive for β close (or equal) to β^0. Let $\beta^1 = \max\{\beta | h^0(\beta) = 0$ and $h^0(\beta - \varepsilon) < 0$ for any sufficiently small $\varepsilon > 0\}$, and let C^1 denote the corresponding cost (as before, in case of ties, choose the lowest such cost). If there exists no such β^1 above $\underline{\beta}$ or if there exists no $C < C^0$ (so that h^0 is not defined), then the equilibrium is a pure pooling one. Assume that $\beta^1 > \underline{\beta}$.

Let us observe that if in (A9.12) we maximized over $C \geq C^0$ rather than over $C < C^0$, $h^0(\beta)$ would always be positive: We have

$$t^0 - \psi(\beta - C^0) + \delta U(\beta | [\underline{\beta}, \beta^0]) \geq t^0 - \psi(\beta - C^0).$$

But for all C, from the definition of C^0,

$$t^0 - \psi(\beta^0 - C^0) \geq t(C) - \psi(\beta^0 - C).$$

Using $\beta \leq \beta^0$, $C \geq C^0$, and the convexity of ψ, we obtain

$$t^0 - \psi(\beta - C^0) \geq t(C) - \psi(\beta - C).$$

Thus, in our quest for β^1, we can restrict ourselves to costs under C^0. This property (with the same proof) will hold at each stage of our algorithm.

Next define the function $h^1(\beta)$:

$$h^1(\beta) = t^1 - \psi(\beta - C^1) + \delta U(\beta | [\underline{\beta}, \beta^1]) - \max_{C<C^1} \{t(C) - \psi(\beta - C)\}.$$

h^1 is continuous, and from the construction of C^1, h^1 is strictly positive for β slightly under β^1. Let $\beta^2 \equiv \max\{\beta \leq \beta^1 | h^1(\beta) = 0$ and $h^1(\beta - \varepsilon) < 0$ for any sufficiently small $\varepsilon\}$, and let C^2 denote the corresponding cost (in case of ties, choose the lowest such cost). (β^k, C^k) is then constructed by induction until either there exists no $\beta^k \geq \underline{\beta}$ that satisfies $h^k(\beta^k) = 0$ and $h^k(\beta^k - \varepsilon) < 0$ for small ε or there is no allowed cost level left.

The partition equilibrium we propose has type β in (β^{k+1}, β^k) choose cost C^k (the zero-probability cutoff types are indifferent between two cost levels). When a cost C that has probability zero on the equilibrium path is played, Bayes's rule does not pin down posterior beliefs. We will assume that the regulator then believes that the firm has type $\underline{\beta}$ (the reader who worries about the plausibility of this conjecture should remember that the regulator is always free not to allow such cost levels, i.e., the regulator can penalize the firm an infinite amount, so the problem does not arise).

Let us first show that a type β in $[\beta^{k+1}, \beta^k]$ does not prefer a cost $C < C^k$. From the construction of β^{k+1}, we know that

$$t^k - \psi(\beta^{k+1} - C^k) + \delta U(\beta^{k+1} | [\beta^{k+1}, \beta^k]) = \max_{C} \{t(C) - \psi(\beta^{k+1} - C)\}.$$

Now define for $\beta \in [\beta^{k+1}, \beta^k]$,

$$\Delta_k(\beta) \equiv t^k - \psi(\beta - C^k) + \delta U(\beta | [\beta^{k+1}, \beta^k]) - \max_{C<C^k} \{t(C) - \psi(\beta - C)\}.$$

Thus $\Delta_k(\beta^{k+1}) = 0$. Let us show that $\Delta_k'(\beta) \geq 0$:

$$\Delta_k'(\beta) = -\psi'(\beta - C^k) + \delta U'(\beta | [\beta^{k+1}, \beta^k]) + \psi'(\beta - C),$$

for some $C < C^k$.

Next $U'(\beta | [\beta^{k+1}, \beta^k])$ is equal to minus the marginal disutility of effort of type β in the second period. Since the posterior beliefs are the truncated prior on $[\beta^{k+1}, \beta^k]$, assumption 1.2 (monotone hazard rate) is satisfied. The marginal disutility of effort is lower than 1. Thus

$$\Delta_k'(\beta) \geq -\delta + \alpha(C^k - C) \geq 0,$$

since the distance between the allowed costs exceeds δ/α.

Second, we must show that a type β in $[\beta^{k+1}, \beta^k]$ does not prefer a cost $C > C^k$. We prove this by "backward induction" from $\bar{\beta}$. Let us suppose that we have shown that for any β in $[\beta^k, \bar{\beta}]$, β prefers to play its presumed optimal cost to playing a higher cost. (To start the induction, remember that this property holds on $[\beta^1, \bar{\beta}]$, by definition of β^1.) Define on $[\beta^{k+1}, \beta^k]$ and for $C > C^k$,

$$\Lambda_k(\beta, C) \equiv \{t^k - \psi(\beta - C^k) + \delta U(\beta | [\beta^{k+1}, \beta^k])\}$$
$$- \{t(C) - \psi(\beta - C) + \delta U(\beta | C)\},$$

where $U(\beta|C)$ is type β's second-period rent when it chooses cost C in the first period. Notice that, by induction and from the fact that C^k is an optimal strategy for β^k,

$$\Lambda_k(\beta^k, C) \geq 0.$$

To prove our property, it suffices to show that $\Lambda_k'(\beta, C) \leq 0$ on $[\beta^{k+1}, \beta^k]$. But we have

$$\Lambda_k'(\beta, C) \leq -\psi'(\beta - C^k) + \psi'(\beta - C) - \delta U'(\beta | C).$$

If C does not belong to the equilibrium path, from our updating rule we have $U'(\beta|C) = 0$. If C belongs to the equilibrium path, $C = C^l$, with $l < k$ and

$$U'(\beta|C) = -\psi'(e^* - (\beta^{l+1} - \beta)) \geq -1$$

(type β mimics the cost chosen by the lowest possible type given the second-period posterior beliefs). In both cases $U'(\beta|C) \geq -1$ so that

$$\Lambda_k'(\beta, C) \leq \delta - \alpha(C - C^k) \leq 0.$$

Thus type β does not want to choose $C > C^k$ either. ∎

A9.5 Example of the Inexistence of a Partition or Pooling Equilibrium

Let us assume that ψ is quadratic, $\psi = e^2/2$, and that β is uniformly distributed on [1, 2]. Suppose that the regulator offers two cost-transfer pairs $\{C^0, t^0\}$ and $\{C^1, t^1\}$. Assume that without loss of generality $C^0 > C^1$. If $C^0 - C^1 < \delta$, we know from proposition 9.3 that a (nondegenerate) partition equilibrium does not exist. Let us now show that the parameters can be chosen so that a pooling equilibrium does not exist either. Assume that the transfers satisfy

$$t^0 - \psi(2 - C^0) = t^1 - \psi(2 - C^1) + \varepsilon, \tag{A9.13}$$

where ε is strictly positive and small. Equation (A9.13) says that type $\bar{\beta} = 2$ slightly prefers C^0 (remember that this type never enjoys a second-period rent). Thus a full pooling equilibrium must be at cost C^0.

To give the full pooling equilibrium at C^0 its best chance, let us assume that when the firm plays C^1 (a zero-probability event), the regulator believes that the firm has type $\underline{\beta} = 1$, so the firm does not enjoy a second-period rent. Let $U(\beta|[1, 2])$ denote type β's rent when the posterior coincides with the prior, and define

$$\Delta(\beta) \equiv \{t^0 - \psi(\beta - C^0) + \delta U(\beta|[1,2])\} - \{t^1 - \psi(\beta - C^1)\}$$

to be the difference in intertemporal payoffs for type β. We know that $\Delta(2) = \varepsilon$. We have

$$\Delta'(\beta) = (C^0 - C^1) + \delta U'(\beta|[1,2])$$
$$= C^0 - C^1 - \delta\left(1 - \frac{\lambda}{1+\lambda}(\beta - 1)\right).$$

In particular

$$\Delta'(2) = C^0 - C^1 - \frac{\delta}{1+\lambda}.$$

Thus, for $\delta > (C^0 - C^1) > \delta/(1 + \lambda)$, there exists ε sufficiently small such that $\Delta(\beta)$ becomes negative to the left of 2. Then there is no pooling equilibrium at C^0 either. ■

A9.6 Proof of Proposition 9.1′

Consider a finite number of costs C^k that are chosen on the equilibrium path. Let $\overline{\beta}^k = \sup(\beta|\beta$ produces at cost C^k and is active in the second period). Note that $\overline{\beta}^k$ obtains a zero surplus in the second period if it plays C^k. So for all (k,l), with obvious notation, we have

$$t^k - \psi(\overline{\beta}^k - C^k) \geq t^l - \psi(\overline{\beta}^k - C^l) \quad \text{(A9.14)}$$

and

$$t^l - \psi(\overline{\beta}^l - C^l) \geq t^k - \psi(\overline{\beta}^l - C^k). \quad \text{(A9.15)}$$

Adding (A9.14) and (A9.15) gives

$$\psi(\overline{\beta}^k - C^l) + \psi(\overline{\beta}^l - C^k) - \psi(\overline{\beta}^k - C^k) - \psi(\overline{\beta}^l - C^l) \geq 0. \quad \text{(A9.16)}$$

Inequality (A9.16) and the convexity of ψ imply that

$$\overline{\beta}^k < \overline{\beta}^l \Rightarrow C^k \leq C^l. \quad \text{(A9.17)}$$

So there is an increasing relationship between the cost levels chosen on the equilibrium path, and the suprema of the types that choose these costs.

Now consider two "adjacent" cost levels belonging to the equilibrium path $C^k < C^{k+1}$. We have

$$t^{k+1} - \psi(\overline{\beta}^{k+1} - C^{k+1}) \geq t^k - \psi(\overline{\beta}^{k+1} - C^k). \quad \text{(A9.18)}$$

Furthermore we can refine (A9.14): Type $\overline{\beta}^k$, after deviating to C^{k+1}, can always mimic what type $\overline{\beta}^{k+1}$ does in the second period. Given that the latter has a zero surplus and that it makes some effort $e_2(\overline{\beta}^{k+1})$, we get

$$t^k - \psi(\overline{\beta}^k - C^k) \geq t^{k+1} - \psi(\overline{\beta}^k - C^{k+1})$$
$$+ \delta[\psi(e_2(\overline{\beta}^{k+1})) - \psi(e_2(\overline{\beta}^{k+1}) - \Delta\beta^k)], \quad \text{(A9.19)}$$

where $\Delta\beta^k \equiv \overline{\beta}^{k+1} - \overline{\beta}^k$. Adding (A9.18) and (A9.19), we have

$$-\psi(\bar{\beta}^k - C^k) + \psi(\bar{\beta}^{k+1} - C^k) - \psi(\bar{\beta}^{k+1} - C^{k+1}) + \psi(\bar{\beta}^k - C^{k+1})$$
$$\geq \delta[\psi(e_2(\bar{\beta}^{k+1})) - \psi(e_2(\bar{\beta}^{k+1}) - \Delta\beta^k)]. \tag{A9.20}$$

Now assume that the equilibrium is a separating equilibrium. Then we know that $e_2(\bar{\beta}^{k+1}) = e^*$; that is, $\psi'(e_2(\bar{\beta}^{k+1})) = 1$. It is clear that the right-hand side of (A9.20) is of the first order in $\Delta\beta^k$. Thus, if $(C^{k+1} - C^k)$ is not bounded away from zero, the left-hand side cannot exceed the right-hand side (take a Taylor expansion for $\Delta\beta^k$ small). Therefore, as the grid size goes to zero, the range of costs must become infinite. ■

A9.7 Proof of Proposition 9.5

Fix $n > 0$. Let us prove lemma 9.2:

Lemma 9.2 Suppose that the regulator knows β_1 perfectly (but not β_2). In the second period the probability that the firm does not operate or that $|\psi'(e_2(\beta_2)) - 1| > 1/n$ tends to zero, as well as the firm's expected second-period rent, as n tends to infinity (where probabilities and expectations are with respect to β_2 knowing β_1).

Proof The second-period expected welfare is equal to

$$E_{\{\beta_2|\text{firm operates}\}}\{S - (1 + \lambda)(\beta_2 + \psi(e_2(\beta_2)) - e_2(\beta_2)) - \lambda U_2(\beta_2)\}.$$

Expected welfare under full information over β_2 is equal to

$$E_{\beta_2}\{S - (1 + \lambda)(\beta_2 + \psi(e^*) - e^*)\}.$$

Hence, if the conditions of the lemma are not satisfied, the distortion relative to the full information solution does not converge to zero (i.e., "remains finite"). But, by choosing a full pooling contract, the regulator can induce this distortion to converge to zero as n tends to infinity. Such a contract (which is not optimal in the class of full pooling contracts) is given by the cost target $C_2 = \beta_1 + \varepsilon(n) - e^*$ and the transfer $t_2 = \psi(e^*)$. Expected welfare for this pooling contract is

$$E_{\{\beta_2 \leq \beta_1 + \varepsilon(n)\}}\{S - (1 + \lambda)(\beta_1 + \varepsilon(n) - e^*$$
$$+ \psi(e^* - (\beta_1 + \varepsilon(n) - \beta_2))) - \lambda(\psi(e^*)$$
$$- \psi(e^* - (\beta_1 + \varepsilon(n) - \beta_2)))\}.$$

Because $G^n(\beta_1 + \varepsilon(n)|\beta_1) - G^n(\beta_1 - \varepsilon(n)|\beta_1)$ converges to 1, the distortion converges to 0. ■

Now fix two types β_1 and β_1' with $\beta_1' - \beta_1 = k > 0$. Suppose that type β_1 chooses C_1 in the first period and that β_1' chooses C_1'. Assume furthermore that C_1 and C_1' fully reveal the firm's type (separating equilibrium). From the lemma we know that the expected second-period rent of type β_1 when choosing C_1 converges to zero as n tends to infinity. A fortiori this is true for type β_1' if it chooses C_1. This also holds when β_1' chooses C_1'. Last, if type β_1 chooses C_1', the lemma tells us that its second-period rent is approximately $\psi(e^*) - \psi(e^* - k)$. The two first-period incentive constraints are thus, ignoring the terms that converge to zero as n tends to infinity,

$$t_1 - \psi(\beta_1 - C_1) \gtrsim t_1' - \psi(\beta_1 - C_1') + \delta(\psi(e^*) - \psi(e^* - k))$$

and

$$t_1' - \psi(\beta_1' - C_1') \gtrsim t_1 - \psi(\beta_1' - C_1).$$

To complete the proof, first, add the two incentive constraints together, and then assume that k is small (but still fixed, it does not change with n), and perform a first-order Taylor expansion to obtain

$$\psi'(\beta_1 - C_1) - \psi'(\beta_1 - C_1') \gtrsim \delta\psi'(e^*)$$

(after dividing by k). This shows that there exists $k' > 0$ such that $C_1' - C_1 \geq k'$ independently of k. In particular, by choosing a "grid" k sufficiently small, we can find n sufficiently large such that the first-period costs are arbitrarily large or small (so that the effort distortion is arbitrarily large) for a nonnegligible set of types. Hence the distortion imposed by a revealing equilibrium relative to the full information case tends to infinity as n tends to infinity. It is clear that the regulator can do better by imposing a cost target (full pooling). ■

A9.8 Proof of Proposition 9.6

Lemma 9.3 All contracts selected in the first period by the inefficient type with positive probability are on the inefficient type's same static indifference curve.

Proof The inefficient type will have no rent in period 2, whatever the posterior distribution. Therefore all contracts selected in the first period must be equivalent from the first-period point of view. ■

Lemma 9.4 There exists at most one contract that lies strictly below the inefficient type's equilibrium indifference curve.

Proof Suppose there are at least two such contracts A^0 and $A^{0\prime}$. The efficient type by selecting such a contract reveals its type and obtains no rent in period 2. Therefore A^0 and $A^{0\prime}$ must be on the same indifference curve of the efficient type and lie below the indifference curve of the inefficient type. By the same reasoning as in chapter 1, we know that A^0 and $A^{0\prime}$ must coincide since they are both associated with cost $C^* = \underline{\beta} - e^*$. ■

Lemma 9.5 There exists at most one contract (A^k) which is selected by the efficient type with probability 0 and by the inefficient type with positive probability.

Proof Suppose that there are two such contracts A^k and A^l, for instance, with

$$\Delta = (1 + \lambda)[(e^k - \psi(e^k)) - (e^l - \psi(e^l))] > 0,$$

Delete contract A^l, and let the inefficient type choose A^k with probability $(y^k + y^l)$ instead of y^k. The continuation equilibrium is otherwise unchanged. The two types' utility levels are unaltered, but welfare has increased by $(1 - v_1)y^l\Delta > 0$. ■

Therefore,

$$x^k > 0, \qquad k = 0, \ldots, K - 1 \text{ and } x^K \geq 0,$$

$$y^k > 0, \qquad k = 1, \ldots, K \text{ and } y^0 \geq 0.$$

The posterior distributions are

$$\nu^0 \leq 1,$$

$$\nu^1 = \frac{x^1 \nu_1}{x^1 \nu_1 + y^1(1 - \nu_1)},$$

$$\vdots$$

$$\nu^k = \frac{x^k \nu_1}{x^k \nu_1 + y^k(1 - \nu_1)},$$

$$\vdots$$

$$\nu^{K-1} = \frac{x^{K-1} \nu_1}{x^{K-1} \nu_1 + y^{K-1}(1 - \nu_1)},$$

$$\nu^K \geq 0.$$

Let $\mathscr{U}(\nu^k)$ be the associated second-period rent for the efficient type:

$$\mathscr{U}(\nu^k) = \Phi(\bar{e}_{\nu^k}),$$

with

$$\psi'(\bar{e}_{\nu^k}) = 1 - \frac{\lambda}{1+\lambda}\frac{\nu^k}{1-\nu^k}\psi''(\bar{e}_{\nu^k}).$$ ■

A9.9 Simulations

Under complete information and the quadratic case a utilitarian regulator would solve, in each period τ

$$\max\left\{S - (1+\lambda)(t_\tau + \beta - e_\tau) + \left(t_\tau - \frac{\alpha}{2}[\max(e_\tau, 0)]^2\right)\right\}$$

subject to

$$t_\tau - \frac{\alpha}{2}[\max(e_\tau, 0)]^2 \geq 0.$$

Assuming that S is large enough so that the project is always desirable, the optimal regulatory rule is then

$$e_\tau = \frac{1}{\alpha}, \quad t_\tau = \frac{1}{2\alpha}, \quad \tau = 1, 2.$$

Aggregate social welfare is

$$(1+\delta)\left[S - (1+\lambda)\left(\beta - \frac{1}{2\alpha}\right)\right].$$

We assume now that the regulator does not know β in the one-period model. We allow corner solutions. The incentive compatibility constraints (see chapter 1) are

$$\underline{t} - \left(\frac{\alpha}{2}\right)\max(0, (\underline{\beta} - \underline{C}))^2 \geq \bar{t} - \left(\frac{\alpha}{2}\right)\max(0, (\underline{\beta} - \bar{C}))^2, \tag{A9.21}$$

$$\bar{t} - \left(\frac{\alpha}{2}\right)\max(0, (\bar{\beta} - \bar{C}))^2 \geq \underline{t} - \left(\frac{\alpha}{2}\right)\max(0, (\bar{\beta} - \underline{C}))^2. \tag{A9.22}$$

The individual rationality constraints are

$$\bar{t} - \left(\frac{\alpha}{2}\right)\max(0, (\bar{\beta} - \bar{C}))^2 \geq 0, \tag{A9.23}$$

$$\underline{t} - \left(\frac{\alpha}{2}\right)\max(0, (\underline{\beta} - \underline{C}))^2 \geq 0. \tag{A9.24}$$

Any fourtuple $(\underline{t}, \underline{C}; \bar{t}, \bar{C})$ satisfying (A9.21) through (A9.24) is an admissible incentive mechanism. The optimal mechanism for the regulator with belief ν is obtained from the program

$$\max\{\nu[S - (1 + \lambda)\underline{C} - \lambda\underline{t} - \left(\frac{\alpha}{2}\right)\max(0, (\underline{\beta} - \underline{C})^2)]$$

$$+ (1 - \nu)[S - (1 + \lambda)\bar{C} - \lambda\bar{t} - \left(\frac{\alpha}{2}\right)\max(0, (\bar{\beta} - \bar{C}))^2]\} \tag{A9.25}$$

subject to (A9.21), (A9.22), (A9.23), (A9.24).

In equilibrium we have

$$\underline{\beta} - \underline{C} = \underline{e} \geq 0,$$

$$\bar{\beta} - \bar{C} = \bar{e} \geq 0.$$

Therefore $\bar{\beta} - \underline{C} = \bar{\beta} - \underline{\beta} + \underline{e} > 0$. Equations (A9.21) and (A9.22) simplify to

$$\underline{t} - \left(\frac{\alpha}{2}\right)(\underline{\beta} - \underline{C})^2 \geq \bar{t} - \left(\frac{\alpha}{2}\right)\max(0, (\underline{\beta} - \bar{C}))^2, \tag{A9.26}$$

$$\bar{t} - \left(\frac{\alpha}{2}\right)(\bar{\beta} - \bar{C})^2 \geq \underline{t} - \left(\frac{\alpha}{2}\right)(\bar{\beta} - \underline{C})^2. \tag{A9.27}$$

Since it is always in the interest of the regulator to decrease $\underline{t}$ and $\bar{t}$, at least two of the four constraints are binding. Equations (A9.22) and (A9.23) imply (A9.24). As is usual, $\bar{C} \geq \underline{C}$. Therefore the two binding constraints are (A9.21) and (A9.23). Three cases must be distinguished.

Case 1. Two contracts are offered, and $\bar{e} \geq \Delta\beta$.

Case 2. Two contracts are offered. But since $\bar{e} < \Delta\beta$, when the efficient type imitates the inefficient type, it chooses a negative effort level. The disutility of effort has then a different form than in case 1 because $\psi(e) = \alpha(\max(0, e))^2/2$.

Case 3. One contract is offered to attract only the efficient type.

Let μ and ρ, respectively, be the lagrange multipliers of the binding constraints (A9.21) and (A9.23) in program (A9.25). We must distinguish two cases according to the sign of $\bar{e} - \Delta\beta$: If $\bar{e} \geq \Delta\beta$, $\underline{\beta} - \bar{C} = \bar{e} - \Delta\beta \geq 0$ and (A9.26) become

$$\underline{t} - \left(\frac{\alpha}{2}\right)(\underline{\beta} - \underline{C})^2 \geq \bar{t} - \left(\frac{\alpha}{2}\right)(\underline{\beta} - \bar{C})^2. \tag{A9.28}$$

If $\bar{e} < \Delta\beta$, (A9.26) is

$$\underline{t} - \left(\frac{\alpha}{2}\right)(\underline{\beta} - \underline{C})^2 \geq \bar{t}. \tag{A9.29}$$

Consider first the case where $\bar{e} \geq \Delta\beta$. The first-order conditions of the regulator's program are

$$-\lambda v + \mu = 0, \tag{A9.30}$$

$$-\lambda(1 - v) - \mu + \rho = 0, \tag{A9.31}$$

$$-v(1 + \lambda) + v\alpha(\underline{\beta} - \underline{C}) + \mu\alpha(\underline{\beta} - \underline{C}) = 0, \tag{A9.32}$$

$$-(1 - v)(1 + \lambda) + (1 - v)\alpha(\bar{\beta} - \bar{C}) - \mu\alpha(\underline{\beta} - \bar{C}) + \rho\alpha(\bar{\beta} - \bar{C}) = 0. \tag{A9.33}$$

Equations (A9.30) and (A9.32) give

$$\underline{e} = \underline{\beta} - \underline{C} = \frac{1}{\alpha}. \tag{A9.34}$$

Equation (A9.33) yields

$$\bar{e} = \frac{1}{\alpha} - \frac{\lambda v \Delta\beta}{(1 + \lambda)(1 - v)}. \tag{A9.35}$$

From (A9.23) we have

$$\bar{t} = \left(\frac{\alpha}{2}\right)\bar{e}^2. \tag{A9.36}$$

From (A9.21), we have

$$\underline{t} = \left(\frac{\alpha}{2}\right)[\underline{e}^2 + 2\Delta\beta\bar{e} - \Delta\beta^2]. \tag{A9.37}$$

The efficient type's rent is

$$\mathscr{U}(v) = \Delta\beta - \left\{\frac{1}{2} + \frac{\lambda v}{(1 + \lambda)(1 - v)}\right\}\alpha\Delta\beta^2. \tag{A9.38}$$

The expected welfare is, as a function of the prior,

$$W_1^{AI}(v) = S - v\left[\left(\frac{\lambda\alpha}{2}\right)(2\Delta\beta\bar{e} - \Delta\beta^2) + (1 + \lambda)\left(\underline{\beta} - \underline{e} + \left(\frac{\alpha}{2}\right)\underline{e}^2\right)\right]$$
$$- (1 - v)(1 + \lambda)\left(\bar{\beta} - \bar{e} + \left(\frac{\alpha}{2}\right)\bar{e}\right)^2. \tag{A9.39}$$

For case 1 to hold, we must have $\bar{e} \geq \Delta\beta$:

$$\frac{1}{\alpha} \geq \frac{\Delta\beta(1 - v + \lambda)}{(1 - v)(1 + \lambda)}. \tag{A9.40}$$

In case 2, $\bar{e} < \Delta\beta$; similar calculations give

$$\underline{e} = \frac{1}{\alpha}, \tag{A9.41}$$

$$\bar{e} = \frac{(1-v)(1+\lambda)}{\alpha(1-v+\lambda)}, \tag{A9.42}$$

$$\bar{t} = \left(\frac{\alpha}{2}\right)\bar{e}^2, \tag{A9.43}$$

$$\underline{t} = \left(\frac{\alpha}{2}\right)(\underline{e}^2 + \bar{e}^2), \tag{A9.44}$$

$$\mathscr{U}(v) = \frac{1}{2\alpha}\frac{(1-v)^2(1+\lambda)^2}{(1-v+\lambda)^2}, \tag{A9.45}$$

$$W_2^{AI}(v) = S - (1+\lambda)(v\underline{\beta} + (1-v)\bar{\beta}) + \frac{(1+\lambda)}{2\alpha} - \frac{(1+\lambda)}{2\alpha}\frac{(1-v)v\lambda}{1-v+\lambda}. \tag{A9.46}$$

This case holds if (A9.40) does not hold.

Always carrying out the project (i.e., even when the firm is inefficient), as we have implicitly assumed up to now, forces the regulator to give a rent to the efficient type. When the probability v that the firm is efficient is high enough, it is no longer worth keeping the inefficient type. A scheme is offered that is accepted only by the efficient type. The optimum is then

$$\underline{e} = \frac{1}{\alpha}, \tag{A9.47}$$

$$\underline{t} = \left(\frac{\alpha}{2}\right)\underline{e}^2, \tag{A9.48}$$

$$\mathscr{U}(v) = 0, \tag{A9.49}$$

$$W_3^{AI}(v) = v\left[S - (1+\lambda)\left(\underline{\beta} - \frac{1}{2\alpha}\right)\right]. \tag{A9.50}$$

To sum up, the optimal expected welfare is obtained as follows:

$$\text{if} \quad \frac{1}{\alpha} \geq \frac{\Delta\beta(1-v+\lambda)}{(1-v)(1+\lambda)}, \quad W^{AI}(v) = \max[W_1^{AI}(v), W_3^{AI}(v)],$$

$$\text{if} \quad \frac{1}{\alpha} < \frac{\Delta\beta(1-v+\lambda)}{(1-v)(1+\lambda)}, \quad W^{AI}(v) = \max[W_2^{AI}(v), W_3^{AI}(v)].$$

Consider now the two-period model. As explained in subsection 9.4.2 we have three types of equilibria.

Equilibrium of Type I: Two Contracts, Incentive Constraint of Only Efficient Type Binding

One way of describing a type I equilibrium is that type $\underline{\beta}$ can randomize over the two strategies $\bar{\beta}$ and $\underline{\beta}$. Let x^0 be the probability that type $\underline{\beta}$ announces truthfully. $x^0 = 1$ corresponds to a separating equilibrium. In a perfect Bayesian equilibrium the regulator interprets the announcement $\underline{\beta}$ as the fact that the firm is of type $\underline{\beta}$. At the beginning of period 2, the regulator knows the firm's type and can force it to the first-best level of effort $e^* = 1/\alpha$, with a transfer $t = 1/2\alpha$ [if the cost is $(\underline{\beta} - 1/\alpha)$] and leave it no rent. In that case welfare is in period 2,

$$\underline{W}_2 = S - (1+\lambda)(\underline{\beta} - 1/2\alpha). \tag{A9.51}$$

From the regulator's point of view at date 1, this case will occur with probability $\nu_1 x^0$.

If told $\bar{\beta}$ in period 1 (this case will occur with probability $1 - \nu_1 x^0$ from the regulator's point of view), the regulator revises his or her beliefs according to Bayes's rule, so that the regulator's posterior probability of type $\underline{\beta}$ at the beginning of period 2 is

$$\nu_1(x^0) = \frac{(1 - x^0)\nu_1}{1 - \nu_1 x^0} \leq \nu_1. \tag{A9.52}$$

We also know that in period 2 type $\underline{\beta}$ exerts an effort level $1/\alpha$ and type $\bar{\beta}$ exerts effort level

$$\frac{1}{\alpha} - \left(\frac{\lambda}{1 + \lambda}\right)\frac{\nu_1(x^0)\Delta\beta}{[1 - \nu_1(x^0)]}.$$

Welfare is then $W^{AI}(\nu^1(x^0))$. So expected welfare for period 2 is in period 1,

$$\delta[\nu_1 x^0 \underline{W}_2 + (1 - \nu_1 x^0) W^{AI}(\nu^1(x^0))].$$

To have an equilibrium of type I, type $\underline{\beta}$ must be indifferent between announcing either $\underline{\beta}$ or $\bar{\beta}$ and type $\bar{\beta}$ must prefer to announce $\bar{\beta}$. Type $\underline{\beta}$ will receive in period 2 rent $\mathscr{U}(\nu^1(x^0))$ if it announces $\bar{\beta}$ in period 1, and 0 if it announces $\underline{\beta}$ in period 1. By announcing $\bar{\beta}$ in period 1 it loses, in period 1,

$$\begin{aligned} L &= \underline{t}^1 - \left(\frac{\alpha}{2}\right)(\underline{\beta} - \underline{C}^1)^2 - \left[\bar{t}^1 - \left(\frac{\alpha}{2}\right)(\underline{\beta} - \bar{C}^1)^2\right] \\ &= \underline{t}^1 - \left(\frac{\alpha}{2}\right)(\underline{e}^1)^2 - \left[\bar{t}^1 - \left(\frac{\alpha}{2}\right)(\bar{e}^1 - \Delta\beta)^2\right]. \end{aligned}$$

Type $\underline{\beta}$ is indifferent between both strategies iff[18]

$$L = \delta\mathscr{U}(\nu^1(x^0)),$$

or

$$\underline{t}^1 - \left(\frac{\alpha}{2}\right)(\underline{e}^1)^2 = \delta\mathscr{U}(\nu^1(x^0)) + \bar{t}^1 - \left(\frac{\alpha}{2}\right)(\bar{e}^1 - \Delta\beta)^2. \tag{A9.53}$$

Type $\bar{\beta}$ has always its minimum utility level in period 2. It prefers to announce truthfully iff

$$\bar{t}^1 - \left(\frac{\alpha}{2}\right)(\bar{e}^1)^2 > \underline{t}^1 - \left(\frac{\alpha}{2}\right)(\Delta\beta + \underline{e}^1)^2. \tag{A9.54}$$

Expected welfare in period 1 is obtained as follows: With probability $(1 - \nu_1)$ the firm has type $\bar{\beta}$ and announces $\bar{\beta}$. Welfare is then

$$\bar{W}^1 = S - \lambda\bar{t}^1 - (1 + \lambda)(\bar{\beta} - \bar{e}^1) - \left(\frac{\alpha}{2}\right)(\bar{e}^1)^2.$$

With probability $\nu_1 x^0$ the firm has type $\underline{\beta}$ and announces $\underline{\beta}$. Welfare is then

18. Since $\mathscr{U}(\nu^1(x))$ is monotonic in x, there is a unique such equilibrium for a given incentive scheme.

$$\underline{\underline{W}}^1 = S - \lambda \underline{t}^1 - (1 + \lambda)(\underline{\beta} - \underline{e}^1) - \left(\frac{\alpha}{2}\right)(\underline{e}^1)^2.$$

With probability $v_1(1 - x^0)$ the firm has type $\underline{\beta}$ and announces $\overline{\beta}$. Welfare is then

$$\underline{\overline{W}}^1 = S - \lambda \overline{t}^1 - (1 + \lambda)(\overline{\beta} - \overline{e}^1) - \left(\frac{\alpha}{2}\right)(\overline{e}^1 - \Delta\beta)^2.$$

Total expected welfare in period 1 is

$$(1 - v_1)\overline{W}^1 + v_1[x^0 \underline{\underline{W}}^1 + (1 - x^0)\underline{\overline{W}}^1] + \delta[v_1 x^0 \overline{W}^2 + (1 - v_1 x^0) W^{AI}(v^1(x^0))]. \tag{A9.55}$$

Since this expression is decreasing in $\overline{t}^1$, $\underline{t}^1$, and since individual rationality must be preserved for type $\overline{\beta}$, we set

$$\overline{t}^1 = \frac{\alpha}{2}(\overline{e}^1)^2. \tag{A9.56}$$

Equation (A9.53) becomes

$$\underline{t}^1 = \left(\frac{\alpha}{2}\right)(\underline{e}^1)^2 + \alpha \overline{e}^1 \Delta\beta + \delta \mathcal{U}(v^1(x^0)) - \left(\frac{\alpha}{2}\right)\Delta\beta^2. \tag{A9.57}$$

We can substitute (A9.56) and (A9.57) into (A9.55), and since the objective function of the regulator is then concave in $(\overline{e}^1, \underline{e}^1)$, we maximize with respect to $\overline{e}^1$ and $\underline{e}^1$ analytically. We obtain

$$\underline{e}^1 = \frac{1}{\alpha}, \tag{A9.58}$$

$$\overline{e}^1 = \frac{1}{\alpha} - \frac{v_1[\lambda x^0 - 1 + x^0]\Delta\beta}{(1 + \lambda)(1 - v_1 x^0)}. \tag{A9.59}$$

Substituting (A9.58) and (A9.59) into (A9.55), we finally maximize numerically with respect to $x^0 \in [0, 1]$.[19] If $x^{0*} = 1$, we have a separating equilibrium. If $x^{0*} = 0$, we have a pooling equilibrium. If $x^{0*} \in (0, 1)$ it is a semiseparating equilibrium. However, this procedure is correct only if (A9.54) is satisfied. If (A9.54) is not satisfied, both incentive constraints are binding, and we obtain a type III equilibrium.

Equilibrium of Type II: Two Contracts, Incentive Constraint of Only Inefficient Type Binding

Lemma 9.1 in the text shows that type II equilibria cannot be optimal. Yet it is instructive to go through the derivations of such equilibria. In particular it will be shown that the inefficient type faces a more powerful incentive scheme than in the complete information (i.e., first-best) benchmark. Consider an equilibrium in which the inefficient type randomizes and the efficient type tells the truth. Let y^0 be the probability that the type $\overline{\beta}$ says $\underline{\beta}$. The posterior distribution of the regulator is

19. We maximize with respect to x^0 only as a matter of practical convenience; x^0 is determined by (A9.53) for a given incentive scheme, and the regulator maximizes with respect to incentive schemes.

$$v^0(y^0) = \frac{v_1}{v_1 + y^0(1 - v_1)} \geq v_1 \qquad \text{if told } \underline{\beta},$$

$$v^1(y^0) = 0 \qquad \text{if told } \overline{\beta}.$$

Since type $\overline{\beta}$ is always at the zero-utility level in period 2, type $\overline{\beta}$ must be indifferent between saying $\overline{\beta}$ or $\underline{\beta}$ on the basis of the first-period payoffs only. Hence

$$\overline{t}^1 - \left(\frac{\alpha}{2}\right)(\overline{e}^1)^2 = \underline{t}^1 - \left(\frac{\alpha}{2}\right)(\Delta\beta + \underline{e}^1)^2 \geq 0. \tag{A9.60}$$

Consider now type $\underline{\beta}$. If it says $\underline{\beta}$, it gets

$$\underline{t}^1 - \left(\frac{\alpha}{2}\right)(\underline{e}^1)^2 + \delta\mathscr{U}(v^0(y^0)).$$

If it says $\overline{\beta}$, it gets

$$\overline{t}^1 - \left(\frac{\alpha}{2}\right)(\overline{e}^1 - \Delta\beta)^2 + \delta\mathscr{U}(0).$$

In this equilibrium we must have

$$\underline{t}^1 - \left(\frac{\alpha}{2}\right)(\underline{e}^1)^2 + \delta\mathscr{U}(v^0(y^0)) > \overline{t}^1 - \left(\frac{\alpha}{2}\right)(\overline{e}^1 - \Delta\beta)^2 + \delta\mathscr{U}(0). \tag{A9.61}$$

From the same argument as above we have

$$\overline{t}^1 = \left(\frac{\alpha}{2}\right)(\overline{e}^1)^2. \tag{A9.62}$$

Then from (A9.60)

$$\underline{t}^1 = \left(\frac{\alpha}{2}\right)(\Delta\beta + \underline{e}^1)^2, \tag{A9.63}$$

and (A9.61) can be rewritten

$$\overline{e}_1 - \underline{e}^1 < \Delta\beta + \left(\frac{\delta}{\alpha\Delta\beta}\right)[\mathscr{U}(v^0(y^0)) - \mathscr{U}(0)]. \tag{A9.64}$$

Substituting (A9.62) and (A9.63) in the objective function, we obtain

$$S - v_1\left[\lambda\left(\frac{\alpha}{2}\right)(\underline{e}^1 + \Delta\beta)^2 + (1+\lambda)\left(\underline{\beta} - \underline{e}^1 + \left(\frac{\alpha}{2}\right)(\underline{e}^1)^2\right)\right] - (1 - v_1)$$
$$\times\left[(1 - y^0)(1+\lambda)\left(\overline{\beta} - \overline{e}^1 + \left(\frac{\alpha}{2}\right)(\overline{e}^1)^2\right)\right.$$
$$\left. + y^0(1+\lambda)\left(\underline{\beta} - \underline{e}^1 + \left(\frac{\alpha}{2}\right)(\underline{e}^1 + \Delta\beta)^2\right.\right]$$
$$+ \delta\left[(1 - y^0)(1 - v_1)\left[S - (1+\lambda)\left(\overline{\beta} - \frac{1}{2\alpha}\right)\right.\right.$$
$$\left. + (1 - (1 - y^0)(1 - v_1))W^{AI}(v^0(y^0))\right].$$

The maximization with respect to $\bar{e}^1$, $\underline{e}^1$ gives

$$\bar{e}^1 = \frac{1}{\alpha}, \tag{A9.65}$$

$$\underline{e}^1 = \frac{1}{\alpha} - \Delta\beta \frac{\lambda v_1 + (1+\lambda)(1-v_1)y^0}{(1+\lambda)[v_1 + (1-v_1)y^0]}. \tag{A9.66}$$

Notice that in such an equilibrium, the inefficient type works harder than in the first best with probability y^0:

$$\underline{e}^1 + \Delta\beta > \bar{e}^1 = \frac{1}{\alpha} \tag{A9.67}$$

(and always at least as much). We then maximize with respect to y^0 to have a type II equilibrium.

Equilibrium of Type III: Both Types' Incentive Constraints Binding

Let x^0 be the probability that the efficient type says that it is efficient, and let y^0 be the probability that the inefficient type says that it is efficient. Then the ex post probability that the firm is efficient given that "efficient" is told is

$$v^0(x^0, y^0) = \frac{x^0 v_1}{x^0 v_1 + y^0(1 - v_1)}.$$

Similarly the probability that the firm is efficient given that it announces it is inefficient is

$$v^1(x^0, y^0) = \frac{(1 - x^0)v_1}{(1 - x^0)v_1 + (1 - y^0)(1 - v_1)}.$$

In equilibrium both are indifferent between both announcements:

$$\bar{t}^1 - \left(\frac{\alpha}{2}\right)(\bar{e}^1)^2 = \underline{t}^1 - \left(\frac{\alpha}{2}\right)(\underline{e}^1 + \Delta\beta)^2 = 0, \tag{A9.68}$$

$$\underline{t}^1 - \left(\frac{\alpha}{2}\right)(\underline{e}^1)^2 + \delta\mathscr{U}(v^0(x^0, y^0)) = \bar{t}^1 - \left(\frac{\alpha}{2}\right)(\bar{e}^1 - \Delta\beta)^2 + \delta\mathscr{U}(v^1(x^0, y^0)). \tag{A9.69}$$

Hence

$$\bar{e}^1 = \underline{e}^1 + \Delta\beta + \left(\frac{\delta}{\alpha\Delta\beta}\right)[\mathscr{U}(v^0(x^0, y^0)) - \mathscr{U}(v^1(x^0, y^0))].$$

The best contract is obtained from the maximization of

$$S + v_1\left[x^0\left(-\lambda\underline{t}^1 - (1+\lambda)(\underline{\beta} - \underline{e}^1) - \left(\frac{\alpha}{2}\right)(\underline{e}^1)^2\right)\right.$$

$$\left. + (1 - x^0)\left(-\lambda\bar{t}^1 - (1+\lambda)(\bar{\beta} - \bar{e}^1) - \left(\frac{\alpha}{2}\right)(\bar{e}^1 - \Delta\beta)^2\right)\right]$$

$$+ (1 - v_1)\left[y^0\left(-\lambda\underline{t}^1 - (1+\lambda)(\underline{\beta} - \underline{e}^1) - \left(\frac{\alpha}{2}\right)(\underline{e}^1 + \Delta\beta)^2\right)\right.$$

$$+ (1 - y^0)\left(-\lambda \bar{t}^1 - (1 + \lambda)(\bar{\beta} - \bar{e}^1) - \left(\frac{\alpha}{2}\right)(\bar{e}^1)^2\right]$$

$$+ \delta[[v_1 x^0 + (1 - v_1)y^0] W^{AI}(v^0(x^0, y^0))$$

$$+ [v_1(1 - x^0) + (1 - v_1)(1 - y^0)] W^{AI}(v^1(x^0, y^0))]$$

under the constraints (A9.68) and (A9.69).

We can substitute $\underline{t}^1, \bar{t}^1, \bar{e}^1$ as functions of $\underline{e}^1$, differentiate to obtain the best $\underline{e}^1$ as a function of x^0 and y^0.

$$\underline{e}^1 = \frac{1}{\alpha} - \Delta\beta\left(1 - \frac{v_1}{1 + \lambda}\right) - \left(\frac{\delta}{\alpha\Delta\beta}\right)[v_1(1 - x^0) + (1 - v_1)(1 - y^0)]$$

$$\times [\mathscr{U}(v^0(x^0, y^0)) - \mathscr{U}(v^1(x^0, y^0))].$$

Then we optimize numerically with respect to x^0 and y^0. ■

A9.10 Proof of Proposition 9.9 (Full Separation Is Optimal for δ Small)

Let the regulator offer a menu $\mathscr{C}$ of costs that are used in equilibrium. Since we look first for an upper bound on welfare, we can assume that all costs in $\mathscr{C}$ are chosen on the equilibrium path.

For technical reasons we will assume that the menu $\mathscr{C}$ is countable: $\mathscr{C} = \{C^k\}$. Let x^k (resp. y^k) denote the *unconditional* probability that the firm has type $\underline{\beta}$ (resp. $\bar{\beta}$) *and* chooses cost C^k [so $\sum_k (x^k + y^k) = 1$]. Let $W(v)$ denote the second-period welfare for posterior beliefs v; $W(\cdot)$ has been determined in chapter 1. Note that

$$(x^k + y^k)\, W\left(\frac{x^k}{x^k + y^k}\right) < x^k W(0) + y^k W(1) \qquad \text{unless } x^k y^k = 0$$

(i.e., the regulator is better off under full information). Intertemporal welfare can be written

$$\mathscr{W} = S - \sum_k [(1 + \lambda)(x^k(C^k + \psi(\underline{\beta} - C^k)) + y^k(C^k + \psi(\bar{\beta} - C^k))$$

$$+ \lambda x^k \Phi(\bar{\beta} - C^k)]$$

$$+ (x^k + y^k) W\left(\frac{x^k}{x^k + y^k}\right)\Bigg].$$

We make the following convention: That a population (x^k or y^k) is "moved to cost C" means that either this population now chooses cost C if $C \notin \mathscr{C}$, or if $C \in \mathscr{C}$, chooses a cost arbitrarily close to C but *not in* $\mathscr{C}$. (In the latter case we will write payoffs as if C was chosen. This is without loss of generality because we will make only strict comparisons.) Note that because $\mathscr{C}$ is countable, one can approximate any cost C by costs not in $\mathscr{C}$ arbitrarily closely.

For the above allocation to dominate the fully separating allocation, it must be the case that for all $C^k \in \mathscr{C}$ such that $y^k > 0: C^k \geq \bar{\beta} - \bar{e}(v_1) - \varepsilon(\delta)$, where $\lim_{\delta \to 0} \varepsilon(\delta) = 0$ and $\bar{e}(v_1)$ is type $\bar{\beta}$'s effort at the static optimum. If this were not the case, type $\underline{\beta}$'s rent, which exceeds $\Phi(\bar{\beta} - \inf C^k)$ would remain uniformly bounded away from, and exceeding, $\Phi(\bar{e}(v_1))$, and the allocation would be dominated by the fully separating one, whose welfare converges to the commitment welfare as δ tends to 0.

Move the population of types $\underline{\beta}$ (in number x^k) from C^k to $\underline{\beta} - e^*$ so as to maintain the same utility and thus not upset the overall equilibrium. That is, if C^k is such that $x^k > 0$, the transfer t for the new cost must satisfy

$$t - \psi(e^*) = t^k - \psi(\underline{\beta} - C^k) + \delta\mathcal{U}\left(\frac{x^k}{x^k + y^k}\right).$$

Similarly move the population of types $\overline{\beta}$ (in number y^k) from C^k to $\tilde{C}$ such that

$$\Phi(\overline{\beta} - C^k) + \delta\mathcal{U}\left(\frac{x^k}{x^k + y^k}\right) = \Phi(\overline{\beta} - \tilde{C})$$

(implying $\tilde{C} \leq C^k$). That is, types $\overline{\beta}$, like types $\underline{\beta}$, who were choosing C^k now separate. $\tilde{C}$ is chosen so that type $\underline{\beta}$'s rent is kept constant, and thus the equilibrium is unaffected.

Since the fraction $(x^k + y^k)$ concerned now separates, second-period welfare is higher: Recall that

$$x^k W(0) + y^k W(1) > (x^k + y^k) W\left(\frac{x^k}{x^k + y^k}\right).$$

The gain in first-period welfare is

$$G = x^k\left[(1 + \lambda)[-(\underline{\beta} - e^* + \psi(e^*)) + (C^k + \psi(\underline{\beta} - C^k)]\right.$$
$$\left. - \lambda\delta\mathcal{U}\left(\frac{x^k}{x^k + y^k}\right)\right] + y^k(1 + \lambda)[(C^k + \psi(\overline{\beta} - C^k)) - (\tilde{C} + \psi(\overline{\beta} - \tilde{C}))].$$

For δ small, $\lambda\delta\mathcal{U}[x^k/(x^k + y^k)] \leq \lambda\delta\mathcal{U}(0) \to 0$, and because C^k is close to $\overline{\beta} - \bar{e}(v_1)$, the coefficient of x^k is strictly positive. Also for δ small, if $y^k > 0$, $\overline{\beta} - e^* < \tilde{C} \leq C^k$, and therefore the coefficient of y^k is positive. Hence the initial allocation cannot deliver the upper bound on the principal's welfare.

Last, note that the upper bound (which is given by the separating equilibrium) can be implemented through a menu with a unique continuation equilibrium. (It suffices to give the menu $\{(\underline{C} = \underline{\beta} - e^*, t = \psi(e^*) + \Phi(\bar{e}(v_1)) + \delta\Phi(e^*) + \varepsilon), (\overline{C} = \overline{\beta} - \bar{e}(v_1), \bar{t} = \psi(\bar{e}(v_1)) + \varepsilon^2)\}$ for ε positive and tending to zero). ∎

REFERENCES

Aghion, P., and P. Bolton. 1987. Contracts as a barrier to entry. *American Economic Review* 77:388–401.

Anton, J., and D. Yao. 1987. Second-sourcing and the experience curve: Price competition in defence procurement. *Rand Journal of Economics* 18:57–76.

Armstrong, M., Rees, R. and J. Vickers. 1991. Optimal regulatory lag under price caps regulation. Mimeo, Oxford University.

Aron, D. 1987. Worker reputation and productivity incentives. *Journal of Labor Economics* 5:S87–S106.

Baron, D., and D. Besanko. 1987. Commitment and fairness in a dynamic regulatory relationship. *Review of Economic Studies* 54:413–436.

Crawford, V., and J. Sobel. 1982. Strategic information transmission. *Econometrica* 50:1431–1452.

Croker, K., and K. Reynolds. 1989. Efficient contract design in long-term relationships: The case of air force engine procurement. WP 10-89-1, Penn State University.

Dearden, J. 1990. Short-term and commitment contracting in long-term relationships. Mimeo, Lehigh University.

Diamond, D. 1992. Bank loan maturity and priority when borrowers can refinance. Mimeo, University of Chicago.

Fellingham, J., D. Newman, and Y. Suh. 1985. Contracts without memory in multiperiod agency models. *Journal of Economic Theory* 37:340–355.

Fernandez-Arias, E., and A. Kofman. 1989. Equilibrium characterization in finite-horizon games of reputation. Mimeo, University of California, Berkeley.

Freixas, X., R. Guesnerie, and J. Tirole. 1985. Planning under incomplete information and the ratchet effect. *Review of Economic Studies* 52:173–192.

Fudenberg, D., B. Holmström, and P. Milgrom. 1990. Short-term contracts and long-term agency relationships. *Journal of Economic Theory* 51:1–31.

Gibbons, R. 1987. Piece-rate incentive schemes. *Journal of Labor Economics* 5:413–429.

Gilbert, R., and D. Newbery. 1988. Regulation games. WP 8879, University of California, Berkeley.

Grossman, S., and O. Hart. 1986. The costs and benefits of ownership: A theory of vertical and lateral integration. *Journal of Political Economy* 94:691–719.

Hart, O., and J. Tirole. 1988. Contract renegotiation and coasian dynamics. *Review of Economic Studies* 55:509–540.

Hermalin, B. 1988. Adverse selection and contract length. Chapter 1, Ph.D. dissertation, Massachusetts Institute of Technology.

Holmström, B. 1982. Managerial incentive problems: A dynamic perspective. In *Essays in Economics and Management in Honor of Lars Wahlbeck*. Helsinki: Swedish School of Economics.

Ickes, B., and L. Samuelson. 1987. Job transfers and incentives in complex organizations: Thwarting the ratchet effect. *Rand Journal of Economics* 18:275–286.

Kanemoto, Y., and B. Macleod. 1990. The ratchet effect and the market for second-hand workers. Mimeo, University of Tokyo and Queen's University.

Litwack, J. 1987. Incentives and coordination problems in centrally planned economies: A theoretical study with applications to the USSR. Ph.D. dissertation, University of Pennsylvania.

Malcomson, J., and F. Spinnewyn. 1988. The multiperiod principal-agent problem. *Review of Economic Studies* 55:391–407.

Olsen, T., and G. Torsvik. 1991. The ratchet effect in common agency. Mimeo, Norwegian Center for Research in Organization and Management, Bergen.

Rey, P., and B. Salanié. 1990. Long-term, short-term and renegotiation: On the value of commitment in contracting. *Econometrica* 58:597–619.

Richardson, T. 1989. Bilateral incomplete information and the ratchet effect. Mimeo, Columbia University.

Riordan, M., and D. Sappington. 1988. Commitment in procurement contracting. *Scandinavian Journal of Economics* 90:357–372.

Salant, D., and G. Woroch. 1988. Trigger price regulation. Mimeo, GTE Laboratories, Waltham.

Schmidt, K. 1990. Commitment through incomplete information in a simple repeated bargaining model. Mimeo, University of Bonn.

Sen, A. 1991 Intertemporal contractual relationships with agent switching. Mimeo, Princeton University.

Skillman, G. 1988. Ratchet effect dynamics in finitely repeated principal-agent relationships. Mimeo, Crown University.

Vincent, D. 1989. Bilateral monopoly, non-durable goods and dynamic trading relationships. Mimeo, Northwestern University.

Weitzman, M. 1980. The ratchet principle and performance incentives. *Bell Journal of Economics* 11:302–308.

Yao, D. 1988. Strategic responses to automobile emissions control: A game-theoretic analysis. *Journal of Environmental Economics and Management* 15:419–438.

Zhou, H. 1986. Dynamic effects of incentive schemes in economic planning. Ph.D. dissertation, Northwestern University.

Zou, L. 1989. Target-incentive system vs. price-incentive system under adverse selection and ratchet effect. Mimeo, Center, Tilburg University.

10 COMMITMENT AND RENEGOTIATION

10.1 Some Background

This chapter continues the study of long-term relationships undertaken in chapter 9. Now instead of assuming that the regulatory relationship is run by a series of short-term contracts, we allow commitment to a long-term contract. We analyze situations where there are no impediments (unforeseeability of contingencies or legal constraints) to commitment. Commitment, however, does not mean that the parties will abide by their contract in the future, but only that the contract will be implemented if at least one of them wishes so. The parties are always free to agree to modify the contract to their mutual advantage. Indeed full commitment in which the parties cannot renegotiate is an idealized case. The optimal contract derived under the assumption that the parties are unable to renegotiate, is in general not sequentially optimal or renegotiation-proof. That is, in the process of implementing a long-term contract, all parties may be better off modifying the initial contract (while renegotiation is ex post mutually beneficial, the regulator would ex ante like to be able to commit not to renegotiate). The commitment modeling so common in economic theory at best describes an extreme case in which the physical costs of recontracting are important or in which one of the parties can develop a reputation for refraining from signing mutually advantageous contracts.

This chapter investigates the implications of renegotiation in the twice-repeated version of the model of chapter 1 (set up in section 10.2). In each period the firm realizes a project for the regulator. The project's cost in that period depends on the time-invariant type (the firm's state of technology) and on the cost-reducing effort. The only commonly observable variable is the realized cost in the period. Recall from chapter 1 that in a static (one-period) framework the optimal incentive scheme trades off the two conflicting concerns of extracting the firm's informational rent and giving the latter appropriate incentives to reduce cost, and it specifies a reward that decreases with realized cost. With two possible types (the case considered in most of this chapter), the incentive constraint is binding "upward" only. The issue is to induce the efficient type not to mimic the inefficient type. For the optimal incentive scheme under asymmetric information, the efficient type produces at its socially optimal cost, while the inefficient type's cost exceeds its socially optimal cost in order to reduce the efficient type's rent.

In the twice-repeated relationship the regulator would optimally commit to repeat twice the optimal static scheme (see section 1.10). That is, he or she ought to commit not to alter the first-period incentive scheme in the second period. However, this optimal commitment incentive scheme is not renegotiation-proof. Suppose that the firm has produced at the high cost in the first period, demonstrating that the technology is unfavorable. While the initial contract induces the same inefficiently high cost in the second period, it has become common knowledge that this contract can be renegotiated to benefit both parties by giving more incentives to the firm. But this renegotiation with the inefficient type toward higher incentives raises the rent of the efficient type, if the latter mascarades as an inefficient type in the first period. It makes the efficient type's incentive compatibility constraint in the first period harder to satisfy.

In chapter 9 we assumed that the regulator can commit only to one-period incentive schemes. Then in the second period the regulator selects his or her preferred contract conditional on the information learned in the first period. Such short-term contracts are trivially renegotiation-proof. A main focus of this analysis was the ratchet effect: The fact that the firm is concerned about the expropriation of its informational rent in the second period makes separation of types costly, and even infeasible in the case of a continuum of types. The analysis of short-term contracting is complex because an inefficient type may adopt the take-the-money-and-run strategy: To induce an efficient type to reveal some information in the first period, the first-period contract must offer this type a deal that would make it optimal for an inefficient type to mimic an efficient type in the first period and quit the relationship in the second period. Thus the first-period incentive constraints may be binding upward and downward.

In the chapter we make an assumption about commitment abilities of the parties being intermediate between full intertemporal commitment and no intertemporal commitment. We refer to this as "commitment and renegotiation." We allow commitment in that the two parties sign a long-term contract that is enforced as long as one of the parties wants it to be enforced. Nothing prevents the parties from agreeing to alter the initial contract. While the optimal contract can, without loss of generality, be designed so as not to be renegotiated in the second period, the renegotiation-proofness (RP) requirement restricts the set of allowable second-period contracts. The analysis shares with the commitment case the simplicity associated with the incentive constraint being binding upward only and yet exhibits a form of ratcheting similar to that of the no-commitment case. The ability to commit eliminates the possibility of the take-the-money-and-run strategy by making all payments conditional on the firm's participation in period 2.

Section 10.3 demonstrates that there are three kinds of renegotiation-proof contracts. In all kinds the efficient type produces at its socially optimal cost level. In the first kind the second-period allocation is that of a *sell-out* or *fixed-price contract*; that is, the firm, whatever its type, behaves as if it were residual claimant for its cost savings and produces at its (type-contingent) socially optimal cost. The second kind is the *conditionally optimal contract*. That is, the firm faces the same incentive contract it would face if the regulator were not bound by a previous contract and offered the optimal static contract given his or her posterior beliefs about the firm's type. The third kind is the intermediate class of *rent-constrained contracts* in which the inefficient type produces at a cost that lies between its socially optimal cost and its cost in the optimal static contract given the regulator's posterior beliefs (the conditionally optimal contract is thus an extreme rent-constrained contract). The regulator would like to increase the inefficient type's cost to reduce the efficient type's rent but is unable to do so because of the rent level previously offered the efficient type.

Section 10.4 characterizes the optimal intertemporal contract. The second-period contract is conditionally optimal (the second kind of renegotiation-proof contract). In the first period only the efficient type's incentive compatibility constraint is binding (as in the full commitment case but not in the noncommitment case). The efficient type is indifferent between revealing its type and mascarading as inefficient. The optimal contract is therefore rather simple. Incentive constraints are binding as usual, and the contract offered in period 2 is conditionally optimal (i.e., is not distorted by the regulator's ability to commit to rents). However, none of these results is obvious. Limits on commitment might, as in chapter 9, lead to incentive constraints binding in both directions. What is more, the ability to commit to rents to mitigate the first-period incentive constraints might lead to distortions in second-period contracts away from conditionally optimal contracts.

Section 10.5 shows that the equilibrium is a separating one only if the discount factor is small. The equilibrium probability that the efficient type pools with the inefficient type increases with the discount factor and converges to one (without ever reaching this value) when the parties become very patient. Section 10.6 analyzes the case of a continuum of types. It shows that fully separating the types is feasible but never optimal for the regulator. Section 10.7 concludes the chapter with a fairly extensive comparison of the findings with those for the same model when the relationship involves a series of short-term contracts. Also explored is whether the outcome under commitment and renegotiation is intermediate between those attained under full commitment and under noncommitment.

The chapter does not make predictions as to whether contract renegotiation is likely to be observed. On the one hand, the renegotiation-proofness principle claims that the regulator can restrict attention to contracts that are not renegotiated. On the other, the chapter shows that in the case of two types an alternative optimal scheme for the regulator is to offer a menu of two contracts in period 1 that can be renegotiated with some probability: a long-term fixed-price contract (which is not renegotiated) and a short-term contract.

It is often claimed that in procurement high-powered incentive schemes (e.g., a fixed-price contract) are impractical because they are likely to be renegotiated. But, contrary to conventional wisdom, high-powered incentive schemes do yield efficient production, and consequently they are less subject to renegotiation than low-powered schemes, which are designed to limit the firm's rent. Indeed, comparing full commitment to commitment and renegotiation, the threat of renegotiation induces more powerful incentive schemes in the second period. (The effects of renegotiation on the first period are more ambiguous. The efficient type's incentives go down, while the inefficient type's go up.) If there are any merits to the conventional wisdom, they must stem from factors not captured by our modeling, such as ex post cost uncertainty combined with bankrupty or political reasons for the regulator not to commit even to the original contract.

10.2 The Model

10.2.1 The Commitment Framework

Recall the two-type, two-period model setup of section 9.4. The firm must in each period realize a project with a cost structure

$$C_\tau = \beta - e_\tau, \qquad \tau = 1, 2,$$

where e_τ is the level of effort exerted by the firm's manager in period τ and β is a parameter known only by the manager, which can take two values $\underline{\beta}$ ("efficient type") and $\bar{\beta}$ ("inefficient type"), with $\bar{\beta} > \underline{\beta}$. Let $\Delta\beta \equiv \bar{\beta} - \underline{\beta}$.

Each period τ the firm's utility level is $U \equiv t_\tau - \psi(e_\tau)$, where t_τ is the net (i.e., in addition to cost) monetary transfer it receives from the regulator and $\psi(e_\tau)$ is its disutility of effort, where $\psi(0) = 0$, $\psi' > 0$, $\psi'' > 0$, $\psi''' \geq 0$. Let e^* denote the socially optimal level of effort, defined by the equality between the marginal disutility of effort and the marginal cost savings:

$$\psi'(e^*) = 1.$$

The socially optimal cost level is type contingent and is equal to $\beta - e^*$.

The regulator observes cost but not the effort level or the value of the parameter β. The regulator has a prior about β characterized by $\nu_1 = \text{Prob}(\beta = \underline{\beta})$. This probability is common knowledge.

Let S be, each period, the social utility of the project. The project can be viewed for simplicity as the production of a public good not sold on the market. The gross payment made by the regulator to the firm is $t_\tau + C_\tau$. Letting λ denote the shadow cost of public funds, consumers' welfare in period τ is

$$S - (1 + \lambda)(t_\tau + C_\tau).$$

Let δ be the firm's and the regulator's discount factor. Note that δ may exceed 1 because it reflects the relative lengths of the accounting periods or the relative importance of the first- and second-period projects.

Under *complete information* a utilitarian regulator would solve in each period τ

$$\max_{\{e_\tau, t_\tau\}} \{S - (1 + \lambda)(t_\tau + \beta - e_\tau) + t_\tau - \psi(e_\tau)\}$$

subject to

$$t_\tau - \psi(e_\tau) \geq 0.$$

The individual rationality constraint $t_\tau - \psi(e_\tau) \geq 0$ says that the firm's utility level must be positive to obtain its participation (the complete information problem being stationary, the allocation is the same at each period).

We assume that S is large enough so that the project is always desirable. The optimal regulatory allocation is then

$$e_\tau = e^* \quad \text{and} \quad t_\tau = \psi(e^*), \qquad \tau = 1, 2.$$

Welfare is

$$(1 + \delta)[S - (1 + \lambda)(\psi(e^*) + \beta - e^*)].$$

Under *asymmetric information* (in a one-period relationship, or from section 1.10 in the two-period relationship under full commitment), the regulator offers a menu $(\underline{t}, \underline{C})$ for type $\underline{\beta}$, and $(\bar{t}, \bar{C})$ for type $\bar{\beta}$. Recall from section 1.3 that the efficient type's rent is $\Phi(\bar{e})$, where $\bar{e} \equiv \bar{\beta} - \bar{C}$ and $\Phi(e) \equiv \psi(e) - \psi(e - \Delta\beta)$. The function Φ is increasing and convex. Replacing t by $U + \psi(e)$ and (from now on) ignoring the constant surplus S, the regulator's program is

$$\min E_\beta[(1 + \lambda)(\psi(e) + C) + \lambda U]. \tag{10.1}$$

Note that welfare is expressed in terms of *efficiency* $E_\beta[(1 + \lambda)(\psi(e) + C)]$ and *rent* $E_\beta(\lambda U)$. (In this chapter the method for improving on a given contract will be either to increase efficiency, keeping rent constant, or to increase both efficiency and rent.) That is, the total cost for a given type is $\psi(e) + C$, which has shadow cost $1 + \lambda$, to which must be added the shadow cost of the firm's rent.

Program I

$$\min_{\{\underline{e}, \bar{e}\}} \{\nu_1[(1+\lambda)(\psi(\underline{e})+\underline{\beta}-\underline{e})+\lambda\Phi(\bar{e})]+(1-\nu_1)(1+\lambda)(\psi(\bar{e})+\bar{\beta}-\bar{e})\}.$$

The efficient type's cost is socially optimal:

$$\underline{e} = e^*. \tag{10.2}$$

However, the inefficient type's cost is inflated so as to reduce the efficient type's rent:

$$\psi'(\bar{e}) = 1 - \frac{\lambda \nu_1}{(1+\lambda)(1-\nu_1)} \Phi'(\bar{e}) < 1. \tag{10.3}$$

We let $\bar{e}(\nu_1)$ denote the unique solution to equation (10.3). It is easily verified that $\bar{C}(\nu_1) \equiv \bar{\beta} - \bar{e}(\nu_1)$ exceeds the socially optimal cost $\bar{\beta} - e^*$ (unless $\nu_1 = 0$) and that it increases with ν_1. Proposition 10.1 summarizes this recap of section 1.3.

Proposition 10.1 The optimal (static or dynamic) commitment solution is characterized by

$$\underline{C}(\nu_1) = \underline{\beta} - e^* \quad \text{or} \quad \underline{e}(\nu_1) = e^*,$$

$$\bar{C}(\nu_1) > \bar{\beta} - e^* \quad \text{or} \quad \bar{e}(\nu_1) < e^*,$$

$$\frac{d\bar{C}}{d\nu_1} > 0 \quad \text{or} \quad \frac{d\bar{e}}{d\nu_1} < 0,$$

and

$$\mathcal{U}(\nu_1) = \Phi(\bar{e}(\nu_1)).$$

We implicitly assumed in the previous analysis that the probability of the inefficient type is not too small, for above some cutoff level of ν_1 the regulator would choose not to let the inefficient type produce at all. We will henceforth assume that $1 - \nu_1$ is sufficiently high so that the regulator does not choose to ignore the inefficient type.[1]

For further reference we also derive the optimal *pooling* allocation. Suppose that the regulator is constrained to pick a single-cost target C for both types [in the full commitment case the regulator would never choose to do so (see proposition 10.1), but this thought experiment will be useful later on, for the solution under commitment and renegotiation may involve pooling in the first period]. The regulator pays a transfer equal to $\psi(\bar{\beta} - C)$ so as to satisfy the inefficient type's individual rationality constraint. The cost is thus $\psi(\bar{\beta} - C) + C$, regardless of the firm's type. The efficient type's rent is $\Phi(\bar{\beta} - C)$. Hence the regulator chooses C so as to solve

$$\min_{\{C\}} \{(1+\lambda)E_\beta[(\psi(\bar{\beta} - C) + C)] + \lambda \nu_1 \Phi(\bar{\beta} - C)\}$$

$$= \{(1+\lambda)[\nu_1(\psi(\underline{\beta} - C) + C) + (1-\nu_1)(\psi(\bar{\beta} - C) + C)] + \lambda \nu_1 \Phi(\bar{\beta} - C)\}. \tag{10.4}$$

1. The reader may wonder whether this assumption can be made for a dynamic model. Indeed the second-period beliefs ν_2 can be close to 1 even though the prior beliefs ν_1 are assumed not to. However, we will show that along the equilibrium path either $\nu_2 \leq \nu_1$ (and then our assumption implies that both types should be retained) or $\nu_2 = 1$ (and then only the efficient type is relevant). It can be shown that for any ν_1 under some cutoff level, the equilibrium is as described in this chapter.

The solution of this strictly convex program $C^P(v_1)$ lies between the two types' socially optimal costs,

$$\underline{\beta} - e^* < C^P(v_1) < \bar{\beta} - e^*,$$

and decreases with the probability of the efficient type,

$$\frac{dC^P}{dv_1} < 0. \tag{10.5}$$

10.2.2 The Renegotiation Game

We now assume that the parties sign a long-term contract at date 1 but that the regulator can, at date 2, offer to renegotiate the initial contract. The regulator puts prior beliefs v_1 on the firm's having the efficient type. The two parties are initially bound by the "null contract," which specifies no production and no transfer in either period. At the beginning of period 1, the regulator offers a long-term contract $\{t_1(C_1), t_2^0(C_1, C_2)\}$.[2] This contract is called a short-term contract if t_2^0 is the (second-period) null contract. After observing the firm's performance C_1, the regulator updates his or her beliefs to v_2 and offers a new second-period contract, which the firm accepts or refuses.[3] At every stage the parties abide by the contract in force if the firm rejects the new contract offer. The old contract is superseded by the new one if the firm accepts the new contract. Last, since both parties have rational expectations, the contract offered in period 1 may be restricted to be renegotiation-proof in period 2.

10.3 Renegotiation-Proof Second-Period Contracts

Suppose that at the beginning of date 2, beliefs are $v_2 = v$. Two cases must be considered, depending on whether the regulator wants to keep the

2. Equivalently in the two-type case a long-term contract is the offer of two incentive schemes, A and B, between which the firm selects. Both A and B are of the form $\{(C_1, t_1); (\underline{C}_2, \underline{t}_2), (\bar{C}_2, \bar{t}_2)\}$. That is, the firm chooses (C_1, t_1) in period 1 and then announces its type in period 2 to pick either $(\underline{C}_2, \underline{t}_2)$ or $(\bar{C}_2, \bar{t}_2)$. Lemma 10.1 shows that there is no gain in having the firm reveal more information in period 1 than is necessary to determine the first-period allocation [i.e., if A and B specified the same (C_1, t_1) and differed in some first-period announcement by the firm, A and B could be merged in a single incentive scheme at no loss for the regulator] and that there is no gain in introducing more than two incentive schemes.

3. Note that we model renegotiation with the uninformed party making the offer. The analysis is more complex if the informed party (here the firm) makes the offer in the renegotiation, since we must worry about the information transmitted by this offer. The difficulty comes from the multiplicity of perfect Bayesian equilibria in the game where the firm makes an offer that the regulator accepts or rejects. However, if we used the notion of strong renegotiation proofness of Maskin and Tirole (1992) (a contract is strongly renegotiation-proof if it is not renegotiated in any equilibrium of the renegotiation game), we would obtain the same result as here for this different extensive form for renegotiation.

inefficient type in period 2. If the regulator does not wish to keep the inefficient type, then a renegotiation-proof contract specifies the first-best cost of the efficient type $\underline{\beta} - e^*$ and some level of rent $\underline{U}$.

If the regulator wishes to keep the inefficient type, let $\underline{U}^0$ and $\overline{U}^0$ be the second-period rents of the efficient and inefficient types (not including the forgone first-period transfer and disutility of effort) specified by the initial contract binding the parties. Without loss of generality, we assume that $\overline{U}^0 = 0$ by adjusting, if necessary, the first-period transfers (the reader can check that the analysis below is unaffected if we choose a different normalization). The regulator offers a new contract, yielding second-period costs $\{\underline{C}, \overline{C}\}$ and rents $\{\underline{U}, \overline{U}\}$ for the two types:

Program II

$$\min_{\{\underline{e},\bar{e},\underline{U},\overline{U}\}} \{\nu[(1+\lambda)(\psi(\underline{e}) + \underline{\beta} - \underline{e}) + \lambda \underline{U}] + (1-\nu)[(1+\lambda)(\psi(\bar{e}) + \bar{\beta} - \bar{e}) + \lambda \overline{U}]\}$$

subject to

$$\underline{U} \geq \overline{U} + \Phi(\bar{e}), \tag{10.6}$$

$$\overline{U} \geq 0, \tag{10.7}$$

$$\underline{U} \geq \underline{U}^0. \tag{10.8}$$

The levels of rent committed to, $\underline{U}^0$ and $\overline{U}^0 = 0$, are renegotiation-proof if the solution to program II involves $\underline{U} = \underline{U}^0$ and $\overline{U} = \overline{U}^0$. One can always choose to realize these levels of rent by allocations that are the solutions to program II and appropriate transfers.

Note that program II includes only the efficient type's IC constraint (10.6). As before the ignored IC constraint for the inefficient type ($\overline{U} \geq \underline{U} - \Phi(\underline{e} + \Delta\beta)$) is checked ex post. The only difference between programs I and II is the presence of the extra IR constraint (10.8). That is, the efficient type may have been promised a higher second-period rent than in program I (see proposition 10.1).

The solution to program II clearly involves $\overline{U} = 0$ (no new rent for the inefficient type) and $e = e^*$ (the efficient type's cost is socially optimal). Let us simplify the optimization program:

Program III

$$\min_{\{\bar{e},\underline{U}\}} \{\nu[(1+\lambda)(\psi(e^*) + \underline{\beta} - e^*) + \lambda \underline{U}] + (1-\nu)[(1+\lambda)(\psi(\bar{e}) + \bar{\beta} - \bar{e})]\}$$

subject to

$$\underline{U} \geq \Phi(\bar{e}) \qquad (\gamma_1), \tag{10.9}$$

$$\underline{U} \geq \underline{U}^0 \qquad (\gamma_2). \tag{10.10}$$

Three cases can be distinguished according to which constraints are binding in program III. The lagrangian of this convex program reduces to

$$L = \nu\lambda\underline{U} + (1-\nu)(1+\lambda)(\psi(\bar{e}) + \bar{\beta} - \bar{e}) - \gamma_1(\underline{U} - \Phi(\bar{e})) - \gamma_2(\underline{U} - \underline{U}^0) \tag{10.11}$$

with first-order conditions

$$\psi'(\bar{e}) = 1 - \frac{\gamma_1}{(1-\nu)(1+\lambda)}\Phi'(\bar{e}), \tag{10.12}$$

$$\gamma_1 + \gamma_2 = \nu\lambda \qquad \text{with } \gamma_1 \geq 0, \gamma_2 \geq 0. \tag{10.13}$$

In *case 1*, $\underline{U}^0$ is small so that (10.10) is not binding ($\gamma_2 = 0$). From (10.12) and (10.13),

$$\psi'(\bar{e}) = 1 - \frac{\nu}{1-\nu}\frac{\lambda}{1+\lambda}\Phi'(\bar{e}). \tag{10.14}$$

We obtain the same result as in proposition 10.1. The solutions to programs I and III coincide except that ν_1 is replaced by $\nu = \nu_2$. The allocation is optimal for the regulator conditionally on his or her posterior beliefs. The contract is called *conditionally optimal.* From proposition 10.1 $\underline{U} = \Phi(\bar{e}(\nu))$. This case is therefore valid for $\underline{U}^0 \leq \Phi(\bar{e}(\nu))$. Actually, for the first-period contract to be renegotiation-proof, we must have $\underline{U}^0 = \Phi(\bar{e}(\nu))$.

In *case 2*, $\underline{U}^0$ is increased just beyond $\Phi(\bar{e}(\nu))$. Then both constraints are binding. So $\underline{U} = \underline{U}^0$ and $\bar{e}$ is defined by $\underline{U}^0 = \Phi(\bar{e})$. This case ceases to be valid when $\underline{U}^0$ is so large that the incentive constraint (10.9) ceases to be binding, implying that $\gamma_1 = 0$; then $\psi'(\bar{e}) = 1$ or $\bar{e} = e^*$, the socially optimal level. The second case holds for $\underline{U}^0$ between $\Phi(\bar{e}(\nu))$ and $\Phi(e^*)$, indicating a cost $\bar{C}$ between $\bar{\beta} - e^*$ and $\bar{C}(\nu)$. A contract specifying $\{\underline{C} = \underline{\beta} - e^*; \bar{\beta} - e^* \leq \bar{C} \leq \bar{C}(\nu); \underline{U} = \Phi(\bar{e})\}$ is called *rent constrained* and is renegotiation-proof for $\underline{U}^0 = \underline{U}$. The regulator would want to lower the efficient type's rent but cannot do so because of the existence of the initial contract. This loss in rent is partially compensated by the fact that the cost of the inefficient type can be brought closer to the efficient level while still satisfying the efficient type's incentive constraint. Clearly *in the second period* the regulator would prefer a lower value of $\underline{U}^0$ which yields a conditionally optimal contract. However, this does not mean that the regulator is better off committing to the conditionally optimal contract, because the value of $\underline{U}^0$ affects the first-period incentive constraint.

Finally, in *case 3*, $\underline{U}^0$ lies between $\Phi(e^*)$ and $\Phi(e^* + \Delta\beta)$;[4] (10.10) is binding and (10.9) is not. As observed above, the solution is then such that $\bar{C} = \bar{\beta} - e^*$. That is, the two cost levels are socially optimal. The cost allocation is identical to that under a *sell out* or *fixed-price contract* in which the firm is the residual claimant for its cost savings. It is renegotiation-proof if it corresponds to the rent $\underline{U}^0$ for the efficient type. Note that all sellout contracts have the same *efficiency* $E_\beta(1 + \lambda)(\psi(e^*) + \beta - e^*)$. They differ only by the efficient type's rent. From a second-period viewpoint, the regulator prefers the one with the lowest rent in this third class of renegotiation-proof contracts.

We gather our analysis in a proposition and four corollaries.

Proposition 10.2 Normalizing $\bar{U} = 0$, renegotiation-proof contracts that keep both types in period 2 can be indexed by a single parameter, the efficient type's rent $\underline{U}$, with $\underline{U} \in [\Phi(\bar{e}(v)), \Phi(e^* + \Delta\beta)]$.

i. Case 1: For $\underline{U} = \Phi(\bar{e}(v))$, it is the conditionally optimal contract

$\underline{e} = e^*; \bar{e} = \bar{e}(v)$.

ii. Case 2: For $\Phi(\bar{e}(v)) < \underline{U} < \Phi(e^*)$, it is a rent-constrained contract

$\underline{e} = e^*; \bar{e}(v) \leq \bar{e} \leq e^*$.

iii. Case 3: For $\Phi(e^*) \leq \underline{U} \leq \Phi(e^* + \Delta\beta)$, it is a sellout contract

$\underline{e} = \bar{e} = e^*$.

Corollary 10.1 In a renegotiation-proof contract the efficient type's rent is at least as large as that in a conditionally optimal contract: $\underline{U} \geq \underline{U}(v) \equiv \Phi(\bar{e}(v))$.

Corollary 10.2 The regulator's second-period welfare is strictly and continuously decreasing with the (efficient type's) rent $\underline{U}$, which indexes the set of renegotiation-proof contracts. The efficiency of the allocation increases with the rent on $[\Phi(\bar{e}(v)), \Phi(e^*)]$ (rent-constrained contracts) and does not depend on the rent on $[\Phi(e^*), \Phi(e^* + \Delta\beta)]$ (sellout contracts).

Corollary 10.3 A rent-constrained contract indexed by $\underline{U}$, which is renegotiation-proof for beliefs v, remains renegotiation-proof for beliefs $v' > v$.

Proof From proposition 10.2, $e^* \geq \Phi^{-1}(\underline{U}) \geq \bar{e}(v)$. From proposition 10.1, $d\bar{e}/dv < 0$. Therefore we still have $e^* \geq \Phi^{-1}(\underline{U}) \geq \bar{e}(v')$. ■

4. Giving up a rent higher than $\Phi(e^* + \Delta\beta)$ to the efficient type is impossible because this would violate the inefficient type's IC constraint. There is actually a fourth type of renegotiation-proof contract in which only the inefficient type's IC constraint is binding, $\underline{e} > e^*$, and $\bar{e} = e^*$. It is easy to show that such contracts are ex ante suboptimal.

Last, corollary 10.2 implies corollary 10.4.

Corollary 10.4 For any renegotiation-proof contract that is not conditionally optimal, there exists an arbitrary close renegotiation-proof contract with a (slightly) lower rent for the efficient type and a (slightly) higher welfare for the regulator in period 2.

10.4 Characterization of the Optimal Contract

In this section we partially characterize the optimal contract. Section 10.5 completes the characterization.

Proposition 10.3 The regulator offers the firm a choice between two contracts in the first period. The first is picked by the efficient type only and yields the efficient cost in both periods. In the second contract both types produce at the same cost level in the first period, and the second-period allocation is the conditionally optimal one, given posterior beliefs ν_2 in $[0, \nu_1]$.

To prove proposition 10.3, we first show that the relevant IC constraint in the first period is the efficient type's.

Lemma 10.1 Without loss of welfare, the regulator can offer the firm a choice between two contracts, one chosen by the efficient type and the other chosen by the inefficient type and possibly by the efficient type.

Proof See appendix A10.1.

Despite the renegotiation-proofness condition the ability to commit enables the regulator to neglect the inefficient type's incentive constraint. The noncommitment analysis provides the intuition for this result. As noted in sections 9.1 and 9.4, under noncommitment the inefficient type's incentive constraint may be binding: The efficient type must be given a high transfer to reveal information (produce at a low cost) in the first period, which may induce the inefficient type to mimic the efficient type in period 1 and quit the relationship in period 2. This take-the-money-and-run strategy, illustrated in figure 9.1, can be prevented under commitment and renegotiation, since the firm can commit to produce in period 2 if it produces at a low cost in period 1. Indeed, as we will later show, the firm is required to duplicate a low first-period cost in period 2. Interestingly lemma 10.1 and the subsequent analysis still hold when only the regulator can commit intertemporally. As is easily seen, the regulator can delay transfers so as to ensure that the firm's second-period utility level is nonnegative whenever the firm is active.

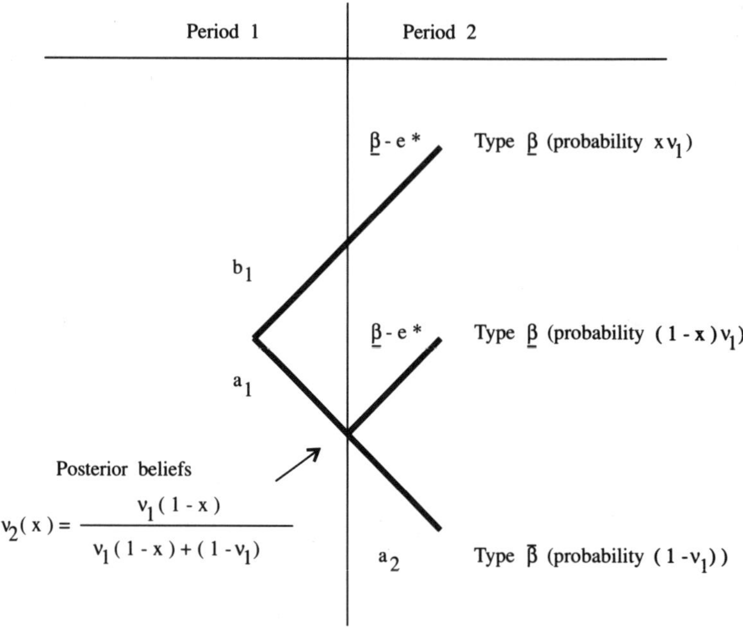

Figure 10.1
At the optimum only the efficient type randomizes

Lemma 10.1 implies that the overall optimal contract can be described as in figure 10.1, where the indices of the branches $(a_1, a_2, \ldots)$ refer to the costs requested in the associated contracts. The top branch in figure 10.1 represents the first contract and is chosen by the efficient type with probability x. The low and middle branches in period 2 represent the second contract. The middle branch is chosen by the efficient type with probability $1 - x$. The low branch is always chosen by the inefficient type.

Let $\underline{U}_2$ denote the second-period rent that the efficient type is promised if it chooses a_1 in period 1. From corollary 10.2, $\underline{U}_2 \geq \Phi(\bar{\beta} - a_2)$. The second-period cost following cost b_1 is the socially efficient one: $b_2 = \underline{\beta} - e^*$, since it has become common knowledge from the observation of the first-period cost b_1 that the firm has type $\underline{\beta}$. The efficient type must be given a rent in the first contract that is sufficient not to induce it to choose the second contract. The best way to do this is to ask the firm to produce efficiently, $b_1 = \underline{\beta} - e^*$, and to promise it a total rent

$$\underline{U} = \Phi(\bar{\beta} - a_1) + \delta \underline{U}_2. \tag{10.15}$$

It remains to determine the optimal pooling cost a_1, the inefficient type's second-period cost a_2, and the optimal x. The determination of the probability x that the efficient type reveals its type (separates) is tackled in section 10.5. For a given x the regulator's welfare is obtained by solving

$$\min_{\{a_1,a_2,\underline{U}_2\}} \{(1+\lambda)[v_1 x(\psi(e^*)+\underline{\beta}-e^*) + v_1(1-x)(\psi(\underline{\beta}-a_1)+a_1)+(1-v_1)(\psi(\bar{\beta}-a_1)+a_1)] + \lambda v_1 \Phi(\bar{\beta}-a_1) + \delta[(1+\lambda)[v_1(\psi(e^*)+\underline{\beta}-e^*) + (1-v_1)(\psi(\bar{\beta}-a_2)+a_2)] + \lambda v_1 \underline{U}_2]\} \tag{10.16}$$

subject to the incentive and renegotiation-proofness conditions

$$\underline{U}_2 \geq \Phi(\bar{\beta}-a_2), \tag{10.17}$$

$$\bar{\beta}-e^* \leq a_2 \leq \bar{C}(v_2). \tag{10.18}$$

We first note that (10.17) is binding:

Lemma 10.2 $\underline{U}_2 = \Phi(\bar{\beta}-a_2)$.

Proof The second-period contract must be a rent-constrained contract (including the two extremes in this class): If the second-period contract were a sellout one with rent exceeding $\Phi(e^*)$, the regulator could specify a slightly lower rent for the efficient type while keeping efficiency constant and thus increase welfare. ■

The intuition for the result that second-period contracts are rent constrained is that any increase of the rent beyond $\Phi(\bar{\beta}-a_2)$ serves no purpose in period 2 and moreover requires a further increase of the rent of the efficient type when it reveals its type because the incentive constraint of the efficient type is binding. The optimization program (10.16) can be broken down in two separate optimizations: minimization of first-period costs with respect to a_1 and minimization of second-period costs with respect to a_2 subject to (10.17) and (10.18).

To complete the proof of proposition 10.3, we consider the second minimization, which is rewritten

$$\min_{\{a_2\}} \{(1+\lambda)(1-v_1)(\psi(\bar{\beta}-a_2)+a_2)+\lambda v_1 \Phi(\bar{\beta}-a_2)\} \tag{10.19}$$

subject to

$$\bar{\beta}-e^* \leq a_2 \leq \bar{C}(v_2). \tag{10.20}$$

Lemma 10.3 The optimal a_2 equals $\bar{C}(v_2)$.

Proof Consider first the unconstrained minimization. The problem is analogous to a one-period problem with the prior v_2. From the Bayesian revision of expectations, $v_2 \leq v_1$. So the optimal solution of the unconstrained problem $\bar{C}(v_1)$ is no smaller than $\bar{C}(v_2)$ (from the first-order condition). Since the objective function (10.19) is strictly convex in a_2, the optimal solution of the constrained problem is $\bar{C}(v_2)$. ■

From lemma 10.3 we know that the second-period contract is conditionally optimal given v_2. Minimization of (10.16) with respect to a_1 yields

$$\frac{(1-v_1)\psi'(\bar{\beta}-a_1)+(1-x)v_1\psi'(\underline{\beta}-a_1)}{(1-v_1)+(1-x)v_1}$$
$$=1-\frac{\lambda}{1+\lambda}\frac{v_1}{1-v_1 x}[\psi'(\bar{\beta}-a_1)-\psi'(\underline{\beta}-a_1)]. \quad (10.21)$$

The optimization problem is here identical to that determining the optimal pooling contract [see (10.4)], but for the fact that only a fraction $(1-x)$ of the efficient types produce at cost a_1. The two programs coincide when $x=0$. When $x=1$, (10.16) coincides with the commitment (separating) program (program I). Letting $a_1=C_1(x)$ denote the solution of (10.21), we obtain immediately proposition 10.4.

Proposition 10.4 The first-period cost in the pooling branch $C_1(x)$ is independent of the discount factor (for a given x) and is an increasing function of the probability x that the efficient type separates in the first period. In a pooling equilibrium ($x=0$), $C_1(0)=C^P(v_1)$, and in a separating equilibrium ($x=1$), $C_1(1)=\bar{C}(v_1)$.

Propositions 10.3 and 10.4 reduce the computation of the optimal contract to the choice of a single number x in [0, 1] and are summarized in figure 10.2.

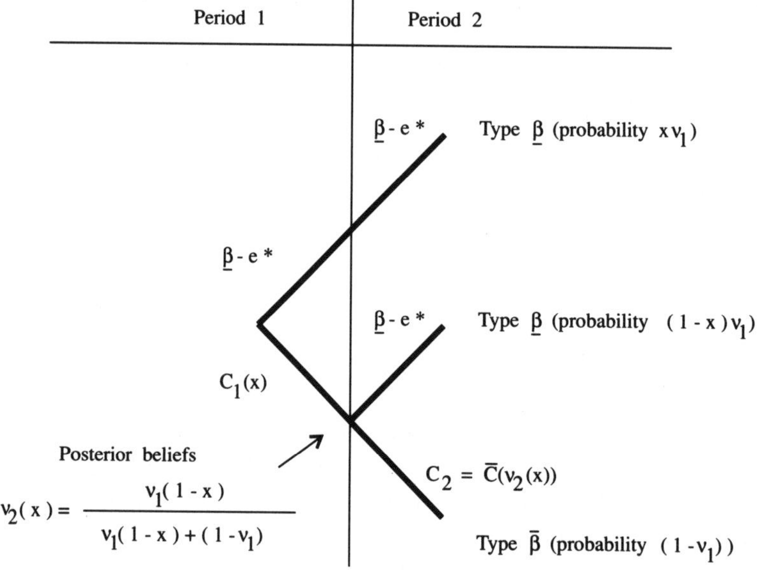

Figure 10.2
The optimal contract

Remark 1 We observe that the rent given to the efficient type in the case of commitment and renegotiation is strictly higher than in the case of commitment; that is, $\Phi(\bar{\beta} - C_1(x)) + \delta\Phi(\bar{e}(v_2)) > \Phi(\bar{e}(v_1)) + \delta\Phi(\bar{e}(v_1))$. This inequality results from the facts that $\bar{\beta} - C_1(x) \geq \bar{e}(v_1)$ and that $\bar{e}(v_2) > \bar{e}(v_1)$ from $v_2 < v_1$. The inequality $v_2 < v_1$ is strict from proposition 10.5 below.

Remark 2 The regulator's behavior is equivalent to the offering of a choice between a long-term and a short-term contract. The acceptance of the short-term contract [to produce at the cost target $C_1(x)$ in the first period] is followed by the second-period conditionally optimal contract. As we will see in section 10.7, the main difference with the noncommitment case is that the regulator can sign a long-term contract with the efficient type to which the inefficient type would be committed if it were to sign the contract.

10.5 How Much Pooling?

This section completes the derivation of the optimal contract by determining the probability x that the efficient type separates in the first period as a function of the discount factor. The regulator's optimization program over x may not be concave, for we have little information about the curvature of the functions $C_1(x)$ and $C_2(x) \equiv \bar{C}(v_2(x))$. If the solution is not unique, the following properties hold for any optimizing value. For notational simplicity we will write $x(\delta)$ as if it were unique. For instance, "$x(\delta)$ is nonincreasing with δ" means "if x an optimum for δ and $\tilde{x}$ is an optimum for $\tilde{\delta} > \delta$, then $x \geq \tilde{x}$."

Proposition 10.5

i. The efficient type's probability of separation x is nonincreasing with the discount factor δ.

ii. There exists $\delta_0 > 0$ such that for all $\delta \leq \delta_0$, the optimal contract is a separating one ($x = 1$).

iii. When δ becomes large ($\delta \to \infty$), the optimal contract tends toward a pooling contract ($x \to 0$). However, a pooling contract is never optimal ($x > 0$ for all δ).

Thus, when the discount factor increases, the optimal allocation moves from full revelation to full pooling. While full separation is optimal for small discount factors, full pooling is optimal only in the limit of large discount factors. Recall that large discount factors (above 1) need not be absurd, since the discount factor reflects the relative lengths of the accounting periods (or the relative importance of the first- and second-period projects).

Proof

i. Let $W(x, \delta, C_1, C_2)$ denote the regulator's welfare, where C_1 denotes the first-period cost in the pooling branch and C_2 the second-period cost of the inefficient type. At the optimum C_1 and C_2 are functions of x, but not of δ: Proposition 10.3 implies that $C_2 = C_2(x) \equiv \bar{C}(v_2(x))$, and proposition 10.4 yields $C_1 = C_1(x)$. We have

$$W(x, \delta, C_1, C_2) = G(x, C_1) + \delta H(C_2), \tag{10.22}$$

where

$$G(x, C_1) \equiv S - (1 + \lambda)[v_1 x(\psi(e^*) + \underline{\beta} - e^*) + v_1(1 - x)(\psi(\underline{\beta} - C_1) + C_1) + (1 - v_1)(\psi(\bar{\beta} - C_1) + C_1)] - \lambda v_1 \Phi(\bar{\beta} - C_1) \tag{10.23}$$

is the "first-period welfare" and

$$H(C_2) \equiv S - (1 + \lambda)[v_1(\psi(e^*) + \underline{\beta} - e^*) + (1 - v_1)(\psi(\bar{\beta} - C_2) + C_2)] - \lambda v_1 \Phi(\bar{\beta} - C_2) \tag{10.24}$$

is the "second-period welfare."

Consider two discount factors $\delta < \tilde{\delta}$, and let $\{x, C_1 = C_1(x), C_2 = C_2(x)\}$ and $\{\tilde{x}, \tilde{C}_1 = C_1(\tilde{x}), \tilde{C}_2 = C_2(\tilde{x})\}$ denote associated optimal allocations. Since renegotiation proofness depends only on the separating probability and the second-period cost, and not on the discount factor, the regulator could have chosen the allocation $\{\tilde{x}, \tilde{C}_1, \tilde{C}_2\}$ when facing discount factor δ. Hence:

$$W(x, \delta, C_1, C_2) \geq W(\tilde{x}, \delta, \tilde{C}_1, \tilde{C}_2). \tag{10.25}$$

Similarly

$$W(\tilde{x}, \tilde{\delta}, \tilde{C}_1, \tilde{C}_2) \geq W(x, \tilde{\delta}, C_1, C_2). \tag{10.26}$$

Adding (10.25) and (10.26), using (10.23) and (10.24), yields

$$(\tilde{\delta} - \delta)\{[(1 + \lambda)(1 - v_1)(\psi(\bar{\beta} - C_2) + C_2) + \lambda v_1 \Phi(\bar{\beta} - C_2)] - [(1 + \lambda)(1 - v_1)(\psi(\bar{\beta} - \tilde{C}_2) + \tilde{C}_2) + \lambda v_1 \Phi(\bar{\beta} - \tilde{C}_2)]\} \geq 0. \tag{10.27}$$

Recall that the function $(1 + \lambda)(1 - v_1)[\psi(\bar{\beta} - C) + C] + \lambda v_1 \Phi(\bar{\beta} - C)$, which is nothing but the objective function under commitment, is convex in C and takes its minimum value at $C = \bar{C}(v_1)$ by definition of $\bar{C}(v_1)$. Recall further that $C_2 = \bar{C}(v_2(x))$ and that $\tilde{C}_2 = \bar{C}(v_2(\tilde{x}))$, where $v_2(x)$ and $v_2(\tilde{x})$ are lower than v_1, implying that C_2 and $\tilde{C}_2$ are lower than $\bar{C}(v_1)$ (proposition 10.1). Equation (10.27), together with $\tilde{\delta} > \delta$, implies that $C_2 \leq \tilde{C}_2$, which (again from proposition 10.1) implies that $v_2(x) \leq v_2(\tilde{x})$ or $x \geq \tilde{x}$.

ii. Let us first show that as δ tends to 0, $x(\delta)$ tends toward 1. If it does not, there exists a subsequence of discount factors tending to 0 and associated values of $x(\delta)$ such that $1 - x(\delta) \geq \alpha > 0$. Along this subsequence the efficient type produces, with probability α at least, at a first-period cost exceeding $C^P(v_1)$ (proposition 10.4) and thus bounded away from $\underline{\beta} - e^*$. Thus the welfare loss relative to the commitment solution does not converge to 0. But choosing $\{x = 1, C_1 = \overline{C}(v_1), C_2 = \overline{C}(0) = \overline{\beta} - e^*\}$ yields a welfare $W(x, \delta, C_1, C_2)$ that converges to the welfare under commitment when δ tends to 0 [see (10.22)], a contradiction.

Second, at $\delta = 0$, the optimum is the static optimum and thus involves full separation ($x = 1$). Furthermore

$$\begin{aligned}\frac{d}{dx}(W(x, \delta, C_1(x), C_2(x)))\bigg|_{\{\delta=0,x=1\}} &= \frac{d}{dx}(G(x, C_1(x)))\bigg|_{x=1} \\ &= v_1(1+\lambda)[(\psi(\underline{\beta} - \overline{C}(v_1)) + \overline{C}(v_1)) \\ &\quad - (\psi(e^*) + \underline{\beta} - e^*)] \\ &> 0, \end{aligned} \tag{10.28}$$

where use is made of the envelope theorem. Hence $W(1, \delta, C_1(1), C_2(1)) > W(x, \delta, C_1(x), C_2(x))$ for all x close to (but lower than) 1 and all δ close to 0.

The intuition behind this proof is that if ε $(= 1 - x)$ is the probability of pooling, the first-period loss in welfare due to pooling is proportional to ε, while the second-period gain due to a reduction in the efficient type's rent is proportional to $\delta\varepsilon$.

iii. When δ tends to $+\infty$, the (normalized) welfare under pooling $[W(0, \delta, C_1(0), C_2(0))]/(1 + \delta)$ tends to the (normalized) welfare under commitment. So must the optimal (normalized) welfare. From (10.24), $C_2(x(\delta))$ must converge to $C_2(0) = \overline{C}(v_1)$, which implies that $v_2(x(\delta))$ converges to v_1 or $x(\delta)$ converges to 0 (for δ large, G becomes negligible relative to δH).

Next, fix δ. Let us show that $x = 0$ cannot be optimal:

$$\frac{d}{dx}(W(x, \delta, C_1(x), C_2(x)))\bigg|_{x=0} = \frac{\partial}{\partial x}(W(x, \delta, C_1(x), C_2(x)))\bigg|_{x=0}, \tag{10.29}$$

where again use is made of the envelope theorem, $\partial W/\partial C_1 = 0$ for all x and $\partial W/\partial C_2 = 0$ for $x = 0$, since the second-period cost $C_2(0)$ is the commitment one $\overline{C}(v_1)$ (note that for $x > 0$, $\partial W/\partial C_2 > 0$; i.e., the regulator is constrained by renegotiation proofness in choosing C_2). Hence

$$\frac{d}{dx}(W(x, \delta, C_1(x), C_2(x)))\bigg|_{x=0} = \frac{\partial G}{\partial x}\bigg|_{x=0} > 0. \tag{10.30}$$

Thus full pooling cannot be optimal.

The intuition here is that at the full pooling allocation, small changes in C_2 have only second-order effects because the second-period allocation is the commitment one. A small decrease in C_2 allows x to become positive without violating renegotiation proofness, and the first-period allocation is improved to the first order in x. ■

10.5.1 Unique Implementation by a Long-Term Fixed-Price Contract and a Short-Term Contract

We can without loss of generality assume that when the regulator offers the optimal renegotiation-proof contract (depicted in figure 10.2 for the optimal x characterized in proposition 10.5), the efficient type randomizes according to probability x (i.e., the maximal probability that makes the optimal contract renegotiation-proof). The reader may wonder how the regulator can guarantee that the efficient type chooses x. Since the efficient type is indifferent between two contracts, it has no particular incentive to do so. Indeed for this optimal renegotiation-proof contract there are other continuation equilibria (the reader should check that any $y \leq x$ corresponds to a continuation equilibrium and does not give rise to renegotiation). However, we can show that the regulator can obtain his or her maximal payoff without encountering this issue of multiplicity of continuation equilibria following the contract offer. To do so, the regulator must offer a *contract that is renegotiated.*[5] Suppose that in period 1 the regulator offers two contracts: a *long-term contract* specifying production at cost $(\underline{\beta} - e^*)$ in each period and intertemporal transfer $[(1 + \delta)\psi(e^*) + \Phi(\bar{\beta} - C_1(x)) + \delta\Phi(\bar{\beta} - \bar{C}(v_2(x)))]$, and a *short-term contract* specifying production at cost $C_1(x)$ and transfer $\psi(\bar{\beta} - C_1(x))$ for the first period (and nothing for the second period). First, note that the inefficient type never chooses the long-term contract because it would get a strictly negative payoff (even if the contract were renegotiated in period 2, since renegotiation never raises the inefficient type's welfare). Hence the long-term contract is chosen only by the efficient type, who obtains rent $[\Phi(\bar{\beta} - C_1(x)) + \delta\Phi(\bar{\beta} - \bar{C}(v_2(x)))]$, and this contract is not renegotiated. Let y denote the probability that the efficient type chooses the long-term contract. Second, if the firm chooses the short-term contract, the regulator is not committed in period 2 and offers the optimal static contract for beliefs $v_2(y)$ characterized in proposition 10.1. In particular the efficient type's second-period rent is $\Phi(\bar{\beta} - \bar{C}(v_2(y)))$, so its intertemporal rent from choosing the short-term contract is $[\Phi(\bar{\beta} - C_1(x)) + \delta\Phi(\bar{\beta} - \bar{C}(v_2(y)))]$. We claim that in equilibrium $y = x$. Suppose that $y > x$, implying that $v_2(y) < v_2(x)$. From proposition 10.1, $\bar{C}(v_2(y)) < \bar{C}(v_2(x))$. Since $\Phi(\cdot)$ is increasing, the efficient type's intertemporal rent when choosing the short-term contract strictly exceeds that when choosing the long-term contract. Hence $y = 0$, a contradiction. The

5. The following argument is similar to one in Fudenberg and Tirole (1990).

proof that $y < x$ is impossible is the same. We conclude that (1) the equilibrium of the overall game is unique and (2) the regulator can obtain his or her equilibrium payoff by offering a (renegotiated) contract with a unique continuation equilibrium.[6]

10.5.2 Small Uncertainty

Last, it is instructive to consider the case of small uncertainty ($\Delta\beta = \bar{\beta} - \underline{\beta}$ small). Under noncommitment (see chapter 9) the welfare distortion relative to commitment is of the first order in $\Delta\beta$ (i.e., proportional to $\Delta\beta$) for the best pooling contract. In contrast, it remains finite (i.e., does not converge to 0 with $\Delta\beta$) for the best separating contract (so that full pooling always dominates full separation for $\Delta\beta$ small). Under commitment and renegotiation the welfare loss relative to commitment under both the best full pooling and the best full separating contracts (as well as contracts corresponding to intermediate x's) turns out to be of the second order in $\Delta\beta$. To see this, note first that for $x = 1$ (separating contract), the allocation differs from the commitment one only with respect to the inefficient type's second-period cost, which is equal to $\bar{\beta} - e^*$ instead of $\bar{C}(v_1)$. Let W^c denote the social welfare under commitment. So the welfare loss under the best separating equilibrium is

$$\begin{aligned} L^s &\equiv W^c - W(1, \delta, \bar{C}(v_1), \bar{\beta} - e^*) \\ &= \delta\{[(1+\lambda)(1-v_1)(\psi(\bar{\beta} - \bar{C}(v_1)) + \bar{C}(v_1)) + \lambda v_1 \Phi(\bar{\beta} - \bar{C}(v_1))] \\ &\quad - [(1+\lambda)(1-v_1)(\psi(e^*) + \bar{\beta} - e^*) + \lambda v_1 \Phi(e^*)]\}. \end{aligned}$$

But, from (10.3), the difference between $\bar{C}(v_1)$ and $(\bar{\beta} - e^*)$ is proportional to $\Delta\beta$ for $\Delta\beta$ small. Furthermore $\bar{C}(v_1)$ minimizes the commitment cost, so small variations around $\bar{C}(v_1)$ have only second-order effects. Hence L^s is proportional to $(\Delta\beta)^2$.

The proof that the loss under pooling $L^P \equiv W^c - W(0, \delta, C^P(v_1), \bar{C}(v_1))$ is proportional to $(\Delta\beta)^2$ as well is similar. It suffices to note that the best pooling contract differs from the commitment allocation only with respect to the first-period cost, which is equal to $C^P(v_1)$ instead of $\underline{\beta} - e^*$ for type $\underline{\beta}$ and $\bar{C}(v_1)$ for type $\bar{\beta}$.[7] We conclude that the best pooling contract and

6. The regulator can guarantee his or her maximal payoff through a renegotiation-proof contract without relying on the "right mixing" by the efficient type if the efficient type's strategy can be purified. In the spirit of Fudenberg and Tirole (1990) and standard purification arguments, suppose that the firm's preferences are characterized by another private information parameter than β and that this second parameter has a continuous distribution. Then under some weak assumptions, the regulator can offer a renegotiation proof contract such that (1) the efficient type ($\underline{\beta}$) plays a pure strategy (with probability 1 over its second parameter) and (2) the probability of the efficient type's revealing its β converges to x and the regulator's payoff converges to that characterized in the text when the second private information parameter converges to a mass point.

7. The best pooling contract dominates the pooling contract specifying $C_1 = \underline{\beta} - e^*$ for both types. But since $\bar{C}(v_1) - (\underline{\beta} - e^*)$ is proportional to $\Delta\beta$ for $\Delta\beta$ small, the welfare distortion of this alternative pooling contract relative to commitment is itself of the second order.

the best separating contract involve little loss for $\Delta\beta$ small under commitment and renegotiation contrary to the noncommitment case.[8]

10.6 Continuum of Types

We now assume that the firm's type β belongs to an interval $[\underline{\beta}, \bar{\beta}]$ and is distributed according to the cumulative distribution function $F(\cdot)$ with continuous positive density $f(\cdot)$. We make the monotone-hazard-rate assumption: $F(\beta)/f(\beta)$ is a nondecreasing function of β.

Chapter 9 studied this continuum model under the noncommitment assumption (the relationship is run by two consecutive short-term contracts). Recall that separation is not feasible, let alone desirable. That is, there exists no separating first-period incentive scheme $t_1(C_1)$ (even a suboptimal one); for any $t_1(\cdot)$ the equilibrium function $C_1(\cdot)$ does not fully reveal the firm's type. We investigate whether separation is feasible and desirable under renegotiable commitment. The answer is found in proposition 10.6.

Proposition 10.6

i. There exist separating (first-period) incentive schemes. The optimal contract in the class of separating schemes yields the commitment allocation in period 1 and the socially efficient cost in period 2.

ii. A separating contract is never optimal for the regulator.

Proof

i. In a separating equilibrium the firm's type is common knowledge at the beginning of period 2. The possibility of renegotiation implies that the firm's second-period effort is socially optimal: $e_2(\beta) = e^*$. Hence the firm's second-period rent $U_2(\beta)$ grows one to one with the firm's efficiency: $\dot{U}_2(\beta) = -1$ or $U_2(\beta) - U_2(\bar{\beta}) = \bar{\beta} - \beta$. Thus, fixing $U_2(\bar{\beta}) = 0$ w.l.o.g., both the firm's effort and its rent, and therefore the regulator's second-period welfare, are the same in all separating contracts. We call the second-period contract the "sellout contract."

The regulator, if constrained to choose a separating contract, thus maximizes his or her first-period welfare. But, by definition, the welfare optimal scheme is the commitment scheme. The commitment scheme is computed for a continuous distribution in section 1.4. Under the monotone-hazard-rate assumption, the firm produces at cost $C_1(\beta) = C^*(\beta)$, where $C^*(\beta) \geq \beta - e^*$ (with strict inequality except at $\beta = \underline{\beta}$) is defined by equation (1.44), and $C^*(\beta)$ is a strictly increasing function of β. Conversely, suppose that

8. The best separating contract dominates the best pooling contract for δ small, and the converse holds for δ larger (by the same reasoning as in the proof of proposition 10.5, but with the choice of x restricted to two values, 0 and 1).

the regulator offers the following contract: "The firm can choose first-period cost in the interval $[C^*(\underline{\beta}), C^*(\overline{\beta})]$. If it has produced at cost C_1 in the first period, it must produce at cost $(C^{*-1}(C_1) - e^*)$ in the second, and receives intertemporal transfer $[\psi(C^{*-1}(C_1) - C_1) + \delta\psi(e^*) + (\int_{C^{*-1}(C_1)}^{\overline{\beta}} \psi'(\beta - C^*(\beta))d\beta + \delta(\overline{\beta} - C^{*-1}(C_1))]$." The regulator thus asks for the efficient effort e^* in period 2. The first part of the transfer is the compensation for the intertemporal disutility of effort. The second part corresponds to the rent in the commitment contract, plus the second-period rent. By construction, this contract yields the commitment welfare in the first period and the sellout welfare in the second. The firm's local incentive compatibility constraint is satisfied by construction; checking that the global incentive compatibility constraint holds as well is routine.

ii. The nonseparation result is proved in appendix A10.2. The intuition is the following. In the best separating equilibrium (characterized in part i of proposition 10.6), the first-period allocation is the commitment one. That is, it maximizes ex ante welfare subject to the informational constraints. This implies that any change in the first-period allocation has a second-order effect. In contrast, the second-period allocation is not optimal from the point of view of the *ex ante* informational structure. This implies that changes in the corresponding allocation have first-order effects on welfare.

From part i of the proposition we know that the only way to change the second-period allocation is to create some pooling in the first period. Our proof shows that starting from the best separating contract, the regulator can force the less efficient types to pool in the first period and thus increase intertemporal welfare. More precisely suppose that the regulator penalizes the firm heavily if the latter's cost exceeds $C^*(\overline{\beta} - \varepsilon)$, where ε is positive and small, and the regulator keeps the same transfers for costs in $[C^*(\underline{\beta}), C^*(\overline{\beta} - \varepsilon)]$ as in the commitment solution. The "inefficient types" (i.e., those in $[\overline{\beta} - \varepsilon, \overline{\beta}]$) now pool at cost $C^*(\overline{\beta} - \varepsilon)$. This increases the inefficient types' efficiency (because C_1 is brought closer to its efficient level for those types. Recall that $C^*(\beta) > \beta - e^*$) but increases all types' rent [because $\dot{U}_1(\beta) = -\psi'(\beta - C_1(\beta))$ and $U_1(\overline{\beta}) = 0$]. Overall the change decreases first-period welfare only to the third order in ε: to the second order times the length ε over which the change operates. In contrast, in period 2 the pooling of the inefficient types goes in the right direction from an ex ante point of view. Since the regulator offers the conditionally optimal contract given truncated beliefs on $[\overline{\beta} - \varepsilon, \overline{\beta}]$, the cost of each inefficient type (but type $\overline{\beta} - \varepsilon$) is raised a bit (in a credible way). This moves the allocation in the direction of the commitment solution. The welfare gain is second order in ε: first order times the length ε over which the change operates. ■

Proposition 10.6 shows that commitment with renegotiation is intermediate between full commitment (for which separation is optimal) and noncommitment (for which separation is not feasible). Here separating contracts exist but are not optimal.

10.7 Commitment, Renegotiation, and Noncommitment

Chapter 9 studied the model of this chapter under the assumption that the relationship is run by a series of two short-term contracts (the noncommitment case). That is the regulator offers a first-period incentive scheme $t_1(C_1)$, observes C_1, and offers in period 2 the contract $t_2(C_2, C_1)$ that is conditionally optimal given posterior beliefs. As discussed earlier, we view the analysis of commitment with renegotiation and noncommitment as complementary. The first refers to a complete contract situation and the second to a situation in which the parties cannot commit, either because of legal constraints (as may be the case for public procurement) or because the second-period contingencies are hard to foresee or costly to include in the initial contract. Alternatively, when complete contracts can be signed, the difference between the two is a measure of the value of commitment. Table 10.1 gathers some results from chapters 1, 9, and 10 and compares commitment, commitment and renegotiation, and noncommitment.

The renegotiation case technically resembles the commitment case in that the IC constraints are well-behaved: In the two-type case only the efficient type's IC constraint is binding. Under noncommitment the efficient type must receive a high first-period reward to reveal its information because ratcheting makes such revelation costly to the firm. The inefficient type may then be tempted to "take the money and run," that is, to mimic the efficient type in the first period, get the high reward, and refuse to produce in the second period (this strategy is particularly tempting if δ is high because the efficient type values the future much and therefore must be bribed more to reveal its type). This possibility makes the inefficient type's IC constraint binding if the discount factor is not too small. The take-the-money-and-run strategy can be prevented under commitment (even with renegotiation) by forcing the firm to repeat its first-period performance if that performance was excellent (i.e., equal to $\underline{\beta} - e^*$) assuming that the firm can commit to stay in the relationship. If the firm cannot commit, the take-the-money-and-run strategy can still be prevented by delaying payments.

In both the renegotiation and noncommitment cases, the first-period contract involves pooling if the discount factor is not too small. Recall that the second-period contract is conditionally optimal. In a sense the main difference between these two cases is the possibility for the regulator

Table 10.1
Comparison of commitment, noncommitment, and renegotiation

	Nature of commitment		
Nature of equilibrium	Full commitment (c)	Commitment and renegotiation (r)	Non-commitment (nc)
Two types			
Binding IC constraint in first period	Efficient type's	Efficient type's	Efficient type's, or both
First-period revelation	Full separation	Randomization[a] by efficient type	Randomization[a] by one or the two types
Equilibrium for small δ	Full separation	Full separation	Full separation
Equilibrium for large δ	Full separation	Tends to full pooling	Tends to full pooling
Second-period contract conditionally optimal?	No	Yes	Yes
Efficient type's rent ($\underline{U}^c, \underline{U}^r, \underline{U}^{nc}$)	$\underline{U}^c$	$\underline{U}^r > \underline{U}^c$ $(\underline{U}^r - \underline{U}^c)/\delta \to 0$ as $\delta \to +\infty$[b]	$\underline{U}^{nc} = \underline{U}^r > \underline{U}^c$ for δ small; $\underline{U}^{nc} \gtrless \underline{U}^c$ in general[c]
Regulator's expected welfare (W^c, W^r, W^{nc})	W^c	$W^r < W^c$	$W^{nc} = W^r$ for δ small $W^{nc} < W^r$ otherwise[d]
Continuum of types			
Full separation feasible?[e]	Yes	Yes[f]	No
Full separation desirable?[e]	Yes	No	No ("much pooling")

a. The "randomization" can be degenerate, as in the case of full separation.
b. $\underline{U}^r = \Phi(\bar{\beta} - C_1(x)) + \delta\Phi(\bar{\beta} - \bar{C}(v_2(x)))$ is equal to $\Phi(\bar{\beta} - \bar{C}(v_1)) + \delta\Phi(e^*) > (1+\delta)\Phi(\bar{\beta} - \bar{C}(v_1)) = U^c$ for δ small. When δ tends to infinity, $\underline{U}^r/\delta \simeq \Phi(\bar{\beta} - \bar{C}(v_1)) = \underline{U}^c/\delta$.
c. For δ small, the noncommitment equilibrium is separating, and the rent is $\underline{U}^{nc} = \Phi(\bar{\beta} - \bar{C}(v_1)) + \delta\Phi(e^*) = \underline{U}^r$.
d. In general $W^{nc} \leq W^r$ because under commitment and renegotiation the regulator can always offer a short-term contract in the first-period and thus duplicate the noncommitment solution. The two welfares coincide only when the inefficient type's IC constraint is not binding in the noncommitment case (i.e., when δ is small). See also the comments in the text.
e. "Full separation" means that the regulator learns the firm's type at the end of the first period. "Feasibility" refers to the existence of a (not necessarily optimal) contract that separates the types. "Desirability" refers to the optimal contract.
f. The regulator can fully separate the types by offering a sellout contract from date 1 on [i.e., offering $t_1(C) = t_2(C) = (\psi(e^*) + \bar{\beta} - e^*) - C$, where $\bar{\beta}$ is the upper bound of the interval of types].

under commitment and renegotiation to prevent the take-the-money-and-run strategy. This empowers the regulator to give the efficient type more incentives to separate, while preventing the inefficient type from mimicking the efficient type in the first period. Since the take-the-money-and-run strategy is not optimal for the inefficient type for small discount factors, it is not surprising that the renegotiation and noncommitment solutions coincide for small discount factors. An apparent lesson of the three chapters and of table 10.1 is that the renegotiation case is somewhat intermediate between the commitment and noncommitment paradigms.

BIBLIOGRAPHIC NOTES

B10.1 Commitment and Renegotiation

The idea that optimal long-term contracts are in general not renegotiation-proof in adverse-selection contexts originates in Dewatripont (1986). The work most closely related to this chapter is that of Hart and Tirole (1988), which considers a T-period model of intertemporal price discrimination by a monopolist. The seller (the principal, the regulator) offers each period a long-term contract to the buyer (the agent, the firm). Trade is discrete (0 or 1 unit in each period); in contrast, cost levels in this chapter can take on a continuum of values. Section B10.2 shows how this chapter extends Hart-Tirole by reinterpreting our model as one of multiple-unit two-period Coasian price discrimination.

We should also mention that the effects of renegotiation of long-term contracts have been studied for the case of symmetric but nonverifiable information (Aghion, Dewatripont, and Rey 1990; Green and Laffont 1988, 1992; Hart and Moore 1988; Maskin and Moore 1989); and in moral hazard contexts (Fudenberg and Tirole 1990; Ma 1991). There is also a quite distinct literature on noncontractual renegotiation in supergames (e.g., Farrell and Maskin 1989; Pearce 1987); "renegotiation" is there a misnomer, since there is no contract to be renegotiated ("recoordination" would be more appropriate).

Rey and Salanié (1990), in the first part of their paper, find general conditions under which commitment and renegotiation does not improve upon noncommitment (see section 10.7).

B10.2 Application to Intertemporal Price Discrimination

After substitution of effort $e = \beta - C$, our model is one of adverse selection with type β and screening variable C. The conclusions obtained in this chapter apply to alternative adverse-selection models. An obvious candidate for this transposition is the repeated version of the monopoly price (or quality) discrimination paradigm. Consider the following static two-type model (see. e.g., Maskin and Riley 1984). A monopolist produces a good at marginal cost γ and supplies an amount q to a buyer, who derives a surplus $V(q,b)$ from its consumption, where $V_q > 0$, $V_{qq} < 0$, $V_b > 0$, $V_{qb} > 0$, $V_{qqb} \geq 0$. The taste parameter b is private information to the buyer and can take two values: $\underline{b}$ ("bad type" or "low valuation buyer") with probability $1 - \nu_1$ and $\bar{b}$ ("good type" or "high-valuation buyer") with probability ν_1. Let $\bar{q}^*$ and $\underline{q}^*$ denote the complete information or socially optimal consumptions: $V_q(\bar{q}^*, \bar{b}) = V_q(\underline{q}^*, \underline{b}) = \gamma$ (with $\bar{q}^* > \underline{q}^*$).

We now assume that the seller has incomplete information about b. Let $\Phi(q) \equiv V(q,\bar{b}) - V(q,\underline{b})$ with $\Phi' > 0$ and $\Phi'' \geq 0$. The monopolist chooses an optimal nonlinear price subject to the buyer's IR and IC constraints so as to maximize its profit. In a single-period context, the good type's consumption is socially optimal, $\bar{q} = \bar{q}^*$, while the bad type's consumption, $\underline{q} = \underline{q}(\nu_1)$ which is lower than $\underline{q}^*$, maximizes the social surplus for this type minus the good type's rent:

$$\underline{q}(\nu_1) = \arg\max_{q} \{(1 - \nu_1)[V(q,\underline{b}) - \gamma q] - \nu_1 \Phi(q)\}. \tag{B10.1}$$

[(B10.1) is the analogue of program I in section 10.2.]

This price discrimination model is formally identical to ours (b corresponds to minus β, q to minus C, etc.).[9] Hence we can apply our results to its twice repeated version. Assume that the seller leases the good to the buyer in each of two periods. $V(\cdot,\cdot)$ and γ are then per-period surplus and marginal cost. [The good can either be a perishable, i.e., one-period-lived, good with production cost γ or a good that last two periods and costs $\gamma(1 + \delta)$ to produce. In the latter case, to ensure that the second-period opportunity cost is γ, we must assume either that there exist overlapping generations of two-period-lived consumers and that the firm can price-discriminate between generations or that a one-period lived version can be produced at cost γ as well.] The seller offers in period 1 a long-term leasing contract, which he or she can offer to renegotiate in period 2. The solution will be called the "LT contracting solution" (where LT stands for "long-term," and the possibility of renegotiation under LT contracting is im-

9. Consider the following model, which is slightly more general than the one in this chapter: (After normalization) the regulator has utility $W = Y(C,\beta) - t$, and the firm $U = Z(C,\beta) + t$. Assume that $Y_{CC} \leq 0$, $Y_{C\beta} \geq 0$; $Z_C > 0$, $Z_\beta < 0$, $Z_{CC} < 0$, $Z_{\beta C} > 0$, and $Z_{CC\beta} \geq 0$. The last two inequalities ensure that $\Lambda(C) \equiv Z(C,\underline{\beta}) - Z(C,\bar{\beta})$ satisfies $\Lambda' < 0$, $\Lambda'' \geq 0$. These properties are the only ones used in the chapter, and the results carry over to this superficially more general model. The good type ($\bar{b}$) corresponds to the efficient type ($\underline{\beta}$) of the regulation model.

Now, consider the price discrimination model. The seller's utility is $W = p - \gamma q$, where p is the price, γ the marginal cost of production, and q the quantity; the buyer's utility is $U = V(q,b) - p$. To see that the price discrimination model is a special case of the above model, set $C \equiv -q$, $\beta \equiv -b$, $p \equiv -t$, $Y(C,\beta) \equiv \gamma C$, $Z(C,\beta) \equiv V(-C,-\beta)$. The five assumptions on $V(\cdot,\cdot)$ made above translate into the five required assumptions on $Z(\cdot,\cdot)$.

plicit.) In the optimal contract the seller offers the buyer a choice between two consumption levels in period 1: $\bar{q}^*$, which is chosen by the good type only, and is followed by the same consumption in period 2; and $q_1(x)$, which is chosen by the bad type and possibly by the good type and is given by the analogue of the maximization of (10.16) with respect to a_1:

$$q_1(x) = \arg\max_q \{v_1(1-x)(V(q,\bar{b})-\gamma q)+(1-v_1)(V(q,\underline{b})-\gamma q)-v_1\Phi(q)\}, \tag{B10.2}$$

where $(1 - x)$ is the probability that the good type pools with the bad type. This pooling consumption is followed by the conditionally optimal price discrimination scheme, yielding consumptions $\bar{q}^*$ and $\underline{q}(v_2(x))$ to the good and bad types [where $v_2(x) \equiv v_1(1 - x)/(v_1(1 - x) + 1 - v_1)$].

Hart and Tirole (1988) solved this model of long-term leasing with renegotiation in a T-period framework for the case of unit demand ($q = 0$ or 1).[10] A main result of their paper is that the equilibrium LT contract is equivalent to the Coasian durable-good equilibrium. In Coase's durable-good model, buyers have unit demands for a perfectly durable good. They differ in their valuations for the good. At each date τ the seller offers a new price p_τ for the purchase of the good. Equilibrium is characterized by a decreasing sequence of price offers. The seller screens low-valuation buyers through their willingness to delay their purchase and wait for a lower price. In contrast, in Hart-Tirole the seller offers buyers long-term leasing contracts that are renegotiated if the concerned buyer and the seller find it mutually advantageous. Yet the outcome in the rental model under commitment and renegotiation is the same as that in the sale model under noncommitment. One may wonder whether an analogous result holds in the multiunit case.[11] Before tackling this problem, we make three remarks. First, the durable-good model has not yet been studied with multiunit consumption, to the best of our knowledge. Second, if such an equivalence result is to hold, we must consider nonlinear pricing in each period in the durable-good model. Third, to make things comparable, we assume that supplying in period 1 a good that lasts for two periods costs $(1 + \delta)\gamma$, that is, $(1 + \delta)$ as much as supplying a single-period-lived product.

It is straightforward to show that the seller cannot obtain more in the durable-good model than under a LT contract. In the LT contract framework the seller can offer the consumption pattern corresponding to the

10. The unit demand assumption simplifies matters in many respects. First, the socially optimal consumption is not type contingent (which implies, e.g., that there exists a single sellout contract instead of a continuum of them). Second, although some continuous consumption choice is introduced into the unit demand model by considering a probability that the buyer consumes in each period, the nature of the proof has a simple bang-bang flavor (e.g., the critical beliefs for a socially inefficient contract to be renegotiation-proof in period 2 are independent of the bad type's probability of consumption, while they depend on C_2 in this chapter).

11. We are grateful to Oliver Hart for suggesting this question.

durable-good equilibrium. In period 2 the buyer's consumption pattern is conditionally optimal for the seller (since the durable-good model has no commitment, the seller optimizes in the second period) and is thus renegotiation-proof.[12]

Conversely, the LT contract outcome can be achieved by the durable-good monopolist subject to the caveat described below. A central result of this chapter (transposed to price discrimination) is that following the pooling consumption, the seller uses the conditionally optimal price discrimination (see proposition 10.3). With regard to this, consider the following strategies in the durable-good model: In period 1 the seller offers for sale the quantities $q_1(x)$ at price $V(q_1(x),\underline{b})(1+\delta)$, and $\bar{q}^*$ at price $V(\bar{q}^*,\bar{b})(1+\delta) - \Phi(q_1(x)) - \delta\Phi(\underline{q}(v_2(x)))$, where x is the equilibrium probability under LT contracting and $q_1(x)$ is given by (B10.2). In period 2 no further offer is made if the buyer has purchased $\bar{q}^*$ in period 1. If the buyer has bought $q_1(x)$ in period 1, the seller offers quantities $\bar{q}^* - q_1(x)$ at price $V(\bar{q}^*,\bar{b}) - V(q_1(x),\underline{b}) - \Phi(\underline{q}(v_2(x)))$, and $\underline{q}(v_2(x)) - q_1(x)$ at price $V(\underline{q}(v_2(x)),\underline{b}) - V(q_1(x),\underline{b})$. The low-valuation buyer purchases $q_1(x)$ in the first period. The high-valuation buyer purchases $\bar{q}^*$ with probability x and $q_1(x)$ with probability $1-x$ in the first period. Given the first-period sale offers, the seller's and the buyer's behaviors clearly form a continuation equilibrium of the durable-good game. Furthermore the first-period sale offers are optimal for the seller because, from our earlier result, the seller's profit in the durable-good model cannot exceed that for the optimal LT contract.

The caveat is apparent in the previous proof. For the equivalence result to hold, the buyer's consumption under LT contracting must be nondecreasing. This amounts to the condition $q_1(x) \leq \underline{q}(v_2(x))$. This condition holds for discount factors under some threshold level from proposition 10.5.[13] For instance, for small discount factors, the equilibrium is separating ($x = 1$) so that $q_1(x) = \underline{q}(v_1) < \underline{q}(v_2(x)) = \underline{q}^*$. But for discount factors above the threshold level, $q_1(x)$ exceeds $\underline{q}(v_2(x))$, and the durable-good monopolist's profit is strictly lower than the profit under LT contracting (because LT contracting allows decreasing consumption paths).

To summarize our study of the two-period framework, the equivalence between Coasian durable-good dynamics and LT contracting holds as long as the discount factor is lower than some threshold value (i.e., as long as the low-valuation buyer's consumption under long-term contracting is time increasing). Alternatively, our work can be viewed as generalizing the durable-good model to, and deriving the equilibrium for, multiunit consumption.

12. This simple reasoning holds only in the two-period model. With more than two periods, a more elaborate argument is needed. See Hart and Tirole (1988) for the unit demand case.
13. Proposition 10.5 implies that x is a nonincreasing function of δ. Furthermore $\underline{q}(v_2(x))$ is increasing in x while $q_1(x)$ decreases with x.

Proposition 10.7 Consider the two-period, two-type price discrimination (rental) model with commitment and renegotiation.

i. In the first period the buyer chooses between consumptions $\overline{q}^*$ and $q_1(x)$, where $\overline{q}^* > q_1(x)$. Consumption $\overline{q}^*$, which is chosen by the high-valuation consumer with probability x, is repeated in period 2. With probability $1 - x$, the high-demand consumer pools with the low-demand consumer and consumes $q_1(x)$ in period 1. They then consume $\overline{q}^*$ and $\underline{q}(v_2(x))$, respectively, in period 2.

ii. There exists a discount factor $\delta_0 > 0$ such that the outcome in the rental model under commitment and renegotiation (characterized in part i) is the same as that in the sale model under noncommitment if and only if $\delta \leq \delta_0$.

APPENDIXES

A10.1 Proof of Lemma 10.1

We first assume that the regulator offers two contracts A and B in the first period (see footnote 2). We will later show that the use of more than two contracts does not increase the regulator's welfare. The inefficient type's intertemporal utility may be set equal to zero (if it were equal to a strictly positive number, the regulator could uniformly reduce all rents by this number and reach a higher welfare without perturbing any of the IR, IC, and RP constraints). Furthermore we can choose the intertemporal structure of transfers to put the inefficient type's utility equal to zero in each period.

Let a_1 and b_1 denote the first-period costs in these two contracts, and a_2 and b_2 the corresponding inefficient type's second-period costs (proposition 10.2 implies that the efficient type's second-period cost in both contracts is $\underline{\beta} - e^*$). Let A_1 and A_2 and B_1 and B_2 denote the efficient type's first- and second-period rents (i.e., its utility levels since the IR levels of the inefficient type are normalized at zero) in contracts A and B.

Let x (resp. $1 - x$) denote the probability that the efficient type chooses contract B (resp. A). Similarly y is the probability that the inefficient type chooses contract A. We assume that $1 > x, y > 0$, so that we have "double randomization."[14] Our goal is to show that the regulator can do as well with randomization by one type only or no type at all. The efficient type randomizes between the two contracts only if it obtains the same intertemporal rent in both:

$$A_1 + \delta A_2 = B_1 + \delta B_2. \tag{A10.1}$$

Equation (A10.1) will be called the (first-period) incentive compatibility constraint.

14. We assume that the regulator keeps both types in both contracts. As noted in the text, if the regulator kept only the efficient type in period 2 in contract B, the contract B second-period cost would be the socially optimal one for the efficient type. The following proof shows that the regulator is better off if the inefficient type ceases to randomize and chooses contract A with probability 1 (i.e., produces with probability 1 in period 2).

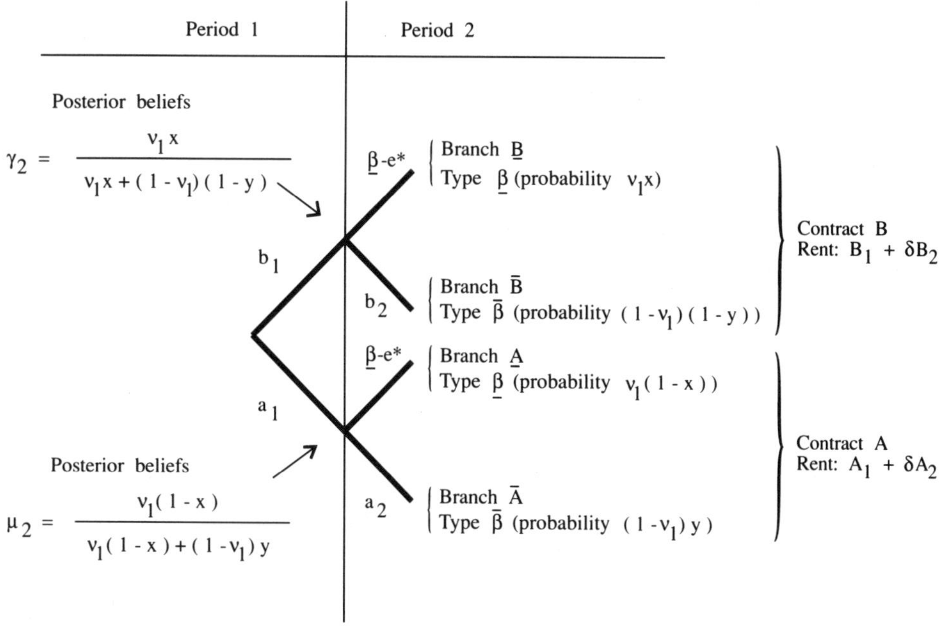

Figure 10.3
Double randomization

Last, let γ_2 denote the posterior probability that the firm has type $\underline{\beta}$ given that first-period cost was b_1 (i.e., contract B was chosen). Similarly μ_2 is the posterior probability following cost a_1. Figure 10.3 summarizes the situation.

From our normalization (the rent of the inefficient type is zero in each period), the rent of the efficient type in period 1 is the static rent $\Phi(\bar{\beta} - b_1)$ for contract B and $\Phi(\bar{\beta} - a_1)$ for contract A. Consequently we obtain the following claim:

Claim 1 $A_1 = \Phi(\bar{\beta} - a_1)$ and $B_1 = \Phi(\bar{\beta} - b_1)$.

From corollary 10.1 we know that $A_2 \geq \mathscr{U}(\mu_2)$ and $B_2 \geq \mathscr{U}(\gamma_2)$. We next show that both second-period contracts are rent-constrained contracts and that one of the two is a conditionally optimal contract:

Claim 2

i. Either $A_2 = \mathscr{U}(\mu_2)$ or $B_2 = \mathscr{U}(\gamma_2)$.

ii. $A_2 = \Phi(\bar{\beta} - a_2)$ and $B_2 = \Phi(\bar{\beta} - b_2)$.

Proof

i. Suppose that $A_2 > \mathscr{U}(\mu_2)$ and $B_2 > \mathscr{U}(\gamma_2)$. From corollary 10.4, the regulator could in the first-period offer contracts that reduce A_2 and B_2 slightly and increase welfare. If A_2 and B_2 are reduced in equal amounts (which is feasible because they can be lowered continuously), the IC constraint (A10.1) is kept satisfied and the randomizing probabilities and the first-period allocations can be kept the same.

ii. Suppose without loss of generality that $A_2 = \mathscr{U}(\mu_2)$ and that B specifies a sellout contract in period 2. From proposition 10.2 the sellout contract is renegotiation-proof for any posterior γ_2. This implies that we can change the probabilities x and y without perturbing the renegotiation proofness of contract B.

Corollary 10.3 implies that renegotiation proofness of contract A is preserved if the new probabilities $\tilde{x}$ and $\tilde{y}$ are chosen so that the induced posterior $\tilde{\mu}_2$ is at least as large as μ_2:

$$\frac{(1-\tilde{x})v_1}{v_1(1-\tilde{x})+(1-v_1)\tilde{y}} \geq \mu_2 \tag{A10.2}$$

or

$$v_1(1-\mu_2)(1-\tilde{x}) \geq (1-v_1)\mu_2\tilde{y}. \tag{A10.3}$$

The regulator's welfare $W(\tilde{x}, \tilde{y})$ is linear in $\tilde{x}$ and $\tilde{y}$, keeping contracts (i.e., a_1, a_2, b_1, and b_2) constant. Its maximization with respect to $\tilde{x}$, $\tilde{y}$ under (A10.3) and $0 \leq \tilde{x} \leq 1$ and $0 \leq \tilde{y} \leq 1$ yields corner solutions. Consequently at least one of the $\tilde{x}$ and $\tilde{y}$ is 0 or 1 and the maximum of the regulator's welfare can be reached without double randomization by the firm, a contradiction. ■

Claim 2 implies that (A10.1) can be rewritten in the following way:

$$\Phi(\bar{\beta}-a_1)+\delta\Phi(\bar{\beta}-a_2)=\Phi(\bar{\beta}-b_1)+\delta\Phi(\bar{\beta}-b_2). \tag{A10.4}$$

Let us assume w.l.o.g. that $a_1 \geq b_1$. Then $\Phi(\bar{\beta}-a_1) \leq \Phi(\bar{\beta}-b_1)$, and therefore $a_2 \leq b_2$ from (A10.4).

Claim 3 $C^P(\gamma_2) \leq C^P(\mu_2)$.

Proof From (10.5), this amounts to showing that $\gamma_2 \geq \mu_2$. From claim 2 we have two cases to consider:

Case i. $a_2 = \bar{C}(\mu_2)$ and $b_2 \leq \bar{C}(\gamma_2)$. The inequality $a_2 \leq b_2$ implies that $\bar{C}(\mu_2) \leq \bar{C}(\gamma_2)$, which from proposition 10.1 yields $\mu_2 \leq \gamma_2$.

Case ii. $b_2 = \bar{C}(\gamma_2)$ and $a_2 < \bar{C}(\mu_2)$. From the strict concavity of the objective function in the commitment case, raising a_2 slightly strictly increases welfare. But to keep (A10.4) satisfied, a_1 must be reduced slightly. This also increases welfare (or has a second-order effect) if $a_1 \geq C^P(\mu_2)$. Hence we have $a_1 < C^P(\mu_2)$.

Next, since b_2 is conditionally optimal, a small reduction in b_2 has only a second-order effect on the second-period welfare and from proposition 10.2, preserves renegotiation proofness of contract B. So it must be the case that a slight increase in b_1 [so as to keep (A10.4) satisfied] does not raise first-period welfare. Hence $b_1 \geq C^P(\gamma_2)$. But since $a_1 \geq b_1$, $C^P(\mu_2) > C^P(\gamma_2)$ and $\mu_2 < \gamma_2$. ■

The next result unveils two different cases.

Claim 4 Either

$$C^P(\gamma_2) \leq b_1 \leq a_1 \leq C^P(\mu_2) \qquad \text{(case 1)},$$

or

$$b_1 < C^P(\gamma_2) \leq C^P(\mu_2) < a_1 \qquad \text{(case 2)}.$$

Proof Suppose first that $b_1 \leq C^P(\gamma_2) \leq a_1 \leq C^P(\mu_2)$, with $b_1 < C^P(\gamma_2)$ or $a_1 < C^P(\mu_2)$ (or both). Raising slightly a_1 and b_1 so as to keep $\Phi(\bar{\beta}-b_1)-\Phi(\bar{\beta}-$

a_1) constant [and thus (A10.4) satisfied] raises welfare to the first order by bringing the first-period costs toward the optimal pooling costs corresponding to the mix of types associated with each contract. [This again results from the strict concavity of the pooling objective function. When, e.g., $b_1 = C^P(\gamma_2)$, a slight increase in b_1 has only second-order effects on welfare.] The proof is identical when $C^P(\gamma_2) \leq b_1 \leq C^P(\mu_2) \leq a_1$, with $C^P(\gamma_2) < b_1$ or $C^P(\mu_2) < a_1$ (or both). It then suffices to reduce b_1 and a_1 slightly keeping (A10.4) satisfied. ∎

We consider the two cases defined in claim 4 sequentially:

Case 1. Let us show that a slight increase in x raises welfare. An increase in x amounts to a displacement of the "efficient type population" from branch $\underline{A}$ to branch $\underline{B}$. The efficient type's rent is unaffected if renegotiation-proofness is preserved; so is the second-period efficiency (because the efficient type produces at $\underline{\beta} - e^*$ in both cases). The first-period efficiency strictly increases if $b_1 < a_1$. [The case $b_1 = a_1$ is uninteresting since (A10.4) then implies that $b_2 = a_2$, and thus the two contracts are identical and can be merged. Renegotiation proofness is preserved in the merger because the new posterior beliefs, equal to ν_1, are a convex combination of μ_2 and γ_2, because of the fact that $\overline{C}(\nu_1) \leq \overline{C}(\gamma_2)$ and because of corollary 10.3.] Indeed from (10.5),

$$\underline{\beta} - e^* < C^P(\gamma_2) \leq b_1 < a_1.$$

By strict concavity of the objective function under commitment, a reduction in the efficient type's cost above $\underline{\beta} - e^*$ raises welfare.

The next question is whether the increase in x maintains renegotiation proofness. It clearly does for contract B from corollary 10.3. It also does for contract A unless $A_2 = \mathscr{U}(\mu_2)$ (also from corollary 10.3). So assume that $A_2 = \mathscr{U}(\mu_2)$. A small increase in x requires a slight upward adjustment in A_2 (i.e., a slight downward adjustment in a_2) to preserve renegotiation proofness. But this increase in A_2 has only a second-order welfare effect because the initial contract is conditionally optimal. Next this decrease in a_2 requires a small increase in a_1 to keep (A10.4) satisfied. But $a_1 \leq C^P(\mu_2)$ implies that an increase in a_1 raises first-period welfare (or does not affect it to the first order).

We can conclude that a slight increase in x, together with small changes in a_1 and a_2 so as to keep renegotiation proofness and (A10.4) satisfied, strictly increases welfare, a contradiction.

Case 2. First suppose that $B_2 = \mathscr{U}(\gamma_2)$. Then any small reduction in b_2 has a second-order effect on welfare and preserves renegotiation proofness by proposition 10.2. A small increase in b_1 to keep (A10.4) satisfied strictly increases welfare because $b_1 < C^P(\gamma_2)$. Hence $B_2 > \mathscr{U}(\gamma_2)$ [and therefore $A_2 = \mathscr{U}(\mu_2)$].

Keeping everything else (costs) constant, let $W(\tilde{x}, \tilde{y})$ denote the regulator's welfare when the randomizing probabilities are $\tilde{x}$ and $\tilde{y}$. W is linear in $\tilde{x}$ and $\tilde{y}$. From corollary 10.3 any $(\tilde{x}, \tilde{y})$ satisfying

$$\nu_1(1 - \mu_2)(1 - \tilde{x}) \geq \mu_2(1 - \nu_1)\tilde{y} \tag{A10.5}$$

yields posterior beliefs $\tilde{\mu}_2 \geq \mu_2$ in contract A and thus preserves renegotiation proofness in this contract. In the $(\tilde{x}, \tilde{y})$ space the solution of the maximization of the linear objective function W over the half-space defined by (A10.5) and over the constraints that $\tilde{x}$ and $\tilde{y}$ belong to $[0, 1]$ and that $B_2 \geq \mathscr{U}(\gamma_2(\tilde{x}, \tilde{y}))$ (renegotiation proofness on contract B) is a corner solution. Either $B_2 = \mathscr{U}(\gamma_2(\tilde{x}, \tilde{y}))$ and our previous condition is violated, or $\tilde{x}$ or $\tilde{y}$ (or both) is equal to 0 or 1, and the double randomization assumption is violated.

We thus conclude that in both cases maximal welfare can be reached without double randomization. That is, there exists a renegotiation-proof contract that yields the same intertemporal rent to the efficient type, and at least as much welfare to the regulator, and that involves randomization by at most a single type. Note in passing that this shows also that there is no point considering more than two contracts. With more than two contracts, one can apply the above reasoning to any pair of pooling contracts. Since it is possible to keep the firm's rent constant in the inductive reduction process, there is at most one pooling contract.

The next step in the proof of lemma 10.1 consists in showing that randomization by the inefficient type only cannot be optimal for the regulator. Suppose that $x = 1$ and $0 < y < 1$. Then $a_2 = \bar{\beta} - e^*$ because, following a_1, it is common knowledge that the firm's type is $\bar{\beta}$.

Suppose, first, that

$$A_1 + \delta A_2 < B_1 + \delta B_2. \tag{A10.6}$$

Then $a_1 = \bar{\beta} - e^*$, moving a_1 toward $\bar{\beta} - e^*$ raises efficiency and affects neither the incentive constraint (A10.6) nor the efficient type's rent. Since branch $\bar{A}$ is efficient (the inefficient type produces at the efficient cost in each period), an increase in y raises efficiency and preserves renegotiation proofness of contract B by raising γ_2 (from corollary 10.3). Thus there exists a dominating separating equilibrium (with $y = 1$).

Second, suppose that

$$A_1 + \delta A_2 = B_1 + \delta B_2. \tag{A10.7}$$

Let $W(y)$ denote the regulator's welfare when y varies, everything else being kept constant. It is linear in y. If $W_y \geq 0$, one can increase y without reducing welfare and keep renegotiation proofness in contract B. If $W_y < 0$, a slight decrease in y strictly raises welfare. However, it lowers γ_2, and to preserve renegotiation proofness in contract B, the regulator must increase B_2 (i.e., lower b_2) slightly. Since the second-period contract following b_1 is conditionally optimal, this adjustment has only a second-order effect on welfare. Hence the upper bound cannot be reached by having only the inefficient type randomize, which completes the proof of lemma 10.1. ■

A10.2 Proof of Proposition 10.6: Separation Is Not Optimal with a Continuum of Types

Recall from chapter 1 that the optimal static mechanism is the solution of

$$\max_{\{e(\cdot),U(\cdot)\}} \int_{\underline{\beta}}^{\bar{\beta}} [S - (1+\lambda)(\beta - e(\beta) + \psi(e(\beta))) - \lambda U(\beta)]\, dF(\beta) \quad \text{(program IV)},$$

$$\dot{U}(\beta) = -\psi'(e(\beta)) \quad \text{a.e.}, \tag{A10.8}$$

$$U(\bar{\beta}) \geq 0, \tag{A10.9}$$

$$\dot{e}(\beta) \leq 1. \tag{A10.10}$$

Maximizing the hamiltonian with respect to the control e gives

$$\psi'(e^*(\beta)) = 1 - \frac{\lambda}{1+\lambda}\frac{F(\beta)}{f(\beta)}\psi''(e^*(\beta)). \tag{A10.11}$$

The rent of type β is [integrating (A10.8)]

$$U(\beta) = \int_{\beta}^{\bar{\beta}} \psi'(e^*(x))\,dx.$$

Replacing $e^*(\beta)$ by $\beta - C^*(\beta)$ in (A10.11) and differentiating yields

$$\frac{dC^*}{d\beta} \equiv A(\beta) = 1 + \frac{[\lambda/(1+\lambda)]\psi''(e^*(\beta))[d(F(\beta)/f(\beta))/d\beta]}{\psi''(e^*(\beta)) + [\lambda/(1+\lambda)](F(\beta)/f(\beta))\psi'''(e^*(\beta))}. \tag{A10.12}$$

Now consider the small change described in the text, namely that the types in $[\bar{\beta}-\varepsilon, \bar{\beta}]$ pool at cost $C^*(\bar{\beta}-\varepsilon)$ in the first period. Following $C^*(\bar{\beta}-\varepsilon)$, the regulator offers the commitment contract for the truncated distribution $(F(\beta) - F(\bar{\beta}-\varepsilon))/(1 - F(\bar{\beta}-\varepsilon))$ for $\beta \geq \bar{\beta}-\varepsilon$. It is straightforward to check that the new allocation is incentive compatible (this is due to the fact that the first- and second-period efforts of type $\bar{\beta}-\varepsilon$ are unchanged and that, by concavity of the firm's utility function, the types in $[\underline{\beta}, \bar{\beta}-\varepsilon]$ would pool with type $\bar{\beta}-\varepsilon$ if they were forced to pool with a type in $[\bar{\beta}-\varepsilon, \bar{\beta}]$ in the optimal static mechanism. The change in first-period welfare ΔW_1 is given by

$$\Delta W_1 \equiv G_1 - L_1, \tag{A10.13}$$

where G_1 is the gain in efficiency and L_1 the loss due to the increase in the firm's rent. We have

$$G_1 = \int_{\bar{\beta}-\varepsilon}^{\bar{\beta}} (1+\lambda)[\psi(\beta - C^*(\beta)) + C^*(\beta) - \psi(\beta - C^*(\bar{\beta}-\varepsilon)) - C^*(\bar{\beta}-\varepsilon)]f(\beta)\,d\beta$$

$$\simeq \int_{\bar{\beta}-\varepsilon}^{\bar{\beta}} (1+\lambda)(C^*(\beta) - C^*(\bar{\beta}-\varepsilon))(1 - \psi'(\bar{\beta} - C^*(\bar{\beta})))f(\beta)\,d\beta. \tag{A10.14}$$

But from (A10.11) and $F(\bar{\beta}) = 1$.

$$1 - \psi'(\bar{\beta} - C^*(\bar{\beta})) = \frac{\lambda}{(1+\lambda)} \frac{\psi''(e^*(\bar{\beta}))}{f(\bar{\beta})}, \tag{A10.15}$$

and from (A10.12),

$$C^*(\beta) - C^*(\bar{\beta}-\varepsilon) \simeq A(\bar{\beta})(\beta - \bar{\beta} + \varepsilon). \tag{A10.16}$$

Substituting (A10.15) and (A10.16) into (A10.14) yields

$$G_1 \simeq \int_{\bar{\beta}-\varepsilon}^{\bar{\beta}} (1+\lambda)A(\bar{\beta})(\beta - \bar{\beta} + \varepsilon)\frac{\lambda}{1+\lambda}\psi''(e^*(\bar{\beta}))\frac{f(\beta)}{f(\bar{\beta})}\,d\beta \tag{A10.17}$$

or

$$G_1 = \lambda A(\bar{\beta})\psi''(e^*(\bar{\beta}))\frac{\varepsilon^2}{2} + 0(\varepsilon^3). \tag{A10.18}$$

Next we compute L_1. Since $e_1(\beta)$ is unchanged for $\beta \leq \bar{\beta}-\varepsilon$, the rent of each type $\beta \leq \bar{\beta}-\varepsilon$ increases by the same amount as that of type $\bar{\beta}-\varepsilon$ [the increase in the rents of types $\beta > \bar{\beta}-\varepsilon$ is socially negligible (i.e., of order $0(\varepsilon^3)$) relative to that of types $\beta \leq \bar{\beta}-\varepsilon$, since the former types have negligible weight relative to the latter types for ε small]. The increase in the rent of type $\bar{\beta}-\varepsilon$ is given by

$$\begin{aligned}\Delta U(\bar{\beta}-\varepsilon) &= \int_{\bar{\beta}-\varepsilon}^{\bar{\beta}} [\psi'(\beta - C^*(\bar{\beta}-\varepsilon)) - \psi'(\beta - C^*(\beta))]\,d\beta \\ &\simeq \int_{\bar{\beta}-\varepsilon}^{\bar{\beta}} \psi''(\bar{\beta} - C^*(\bar{\beta}))(C^*(\beta) - C^*(\bar{\beta}-\varepsilon))\,d\beta \\ &\simeq \int_{\bar{\beta}-\varepsilon}^{\bar{\beta}} \psi''(\bar{\beta} - C^*(\bar{\beta}))A(\bar{\beta})(\beta - \bar{\beta} + \varepsilon)\,d\beta \\ &= A(\bar{\beta})\psi''(\bar{\beta} - C^*(\bar{\beta}))\frac{\varepsilon^2}{2}. \end{aligned} \tag{A10.19}$$

But

$$\begin{aligned} L_1 &= \int_{\underline{\beta}}^{\bar{\beta}-\varepsilon} \lambda \Delta U(\bar{\beta}-\varepsilon) f(\beta)\,d\beta \\ &\simeq \lambda \Delta U(\bar{\beta}-\varepsilon) = \lambda A(\bar{\beta})\psi''(\bar{\beta} - C^*(\bar{\beta}))\frac{\varepsilon^2}{2} + 0(\varepsilon^3) = G_1 + 0(\varepsilon^3). \end{aligned} \tag{A10.20}$$

As claimed in the text, we have

$$\Delta W_1 = 0(\varepsilon^3). \tag{A10.21}$$

Let us now consider the second period. The change in welfare is given by $\delta \Delta W_2$, where

$$\Delta W_2 = G_2 - L_2, \tag{A10.22}$$

G_2 is the gain coming from the reduction in the firm's rent, and L_2 is the loss in efficiency. The computation of G_2 is identical to that of L_1, except that the effort of the high type is in the second period e^* and not $e^*(\bar{\beta})$ as in period 1. As can easily be checked, this implies that the new $A(\bar{\beta})$, computed from the new effort e^* and from the truncated distribution, is equal to 1. Hence

$$G_2 = \lambda \psi''(e^*)\frac{\varepsilon^2}{2} + 0(\varepsilon^3). \tag{A10.23}$$

In contrast, L_2 is of the third order in ε, since the initial allocation is cost efficient. More formally

$$L_2 = \int_{\bar{\beta}-\varepsilon}^{\bar{\beta}} (1+\lambda)[\psi(\beta - \tilde{C}(\beta)) + \tilde{C}(\beta) - \psi(e^*) - \beta + e^*] f(\beta)\,d\beta, \tag{A10.24}$$

where $\tilde{C}(\beta)$ is the commitment solution for the truncated distribution

$$\psi'(\beta - \tilde{C}(\beta)) = 1 - \frac{\lambda}{1+\lambda}\,\frac{F(\beta) - F(\bar{\beta}-\varepsilon)}{f(\beta)}\,\psi''(\beta - \tilde{C}(\beta)). \tag{A10.25}$$

Note that for ε small,

$$\psi(\beta - \tilde{C}(\beta)) - \psi(e^*) = [\beta - \tilde{C}(\beta) - e^*] + \tfrac{1}{2}\psi''(e^*)[\beta - \tilde{C}(\beta) - e^*]^2 + 0(\varepsilon^3), \tag{A10.26}$$

using $\psi'(e^*) = 1$. Hence (A10.24) can be rewritten as

$$L_2 = \int_{\bar{\beta}-\varepsilon}^{\bar{\beta}} \frac{1+\lambda}{2}\psi''(e^*)[\beta - \tilde{C}(\beta) - e^*]^2 f(\beta)\,d\beta. \tag{A10.27}$$

But from (A10.25) and $1 = \psi'(e^*)$,

$$\beta - \tilde{C}(\beta) - e^* \simeq -\frac{\lambda}{1+\lambda}(\beta - \bar{\beta} + \varepsilon). \tag{A10.28}$$

Equations (A10.27) and (A10.28) yield

$$L_2 \simeq \frac{\lambda^2}{6(1+\lambda)}\psi''(e^*)f(\bar{\beta})\varepsilon^3 = 0(\varepsilon^3). \tag{A10.29}$$

We conclude that

$$\Delta W_1 + \delta \Delta W_2 \simeq \delta G_2 > 0.$$ ∎

REFERENCES

Aghion, P., M. Dewatripont, and P. Rey. 1990. Renegotiation design under symmetric information. Forthcoming, *Econometrica.*

Baron, D., and D. Besanko. 1984. Regulation and information in a continuing relationship. *Information Economics and Policy* 1:447–470.

Dewatripont, M. 1986. Renegotiation and information revelation over time in optimal labor contracts. Chap. 1 in *On the Theory of Commitment, with Applications to the Labor Market*, Ph.D. dissertation, Harvard University. Also in *Quarterly Journal of Economics* 104 (1989): 589–620.

Farrell, J., and E. Maskin. 1989. Renegotiation in repeated games. *Games and Economic Behavior.* 1:327–360.

Fudenberg, D., and J. Tirole. 1990. Moral hazard and renegotiation in agency contracts. *Econometrica* 58:1279–1320.

Green, J., and J. -J. Laffont. 1988. Contract renegotiation and the underinvestment effect. Mimeo.

Green, J., and J.-J. Laffont. 1992. Renegotiation and the form of efficient contracts. *Annales d'Economie et Statistique* 25/26:123–150.

Hart, O., and J. Tirole. 1988. Contract renegotiation and coasian dynamics. *Review of Economic Studies* 55:509–540.

Ma, A. 1991. Adverse selection in a dynamic moral hazard. *Quarterly Journal of Economics* 106:255–276.

Maskin, E., and J. Moore. 1989. Implementation with renegotiation. Mimeo. Harvard University.

Maskin, E., and J. Riley. 1984. Monopoly with incomplete information. *Rand Journal of Economics* 15:171–196.

Maskin, E., and J. Tirole. 1992. The principal-agent relationship with an informed principal. II: Common values. *Econometrica* 60:1–42.

Pearce, D. 1987. Renegotiation-proof equilibria: Collective rationality and intertemporal cooperation. *Cowles Foundation DP 855.*

Rey, P., and B. Salanié. 1990. Long-term, short-term and renegotiation: On the value of commitment with asymmetric information. Mimeo, INSEE, Paris.

Roberts, K. 1983. Long term contracts. Mimeo, University of Warwick.

V THE POLITICS OF REGULATION

11 REGULATORY CAPTURE

11.1 Some Background

A major task of economics and political science is to explain the pattern of government intervention in industries. Two main theories have been proposed to this effect. The "public interest" theory emphasizes the government's role in correcting market imperfections such as monopoly pricing and environmental externalities. While regulatory agencies may face informational constraints, they are viewed as benevolent maximizers of social welfare. Up to this chapter we have embraced this public interest paradigm. The "capture" or "interest group" theory emphasizes the role of interest groups in the formation of public policy. Its origin can be traced back to Marx's view that big business controls institutions and to the early twentieth-century political scientists. Stigler's work (1971) considerably extended this paradigm by noting that the regulatory process can be captured by small business industries as well, and by using Olson's (1965) theory of collective action[1] as a building block to explain how "regulation is acquired by the industry and is designed and operated primarily for its benefit" (p. 3).[2] Olson's logic of collective action implies that for a given issue, the smaller the group, the higher the per-capita stake, and therefore the incentive of its members to affect the regulatory outcomes. Stigler inferred that members of an industry have more incentives than dispersed consumers with a low per-capita stake to organize to exercise political influence. The emergence of some powerful consumer groups and the regulatory experience of the 1970s led Peltzman (1976) and the academic profession to take a broader view of Stigler's contribution that allows government officials to arbitrate among competing interests, and not always in favor of business.[3]

The positive models developed in the last two decades by the Chicago school (Stigler, Peltzman, Becker) and the Virginia school (Tollison, Tullock) suffer from two methodological limitations. First, they are not agency theoretic in that they ignore informational asymmetries. In the absence of such asymmetries, regulated firms would be unable to extract rents and therefore would have no incentive to influence regulatory outcomes. Similarly voters and legislators would be able to control their agents (members of committees and agencies) who thus could not get away with policies favoring interest groups over the common good. In contrast, an agency-theoretic framework can explain why regulators have discretion and why interest groups have stakes and power. Second, the

1. See also Buchanan (1965).
2. Stigler also offered the view that there is a market for regulation, in which outcomes are determined by supply and demand. See Peltzman (1976) and Becker (1983, 1985) for complete information voting models of regulatory behavior.
3. For reviews of the capture argument, see the second part of Moe (1986), Noll (1983, 1985), Posner (1974), and Wilson (1980).

Chicago and Virginia schools have focused on the "demand side" in their study of political and regulatory decision making, in that all the action takes place on the side of interest groups. By "black-boxing" the "supply side" (the political and regulatory institutions), they have ignored a crucial agency relationship between politicians and their delegates in the bureaucracy. In this and the next three chapters, we bring together the demand and the supply side in an agency-theoretic framework.

Interest groups try to capture government decision making because it affects the industry and the consumers' welfare. Interest groups have means to influence public decision makers: (1) Monetary bribes are feasible, although not common due to their illegality.[4] (2) More pervasive are the hoped-for future employment for commissioners and agency staff with the regulated firms or their law firms or with public-interest law firms.[5] (3) Personal relationships provide incentives for government officials to treat their industry partners kindly.[6] (4) The industry may cater to the agency's concern for tranquility by refraining from criticizing publicly the agency's management. (5) Last, but not least, the industry can also operate indirect transfers through a few key elected officials who have influence over the agency. These include monetary contributions to political campaigns (Political Action Committees),[7] as well as the votes and lobbying of the

4. Note that some monetary bribes are legal however. For instance, the U.S. Department of Defense directive 55007 allows gratuities when they are a part of a "customary exchange of social amenities between personal friends and relatives when motivated by such relationships and extended on a personal basis" (Adams 1981, p. 177).

5. Breyer and Steward (1979, pp. 141–142) and Adams (1981) contain extensive descriptions of the "revolving door" phenomenon. Two quotations from Adams (pp. 82–83) illustrate the point nicely:

> The availability of jobs in industry can have a subtle, but debilitating effect on an officer's performance during his tour of duty in procurement management assignment. If he takes too strong a hand in controlling contractor activity, he might be damaging his opportunity for a second career following retirement. Positions are offered to those officers who have demonstrated their appreciation for industry's particular problems and commitments. (former Assistant Secretary of Defense J. Ronald Fox)

> The greatest public risks arising from post-employment conduct may well occur during the period of Government employment, through the dampening of aggressive administration of Government policies. (New York Bar)

Postemployment restrictions are costly because of the tight market for managerial expertise in industries (Breyer and Steward 1979, pp. 142–144).

6. The full circle revolving door between government and industry is obviously conducive to the development of such relationships. The 1978 U.S. Ethics in Government Act aimed at restricting postemployment contacts between former top-level administrators and their former agencies. But as Warren (1982, p. 205) notes: "Conflicts of interest laws are virtually impossible to enforce unless governmental employees flagrantly violate them." (On this, see also Adams 1981, p. 79.) Contacts occur in various manners, including committees between government and private sector representatives; for instance, there were 820—mainly closed doors—committees in the defense sector in 1979 (Adams 1981, p. 165).

7. See, for example, Adams (1981, pp. 8, 9) for a list of political contributions by defense contractors to the members of the Senate and House Defense Appropriations and Armed Services Committees.

"Grass Roots" (employees, shareholders, suppliers, citizens of communities where plants are located).

Such attempts at capturing the supervisory decision making through collusive activities are likely to be only the "tip of the iceberg." That is, the hidden and bigger part of the iceberg is the organizational response to prevent collusion, in this case the rules and policies whose raison d'être is the potential for regulatory capture and their effect on industry performance.

This chapter depicts the regulation of a natural monopoly (or alternatively a cohesive industry[8]). The regulatory structure regulates the firm's rate of return and price. The firm (the "agent") has private information about a technological parameter and chooses an unobserved level of cost reduction. Its private knowledge of technology allows it to enjoy an informational rent. The regulatory structure is two-tiered: agency (the "supervisor") and Congress (the "principal"). In contrast to Congress, the agency has the time, resources, and expertise to obtain information about the firm's technology.[9] Congress relies on information supplied by the agency. The agency's expertise allows it to hide information from Congress in order to identify either with the industry or with consumer groups affected by the price (output) decision. That is, these interest groups can bribe the agency to retain specific kinds of information. To keep the model tractable, we assume that a monetary equivalent of \$1 received by the agency costs $\$(1 + \lambda_i)$ to interest group i. The shadow price of transfers λ_i has two facets: First it reflects the fact that transfers to an agency are not fully efficient (a monetary bribe exposes the parties to the possibility of legal sanctions, government officials would prefer to receive the monetary equivalent of entertainment expenses, catering to specific interests goes against the agency's concern for "public service," etc.). Second, it embodies organizational costs. While the latter are likely to be small for a firm, they can be substantial for consumers; following Olson (1965), one would expect small

8. Any free riding in lobbying within an interest group is described in reduced form through the interest group's shadow price of transfers.

9. For instance, Barke and Riker (1982, p. 77) note:

> Administrators within a particular system are, however, full-time employees, devoting all their professional attention to the rules and cases before them. Their role renders them better informed than legislators and at the same time wholly identifies their interests with the condition of the regulatory scheme.

This view is shared by Warren (1982, p. 51):

> Bureaucracy, as Max Weber and other organizational theorists have recognized, is able to maintain its power position, despite challenges, because the bureaucrats are able to make themselves the real experts by keeping and controlling virtually all of the information.

and by Breyer and Stewart (1979, p. 144):

> At present, Congress usually gets only an agency's official view of its activities—a view which may filter out unfavorable, though potentially important, information.

consumer groups with a high per-capita stake to have a smaller cost of organizing than the group of all taxpayers for instance. The legal environment (Ethics Acts, appropriations for intervenors programs) and other "exogenous" variables (rise of consumerism or of environmental awareness) affect the transfer costs and the relative influence of the interest groups.[10]

To use standard agency methodology, we assume that side contracts between the agency and the interest groups are enforceable. Side contracts should not in general be thought of as being enforced by a court (and therefore might be best labeled "quasi-enforceable"). Rather, enforcement comes from the parties' willingness to abide by their promise to cooperate. This interpretation may cover a spectrum of cases. First, the parties may pledge their word and be loathe to cheat on agreements with other parties even in a one-shot relationship ("word-of-honor" case). Second, a variation on this theme (not formally equivalent to the word-of-honor hypothesis, but having the same flavor) is that the agency and the interest groups over time develop reputations for not breaching side contracts even if they have no aversion to cheating on the agreements.[11] Third, there may be situations in which the benefits from a collusive agreement accrue as a flow and in which adherence to the agreement is ensured by the threat that the flow of benefits and the associated flow of side transfers will stop if anyone cheats on the agreement. The enforceability-of-side-contracts hypothesis is a good description of cases in which collusion works well (e.g., the idealized word-of-honor and self-enforcement interpretations); it does not do full justice to intermediate cases (e.g., the reputation interpretation) in which collusion is feasible but not fully effective. We do, however, think that our analysis sheds light on such intermediate cases because it focuses on when collusion is likely to be an issue and on how agency discretion can be reduced to prevent collusion.

Congress has the means to reward or punish the agency.[12] It maximizes a social welfare function that adds consumer, agency, and producer sur-

10. Most of our results still hold when, more generally, the maximum amount of resources that can be channeled to the agency by interest group i, when the latter has stake Δ_i in the agency's decision, can be written $\rho^i(\lambda_i, \Delta_i)$ with $\rho^i_{\lambda_i} < 0$, $\rho^i_{\Delta_i} > 0$, and $\rho^i_{\lambda_i \Delta_i} \leq 0$. Here $\rho^i(\lambda_i, \Delta_i) = \Delta_i/(1 + \lambda_i)$. But one could think of other functional forms. For instance, if there are n members in the interest group, and there is a fixed per-capita cost f of collecting funds, the resource function might be $\rho^i = \Delta_i - nf$. Defining $\lambda_i = n$ yields a function that satisfies the assumptions above.

11. See Tirole (1990) for examples.

12. The U.S. Congress can abolish or reorganize an agency, change its jurisdiction, cut its appropriations, and conduct embarrassing investigations. Weingast (1984) and Weingast and Moran (1983) have shown in specific instances that Congress has a substantial influence on agencies.

The focus on Congress as the external monitor may be a good first approximation in the United States. The president has theoretical, but small actual control over the bureaucracy (Fiorina 1981), and courts are often limited to the punishment of clear deviations from vague legislative mandates and are also constrained to taking universalistic decisions (Warren 1982).

pluses. The assumption that Congress is a benevolent maximizer of a social welfare function is clearly an oversimplification, as its members are themselves subject to interest group influence. There are three justifications for making this assumption. First, ignoring the politics of Congress and focusing on the politics of the agency is a first step toward a more general theory of regulatory politics, yet it allows the derivation of a rich set of insights. Second, the model may admit alternative interpretations; in particular the "agency" in the model might represent the coalition of a government agency and the members of the relevant congressional oversight committee, and "Congress" the rest of the legislature. Third, and most important, our methodology can be straightforwardly applied to cases in which Congress does not maximize social welfare but tries to control the regulatory outcome. Our model is thus mainly one of control of agencies by their political principals.[13] Since interest groups have a stake in the agency's behavior, congressional oversight of the agency and the industry must respond to the potential for collusion between the agency and the interest groups.

This simple model permits the study of several central issues in the theory of regulation: (1) the determinants of interest group power (an interest group has power if its potential for organizing triggers a regulatory response; we will show that because of the latter response an interest group can be hurt by its own power); (2) the effect of regulatory politics on the agency's incentive structure and discretion (in this model, discretion is measured by the sensitivity of regulatory decisions to agency reports); (3) the effect of regulatory politics on the regulated firm's incentives, rent, and pricing; (4) the dependency of these effects on the power of interest groups and on the amount of resources appropriated to the agency; (5) whether interest groups' pressures offset or add up, and how interest groups affect each other's welfare (does an improved organization of consumers hurt or benefit the industry?).

Section 11.2 introduces the model. Sections 11.3 through 11.5 consider the case in which production is essential (the firm cannot be shut down), and solve the model in an increasing order of generality: Section 11.3 considers the benchmark in which interest groups are powerless, section 11.4 studies "producer protection," and section 11.5 allows multiple inter-

Note that there is no conflict between the observations that "monitoring and sanctions do not comprise a perfect solution to the problem of bureaucratic compliance" (McCubbins et al. 1987, p. 253), and studies showing that agencies tend to be obedient to Congress (e.g., Barke and Riker 1982; Joskow 1972; McFadden 1976). In our model Congress can dictate regulatory policy but is dependent on the agency for information.

13. It cannot, however, explain rules that constrain the regulatory process and decision making (the definition of the scope of regulation, the limitations on transfers to the industry, etc.). Restraining the choice set of a benevolent Congress can only reduce welfare in our setup. In contrast, in the absence of any benevolent party, it may pay to design regulatory institutions so as to limit the regulatory structure's scope of authority. See chapters 15 through 17.

est groups. Section 11.6 discusses the case in which the firm can be shut down when it has an inefficient technology. Section 11.7 proposes a political theory of cross-subsidization in the spirit of the previous sections, and section 11.8 summarizes the main economic insights.

11.2 The Model

We consider a three-tier hierarchy: firm/agency/Congress. All parties are risk neutral.

11.2.1 The Firm

The firm produces a marketable output q at cost

$$C = (\beta - e)q. \tag{11.1}$$

The cost or technology parameter β can take one of two values: "low" or "efficient" ($\underline{\beta}$), with probability ν, and "high" or "inefficient" ($\bar{\beta}$), with probability $1 - \nu$. We follow the notation of chapter 2. Letting t denote the (net) transfer from Congress to the firm, the firm's utility or rent is

$$U = t - \psi(e) \geq 0. \tag{11.2}$$

11.2.2 The Agency

The agency receives income s from Congress and derives utility from its relationship with Congress: $V(s) = s - s^*$. That is, its reservation income (the income below which its employees refuse to participate) is s^*. For simplicity we assume that the agency is indispensable (Congress needs the agency to regulate the firm's price and cost). Thus Congress must pay at least s^* to the agency in each state of nature:

$$V(s) = s - s^* \geq 0. \tag{11.3}$$

[The remark below discusses this ex post formalization of the agency's individual rationality constraint.] The agency obtains information (a signal σ) about the firm's technology. With probability ζ, the agency learns the true β ($\sigma = \beta$); with probability $1 - \zeta$, the agency learns "nothing" ($\sigma = \emptyset$). There are thus four states of nature: With probability $\zeta\nu$, the technology and the signal are $\underline{\beta}$; with probability $(1 - \zeta)\nu$, the technology is $\underline{\beta}$, but the agency does not know it and therefore still puts probability ν on the firm being efficient; and so on. The signal is hard evidence in the sense that the agency is able to reveal the true technology to Congress if $\sigma = \beta$. For simplicity we assume that the interest groups (the firm, consumer groups) learn what signal the agency receives.[14] Note also that ζ is

14. Alternatively, one could assume that when the agency has an incentive to collude with an interest group, it can go to this interest group and disclose the signal it has received.

exogenous (we take the agency's effort to discover the technology as given); ζ can be thought of as entirely determined by the agency's budget for investigation.

The agency reports $r \in \{\sigma, \varnothing\}$ to Congress. If it has learned nothing ($\sigma = \varnothing$), it can only say so ($r = \varnothing$). If it has learned the truth ($\sigma = \beta$), it can either tell the truth ($r = \beta$) or claim its search for information was unfruitful ($r = \varnothing$).

11.2.3 Congress

As discussed in the introduction, Congress's utility is the sum of producer, agency, and consumer surpluses. According to our usual notation,

$$W = U + V + [S(q) - P(q)q - (1 + \lambda)(s + t + (\beta - e)q - P(q)q)],$$

or

$$W = [S(q) + \lambda P(q)q] - (1 + \lambda)(s^* + (\beta - e)q + \psi(e)) - \lambda U - \lambda V. \tag{11.4}$$

In words, from the "generalized consumer surplus," $S(q) + \lambda P(q)q$, must be subtracted $1 + \lambda$ times the total cost of the project, $s^* + (\beta - e)q + \psi(e)$, and λ times the rents left to the firm and the agency. The important property of (11.4) for our analysis is that Congress dislikes leaving a rent to the firm and to the agency. Note also that W does not incorporate any deadweight loss associated with side transfers. It turns out that (except in section 11.7) optimal contracts can be designed so as to leave no scope for side transfers (see appendix A11.1).

Congress observes neither β nor σ. It observes the cost C, the output q [or the price $p = P(q)$], and receives the agency's report r. Congress designs incentive schemes $s(C, q, r)$ and $t(C, q, r)$ for the agency and the firm so as to maximize expected social welfare EW (where expectations are taken over the four states of nature).[15]

The timing is as follows: At date 0, all parties learn their information simultaneously: They all learn the nature of the project; Congress learns that β belongs to $\{\underline{\beta}, \bar{\beta}\}$, the agency and the interest groups learn σ, and the firm learns β. The probability distributions are common knowledge. Then Congress designs incentives schemes for the agency and the firm. The agency can then sign side contracts (see below) with the interest groups. Next the agency makes its report, and the firm chooses its effort and price (the exact timing in this stage turns out to be irrelevant). Last, transfers are operated as specified in the contracts.

15. More complex mechanisms (including, e.g., announcements by the firm and the agency) would not raise welfare in this model with collusion; see appendix A11.1.

Remark The formulation implicitly assumes that the project is too ill-defined before date 0 for the parties to be able to sign relevant contracts before that date. Alternatively, we could assume that the project is well defined before date 0 so that the parties can sign complete contracts before obtaining their information, as in Tirole (1986). Most results (on the effect of collusion on incentive schemes, on pricing, and on the circumstances under which an interest group has power) are qualitatively unaffected if the firm and the agency are risk averse and attention is restricted to deterministic contracts; the difference is that the agency and the firm then have no ex ante rent, unless an ex post no slavery or limited-liability constraint is imposed. The analysis is a bit more cumbersome than in the case in which there is no contract prior to date 0, except when the agency and the firm are infinitely risk averse (see section 11.4).

11.2.4 Consumer Groups

When consumers cannot organize (sections 11.3 and 11.4), it does not matter how the net surplus, $S(q) - P(q)q$, and the taxes, $(1 + \lambda)(s + t + C - P(q)q)$, are allocated among consumers. In contrast, when they can influence policy decisions (section 11.5), the distribution of costs and benefits among consumers becomes important, since consumers have different marginal rates of substitution between consumption of the good and taxes. To simplify computations without losing insights, we will assume in section 11.5 that there are two groups of consumers: those that pay all taxes and those that receive the entire net surplus. Let us give three examples: (1) q is the output of an intermediate good used by another industry, or else the output of a final good consumed by a small group of consumers; taxes are paid by the general taxpayer. (2) q is the level of welfare benefits enjoyed by the poor; taxes are paid by the rich. (3) q is the level of pollution or pollution abatement that affects local residents; taxes are paid by the federal taxpayers. (In these last two examples, the objective functions must be changed slightly since the good is not marketed, but this is inconsequential.)

11.3 Collusion-Free Regulation

In this section we analyze the benchmark in which interest groups have no influence on the agency (their transfer costs are infinite). We sketch the solution, and summarize the relevant points for subsequent analysis.

Congress optimally offers the agency a constant income equal to its reservation income: $s = s^*$. The agency then has no incentive to misreport the signal. Hence, at social cost $(1 + \lambda)s^*$, Congress has the same information structure as the agency.

Next we consider optimal regulation of the firm when Congress has full information (FI) and asymmetric information (AI). (The following is a summary of section 2.3.)

11.3.1 Full Information ($\sigma = \beta$)

Congress knows the firm's technology parameter and can deprive it of its rent (we index variables by a star to indicate the socially optimal policy under full information):

$$U(\beta) = U^*(\beta) = 0 \qquad \text{for all } \beta. \tag{11.5}$$

The effort $e^*(\beta)$ and output $q^*(\beta)$ or price $p^*(\beta)$ [which we will write $(\underline{e}^*, \underline{q}^*, \underline{p}^*)$ for the efficient type and $(\bar{e}^*, \bar{q}^*, \bar{p}^*)$ for the inefficient type] are set so as to maximize the full information welfare, $[S(q) + \lambda P(q)q] - (1+\lambda)[s^* + (\beta - e)q + \psi(e)]$. Hence, for all β, $\{e^*(\beta), p^*(\beta)\}$ solves[16]

$$\psi'(e) = q \tag{11.6}$$

and

$$\frac{p - (\beta - e)}{p} = \frac{\lambda}{1+\lambda}\frac{1}{\eta(p)}, \quad \text{or} \quad p \equiv R(\beta - e). \tag{11.7}$$

Equation (11.6) states that the marginal cost and benefit of effort are equal. Equation (11.7) shows that price is given by a simple Ramsey formula. $R(c)$ is called the Ramsey price for marginal cost c. Since the cost function satisfies the condition for the dichotomy given in proposition 3.4, the formula giving the price as a function of marginal cost turns out to be independent of informational asymmetries (see subsection 11.3.2). We let $\underline{q}^*(e)$ and $\bar{q}^*(e)$ denote the Ramsey outputs given by (11.7) contingent on marginal cost being $\underline{\beta} - e$ or $\bar{\beta} - e$. Clearly $\underline{q}^*(\cdot)$ and $\bar{q}^*(\cdot)$ are nondecreasing functions of e.[17]

Shortly we will show that under asymmetric information the efficient type's allocation is unchanged relative to symmetric information [it is equal to $(\underline{e}^*, \underline{q}^*)$]. The inefficient type's output $\bar{q}$ is still conditionally optimal given the inefficient type's effort $\bar{e}$ [i.e., $\bar{q} = \bar{q}^*(\bar{e})$]. The focus of the analysis will thus be on how $\bar{e}$ differs from the full information level $\bar{e}^*$. This suggests singling out the inefficient type's effort for the purpose of the analysis. Let $W^{FI}(\bar{e})$ denote the expected social welfare (i.e., social welfare when Congress has not yet learned β but knows that it will do so before regulating) given that the efficient type's allocation is at its full information level, the inefficient type's output is conditionally (Ramsey) optimal, but the inefficient type's effort is an arbitrary $\bar{e}$:

16. Throughout this chapter we will assume that optimization programs have interior solutions.
17. See section 2.3.

$$W^{FI}(\bar{e}) \equiv \nu[S(\underline{q}^*) + \lambda P(\underline{q}^*)\underline{q}^* - (1+\lambda)(s^* + (\underline{\beta} - \underline{e}^*)\underline{q}^* + \psi(\underline{e}^*))] + (1-\nu)[S(\bar{q}^*(\bar{e})) + \lambda P(\bar{q}^*(\bar{e}))\bar{q}^*(\bar{e}) - (1+\lambda)(s^* + (\bar{\beta} - \bar{e})\bar{q}^*(\bar{e}) + \psi(\bar{e}))]. \tag{11.8}$$

We assume that $W^{FI}(\cdot)$ is strictly concave.[18] The expected social welfare W^{FI} is by definition obtained by choosing $\bar{e} = \bar{e}^*$:

$$W^{FI} \equiv W^{FI}(\bar{e}^*). \tag{11.9}$$

11.3.2 Asymmetric Information ($\sigma = \varnothing$)

We let $(\underline{e}, \underline{q}, \underline{t})$ and $(\bar{e}, \bar{q}, \bar{t})$ denote the efforts, output levels, and transfers for types $\underline{\beta}$ and $\bar{\beta}$ under the optimal incentive scheme when the firm has an informational advantage over Congress. The regulatory issue is to prevent the efficient type from claiming that it is inefficient. That is, we must add an incentive constraint to the full information program:

$$\underline{t} - \psi(\underline{e}) \geq \bar{t} - \psi(\bar{e} - \Delta\beta). \tag{11.10}$$

(The efficient type can produce at cost $\bar{\beta} - \bar{e}$ by exerting effort $\bar{e} - \Delta\beta$ and obtain transfer $\bar{t}$.)

The inefficient type obtains no rent, $\bar{t} = \psi(\bar{e})$. The efficient type's rent under asymmetric information will be denoted by $\underline{U}$. Since (11.10) is binding at the optimum, we have

$$\underline{U} \equiv \underline{t} - \psi(\underline{e}) = \bar{t} - \psi(\bar{e} - \Delta\beta) = \psi(\bar{e}) - \psi(\bar{e} - \Delta\beta), \tag{11.11}$$

or

$$\underline{U} = \Phi(\bar{e}), \tag{11.12}$$

where

$$\Phi(e) \equiv \psi(e) - \psi(e - \Delta\beta). \tag{11.13}$$

Under our assumptions the function Φ is increasing and convex. Note that when $\bar{e}$ increases (i.e., when the inefficient type is given "more incentives"), the efficient type's rent increases.

Congress maximizes expected social welfare:

$$\max_{\{\underline{q}, \underline{e}, \bar{q}, \bar{e}\}} \{\nu[S(\underline{q}) + \lambda P(\underline{q})\underline{q} - (1+\lambda)(s^* + (\underline{\beta} - \underline{e})\underline{q} + \psi(\underline{e})) - \lambda\Phi(\bar{e})] + (1-\nu)[S(\bar{q}) + \lambda P(\bar{q})\bar{q} - (1+\lambda)(s^* + (\bar{\beta} - \bar{e})\bar{q} + \psi(\bar{e}))]\} \tag{11.14}$$

A simple inspection reveals that $\underline{q} = \underline{q}^*$, $\underline{e} = \underline{e}^*$, and $\bar{q} = \bar{q}^*(\bar{e})$, as announced. The absence of distortion of $(\underline{q}, \underline{e})$ and of conditional distortion of $\bar{q}$ is not surprising. The incentive constraint (11.12) tells us that only $\bar{e}$

18. Sufficient conditions are λ small or decreasing marginal revenue.

should be distorted:

$$\psi'(\bar{e}) = \bar{q}^*(\bar{e}) - \frac{\lambda v}{(1+\lambda)(1-v)}\Phi'(\bar{e}), \tag{11.15}$$

yielding[19]

$$\bar{e} < \bar{e}^*. \tag{11.16}$$

Thus the inefficient type's effort $\bar{e}$ is distorted downward in order to reduce the efficient type's rent.

Since the Ramsey output $\bar{q}^*(\cdot)$ is increasing, (11.16) implies that

$$\bar{q} < \bar{q}^*. \tag{11.17}$$

Let $W^{AI}(e)$ denote the expected welfare under asymmetric information when the inefficient type's effort is exogenously fixed at e [and (11.14) is maximized with respect to the other variables]. Note that

$$W^{AI}(e) = W^{FI}(e) - \lambda v \Phi(e). \tag{11.18}$$

$W^{AI}(\cdot)$ is strictly concave when $W^{FI}(\cdot)$ is strictly concave.

The expected social welfare under asymmetric information can be rewritten

$$W^{AI} = \max_{e} \{W^{FI}(e) - \lambda v \Phi(e)\} = W^{FI}(\bar{e}) - \lambda v \Phi(\bar{e}). \tag{11.19}$$

Let us summarize the relevant points for what follows. Congress obtains the agency's information by giving it a constant income s^*. The expected social welfare under full and asymmetric information can be written as strictly concave functions of the inefficient type's effort e: $W^{FI}(e)$ and $W^{AI}(e) = W^{FI}(e) - \lambda v \Phi(e)$, where $\Phi(e)$ is the efficient type's rent under asymmetric information and is an increasing function. The optimization with respect to e therefore implies that the inefficient type is given a less powerful incentive scheme under asymmetric information ($\bar{e} < \bar{e}^*$) in order to extract some of the efficient type's rent. The corresponding market price is higher than under full information.

11.4 Producer Protection

In this section we allow the firm to collude with the agency. More precisely, the firm can give a transfer $\tilde{s}$ to the agency (so that the agency's

19. The proof of (11.16) is a standard revealed preference argument. Recalling that $\underline{q} = \underline{q}^*$ and $\underline{e} = \underline{e}^*$ under both full and asymmetric information, $\{\bar{e}, \bar{q}^*(\bar{e})\}$ yields a higher maximand in (11.14) than $\{\bar{e}^*, \bar{q}^*(\bar{e}^*)\}$. Conversely, in the full information program [which is the same as (11.14) except that there is no $(-v\lambda\Phi(\bar{e}))$ term], $\{\bar{e}^*, \bar{q}^*(\bar{e}^*)\}$ yields a higher maximand than $\{\bar{e}, \bar{q}^*(\bar{e})\}$. Adding up these two inequalities yields $v\lambda(\Phi(\bar{e}^*) - \Phi(\bar{e})) > 0$ (the inequality is strict, since maximands are strictly convex and (11.15) implies that $\bar{e} \neq \bar{e}^*$). Since $\Phi(\cdot)$ is strictly increasing, $\bar{e}^* > \bar{e}$.

income equivalent becomes $s + \tilde{s}$) at cost $(1 + \lambda_f)\tilde{s}$, where $\lambda_f \geq 0$ denotes the shadow cost of transfers for the firm [equivalently the agency attributes monetary value $1/(1 + \lambda_f)$ per dollar of the firm's collusive activity; see the introduction for a general discussion of transfer costs]. We here content ourselves with a heuristic derivation of the equilibrium outcome under collusion with the firm. Appendix A11.1 offers a complete proof. In particular it shows that (1) Congress can, without loss of generality, restrict attention to "collusion-proof" schemes, namely schemes that do not induce the agency and the firm to collude and lead the agency to report truthfully, and hence there is no welfare loss in requiring that there be no bribes in equilibrium;[20] (2) the agency's income depends only on its report. We let $\underline{s}_1$, $\bar{s}_1$, and s_0 denote the agency's income when $r = \underline{\beta}$, $r = \bar{\beta}$, and $r = \varnothing$, respectively.

Collusion occurs when the agency has an incentive to hide information from Congress. The analysis in section 11.3 suggests the following intuition: Collusion can arise only if the retention of information benefits the firm. If the signal is $\bar{\beta}$, the firm has no stake in the agency's report, since it obtains no rent under either full information or asymmetric information. In contrast, when the signal is $\underline{\beta}$, the firm has a stake, since the revelation of the truth lowers its rent from $\Phi(e)$ (where e is the inefficient type's effort under asymmetric information) to 0. To prevent the firm from bribing the agency, the cost to the firm of compensating the agency by the income $\underline{s}_1 - s_0$ lost by not reporting must exceed its stake:

$$(1 + \lambda_f)(\underline{s}_1 - s_0) \geq \Phi(e). \tag{11.20}$$

From the agency's individual rationality constraint, we know that $\underline{s}_1$, $\bar{s}_1$, s_0 all exceed s^*. Since revelation is not an issue when $\sigma = \bar{\beta}$ or $\sigma = \varnothing$, and since income given to the agency is socially costly, we have $\bar{s}_1 = s_0 = s^*$. We can thus rewrite (11.20) as

$$(1 + \lambda_f)(\underline{s}_1 - s^*) \geq \Phi(e). \tag{11.21}$$

Since income given to the agency is socially costly, (11.21) holds with equality at the optimal policy:

$$\underline{s}_1 = s^* + \frac{\Phi(e)}{1 + \lambda_f}. \tag{11.22}$$

Equation (11.22), which depends only on e and $\underline{s}_1$, suggests that Congress

20. Equilibrium collusion may be unavoidable in situations in which Congress has incomplete information about the agency's cost of colluding. Suppose, for instance, that $\lambda_f = +\infty$ with probability 0.99 and $\lambda_f = 0$ with probability 0.01 (the firm and the agency know λ_f, but Congress does not). Then Congress may find it cheaper to let collusion occur with probability 0.01 (i.e., when $\lambda_f = 0$) than to ensure that the coalition incentive constraint [equation (11.20) below] is satisfied when $\lambda_f = 0$, which yields the rent given by (11.22) to the agency even when the agency would not have colluded anyway ($\lambda_f = +\infty$). A similar remark is made in Kofman and Lawarrée (1989) and in chapter 16.

should give lower incentives to an inefficient firm under asymmetric information but that it should leave the other variables (except $\underline{s}_1$) unchanged. In other words, the efficient type's allocations under full and asymmetric information and the inefficient type's allocation under symmetric information are still the socially optimal ones $(\underline{e}^*, \underline{q}^*)$ and $(\bar{e}^*, \bar{q}^*)$. Furthermore, under asymmetric information, the inefficient type's output is the Ramsey level $\bar{q}^*(e)$ relative to effort e. That these properties indeed hold is verified in appendix A11.1.

Congress chooses e so as to maximize expected social welfare:

$$EW = \max_{e} \left\{ \zeta W^{FI} + (1 - \zeta) W^{AI}(e) - \zeta \nu \lambda \frac{\Phi(e)}{1 + \lambda_f} \right\}, \tag{11.23}$$

where the last term reflects the fact that the agency's rent has social cost λ from (11.4). Using the fact that the objective function in (11.23) is strictly concave, the envelope theorem and the first-order condition in (11.23) yield proposition 11.1.

Proposition 11.1 Under producer protection

i. collusion reduces social welfare, $\partial(EW)/\partial\lambda_f > 0$,

ii. the firm is given a low-powered incentive scheme, $e < \bar{e}$,

iii. output is still Ramsey optimal but is lowered from $\bar{q}^*(\bar{e})$ to $\bar{q}^*(e)$ under asymmetric information for the inefficient type,

iv. the agency is given an incentive scheme, $\underline{s}_1 > \bar{s}_1 = s_0$,

v. the efficient type enjoys a lower rent than in the absence of collusion, $\Phi(e) < \Phi(\bar{e})$,

vi. e [and therefore $\Phi(e)$ and $\bar{q}^*(e)$] increase with λ_f.

To prevent collusion, Congress *reduces the stakes* (i.e., the efficient type's rent under asymmetric information). To this purpose the inefficient type is given an incentive scheme under asymmetric information that is even less powerful than the corresponding scheme in the absence of collusion. Since the other states of nature are unaffected, producer protection can only reduce incentives. Note also that since $\bar{q}^*(\cdot)$ is increasing, the price is higher, and the transfer to the firm is lower than in the absence of collusion, under asymmetric information, and for type $\bar{\beta}$.

Remark What happens if the project is sufficiently well-defined before date 0 so that contracts can be signed before date 0? (Appendix A11.1 contains some of the details of the following discussion.) As mentioned above, the results are quite similar if the agency and the firm are risk averse and attention is restricted to deterministic contracts. Suppose, for instance, that before date 0 the firm and the agency have objective functions min U and min V (they are infinitely risk averse). Thus U and V must be nonnegative for any realization of uncertainty at date 0. The coalition incentive constraint is still (11.20). What is modified relative to our analysis is the expression of the social welfare function. At the optimum, min U = min $V = 0$. Furthermore ex post rents ($U > 0$, $V > 0$) have no ex ante social value because they are not "enjoyed" by the parties. Therefore they have unit cost $1 + \lambda$ instead of λ. So (11.23) is replaced by

$$EW = \max_e \left\{ \zeta W^{FI} + (1-\zeta)W^{AI}(e) - \zeta v(1+\lambda)\frac{\Phi(e)}{1+\lambda_f} - (1-\zeta)v\Phi(e) \right\}, \tag{11.24}$$

where W^{FI} is defined by (11.9) and $W^{AI}(e)$ is defined by (11.18). Clearly the results are qualitatively similar. The main difference is that the agency and the firm may enjoy an ex post rent but do not have any ex ante rent.[21]

11.5 Multiple Interest Groups

To illustrate the effects of multiple interest groups, we now consider a specification of our model in which the firm's output affects the environment. Suppose that the total gross surplus associated with a level of production q is equal to the gross consumer surplus $\tilde{S}(q)$ associated with consumption of the good, minus an increasing and convex pollution damage $D(q)$ born by a fraction of the population called "environmentalists" or "local residents":

$$S(q) = \tilde{S}(q) - D(q). \tag{11.25}$$

Suppose also that the environmentalists do not purchase the good and do not pay the taxes associated with the regulation of the industry (as discussed in section 11.2, this assumption simplifies computations and does not affect qualitative results; what matters for our theory is that the environmentalists' marginal rate of substitution between output and taxes exceeds that of the rest of the public).

In a first step we assume that among the nonindustry groups only the environmentalists can organize. They can transfer $\tilde{s}$ to the agency at cost

21. If the agency is very risk averse, and the firm is less risk averse, it may pay for Congress to commit to leave an ex post rent $U > 0$ when the agency announces $r = \underline{\beta}$. The reason for this is that leaving such a rent relaxes the coalition incentive constraint, which becomes $(1 + \lambda_f)(\underline{s}_1 - s_0) \geq \Phi(e) - U$, which allows Congress to reduce $\underline{s}_1$. Reducing $\underline{s}_1$ is socially important because Congress cannot reduce much the agency's utility in other states of nature if $\underline{s}_1$ is large and the agency is very risk averse. On the other hand, leaving a rent to the firm is costly. But this cost is small if the firm is not too risk averse because Congress can reduce the firm's utility in other states of nature while keeping the firm's individual rationality constraint satisfied in expectation. So *it may pay for Congress to somewhat renounce the pursuit of the extraction of the firm's ex post rent.* Then the agency acts not only as a potential advocate for the firm but also as an effective advocate.

$(1 + \lambda_e)\tilde{\tilde{s}}$ (so that the agency's income equivalent becomes $s + \tilde{s} + \tilde{\tilde{s}}$, where $\tilde{s}$ is the firm's transfer to the agency). We assume that public collection of funds is more efficient than the private collection of funds (where the latter cost takes account of the inefficiency of transfers to the agency; see the introduction): $\lambda_e \geq \lambda$. This assumption allows us to focus on collusion-proof incentive schemes. [The intuition for this property, which is proved in appendix A11.2, is that if the optimal allocation involved actual transfers from the environmentalists to the agency, it would be socially cheaper to have Congress substitute for the environmentalists and give these transfers to the agency. If $\lambda_e < \lambda$, it may be optimal to let the agency be rewarded by bribes, since private collection is more efficient than public collection. We believe that the assumption $\lambda_e \geq \lambda$ is reasonable for developed economies, where λ is relatively small (of the order of 0.3 for the United States from econometric studies).] Again, we give an informal treatment. Complete proofs are relegated to appendix A11.2.

Congress must ensure that the agency colludes neither with the firm nor with the environmentalists. Since Congress's optimization program has more coalition incentive constraints than when $\lambda_e = +\infty$, social welfare cannot exceed the level obtained for $\lambda_e = +\infty$.[22] We show that environmentalists affect the regulatory outcome.

For intuition about which coalition incentive constraints are binding, it is useful to go back to proposition 11.1. When $\sigma = \underline{\beta}$, the firm has a stake in regulation. To preserve its rent, it is willing to bribe the agency up to the level $\Phi(e)$, where e denotes the inefficient type's effort if $r = \emptyset$. In contrast, the environmentalists have no stake in the agency's report because output is the same for both reports. Thus the only coalition incentive constraint, when $\sigma = \underline{\beta}$, is

$$(1 + \lambda_f)(\underline{s}_1 - s_0) \geq \Phi(e). \tag{11.26}$$

When $\sigma = \bar{\beta}$, the firm enjoys no rent and has no stake in the agency's report. In contrast, the agency's hiding its information induces asymmetric information and reduces output (proposition 11.1). Let (e, q) and $(\tilde{e}, \tilde{q})$ denote the inefficient type's effort and output when $r = \emptyset$ and $r = \bar{\beta}$, respectively. We must add a second coalition incentive constraint:[23]

$$(1 + \lambda_e)(\bar{s}_1 - s_0) \geq D(\tilde{q}) - D(q). \tag{11.27}$$

The optimal policy implies that $s_0 = s^*$. Therefore (11.26) and (11.27) (which hold with equality at the optimum) can be rewritten

22. In our model a reduction in λ_e—through a better organization, the advent of consumer activism, or government subsidies—always reduces welfare. If consumers play a substantial role as watchdogs, that is, if they bring information about the industry and products and check the agency, a reduction in their organization costs may improve social welfare; see chapter 15.

23. Note that this constraint does not in general define a convex set.

$$\underline{s}_1 = s^* + \frac{\Phi(e)}{1 + \lambda_f} \tag{11.28}$$

and

$$\bar{s}_1 = s^* + \frac{D(\tilde{q}) - D(q)}{1 + \lambda_e}. \tag{11.29}$$

This suggests (and it can be verified) that e, q, and $\tilde{q}$ are distorted at the optimal allocation so as to reduce the agency costs. More precisely let $W^{FI}(\tilde{q}, \tilde{e})$ and $W^{AI}(q, e)$ denote the expected welfares under full information and under asymmetric information when the inefficient type's allocation is $(\tilde{q}, \tilde{e})$ and (q, e), respectively, and when the efficient type's allocation is undistorted ($\underline{q} = \underline{q}^*, \underline{e} = \underline{e}^*$). Using (11.28) and (11.29), Congress maximizes expected social welfare:

$$EW = \max_{\{\tilde{q}, \tilde{e}, q, e\}} \Bigg\{ \zeta W^{FI}(\tilde{q}, \tilde{e}) + (1 - \zeta) W^{AI}(q, e) - \zeta \nu \lambda \frac{\Phi(e)}{1 + \lambda_f} - \zeta(1 - \nu)\lambda \frac{D(\tilde{q}) - D(q)}{1 + \lambda_e} \Bigg\}. \tag{11.30}$$

We will assume that the maximand in (11.30) is strictly concave (for this it suffices that λ be small or that λ_e be large): A straightforward analysis of (11.30) yields proposition 11.2.

Proposition 11.2

i. The environmentalists have an influence on regulation.

ii. $\underline{s}_1$ and, when $\tilde{q} > q$, $\bar{s}_1$ strictly exceed $s_0 = s^*$.

iii. A decrease in λ_e raises e and therefore raises the firm's rent $\Phi(e)$. It lowers $\tilde{e}$, and it lowers $\tilde{q}$ and raises q; therefore it reduces $(\tilde{q} - q) \geq 0$ toward 0.[24]

iv. A decrease in λ_f decreases q and therefore raises the environmentalists' welfare.

The intuition behind proposition 11.2 is simple. To relax the environmentalists' coalition incentive constraint [see (11.27)], Congress lowers $\tilde{q}$ and raises q, so that the environmentalists' stake $D(\tilde{q}) - D(q)$ in regulation is reduced. Since q increases, marginal cost reduction becomes more valuable when $\sigma = \varnothing$ and $\beta = \bar{\beta}$. Hence e increases. The striking conclusion is that *the more powerful the environmentalists, the higher is the firm's rent*. This is not altogether surprising. In this economy the firm and the environmentalists are "objective accomplices" in that they both have a stake in making regulation inefficient. The firm wants Congress to be

24. For λ_e small enough, it may be the case that $q = \tilde{q}$ (a corner solution).

uninformed in order to enjoy a rent. The environmentalists want Congress to be uninformed in order to reduce output and thus pollution. We will see in section 11.6 that this coincidence of interests heavily relies on the assumption that production is essential. An increase in the environmentalists' power may well hurt the firm if shutdown is a relevant option.

As we mentioned earlier, environmentalists are powerful here because their interest lies in inefficient regulation. Note also that the effects of multiple interest groups do not cancel but rather add up. What is more, as in section 11.4, the agency must be rewarded for cooperating with Congress.

We have assumed that neither the consumers of the good nor the taxpayers can organize (presumably because their per-capita stakes are too small). Let us now show that even if the consumers of the good (henceforth, the "consumers") could organize, they would have no influence on the regulatory outcome. Without loss of generality, we assume that the consumers enjoy net surplus $\tilde{S}^n(q) \equiv \tilde{S}(q) - P(q)q$ and that they do not pay the taxes or bear the pollution cost associated with the project. They have a cost of transfer $\lambda_c \geq \lambda$. We can now state proposition 11.3.

Proposition 11.3 Whether the environmentalists can organize or not, the consumers have no political power. That is, the regulatory outcome is the same as if λ_c were infinite (as given by proposition 11.2).

The proof of proposition 11.3 is straightforward. Introducing the possibility of collusion between consumers and the agency cannot raise welfare, since the number of constraints facing Congress increases. Conversely, suppose that Congress adopts the regulatory policy that is optimal when consumers cannot organize. When $\sigma = \underline{\beta}$, the output is at its socially efficient level $\underline{q}^*$, regardless of whether the agency reports the truth ($r = \underline{\beta}$) or not ($r = \varnothing$). Hence the consumers have no stake in the report. When $\sigma = \bar{\beta}$, the consumers do have a stake. The output is $\tilde{q}$ if the agency reports the truth ($r = \bar{\beta}$) and $q \leq \tilde{q}$ if the agency lies ($r = \varnothing$). Hence, by bribing the agency to hide its information, the consumers can only raise the price. Therefore they have no incentive to bribe the agency.[25]

The intuition behind proposition 11.3 is that consumers favor high outputs. Since asymmetric information between Congress and the firm leads to low-powered incentives and hence to low quantities (section 11.3), a high output requires full information. But the potential power of con-

25. One might conjecture that the agency could extract a bribe from the consumers by threatening them to hide the information $\sigma = \bar{\beta}$. However, such a threat is not "subgame perfect": When the day comes at which the agency must report to Congress, the agency has an incentive to tell the truth, as $\bar{s}_1 > s_0$ from proposition 11.2.

Only in the case in which the agency can develop a reputation for being tough (lose income to hurt consumers) can such a threat be effective. Such a reputation might develop in organizations where the supervisor monitors a large number of subordinates.

sumers (as well as of other interest groups) lies in inducing the agency to hide information from Congress.

Last, we can consider what happens when taxpayers, who want to minimize taxes $(1 + \lambda)[s + t + C - P(q)q]$, can organize, although their high cost of organization in many situations makes this analysis irrelevant. We were unable to give a general characterization of whether taxpayers have influence on regulation. However, there is a case of interest in which the answer is straightforward. Suppose that the taxpayers and the consumers are the same people so that they form a single group, with objective function $\tilde{S}^n(q) - (1 + \lambda)[s + t + C - P(q)q]$. When $\sigma = \underline{\beta}$, this group's interest lies in rent extraction (i.e., in the truth being reported).[26] Hence the group has no incentive to bribe the agency to misreport. Similarly, when $\sigma = \bar{\beta}$, it can be shown that the group prefers that the agency report the truth.[27] Hence the taxpayers-consumers group has no political power in this model.

A New Determinant of Interest Group Power

An important principle emerging from this section is that *the power of an interest group depends not only on its stake and its transfer cost but also on what kind of influence it wants to exert. An interest group has more political power when its interest lies in inefficient rather than efficient regulation,* since the agency's discretion lies in hiding information from Congress and asymmetries in information makes regulation less efficient.

This principle can be transposed to other examples:

Example 1 (Pollution Abatement versus Production-Embodied Pollution) Proposition 11.2 shows that environmentalists are powerful when pollution is tied to production. We now show that they may have no power in other circumstances. Let the firm's output be fixed at some level q_0. The firm can reduce its pollution level by an amount q at abatement cost $C = (\beta - e)q$ (which comes on top of a given cost C_0 of producing q_0). C can be thought of as the cost of buying and installing a new pollution-reducing technology. β here denotes a technology parameter that affects the marginal cost of pollution abatement, and e the effort to reduce the abatement cost. The reduction in pollution yields benefits $B(q)$ to the "environmentalists" [$B(\cdot)$ is assumed increasing and concave]. Ignoring the constant cost of producing q_0 and the generalized consumer surplus,

26. Consider the solution described in proposition 11.2 (which includes that described in proposition 11.1 as a special case). As $\Phi(e) = (1 + \lambda_f)(\underline{s}_1 - s_0)$, $\underline{s}_1 - s_0 < \Phi(e)$ so that the total wage bill $s + t$ is lower when the report is $r = \underline{\beta}$ (the cost and the output are independent of the report).

27. Again, consider the solution described in proposition 11.2. Since Congress can always duplicate the outcome for $r = \varnothing$ and $\beta = \bar{\beta}$ when $r = \bar{\beta}$, social welfare is at least as high in the latter case as in the former. But the firm has no rent in either case and the environmentalists prefer the former case to the latter from proposition 11.2. Hence the remaining group (consumers plus taxpayers) strictly prefers the latter to the former.

$S(q_0) + \lambda P(q_0)q_0$, the social welfare function is

$$W = B(q) - (1 + \lambda)[s^* + C + \psi(e)] - \lambda U - \lambda V. \tag{11.32}$$

Replacing $S(q) + \lambda P(q)q$ by $B(q)$, the analysis of sections 11.3 and 11.4 can be directly transposed to the pollution-abatement model. However, the environmentalists have no power here, since they resemble the "consumers" of the production-embodied pollution model: Their interest lies in high pollution abatements (high qs). That the environmentalists have power in one case and not the other is not surprising. They favor inefficient regulation in the production-embodied pollution model and efficient regulation in the pollution-abatement model.

Example 2 (Welfare Benefits) Consider a two-class economy (rich/poor), and suppose that the poor are the recipients of a quantity q of welfare benefits financed by taxes on the rich. The poor have an interest in efficient regulation, since the latter is conducive to higher benefits, and they therefore have less power than the rich, who save on taxes when inefficient regulation limits the level of welfare benefits.

11.6 Shutdown of the Regulated Firm

The analysis in sections 11.3 through 11.5 proceeded under the assumption that the firm is essential. That is, it must produce even if it is inefficient (has type $\bar{\beta}$). This is the case if the consumer surplus is sufficiently large, so Congress cannot run the risk of forgoing production (shutting the firm down when it has type $\bar{\beta}$ and allowing production by type $\underline{\beta}$ only). This sounds like a reasonable assumption for many regulated firms. In some instances, however, shutdown is a relevant option.

Shutting down type $\bar{\beta}$ is a simple policy in our two-type model. Type $\underline{\beta}$ has now no rent because mimicking type $\bar{\beta}$ brings none. Congress has full information on the technology conditionally on the firm's choosing to produce. This implies that the optimal policy in the collusion-free environment in the shutdown option is still collusion-proof when the interest groups can organize.[28] This result, together with the results in sections 11.4 and 11.5, implies that the more powerful the interest groups (i.e., the lower their transfer costs), the more attractive the shutdown policy is relative to the no-shutdown policy.

The possibility of shutdown reinforces most of our insights. For instance, in our model it corresponds to an extreme absence of agency

28. The optimal shutdown policy consists in requiring that the firm produce $q = \underline{q}^*$ at cost $\underline{C}^* = (\underline{\beta} - \underline{e}^*)\underline{q}^*$ and in giving transfer $\underline{t}^* = \psi(\underline{e}^*)$ (the efficient type has no rent).

Note that the agency has no role in the two-type model under the shutdown policy. With more than two types, the agency would bring information that helps Congress to distinguish those types that are not shut down. The features discussed in this section would still be relevant in the many-type model as long as the shutdown option is a relevant one.

discretion. Furthermore the shutdown of the firm can be viewed as an extreme case of low-powered incentive scheme.

There is a result, however, that relies heavily on the essentiality of production. In section 11.5 we observed that the better organized the environmentalists, the higher is the firm's rent. This may not be so when shutdown is a relevant option. A decrease in the environmentalists' transfer cost reduces the welfare associated with the no-shutdown policy. So it may induce Congress to switch to the shutdown policy, which would annihilate the firm's rent.

11.7 A Political Theory of Cross-subsidization

Our methodology can be applied to study whether interest group pressure would lead to cross-subsidization by a multiproduct firm. To this purpose, we consider a variant of the model of section 11.2, in which none of the types of cross-subsidizations listed in chapter 3 applies. In this variant, cross-subsidization might be an optimal response to the political activities of some customers of the regulated firm. [One could, for instance, think of the captive coal shippers' successful fight against unrestrained price discrimination by railroad monopolies.]

Suppose that there are two classes of consumers, $k = 1, 2$, with identical demands. Let $S(q_k)$ and $S^n(q_k) \equiv S(q_k) - P(q_k)q_k$ denote the gross and net surpluses of class k, where $P(\cdot)$ is the inverse demand function. We let $\eta(p_k)$ denote the elasticity of demand at price p_k.

The regulated firm's cost is

$$C = (\beta - e)(q_1 + q_2) + d(q_2 - q_1)\chi, \tag{11.32}$$

where $\chi = 1$ or -1 with equal probabilities and $d > 0$. The parameter χ indicates which category of consumers is cheaper to serve (the marginal cost of serving one category is $2d$ lower than the marginal cost of serving the other category). The "cost-differential parameter" d is common knowledge.

To simplify the analysis, we assume that the agency does not learn χ and therefore has no role (this involves no loss in insight; see below). Therefore Congress regulates the firm directly. Since in this section our focus is on cross-subsidization, we assume that β is known to Congress.

If Congress knows that $\chi = 1$ (without loss of generality), from chapter 3 the optimal regulation specifies Ramsey pricing:

$$L_1 \equiv \frac{p_1 - (\beta - e - d)}{p_1} = R_1 \equiv \frac{\lambda}{1+\lambda}\frac{1}{\eta(p_1)}, \tag{11.33}$$

$$L_2 \equiv \frac{p_2 - (\beta - e + d)}{p_2} = R_2 \equiv \frac{\lambda}{1+\lambda}\frac{1}{\eta(p_2)}. \tag{11.34}$$

The marginal disutility of effort is equal to marginal cost savings:

$$\psi'(e) = q_1 + q_2. \tag{11.35}$$

R_1 and R_2 are the Ramsey terms. When we allow collusion, we say that there is cross-subsidization of good 2 by good 1 if $L_1 > R_1$ and $L_2 < R_2$. Note that (11.33) and (11.34) imply that $p_1 < p_2$, $q_1 > q_2$, and $L_1 = R_1 < L_2 = R_2$.

From now on we assume that the firm, but not Congress, knows χ. Furthermore χ is "soft information." That is, the firm cannot "prove" to Congress that χ is equal to 1 or -1 but can only announce it ($\hat{\chi}$); in other words, Congress knows that the firm knows χ but cannot subpoena the firm to supply evidence that substantiates its announcement $\hat{\chi}$. The softness of information is not crucial to the analysis of cross-subsidization. Last, we assume for simplicity that the consumers also know χ.[29]

If Congress does not know χ, and there is no collusion between the firm and any group of consumers, the solution is unchanged, since the firm has no incentive to misreport χ. Indeed lying about χ would only lead Congress to switch the roles of goods 1 and 2 and to increase the firm's cost by $2(q_1 - q_2)d$, and therefore the firm's effort by $[2(q_1 - q_2)d]/(q_1 + q_2)$ without any gain.

On the other hand, suppose that type 2 consumers can organize and make a take-it-or-leave-it offer to the firm, when $\chi = 1$, to induce the firm to announce $\hat{\chi} = -1$. This leads Congress to quote a low price for good 2 and a high price for good 1, which benefits type 2 consumers and hurts type 1 consumers.

Let us assume that the two classes of consumers have transfer costs λ_c with $\lambda_c \geq \lambda$.[30] In a first step we assume that it is optimal for Congress to structure incentives so as to prevent collusion. We then relax this assumption and show that collusion proofness is optimal only for a subset of parameters. To avoid collusion with type 2 consumers when $\chi = +1$, the gain for type 2 consumers of a misreport of χ, $S^n(q_1) - S^n(q_2)$, must be lower than the extra disutility of effort, $\psi(e + [2(q_1 - q_2)d/(q_1 + q_2)]) - \psi(e)$, valued at the transfer cost between the type 2 consumers and the firm. The coalition incentive constraint is thus[31]

$$(1 + \lambda_c)\left[\psi\left(e + \frac{2d(q_1 - q_2)}{q_1 + q_2}\right) - \psi(e)\right] \geq S^n(q_1) - S^n(q_2). \tag{11.36}$$

29. The analysis is qualitatively the same when the consumers do not know χ; the main difference is that there is less incentive to collude, and therefore a lower likelihood of cross-subsidization when the consumers have incomplete information about χ.

30. As before, assuming that $\lambda_c \geq \lambda$ is meant to rule out the possibility that side transfers occur only because an interest group is a better collector of funds than Congress.

31. This constraint does not define a convex set.

Using the symmetry of the model, we look for a symmetric solution. It is easily seen that the firm, which has no private information about β, enjoys no rent. Congress's optimization program is

$$\max_{\{q_1, q_2, e\}} \{S(q_1) + S(q_2) - (1 + \lambda)[(\beta - e)(q_1 + q_2)$$
$$+ d(q_2 - q_1) + \psi(e)] + \lambda[P(q_1)q_1 + P(q_2)q_2]\} \tag{11.37}$$

subject to (11.36).

We can now state proposition 11.4.

Proposition 11.4 For the solution to the collusion-proof program (11.37) (assuming that $\chi = 1$; for $\chi = -1$, indices are permuted), there exist $d_1 > 0$ and $d_2 > d_1$ ($d_2 \leq +\infty$) such that

i. if $d < d_1$, pricing is uniform ($p_1 = p_2 = p$; $q_1 = q_2 = q$, and the values of p and q are intermediate between the ones that prevail under symmetric information about χ), and cross-subsidization occurs ($L_1 > R_1$ and $L_2 < R_2$);

ii. if $d_1 < d < d_2$, price discrimination occurs, and the threat of collusion is socially costly;

iii. if $d \geq d_2$, the threat of collusion is socially costless [i.e., the solution is given by equations (11.33) through (11.35)].

The proof of proposition 11.4 is relegated to appendix A11.3. An interesting conclusion is that for small d, the stakes in collusion, $S^n(q_1) - S^n(q_2)$, are not only reduced at the optimum, they totally disappear. Congress imposes uniform pricing, an extreme form of cross-subsidization. The intuition for this result is as follows: The welfare loss due to collusion is at most of order d when d is small, since Congress can adopt uniform pricing which is collusion-proof and involves only a loss of order at most d. Hence a policy in which $q_1 - q_2$ is not of order at most d is suboptimal, for it involves a distortion relative to the full information case that does not converge to 0 at rate d or faster. Now consider the collusion incentive constraint (11.36). As a first approximation, the left-hand side is proportional to $(q_1 - q_2)d$ and the right-hand side is of order $q_1 - q_2$. Hence the constraint cannot be satisfied unless $q_1 = q_2$. In words, the consumers' stake is proportional to the difference in outputs, while the firm's cost of lying is proportional to this difference times the marginal cost of switching outputs and is therefore smaller for d small.

For a large d the firm's cost of lying is very large, and constraint (11.36) is satisfied by the solution to (11.33) through (11.34) in the case of $d_2 < +\infty$. For an intermediate d the analysis is complex, and we were not able to get specific results. This is due to the fact that lowering the differential $q_1 - q_2$ reduces the consumers' stake $S^n(q_1) - S^n(q_2)$ but also makes it less costly for the firm to lie.

We now investigate the possibility that bribes are socially optimal *in equilibrium.*[32] To see why bribes may be optimal, suppose that $\chi = 1$ and that there is price discrimination: $q_1 > q_2$. The type 2 consumers are willing to pay $S^n(q_1) - S^n(q_2)$ to the firm. Let

$$\Delta \equiv \frac{S^n(q_1) - S^n(q_2)}{1 + \lambda_c} - \left[\psi\left(e + \frac{2d(q_1 - q_2)}{q_1 + q_2}\right) - \psi(e)\right] \tag{11.38}$$

denote the bribe that the firm must receive from type 1 consumers to tell the truth if equation (11.36) is not satisfied ($\Delta > 0$). It is in the interest of type 1 consumers to bribe the firm to tell the truth if and only if[33]

$$S^n(q_1) - S^n(q_2) \geq (1 + \lambda_c)\Delta, \tag{11.39}$$

or

$$\psi\left(e + \frac{2d(q_1 - q_2)}{q_1 + q_2}\right) - \psi(e) \geq 0. \tag{11.40}$$

Note, for instance, that for $q_1 > q_2$ equation (11.40) is not binding. So price discrimination is feasible even for a small d. But there is a cost of having type 1 consumers transfer Δ to the firm, equal to $(\lambda_c - \lambda)\Delta$. There is a trade-off between relaxing the collusion-proofness constraint by having the type 1 consumers bribe the firm and creating costly side transfers.

Congress must choose between two regimes. The "*no-side-transfer regime*" corresponds to $\Delta \leq 0$; it has already been studied. The "*side-transfer regime*" corresponds to $\Delta > 0$. In the side-transfer regime there is no collusion-proofness constraint, and the social welfare function is given by

$$\begin{aligned}\max_{\{q_1, q_2, e\}} \Bigg\{ & S(q_1) + S(q_2) - (1 + \lambda)[(\beta - e)(q_1 + q_2) + d(q_2 - q_1) + \psi(e)] \\ & + \lambda[P(q_1)q_1 + P(q_2)q_2] \\ & - (\lambda_c - \lambda)\left[\frac{S^n(q_1) - S^n(q_2)}{1 + \lambda_c} - \psi\left(e + \frac{2d(q_1 - q_2)}{q_1 + q_2}\right) + \psi(e)\right]\Bigg\},\end{aligned} \tag{11.41}$$

where the last term takes into account the reduction in Congress's transfer to the firm in amount equal to the bribe received. When λ_c is close to λ, Congress can reach almost the collusion-free welfare in program (11.41), while it cannot in program (11.37). Hence the side-transfer regime is optimal.

32. The following discussion has benefited from discussions with Bengt Holmström, who, in another context, suggested to us that it may be socially optimal to allow bribes between two members of an organization who share soft information.

33. We are here envisioning an auction between the two groups of consumers. The firm announces the $\hat{\chi}$ which is favorable to the highest bidder, where the bid of the expensive-to-serve consumers is deflated by the extra disutility of effort engendered by lying.

Fixing $\lambda_c > \lambda$, when d tends to 0, the no-side-transfer regime (which we know, from proposition 11.4, involves uniform pricing) is optimal. To show this, it suffices to take the derivatives of (11.41) with respect to q_1 and q_2 and to note that $q_1 - q_2$ becomes negative as d tends to 0^+ while $q_1 \geq q_2$ for constraint (11.40) to be satisfied. The intuition for this result can be obtained from (11.41): Choosing $q_1 - q_2$ positive and of order d yields two gains that are second order in d—cost savings $(1 + \lambda)d(q_1 - q_2)$ and cost for the firm of lying $\simeq \psi'(e)2d(q_1 - q_2)/(q_1 + q_2)$—and imposes a first-order loss $\simeq (\lambda_c - \lambda)p(q_1 - q_2)/(1 + \lambda_c)$ due to an inefficient side transfer.

Proposition 11.5 Assume that $\lambda_c > \lambda$.

i. When λ_c is close to λ, it is socially optimal to practice price discrimination and to let consumers that are cheap to serve bribe the firm.

ii. When d is small, uniform pricing and the absence of side transfers are optimal.

A striking conclusion is that equilibrium side transfers can arise. Type k consumers are then used as a countervailing force to type l consumers. Recall that the collusion proofness principle obtained for the hard information model of sections 11.2 through 11.6. The interest groups could bribe the agency to report or misreport its piece of hard information; but Congress could duplicate this bribe at a lower transfer cost. Here, Congress does not know whether $\hat{\chi} = 1$ is a true report because of the softness of information, while the consumers are able to base their transfers on both the announcement and the truth.[34]

Last, we have assumed that there was no agency. Alternatively one could assume that the agency colludes with the firm. Suppose for instance that the agency learns χ (soft information) and announces it. While the outcome is similar to the one obtained above, this more complex framework allows the possibility that the consumers' side transfers be directed to the agency rather than directly to the firm.

11.8 Concluding Remarks

This chapter has shown that interest-group politics can be comprehended in a tractable agency framework. It has yielded a number of general insights:

1. The organizational response to the possibility of agency politics is to reduce the stakes interest groups have in regulation.

34. This shows that the possibility of equilibrium bribes is linked with our assumption that consumers know the true value of χ. If consumers do not know χ, then the collusion-proofness principle holds, since Congress can duplicate the consumers' side transfers.

2. The threat of producer protection leads to low-powered incentive schemes. That is, the theory predicts contracts that are somewhat closer to cost-plus contracts than a theory ignoring the possibility of producer protection.

3. The agency's discretion to choose among price levels, pollution levels, and more generally variables affecting the other interest groups than the regulated industry is reduced when the latter become better organized.

4. Our approach refines the view that there is a market for regulatory decisions. First, the regulatory inefficiencies associated with the pressures of several interest groups may compound rather than cancel. For instance, an industry (eager to extract a rent) and an environmental group (eager to limit production to curb pollution) may have a common interest in Congress's not being informed about the production technology. Second, the power of an interest group depends not only on its willingness to pay (i.e., on the combination of its stake in the regulatory decision and of its cost of organizing and of influencing government) but also on the kind of influence it wants to exert. The group has more power when its interest lies in inefficient rather than efficient regulation, where inefficiency is measured by the degree of informational asymmetry between the regulated industry and Congress.

5. In contrast with the conventional wisdom on interest-group politics, an interest group can be hurt by its own power.

6. Congress must reward the agency for "cooperating," that is, for supplying information.

The more specific insights are

7. In our production-embodied pollution model (section 11.5) the better organized the environmentalists, the higher is the firm's rent if the firm's production is essential. In contrast, if production is not essential so that shutdown is a relevant policy, the environmentalists' pressure may hurt the firm.

8. The methodology developed in this paper is extended to yield a political theory of cross-subsidization. Interest-group politics may yield uniform pricing by regulated multiproduct firms.

9. The optimal allocation can be implemented without side transfers when the supervisory information is hard. Soft supervisory information could make equilibrium side-transfers desirable; that is, Congress could set up one interest group against another interest group.

Because of their complexity, hierarchical models such as the one in this chapter must be highly stylized. It is therefore worth commenting on which results are likely to extend to other models. The strong intuition behind the general insights gives us confidence in their robustness. Insights

1 through 3, on the desirability of reducing the interest groups' stakes in regulation, are likely to carry over to other models in which interest groups only try to capture but do not contribute positively to the regulatory process. In contrast, if interest groups can bring new information about the agency's activity, it may be socially desirable to increase their stakes in regulatory decisions so as to induce them to acquire information and make regulation more efficient (chapter 15). Insight 2, on the optimality of low-powered incentive schemes, will carry over to the other situations in which the agency brings *technical expertise* to the political principal; high-powered incentive schemes are bound to leave high potential rents to the industry and thus to create high payoffs to collusion. A different situation arises when the agency performs the role of an *accounting office*. Then stakes in collusion may be reduced by the use of high-powered incentive schemes; in particular fixed-price contracts remove agency discretion by suppressing cost accounting by the agency (chapter 12). Insight 4, linking interest group power and gain from inefficient regulation, is a natural conclusion in models of hard information, in which the agency's degree of freedom is necessarily to hide information from Congress. Insight 5 is akin to the classic point in game theory that a player can lose from having more options in a multiplayer situation. Insight 6 conforms to standard agency theory. Although in this chapter agency incentives are provided by rewards, they might alternately be provided by punishments inflicted when the agency is caught colluding with interest groups (chapter 15) or by the threat of dismissal or nonreelection if collusion is suspected (chapter 16). Last, insights 7 through 9, while making sense, are quite special, and their extension to more general frameworks is an important line for future research.

BIBLIOGRAPHIC NOTES

This chapter relates to two large literatures, political science and political economy. Since it would be presumptuous to summarize them in a few pages, the purpose of the bibliographic notes of this chapter is to alert the reader to a few standard references[35] and to locate this chapter in these literatures.

B11.1 Political Science and the Organization of Government

Whether governments can be trusted to serve the public good has long been a central issue in political science. As discussed in the introduction of

35. Surveys with different coverage than these notes include Noll (1987), Romer and Rosenthal (1986), and Wilson (1980).

the chapter, authors as diverse as Montesquieu, the American Federalists, Marx, Truman (1951), and Bernstein (1955) have been concerned by the potential for capture. They have discussed why and how governments may favor specific interest groups and have emphasized the necessity of building a system of checks and balances.

The Political Control of Bureaucracies

Some of the recent political science literature takes a disaggregated view of government by distinguishing among its branches. In particular it studies the control of self-interested government agencies by elected officials. Niskanen (1971) stresses the asymmetry of information between agencies and their political principal. Political principals, so goes the argument, can hardly control agencies and must leave them rents.[36] On the other hand, another strand of the political science literature shows that political principals can impose their will on agencies. For instance, Weingast and Moran (1983) find evidence that Congress can substantially influence the Federal Trade Commission.

These seemingly opposing views are actually quite consistent. Political principals may be able to dictate decisions when informed, but they are at the mercy of better-informed agencies. (This reconciliation actually is embodied in our modeling. In this chapter agency discretion is entirely due to the privacy of its information.)

More generally the extent of agency discretion depends not only on the asymmetry of information but also on the allocation of residual rights of control over the industry between the agency and its political principal. This chapter assumes that residual rights of control lie with the political principal. The political principal de facto regulates the industry, and the agency only reports information to the political principal. However, political scientists, most notably Fiorina (1981, 1982), have pointed out that there is some variation in the extent to which agencies must comply with the political principal's instructions.[37] Indeed we observe a wide spectrum of delegation, from almost independent agencies (e.g., some central banks) to very constrained agencies (e.g., some branches of ministries). Fiorina argues in particular that politicians grant agencies some independence when this can help shift the blame for poor policy onto agencies. We are not aware of a formal analysis of why rational voters would on average be more complacent toward politicians that delegate their powers to agencies.

36. See, for example, Kaufman (1961) and Wilson (1980) for similar views. Banks (1989) and Banks and Weingast (1989) develop formal two-tier models in which the agency is better informed than its political principal. The agency's rent is higher, the higher the cost of audit by the political principal.
37. See also Truman (1951).

Lenoir (1991) takes a different approach to agency independence. She considers a three-tier model similar to the one in this chapter, except that the political principal rather than the agency may collude with the industry. Under "agency dependence" the political principal sets the agency's budget, while under "agency independence" the budget is set by some exogenous rule. Agency independence is suboptimal when politicians are honest (i.e., do not collude with the industry) because politicians can fine-tune the agency's budget to its needs. Agency independence fares better when politicians are prone to protect the industry. Politicians can then use their discretion to pressure the agency when they want to collude with the industry. The politicians can offer a high budget and thereby grant a rent to the agency, when its needs are modest, in exchange for the agency's keeping a low profile. The agency in Lenoir's model is self-interested (but cannot easily collude with the industry) and therefore prefers to receive a high budget to displeasing the political principal by revealing to a court or to the public that the political principal leaves excessive rents to the industry.

Information Acquisition by the Political Principal

Some of the recent political science literature has used the disaggregated view of government to further explore the institutional restraints on capture emphasized by the older literature. For instance, McCubbins and Schwartz (1984) have asked how a couple of hundred elected officials can effectively monitor millions of bureaucrats. Elected officials often lack the competence, the time, and even the incentive to carefully scrutinize agencies. McCubbins and Schwartz argue that the political system does not go completely awry because the elected officials' constituents mitigate problems associated with asymmetric information. For example, the U.S. Congress to a large extent reacts to information supplied by the constituents. Regulatory hearings are driven by the same engine. Thus political oversight of agencies is often characterized more by "fire alarm" than by "police patrol" activity, to use a phase coined by McCubbins and Schwartz. We will build a formal analysis of the role of constituents in checking on agencies in chapter 15.

Another implication of informational asymmetries for the design of government is that political principals need to specialize. This idea underlies the existence of committees in Congress. Committee members are better informed than the rest of the legislature. It is therefore not surprising that, like agencies, they often make strategic use of their information.[38]

38. See Krehbiel (1990, ch. 3) for references. There is also a large literature in political science, starting with Fenno's (1966) observations, analyzing the power of committees in congressional decision making. This literature emphasizes the role of committees in setting the agenda and manipulating the voting process rather than in hiding information. For models in which institutions determine political influence, see Shepsle (1979), Shepsle and Weingast (1981), and Baron and Ferejohn (1988).

Like agencies, they may also develop cozy relationships with the interest groups affected by their decisions. (In this respect there is both anecdotal evidence on collusion and Shepsle's 1978 indirect evidence about the self-selection process in committees—the farming committees are populated by representatives of agricultural states or districts who can grant favors to their constituents, etc.)

Further Topics

Many fascinating normative and positive questions related to the organization of government by and large have not been confronted with formal economic modeling. Here are a few of them.

The analyses in parts V and VI of this book suppose that benevolent lawmakers or founders develop optimal incentive structures or constitutions. Often, though, designers of the political system have vested interests. While our analysis can be extended to allow nonbenevolent designers, it would be desirable to pursue such an extension in some detail. Future research along these lines may shed light on some standard issues in political science: How do politicians decide which agencies to create (Fiorina 1985; McCubbins 1985)? How does regulation or deregulation come about (e.g., Derthick and Quirk 1985; Peltzman 1989; Wilson 1980)?

Another area of considerable interest for the study of regulation is the multiprincipal structure of government. How should residual rights of control over industries be allocated among the executive, legislative, and judiciary branches of government? What control should these branches exert over agencies? Should powers be divided within a branch (e.g., between the Senate and the House, or between the ministry of industry and the ministry of finance)?

B11.2 The Political Economy Approach: The Chicago and Virginia Schools

The tenet of the Chicago school's approach to regulatory capture, starting with Stigler (1971), is that the political system is rationally employed by the actors. In particular interest groups choose to influence government at a level where marginal benefit is equal to marginal cost.

Stigler, like Marx, but unlike subsequent Chicago school contributors, focused on producer protection. While Marx was mainly concerned with the protection of big industry, Stigler emphasized that seemingly competitive industries (e.g., trucking, farming, or some professions) can successfully organize to influence government. Following the earlier political science literature (in particular Olson), Stigler discusses the costs of organization and views them as a crucial determinant of industry (and more generally interest group) influence.

Stigler's second contribution is to argue that industries try to influence policies for which they have a high stake. He identifies four classes of policies an industry may want to affect. The first is direct government subsidies to the industry. Stigler argues that this category is often not the primary target of the lobbying activity because the benefits of subsidies attract new entrants and create a countervailing effect on industry profit (to illustrate this, consider the extreme case of a free-entry, contestable market. Profits are then equal to zero regardless of the level of subsidy). In other words, subsidies must be shared among too many firms (this argument of course has more force in atomistic industries than in the natural monopoly situations considered in this book). This observation brings us to Stigler's second category, government-created barriers to entry. Preventing entry by new rivals through licensing, biased standards, import quotas, or tariffs guarantees rents to the existing firms. Stigler's third and related category concerns policies that affect substitutes or complements to the industry under consideration. For instance, the airline industry will support government subsidies to airports. The fourth category is the government's fixing the price to prevent price competition in the industry (as in the case of the prohibition of interest payments on checking accounts by banks to depositors).

While much of the modern political science literature takes a disaggregated view of the regulatory system, the Chicago school makes little distinction between agencies and political principals. When it does, it focuses mainly on the capture of politicians. Peltzman (1976) and Becker (1983, 1985) develop formal models of political influence of interest groups. For instance, Becker assumes that interest groups compete to shift political favors in their favor. Each group chooses a level of "pressure"; exerting pressure is costly to the interest group. A higher level of of pressure raises the probability of a policy favorable to the interest group and unfavorable (at least on average) to the other interest groups. He looks at a Nash equilibrium in pressure levels and derives comparative statics.

Becker's model treats the political system as a black box describing the probabilities of benefiting each group as a function of all pressure levels. Baron (1989) opens the black box by expliciting the agency relationship between the interest groups (the principals) and the politicians (their agents). In Baron, candidates in an election promise favors to interest groups and receive money in exchange. The probability of the candidate being elected depends on the relative size of campaign contributions of all candidates.[39] Candidates receive private benefits of being in office and therefore are eager to receive campaign contributions. Baron analyzes the agency problem between interest groups and candidates. The candidate

39. For empirical analyses of the effect of campaign contributions on political behavior and on election outcomes, see Edelman (1990), Snyder (1990), and the references therein.

learns his cost of providing the services to the interest groups after being elected. Pledged campaign contributions that will increase the candidate's probability of being reelected are used to build an incentive-compatible revelation of the cost of providing the services.

Baron's model does not focus on competition among interest groups to obtain favors.[40] Closer in spirit to Becker's analysis of competition among interest groups is Spiller's (1990) model. In Spiller, the decision maker is an agency. The agency responds to two principals, Congress and the industry. Both announce rewards to the agency that depend on some realized variable (industry price or pollution level) that results from the agency's activity and over which Congress and the industry have conflicting preferences. The agency's unobservable effort increases the probability of a low price or of a low pollution level. Viewing Congress as an interest group yields a theory of competition for agency favors. The papers by Baron and Spiller thus improve on the previous literature by, among other things, expliciting the agency relationship between interest groups and public decision makers.

Another school of thought, often referred to as the Virginia school (Buchanan 1980; Tollison 1982; Tullock 1967),[41] studies how politicians or bureaucrats compete for the rents associated with bribes and kickbacks. Bureaucrats have the power to generate rents, for instance, by creating or preserving a monopoly position. Accordingly the private sector lobbies to obtain those rents.[42] In turn would-be politicians and bureaucrats compete to become rent granters, and within government, rent granters compete among themselves for the right to distribute rents and thereby receive favors from interest groups. The deadweight losses associated with these activities must be added to the original deadweight loss associated with the original rent, such as monopoly pricing, in order to obtain a complete assessment of social cost.

Note that our model exhibits a cost of leaving rents to the agency because of the existence of the shadow cost of public funds. We could also introduce competition for these rents. This would increase the deadweight loss associated with the existence of potential agency rents and would further call for low-powered incentive schemes to reduce potential industry rents, and thereby potential agency rents and wasteful rent seeking.

A different approach to rent seeking is offered by Milgrom (1988) and Milgrom and Roberts (1988). They are particularly concerned with the time and effort spent by the members of an organization to influence

40. There is a different kind of interaction among interest groups, in that the candidate's probability of election depends on his or her total campaign contributions across all industries.

41. See, for example, Tollison (1982) and Delorme and Snow (1990) for other references. In particular the papers by Bhagwati (1982) and Krueger (1974) have been quite influential.

42. The books by Jacoby et al. (1977) and Klitgaard (1988) are particularly instructive in this respect.

decision makers. They develop formal models in which employees choose the amount of time dedicated to manipulating the information received by the decision maker.[43] This approach contrasts with the Chicago and Virginia school approaches in that (1) it does not emphasize the quid pro quo between rent granter and rent seeker, but (2) it opens the black box of the rent-seeking activity and fully explicates its nature. We refer to the papers for implications, which are mainly developed in an internal organization context.

B11.3 Contract Theory and Collusion

There exists a small, but expanding literature formalizing organizations as nexus of contracts. We will not review this literature and will simply refer to Tirole (1990) for a discussion.

APPENDIXES

A11.1 Producer Protection

Let us index the four states of nature in the following way: State 1: $\{\beta = \underline{\beta}, \sigma = \underline{\beta}\}$; state 2: $\{\beta = \underline{\beta}, \sigma = \varnothing\}$; state 3: $\{\beta = \bar{\beta}, \sigma = \varnothing\}$; state 4: $\{\beta = \bar{\beta}, \sigma = \bar{\beta}\}$. We let x_i denote the probability of state i (e.g., $x_1 = \zeta\nu$). A contract offered by Congress may lead to a side contract between the agency and the firm, and yields some equilibrium allocation. We index the *final* incomes and utilities (which include the equilibrium bribes, if any) by a caret: $\{\hat{t}_i, \hat{s}_i, \hat{U}_i, \hat{V}_i\}_{i=1}^4$. The actual transfers from Congress to the agency and to the firm are denoted s_i and t_i in state i. Letting $\tilde{s}_i$ denote the firm's bribe to the agency, we have[44]

$$\hat{s}_i = s_i + \tilde{s}_i, \tag{A11.1}$$

$$\hat{t}_i = t_i - (1 + \lambda_f)\tilde{s}_i, \tag{A11.2}$$

$$\tilde{s}_i \geq 0, \tag{A11.3}$$

$$\hat{U}_i = \hat{t}_i - \psi(e_i), \tag{A11.4}$$

$$\hat{V}_i = \hat{s}_i - s^*. \tag{A11.5}$$

(We will assume that the final allocation is deterministic. The reasoning is easily extended to random final allocations.)

We want to prove that there is no loss of generality in assuming that (1) the agency reports σ truthfully; (2) transfers are based on (q, C, r) only (in particular more complex mechanisms, e.g., announcement games, do not raise welfare); (3)

43. An early paper on the strategic manipulation of information in labor markets is Holmström's paper on career concerns discussed in the bibliographic notes B9.6 of chapter 9.

44. We allow only positive bribes for simplicity. Negative bribes [bribes $\tilde{t}_i$ from the agency to the firm, which would cost $(1 + \lambda_a)\tilde{t}_i$] can be shown to be suboptimal as long as $\lambda_a \geq 0$. (The reasoning is the same as the reasoning below.)

the agency's income depends only on its report; (4) there is no side transfer in equilibrium ($\tilde{s}_i = 0$ for all i). The strategy of proof is the following: First, we derive an upper bound on expected welfare. To do so, we derive a couple of necessary conditions that must be satisfied by the final allocation in any equilibrium. We then write welfare as a function of the final allocation and equilibrium bribes, and maximize it subject to this limited set of constraints. We find in particular that optimal bribes are equal to zero. Second, we show that this upper bound can indeed be reached by an incentive scheme that satisfies properties 1 through 4 (and in particular is collusion-proof). It is then straightforward to check that the optimization program is equivalent to (11.23).

First, we claim that for all i,

$$\hat{s}_i \geq s^*, \tag{A11.6}$$

$$\hat{U}_i \geq 0. \tag{A11.7}$$

If either of these inequalities is violated, one of the parties refuses to participate in the regulatory process because it rationally anticipates that its final utility will be lower than its reservation utility. Next we claim that

$$\hat{U}_2 \geq \hat{U}_3 + \Phi(e_3). \tag{A11.8}$$

Since in state 2 the firm is the only one to know that $\beta = \underline{\beta}$, it can mimic the behavior of type $\bar{\beta}$ and get utility $\hat{U}_3 + \Phi(e_3)$. Last,

$$(1 + \lambda_f)(\hat{s}_1 - \hat{s}_2) \geq \hat{U}_2 - \hat{U}_1. \tag{A11.9}$$

If (A11.9) were violated, the agency and the firm would be better off signing a different side contract in state of nature 1. The crucial point here is that any messages m_2 that are sent by both parties in state of nature 2 can also be sent in state 1 (the converse is not true, as in state 2 the agency cannot substantiate a report that $\sigma = \underline{\beta}$). So the two parties can agree to send the messages m_2, and specify a large side transfer from a party that defects from these messages to the other party.[45]

The expected social welfare is

$$\mathscr{W} = \sum_{i=1}^{4} x_i\{S(q_i) + \lambda P(q_i)q_i - (1 + \lambda)[s_i + t_i + (\beta_i - e_i)q_i] + \hat{U}_i + \hat{V}_i\}, \tag{A11.10}$$

or using (A11.1), (A11.2), (A11.4), and (A11.5),

$$\mathscr{W} = \sum_{i=1}^{4} x_i\{S(q_i) + \lambda P(q_i)q_i - (1+\lambda)[s^* + \lambda_f\tilde{s}_i + \psi(e_i) + (\beta_i - e_i)q_i] - \lambda\hat{U}_i - \lambda(\hat{s}_i - s^*)\}. \tag{A11.11}$$

We now find an upper bound $\mathscr{W}^{\max}$ for $\mathscr{W}$ when the constraints (A11.3), and (A11.6) through (A11.9) are imposed on the control variables $\{q_i, e_i, \tilde{s}_i, \hat{s}_i, \hat{U}_i\}_{i=1}^4$. That is, we ignore other potential constraints for the moment.

45. We are here assuming that to be enforceable, the transfers from Congress to the agency and the firm, the price level, and the cost targets are based on observable messages. But the analysis can be extended to cases in which the messages are not observed by all parties (under risk neutrality the parties can design side transfers based on the observable transfers, price, and cost target that deter any party from deviating from m_2).

Since rents are costly, the solution must satisfy

$$\hat{s}_i = s^* \qquad \text{for } i = 2, 3, 4, \tag{A11.12}$$

$$\hat{U}_3 = \hat{U}_4 = 0. \tag{A11.13}$$

Furthermore (A11.8) and (A11.9) are satisfied with equality. Next, since the problem is separable between bribes and other variables,

$$\tilde{s}_i = 0 \qquad \text{for all } i. \tag{A11.14}$$

Last, we must show that $\hat{U}_1 = 0$. To do so, note that (A11.8) and (A11.9) imply that

$$(1 + \lambda_f)(\hat{s}_1 - s^*) = \Phi(e_3) - \hat{U}_1. \tag{A11.15}$$

Thus maximizing $\mathscr{W}$ with respect to $\hat{U}_1$ is equivalent to maximizing

$$\left\{-\lambda\hat{U}_1 - \lambda\left(-\frac{\hat{U}_1}{1 + \lambda_f}\right)\right\}$$

subject to $\hat{U}_1 \geq 0$.

Thus $\hat{U}_1 = 0$. The maximizations with respect to q_i and e_i are as announced in section 11.4: Output q_i is Ramsey optimal given marginal cost $(\beta_i - e_i)$: $q_i = R(\beta_i - e_i)$. Effort is socially optimal ($\psi'(e_i) = q_i$) except in state 3, in which

$$\psi'(e_3) = q_3 - \frac{\lambda}{1 + \lambda}\left[\frac{x_2}{x_3} + \frac{x_1}{x_3(1 + \lambda_f)}\right]\Phi'(e_3), \tag{A11.16}$$

using (A11.8) and (A11.9). [That is, e_3 is the arg max of (11.23)].

The second step of the proof consists in showing that the upper bound can be reached (i.e., in the notation of the text, $EW = \mathscr{W}^{\max}$). To do so, suppose that Congress offers the following incentive schemes: The agency makes a report r and the firm announces its type $\hat{\beta}$ (equivalently the firm could be rewarded on the basis of r and C/q). Letting $i = 1$ denote the state in which $r = \underline{\beta}$ and $\hat{\beta} = \underline{\beta}$, and so on, Congress gives transfers

$$t_i = \hat{U}_i + \psi(e_i), \tag{A11.17}$$

$$s_i = \hat{s}_i, \tag{A11.18}$$

and imposes cost target

$$C_i = (\hat{\beta} - e_i)q_i \tag{A11.19}$$

and price

$$p_i = R(\hat{\beta} - e_i), \tag{A11.20}$$

where $\{q_i, e_i, \hat{s}_i, \hat{U}_i\}_{i=1}^4$ are the solutions to the maximization (A11.11) and $p_i \equiv P(q_i)$. (If the agency's report and the firm's announcement are inconsistent, or if the cost target is not reached, Congress imposes a large penalty on the other two parties.) Now it is straightforward to check that in no state of nature do the agency and the firm have an incentive to collude against this scheme, nor to individually misreport or lie. Thus the upper bound can be reached by a pair of contracts that satisfy properties 1 through 4, as claimed above.

Last, we say a few words about the case in which the parties can sign a contract before the agency and the firm (simultaneously) get their information. We assume that both the agency and the firm are infinitely risk averse, so they care only about their worst payoff. It is clear that for the optimal contract both the agency and the firm are put at their reservation utilities, s^* and 0 (otherwise, transfers could be reduced uniformly for at least one party, without any incentive effect). We focus on *deterministic* contracts. The social welfare function is slightly different from $\mathscr{W}$, since ex post rents have no longer a social value:

$$\tilde{\mathscr{W}} = \sum_{i=1}^{4} x_i\{S(q_i) + \lambda P(q_i)q_i - (1+\lambda)[s_i + t_i + (\beta_i - e_i)q_i]\}, \tag{A11.21}$$

or

$$\tilde{\mathscr{W}} = \sum_{i=1}^{4} x_i\{S(q_i) + \lambda P(q_i)q_i - (1+\lambda)[\hat{s}_i + \lambda_f \tilde{s}_i + \hat{U}_i + (\beta_i - e_i)q_i + \psi(e_i)]\}. \tag{A11.22}$$

To show that the analysis is (qualitatively) identical to that of the no-prior-contract case, it suffices to note that the minimal set of constraints {(A11.3), (A11.6) through (A11.9)} is still a set of necessary conditions when the parties are infinitely risk averse and contracts are signed prior to the revelation of information. ■

A11.2 Multiple Interest Groups

The reasoning is the same as in appendix A11.1, so we will skip the details. Let $\tilde{\tilde{s}}_i$ denote the environmentalists' transfer to the agency in state of nature i. To show that $\tilde{\tilde{s}}_i = 0$ for all i in equilibrium, we proceed as in appendix A11.1, by writing the social welfare function as a function of the final allocations and bribes and showing that there is a corner solution for bribes. An intuitive argument is the following: A bribe $\tilde{\tilde{s}}_i$ allows Congress to reduce s_i by $\tilde{\tilde{s}}_i$ for a given final income $\hat{s}_i$ (as in appendix A11.1, the optimization problem is separable between bribes and the final allocations, so we must hold the final allocation as fixed). The social gain is $(1+\lambda)\tilde{\tilde{s}}_i$. But the environmentalists' welfare is reduced by $(1+\lambda_e)\tilde{\tilde{s}}_i$. Then the net welfare gain is equal to $(\lambda - \lambda_e)\tilde{\tilde{s}}_i \leq 0$ if $\lambda_e \geq \lambda$.

The social welfare function is (using the notation of appendix A11.1)

$$\mathscr{W} = \sum_{i=1}^{4} x_i\{S(q_i) + \lambda P(q_i)q_i - (1+\lambda)[s_i + t_i + (\beta_i - e_i)q_i] + \hat{U}_i + \hat{V}_i\}. \tag{A11.23}$$

Using (11.28), (11.29), and the fact that $\tilde{s}_i = \tilde{\tilde{s}}_i = 0$ for all i,

$$\mathscr{W} = \sum_{i=1}^{4} x_i\{S(q_i) + \lambda P(q_i)q_i - (1+\lambda)[s^* + \psi(e_i) + (\beta_i - e_i)q_i]\} - \lambda\left[x_2\Phi(e_3) + x_1\frac{\Phi(e_3)}{1+\lambda_f} + x_4\frac{D(q_4) - D(q_3)}{1+\lambda_e}\right]. \tag{A11.24}$$

(In the notation of section 11.5, $q_4 = \tilde{q}$, $e_4 = \tilde{e}$, $q_3 = q$, $e_3 = e$.) We thus obtain

$$(1+\lambda)[P(q_i) - (\beta_i - e_i)] + \lambda q_i P'(q_i) = 0, \qquad i = 1, 2, \tag{A11.25}$$

$$(1+\lambda)[P(q_3) - (\bar{\beta} - e_3)] + \lambda q_3 P'(q_3) = -\lambda\frac{x_4}{x_3}\frac{D'(q_3)}{1+\lambda_e}, \tag{A11.26}$$

$$(1 + \lambda)[P(q_4) - (\bar{\beta} - e_4)] + \lambda q_4 P'(q_4) = \lambda \frac{D'(q_4)}{1 + \lambda_e}, \tag{A11.27}$$

$$\psi'(e_i) = q_i, \qquad i = 1, 2, 4, \tag{A11.28}$$

$$\psi'(e_3) = q_3 - \frac{\lambda}{1 + \lambda}\left[\frac{x_2}{x_3} + \frac{x_1}{x_3(1 + \lambda_f)}\right]\Phi'(e_3). \tag{A11.29}$$

The price is distorted away from the Ramsey price in states 3 and 4, and effort is distorted downward in state 3. Now, using our assumption that the program is concave (as we mentioned earlier, a sufficient condition for this is that λ not be too big), equations (A11.26) and (A11.27) imply that

$$\frac{\partial q_3}{\partial \lambda_e} < 0, \quad \frac{\partial q_4}{\partial \lambda_e} > 0.$$

Note that it may happen that the solution above satisfies $q_4 < q_3$. In this case the solution is a corner solution: $q_4 = q_3$ [because $q_4 = \tilde{q}$ and $q_3 = q$ in the coalition incentive constraint (11.27), (11.27) is no longer binding if $q_4 \leq q_3$; hence the term in $D(q_4) - D(q_3)$ must be omitted in the expression of $\mathscr{W}$, which yields $q_4 > q_3$, a contradiction]. ■

A11.3 Proof of Proposition 11.4

Let κ be the Kuhn-Tucker multiplier associated with (11.36). The first-order condition for program (11.37) for an interior solution is

$$L_1 = \frac{p_1 - (\beta - e - d)}{p_1} = \frac{\lambda}{1 + \lambda}\frac{1}{\eta(p_1)} + \frac{\kappa}{1 + \lambda}\left[\frac{1}{\eta(p_1)} - \frac{1 + \lambda_c}{p_1}\frac{4dq_2}{(q_1 + q_2)^2}\psi'\left(e + \frac{2d(q_1 - q_2)}{q_1 + q_2}\right)\right], \tag{A11.30}$$

$$L_2 = \frac{p_2 - (\beta - e + d)}{p_2} = \frac{\lambda}{1 + \lambda}\frac{1}{\eta(p_2)} - \frac{\kappa}{1 + \lambda}\left[\frac{1}{\eta(p_2)} - \frac{1 + \lambda_c}{p_2}\frac{4dq_1}{(q_1 + q_2)^2}\psi'\left(e + \frac{2d(q_1 - q_2)}{q_1 + q_2}\right)\right], \tag{A11.31}$$

$$\psi'(e) = q_1 + q_2 + \frac{\kappa(1 + \lambda_c)}{1 + \lambda}\left[\psi'\left(e + \frac{2d(q_1 - q_2)}{q_1 + q_2}\right) - \psi'(e)\right]. \tag{A11.32}$$

i. Let us first assume that d is small. We see that $\{q_1 = q_2 = q, p_1 = p_2 = p, e, \kappa\}$ satisfy (A11.30) through (A11.32) if

$$\frac{p - (\beta - e)}{p} = \frac{\lambda}{1 + \lambda}\frac{1}{\eta(p)}, \tag{A11.33}$$

$$\psi'(e) = 2q, \tag{A11.34}$$

$$\kappa = \frac{(1 + \lambda)d}{[-P'(q)q] - 2(1 + \lambda_c)d}. \tag{A11.35}$$

Note that p, q, and e are independent of d. The proof that uniform pricing is optimal proceeds in two steps. First, $q_1 < q_2$ is dominated by uniform pricing from the concavity of the social welfare function in a collusion-free world. Furthermore uniform pricing is collusion free. Second, for any $\varepsilon > 0$, there exists $d_0 > 0$ such that for any $d < d_0$, the optimal q_1 and q_2 satisfy $\max(|q_1 - q|, |q_2 - q|) < \varepsilon$, where q is the solution to (A11.33) and (A11.34) and is the optimal output for each category of consumers when $d = 0$. If this property were not satisfied, for some $\varepsilon > 0$, there would exist a sequence $d^n \to 0$ with optimal (q_1^n, q_2^n) such that for all n, $\max(|q_1^n - q|, |q_2^n - q|) > \varepsilon$. Since in the absence of collusion outputs must tend to q when d^n tends to zero, welfare along this sequence would be bounded away from the collusion-free welfare. But the difference between the collusion-free welfare and the welfare obtained under uniform pricing tends to zero as d^n tends to zero. Hence (q_1^n, q_2^n) must be strictly dominated by uniform pricing for n large, a contradiction. Last, now that we have established that $q_1 - q_2$ tends to zero when d^n tends to zero, which implies that κ tends to zero, we can make a first-order Taylor expansion of the coalition incentive constraint. Using (A11.32), the left-hand side of (11.36) is equal to $(1 + \lambda_c)2d(q_1 - q_2)$ to the first order, and the right-hand side of (11.36) is equal to $(-P'(q)q)(q_1 - q_2)$ to the first order. Hence, if $q_1 > q_2$ and $d \leq (-P'(q)q)/(1 + \lambda_c)$, (11.36) is not satisfied. If $q_1 < q_2$, (11.36) is not binding, implying that $\kappa = 0$ and, from (A11.30) and (A11.31), that $q_1 > q_2$, a contradiction.

ii. Consider the case in which the solution to (11.33) through (11.35) does not satisfy (11.36) for any d (so that $d_2 = +\infty$). We want to show that uniform pricing is not optimal for a large d (note that large d's raise the possibility that marginal costs become negative. We will assume that β is large enough so that this does not occur).

To this purpose, suppose that optimal pricing at p, yielding demand q, is optimal. Consider a small deviation around uniform pricing: $q_1 - q_2 = \varepsilon > 0$. The left-hand side of (11.36) is equal to $(1 + \lambda_c)\psi'(e)(2d\varepsilon/2q) = 2(1 + \lambda_c)d\varepsilon$ to the first approximation, where use is made of (A11.32) and (A11.35). Similarly the right-hand side of (11.36) is $[-P'(q)q]\varepsilon$ and is independent of d from (A11.31) and (A11.32). Hence, for d large enough, (11.36) is satisfied for small amounts of price discrimination. From the concavity of the social welfare function in the collusion-free world, a small amount of price discrimination, which, we just saw, is feasible, is preferable to uniform pricing.

Next consider the case in which there exist d's such that (11.36) is not binding for the collusion-free solution [given by (11.33) through (11.35)]. Let d_2 denote the smallest such d. We claim that for $d = d_2 - \varepsilon$ (where ε is positive and small) pricing is discriminatory. We know that at d_2, (11.36) is just binding. Because ψ is convex, e can be increased to $e + \eta$, where η is small such that

$$\psi\left(e + \eta + \frac{2(d_2 - \varepsilon)(q_1 - q_2)}{q_1 + q_2}\right) - \psi(e + \eta) = \psi\left(e + \frac{2d_2(q_1 - q_2)}{q_1 + q_2}\right) - \psi(e).$$

Equation (11.36) is still satisfied for the collusion-free levels q_1 and q_2. This implies that Congress can obtain almost the collusion-free level of welfare when d is close to d_2, which obviously is impossible under uniform pricing.

Next we observe that if (11.36) is satisfied for the collusion-free levels and parameter d, it is also satisfied for the collusion-free levels and parameter $d' > d$. This means that the set of parameters for which the collusion-free solution obtains is indeed the open interval $[d_2, +\infty)$.

Last, we want to show that there exists d_1 such that uniform pricing obtains on $[0, d_1]$ and not elsewhere. To this purpose, note that the welfare under uniform pricing is independent of d. More generally the envelope theorem shows that the derivative of the social welfare function with respect to d is equal to

$$-(1+\lambda)(q_2-q_1)+\kappa(1+\lambda_c)\psi'\left(e+\frac{2d(q_1-q_2)}{q_1+q_2}\right)\frac{2(q_1-q_2)}{q_1+q_2}>0$$

for price discrimination $q_1 > q_2$. Hence the region with discriminatory pricing and binding collusion is exactly an interval (d_1, d_2). ■

REFERENCES

Adams, G. 1981. *The Politics of Defense Contracting—The Iron Triangle.* New Brunswick: Transaction Books.

Bhagwati, J. N. 1982. Directly unproductive, profit-seeking (DUP) activities. *Journal of Political Economy* 90:988–1002.

Banks, J. 1989. Agency budgets, cost information, and auditing. *American Journal of Political Science* 50:670–699.

Banks, J., and B. Weingast. 1989. The political control of bureaucracies under asymmetric information. Mimeo, University of Rochester and Stanford University.

Barke, R., and W. Riker. 1982. A political theory of regulation with some observations on railway abandonments. *Public Choice* 39:73–106.

Baron, D. 1989. Service-induced campaign contributions and the electoral equilibrium. *Quarterly Journal of Economics* 104:45–72.

Baron, D., and J. Ferejohn. 1988. The power to propose. Mimeo, Stanford University.

Becker, G. 1983. A theory of competition among pressure groups for political influence. *Quarterly Journal of Economics* 98:371–400.

Becker, G. 1985. Public policies, pressure groups, and deadweight costs. *Journal of Public Economics* 28:329–47.

Bernstein, M. 1955. *Regulating Business by Independent Commission.* Princeton, NJ: Princeton University Press.

Breyer, S., and R. Steward. 1979. *Administrative Law and Regulatory Policy.* Boston: Little, Brown and Company.

Buchanan, J. 1965. An economic theory of clubs. *Econometrica* 33:1–14.

Buchanan, J. M. 1980. Rent-seeking under external diseconomies. In *Toward a Theory of the Rent-Seeking Society,* ed. J. M. Buchanan, R. D. Tollison, and G. Tullock. College Station: Texas A&M Press.

Delorme, C., and A. Snow. 1990. On the limits to rent-seeking waste. *Public Choice* 67:129–154.

Demski, J., and D. Sappington. 1987. Hierarchical regulatory control. *Rand Journal of Economics* 28:369–383.

Derthick, M., and P. Quirk. 1985. *The Politics of Deregulation.* Washington, DC: Brookings Institution.

Edelman, S. 1990. Gotcha! Campaign contributions, political action and house incumbents. Mimeo, Columbia University.

Fenno, R. 1966. *Power of the Purse.* Boston: Little, Brown.

Fiorina, M. 1981. Congressional control of the bureaucracy: A mismatch of incentives and capabilities. In *Congress Reconsidered,* ed. L. Dodd and B. Oppenheimer, 2d ed. Washington: Congressional Quarterly Press.

Fiorina, M. 1982. Legislative choice of regulatory forms: Legal process or administrative process? *Public Choice* 39:33–66.

Fiorina, M. 1985. Group concentration and the delegation of legislative authority. In *Regulatory Policy and the Social Sciences*, ed. Roger G. Noll. Berkeley: University of California Press.

Grossman, S., and O. Hart. 1983. An analysis of the principal-agent problem. *Econometrica* 51:7–46.

Jacoby, N., P. Nehemkis, and R. Eells. 1977. *Bribery and Extortion in World Business*. New York: Macmillan.

Joskow, P. 1972. The determination of the allowed rate of return in a formal regulatory hearing. *Bell Journal of Economics* 3:632–644.

Kaufman, H. 1961. Why organizations behave as they do: An outline of a theory. *Administrative Theory*, pp. 37–72.

Kofman, F., and J. Lawarrée. 1990. On the optimality of allowing collusion. Mimeo, University of California, Berkeley.

Klitgaard, R. 1988. *Controlling Corruption*. Berkeley: University of California Press.

Krehbiel, K. 1990. *Informational Theories and Legislative Organization*. Unpublished manuscript.

Krueger, A. O. 1974. The political economy of the rent-seeking society. *American Economic Review* 64:291– 303.

Lenoir, N. 1991. Optimal structure of regulatory agencies facing the threat of political influence. Master's thesis in the Science of Transportation, Massachusetts Institute of Technology.

McCubbins, M. 1985. Legislative design of regulatory structure. *American Journal of Political Science* 29:721–48.

McCubbins, M., R. Noll, and B. Weingast. 1987. Administrative procedures as instruments of political control. *Journal of Law, Economics, and Organization* 3:243–277.

McCubbins, M., and T. Schwartz. 1984. Congressional oversight overlooked: Police patrols vs. fire alarms. *American Journal of Political Science* 28:165–179.

McFadden, D. 1976. The revealed preferences of a government bureaucracy: empirical evidence. *Bell Journal of Economics* 6:55–72.

Milgrom, P. 1988. Employment contracts, influence activities and organization design. *Journal of Political Economy* 96:42–60.

Milgrom, P., and J. Roberts. 1988. An economic approach to influence activities in organizations. *American Journal of Sociology* 94:S154–S179.

Moe, T. 1986. Interests, institutions, and positive theory: The policies of the NLRB. Mimeo, Stanford University.

Niskanen, W. 1971. *Bureaucracy and Representative Government*. Chicago, IL: Aldine Press.

Noll, R. 1983. The political foundations of regulatory politics. *Journal of Institutional and Theoretical Economics* 139:377–404. Reprinted in *Congress*, ed. M. McCubbins and T. Sullivan. Cambridge: Cambridge University Press, 1987.

Noll, R. 1985. Behavior of administrative agencies. In *Regulation and the Social Sciences*, ed. R. Noll. Berkeley: University of California Press.

Noll, R. 1989. Economic perspectives on the politics of regulation. In *The Handbook of Industrial Organization*, ed. R. Schmalensee and R. Willig. Amsterdam: North-Holland.

Olson, M. 1965. *The Logic of Collective Action*. Cambridge, Ma: Harvard University Press.

Peltzman, S. 1976. Toward a more general theory of regulation. *Journal of Law and Economics* 19:211–240.

Peltzman, S. 1989. The economic theory of regulation after a decade of deregulation. *Brookings Papers on Economic Activity, Microeconomics*, 1–60.

Posner, R. 1974. Theories of economic regulation. *Bell Journal of Economics* 5:335–358.

Romer, T., and H. Rosenthal. 1986. Modern political economy and the study of regulation. In *Public Regulation: New Perspectives on Institutions and Policies*, ed. E. Bailey. Cambridge: Cambridge University Press.

Shepsle, K. 1978. *The Giant Jigsaw Puzzle: Democratic Committee Assignments in the Modern House.* Chicago, IL: University of Chicago Press.

Shepsle, K. 1979. Institutional arrangements and equilibrium in multidimensional voting models. *Public Choice* 37:503–520.

Shepsle, K., and B. Weingast. 1981. Structure induced equilibrium and legislative choice. *Public Choice* 37:503–520.

Snyder, J. 1990. Campaign contributions as investments: The US house of representatives, 1980–86. Mimeo, University of Chicago.

Spiller, P. 1990. Politicians, interest groups, and regulators: A multi-principals agency theory of regulation (or "let them be bribed"). *Journal of Law and Economics* 33:65–101.

Stigler, G. 1971. The economic theory of regulation. *Bell Journal of Economics* 2:3–21.

Tirole, J. 1986. Hierarchies and bureaucracies. *Journal of Law, Economics, and Organization* 2:181–214.

Tirole, J. 1990. Collusion and the theory of organizations. In *Advances in Economic Theory: Proceedings of the Sixth World Congress of the Econometric Society*, ed. J.-J. Laffont. Cambridge: Cambridge University Press.

Tollison, R. D. 1982. Rent seeking: A survey. *Kyklos* 35:575–602.

Truman, D. 1951. *The Governmental Process.* New York: Knopf.

Tullock, G. 1967. The welfare costs of tariffs, monopoly, and theft. *Western Economic Journal* 5:224–232.

Warren, K. 1982. *Administrative Law in the American Political System.* St. Paul, Minn.: West Publishing Company.

Weingast, B. 1984. The congressional-bureaucratic system: a principal-agent perspective (with applications to the SEC). *Public Choice* 44:147–192.

Weingast, B., and M. Moran. 1983. Bureaucratic discretion on congressional control: Regulatory policymaking by the federal trade commission. *Journal of Political Economy* 91:765–800.

Wilson, J. Q. 1980. The politics of regulation. In *The Politics of Regulation*, ed. J. Q. Wilson. New York: Basic Books.

12 COST PADDING, AUDITING, AND COLLUSION

12.1 Some Background

Manipulation of accounting is a serious concern in procurement and regulation,[1] as well as in large organizations, because this reduces the information value of cost data and thus the effectiveness of management control systems. The purpose of this chapter is, first, to study the effect of accounting contrivances and auditing on the power of incentive schemes, and, second, to analyze the scope for collusion between the auditor and the auditee.

The model of this book, in which cost depends on technology and effort, is a polar case where accounting manipulations that transfer money to the firm or its managers—cost padding—are perfectly and costlessly monitored. In practice there are many ways for a firm to divert money: subsidization of R&D with commercial purposes or advertising for corporate image charged to the project; transfer of funds among divisions with different cost-reimbursement rules;[2] compensation for personal services, salaries, and stock options of managers; charges for depreciated assets, royalties, bad debts, or losses on other contracts. Substantial resources are committed to audit nonallowable expenses. There further is concern not only that regulated firms unduly charge the government but also that their auditors are too lenient. For years the U.S. General Accounting Office has reported to the Congress on alleged overpricing of defense contracts and argued that the Department of Defense ought to conduct stricter audits and be harsher if the contractor submits defective data.[3] Similarly the regulatory agencies' actions to check cost padding are under surveillance.

The effect of cost padding on incentives can be apprehended by, first, recalling the basic conflict between incentives and the extraction of the firm's informational rent, and, second, noting that the existence of cost padding is closely connected to the regulator's desire to extract the rent. As we saw earlier, incentives for cost reduction (effort) are best provided

1. On procurement, see, for example, DeSouza (1985), McAfee-McMillan (1988, pp. 85–86), Overly (1987), Pace (1970), Rogerson (1990), and Trueger (1966). On regulation, see, for example, Berg and Tschirhart (1988) and Kahn (1971).

2. Differences in cost-reimbursement rules arise often in the context of defense contractors or regulated firms with commercial activities. The firm is then tempted to charge commercial costs to government contracts. The regulated and commercial divisions may be vertically related (as in the case of AT&T and Western Electric) or unrelated. Among many accounting contrivances, Sundstrand, a defense contractor, pleaded guilty in 1988 to commingling government and commercial costs. The fraud led to reparations in excess of $200 million (see *Business Week*, Jan. 23, 1989); unfortunately it is indicative of not so unusual accounting practices in procurement. Normanton (1966, chs. 7, 8) contains an extensive discussion of state audits.

3. The potential for capture creates scope for auditing by multiple, "internal" and "external," auditors as in Kofman and Lawarrée (1989). In this respect it is interesting to note that most countries have some independent or external auditor (e.g., General Accounting Office in the United States, Exchequer and Audit Department in Britain, Cour des Comptes in France, Bundesrechnungshof in Germany).

by high-powered schemes, in particular by the fixed-price contract in which the firm is residual claimant for its cost savings. High-powered schemes, however, allow large rents, which may be reduced by cost sharing between the government and the firm. Cost padding would never arise if rent extraction were not a regulatory concern: The regulator would offer a fixed-price contract, and the firm would have no incentive to engage in cost padding because it would pay the entirety of each dollar diverted. The rent extraction motive, by leading to cost sharing, breeds cost padding.

A useful observation for the analysis of cost padding is that *at a given cost* (claimed, but not necessarily allowed) efficient types engage in more cost padding than inefficient ones. This results from the fact that, to reach the same cost (i.e., actual cost plus cost padding), cost padding must be offset by more effort, which is cheaper for the efficient types to provide. (But beware: This property holds only for a given cost level. In equilibrium different types produce at different costs, and as we will see, more efficient types choose more powerful incentive schemes and engage in *less* cost padding.) Hence a deterioration in the audit of cost padding makes it more difficult to extract rent and privileges incentives over rent extraction. As intuition would suggest, incentive schemes move toward fixed-price contracts when cost padding becomes harder to detect.

The incentive effect of collusion between the auditor and the firm is more subtle. On the one hand, collusion impairs audits, which, as we have seen, raises the desirability of high-powered schemes. On the other hand, high-powered schemes induce more cost-reducing effort, which must be compensated by high transfers to the firm. These high transfers raise the stakes in collusion because the firm loses more when the auditor reveals cost padding. Thus the threat of collusion calls for low-powered schemes to reduce the stakes. Either of these two effects may dominate, so collusion may increase or decrease the power of incentive schemes.

An interesting by-product of the analysis is that maximal penalties may not be optimal even though the firm is risk neutral. High penalties create scope for collusion, and it may be cheaper to reduce penalties than pay the auditor large amounts for truthful reporting.

Our model has two moral hazard variables and studies the effect of auditing one—cost padding—on the other—cost-reducing effort. While cost padding represents the accounting transfers discussed above, the cost-reducing activity stands for the decisions that determine the real (as opposed to measured) cost: length and intensity of work, avoidance of leisurely meetings, lunches, or discussions with colleagues, willingness to learn new techniques or tackle new and challenging ideas, and so on. It is important to note that this distinction between real costs and transfers is for convenience only. In practice there is a continuum of moral hazard variables that, together with the exogenous technological conditions, determine cost. For instance, first-class travel by employees, nice offices, and entertainment expenditures fall in between these two stereotypes of cost padding and cost-reducing efforts. Where they fall depends on, first, the deadweight loss associated with the activity (would employees have flown first class anyway?) and, second, on the ease with which they are audited. The primary distinction among moral hazard variables for the purpose of this chapter is the ease of their auditing; in particular we investigate the effect of the auditing of one moral hazard variable (cost padding) on another moral hazard variable that is harder to audit (effort). The deadweight loss distinction is only a secondary concern of the analysis, but we should point out that cost padding, being based on accounting contrivances, often generates less deadweight losses than shirking.

After developing the analysis of cost padding in section 12.3, we study in section 12.4 the effect of monitoring the effort. While the monitoring of effort is in practice more difficult than the audit of cost padding (at least in the regulatory context), auditors do find evidence of low effort. They sometimes are able to obtain reliable measures of material and staff needs. They unveil overruns due to improper work supervision or to the managers' failure to read available technical reports. They find instances in which an asset is sold by the firm at a price that is revealed to be much lower than the market price by a resale on the private market a few months later. In addition to being of economic interest, the analysis of the monitoring of effort also serves as a useful reference. It is shown that, in contrast with the audit of cost padding, the monitoring of effort raises the power of incentive schemes.

12.2 The Benchmark (No Cost Padding, No Auditing)

This section is a brief reminder of the analysis in section 1.3. A project valued S by the consumers can be realized by a firm with technology

$$C = \beta - e_1. \tag{12.1}$$

Cost is determined by an efficiency parameter $\beta \in \{\underline{\beta}, \bar{\beta}\}$, $\bar{\beta} > \underline{\beta}$, known only to the firm and by an effort level e_1 which brings a disutility to the firm of $\psi(e_1)$ expressed in monetary terms, $\psi' > 0$, $\psi'' > 0$, $\psi''' \geq 0$. The regulator has prior probability ν that $\beta = \underline{\beta}$. (Since we ignore collusion in a first step, we make no distinction between the regulator and his superior.) We let $\Delta\beta = \bar{\beta} - \underline{\beta}$.

Making the accounting convention that the regulator reimburses the cost and pays in addition a net transfer t, the firm's utility level is

$$U = t - \psi(e_1). \tag{12.2}$$

Letting $1 + \lambda$ ($\lambda > 0$) denote the opportunity cost of public funds, the consumers' net utility is

$$S - (1 + \lambda)(t + \beta - e_1). \tag{12.3}$$

For a utilitarian regulator, social welfare is

$$\begin{aligned} & S - (1 + \lambda)(t + \beta - e_1) + t - \psi(e_1) \\ & \quad = S - (1 + \lambda)[\beta - e_1 + \psi(e_1)] - \lambda U. \end{aligned} \tag{12.4}$$

Under complete information about β and e_1, the regulator maximizes social welfare under the individual rationality (IR) constraint of the firm:

$$U = t - \psi(e_1) \geq 0. \tag{12.5}$$

Optimal regulation under symmetric information entails $e_1 = e^*$ with $\psi'(e^*) = 1$—namely effort is optimal (marginal cost of effort equals marginal benefit of effort)—and $t = \psi(e^*)$—namely no rent is left to the firm. We make the maintained assumption that S is sufficiently large that the regulator never wants to shut down the firm.

Assume now that the regulator does not know β and does not observe e_1. Let $(\underline{t}, \underline{C})$, $(\bar{t}, \bar{C})$ denote a pair of contracts for types $\underline{\beta}$ and $\bar{\beta}$. Incentive compatibility requires that the efficient type not gain by behaving like an inefficient one:

$$\underline{U} \equiv \underline{t} - \psi(\underline{\beta} - \underline{C}) \geq \bar{t} - \psi(\underline{\beta} - \bar{C}). \tag{12.6}$$

(We ignore the incentive compatibility constraint for the inefficient type. As is customary, it can be checked ex post that this constraint is not binding.) The individual rationality constraint for the inefficient type is

$$\bar{t} - \psi(\bar{\beta} - \bar{C}) \geq 0. \tag{12.7}$$

At the regulator's optimum, (12.6) and (12.7) are binding, and the efficient type's rent is $\underline{U} = \Phi(\bar{e}_1) = \Phi(\bar{\beta} - \bar{C})$, where

$$\Phi(e_1) \equiv \psi(e_1) - \psi(e_1 - \Delta\beta). \tag{12.8}$$

The regulator maximizes expected social welfare

$$\begin{aligned} W = {} & S - \nu[(1 + \lambda)(\underline{\beta} - \underline{e}_1 + \psi(\underline{e}_1)) + \lambda\Phi(\bar{e}_1)] \\ & - (1 - \nu)(1 + \lambda)(\bar{\beta} - \bar{e}_1 + \psi(\bar{e}_1)) \end{aligned} \tag{12.9}$$

with respect to $\underline{e}_1$ and $\bar{e}_1$, yielding

$$\psi'(\underline{e}_1) = 1 \quad \Leftrightarrow \quad \underline{e}_1 = e^* \tag{12.10}$$

and

$$\psi'(\bar{e}_1) = 1 - \frac{\lambda}{1 + \lambda}\frac{\nu}{1 - \nu}\Phi'(\bar{e}_1) \quad \Rightarrow \quad \bar{e}_1 \equiv \bar{e}_0 < e^*. \tag{12.11}$$

The efficient type's effort is not distorted by asymmetric information. The effort of the inefficient type is reduced relative to the full information optimum in order to limit the efficient type's rent: Rent extraction concerns lead to low-powered incentives.

In the entire chapter it will be optimal for the principal not to distort the efficient type's effort. The power of the optimal incentive scheme will thus be measured by the effort level of the inefficient type.

12.3 Audit of Cost Padding

12.3.1 Benevolent Audit of Cost Padding

We now let the manager engage in two activities: cost reduction ($e_1 \geq 0$) and cost padding ($e_2 \geq 0$). The cost function is

$$C = \beta - e_1 + e_2. \tag{12.12}$$

We ignore monitoring of effort (see section 12.4) and focus on the audit of cost padding. We formalize the audit technology in the following way: Given a level of cost padding e_2, the auditor receives a signal (or measured cost padding) e_2^m with conditional distribution $G(e_2^m|e_2)$ on $[0, +\infty)$. We let $T(C, e_2^m, e_2)$ denote the firm's net income when producing at cost C and choosing cost padding e_2 and when the outcome of the audit is e_2^m. The function $T(\cdot,\cdot,\cdot)$ depends on (1) the incentive scheme set up by the principal, (2) the level of limited liability of the firm, in particular whether part or all of the cost padding can be recouped by the principal when it is discovered, and (3) the deadweight loss involved in engaging in cost padding. We will later assume for concreteness that the firm consumes the level of cost padding before the audit, so the regulator cannot recoup any fraction. Then $T(C, e_2^m, e_2) = t(C, e_2^m) + h(e_2)$, where $t(\cdot,\cdot)$ is the net transfer following the audit and satisfies $t(\cdot,\cdot) \geq 0$ (from limited liability) and $0 \leq h(e_2) \leq e_2$ [so $e_2 - h(e_2)$ is the deadweight loss associated with the diversion of funds]. But at this stage we want to keep the formulation as general as possible.

For a given cost C the firm chooses a level of cost padding so as to solve

$$\max_{e_2} \int [T(C, e_2^m, e_2) - \psi(\beta - C + e_2)] dG(e_2^m|e_2). \tag{12.13}$$

Cost padding requires the firm to exert more effort to reach a given cost. This suggests that for a given cost a more efficient type will engage in more cost padding, as the marginal disutility of reducing cost is lower:

Proposition 12.1 Fix a cost C, and consider two types $\beta < \tilde{\beta}$. If e_2 and $\tilde{e}_2$ are optimal levels of cost padding for β and $\tilde{\beta}$, respectively, $e_2 \geq \tilde{e}_2$.

Proof The proof uses a simple revealed preference argument. Let $\overline{T}(C,e_2) \equiv \int T(C,e_2^m,e_2)dG(e_2^m|e_2)$. Revealed preference implies that

$$\overline{T}(C,e_2) - \psi(\beta - C + e_2) \geq \overline{T}(C,\tilde{e}_2) - \psi(\beta - C + \tilde{e}_2) \tag{12.14}$$

and

$$\overline{T}(C,\tilde{e}_2) - \psi(\tilde{\beta} - C + \tilde{e}_2) \geq \overline{T}(C,e_2) - \psi(\tilde{\beta} - C + e_2). \tag{12.15}$$

Adding up (12.14) and (12.15) and using the convexity of $\psi(\cdot)$ shows that $e_2 \geq \tilde{e}_2$. ■

Remark Although proposition 12.1 asserts that efficient types do more cost padding for a given cost level, it does not imply that efficient types do more cost padding *in equilibrium*, since in general they produce at different cost levels. Indeed we will see that in the two-type case $\underline{\beta} < \overline{\beta}$, the efficient type exerts the socially efficient level of cost-reducing effort (that which would result from a fixed-price contract) and the inefficient type exerts a suboptimal effort. Since the efficient type's marginal disutility of effort is equal to one, each dollar diverted through cost padding requires an extra effort, with monetary disutility equal to one; the efficient type thus does not engage in cost padding. In contrast, the inefficient type's marginal disutility of effort is lower than one, which may give it an incentive to engage in cost padding.

Let us now consider the two polar cases of perfect and no audit of cost padding. We will later analyze the richer case of imperfect audit.

Perfect Audit

If cost padding is perfectly observable while cost reducing effort is not observable, the principal can require $e_2 = 0$ and thus obtain the level of welfare determined in section 12.2. In particular type $\overline{\beta}$'s effort is equal to $\overline{e}_0$.

No Audit

In contrast, suppose that $e_2^m = 0$ for any e_2 (the signal is uninformative) and that the firm's utility is equal to $\{t(C) + e_2 - \psi(\beta - C + e_2)\}$, where $t(C)$ is the transfer for realized cost C. Note that this formulation of "no audit" embodies the assumption that there is no deadweight loss associated with cost padding; that is, the firm derives utility \$1 from padding cost by \$1.

Since the firm chooses e_2 so as to maximize its utility, it seems intuitive that only effort $e_1 = e^*$ (the effort corresponding to a fixed-price contract) can be implemented. Things are slightly more complicated than intuition suggests if we impose the nonnegativity constraint $e_2 \geq 0$. The maximization of the firm's utility with respect to e_2 only implies that for any β and C chosen by type β,

$$1 \leq \psi'(\beta - C + e_2) \quad \text{and} \quad e_2 = 0 \qquad \text{if } \psi'(\beta - C + e_2) > 1. \tag{12.16}$$

Let $(\bar{C}, \bar{e}_2)$ denote type $\bar{\beta}$'s equilibrium choices. Note that type $\underline{\beta}$ can mimic cost level $\bar{C}$. We claim that when doing so, it obtains at least rent $\Delta\beta$:

$$\underline{U} \geq \Delta\beta. \tag{12.17}$$

To see this, assume first that $\underline{\beta} - \bar{C} + \bar{e}_2 \geq e^*$. Then $\bar{\beta} - \bar{C} + \bar{e}_2 > e^*$, so $\bar{e}_2 = 0$ from (12.16). Furthermore type $\underline{\beta}$ can mimic both cost level $\bar{C}$ and cost padding 0, and obtain

$$\Phi(\bar{\beta} - \bar{C}) = \psi(\bar{\beta} - \bar{C}) - \psi(\underline{\beta} - \bar{C}) \geq \Delta\beta,$$

since $\underline{\beta} - \bar{C} \geq e^*$, $\psi'(e^*) = 1$, and $\psi(\cdot)$ is convex. Second, suppose that $\underline{\beta} - \bar{C} + \bar{e}_2 < e^*$ [while $\bar{\beta} - \bar{C} + \bar{e}_2 \geq e^*$ from (12.16)]. Then, when mimicking $\bar{C}$, type $\underline{\beta}$ engages in cost padding $e_2 > \bar{e}_2$, where $\underline{\beta} - \bar{C} + e_2 = e^*$. Its utility is equal to

$$[e_2 - \bar{e}_2] + [\psi(\bar{\beta} - \bar{C} + \bar{e}_2) - \psi(e^*)] \geq [e^* + \bar{C} - \underline{\beta} - \bar{e}_2]$$
$$+ [\bar{\beta} - \bar{C} + \bar{e}_2 - e^*] = \Delta\beta.$$

Now (12.17) implies that the principal's welfare is bounded above by

$$W = \max_{\{\underline{e}_1, \bar{e}_1\}} \{\nu[S - (1 + \lambda)(\underline{\beta} - \underline{e}_1 + \psi(\underline{e}_1)) - \lambda\Delta\beta]$$
$$+ (1 - \nu)[S - (1 + \lambda)(\bar{\beta} - \bar{e}_1 + \psi(\bar{e}_1))]\}. \tag{12.18}$$

Note that this maximum is reached for $\underline{e}_1 = \bar{e}_1 = e^*$. Conversely, this upper bound can be obtained by offering the fixed-price contract $t(C) = \psi(e^*) - [C - (\bar{\beta} - e^*)]$. Since the firm is residual claimant for its cost savings, it chooses $e_1 = e^*$ and $e_2 = 0$ for any type. We thus have proposition 12.2.

Proposition 12.2

i. Under perfect audit of cost padding, the outcome is the same as in the absence of cost padding (i.e., the same as determined in section 12.2). Type $\bar{\beta}$'s effort is $\bar{e}_0$.

ii. In the absence of audit of cost padding, the principal forgoes rent extraction and offers a single fixed-price contract. In particular type $\bar{\beta}$'s effort is equal to $e^* > \bar{e}_0$.

This proposition gives a simple illustration of the idea that unfettered cost padding leads to an increase in the power of incentive schemes.

Imperfect Auditing

We now study a simple model with two levels of cost padding: $e_2 = 0$ and $e_2 = \alpha > 0$. The audit yields one of two signals: $e_2^m = 0$ and $e_2^m = \alpha$. We let $x = \text{Prob}(e_2^m = 0 | e_2 = 0)$ and $y = \text{Prob}(e_2^m = 0 | e_2 = \alpha)$, and assume that

$1 > x > y > 0$.[4] That is, we allow for the possibility of mistakes, and we assume that the auditing technology satisfies the monotone likelihood ratio property (MLRP) that actual cost padding makes a cost-padding signal more likely.

For a given cost $C = \beta - e_1 + e_2$, the principal gives transfers to the firm, t_0 when $e_2^m = 0$ and t_α when $e_2^m = \alpha$. The firm's expected utility is then

$$U = \begin{cases} xt_0 + (1-x)t_\alpha - \psi(\beta - C) & \text{if } e_2 = 0, \\ yt_0 + (1-y)t_\alpha + \alpha' - \psi(\beta - C + \alpha) & \text{if } e_2 = \alpha. \end{cases}$$

We impose the limited liability constraints $t_0,\ t_\alpha \geq 0$, and assume that $0 \leq \alpha' \leq \alpha$. Several comments are in order. First, we allow cost padding to create a deadweight loss ($\alpha' < \alpha$). For instance, transfers of money from one account under contract into an unregulated account involve no deadweight loss ($\alpha' = \alpha$) if they are routine accounting manipulations, but such account transfers do impose a deadweight loss if they require a substantial amount of accounting expertise and time. Similarly cost padding through increases in managerial compensation creates a deadweight loss if the need to hide these increases creates an inefficient structure of managerial compensation. Second, we assume that α' is consumed by the firm before the audit and cannot be recouped by the principal. It is straightforward to extend the model to allow partial or full recovery of the money set aside.

Assuming auditing is costless, the regulator's objective function is

$$\begin{aligned} W &= S - (1+\lambda)(C + Et) + U \\ &= \begin{cases} S - (1+\lambda)(\beta - e_1 + \psi(e_1)) - \lambda U & \text{if } e_2 = 0, \\ S - (1+\lambda)(\beta - e_1 + \alpha - \alpha' + \psi(e_1)) - \lambda U & \text{if } e_2 = \alpha. \end{cases} \end{aligned} \tag{12.19}$$

In a first step we assume that the auditor does not collude with the firm, and consider several regimes. (The appendix to this chapter contains more detailed arguments.)

In the *cost-padding regime* type $\bar{\beta}$ engages in cost padding ($e_2 = \alpha$), and so would type $\underline{\beta}$ if it were to mimic type $\bar{\beta}$ (from proposition 12.1). The regulatory outcome is then the same as in the absence of cost padding (see section 12.2), except for the deadweight loss $(1-\nu)(1+\lambda)(\alpha - \alpha')$.[5] This

4. Note that we do not optimize on the auditing technology. Also we restrict attention to two levels of cost padding to avoid possible nonconcavities in the choice among a continuum of levels.

5. The intuition for this result is as follows: The inefficient type's allocation of effort is distorted to limit the efficient type's rent of asymmetric information $\underline{U}$. This rent, which equals the efficient type's utility level when it mimics the inefficient type, is as in section 12.2:

$$\begin{aligned} \underline{U} &= y\bar{t}_0 + (1-y)\bar{t}_\alpha + \alpha' - \psi(\underline{\beta} - \bar{C} + \alpha) \\ &= \psi(\bar{\beta} - \bar{C} + \alpha) - \psi(\underline{\beta} - \bar{C} + \alpha) \\ &= \psi(\bar{e}_1) - \psi(\bar{e}_1 - \Delta\beta) = \Phi(\bar{e}_1). \end{aligned}$$

regime is optimal if either cost padding is hard to detect (y close to x) or harmless (α' close to α).

We now study more interesting regimes, in which type $\bar{\beta}$ does not engage in cost padding. Let $\bar{C} = \bar{\beta} - \bar{e}_1$ denote the cost realized by type $\bar{\beta}$ and $(\bar{t}_0, \bar{t}_\alpha)$ the associated transfers. We have

$$\bar{U} = x\bar{t}_0 + (1 - x)\bar{t}_\alpha - \psi(\bar{e}_1) = 0. \tag{12.20}$$

Type $\underline{\beta}$'s rent is determined by its possibility of mimicking type $\bar{\beta}$. When choosing cost $\bar{C}$, it can choose either $e_2 = 0$ or $e_2 = \alpha$. Therefore, using (12.20), we obtain two lower bounds for its rent according to the way it mimics the inefficient type:

$$\underline{U} \geq \Phi(\bar{e}_1) \tag{12.21}$$

and

$$\underline{U} \geq y\bar{t}_0 + (1 - y)\bar{t}_\alpha + \alpha' - \psi(\bar{e}_1 - \Delta\beta + \alpha) = \Gamma(\bar{e}_1, \bar{t}_\alpha), \tag{12.22}$$

where

$$\Gamma(\bar{e}_1, \bar{t}_\alpha) \equiv \left[\frac{y}{x}\psi(\bar{e}_1) - \psi(\bar{e}_1 - \Delta\beta + \alpha)\right] + \left[(1 - y) - y\frac{(1 - x)}{x}\right]\bar{t}_\alpha + \alpha'. \tag{12.23}$$

We can now define the *classical regime* in which (12.22) is not binding. In this case the optimal regulatory outcome is the same as when cost padding is infeasible and is determined in section 12.2.[6] A necessary and sufficient condition for the classical regime to obtain is that type $\underline{\beta}$ does not want to deviate to cost $\bar{C}$ and cost padding α. That is, using (12.20),

$$\Phi(\bar{e}_0) \geq \left[\frac{y}{x}\psi(\bar{e}_0) - \psi(\bar{e}_0 - \Delta\beta + \alpha)\right] + \alpha' \tag{12.24}$$

[since $x > y$, $\Gamma(\bar{e}_0, \cdot)$ is minimized at $\bar{t}_\alpha = 0$]. Recalling that $\Phi(\bar{e}_0) = \psi(\bar{e}_0) - \psi(\bar{e}_0 - \Delta\beta)$, and that ψ is convex, we conclude that the classical regime obtains if cost padding can be detected well (y/x small) or if it entails a substantial deadweight loss (α' much smaller than α).

The third regime, the *repressed cost-padding regime*, defined by the conditions that type $\bar{\beta}$ does not engage in cost padding but (12.22) is binding, is the only nontrivial regime. Let κ and ζ denote the Lagrange multipliers of constraints (12.21) and (12.22). The principal maximizes

$$\begin{aligned} W = {} & \nu[S - (1 + \lambda)(\underline{\beta} - e^* + \psi(e^*)) - \lambda\underline{U}] \\ & + (1 - \nu)[S - (1 + \lambda)(\bar{\beta} - \bar{e}_1 + \psi(\bar{e}_1))] \\ & + \kappa[\underline{U} - \Phi(\bar{e}_1)] + \zeta[\underline{U} - \Gamma(\bar{e}_1, \bar{t}_\alpha)]. \end{aligned} \tag{12.25}$$

6. The reasoning is the same as in footnote 5, except that $\bar{e}_2 = 0$ instead of $\bar{e}_2 = \alpha$.

As before, the monotone likelihood ratio property implies that punishments are maximal: $\bar{t}_\alpha = 0$. The derivatives of W with respect to $\underline{U}$ and $\bar{e}_1$ are

$$-\lambda v + \kappa + \zeta = 0, \tag{12.26}$$

$$(1 - v)(1 + \lambda)[1 - \psi'(\bar{e}_1)] - \kappa\Phi'(\bar{e}_1) - \zeta\frac{\partial\Gamma}{\partial\bar{e}_1}(\bar{e}_1, 0) = 0, \tag{12.27}$$

and therefore

$$\psi'(\bar{e}_1) = 1 - \frac{\lambda v}{(1 + \lambda)(1 - v)}\Phi'(\bar{e}_1) + \frac{\zeta}{(1 + \lambda)(1 - v)}\left[\Phi'(\bar{e}_1) - \frac{\partial\Gamma}{\partial\bar{e}_1}(\bar{e}_1, 0)\right]. \tag{12.28}$$

Equation (12.28) and the fact that $\Phi'(e_1) > \partial\Gamma(e_1, 0)/\partial e_1$ for all $e_1 \geq 0$ yield our main conclusion: Incentives are more powerful under imperfect auditing than under perfect auditing. A corollary is that the efficient type's rent is higher under imperfect auditing than under perfect auditing.

The intuition for this result is that increasing $\bar{e}_1$ is more attractive under cost padding for two reasons. First, increasing $\bar{e}_1$ raises the transfer $\psi(\bar{e}_1)/x$ to the inefficient type when no cost padding is discovered. Since, from proposition 12.1, the efficient type tends to do more cost padding, cost padding (which raises the probability of not receiving the transfer) becomes more costly to the efficient type, which reduces its rent. Second, cost padding raises the marginal disutility $\psi'(\bar{e}_1 - \Delta\beta + e_2)$ of the efficient type to mimic the inefficient type. Again an increase in $\bar{e}_1$ increases the efficient type's rent by less than in the absence of cost padding.

Proposition 12.3 In the absence of collusion, punishments are maximal ($\bar{t}_\alpha = 0$). The inefficient type's effort exceeds that under perfect auditing of cost padding: $\bar{e}_1 \geq \bar{e}_0$ (and the efficient type's effort is still the socially optimal one).

12.3.2 Collusion in Auditing

Let us now allow collusion between the firm and the auditor. We assume that the auditor's utility function is $V(s) = s$, where $s \geq 0$ is his or her income. (The benevolent auditor case of section 12.3.1 thus corresponds to a flat wage $s \equiv 0$ inducing truthful revelation of the outcome of the audit.) The auditor may be captured by the firm. Let $1 + \lambda_f$ be the marginal cost of internal side payments in the auditor-firm coalition ($\lambda_f \geq 0$ can be thought of as an organization or distribution cost; see chapter 11). Suppose that when $e_2^m = \alpha$, the auditor can pretend that no cost padding has been observed. That is, the auditor's report satisfies $r(\alpha) \in \{0, \alpha\}$ [while $r(0) = 0$; the report "0" corresponds to the report "$\varnothing$" in chapter 11, in that both claim ignorance]. To prevent collusion, the principal must give income s_α to the auditor when $r = \alpha$ that satisfies

$$s_\alpha \geq \frac{\bar{t}_0 - \bar{t}_\alpha}{1 + \lambda_f}, \tag{12.29}$$

where λ_f is the organization cost. We assume that the auditor has the bargaining power; that is, the auditor makes a take-it-or-leave-it offer of a collusive arrangement to the firm.

Welfare in the *cost-padding regime* is not affected by the possibility of collusion because the principal, who allows cost padding by type $\bar{\beta}$, may as well choose $\bar{t}_0 = \bar{t}_\alpha$ [$= \psi(\bar{e}_1) - \alpha'$]. Therefore $s_\alpha = 0$ does not give rise to collusive behavior. In the classical and repressed cost-padding regimes, neither type engages in cost padding. But s_α must be paid with the probability $(1 - \nu)(1 - x)$ of mistake in the repressed cost-padding regime. Hence $\lambda(1 - \nu)(1 - x)s_\alpha$ must be subtracted from the social welfare function.[7]

The *classical regime* prevails for a smaller set of parameters than in the absence of collusion. It requires the constraint

$$\Phi(\bar{e}_1) \geq y\bar{t}_0 + (1 - y)\bar{t}_\alpha + \alpha' - \psi(\bar{e}_1 - \Delta\beta + \alpha), \tag{12.30}$$

to be nonbinding. Since this constraint is nonbinding, $\bar{t}_\alpha = \bar{t}_0$ (in order to reduce s_α), $\bar{e}_1 = \bar{e}_0$, and therefore a necessary and sufficient condition for the classical regime to prevail is

$$\Phi(\bar{e}_0) \geq \psi(\bar{e}_0) - \psi(\bar{e}_0 - \Delta\beta + \alpha) + \alpha', \tag{12.31}$$

or

$$\psi(\bar{e}_0 - \Delta\beta + \alpha) - \psi(\bar{e}_0 - \Delta\beta) \geq \alpha', \tag{12.32}$$

which holds for a smaller set of parameters than (12.24). The classical regime thus prevails if α' is much smaller than α.

Last, we turn to the *repressed cost-padding regime*. The constraints are still (12.21) and (12.22), together with

$$s_\alpha \geq \frac{\psi(\bar{e}_1) - \bar{t}_\alpha}{x(1 + \lambda_f)}, \tag{12.33}$$

where use is made of the individual rationality constraint (12.20). Letting κ and ζ denote the shadow prices of (12.21) and (12.22) for the new program, the principal maximizes

$$\tilde{W} = W - \lambda(1 - \nu)(1 - x)\frac{\psi(\bar{e}_1) - \bar{t}_\alpha}{x(1 + \lambda_f)}, \tag{12.34}$$

7. This results from our assumption that the regulator cannot impose negative transfers to the auditor when no cost padding is found. The auditor's limited liability (or, similarly, risk aversion) ensures that the regulator cannot perfectly recoup expected rewards through an ex ante contract.

where W is given in (12.25), with respect to $\bar{e}_1$, and

$$\bar{t}_\alpha \in \left[0, \frac{x(\psi(\bar{e}_1 + \alpha) - \alpha') - y\psi(\bar{e}_1)}{x - y}\right],$$

where the upper bound in this interval reflects the constraint that type $\bar{\beta}$ does not engage in cost padding. For a given $\bar{e}_1$, $\tilde{W}$ is linear in $\bar{t}_\alpha$. The solution is therefore a corner solution. The coefficient of $\bar{t}_\alpha$ is

$$\frac{\lambda(1 - x)}{x(1 + \lambda_f)} - \zeta\left[(1 - y) - (1 - v)y\left(\frac{1 - x}{x}\right)\right],$$

which may be positive or negative depending on the values of the parameters (recall that $\zeta = \lambda v - \kappa$). In particular optimal penalties may be limited (but not equal to zero, unlike in the full cost-padding regime).

If the optimum specifies $\bar{t}_\alpha = 0$ (maximal penalty), then the maximization of $\tilde{W}$ with respect to $\bar{e}_1$ shows that $\bar{e}_1$ is smaller than in the absence of collusion (as can be shown by a simple revealed preference argument). On the contrary, when the optimum specifies $\bar{t}_\alpha \neq 0$ (and this happens for low values of λ_f), the effect on $\bar{e}_1$ is ambiguous. Last, we note that the welfare in the repressed-cost-padding regime increases with λ_f, while that in the cost-padding region is independent of λ_f. Therefore the set of parameters such that the repressed-cost-padding regime is optimal shrinks.

We have seen that $\bar{e}_1$ is altered by collusion in the repressed-cost-padding regime and is unaffected in the other two regimes. What remains to be analyzed is the effect on $\bar{e}_1$ of a regime switch induced by collusion. If the regime switches from classical to repressed cost padding, $\bar{e}_1$ increases, and it decreases when the regime switches from repressed cost padding to cost padding, when parameters are such that maximal penalties are used.

We gather our main results in the next proposition:

Proposition 12.4 When collusion becomes easier ($\lambda_f \downarrow$),

i. the classical region shrinks,

ii. the cost-padding region expands,

iii. limited but nonzero penalties may be optimal,

and, when maximal penalties are used,

iv. the power of incentive schemes decreases in the repressed-cost-padding regime when maximal penalties (resp. when limited penalties) are optimal, and remains unchanged in the classical and cost-padding regimes,

v. the power of incentive schemes decreases if the regime switches from repressed cost padding to cost padding, and increases when the regime switches from classical to repressed cost padding.

Figure 12.1 describes how the inefficient type's level of effort is affected by

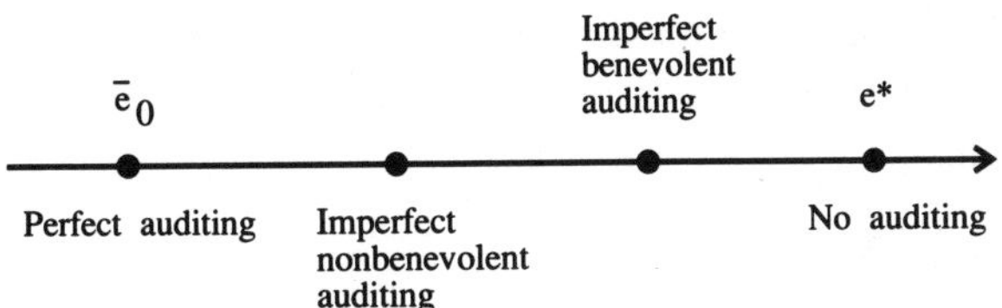

Figure 12.1
Effect of auditing on the power of the incentive scheme

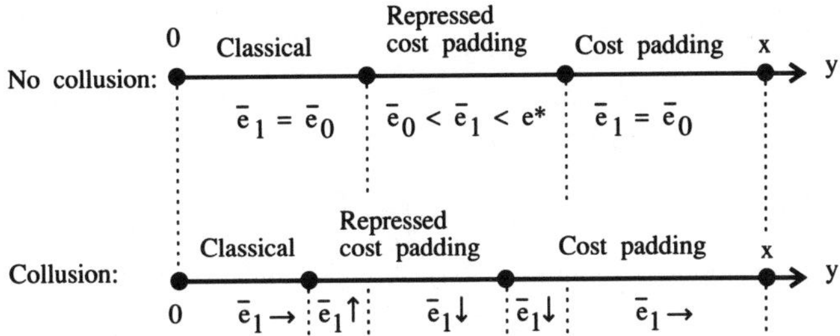

Figure 12.2
Effect of the probability of undetected cost padding on the power of the incentive scheme

cost padding in the repressed-cost-padding regime when maximal penalties are used. Figure 12.2 summarizes proposition 12.4, taking the probability y as variable (similar figures could be drawn for other parameters, e.g., α').

When the probability of catching cost padding is very low (y high) cost padding occurs for type $\bar{\beta}$: This is the cost-padding regime. The effort level of type $\bar{\beta}$ is the same as without cost padding. The marginal disutility of effort for type $\underline{\beta}$ is equal to 1, and therefore type $\underline{\beta}$ has no incentive for cost padding.

When the probability of catching cost padding increases, type $\bar{\beta}$ no longer engages in cost padding. This first gives rise to the repressed-cost-padding regime in which type $\underline{\beta}$ might want to do some cost padding if it were mimicking type $\bar{\beta}$. To make this mimicking more costly, the effort level of type $\bar{\beta}$ is increased, decreasing the rent that type $\underline{\beta}$ would obtain from engaging in cost padding and mimicking type $\bar{\beta}$. In equilibrium type $\underline{\beta}$ exerts the efficient level of effort and does no cost padding.

When the probability of catching cost padding becomes even higher, we switch to the classical regime in which type $\underline{\beta}$ would not pad costs if it were to mimic type $\bar{\beta}$. The effort level of type $\bar{\beta}$ and the rent of type $\underline{\beta}$ return to the levels that obtain when cost padding is impossible.

12.4 Monitoring of Effort

Last, we study the regulator's monitoring of the firm's effort. For clarity we assume away cost padding ($e_2 = 0$, which implies that monitoring of effort is equivalent to monitoring of the technology). Accordingly we will drop the subscript "1" from the effort variable, since there is no possibility of confusion.

12.4.1 Benevolent Monitoring of Effort

With probability z, the regulator perfectly observes the effort exerted by the firm, and with probability $1 - z$, the regulator obtains no new information. When an inappropriate level of effort is discovered, the regulator can impose a penalty as large as the net transfer, but no larger since the firm is protected by limited liability.

Let $(\underline{t}, \underline{C})$, $(\bar{t}, \bar{C})$ denote a pair of contracts for types $\underline{\beta}$ and $\bar{\beta}$. The generalization of the incentive compatibility condition (12.6) is

$$\underline{t} - \psi(\underline{\beta} - \underline{C}) \geq (1 - z)[\bar{t} - \psi(\underline{\beta} - \bar{C})] - z\psi(\underline{\beta} - \bar{C}). \tag{12.35}$$

This formulation presumes the obvious facts that (in the absence of collusion) the efficient type faces the maximal penalty when it is caught lying about its effort level and that the inefficient type's incentive compatibility constraint is not binding.

The individual rationality constraints are

$$\underline{t} - \psi(\underline{\beta} - \underline{C}) \geq 0, \tag{12.36}$$

$$\bar{t} - \psi(\bar{\beta} - \bar{C}) \geq 0. \tag{12.37}$$

The regulator maximizes expected social welfare

$$W = \nu\{S - (1 + \lambda)[\underline{C} + \psi(\underline{\beta} - \underline{C})] - \lambda[(1 - z)\psi(\bar{\beta} - \bar{C}) - \psi(\underline{\beta} - \bar{C})]\}$$
$$+ (1 - \nu)\{S - (1 + \lambda)[\bar{C} + \psi(\bar{\beta} - \bar{C})]\}, \tag{12.38}$$

which is obtained from (12.35) and (12.37). We ignore (12.36) [if z is sufficiently large, the right-hand side of (12.35) is negative, and (12.36) must be reintroduced]. That is, we assume that monitoring of effort does not solve the rent extraction problem perfectly.

An interior maximum must satisfy[8]

$$\psi'(\underline{e}) = \psi'(\underline{\beta} - \underline{C}) = 1 \quad \Leftrightarrow \quad \underline{e} = e^*, \tag{12.39}$$

$$\psi'(\bar{e}) = \psi'(\bar{\beta} - \bar{C}) = 1 - \frac{\lambda}{1 + \lambda}\frac{\nu}{1 - \nu}[\Phi'(\bar{e}) - z\psi'(\bar{e})] \quad \Rightarrow \quad \bar{e} > \bar{e}_0. \tag{12.40}$$

As z increases, $\bar{e}$ increases from $\bar{e}_0$ and reaches e^* for

$$z^* = 1 - \frac{\psi'(e^* - \Delta\beta)}{\psi'(e^*)}. \tag{12.41}$$

8. We assume that z does not interfere with the concavity of social welfare in $\bar{e}$ (e.g., which is the case if $\nu \leq \frac{1}{2}$).

Monitoring of effort enables the regulator to reduce the informational rent and consequently leads to a smaller distortion of effort for the inefficient type. If $\Lambda(z)$ is the (increasing and convex) monetary cost of a monitoring scheme with parameter z, the optimal z is defined by

$$(1 + \lambda)\Lambda'(z) = \lambda\nu\psi(\bar{e}), \tag{12.42}$$

from the envelope theorem.

12.4.2 Collusion in Monitoring of Effort

So far we have assumed that the monitoring of effort was costly but benevolent. Suppose now that the monitoring is realized by a supervisor who can claim that she did not observe the effort level even if she did. As in subsection 12.3.2 we assume that the supervisor's utility function is $V(s) = s$, $s \geq 0$, where s is her income. When she observes the effort level, this is hard information and she cannot lie about its level. The supervisor may now be captured by the firm. Let $(1 + \lambda_f)$ be the marginal cost of transfers from the firm to the supervisor. Suppose that the supervisor is given income:

$$s \geq \frac{\bar{t}}{1 + \lambda_f} = \frac{\psi(\bar{e})}{1 + \lambda_f}, \tag{12.43}$$

when revealing that the firm lied about its effort and 0 otherwise. Suppose further that the incentive scheme for the firm is unchanged. In particular the firm receives no transfer when caught lying. Then collusion does not occur, since the efficient firm does not lie in equilibrium, the income s is never paid, and collusion can be fended off costlessly.

However, suppose that the supervisor can ex ante give the efficient type a side payment to produce at cost $\overline{C}$, that is, to exert a low effort level. Let $1 + \lambda_a$ be the marginal cost of transfers from the supervisor to the firm. Suppose that the firm has all the bargaining power. To prevent this type of collusion, the firm's rent must now be[9]

$$\underline{U} = \Phi(\bar{e}) - z\psi(\bar{e}) + z\frac{\psi(\bar{e})}{(1 + \lambda_f)(1 + \lambda_a)}. \tag{12.44}$$

This creates an additional social loss of

$$\nu\lambda z\frac{\psi(\bar{e})}{(1 + \lambda_f)(1 + \lambda_a)},$$

leading to an optimal effort level defined by

9. We assume here that (for $\beta = \underline{\beta}$) this type of collusion occurs only when the supervisor discovers the effort level, that is, with probability z, hence the additional rent $z(\psi(\bar{e}))/[(1 + \lambda_f)(1 + \lambda_a)]$. However, it is never in the interest of the firm to provide verifiable information about the effort level to the supervisor.

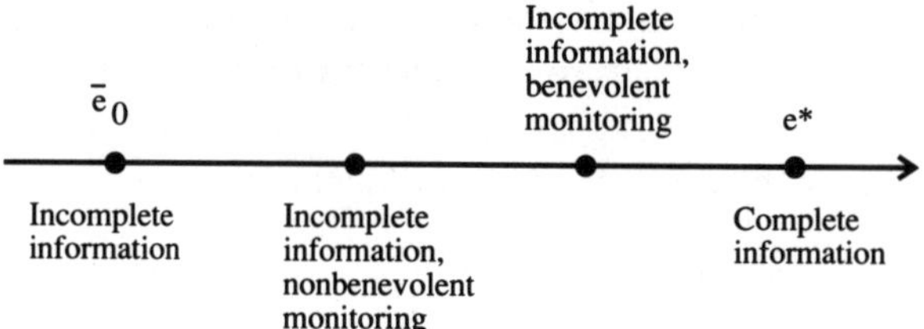

Figure 12.3
Information, collusion, and the power of the incentive scheme

$$\psi'(\bar{e}) = 1 - \frac{\lambda}{1+\lambda}\frac{\nu}{1-\nu}\left\{\Phi'(\bar{e}) - z\psi'(\bar{e})\left[1 - \frac{1}{(1+\lambda_f)(1+\lambda_a)}\right]\right\}. \quad (12.45)$$

The threat of collusion reduces the value of monitoring for the principal and induces a move toward the optimal contract without monitoring. The optimal level of monitoring is now defined by

$$(1+\lambda)\Lambda'(z) = \lambda\nu\psi(\bar{e})\left[1 - \frac{1}{(1+\lambda_f)(1+\lambda_a)}\right]. \quad (12.46)$$

Straightforward revealed preference arguments lead to proposition 12.5.

Proposition 12.5 For an interior optimum,

i. when the costs of side transfers (λ_a or λ_f) increase, monitoring expenditures (as measured by z) increase, and incentives schemes become more powerful.

ii. when the marginal cost of monitoring increases, incentive schemes become less powerful, and monitoring expenditures decrease.

iii. when uncertainty increases ($\Delta\beta\uparrow$), incentive schemes become less powerful, and there is less monitoring.

The intuition for these results of proposition 12.5 is as follows: The cross-partial derivative of the social welfare function with respect to z and $\bar{e}$ [which is equal to $\nu\lambda(1 - [1/(1+\lambda_f)(1+\lambda_a)])\psi'(\bar{e})$] is positive. Thus, ceteris paribus, an increase in monitoring raises the desirability of powerful incentives, and powerful incentives raise the benefit of monitoring. Another way of looking at this is to note that monitoring and low incentives are substitute instruments to extract the firm's rent. An increase in the use of one instrument makes the other instrument less attractive. The analysis is summarized in figure 12.3 which describes the inefficient type's effort level.

BIBLIOGRAPHIC NOTES

B12.1 Auditing Models

There is a vast literature (e.g., see Antle 1982, 1984; Fellingham and Newman 1985; Kumar 1989; Wilson 1983) on the analysis of auditing in a principal-agent framework. Bolton (1986), Guasch and Weiss (1982), Mirrlees (1974), Nalebuff and Scharfstein (1987), and Polinsky and Shavell (1979) study testing with adverse selection when there is no limited liability constraint. In contrast, some of the literature on crime deterrence (see Malik 1990 for a recent contribution) assumes risk neutrality and limited liability. Fudenberg and Tirole (1992) attribute intertemporal manipulations of income reports to career concerns.

A difference between subsection 12.4.1 and the literature on auditing of private information parameters or of effort (Baron and Besanko 1984; Kofman and Lawarrée 1989) is that the maximal penalty is endogenous. While this literature assumes a transfer-independent penalty, we interpret limited liability as the regulator's inability to extract money from the agent, implying that the maximal penalty is the retention of the transfer. The results are accordingly different. Baron and Besanko and Kofman and Lawarrée prove a "separation property": When the quality of monitoring improves (z increases in our model), the principal first extracts more and more informational rents and does not change the allocation (effort, output). Only when informational rents are extracted is the allocation affected. In contrast, our assumption that the penalty is the absence of reward implies that both the allocation (here, effort) and the informational rent are affected simultaneously.[10]

Little has been written on the interaction between the power of incentive schemes and auditing. An exception is Lewis (1990; see review problem 4), who develops a model of cost inflation in which the regulated firm engages in two activities. In our notation the firm's utility is $U = t(C) + e_2 - \zeta e_2^2 - \gamma(\beta - C + e_2)^2$. That is, any cost inflation is consumed by the firm (with some deadweight loss). There is no (explicit) audit. Lewis shows that $e_2 > 0$ except for the most efficient type, that e_2 is positively correlated with actual costs $(C - e_2)$, that the regulator can use a menu of linear contracts, and that incentive schemes become less powerful with increases in ζ.

10. At the end of their paper Kofman and Lawarrée break the separation result in another way, by assuming that the principal cannot commit not to renegotiate.

B12.2 Collusion and Nonmaximal Penalties

Subsection 12.3.2 shows that it may be strictly optimal to choose a penalty intermediate between no penalty and the maximal penalty. Kofman and Lawarrée (1989) exhibit a situation in which the principal is indifferent between the maximal penalty or a lower penalty when the auditor and the agent can collude. As they show, this weak optimality of nonmaximal penalties can be made strict by assuming that the auditor pays a fee for the right to audit.

APPENDIX

Proof of Proposition 12.3

Four types of optima are possible:

Type 1. There is no cost padding.

Type 2. There is cost padding by the inefficient type only.

Type 3. There is cost padding by the efficient type only.

Type 4. There is cost padding by both types.

Lemma 12.1 For each type of optimum, the efficient type faces a fixed price contract and therefore does not engage in cost padding.

Proof For each type of optimum, the proof is similar to the one in section 12.2. The key observation is that the regulator's welfare is affected by incomplete information only through the rent of the efficient type. This rent depends only on the effort level of the inefficient type. So the maximization with respect to the efficient type's effort level is as under complete information. ■

From Lemma 12.1 we can restrict attention to equilibria of types 1 and 2.

Lemma 12.2 Penalties can always be chosen to be maximal.

Proof The two binding constraints are the inefficient type's IR constraint and the efficient type's IC constraint. Moreover transfers are costly. The IR constraint can be satisfied at the same expected cost with $\bar{t}_\alpha = 0$ by adjusting appropriately $\bar{t}_0$.

In a type 2 optimum, where the bad type engages in cost padding, we know from proposition 12.1 that the efficient type will want to pad costs as well when mimicking the inefficient type. Choosing $\bar{t}_\alpha = 0$ thus does not affect the incentive constraint. The situation is similar in the type 1 optimum when the efficient type decides not to pad costs when mimicking the inefficient type.

In the type 1 optimum, when the efficient type desires to pad costs when mimicking the inefficient type, choosing $\bar{t}_\alpha = 0$ relaxes the IC constraint because of the MLRP property: The IC constraint is then

$$\underline{U} \geq y\bar{t}_0 + (1-y)\bar{t}_\alpha - \psi(\bar{e}_1 - \Delta\beta + \alpha) + \alpha'$$
$$= \frac{y}{x}\psi(\bar{e}_1) - \psi(\bar{e}_1 - \Delta\beta + \alpha) + \left[(1-y) - y\frac{(1-x)}{x}\right]\bar{t}_\alpha + \alpha',$$

which is obtained from the inefficient type's IR constraint. From the MLRP property $1 - y - y[(1-x)/x] > 0$. ■

Now consider type 2 equilibria. From proposition 12.1 we know that the efficient type will pad costs when mimicking the inefficient type. The IC constraint, which defines the efficient type's rent, is therefore

$$\underline{U} = y\bar{t}_0 + (1-y)\bar{t}_\alpha + \alpha' - \psi(\bar{e}_1 - \Delta\beta). \quad \text{(A12.1)}$$

The other binding constraint is the inefficient type's IR constraint:

$$y\bar{t}_0 + (1-y)\bar{t}_\alpha + \alpha' = \psi(\bar{e}_1). \quad \text{(A12.2)}$$

Using (A12.2) the efficient type's rent can be written

$$\underline{U} = \psi(\bar{e}_1) - \psi(\bar{e}_1 - \Delta\beta).$$

The regulator's program is then

$$\max_{\{\bar{e}_1, \underline{e}_1\}} \{\nu[S - (1+\lambda)(\underline{\beta} - \underline{e}_1 + \psi(\underline{e}_1)) - \lambda(\psi(\bar{e}_1) - \psi(\bar{e}_1 - \Delta\beta))]$$
$$+ (1-\nu)[S - (1+\lambda)(\bar{\beta} - \bar{e}_1 + \psi(\bar{e}_1))] - (1-\nu)(1+\lambda)(\alpha - \alpha')\},$$

where $\alpha - \alpha'$ is the effective cost increase due to (inefficient) cost padding. Type $\bar{\beta}$ increases cost by α but benefits only by α' (which is therefore the maximal amount by which its transfer can be decreased while still respecting its IR constraint).

This program differs from the no-cost-padding model only through the constant $-(1-\nu)(1+\lambda)(\alpha - \alpha')$, which leads to $\underline{e}_1 = e^*$ and $\bar{e}_1 = \bar{e}_0$. This case occurs when type $\bar{\beta}$ desires to pad costs, that is, when $yt_0 + \alpha' - \psi(\bar{e}_0) \geq xt_0 - \psi(\bar{e}_0 - \alpha)$ or, using the IR constraint, $yt_0 + \alpha' - \psi(\bar{e}_0) = 0$:

$$0 \geq \frac{x}{y}[\psi(\bar{e}_0) - \alpha'] - \psi(\bar{e}_0 - \alpha).$$

Therefore cost padding by type $\bar{\beta}$ occurs for y close to x and α' close to α, that is, when cost padding is difficult to detect or not socially costly. We refer to this case as the cost-padding regime.

Consider now type 1 equilibria. The inefficient type does not engage in cost padding. We must distinguish between two subcases. The rent of the efficient type must be such that it does not wish to mimic the inefficient type either without cost padding,

$$\underline{U} \geq \Phi(\bar{e}_1), \quad \text{(A12.3)}$$

or with cost padding,

$$\underline{U} \geq y\bar{t}_0 + (1-y)\bar{t}_\alpha + \alpha' - \psi(\bar{e}_1 - \Delta\beta + \alpha). \quad \text{(A12.4)}$$

Moreover the inefficient type's IR constraint must be binding:

$$\bar{U} = x\bar{t}_0 + (1-x)\bar{t}_\alpha - \psi(\bar{e}_1) = 0. \quad \text{(A12.5)}$$

If (A12.4) is not binding, then $\underline{U} = \Phi(\bar{e}_1)$ as in the case where cost padding is not feasible. The optimal regulation is as in section 12.2. We call this regime the *classical regime*, and it obtains if type $\underline{\beta}$ does not want to pad costs when mimicking the inefficient type:

$$\Phi(\bar{e}_0) \geq \frac{y}{x}\psi(\bar{e}_0) - \psi(\bar{e}_0 - \Delta\beta + \alpha) + \alpha',$$

where use is made of (A12.5). If (A12.4) is binding, we get the repressed-cost-padding regime (see the text). ■

REFERENCES

Antle, R. 1982. The auditor as an economic agent. *Journal of Accounting Research*, Autumn, Part II.

Antle, R. 1984. Auditor independence. *Journal of Accounting Research*, Spring.

Baron, D., and D. Besanko. 1984. Regulation, asymmetric information, and auditing. *Rand Journal of Economics* 15:447–470.

Berg, S., and J. Tschirhart. 1988. *Natural Monopoly Regulation.* Cambridge: Cambridge University Press.

Bolton, P. 1986. Random inspection in the principal-agent relationship. Chapter 1, Ph.D. dissertation, London School of Economics.

DeSouza, P. 1985. Regulating fraud in military procurement: A legal process model. *Yale Law Journal* 95:390–413.

Fellingham, J., and D. P. Newman. 1985. Strategic considerations in auditing. *Accounting Review*, October, 634–650.

Fudenberg, D., and J. Tirole. 1992. A theory of income and dividend smoothing based on incumbency rents. Mimeo, Massachusetts Institute of Technology and Institut d'Économie Industrielle, Toulouse.

Guasch, J. L., and A. Weiss. 1982. Existence of an optimal random monitor: the labour market case. Mimeo, University of California, San Diego.

Kahn, A. 1971. *The Economics of Regulation: Principles and Institutions.* New York: Wiley. Reprint Cambridge, MA: MIT Press, 1988.

Kofman, A., and J. Lawarrée. 1989. Collusion in hierarchical agency. Mimeo, University of California, Berkeley. Forthcoming, *Econometrica.*

Kumar, P. 1989. The generalized principal-agent problem and optimal monitoring: A first-order approach. Mimeo, Carnegie-Mellon University.

Lewis, T. 1990. Notes on cost inflating. Mimeo, University of California, Davis.

McAfee, R. P., and J. McMillan. 1988. *Incentives in Government Contracting.* Toronto: University of Toronto Press.

Malik, A. 1990. Avoidance, screening and optimum enforcement. *Rand Journal of Economics* 21:341–353.

Mirrlees, J. 1974. Notes on welfare economics, information and uncertainty. In *Essays on Economic Behavior under Uncertainty*, ed. M. Balch, D. McFadden, and S. Wu. Amsterdam: North-Holland.

Nalebuff, B., and D. Scharfstein. 1987. Testing in models of asymmetric information. *Review of Economic Studies* 54:265–277.

Normanton, E. 1966. *The Accountability and Audit of Governments: A Comparative Study.* Manchester: Manchester University Press.

Overly, S. 1987. Government contractors, beware: Civil and criminal penalties abound for defective pricing. *Loyola of Los Angeles Law Review* 20:597–641.

Pace, D. F. 1970. *Negotiation and Management of Defense Contracts.* New York: Wiley.

Polinsky, A. M., and S. Shavell. 1979. The optimal tradeoff between the probability and magnitude of fines. *American Economic Review* 69:880–891.

Rogerson, W. 1990. Overhead allocation and incentives for cost minimization in defense procurement. Mimeo, Northwestern University.

Trueger, P. 1966. *Accounting Guide for Defense Contracts.* New York: Commerce Clearing House.

Wilson, R. 1983. Auditing: Perspectives from multiperson decision theory. *Accounting Review*, April.

13 CARTELIZATION BY REGULATION

13.1 Some Background

Many economists favor competition more because they fear abuse of its control by regulators than because of its intrinsic virtues. The case against free market outcomes is well-known. Unregulated industries are technologically inefficient (e.g., they may lead to a duplication of fixed costs), offer socially suboptimal selection of products and qualities, yield inadequate prices, give rise to externalities, and so on. Yet most, if not all, economists would be reluctant to give free reign to agencies to restrict entry and regulate industries. Since Marx (1867), and especially Stigler's (1971) fundamental contribution to the capture argument, it has been well understood that regulation is often motivated or controlled by the industries to be regulated. Stigler (1971) distinguishes four ways by which a regulated industry will try to draw benefits from the state: direct monetary subsidies, constraints or subsidies on substitutes or complements of the commodities produced by the industry, price fixing, and, most prominently, control over entry by new rivals.

In this chapter we focus on control over entry as a way to cartelize the industry. There is ample evidence and agreement that "the power to license becomes the power to exclude" (to use a phrase of Adams 1975). For instance, as Stigler (1971) observed, "the Civil Aeronautics Board has not allowed a single new trunk line to be launched since it was created in 1938. The power to insure new banks has been used by the Federal Deposit Insurance Corporation to reduce the rate of entry into commercial banking by 60%. The interstate motor carrier history is in some respects even more striking because no even ostensibly respectable case for restriction on entry can be developed on grounds of scale economies." Or as Kahn (1988, II, p. 1) so succinctly phrased it in his retrospective study,[1] "Regulation has consisted largely in the imposition and administration of restrictions on entry and on what might otherwise have been independent and competitive price and output decisions." What is more, to achieve this control over entry, it is well-known that industries can "bribe" politicians, in particular key members of the legislature in charge of overseeing the relevant agencies through campaign contributions, votes, or extrapolitical payments to legislators' law firms, and regulators through entertainment expenditures, job prospects in the industry, or absence of complaints.

1. Similar opinions are expressed by Adams and Gray:

> I think, first, that regulatory commissions tend to develop an undue identification with the industries they are supposed to regulate. More often than not, they seem to protect the regulated industries from competition rather than the public from exploitation. (Walter Adams 1975)

> The public utility status was to be the haven of refuge for all aspiring monopolists who found it too difficult, too costly or too precarious to secure and maintain monopoly by private action alone. (H. Gray in Kahn 1988, II, p. 2)

In chapter 11 we argued that a proper analysis of regulatory capture must account for informational asymmetries. In the absence of such asymmetries regulated industries would be unable to extract rents and therefore would have no incentive to influence regulatory outcomes. Similarly voters and legislatures would have no difficulty controlling their agents—members of committees and agencies—who thus would not get away with policies favoring interest groups over the common good. An agency-theoretic framework, however, can explain why the firms have a stake in regulation and why regulation can be captured. The incorporation of informational asymmetries into the theory points at key determinants of interest group power (whether information substantially affects regulatory outcomes and whether it can be manipulated to the benefit of the interest group), and it indicates the likely institutional response to the threat of regulatory capture. In this chapter we extend this methodology to the case where the protection of rents by a captured regulatory agency is achieved by manipulation of the entry decision. It enables us to formalize and study the argument of cartelization of industries through captured agencies.

Section 13.2 sets up a model of a single-product regulated incumbent with private information about its technology. An "agency" (possibly interpreted as the regulatory agency plus the members of congressional committees in charge of overseeing it) can affect entry by the producer of a differentiated commodity. The agency may or may not have information about the value to consumers of introducing the new commodity. Entry may be socially efficient because it enhances product diversity, or inefficient because it creates a duplication of fixed costs. The "political principal" or "Congress" (possibly interpreted as the rest of the legislature) has no such information and must rely on the agency to decide whether to allow entry. Section 13.3 studies the benchmark case of a benevolent agency (an agency that always releases its information to Congress).

Section 13.4 allows the agency to collude with the incumbent (collusion with the entrant is inoperative in our model) and analyzes the institutional response to the threat of regulatory capture. Since the incumbent's informational rent is higher when entry is prohibited, the agency will tend to prohibit entry; this limited entry formalizes the cartelization argument. Thus, with a naive or passive political principal, entry is reduced. However, with a rational and activist political principal, the threat of regulatory capture *increases* the likelihood of entry. This result, which illustrates the importance of endogenizing the response to the threat of regulatory capture, is due to the fact that collusion makes it costly to give the agency discretion over the entry decision. That nonagency participants may play a substantial, though nonexclusive, role in fostering competition fits well with the recent deregulatory experience in that the United States Congress (or part of it) has been active in forcing DOD to use competition in the production of major weapon systems (as requested by the Armed Services Procurement Act of 1947 but not applied by DOD[2]), and in the deregulation of the trucking and airline industries. And the judiciary has played a preponderant role in the divestiture of A&T and the broadening of access to the local network to A&T's competitors.[3]

Another concern of section 13.4 is the influence of regulatory capture on the power of regulatory incentive schemes (i.e., on the share of cost savings retained by the incumbent). The threat of collusion implies that the incumbent is given a more powerful incentive scheme and gets a higher informational rent when the agency reports a proentry signal, and is given a less powerful incentive scheme and gets a lower informational rent when the agency claims it lacks information about demand.

Section 13.5 summarizes the results and discusses extensions of the model. In particular it argues that if the entrants can earn substantial rents or if powerful customers can derive substantial benefits from increased competition, nonbenevolent regulators may become procompetitive. This point naturally leads to a discussion of when competition destroys or creates industry rents. Agency theory thus yields a rich approach to the question of whether cartelization is likely to occur in a regulatory environment.

Last, the regulatory model of this chapter emphasizes the trade-off between product diversity and duplication of fixed costs. Appendix A13.3 shows that its methodology and implications can be straightforwardly extended to a procurement situation in which the benefit of competition is yardstick competition.

2. The 1984 Competition in Contracting Act requires DOD to use "full and open competition." It directs each executive agency to establish a "competition advocate" to promote competition in procurement and strengthen appeal procedures. The 1986 Defense Authorization Act and the 1987 DOD Appropriations Act put further constraints on the executive branch in using sole source procurement. For more details on and a discussion of the reform of U.S. procurement policy, see Burnett and Kovacic (1989). In 1969 the Subcommittee on Priorities and Economy in Government of the Joint Economic Committee reported that "the Subcommittee once again makes its longstanding recommendation that DOD make greater use of true competitive bidding in military procurement, and that the tendency to award contracts through noncompetitive negotiation be reversed." Yuspeh (1976) notes that in 1973, 56.7% of all DOD contracts were sole source (i.e., resulted from negotiation of DOD with a single producer). Among the other contracts only 10.3% were formally "advertised" (i.e., were procured through an auction in which no negotiations are permitted and DOD must accept the lowest bid). He also lists some reasons given by DOD for not using competition more widely. See chapter 14 for an analysis of favoritism in auctions.

3. This chapter does not attempt to explain why deregulation took place in the 1970s and 1980s. Further research ought to investigate whether changes in the supply and demand conditions, in the information structure or in the organization of interest groups have influenced the timing of regulation and deregulation. We here content ourselves with noting that nonagency participants may want to foster competition beyond the level chosen by the agency (see the discussion in section 13.4).

13.2 The Model

The regulatory structure is a three-tier hierarchy: incumbent/agency/political principal (e.g., Congress). All parties are risk neutral. The regulated incumbent produces output q_1 of commodity 1 at cost:

$$C = (\beta - e)q_1. \tag{13.1}$$

A known fixed cost can be added in (13.1), but we ignore it for notational simplicity. The cost parameter β takes its value in $\{\underline{\beta}, \overline{\beta}\}$. The incumbent knows β; the other parties only know that $\beta = \underline{\beta}$ with probability ν and $\beta = \overline{\beta}$ with probability $1 - \nu$. The firm's managers incur an increasing and convex disutility (in terms of the numéraire) $\psi(e)$ (with $\psi' > 0$, $\psi'' > 0$, $\psi''' \geq 0$) by exerting effort e to reduce cost.

In the absence of entry, the gross consumer surplus is denoted $S(q_1, 0)$, an increasing and concave function, and the inverse demand function is $P_1(q_1)$. A potential entrant can produce a differentiated commodity (commodity 2) in quantity q_2. Gross consumer surplus is then $S(q_1, \theta q_2)$, $S_1 > 0$, $S_2 > 0$, where θ is a taste parameter that can take one of two values $\{\underline{\theta}, \overline{\theta}\}$. Let $\alpha = \text{Prob}(\theta = \overline{\theta})$, and let

$$P_1(q_1, \theta q_2) = \frac{\partial S}{\partial q_1}(q_1, \theta q_2), \tag{13.2}$$

$$P_2(q_1, \theta q_2) = \frac{\partial S}{\partial q_2}(q_1, \theta q_2), \tag{13.3}$$

denote the inverse demand functions.

To simplify the algebra, we make the following assumption on the parametrization of tastes. There exists $\tilde{\theta} \in (\underline{\theta}, \overline{\theta})$ such that

$$S(q_1, \tilde{\theta} q_2) = \alpha S(q_1, \overline{\theta} q_2) + (1 - \alpha) S(q_1, \underline{\theta} q_2) \tag{13.4}$$

for all (q_1, q_2). This assumption [which holds if $S(q_1, \theta q_2) = H(q_1) + J(q_1)(\theta q_2)^{\gamma}$] implies that the absence of information about θ is equivalent to complete information about an intermediate value $\tilde{\theta}$, as far as marginal utilities of consumers are concerned.

When the regulator has information $\sigma = \varnothing$ (does not know θ), his or her perceived inverse demand functions are

$$\frac{\partial S}{\partial q_1}(q_1, \tilde{\theta} q_2) \quad \text{and} \quad \frac{\partial S}{\partial q_2}(q_1, \tilde{\theta} q_2),$$

which we denote $P_1(q_1, \tilde{\theta} q_2)$ and $P_2(q_1, \tilde{\theta} q_2)$ for convenience. We will often identify $\tilde{\theta}$ and $\varnothing$. Finally, one may wonder why prices clear the market when $\sigma = \varnothing$. We have in mind the following timing: Firms choose their production levels q_1 and q_2. Then the uncertainty about θ is resolved.

Market-clearing prices p_1 and p_2 are then chosen by the firms (or by the regulator). The economic interpretation of this timing is that the q_i are capacities or output levels that are committed before the goods are marketed. Note that choosing market-clearing prices is socially optimal.

We also assume that $S_{12} < 0$, namely that the entrant's and the incumbent's goods are substitutes (most of our conclusions would be reversed with complements). We let $\eta_{kl} = (\partial q_k/\partial p_l)(p_l/q_k)$ and $\eta_k \equiv -\eta_{kk}$ denote the cross and own demand elasticities, and we let $R_k \equiv p_k q_k$ denote the revenue on good k.

The revenue from the incumbent's output is $P_1(q_1, \theta q_2)q_1$. Our accounting convention is that Congress pays the incumbent's (observable) cost and receives the revenue. Letting t denote the (net) transfer from Congress to the incumbent, the incumbent's rent is

$$U = t - \psi(e). \tag{13.5}$$

We normalize the incumbent's reservation utility at 0 so that the incumbent's participation or individual rationality constraint is

$$U \geq 0. \tag{13.6}$$

The entrant's technology is characterized by a commonly known cost function:

$$\begin{cases} d(q_2) + k & \text{if } q_2 > 0, \\ 0 & \text{if } q_2 = 0, \end{cases} \tag{13.7}$$

with $d(0) = 0$, $d'(0) = 0$, $d' > 0$, and $d'' > 0$ for $q_2 > 0$.

For simplicity, we will assume that the entrant is regulated. This implies that both the incumbent's and the entrant's revenues and costs have shadow value or cost $1 + \lambda$, where $\lambda > 0$ is the shadow cost of raising public funds through distortionary taxation. (It is straightforward to extend the analysis to the case in which the entrant is not regulated and a fraction τ of its profit is levied by Congress: Letting $\lambda_e \equiv \tau\lambda$, it suffices to replace λ by λ_e in front of the entrant's profit in the social welfare function.)

The agency receives income s from the political principal and derives utility $V(s) = s - s^*$. Its reservation utility is s^*. For simplicity we assume that the agency is indispensible (i.e., the political principal needs the agency to regulate the incumbent's price and cost). We further assume that the political principal must pay at least s^* to the agency in each state of nature:

$$V(s) = s - s^* \geq 0. \tag{13.8}$$

The agency obtains information (a signal σ) about the consumers' tastes. With probability ξ, the agency learns the true $\bar{\theta}(\sigma = \theta)$; with probability $1 - \xi$, the agency learns nothing ($\sigma = \emptyset$). There are thus four states of nature concerning demand: with probability $\xi\alpha$, the taste parameter and the signal are $\bar{\theta}$; with probability $(1-\xi)\alpha$, the parameter is $\bar{\theta}$ but the agency does not know it and puts probability α that it is $\bar{\theta}$; and so forth.

We assume that the signal is hard evidence in the sense that the agency can prove to the political principal that $\sigma = \bar{\theta}$ or that $\sigma = \underline{\theta}$ if this is indeed the case.[4] The ability to claim it is uniformed is its dimension of discretion. The agency reports $r \in \{\sigma, \varnothing\}$ to Congress. The political principal is utilitarian and attempts to maximize the sum of producer's, agency's and consumers' surpluses. Social welfare is

$$\begin{aligned} W = U + V + S(q_1, \theta q_2) - P_1(q_1, \theta q_2)q_1 - P_2(q_1, \theta q_2)q_2 \\ - (1+\lambda)[s + t + (\beta - e)q_1 - P_1(q_1, \theta q_2)q_1] \\ + (1+\lambda)[P_2(q_1, \theta q_2)q_2 - d(q_2) - k\chi(q_2)], \end{aligned} \tag{13.9}$$

where $\chi(q_2) = 1$ for $q_2 > 0$, and $\chi(q_2) = 0$ for $q_2 = 0$ (χ is thus an entry dummy). Equation (13.9) can be rewritten

$$\begin{aligned} W = [S(q_1, \theta q_2) + \lambda P_1(q_1, \theta q_2)q_1 + \lambda P_2(q_1, \theta q_2)q_2] \\ - (1+\lambda)[s^* + (\beta - e)q_1 + \psi(e) + d(q_2) + k\chi(q_2)] \\ - \lambda U - \lambda V. \end{aligned} \tag{13.10}$$

From the generalized consumer surplus $[S(q_1, \theta q_2) + \lambda P_1(q_1, \theta q_2)q_1 + \lambda P_2(q_1, \theta q_2)q_2]$ must be subtracted $1 + \lambda$ times the total cost of the incumbent's activity, $1 + \lambda$ times the total cost of the entrant, and λ times the rents left to the incumbent and the agency.

Remark This chapter focuses on the control of an agency by benevolent higher levels, labeled the "political principal." Needless to say, the political principal (in particular Congress) may also identify with interest groups and not be benevolent. In this case the institutional response may differ from the one described here. But the very logic of the chapter can be applied one step up. That the entry decision may be manipulated by whoever is in charge of regulating the industry implies that some institutional response (constitutional or judicial for instance) is desirable.

Let us summarize the timing. First, the agency learns the signal about demand and the firm learns β. The political principal designs incentive schemes or contracts for both the firm and the agency. Then side contracting might take place. The agency reports r (about demand) and the firm reports $\hat{\beta}$ (about its efficiency). On the basis of these reports and agreed-upon contracts, the political principal decides whether to let the

4. For simplicity we assume that the incumbent learns what signal the agency receives. This eliminates informed principal issues in the collusion activities.

entrant in and chooses the output levels. The true level of demand is then revealed and prices clear the markets.

To restrict the number of cases to be considered, we assume that k belongs to an interval $[k_0, k_1]$ such that entry should always occur (i.e., for all β) when $\theta = \bar{\theta}$ and entry should never occur (i.e., for no β) when $\theta = \underline{\theta}$. This assumption is made in the three cases to be considered: full information (FI), asymmetric information (AI) with a benevolent agency, and asymmetric information with collusion (C). This assumption means that the uncertainty about demand for the substitute product is sufficiently large (relative to the uncertainty about β). It is not innocuous, as we later discuss.

Therefore entry is an issue only for $r = \varnothing$. We will denote by $k^{\mathrm{FI}}(\beta)$, $k^{\mathrm{AI}}(\beta)$. $k^{\mathrm{C}}(\beta)$ the critical values of k beyond which entry should be prohibited when $r = \varnothing$, in the three cases. As a benchmark we first derive the optimal regulation when the agency is benevolent and the political principal observes β (and therefore, indirectly, e):

Proposition 13.1 With a benevolent agency and under complete information about the incumbent's technology, optimal regulation satisfies four conditions:

i. The incumbent's marginal disutility of effort is equal to marginal cost savings, $\psi'(e) = q_1$.

ii. For each β there exists a level $k^{\mathrm{FI}}(\beta) > 0$ of the entrant's fixed cost such that if $k < k^{\mathrm{FI}}(\beta)$, optimal pricing and entry decisions are defined as follows: For $\sigma = \underline{\theta}$, entry does not occur, and

$$\frac{p_1 - (\beta - e)}{p_1} = \frac{\lambda}{1 + \lambda} \frac{1}{\eta_1} \quad \text{(monopoly Ramsey pricing).} \tag{13.11}$$

For $\sigma = \varnothing$ or $\bar{\theta}$, entry does occur, and

$$\frac{p_1 - (\beta - e)}{p_1} = \frac{\lambda}{1 + \lambda} \frac{1}{\hat{\eta}_1}, \tag{13.12}$$

$$\frac{p_2 - d'(q_2)}{p_2} = \frac{\lambda}{1 + \lambda} \frac{1}{\hat{\eta}_2} \quad \text{(competitive Ramsey pricing),} \tag{13.13}$$

with superelasticities $\hat{\eta}_k$ corresponding in each case to the appropriate demand function (see appendix A13.1). But if $k > k^{\mathrm{FI}}(\beta)$, optimal pricing and entry decisions are the same as before, except that there is no entry when $\sigma = \varnothing$.

iii. $U = V = 0$.

iv. $k^{\mathrm{FI}}(\bar{\beta}) > k^{\mathrm{FI}}(\underline{\beta})$; that is, there is less entry when the incumbent is efficient.

Proof See appendix A13.1.

To sum up, when fixed costs are low enough $[k < k^{\mathrm{FI}}(\beta)]$, entry occurs if the taste parameter is high or unknown, and entry occurs only if the taste parameter is known to be high when fixed costs are high $[k > k^{\mathrm{FI}}(\beta)]$. Prices are given by the familiar Ramsey formula (13.11) or by the superelasticity Ramsey formulas (13.12) and (13.13). This comes from the fact that the incumbent's cost function satisfies the separability property that yields the dichotomy property (see chapter 3): Prices are not used to correct incentives, so the Lerner index is equal to the Ramsey index. Formulas (13.11) (if no entry occurs) and (13.12)–(13.13) (if entry occurs) will hold throughout the chapter because of the separability property and will not be repeated.

Corollary 13.1 Denoting $q_1^\sigma(\beta)$ the incumbent's production in state of information σ, we have for any β,

$$q_1^{\underline{\theta}}(\beta) > q_1^{\varnothing}(\beta) > q_1^{\bar{\theta}}(\beta) \qquad \text{if } k < k^{\mathrm{FI}}(\beta),$$

$$q_1^{\underline{\theta}}(\beta) = q_1^{\varnothing}(\beta) > q_1^{\bar{\theta}}(\beta) \qquad \text{if } k > k^{\mathrm{FI}}(\beta).$$

Since $\psi'(e) = q_1$, corollary 13.1 implies that for $k < k^{\mathrm{FI}}(\beta)$, $e^{\underline{\theta}}(\beta) > e^{\varnothing}(\beta) > e^{\bar{\theta}}(\beta)$ and for $k > k^{\mathrm{FI}}(\beta)$, $e^{\underline{\theta}}(\beta) = e^{\varnothing}(\beta) > e^{\bar{\theta}}(\beta)$. In particular the incumbent's effort level is higher when the agency is uninformed than when it is informed and $\theta = \bar{\theta}$. Indeed, if it is known that entry is particularly desirable ($\theta = \bar{\theta}$), the production level of the incumbent is low, and therefore effort should be low.

13.3 Benevolent Agency and Incomplete Information about the Incumbent's Technology

A benevolent agency truthfully reveals its signal to Congress, even if it faces a flat income scheme $s \equiv s^*$. Its rent $V^\sigma(\beta)$ is zero for any (σ, β). The incumbent enjoys an informational rent when it is efficient. Let $t^\sigma(\beta)$, $C^\sigma(\beta)$, $q_1^\sigma(\beta)$, $q_2^\sigma(\beta)$, $e^\sigma(\beta)$, and $U^\sigma(\beta)$ denote the transfer, total cost, productions, effort, and rent in state of nature (σ, β). Finally, let $c^\sigma(\beta) = C^\sigma(\beta)/q_1^\sigma(\beta)$ be the incumbent's average cost.

As is customary, the incentive compatibility constraint is binding only for the efficient type and the individual rationality constraint is binding only for the inefficient type:

$$t^\sigma(\underline{\beta}) - \psi(\underline{\beta} - c^\sigma(\underline{\beta})) = t^\sigma(\bar{\beta}) - \psi(\underline{\beta} - c^\sigma(\bar{\beta})), \tag{13.14}$$

$$t^\sigma(\bar{\beta}) - \psi(\bar{\beta} - c^\sigma(\bar{\beta})) = 0. \tag{13.15}$$

The efficient type's rent is

$$\begin{aligned} U^\sigma(\underline{\beta}) &= t^\sigma(\underline{\beta}) - \psi(\underline{\beta} - c^\sigma(\underline{\beta})) = t^\sigma(\bar{\beta}) - \psi(\underline{\beta} - c^\sigma(\bar{\beta})) \\ &= \psi(\bar{\beta} - c^\sigma(\bar{\beta})) - \psi(\underline{\beta} - c^\sigma(\bar{\beta})) \\ &= \psi(e^\sigma(\bar{\beta})) - \psi(e^\sigma(\bar{\beta}) - \Delta\beta) \\ &\equiv \Phi(e^\sigma(\bar{\beta})), \qquad \Phi' > 0, \Phi'' > 0. \end{aligned} \tag{13.16}$$

Thus, in information state σ, type $\underline{\beta}$, which has probability ν, enjoys rent $\Phi(e^\sigma(\bar{\beta}))$, which has expected social cost $\lambda\nu\Phi(e^\sigma(\bar{\beta}))$.

Expected social welfare is

$$\begin{aligned} &E_\beta\{S(q_1^\sigma(\beta), \sigma q_2^\sigma(\beta)) + \lambda q_1^\sigma(\beta)P_1(q_1^\sigma(\beta), \sigma q_2^\sigma(\beta)) + \lambda q_2^\sigma(\beta)P_2(q_1^\sigma(\beta), \sigma q_2^\sigma(\beta)) \\ &\quad - (1+\lambda)[(\beta - e^\sigma(\beta))q_1^\sigma(\beta) + \psi(e^\sigma(\beta)) + s^*] \\ &\quad - (1+\lambda)[d(q_2^\sigma(\beta)) + k\chi^\sigma(\beta)]\} - \lambda\nu\Phi(e^\sigma(\bar{\beta})), \end{aligned} \tag{13.17}$$

where

$$\chi^\sigma(\beta) = \begin{cases} 1 & \text{if } q_2^\sigma(\beta) > 0, \\ 0 & \text{if } q_2^\sigma(\beta) = 0. \end{cases}$$

The first-order conditions with respect to effort levels are

$$\psi'(e^\sigma(\bar{\beta})) = q_1^\sigma(\bar{\beta}) - \frac{\lambda}{1+\lambda}\frac{\nu}{1-\nu}\Phi'(e^\sigma(\bar{\beta})), \tag{13.18}$$

$$\psi'(e^\sigma(\underline{\beta})) = q_1^\sigma(\underline{\beta}). \tag{13.19}$$

Prices are still given by (13.11) through (13.13). Last, the optimal entry decision is as follows:

When $\sigma = \bar{\theta}$, entry occurs always.

When $\sigma = \underline{\theta}$, entry never occurs.

When $\sigma = \varnothing$, the change in the entry decision due to asymmetric information depends on β:

The entry decision is unchanged if $\beta = \underline{\beta}$; that is, $k^{\mathrm{AI}}(\underline{\beta}) = k^{\mathrm{FI}}(\underline{\beta})$.

There is more entry for incentive reasons if $\beta = \bar{\beta}$; that is, $k^{\mathrm{AI}}(\bar{\beta}) > k^{\mathrm{FI}}(\bar{\beta})$.

We summarize our results in proposition 13.2.

Proposition 13.2 With a benevolent agency and incomplete information about the incumbent's technology, optimal regulation is defined as in proposition 13.1 except that for any σ,

i. effort is suboptimal for the inefficient type in order to reduce the efficient type's informational rent,

$$\psi'(e^\sigma(\bar{\beta})) = q_1^\sigma(\bar{\beta}) - \frac{\lambda}{1+\lambda}\frac{\nu}{1-\nu}\Phi'(e^\sigma(\bar{\beta}));$$

ii. $V^\sigma(\beta) = 0$ for all (σ, β), $U^\sigma(\bar{\beta}) = 0$ for all σ, $U^\sigma(\underline{\beta}) = \Phi(e^\sigma(\bar{\beta}))$ for all σ;

iii. for $\sigma = \varnothing$ entry is more likely than under complete information for $\beta = \bar{\beta}$, whereas for $\beta = \underline{\beta}$ or for $\sigma \in \{\underline{\theta}, \bar{\theta}\}$ the entry criterion is unchanged.

Proof See appendix A13.2.

Asymmetric information increases the incumbent's rent of asymmetric information more when entry is not allowed than when entry is allowed (this is due to the fact that the rent is increasing in the inefficient type's effort and therefore production level). Consequently the incumbent's cost is increased more without entry than with entry, and entry becomes more attractive. This conclusion is familiar in asymmetric information models (see, e.g., Demski, Sappington, and Spiller 1987; Scharfstein 1988).

Corollary 13.2
For $k < k^{\mathrm{AI}}(\beta)$, $q_1^{\underline{\theta}}(\beta) > q_1^{\varnothing}(\beta) > q_1^{\bar{\theta}}(\beta)$ and $e^{\underline{\theta}}(\beta) > e^{\varnothing}(\beta) > e^{\bar{\theta}}(\beta)$.
For $k > k^{\mathrm{AI}}(\beta)$, $q_1^{\underline{\theta}}(\beta) = q_1^{\varnothing}(\beta) > q_1^{\bar{\theta}}(\beta)$ and $e^{\underline{\theta}}(\beta) = e^{\varnothing}(\beta) > e^{\bar{\theta}}(\beta)$.

The main implication of corollary 13.2 is that efficient type's rent is higher when the agency is uninformed about θ than when $\theta = \bar{\theta}$. For $k > k^{\mathrm{AI}}(\beta)$ this is because entry is prevented, and for $k < k^{\mathrm{AI}}(\beta)$ this is only because production is higher (since consumers' "expected" marginal utility for the competing product is lower). Accordingly the incumbent has a stake in an inefficient regulation in which the agency would hide its signal when $\sigma = \bar{\theta}$. We derive the implications of this observation in the next section.

Remark What we call "entry" may sometimes be interpreted more broadly. For example, entry may be the production of another service by the incumbent. If this alternative service generates small informational rents to the regulated firm and if it competes with an existing service for which large informational rents are available, the regulated firm will be reluctant to introduce the alternative service.

13.4 Cartelization

We now allow the incumbent to collude with the agency. The incumbent can give a transfer $\tilde{s}$ to the agency at cost $(1 + \lambda_f)\tilde{s}$ (so that the agency's total income equivalent is $s + \tilde{s}$). The parameter $\lambda_f \geq 0$ denotes the shadow cost of transfers for the firm (equivalently the agency attributes monetary value $1/(1 + \lambda_f)$ per dollar of the incumbent's collusive activity); it reflects the deadweight loss associated with side transfers.

Because the agency's information is hard, and because the incumbent has no incentive to induce the agency to conceal signal $\sigma = \underline{\theta}$, collusion can only consist in the agency's reporting $r = \varnothing$ when $\sigma = \bar{\theta}$, where r is the agency's report. Let $k^{C}(\beta)$ be such that when $r = \varnothing$, the political principal allows entry if $k < k^{C}(\beta)$ and prohibits entry if $k > k^{C}(\beta)$. Reporting $r = \varnothing$ when $\sigma = \bar{\theta}$ prevents entry if $k > k^{C}(\beta)$ and reduces the entrant's output when $k < k^{C}(\beta)$.

Type $\underline{\beta}$'s gain from collusion is $\Phi(e^{\varnothing}(\bar{\beta})) - \Phi(e^{\bar{\theta}}(\bar{\beta}))$. The regulator must give incentives to the agency not to collude with the incumbent. Namely collusion may be profitable when $\beta = \underline{\beta}$ and $\sigma = \bar{\theta}$ (the firm enjoys a rent and this rent is reduced by the signal that entry is desirable). Let $\hat{s}$ denote the agency's income from the political principal when $r = \bar{\theta}$ and $\hat{\beta} = \underline{\beta}$. For all other $(r, \hat{\beta})$, give the agency its reservation income s^*.

A necessary condition for collusion between the agency and the firm not to occur is[5]

$$\hat{s} - s^* \geq \frac{\Phi(e^{\varnothing}(\bar{\beta})) - \Phi(e^{\bar{\theta}}(\bar{\beta}))}{1 + \lambda_f} \qquad \text{for } e^{\varnothing}(\bar{\beta}) \geq e^{\bar{\theta}}(\bar{\beta}). \tag{13.20}$$

We later will need to check that (13.20) is sufficient to prevent collusion in other states of nature. Expected social welfare in information state σ (gross of the agency's extra income) is

$$\begin{aligned} W^{\sigma} \equiv E_{\beta}[&S(q_1^{\sigma}(\beta), \sigma q_2^{\sigma}(\beta)) + \lambda q_1^{\sigma}(\beta) P_1(q_1^{\sigma}(\beta), \sigma q_2^{\sigma}(\beta)) \\ &+ \lambda q_2^{\sigma}(\beta) P_2(q_1^{\sigma}(\beta), \sigma q_2^{\sigma}(\beta)) \\ &- (1 + \lambda)((\beta - e^{\sigma}(\beta)) q_1^{\sigma}(\beta) + \psi(e^{\sigma}(\beta)) + d(q_2^{\sigma}(\beta)) \\ &+ k\chi^{\sigma}(\beta) + s^*)] - \lambda\nu\Phi(e^{\sigma}(\bar{\beta})). \end{aligned} \tag{13.21}$$

The new feature introduced by the possibility of collusion is that the optimizations in the various states of information about demand are interdependent. That is, the optimal incentive scheme solves

$$\max\{\xi[\alpha W^{\bar{\theta}} + (1 - \alpha) W^{\underline{\theta}}] + (1 - \xi) W^{\varnothing} - \lambda\nu\xi\alpha[\hat{s} - s^*]\} \tag{13.22}$$

subject to (13.20).

Note in (13.22) that because the extra cost due to collusion depends only on $\{e^{\varnothing}(\bar{\beta}), e^{\bar{\theta}}(\bar{\beta})\}$, the other efforts are as given in section 13.3. Furthermore the Ramsey pricing rules (13.11) through (13.13) still apply. Thus we can content ourselves with analyzing the effect of collusion on $\{e^{\varnothing}(\bar{\beta}), e^{\bar{\theta}}(\bar{\beta})\}$ and on the critical $k^{C}(\beta)$ under which entry is allowed for signal $\sigma = \varnothing$. Since the new constraints do not involve $\underline{\beta}$, $k^{C}(\underline{\beta}) = k^{AI}(\underline{\beta})$ and nothing is changed for type $\underline{\beta}$ (except for the size of rents) with respect to section 13.3. We must distinguish two regimes in the solution of program (13.22).

5. See chapter 11 for a proof that there is no loss in focusing on incentive schemes for which collusion does not arise.

Regime 1: $e^{\varnothing}(\bar\beta) > e(\bar\beta)$

In this case we substitute (13.20) in (13.22) and differentiate (13.22) with respect to $e^{\varnothing}(\bar\beta)$ and $e^{\bar\theta}(\bar\beta)$ to obtain

$$\psi'(e^{\varnothing}(\bar\beta)) = q_1^{\varnothing}(\bar\beta) - \frac{\lambda}{1+\lambda}\frac{\nu}{1-\nu}\left(1 + \frac{\xi\alpha}{(1-\xi)(1+\lambda_f)}\right)\Phi'(e^{\varnothing}(\bar\beta)), \tag{13.23}$$

and

$$\psi'(e^{\bar\theta}(\bar\beta)) = q_1^{\bar\theta}(\bar\beta) - \frac{\lambda}{1+\lambda}\frac{\nu}{1-\nu}\frac{\lambda_f}{(1+\lambda_f)}\Phi'(e^{\bar\theta}(\bar\beta)). \tag{13.24}$$

As one would expect, $e^{\sigma}(\bar\beta)$, and therefore the efficient type's rent, is decreased when the agency reports ignorance ($r = \varnothing$) and is increased when the agency reports the proentry signal ($r = \bar\theta$), as is needed to fight collusion. An interesting implication of (13.24) is that when the agency and the firm can perfectly collude ($\lambda_f = 0$), there is no distortion of effort for type $\bar\beta$ when $r = \bar\theta$. The intuition for this result is that giving up rent to the efficient type when $\theta = \bar\theta$ is socially costless because the transfer to the agency required to prevent collusion can be lowered by an equal amount.

Regime 2: $e^{\varnothing}(\bar\beta) = e^{\bar\theta}(\bar\beta)$

Here $\hat s = s^*$. Let κ the multiplier of the constraint $e^{\varnothing}(\bar\beta) \geq e^{\bar\theta}(\bar\beta)$. The optimal allocation is determined by the equality of the two efforts, by the pricing equations and

$$\psi'(e^{\varnothing}(\bar\beta)) = q_1^{\varnothing}(\bar\beta) - \frac{\lambda}{1+\lambda}\frac{\nu}{1-\nu}\Phi'(e^{\varnothing}(\bar\beta)) - \frac{\kappa}{(1-\xi)(1+\lambda)(1-\nu)} \tag{13.23'}$$

and

$$\psi'(e^{\bar\theta}(\bar\beta)) = q_1^{\bar\theta}(\bar\beta) - \frac{\lambda}{1+\lambda}\frac{\nu}{1-\nu}\Phi'(e^{\bar\theta}(\bar\beta)) + \frac{\kappa}{\xi\alpha(1-\nu)(1+\lambda)}. \tag{13.24'}$$

In this case no rent is given up to the agency. Regulation is sufficiently distorted to nullify the incumbent's stake in collusion.

Next we determine the critical $k^{C}(\bar\beta)$ under which entry is allowed when $\sigma = \varnothing$ and $\beta = \bar\beta$. We index the cases of entry and no-entry by $+$ and $-$. Let W^+ and W^- denote the maximum expected social welfares given by (13.22) when entry is exogenously allowed in state $\{\varnothing, \bar\beta\}$ ($\chi^{\varnothing}(\bar\beta) = 1$) and when it is exogenously prohibited $\{\chi^{\varnothing}(\bar\beta) = 0\}$. By definition of k^{C}, $W^+ = W^-$ when $k = k^{C}$. Applying the envelope theorem to (13.22) yields in regime 1,

$$\frac{d(W^+ - W^-)}{d\lambda_f} = \frac{\lambda\nu\xi\alpha}{(1+\lambda_f)^2}[\Phi(e_+^{\varnothing}(\bar\beta)) - \Phi(e_-^{\varnothing}(\bar\beta))]. \tag{13.25}$$

Then $e_+^{\varnothing}(\bar{\beta}) < e_-^{\varnothing}(\bar{\beta})$ because $\{e_+^{\varnothing}(\bar{\beta}), q_{1+}^{\varnothing}(\bar{\beta})\}$ are determined by (13.23) and (13.12) and $\{e_-^{\varnothing}(\bar{\beta}), q_{1-}^{\varnothing}(\bar{\beta})\}$ are determined by (13.23) and (13.11). Since $\Phi(\cdot)$ is increasing, $d(W^+ - W^-)/d\lambda_f < 0$. Last, since a benevolent agency corresponds to $\lambda_f = +\infty$, entry becomes relatively more attractive under a nonbenevolent agency and thus $k^{\mathrm{C}}(\bar{\beta}) > k^{\mathrm{AI}}(\bar{\beta})$. As λ_f decreases, $k^{\mathrm{C}}(\bar{\beta})$ decreases until $\lambda_f = \overline{\lambda_f}$, at which point regime 2 holds and k^{C} becomes constant.

So far we have implicitly assumed that no transfer from the agency to the firm was possible. Let λ_a finite be the shadow cost of such transfers. The only serious issue in checking that the solution to (13.22) satisfies collusion proofness in each state of nature $\{\sigma, \beta\}$ is the following: The agency in state of nature $\{\bar{\theta}, \bar{\beta}\}$ might want to bribe the firm to announce $\hat{\beta} = \underline{\beta}$ in order to increase the agency's income by $(\hat{s} - s^*)$. Now the agency may not know that $\beta = \bar{\beta}$, but a sufficient condition for eliminating this issue is that even if it knew that $\beta = \bar{\beta}$ (symmetric information), which is the most favorable case for gains from trade from collusion to be realized, it would not want to bribe the firm. The loss for the firm of claiming that it is more efficient than it really is, $-U^{\bar{\theta}}(\underline{\beta}) + [\psi(e^{\bar{\theta}}(\underline{\beta}) + \Delta\beta) - \psi(e^{\bar{\theta}}(\underline{\beta}))] = \Phi(e^{\bar{\theta}}(\underline{\beta}) + \Delta\beta) - \Phi(e^{\bar{\theta}}(\bar{\beta}))$, must exceed the income that the agency is willing to give to the firm to lie. We need to check that

$$\frac{1}{(1 + \lambda_f)(1 + \lambda_a)}[\Phi(e^{\varnothing}(\bar{\beta})) - \Phi(e^{\bar{\theta}}(\bar{\beta}))] \leq \Phi(e^{\bar{\theta}}(\bar{\beta}) + \Delta\beta) - \Phi(e^{\bar{\theta}}(\bar{\beta})). \tag{13.26}$$

The inequality (13.26) is always satisfied in regime 2 because the left-hand side is equal to zero. In regime 1 it may require $\lambda_a \geq \overline{\lambda_a}$, for some $\overline{\lambda_a}$ because $e^{\varnothing}(\bar{\beta})$ may be larger than $e^{\bar{\theta}}(\underline{\beta}) + \Delta\beta$. When $\lambda_a < \overline{\lambda_a}$, giving an extra income $\hat{\hat{s}}$ to the agency in state of nature $\{\bar{\theta}, \underline{\beta}\}$ such that $\{[(\Phi(e^{\varnothing}(\bar{\beta})) - \Phi(e^{\bar{\theta}}(\bar{\beta})))/(1 + \lambda_f)] - \hat{\hat{s}}\}/(1 + \lambda_a) \leq \Phi(e^{\bar{\theta}}(\underline{\beta}) + \Delta\beta) - \Phi(e^{\bar{\theta}}(\bar{\beta}))$ suffices to preserve collusion-proofness. We have not analyzed the optimal policy in this case.

We gather our main results in the next proposition.

Proposition 13.3 With a nonbenevolent agency and incomplete information about the monopoly's characteristics, optimal regulation is as in proposition 13.2, except that

i. in state $\bar{\theta}$, type $\bar{\beta}$'s effort level is higher and in state $\varnothing$, type $\bar{\beta}$'s effort level is lower;

ii. in regime 1, one of the two possible regimes, the agency is given income $\hat{s}$ when $\sigma = \bar{\theta}$ and $\beta = \underline{\beta}$; this income $\hat{s}$ is greater when entry is not allowed $[k > k^{\mathrm{C}}(\bar{\beta})]$ than when it is allowed $[k < k^{\mathrm{C}}(\bar{\beta})]$; for λ_f small enough [and $k < k^{\mathrm{C}}(\bar{\beta})$], a regime 2 may appear in which the agency is given a flat income s^* and type $\bar{\beta}$'s effort levels in states $\bar{\theta}$ and $\varnothing$ are equated;

iii. when $\sigma = \varnothing$ and $\beta = \bar{\beta}$, entry occurs more often than with a benevolent agency, $k^{C}(\bar{\beta}) > k^{AI}(\bar{\beta}) > k^{FI}(\bar{\beta})$.

The regulatory response to collusion is composed of three parts:

1. Efforts are distorted in order to decrease the stake of collusion, namely the incumbent's gain from withholding of information by the agency. A more powerful incentive scheme is given to the incumbent when the agency's report is $\bar{\theta}$ and a less powerful one when the report is $\varnothing$.

2. If the distortions of efforts mentioned in regulatory response 1 do not nullify the stake of collusion, the agency is given a reward for releasing procompetitive information.

3. The entry rule is distorted so as to leave less discretion to the agency. It is distorted toward more entry in order to decrease the stake of collusion (which is higher when entry is prevented rather than when it is not).

Remark The conclusion that the institutional response to the threat of cartelization is to increase the likelihood of entry depends on our assumption that entry is not an issue in the high state of demand. Suppose that under a benevolent regulator entry occurs for $\sigma = \bar{\theta}$ and $\beta = \bar{\beta}$ only when $k < k^{AI}(\bar{\beta})$ but that it never occurs for $\sigma = \varnothing$ or $\underline{\theta}$. The threat of collusion may induce the political principal to set $k^{C}(\bar{\beta}) < k^{AI}(\bar{\beta})$ to decrease the agency's discretion over the entry decision. That is, to reduce the temptation to collude, the political principal may decide that entry occurs less often in the high state of demand. Thus it seems that in a more general model entry would be reduced in high states of demand and increased when the state of demand is unknown. Quite generally the agency's discretion over the entry decision is reduced. The way this discretion is reduced is an empirical matter. For example, the institutional response described in proposition 13.3 seems consistent with the recent evolution in regulation and procurement in the United States.

13.5 Pro- and Anticompetition Agencies

13.5.1 Summary of the Argument

A regulated firm is adversely affected by entry and therefore has an incentive to induce the agency to prevent new firms from entering the industry. If, first, the incumbent firm is the only organized interest group, and, second, the political principal (e.g., Congress) is passive and does not control the agency, regulation contributes to the cartelization (here, monopolization) of the industry. This scenario would be relevant for the CAB, FDIC, and ICC episodes mentioned in the introduction.

Dropping the assumption that the political principal is inactive may lead precisely to the opposite conclusion. In our model the institutional response to the threat of capture of the agency by the incumbent is to induce more entry. The logic of the argument is straightforward: The agency's discretion resides in concealing information about the desirability of entry from the political principal. Because the incumbent has a stake in *favorable* information about entry being hushed, the threat of collusion with the agency is reduced by the political principal giving the "benefit of the doubt" to the proentry position when it is uninformed. This makes entry more likely. This logic is well illustrated by a rule under the Armed Services Procurement Regulations that a service can forgo competitive bids in favor of negotiations with a single contractor only if the service can demonstrate its necessity in preserving industrial capacity (understand: "in competition being socially undesirable"). It is also implicit in the general feeling that various programs aimed at promoting competition in procurement[6] may be very expensive. Yet the benefit-of-the-doubt argument may vindicate the high costs of fostering competition. This logic may also show up in some of the recent deregulatory experience mentioned in the introduction.

13.5.2 Agency-Entrant and Agency-Customer Collusion and Entry

When the incumbent firms are the only organized interest group, agencies tend to take an anticompetition stance. It is important to realize that powerful customers or entrants could make the agency procompetitive. Suppose, first, that in our model customers are well organized (e.g., they form a large group). Because entry may increase their net surplus, or at least the net surplus of the subgroup of organized customers,[7] the customers may try to induce the agency to conceal information *unfavorable* to entry ($\sigma = \underline{\theta} > 0$) from the political principal.[8] This gives rise to an interesting situation in which the firm (when it is efficient, i.e., $\beta = \underline{\beta}$) and the customers have conflicting preferences and compete to capture the agency. Similarly, when the agency has information favorable to entry ($\sigma = \bar{\theta}$), the customers will try to prevent the firm from capturing the agency and avoiding entry. In both cases the political principal might pit the two interest groups against each other.[9]

6. In the United States the DOD pays for a fraction of defense firms' expenditures on independently chosen and conducted research programs, production-inefficient educational buys, competitive auctioning with substantial administrative costs, costly licensing, and so on.

7. One case is when $\theta > 0$, and good 2 is primarily consumed by a small group of industrial customers who value it over good 1. In this case the organized subgroup of customers benefits from entry while the other (powerless) customers are hurt by entry because the production of good 1 is subject to increasing returns to scale (through the cost-reducing effort).

8. Note that, as in section 11.7, Ramsey pricing is no longer optimal when customers are organized. One way to lower the customers' incentive to capture the agency is to charge a price under the Ramsey price when no entry occurs, and above the Ramsey price when entry occurs.

9. This argument is couched in a regulatory framework. In procurement the DOD is the customer. This argument suggests that DOD would be torn between an incentive to create

Second, consider the entrant(s). In our model the entrant is regulated and has no private information. Therefore the entrant has no rent and no stake in the entry decision. Had it private information or were it left unregulated after entry (for legal or other reasons), the entrant would join the customers to defend the proentry position. In particular the entrant and the incumbent would compete to capture the agency. If the entrant is better organized or has higher potential rent than the incumbent, we would expect the agency to take an excessively proentry stance.

We would, however, expect incumbents to often have more power than entrants. They may be better organized (especially if there are multiple entrants) and have a closer relationship to regulators. Mainly competition tends to destroy rents.[10] Therefore an incumbent may have more incentive to remain a monopolist than an entrant has to become a duopolist. This point is best illustrated by the yardstick competition model of appendix A13.3. There the entrant has the same private information as the incumbent, and while a monopolist enjoys an informational rent, yardstick competition in duopoly fully dissipates any such rent.

We thus obtain a rich theory of the effect of regulatory capture on entry. Whether cartelization or excessive entry occurs depends on (1) the pro- or anticompetition nature of the agency's information, (2) whether the political principal is active or passive, (3) who among incumbents, entrants, and customers is best organized, and (4) whether competition destroys industry rents. The question of whether agencies favor or discourage entry thus cannot be resolved on purely theoretical grounds. Only a detailed industry study can indicate the relevance of each factor. The purpose of this chapter has been to supply a conceptual framework to conduct such industry studies.

APPENDIXES

A13.1 Proof of Proposition 13.1

Fix a signal σ, and suppose first that entry occurs. Because of its information and of the agency's benevolence, the political principal leaves no rent to the incumbent and the agency. The political principal maximizes

competition to obtain lower prices and the desire to identify with incumbents. This may be so, but we should note that the DOD is much less price sensitive than customers in the regulatory context. A guess is that DOD as a customer takes a procompetitive stance mainly when competition increases weapons quality, which is not a forgone conclusion.

10. This is a transposition to a regulatory environment of the well-known "efficiency effect" in industrial organization, according to which competition destroys profits in an homogeneous good industry. The usual qualification that competition may raise industry profit if the entrant produces a differentiated good here takes the form that industry rents may increase if the firms have uncorrelated ("differentiated") technological information.

$$S(q_1(p_1,\sigma p_2),\sigma q_2(p_1,\sigma p_2)) + \lambda p_1 q_1(p_1,\sigma p_2) + \lambda p_2 q_2(p_1,\sigma p_2)$$
$$- (1+\lambda)[(\beta - e)q_1(p_1,\sigma p_2) + \psi(e)]$$
$$- (1+\lambda)[d(q_2(p_1,\sigma p_2)) + k\chi^\sigma(\beta)]. \tag{A13.1}$$

The first-order conditions are

$$\psi'(e) = q_1, \tag{A13.2}$$

$$S_1\frac{\partial q_1}{\partial p_1} + \sigma S_2\frac{\partial q_2}{\partial p_1} + \lambda q_1 + \lambda p_1\frac{\partial q_1}{\partial p_1} + \lambda p_2\frac{\partial q_2}{\partial p_1} - (1+\lambda)(\beta - e)\frac{\partial q_1}{\partial p_1}$$
$$- (1+\lambda)d'(q_2)\frac{\partial q_2}{\partial p_1} = 0, \tag{A13.3}$$

$$S_1\frac{\partial q_1}{\partial p_2} + \sigma S_2\frac{\partial q_2}{\partial p_2} + \lambda p_1\frac{\partial q_1}{\partial p_2} + \lambda q_2 + \lambda p_2\frac{\partial q_2}{\partial p_2} - (1+\lambda)(\beta - e)\frac{\partial q_1}{\partial p_2}$$
$$- (1+\lambda)d'(q_2)\frac{\partial q_2}{\partial p_2} = 0. \tag{A13.4}$$

Since $S_1 = p_1$ and $\sigma S_2 = p_2$, (A13.3) and (A13.4) become

$$\begin{bmatrix} \dfrac{\partial q_1}{\partial p_1} & \dfrac{\partial q_2}{\partial p_1} \\ \dfrac{\partial q_1}{\partial p_2} & \dfrac{\partial q_2}{\partial p_2} \end{bmatrix} \begin{bmatrix} (1+\lambda)[p_1 - (\beta - e)] \\ (1+\lambda)[p_2 - d'(q_2)] \end{bmatrix} = \begin{bmatrix} -\lambda q_1 \\ -\lambda q_2 \end{bmatrix}. \tag{A13.5}$$

To validate the focus on the first-order condition, the welfare function given by (A13.1) must be concave. This requires first that the matrix of second derivatives with respect to (q_1, q_2, e) be negative definite. This is achieved under the conditions of our one-good analysis (chapter 2), that is, S concave in q_1, $S_{11}\psi'' + 1 < 0$ and λ not too large. Denoting Δ the (positive) jacobian of this matrix, we must also have $[\sigma^2 S_{22} - (1+\lambda)d''(q_2)]\Delta + \sigma^2 S_{12}(1+\lambda)\psi'' \leq 0$, which is always true under our assumptions [concavity of S in (q_1, q_2), $d''(q_2) > 0$, and substitute goods].

Solving (A13.5), we get

$$L_1 = \frac{p_1 - (\beta - e)}{p_1} = \frac{\lambda}{1+\lambda}\frac{1}{\eta_1}\left[\frac{1 + (R_2/R_1)(\eta_{21}/\eta_2)}{1 - (\eta_{12}\eta_{21}/\eta_1\eta_2)}\right] \equiv \frac{\lambda}{1+\lambda}\frac{1}{\hat{\eta}_1} \tag{A13.6}$$

and

$$L = \frac{p_2 - d'(q_2)}{p_2} = \frac{\lambda}{1+\lambda}\frac{1}{\eta_2}\left[\frac{1 + (R_1/R_2)(\eta_{12}/\eta_1)}{1 - (\eta_{12}\eta_{21}/\eta_1\eta_2)}\right] \equiv \frac{\lambda}{1+\lambda}\frac{1}{\hat{\eta}_2}. \tag{A13.7}$$

When there is no entry, we simply get

$$\psi'(e) = q_1, \tag{A13.8}$$

with

$$\frac{p_1 - (\beta - e)}{p_1} = \frac{\lambda}{1+\lambda}\frac{1}{\eta_1},$$

and

$$p_1 = P_1(q_1) = \frac{\partial S}{\partial q_1}(q_1, 0).$$

Recall that we made assumptions such that for $\sigma = \underline{\theta}$, entry should not occur and for $\sigma = \bar{\theta}$, it should. When $\sigma = \varnothing$, social welfare without entry is independent of k, and social welfare with entry is decreasing in k. Therefore there exists $k^{\mathrm{FI}}(\beta)$ such that for $k < k^{\mathrm{FI}}(\beta)$ the entrant should enter and for $k > k^{\mathrm{FI}}(\beta)$ it should not. $k^{\mathrm{FI}}(\beta)$ is defined by the equality of expected optimal social welfare with and without entry for $\sigma = \varnothing$.

Finally, straightforward differentiation of the first-order conditions [when the social welfare function in the entry case is maximized with respect to (q_1, q_2, e)] shows that $dq_1/d\theta < 0$. Therefore for $k < k^{\mathrm{FI}}(\beta)$ entry should occur for $\sigma = \varnothing$ and $q_1^{\underline{\theta}}(\beta) > q_1^{\varnothing}(\beta) > q_1^{\bar{\theta}}(\beta)$. For $k > k^{\mathrm{FI}}(\beta)$ entry should not occur for $\sigma = \varnothing$ and $q_1^{\underline{\theta}}(\beta) = q_1^{\varnothing}(\beta) > q_1^{\bar{\theta}}(\beta)$. ■

A13.2 Proof of Proposition 13.2

Let $\sigma = \varnothing$. Note that if $v = 0$, the incomplete information case coincides with the complete information case. Let $W^+(v, \beta)$ (resp. $W^-(v, \beta)$) be the optimal (expected) social welfare with (resp. without) entry (where, by convention, the efficient type's rent $-\lambda v \Phi(e_+^{\varnothing}(\bar{\beta}))$, though paid as a transfer when $\beta = \underline{\beta}$, is included in $W^+(v, \bar{\beta})$ in order to apply the envelope theorem below). Let us index all variables by $+$ or $-$ according to the case considered.

To study the position of $k^{\mathrm{AI}}(\beta)$ with respect to $k^{\mathrm{FI}}(\beta)$, it is enough to sign unambiguously $d[W^+(v, \beta) - W^-(v, \beta)]/dv$. Using the envelope theorem [maximization of (13.17)], we have

$$\frac{d}{dv}[W^+(v, \underline{\beta}) - W^-(v, \underline{\beta})] = 0,$$

and

$$\frac{d}{dv}[W^+(v, \bar{\beta}) - W^-(v, \bar{\beta})] = -\lambda[\Phi(e_+^{\varnothing}(\bar{\beta})) - \Phi(e_-^{\varnothing}(\bar{\beta}))] > 0$$

because $e_+^{\varnothing}(\bar{\beta}) < e_-^{\varnothing}(\bar{\beta})$ given that the incumbent's production is higher if there is no entry. ■

A13.3 A Model of Dual Sourcing in Procurement

The political principal wants to buy one unit of a commodity. It may be produced by an incumbent firm with the technology $C = \beta - e$, $\beta \in \{\underline{\beta}, \bar{\beta}\}$, $\mathrm{Prob}(\beta = \underline{\beta}) = v$. The incumbent's utility function is

$$U = \begin{cases} t - \psi(e) & \text{if } t - \psi(e) \geq 0, \\ -\infty & \text{otherwise,} \end{cases}$$

with $\psi' > 0$, $\psi'' > 0$, $\psi''' \geq 0$. The political principal has also the ability to subsidize through an agency the entry of a competitor with the same technology as the incumbent and the same disutility of effort. However, for entry to occur, expenses

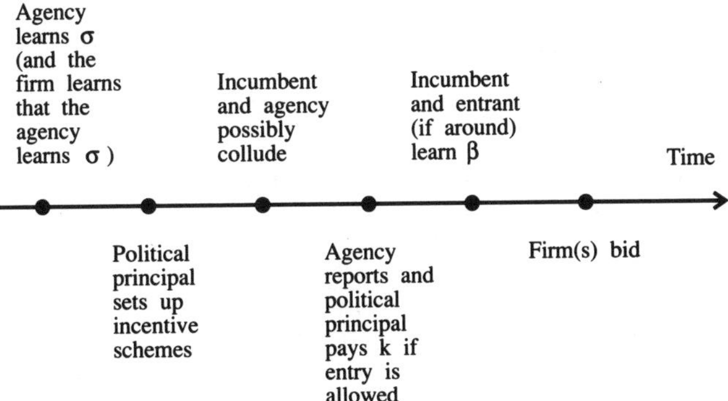

Figure 13.1
Timing of cartelization game

k must be incurred by the political principal (e.g., subsidization of R and D or cost of an educational buy). The needed expenses are either $k = 0$ or $k = \bar{k}$ and $\text{Prob}(k = 0) = \alpha$.

The parameter k is unknown to the political principal, but an agency can be created to learn the value of k. We assume that the agency learns with probability ξ the value of k (hard information). Let σ be its signal: $\sigma = 0$ if $k = 0$ and $\sigma = \bar{k}$ if $k = \bar{k}$, if the agency learns the value of k, and $\sigma = \varnothing$ if no information is learned by the agency.

We assume that if both firms are present, the optimal auction is set up ex post. Since the two firms have the same technology, this implies that no rent is given up and the optimal effort levels are achieved. The timing of the model is described in figure 13.1.

To simplify the exposition we assume that the incumbent learns its technology only after the entry decision; this is not an unreasonable assumption in the case of procurement where k represents the cost of subsidizing R and D or keeping a second source alive through small production runs before contracts on new systems are signed. [One could let the incumbent learn β before the entry decision, with little change in the conclusions. Our previous assumption that the incumbent is infinitely risk averse under zero utility guarantees that the incumbent enjoys a positive expected rent even though the regulatory contract is signed under symmetric information (however, the entry decision could now be a function of the report on β).] The incumbent thus has a stake in the agency's report of k. Last, collusion contracts between the incumbent and the agency take the form of a transfer from the firm to the agency conditionally on the agency hiding its information $\sigma = 0$. (It is straightforward to check that we need not worry about other forms of collusion.)

With a benevolent agency, social welfare in information state σ is, if entry takes place:

$$W_\sigma^e = S - \nu(1+\lambda)[\underline{\beta} - e^* + \psi(e^*)] - (1-\nu)(1+\lambda)[\bar{\beta} - e^* + \psi(e^*)] - (1+\lambda)k_\sigma$$

with

$$k_\sigma = 0 \qquad \text{if } \sigma = 0,$$

$$k_\sigma = \bar{k} \qquad \text{if } \sigma = \bar{k},$$

$$k_\sigma = (1-\alpha)\bar{k} \qquad \text{if } \sigma = \varnothing.$$

In particular yardstick (Bertrand) competition guarantees that the efficient outcome (including rent extraction) prevails ex post. In the absence of entry, the incumbent enjoys rent $\Phi(\bar{e}_\sigma)$ when having type $\underline{\beta}$. Thus expected welfare is equal to

$$W_\sigma^{ne} = S - \nu(1+\lambda)[\underline{\beta} - e^* + \psi(e^*)] - (1-\nu)(1+\lambda)[\bar{\beta} - \bar{e}_\sigma + \psi(\bar{e}_\sigma)] - \nu\lambda\Phi(\bar{e}_\sigma)$$

with $\Phi(e) = \psi(e) - \psi(e - \Delta\beta)$. $\bar{e}_\sigma$ is determined by maximizing W_σ^{ne}; namely it is defined by

$$\psi'(\bar{e}_\sigma) = 1 - \frac{\lambda}{(1+\lambda)}\frac{\nu}{(1-\nu)}\Phi'(\bar{e}_\sigma).$$

Note that $\bar{e}_\sigma$ is independent of σ in the absence of collusion. We therefore omit this subscript. Expected utility before deciding on entry is

$$W_\sigma^{e} = S - \nu(1+\lambda)[\underline{\beta} - e^* + \psi(e^*)] - (1-\nu)(1+\lambda)[\bar{\beta} - e^* + \psi(e^*)] - (1+\lambda)k_\sigma$$

if the agency reports σ and entry is allowed, or

$$W^{ne} = S - \nu(1+\lambda)[\underline{\beta} - e^* + \psi(e^*)] - (1-\nu)(1+\lambda)[\bar{\beta} - \bar{e} + \psi(\bar{e})] - \nu\lambda\Phi(\bar{e})$$

if no entry is allowed. We assume that $\bar{k}$ is large enough so that there is a value α^{AI} such that when $\sigma = \varnothing$, for $\alpha < \alpha^{\mathrm{AI}}$ entry is not allowed, and for $\alpha > \alpha^{\mathrm{AI}}$ entry is allowed.

If the agency is not benevolent, we must add the collusion-proof constraint (see the main text):

$$\hat{s} - s^* \geq \frac{1}{1+\lambda_f}\Phi(\bar{e}_\varnothing)$$

when entry is not allowed for report $\varnothing$, where $\hat{s}$ is the transfer received by the agency if the report is $k = 0$ and efficiency turns out to be $\underline{\beta}$. When entry is not allowed for report $\varnothing$, this reduces expected social welfare by $\nu\lambda\alpha\xi\Phi(\bar{e}_\varnothing)/(1+\lambda_f)$. When entry is allowed for report $\varnothing$, no collusion-proofness constraint needs to be considered because the incumbent does not benefit from the agency's hiding information $k = 0$.

Optimal regulation is as in the absence of collusion except that

1. the effort of the inefficient type, when no entry is allowed and the message of the agency is $\varnothing$, is defined by

$$\psi'(\bar{e}_\varnothing) = 1 - \frac{\nu}{1-\nu}\frac{\lambda}{1+\lambda}\left(1 + \frac{\xi\alpha}{(1-\xi)(1+\lambda_f)}\right)\Phi'(\bar{e}_\varnothing),$$

2. there is more dual sourcing [since the entry regime is more costly, the value α^{C} below which entry is allowed is higher $(\alpha^{\mathrm{C}} > \alpha^{\mathrm{AI}})$].

REFERENCES

Adams, W. 1975. *Public Utility Regulation*, ed. W. Sichel and T. Gies. Lexington, MA: D.C. Heath, Lexington Books, ch. 2.

Burnett, W. and W. Kovacic. 1989. Reform of United States acquisition policy: Competition, teaming agreements, and dual sourcing. *Yale Journal of Regulation* 6:249–317.

Demski, J., Sappington, D., and P. Spiller. 1987. Managing supplier switching. *Rand Journal of Economics* 18:77–97.

Kahn, A. 1988. *The Economics of Regulation*. Cambridge, MA: MIT Press.

Marx, K. [1867]. 1967. *Capital: A Critique of Political Economy*, ed F. Engels (transl. of third German edition by S. Moore and E. Aveling). New York: International Publishers.

Scharfstein, D. 1988. The disciplinary role of takeovers. *Review of Economic Studies* 55:185–200.

Stigler, G. 1971. The economic theory of regulation. *Bell Journal of Economics* 2:3–21.

Subcommittee on Economy in Government Report. 1969. *The Economics of Military Procurement*. Joint Executive Committee. Washington: Government Printing Office.

Yuspeh, L. 1976. A case for increasing the use of competitive procurement in the Department of Defense. In *Bidding and Auctionning for Procurement and Allocation*, ed. Y. Amihud. New York: New York University Press.

14 AUCTION DESIGN AND FAVORITISM

14.1 Some Background

The economic theory of auctions has analyzed the design of bidding procedures that maximize the principal's expected revenue. It has ignored the fact that the auction designer generally is not the principal but its agent.[1] An auction house's duty is to sell at the best terms for the principal, a contractor may select a subcontractor on behalf of the buyer, and the Department of Defense acts as an agent for Congress or the public when soliciting and evaluating offerors' proposals for weapons acquisitions. There has been much concern that the auction designer may prefer or collude with a specific buyer. Indeed most military or governmental markets acquisition regulations[2] go at great length to impose rules aimed at curbing favoritism. Similarly the European Economic Commission, alarmed by the abnormaly large percentage (above 95% in most countries) of government contracts awarded to domestic firms, is trying to design rules that would foster fairer competition between domestic and foreign suppliers and that would fit better than recent experience with the aim of fully opening borders.

In our view the importance of the threat of collusion between auction designers and specific bidders depends much on what is being auctioned off. When the object of bidding is simple, as is often the case in the auction house example, the principal (the seller) may conciliate the goal that the auctioneer enjoys little discretion and that the good must be sold at the best terms; this results from the fact that under some circumstances[3] the seller's expected revenue is maximized by auction procedures (first- or

1. See chapter 7 for references to the theory of auctions. However, favoritism in auctions is a familiar theme in the economics of corruption (e.g., Rose-Akerman 1975).
2. See, for example, the U.S. Air Force Regulation 70-15, Department of the Air Force, Washington, or the Instruction pour l'Application du Code des Marchés Publics (*Journal Officiel de la République Française*, 1976). Constraints on acquisition procedures have a long history. For instance, the early twentieth century state and federal regulations in the United States required that gas and electric utilities and some agencies (e.g., ICC) secure competitive bids for their purchases.
3. We are here alluding to the revenue equivalence theorem (Vickrey 1961; Myerson 1981). Roughly, if the bidders' valuations for the good are private, independent, and drawn from the same distribution, and if the bidders are risk neutral, the first- and second-bid auctions maximize the seller's expected revenue. In this respect it is interesting to note that the detailed procedures of the U.S. Air Force Regulation 70-15 "do not apply if the contract is awarded primarily on the basis of price competition." When the valuations exhibit common values, or when the bidders are asymmetric or risk averse, such simple auctions are no longer optimal (Milgrom and Weber 1982; Maskin and Riley 1984). For instance, under some regularity conditions more eager buyers should be discriminated against (Myerson 1981); if the auction designer has private information about who is more eager to buy, phenomena such as those described in this chapter may arise. Last, we do not claim that first- and second-bid auctions are completely immune to collusion between the agency and specific bidders (e.g., many regulations that specify that a contract be awarded at the lowest price offer ensure that no communication of the maximum price, of the competitors' bids, or of secret information held by the principal to a specific bidder occurs; also the auction designer may manipulate the specifications to favor one of the bidders); rather such auctions are collusion-proof under some circumstances.

second-bid auctions) that require no decentralized information and therefore can be perfectly controlled by the principal.

The procurement examples demonstrate that the stake of bidding can be multidimensional (while, in placing a good for sale, the seller is generally interested only in the price). For a given project the incentive scheme includes at least a fixed fee and a coefficient of cost sharing by the principal. Furthermore the principal generally cares about other attributes of the trade with the winning bidder, including quality and reliability of service, date of delivery, probability of bankruptcy of the supplier, reputation for fairness and competency in dealing with contingencies not foreseen by the contract, and level of pollution associated with the production by this specific firm. This raises two related concerns. First, the contract designer must assign relative weights to the observable characteristics of the bids, that is, determine the monetary values of units of some dimensions of performance, and the optimal choice of weights is likely to depend on information held by the contract designer. Second, some of these characteristics may not be observable by the principal and must be assessed by the contract designer. In both cases the information held by the contract designer about the principal's optimal source selection may give rise to collusion between the contract designer and some bidders.[4] By choosing weights appropriately or by misrepresenting the quality of projects, the auction designer may favor one firm over the others.[5] We will say that the auction designer engages in *unfair* discrimination.

The purchase of power by U.S. electric utilities from qualifying cogeneration and small power production facilities is a good case in point. In their interpretation of the 1978 PURPA Act, many states have forced electric utilities to use competitive bidding procedures to purchase power rather than buy internally. A typical request for proposal (RFP) specifies a fixed quantity to be supplied (number of megawatts) and contains a detailed scoring system for proposals. With each bid a score is given for each broad category (itself an aggregation of more detailed attributes): among these, price factor, "system optimization factor" (location of facilities, maintenance, power for the utility to dispatch, i.e., to have operating control over the amount and the timing of electricity supplies by the qualifying facility, etc.), "economic confidence factor" (probability of bankruptcy and financial structure of the qualifying facility, etc.), and "project development factor" (technical characteristics, experience of seller, etc.). The weights among the different factors are fixed in advance in the RFP.

4. Our model is one of unobservable quality, and not one of weights to be determined, but the same principles would apply to both situations.

5. The potential discretion of contract designers appears clearly in the vague objectives set up by acquisition regulations: For instance, "the principal objective of the major source selection process is to select the source whose proposal has the highest degree of credibility and whose performance can be expected to best meet the government's requirements at an affordable cost" (U.S. Air Force regulation 70-15, p. 3).

While the states have imposed competitive bidding on electric utilities, the latter have kept substantial discretion despite the seemingly objective scoring systems. First, the weights among various factors can vary substantially. For instance, Virginia Power puts weight 70% on economic factors, while Boston Edison puts less weight on such factors (25% on "price factor," plus some weight put on quasi-monetary factors such as dispatchability). Second, the utility evaluates the levels of subjective characteristics such as the reputation or probability of bankruptcy of the qualifying facilities and the value of dispatching rights (which depends on the utility's own resources and on other bids if the contract is shared among several qualifying facilities).[6] Very similar observations can be made concerning the scoring systems used by the Department of Defense.[7]

This chapter is an exploration of the control of auction designers by principals.[8] Section 14.2 sets up the model. Two suppliers, the "agents," compete for a procurement contract for the "principal" (a government or a commission of the European Community). A contract specifies a monetary transfer to the winning agent and an obligation to reach a cost target. An agency, the "supervisor," has more information than the principal about the social surplus—henceforth "quality"—brought about by each potential supplier. One can think of "quality" as reflecting the quality of the supplier's output, its probability of bankruptcy, or the likelihood of being fair in unforeseen contingencies. We first assume that the supervisor is benevolent (truthfully reveals its information, if any, to the principal) and that the firm's technologies are commonly known. The principal then compares the quality differential and the cost differential between the agents. Depending on the parameters, the cost differential or the quality differential may be "decisive" in the principal's selection (if each firm has an advantage in one dimension and a disadvantage in the other; if both criteria agree, the choice between the agents is trivial).

We next relax the assumption that the firms' technologies are commonly known. If firms have private information about their costs, the cost differential is more likely to be decisive (section 14.3). This result can be explained as follows: To limit the firms' informational rents, the principal reduces the power of incentive schemes for intrinsically high-cost types.

6. In some states the utility retains one more degree of freedom. For instance, New York State Electric and Gas Corporation uses a scoring system only to select an "initial award group." The utility uses its judgment to select among the screened sellers in order to "maintain flexibility" (Executive Summary, p. 2). The utility can reject any or all proposals and can consider a substitution in favor of "nonbid alternatives" (including construction of a plant by the utility itself).

7. The DOD's RFPs put scores on price, schedules, logistics, management, past experience, technological characteristics (e.g., range, maneuverability, takeoff/landing distance, cruise speed, for an airplane), and so on.

8. In most of the chapter, we ignore the important issue of collusion among bidders. For analyses of bid rigging, see Graham and Marshall (1987), McAfee and MacMillan (1988), and Mailath and Zemsky (1989). See also section 14.4.

This lowers their cost-reducing activity and increases the realized cost differentials. Another way of putting it is that by favoring cost over quality, the principal reduces the probability that a high-cost firm will be chosen and thus the temptation for a low-cost firm to pretend that its cost is intrinsically high.

Last, the chapter also relaxes the assumption that the supervisor is benevolent and does not collude with bidders. The potential for collusion stems from the agents' stake in the supervisor's report about quality (they enjoy a rent from their technological knowledge if selected). When the supervisor's information about quality is "soft" (i.e., is not verifiable by the principal), the principal imposes a symmetric auction, even though the supervisor's information about quality would vindicate discrimination between the two bidders (section 14.4).

The analysis of the case of "hard" information (information that is verifiable if communicated to the principal) is more difficult. We carry it first only in the special case in which the agency can collude only with one bidder (section 14.5). This assumption may be appropriate for auctions between a domestic and a foreign firm; the supervisor (the domestic government or agency in this application) may be able to trade favors with the domestic firm but not with the foreign firm.[9] The principal (the European Community) relies on the supervisor for the provision of hard information (about the quality or fit of the agents with the needs), giving reasons to discriminate between the domestic agent and the foreign agent.[10] The main conclusion is that the foreign firm should be favored when no information about quality is disclosed (then in our two-type model no welfare loss is imposed on the principal by the threat of collusion).

The case of symmetric collusion is taken up in section 14.6 where only an exploratory analysis is provided, for developing techniques to study collusion with several informed parties is outside the scope of this chapter. We find that two cases must be considered. If the quality differentials are high enough, collusion-proofness is ensured by appropriately motivating the agency, and the auction is similar to that in section 14.3 but with weaker incentive schemes. If the quality differentials are low, the agency faces a flat incentive scheme, and the stakes in collusion are reduced by altering the auction toward a more symmetric auction and by decreasing the power of incentive schemes for firms.

9. A comparable situation may arise in the case of a division of a firm choosing between an internal and an external supplier, or in the case of a department choosing between an insider and an outsider for a tenured position in a given field.

10. We here take the view that the European Community has the power to dictate auctioning procedures or to ex post punish governments if these are not respected. This assumption has proved unrealistic despite the 1971 and 1976 directives to create a "Europe of governmental markets." But the European Community is currently studying how to regulate governmental contracts in a more effective way than in the past. We should also note that the Court of Justice and the European Community have means of enforcing the directives of fair competition, including legal procedures and cancellation of financial loans or of subsidies.

14.2 The Model

For simplicity we assume that only two firms can participate in the auction. Each firm i, $i = 1, 2$, is able to realize an indivisible public project at cost:

$$C^i = \beta^i - e^i, \qquad i = 1, 2,$$

where β^i is firm i' s efficiency parameter and e^i is manager i's effort level (which is incurred only if this firm is selected).

The firms' efficiency parameters are independently drawn from a common-knowledge, two-point probability distribution on $\{\underline{\beta}, \bar{\beta}\}$. Let $\nu = \text{Prob}(\beta^i = \underline{\beta})$ and $\Delta\beta = \bar{\beta} - \underline{\beta}$. Firm i, $i = 1, 2$, has utility

$$U^i = t^i - \psi(e^i), \qquad i = 1, 2,$$

where t^i is the net (i.e., in addition to the reimbursement of cost) monetary transfer that it receives from the regulator and $\psi(e^i)$ is its disutility of effort with $\psi' > 0$, $\psi'' > 0$, $\psi''' \geq 0$. Moreover each firm's outside opportunity level (individual rationality, IR) is normalized at 0.

The consumers' valuation of the project can take one of two values $\{\bar{S}, \underline{S}\}$ with $\bar{S} > \underline{S}$, according to the quality of the firm. S^i denotes the valuation when firm i realizes the project. Again, to simplify the analysis, we assume that either $S^1 = \bar{S}$, $S^2 = \underline{S}$ or $S^1 = \underline{S}$, $S^2 = \bar{S}$ and that $\text{Prob}(S^1 = \bar{S}, S^2 = \underline{S}) = \frac{1}{2}$. We will refer to the firm with the $\bar{S}$ value as the high-quality firm. Let $\Delta S = \bar{S} - \underline{S}$.

These values of the project cannot be contracted upon, but ex ante an agency may learn these values. We assume that the agency can be in one of three states of information σ:

$$\sigma = 1 \quad \Leftrightarrow \quad S^1 = \bar{S}, S^2 = \underline{S},$$

$$\sigma = 2 \quad \Leftrightarrow \quad S^1 = \underline{S}, S^2 = \bar{S},$$

$$\sigma = 0 \quad \Leftrightarrow \quad \emptyset.$$

In state $\emptyset$ the agency learns nothing. In the other two states the agency learns the identity of the high-quality firm. Let $\xi = \text{Prob}(\sigma = 1) = \text{Prob}(\sigma = 2) \leq \frac{1}{2}$.

The agency receives income s from the principal, has utility function $V(s) = s$ for $s \geq s^*$, and its ex post utility level cannot be lower than s^*. The principal's objective function is the sum of welfares in society. Its ex post value is

$$\begin{aligned} W &= S - (1 + \lambda)(C + t + s) + U + (s - s^*) \\ &= S - (1 + \lambda)(C + \psi(e)) - \lambda(U + (s - s^*)) - (1 + \lambda)s^*, \end{aligned}$$

where $\lambda > 0$ is the social cost of public funds, t is the total transfer to firms,

U the sum of the firms' utilities, and C and e the cost and effort of the selected firm.

Full Information

As a benchmark case we derive the optimal regulatory scheme for a utilitarian principal when a benevolent agency knows σ, the values of the β^i and can observe costs. Let $x_\sigma^i(\beta^1, \beta^2)$ denote the probability of selecting firm i in the state of information σ for the values β^1 and β^2 of the efficiency parameters. We need to distinguish two cases in order to determine the optimal values of $x_\sigma^i(\cdot)$:

Case 1: $\Delta S \leq (1 + \lambda)\Delta\beta$

This condition means that choosing the more efficient firm is more important than choosing the better quality firm. We will say that *cost considerations are decisive.* Straightforward reasoning shows that

$$x_1^1(\underline{\beta}, \bar{\beta}) = 1, \quad x_1^1(\bar{\beta}, \underline{\beta}) = 0, \quad x_1^1(\underline{\beta}, \underline{\beta}) = x_1^1(\bar{\beta}, \bar{\beta}) = 1,$$

$$x_2^1(\underline{\beta}, \bar{\beta}) = 1, \quad x_2^1(\bar{\beta}, \underline{\beta}) = 0, \quad x_2^1(\underline{\beta}, \underline{\beta}) = x_2^1(\bar{\beta}, \bar{\beta}) = 0,$$

$$x_0^1(\underline{\beta}, \bar{\beta}) = 1, \quad x_0^1(\bar{\beta}, \underline{\beta}) = 0,$$

$x_0^1(\underline{\beta}, \underline{\beta})$ and $x_0^1(\bar{\beta}, \bar{\beta})$ are indeterminate in $[0, 1]$.

Clearly the low cost firm is always selected. At equal cost the better quality firm is selected, and if there is no information about quality, any random selection will do.

The social cost of the project is

$$(1 + \lambda)[\beta - e + \psi(e)].$$

Effort minimizes cost if $\psi'(e) = 1$ or $e = e^*$. Optimal regulation leads to $e = e^*$ and to the $x_\sigma^1(\cdot)$ function defined above. Accordingly expected social welfare is

$$W_1^{FI} = 2\xi(\bar{S} - \nu(1 - \nu)\Delta S) + (1 - 2\xi)\left(\frac{\bar{S} + \underline{S}}{2}\right)$$
$$- (1 + \lambda)[\underline{\beta} - e^* + \psi(e^*) + s^*] - (1 - \nu)^2(1 + \lambda)\Delta\beta.$$

Case 2: $\Delta S > (1 + \lambda)\Delta\beta$

We will say that *quality considerations are decisive.* Straightforward reasoning shows that

$$x_1^1(\underline{\beta}, \bar{\beta}) = x_1^1(\bar{\beta}, \underline{\beta}) = x_1^1(\underline{\beta}, \underline{\beta}) = x_1^1(\bar{\beta}, \bar{\beta}) = 1,$$

$$x_2^1(\underline{\beta}, \bar{\beta}) = x_2^1(\bar{\beta}, \underline{\beta}) = x_2^1(\underline{\beta}, \underline{\beta}) = x_2^1(\bar{\beta}, \bar{\beta}) = 0,$$

$$x_0^1(\underline{\beta}, \bar{\beta}) = 1, \quad x_0^1(\bar{\beta}, \underline{\beta}) = 0,$$

$x_0^1(\underline{\beta}, \underline{\beta})$ and $x_0^1(\bar{\beta}, \bar{\beta})$ are indeterminate in $[0, 1]$.

As in case 1 we define welfare

$$W_2^{FI} = 2\xi\bar{S} + (1 - 2\xi)\left(\frac{\bar{S} + \underline{S}}{2}\right) - (1 + \lambda)[\underline{\beta} - e^* + \psi(e^*) + s^*]$$
$$- (1 + \lambda)[2\xi\nu(1 - \nu) + (1 - 2\xi)(1 - \nu)^2]\Delta\beta.$$

14.3 Optimal Auction with a Benevolent Agency

In this section we maintain the assumption that the agency is benevolent (does not collude, i.e., truthfully reveals its information to the principal), but we recognize the asymmetry of information between the agency and the firms concerning the efficiency parameters. Specifically β^i is known to firm i only, and costs are ex post observable by the agency. The analysis generalizes that of section 7.2 to quality differences between the two firms.

For each state σ of its information the agency organizes an auction of contracts. From the revelation principle we know that such an auction is equivalent to a revelation mechanism. For each value of σ, let $\{t_\sigma^1(\beta^1, \beta^2), C_\sigma^1(\beta^1, \beta^2), t_\sigma^2(\beta^1, \beta^2), C_\sigma^2(\beta^1, \beta^2), x_\sigma^1(\beta^1, \beta^2), x_\sigma^2(\beta^1, \beta^2)\}$ be a revelation mechanism that specifies transfers to firm i, $t_\sigma^i(\beta^1, \beta^2)$, a cost target for firm i if selected, $C_\sigma^i(\beta^1, \beta^2)$, and a probability of selecting firm i, $x_\sigma^i(\beta^1, \beta^2) \in [0, 1]$ for each announcement β^1, β^2 of cost characteristics. Under the natural monopoly assumption, $x_\sigma^1 + x_\sigma^2 \leq 1$ (and at the optimum, $x_\sigma^1 + x_\sigma^2 = 1$ if the surpluses are sufficiently large, which we will assume).

Incentive compatibility in the auction requires for firm 1, when it has type $\underline{\beta}$, that

$$E_{\beta^2} t_\sigma^1(\underline{\beta}, \beta^2) - E_{\beta^2} x_\sigma^1(\underline{\beta}, \beta^2)\psi(\underline{\beta} - C_\sigma^1(\underline{\beta}, \beta^2))$$
$$\geq E_{\beta^2} t_\sigma^1(\bar{\beta}, \beta^2) - E_{\beta^2} x_\sigma^1(\bar{\beta}, \beta^2)\psi(\underline{\beta} - C_\sigma^1(\bar{\beta}, \beta^2)) \qquad (\mathrm{IC}_1).$$

Similarly incentive compatibility for firm 2, when it has type $\underline{\beta}$, requires that

$$E_{\beta^1} t_\sigma^2(\beta^1, \underline{\beta}) - E_{\beta^1} x_\sigma^2(\beta^1, \underline{\beta})\psi(\underline{\beta} - C_\sigma^2(\beta^1, \underline{\beta}))$$
$$\geq E_{\beta^1} t_\sigma^2(\beta^1, \bar{\beta}) - E_{\beta^1} x_\sigma^2(\beta^1, \bar{\beta})\psi(\underline{\beta} - C_\sigma^2(\beta^1, \bar{\beta})) \qquad (\mathrm{IC}_2).$$

Individual rationality for firms 1 and 2 when having type $\bar{\beta}$ requires that

$$E_{\beta^2} t_\sigma^1(\bar{\beta}, \beta^2) - E_{\beta^2} x_\sigma^1(\bar{\beta}, \beta^2)\psi(\bar{\beta} - C_\sigma^1(\bar{\beta}, \beta^2)) \geq 0 \qquad (\mathrm{IR}_1),$$
$$E_{\beta^1} t_\sigma^2(\beta^1, \bar{\beta}) - E_{\beta^1} x_\sigma^2(\beta^1, \bar{\beta})\psi(\bar{\beta} - C_\sigma^2(\beta^1, \bar{\beta})) \geq 0 \qquad (\mathrm{IR}_2).$$

From incentive theory we guess that we can ignore the other incentive and individual rationality constraints and check ex post that they are satisfied by the solution to the subconstrained problem. Since transfers are costly, the above IC and IR constraints are tight. We can henceforth obtain the rents of asymmetric information that must be given up to the efficient types:

$$\begin{aligned}U_\sigma^1(\underline{\beta}) &= E_{\beta^2}t_\sigma^1(\underline{\beta},\beta^2) - E_{\beta^2}x_\sigma^1(\underline{\beta},\beta^2)\psi(\underline{\beta} - C_\sigma^1(\underline{\beta},\beta^2))\\ &= E_{\beta^2}x_\sigma^1(\bar{\beta},\beta^2)\{\psi(\bar{\beta} - C_\sigma^1(\bar{\beta},\beta^2)) - \psi(\underline{\beta} - C_\sigma^1(\bar{\beta},\beta^2))\}\\ &= \nu x_\sigma^1(\bar{\beta},\underline{\beta})\{\psi(\bar{\beta} - C_\sigma^1(\bar{\beta},\underline{\beta})) - \psi(\underline{\beta} - C_\sigma^1(\bar{\beta},\underline{\beta}))\}\\ &\quad + (1-\nu)x_\sigma^1(\bar{\beta},\bar{\beta})\{\psi(\bar{\beta} - C_\sigma^1(\bar{\beta},\bar{\beta})) - \psi(\underline{\beta} - C_\sigma^1(\bar{\beta},\bar{\beta}))\}\\ &= \nu x_\sigma^1(\bar{\beta},\underline{\beta})\Phi(e_\sigma^1(\bar{\beta},\underline{\beta})) + (1-\nu)x_\sigma^1(\bar{\beta},\bar{\beta})\Phi(e_\sigma^1(\bar{\beta},\bar{\beta})),\end{aligned}$$

where

$$\begin{aligned}e_\sigma^1(\bar{\beta},\underline{\beta}) &= \bar{\beta} - C_\sigma^1(\bar{\beta},\underline{\beta}),\\ e_\sigma^1(\bar{\beta},\bar{\beta}) &= \bar{\beta} - C_\sigma^1(\bar{\beta},\bar{\beta}),\\ \Phi(e) &= \psi(e) - \psi(e - \Delta\beta).\end{aligned}$$

Similarly

$$U_\sigma^2(\underline{\beta}) = \nu x_\sigma^2(\underline{\beta},\bar{\beta})\Phi(e_\sigma^2(\underline{\beta},\bar{\beta})) + (1-\nu)x_\sigma^2(\bar{\beta},\bar{\beta})\Phi(e_\sigma^2(\bar{\beta},\bar{\beta})).$$

Let S_σ^i denote the expected valuation of the project done by firm i conditional on the information σ:

$$S_1^1 = \bar{S},\quad S_2^1 = \underline{S},\quad S_0^1 = \frac{\bar{S}+\underline{S}}{2},$$

$$S_1^2 = \underline{S},\quad S_2^2 = \bar{S},\quad S_0^2 = \frac{\bar{S}+\underline{S}}{2}.$$

In state of information σ expected social welfare is

$$\begin{aligned}W_\sigma = E_{\beta^1,\beta^2}\{&S_\sigma^1 - (1+\lambda)(\beta^1 - e_\sigma^1(\beta^1,\beta^2)\\ &+ \psi(e_\sigma^1(\beta^1,\beta^2)) + s^*)\}x_\sigma^1(\beta^1,\beta^2) - \lambda\nu U_\sigma^1(\underline{\beta})\\ + E_{\beta^1,\beta^2}\{&S_\sigma^2 - (1+\lambda)(\beta^2 - e_\sigma^2(\beta^1,\beta^2)\\ &+ \psi(e_\sigma^2(\beta^1,\beta^2)) + s^*)\}(1 - x_\sigma^1(\beta^1,\beta^2)) - \lambda\nu U_\sigma^2(\underline{\beta}).\end{aligned} \tag{14.1}$$

Maximizing expected social welfare with respect to $(e_\sigma^i(\cdot), x_\sigma^i(\cdot))$ yields proposition 14.1.

Proposition 14.1 When the agency is benevolent, the optimal auction is characterized by the following conditions for $\sigma = 1, \sigma = 2, \sigma = 0$:

i. If $\sigma = 1$,

$x_1^1(\bar{\beta},\bar{\beta}) = x_1^1(\underline{\beta},\bar{\beta}) = x_1^1(\underline{\beta},\underline{\beta}) = 1.$

$x_1^1(\bar{\beta},\underline{\beta}) = 1$ if

$$\Delta S - (1+\lambda)\Delta\beta > (1+\lambda)[\psi(\hat{e}) - \hat{e} + \frac{\lambda}{1+\lambda}\frac{v}{1-v}\Phi(\hat{e}) - \psi(e^*) + e^*] > 0.$$

$x_1^1(\bar{\beta}, \underline{\beta}) = 0$ if the inequality is reversed, and $x_1^1(\bar{\beta}, \underline{\beta})$ is indeterminate in $[0, 1]$ otherwise.

ii. If $\sigma = 2$,

$x_2^2(\bar{\beta}, \bar{\beta}) = x_2^2(\bar{\beta}, \underline{\beta}) = x_2^2(\underline{\beta}, \underline{\beta}) = 1.$

$x_2^2(\underline{\beta}, \bar{\beta}) = 1$ if

$$\Delta S - (1+\lambda)\Delta\beta > (1+\lambda)[\psi(\hat{e}) - \hat{e} + \frac{\lambda}{1+\lambda}\frac{v}{1-v}\Phi(\hat{e}) - \psi(e^*) + e^*] > 0.$$

$x_2^2(\underline{\beta}, \bar{\beta}) = 0$ if the inequality is reversed, and $x_2^2(\underline{\beta}, \bar{\beta})$ is indeterminate in $[0, 1]$ otherwise.

iii. If $\sigma = 0$,

$x_0^1(\bar{\beta}, \bar{\beta})$ and $x_0^1(\underline{\beta}, \underline{\beta})$ indeterminate in $[0, 1]$,

$x_0^1(\underline{\beta}, \bar{\beta}) = 1$ and $x_0^1(\bar{\beta}, \underline{\beta}) = 0.$

The effort level of a $\underline{\beta}$ firm if selected is the efficient level e^*. The effort level of a $\bar{\beta}$ firm, if selected, is $\hat{e}$ defined [as in equation (1.23)] by

$$\hat{e} = \arg\min_e \left\{\psi(e) - e + \frac{\lambda}{1+\lambda}\frac{v}{1-v}\Phi(e)\right\}.$$

Proof See appendix A14.1.

The intuition for the optimal auction is clear. If the regulator is informed about quality, the preference is given to the high-quality firm when it is at least as efficient as the low-quality firm. When the high-quality firm is less efficient than the low-quality firm, it is still favored as long as ΔS is larger than

$$(1+\lambda)\Delta\beta + (1+\lambda)\left[\left\{\psi(\hat{e}) - \hat{e} + \frac{\lambda}{1+\lambda}\frac{v}{1-v}\Phi(\hat{e})\right\} - \{\psi(e^*) - e^*\}\right]. \tag{14.2}$$

The first term is the cost disadvantage already present under complete information, and the second is the increase in cost of the less efficient type due to asymmetric information. Effort is not optimal ($\hat{e} \neq e^*$) because using the $\bar{\beta}$ firm increases the rent that must be given up to a $\underline{\beta}$ firm when selected, which has expected social cost $\lambda[v/(1-v)]\Phi(\hat{e})$. *Under incomplete information the quality advantage is decisive less often than under complete information.* Last, an uninformed agency may use a symmetric auction (choose $x_0^1(\bar{\beta}, \bar{\beta}) = x_0^1(\underline{\beta}, \underline{\beta}) = \frac{1}{2}$).

Remark First, we check that the ignored incentive constraints for the $\bar{\beta}$ types are satisfied by the auction defined in proposition 14.1. This results directly from the facts that $x_\sigma^1(\underline{\beta}, \beta^2) \geq x_\sigma^1(\bar{\beta}, \beta^2)$ and $e_\sigma^1(\underline{\beta}, \beta^2) \geq e_\sigma^1(\bar{\beta}, \beta^2)$ for all β^2 and σ and that the IC constraints for the $\underline{\beta}$ types are binding, and symmetrically for firm 2 (allocations are "monotonic" in the firm's type). Second, firm i's rent is highest for signal $\sigma = i$, as one would expect. It is weakly higher under signal $\sigma = 0$ than under signal $\sigma = j \neq i, 0$. Third, the separability exhibited in chapter 7 also holds here: The effort levels of the selected firm are identical to those which would be obtained if the regulator was facing a single firm and are defined by e^* for a $\underline{\beta}$ firm and $\hat{e}$ by for a $\bar{\beta}$ firm. Proposition 14.1 defines the optimal effort levels and the optimal selection variables x. The efficient type's rent associated with the optimal auction is for firm 1,

$$U_\sigma^1(\underline{\beta}) = \nu x_\sigma^1(\bar{\beta}, \underline{\beta})\Phi(e_\sigma^1(\bar{\beta}, \underline{\beta})) + (1 - \nu)x_\sigma^1(\bar{\beta}, \bar{\beta})\Phi(e_\sigma^1(\bar{\beta}, \bar{\beta})),$$

and the optimal expected transfers are

$$t_\sigma^1(\underline{\beta}) = U_\sigma^1(\underline{\beta}) + \psi(e^*)E_{\beta^2}x_\sigma^1(\underline{\beta}, \beta^2),$$

$$t_\sigma^1(\bar{\beta}) = \psi(\hat{e})E_{\beta^2}x_\sigma^1(\bar{\beta}, \beta^2),$$

and similarly for firm 2. The ex post transfers $t_\sigma^1(\beta^1, \beta^2)$ are not determined; only their expectations are.

14.4 Collusion and Soft Information

14.4.1 Description of Collusion

From now on we allow the agency to collude with specific bidders. We first remind the reader of the distinction between soft and hard information, a distinction that was irrelevant in the absence of collusion. Hard information is information that can be substantiated. That is, the principal can verify the agency's information, if transmitted. The agency's degree of freedom then stems from the possibility of retaining information (reporting $r = 0$ when $\sigma = 1$ or 2). Formally $r \in \{\sigma, 0\}$.

In contrast, soft information cannot be verified. For any realized signal the agency can claim to have received any of the three possible signals without being detected. In the case of hard information, we will assume that only the agency can bring evidence about which firm the principal prefers. For simplicity we will also assume that even though the firms cannot bring hard evidence on the quality parameter, they learn the signal received by the agency; this assumption limits asymmetries of information in the design of side contracts (see below) and is not crucial: It is easily seen that if the agency wants to collude with a specific firm not to disclose its

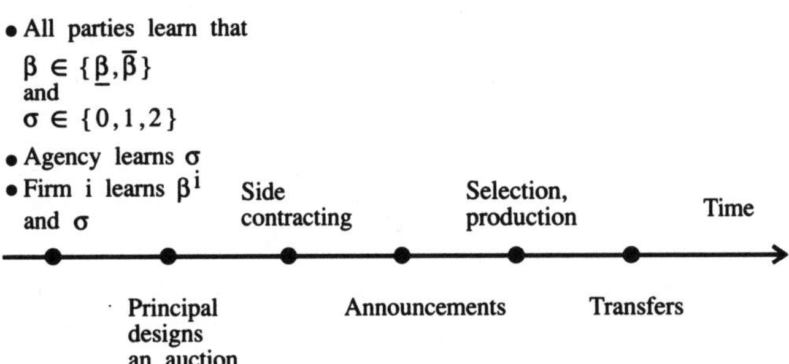

Figure 14.1
Timing of auction and collusion

signal, it is in its interest to show this (hard) information to the firm to convince it of the benefit of colluding.

Next, we assume the following timing: First, the principal publicly offers primary contracts (an auction) to the agency and the firm. These contracts specify the winner and primary transfers from the principal to the agency and the firm as functions of all (simultaneous) announcements (report of signal by the agency and announcements of technological parameters by the firms) and the winner's realized cost. Second, side contracting occurs. A side contract specifies a secondary or side transfer between the two concerned parties. The side transfer may be contingent on all announcements and on the winner's realized cost. Each firm's side contract is not observed by the other firm (in section 14.5 we do not make specific assumptions on the collusion game, that is, on who makes the offers for side contracts. In subsection 14.4.3 and section 14.6 we specialize the collusion game by assuming that the firms make take-it-or-leave-it offers to the agency for side contracts). Third, announcements are made, the winner is selected as specified in the auction set up by the principal, and production and primary and side transfers occur. The timing can be summarized as shown in figure 14.1.

We allow side transfers to be costly. An income equivalent of \$1 transferred by firm i to the agency costs \$ $(1 + \lambda^i)$ of firm i. The parameter $\lambda^i \geq 0$ is a measure of the deadweight loss of collusive transfers for the two parties. In sections 14.5 and 14.6 we will focus on two cases with hard information: *asymmetric collusion* in which $\lambda^1 \equiv \lambda_f < +\infty$ and $\lambda^2 = +\infty$ (only firm 1 can collude with the agency), and *symmetric collusion* in which $\lambda^1 = \lambda^2 \equiv \lambda_f$.

14.4.2 Soft Information

The case of soft information has a simple implication in our context. Since quality does not enter the agency's and the firms' objective functions, for a given set of primary contracts (auction), the set of equilibria of the collusion and announcements continuation game is independent of the realization of the quality signal. We will adhere to the "Markov principle" that strategically equivalent games or subgames should have the same equilibrium. This principle implies that the same continuation equilibrium prevails for all possible *quality signals received by the agency*[11] and thus that quality differentials are never decisive; the agency has no discretion in that its announcement has no effect on selection.

This assumption implies that the final allocation is insensitive to the quality signal for a given auction. Therefore the outcome can be implemented without paying attention to the agency's information. We are thus in the case $\sigma = 0$ of section 14.3, except that we can allow side transfers between the agency and the firms. Since side transfers involve a deadweight loss, all transfers are cheaper to achieve through the principal. We can conclude that the optimal auction is the symmetric auction corresponding to signal $\sigma = 0$. *Quality differentials are never decisive* because no attention is paid to the quality signal; the agency has no discretion in that its announcement has no effect on selection.

Remark 1 The case of soft information is meant to illustrate some potentially extreme implications of collusion for auction design. It by no means implies that soft information always leads to a rigid auction in which decentralized information about quality is systematically ignored. Consider the case where quality affects the agency's utility as well as the principal's (as is particularly relevant in the example of the European Community). Then even soft information can be used in the presence of collusion. The point is that the agency's report can be made incentive compatible through appropriate transfers because it affects its utility. (For a technically similar example in which soft information conditions the equilibrium allocation, see chapter 11.)

Remark 2 We have observed that if we adhere to the viewpoint that strategically equivalent games or subgames should have the same equilibrium, no use can be made of the agency's signal. This does not imply that the agency has no role, for it may perform other tasks than collecting information about quality. This also does not imply that the principal can guarantee him- or herself the collusion-proof payoff for $\sigma = 0$: While we have deliberately ignored collusion between the two bidders (bid rigging) to focus on favoritism, bid rigging can still arise in a roundabout way through side contracts between the agency and the firms. For instance, the agency could act as a "cartel ringmaster" (to use a phrase employed by Krattenmaker and Salop 1986 in a vertical restraints context) and induce each firm to announce "high" $\bar{\beta}$ and be rewarded by both. This

11. In other words, we do not allow the quality signal to play the role of a "correlating device" or "sunspot." For a general definition of Markov perfect equilibrium, see Maskin and Tirole (1992). (The reason why the allocation was responsive to even soft information in section 14.3 is that the level of quality entered the benevolent agency's preferences.)

point is vague, since we have not described how collusion can be implemented through side contracts; we bring it up only to illustrate the possibility of indirect bid rigging. We will investigate this possibility in the next subsection.

14.4.3 Indirect Bid Rigging

The study of collusion with several informed parties is complex. The outcome depends on the bargaining process for collusion as well as possibly on the equilibrium selection. In this section we derive an upper bound on welfare under collusion and soft information. The upper bound, which turns out to be equal to the one mentioned in the previous subsection, is obtained when the agency cannot coordinate collusion between the two firms and thus does not act as a cartel ringmaster.

We observed above that the principal can obtain at most W_0. That this upper bound may be reached for some bargaining process for collusive contracts can be seen as follows: Suppose that the firms simultaneously make take-it-or-leave-it offers of side contracts to the agency. One might imagine that the firms bargain secretly with the agency and have all the bargaining power. Let the principal offer the symmetric auction for $\sigma = 0$ characterized in proposition 14.1.

We claim that an equilibrium exists in which both firms offer "no side contract" (i.e., the side contract that specifies zero side transfers whatever happens) and announce their technological parameters truthfully: Suppose that firm i expects firm j and the agency not to enter a side contract and firm j to announce its parameter truthfully. Then from incentive compatibility of the auction, firm i cannot do better than announce the truth, and there is nothing the agency can do to improve its welfare. (In section 14.6 we will give a more general definition of "bilaterally interim-efficient allocations," which are allocations that are interim efficient from the point of view of a firm and the agency taking as given the behavior of the other firm. Such allocations cannot give rise only to unilateral collusion; they require multiple collusive arrangements to be upset.) Thus an optimal strategy for firm i is to offer no side contract and tell the truth (if firm i were to do strictly better than in the allocation of proposition 14.1, then by bilateral interim efficiency the agency would lose, which is impossible because it can guarantee itself s^* by not entering side contracts).

What is allowing the upper bound to be reached is clear. Coordination to announce high-cost parameters might not be possible if firms offer side contracts. It is relatively straightforward to derive the principal's welfare when firms collude as if they had complete information about each other. However, we feel that this approach fails to recognize the major difficulty of bargaining under incomplete information. Therefore we leave open the problem of characterizing the optimal auction when bid rigging is possible.

14.5 Asymmetric Collusion and Hard Information

Suppose now that the agency's information is hard and that the agency can collude only with firm 1. We first claim that the principal can obtain the same welfare as under a benevolent agency by adequately picking a variable left indeterminate in proposition 14.1. Suppose that the auction is defined as in proposition 14.1 except that $x_0^1(\bar{\beta},\bar{\beta}) = 0$ ($x_0^1(\underline{\beta},\underline{\beta})$ is still indeterminate in $[0,1]$). We now show that this auction does not give rise to a side contract between the agency and firm 1 and therefore yields the same welfare to the principal as in the absence of collusion. On the one hand, only type $\underline{\beta}$ of firm 1 may want to bribe the agency to hide its information, since type $\bar{\beta}$ gets a zero rent in each state of nature. On the other hand, type $\underline{\beta}$'s rent, in expectation over firm 2's technological parameter, is the following function of the report r:

$$(1 - \nu)x_r^1(\bar{\beta},\bar{\beta})\Phi(e_r^1(\bar{\beta},\bar{\beta})) + \nu x_r^1(\bar{\beta},\underline{\beta})\Phi(e_r^1(\bar{\beta},\underline{\beta})),$$

which, for the auction specified by proposition 14.1 [with $x_0^1(\bar{\beta},\bar{\beta}) = 0$], is equal to

$$\begin{cases} [(1-\nu) + \nu x_1^1(\bar{\beta},\underline{\beta})]\Phi(\hat{e}) > 0 & \text{if } r = 1, \\ 0 & \text{if } r = 2, \\ 0 & \text{if } r = 0. \end{cases}$$

Since under hard information the agency can only hide information away from the principal, firm 1 cannot gain from inducing the agency to retain information (to induce $r = 0$). We thus conclude that the auction specified in proposition 14.1, with $x_0^1(\bar{\beta},\bar{\beta}) = 0$ is collusion-proof, and clearly it is optimal in the class of collusion-proof auctions.

Second, we claim that the principal cannot do better with an auction that gives rise to a side contract. The proof of this is very similar to the proof of the collusion-proofness principle for a single firm and hard information in chapter 11 and is omitted. The reason for this similarity is that firm 2 cannot collude and is therefore much like a dummy firm. Once the incentive cost is included to obtain firm 2's generalized cost, firm 2 can be regarded as a backstop technology. The asymmetric collusion model is really a one-firm model. We thus obtain proposition 14.2.

Proposition 14.2 Suppose that the agency can collude only with firm 1 and that information is hard. The threat of collusion imposes no welfare loss on the principal as long as firm 2 is favored at equal cost when no information about quality is transmitted to the principal.

The main conclusion in proposition 14.2 is that firm 2 should be favored when no information about quality is disclosed, in order to induce the agency to reveal information unfavorable to firm 1. The conclusion that asymmetric collusion imposes no welfare loss is less robust. Suppose that the β^i are drawn from a continuous distribution. Then the indeterminacy of $x_0^1(\beta^i, \beta^j)$ when $\beta^i = \beta^j$ under no collusion has probability 0 over the set of (β^i, β^j). Resolving this indeterminacy in favor of firm 2 apparently does not suffice to yield collusion proofness of the optimal no-collusion auction.[12]

Note also that since the agency can collude with only one firm, we do not need to consider indirect bid rigging, and that in the EEC example the costs envisioned here could be "generalized costs" if the government attaches some value to the domestic firm's being selected, say, for secrecy reasons.

14.6 Symmetric Collusion and Hard Information

We now allow the agency to collude with the two firms (symmetric collusion). This section is to a large extent exploratory because the development of techniques to study collusion with several informed parties is outside the scope of this chapter. We will content ourselves with requiring that the auction offered by the principal (1) induces truth telling by the three parties in the absence of collusion and (2) is "bilaterally interim efficient." We will say that an allocation is bilaterally interim efficient if there exist no vector of side transfers between the agency and a firm i and no announcement strategy by the agency and this firm that is incentive compatible given the original auction and the side transfers and that yields a Pareto superior allocation for the agency and firm i, *taking firm j's announcement strategy* (*i.e., telling the truth*) *as given.*

We do not offer a complete defense of this requirement, but we make the following points. Assume that the extensive form for the collusion game has the firms make take-or-leave-it offers of side contracts to the agency (and that these offers are secret), and suppose that the principal offers a bilaterally interim-efficient allocation. Then the absence of collusion (each firm's offering the null contract) followed by truth telling is an equilibrium: Knowing that the other firm does not offer a side contract and subsequently tells the truth, each firm has no incentive to offer a side contract, since by bilateral interim efficiency it either loses expected utility or the agency loses expected utility, in which case the agency turns the side contract down.

In our context bilateral interim efficiency is equivalent to imposing the extra requirement that no firm has an incentive to bribe the agency to

12. It is worth mentioning why we chose to work with a two-type space. With two types, collusive activities necessarily stem from type $\underline{\beta}$ because type $\overline{\beta}$ gets no rent. With more than two types, the agency must screen in a more subtle way the firm's willingness to pay for collusion.

hide its information [conditions (14.3) and (14.4) below]. If either condition is violated, then the firms' offering the null side contract and truth telling by all parties is not an equilibrium.

To obtain bilateral interim efficiency, it must be the case that if firm i has cost parameter $\underline{\beta}$ (and therefore enjoys a rent) and the agency receives the signal that firm $j \neq i$ offers a higher quality, firm i has no incentive to induce the agency to retain its information. Let s_j $(j = 1, 2)$ denote the agency's income when it reports $r = j$ and firm $i \neq j$ announces $\hat{\beta}^i = \underline{\beta}$. As is easily seen, the other contingent incomes for the agency are optimally set at s^*, since the threat of collusion operates only in the above case.

Let

$$\begin{aligned} A_1 \equiv s_1 - s^* - \frac{1}{1+\lambda_f}[&(1-\nu)x_0^2(\bar{\beta},\bar{\beta})\Phi(e_0^2(\bar{\beta},\bar{\beta})) \\ &+ \nu x_0^2(\underline{\beta},\bar{\beta})\Phi(e_0^2(\underline{\beta},\bar{\beta})) - (1-\nu)x_1^2(\bar{\beta},\bar{\beta})\Phi(e_1^2(\bar{\beta},\bar{\beta})) \\ &- \nu x_1^2(\underline{\beta},\bar{\beta})\Phi(e_1^2(\underline{\beta},\bar{\beta}))], \end{aligned} \tag{14.3}$$

$$\begin{aligned} A_2 \equiv s_2 - s^* - \frac{1}{1+\lambda_f}[&(1-\nu)x_0^1(\bar{\beta},\bar{\beta})\Phi(e_0^1(\bar{\beta},\bar{\beta})) \\ &+ \nu x_0^1(\bar{\beta},\underline{\beta})\Phi(e_0^1(\bar{\beta},\underline{\beta})) - (1-\nu)x_2^1(\bar{\beta},\bar{\beta})\Phi(e_2^1(\bar{\beta},\bar{\beta})) \\ &- \nu x_2^1(\bar{\beta},\underline{\beta})\Phi(e_2^1(\bar{\beta},\underline{\beta}))]. \end{aligned} \tag{14.4}$$

Bilateral interim efficiency is equivalent to $A_1 \geq 0$, $A_2 \geq 0$. Indeed the only case when collusion between the agency and firm 2 is valuable is $\sigma = 1$, $\beta_2 = \underline{\beta}$. Then, if the agency withholds its information ($r = 0$), type $\underline{\beta}$ of firm 2 may obtain a rent. $A_1 \geq 0$ says that from $r = 1$ to $r = 0$, the expected rent increase of firm 2 (when it is of type $\underline{\beta}$ and claims that it is of type $\bar{\beta}$), appropriately discounted to take into account that internal transfers within the coalition are costly, is inferior to the loss that the agency would incur from such an untruthful report. Colluding and claiming that $\beta = \bar{\beta}$ would not be more valuable since, with binding incentive contraints, a type $\underline{\beta}$ firm is indifferent between announcing $\beta = \underline{\beta}$ or $\beta = \bar{\beta}$. Similarly for $A_2 \geq 0$. The principal wishes to maximize

$$\xi W_1 + \xi W_2 + (1-2\xi)W_0 - \lambda\nu\xi(s_1 - s^*) - \lambda\nu\xi(s_2 - s^*) \tag{14.5}$$

under the constraints

$$A_1 \geq 0, \quad A_2 \geq 0, \quad s_1 \geq s^*, \quad s_2 \geq s^*$$

where W_σ is defined in equation (14.1).

Lemma 14.1 At the optimum of program (14.5) $A_1 = 0$ and $A_2 = 0$.

Proof Suppose that $A_1 > 0$. Then the shadow price of constraint (14.3) is equal to zero and $s_1 = s^*$. The maximization is the same as that in section

14.5 where only firm 1 can collude. We know that the solution involves $x_0^1(\bar{\beta},\bar{\beta}) = 0$ and $s_2 = s^*$. Then $A_2 = 0$, but $A_1 < 0$, a contradiction, and similarly if $A_2 > 0$. ■

We now give a full description of the optimal bilaterally interim-efficient auction, and later interpret its findings. Let $\hat{\hat{e}}$ and $\check{e}(e^* > \hat{\hat{e}} > \hat{e} > \check{e})$ be defined by

$$\hat{\hat{e}} = \arg\min_e \left\{\psi(e) - e + \frac{\lambda}{1+\lambda}\frac{\nu}{1-\nu}\frac{\lambda_f}{1+\lambda_f}\Phi(e)\right\},$$

$$\check{e} = \arg\min_e \left\{\psi(e) - e + \frac{\lambda}{1+\lambda}\frac{\nu}{1-\nu}\left[1 + \frac{\xi}{(1-2\xi)(1+\lambda_f)}\right]\Phi(e)\right\}.$$

Let $\{\hat{\hat{e}}(\Delta S), \mu(\Delta S)\}$ be the solution $\{e, \mu\}$ of

$$\Delta S = (1+\lambda)\left[\left\{\psi(\hat{e}) - \hat{e} + \frac{\lambda}{1+\lambda}\frac{\nu}{1-\nu}\Phi(\hat{e})\right\} - \left\{\psi(e) - e + \left[\frac{\lambda}{1+\lambda}\frac{\nu}{1-\nu} - \frac{\mu}{\xi(1-\nu)(1+\lambda)}\right]\Phi(e)\right\}\right]$$

and

$$\psi'(e) = 1 - \left[\frac{\lambda}{1+\lambda}\frac{\nu}{1-\nu} - \frac{\mu}{\xi(1-\nu)(1+\lambda)}\right]\Phi'(e).$$

Let $\check{e}(\Delta S)$ be defined by

$$\psi'(\check{e}(\Delta S)) = 1 - \left(\frac{\lambda}{1+\lambda}\frac{\nu}{1-\nu} + \frac{\mu(\Delta S)}{(1-2\xi)(1-\nu)(1+\lambda)}\right)\Phi'(\check{e}(\Delta S)).$$

Proposition 14.3 The solution to program (14.5) is characterized by the following two cases:

Case 1

$$\Delta S > (1+\lambda)\left[\left\{\psi(\hat{e}) - \hat{e} + \frac{\lambda}{1+\lambda}\frac{\nu}{1-\nu}\Phi(\hat{e})\right\} - \left\{\psi(\hat{\hat{e}}) - \hat{\hat{e}} + \frac{\lambda}{1+\lambda}\frac{\nu}{1-\nu}\frac{\lambda_f}{1+\lambda_f}\Phi(\hat{\hat{e}})\right\}\right].$$

ia. If $\sigma = 1$,

$$x_1^1(\bar{\beta},\bar{\beta}) = x_1^1(\underline{\beta},\underline{\beta}) = x_1^1(\underline{\beta},\bar{\beta}) = 1,$$

$$x_1^1(\bar{\beta},\underline{\beta}) = 1$$

if $\Delta S - (1+\lambda)\Delta\beta > (1+\lambda)\left[\left\{\psi(\hat{e}) - \hat{e} + \frac{\lambda}{1+\lambda}\frac{\nu}{1-\nu}\Phi(\hat{e})\right\} - \{\psi(e^*) - e^*\}\right],$

$$x_1^1(\bar{\beta},\underline{\beta}) = 0 \quad \text{if the inequality is reversed, and}$$

$$x_1^1(\bar{\beta},\underline{\beta}) \quad \text{is indeterminate in } [0,1] \text{ otherwise,}$$

$$e_1^1(\bar{\beta},\bar{\beta}) = e_1^1(\bar{\beta},\underline{\beta}) = \hat{e}, \quad e_1^2(\underline{\beta},\bar{\beta}) = \hat{\hat{e}} = e_1^2(\bar{\beta},\bar{\beta}),$$

$$e_1^1(\underline{\beta},\bar{\beta}) = e_1^1(\underline{\beta},\underline{\beta}) = e_1^2(\bar{\beta},\underline{\beta}) = e_1^2(\underline{\beta},\underline{\beta}) = e^*.$$

ib. If $\sigma = 2$, the solution is symmetric.

ic. If $\sigma = 0$,

$$x_0^1(\bar{\beta},\underline{\beta}) = x_0^2(\underline{\beta},\bar{\beta}) = 0,$$

$$x_0^1(\underline{\beta},\underline{\beta}) \quad \text{and} \quad x_0^1(\bar{\beta},\bar{\beta}) \quad \text{indeterminate in } [0,1],$$

$$e_0^1(\underline{\beta},\bar{\beta}) = e_0^2(\bar{\beta},\underline{\beta}) = e_0^1(\underline{\beta},\underline{\beta}) = e_0^2(\underline{\beta},\underline{\beta}) = e^*,$$

$$e_0^1(\bar{\beta},\underline{\beta}) = e_0^2(\underline{\beta},\bar{\beta}) = e_0^1(\bar{\beta},\bar{\beta}) = e_0^2(\bar{\beta},\bar{\beta}) = \check{e}.$$

id.

$$s_1 = s^* + \frac{1-v}{1+\lambda_f} x_0^2(\bar{\beta},\bar{\beta})\Phi(\check{e}),$$

$$s_2 = s^* + \frac{1-v}{1+\lambda_f} x_0^1(\bar{\beta},\bar{\beta})\Phi(\check{e}).$$

Case 2

$$\Delta S < (1+\lambda)\left[\left\{\psi(\hat{e}) - \hat{e} + \frac{\lambda}{1+\lambda}\frac{v}{1-v}\Phi(\hat{e})\right\} - \left\{\psi(\hat{\hat{e}}) - \hat{\hat{e}} + \frac{\lambda}{1+\lambda}\frac{v}{1-v}\frac{\lambda_f}{1+\lambda_f}\Phi(\hat{\hat{e}})\right\}\right]$$

iia. $s_1 = s_2 = s^*$.

iib. The solution is as in case 1 except that

$\hat{\hat{e}}$ is replaced by $\hat{\hat{e}}(\Delta S)$,

$\check{e}$ is replaced by $\check{e}(\Delta S)$,

$$x_1^2(\bar{\beta},\bar{\beta}) = \frac{\Phi(\check{e}(\Delta S))}{\Phi(\hat{\hat{e}}(\Delta S))} x_0^2(\bar{\beta},\bar{\beta}),$$

$$x_2^1(\bar{\beta},\bar{\beta}) = \frac{\Phi(\check{e}(\Delta S))}{\Phi(\hat{\hat{e}}(\Delta S))} x_0^1(\bar{\beta},\bar{\beta}),$$

with $x_0^2(\bar{\beta},\bar{\beta}) + x_0^1(\bar{\beta},\bar{\beta}) = 1$.

A symmetric solution is obtained with $x_0^2(\bar{\beta},\bar{\beta}) = x_0^1(\bar{\beta},\bar{\beta}) = \frac{1}{2}$.

Proof See appendix A14.2.

Two different ways of satisfying the collusion constraints are described in cases 1 and 2. In case 1 the constraint is satisfied by motivating the agency with appropriate transfers. This is the case where the agency's information is valuable (ΔS large) and therefore worth obtaining. A necessary condition for case 1 to obtain is that quality differentials be decisive in the absence of collusion. The allocation (selection rule, effort) is the same as is the absence of collusion when $\sigma = 1$ or 2, but incentives are lowered when $\sigma = 0$.

In case 2 (low ΔS) the agency is not motivated, but the stakes of collusion are nullified by making the auction closer to a symmetric auction when $(\beta_1, \beta_2) = (\bar{\beta}, \bar{\beta})$ and by decreasing the effort levels of the inefficient types (and consequently lowering the power of the incentive schemes). If we choose $x_0^1(\bar{\beta}, \bar{\beta}) = x_0^2(\bar{\beta}, \bar{\beta}) = \frac{1}{2}$, as $\Delta S \to 0$, $\mu \to 0$, $\check{e}(\Delta S) \to \hat{e}$, $\hat{\hat{e}} \to \hat{e}$, and $x_1^2(\bar{\beta}, \bar{\beta}) = x_2^1(\bar{\beta}, \bar{\beta}) \to \frac{1}{2}$. We obtain a *strictly symmetric auction in the limit when quality differentials become small.* Note that when the costs of collusion (λ_f) increase, we are more likely to be in case 1 where quality differentials matter in awarding a contract because the agency is motivated to be truthful.

Last, to completely prevent collusion, it must be the case that the agency when it has signal $\sigma = i$ has no incentive to bribe the $\bar{\beta}$ firm j to claim $\hat{\beta}^j = \underline{\beta}$. In case 2 this condition is automatically satisfied since the agency's income is always s^*. In case 1 let $1 + \lambda_a$ be the cost of transfers from the agency to a firm. The no-collusion constraint when $\sigma = 1$ is that the agency does not want to offer more than the loss incurred by firm 2:

Either

$$\frac{1}{1+\lambda_a}\frac{(1-\nu)^2}{1+\lambda_f}x_0^2(\bar{\beta}, \bar{\beta})\Phi(\check{e}) \le 0$$

if

$$\Delta S - (1+\lambda)\Delta\beta > (1+\lambda)\left[\left\{\psi(\hat{e}) - \hat{e} + \frac{\lambda}{1+\lambda}\frac{\nu}{1-\nu}\Phi(\hat{e})\right\} - \{\psi(e^*) - e^*\}\right].$$

The right-hand side is zero since firm 2 does not produce in that case whatever its β. So $\lambda_a = \infty$ is needed to prevent collusion. If λ_a is not infinite, then the policy described in case 1 of proposition 14.3 must be altered. For instance, if λ_a is large but finite, $x_1^1(\bar{\beta}, \underline{\beta})$ can be brought a bit below 1 so that the expected cost for type $\bar{\beta}$ of firm 2 is strictly positive. Thus the conclusions of proposition 14.3 remain approximately valid if λ_a is large but finite:

Or

$$\frac{1}{1+\lambda_a}\frac{(1-\nu)^2}{1+\lambda_f}x_0^2(\bar{\beta},\bar{\beta})\Phi(\check{e}) < (1-\nu)\Phi(e^*+\Delta\beta)$$

if

$$\Delta S-(1+\lambda)\Delta\beta<(1+\lambda)\left[\left\{\psi(\hat{e})-\hat{e}+\frac{\lambda}{1+\lambda}\frac{\nu}{1-\nu}\Phi(\hat{e})\right\}-\{\psi(e^*)-e^*\}\right],$$

where $x_0^2(\bar{\beta},\bar{\beta})=\frac{1}{2}$ if a symmetric solution is chosen.

If λ_a (or $\Delta\beta$) is large enough, this condition and a symmetric condition when $\sigma=2$ obtain. Otherwise, the auction must be altered by decreasing the transfers to the agency and modifying appropriately effort levels to satisfy all collusion constraints. (The left-hand sides of these equations reflect the fact that the transfer must be made indiscriminately to types $\underline{\beta}$ and $\bar{\beta}$ of firm 2 even though the agency tries to influence only type $\bar{\beta}$'s report.)

14.7 Concluding Remarks

We first summarize the main implications of our analysis and state some caveats. We then discuss instruments for fighting favoritism that are ignored in the model. Bidders' private information generates rents that are sensitive to the nature of the auction. Bidders suffer from being discriminated against because a lower probability of winning reduces their expected informational rent; their interest lies in being favored by the agency. Our analysis predicts that the threat of collusion between the agency and specific bidders tends to reduce the former's discretion in devising an optimal bidding rule. First, acquisition procedures can impose rules on the agency: obligate it to widely publicize the auction to reach all potential bidders, to clearly define the object for bid, and to publicly disclose actual bids so that the principal can control the selection process. Second, and more specifically the focus of this chapter, the bidding game is modified by the possibility of collusion. In extreme cases (see section 14.4) the principal forces the agency to set up a symmetric auction even if the latter has information that would warrant discrimination. For instance, if the winner's ex post cost is unobservable so that only a fixed-price contract can be signed,[13] the contract will be awarded to the lowest bidder despite possible differences in quality among bidders (this procedure cor-

13. A fixed-price contract makes the winning firm the residual claimant for its cost savings. Our model considers the more general case in which the winner's cost is observable. The case in which this cost is unobservable corresponds to a linear specification of the disutility of effort function: $\psi(e)=e$. Negative effort is then equivalent to theft, and cost reimbursement is undesirable.

responds to the *marchés par adjudication* in France). On the other hand, the principal could leave some discretion to the agency but require it to supply substantiated evidence to vindicate discriminatory decisions. In this respect the procedure differs from the French *marchés sur appel d'offre* in which the selection committee picks the bidder it prefers and is not required to explain its choice. It is more akin to the U.S. Air Force acquisition procedures in which the source selection authorities must produce ratings by the (in principle separate) source selection evaluation board on factors such as price, reliability of firms, or technical merit of the projects.[14] Similarly, since 1988, the European Commission requires governments to provide evidence in support of the use of restricted auctions; it also requires disclosure of information so that firms that feel unfairly discriminated against can appeal.

When the agency can collude only with one bidder, the issue is to encourage it to disclose information that is favorable to rival bidder(s). To this end it is optimal to favor the rival bidder (choose it when costs are roughly the same) when no evidence is provided. Asymmetric possibilities of collusion can thus move optimal auctions away from symmetric auctions. Next, if the agency provides evidence in favor of the colluding bidder, and if the quality differential is big enough, the agency is allowed to use a restricted "auction" with only this bidder. When the principal can collude with any of the bidders equally well, the threat of collusion moves the auction toward a symmetric auction. Quality differentials are less likely to be decisive than in the absence of collusive threat.

To conclude, we would like to discuss some limitations of these results and to mention some alternative instruments to fight favoritism. First, we assumed that the principal costlessly organizes the auction and the agency contents itself with announcing its information about project quality. In practice the principal often does not have the resources to organize each and every auction. Rather, as in the case of the European Community, it may give directives on how to design auctions and rely on agents to complain about abuses. In such cases it exerts ex post rather than ex ante control. This raises the question of whether the appeal procedure is costless for the firms that are unfairly discriminated against.[15] Sometimes such

14. In this respect it is interesting to note that a DOD contracting officer who does not select a lowest bidder is supposed to write up a comprehensive justification, defend it, and be prepared to face a protest. While such procedures impose lots of extra work and potential delays, they may be welfare enhancing, as suggested by this chapter. It is also worth noting that the reduction in discretion of the auction designer emphasized by our theory has its counterpart in defense contracting. It is often felt (see Fox 1974, ch. 13) that the General Accounting Office and Congress looking over the shoulder of the project managers cause them to do what is apparently safe: make awards on the basis of objective variables (lowest cost estimate, shortest schedule, etc.) rather than on subjective ones.

15. Marshall, Meurer, and Richard (1989) analyze the role of an appeal procedure in defense contracting. They argue that successful protests reduce the return to lobbying, thereby di-

firms refrain from complaining because they are afraid of being unfairly discriminated against in the future. Further analysis is required to describe the mechanism by which the long-term benefit from having a reputation for not complaining may outweigh the short-term gain from obtaining compensatory damages. But we should note that the European Community is considering making the grievance procedure anonymous. It of course remains to be seen how anonymity can be made compatible with efficient fact finding.

Second, in some industries the enforcement of fairness rules presents the same problem as the enforcement of the prohibition of some vertical restraints. The buyer might integrate vertically in order to withdraw transactions from the legal realm. This could happen when the buyer is not legally an agent for the principal (as in the case when the principal is a legislative or a legal body) and when the buyer itself is a producer. Then the principal would not be able to prevent vertical integration.

This chapter has focused on how auctions of incentive contracts are distorted to thwart favoritism and took the collusion technology as given. There exist complementary methods of fighting favoritism that raise the cost of collusion (λ_f in our model). On the one hand, the principal could put restrictions on the interface between auction designer and bidders.[16] The principal could (and usually does) select agencies that do not exhibit conflicts of interest. On the other hand, he or she could divide tasks in the selection process so as to reduce the possibility of collusion. For instance, the theoretical division of labor in the U.S. Air Force acquisition procedures is as follows: The teams of the source selection evaluation board rate the various components of bids. The source selection authority, who has solicited proposals, selects the winner. The source selection advisory council checks that competition has been obtained in the selection process, and reviews and approves evaluation standards. The limits of the division of labor are obvious: It is costly to employ several bodies with high technological competence in the same area, and it must be the case that these bodies do not collude among themselves. But to the extent that

minishing the incentive to invest in it, and that since protests are invoked by a firm that uses its superior information, they may be a more appealing device for regulating procurement officials than auditing.

In 1984 Congress passed the Competition in Contracting Act that offers firms the opportunity to protest to the General Accounting Office in a quasi-judicial hearing—Marshall et al. note that there have been over 3,000 protests a year and that many protesters have received large settlement awards from the winning bidders in exchange for a promise to drop their protest.

16. According to the U.S. Air Force acquisition procedure 70-15 (pp. 8–9), "the objectivity of the source selection process may be impaired by contacts between prospective contractors related to acquisitions in source selection and senior Department personnel during the period between the release of solicitation and announcement of source selection decision. Contacts with prospective contractors must be avoided except for personnel directly responsible for participating in the contract negotiations."

they can be kept reasonably independent, the division of labor can reduce collusion.[17]

Last, when the agency handles many independent auctions and can collude with only one category of bidders, the principal can use the "law of large numbers" to detect collusion. It is interesting in this respect to note that the 1976 directive of the Commission of the European Community requires each country to publish the percentage (in numbers and value) of contracts going to domestic firms.

APPENDIXES

A14.1 PROOF OF PROPOSITION 14.1

When $\sigma = 1$, expected social welfare is [ignoring the constant term $-(1 + \lambda)s^*$]

$$\begin{aligned}
&v^2[\bar{S} - (1 + \lambda)(\underline{\beta} - e_1^1(\underline{\beta}, \underline{\beta}) + \psi(e_1^1(\underline{\beta}, \underline{\beta})))]x_1^1(\underline{\beta}, \underline{\beta}) \\
&+ v^2[\underline{S} - (1 + \lambda)(\underline{\beta} - e_1^2(\underline{\beta}, \underline{\beta}) + \psi(e_1^2(\underline{\beta}, \underline{\beta})))](1 - x_1^1(\underline{\beta}, \underline{\beta})) \\
&+ v(1 - v)[\bar{S} - (1 + \lambda)(\underline{\beta} - e_1^1(\underline{\beta}, \bar{\beta}) + \psi(e_1^1(\underline{\beta}, \bar{\beta})))]x_1^1(\underline{\beta}, \bar{\beta})) \\
&+ v(1 - v)[\underline{S} - (1 + \lambda)(\bar{\beta} - e_1^2(\underline{\beta}, \bar{\beta}) + \psi(e_1^2(\underline{\beta}, \bar{\beta}))](1 - x_1^1(\underline{\beta}, \bar{\beta})) \\
&+ v(1 - v)[\bar{S} - (1 + \lambda)(\bar{\beta} - e_1^1(\bar{\beta}, \underline{\beta}) + \psi(e_1^1(\bar{\beta}, \underline{\beta})))]x_1^1(\bar{\beta}, \underline{\beta}) \\
&+ v(1 - v)[\underline{S} - (1 + \lambda)(\underline{\beta} - e_1^2(\bar{\beta}, \underline{\beta}) + \psi(e_1^2(\bar{\beta}, \underline{\beta})))](1 - x_1^1(\bar{\beta}, \underline{\beta})) \\
&+ (1 - v)^2[\bar{S} - (1 + \lambda)(\bar{\beta} - e_1^1(\bar{\beta}, \bar{\beta}) + \psi(e_1^1(\bar{\beta}, \bar{\beta})))]x_1^1(\bar{\beta}, \bar{\beta}) \\
&+ (1 - v)^2[\underline{S} - (1 + \lambda)(\bar{\beta} - e_1^2(\bar{\beta}, \bar{\beta}) + \psi(e_1^2(\bar{\beta}, \bar{\beta})))](1 - x_1^1(\bar{\beta}, \bar{\beta})) \\
&- \lambda v[v x_1^1(\bar{\beta}, \underline{\beta})\Phi(e_1^1(\bar{\beta}, \underline{\beta})) + (1 - v)x_1^1(\bar{\beta}, \bar{\beta})\Phi(e_1^1(\bar{\beta}, \bar{\beta}))] \\
&- \lambda v[v(1 - x_1^1(\underline{\beta}, \bar{\beta}))\Phi(e_1^2(\underline{\beta}, \bar{\beta})) + (1 - v)(1 - x_1^1(\bar{\beta}, \bar{\beta}))\Phi(e_1^2(\bar{\beta}, \bar{\beta})].
\end{aligned} \tag{A14.1}$$

Rewriting, we get

$$\begin{aligned}
&v^2[\bar{S} - (1 + \lambda)(\underline{\beta} - e_1^1(\underline{\beta}, \underline{\beta}) + \psi(e_1^1(\underline{\beta}, \underline{\beta})))]x_1^1(\underline{\beta}, \underline{\beta}) \\
&+ v^2[\underline{S} - (1 + \lambda)(\underline{\beta} - e_1^2(\underline{\beta}, \underline{\beta}) + \psi(e_1^2(\underline{\beta}, \underline{\beta})))](1 - x_1^1(\underline{\beta}, \underline{\beta})) \\
&+ v(1 - v)[\bar{S} - (1 + \lambda)(\underline{\beta} - e_1^1(\underline{\beta}, \bar{\beta}) + \psi(e_1^1(\underline{\beta}, \bar{\beta})))]x_1^1(\underline{\beta}, \bar{\beta}) \\
&+ v(1-v)[\underline{S}-(1+\lambda)(\bar{\beta}-e_1^2(\underline{\beta}, \bar{\beta})+\psi(e_1^2(\underline{\beta}, \bar{\beta})))-\frac{\lambda v}{1-v}\Phi(e_1^2(\underline{\beta}, \bar{\beta}))](1-x_1^1(\underline{\beta}, \bar{\beta})) \\
&+ v(1-v)[\bar{S}-(1+\lambda)(\bar{\beta}-e_1^1(\bar{\beta}, \underline{\beta})+\psi(e_1^1(\bar{\beta}, \underline{\beta}))) - \frac{\lambda v}{1-v}\Phi(e_1^1(\bar{\beta}, \underline{\beta}))]x_1^1(\bar{\beta}, \underline{\beta}) \\
&+ v(1 - v)[\underline{S} - (1 + \lambda)(\underline{\beta} - e_1^2(\bar{\beta}, \underline{\beta}) + \psi(e_1^2(\bar{\beta}, \underline{\beta})))](1 - x_1^1(\bar{\beta}, \underline{\beta}))
\end{aligned}$$

17. Similarly in Japan a body different from the auction designer ranks firms in categories A, B, C, which define the types of auctions in which they can participate.

$$+ (1-\nu)^2[\bar{S}-(1+\lambda)(\bar{\beta}-e_1^1(\bar{\beta},\bar{\beta}) + \psi(e_1^1(\bar{\beta},\bar{\beta}))) - \frac{\lambda\nu}{1-\nu}\Phi(e_1^1(\bar{\beta},\bar{\beta}))]x_1^1(\bar{\beta},\bar{\beta})$$

$$+ (1-\nu)^2[\underline{S}-(1+\lambda)(\bar{\beta}-e_1^2(\bar{\beta},\bar{\beta})+\psi(e_1^2(\bar{\beta},\bar{\beta})))-\frac{\lambda\nu}{1-\nu}\Phi(e_1^2(\bar{\beta},\bar{\beta}))](1-x_1^1(\bar{\beta},\bar{\beta})).$$

(A14.2)

Since the x_1^i are between 0 and 1, the maximization of this expression requires the maximization of each term between brackets and then the choice of $x_1^1 = 1$ or $x_1^2 = 1$ according to the magnitude of the terms between brackets.

Take the first two terms. Maximization with respect to effort leads to

$$e_1^1(\underline{\beta},\underline{\beta}) = e^*, \quad e_1^2(\underline{\beta},\underline{\beta}) = e^*.$$

Since $\bar{S} > \underline{S}$, we must choose $x_1^1(\underline{\beta},\underline{\beta}) = 1$. Take then the next two terms. We get

$$e_1^1(\underline{\beta},\bar{\beta}) = e^*,$$

$$e_1^2(\underline{\beta},\bar{\beta}) = \hat{e} < e^*,$$

where $\hat{e}$ is the solution of

$$\psi'(e) = 1 - \frac{\lambda}{1+\lambda}\frac{\nu}{1-\nu}\Phi'(e),$$

and as $\underline{S} < \bar{S}$, clearly $x_1^1(\underline{\beta},\bar{\beta}) = 1$. Taking the last two terms we get similarly

$$e_1^1(\bar{\beta},\bar{\beta}) = e_1^2(\bar{\beta},\bar{\beta}) = \hat{e}$$

and

$$x_1^1(\bar{\beta},\bar{\beta}) = 1.$$

The interesting piece is composed of the fifth and sixth terms where we get

$$e_1^1(\bar{\beta},\underline{\beta}) = \hat{e},$$

$$e_1^2(\bar{\beta},\underline{\beta}) = e^*,$$

and

$$x_1^1(\bar{\beta},\underline{\beta}) = 1 \quad \Leftrightarrow \quad \Delta S - (1+\lambda)\Delta\beta$$

$$\geq (1+\lambda)[\psi(\hat{e}) - \hat{e} + \frac{\lambda}{1+\lambda}\frac{\nu}{1-\nu}\Phi(\hat{e}) - (\psi(e^*) - e^*)].$$

Similar arguments apply when $\sigma = 2$ or $\sigma = 0$. ■

A14.2 Proof of Proposition 14.3

Suppose first that the constraints $s_1 \geq s^*$ and $s_2 \geq s^*$ are nonbinding. As $A_1 = A_2 = 0$ from lemma 14.1, s_1 and s_2 can be substituted into the objective function. The maximization problem becomes [ignoring the constant term $-(1+\lambda)s^*$]

$$\max \xi[\nu^2\{\bar{S} - (1+\lambda)(\underline{\beta} - e_1^1(\underline{\beta},\underline{\beta}) + \psi(e_1^1(\underline{\beta},\underline{\beta})))\}x_1^1(\underline{\beta},\underline{\beta})$$

$$+ \nu^2\{\underline{S} - (1+\lambda)(\underline{\beta} - e_1^2(\underline{\beta},\underline{\beta}) + \psi(e_1^2(\underline{\beta},\underline{\beta})))\}(1 - x_1^1(\underline{\beta},\underline{\beta}))$$

$$+ \nu(1-\nu)\{\bar{S} - (1+\lambda)(\bar{\beta} - e_1^1(\bar{\beta},\underline{\beta}) + \psi(e_1^1(\bar{\beta},\underline{\beta}))$$

$$+ \frac{\lambda}{1+\lambda}\frac{\nu}{1-\nu}\Phi(e_1^1(\bar{\beta},\underline{\beta})))\}x_1^1(\bar{\beta},\underline{\beta})$$

$$+ \nu(1-\nu)\{\underline{S} - (1+\lambda)(\underline{\beta} - e_1^2(\bar{\beta},\underline{\beta}) + \psi(e_1^2(\bar{\beta},\underline{\beta})))\}(1 - x_1^1(\bar{\beta},\underline{\beta}))$$

$$+ \nu(1-\nu)\{\bar{S} - (1+\lambda)(\underline{\beta} - e_1^1(\underline{\beta},\bar{\beta}) + \psi(e_1^1(\underline{\beta},\bar{\beta})))\}x_1^1(\underline{\beta},\bar{\beta})$$

$$+ \nu(1-\nu)\{\underline{S} - (1+\lambda)(\bar{\beta} - e_1^2(\underline{\beta},\bar{\beta}) + \psi(e_1^2(\underline{\beta},\bar{\beta}))$$

$$+ \frac{\lambda}{1+\lambda}\frac{\nu}{1-\nu}\frac{\lambda_f}{(1+\lambda_f)}\Phi(e_1^2(\underline{\beta},\bar{\beta})))\}x_1^2(\underline{\beta},\bar{\beta})$$

$$+ (1-\nu)^2\{\bar{S} - (1+\lambda)(\bar{\beta} - e_1^1(\bar{\beta},\bar{\beta}) + \psi(e_1^1(\bar{\beta},\bar{\beta}))$$

$$+ \frac{\lambda}{1+\lambda}\frac{\nu}{1-\nu}\Phi(e_1^1(\bar{\beta},\bar{\beta})))\}x_1^1(\bar{\beta},\bar{\beta})$$

$$+ (1-\nu)^2\{\underline{S} - (1+\lambda)(\bar{\beta} - e_1^2(\bar{\beta},\bar{\beta}) + \psi(e_1^2(\bar{\beta},\bar{\beta}))$$

$$+ \frac{\lambda}{1+\lambda}\frac{\nu}{1-\nu}\frac{\lambda_f}{(1+\lambda_f)}\Phi(e_1^2(\bar{\beta},\bar{\beta})))\}x_1^2(\bar{\beta},\bar{\beta})]$$

$$+ \xi[\nu^2\{\bar{S} - (1+\lambda)(\underline{\beta} - e_2^2(\underline{\beta},\underline{\beta}) + \psi(e_2^2(\underline{\beta},\underline{\beta})))\}x_2^2(\underline{\beta},\underline{\beta})$$

$$+ \nu^2\{\underline{S} - (1+\lambda)(\underline{\beta} - e_2^1(\underline{\beta},\underline{\beta}) + \psi(e_2^1(\underline{\beta},\underline{\beta})))\}(1 - x_2^2(\underline{\beta},\underline{\beta}))$$

$$+ \nu(1-\nu)\{\bar{S} - (1+\lambda)(\underline{\beta} - e_2^2(\bar{\beta},\underline{\beta}) + \psi(e_2^2(\bar{\beta},\underline{\beta})))\}x_2^2(\bar{\beta},\underline{\beta}))$$

$$+ \nu(1-\nu)\{\underline{S} - (1+\lambda)(\bar{\beta} - e_2^1(\bar{\beta},\underline{\beta}) + \psi(e_2^1(\bar{\beta},\underline{\beta}))$$

$$+ \frac{\lambda}{1+\lambda}\frac{\nu}{(1-\nu)}\frac{\lambda_f}{1+\lambda_f}\Phi(e_2^1(\bar{\beta},\underline{\beta})))\}(1 - x_2^2(\bar{\beta},\underline{\beta}))$$

$$+ \nu(1-\nu)\{\bar{S} - (1+\lambda)(\bar{\beta} - e_2^2(\underline{\beta},\bar{\beta}) + \psi(e_2^2(\underline{\beta},\bar{\beta}))$$

$$+ \frac{\lambda}{1+\lambda}\frac{\nu}{1-\nu}\Phi(e_2^2(\underline{\beta},\bar{\beta})))\}x_2^2(\underline{\beta},\bar{\beta})$$

$$+ \nu(1-\nu)\{\underline{S} - (1+\lambda)(\underline{\beta} - e_2^1(\underline{\beta},\bar{\beta}) + \psi(e_2^1(\underline{\beta},\bar{\beta})))\}(1 - x_2^2(\underline{\beta},\bar{\beta}))$$

$$+ (1-\nu)^2\{\bar{S} - (1+\lambda)(\bar{\beta} - e_2^2(\bar{\beta},\bar{\beta}) + \psi(e_2^2(\bar{\beta},\bar{\beta}))$$

$$+ \frac{\lambda}{1+\lambda}\frac{\nu}{1-\nu}\Phi(e_2^2(\bar{\beta},\bar{\beta})))\}x_2^2(\bar{\beta},\bar{\beta})$$

$$+ (1-\nu)^2\{\underline{S} - (1+\lambda)(\bar{\beta} - e_2^1(\bar{\beta},\bar{\beta}) + \psi(e_2^1(\bar{\beta},\bar{\beta}))$$

$$+ \frac{\lambda}{1+\lambda}\frac{\nu}{1-\nu}\frac{\lambda_f}{1+\lambda_f}\Phi(e_2^1(\bar{\beta},\bar{\beta})))\}(1 - x_2^2(\bar{\beta},\bar{\beta}))]$$

$$+ (1-2\xi)[\nu^2\left(\frac{\bar{S}+\underline{S}}{2} - (1+\lambda)(\underline{\beta} - e_0^1(\underline{\beta},\underline{\beta}) + \psi(e_0^1(\underline{\beta},\underline{\beta})))\right)x_0^1(\underline{\beta},\underline{\beta})$$

$$+ \nu^2\left(\frac{\bar{S}+\underline{S}}{2} - (1+\lambda)(\underline{\beta} - e_0^2(\underline{\beta},\underline{\beta}) + \psi(e_0^2(\underline{\beta},\underline{\beta})))\right)(1 - x_0^1(\underline{\beta},\underline{\beta}))$$

$$+ \nu(1-\nu)\left(\frac{\bar{S}+\underline{S}}{2} - (1+\lambda)(\bar{\beta} - e_0^1(\bar{\beta},\underline{\beta}) + \psi(e_0^1(\bar{\beta},\underline{\beta}))\right.$$

$$\left. + \frac{\lambda}{1+\lambda}\frac{\nu}{1-\nu}(1 + \frac{\xi}{(1+\lambda_f)(1-2\xi)})\Phi(e_0^1(\bar{\beta},\underline{\beta})))\right) x_0^1(\bar{\beta},\underline{\beta})$$

$$+ \nu(1-\nu)\left(\frac{\bar{S}+\underline{S}}{2} - (1+\lambda)(\underline{\beta} - e_0^1(\underline{\beta},\bar{\beta}) + \psi(e_0^1(\underline{\beta},\bar{\beta})))\right) x_0^1(\underline{\beta},\bar{\beta}))$$

$$+ \nu(1-\nu)\left(\frac{\bar{S}+\underline{S}}{2} - (1+\lambda)(\underline{\beta} - e_0^1(\underline{\beta},\bar{\beta}) + \psi(e_0^1(\underline{\beta},\bar{\beta})))\right) x_0^1(\underline{\beta},\bar{\beta}))$$

$$+ \nu(1-\nu)\left(\frac{\bar{S}+\underline{S}}{2} - (1+\lambda)(\bar{\beta} - e_0^2(\underline{\beta},\bar{\beta}) + \psi(e_0^2(\underline{\beta},\bar{\beta}))\right.$$

$$\left. + \frac{\lambda}{1+\lambda}\frac{\nu}{1-\nu}(1 + \frac{\xi}{(1-2\xi)(1+\lambda_f)})\Phi(e_0^2(\underline{\beta},\bar{\beta})))\right)(1 - x_0^1(\underline{\beta},\bar{\beta}))$$

$$+ (1-\nu)^2\left(\frac{\bar{S}+\underline{S}}{2} - (1+\lambda)(\bar{\beta} - e_0^1(\bar{\beta},\bar{\beta}) + \psi(e_0^1(\bar{\beta},\bar{\beta}))\right.$$

$$\left. + \frac{\lambda}{1+\lambda}\frac{\nu}{1-\nu}(1 + \frac{\xi}{(1-2\xi)(1+\lambda_f)})\Phi(e_0^1(\bar{\beta},\bar{\beta})))\right) x_0^1(\bar{\beta},\bar{\beta}))$$

$$+ (1-\nu)^2\left(\frac{\bar{S}+\underline{S}}{2} - (1+\lambda)(\bar{\beta} - e_0^2(\bar{\beta},\bar{\beta}) + \psi(e_0^2(\bar{\beta},\bar{\beta}))\right.$$

$$\left. + \frac{\lambda}{1+\lambda}\frac{\nu}{1-\nu}(1 + \frac{\xi}{(1-2\xi)(1+\lambda_f)})\Phi(e_0^2(\bar{\beta},\bar{\beta})))\right)(1 - x_0^1(\bar{\beta},\bar{\beta})).$$

If $\sigma = 1$,

$$e_1^1(\underline{\beta},\underline{\beta}) = e^* = e_1^2(\underline{\beta},\underline{\beta}), \quad x_1^1(\underline{\beta},\underline{\beta}) = 1,$$

$$e_1^1(\bar{\beta},\underline{\beta}) = \hat{e}, \quad e_1^2(\bar{\beta},\underline{\beta}) = e^*, \quad \text{and}$$

$$x_1^1(\bar{\beta},\underline{\beta}) = 1 \Leftrightarrow \Delta S - (1+\lambda)\Delta\beta$$

$$> (1+\lambda)\left\{\left(\psi(\hat{e}) - \hat{e} + \frac{\lambda}{1+\lambda}\frac{\nu}{1-\nu}\Phi(\hat{e})\right) - (\psi(e^*) - e^*)\right\},$$

$$e_1^1(\underline{\beta},\bar{\beta}) = e^*, \quad e_1^2(\underline{\beta},\bar{\beta}) = \hat{\hat{e}}, \quad \text{and} \quad x_1^1(\underline{\beta},\bar{\beta}) = 1,$$

with

$$\hat{\hat{e}} \in \arg\min_e \left\{\psi(e) - e + \frac{\lambda}{1+\lambda}\frac{\nu}{1-\nu}\frac{\lambda_f}{1+\lambda_f}\Phi(e)\right\},$$

$$e_1^1(\bar{\beta},\bar{\beta}) = \hat{e}, \quad e_1^2(\bar{\beta},\bar{\beta}) = \hat{\hat{e}},$$

$$x_1^1(\bar{\beta},\bar{\beta}) = 1 \Leftrightarrow \Delta S > (1+\lambda)\left\{\left(\psi(\hat{e}) - \hat{e} + \frac{\lambda}{1+\lambda}\frac{\nu}{1-\nu}\Phi(\hat{e})\right)\right.$$

$$\left. - \left(\psi(\hat{\hat{e}}) - \hat{\hat{e}} + \frac{\lambda}{1+\lambda}\frac{\nu}{1-\nu}\frac{\lambda_f}{1+\lambda_f}\Phi(\hat{\hat{e}})\right)\right\} > 0.$$

If $\sigma = 2$, the solution is symmetric.
If $\sigma = 0$,

$$e_0^2(\underline{\beta},\underline{\beta}) = e_0^1(\underline{\beta},\underline{\beta}) = e^* \quad \text{and} \quad x_0^1(\underline{\beta},\underline{\beta}) \in [0,1],$$

$$e_0^1(\bar{\beta},\underline{\beta}) = \check{e},$$

with

$$\check{e} \in \arg\min_e \left\{\psi(e) - e + \frac{\lambda}{1+\lambda}\frac{\nu}{1-\nu}\left[1 + \frac{\xi}{(1+\lambda_f)(1-2\xi)}\right]\Phi(e)\right\},$$

$$e_0^2(\bar{\beta},\underline{\beta}) = e^* \quad \text{and} \quad x_0^1(\bar{\beta},\underline{\beta}) = 0,$$

$$e_0^1(\underline{\beta},\bar{\beta}) = e^*, \quad e_0^2(\underline{\beta},\bar{\beta}) = \check{e}, \quad \text{and} \quad x_0^1(\underline{\beta},\bar{\beta}) = 1,$$

$$e_0^1(\bar{\beta},\bar{\beta}) = \check{e} = e_0^2(\bar{\beta},\bar{\beta}),$$

$$\text{and} \quad x_0^1(\bar{\beta},\bar{\beta}) \in [0,1].$$

From $A_1 = A_2 = 0$,

$$s_1 = s^* + \frac{1-\nu}{1+\lambda_f}[x_0^2(\bar{\beta},\bar{\beta})\Phi(\check{e}) - x_1^2(\bar{\beta},\bar{\beta})\Phi(\hat{\hat{e}})],$$

with $\check{e} < \hat{\hat{e}}$, and

$$s_2 = s^* + \frac{1-\nu}{1+\lambda_f}[x_0^1(\bar{\beta},\bar{\beta})\Phi(\check{e}) - x_2^1(\bar{\beta},\bar{\beta})\Phi(\hat{\hat{e}})].$$

Since $x_0^2(\bar{\beta},\bar{\beta}) + x_0^1(\bar{\beta},\bar{\beta}) = 1$ and $\check{e} < \hat{\hat{e}}$, the constraints $s_1 \geq s^*$ and $s_2 \geq s^*$ cannot hold unless

$$\Delta S > (1+\lambda)\left[\left\{\psi(\hat{e}) - \hat{e} + \frac{\lambda}{1+\lambda}\frac{\nu}{1-\nu}\Phi(\hat{e})\right\}\right.$$
$$\left. - \left\{\psi(\hat{\hat{e}}) - \hat{\hat{e}} + \frac{\lambda}{1+\lambda}\frac{\nu}{1-\nu}\frac{\lambda_f}{1+\lambda_f}\Phi(\hat{\hat{e}})\right\}\right], \tag{A14.3}$$

which we refer to as case 1.

If (A14.3) does not hold, we have necessarily $s_1 = s_2 = s^*$. Then we must solve

$$\max\{\xi W_1 + \xi W_2 + (1-2\xi)W_0\}$$

subject to

$$(1-\nu)x_0^2(\bar{\beta},\bar{\beta})\Phi(e_0^2(\bar{\beta},\bar{\beta})) + \nu x_0^2(\underline{\beta},\bar{\beta})\Phi(e_0^2(\underline{\beta},\bar{\beta}))$$
$$- (1-\nu)x_1^2(\bar{\beta},\bar{\beta})\Phi(e_1^2(\bar{\beta},\bar{\beta})) - \nu x_1^2(\underline{\beta},\bar{\beta})\Phi(e_1^2(\underline{\beta},\bar{\beta})) \leq 0,$$

$$(1-\nu)x_0^1(\bar{\beta},\bar{\beta})\Phi(e_0^1(\bar{\beta},\bar{\beta})) + \nu x_0^1(\bar{\beta},\underline{\beta})\Phi(e_0^1(\bar{\beta},\underline{\beta}))$$
$$- (1-\nu)x_2^1(\bar{\beta},\bar{\beta})\Phi(e_2^1(\bar{\beta},\bar{\beta})) - \nu x_2^1(\bar{\beta},\underline{\beta})\Phi(e_2^1(\bar{\beta},\underline{\beta})) \leq 0.$$

Let μ_1 and μ_2 be the Lagrange multipliers of the constraints $A_1 \geq 0$ and $A_2 \geq 0$. Since $\mu_1 \geq 0$, $\mu_2 \geq 0$, we still have $x_0^1(\bar{\beta},\underline{\beta}) = 0$ and $x_0^2(\underline{\beta},\bar{\beta}) = 0$. By lemma 14.1 both constants must be binding at the optimum. The constraints are reduced to

$$x_0^2(\bar\beta,\bar\beta)\Phi(e_0^2(\bar\beta,\bar\beta)) - x_1^2(\bar\beta,\bar\beta)\Phi(e_1^2(\bar\beta,\bar\beta))$$

$$-\frac{\nu}{1-\nu}x_1^2(\underline\beta,\bar\beta)\Phi(e_1^2(\underline\beta,\bar\beta)) \le 0,$$

$$x_0^1(\bar\beta,\bar\beta)\Phi(e_0^1(\bar\beta,\bar\beta)) - x_2^1(\bar\beta,\bar\beta)\Phi(e_2^1(\bar\beta,\bar\beta))$$

$$-\frac{\nu}{1-\nu}x_2^1(\bar\beta,\underline\beta)\Phi(e_2^1(\bar\beta,\underline\beta)) \le 0.$$

Both constraints can be satisfied only when either $x_1^2(\bar\beta,\bar\beta)$ or $x_2^1(\bar\beta,\bar\beta)$ is strictly positive. From the first-order conditions, this implies that

$$\Delta S = (1+\lambda)\Bigg[\left\{\psi(\hat e) - \hat e + \frac{\lambda}{1+\lambda}\frac{\nu}{1-\nu}\Phi(\hat e)\right\} - \left\{\psi(\hat{\hat e}(\Delta S)) - \hat{\hat e}(\Delta S) + \left[\frac{\lambda}{1+\lambda}\frac{\nu}{1-\nu} - \frac{\mu(\Delta S)}{\xi(1-\nu)(1+\lambda)}\right]\Phi(\hat{\hat e}(\Delta S))\right\}\Bigg],$$

where $\hat{\hat e}(\Delta S)$ is defined by

$$\psi'(\hat{\hat e}(\Delta S)) = 1 - \left[\frac{\lambda}{1+\lambda}\frac{\nu}{1-\nu} - \frac{\mu(\Delta S)}{\xi(1-\nu)(1+\lambda)}\right]\Phi'(\hat{\hat e}(\Delta S)), \tag{A14.5}$$

and $\mu(\Delta S)$ is the (symmetric) multiplier of the constraints. $\{\hat{\hat e}(\Delta S), \mu(\Delta S)\}$ denotes the solution of (A14.4) and (A14.5); $\hat{\hat e} \ge \hat{\hat e}(\Delta S) \ge \hat e$.

Let $\breve e(\Delta S)$ be the solution of

$$\psi'(\breve e(\Delta S)) = 1 - \left[\frac{\lambda}{1+\lambda}\frac{\nu}{1-\nu} + \frac{\mu(\Delta S)}{(1-2\xi)(1-\nu)(1+\lambda)}\right]\Phi'(\breve e(\Delta S)).$$

We still have $\breve e(\Delta S) \le \hat{\hat e}(\Delta S)$. Choosing

$$x_1^2(\bar\beta,\bar\beta) = x_2^1(\bar\beta,\bar\beta) = \frac{1}{2}\frac{\Phi(\breve e(\Delta S))}{\Phi(\hat{\hat e}(\Delta S))} < \frac{1}{2},$$

the collusion constraints are satisfied. From the constrained maximization, $e_0^2(\bar\beta,\bar\beta) = e_0^1(\bar\beta,\bar\beta) = \breve e(\Delta S)$ and $e_1^2(\bar\beta,\bar\beta) = e_2^1(\bar\beta,\bar\beta) = e_1^2(\underline\beta,\bar\beta) = e_2^1(\bar\beta,\underline\beta) = \hat{\hat e}(\Delta S)$. Equation (A14.4) further implies that $x_1^2(\bar\beta,\bar\beta)$ and $x_2^1(\bar\beta,\bar\beta)$ is unrestricted in $[0,1]$. Therefore the constraints are satisfied by setting

$$x_2^1(\bar\beta,\bar\beta) = \frac{\Phi(\breve e(\Delta S))}{\Phi(\hat{\hat e}(\Delta S))}x_0^1(\bar\beta,\bar\beta)$$

and

$$x_1^2(\bar\beta,\bar\beta) = \frac{\Phi(\breve e(\Delta S))}{\Phi(\hat{\hat e}(\Delta S))}x_0^2(\bar\beta,\bar\beta)$$

for some choice of $x_0^1(\bar\beta,\bar\beta)$ and $x_0^2(\bar\beta,\bar\beta) \in [0,1]$ such that $x_0^1(\bar\beta,\bar\beta) + x_0^2(\bar\beta,\bar\beta) = 1$. A symmetric solution is obtained by setting $x_0^1(\bar\beta,\bar\beta) = x_0^2(\bar\beta,\bar\beta) = \frac{1}{2}$. As $\breve e(\Delta S) \le \hat{\hat e}(\Delta S)$, $x_1^2(\bar\beta,\bar\beta) = x_2^1(\bar\beta,\bar\beta) \le \frac{1}{2}$. ■

REFERENCES

Fox, R. 1974. *Arming America.* Division of Research, Graduate School of Business Administration, Harvard University.

Graham, D., and R. Marshall. 1987. Collusive bidder behavior at single-object second price and English auctions. *Journal of Political Economy* 95:1217–1239.

Holmström, B., and R. Myerson. 1983. Efficient and durable decision rules with incomplete information. *Econometrica* 51:1799–1818.

McAfee, R. P., and J. McMillan. 1988. Bidding rings. Mimeo, University of Western Ontario.

McAfee, R. P., and J. McMillan. 1987. Auctions and bidding. *Journal of Economic Literature* 25:708–747.

Mailath, G., and P. Zemsky. 1989. Collusion in second price auctions with heteregeneous bidders. *CARESS WP* 89-02.

Marshall, R., Meurer, M., and J. F. Richard. 1989. Delegated procurement and the protest process. Mimeo, Duke University.

Maskin, E., and J. Riley. 1984. Optimal auctions with risk averse buyers. *Econometrica* 6:1473–1518.

Maskin, E., and J. Tirole. 1992. Markov perfect equilibria. Mimeo.

Milgrom, P. R. 1987. Auction theory. In *Advances in Economic Theory—Fifth World Congress*, ed. T. Bewley. Cambridge: Cambridge University Press.

Milgrom, P., and R. Weber. 1982. A theory of auctions and competitive bidding. *Econometrica* 50:1089–1122.

Myerson, R. 1981. Optimal auction design. *Mathematics of Operations Research* 6:58–73.

Rose-Ackerman, S. 1975. The economics of corruption. *Journal of Public Economics* 4:187–203.

Vickrey, N. 1961. Counterspeculation, auctions, and competitive sealed tenders. *Journal of Finance* 16:8–37.

VI REGULATORY INSTITUTIONS

15 REGULATORY INSTRUMENTS, HEARINGS, AND INTEREST GROUP MONITORING

15.1 Welfare Foundations of Institutions

Because the philosophy of part VI differs somewhat from that of the theoretical literature on regulation, we take the liberty of discussing its approach in a lengthy introduction. The ideas developed in this section are not new. Indeed they are central in political science.[1] Our goal is to recast them in a form and vocabulary familiar in economic analysis.

An idealized, but illuminating, view of regulatory institutions is that they result from a constitution drafted by some benevolent "founders" or "social planners" behind a veil of ignorance. The writers of the constitution have some assessment of social welfare, for example, the sum of utilities in society. They must delegate actual social choices to other agents, broadly labeled "public decision makers," and they design a set of institutions or rules of the game that as much as is feasible induce these public decision makers to behave as if their two assessments of welfare coincided.

This view of institutions can be enriched in several directions. First, one might note that the veil of ignorance is often an abstraction. The founders (or their descendants) may have vested interests in the design of the constitution. Their assessment of social welfare then differs from that of impartial social planners. Second, institutions may not be associated with a constitution. They can also result from a law or even from durable tradition and social norms. Allowing for these two alterations of the previous view preserves its main points of separation between planning and control or between intentions and actual decision making, and of the concomitant need to constrain the executants.[2] While we will henceforth assume that founders draft a constitution, the notion of "constitution" should be interpreted broadly: The "founders" might stand for lawmakers (Congress, state legislatures; see section 15.4) or tradition, and the so-called social welfare function could be generalized to account for potentially partial goals of the founders.

1. They are also implicit in some models of public finance. For instance, Brennan and Buchanan (1977) argue that institutions are "uncontrollable" once they are established and study a model in which the government maximizes revenue subject to tax constraints imposed by the constitution. The recent literature on the political economy of public debt management (Aghion and Bolton 1990; Alesina and Tabellini 1987a, b; Persson and Svensson 1989) has emphasized the idea that an a priori suboptimal balanced-budget rule may improve welfare when governments are primarily concerned by their reelection. Sappington (1986) argues that an institution that prevents a regulator from observing the regulated firm's true cost may be optimal when the regulated firm sinks some noncontractible investment and the regulator cannot commit to future incentive schemes. The absence of cost observation partly protects the firm from expropriation of its investment.

2. A good case in point is deck-stacking (e.g., through administrative procedures and assignment of the burden of proof) which enables a legislature to ensure that agencies "operate to mirror the political forces that gave rise to the agency's legislative mandate long after the coalition behind the legislation has disbanded" (McCubbins, Noll, and Weingast 1987, p. 262).

The design of a constitution is trivial when the founders can design a mechanism that assembles a group of public decision makers whose preferences coincide with their own. The optimal constitution then consists in delegating all authority to these benevolent public decision makers. (Benevolence of course does not imply that regulatory outcomes will conform to the founders' and the public decision makers' best-of-all-worlds. The public decision makers might have poor information about the economy. To elicit information, they must design costly incentive schemes for the economic agents and set up regulatory agencies to reduce the informational asymmetries with these economic agents.) The benevolent-public-decision-makers paradigm is the natural first step in analyzing the politics of regulation. It focuses on the public decision makers' (e.g., Congress's) control over agencies and economic agents, and it derives the organizational response to the agencies' natural tendency to identify with interest groups.[3]

A serious drawback of the benevolent-public-decision-makers paradigm is that it cannot explain limitations on the scope of authority conferred on public decision makers by the constitution: Any restriction imposed by the founders on the benevolent public decision makers amounts to a self-mutilation and can only be welfare reducing.[4] In practice the scope of authority of public decision makers is limited. First, they have a mandate to regulate some firms, industries, or activities but not others. Second, they are constrained to conduct regulatory hearings and to disseminate the information they obtain. Third, they are given a limited set of instruments to regulate. In the United States, agencies regulating the electric utilities or the telecommunications industry are prohibited from operating monetary transfers to the regulated firms. Similarly the Environmental Protection Agency is constrained to use bans or technology standards on some chemical products and is allowed to use warning labels, instructions, or tax incentives for others. Fourth, there are restrictions on how much the current administration may commit future administrations.[5]

The benevolent-public-decision-maker paradigm also has little to say about Montesquieu's well-established vision of separation of powers among branches of government (e.g., executive, legislative, and judiciary) because it implies that there is no need to keep a delicate set of controls between branches of government; nor can it fully account for the watchdog role of nongovernmental groups (consumers, mass media) in public decision making. The paradigm thus misses some economic aspects of

3. See part V.

4. An exception to this is when a benevolent regulator lacks commitment power in a multiperiod setting. For instance, a constitutional upper bound on the rate of growth of money supply may prevent a welfare-reducing inflationary spiral that may arise even under welfare-maximizing monetary authorities. Similarly regulatory lags may alleviate the welfare-reducing ratchet effect that may arise even under a benevolent regulator.

5. See McCubbins (1985) for a discussion of constraints on bureaucratic decision making.

government decision making and probably most of the interesting issues in political science.

The first key to understanding the development of institutions is to envision a conflict between the founders and the public decision makers. The public decision makers cannot be trusted to perfectly implement the founders' intent because they are self-interested, have an intrinsically different view of social welfare, or, as will be assumed in this chapter, have an incentive to identify with specific interest groups.[6] The founders must "stack the deck" in favor of their own objectives by constraining the public decision makers.

The second is to take the notion of "veil of ignorance" literally. We must assume that the founders are unable to design a "complete constitution" in which all future contingencies are perfectly foreseen and costlessly described.[7] If they could write such a complete constitution, public decision making would amount to the implementation of a precise mandate—formally the implementation of a revelation mechanism in which all economic agents announce their information when they receive it. The founders would only set up a court that would ensure that their *desiderata* are implemented.[8] The only branch of government would be the judicial branch. In contrast, public decision makers have a nontrivial role when given a vague mandate, namely a mandate that incompletely describes the set of states of nature. Government is then divided into the judiciary branch whose role is to ensure that the instructions that have been included in the constitution are fulfilled and a more activist branch (which itself can be divided into several subbranches, e.g., legislative and executive) that has the authority to fill in the details when contingencies that have not been included in the constitution occur. Note here the resemblance to Williamson's (1975, 1985) and Grossman and Hart's (1986) seminal work on vertical integration. Grossman and Hart define authority as the residual rights of control conferred by ownership; that is, one of the parties to a transaction is given power to impose decisions in states of nature not specified in the original contract. In the same spirit we offer to view the constitution as an incomplete (social) contract.

Williamson and Grossman-Hart emphasize the effects on economic decisions of the distribution of authority between a buyer and a seller.[9] Similarly, in the political arena, authority over economic transactions to

6. Empirically it may be difficult to distinguish between the public decision makers' intrinsic preferences and the ones that are induced by their belonging to a social class or by the collusion with interest groups.

7. The complete constitution is the analog of a complete or comprehensive contract in contract theory (except that it is not written by the parties who will implement it).

8. The court would then be the analog of Myerson's (1986) "mediator." See Laffont and Maskin (1982) and Myerson (1986) for general abstract models of complete contracting.

9. See Hart and Moore (1990) for a more general theory of distribution of authority among n parties.

be regulated is distributed among the various branches of government through rules of procedures, precedence between executive and legislative, and so forth. As in a contract between economic agents, the range of decisions and instruments for the party on which authority is bestowed can be constrained ex ante.

What prevents the public decision makers from abusing their authority to achieve their own goals or the goals of the interest groups with which they identify?[10] One safeguard is the division of authority among branches of government. A constitution ought to create a viable system of checks and balances (which should not jeopardize flexibility in public decision making). For instance, an agency may be independent in its decision making, but Congress may in the long run exert indirect control through the appropriations procedure. Similarly the Senate and the House may exert reciprocal control. But ultimately what exerts control over the public decision makers is the existence of courts and of a constitution. Note that we are here taking a passive view of the role of courts. That is, they act on hard information transmitted by various parties (whistle-blowers, consumers, mass media, discontented or idealistic civil servants, etc.)[11] and content themselves with correcting deviations from what is specified in the constitution.[12]

The agenda set above—to develop an incomplete-contract approach to public decision making—has wide scope, and it would be presumptuous to claim that we have got a good handle even on a small subset of issues. The purpose of this chapter is to illustrate some of the above ideas in a particular context. In the process of building an example, we will discuss some modeling issues that are likely to be relevant in other models of institution design. The reader should be warned that we do not possess a fully satisfactory formalization of incomplete contracting. The formidable task of developing the corresponding theoretical apparatus is beyond the

10. In the United States the concern about the usurpation of government by powerful interest groups dates back to Madison (1788). The 1946 Administrative Procedures Act was to a large extent a response to this concern about capture. More recently the courts have referred to industry influence to vindicate judicial review of agency decisions (e.g., in *State Farm*, 463US29, 1983). For a more complete discussion of this, see Sunstein (1986).

11. Under some legislations only affected parties (firms, consumers) have the "standing" to address the courts directly. Whistle-blowers and civil servants then transmit the information indirectly to courts.

12. Courts may exert a more activist role and act on the basis of soft information. They then have discretionary power and compete with the executive and legislative branches in filling in unforeseen contingencies (Shapiro 1986). Hamilton (1788), in the spirit of Montesquieu, argued that "the judiciary is beyond comparison the weakest of the three departments of power," that its duty is "to declare all acts contrary to the manifest tenor of the constitution void," and that discretion in the courts should be limited. In a similar spirit the 1984 *Chevron* decision of the U.S. Supreme Court sharply restricted the scope of judicial review of agency decisions. The Supreme Court stated that the agency was due considerable deference if Congress had not directly addressed the precise question at issue. Our adhesion to a passive view of courts is not a value judgment, but rather a convenient as well as realistic expositional device.

limited scope of the chapter. We content ourselves with comparing two standard institutions, and (notwithstanding some loose comments in section 15.4) we do not inquire into the optimality of these two institutions in the larger class of institutions that are feasible given the information and the transaction costs of writing the constitution at the date it is enacted.

Section 15.2 develops a model of a natural monopoly in which the constitution and a countervailing power (consumers) put limits on the discretion of nonbenevolent public decision makers. The central theme of this illustration is that different institutions give different incentives for watchdogs to monitor the government. A choice among constitutions must therefore take into account not only the cost associated with restricting regulatory instruments but also the effect on rent seeking and monitoring. Section 15.3 solves the model and obtains the comparative statics results. Section 15.4 discusses the limitations of our analysis; in particular it discusses alternative ways of enlisting monitors. The section also relates our analysis to that of McCubbins and Schwartz (1984) on Congress's preference for "fire alarm" over "police patrol" oversight of the bureaucracy. Section 15.5 concludes.

15.2 The Model

15.2.1 Components

The starting point for this research was the intriguing fact that in some countries and industries, regulators are legally prevented from transferring money to regulated firms, which must then cover their costs entirely through charges to customers. One might adopt the view that this institution survives only because of a general lack of understanding of the basic economic principle that the regulated firm's fixed cost should not affect the consumers' decision of how much to buy. This may be, but before hastily jumping to the conclusion that the institution is irrational, we might wonder whether there do not exist basic underlying economic forces. As discussed in section 15.1, a mistrust of regulators should be the foundation for a rational theory of restrictions in the scope of their authority, of the prohibition of transfers in this particular context. We argue that this institution results from the need to involve parties outside the government (consumers, mass media) to perform the role of watchdogs and to prevent abuse of the government's discretionary power.

In a nutshell we assume that there is a single public decision maker—the "agency"—and a single-product regulated firm that is a natural monopoly. The "constitution" (or Congress or state legislature) gives the agency the vague mandate of maximizing social welfare, namely, of extracting the firm's rent and of pricing its product efficiently. We compare two institutions. In the first, labeled "marginal cost pricing" or "transfer," the agency can use the full set of instruments: monetary transfer to the firm and price control. Maximizing social welfare then consists in charging marginal cost, or rather, as in chapter 2, the appropriate version of marginal cost in the presence of a shadow cost of public funds, and in choosing transfers so as to extract the firm's rent. In the second institution, labeled "average cost pricing" or "no transfer," the agency is limited to price controls and is not allowed to transfer money to the firm. Maximizing social welfare subject to this constraint yields average cost pricing. The firm's price is as low as is consistent with balance of the firm's budget, where the firm's cost includes its managers' compensation.

Whatever its mandate, the agency, which for simplicity knows the firm's technology, may identify with producer interests. What might prevent such collusion is that consumers (or the mass media which is indirectly rewarded by consumers through an increase in circulation or ratings, or proxy advocates such as a state attorney general or a consumer council) could find it in their interest to investigate the agency's activities. If they find hard evidence of wrongdoing, that is, if they can prove that the agency defended the firm's interests by allowing a high price, they can ask the judicial system to overrule the agency's decision and to punish the agency.

Obviously marginal cost pricing, which gives full freedom to the agency, dominates average cost pricing when the agency is benevolent. However, the two institutions respond differently to the perversion of public decision making. Their comparison hinges on the stake in collusion they create for the firm and the agency and on the incentives they give to the public to be effective watchdogs.[13]

To illustrate this idea, suppose that there is uncertainty about the regulated firm's fixed cost, which is known to the agency and the firm but not to other parties. Under marginal cost pricing an overreport of this fixed cost is passed on to taxpayers. Under average cost pricing it is passed on to consumers in the form of higher prices. If consumers are better organized than taxpayers, average cost pricing induces more monitoring of the agency's activity. The absence of transfers pits the consumers against the agency and the industry. True, in a complete contract setup there would be better ways of enlisting a monitor than by distorting consumer prices, but creating this simple conflict behind the veil of ignorance is an easy way to guarantee some monitoring.[14]

13. The public in our model plays the role of an "external monitor" (although it is not under contract to check on the "internal monitor"—the agency). Kofman and Lawarrée (1989) develop an interesting model of internal and external auditing of management.

14. See Freixas and Laffont (1985) for different considerations on the choice between average and marginal cost pricing. Section 3 of the introductory chapter reviews still other considerations, due to Coase, for the choice between these two institutions. Last, review problem 12 argues that the average cost pricing institution may allow the government to commit to a "hard budget constraint."

It is interesting to note that the theoretical literature on regulation reflects the two institutional arrangements. Most of the literature on asymmetric information and incentives in regulation assumes that the regulator can operate transfers to the regulated sector. In contrast, the literature on cost-of-service (Boiteux) pricing, multiproduct firms, and contestability assumes away transfers. We feel uneasy about *exogenously* ruling out transfers. While this assumption is realistic in some industries on legal grounds, it may mislead the researcher when formalizing the regulator's objectives. As mentioned above, a rational theory of regulation implies that the prohibition is motivated by a mistrust of the regulator. There is thus a tension between the two assumptions that the regulators maximize social welfare and that they are not given free rein.

We now spell out the model in more detail. It considers a four-party hierarchy: founders/agency/firm/consumers.

The Firm

The firm produces a marketable output $q = D(p)$ at cost

$$C = (\beta - e) + cq. \tag{15.1}$$

The cost or technology parameter β can take one of two values: "low" or "efficient" ($\underline{\beta}$) with probability ν and "high" or "inefficient" ($\bar{\beta}$) with probability $1 - \nu$. The firm and the agency know the realization of β. Let $\Delta\beta \equiv \bar{\beta} - \underline{\beta} > 0$. The firm's manager incurs an increasing and convex (monetary) disutility $\psi(e)$ ($\psi' > 0, \psi'' > 0$) by exerting effort e to reduce cost. Note that we put all technological uncertainty on the fixed cost. This is an important assumption which will be discussed later.

In our usual notation the IR constraint of the firm is

$$U = t - \psi(e) \geq 0. \tag{15.2}$$

We will actually assume that the firm faces limited punishment, so U must always be nonnegative.[15]

The Agency

The agency receives income s from the state and has the utility function

$$V(s) = s. \tag{15.3}$$

We assume that the income s is received if and only if it is not proved that the agency has violated the constitution. If the consumers find hard evidence that the agency cheated, the agency is punished. Limited liability limits the punishment of the agency to a zero income. We assume for

15. We thus assume either that consumers can (or have incentives to) search only during the hearing period [so that the firm cannot end up with utility $-\psi(e)$ after choosing e and later be denied any payment], or that the firm has utility function $V(U) = U$ for $U \geq 0$ and $V(U) = -\infty$ for $U < 0$ and there is an arbitrarily small probability that the evidence found by consumers (see below) is inaccurate.

notational simplicity that the agency's reservation income (and utility) is equal to 0.[16] Last, we assume for simplicity that the income s received in the absence of evidence of wrongdoing is fixed by the constitution.

The agency learns β. This signal is soft information, so it can misreport β if it chooses to (the signal could be hard information in the sense of chapter 11 without any change in the results).

The Founders

The utility of the founders is the sum of the utilities of all parties in the economy, where the utility of the public is equal to their net surplus $[S(q) - P(q)q]$ minus the taxpayers' expenditure on the regulated industry $[s + t + C - P(q)q]$ times the shadow cost λ of raising public funds through distortionary taxation, or

$$W = [S(q) + \lambda P(q)q] - (1 + \lambda)[\beta - e + cq + \psi(e)] - \lambda U - \lambda V. \qquad (15.4)$$

That is, from the "generalized consumer surplus" $S(q) + \lambda P(q)q$ must be subtracted $1 + \lambda$ times the total cost of the project $\beta - e + cq + \psi(e)$ and λ times the rents left to the firm and the agency. The important property of (15.4) for our analysis is that the founders dislike leaving a rent to the firm and the agency.

It is too costly for the founders to describe the technology when they draft the constitution. Instead, they give the mandate to maximize the sum of utilities over a specified set of instruments. This mandate is implemented by the agency and is enforced by the courts. The courts, if called upon by some party, can find out the parameters of the economic environment by itself, except for β whose value can only be learned from consumers. The courts enforce the welfare-maximizing policy conditional either on the announcement $\hat{\beta}$ of β by the agency, or on the true value of β if it differs from $\hat{\beta}$ and is discovered by the consumers.

The Consumers

The consumers, who enjoy net surplus $S(q) - P(q)q$ and who also have prior v on β being $\underline{\beta}$, can spend 0 (no search) or E (search) to investigate. They find the true β if they search and do not learn anything if they do not search. We assume that taxpayers are too dispersed and do not intervene in the regulatory process. Our model thus reflects the fact that in practice interveners often represent a subset of interested parties and stress increasing their fraction of the pie.

16. We could, with little change, allow positive reservation utilities as in chapter 11 (indeed we do so in some simulations in the section on alternative cost technologies).

We could consider slight variants in which the agency is rewarded differently when there is no wrongdoing depending on whether consumers find evidence. The qualitative results would be unchanged. Note also that it can be argued that in the presence of intervention costs, consumers will intervene only if there is wrongdoing, so our assumption is not too unrealistic.

15.2.2 Benevolent Agency Benchmark

Let us begin with the benchmark in which the agency cannot collude with the firm. The consumers have no incentives to search in this case because the agency tells the truth.

Marginal Cost Pricing

Suppose that the agency can use all instruments (t, p). The optimal policy has $V = 0$ and $U = 0$, since the firm's rent is extracted whatever the technology. W is maximized under full information. Cost minimization requires that the marginal disutility of effort be equal to the marginal cost savings:

$$\psi'(e) = 1 \quad \text{or} \quad e \equiv e^* \qquad \text{for all } \beta. \tag{15.5}$$

The price is given by a simple Ramsey formula:

$$\frac{p - c}{p} = \frac{\lambda}{1 + \lambda}\frac{1}{\eta(p)} \quad \text{or} \quad p \equiv p^{MC} \qquad \text{for all } \beta. \tag{15.6}$$

The Lerner index (price–marginal cost margin) is inversely proportional to the elasticity of demand (since public funds are costly, revenue is socially valuable, and pricing is intermediate between marginal cost and monopoly pricing). Note that the price is entirely determined by the marginal cost (indeed, for $\lambda = 0$, $p^{MC} = c$) and that it is independent of β. Because price is determined by the marginal cost and not by the fixed cost, we call it the marginal cost price even though this is really a Ramsey price. The net transfer to the firm is $t^{MC} = \psi(e^*)$. Let

$$W^{MC}(\beta) \equiv [S(D(p^{MC})) + \lambda p^{MC} D(p^{MC})] - (1 + \lambda)[\beta - e^* + cD(p^{MC}) + \psi(e^*)] \tag{15.7}$$

be the optimal welfare and

$$\underline{W}^{MC} \equiv W^{MC}(\underline{\beta})$$

and

$$\overline{W}^{MC} \equiv W^{MC}(\overline{\beta}) = \underline{W}^{MC} - (1 + \lambda)(\overline{\beta} - \underline{\beta}). \tag{15.8}$$

Average Cost Pricing

Although the institution is dominated by the previous one (which is socially optimal) when the agency is benevolent, let us assume that the agency is not allowed to transfer money to the firm. The firm's price is then given by the smallest price that yields a balanced budget:[17]

17. We will for simplicity assume that (15.9) has a solution and that there exists a unique solution that is lower than the monopoly price. A sufficient condition for the latter assumption is that $(p - c)D(p)$ be quasi-concave or $2D'^2 \geq DD''$.

$$pD(p) = \beta - e^* + cD(p) + \psi(e^*) \quad \text{or} \quad p \equiv p^{AC}(\beta). \tag{15.9}$$

The firm's revenue $pD(p)$ must cover the firm's cost $\beta - e + cD(p)$ as well as the managers' compensation $\psi(e)$ which, like the cost, cannot be paid from public funds. The benevolent agency, knowing β, can control e (by disallowing excessive cost). The desired level of effort minimizes $\psi(e) - e$ and is therefore the same as under marginal cost pricing. Note that the firm's price is now an increasing function of β.

Since the state operates no transfer, and the agency and the firm have no rent, social welfare is

$$W^{AC}(\beta) = S^n(q^{AC}(\beta)), \tag{15.10}$$

where

$S^n(q) \equiv S(q) - P(q)q$ denotes the net surplus,

$q^{AC}(\beta) \equiv D(p^{AC}(\beta))$.

We let

$$\underline{W}^{AC} \equiv W^{AC}(\underline{\beta}) \quad \text{and} \quad \overline{W}^{AC} \equiv W^{AC}(\overline{\beta}). \tag{15.11}$$

15.2.3 Collusive Agency

From now on we allow the agency to collude with the firm. We assume that transferring an income equivalent $\tilde{s}$ to the agency costs $(1 + \lambda_f)\tilde{s}$ to the firm, where $\lambda_f \geq 0$ measures the deadweight loss (or transaction cost) associated with the transfer. The agency's income equivalent is then $s + \tilde{s}$. For simplicity we assume that the agency makes a take-it-or-leave-it offer, according to which the firm must transfer a certain amount of income equivalent (conditional on the decision not being reversed by the courts) to the agency if the latter reports some $\hat{\beta}$. More generally we could allow bargaining and rent sharing between the firm and the agency.

The timing is as follows:

1. The founders choose between the two institutions: $i = MC$ or AC and determine the income of the agency s.

2. Society (firm, agency, consumers, courts if they are addressed; see stage 6 below) learns the nature of the relevant product and the demand function, and that β is either $\underline{\beta}$ or $\overline{\beta}$. The only remaining piece of private (and soft) information is β, which is learned by the firm and the agency.

3. The agency can offer a side contract to the firm, which specifies a side transfer (conditional on $\hat{\beta} \neq \beta$ not being found out) if the agency announces $\hat{\beta} \neq \beta$.

4. The agency announces its intended policy, which is equivalent to announcing $\hat{\beta}$. It de facto proposes the socially optimal allocation (p^{MC}, t^{MC})

or $p^{AC}(\hat{\beta})$ for parameter $\hat{\beta}$ under whatever institution MC or AC is relevant (this allocation was determined in subsection 15.2.2).

5. Learning $\hat{\beta}$, the consumers decide whether to search or not.

6. If consumers do not search and therefore do find any hard information, or if they find that $\beta = \hat{\beta}$, the agency's proposed allocation is implemented. If the consumers find out that $\beta \neq \hat{\beta}$, they can ask for a correction of the proposed policy; in this case the allocation implemented is the socially optimal one for parameter β and the relevant institution.

7. Production (and possibly transfers) take place.

Stage 1 is that of constitutional design. Stage 4 corresponds to a regulatory hearing. It is consistent with the constraints of due process imposed in the Administrative Procedures Act in the United States, according to which an agency cannot announce a policy without warning but must give notice and solicit comments. As argued by McCubbins et al. (1987) and formalized here, this procedure provides nonagency participants with a chance to submit viewpoints for the purpose of altering the proposed rule. Stage 6 assumes weak evidentiary standards in administrative law (here, the constitution) that give the agency flexibility (its proposed policy is implemented unless consumers come up with hard evidence).

By abuse of notation, we let s denote the agency's (observable) income when there is no evidence of wrongdoing. The agency receives 0 if the consumers find out that $\hat{\beta} \neq \beta$ and report it to the court.

Clearly the agency and the firm have no incentive to collude when $\beta = \overline{\beta}$. The agency then announces the truth: $\hat{\beta} = \overline{\beta}$. When $\beta = \underline{\beta}$, announcing $\hat{\beta} = \overline{\beta}$ allows the firm to reduce its effort. More precisely it can choose effort e such that $\underline{\beta} - e = \overline{\beta} - e^*$ or $e = e^* - \Delta\beta$. Cost accounting does not reveal that the agency cheated, and the firm, which receives compensation $\psi(e^*)$ under either regime, enjoys rent

$$\underline{U} = \Delta_f \equiv \Phi(e^*) \equiv \psi(e^*) - \psi(e^* - \Delta\beta). \tag{15.2}$$

Δ_f will be called "the firm's stake" in collusion. Note that it is independent of the institution (this does not generalize to more general technologies; see below). The agency can thus ask $\tilde{s} = \Delta_f/(1 + \lambda_f)$ from the firm in exchange for the policy corresponding to $\beta = \overline{\beta}$ being implemented.

Let Δ_c denote the consumers' stake, that is, the increase in their net surplus when they can rectify the policy corresponding to $\hat{\beta} = \overline{\beta}$ into that for $\beta = \underline{\beta}$ (we assume that consumers are only a small fraction of taxpayers so that they neglect the reduction s in the agency's income. This assumption can be trivially relaxed). Under institution i,

$$\Delta_c^i = S^n(q^i(\underline{\beta})) - S^n(q^i(\overline{\beta})). \tag{15.13}$$

We assume the following:

Assumption 15.1 $E \leq v\Delta_c^{AC}$.

Assumption 15.1 guarantees that if the agency always cheats (reports $\overline{\beta}$ when the truth is $\underline{\beta}$), the consumers have an incentive to search under average cost pricing. (They have no incentive to search under marginal cost pricing, since the price is insensitive to the level of β.)

Last, let x denote the probability that the agency cheats; y the probability that the consumers search (when $\hat{\beta} = \overline{\beta}$; they have no incentive to search when $\hat{\beta} = \underline{\beta}$). The expected social welfare under institution $i \in \{MC, AC\}$ is given by

$$W^i \equiv (1 - v)[\overline{W}^i - \lambda s - y^i E] + v(1 - x^i)[\underline{W}^i - \lambda s]$$
$$+ vx^i\left[(1 - y^i)\left(\overline{W}^i + \frac{\Delta_f}{1 + \lambda_f} - \lambda s\right) + y^i\underline{W}^i - y^i E\right]. \tag{15.14}$$

The first term on the right-hand side of (15.14) is social welfare when $\beta = \overline{\beta}$ minus the social cost λs of the agency's income (the agency does not misreport in this state of nature) minus the expected search cost for consumers (which obviously is incurred in vain). Suppose next that $\beta = \underline{\beta}$. With probability $1 - x^i$, the agency does not cheat, and the consumers do not search. The only cost relative to the benevolent agency case is that associated with the agency's income, which explains the second term. With probability x^i, the agency announces $\hat{\beta} = \overline{\beta}$. The consumers search with probability y^i. If they search, they discover the deception, and welfare (gross of search costs) is the welfare under a benevolent agency. If they do not search, everything is as if the agency were benevolent and as if the true value of β were $\overline{\beta}$, except that the agency receives income s and enjoys rent $\Delta_f/(1 + \lambda_f)$ appropriated from the firm (it can be checked that $\overline{W}^i + \Delta_f/(1 + \lambda_f) < \underline{W}^i$ for $i \in \{MC, AC\}$).

15.3 The Solution

We first determine the equilibrium probabilities of cheating (x^i) and searching (y^i) in the "inspection game" that arises when $\hat{\beta} = \overline{\beta}$. Substituting into (15.14) and maximizing over s then yields the expected social welfare under the two institutions. Next we determine how the founders' choice between the two institutions is affected by a few parameters.

15.3.1 Average Cost Pricing

Since $E < \Delta_c^{AC}v$, the consumers would search if the agency cheated with probability one when $\beta = \underline{\beta}$, and therefore the agency would not cheat. On the other hand, the agency cheats if the consumers do not search. Hence the equilibrium must be a mixed-strategy equilibrium where the probability of cheating of the agency x is determined by

$$E = \Delta_c^{AC} v x. \tag{15.15}$$

The probability of the consumers' searching y is determined by

$$(1 - y)\frac{\Delta_f}{1 + \lambda_f} = ys. \tag{15.16}$$

Equation (15.16) can be written

$$y = \frac{\Delta_f}{\Delta_f + s(1 + \lambda_f)}. \tag{15.17}$$

Equation (15.17) highlights a trade-off between the two checks on collusion. One check is consumer search. The other consists of giving an "efficiency income," namely an income greater than the reservation income, to the agency in order to reduce the temptation to collude. Equation (15.17) shows that any increase in agency income reduces search by consumers.

We maximize social welfare:

$$W^{AC} = [1 - v + vx(1 - y)]\overline{W}^{AC} + v(1 - x + xy)\underline{W}^{AC} - [(1 - v)y + vxy]E - [1 - vxy]\lambda s + vx(1 - y)\frac{\Phi(e^*)}{1 + \lambda_f}, \tag{15.18}$$

subject to (15.15), (15.17), and $s \geq 0$. Substituting (15.15) and (15.17) into (15.18) eliminates x and y; we leave it to the reader to check that the resulting objective function $W^{AC}(s)$ is strictly quasi-concave in s. The optimal agency income s is determined, when it is an interior solution, by

$$\lambda(1 - vxy) = \frac{(1 + \lambda_f)\Delta_f}{[(1 + \lambda_f)s + \Delta_f]^2}\left[(1 - v + vx)E - vx\lambda s - vx\left(\underline{W}^{AC} - \overline{W}^{AC} - \frac{\Phi(e^*)}{1 + \lambda_f}\right)\right], \tag{15.19}$$

where

$$x = x^{AC} = \frac{E}{\Delta_c^{AC} v}$$

and

$$y = \frac{\Delta_f}{\Delta_f + s(1 + \lambda_f)}.$$

If at $s = 0$, the left-hand side of (15.19) exceeds the right-hand side, we have a corner solution $s = 0$. The agency cheats, and y is equal to 1.

15.3.2 Marginal Cost Pricing

Under MC pricing the price is independent of β because the marginal cost is certain [see (15.6)], and therefore the consumers have no stake in the regulatory decision and do not search ($y = 0$). Consequently the agency always cheats ($x = 1$), its income is optimally set equal to zero, and social welfare can be written

$$W^{MC} = \overline{W}^{MC} + v\frac{\Phi(e^*)}{1 + \lambda_f}. \tag{15.20}$$

15.3.3 Optimal Institutions

We show that either institution can be optimal depending on the values of the parameters:

Proposition 15.1 MC pricing dominates AC pricing for small uncertainty.

Proof When $\Delta\beta \to 0$, $W^{MC} \to W^{FI}$ (full information social welfare, which would be obtained under a benevolent agency and marginal cost pricing) since $\overline{W}^{MC} \to \underline{W}^{MC}$ and $\Phi(e^*) \to 0$. On the other hand, W^{AC} is bounded away from W^{FI}, because pricing, which includes the fixed cost, is inadequate. ■

More interestingly AC pricing can dominate MC pricing. For example, we have proposition 15.2.

Proposition 15.2 AC pricing will dominate MC pricing when the search costs E are low enough and the cost of collusion λ_f high enough.

Proof When E tends to 0, the probability of cheating x under AC pricing tends to 0 from (15.15). Equation (15.19) actually indicates a corner solution: $s = 0$ for E sufficiently small. This and equation (15.16) imply that the consumers always search: $y = 1$. The absence of an efficiency wage (a wage that exceeds the reservation wage) implies that the agency continues cheating even though consumers search with probability 1. Thus, as $E \to 0$,

$$W^{AC} - W^{MC} \to (\overline{W}^{AC} - \overline{W}^{MC}) + v\left[\underline{W}^{AC} - \overline{W}^{AC} - \frac{\Phi(e^*)}{1 + \lambda_f}\right].$$

Now we can adjust the parameters such that $\overline{W}^{AC} = \overline{W}^{MC}$. Indeed we know that

$$p^{MC} = c - \frac{\lambda}{1 + \lambda}\frac{D(p^{MC})}{D'(p^{MC})} > c$$

and that

$$\bar{p}^{AC} = c + \frac{\bar{\beta} + \psi(e^*) - e^*}{D(\bar{p}^{AC})}.$$

We can choose the parameters so that $\bar{p}^{AC} = p^{MC}$. Then $\overline{W}^{AC} = \overline{W}^{MC}$ because the budget is balanced even under marginal cost pricing. Hence, as E tends to 0,

$$W^{AC} - W^{MC} \to v\left[\underline{W}^{AC} - \overline{W}^{AC} - \frac{\Phi(e^*)}{1+\lambda_f}\right].$$

Now let λ_f increase until $\Phi(e^*)/(1+\lambda_f)$ becomes less than $\underline{W}^{AC} - \overline{W}^{AC}$ (which is independent of λ_f). ■

Intuitively, when E becomes small, the probability of cheating becomes small. If the AC price for $\beta = \bar{\beta}$ is identical to the MC price (which is possible because of the shadow cost of public funds), the comparison of welfares reduces to that when $\beta = \underline{\beta}$. The welfare loss when $\beta = \underline{\beta}$ is due to collusion under MC pricing and to the inclusion of the fixed cost in the price under AC pricing. The first loss is

$$L^{MC} = \underline{W}^{MC} - \overline{W}^{MC} - \frac{\Phi(e^*)}{1+\lambda_f}$$

(efficiency loss minus rent to agency) and the second is

$$L^{AC} = \underline{W}^{MC} - \underline{W}^{AC}$$

(efficiency loss). So when $\overline{W}^{MC}$ equals $\overline{W}^{AC}$,

$$L^{MC} - L^{AC} = \underline{W}^{AC} - \overline{W}^{AC} - \frac{\Phi(e^*)}{1+\lambda_f} > 0$$

for a high λ_f.

It is convenient to write the difference in welfare between the two institutions as

$$\begin{aligned}\Delta W \equiv W^{AC} - W^{MC} &= \overline{W}^{AC} - \overline{W}^{MC} + v[\underline{W}^{AC} - \overline{W}^{AC}](1 - x + xy) \\ &\quad - [(1-v)y + vxy]E - [1 - vxy]\lambda s \\ &\quad - v(1 - x(1-y))\frac{\Phi(e^*)}{1+\lambda_f},\end{aligned} \tag{15.21}$$

where x, y, and s are the values under AC pricing [see (15.15), (15.17), and (15.19)].

Proposition 15.3

i. $\partial(\Delta W)/\partial\lambda_f > 0$.

ii. $\partial(\Delta W)/\partial E < 0$.

Proof See appendix A15.1.

When the monitoring cost E decreases, the probability of cheating under AC pricing decreases [from (15.15)]. The lower monitoring cost and probability of cheating both raise welfare and the desirability of AC pricing. Thus proposition 15.3 suggests that the prohibition of transfers is more likely to be observed in countries or industries where consumer groups are well organized to investigate whether regulated prices are justified.

An increase in the cost of collusion λ_f has two effects. First, it reduces the income $\Delta_f/(1+\lambda_f)$ received by the agency when it cheats and is not discovered. Since there is more cheating and less monitoring by consumers (and therefore more income received by the agency) under MC pricing, an increase in λ_f favors AC pricing. Second, an increase in λ_f reduces the attractiveness of cheating for the agency and therefore lowers the probability y that consumers search under AC pricing. But a decrease in y, with s kept constant, is socially beneficial ($\partial(\Delta W)/\partial y < 0$) because, at the optimal s, monitoring is encouraged beyond the efficient point in order to reduce s. Thus both effects have the same sign.

The conclusion on the role of λ_f in the choice between institutions relies both on our choice of technology and on the consumers' being the only "outside monitor" (the agency is the "inside monitor"). First, as we will note below, an increase in λ_f may favor the MC pricing institution when the uncertainty affects marginal cost as well. Second, the assumption that the consumers are the only outside monitor implies that there is absolutely no check on collusion under the MC pricing institution when the uncertainty affects only the fixed cost. The agency always colludes with the industry and is never caught. In such circumstances there would be great demand for the creation of an additional outside monitor such as a public auditor.[18] With public auditors now in the picture, the analysis under MC pricing becomes qualitatively similar to that under AC pricing: The equilibrium of the inspection game between the public auditors and the agency is in mixed strategy as long as the public auditors have enough incentive to monitor [equations (15.15) and (15.16) hold with Δ_c^{AC} and E replaced by the public auditors' incentive and cost of auditing]. An increase in λ_f then reduces the equilibrium probability and thus the cost of inspection by public auditors under MC pricing and may favor the MC pricing institution. For these two reasons we do not find it implausible

18. In particular, state-owned enterprises are often subject to financial audits. Such audits not only check that the firm's accounting is properly performed, but also report unprofitable activities and waste. Such audits, while useful, are very imperfect instruments of control. In the United States the corporation audits created by the Government Corporation Control Act of 1945 are performed only once every three years since 1974. Similarly the French national audit body (Cour des Comptes), while having substantial audit powers, is seriously short of staff. Another issue is that public controllers may become the advocates of the state-owned enterprise in the ministry (e.g., see the 1967 Nora report in France). We will say more about outside monitors in section 15.4.

that transfers are less likely to be prohibited when public decision makers are less prone to collude with the regulated industry.[19]

Proposition 15.3 characterizes the effect of the collusion and monitoring variables on the choice between the two institutions. The effect of the traditional variables (cost and demand variables, and shadow price of public funds) is more complex to study and is likely to be ambiguous.

We now study the optimal agency income under AC pricing.

Proposition 15.4 Under AC pricing,

i. the agency's income is nonincreasing in the shadow cost of public funds,

ii. if $v\Delta_c^{AC} \geq E + \Delta_f/(1+\lambda_f)$, the agency's income is equal to zero for all λ; if $v\Delta_c^{AC} < E + \Delta_f/(1+\lambda_f)$, the agency's income strictly decreases with λ on $[0, \lambda_0]$ and is equal to 0 for $\lambda \in [\lambda_0, +\infty)$, for some $\lambda_0 > 0$.

Proof

i. We earlier noted that $W^{AC}(s, \lambda)$ is strictly quasi-concave in s. It thus suffices to show that $\partial(\partial W^{AC}/\partial s)/\partial\lambda < 0$. We have

$$\frac{\partial^2 W^{AC}}{\partial\lambda\partial s} = -(1 - vxy) + \frac{\partial y}{\partial s} vxs < 0,$$

since $\overline{W}^{AC}$ and $\underline{W}^{AC}$ do not depend on λ and $\partial y/\partial s < 0$.

ii.

$$\left.\frac{\partial W^{AC}}{\partial s}\right|_{\lambda=0} = \frac{\partial y}{\partial s}\left(vx\left(\underline{W}^{AC} - \overline{W}^{AC} - \frac{\Delta_f}{1+\lambda_f}\right) - (1 - v + vx)E\right).$$

Therefore, for the optimal s to be positive, it must be the case that this expression be positive at $s = 0$, or since $\partial y/\partial s < 0$,

$$\underline{W}^{AC} - \overline{W}^{AC} - \frac{\Delta_f}{1+\lambda_f} < E + \frac{1-v}{vx}E.$$

The facts that $\underline{W}^{AC} - \overline{W}^{AC} = \Delta_c^{AC}$ and $vx\Delta_c^{AC} = E$ yield the result. ■

When λ grows, it becomes more and more costly to reward the agency, and the efficiency-income method of avoiding collusion ($s > 0$) becomes less attractive relative to the method of letting the consumers monitor (part i of proposition 15.4). When E is small, consumer search is cheap and allows a better allocative efficiency. Increasing s beyond 0 would be detri-

19. That is, when λ_f is high. A high λ_f might stem from the civil servants' being "public minded" (their having a high psychological cost of receiving transfers), from a frequent rotation among regulatory jobs (which makes trust between agency personnel and regulated firms harder to develop), or from other factors. These considerations (together with the difference in the organization of consumer groups—represented by the parameter E in our model) might, for instance, be reflected in the different treatments of transfers in the regulation of electric utilities and telephone companies in France (transfers sometimes allowed) and the United States (transfers prohibited).

mental because it would reduce consumer search. In contrast, when E is larger (but still satisfies assumption 15.1: $v\Delta_c^{AC} \geq E$), it is optimal to give an efficiency income to the agency to reduce the extent of search.

15.3.4 Subsidies for Intervener Programs

In the United States, Congress and state legislatures have authorized funds for intervenor programs. On the one hand, such funds allow public representatives (attorney general, independent public staff in regulatory commissions, public advocates) to intervene on behalf of consumers. On the other hand, recognized private intervenors can apply for a refund of their monetary costs.

Assume that a fraction $\bar{\alpha} \in [0, 1]$ of the consumers' expenses is observable or verifiable. Suppose that the constitution or law specifies that the state pay αE to the consumers if the latter decide to search (and discover), where $\alpha \in [0, \bar{\alpha}]$ is a choice variable in the optimal constitution (the previous analysis thus assumed that $\bar{\alpha} = 0$). The feasibility of an intervener program does not affect the marginal cost regime because the consumers have no incentive to search even if they are subsidized. Social welfare is $\tilde{W}^{MC} = W^{MC}$.

Under AC pricing the new welfare $\tilde{W}^{AC}$ $(\geq W^{AC})$ must take into account the fact that the shadow cost of public funds makes subsidies socially costly. The social cost of subsidies is $\lambda(\alpha E)$ and is incurred with probability $(1 - v)y + vxy$. Thus

$$\tilde{W}^{AC} = W^{AC} - [(1 - v)y + vxy]\lambda\alpha E, \tag{15.22}$$

where W^{AC} is given in (15.18), but with a different x, as discussed below. Subsidies also encourage consumers to search, which in this model means that the probability of cheating by the agency that makes consumers indifferent between searching and not searching goes down. Equation (15.15) is replaced by

$$(1 - \alpha)E = \Delta_c^{AC} vx. \tag{15.23}$$

Last, equation (15.17) remains valid. Substituting x from (15.23) and y from (15.17) into (15.22) shows that $\tilde{W}^{AC}$, for an s given, is quadratic and convex in α. The convexity implies that for any s the optimal α is a corner solution: $\alpha = 0$ or $\alpha = \bar{\alpha}$.

Proposition 15.5 Suppose that the law can specify that a fraction $\alpha \in [0, \bar{\alpha}]$ of consumer expenses can be subsidized by the state.

i. There exist shadow costs of public funds λ_1 and λ_2 with $0 < \lambda_1 < \lambda_2 < +\infty$ such that $\alpha = \bar{\alpha}$ is socially optimal if $\lambda \leq \lambda_1$ and $\alpha = 0$ is socially optimal if $\lambda \geq \lambda_2$.

ii. The agency's income (rent) may be reduced or increased by the feasibility of subsidies for intervener programs.

Proof See appendix A15.2.

Part i of proposition 15.5 is quite intuitive. Subsidies reduce the probability of cheating by the agency and are socially inexpensive when the shadow cost of public funds is low. Part ii came more as a surprise to us. We would have expected that the rent would be reduced by the existence of subsidies that reduce consumer search costs.[20]

15.3.5 Alternative Technologies

We assumed that technological uncertainty affects the firm's fixed cost. For instance, the agency may report an inflated cost of the firm's equipment. Focusing on fixed-cost uncertainty is natural when deriving rational foundations for average cost pricing. However, it would be worth developing the theory for general cost functions. Here we content ourselves with giving a few elements for the other polar case in which the technological uncertainty affects marginal cost:

$$C = (\beta - e)q + \alpha, \tag{15.24}$$

where α is a known fixed cost.

In the marginal cost pricing regime the agency is instructed to maximize social welfare over the instruments $\{t, p\}$:

$$\max\{S(q) + \lambda P(q)q - (1 + \lambda)[t + (\beta - e)q + \alpha]\},$$

where $t = \psi(e)$ (because the agency has full information about the firm). This yields

$$\psi'(e) = q \tag{15.25}$$

and

$$\frac{p - (\beta - e)}{p} = \frac{\lambda}{1 + \lambda}\frac{1}{\eta(p)}, \tag{15.26}$$

where $\eta(p)$ is the elasticity of demand. Substituting $p = P(q)$ yields $q^{MC}(\beta)$ and $e^{MC}(\beta)$.

In the average cost pricing regime the agency is instructed to set the price so that

$$p = \frac{\psi(e) + (\beta - e)q + \alpha}{q}, \tag{15.27}$$

where the managerial compensation $t = \psi(e)$ is included in the total cost of the firm. To obtain the lowest price, the agency sets e so that

20. In our model the agency is assumed to obtain the full rent attached to collusion. It is straightforward to modify the model so that the firm has some bargaining power and shares the rent with the agency. The observation that appropriations for intervener programs are often lobbied against by the regulated industry suggests that the most likely case in part ii of proposition 15.5 is that the agency's rent decreases with the feasibility of such programs.

$$\psi'(e) = q. \tag{15.28}$$

Equations (15.27) and (15.28) yield $q^{AC}(\beta)$ and $e^{AC}(\beta)$.

In both regimes the agency may collude with the firm. The firm's stake in regime i is $\Delta_f^i = \psi(e^i(\overline{\beta})) - \psi(e^i(\overline{\beta}) - \Delta\beta)$. The consumers' gain when reversing the regulatory decision is $\Delta_c^i = S^n(q^i(\underline{\beta})) - S^n(q^i(\overline{\beta}))$. Equation (15.14) and, assuming that $E \leq \min_i(v\Delta_c^i)$, equations (15.15) and (15.17) are valid in both regimes as long as Δ_f and Δ_c are indexed by i. Both regimes are treated like the AC regime in the previous analysis.

Computer simulations reveal that either regime may be optimal. Furthermore the effect of λ_f on the choice between regimes is now ambiguous. In particular an increase in λ_f could make the marginal cost institution desirable. See appendix A15.3.

15.3.6 Standards of Judicial Review

Another issue worth studying is that of standards of judicial review. We assumed that consumers come up with either perfect evidence or no evidence. Suppose more generally that search yields the observation of $\tilde{\beta} \in \{\underline{\beta}, \overline{\beta}\}$ that has correlation $\rho \in (\frac{1}{2}, 1)$ with β (assume that this is still hard information: $\tilde{\beta}$ can be credibly communicated to the court). The court knows the accuracy ρ of the evidence. A standard of judicial review might be characterized by a cutoff parameter ρ^* such that the court overrules the agency's proposed policy if and only if $\rho \geq \rho^*$. Defining a lower standard (lowering ρ^*) encourages consumers to search but increases the probability of incorrect reversals of proposed policies. We have not formalized these arguments.

15.4 Choice of Watchdog

Our stylized model assumes a single public decision maker (agency) and a single watchdog/outside monitor (consumers). A crucial assumption of our analysis is thus that other potential watchdogs ignored in our model only imperfectly oversee the agency. In reality there are other parties within and outside the government that can and do perform an oversight role, such as Congress, public auditors, independent boards set up to review the agency, and whistle-blowers.[21] If these parties can be given adequate incentives to investigate the agency's activity and to release their findings, constraining regulatory instruments to encourage consumers to oversee the agency ought to be welfare reducing. There are two reasons why these alternative watchdogs perform their function imperfectly.

First, rewarding these watchdogs is costly. Furthermore it is hard to ex ante specify an adequate reward for a "finding that reverses an agency

21. To this list might be added the president and activist courts.

decision." The finding that an agency is not buying the appropriate brand of pencils is not commensurate with the discovery that the agency inflates prices or sides up with regulated firms on major technological choices. Making the reward commensurate with the importance of major discoveries would be very costly as it is also claimed for minor discoveries. The point made here is the same as the argument that a patent law—an a priori suboptimal system of rewards for innovations because it creates monopoly power—is judged preferable to a direct price or reward system, which would be superior in an environment in which all potential innovations could be costlessly described beforehand. In our model the consumers' stake Δ_c^{AC} reflects (imperfectly) the size of the issue, in the same way that the monopoly profit accruing from a patent reflects (imperfectly) the increase in social surplus brought about by the innovation.

Second, the watchdogs may themselves engage in collusive activity. They may be bribed either not to search for information or not to make their discoveries public (e.g., congressional oversight committees are often captured by special interests or the agency). In this case they should not be trusted to bring information that leads to the overruling of agency decisions and to punishments. This raises the well-known question of "who will take care of the caretakers?"

The possibility of collusion also sheds some light on why the court's estimating the value of evidence found by watchdogs would most likely be subject to abuse. We argued that as in the case of a patent, the court would have much discretion in determining the value of information supplied. One could object to this argument on the basis that courts sometimes do produce such assessments. In particular under U.S. antitrust laws plaintiffs who win their case are entitled to treble damages, which are determined by the court. In a sense, however, this antitrust institution obeys the same principle as the institution of not assessing and granting monetary rewards for evidence of agency wrongdoing. Pitting one organized interest group against another (plaintiff against defendant, consumers against agency and firm) and not letting a poorly organized third party (taxpayers) act as a source of funds limits the scope for abuse.

While these two factors put limits on the efficiency of oversight by Congress, review boards, public auditors, and whistle-blowers, they can apply to consumer groups as well. We already argued that the first factor has less force for consumers because their reward (the increase in net consumer surplus) is "proportional to" the social value of discovering agency wrongdoing. In a sense consumers signal the value to them of altering the decision by searching. An interesting question is whether the second factor applies less for consumers, that is, whether the delegates of the consumer groups are less prone to colluding with the agency and the firm than the other watchdogs.

While we are not satisfied by the exogeneity of our assumptions that consumers (and their allies) are the only watchdogs and that their rewards are fully identified with their influence on regulatory decisions, rather than with direct monetary transfers, we feel that our model captures many salient features of reality. For instance, McCubbins and Schwartz (1984) argue that what appears to be a neglect of oversight of agencies by Congress is really a preference by members of Congress for "fire-alarm" over "police-patrol" oversight (i.e., for reacting to the whistle blowers over conducting their own investigations):

> Instead of examining a sample of administrative decisions, looking for violations of legislative goals, Congress establishes a system of rules, procedures, and informal practices that enable individual citizens and organized interest groups to examine administrative decisions (sometimes in prospect) to charge executive agencies with violating congressional goals, and to seek remedies from agencies, courts, and Congress itself. (p. 166)

McCubbins and Schwartz go on to argue that Congress's role consists of creating this decentralized system and that members of Congress have little incentive to engage in police-patrol oversight because they must spend much time detecting agency violations and yet receive scant credit for their discoveries. The McCubbins and Schwartz theory reflects the difficulty of designing adequate rewards for a direct oversight of agencies. Reinterpreting the founders of our model as members of Congress and the constitution as the law or congressional intents, our model seems a good description of their view of congressional oversight activity.

15.5 Concluding Remarks

Institutions may be viewed as resulting from an incomplete constitution (or law or tradition). Since the public decision makers who are conferred discretionary power need not be benevolent, the comparison of institutions must take into account the incentives they give to the public decision makers to identify with interest groups and to counter forces to oversee the public decision makers.

Our very stylized model aimed at finding rational foundations for the prohibition of transfers observed in some industries and traced this institution to a mistrust of regulators. It compared the mandate of average cost pricing (associated with the absence of transfers) with that of marginal cost pricing (associated with the possibility of transfers), and it showed that average cost pricing can dominate marginal cost pricing. This type of analysis is definitely not intended to support the prohibition of transfers, but rather it aims to point out some elements that make the observation of such a prohibition more likely.

Our model is consistent with the thesis developed in McCubbins et al. (1987) that administrative procedures such as hearings can serve as instruments of agency control, and it argues that the absence of transfers (outside source) pits the consumers against the agency and the industry. More generally the creation of conflicts between agents plays a central role in the collection of information and the provision of incentives in public life as well as in private organization. (This comment has much benefited from discussions with Bengt Holmström.) Consider the institution of cost-plus–profit-markup transfer pricing between two divisions of a firm, which specifies that the selling profit center charges the cost of producing an intermediate good plus a gross margin to the buying profit center. Eccles and White (1988, p. 538) argue that this transfer-pricing rule induces monitoring of the selling profit center by the buying profit center and creates valuable information available to the central office (higher levels of management), helping it to "obviate the loss of control associated with hierarchies without interfering with the prerogatives of these middle managers." This internal organization institution is analogous to the average cost pricing mandate of our model. First, cost-plus–transfer pricing provides the selling profit center with poor incentives for cost reduction, while average cost pricing discourages the use of the regulated firm's product by consumers. Second, cost-plus–transfer pricing induces the buying profit center to collect information about production and transmit it to the central office, while average cost pricing may induce consumer groups to scrutinize the production of regulated goods and appeal to the courts (or Congress). Last, in these two institutions, the absence of transfers from a third party (central office, government) pits one interest group against another interest group. The relative robustness of "sourceless" or "balanced-budget" mechanisms to collusive activities is the key to understanding the widespread use of these otherwise suboptimal mechanisms.

APPENDIXES

A15.1 Proof of Proposition 15.3

As we saw in the proof of proposition 15.2, the solution is a corner solution ($s = 0$) for E small. In this case W^{AC} is (locally) independent of λ_f and decreases with E, while W^{MC} decreases with λ_f and is independent of E. So proposition 15.3 is trivially satisfied. Next we assume an interior solution for s.

i. Using the fact that s maximizes W^{AC} (the envelope theorem), we have

$$\frac{\partial(\Delta W)}{\partial \lambda_f} = v(1 - x + xy)\frac{\Phi(e^*)}{(1 + \lambda_f)^2} + A\frac{\partial y}{\partial \lambda_f},$$

where

$$A \equiv \frac{\partial W^{AC}}{\partial y} = vx\left(\underline{W}^{AC} - \overline{W}^{AC} - \frac{\Phi(e^*)}{1+\lambda_f}\right) - (1 - v + vx)E + vx\lambda s.$$

Equation (15.19) can be rewritten $A(\partial y/\partial s) - \lambda(1 - vxy) = 0$. Since $\partial y/\partial s < 0$, $A < 0$. Moreover $\partial y/\partial \lambda_f < 0$. We conclude that $\partial(\Delta W)/\partial \lambda_f < 0$.

ii. Again, using the envelope theorem yields

$$\frac{\partial(\Delta W)}{\partial E} = -[(1-v)y + vxy] + \frac{1}{v\Delta_c^{AC}}\frac{\partial(\Delta W)}{\partial x}.$$

But

$$\frac{\partial(\Delta W)}{\partial x} = -v\theta + vy(\theta - (E - \lambda s)),$$

where

$$\theta \equiv \underline{W}^{AC} - \overline{W}^{AC} - \frac{\Phi(e^*)}{1+\lambda_f}.$$

From i, we have $A < 0$ or $vx(\theta - (E - \lambda s)) < (1-v)E$. Recall now that $E = \Delta_c^{AC} vx$. Thus

$$\frac{\partial(\Delta W)}{\partial E} < -[(1-v)y + vxy] - \frac{\theta}{\Delta_c^{AC}} + y(1-v) < -vxy - \frac{\theta}{\Delta_c^{AC}} < 0. \qquad \blacksquare$$

A15.2 Proof of Proposition 15.5

i. Social welfare is given by

$$\begin{aligned}\tilde{W}^{AC}(s,\alpha) = {} & (1 - v + v\tilde{x}(1-y))\overline{W}^{AC} + v(1 - \tilde{x} + \tilde{x}y)\underline{W}^{AC} \\ & - (1 - v + v\tilde{x})y(1+\alpha\lambda)E - (1 - v\tilde{x}y)\lambda s \\ & + v\tilde{x}(1-y)\frac{\Phi(e^*)}{1+\lambda_f},\end{aligned}$$

where

$$\tilde{x} = \tilde{x}(\alpha) = \frac{E(1-\alpha)}{v\Delta_c^{AC}}$$

and

$$y = y(s) = \frac{\Delta_f}{\Delta_f + s(1+\lambda_f)}.$$

Thus

$$\begin{aligned}\frac{\partial \tilde{W}^{AC}}{\partial \alpha} = {} & -\frac{E}{v\Delta_c^{AC}}\left[-v(1-y)\left(\underline{W}^{AC} - \overline{W}^{AC} - \frac{\Phi(e^*)}{1+\lambda_f}\right)\right. \\ & \left. + \lambda vys - vyE(1+\alpha\lambda)\right] \\ & - (1 - \tilde{v} + vx)y\lambda E.\end{aligned}$$

When λ tends to zero, $\partial W^{AC}/\partial\alpha$ is positive [using the fact that $\underline{W}^{AC} - \overline{W}^{AC} - \Phi(e^*)/(1 + \lambda) > 0$], unless s tends to infinity, which is impossible from (15.19). When λ tends to $+\infty$, $\partial W^{AC}/\partial\alpha$ is negative, and therefore $\alpha = 0$ at the optimum.

ii. Since $\tilde{W}^{AC}(s, \alpha)$ is strictly quasi-concave in s, to see how s varies with α, it suffices to study $\partial(\partial\tilde{W}^{AC}/\partial s)/\partial\alpha$:

$$\frac{\partial^2 \tilde{W}^{AC}}{\partial\alpha\partial s} = \frac{\partial x}{\partial\alpha}\left\{\frac{\partial y}{\partial s}\left[\left(\underline{W}^{AC} - \overline{W}^{AC} - \frac{\Phi(e^*)}{1 + \lambda_f}\right)v + \lambda v s - vE(1 + \alpha\lambda)\right] + \lambda v y\right\}$$

$$- \frac{\partial y}{\partial s}(1 - v + vx)\lambda E.$$

For λ small, $\partial x/\partial\alpha < 0$ and $\partial y/\partial s < 0$ imply that

$$\text{sign}\left(\frac{\partial^2 \tilde{W}^{AC}}{\partial\alpha\partial s}\right) = \text{sign}\left(\Delta_c^{AC} - \frac{\Delta_f}{1 + \lambda_f} - E\right).$$

From part ii of proposition 15.4, we know that the optimal agency income is strictly positive when $\alpha = 0$ and λ is small if and only if $v\Delta_c^{AC} < E + \Delta_f/(1 + \lambda_f)$. Assuming this condition holds, the sign of $\partial^2 \tilde{W}^{AC}/\partial\alpha\partial s$ is negative if v is close to 1, and positive if v is smaller (from assumption 15.1). Furthermore, from part i of proposition 15.5, $\alpha = \bar{\alpha}$ is optimal for λ small. Thus the agency income is lowered by the feasibility of intervener programs if v is close to one and increased if v is smaller. ■

A15.3 Uncertainty about the Marginal Cost

To compare AC pricing and MC pricing for the technology $C = (\beta - e)q + \alpha$, we ran a couple of simulations for the values: $\psi(e) = \frac{3}{2}e^2$, $\alpha = 0$, $p = P(q) = 12 - q$, $\underline{\beta} = 9$, $\overline{\beta} \equiv 10$, $v = \frac{1}{2}$. Moreover we assume that the agency's reservation income s^* is equal to 1. It was normalized at 0 in the text; changing the formulas to allow $s^* = 1$ is immediate. The new feature associated with $s^* > 0$ is that the punishment —the loss of s^* when wrongdoing is discovered—becomes strictly positive. This introduces no qualitative change but affects the level of incentive to cheat. In the range of parameters described below, we obtained a corner solution $s = 1$ for the agency's income.

Proposition 15.1′ *MC* pricing can dominate *AC* pricing.
For example, $E = 1.25$, $\lambda = 0.1$, $\lambda_f = 0.1$, $W^{AC} - W^{MC} = -0.180$.

Proposition 15.2′ *AC* pricing can dominate *MC* pricing.
For example, $E = 1.25$, $\lambda = 0.3$, $\lambda_f = 0.3$, $W^{AC} - W^{MC} = 0.137$.

Contrary to proposition 15.3 in section 15.3, $\Delta W = W^{AC} - W^{MC}$ need not be monotonic in λ_f and E. Consider the following tables:

1. For $\lambda = 0.1$, $E = 1.25$,

λ_f	0.1	0.2	0.3	0.4	0.5	0.6	0.7
ΔW	−0.180	−0.184	−0.188	−0.191	−0.194	−0.197	−0.199

2. For $\lambda = 0.3$, $E = 1.25$,

λ_f	0.3	0.4	0.5	0.6	0.7	0.8	0.9
ΔW	0.137	0.140	0.142	0.145	0.147	0.149	0.150

3. For $\lambda = 0.1$, $\lambda_f = 1$,

E	0.1	0.2	0.3	0.4	0.5	0.6	0.7
ΔW	−0.052	−0.065	−0.078	−0.091	−0.104	−0.118	−0.131

4. For $\lambda = 0.3$, $\lambda_f = 1$,

E	0.2	0.3	0.4	0.5	0.6	0.7	0.8
ΔW	0.001	0.015	0.030	0.044	0.059	0.073	0.087

REFERENCES

Aghion, P., and P. Bolton. 1990. Government domestic debt and the risk of default: A political-economic model of the strategic role of debt. In *Public Debt Management: Theory and History*, ed. R. Dornbusch and M. Draghi. Cambridge: Cambridge University Press.

Alesina, A., and G. Tabellini. 1987a. A political theory of fiscal deficits and government debt in a democracy. National Bureau for Economic Research Working Paper 2308.

Alesina, A., and G. Tabellini. 1987b. External debt, capital flights and political risk. Mimeo, Harvard University.

Brennan, G., and J. Buchanan. 1977. Towards a tax constitution for Leviathan. *Journal of Public Economics* 8:255–273.

Eccles, R., and H. White. 1988. Price and authority in inter-profit center transactions. *American Journal of Sociology* 94:517–551.

Freixas, X., and J.-J. Laffont. 1985. Average cost pricing versus marginal cost pricing under moral hazard. *Journal of Public Economics* 26:135–146.

Grossman, S., and O. Hart. 1986. The costs and benefits of ownership: A theory of lateral and vertical integration. *Journal of Political Economy* 94:691–719.

Hamilton, A. [1788] 1986. *The Federalist No. 78*. Reprinted in *The Origins of the American Constitution*, ed. M. Kammen. Harmondsworth: Penguin.

Hart, O., and J. Moore. 1990. Property rights and the nature of the firm. *Journal of Political Economy* 98:1119–1158.

Kofman, F., and J. Lawarrée. 1989. Collusion in hierarchical agency. Mimeo, University of California, Berkeley. Forthcoming, *Econometrica*.

Laffont, J.-J., and E. Maskin. 1982. The theory of incentives: an overview. In *Advances in Economic Theory*, ed. W. Hildenbrand. Cambridge: Cambridge University Press.

McCubbins, M. 1985. Legislative design of regulatory structure. *American Journal of Political Science* 29:721–748.

McCubbins, M., R. Noll, and B. Weingast. 1987. Administrative procedures as instruments of political control. *Journal of Law, Economics and Organization* 3:243–277.

McCubbins, M., and T. Schwartz. 1984. Congressional oversight overlooked: Police patrols versus fire alarms. *American Journal of Political Science* 2:165–179.

Madison, J. [1788] 1986. *The Federalist No. 10* (47–51). Reprinted in *The Origins of the American Constitution*, ed. M. Kammen. Harmondsworth: Penguin.

Myerson, R. 1986. Multistage games with communication. *Econometrica* 54:323–358.

Persson, T., and L. Svensson. 1989. Why a stubborn conservative would run a deficit: Policy with time-inconsistent preferences. *Quarterly Journal of Economics* 65:325–346.

Sappington, D. 1986. Commitment to regulatory bureaucracy. *Information Economics and Policy* 2:243–258.

Shapiro, M. 1986. APA: Past, present and future. *Virginia Law Review* 72:447–492.

Spiller, P. 1990. Politicians, interest groups, and regulators: A multiple-principals agency theory of regulation (or "let them be bribed"). *Journal of Law and Economics* 33:65–101.

Sunstein, C. 1986. Factions, self-interest, and the APA: Four lessons since 1946. *Virginia Law Review* 72:271–296.

Williamson, O. 1975. *Markets and Hierarchies: Analysis and Antitrust Implications.* New York: The Free Press.

Williamson, O. 1985. *The Economic Institutions of Capitalism.* New York: The Free Press.

16 COMMITMENT AND POLITICAL ACCOUNTABILITY

16.1 Some Background

Governments commit the nation in the long run by issuing treasury bonds, signing international treaties, and investing in infrastructure. Yet the settings of budgets, money supply, or regulatory prices show that governments also often do not commit beyond a short horizon.[1] Such short-run commitments are perceived to create inefficiencies. For instance, the lack of commitment to a monetary policy can give rise to inflationary expectations. Similarly reviews updating the prices of regulated firms tend to adjust prices to perceived current cost conditions and thus to expropriate the firm's investments; or, as we have seen in chapter 9, reviews can also induce regulated firms to pretend to be inefficient.

The extent to which governments ought to be able to commit the nation over the long run has always been subject to lively debates. Should the central bank be constrained by rules governing the evolution of the money supply, the interest rate, or the exchange rate? Should federal or state governments be required to balance their budget every year? Should procurement officials be allowed to commit through multiyear procurement? Should regulators be prevented from adjusting prices for a fixed number of years?[2]

There are two basic reasons why governments do not commit. The first cause of noncommitment is the difficulty of signing complete state-contingent contracts in an uncertain environment. The central bank will want to expand monetary supply if signals indicate a forthcoming recession, yet those signals may be difficult to describe in detail today. So the central bank may want to keep a free hand rather than abide by a rule that sometimes is inappropriate. Similarly regulators may not commit today because they are unable to set the exact characteristics of the goods to be produced tomorrow or because they may learn tomorrow technological information that cannot be described today.

We believe that such transaction costs are an important explanation of short-run commitments. Yet they cannot fully account for the limited use of commitment along some policy dimensions. They cannot explain why regulators often feel that their hands are tied and that they cannot implement Pareto-improving policies because they are constrained to short-run policies. In other words, transaction costs cannot by themselves account

1. Note that the nonindexation of government bonds makes the commitment associated with public debt uncertain.

2. The length of commitment is, as we have seen, a central feature of the debate about price caps and cost-of-service regulation. Price caps are akin to cost-of-service regulation in that prices are determined by the regulator and free from regulatory intervention for some period of time. The proponents of price caps have emphasized the longer length of commitment—four to five years—as one of their distinguishing features. (Another point of departure is the downward price flexibility for the firm under price caps. In particular, when caps affect a basket of goods, regulated firms can adjust the structure of relative prices in this basket.)

for the array of constitutional and administrative rules that prohibit long-term commitment. The purpose of this chapter is to investigate a second foundation for noncommitment. The idea is that nonbenevolent governments can do more harm if they are allowed to commit. Short commitments allow wrong policies to be corrected by future administrations.

To keep with the theme of this book, we illustrate the commitment issue in a regulatory context. A regulator may or may not be able to commit in the long term (two periods in our model). The benefit of commitment is that the regulated firm's investment is not expropriated.[3] The cost of commitment is that the government may identify with the firm and bind the nation to a bad outcome over the long run.[4]

We investigate the cases where the governments are short-lived (i.e., are automatically replaced after one period) and where politicians have career concerns. In the latter case we examine a rational (re)election model: Voters correctly update their beliefs about the current government's integrity on the basis of its policy record. The government trades off its desire to identify with the industry and its career concern.

This chapter is organized as follows: Section 16.2 assumes that regulators are short-lived and examines the optimal choice of a constitution. It illustrates the trade-off between encouraging investment through commitment and correcting wrong policies through noncommitment. This section, along the lines of chapter 15, assumes that the constitution can only give a rough mandate, namely "commitment" or "noncommitment."

Section 16.3 tests the robustness of the ideas to more complete mandates. Following the lines of chapter 11, it looks at the polar case in which the constitution (or a political principal) can specify a complete incentive contract for the regulator and the firm. Formally the optimal contract with the firm is a long-term contract, but we show that its potential flexibility to reflect the position of future regulators leads to the same trade-off between the promotion of investment and the rectification of wrong policies as in section 16.2. Indeed, for a set of parameters, focusing on the two constitutions studied in section 16.2 involves no loss of generality. For the complementary set of parameters, the optimal complete contract strictly dominates the optimal constitution, but the optimal allocation can be obtained through either a long-term or a short-term contract with the firm. These robustness results are reassuring in view of the strong assumptions made in section 16.2.

The intuition for this robustness is as follows: When the second administration observes that the firm's cost is low, it may not know whether the firm has invested to reduce its cost or whether the firm's cost was

3. See sections 1.8 and 1.9 for a discussion of regulatory expropriation of investment.

4. The cause of nonbenevolence is thus collusion with an interest group in this model. Alternatively, the government could have a hidden ideological bias relative to its electorate, or else be incompetent.

intrinsically low and the previous administration was not demanding enough. In other words, giving the second administration the possibility of adjusting price (short-term contracting is one way of doing so) raises the issue of selective intervention. The second administration, if given the power to correct wrongful pricing by the previous administration, will not reward the firm for investing.

Section 16.4 generalizes the model of section 16.2 by allowing regulators to have career concerns, and solves for optimal behavior by regulators and Bayesian inference by the voters. Section 16.5 summarizes the main insights and discusses the attributes of policies for which governmental commitments are likely to be constrained.

16.2 Short-lived Regulators and the Optimal Constitution

16.2.1 The Model

There are two periods, $\tau = 1, 2$. The discount factor between the two periods will be denoted by δ. In each period a natural monopoly can realize an indivisible project for the government. The gross surplus S generated by each of these projects is large enough that it is never optimal not to implement them. The shadow price of public funds is $1 + \lambda (\lambda > 0)$.

The firm is long-lived and has *private* cost $\beta \in \{\underline{\beta}, \overline{\beta}\}$ of realizing the project in a given period. [Note that this assumption can be regarded as a special case of the general framework of this book. From chapter 1 we know that for disutility of effort $\psi(e) \equiv e$, cost is de facto unobservable and that focusing on fixed-price contracts involves no loss of generality. It is not difficult to extend the model to allow cost observability and moral hazard, but we prefer to keep the exposition as simple as possible.] This cost is known to the firm at the beginning of period 1. Because we later allow the firm to invest to reduce its cost from $\overline{\beta}$ to $\underline{\beta}$, we let β_τ denote the firm's cost at date τ (so $\beta_1 = \beta$).

The governments are short-lived. To simplify the exposition, we assume that its members live for a single period.[5] Government G_τ, $\tau = 1, 2$, receives a hard signal σ_τ that perfectly reveals the firm's current cost. This signal is $\sigma_\tau = \underline{\beta}$ when $\beta_\tau = \underline{\beta}$, and $\sigma_\tau = \emptyset$ when $\beta_\tau = \overline{\beta}$. That is, the basic technology, which allows the firm to produce at private cost $\overline{\beta}$, is known to everyone. G_1 learns whether the firm benefits from an exogenous technological improvement reducing the private cost to $\underline{\beta}$. G_2 learns whether the firm benefits from an exogenous technological improvement or else

5. What matters for our results is that penalties in the second period be limited. To obtain our results with two-period lived rulers (who govern for a single period), one can assume either limited liability, or an infinitesimal probability that the firm's type exogenously changes between the two periods together with an infinite disutility for the rulers under zero income.

has reduced its cost (but G_2 may not be able to distinguish between the two causes). Government G_τ can, however, conceal the observation of an improvement. That is, it can report $r_\tau \in \{\underline{\beta}, \varnothing\}$ when $\beta_\tau = \underline{\beta}$, while it can only report $r_\tau = \varnothing$ when $\beta_\tau = \overline{\beta}$. Government G_τ learns σ_τ after taking its functions. The rest of society (including the court; see below) only knows that $\beta = \underline{\beta}$ with probability v and that $\beta = \overline{\beta}$ with probability $1 - v$.

Government G_τ has reservation utility 0 and has utility from income s, $V(s) = s$ for $s \geq 0$, and $V(s) = -\infty$ for $s < 0$. In this section we assume that the government always receives its reservation income 0 from the taxpayers; that is, we assume that there is no principal above the government who could design an incentive scheme for releasing information about the firm's efficiency. The only control over the government is exerted by an administrative court that severely punishes the government if the latter implemented a regulatory policy inconsistent with its reported information or with the constitutional allowance of commitment. (As mentioned in the previous section, we later consider the other polar case in which contracting is complete and in particular the government can be rewarded on the basis of its reported information.)

It should also be noted that government G_τ is treated as a single actor. In practice, splitting the power to commit public funds among several government officials could strengthen the case for commitment to the extent these officials do not perfectly collude. For instance, French ministries are subject to constant control by the ministry of finance.[6] No document of a ministry creating a commitment is valid without the visa of the *contrôleur financier*,[7] and contracts are scrutinized by a Commission Consultative Centrale des Marchés.

When $\beta = \overline{\beta}$, the firm can, while producing in period 1, reduce its second-period cost to $\underline{\beta}$ by committing unobservable private investment δI in period 1 (with period 2 equivalent cost I). We assume that $I < \Delta\beta \equiv \overline{\beta} - \underline{\beta}$, so investment is socially desirable.[8]

The firm receives t_τ in period τ and gives side transfer $s_\tau \geq 0$ to G_τ. Its utility is thus

$$t_1 - s_1 + \delta(t_2 - s_2) - (1 + \delta)\underline{\beta} \qquad \text{if } \beta = \underline{\beta},$$

and,

$$t_1 - s_1 + \delta(t_2 - s_2) - (1 + \delta)\overline{\beta} + \delta(\Delta\beta - I)x \qquad \text{if } \beta = \overline{\beta},$$

6. In this they differ from their English counterparts. See Normanton (1966, pp. 91–101) for a cross-country comparison of controls of commitments.

7. The *contrôleur financier* exerts a priori control and must be distinguished from the Cour des Comptes inspector who controls a posteriori. The two tasks are separated to reduce the incentive for cover ups.

8. So $\beta_2 = \beta$ if $\beta = \underline{\beta}$, or if $\beta = \overline{\beta}$ and no investment is made; $\beta_2 = \underline{\beta}$ if $\beta = \overline{\beta}$, and the investment is made.

where $x = 1$ if the investment is made, and $x = 0$ otherwise. The firm's reservation utility is 0.

With probability α, government G_τ is honest and always reveals its information truthfully; with probability $1 - \alpha$, government G_τ is dishonest and colludes with the firm. The firm knows whether the government is honest or dishonest. We assume that the government has all the bargaining power and proposes both an official contract and a side contract. This distribution of bargaining power implies that the firm never enjoys a rent and simplifies the computations. Letting λ_f denote the deadweight loss incurred when transferring \$1 of income equivalent to the government, a dishonest G_τ receives $\underline{U}_\tau/(1 + \lambda_f)$ when $\beta_\tau = \underline{\beta}$, where $\underline{U}_\tau$ is the firm's stake at date τ in inducing G_τ to conceal the information that it is efficient (this stake will be determined endogenously). Two points are worth making. First, the probability of honesty could depend on time and other factors (indeed it will depend on the policy record in section 16.4, where governments are long-lived). Second, "honesty" can be given two interpretations. Either the government is intrinsically benevolent and maximizes social welfare (in this model, releasing information that $\beta_\tau = \underline{\beta}$ will always guarantee the first-best level of welfare from date τ on). Or the government is self-interested but cannot receive bribes from the firm (its λ_f is equal to infinity). The distinction between these two interpretations matters when governments are long-lived as in section 16.4.

The constitution gives the government its reservation wage and also allows or disallows the government to sign a long-term contract with the firm. A *short-term contract* is a transfer or price t_1 for the realization of the project in period 1. The contract signed by G_1 is consistent with reported information if $t_1 = \underline{\beta}$ when $r_1 = \underline{\beta}$ and $t_1 = \bar{\beta}$ when $r_1 = \varnothing$. Under short-term contracting G_2 has the responsibility to determine the second-period price t_2, which itself must be consistent with available reports: $t_2 = \bar{\beta}$ if $r_1 = r_2 = \varnothing$ and $t_2 = \underline{\beta}$ otherwise. We assume that under short-term contracting the administrative court requires that G_2 offer at date 2 the contract that is socially optimal *at date 2* given the reported information. In particular, if $r_1 = \varnothing$ and $r_2 = \underline{\beta}$, it does not try to ask the government not to expropriate the firm's (possible) investment. Allowing the court to implement more subtle policies brings us into the realm of complete long-term contracts, which we will study in section 16.3. Note also that G_2 cannot recover t_1 if $r_1 = \varnothing$ and $r_2 = \underline{\beta}$.[9]

A *long-term contract* specifies at date 1 prices t_1 and t_2 for the realization of the projects in periods 1 and 2. The long-term contract must be consistent with the reported information r_1: If $r_1 = \underline{\beta}$, then $t_1 = t_2 = \underline{\beta}$; if $r_1 = \varnothing$, then G_1 offers the socially optimal fixed price to the firm: $t =$

9. There are several ways of justifying this. Here is one: There is an infinitesimal probability that $\beta_2 = \underline{\beta}$ when $\beta_1 = \bar{\beta}$ and $x = 0$. Furthermore the firm's utility is minus infinity when its income minus its private cost falls below 0.

$t_1 + \delta t_2 = (1 + \delta)\overline{\beta} - \delta(\Delta\beta - I)$ [under a fixed price the firm will undertake the investment and gain private cost $\delta(\Delta\beta - I)$]. This consistency assumption depicts the idea that G_2 is bound by the contract signed by G_1 and cannot affect the second-period price. If, instead, the long-term contract specified that $t_2 = \overline{\beta}$ if $r_2 = \varnothing$ and $t_2 = \underline{\beta}$ if $r_2 = \underline{\beta}$, the long-term contract would be equivalent to the short-term contract.

The constitution either allows commitment, in which case G_1 must sign a long-term contract, or prohibits it, forcing G_1 to sign a short-term contract. We will derive the optimal constitution. There is no loss of generality involved in ruling out the constitution in which G_1 can choose between a short-term and a long-term contract. This third constitution, however, could be optimal once G_1 has career concerns (section 16.4).

Last, we summarize the timing. At date 0, benevolent founders choose the constitution ("commitment" or "noncommitment"). At date 1, the firm and G_1 learn β. Monitored by a court, G_1 then reports its information or, equivalently, offers the optimal contract given this reported information and the length of public contracts specified by the constitution. At date 2, G_2 learns the new technological parameter β_2 ($\beta_2 = \underline{\beta}$ if $\beta = \overline{\beta}$ and $x = 1$, $\beta_2 = \beta$ otherwise), and reports its information, which under noncommitment is used to determine the second-period price.

16.2.2 Commitment

Suppose first that the constitution imposes long-term contracting.

Honest G_1

With probability α, G_1 is honest (H) and offers

$$t = t_1 + \delta t_2 = (1 + \delta)\underline{\beta} \qquad \text{if } \beta = \underline{\beta}$$

and

$$t = t_1 + \delta t_2 = (1 + \delta)\overline{\beta} - \delta(\Delta\beta - I) \qquad \text{if } \beta = \overline{\beta}.$$

Since $\Delta\beta > I$, the firm invests when $\beta = \overline{\beta}$, and social welfare is

$$W_H^c = (1 + \delta)S - (1 + \lambda)\{\nu(1 + \delta)\underline{\beta} + (1 - \nu)[(1 + \delta)\overline{\beta} - \delta(\Delta\beta - I)]\}.$$

(Note that the firm accepts G_1's offer even though it gets no rent and there is a probability that G_2 is dishonest. Because of our assumption on the bargaining power, the firm obtains no second-period rent either.)

Dishonest G_1

With probability $1 - \alpha$, G_1 is dishonest (D). Whatever the firm's technology, G_1 offers the long-term price $t = (1 + \delta)\overline{\beta} - \delta(\Delta\beta - I)$, that is, reports $r_1 = \varnothing$. The firm accepts. If $\beta = \overline{\beta}$, the firm invests. If $\beta = \underline{\beta}$, it gives its potential rent

$$\underline{U}_1 = \Delta\beta + \delta I$$

to G_1 (the second-period rent is I because the inefficient type invests I to reduce its cost to $\underline{\beta}$). Social welfare is then

$$W_D^c = (1+\delta)S - (1+\lambda)[(1+\delta)\bar{\beta} - \delta(\Delta\beta - I)] + v\left(\frac{\Delta\beta + \delta I}{1+\lambda_f}\right),$$

where the last term is G_1's rent when $\beta = \underline{\beta}$. Expected welfare under commitment is thus

$$W^c = \alpha W_H^c + (1-\alpha) W_D^c.$$

16.2.3 Noncommitment

Under short-term contracts the firm never invests because it always receives zero utility in period 2 whatever its efficiency and the type of government.

Honest G_1

If G_1 is honest, welfare is

$$W_H^{nc} = (1+\delta)S - (1+\lambda)[v(1+\delta)\underline{\beta} + (1-v)(1+\delta)\bar{\beta}].$$

Thus

$$W_H^c - W_H^{nc} = (1+\lambda)(1-v)\delta(\Delta\beta - I) > 0.$$

As we expected, welfare is higher under commitment if G_1 is honest, since noncommitment suppresses investment.

Dishonest G_1

If $\beta = \bar{\beta}$, then $r_1 = \varnothing$, $t_1 = \bar{\beta}$, and $x = 0$. Therefore $\beta_2 = \bar{\beta}$, $r_2 = \varnothing$, and $t_2 = \bar{\beta}$. If $\beta = \underline{\beta}$, the firm transfers $\Delta\beta$ (the most it is willing to pay for $r_1 = \varnothing$, given that the firm will not enjoy a second period rent) to G_1 and does not invest. With probability α, G_2 is honest and reveals that $\beta = \underline{\beta}$; with probability $1-\alpha$, G_2 is dishonest and the allocation is the same as in period 1. Welfare is thus

$$W_D^{nc} = (1+\delta)S - (1+\lambda)\{v[(1+\delta(1-\alpha))\bar{\beta} + \delta\alpha\underline{\beta}] + (1-v)(1+\delta)\bar{\beta}\}$$
$$+ v(1+\delta(1-\alpha))\frac{\Delta\beta}{1+\lambda_f},$$

where the last term is the expected rents of G_1 and G_2. Note that

$$W_D^c - W_D^{nc} = \delta\left\{\left(1+\lambda - \frac{v}{1+\lambda_f}\right)(\Delta\beta - I) - v\alpha\left(1+\lambda - \frac{1}{1+\lambda_f}\right)\Delta\beta\right\}.$$

This comparison of commitment and noncommitment under a dishonest G_1 has a straightforward interpretation. Noncommitment allows the second-period recovery of the firm's rent $\Delta\beta$ when it is efficient (which has probability v) and G_2 is honest (which has probability α); the unit social value of this capture of the rent is the shadow cost of public funds $1 + \lambda$ minus the social value $1/(1 + \lambda_f)$ of rents transferred to G_1. On the other hand, commitment encourages investment. Investment reduces the price to be paid by the government by $\Delta\beta - I$ (whatever the firm's type as the dishonest government does not price discriminate), which has social value $(1 + \lambda)(\Delta\beta - I)$. The inefficient type's investment also reduces the efficient type's potential second-period rent by $\Delta\beta - I$, which lowers the governments' expected rent by $v(\Delta\beta - I)/(1 + \lambda_f)$.

Note that when investment is not important ($\Delta\beta - I$ is small), $W_D^{nc} > W_D^c$. The social welfare under noncommitment is

$$W^{nc} = \alpha W_H^{nc} + (1 - \alpha) W_D^{nc}.$$

16.2.4 Optimal Constitution

We have

$$W^c - W^{nc} = \delta\left\{\left[1 + \lambda - v\left(\alpha + \frac{1 - \alpha}{1 + \lambda_f}\right)\right](\Delta\beta - I) - (1 - \alpha)v\alpha\left[1 + \lambda - \frac{1}{1 + \lambda_f}\right]\Delta\beta\right\}.$$

Proposition 16.1

i. Noncommitment is optimal if and only if, ceteris paribus,

investment yields low benefits (I large),
the firm is likely to be efficient (v high),
collusion is difficult (λ_f large).[10]

ii. There exists $\alpha^* \in [0, 1]$ such that $W^c - W^{nc}$ decreases on $[0, \alpha^*]$ and increases on $[\alpha^*, 1]$.

It may seem surprising that noncommitment becomes more appealing when collusion is more difficult. But recall that collusion always occurs under a dishonest government because the constitution does not provide penalties or rewards to prevent it. Therefore the choice of constitution has no impact on the probability of collusion in period 1. The point is rather that the rent is smaller under commitment than under noncommitment because investment by the inefficient type (which is fostered by commitment) reduces the second-period rent of the efficient type. Therefore a decrease in the deadweight loss of transferring the rent to the government has more impact in the noncommitment case. Proposition 16.2 will show

10. To show this, note that $\partial(W^c - W^{nc})/\partial\lambda_f \propto -[\alpha\Delta\beta - (\Delta\beta - I)]$. Now, if $\Delta\beta - I > \alpha\Delta\beta$, then W^c always exceeds W^{nc}, and in this case the set of λ_f such that noncommitment is optimal is empty. Thus, for the set of parameters for which noncommitment may be optimal, it is optimal for λ_f large.

that short-term contracts become *less* appealing when collusion is more difficult if penalties or rewards are given to prevent collusion.

It is interesting to note that the other comparative statics exercises yield ambiguous conclusions. Consider, first, an increase in the probability α that governments are honest. The higher probability of honesty of G_1 pushes the constitution toward allowing commitment, but the higher probability of honesty of G_2 increases the probability that a wrong price be corrected and raises the desirability of noncommitment. It is worth noting in this respect that under full honesty ($\alpha = 1$) or full dishonesty ($\alpha = 0$) commitment is always optimal. Similarly an increase in the shadow cost of public funds makes it more costly to leave rents, favoring noncommitment, but also makes it more desirable to encourage investment in order to reduce prices, which favors commitment.

16.3 Short-lived Regulators and Complete Contracting

To test the robustness of the results of section 16.2 to more sophisticated constitutions or courts, we now consider the case of complete incentive contracts. The "government" of section 16.2 is now called an "agency" subject to the careful control of a benevolent political principal (alternatively, it could be a government subject to a careful control of courts, voters, or detailed constitutions). The setup is thus similar to that of chapter 11 except that agencies are short-lived.

The firm is described as in section 16.2. Agencies A_1 and A_2 have the preferences of the players G_1 and G_2 described in section 16.2. Their role consists of learning the firm's technology and reporting it to the political principal. Agency A_τ is honest with probability α and dishonest with probability $1 - \alpha$. The benevolent political principal can indifferently be short-lived or long-lived. The only difference with section 16.2 is that we allow the political principal (the "constitution" in section 16.2) to write a complete long-term incentive contract for the regulators and the firm rather than to write a rough mandate on commitment and let a court check that the regulatory contract is consistent with commitment power and reported information.

Let s_1 denote agency A_1's reward from the political principal when reporting $r_1 = \underline{\beta}$; let s_2 denote agency A_2's reward when $r_1 = \varnothing$ and $r_2 = \underline{\beta}$; it is easy to see that all other rewards are equal to zero and that eliciting the firm's information is useless (either the agency is honest and reports the true cost level, or it is dishonest and coordinates its report with the firm's if the two collude). Because of complete contracting there is no loss of generality in assuming long-term contracts (as long as, unlike in section 16.2, we allow them to be sensitive to the second-period report). The thrust of the analysis is thus to see to what extent the allocation resulting from the optimal long-term contract can alternatively be implemented by a short-term one, and possibly by a simple constitution as in section 16.2. Let $t_1(r_1)$ and $t_2(r_1, r_2)$ denote the prices paid to the firm. We assume that the firm must obtain a nonnegative utility in each period (see section 16.2 for foundations for this assumption). We consider optimal long-term incentive contracts that induce investment by the inefficient type ($x = 1$) or do not induce investment ($x = 0$).

16.3.1 Investment Induced

Note, first, that when investment takes place, the firm's second-period cost is independent of its original type. Hence the second-period report is useless and collusion with A_2 is irrelevant along the equilibrium path. Second, the efficient type's potential rent is $\Delta\beta + \delta I$. Thus the political principal has the choice between preventing collusion with A_1 by paying $s_1 = (\Delta\beta + \delta I)/(1 + \lambda_f)$ or allowing collusion when A_1 is dishonest by paying $s_1 = 0$ (any other s_1 is dominated).

No Collusion

The social cost of paying s_1 for report $r_1 = \underline{\beta}$ is λs_1, and it is incurred with probability v. Welfare, when investment is induced and collusion with A_1 avoided, is thus

$$\tilde{W}^c = W_H^c - \lambda v \frac{\Delta\beta + \delta I}{1 + \lambda_f} = W_D^c + (1 + \lambda) v \lambda_f \frac{\Delta\beta + \delta I}{1 + \lambda_f}.$$

Collusion

Alternatively, the political principal could tolerate collusion between the firm and the dishonest A_1 in order to save the first period reward of inducing honesty. With $s_1 = 0$, we are back to the case of a constitution studied in section 16.2. That is, welfare is

$$W^c = \alpha W_H^c + (1 - \alpha) W_D^c.$$

Note that the levels of welfare $\tilde{W}^c$ and W^c can be obtained. It suffices to offer the following contracts: $\{t_1(\underline{\beta}) = \underline{\beta}; t_1(\varnothing) = \bar{\beta}; t_2(\underline{\beta}, \cdot) = \underline{\beta}; t_2(\varnothing, \cdot) = \underline{\beta} + I\}$ to the firm, and $\{s_2(\cdot, \cdot) = 0; s_1(\varnothing) = 0; s_1(\underline{\beta}) = (\Delta\beta + \delta I)/(1 + \lambda_f)$ (to obtain $\tilde{W}^c$), $s_1(\underline{\beta}) = 0$ (to obtain W^c)$\}$ to the agencies. We can conclude that it is optimal to prevent collusion if α is small, and to allow it if α is large. In the latter case complete contracting does not improve on the commitment mandate studied in section 16.2.

16.3.2 No Investment

Suppose now that the political principal chooses incentive schemes such that type $\bar{\beta}$ does not invest whatever A_1's type.[11] Type $\underline{\beta}$'s potential rent is

11. Note that the incentive to invest is independent of A_1's type and that the first period report is necessarily $r_1 = \varnothing$.

then $(1 + \delta)\Delta\beta$. But, because of our assumption on bargaining powers, the firm obtains no rent in period 2 and thus is not willing to transfer more than $\Delta\beta$ to A_1. The reward $s_1 = \Delta\beta/(1 + \lambda_f)$ thus suffices to prevent collusion. It is interesting to note that it is easier to prevent collusion when investment is not induced than when it is, despite the fact that the firm's potential rent is higher. The reason for this is that if investment does not occur, part of the firm's rent accrues in period 2; since A_1 does not internalize the negative externality on A_2 associated with the revelation that the firm is efficient, the political principal needs only reward A_1 for an amount corresponding to the first-period rent. Again we consider the two cases where collusion is allowed and where it is not.

No Collusion
Welfare in this case is

$$\tilde{W}^{nc} = W_H^{nc} - \lambda v \frac{\Delta\beta}{1 + \lambda_f}.$$

This welfare can be obtained by offering, for instance,

$$\{t_1(\underline{\beta}) = t_2(\underline{\beta}, \cdot) = \underline{\beta};\ t_1(\varnothing) = t_2(\varnothing, \varnothing) = \bar{\beta};\ t_2(\varnothing, \underline{\beta}) = \underline{\beta}\}$$

and

$$\left\{s_1(\underline{\beta}) = \frac{\Delta\beta}{1 + \lambda_f};\ s_1(\varnothing) = 0;\ s_2(\cdot, \cdot) = 0\right\}.$$

Collusion
Alternatively, the political principal can let the dishonest A_1 collude with the firm by offering $s_1(\cdot) \equiv 0$. He or she can further let the dishonest A_2 collude with the firm by offering $s_2(\cdot) \equiv 0$, resulting in welfare

$$\begin{aligned} W^{nc} &= \alpha W_H^{nc} + (1 - \alpha) W_D^{nc} \\ &= W_H^{nc} - (1 - \alpha)v(1 + \delta(1 - \alpha))\left(1 + \lambda - \frac{1}{1 + \lambda_f}\right)\Delta\beta; \end{aligned}$$

or offer $s_2(\varnothing, \underline{\beta}) = \Delta\beta/(1 + \lambda_f)$ to prevent the dishonest A_2 from colluding, which yields welfare

$$\begin{aligned} \hat{W}^{nc} &= (1 + \delta)S - \alpha(1 + \delta)(1 + \lambda)(v\underline{\beta} + (1 - v)\bar{\beta}) - (1 - \alpha) \\ &\quad \times \left\{(1 + \lambda)\bar{\beta} - v\frac{\Delta\beta}{1 + \lambda_f} + \delta\left[(1 + \lambda)(v\underline{\beta} + (1 - v)\bar{\beta}) + \lambda v\frac{\Delta\beta}{1 + \lambda_f}\right]\right\} \\ &= W_H^{nc} - (1 - \alpha)\left[v\left(1 + \lambda - \frac{1}{1 + \lambda_f}\right)\Delta\beta + \delta\lambda v\frac{\Delta\beta}{1 + \lambda_f}\right] \\ &\leq \max\{\tilde{W}^{nc}, W^{nc}\}. \end{aligned}$$

It is thus optimal to prevent collusion or else to allow collusion in both periods (this result depends on the stationarity of the probability of honesty). Again we find that the optimal allocation under complete contracts is the same as under a rough mandate (here of noncommitment) if α is large.

We now determine the optimal allocation under complete contracts. Optimal welfare is $\max\{\tilde{W}^c, W^c, \tilde{W}^{nc}, W^{nc}\}$. We obtain proposition 16.2.

Proposition 16.2 There exists $\hat{\alpha} \in (0, 1)$ such that

i. for $\alpha \geq \hat{\alpha}$, it is not optimal to try to prevent collusion. The optimal complete contract then does not improve on the best constitution derived in section 16.2. It may thus yield either the commitment outcome W^c or the noncommitment outcome W^{nc}.

ii. for $\alpha < \hat{\alpha}$, the optimal complete contract improves on the best constitution by preventing collusion. If $\tilde{W}^c > \tilde{W}^{nc}$ the optimal allocation, which involves investment, can be obtained by committing not to extract the firm's rent if the firm lowers its cost. If $\tilde{W}^{nc} > \tilde{W}^c$, the optimal allocation, which involves no investment, can be obtained through a short-term contract with the firm. Furthermore (for $\alpha < \hat{\alpha}$), $\tilde{W}^{nc} \geq \tilde{W}^c$ if investment yields low benefits (I large) or if the firm is likely to be efficient (ν large).

The principal can prevent collusion with appropriate transfers. If the transfers for the principal are too costly, collusion occurs and the analysis is the same as in section 16.2. If the principal decides to prevent collusion, a new effect appears: The transfers needed to prevent collusion are higher in the commitment case. Accordingly the effect of an increase in λ_f differs from that in section 16.2.

Unlike in proposition 16.1, long-term contracts may become more attractive when collusion becomes more difficult. To see this, consider the case of a small probability of honesty (part ii of proposition 16.2.) It is then optimal to prevent collusion. A long-term contract enables agency A_1 to extract more rent by colluding with the firm. It is therefore more costly to prevent collusion under a long-term contract. In contrast, when it is optimal not to prevent collusion (part i of proposition 16.2), which corresponds to the analysis of section 16.2, the regime that leaves more rent to A_1 (i.e., long-term contracting) becomes more appealing when the deadweight loss of transfers decreases.

16.4 Elections, Career Concerns, and Commitment

We now generalize the model of section 16.2 by endogenizing G_1's probability of being reelected (which was equal to 0 up to now). Let α_2 denote the voters' posterior probability at the beginning of period 2 that G_1 is honest given its policy record; let $g(\alpha_2) \in [0, 1]$ denote the probability that G_1 is reelected. An implicit assumption is that the probability of reelection does not depend on side transfers received by G_1 in period 1. That is, side transfers are to be thought of as monetary bribes, consulting contracts, friendship, or promise of future jobs but not as PACs. We will comment on the financing of political campaigns later. Except for this important restriction, the function $g(\cdot)$, which we assume is increasing, can accommodate many rational voting models.[12] Since we wish to keep $g(\cdot)$ quite general, we will perform only positive analysis (study G_1's incentive to collude) and will abandon the normative analysis, which would require a more specific voting model.

We assume that G_1, whatever its type, has private value $V \geq 0$ of being reelected (to which second-period side transfers from the firm may be added). In particular in this section we interpret "honest government" as "self-interested government with $\lambda_f = +\infty$," and not as "benevolent government." Note that an honest G_1 has a simple strategy when $\beta = \underline{\beta}$: Report whichever of $r_1 = \underline{\beta}$ and $r_1 = \emptyset$ results in the highest posterior beliefs. In contrast, a dishonest G_1 must trade off its reputation and the side transfer it receives from the firm. We let $\alpha_2(r_1)$ denote the posterior beliefs.

We will assume that the honest G_1 always reports $r_1 = \underline{\beta}$ when $\beta = \underline{\beta}$.[13] Let $\gamma \in [0, 1]$ denote the probability that the dishonest G_1 colludes, that is, reports $r_1 = \emptyset$ when $\beta = \underline{\beta}$ (γ was equal to 1 in section 16.2). In equilibrium $\gamma > 0$; for if the equilibrium were a pooling equilibrium ($\gamma = 0$), then both reports $r_1 = \underline{\beta}$ and $r_1 = \emptyset$ would be uninformative [$\alpha_2(\underline{\beta}) = \alpha_2(\emptyset) = \alpha$], and it would therefore be optimal for the dishonest G_1 to collude with probability 1. We now consider three constitutions: the commitment and noncommitment constitutions of section 16.2, and the hybrid constitution that lets G_1 choose between a long-term contract and a short-term contract.[14]

16.4.1 Commitment Constitution

As in section 16.2 the firm's long-term contract specifies a price $t = (1 + \delta)\underline{\beta}$ when $r_1 = \underline{\beta}$, and $t = (1 + \delta)\bar{\beta} - \delta(\Delta\beta - I)$ when $r_1 = \emptyset$. We first

12. For instance, the median voter's preferences can be randomly located. This median voter takes into account, in addition to his or her beliefs about integrity, the distance between his or her "bliss point," and the candidates' platform or personality.

13. This behavior can be obtained endogenously by invoking Banks-Sobel's D1 criterion. Once the bribes associated with concealing evidence are factored into G_1's utility function, the game is transformed into a monotonic signaling game. The dishonest G_1 values reporting $r_1 = \emptyset$ when $\beta = \underline{\beta}$ more than the honest one, since it has a positive valuation for the bribe.

14. This third constitution was irrelevant with shortsighted G_1. Under this constitution the dishonest G_1 would have chosen the long-term contract as this would yield him the highest bribe. The constitution would then have been equivalent to the commitment constitution.

find a condition under which the dishonest G_1 always colludes ($\gamma = 1$). In doing so, G_1 receives bribe $(\Delta\beta + \delta I)/(1 + \lambda_f)$ from type $\underline{\beta}$. However, this reduces G_1's probability of reelection. While report $r_1 = \varnothing$ is no foolproof evidence that G_1 is dishonest, it suggests that it is likely to be. Indeed the posterior beliefs (for an equilibrium in which $\gamma = 1$) are $\alpha_2(\underline{\beta}) = 1$ and $\alpha_2(\varnothing) = \alpha(1 - \nu)/(1 - \alpha\nu) < \alpha$.

Thus the necessary and sufficient condition for the dishonest G_1 to always collude under the commitment constitution is

$$\frac{\Delta\beta + \delta I}{1 + \lambda_f} \geq \delta\left[g(1) - g\left(\frac{\alpha - \alpha\nu}{1 - \alpha\nu}\right)\right]V, \tag{16.1}$$

where use is made of the fact that the dishonest G_1 can no longer extract rents from the firm in period 2 even if it is reelected (since, regardless of its first-period cost, the firm's second-period cost is $\underline{\beta}$).

If condition (16.1) is not satisfied, the equilibrium is also unique and involves mixing by the dishonest G_1 between colluding and not colluding. From Bayes's rule, $\alpha_2(\underline{\beta}) = \alpha/[1 - (1 - \alpha)\gamma]$ and $\alpha_2(\varnothing) = \alpha(1 - \nu)/[1 - \nu + (1 - \alpha)\nu\gamma]$; the probability γ is thus uniquely defined by

$$\frac{\Delta\beta + \delta I}{1 + \lambda_f} = \delta\left[g\left(\frac{\alpha}{1 - (1 - \alpha)\gamma}\right) - g\left(\frac{\alpha(1 - \nu)}{1 - \nu + (1 - \alpha)\nu\gamma}\right)\right]V.$$

We can conclude that career concerns may reduce the government's incentive to collude.

16.4.2 Noncommitment Constitution

As in section 16.2 the firm's short-term contract specifies price $t_1 = \underline{\beta}$ if $r_1 = \underline{\beta}$ and $t_1 = \bar{\beta}$ if $r_1 = \varnothing$. The analysis is very similar to that of the commitment constitution. There are two differences stemming from the fact that the firm does not invest. First, the dishonest G_1 extracts rent $\Delta\beta/(1 + \lambda_f)$ when colluding in period 1. Second, if reelected, G_1 will be able to extract the same rent in period 2 as well.

The necessary and sufficient condition for the dishonest G_1 to always collude ($\gamma = 1$) is thus

$$\frac{\Delta\beta}{1 + \lambda_f} + \delta g\left(\frac{\alpha - \alpha\nu}{1 - \alpha\nu}\right)\left(V + \frac{\Delta\beta}{1 + \lambda_f}\right) \geq \delta g(1)V,$$

or

$$\left[1 + \delta g\left(\frac{\alpha - \alpha\nu}{1 - \alpha\nu}\right)\right]\frac{\Delta\beta}{1 + \lambda_f} \geq \delta\left[g(1) - g\left(\frac{\alpha - \alpha\nu}{1 - \alpha\nu}\right)\right]V. \tag{16.2}$$

If (16.2) is not satisfied, then the unique equilibrium involves the dishonest G_1 mixing between colluding and not colluding in such a way that

$$\left[1 + \delta g\left(\frac{\alpha(1-\nu)}{1-\nu+(1-\alpha)\nu\gamma}\right)\right]\frac{\Delta\beta}{1+\lambda_f}$$
$$= \delta\left[g\left(\frac{\alpha}{1-(1-\alpha)\gamma}\right) - g\left(\frac{\alpha(1-\nu)}{1-\nu+(1-\alpha)\nu\gamma}\right)\right]V.$$

Proposition 16.3

i. The government's probability of colluding can be bigger under the commitment constitution or under the noncommitment constitution. Noncommitment raises total rents. But commitment allows the government to grant all rents in the first period, and thus to capture a higher fraction of the rents.

ii. Consider two functions g and $\tilde{g}$. We will say that consumers are better informed under g than under $\tilde{g}$ if for all x, y such that $x \geq y$, $g(x) - g(y) \geq \tilde{g}(x) - \tilde{g}(y)$.[15] Under either constitution the probability of collusion decreases weakly when consumers are better informed. It also decreases weakly with the private value V of remaining in office.

The condition linking an increase in the posterior beliefs to the probability of reelection is interpreted in proposition 16.3 as a measure of the number of consumers who know the policy record. Alternatively, one could interpret it as a measure of how sensitive the voters' beliefs are to the policy record in this particular industry. A small sensitivity then means that voters do not pay much attention to the industry record relative to the overall record.

16.4.3 Flexibility-on-Commitment Constitution

Suppose now that G_1 is allowed by the constitution to choose between a short-term contract and a long-term contract. We still assume that the honest G_1 reports $r_1 = \underline{\beta}$ when $\beta = \underline{\beta}$.[16] Our purpose is to illustrate that even under this assumption, multiple equilibria may exist. The point is that when $\beta = \bar{\beta}$, it is not clear whether the honest type builds a better reputation by committing or not.

First, we look for an equilibrium in which the dishonest G_1 colludes ($\gamma = 1$) and furthermore report $r_1 = \varnothing$ is always accompanied by the decision not to commit. It is easy to ensure that the honest G_1 does not deviate; it suffices that the out-of-equilibrium behavior of reporting $r_1 = \varnothing$ and committing be interpreted as being chosen by a dishonest type. To ensure that the dishonest G_1 does not deviate when $\beta = \underline{\beta}$, one must make sure, first, that G_1 wants to collude and, second, that it does not benefit

15. For instance, one could assume that a fraction κ of voters look at the policy record and update their beliefs about G_1 to $\alpha_2(r_1)$. A fraction $1 - \kappa$ is uninformed and has posterior beliefs α. Consumers are better informed when κ is higher.

16. Whether the contract is then short or long is irrelevant. In both cases the firm receives $(1 + \delta)\underline{\beta}$.

from colluding and committing. This requires that

$$\frac{\Delta\beta}{1+\lambda_f} + \delta g\left(\frac{\alpha - \alpha\nu}{1-\alpha\nu}\right)\left(V + \frac{\Delta\beta}{1+\lambda_f}\right)$$

$$\geq \max\left\{\frac{\Delta\beta + \delta I}{1+\lambda_f} + \delta g(0)V; \delta g(1)V\right\}.$$

Second, we look for an equilibrium in which the dishonest G_1 colludes ($\gamma = 1$) and furthermore report $r_1 = \varnothing$ is always accompanied by the decision to commit. Again it is easy to ensure that the honest G_1 does not deviate; it suffices that the out-of-equilibrium behavior of reporting $r_1 = \varnothing$ and not committing be interpreted as being chosen by a dishonest type. To ensure that the dishonest G_1 does not deviate when $\beta = \underline{\beta}$, one must make sure, first, that G_1 wants to collude, and second, that it does not benefit from colluding and not committing. This requires that

$$\frac{\Delta\beta + \delta I}{1+\lambda_f} + \delta g\left(\frac{\alpha - \alpha\nu}{1-\alpha\nu}\right)V \geq \max\left\{\frac{\Delta\beta}{1+\lambda_f} + \delta g(0)\left(V + \frac{\Delta\beta}{1+\lambda_f}\right); \delta g(1)V\right\}.$$

It can be seen that these two inequalities are not inconsistent, so that the two perfect Bayesian equilibria may coexist. The first equilibrium, in which the honest G_1 does not commit, is of particular interest in view of casual remarks made to us by a regulated firm that the government could commit more than it does but does not want to.

16.4.4 Campaign Contributions

We have assumed that the probability of being reelected depends on the policy record but not on side transfers. There is no technical difficulty in extending the analysis to probabilities of reelection $g(\alpha_2, s)$, where s is the income received by G_1 from the industry (e.g., through political action committees). But we leave this extension for future research, for two reasons.

First, we would need to sign the derivative of g with respect to s. Empirical evidence as well as the fact that politicians eagerly accept campaign contributions suggest strongly that the probability of reelection increases with the level of campaign contributions. The theoretical argument for why this is so is less clear. A rational voter who observes that a politician has received large campaign contributions (or infers it from the large scale of his or her political advertising) might well deduct that this politician has sold out to interest groups. In this case the voter is likely to vote for candidates with low contributions, which they take to be a signal of honesty. Certainly we can think of stories in which the voter draws the opposite inference. For instance, politicians who raise money from interest groups might be the most able or energetic ones, and even if there is a risk that they sell out, it might be worth voting for them. For instance, if (as in chapter 11) the regulator may or may not learn the firm's true technology, and if the probability of learning it depends on the regulator's ability, a high campaign contribution (which in our model can only result from the discovery that $\beta = \underline{\beta}$) might still be positively correlated with the probability of being reelected. Another reason why g might increase with s is that more political advertising might allow the politician to better explain his or her policy stance to voters. We have not as yet assessed the relevance of these two explanations.

Another hurdle to the inclusion of a rational theory of campaign contributions in our model is that if we later perform the normative analysis, we must explain why such campaign contributions are legal in the first place. Again we can think of normative stories that vindicate their legality. For instance, it might be the case that unscrupulous politicians would be able to illegally raise money from interest groups anyway, while the legal prohibition would prevent more scrupulous or more risk-averse politicians from doing so. A constitution making campaign contributions illegal would then favor those politicians who find ways to cheat the system. But, in our opinion, a main reason why campaign contributions are still legal is that they favor incumbents who are precisely those politicians who have the power to enact a law prohibiting the contributions. That is, the paradigm of benevolent founders may not apply well to the issue of campaign contributions because the legislators have a vested interest in not modifying the current law.

16.5 Concluding Remarks

We argued that the benefit of letting governments commit is that the regulated sector has more incentives to invest (or not to behave inefficiently) and that the benefit of noncommitment is the flexibility in rectifying wrongful decisions by previous administrations. Our analysis yields several implications as to when administrations ought to be able to commit:

1. when the probability of honesty is either very high or very low,

2. when their informational advantage relative to the public (courts, media, etc.) is small,

3. when the regulated sector is especially worried about the expropriation of its investments.

We also noted that both a higher private value of remaining in office and better voters' information about the government's policy record reduce the probability of producer protection, but we expect them to have ambiguous implications for the choice between commitment and noncommitment. The extent to which administrations ought to be able to commit the nation is an important topic in political economy, and we hope that extensive theoretical and empirical investigations will be conducted in the near future.

BIBLIOGRAPHIC NOTES

This chapter has benefited much from the unpublished notes by An-Jen Tai (1990). Tai considers the trade-off between commitment and noncommitment in a ratchet model similar to that of chapter 9. The gain of commitment is that the firm does not worry about revealing its information. The cost of commitment is, as in this chapter, that the first-period government may not act in the interest of society.

Another (less related) paper is that of Lewis and Sappington (1990). They consider a model of short-lived regulators who maximize the level of consumer welfare during their tenure. They consider several possible constitutions. Allowing current regulators to commit may not be optimal because they may pass on some costs to second-period consumers.

In Baron (1988) a benevolent regulator can commit. However, this commitment is reversed with some probability through political action by a consumer interest group. The idea is thus that commitment can always be undone by the politicians who take precedence over courts. In Baron's model, whether commitment is undone depends on the interest group's effort. The regulator tries to reduce the interest group's incentive to take political action.

REFERENCES

Baron, D. 1988. Regulatory incentive mechanisms, commitment, and political action. Research Paper 1028, Stanford University Graduate School of Business.

Lewis, T., and D. Sappington. 1990. Sequential regulatory oversight. *Journal of Regulatory Economics* 2:327–348.

Normanton, E. 1966. *The Accountability and Audit of Governments: A Comparative Study.* Manchester: Manchester University Press.

Tai, A. J. 1990. Commitment in repeated hierarchical relationships. Mimeo, Massachusetts Institute of Technology.

17 PRIVATIZATION AND INCENTIVES

17.1 Some Background

Is public or private ownership more likely to promote social welfare? This ancient and central question in economics has generated a fair amount of conventional wisdom on the benefits and costs of public production of goods and services. However, the arguments underlying this conventional wisdom are often delicate. The first goal of this exploratory chapter is to recast some of these arguments in the framework of modern agency theory.[1] This chapter will remain almost as superficial as the conventional wisdom it criticizes and will only try to suggest that recent research in agency theory may start offering clues to a more satisfactory analysis of comparative ownership structures.

The second goal of this chapter is to analyse a specific trade-off between a public enterprise and a private regulated firm. In order not to exogenously presume the superiority of one ownership structure, we trace differences in efficiency not to intrinsic taste differences of managers and supervisors of public and private enterprises but rather to different institutional arrangements and incentives. In our model *the cost of public ownership is a suboptimal investment by the firm's managers in those assets that can be redeployed to serve social goals pursued by the public owners.* While such a reallocation of investment away from profit-enhancing uses may be ex post socially optimal, it constitutes an expropriation of the firm's investment. This expropriation is less likely to take place under private ownership because the shareholders, like the managers, derive their monetary rewards from high profits. *The cost of private ownership in our model is that the firm's managers must respond to two masters, the regulators and the shareholders.* Conflicts between the regulators and the shareholders' goals have been perceived as a source of inefficiency in regulated industries. In our model we focus on the conflict over managerial incentive schemes. The multiprincipal situation dilutes incentives and yields low-powered managerial incentive schemes and low managerial rents. (Technically the multiprincipal distortion is very similar to the classic double marginalization on two complementary goods sold by noncooperative monopolists.) This conclusion fits with very anecdotal evidence that U.S. regulators complain about low managerial incentives in public utilities.[2] While we are comfortable with the idea that each principal suffers from the other principal's providing too few incentives to the firm, we do not want to rely on this

1. See Sappington and Stiglitz (1987), Riordan (1988), Vickers and Yarrow (1988, 1991) for interesting discussions of theoretical issues related to privatization.

2. In a recent case in point, regulators in Syracuse tried to force a utility to raise managerial incentives. Smiley (1987) has emphasized the conflict of objectives between regulators and shareholders in regulated industries and has advocated the use of more powerful incentive schemes for management, and not only more performance-related rewards for stockholders.

particular conflict and simply take it as an example of inefficiency created by the divergence of objectives among principals.

Our methodology is to merge two strands of the contract literature. First, we presume contract incompleteness in that the government cannot commit to detailed incentive contracts when nationalizing or privatizing the firm (the absence of commitment may be due either to transaction costs or to political constraints). This contract incompleteness is the foundation for the cost of public ownership. The tighter congruence of managerial and ownership goals in a private firm offers a better protection of managerial investments against ex post expropriation. Contract incompleteness also underlies the cost of private ownership. Private ownership implies a more diffuse allocation of residual rights of control and generates externalities among the parties exerting these rights. To illustrate this conflict, we consider the distortions associated with the firm's superior information about its technology. The regulator trades off allocative efficiency and leaving a rent to the firm. Allowing several parties to extract the firm's informational rent transforms a second-best situation into a third-best one (except in the case of symmetric information, in which there is no such distortion under either governance structure, and private ownership therefore always dominates public ownership).

In the remainder of the introduction we develop a taxonomy of ownership structures. We recall and criticize the conventional wisdom, and we recast the debate in a framework of residual rights of control. Section 17.2 sets up a model which is analyzed in sections 17.3, 17.4, and 17.5. Concluding remarks are gathered in section 17.6.

17.1.1 Public Enterprise, Private Regulated Firm, and Unregulated Firm

Government intervention in production gives rise to a continuum of governance structures. For expositional convenience we distinguish between two scopes of control to obtain three stylized ownership patterns. The government can exercise external and internal control of the firm, or one of the two, or none.

External control is the control of all variables that link the firm with outsiders: consumers (regulation of prices, quality, product selection, etc.), competitors (regulation of entry, access pricing, etc.), taxpayers or ratepayers (cost auditing). *Internal control* is the control of the firm's inputs and cost minimization process, including influence on managerial inputs through managerial incentive schemes, intervention in the decisions concerning employment, level, location, and type of investments, and borrowing.

We define a public enterprise as a firm whose assets are in majority owned by the government who therefore performs both internal and external control. In a private regulated firm, ownership belongs to the private sector which has residual rights over the firm's management. So the government contents itself with external control and the shareholders exercise internal control. A private unregulated firm is subject to neither external nor internal control by the government.

Clearly there are other governance structures. For instance, in a franchised firm (e.g., naval dockyards in Britain) the government owns the assets and delegates operational tasks to the private sector. Futhermore each of the above governance stuctures admits several variants. There exist public enterprises (e.g., Renault in France) whose market is relatively unregulated and in which internal control may be as important as external control. In the regulated sector the division of residual rights between agencies and the shareholders fluctuates across industries and over time; for instance, the U.S. Supreme Court has moved toward allowing more agency discretion. Last, we could argue that there is no such thing as a "private unregulated firm." Most private firms are subject to antitrust laws and are affected by tariffs, subsidies, and other government decisions. A "private unregulated firm" must thus be thought of as a firm not subject to "personalized regulation" but only to general rules.

Another difficulty with such a simplistic taxonomy relates to the legal nature of ownership. After all the government can change the law and affect the distribution of control. For instance, it is common during wars for governments to intervene in the business of private firms. Since governments can change the distribution of control, the relevant governance structure does not depend only on the formal allocation of residual rights of control but also on the sociopolitical conditions that determine the government's cost of breaching contracts, altering ownership structures and interfering with private property. For instance, in a country in which the cost for the government of taking private property is small, public ownership is likely to be the only efficient or viable structure. From now on, we will ignore this issue and assume that because of strong legal institutions and a high political cost of altering ownership structures, the government is able to abide by its contracts and to respect the ownership structures once these have been determined.

17.1.2 Conventional Wisdom about Privatizations

Although we will occasionally mention private unregulated firms, the interesting comparison for many instances of privatization in capitalist economies is that between public enterprises and private regulated firms, henceforth called "regulated firms."

The conventional wisdom (CW) has noted some analogies between a private firm and a public enterprise. Both face agency problems associated with the separation of ownership and control. Both have "boards of directors" meant to represent dispersed ownership. Boards of directors are known to exert insufficient control over the firm either because they receive too little relevant information from the firm or because they collude with its managers (see Stigler 1971 for a discussion of regulatory capture which, though cast in a regulatory framework, is relevant for a public enterprise and Mace 1971 for similar complaints about the control of private firms by their board of directors). Last, in both cases takeovers (in the private sector; elections or administrative upheaval in the public sector) are known to be imperfect mechanisms for controlling the firm and its board of directors.

The conventional wisdom has identified the following costs and benefits of public ownership (a "minus" indexes a cost, a "plus" a benefit):

CW 1^- (*absence of capital market monitoring*).

The managers of a public enterprise may mismanage its assets. First, they invest too little, since they are not given the stocks and stock options that would encourage them to take a long-term perspective. Stock market prices contain information about the firm's future prospects and thus about the managers' long-term decisions. By retiring the firm's stock, a public enterprise deprives itself of a measure of managerial performance and reduces managerial incentives. Second, a public enterprise is not subject to takeovers, and its managers are therefore less concerned about losing their jobs.

The first argument in CW 1^- is not as straightforward as it seems. First, the government may, and sometimes does, retire only a fraction of the firm's stocks when nationalizing. A further argument is needed to explain why the stock price in a mixed firm (e.g., in which the government would hold 51% of the shares) would be less informative about managerial performance than that of the same private firm. Second, economists have never demonstrated that the stock market is the only instrument, or even the most efficient instrument, to obtain outside information about a firm's health.

The absence-of-financial-takeovers argument is clearer but not conclusive either. First, managers of public enterprises are fired, and political takeovers occur. Second, this argument has little relevance in countries or in periods in which, for legal or other reasons, corporate takeovers have played a minor role. Furthermore takeovers of public utilities are quite rare even in periods of active takeover activity in other industries.

CW 2^- (*soft budget constraint*).

A public enterprise is not subject to the discipline of the bankruptcy process because the government always bails it out in case of difficulty. This reduces managerial incentives.

One difficulty with CW 2^- is that public enterprises can be shut down (although one would expect that this would occur less frequently than if the firm were private.) Another difficulty is that regulators do bail out private regulated firms in difficulty, by raising allowed prices, for instance (sometimes bankruptcy is even the cause of nationalization). Thus CW 2^- does not distinguish clearly between a public enterprise and a regulated firm.

CW 3^- (*expropriation of investments*).

Managers of public enterprises refrain from investing because, once investments are sunk, the government may use these investments for purposes they were not intended to serve. Hence managerial investments may be expropriated.

The argument in CW 3^- is appealing in situations in which managerial incentive contracts are incomplete, so the government's residual rights of control over the firm would help it to ex post expropriate the managers' investments. However, as the argument stands, it fails to distinguish between public and private ownership. Why shouldn't the shareholders of a private firm expropriate managerial investments in similar situation?

CW 4^- (*lack of precise objectives*).

The multiplicity, fuzziness, and changing character of government objectives exarcerbates the problem of managerial control in public enterprises.

CW 4^- also fails to distinguish among ownership structures. Government goals that are complex and vary over time will also affect the behavior of regulated firms.

CW 5^- (*lobbying*)

Governments are subject to the pressure of interest groups to direct the behavior of public enterprises to enhance the welfare of these groups.

An obvious objection to CW 5^- is that interest groups successfully lobby governments to control regulated firms to their benefit as well.

There are two arguments concerning the benefits of public ownership:

CW 1^+ (*social welfare*)

Public ownership gives governments the means to achieve social goals that include, but are not confined to, profit maximization.

While this argument is well-taken, it does not explain why the government cannot achieve the same social goals in a regulatory framework.

CW 2^+ (*centralized control*)

By letting the government be responsible for both internal and external control, a nationalization prevents conflicts of objectives of the firm's regulators and owners.

While CW 2^+ suggests a potential inefficiency associated with the multimasters feature of private regulated firms, it remains vague about the nature of the inefficiency.

17.1.3 Residual Rights Considerations

The previous subsection has discussed some difficulties with the conventional wisdom. This subsection hardly scratches the surfaces of the ownership puzzle but tries to point at ways to look at the issues. As emphasized by Williamson (1985) and Grossman and Hart (1986), the ownership structure does not matter if complete contracts can be written. Therefore, if we are to distinguish between public enterprises and regulated firms, we must point at some contract incompleteness. Our goal is to examine where in the logic of the arguments incompleteness arises.

We argue that the ownership structure matters in two basic respects, which in turn imply further distinctions. *First, (even partial) public ownership reduces the acquisition of (noncontractible) information about the firm's managers' activity by outsiders, namely stock market participants. Second, public and private ownerships imply owners with different objectives and therefore different behaviors in case of contract incompleteness.*

Acquisition of Information about Managerial Activity

The separation of ownership and control creates a problem of managerial discipline. One of the crucial roles of a stock market is to give managers incentives beyond those provided by reward schemes based on accounting data.

First, stock market participants, including investment bankers, lured by the prospect of speculative gains, analyze the firm's health and, to the extent that their knowledge is at least partly reflected in the stock price, convey information about the level and quality of managerial investments. Stocks and stock options accordingly induce managers to invest. The information conveyed by the stock price about the value of the firm disappears when the stock is retired, as in the case of (pure) public firm. In this respect pure public firms have a hard time disciplining their managers. However, we mentioned above that the government could take control only of a majority of shares and have an active stock market for the remaining shares. The information value of 20% of the shares, say, is a priori the same as that of 100% of the shares. This might suggest that managerial incentives are unaffected when the government takes control, but does not retire the entire stock. Holmström and Tirole (1991) nevertheless argue that the ownership structure matters because market liquidity is affected. Stock market participants have low incentives to acquire information in the illiquid market created by high government stakes. The stock price is then a very garbled measure of managerial performance.

A limitation of the Holmström-Tirole analysis is that it takes for granted that a stock market is an (approximately) optimal institution to induce outsiders to acquire information about the firm's prospects. No such proposition has ever been proved. Since the information held by outsiders is often not contractible (verifiable in the language of information economics), it is likely that incentives given to outsiders must be (positively or negatively) correlated with the firm's future performance, as an incentive-compatible way for outsiders to "prove" that they have acquired relevant (favorable or unfavorable) information about the firm. This is exactly what speculation in the stock market does. However, one could think about disconnecting shareholding and property rights. For instance, absent legal constraints, a pure public enterprise could issue shares with nonvoting rights. The speculator could still supply useful information about the firm by buying and selling such shares while leaving ownership to the government. Therefore the puzzle seems to find an explanation for the cost of depriving shares of their voting rights. We have little to offer on this issue beyond some superficial remarks. The government may be tempted to expropriate shareholders with nonvoting shares (as well as minority shareholders with voting rights). Expropriation, which may take the form of sales of the firm's assets or products at artificially low prices to firms or interest groups favored by the government, may entail deadweight losses (e.g., result in suboptimal use of the assets or excessive consumption of the products). Expropriation also reduces the value of the shares and thus the incentives for speculators to search for information (think of the extreme case in which everything is expropriated); in this respect it has consequences similar to those of a reduction in market liquidity.

Second, stock market participants may intervene in management through a proxy fight or a takeover. Such interventions disappear under (pure or partial) public ownership. To be certain, there are also political takeovers. Ministry personnel changes or, more drastically, the entire administration may change. Political takeovers, however, have two drawbacks. First, they tend to be global, in that the change of ministry officers or of an entire administration is triggered by a whole set of regulatory issues and not by the regulation of a particular public enterprise; in contrast, a financial takeover focuses on a specific mismanaged firm. Second, civil servants may not always have enough incentives to invest in acquiring information about mismanagement or potential synergies, while corporate raiders have financial incentives.

Owner's Objectives

A government naturally has other objectives than profit maximization: prevent monopoly pricing; control quality; reduce negative externalities; encourage sectoral policies, national independence, investment, and employment in recessions, and so on. The problem with many government objectives is that, unlike profit maximization, they are hard to contract upon. It may be costly, for instance, to describe the state-contingent shadow price of employment in a contract with the firm. Also, since the weights among objectives can change between successive administrations, legal limitations on the power to commit must be introduced (this concern does not arise in a private firm, whose objective—value maximization—stays the same over time). This could explain why it is often felt that regulators have fuzzy and time-varying objectives (CW 4^-).

This observation per se does not shed light on the privatization issue, as it pertains to both public ownership and regulation. Where ownership makes a difference is when contingencies occur that are not covered by the contract between the government and the firm. Residual rights of control determine who can dispose of the assets in such contingencies. We should thus not expect the same response under public and private ownership.

First, a benefit from public ownership (CW 1^+) is that the government can impose socially desirable adjustments to the firm in unforeseen contingencies, while it must bargain with a private firm.[3] Second, public ownership can lead to an expropriation of managerial investments (see the model in section 17.2). Suppose that the manager invests today in nonverifiable capital that permits cost reduction and profit enhancement tomorrow. Tomorrow the government could reallocate this investment to an alternative use for which the manager is not rewarded. Even if such a reallocation is ex post socially optimal, it reduces the managers' incentive to invest and leads to a situation in which private ownership (in which managers are induced by incentive schemes and in which shareholders have no reason to ex post intervene to reduce profit) is superior, even though it may make the socially wrong use of assets ex post (CW 3^-).

The case against public enterprise might be even stronger when the government does not maximize social welfare. As is well-known, government decision making can be captured by interest groups. The increase in a nonbenevolent government's power associated with a nationalization could thus reduce welfare (CW 5^-). An example is the frequent pressure of governments on public enterprises in the military sector not to compete with private firms on civilian markets, even if the public enterprises have idle capacity and the machinery and expertise to produce the civilian goods.

Last, the divergence of objectives between government and shareholders may explain why the U.S. public utilities' shareholders have the right of control over their managers' incentive schemes. A possible explanation is that it is difficult for the government and the shareholders to agree contractually on the details of managerial incentive schemes and that a government that has residual rights of control over managerial incentive schemes might not induce managers to properly maintain the shareholders' assets and to make the profit-maximizing investment decisions (this is

3. In particular, if bargaining takes place under asymmetric information, inefficiencies will typically result, as pointed out in Milgrom and Roberts (1990) and Holmström and Tirole (1989).

yet another variant on the theme that expropriation might occur if private shareholders leave residual rights of control to the government). We have little more to offer than this conjecture, and much more work will be required to explain the fact.

17.2 The Model

A government wants to realize an indivisible project with social value S. A single firm can realize this project at cost

$$C = \beta - e, \tag{17.1}$$

where $\beta \in (\underline{\beta}, \overline{\beta})$ parameterizes the firm's efficiency, and e is managerial effort. β is known to the firm's manager only. Other parties have prior cumulative distribution $F(\cdot)$ over β with a strictly positive density f. We make the usual monotone-hazard-rate assumption $d(F(\beta)/f(\beta))/d\beta > 0$ to avoid bunching in optimal incentive schemes. Managerial effort creates a disutility $\psi(e)$ in monetary units with $\psi' > 0$, $\psi'' > 0$, $\psi''' \geq 0$.

Moreover the manager can commit some nonmonetary and noncontractible investment $\tilde{I} \in \{0, I\}$. I is a nonmonetary cost for the manager and is to be added to $\psi(e)$. Not investing ($\tilde{I} = 0$) yields no benefit. If the investment is made ($\tilde{I} = I$), it has one of two alternative uses. Its internal use yields private (nonmonetary) benefit $D > I$ to the firm's insiders (formalized by the manager) and 0 to outsiders. Its external use yields private benefit $D' > D$ to outsiders and 0 to insiders. Investment and accrual of benefit take place during the single period of the model. The benefit, like the investment, is not contractible (not verifiable) and therefore cannot be sold. Let $\Delta = D - I$. Two ownership structures will be considered: public ownership and the regulated private firm.

17.2.1 Public Ownership

The government owns the firm and gives to the firm's manager an incentive scheme based on the realization of cost $t(C)$. Making the accounting convention that costs are paid by the government the manager's utility level is

$$U = t - \psi(e).$$

Since the investment and its benefit are not contractible, the government cannot commit not to expropriate the manager's investment in order to maximize ex post public use of the investment.[4] Anticipating this behav-

4. Here the investment yields higher benefits if controlled by the government than if controlled by shareholders, because it is expropriated by the government under public ownership. One could think of cases in which the incentives to invest are higher under government

ior, the manager does not invest. Let us give simple examples of such behavior. The management of a government-owned firm will be reluctant to invest in facilities (e.g., cafeteria, theater, or holiday resort) or machines if it knows that access to those will be later granted to the general population by the government. More important, the government could reduce the return on a new plant by forcing it to keep excess labor in bad states of demand or to buy domestically produced inputs. Still another investment that might be expropriated (through tasks and duties reassignments) is the manager's human capital. In all these examples the government's action may be ex post optimal but represents an expropriation of the firm's investment.

Accordingly, the objective function of a utilitarian government is

$$W = S - (1 + \lambda)(t + C) + U, \tag{17.2}$$

where $(t + C)$ is total regulatory cost.

17.2.2 The Regulated Private Firm

Suppose now that the government privatizes and regulates the firm.[5] We assume the following timing: First, the government sells the firm at price p to the public. Second, the government regulates the firm for the relevant project, and the shareholders offer an incentive scheme to the manager. The tax rate $\tau < 1$ on profits[6] can be determined in either stage; for concreteness we assume it is chosen in the first stage. The assumption that the government does not commit to a regulatory scheme when privatizing reflects the idea that privatizations are long-term decisions whose effects cover several periods. If the government could commit to a regulatory scheme at the privatization stage, it could sell the social surplus associated with the owners' decisions to them and multiprincipal conflicts would not arise. Privatization would always be optimal.

In a regulated firm private shareholders select managerial incentive schemes. Shareholders are taxed at rate τ. Let w denote the manager's reward (including perks) provided by the stockholders. The firm realizes the project and receives its income from the government.

We assume that the government observes only cost C but not w. This assumption makes particular sense in a multiproduct firm in which the government observes only the cost of the product line it is interested in and is unable to measure various components (including perks) of mana-

ownership than under private ownership. This would occur, for instance, if socially conscious managers were to make investments that would be redirected by the shareholders away from their original purpose to enhance profits. The case we consider seems, however, more realistic in many situations.

5. One could consider the converse experiment in which the firm is initially private and is nationalized by the government. The analysis is unchanged.

6. See our (1991) paper for a discussion of when $\tau < 1$ is a natural assumption once incentives of the capital market are accounted for.

gerial compensation that enter the firm's global accounting. The assumption also fits with the legal reality that governments are not permitted to interfere with managerial incentive schemes in private firms. The government makes a transfer to the firm $z(C)$, and its objective function is again the sum of surpluses in society:

$$W = S - (1 + \lambda)[z + C - \tau(z - w)] + U + (1 - \tau)(z - w) + \lambda p, \qquad (17.3)$$

where $U = w - \psi(e) + \Delta$.[7] Note that now the shareholders have no incentive to reallocate the benefits of the investment to outsiders, and knowing this, the manager invests and reaps net private benefits Δ.[8]

We assume that the government and the shareholders make simultaneous contract offers. The government offers $z(C)$ to the firm, and the shareholders offer $w(C)$ to the managers. The manager produces only if he or she accepts both offers. Clearly the advantage of private ownership is to make credible the commitment of nonexpropriation of managerial investments. The cost will come from the multiprincipal structure of regulation and the inability of the government to fully tax stockholders' profits.

Before studying optimal regulation under the different ownership structures, let us determine the optimal allocation of resources under complete information: The investment should be made and allocated ex post to outsiders. The marginal disutility of effort should equate with its marginal utility, $\psi'(e^*) = 1$, and the transfer to the manager should saturate his or her individual rationality (IR) constraint. If S is large enough, the project should always be realized.

17.3 Optimal Regulation with Public Ownership

Under public ownership the manager does not invest. The manager's utility level is

$$U = t - \psi(e) = t - \psi(\beta - C). \qquad (17.4)$$

7. Note that in equilibrium $p = E_\beta(1 - \tau)(z - w)$. However, it is important to treat it as a sunk revenue for the government. That is, by changing its regulatory process today, the government does not affect the price that the public paid for the shares.

8. Under our assumption, the stockholders are actually indifferent between ordering the manager to reallocate or not. It seems reasonable to assume that they favor their manager, which they would strictly prefer if the internal use of the investment had any direct or indirect monetary value to the firm. Note also that it is assumed that the firm and the government do not contract for the (more efficient) use of the investment by outsiders. The analysis would carry through if they did contract (the benefit of investment to the firm would lie between $D - I$ and $D' - I$ depending on the relative bargaining powers).

By assuming Δ to be exogenous and not monetary, we completely separate the costs and the benefits of privatization. As this section clearly shows, the same model would obtain if we made the assumption that the government cannot commit not to expropriate the manager's investment, whereas stockholders can. Therefore a political theory of differences in commitment abilities could be substituted for the incomplete contract theory that we rely upon here.

Incentive compatibility (IC) requires that

$$\dot{U}(\beta) = -\psi'(e(\beta)) \qquad \text{for all } \beta \in (\underline{\beta}, \beta_P^*), \tag{17.5}$$

where β_P^* is the largest value of β for which the project is undertaken, and

$$\dot{C}(\beta) \geq 0 \qquad \text{for all } \beta \in [\underline{\beta}, \beta_P^*]. \tag{17.6}$$

Using (17.5), the IR constraint $[U(\beta) \geq 0$ for any $\beta \in [\underline{\beta}, \beta_P^*]]$ can be rewritten

$$U(\beta_P^*) \geq 0. \tag{17.7}$$

A utilitarian government maximizes, under the IC and IR constraints (17.5), (17.6), and (17.7), expected social welfare:

$$\int_{\underline{\beta}}^{\beta_P^*} \{S - (1 + \lambda)[\beta - e(\beta) + \psi(e(\beta))] - \lambda U(\beta)\}\, dF(\beta). \tag{17.8}$$

Proposition 17.1 (See chapter 1.) The optimal regulatory outcome under public ownership is given by

$$\psi'(e_P(\beta)) = 1 - \frac{\lambda}{1 + \lambda} \frac{F(\beta)}{f(\beta)} \psi''(e_P(\beta)), \tag{17.9}$$

$$U(\beta) = \int_{\beta}^{\beta_P^*} \psi'(e_P(\tilde{\beta}))d\tilde{\beta}; \tag{17.10}$$

either

$$S - (1 + \lambda)[(\beta_P^* - e_P(\beta_P^*)) + \psi(e_P(\beta_P^*))] - \lambda \frac{F(\beta_P^*)}{f(\beta_P^*)} \psi'(e_P(\beta_P^*)) = 0 \tag{17.11}$$

or

$$\beta_P^* = \bar{\beta}.$$

Equation (17.10) defines the rent of asymmetric information captured by a firm with efficiency β. Equation (17.9) describes the optimal distortion from efficiency to mitigate the rent of asymmetric information. Equation (17.11) defines the cutoff point β_P^*. From chapter 1, we know that the optimal mechanism can be implemented by a menu of linear contracts defined by

$$t(C, C^a) = a(C^a) - b(C^a)(C - C^a),$$

where C^a is the announced cost and C the realized cost. The coefficient $b(C^a)$ defines the sharing of overruns and is equal to $\psi'(e_P(\beta))$. For $\beta = \underline{\beta}$, $F(\underline{\beta}) = 0$ and $\psi'(e_P(\underline{\beta})) = 1$; type $\underline{\beta}$ selects a fixed price contract and has the right incentive to minimize cost. Less efficient types have part of their cost, $1 - \psi'(e_P(\beta))$, reimbursed by the regulator and consequently exert a socially suboptimal effort. This distortion in allocative efficiency enables the regulator to decrease the costly rent of asymmetric information.

17.4 Optimal Regulation of a Private Firm

17.4.1 Differentiable Equilibrium

We assume that the government and the shareholders of the private firm simultaneously offer incentive schemes $z(C)$ and $r(C)$ to the manager. The scheme $z(\cdot)$ is a monetary reward to the manager offered by the government and $r(\cdot)$ is a rental contract required by shareholders. Alternatively, one could think of $z(\cdot)$ as being offered to the shareholders who offer $w(\cdot) = z(\cdot) - r(\cdot)$ to the manager. We look for a differentiable Nash equilibrium in these contracts.

Taking $z(\cdot)$ as given, the shareholders maximize their expected profit subject to the manager's incentive compatibility and individual rationality constraints. We allow the shareholders to offer incentive schemes such that some high β types do not want to produce. Let β_R^* denote the "cutoff type," that is, the type who is indifferent between producing and not producing.

The manager receives $w(C)$, as well as the benefit of his or her investment Δ, and incurs a disutility $\psi(e)$. The manager's utility level is

$$U(\beta) = w(C(\beta)) + \Delta - \psi(e(\beta)). \tag{17.12}$$

From the point of view of the manager, $w(\cdot)$ plays the same role as $t(\cdot)$ in section 17.3, and therefore incentive compatibility and individual rationality constraints are as in section 17.3. Accordingly, using $w(C(\beta)) = U(\beta) - \Delta + \psi(e(\beta))$, the shareholders' optimization program is

$$\max_{\{e(\cdot),\beta_R^*\}} (1-\tau)\int_{\underline{\beta}}^{\beta_R^*} [z(\beta - e(\beta)) - U(\beta) + \Delta - \psi(e(\beta))]dF(\beta) \tag{17.13}$$

subject to

$$\dot{U}(\beta) = -\psi'(e(\beta)), \tag{17.14}$$

$$U(\beta_R^*) = 0. \tag{17.15}$$

The first-order conditions of this program are (see appendix A17.1)

$$\psi'(e_R(\beta)) = -z'(\beta - e_R(\beta)) - \frac{F(\beta)}{f(\beta)}\psi''(e_R(\beta)); \tag{17.16}$$

$$\text{either} \quad [z(\beta_R^* - e_R(\beta_R^*)) + \Delta - \psi(e_R(\beta_R^*))]f(\beta_R^*) - F(\beta_R^*)\psi'(e(\beta_R^*)) = 0$$

$$\text{or} \quad \beta_R^* = \bar{\beta}. \tag{17.17}$$

Note that (17.16) differs from the formula (17.9) obtained in the case of public ownership in two ways. First, a unit reduction in cost is valued $(-z')$ by shareholders (which is what the firm receives from the government) instead of 1. Second, the ratio of the cost of transfers to the cost of real expenditures is equal to 1 for the profit-maximizing shareholders instead of $\lambda/(1+\lambda)$ for the welfare-maximizing government.

The government chooses $z(\cdot)$ in order to maximize expected social welfare subject to the manager's incentive compatibility and individual rationality constraints, taking $r(\cdot)$ as given. Ex post social welfare is

$$\begin{aligned} S &- (1+\lambda)[\beta - e(\beta) + z(\beta - e(\beta)) - \tau r(\beta - e(\beta))] + U(\beta) \\ &+ (1-\tau) r(\beta - e(\beta)) + \lambda p \\ &= S - (1+\lambda)[\beta - e(\beta) + \psi(e(\beta)) - \Delta] - \lambda U(\beta) \\ &- \lambda(1-\tau) r(\beta - e(\beta)) + \lambda p \end{aligned} \tag{17.18}$$

when the project is implemented and λp when the project is not implemented. Hence we have the following government's optimization program:

$$\begin{aligned} \max_{\{e(\cdot),\beta_R^{**}\}} \int_{\underline{\beta}}^{\beta_R^{**}} & \{S - (1+\lambda)[\beta - e(\beta) + \psi(e(\beta)) - \Delta] - \lambda U(\beta) \\ & - \lambda(1-\tau) r(\beta - e(\beta))\} dF(\beta) + \lambda p \end{aligned} \tag{17.19}$$

subject to

$$\dot{U}(\beta) = -\psi'(e(\beta)), \tag{17.20}$$

$$U(\beta_R^{**}) = 0. \tag{17.21}$$

The first-order conditions of this program are (see appendix A17.1)

$$\psi'(e_R(\beta)) = 1 + \frac{\lambda}{1+\lambda}(1-\tau) r'(\beta - e_R(\beta)) - \frac{\lambda}{1+\lambda}\frac{F(\beta)}{f(\beta)}\psi''(e_R(\beta)); \tag{17.22}$$

$$\begin{aligned} \text{either}\quad & \{S - (1+\lambda)(\beta_R^{**} - e_R(\beta_R^{**}) - \Delta + \psi(e_R(\beta_R^{**}))) \\ & - \lambda(1-\tau) r(\beta_R^{**} - e_R(\beta_R^{**}))\} f(\beta_R^{**}) \\ & - \lambda F(\beta_R^{**}) \psi'(e_R(\beta_R^{**})) = 0 \\ \text{or}\quad & \beta_R^{**} = \bar{\beta}. \end{aligned} \tag{17.23}$$

From the manager's first-order incentive compatibility condition [written in transfers instead of utilities as in (17.20)], we have

$$-z'(\beta - e(\beta)) + r'(\beta - e(\beta)) = \psi'(e(\beta)). \tag{17.24}$$

Multiplying (17.16) by $[\lambda/(1+\lambda)]$ $(1-\tau)$, adding to (17.22), and using (17.24) yields

$$\psi'(e_R(\beta)) = 1 - \frac{\lambda}{1+\lambda}(2-\tau)\frac{F(\beta)}{f(\beta)}\psi''(e_R(\beta)). \tag{17.25}$$

In equilibrium $\beta_R^* = \beta_R^{**}$. Furthermore from (17.24) and (17.15) we have

$$r(\beta - e_R(\beta)) - z(\beta - e_R(\beta)) = -\int_\beta^{\beta_R^*} \psi'(e_R(\tilde\beta))(1 - \dot e_R(\tilde\beta))d\tilde\beta + \Delta - \psi(e_R(\beta_R^*)). \tag{17.26}$$

An interesting observation is that the shareholders make a positive profit at the cutoff type β_R^*. (The manager has no rent at the cutoff type, just as in the case of a public enterprise.) The reason is obvious: The shareholders would lose nothing from shutting off a type who brings them no profit and would reduce the rent of better types by doing so.[9]

From (17.22), we obtain

$$r(\beta - e_R(\beta)) = \frac{(1+\lambda)}{\lambda(1-\tau)}\int_\beta^{\beta_R^*}\left[1 - \psi'(e_R(\tilde\beta)) - \frac{\lambda}{1+\lambda}\frac{F(\tilde\beta)}{f(\tilde\beta)}\psi''(e_R(\tilde\beta))\right] \times (1 - \dot e_R(\tilde\beta))d\tilde\beta + r(\beta_R^* - e_R(\beta_R^*)). \tag{17.27}$$

From (17.16) and (17.23), we obtain the constants $r(\beta_R^* - e_R(\beta_R^*))$ and $z(\beta_R^* - e_R(\beta_R^*))$, and using (17.15), we determine β_R^*. From (17.16), we obtain

$$z(\beta - e_R(\beta)) = \int_\beta^{\beta_R^*}\left[\psi'(e_R(\tilde\beta)) + \frac{F(\tilde\beta)}{f(\tilde\beta)}\psi''(e_R(\tilde\beta))\right](1 - \dot e_R(\tilde\beta))d\tilde\beta + z(\beta_R^* - e_R(\beta_R^*)). \tag{17.28}$$

Next we must ask whether the first-order conditions for the manager and the two principals are sufficient. The second-order condition for the manager is $\dot C = 1 - \dot e \geq 0$. But (17.25) implies that effort is decreasing with type under our assumptions:

$$\dot e = \frac{[-\lambda/(1+\lambda)](2-\tau)\psi''[d(F/f)/d\beta]}{\psi'' + [\lambda/(1+\lambda)](2-\tau)(F/f)\psi'''} < 0.$$

Hence the manager's global second-order condition is satisfied.

Before turning to the principals' second-order conditions, we derive results of independent interest concerning the curvature of reward functions. Differentiating (17.16), and substituting (17.24) and (17.25), yields

$$r'' = \frac{\psi''}{[\lambda/(1+\lambda)](2-\tau)}\frac{\dot e}{1-\dot e} < 0. \tag{17.29}$$

9. This is the same argument as that showing that a monopolist charges a price above marginal cost.

Differentiating (17.24), using (17.29), gives

$$z'' = \left[1 - \frac{\lambda}{1+\lambda}(2-\tau)\right] r'', \tag{17.30}$$

from which it follows that

$$w'' = z'' - r'' = -\frac{\lambda}{1+\lambda}(2-\tau) r'' > 0. \tag{17.31}$$

The manager's net reward $w(\cdot)$ is convex in cost as in chapter 1. In the single-principal (i.e., public ownership) case, the transfer from the government $t(\cdot)$ is convex in cost, and therefore the regulator can replace his or her reward scheme by a menu of linear contracts. In contrast, $z(\cdot)$ is concave in cost if $\lambda < 1/(1-\tau)$, and the regulator cannot use a menu of linear contracts. The shareholders' reward function $-r(\cdot)$ is convex in cost. However, this does not imply that they can replace their reward scheme $-r(\cdot)$ by a menu of linear contracts. The regulator might want to change his or her own scheme to take advantage of the shareholders' linear sharing of costs by inducing large costs.

We can turn to the principals' second-order conditions. First, if $\lambda < 1/(1-\tau)$, the hamiltonian in program (17.13) is concave in effort. Second, it can be shown that there exists $\lambda_0 > 0$ such that, when $\lambda \leq \lambda_0$, the hamiltonian in program (17.19) is concave in effort. The second-order conditions are then satisfied. Last, using $p \equiv E_\beta[(1-\tau)r(\beta - e(\beta))]$, ex ante social welfare is

$$E_\beta[S - (1+\lambda)(\beta - e + \psi(e) - \Delta) - \lambda U].$$

We now summarize our main conclusions in proposition 17.2.

Proposition 17.2 The necessary conditions for a differentiable regulatory outcome under private ownership is given by equations (17.23), (17.25), (17.27), and (17.28). These conditions are sufficient if $\lambda \leq \min\{\lambda_0, 1/(1-\tau)\}$. The managers' net reward function is convex in cost. The government's net transfer to the firm is concave in cost.

17.4.2 Nondifferentiable Equilibria

We have focused on the equilibrium in which z and r are differentiable functions of C. There also exist nondifferentiable equilibria. (For notational simplicity we will assume that $\Delta = 0$ in the following argument.) Consider the following schemes:

$$z(C) = \begin{cases} \bar{z} & \text{if } C = \bar{C}, \\ -\infty & \text{otherwise,} \end{cases}$$
$$r(C) = \begin{cases} \bar{r} & \text{if } C = \bar{C}, \\ +\infty & \text{otherwise.} \end{cases} \tag{17.32}$$

The manager accepts those schemes iff $\bar{z} - \bar{r} \geq \psi(\beta - \bar{C})$. Can a principal do better than this simple cost target scheme? For this not to be the case, $\bar{r}$ and $\bar{z}$ must satisfy

$$\bar{r} = \arg\max_{r} \{F(\bar{C} + \psi^{-1}(\bar{z} - r))r\} \tag{17.33}$$

and

$$\bar{z} = \arg\max_{z} \left\{ \int_{\underline{\beta}}^{\bar{C} + \psi^{-1}(z - \bar{r})} [S - (1 + \lambda)(\bar{C} + \psi(\beta - \bar{C})) - \lambda[z - \bar{r} - \psi(\beta - \bar{C})] - \lambda(1 - \tau)\bar{r}] f(\beta) d\beta \right\}. \tag{17.34}$$

From (17.34), since transfers to the firm are socially costly [the cost for society of these transfers is $\lambda(z - \tau r)$ with $\tau < 1$ and $z \geq r$ from the manager's individual rationality], z is bounded above, say, by z^*. Therefore r is also bounded above by z^*.

The existence of the pooling equilibrium is guaranteed if $F(\cdot)$ is concave and $f(\cdot)$ bounded below by a positive number. The function defined in (17.33) is strictly concave in r and maps $\bar{z}$ from $[\psi(\underline{\beta} - \bar{C}), z^*]$ into $[0, z^*]$. The function defined in (17.34) is strictly concave in z and maps r from $[0, z^*]$ into $[\psi(\underline{\beta} - \bar{C}), z^*]$. We can apply Brouwer's theorem in the compact space $[0, z^*] \times [\psi(\underline{\beta} - \bar{C}), z^*]$ to obtain the existence of a solution.

17.5 Comparison of Ownership Structures

The main result is that in a differentiable equilibrium, effort is lower in the regulated private firm than in the public firm, as one can check by differentiating (17.25) with respect to e and τ.

Proposition 17.3 $e_R(\beta) < e_P(\beta)$ for any $\beta \in [\underline{\beta}, \min(\beta_R^*, \beta_P^*)]$.

The intuition for the result is straightforward. As program (17.19) shows, the existence of shareholders and the fact that the tax rate is less than 100% create an additional ex post rent. It is therefore more costly to elicit the same effort level as in the public firm and the regulator settles for a lower level of effort.

For S large enough, $\beta_P^* = \beta_R^* = \bar{\beta}$. Furthermore $w(\bar{\beta} - e_R(\bar{\beta})) = \psi(e_R(\bar{\beta})) - \Delta$ from (17.12), but the decomposition of $w(\bar{\beta} - e_R(\bar{\beta}))$ between $z(\bar{\beta} - e_R(\bar{\beta}))$ and (minus) $r(\bar{\beta} - e_R(\bar{\beta}))$ is arbitrary at the Nash equilibrium as long as the left-hand sides in (17.17) and (17.23) are nonnegative. For lower levels of S, β_R^* differs from $\bar{\beta}$ and is (uniquely) defined by

$$S - (1 + \lambda)(\beta_R^* - e_R(\beta_R^*) + \psi(e_R(\beta_R^*))) + (1 + \lambda)\Delta$$
$$= \lambda\left[(2 - \tau)\frac{F(\beta_R^*)}{f(\beta_R^*)}\psi'(e_R(\beta_R^*))\right]. \tag{17.35}$$

In this case $z(\beta_R^* - e_R(\beta_R^*))$ and $r(\beta_R^* - e_R(\beta_R^*))$ are uniquely defined by (17.17) and (17.23). That the principals' transfers are either determinate or defined up to a constant should not surprise the reader familiar with the theory of public goods. In the case of a corner solution ($\beta_R^* = \bar{\beta}$), both principals are responsible for making sure that type $\bar{\beta}$ produces. Reducing the transfer to the agent by one principal, and increasing the one by the other principal by an equal amount, preserves equilibrium as long as the second principal strictly prefers type $\bar{\beta}$ to produce. There is therefore a range of possible transfers to type $\bar{\beta}$ (and therefore to more efficient types) for each principal. The transfer received by the agent, however, is determinate. In the case of an interior solution ($\beta_R^* < \bar{\beta}$), an increase in the transfer that a principal must pay for β_R^* to produce would lead him or her to reduce the cutoff point β_R^* and would induce the other principal to raise the cutoff point, thereby destroying equilibrium.

17.6 Concluding Remarks

Let us first summarize the main insights of the formal analysis:

1. Private regulated firms suffer from the conflict of interest between shareholders and regulators. For instance, each principal fails to internalize the effect of contracting on the other principal and provides socially too few incentives for the firm's insiders.

2. The managers of a private regulated firm invest more in noncontractible investments because they are more likely to benefit from such investments. Public enterprise managers are concerned that they will be forced to redeploy their investments to serve social goals such as containing unemployment, limiting exports, or promoting regional development.

Taken together, these two insights have ambiguous implications for the relative cost efficiency of the public and private sectors; theory alone is thus unlikely to be conclusive in this respect.[10]

This chapter has analyzed at length one aspect of the trade-off between the two ownership structures. There of course are a number of other issues that are crucial for a good grasp of the ownership puzzle. Some of these were discussed at the beginning of the chapter. Among them were market

10. The empirical literature on the relative efficiency of the two ownership structures is itself currently inconclusive. See, for example, Atkinson and Halvorsen (1986), Boardman and Vining (1989), and Teeples and Glyer (1987).

monitoring and takeovers. We chose to assume that regulators are benevolent in order to provide a classical analysis of the expropriation and conflict-among-principals effects. Clearly new issues arise when regulators can be captured by interest groups. The government is likely to be constrained in its use of instruments. For instance, public enterprise employees might be subject to general civil service regulations that limit their wages and incentive schemes.[11] We still need to learn when such restrictions are likely to dominate the effects unveiled in this chapter.

The formalization of the government as a single principal is another oversimplification. In practice the executive, legislative, and judiciary, as well as the interest groups that lean on them, act (or do not act) on behalf of the electorate. A more general approach would confront the division of tasks within the government. The existence of multiple controlling ministries or agencies (e.g., ministry of industry and ministry of finance), and the degree of independence of ministries and agencies from the legislative and judiciary, warrant further investigations. A richer approach than ours would call for a comparative analysis of alternative forms of public entreprises.[12]

BIBLIOGRAPHIC NOTES

This chapter is related to several independent contributions on common agency and on privatization.

B17.1 The Theory of Common Agency

Martimort (1991) and Stole (1990) have developed a much more general theory of common agency than ours. In their model an agent contracts separately with two principals. A contract between principal i ($i = 1, 2$) and the agent specifies a transfer t_i to the agent and level of "trade" x_i. The agent's utility function depends on the total transfer ($t_1 + t_2$), the trades, and the agent's type β, $U(t_1 + t_2, x_1, x_2, \beta)$.

11. It is interesting to note that the common complaint in some countries that it is difficult to pay competitive wages to attract competent civil servants and to give them appropriate incentives has a counterpart, for instance, in the regulated electricity sector in the United States.

12. There are roughly three forms of public enterprise. At one extreme of the spectrum are departmental administrations (e.g., the U.S. post office) whose budgets come from the ministry or from parliamentary appropriations. At the other extreme are private, joint stock companies whose sole or majority shareholder turns out to be the government (Air France, Rolls Royce, and British Leyland before their privatizations). In the middle lie strictly public entreprises that have a separate legal personality (they can be sued, they sign contracts, etc.) and that can borrow either from the ministry of finance or from the private sector under Treasury backing. One rationale for the division of labor between a spending ministry and the ministry of finance is examined in preliminary work by Dewatripont and Tirole (reported in section 7 of Tirole 1992).

Martimort and Stole allow for both contract complements ($\partial^2 U/\partial x_1 \partial x_2 > 0$) and contract substitutes ($\partial^2 U/\partial x_1 \partial x_2 < 0$). Our model can be viewed as studying the special case of perfect complements (here $x_1 = x_2 = C$). We refer to their papers for general analyses.

An early piece on common agency under adverse selection is Baron's (1985) analysis of the joint regulation of electric utilities by a public utility commission and the Environmental Protection Agency. The theory of common agency under moral hazard was developed by Bernheim and Whinston (1986). Spiller (1990) is an application to regulation.

B17.2 Formal Analyses of Privatization

Two other papers by Shapiro and Willig (1990) and by Schmidt (1990) have analyzed the choice between public ownership and the regulation of a private firm.[13] The two papers also emphasize that ownership matters under incomplete contracting. In both papers the cost and benefit of public ownership differ from those studied here. The starting point is that public ownership, by giving the government residual rights over the accounting structure, allows the government to have a more precise information about the firm's cost than it would have in a regulatory context.[14] The benefit of public ownership is thus that the government is better able to extract the firm's informational rent. The cost of public ownership differs between the two papers. Shapiro and Willig allow the government to sometimes be malevolent; one would prefer malevolent governments to be hampered by informational limitations and thus prefer regulation to a public entreprise. Schmidt presumes a benevolent regulator who cannot commit intertemporally. The lack of information associated with private ownership in a sense commits the regulator not to expropriate too much the firm's investment. To illustrate this idea, consider the following simple model, which builds on section 1.9:

1. The government chooses whether to privatize.
2. The firm sinks some noncontractible investment $I \geq 0$.
3. The firm's efficiency parameter β is drawn from the cumulative distribution $F(\beta | I)$. β is observed by the firm and the regulator under public ownership, and by the firm only under private ownership.
4. The regulator offers a contract $t(C)$ to the firm.

13. De Fraja (1991) compares the slacks in a public enterprise and a private unregulated firm.
14. Riordan (1987) and Sappington (1987) have developed models in which the regulator wants to commit to procedures that rely on imperfect monitoring. The idea is that imperfect knowledge about the firm's technology constitutes, in a noncommitment situation, a credible commitment not to extract the firm's rent; this in turn induces more investment by the firm. Another interesting paper in this context is Riordan's (1990) model of vertical integration.

5. The firm produces at cost $C = \beta - e$ (if it accepts the regulator's contract).

Assume for the moment that in case of privatization the manager of the firm owns the shares, that is, is also the owner. Under public ownership, the regulator perfectly extracts the firm's rent [$U(\beta) = 0$ for all β]. The firm, knowing this, does not invest at stage 2 ($I = 0$). Public ownership yields the first best when investment is irrelevant (F is independent of I); however, as in this chapter but for a slightly different reason, public ownership leads to investment expropriation.

Under private ownership, the regulator offers the incomplete information contract derived in section 1.4. The firm's rent $U(\beta)$ increases with efficiency, and the firm has thus an incentive to invest. If rent extraction is irrelevant ($\lambda \simeq 0$) and if investment matters, private ownership dominates public ownership.

If under privatization the manager of the firm does not hold the shares, the previous reasoning breaks down: The manager is expropriated by the private owners under privatization as he or she is under nationalization. Schmidt introduces a nonappropriable private benefit for the manager that increases with the level of output; formally this is equivalent to a private benefit that decreases with cost in our setup. In Schmidt's model public ownership reduces (actually eliminates) the ex post output distortion due to asymmetric information, but it reduces the sensitivity of output to the efficiency parameter and, through the private benefit, reduces the manager's incentive to invest. Thus, in Schmidt as in this chapter, a nationalization decreases managerial investment but reduces allocative inefficiency.

Last, it should be pointed out that we ignored the political economy aspects of privatization. See Vickers (1991).

APPENDIXES

A17.1 Proof of (17.17)

The hamiltonian of program (17.13) is, up to a constant,

$$H = (1 - \tau)[z(\beta - e(\beta)) - U(\beta) + \Delta - \psi(e(\beta))]f(\beta) - \mu(\beta)\psi'(e(\beta)).$$

From the Pontryagin principle we have

$$\dot{\mu}(\beta) = (1 - \tau)f(\beta).$$

Using the transversality condition $\mu(\underline{\beta}) = 0$, we get $\mu(\beta) = (1 - \tau)F(\beta)$. Maximization of the hamiltonian with respect to $e(\cdot)$ gives

$$(1-\tau)[-z'(\beta-e(\beta))-\psi'(e(\beta))]f(\beta)-(1-\tau)F(\beta)\psi''(e(\beta))=0,$$

which is equation (17.15). ■

A17.2 Proof of (17.22)

The hamiltonian of program (17.19) is, up to a constant,

$$H=\{S-(1+\lambda)(\beta-e(\beta))+\psi(e(\beta))-\Delta-\lambda U(\beta)$$
$$-\lambda(1-\tau)r(\beta-e(\beta))\}f(\beta)-\mu(\beta)\psi'(e(\beta)).$$

The first-order conditions are

$$\dot{\mu}(\beta)=-\frac{\partial H}{\partial U}=\lambda f(\beta),$$

$$\mu(\underline{\beta})=0 \quad \Rightarrow \quad \mu(\beta)=\lambda F(\beta),$$

$$\frac{\partial H}{\partial e}=0 \quad \Leftrightarrow \quad \{-(1+\lambda)(\psi'(e(\beta))-1)+\lambda(1-\tau)r'(\beta-e(\beta))\}f(\beta)$$
$$-\lambda F(\beta)\psi'(e(\beta))=0,$$

or

$$\psi'(e(\beta))=1+\frac{\lambda}{1+\lambda}(1-\tau)r'(\beta-e(\beta))-\frac{\lambda}{1+\lambda}\frac{F(\beta)}{f(\beta)}\psi''(e(\beta)).$$ ■

REFERENCES

Atkinson, S., and R. Halvorsen. 1986. The relative efficiency of public and private firms in a regulated environment: The case of U.S. electric utilities. *Journal of Public Economics* 29:281–294.

Baron, D. 1985. Noncooperative regulation of a nonlocalized externality. *Rand Journal of Economics* 16:553–568.

Bernheim, D., and M. Whinston. 1986. Common agency. *Econometrica* 54:923–942.

Boardman, A., and A. Vining. 1989. Ownership and performance in competitive environments: A comparison of the performance of private, mixed, and state-owned enterprises. *Journal of Law and Economics* 32:1–33.

Defraja, G. 1991. Incentive contracts for public firms. Mimeo, University of Bristol.

Grossman, S., and O. Hart. 1986. The costs and benefits of ownership: A theory of lateral and vertical integration. *Journal of Political Economy* 94:691–719.

Holmström, B., and J. Tirole. 1989. The theory of the firm. In *Handbook of Industrial Organization*, vol. 1, ed. R. Schmalensee and R. Willig. Amsterdam: North-Holland, ch. 2.

Holmström, B., and J. Tirole. 1991. Market liquidity and performance monitoring. Mimeo, Yale University and Massachusetts Institute of Technology. Forthcoming, *Journal of Political Economy*.

Laffont, J.-J., and J. Tirole. 1991. Privatization and incentives. *Journal of Law, Economics and Organization* 7:84–105.

Martimort, D. 1991. Multi-principaux avec sélection adverse. Mimeo, Institut d'Économie Industrielle, Toulouse.

Milgrom, P., and J. Roberts. 1990. Bargaining and influence costs and the organization of economic activity. In *Perspectives on Positive Political Economy*, ed. J. Alt and K. Shepsle. Cambridge: Cambridge University Press, ch. 3.

Riordan, M. 1987. Hierarchical control and investment incentives in procurement. Hoover Institution, Working Paper E-87-44, Stanford University.

Riordan, M. 1990. What is vertical integration? In *The Firm as a Nexus of Treaties*, ed. M. Aoki et al. Sage publications.

Sappington, D. 1987. Commitment to regulatory bureaucracy. *Information, Economics and Policy.*

Sappington, D., and J. Stiglitz. 1987. Privatization, information and incentives. *Journal of Policy Analysis and Management* 6:567–582.

Schmidt, K. 1990. The costs and benefits of privatization. DP A-330, University of Bonn.

Shapiro, C., and R. Willig. 1990. Economic rationales for the scope of privatization. DP 41, Princeton University.

Smiley, R. 1987. Management compensation in regulated industries. In *Analyzing the Impact of Regulatory Change in Public Utilities*, ed. M. Crew. Lexington, MA: D.C. Heath, Lexington Books.

Spiller, P. 1990. Politicians, interest groups, and regulators: A multiple-principals agency theory of regulation (or "let them be bribed"). *Journal of Law and Economics* 33:65–101.

Stole, L. 1990. Mechanism design under common agency. Mimeo, Massachusetts Institute of Technology.

Teeples, R., and D. Glyer. 1987. Cost of water delivery systems: Specification and ownership effects. *Review of Economics and Statistics* 69:399–408.

Tirole, J. 1992. The internal organization of government. Hicks lecture. Oxford University. Forthcoming in *Oxford Economic Papers.*

Vickers, J. 1991. Privatization and the risk expropriation. Mimeo, Oxford University.

Vickers, J., and G. Yarrow. 1988. *Privatization: An Economic Analysis.* Cambridge, MA: MIT Press.

Vickers, J., and G. Yarrow. 1991. Economic perspectives on privatization. *Journal of Economic Perspectives* 5:111–132.

Williamson, O. 1985. *The Economic Institutions of Capitalism.* New York: The Free Press.

CONCLUSION

In closing, our intention is to offer some thoughts about a few things we have learned in the process of writing this book and about the (many) areas for future research in procurement and regulation. We will begin by pointing out the wide applicability of the model and of the techniques developed here that extend beyond the primary motivations of the book.

1 Other Applications

Not all chapters are relevant for any given application. Nevertheless, we will consider a few of the other important applications.[1]

• *Managerial and employee incentive schemes.* The rewards of managers and employees are based on accounting data such as cost, profit, output, or productivity or market-based data such as stock prices. The principals are shareholders, boards of directors, chief executive officers, division managers or supervisors, depending on the employee's position. Employees usually have substantial discretion and learn private information before or during the execution of their tasks. Moral hazard and adverse selection are therefore most relevant.

As will be the case for subsequent applications, it would be foolish to apply our theory blindly to the employee context. Some features such as risk aversion are even more relevant here than for regulation and public procurement. Job rotation is also often easier to implement at the employee level than at the firm's level. Consequently job rotation (the counterpart of breakouts) is more often used in labor management than in public procurement or regulation to alleviate the ratchet effect or reduce the impact of collusion. Teamwork, task allocation, and career concerns would require more emphasis than that given in this book in order to get a sharp theoretical picture of managerial incentive schemes.

The purpose of mentioning this application and some others is only to stress that a number of points made in the book apply to the labor context. They include, but are not restricted to, the preference of confident managers for a low fixed reward and a high-powered incentive scheme; the design of incentives based on output, input, and profit data; the treatment of multitask and quality issues; the analysis of managerial myopia, ratcheting, collusion in organizations, and multiprincipals.

• *Private procurement.* Firms contract out many of their activities. The issues stressed in this book—associated with rent extraction and incentives—arise all the same. Note though that less emphasis should be placed on the design of cost-reimbursement rules in some situations. It is some-

1. Note that in most applications described below the cost to the principal of transferring \$1 is \$1 instead of \$$\lambda$ as in this book, where the principal is a benevolent social welfare maximizer who raises money through distortionary taxation.

times too costly for the buyer to audit the subcost of the supplier for the specific intermediate good. In other words, fixed-price contracts may be the only relevant contracts.

• *Cost-based transfer pricing.* Transfer-pricing rules between two divisions of the same firm are the pendant of procurement contracts between two separate firms. A fraction of transfer-pricing rules in practice are based on the cost of the supplying division. Although transfer pricing cannot be subsumed to the design of an optimal complete contract and control rights matter,[2] issues such as rent extraction, incentives for cost reduction, outside sourcing, or ratcheting are quite important in transfer pricing. Furthermore institutional features such as budget balance in the transfer and hierarchical issues developed in the book are also relevant in this context.

• *Sharecropping.* The relationship between a tenant farmer (agent) and a landowner (principal) can be analyzed within our framework. The crop level replaces cost as the main contractual observable. Fixed-price contracts are here rent contracts, cost-plus contracts are wage contracts, while incentive contracts correspond to sharecropping contracts. It would be particularly relevant for this application to further develop the theory to account for the tenant's risk aversion and financial constraints as well as to build incentives for cooperation. Indeed it is often crucial that the landowner be induced to provide good advice to the tenant. Also the need to embed the analysis in a repeated relationship framework is obvious here.

Last, we mention two applications in which incentive schemes are based partly on input data:

• *Loan contracts.* An entrepreneur who borrows money from a lender to finance an investment, and whose final gross profit is observed, can be described as an agent producing a negative output (the loan) and reaching some performance level (the gross profit). The analysis of chapters 2 and 3, for instance, can be applied. As an illustration, suppose that the gross profit is separable between, on the one hand, the borrower's effort and private information about the project and, on the other hand, the loan. Then the dichotomy result states that the size of the loan is not distorted for incentives purposes.[3]

• *Pollution control.* Consider a natural monopoly that produces a private good jointly with a public bad (pollution). Pollution can be viewed as a costly input, and the situation is therefore somewhat similar to the one

2. See Holmström and Tirole (1991) for a discussion of this point.

3. Formally let $\pi(\beta, e, I)$ denote the gross profit as a function of the quality β of the project, the entrepreneur's effort e, and the size of the loan I. Then if $\pi(\beta, e, I) = \Pi(\zeta(\beta, e), I)$, the loan is chosen so as to maximize $\{-I + \pi(\beta, e, I)\}$, whether the lender has complete or incomplete information about the project.

described previously. Formally the firm has two products. The results of chapter 3 can thus be applied.

This view leads to a substantial revision of Pigovian taxes. Incentive corrections are needed when pollution levels affect the rate at which the firm can substitute effort and efficiency in its cost function. Moreover the pollution tax must now be appropriately scaled down given that the firm bears only a fraction of its cost. More generally environmental economics can benefit from the various results provided in this book.

In addition to these specific applications, we believe that the emphasis put in this book on information and incentives is more broadly relevant for fields such as the economics of research and development, strategic international trade, the economics of health and insurance, and agricultural economics. We suspect these fields will benefit from a more careful consideration of information and incentives.

2 A Few Things We Have Learned

It would be presumptuous for us to draw a list of the accomplishments of this book or, for that matter, of those of the new theory of regulation in general. But it is worthwhile to recall the major lessons we (the authors) have learned in writing this book. In doing so, we emphasize the broad lines rather than the specific insights.

• *Trade-off between incentives and rent extraction.* While adverse selection theories always emphasize trade-offs between efficiency and (ex ante) rent extraction (in the same way moral hazard theories are built on the conflict between efficiency and ex post rent extraction, i.e., insurance), the specific trade-off unveiled in this book, between the power of the incentive scheme and the level of rent extraction, seems particularly apt at capturing real-world contracting issues. Its analysis can be generalized to allow for multiple product lines and task allocation and to determine when the observation of subcosts is useful.

We also learned that under some conditions linear incentive schemes are optimal, and therefore optimal contracts are robust to misspecification of the measurement or forecast errors. The linearity result requires strong assumptions on the preferences—in particular risk neutrality—and on the distribution of uncertainty. Even so, it is not robust to extensions of the model. Although optimal contracts were linear in the first eight chapters, they were no longer so once dynamics, political economy, or multiprincipal considerations were thrown in. Despite all this we find the linearity property attractive when it holds. Besides the robustness with respect to the distribution of noise, it also allows us to speak about the power of the incentive schemes in a simple and concise way in terms of slopes.

• *Quality.* When incentives for noncontractible quality are provided by reputational concerns, low-powered incentive schemes are needed to encourage its provision. In contrast, the power of the incentive scheme need not necessarily be distorted in the case of search goods, for which direct incentive schemes based on sales can be designed.

• *Pricing issues.* The determination of pricing and output levels—for example, the issue of whether they are distorted by incentive considerations—is governed by a few principles derived from various aggregation results. The theory can be used to study a wide range of situations by reinterpreting output as contractible investment, quality, or inputs and by applying the multiproduct framework to second- and third-degree price discrimination with or without competition.

• *Allowing competition.* Competition policy comes in at two levels. A regulated firm's output prices determine the level of entry and production by rival firms. So does the choice of an access price when the regulated firm controls an essential facility that is needed by its competitors to produce their final outputs. Competition policy with respect to intermediate and final goods can be examined precisely to weigh the gains of competition in terms of product diversity and increased incentives, and its costs in terms of suboptimal second- and third-degree price discrimination and non-exploitation of returns to scale.

• *One-shot auctioning.* Under some conditions and for a given winner, the power of the incentive scheme in an auction for a natural monopoly position is independent of the presence of competitors. Auctioning only reduces the winning firm's rent by lowering its fixed reward. Of course increasing the number of potential firms through, say, R&D subsidies, raises the winner's efficiency and allows more powerful incentive schemes.

• *Repeated auctioning.* Breaking out is a difficult enterprise for two reasons. First, some investments by an incumbent firm cannot be transferred to an entrant. Second, the incumbent rationally underinvests in those assets that are transferable but for which it is not guaranteed a fair price. To reduce "myopia," one must bias the auctions in favor of incumbents and, as is often observed in procurement, raise the slope of the incentive scheme over time.

• *Ratcheting.* The rent extraction concern gives rise to the celebrated ratchet effect. The regulator infers from a high performance an ability to repeat a similar performance in the future and becomes more demanding. Consequently the firm has an incentive to keep a low profile. The analysis of the ratchet effect is complex, but a few general insights can be gleaned. For instance, the speed of revelation of information decreases with the patience of the two parties. Despite the firm's incentive to keep a low profile, incentives need not be low powered compared to the static context.

• *Capture.* The design of incentive schemes by regulators and politicians ought to be guided by their decentralized information. This feature is the foundation for the possibility of capture. Regulators and politicians may manipulate their information to favor specific interest groups such as incumbent firms, entrants, consumers, and environmentalists.

Several policies can be used to reduce the threat of capture. The first is to limit the stakes interest groups have in decision making. For instance, industry protection is reduced by the adoption of low-powered incentive schemes such as cost-plus contracts and cost-of-service regulation. Such schemes reduce potential rents and regulatory discretion. It should be noted though that by sensitizing the regulated firms to audited costs, they make the control of audits more important.

Examples of reductions of stakes in a competitive context are the emphasis in auctions on tangible variables such as price over nontangible, quality ones in order to avoid favoritism, and a low level of discretion left to regulators in matters of entry, which is generated by a fear of cartelization or excessively proentry policies.

• *Institutions.* Institutions matter because the ultimate principals—the people—cannot design a complete contract or grand mechanism governing the behavior of regulated firms, regulators, politicians, and interest groups. Institutions determine the residual rights of control, that is, who decides on what matters with which instruments. Institutions that a priori ought to reduce welfare by tying the regulators' hands—such as budget balance, restrictions on commitment, or privatization—can be analyzed in this light. Institutions serve to curb regulatory abuse by prohibiting the use of those instruments that are most prone to be misused, by creating checks and balances and by enlisting watchdogs.

3 Looking Forward

The theory developed in this book ought to be enriched in many directions, some technical and some more conceptual. The purpose of this concluding section is to list a number of current limitations. None is inconsistent with the theory, and all extensions suggest directions for future research.

• *Treatment of measurement errors.* As mentioned above, the robustness of the optimal incentive schemes to a misspecification in the measurement and forecast errors is interesting but, we find, too strong a result. The limitation here is due to risk neutrality of the objective functions. To be certain, regulators and firms exhibit some risk aversion. Furthermore firms are usually protected by limited liability. The pure moral hazard paradigm, which ignores adverse-selection issues and emphasizes the role of risk aversion, is a convenient paradigm to analyze the link between measurement errors and the power of optimal incentive schemes,[4] and it is complementary to the analysis developed here. There is no conceptual difficulty in extending our analysis to allow for risk aversion or limited liability. However, such "mixed models" must be made more tractable in order to yield insights that go beyond the union of those generated by each paradigm.

This is not to say that we are completely at ease with a straight assumption of risk-averse preferences. As will be emphasized, the "regulator" and the "firm" are really black boxes for complex organizations. Organizations are not per se risk averse. Their members may be. The degree of risk aversion of decision makers is endogenously determined by the incentive schemes governing their organization.

• *Treatment of yardstick competition and joint production.* A closely related limitation of the model reduces its usefulness in studying yardstick competition and joint production. A general result in incentive theory states that two risk-neutral agents having (however slightly) correlated private information de facto have no private information at all (see bibliographic notes B1.3 of chapter 1). This result seriously reduces the interest of studying optimal common-value auctions of incentive contracts, yardstick competition, and product market competition between two regulated utilities. For instance, under risk neutrality and correlated informations, extracting the firms' rents is costless, and optimal contracts are always fixed-price contracts. One way out of this extreme result[5] is to assume that each firm's technological parameter is the sum of two parameters, an aggregate shock and an idiosyncratic shock, and that each firm knows both parameters and not only the sum of the two. Then, by the previous result, the aggregate shock is de facto not private information and can be elicited costlessly by the regulator. The analysis of this book can then be applied by focusing on the idiosyncratic shocks. For instance, under some conditions contracts become more high powered when the share of the aggregate shock in total technological uncertainty grows. Another way out is, as in the case of measurement errors, to dispose of risk neutrality and introduce risk aversion or limited liability. The drawback here is a potential lack of tractability.

A similar issue arises when an output is produced jointly by several regulated firms. An interesting result in this context is that it does not

4. See Holmström and Milgrom (1991) for a useful application of this paradigm.
5. See Auriol and Laffont (1991).

matter whether the regulator observes the total performance only or each firm's contribution to this performance (see bibliographic notes B1.3 of chapter 1). Again this result is too strong in situations in which the risk neutrality assumption is stretched, that is, when the uncertainty about each partner's technology is large.

• *Technical treatment of dynamics and capture issues.* We saw that the dynamics of regulation are sometimes complex. Yet we would argue that the practical importance of the matter warrants more work in the area. Similarly we have studied capture within the framework of "complete side contracts." This is not the only route, though it is the simplest, to analyze capture. Complementary routes ought to be explored.[6]

• *The firm as a black box.* The firm, which we identified with a manager or homogeneous group of managers, is not a single entity in practice.

First, the firm, if private, has claimholders. Only in chapter 17 did we allow for a conflict of interest between claimholders and managers. Furthermore we contented ourselves there with the analysis of a situation where there was no private role for more than one category of claimholders (the shareholders). More generally private utilities have shareholders, debtholders and possibly other claimholders. The firm's financial structure is subject to regulatory scrutiny because it interacts with regulatory efficiency. For example, a regulator ought to worry about high levels of debt if the market perceives that the government will not let the firm go bankrupt and will bail it out in case of financial hardship. Conversely, in the absence of such a perception, the regulator might object to low debt levels if these lead to a lack of managerial discipline.

Second, the firm is internally composed of employees holding different positions and having different information and interests.

Clearly we would not have written this book had we not believed in the usefulness of the black box view of the firm as a first approximation. Yet this view ought to be investigated more deeply, and this process will generate new insights. For example, it would be worth studying how incentives provided by the regulator trickle down the hierarchy.

• *The government as a black box.* Much of the book assumes a single regulator. Yet government is a complex web of political and administrative powers, of agencies with split control rights and conflicting objectives, and of lobbying interest groups. We made an endeavor to introduce political economy considerations into the new regulatory economics. Much more remains to be done.

As an illustration we can focus on the multiplicity of regulatory agencies overseeing utilities and public enterprises. For instance, Public Utility

6. See Tirole (1992a) for a methodological discussion of the modeling of collusion.

Commissions and the Environmental Protection Agency have authority over U.S. electric utilities. In most developed countries public enterprises must respond to a soft ministry (e.g., of industry) and to a tough ministry of finance. There are many interesting positive issues to be studied in such contexts. But there is also a fundamental normative issue: Why is there more than one regulator in the first place? One possibility is that the multiplicity of regulators makes capture by interest groups more difficult. A second reason may be that the multiplicity of regulators provides an optimal balance of incentives for the firm in the same way debt and equity complement themselves to control managerial behavior in corporations. A third motivation may be that the creation of advocates for the various causes (industry, consumers, taxpayers, environmentalists) generates better information for public decision making.[7]

• *Institutions.* We have studied a few institutions such as budget balance, subsidies to interveners, and limits on public commitment. We certainly have not exhausted the motivations for these institutions. For instance, the balanced-budget requirement may be due at least as much to the fear of abuse of public funds as to the attempt to enlist watchdog groups on the monitoring of all costs, as in chapter 15, or to commit to a hard budget constraint, as in review problem 12.

Nor have we exhausted the whole range of institutions. There are many more ranging from due process requirements to the mixture of congressional, presidential, and judicial oversight. In our view, it will be necessary to develop a more thorough understanding of incomplete contracting and residual rights of control at an abstract level. This aspect of bounded rationality, like other aspects, is high on the profession's research agenda for the years to come.

• *Oligopolies.* Our focus on natural monopolies is clearly excessive. Indeed several crucial regulatory issues are related to competition policy. To be certain, we have touched on product market competition in part II of the book. We see two further avenues of research in this area.

First, we ought to refine existing insights concerning important issues such as access pricing and bypass. We could also investigate the issue of predatory behavior by regulated firms.

Second, and this will require more conceptual headway, we ought to explain and investigate the implications of specific institutions of competition policy. The widespread coexistence of regulated firms and private or partially unregulated ones in the same product market (British Telecom and Mercury, AT&T and Sprint or MCI, public and private schools and hospitals) raises the question of why the whole industry is not fully regu-

7. The second and third reasons are investigated in work by Dewatripont and Tirole (reported in Tirole 1992b and Dewatripont and Tirole 1993, respectively).

lated. Certainly the answer should be that an independent fringe acts as a yardstick against substantial public mismanagement. Such a motivation should be studied thoroughly. In a similar vein we could attempt to explain why regulators are sometimes constrained to a "light regulation," in which they use only limited instruments. Such light regulation is often used in oligopolistic industries (schools, hospitals, airlines). Until now, the new regulatory economics has proved more successful in the study of natural monopolies such as electricity, gas, telephone, water, and transportation than in the study of natural oligopolies.

• *Applicability and empirical work.* Last, but not least, we discuss the application of the theory. A common criticism of the new regulatory economics (and of contract theory more generally) is that the policy recommendations are complex. It is here important to distinguish between formal complexity and informational requirements. Ramsey pricing is formally more complex than marginal cost pricing. Nonlinear incentive schemes are formally more complex than linear cost-reimbursement rules, and so forth. Formal complexity does not seem to be the crux of the matter for two reasons. First, the formal complexity of the optimal cost-reimbursement and pricing rules is quite limited and can be easily clarified to policymakers (this is at least our experience in the French regulatory context). Second, one could look for formally simpler approximations of optimal rules.[8]

Informational requirements seem to be a more crucial issue. One of the merits of the new regulatory economics is precisely to have put these informational requirements to the fore. Still, the new theory posits some Bayesian prior held by the regulator (which, in passing, is often intuitive and not easily transcribed in a cumulative distribution function). To the extent that the economist does not know this prior, discretion must be left to the regulator in the application of the optimal rules. While this discretion can, as in part V, be reduced to limit the risk of capture (or incompetent appplication), there is no escape from this issue.

It also goes without saying that econometric analyses are badly needed in the area. Such studies are not easy to conduct due to the nature of the problem (information asymmetries and incomplete contracting) and the dearth of data (in part due to the life span of contracts and to the natural monopoly aspect. Countries organized as federations of states offer better prospects in this regard). But they could help measure the discrepancy between actual practice and optimal regulation, and they could contribute to the calibration of uncertainty and preferences for further applications. We do wish that such a core of empirical analysis will develop in the years to come.[9]

8. In this spirit, see Schmalensee (1989) and Gasmi et al. (1991).
9. See Wolak (1991) for an example of such a work.

REFERENCES

Auriol, E., and J.-J. Laffont. 1991. Regulation by duopoly. Mimeo, Institut d'Économie Industrielle, Toulouse.

Dewatripont, M., and J. Tirole. 1993. Advocates. Mimeo, ULB, Brussels, and Institut d'Économie Industrielle, Toulouse.

Gasmi, F., Ivaldi, M. and J.-J. Laffont. 1991. Rent extraction and incentives for efficiency in recent regulatory proposals. Mimeo, Institut d'Économie Industrielle, Toulouse. Forthcoming, *Journal of Regulatory Economics.*

Holmström, B., and P. Milgrom. 1991. Multitask principal-agent analyses. *Journal of Law, Economics and Organization* 7:24–52.

Holmström, B., and J. Tirole. 1991. Transfer pricing and organizational form. *Journal of Law, Economics and Organization* 7:201–228.

Schmalensee, R. 1989. Good regulatory regimes. *Rand Journal of Economics* 20:417–436.

Tirole, J. 1992a. Collusion and the theory of organizations. In *Advances in Economic Theory: Proceedings of the Sixth World Congress of the Econometric Society*. ed. J.-J. Laffont. Cambridge: Cambridge University Press, in press.

Tirole, J. 1992b. The internal organization of government. Hicks lecture, Oxford University. To appear in *Oxford Economic Papers.*

Wolak, F. 1991. An econometric analysis of the asymmetric information regulator-utility interaction. Mimeo, Stanford University.

REVIEW EXERCISES

REVIEW PROBLEMS

These review problems were prepared with two objectives in mind. The first is to strengthen intuition about some themes studied in the book. The second is to analyze some topics that were only mentioned in passing or not mentioned at all. Answers to the review problems have been prepared by Peter Klibanoff and are available to instructors from The MIT Press. Review questions are easier and more closely related to the book (and therefore often more appropriate for classroom purposes). The answers to selected review questions can also be found in Peter Klibanoff's solutions manual.

The levels of difficulty of the review exercises are indicated by asterisks, ranging from a single asterisk (*) to three asterisks (***).

Review Problem 1 (Second Sourcing and Access Pricing)**

(a) A regulated firm can produce one unit of a good (yielding gross surplus S) at cost $C = \beta - e$, where the effort e involves a disutility $\psi(e)$. The regulator observes C only. The firm knows its efficiency parameter β before contracting ($\beta = \underline{\beta}$ with probability ν, and $\beta = \bar{\beta}$ with probability $1-\nu$). The regulator wants one unit of the good and can procure it alternatively from a competitive sector at known cost γ. Let λ denote the shadow cost of public funds, $\Phi(e) = \psi(e) - \psi(e - \bar{\beta} + \underline{\beta})$, $\psi'(e^*)=1$, and $W(\bar{e})=S - (1 + \lambda)\nu(\underline{\beta} - e^* + \psi(e^*))-\lambda\nu\Phi(\bar{e})-(1 + \lambda)(1 - \nu)(\bar{\beta} - \bar{e} + \psi(\bar{e}))$. Assume in this question and the next that S is very large, so it is always optimal to produce the good. Show that social welfare is equal to

$$\max\left\{\max_{\bar{e}} W(\bar{e}); S-\nu(1+\lambda)(\underline{\beta}-e^*+\psi(e^*)) -(1-\nu)(1+\lambda)\gamma; S-(1+\lambda)\gamma\right\}.$$

How does the regulated firm's rent change with the degree of competition (as measured by γ)?

(b) Assume, in the model of question (a), that the competitive sector must gain access to resources owned by the regulated firm in order to produce. As in question (a), the regulator orders one unit from either the regulated firm or the competitive sector.

With probability μ, access is infeasible (or prohibitively costly) and only production by the regulated firm is feasible; with probability $1 - \mu$, giving access is costless for the regulated firm. Only the regulated firm knows which prevails. [Also the regulated firm's cost of access (0 or $+\infty$, here) is independent of β.] So the regulated firm has an informational advantage both about β (and therefore its cost function $C = \beta - e$ if it is picked) and about the feasibility of access. Compare the policy of giving access and letting the competitive sector produce the good (for all β) when the regulated firm announces that access is feasible and that of not giving access (for all β) even if the firm announces that access is feasible. (We will ignore the possibility of giving access when feasible for $\beta = \bar{\beta}$ and never giving access for $\beta = \underline{\beta}$. This third policy may be optimal, but considering it does not alter the insights.) Can the *inefficient* type ($\bar{\beta}$) have a rent? Show that welfare is

$$\max\left\{\max_{\bar{e}} \mu W(\bar{e}) + (1-\mu)(S - (1+\lambda)\gamma - \lambda\Phi(\bar{e})); \max_{\bar{e}} W(\bar{e})\right\}.$$

Under which of the two policies are the incentives the least powerful? Explain.

Review Problem 2 (Budget Balance)**

This problem applies the usual techniques to the case in which the government cannot transfer money to the firm, which must cover its cost through direct charges to customers.

A regulated firm has cost $C = cq + \beta - e$ (c = known marginal cost; $\beta \in \{\underline{\beta}, \bar{\beta}\}$ is private information to the firm, and e is a moral hazard variable). The firm has utility $U = t - \psi(e)$, where t is the *income* of its managers. Social welfare is $W = S^n(p) + U$, where S^n is the consumer net surplus (recall that there are no transfers from the government). Let $R(p) \equiv D(p)(p - c)$ denote the firm's revenue net of marginal cost (assume R concave). The budget constraint is

$$R(p) = (\beta - e) + t = \alpha + U, \tag{P2.1}$$

where $\alpha \equiv (\beta - e) + \psi(e)$. Let $p^*(\alpha + U)$ denote the solution to (P2.1) and $\varphi(\alpha + U) \equiv S^n(p^*(\alpha + U))$. Make the usual assumptions.

(a) Assume that the regulator has *full information* about β. What is the optimal effort? Is the price the first-best price? Show that $\varphi' < -1$. Assume that $\min_e(\beta - e + \psi(e)) > 0$. (If you don't succeed in showing $\varphi' < -1$, give the intuition and take the result for granted.)

(b) Assume from now on *asymmetric information.* The regulator cannot observe β or e but observes everything else. Let $\text{Prob}(\beta = \underline{\beta}) = \nu$. The regulator gives a menu $\{(\bar{p}, \bar{e}), (\underline{p}, \underline{e})\}$. Derive type $\underline{\beta}$'s rent as a function of $\bar{e}$.

(c) Compute the optimum for the regulator. Show that it can be written as

$$\psi'(\underline{e}) = 1,$$

$$\psi'(\bar{e}) = 1 - \frac{\nu}{1-\nu}\left(\frac{\varphi' + 1}{\overline{\varphi}'}\right)\Phi'(\bar{e}),$$

where $\Phi(e) \equiv \psi(e) - \psi(e - \bar{\beta} + \underline{\beta})$.

Point out the analogy with the case in which transfers are feasible.

Review Problem 3 (Quality)**

It is often claimed that there is a conflict between quality and cost reduction. Consider the procurement model studied in chapter 1, and introduce a quality level s chosen by the firm. The firm's cost is now $C = \beta - e + s$. The regulator observes only C, so the incentive scheme depends only on this variable: $t(C)$. Quality yields future benefits (from later contracts) $B(s)$ to the firm (with $B' > 0$, $B'' < 0$) and $R(s)$ to the rest of society (with $R' > 0$, $R'' < 0$). The term $R(s)$ includes current benefits enjoyed by society from quality s. The incentive scheme cannot be contingent on these benefits. The firm's utility is $U = t - \psi(e) + B(s)$. The regulator maximizes (the expectation of) $W = S - (1 + \lambda)(t + C) + R(s) + U$.

Suppose that β is distributed according to the continuous cumulative distribution $F(\beta)$ with density $f(\beta)$ on $[\underline{\beta}, \bar{\beta}]$, with F/f increasing. Letting $G(s) \equiv B(s)(1 + \lambda) + R(s)$, show that for the optimal incentive scheme

$$\psi'(e) = 1 - \frac{\lambda F}{(1+\lambda)f}\psi''(e) - \frac{\delta}{f(1+\lambda)}\psi''(e), \tag{P3.1}$$

$$G'(s) - (1 + \lambda) = \frac{-\delta B''(s)}{f}, \tag{P3.2}$$

where δ is a lagrange multiplier. [Hint: $dU/d\beta = -\psi'(e(\beta))$ and $B'(s) = \psi'(e)$.] How do these conditions differ from the full information conditions? How does (P3.1) differ from the case in which quality is verifiable? It can be shown that quality and cost covary positively ($ds/d\beta > 0, dC/d\beta > 0$). How do you explain this?

Review Problem 4 (Cost Padding)**

(The following is drawn from Lewis 1990. See the reference in chapter 12.)

A regulated firm has cost $C = \beta - e$ of realizing a project. The firm can manipulate its cost, so the measured cost C^m differs from C. The (nonmonetary) cost of manipulation for the firm's manager is

$$\Gamma(C, C^m) = \frac{k}{2}(C^m - C)^2.$$

The disutility of effort is

$$\psi(e) = \frac{1}{2}e^2.$$

When it receives net transfer t, the firm has utility

$$U = t + (C^m - C) - \psi(e) - \Gamma(C, C^m).$$

Unlike the firm, the regulator does not know β at the contracting date; β is distributed continuously on $[\underline{\beta}, \overline{\beta}]$ with nondecreasing inverse hazard rate $F(\beta)/f(\beta)$. The regulator offers an incentive scheme $t(C^m)$ so as to maximize the expectation of social welfare

$$W = S - (1 + \lambda)(t + C^m) + U,$$

where S is the surplus associated with the project and λ is the shadow cost of public funds. Assume that S is big enough that the regulator always wants to implement the project.

Solve for the optimal incentive scheme. Show that the regulator can use a menu of linear contracts and that cost padding ($C^m > C$) occurs except for the type that picks a fixed-price contract, and more generally that cost padding increases with actual costs $[d(C^m - C)/dC > 0]$. Interpret.

Hints:

- Show that $\dot{U}(\beta) = -(\beta - C)$ (use the envelope theorem).
- Show that $\dot{C}^m(\beta) \geq 0$ (this is a bit harder). You may, for instance, apply a revealed preference argument, after having posited

$$\hat{\psi}(\beta, C^m) \equiv \min_C \left\{ C + \frac{1}{2}(\beta - C)^2 + \frac{k}{2}(C^m - C)^2 \right\}.$$

What is the sign of $\partial^2\hat{\psi}/\partial\beta\partial C^m$? Ignore this second-order condition in a first step.

- Review the analysis in section 1.4.

Review Problem 5 (Risk Aversion)*

A regulated firm has cost $C = \beta - e + \varepsilon_f$ of realizing a project. The firm knows β and chooses e, but cost is random. The forecast error ε_f has mean 0 and variance σ_f^2. There is also an accounting error. The regulator observes $C^m = C + \varepsilon_a$. The accounting error ε_a has mean 0 and variance σ_a^2. The regulator reimburses C^m and pays net transfer z. The firm's income is thus $t \equiv z + C^m - C$. The firm has mean-variance preferences:

$$U = Et - \frac{r}{2}(\text{var } t) - \psi(e),$$

where $r \geq 0$. The regulator's objective function is the expectation of

$$W = S - (1 + \lambda)(z + C^m) + U.$$

The regulator has prior distribution on $[\underline{\beta}, \overline{\beta}]$ with monotone inverse hazard rate $F(\beta)/f(\beta)$. The firm knows β before contracting.

Constrain the regulator to offer a menu of *linear* incentive schemes (they are optimal for $r = 0$ but not for $r > 0$):

$$z(\hat{\beta}, C^m) = a(\hat{\beta}) - b(\hat{\beta})C^m,$$

where $\hat{\beta}$ is the firm's ex ante announcement.

(a) Derive the optimal menu.

(b) How does the power of the incentive schemes change when

r increases,

σ_f increases,

σ_a increases?

Review Problem 6 (Postcontractual Accrual of Private Information)**

Consider the following timing:

Stage 1: A regulator and a firm sign a contract under *symmetric* information.

Stage 2: The firm learns privately its cost parameter β. Its cost function is $C = \beta - e$, where e is effort. The disutility of effort is $\psi(e)$ ($\psi' > 0, \psi'' > 0, \psi''' \geq 0, \psi(0) = 0$).

Stage 3: The firm exerts effort e and receives a net transfer $t(C)$. The regulator has utility (the expectation of)

$$W = S - (1 + \lambda)(t + C) + U,$$

where S is the surplus from the project and U is the firm's utility.

Consider three von Neumann-Morgenstern utility functions for the firm:

Case 1 (risk neutrality): $U = t - \psi(e)$.

Case 2 (risk neutrality above 0, infinite risk aversion under 0):

$$U = \begin{cases} t - \psi(e) & \text{if } t - \psi(e) \geq 0, \\ -\infty & \text{if } t - \psi(e) < 0. \end{cases}$$

Case 3 (limited liability):

$$U = \begin{cases} t - \psi(e) & \text{if } t \geq 0, \\ -\infty & \text{if } t < 0. \end{cases}$$

(a) Argue that in case 1 the regulator can obtain the first-best allocation by using a fixed-price contract.

(b) Argue that case 2 is formally identical to the situation in which the firm learns its private information before contracting (i.e., when stages 1 and 2 are reversed), and that therefore the analysis of chapter 1 applies.

(c) Argue that the equivalence with chapter 1 in (b) breaks down if cost is garbled by a forecast error.

(d) Solve case 3 (e.g., with two types). Compare to cases 1 and 2.

Review Problem 7 (Development Time)*

The Department of Defense derives gross surplus $S(T)$ when the development time of a new weapons system is T, where $S' < 0$, $S'' < -2S'/T$.

There is a single firm able to develop the new system. It has cost function $C = (\beta - e)/T$. DOD reimburses cost C and pays a reward or penalty t to the firm, whose objective function is $U = t - \psi(e)$ (with $\psi' > 0$, $\psi'' > 0$, $\psi''' \geq 0$). The net transfer t depends on the observables C and T.

The firm has private information about β, which can take value $\underline{\beta}$ (with probability v) and $\bar{\beta}$ (with probability $1 - v$). DOD has objective function $W = S(T) - (1 + \lambda)(t + C) + U$.

(a) Solve for the optimal incentive scheme. (Hint: Use chapter 2.)

(b) How does the firm's rent vary when DOD becomes more sensitive to development time?

Review Problem 8 (Investment)*

A regulated firm has cost $C = \beta - e$ of implementing a project with social value S. There are two possible technologies $\underline{\beta} < \bar{\beta}$. Initially the firm starts with the old technology $\bar{\beta}$, and this is common knowledge. The firm invests in reducing the production cost. The (nonmonetary) investment cost is nonverifiable (i.e., noncontractible). The timing is as follows:

Stage 1: The firm incurs private investment cost $I = I(v)$. It succeeds in obtaining the new and more efficient technology $\underline{\beta}$ with probability v (and is stuck with the old technology with probability $1 - v$). Assume $I' > 0$, $I'' > 0$, $I'(0) = 0$, and $I'(1) = +\infty$. The regulator does not observe the realization of β. The firm does before stage 2.

We can make two assumptions concerning the observability of the investment:

Case 1 (observable investment): The regulator observes I (or, equivalently, v).

Case 2 (unobservable investment): The regulator does not observe I.

Stage 2: The regulator offers a contract $\{(\underline{t}, \underline{C}), (\bar{t}, \bar{C})\}$. The firm has utility $U = t - \psi(e) - I(v)$, where t is the net transfer. The regulator has utility $W = S - (1 + \lambda)(t + C) + U$, where $\lambda > 0$.

Let $\Delta\beta \equiv \bar{\beta} - \underline{\beta}$.

(a) Show that if investment and efficiency were contractible, the optimal investment would maximize $\{v\Delta\beta - I(v)\}$.

(b) Consider case 1. Show that investment is given by

$$\max_{v} \{v\Phi(\bar{e}(v)) - I(v)\},$$

where $\Phi(e) = \psi(e) - \psi(e - \Delta\beta)$, and $\bar{e}(v)$ is given in section 1.3 [equation (1.23)]. Show that investment is lower than that obtained in (a).

(c) Consider case 2. Assume that $I'(v_0) = +\infty$, where v_0 is the cutoff belief such that for $v > v_0$, the regulator shuts down the inefficient type (see section 1.3). Show that there exists a pure strategy equilibrium and that investment is given by

$$\Phi(\bar{e}(v)) = I'(v).$$

Show that investment is intermediate between those in questions (a) and (b). Interpret.

Review Problem 9 (Ratchet Effect)***

Consider the two-period, two-type model of the ratchet effect studied in section 9.4, except that the firm's type is imperfectly correlated over time. The firm's cost is

$$C_\tau = \beta_\tau - e_\tau, \qquad \tau = 1, 2.$$

The timing in each period is as follows: The firm learns β_τ at the beginning of period τ (in particular it does not know β_2 at date 1). The regulator offers a short-term menu covering period τ. The firm then chooses effort e_τ if it accepts (it gets 0 for that period if it refuses). The firm's utility is

$$U = \sum_{\tau=1,2} \delta^{\tau-1}[t_\tau - \psi(e_\tau)].$$

The regulator's utility is

$$W = \sum_{\tau=1,2} \delta^{\tau-1}[S - (1 + \lambda)(t_\tau + C_\tau)] + U.$$

The stochastic structure is as follows: with probability v, $\beta_1 = \underline{\beta}$, and with probability $(1 - v)$, $\beta_1 = \bar{\beta} > \underline{\beta}$. The probability that $\beta_2 = \underline{\beta}$ is equal to x

conditional on $\beta_1 = \underline{\beta}$, and to y conditional on $\beta_1 = \overline{\beta}$, where $v_0 > x > y > 0$ (where v_0 is the cutoff belief defined in section 1.3 over which the regulator shuts down the inefficient type). Let $v' = vx + (1 - v)y$, let $\Phi(e) = \psi(e) - \psi(e - \Delta\beta)$, and let e^* and $\bar{e}(\cdot)$ be types $\underline{\beta}$ and $\overline{\beta}$'s efforts in the static problem (see section 1.3).

(a) Consider the class of separating contracts. Show that there exists δ_0 such that for $\delta \leq \delta_0$, the best first-period contract in this class is the same as the optimal static contract, except that

$$\underline{t} = \psi(e^*) + \Phi(\bar{e}(v)) + \delta x[\Phi(\bar{e}(y)) - \Phi(\bar{e}(x))].$$

(b) Derive the best separating contract when $\delta > \delta_0$ (a diagram might help illustrate the solution).

(c) Compute the best pooling contract.

(d) Consider a reduction in the correlation: The new conditional probabilities that $\beta_2 = \underline{\beta}$ are x' and y', with $x > x' > y' > y$. Use the envelope theorem to show that the range of discount factors for which the best separating equilibrium dominates the best pooling equilibrium becomes larger.

Review Problem 10 (Predation in a Regulated Industry)***

The desire to keep an entrant out or to force out a rival stems, in a regulated industry, from the fact that a higher residual demand for the regulated firm raises the latter's informational rent (see chapter 2). Predation or entry deterrence is achieved by charging low prices or, equivalently, by signaling low costs. This provides the firm with an incentive that countervails the traditional incentive (aggravated by the ratchet effect in a repeated relationship) to claim unfavorable cost conditions. This review problem develops an example of a repeated relationship in which the regulator uses the threat of competition to elicit the firm's information.

A regulated firm has cost $C_\tau = (\beta_\tau - e_\tau)q_\tau$ at dates $\tau = 1, 2$. The firm's type β_τ is positively but imperfectly correlated between the two periods. The firm's first-period efficiency is $\beta_1 = \underline{\beta}$ with probability v and $\beta_1 = \overline{\beta}$ with probability $1 - v$. The firm's second-period cost parameter also belongs to $\{\underline{\beta}, \overline{\beta}\}$ and $\text{Prob}(\beta_2 = \underline{\beta} | \beta_1 = \underline{\beta}) = a > \text{Prob}(\beta_2 = \underline{\beta} | \beta_1 = \overline{\beta}) = b$. The timing in each period τ is as follows: (1) the firm learns β_τ, (2) the regulator offers a contract $\{t_\tau(\hat{\beta}_\tau), C_\tau(\hat{\beta}_\tau), q_\tau(\hat{\beta}_\tau)\}$, and (3) the firm either rejects the current contract and both parties get 0 in the period, or it accepts the contract and announces a type. The firm's date τ welfare is $U_\tau = t_\tau - \psi(e_\tau)$. The common discount factor is δ.

We also assume that the regulator can at the end of date 1 invest $I > 0$ to get costless access to a fixed amount q_2^* of the good from other sources in period 2 (the qualitative analysis would be unchanged if the investment decision were taken by the private sector, as would be required in a theory of predation or entry deterrence). The date 1 and date 2 welfares are

$$W_1 = S(q_1) - (1+\lambda)(t_1 + C_1) + U_1$$

and

$$W_2 = S(q_2 + xq_2^*) - (1+\lambda)\left(t_2 + C_2 + x\frac{I}{\delta}\right) + U_2,$$

where $x = 1$ if the regulator invests and $x = 0$ if he or she doesn't.

Note that the model is the same as the noncommitment model of section 9.4, except that (1) output is variable, (2) there may be entry in the regulated firm's market, and (3) the firm's efficiency is imperfectly correlated over time.

Suppose that a is not too large and that q_2^* is not too big so that the regulator always keeps both types in period 2 for any posterior beliefs $\nu' \le a$ that $\beta_2 = \underline{\beta}$.

(a) Solve the second-period problem when $\nu' \in [b, a]$ and $x = 0$ or 1. Let $U_x(\nu')$ and $W_x(\nu')$ denote the firm's second-period rent when $\beta_2 = \underline{\beta}$ and second-period expected social welfare, respectively, when $\nu' \in [b, a]$ and $x \in \{0, 1\}$.

Use revealed preference arguments to show that

$U_0(\nu') > U_1(\nu')$ (the firm prefers no entry),

$W_1(\nu') > W_0(\nu')$ implies that $W_1(\nu'') > W_0(\nu'')$ for all $\nu'' \le \nu'$ (entry is socially more valuable if the firm is more likely to be inefficient).

From now on, make the following assumptions:

Assumption P10.1 $U_0(a) > U_1(b)$ (the predation effect dominates the ratchet effect).

Assumption P10.2 $W_1(b) > W_0(b)$ and $W_1(a) < W_0(a)$ (under full information about β_1, entry would occur if and only if $\beta_1 = \overline{\beta}$).

Let $W_2^{\text{FI}} \equiv \nu W_0(a) + (1-\nu) W_1(b)$ denote the expected second-period welfare, conditional on learning β_1 before deciding whether to invest. Note that separating the two types in period 1 yields the highest feasible second-period welfare W_2^{FI}.

(b) Consider now the first-period incentive scheme. The first-period expected welfare is given by

$$\nu E[S(\underline{q}_1) - (1+\lambda)(\underline{t}_1 + \underline{C}_1) + \underline{U}_1]$$
$$+ (1-\nu) E[S(\overline{q}_1) - (1+\lambda)(\overline{t}_1 + \overline{C}_1) + \overline{U}_1], \tag{P10.1}$$

where the expectation operators allow the possibility of randomizing behavior.

Solve for the best first-period contract in the class of contracts that fully separate the two types. In particular show that first-period efforts and quantities are as in chapter 2 and that the first-period transfer is lower than the one in the static model. [Hints: Ignore the inefficient type's incentive compatibility constraint and check ex post that it is satisfied. Also assume, in a first step, that the firm is thought of as having type $\bar{\beta}$ if (off the equilibrium path) it rejects the regulator's contract offer. Show that $\underline{U}_1 = \Phi(\bar{e}_1) - \delta a(U_0(a) - U_1(b))$. Note that the efficient type may "buy in" (have negative first-period utility), while the inefficient type does not buy in.]

Discuss the assumption on out-of-equilibrium beliefs as well as the conclusion that the inefficient type does not buy in [it is useful to introduce the beliefs $d \in (a, b)$ such that $W_0(d) = W_1(d)$].

Review Problem 11 (Yardstick Competition)**

We consider an industry producing two commodities that are perfect substitutes. Let $S(q^1 + q^2, \theta)$ be the gross surplus function with $\partial S(q^1 + q^2, \theta)/\partial\theta > 0$. Firm i produces commodity i with the technology

$$C(q^i, \beta^i) = \alpha + \beta^i q^i,$$

where α is a fixed cost which is common knowledge and β^i is private information of firm i.

The stochastic structure of the β^i's is as follows:

$$\beta^i = kb + (1-k)\varepsilon^i, \qquad k \in [0, 1].$$

$$b \in \{\underline{b}, \bar{b}\}; \qquad \text{Prob}(b = \underline{b}) = \nu.$$

ε^1 and ε^2 are stochastically independent with the same distribution $G(\cdot)$ on $[\underline{\varepsilon}, \bar{\varepsilon}]$.

b and ε^i are stochastically independent, for $i = 1, 2$.

$$k\underline{b} + (1-k)\bar{\varepsilon} = k\bar{b} + (1-k)\underline{\varepsilon} = a.$$

The regulator does not observe cost and uses transfers which have a social marginal cost of $1 + \lambda$, $\lambda > 0$.

The choice of the industry structure (monopoly or duopoly) is made in stage 1. In stage 2 firms discover their cost characteristics, and the regulator chooses the regulatory scheme.

(a) Show that the level of fixed cost below which duopoly is preferable under complete information (i.e., the regulator observes the β^i's) is

$$\alpha(k) = \int_{\underline{\beta}}^{\bar{\beta}} q^D(\beta)[F_{\min}(\beta) - F(\beta)]d\beta,$$

where $F(\cdot)$ is the cumulative distribution of β, $F_{\min}(\cdot)$ is the cumulative distribution of $\min(\beta^1, \beta^2)$ and $q^D(\beta)$ is defined by

$$\frac{P(q^D, \theta) - \min(\beta^1, \beta^2)}{P(q^D, \theta)} = \frac{\lambda}{1+\lambda}\frac{1}{\eta(q^D, \theta)},$$

where $P(\cdot, \cdot)$ is the inverse demand function and $\eta(\cdot, \cdot)$ is the price elasticity of demand. We refer to the effect obtained here as the sampling effect of duopoly. Show that $\alpha(k)$ decreases with k if $\underline{b} > \bar{\varepsilon}$ and increases with θ.

(b) Determine the optimal regulation for a monopoly structure (e.g., with firm 1) when $F(\cdot)$ satisfies the monotone-hazard-rate property $d(F(\beta)/f(\beta))/d\beta \geq 0$.

(c) Determine the optimal regulation for a duopoly structure when $G(\cdot)$ satisfies the monotone-hazard-rate property. [Hint: Distinguish two regimes. In regime 1, β^1, $\beta^2 \in [k\underline{b} + (1-k)\underline{\varepsilon}, a] \equiv A_1$; in regime 2, β^1, $\beta^2 \in [a, k\bar{b} + (1-k)\bar{\varepsilon}] \equiv A_2$.]

(d) In the incomplete information case, what is the level of fixed costs $\alpha(k)$ below which duopoly is preferred? Study when incomplete information favors the duopoly structure.

(e) Discuss the special cases $k = 0$ and $k = 1$.

Review Problem 12 (Prohibition of Transfers as a Method of Hardening the Budget Constraint)**

There are many industries in which a regulated firm must balance its budget without receiving subsidies from the government. Chapter 15 suggested one possible explanation: Regulators may not be benevolent and therefore may not be trusted to operate the appropriate transfers to the firm. This review problem develops an alternative explanation: The budget constraint acts as a disciplining device for the firm. If the firm makes poor investments, its high costs are passed through to the consumers; the high prices reduce production and therefore (informational) rents. In contrast, a benevolent regulator, on whom the constitution confers the right to transfer money to the firm, is reluctant to pass through high costs, in particular high fixed costs, and, for allocative reasons, prefers to offset the deficit through a lump-sum transfer. Thus the threat of a demand contraction is less credible in the presence of transfers. In this problem the regulator is benevolent but cannot alone commit to being tough in case of high costs. The constitution prohibits transfers to give the regulator some commitment power.

Consider the following game between a regulated firm and its regulator, with timing:

Date 0: The constitution allows or prohibits transfers from the government to the firm.

Date 1: The managers of the firm make some noncontractible investment that determines the fixed cost $\alpha \in [0, \bar{\alpha}]$ of the firm. They incur private cost $\mathscr{L}(\alpha)$ with $\mathscr{L}' < 0$ and $\mathscr{L}(\bar{\alpha}) = 0$.

Date 2: The regulator observes α. The firm learns privately its marginal cost parameter $\beta \in \{\underline{\beta}, \bar{\beta}\}$. The firm's cost function is thus

$$C = (\beta - e)q + \alpha,$$

where e is effort and q output. $\text{Prob}(\beta = \underline{\beta}) = \nu$. The other assumptions are also the same as in chapter 2.

Date 3: The regulator offers a contract to the firm. The regulator is benevolent and maximizes social welfare subject to, possibly, the constitutional prohibition of transfers.

Note that up to the introduction of the fixed cost α, the setup from date 2 on is the same as that of section 2.2 when transfers are allowed, and the same as (the two-type equivalent of) that of section 2.7 when transfers are prohibited. Note also that the regulator cannot commit to an incentive scheme before date 3. Assume that production is essential (type $\bar{\beta}$ is never shut off for any α).

(a) Observe that if transfers are allowed, the firm's ex post rent when $\beta = \underline{\beta}$ is independent of α. Conclude that $\alpha = \bar{\alpha}$. Show the resemblance to the "soft budget constraint story."

(b) Consider now mandated budget balance. Solve step 3 (for a fixed α). Let $\underline{t}$ and $\bar{t}$ denote the firm's reward when $\beta = \underline{\beta}$ or $\bar{\beta}$, and use similar notation for the other variables. Write the budget balance constraints for the two types and the incentive constraint. Write the social welfare function as a function W of $\bar{e}$ and α. Assuming, for simplicity, that ν is not too large; show that the firm's rent decreases with α. Conclude that the firm now has an incentive to invest and that constitutionally mandated budget balance can be welfare improving if investment is socially important.

(c) Would the same idea apply if production were not essential (e.g., if the regulator could use substitute suppliers)?

Review Problem 13 (Government Contracting When the Supplier Also Engages in Commercial Activities)**

It is often thought that a government contractor also engaged in commercial activities has an incentive to "cross-subsidize" the commercial activities, because the latter are necessarily subject to higher-powered incentives. In addition to accounting manipulations (fraud) that arbitrage between the government and commercial cost-reimbursement rules, the firm may devote more attention (supervision, allocation of best personnel, etc.) to the commercial activities. This review problem looks at the implications of the existence of (unregulated) commercial activities for the power of government incentive schemes.

The Department of Defense contracts with a supplier to develop a new technology. This technology costs

$$C = \beta - e_1,$$

where β is private information to the firm (β is distributed on $[\underline{\beta}, \bar{\beta}]$ according to distribution $F(\cdot)$, which has a monotone-hazard-rate) and where e_1 is the firm's effort allocated to the government project. There is no accounting manipulation, and C is perfectly measured. The firm is also engaged in a secondary commercial activity as a spillover from the primary government activity. (We assume that the commercial activity is not possible without participating in the government activity.) Devoting effort $e_2 \geq 0$ to this activity, the firm makes profit $\pi_2(e_2)$, with $\pi_2' > 0$, $\pi_2'' < 0$. This commercial profit is unregulated. The total disutility of effort is $\psi(e_1 + e_2)$ (with $\psi' > 0$, $\psi'' > 0$, $\psi''' \geq 0$). Ex post social welfare is $S - (1 + \lambda)(C + t) + U$, where $U = t + \pi(e_2) - \psi(e_1 + e_2)$.

(a) Determine the optimal regulation of C given that the firm allocates its effort optimally between activities (assume an interior solution $e_2 > 0$). Show that the incentive scheme is more high powered than in the absence of the commercial activity.

(b) Assume that $\psi(e) = e^2/2$, that $\pi_2(e_2) = ke_2 - e_2^2/2$, and that β is uniformly distributed on $[0, 1]$. Assuming an interior solution ($e_2 > 0$), show that the optimal regulation can take the form of a menu of linear contracts $[t(C) = a - bC]$.

Review Problem 14 (Optimal Forecasting Incentives)**

(This review problem is borrowed from K. Osband 1989, "Optimal Forecasting Incentives," *Journal of Political Economy* 97:1091–1112.)

A planner (the principal) must rely on some estimate Y of a random variable x with known variance σ^2. The loss function is $L(Y, x) = (Y - x)^2$. The principal's expected loss is thus $C = \sigma^2 + p$, where $1/p$ is the precision of the estimate Y of μ. For concreteness assume that $p = 1/n$, where n is the "number of experiments." A forecaster (the agent) chooses the number of experiments and incurs private cost $\beta(n - n_0)$ (so the prior distribution of μ gives n_0 "free experiments"). The forecaster has reservation utility 0. The planner tries to minimize the sum of the expected loss and the transfer t to the forecaster. The outcome x is commonly observable.

(a) Check that the first-best allocation for the planner involves $(1/\sqrt{\beta}) - n_0$ experiments by the forecaster and a transfer $t = \sqrt{\beta} - n_0\beta$.

(b) Show that under symmetric information about preferences, the planner can get the same utility as in (a), even if he or she does not observe the choice of n. (Hint: Let the forecaster internalize the expected loss.)

(c) Replace moral hazard by adverse selection: Suppose that n is observed, but now β is private information to the forecaster. The planner has prior cumulative distribution $F(\beta)$ with density $f(\beta)$ on $[\underline{\beta}, \overline{\beta}]$.

Note that the optimal contract can be chosen, without loss of generality, to be contingent on n only: $t^*(n)$. Solve for the optimal contract. Show that a relabeling of variables transforms the model into one similar to that of section 1.4. Describe the optimal "cost-reimbursement rule." Assume that it can be implemented through a menu of linear schemes (if you are courageous, find conditions under which this is indeed the case).

(d) Now combine adverse selection and moral hazard (neither β nor n are observed). Show that the principal's welfare is as in (c). [Hint: Let $\hat{Y}$ denote the forecaster's announcement of the expectation of the mean. Consider a menu of contracts of the type: $t(\hat{\beta}, \hat{Y}, x) = a(\hat{\beta}) - b(\hat{\beta})(\hat{Y} - x)^2$.]

Review Problem 15 (Regulatory Capture May Alleviate the Underinvestment Problem)*

We noted in section 1.9 that a benevolent regulator in general expropriates too much of the regulated firm's investment in the absence of a long-term contract. This review problem investigates the possibility that producer protection by the regulator may improve incentives for investment, and even welfare.

Consider the three-tier model of chapter 11: benevolent political principal-agency-firm. The firm has type $\underline{\beta}$ or $\overline{\beta}$ with $\overline{\beta} > \underline{\beta}$. The agency receives signal $\sigma = \phi$ if $\beta = \overline{\beta}$ (so $\overline{\beta}$ is the basic technology known to everyone) and $\sigma = \underline{\beta}$ if $\beta = \underline{\beta}$. That is, the agency always learns the truth. However, when $\sigma = \underline{\beta}$, the agency can report either $\underline{\beta}$ or ϕ; that is, it can always claim that it has not observed any improvement on the basic technology (this is a slightly simplified version of the model of chapter 11).

There are two modifications relative to chapter 11: First, as in section 1.9, the firm sinks some investment $I \geq 0$. This investment determines the probability $v(I)$ of finding an improvement and reducing the cost parameter to $\underline{\beta}$. Assume that $v'(I) \equiv dv/dI > 0$, $v'(0) = +\infty$, and $v''(I) < 0$. This investment is not observable by the political principal (it does not matter whether the agency knows it). Second, the agency is "honest" with probability $1 - x$ and "dishonest" with probability x. Honesty means that the agency always reveals its information to the political principal and therefore never colludes with the firm. In contrast, a dishonest agency takes a bribe from the firm if it finds in its interest to do so. We assume that the firm (but not the political principal) knows whether the agency is honest and that in the collusion game (when the agency is dishonest) the firm makes a take-it-or-leave-it offer of a bribe to the agency.

The timing is as follows: The firm invests I and learns its cost parameter $\beta \in \{\underline{\beta}, \bar{\beta}\}$. The political principal then sets up an agency, which is honest with probability $1 - x$. This agency learns β. The agency has reservation wage 0 and cannot receive less than 0 in any state of nature (limited liability). The political principal offers a contract to the firm and the agency (see chapter 11). The agency reports its signal, and the firm chooses its effort e and obtains cost $C = \beta - e$.

(a) Show that if x is small enough, it is optimal not to reward the agency for reporting signal $\underline{\beta}$ and thus to let collusion arise with probability x.

Show that the equilibrium investment by the firm is then determined implicitly by the following two equations:

$$v'(I^*)x\Phi(\bar{e}) = 1$$

and

$$\psi'(\bar{e}) = 1 - \frac{\lambda}{1 + \lambda} \frac{xv(I^*)}{1 - v(I^*)} \Phi'(\bar{e}).$$

[Recall that $\Phi(e) \equiv \psi(e) - \psi(e - (\bar{\beta} - \underline{\beta}))$.] Show that collusion may improve welfare.

(b) Determine the equilibrium conditions when the political principal *can* observe (but not regulate) investment but still does not observe the cost parameter. Do you expect more or less investment than when the political principal observes investment?

Review Problem 16 (Commitment and Investment)**

Consider the investment model of section 1.8, but assume that the regulator can commit to an incentive scheme $C \to t(C)$ *before* the firm sinks its investment I.

(a) Show that if the firm only needs to get zero expected utility (ex ante individual rationality constraint), the regulator can obtain the first best through a long-term contract.

(b) Suppose, in contrast, that the firm must obtain a nonnegative ex post utility for each realization of β [ex post individual rationality constraint;

e.g., the firm's ex ante utility is $V = EU(\beta) - I$, where $U(\beta) = t(\beta) - \psi(e(\beta))$ for $t(\beta) - \psi(e(\beta)) \geq 0$ and $U(\beta) = -\infty$ otherwise]. Show that investment is distorted relative to the first best and that the incentive scheme is more high powered than in the absence of a long-term contract.

Review Problem 17 (Underspecialization of the Firm's Investment in the Presence of a Commercial Activity)*

Section 1.8 pointed out that "outside opportunities" such as a commercial activity of the regulated firm give an incentive for the firm to underspecialize the investment in order to be in a better bargaining position. Here is a simple illustration: Take the symmetric information variant of the model in section 1.8, with the following modifications. First, the level of investment I is fixed (and reimbursed, say). Moral hazard by the firm only affects the "degree of specialization." The firm ex post can supply either the government or a competitive private industry. It cannot supply both because it will only have one unit. Its cost of supplying the government is $C = \beta - e$, and the cost of supplying the private sector is $\tilde{C} = \tilde{\beta} - e$; the disutility of effort is $\psi(e)$ in both cases. The parameters β and $\tilde{\beta}$ are drawn independently from distributions $F_x(\beta)$ and $G_x(\tilde{\beta})$, on $[\underline{\beta}, \overline{\beta}]$, respectively. The subscript x refers to the choice of specialization to the government activity: $x = S$ (specialization) or N (no specialization). Specialization means lower costs of trading with the government: $F_S(\beta) > F_N(\beta)$ for all $\beta \in (\underline{\beta}, \overline{\beta})$ and higher costs of trading with the private sector: $G_S(\tilde{\beta}) < G_N(\tilde{\beta})$ for all $\tilde{\beta} \in (\underline{\beta}, \overline{\beta})$. Assume that the private sector values the good at v, where (1) $v \geq \overline{\beta} - e^* + \psi(e^*)$, with $\psi'(e^*) = 1$, and (2) v is much smaller than the surplus S in the government activity, so it is always optimal to trade with the government.

The timing is as follows: The firm chooses its level of specialization. Then β and $\tilde{\beta}$ are realized and commonly observed. Last, the regulator offers a contract to the firm and the firm decides to supply to the government or to the private sector.

Show that it is socially optimal to specialize the investment and that the firm chooses not to specialize.

Review Problem 18 (Power of Incentive Scheme and Capital Maintenance)**

It is often argued that an increase in the power of the incentive scheme of a regulated firm results in a deterioration of the firm's capital. This review problem examines this argument in the light of the model of section 1.9. A date 0 incentive scheme is added to that model. Consider the timing in figure P18.1

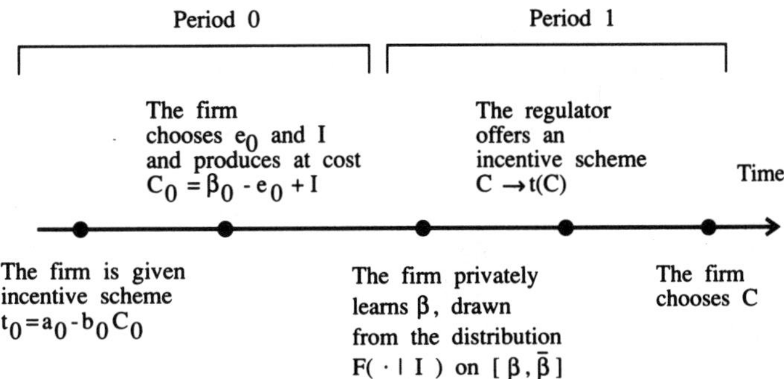

Figure P18.1
Timing of incentive schemes and investment

Note that this is a noncommitment model. Assume that the firm is indispensable (even type $\bar{\beta}$ produces in period 1) and that investment shifts the distribution according to the "more favorable distribution" criterion given in definition 1.1 in section 1.5. Consider two slopes of the date 0 incentive scheme, $\tilde{b}_0 > b_0$. Let $\tilde{I}$ and I denote two corresponding first-period investments. The goal is to show that $I \geq \tilde{I}$.

(a) Argue that an increase in the slope of the incentive scheme gives rise to two opposite effects.

(b) Use a revealed preference argument to show that one effect dominates the other.

(c) Compare the result to those obtained in section 4.6 (a high-powered incentive scheme reduces quality) and in chapter 8 (the regulator should start with a low-powered incentive scheme when there is a possibility of second sourcing).

Review Problem 19 (Regulation of Subcontracting)**

A project is realized by a contractor (firm 1) and a subcontractor (firm 2). The two firms' activities are complementary, in that both must work on the project for the project to be carried out. Firm i's cost is

$$C_i = \beta_i - e_i.$$

The disutility of effort for the managers of firm i is $\psi_i(e_i)$. Firm i has private information about its cost parameter β_i, which is drawn from cumulative distribution $F_i(\cdot)$ with density $f_i(\cdot)$ on $[\underline{\beta}_i, \bar{\beta}_i]$. Ex post social welfare is

$$W = S - (1 + \lambda)[\beta_1 - e_1 + \beta_2 - e_2 + \psi_1(e_1) + \psi_2(e_2)] - \lambda[U_1 + U_2],$$

where $U_i \geq 0$ is the rent of firm i and $\lambda > 0$ is the shadow cost of public funds. Assume that S is sufficiently large that the project is always realized.

(a) Suppose that the procurer regulates both firms. Solve for the optimal incentive schemes.

(b) Suppose now that the regulator contracts only with firm 1 and lets firm 1 subcontract with firm 2. Consider an incentive scheme that gives net transfer $t_1(C_1 + t_2 + C_2) = a_1(\hat{\beta}_1) - b_1(\hat{\beta}_1)(C_1 + t_2 + C_2)$ to firm 1 when firm 1 produces at cost C_1 and pays $t_2 + C_2$ to firm 2 (note that $C_1 + t_2 + C_2$ is the total cost for the project reported by the contractor). Show that the contractor gives an incentive scheme to the subcontractor that is too low powered.

(c) How is your answer to (b) affected if the subcontractor is a foreign firm and its utility does not enter the social welfare function?

(d) Assume that $\psi_2(e_2) = (e_2)^2/2$ and that $F_2(\beta_2) = \beta_2$ on $[0, 1]$. Show that the regulator can costlessly delegate subcontracting to the regulated firm by using a menu of linear incentive schemes

$$t_1 = a_1(\hat{\beta}_1) - b_1(\hat{\beta}_1)[C_1 + t_2 + \hat{C}_2(C_2)],$$

together with a convex scoring rule given by

$$\frac{d\hat{C}_2}{dC_2} = 1 + \frac{1}{1 + 2\lambda}(1 + C_2).$$

REVIEW QUESTIONS

Review Question 1*

A regulated firm has cost $C = \beta - e$ of realizing a project. The regulator observes C only and has objective function (the expectation of) $S - (1 + \lambda)(t + C) + U$, where S is the surplus (if the project is implemented), t the net transfer, U the firm's rent above its reservation utility of zero, and $\lambda > 0$ the shadow cost of public funds. $U = t - \psi(e)$, where $\psi(0) = 0$, $\psi' > 0$, $\psi'' > 0$. Only the firm knows β.

Discuss the general trade-off between rent extraction and incentives. Derive the optimal regulatory scheme in the case of *two types*: $\beta = \underline{\beta}$ with probability ν and $\bar{\beta}$ with probability $1 - \nu$.

Review Question 2*

Assume that a regulator has created an optimal scheme. Would you want to increase or decrease the power of the firm's incentive scheme when

(a) the regulator's information about the firm's technology deteriorates,

(b) the shadow cost of public funds increases,

(c) quality becomes more important,

(d) the regulator may collude with the firm,

(e) there can be accounting manipulations,

(f) there is a second period and, like Williamson, you worry that the threat of second sourcing may affect long-term investment by the first-period incumbent.

In each case explain your reasoning in a short paragraph.

Review Question 3*

Discuss the analogies and differences between cost-of-service and price-cap regulations in the light of incentive regulation.

Review Question 4*

"A regulated firm's price must be distorted relative to its full information level in order to limit the firm's rent": True? False? Depends on what the regulator can observe? Develop briefly, but rigorously, the logic of the argument.

Review Question 5*

Describe in words the "ratchet effect" in repeated relationships run by short-term contracts. Illustrate this ratchet effect for two periods in the model with two types and cost observability (review question 1). Using the notation of review question 1, and letting $\Phi(e) \equiv \psi(e) - \psi(e - (\bar{\beta} - \underline{\beta}))$ and $\psi'(e^*) \equiv 1$, show that the costs $\underline{C}$ and $\bar{C}$ for types $\underline{\beta}$ and $\bar{\beta}$ obtained in the static model of review question 1 cannot be part of a separating equilibrium if the discount factor δ between the two periods exceeds

$$\delta_0 \equiv [\Phi(e^* + \Delta\beta) - \Phi(\bar{\beta} - \bar{C})]/\Phi(e^*).$$

Review Question 6*

A regulator is responsible for two public utilities located in separate geographic areas. Each utility produces a fixed amount of output (normalized at $q = 1$) and has a cost function

$$C_i = \alpha + \beta_i - e_i,$$

where α can be interpreted as some shock common to both firms and β_i is an idiosyncratic shock, with β_i independent of β_j. Social welfare is

$$\sum_i [S - (1 + \lambda)(C_i + t_i) + U_i],$$

where t_i is the net transfer paid by the regulator to firm i, $U_i = t_i - \psi(e_i)$ is firm i's rent, and $\lambda > 0$ is the shadow cost of public funds. The reservation utility of each firm is 0. The effort function can be characterized as $\psi(0) = 0$, $\psi' > 0$, and $\psi'' > 0$. The firm knows both α and β_i when it contracts with the regulator.

(a) (Full information) Assume the regulator observes all components of each cost function. Determine the optimal rents, efforts, and transfers.

(b) (Idiosyncratic shocks) Suppose that $\alpha = 0$ is common knowledge but that the regulator does not observe β_i. Instead the regulator has prior beliefs that $\beta_i = \underline{\beta}$ with probability ν and $\beta_i = \overline{\beta}$ with probability $1 - \nu$. Determine equilibrium efforts, rents, and transfers.

(c) (Common shock) Suppose that $\beta_i = 0$ is common knowledge but that α is known only to the firms. Show that by offering the contract

$$t_i = -(C_i - C_j) + \psi(e^*),$$

where $\psi'(e^*) = 1$ to each firm, the regulator does as well as under full information. Explain.

(d) (Common and idiosyncratic shock) Suppose that both α and β_i are random with β defined as in part (b). Show that the regulator's lack of information about α has no welfare consequences.

(e) Show that the solutions to parts (c) and (d) are vulnerable to collusion between the firms.

Review Question 7*

A regulated firm has cost

$$C = (\beta - e)q + \alpha,$$

where q is output and α is a known fixed cost. The regulator observes C and q. The technology parameter β takes values $\underline{\beta}$ with probability ν and $\overline{\beta}$ with probability $1 - \nu$. The social welfare function is

$$W = S(q) - R(q) - (1 + \lambda)[t + C - R(q)] + U,$$

where $S(q)$ is gross consumer surplus, $R(q)$ is the firm's revenue from selling quantity q and U is the firm's rent.

(a) Determine optimal quantities and effort when the regulator has perfect information. Show that price is determined by a Ramsey-type formula.

How does this formula differ from the Ramsey-Boiteux formulas derived in a general equilibrium context?

(b) Suppose the regulator does not observe the components of C. Argue intuitively that the regulator will regulate marginal cost $c \equiv (C - \alpha)/q$. Infer from this that (for a given marginal cost) price is given by the same Ramsey formula as in (a), but that the marginal cost changes. Show that the firm chooses effort $\underline{e}$ when $\beta = \underline{\beta}$ and $\bar{e}$ when $\beta = \bar{\beta}$, where

$$\psi'(\underline{e}) = \underline{q},$$

$$\psi'(\bar{e}) = \bar{q} - \frac{\lambda\nu}{(1-\nu)(1+\lambda)}\Phi'(\bar{e}),$$

and $\Phi(e) \equiv \psi(e) - \psi(e - \Delta\beta)$.

(c) Would you get a Ramsey formula for pricing in the absence of cost observability (i.e., in the Baron-Myerson model)?

Review Question 8*

This exercise investigates a few variants of Ramsey pricing in a competitive environment in the absence of incentive problems. [The same formulas would hold if the cost function of the regulated firm can be written in a separable way: $C = C(\zeta(\beta, e), q)$ as in review question 7.]

(a) A regulated firm (a railroad, a subway) faces competition from an unregulated and "subsidized" competitor (trucks which do not pay for congestion costs or highway maintenance, cars which do not pay for congestion or pollution costs). The consumer gross surplus is $S(q_1, q_2)$, where q_1 and q_2 are the productions of the regulated and unregulated goods. The (noninternalized) social cost of q_2 is τq_2. The cost of the regulated firm is $C_1(q_1)$. The government faces a shadow price of public funds $\lambda > 0$. Let $\eta_1 \equiv -(\partial q_1/\partial p_1)/(q_1/p_1) > 0$ denote good 1's elasticity of demand and $\eta_{21} \equiv +(\partial q_2/\partial p_1)/(q_2/p_1) > 0$ denote the elasticity of good 2 with respect to the price of good 1. Good 2 is supplied by a competitive sector. Show that

$$L_1 \equiv \frac{p_1 - C_1'}{p_1} = \frac{\lambda}{1+\lambda}\frac{1}{\eta_1} - \frac{\tau q_2}{(p_1 q_1)(1+\lambda)}\frac{\eta_{21}}{\eta_1}. \tag{Q8.1}$$

Interpret equation (Q8.1).

(b) Note that in the absence of subsidy ($\tau = 0$), the regulated firm ought to behave as if it ignored the competitive sector. Suppose now that good two is produced by a *regulated* firm. Argue that (maintaining the assumption $\tau = 0$) $L_1 > [\lambda/(1+\lambda)](1/\eta_1)$. (Do not perform computations; just give the intuition.)

(c) Go back to unsubsidized ($\tau = 0$), competitive, and unregulated producers of good 2. The consumer gross surplus is still $S(q_1, q_2)$. But suppose now that the regulated firm produces an intermediate good q_0 needed to produce q_1 and q_2; its cost function is now $C_1(q_0, q_1)$. The technology is "one for one" so that $q_0 = q_1 + q_2$. The regulated firm must choose two prices: p_0 (the "access price") to sell the intermediate good to the competitive fringe and p_1. We can show that

$$L_1 \equiv \frac{p_1 - \partial C_1/\partial q_1}{p_1} > \frac{\lambda}{1+\lambda}\frac{1}{\eta_1}$$

and that (at least if the competitive fringe has constant returns to scale)

$$L_0 \equiv \frac{p_0 - \partial C_1/\partial q_0}{p_0} > \frac{\lambda}{1+\lambda}\frac{1}{\eta_0}.$$

(Do not compute these expressions.) η_0 is the elasticity of the fringe's demand for the intermediate good with respect to p_0. Give the intuition for these inequalities [Hint: Use (b).] Is an access price in excess of marginal cost socially wasteful?

Review Question 9*

A benevolent regulator chooses an optimal two-part tariff for a firm subject to a budget constraint. The regulator has full information about cost and demand and cannot transfer money to the firm (so this is the Boiteux model with two-part pricing and a single good).

The firm charges $T(q) = A + pq$ ($A \geq 0, p \geq 0$). There is a continuum of consumers, with gross surplus function $S(q, \theta)$ where $\theta \in [0, +\infty)$, and distributed according to cumulative distribution G with density g. Assume that

$$S_q > 0, \quad S_{qq} < 0, \quad S_\theta > 0, \quad S_{q\theta} > 0.$$

(a) Show that there exists a cutoff type θ^* such that consumer θ purchases if and only if $\theta \geq \theta^*$ (assume that $0 < \theta^* < +\infty$). How does the optimal consumption $q^*(p, \theta)$ vary with θ?

(b) The firm has cost $C = cQ + \alpha$, where

$$Q = \int_{\theta^*}^{\infty} q^*(p, \theta) g(\theta) d\theta.$$

The regulator maximizes total net surplus of consumers. Write the first-order conditions for the choice of A and p.

(c) (Showoffs) Prove that the solution in (b) can be viewed as a standard Ramsey prescription, with the firm pricing two goods: access (at price A)

and the physical good (at price p). [Hint: The "marginal cost" of access is $-(p-c)q^*(p,\theta^*)$. The price elasticity of participation is

$$\frac{-(1-G(\theta^*))}{[d(1-G(\theta^*))/d\theta^*](\partial\theta^*/\partial A)A}.]$$

Review Question 10*

(a) Define the "incentive-pricing dichotomy."

(b) Does the incentive-pricing dichotomy hold for the following cost functions:

$$C=\frac{\beta}{e}q \qquad \text{(single output)},$$

$$C=\beta q-e \qquad \text{(single output)},$$

$$C=(\beta-e)q_1+(\beta-e^2)q_2 \qquad \text{(two outputs)},$$

$$C=\min_{e_1+e_2=e}\{(\beta-e_1)^b q_1^2+(\beta-e_2)^b q_2^5\} \qquad \text{(two outputs)}.$$

Review Question 11*

Is a menu of linear contracts still optimal when the cost function $C=\beta-e$ is replaced by cost function $C=\beta/e$ in the analysis of section 1.4?

Review Question 12*

True or False?

(a) The regulated firm AT&T should charge prices under those given by the inverse elasticity rule if its unregulated competitor MCI has market power.

(b) The Boston subway should charge prices under those given by the inverse elasticity rule.

Review Question 13*

Discuss the pros and cons of privatization.

INDEX